Cases
in
Civil Liberties

Robert F. Cushman

with

Susan P. Koniak

Cases
in
Civil Liberties

Sixth Edition

PRENTICE HALL
Englewood Cliffs, New Jersey 07632

Library of Congress Cataloging-in-Publication Data

Cushman, Robert Fairchild, (date)
    Cases in civil liberties / Robert F. Cushman with Susan P.
Koniak. --6th ed.
      p. cm.
    ISBN 0-13-146622-4
    1. Civil rights--United States--Cases.
KF4748.C8 1994
342.73'085'0264--dc 20
[347.302850264]   93-1893
                              CIP

Acquisitions Editor: Charlyce Jones-Owen
Editorial/production Supervision: WordCrafters Editorial Services, Inc.
Cover Design: Karen Salzbach
Manufacturing Buyer: Mary Ann Gloriande
Marketing Manager: M. Divencio

©1994, 1989, 1984, 1979, 1968 by Prentice-Hall, Inc.
A Paramount Communications Company
Englewood Cliffs, New Jersey 07632

Printed in the United States of America
10 9 8 7 6 5 4 3 2 1

ISBN 0-13-146622-4

Prentice-Hall International (UK) Limited, *London*
Prentice-Hall of Australia Pty. Limited, *Sydney*
Prentice-Hall Canada Inc., *Toronto*
Prentice-Hall Hispanoamericana, S.A., *Mexico*
Prentice-Hall of India Private Limited, *New Delhi*
Prentice-Hall of Japan, Inc., *Tokyo*
Simon & Schuster Asia Pte. Ltd., *Singapore*
Editora Prentice-Hall do Brasil, Ltda., *Rio de Janeiro*

Contents

1

Rights in the Early Constitution

EX POST FACTO LAWS

CALDER v. BULL

3 Dallas 386; 1 L. Ed. 648 (1798)

While the original Constitution contained no comprehensive Bill of Rights, it did include a number of provisions designed to protect individuals against governmental action. One of these, the contract clause, was a guarantee against state action only; some, like the guarantee of habeas corpus, were applied to the national government only. Two of them, the clauses forbidding bills of attainder and ex post facto laws, applied to both state and national governments.

There is some historical evidence (not wholly conclusive) that the framers intended the ex post facto clauses to apply to civil as well as criminal retroactive laws, thus protecting property interests from retroactive legislative attack. Any such result was defeated by the Court in Calder v. Bull. In an opinion, most of which is still good law, Justice Chase pointed out that ex post facto laws were only retrospective criminal statutes which operated to the disadvantage of accused persons.

This definition raises difficult problems. What is criminal law? Obviously any law which declares an action to be a crime and provides for its punishment meets the test. But what about statutes that impose so-called civil penalties or disabilities? In the Test Oath Cases, discussed below in connection with bills of attainder, the Court held that to bar a person from a profession was punishment despite the argument that the laws in question were not punitive but merely defined necessary professional qualifications. The grounds for disqualification, the Court found, were irrelevant to the fitness of the individuals to carry on their profession. And since it provided for punishment, the law was considered to be "criminal" within the meaning of the ex post facto and bill of attainder clauses.

In Hawker v. New York (1898) the Court backed away from its stand in the Test Oath Cases. Hawker was a physician who in 1878 had been sent to prison for the crime of performing an abortion. In 1893 New York made it a misdemeanor for anyone who had ever been convicted of a felony to practice medicine. Hawker was convicted under the statute for continuing to practice and appealed to the Supreme Court on the ground that the statute increased the penalty for the original crime and was ex post facto. The Court held, however, that the state was merely setting qualifications for the practice of medicine. Under its police power the state could require good moral character of physicians and could validly make the previous violation of law conclusive evidence of bad moral character. It was unnecessary to look back of the general rule to see if Hawker actually was unfit to practice. The Court followed this doctrine in holding that former Communists could be barred from public employment (Garner v. Los Angeles Board of Public

Works, 1951) and that ex-convicts could not hold union offices on New York's waterfront (De Veau v. Braisted, 1960).

The denaturalization of naturalized citizens and the deportation of aliens are considered civil rather than criminal proceedings. Congress in 1906 provided for the cancellation of naturalization on grounds of fraud, and this was held validly applicable to a person who had been fraudulently naturalized in 1892. See Johannessen v. United States (1912). In the Internal Security Act of 1950, Congress made even "innocent" membership in the Communist Party grounds for deportation. In Galvan v. Press (1954) the Court held that this could validly be applied retroactively, although with obvious misgivings about the justice of the decision. "... Were we writing on a clean slate," said the Court, "... since the intrinsic consequences of deportation are so close to punishment for crime, it might fairly be said also that the ex post facto clause, even though applicable only to punitive legislation, should be applied to deportation. But the slate is not clean." In 1957, in Rowoldt v. Perfetto, the Court overruled the effect of Galvan v. Press by construing the Internal Security Act as requiring proof of "meaningful association" with the Communist party, and in Gastelum-Quinones v. Kennedy (1963) the Court emphasized that such association was not to be inferred from the mere fact that a person paid dues and attended a few meetings.

A state generally has a right to alter its trial procedure and rules of evidence and to make such changes retroactive to crimes already committed. Such changes are not ex post facto unless they "dispense with any of those substantial protections with which the existing law surrounds the person accused of crime." Thus in Thompson v. Utah (1898) the retroactive reduction in the size of the jury from 12 to 8 persons was held ex post facto because it is easier to get 8 jurors to agree to convict than it is 12. On the other hand, in Thompson v. Missouri (1898), where the rules of evidence were altered by law so that letters to Thompson's wife which had previously been excluded became admissible, the Court held that the "substantial rights of the accused" had not been affected. Under the new rule, which was designed merely to give the jury all the light it could get on the disputed facts, both the accused and the state had equal rights to introduce evidence.

In Dobbert v. Florida (1977) the Court held valid as a mere procedural change the enactment of a new death penalty statute (following the commission of the crime) to replace one that had been held unconstitutional following the Court's decision in Furman v. Georgia (1972). What changes there were in the act served to benefit the accused, and since he was on notice that the state could seek the death penalty for murder he was not without warning, despite the invalidity of the statute at the time the murder was actually committed. On the other hand, a statute which reduced retroactively the amount of time to be deducted from a prisoner's sentence for good behavior was held to be a substantive disadvantage to the prisoner and ex post facto; see Weaver v. Graham (1981).

In 1793, as a result of a suit over a contested will, one Calder acquired title to certain property. Two years later the Connecticut legislature passed a law setting aside this decree of the probate court and ordered a new hearing to be held. As a result of the new hearing the property went to Bull. Calder contended that the Connecticut law was ex post facto.

Mr. Justice **Chase** delivered the opinion of the Court, saying in part:

The effect of the resolution or law of Connecticut, above stated, is to revise a decision of one of its inferior courts, called the court of probate for Hartford, and to direct a new hearing of the case by the same court of probate, that passed the decree against the will of Normand Morrison. By the existing law of Connecticut a right to recover certain property had vested in Calder and wife (the appellants) in consequence of a decision of a court of justice, but, in virtue of a subsequent resolution or law, and the new hearing thereof, and the decision in consequence, this right to recover certain property was divested, and the right to the property declared to be in Bull and wife, the appellees. The sole enquiry is, whether this resolution or law of Connecticut, having such operation, is an ex post facto law, within the prohibition of the federal constitution? ...

All the restrictions contained in the constitution of the United States on the power of the state Legislatures, were provided in favor of the authority of the federal government. The prohibition against their making any ex post facto laws was introduced for greater caution, and very probably arose from the knowledge, that the Parliament of Great Britain claimed and exercised a power to pass such laws, under the denomination of bills of attainder, or bills of pains and penalties; the first inflicting capital, and the other less, punishment. These acts were legislative judgments; and an exercise of judicial power. ... The ground for the exercise of such legislative power was this, that the safety of the kingdom depended on the death, or other punishment, of the offender; as if traitors, when discovered, could be so formidable, or the government so insecure! With very few exceptions, the advocates of such laws were stimulated by ambition, or personal resentment, and vindictive malice. To prevent such, and similar, acts of violence and injustice, I believe, the Federal and State Legislatures, were prohibited from passing any bill of attainder; or any ex post facto law. ...

I shall endeavor to show what law is to be considered an ex post facto law, within the words and meaning of the prohibition in the Federal constitution. The prohibition, "that no state shall pass any ex post facto law," necessarily requires some explanation; for naked, and without explanation, it is unintelligible, and means nothing. Literally, it is only that a law shall not be passed concerning, and after the fact, or thing done, or action committed. I would ask, what fact; of what nature, or kind; and by whom done? That Charles 1st king of England, was beheaded; that Oliver Cromwell was Protector of England, that Louis 16th, late king of France, was guillotined, are all facts, that have happened; but it would be nonsense to suppose, that the states were prohibited from making any law after either of these events, and with reference thereto. The prohibition, in the letter, is not to pass any law concerning and after the fact; but the plain and obvious meaning and intention of the prohibition is this; that the Legislatures of the several states shall not pass laws, after a fact done by a subject or citizen, which shall have relation to such fact, and shall punish him for having done it. The prohibition considered in this light, is an additional bulwark in favor of the personal security of the subject, to protect his person from punishment by legislative acts, having a retrospective operation. I do not think it was inserted to secure the citizen in his private rights, of either property, or contracts. The prohibition not to make anything but gold and silver coin a tender in payment of debts, and not to pass any law impairing the obligations of contracts, were inserted to secure private rights; but the restriction not to pass any ex post facto law, was to secure the person of the subject from injury, or punishment, in consequence of such law. If the prohibition against making ex post facto laws was intended to secure personal rights from being affected, or injured, by such laws, and the prohibition is sufficiently extensive for that object, the other restraints I have enumerated, were unnecessary, and therefore improper; for both of them are retrospective.

I will state what laws I consider ex post facto laws, within the words and the intent of the prohibition. 1st. Every law that makes an action done before the passing of the law; and which was innocent when done, criminal; and punishes such action. 2d. Every law that aggravates a crime, or makes it greater than it was, when committed. 3d. Every law that changes the punishment, and inflicts a greater punishment, than the law annexed to the crime, when committed. 4th. Every law that alters the legal rules of evidence, and receives less, or different, testimony, than the law required at the time of the commission of the offense, in order to convict the offender. All these, and similar laws, are manifestly unjust and oppressive. In my opinion, the true distinction is between ex post facto laws, and retrospective laws. Every ex post facto law must necessarily be retrospective; but every retrospective law is not an ex post facto law: The former, only, are prohibited. Every law that takes away, or impairs, rights vested, agreeably to existing laws, is retrospective, and is generally unjust, and may be oppressive; and it is a good general rule, that a law should have no retrospect: but there are cases in which laws may justly, and for the benefit of the community, and also of individuals, relate to a time antecedent to their commencement; as statutes of oblivion, or of pardon. They are certainly retrospective, and literally both concerning, and after, the facts committed. But I do not consider any law ex post facto, within the prohibition, that mollifies the rigor of the criminal law; but only those that create, or aggravate, the crime; or increase the punishment, or change the rules of evidence, for the purpose of conviction. Every law that is to have an operation before the making thereof, as to commence at an antecedent time; or to save time from the statute of limitations; or to excuse acts which were unlawful, and before committed, and the like; is retrospective. But such laws may be proper or necessary, as the case may be. There is a great and apparent difference between making an unlawful act lawful; and the making an innocent action criminal, and punishing it as a crime. The expressions ''ex post facto laws'' are technical, they had been in use long before the Revolution, and had acquired an appropriate meaning, by legislators, lawyers, and authors. The celebrated and judicious Sir William Blackstone in his commentaries, considers an ex post facto law precisely in the same light I have done. His opinion is confirmed by his successor, Mr. Wooddeson; and by the author of the Federalist, whom I esteem superior to both, for his extensive and accurate knowledge of the true principles of government.

I also rely greatly on the definition, or explanation of ex post facto laws, as given by the conventions of Massachusetts, Maryland, and North Carolina; in their several constitutions, or forms of government. . . .

I am of the opinion that the decree of the Supreme Court of Errors of Connecticut be affirmed, with costs.

Judgment affirmed.

Mr. Justice **Paterson,** Mr. Justice **Iredell,** and Mr. Justice **Cushing** each delivered concurring opinions.

BILLS OF ATTAINDER

UNITED STATES v. BROWN

381 U.S. 437; 85 S. Ct. 1707; 14 L. Ed. 2d 484
(1965)

A bill of attainder is a statute which inflicts punishment upon a person without a judicial trial. Where the punishment is for a newly defined offense, which is frequently the case, the law is also ex post facto. This was the situation in the two Test Oath Cases arising out of the Civil War. The Missouri constitution was amended by the Reconstruction government to require all persons wishing to pursue a variety of callings, including teaching, the ministry, and the law, to take an oath that they had among other things never '' 'by act or word' manifested . . . adherence to the cause of the enemies of the United States . . . or . . . sympathy with those engaged in rebellion. . . .'' Cummings, a Catholic priest, was convicted of preaching without taking the oath and fined $500. See Cummings v. Missouri (1867). Ex parte Garland (1867) involved a statute of Congress that forbade anyone to practice law in the courts of the United States unless he took an oath that he had never supported the Confederacy. Garland, who later became Attorney General of the United States, was seeking readmission to practice before the Supreme Court and was unable to take the oath. The Court found in both cases that the deprivation of the right to practice their professions was punishment, and that it was being imposed by legislative act since it in effect declared the guilt of these persons and adjudged their punishment. The acts were therefore bills of attainder. Since some of the acts punished were not already crimes, the statutes were also held to be ex post facto.

The case of United States v. Lovett (1946) involved three federal employees who had been on a list of thirty-nine alleged subversives compiled by the House Committee on Un-American Activities. Congressman Dies, as chairman of the committee, asked that all these men be removed at once from the federal payroll, but the House decided instead to set up a special committee to pass on the charges. This committee heard charges against nine out of the thirty-nine and found that Messrs. Lovett, Watson, and Dodd were subversive and unfit for government service. Whereupon the House passed a rider (§ 304) to an appropriation act which forbade the payment of salaries to these three men, mentioned by name, unless they were renominated by the President and confirmed by the Senate. The three continued to work for a few months and then brought suit for the amount of salary thus earned and not received. The Court found § 304 to be a bill of attainder. The proceedings in the House were analogous to a trial of three named individuals on charges of subversion—in fact, members had spoken of giving each man "his day in court"—and the attempt "permanently to bar them from government service" constituted punishment within the meaning of a bill of attainder. The Court reaffirmed the two Test Oath Cases, noting that "they stand for the proposition that legislative acts, no matter what their form, that apply either to named individuals or to easily ascertainable members of a group in such a way as to inflict punishment on them without a judicial trial are bills of attainder prohibited by the Constitution."

In the light of the Lovett case it was argued that those persons removed for disloyalty under the President's Loyalty Program of 1947 were being punished, and hence should be able to confront their accusers in accordance with due process of law. In Bailey v. Richardson (1950) the court of appeals for the District of Columbia agreed that barring a person from federal service (in this case for three years) was punishment invalidly imposed, but held that dismissal on grounds of loyalty was not. The Supreme Court, dividing four to four, affirmed the decision without opinion.

The present case represents something of a departure from the Court's recent attitude toward the bill of attainder clause. In American Communications Assn. v. Douds (1950), discussed in the case below, the Court had upheld the noncommunist oath provision (§ 9h) of the Taft Hartley Act against the charge that it was a bill of attainder. Then in De Veau v. Braisted, in 1960, it had

held that a state statute barring ex-convicts from holding office in the longshoreman's union was not a bill of attainder, since the intent of the New York legislature was not to punish such persons, but to reform the waterfront. It noted the finding of a Senate subcommittee that criminals "whose long records belie any suggestion that they can be reformed have been monopolizing controlling positions in the International Longshoremen's Association and in local unions. Under their regimes gambling, the narcotics traffic, loansharking, shortganging, payroll 'phantoms', the 'shakedown' in all its forms—and the brutal ultimate of murder—have flourished, often virtually unchecked." It concluded that "duly mindful as we are of the promising record of rehabilitation by ex-felons, and of the emphasis on rehabilitation by modern penological efforts, it is not for this Court to substitute its judgment for that of Congress and the Legislatures of New York and New Jersey regarding the social surgery required by a situation as gangrenous as exposure of the New York waterfront had revealed."

Nor was it considered punishment (and hence a bill of attainder) to deprive deported aliens of their social security benefits; see Flemming v. Nestor (1960). Nestor was a sixty-nine-year-old alien who had resided in the United States for forty-three years, had paid into the social security system for nineteen years, and had been a member of the Communist party from 1933 to 1939. In 1956 he was deported for having been a Communist; and under a statute denying social security benefits to persons deported for this reason, his social security payments were stopped. The Court held that he had no contractual right to social security payments, despite having contributed toward them, and the act was not a bill of attainder since "the presumption of constitutionality with which this enactment, like any other, comes to us" forbade it to read the legislative history of the act as manifesting an intent on the part of Congress to inflict punishment.

Mr. Chief Justice **Warren** delivered the opinion of the Court, saying in part:

In this case we review for the first time a conviction under § 504 of the Labor-Management Reporting and Disclosure Act of 1959, which makes it a crime for a member of the Communist Party to serve as an officer or (except in clerical or custodial positions) as an employee of a labor union. Section 504, the purpose of which is to protect the national economy by minimizing the danger of political strikes, was enacted to replace § 9(h) of the National Labor Relations [Act], as amended by the Taft-Hartley Act, which conditioned a union's access to the National Labor Relations Board upon the filing of affidavits by all of the union's officers attesting that they were not members of or affiliated with the Communist Party.

Respondent has been a working longshoreman on the San Francisco docks, and an open and avowed Communist, for more than a quarter of a century. He was elected to the Executive Board of Local 10 of the International Longshoremen's and Warehousemen's Union for consecutive one-year terms in 1959, 1960, and 1961. On May 24, 1961, respondent was charged in a one-count indictment returned in the Northern District of California with "knowingly and wilfully serv[ing] as a member of an executive board of a labor organization . . . while a member of the Communist Party, in wilful violation of Section 504." It was neither charged nor proven that respondent at any time advocated or suggested illegal activity by the union, or proposed a political strike. The jury found respondent guilty and he was sentenced to six months' imprisonment. The Court of Appeals for the Ninth Circuit, sitting en banc, reversed and remanded with instructions to set aside the conviction and dismiss the indictment, holding that § 504 violates the First and Fifth Amendments to the Constitution. . . .

Respondent urges—in addition to the grounds relied on by the court below—that the statute under which he was convicted is a bill of attainder, and therefore violates Art. I, § 9, of the Constitution. We agree that § 504 is void as a bill of attainder and affirm the decision of the Court of Appeals on that basis. We therefore find it unnecessary to consider the First and Fifth Amendment arguments.

I.

The provisions outlawing bills of attainder were adopted by the Constitutional Convention unanimously, and without debate.

"No Bill of Attainder or ex post facto Law shall be passed [by the Congress]." Art. 1, § 9, cl. 3.

"No State shall . . . pass any Bill of Attainder, ex post facto Law, or Law impairing the Obligation of Contracts. . . ." Art. I, § 10.

A logical starting place for an inquiry into the meaning of the prohibition is its historical background. The bill of attainder, a parliamentary act sentencing to death one or more specific persons, was a device often resorted to in sixteenth, seventeenth and eighteenth century England for dealing with persons who had attempted, or threatened to attempt, to overthrow the government. In addition to the death sentence, attainder generally carried with it a "corruption of blood," which meant that the attainted party's heirs could not inherit his property. The "bill of pains and penalties" was identical to the bill of attainder, except that it prescribed a penalty short of death, e.g., banishment, deprivation of the right to vote, or exclusion of the designated party's sons from Parliament. Most bills of attainder and bills of pains and penalties named the parties to whom they were to apply; a few, however, simply described them. While some left the designated parties a way of escaping the penalty, others did not. The use of bills of attainder and bills of pains and penalties was not limited to England. During the American Revolution, the legislatures of all thirteen States passed statutes directed against the Tories; among these statutes were a large number of bills of attainder and bills of pains and penalties.

While history thus provides some guidelines, the wide variation in form, purpose and effect of ante-Constitution bills of attainder indicates that the proper scope of the Bill of Attainder Clause, and its relevance to contemporary problems, must ultimately be sought by attempting to discern the reasons for its inclusion in the Constitution, and the evils it was designed to eliminate. The best available evidence, the writings of the architects of our constitutional system, indicates that the Bill of Attainder Clause was intended not as a narrow, technical (and therefore soon to be outmoded) prohibition, but rather as an implementation of the separation of powers, a general safeguard against legislative exercise of the judicial function, or more simply—trial by legislature. . . .

[The Court here reviews the theory of the separation of powers and concludes that the bill of attainder provision was intended to keep the legislature from doing judicial work.]

Thus the Bill of Attainder Clause not only was intended as one implementation of the general principle of fractionalized power, but also reflected the Framers' belief that the Legislative Branch is not so well suited as politically independent judges and juries to the task of ruling upon the blameworthiness of, and levying appropriate punishment upon, specific persons.

"Every one must concede that a legislative body, from its numbers and organization, and from the very intimate dependence of its members upon the people which renders them liable to be peculiarly susceptible to popular clamor, is not properly constituted to try with coolness, caution, and impartiality a criminal charge, especially in those cases in which the popular feeling is strongly excited,—the very class of cases most likely to be prosecuted by this mode."

By banning bills of attainder, the Framers of the Constitution sought to guard against such dangers by limiting legislatures to the task of rulemaking. "It is the peculiar province of the legislature to prescribe general rules for the government of society; the application of those rules to individuals in society would seem to be the duty of other departments." Fletcher v. Peck [1810].

II.

It is in this spirit that the Bill of Attainder Clause was consistently interpreted by this Court—until the decision in American Communications Assn. v. Douds [1950], which we shall consider hereafter. In 1810, Chief Justice Marshall, speaking for the Court in Fletcher v. Peck stated that "[a] bill of attainder may affect the life of an individual, or may confiscate his property, or may do both." This means, of course, that what were known at common law as bills of pains and penalties are outlawed by the Bill of Attainder Clause. The Court's pronouncement therefore served notice that the Bill of Attainder Clause was not to be given a narrow historical reading (which would exclude bills of pains and penalties), but was instead to be read in light of the evil the Framers had sought to bar: legislative punishment, of any form or severity, of specifically designated persons or groups. . . .

The approach which Chief Justice Marshall had suggested was followed in the twin post-Civil War cases of Cummings v. Missouri [1867] and Ex parte Garland [1867]. Cummings involved the constitutionality of amendments to the Missouri Constitution of 1865 which provided that no one could engage in a number of specified professions (Cummings was a priest) unless he first swore that he had taken no part in the rebellion against the Union. At issue in Garland was a federal statute which required attorneys to take a similar oath before they could practice in federal courts. This Court struck down both provisions as bills of attainder on the ground that they were legislative acts inflicting punishment on a specific group: clergymen and lawyers who had taken part in the rebellion and therefore could not truthfully take the oath. In reaching its result, the Court emphatically rejected the argument that the constitutional prohibition outlawed only a certain class of legislatively imposed penalties:

"The deprivation of any rights, civil or political, previously enjoyed, may be punishment, the circumstances attending and the causes of the deprivation determining this fact. Disqualification from office may be punishment, as in cases of conviction upon impeachment. Disqualification from the pursuits of a lawful avocation, or from positions of trust, or from the privilege of appearing in the courts, or acting as an executor, administrator, or guardian, may also, and often has been, imposed as punishment."

The next extended discussion of the Bill of Attainder Clause came in 1946, in United States v. Lovett where the Court invalidated § 304 of the Urgent Deficiency Appropriation Act, 1943, which prohibited payment of further salary to three named federal employees, as a bill of attainder.

"[L]egislative acts, no matter what their form, that apply either to named individuals or to easily ascertainable members of a group in such a way as to inflict punishment on them without a judicial trial are bills of attainder prohibited by the Constitution. . . . This permanent proscription from any opportunity to serve the Government is punishment, and of a most severe type. . . . No one would think that Congress could have passed a valid law, stating that after investigation it had found Lovett, Dodd, and Watson 'guilty' of the crime of engaging in 'subversive activities,' defined that term for the first time, and sentenced them to perpetual exclusion from any government employment. Section 304, while it does not use that language, accomplishes that result."

III.

Under the line of cases just outlined, § 504 of the Labor Management Reporting and Disclosure Act plainly constitutes a bill of attainder. Congress undoubtedly possesses power under the Commerce Clause to enact legislation designed to keep from positions affecting interstate commerce persons who may use such positions to bring about political strikes. In § 504, however, Congress has exceeded the authority granted it by the Constitution. The statute does not set forth a generally applicable rule decreeing that any person who commits certain acts or possesses certain characteristics (acts and characteristics which, in Congress' view, make them likely to initiate political strikes) shall not hold union office, and leave to courts and juries the job of deciding what persons have committed the specified acts or possessed the specified characteristics. Instead, it designates in no uncertain terms the persons who possess the feared characteristics and therefore cannot hold union office without incurring criminal liability—members of the Communist Party.

Communist Party v. Subversive Activities Control Board [1961] lends support to our conclusion. That case involved an appeal from an order by the Control Board ordering the Communist Party to register as a "Communist-action organization," under the Subversive Activities Control Act of 1950. The definition of "Communist-action organization" which the Board is to apply is set forth in § 3 of the Act:

"[A]ny organization in the United States . . . which (i) is substantially directed, dominated, or controlled by the foreign government or foreign organization controlling the world Communist movement referred to in section 2 of this title, and (ii) operates primarily to advance the objectives of such world Communist movement. . . ."

A majority of the Court rejected the argument that the Act was a bill of attainder, reasoning that § 3 does not specify the persons or groups upon which the deprivations set forth in the Act are to be imposed, but instead sets forth a general definition. Although the Board had determined in 1953 that the Communist Party was a "Communist-action organization," the Court found the statutory definition not to be so narrow as to insure that the Party would always come within it:

"In this proceeding the Board has found, and the Court of Appeals has sustained its conclusion, that the Communist Party, by virtue of the activities in which it now engages, comes within the terms of the Act. If the Party should at any time choose to abandon these activities, after it is once registered pursuant to § 7, the Act provides adequate means of relief."

The entire Court did not share the view of the majority that § 3's definition constituted rule-making rather than specification. . . . However, language incorporated in the majority opinion indicates that there was agreement on one point: by focusing upon "the crucial constitutional significance of what Congress did when it rejected the approach of outlawing the Party by name and accepted instead a statutory program regulating not enumerated organizations but designated activities," the majority clearly implied that if the Act had applied to the

Communist Party by name, it would have been a bill of attainder:

"The Act is not a bill of attainder. It attaches not to specified organizations but to described activities in which an organization may or may not engage. . . . The Subversive Activities Control Act . . . requires the registration only of organizations which, after the date of the Act, are found to be under the direction, domination, or control of certain foreign powers and to operate primarily to advance certain objectives. This finding must be made after full administrative hearing, subject to judicial review which opens the record for the reviewing court's determination whether the administrative findings as to fact are supported by the preponderance of the evidence."

In this case no disagreement over whether the statute in question designates a particular organization can arise for § 504 in terms inflicts its disqualification upon members of the Communist Party. The moment § 504 was enacted, respondent was given the choice of declining a leadership position in his union or incurring criminal liability.

The Solicitor General points out that in Board of Governors v. Agnew [1947], this Court applied § 32 of the Banking Act of 1933, which provides:

"No officer, director, or employee of any corporation or unincorporated association, no partner or employee of any partnership, and no individual, primarily engaged in the issue, flotation, underwriting, public sale, or distribution, at wholesale or retail, or through syndicate participation, of stocks, bonds, or other similar securities, shall serve the same time as an officer, director, or employee of any member bank except in limited classes of cases in which the Board of Governors of the Federal Reserve System may allow such service by general regulations when in the judgment of the said Board it would not unduly influence the investment policies of such member bank or the advice it gives its customers regarding investments."

He suggests that for purposes of the Bill of Attainder Clause, such conflict-of-interest laws are not meaningfully distinguishable from the statute before us. We find this argument without merit. First, we note that § 504, unlike § 32 of the Banking Act, inflicts its deprivation upon the members of a political group thought to present a threat to the national security. As we noted above, such groups were the targets of the overwhelming majority of English and early American bills of attainder. Second, § 32 incorporates no judgment censuring or condemning any man or group of men. In enacting it, Congress relied upon its general knowledge of human psychology, and concluded that the concurrent holding of the two designated positions would present a temptation to *any* man—not just certain men or members of a certain political party. Thus insofar as § 32 incorporates a condemnation, it condemns all men. Third, we cannot accept the suggestion that § 32 constitutes an exercise in specification rather than rule-making. It seems to us clear that § 32 establishes an objective standard of con-

duct. Congress determined that a person who both (a) held a position in a bank which could be used to influence the investment policies of the bank or its customers, and (b) was in a position to benefit financially from investment in the securities handled by a particular underwriting house, might well be tempted to "use his influence in the bank to involve it or its customers in securities which his underwriting house has in its portfolio or has committed itself to take." In designating bank officers, directors, and employees as those persons in position (a), and officers, directors, partners and employees of underwriting houses as those persons in position (b), Congress merely expressed the characteristics it was trying to reach in an alternative, shorthand way. That Congress was legislating with respect to general characteristics rather than with respect to a specific group of men is well demonstrated by the fact that § 32 provides that the prescribed disqualification should not obtain whenever the Board of Governors determined that "it would not unduly influence the investment policies of such member bank or the advice it gives its customers regarding investments." We do not suggest that such an escape clause is essential to the constitutionality of § 32, but point to it only further to underscore the infirmity of the suggestion that § 32, like § 504, incorporates an empirical judgment of, and inflicts its deprivation upon, a particular group of men.

It is argued, however, that in § 504 Congress did no more than it did in enacting § 32: it promulgated a general rule to the effect that persons possessing characteristics which make them likely to incite political strikes should not hold union office, and simply inserted in place of a list of those characteristics an alternative, shorthand criterion—membership in the Communist Party. Again, we cannot agree. The designation of Communists as those persons likely to cause political strikes is not the substitution of a semantically equivalent phrase; on the contrary, it rests, as the Court in Douds explicitly recognized, upon an empirical investigation by Congress of the acts, characteristics and propensities of Communist Party members. . . . Even assuming that Congress had reason to conclude that some Communists would use union positions to bring about political strikes, "it cannot automatically be inferred that all members shar[e] their evil purposes or participat[e] in their illegal conduct." . . . In utilizing the term "members of the Communist Party" to designate those persons who are likely to incite political strikes, it plainly is not the case that Congress has merely substituted a convenient shorthand term for a list of the characteristics it was trying to reach.

IV.

The Solicitor General argues that § 504 is not a bill of attainder because the prohibition it imposes does not constitute "punishment." In support of this conclusion, he urges that the statute was enacted for preventive rather than retributive reasons—that its aim is not to punish Communists for what they have done in the past, but rather to keep them from positions where they will in the future be able to bring about undesirable events. He relies on American Communications Assn. v. Douds which upheld § 9(h) of the National Labor Relations Act, the predecessor of the statute presently before us. In Douds the Court distinguished Cummings, Garland and Lovett on the ground that in those cases "the individuals involved were in fact being punished for *past* actions; whereas in this case they are subject to possible loss of position only because there is substantial ground for the congressional judgment that their beliefs and loyalties will be transformed into *future* conduct."

This case is not necessarily controlled by Douds. For to prove its assertion that § 9(h) was preventive rather than retributive in purpose, the Court in Douds focused on the fact that members of the Communist Party could escape from the class of persons specified by Congress simply by resigning from the Party:

"Here the intention is to forestall future dangerous acts; there is no one who may not, by a voluntary alteration of the loyalties which impel him to action, become eligible to sign the affidavit. We cannot conclude that this section is a bill of attainder."

Section 504, unlike § 9(h), disqualifies from the holding of union office not only present members of the Communist Party, but also anyone who has within the past five years been a member of the Party. However, even if we make the assumption that the five-year provision was inserted not out of desire to visit retribution but purely out of a belief that failure to include it would lead to pro forma resignations from the Party which would not decrease the threat of political strikes, it still clearly appears that § 504 inflicts "punishment" within the meaning of the Bill of Attainder Clause. It would be archaic to limit the definition of "punishment" to "retribution." Punishment serves several purposes: retributive, rehabilitative, deterrent—and preventive. One of the reasons society imprisons those convicted of crimes is to keep them from inflicting future harm, but that does not make imprisonment any the less punishment.

Historical considerations by no means compel restriction of the bill of attainder ban to instances of retribution. A number of English bills of attainder were enacted for preventive purposes—that is, the legislature made a judgment, undoubtedly based largely on past acts and associations (as § 504 is) that a given person or group was likely to cause trouble (usually, overthrow the government) and therefore inflicted deprivations upon that person or group in order to keep it from bringing about the feared event. It is also clear that many of the early American bills attainting the Tories were passed in order to impede their effectively resisting the Revolution. . . .

We think that the Court in Douds misread United States v. Lovett when it suggested that that case could be distinguished on the ground that the sanction there imposed was levied for purely retributive reasons. In Lovett the Court, after reviewing the legislative history of § 304 of the Urgent Deficiency Appropriation Act, concluded that the statute was the product of a congressional drive to oust from government persons whose (congressionally determined) "subversive" tendencies made their continued employment dangerous to the national welfare: "the purpose of all who sponsored § 304 . . . clearly was to 'purge' the then existing and all future lists of government employees of those whom Congress deemed guilty of 'subversive activities' and therefore 'unfit' to hold a federal job." Similarly, the purpose of the statute before us is to purge the governing boards of labor unions of those whom Congress regards as guilty of subversive acts and associations and therefore unfit to fill positions which might affect interstate commerce.

The Solicitor General urges us to distinguish Lovett on the ground that the statute struck down there "singled out three identified individuals." It is of course true that § 504 does not contain the words "Archie Brown," and that it inflicts its deprivation upon more than three people. However, the decisions of this Court, as well as the historical background of the Bill of Attainder Clause, make it crystal clear that these are distinctions without a difference. It was not uncommon for English acts of attainder to inflict their deprivations upon relatively large groups of people, sometimes by description rather than name. Moreover, the statutes voided in Cummings and Garland were of this nature. We cannot agree that the fact that § 504 inflicts its deprivation upon the membership of the Communist Party rather than upon a list of named individuals takes it out of the category of bills of attainder.

We do not hold today that Congress cannot weed dangerous persons out of the labor movement, any more than the Court held in Lovett that subversives must be permitted to hold sensitive government positions. Rather, we make again the point made in Lovett: that Congress must accomplish such results by rules of general applicability. It cannot specify the people upon whom the sanction it prescribes is to be levied. Under our Constitution, Congress possesses full legislative authority, but the task of adjudication must be left to other tribunals.

This Court is always reluctant to declare that an Act of Congress violates the Constitution, but in this case we have no alternative. . . .

The judgment of the Court of Appeals is
Affirmed.

Mr. Justice **White,** with whom Mr. Justice **Clark,** Mr. Justice **Harlan,** and Mr. Justice **Stewart** join, dissenting, said in part:

. . . When an enactment is challenged as an attainder, the central inquiry must be whether the disability imposed by the act is "punishment" (i.e., is directed at an individual or a group of individuals) or is "regulation" (i.e., is directed at controlling future conduct). . . . Whether a punitive purpose would be inferred has depended in past cases on a number of circumstances, including the nature of the disability, whether it was traditionally regarded as punishment, whether it is rationally connected to a permissible legislative objective, as well as the specificity of the legislature's designation of the persons to be affected. . . .

I.

It is not difficult to find some of the cases and statutes which the necessary implications of the Court's approach which will overrule or invalidate.

American Communications Assn. v. Douds which upheld the predecessor statute to § 504 is obviously overruled. In that case the Court accepted the congressional findings about the Communist Party and about the propensity of Party members "to subordinate legitimate trade union objectives to obstructive strikes when dictated by Party leaders, often in support of the policies of a foreign government." Moreover, Congress was permitted to infer from a person's "political affiliations and beliefs" that such a person would be likely to instigate political strikes. Like § 504, the statute there under consideration did not cover all persons who might be likely to call political strikes. Nevertheless, legislative findings that *some* Communists would engage in illegal activities were sufficient to sustain the exercise of legislative power. The Bill of Attainder Clause now forbids Congress to do precisely what was validated in Douds.

Similarly invalidated are statutes denying positions of public importance to groups of persons identified by their business affiliations, commonly known as conflict-of-interest statutes. . . .

In term of the Court's analysis of the Bill of Attainder Clause, no meaningful distinction may be drawn between § 32 of the Banking Act and § 504. Both sections disqualify a specifically described group, officers and employees of underwriting firms in the one case and members of the Communist Party in the other. Both sections may be said to be underinclusive: others besides underwriters may have business interests conflicting with the duties of a bank director and others than Communists may call political strikes. Equally, both sections may be deemed overinclusive: neither section finds that all members of the group affected would violate their obligations to the office from which they are disqualified; some members would and perhaps others would not. Both sections are based on a probability or likelihood that this would occur. Both sections leave to the courts the task of determining whether particular persons are members of the designated groups and occupy the specified positions.

In attempting to distinguish the two sections, the Court states that in enacting § 32 of the Banking Act Congress made no judgment or condemnation of any specific group of persons. Instead, the Court reasons, "Congress relied upon its general knowledge of human psychology, and concluded that the concurrent holding of the two designated positions would present a temptation to *any* man—not just certain men or members of a certain political party." But § 32 disqualifies only partners and employees of underwriting firms, not other businessmen with conflicting interests. And § 504 applies to *any* man who occupies the two positions of labor union leader and member of the Communist Party. If based upon "its general knowledge of human psychology" Congress may make findings about a group including members and employees of underwriting firms which disqualify such persons from a certain office, why may not Congress on a similar basis make such a finding about members of the Communist Party? "Because of their business connections, carrying as they do certain loyalties, interests and disciplines," § 32 disqualifies members and employees of underwriting firms as posing "a continuing threat of participation in the harmful activities. . . ." Douds. The same might be said about § 504, as was said about its predecessor: "Political affiliations of the kind here involved, no less than business affiliations, provide rational ground for the legislative judgment that those persons proscribed by § 9(h) would be subject to 'tempting opportunities' to commit acts deemed harmful to the national economy. In this respect, § 9(h) is not unlike a host of other statutes which prohibit specified groups of persons from holding positions of power and public interest because, in the legislative judgment, they threaten to abuse the trust that is a necessary concomitant of the power of office."

Conflict-of-interest statutes are an accepted type of legislation. Indeed, our Constitution contains a conflict-of-interest provisions in Art. I, § 6, cl. 2, which prohibits any Congressman from simultaneously holding office under the United States. If the Court would save the conflict-of-interest statutes, which apparently it would, it is difficult to understand why § 504 is stricken down as a bill of attainder.

Other legislative enactments relevant here are those statutes disqualifying felons from occupying certain positions. The leading case is Hawker v. New York [1898], which upheld a provision prohibiting convicted felons from practicing medicine against a claim that, as applied to one convicted before its enactment, it was an ex post facto law. The Court noted that a legislature may establish qualifications for the practice of medicine, and character may be such a qualification. Conviction of a felony, the Court reasoned, may be evidence of character:

"It is not open to doubt that the commission of crime . . . has some relation to the question of character. It is not, as a rule, the good people who commit crime. When the legislature declares that whoever has violated the criminal laws of the State shall be deemed lacking in good moral character it is not laying down an arbitrary or fanciful rule—one having no relation to the subject-matter, but is only appealing to a well recognized fact of human experience. . . .

"It is no answer to say that this test of character is not in all cases absolutely certain, and that sometimes it works harshly. Doubtless, one who has violated the criminal law may thereafter reform and become in fact possessed of a good moral character. But the legislature has power in cases of this kind to make a rule of universal application, and no inquiry is permissible back of the rule to ascertain whether the fact of which the rule is made the absolute test does or does not exist." ...

The Court apparently agrees that the Subversive Activities Control Act was not a bill of attainder with regard to the Communist Party because, as the Court pointed out in Communist Party v. Subversive Activities Control Board, the finding that the Party was a Communist-action organization was not made by the legislature but was made administratively, after a trial-type hearing and subject to judicial review. But this apparently does not settle whether the statute is a bill of attainder with respect to Party members; for under today's approach, a finding about the Party and about some of its members does not cure the vice of overinclusiveness. The Subversive Activities Control Act attaches certain disqualifications to each Party member following the administrative-judicial finding that the Party is a Communist-action organization. Among other things, each Party member is disqualified from holding union office, almost the same disqualification as is involved here. I do not see how this and the other consequences attached to Party membership in that Act could survive examination under the principles announced today.

On the other hand, if the statutes involved in Hawker and Agnew are not bills of attainder, how can the Subversive Activities Control Act be an attainder with respect to members of the Communist Party? In the Communist Party case, the Board found that the "[Party's] principal leaders and a substantial number of its members are subject to and recognize the disciplinary power of the Soviet Union and its representatives. This evidences domination and control over [the Party] by the Soviet Union, and a purpose to advance the objectives of the world Communist movement." ... That finding was expressly sustained by this Court. Certainly, if Hawker and Agnew are to be followed at all, these nonlegislative findings establish a sufficient probability or likelihood with regard to Party members—a sufficient temptation to Party members who are also union officers—to permit the legislature to disqualify Party members from union office as it did in the Subversive Activities Control Act. ...

But how does one prove that a person would be disloyal? The Communist Party's illegal purpose and its domination by a foreign power have already been adjudicated, both administratively and judicially. If this does not in itself provide a sufficient probability with respect to the individual who persists in remaining a member of the Party, or if a probability is in any event insufficient, what evidence with regard to the individual will be sufficient to disqualify him? If he must be apprehended in the act of calling one political strike or in one act of disloyalty before steps can be taken to exclude him from office, there is little or nothing left of the preventive or prophylactic function of § 504 or of the statutes such as the Court had before it in Hawker and Agnew. ...

THE CONTRACT CLAUSE

THE DARTMOUTH COLLEGE CASE: THE TRUSTEES OF DARTMOUTH COLLEGE v. WOODWARD

4 Wheaton 518; 4 L. Ed. 629 (1819)

When the framers of the Constitution forbade the states to pass laws impairing the obligation of contracts, they had in mind the ordinary executory contracts between individuals, which during the "critical period" had so frequently been interfered with by the enactment of "stay laws," legal tender laws, and other legislation for the benefit of insolvent debtors. The first interpretation of the contract clause by the Supreme Court was given in the case of Fletcher v. Peck (1810), which did not relate to this variety of contract at all, but which involved the question of whether an executed contract in the form of a legislative grant of land made by the state itself through its legislature could be later rescinded by the state. The Court held here that the grant of land, even though made under circumstances of the most scandalous corruption, is a contract within the meaning of the constitutional provision and cannot be rescinded by the state after the land in question has passed into the hands of innocent purchasers.

Of far greater significance was the Dartmouth College Case, in which the contract clause was given an even wider application. In 1769 Dartmouth College was chartered by the English Crown. The charter created a college to be governed by a board of trustees but in 1816 the New Hampshire legislature passed a law reorganizing the college as a state university. The trustees of the old college refused to be governed by the law and, undaunted, gathered about them their sympathizers among the professors, hired rooms nearby, and continued to operate as the "college," most of the students remaining loyal to the old regime. The trustees then brought an action to regain control of the college, thus raising the general question of the constitutionality of the reorganizing statute.

The case was argued before the supreme court of New Hampshire in 1817. Little reference was made to the contract clause. The state court decided against the college on the ground that the institution had become public in character and as such was subject to state control. The case was argued before the Supreme Court in 1818. Daniel Webster, a Dartmouth graduate not yet at the height of his fame, represented the college and made an argument which included the now famous quote: "It is a small college and yet there are those who love it." He laid much more emphasis on the necessity of protect-

ing vested rights than upon the contract clause. Rumor has it that the Court was divided in its opinion on the case at the close of the argument and that Marshall, who favored the college, postponed the decision until the next term and in the meantime won over his colleagues to his own position. At the opening of the next term of court the decision was handed down in favor of the college.

The doctrine of this case, that a corporate charter is a contract which may not be impaired by legislative enactment, was criticized because it made it possible for corrupt and ignorant legislatures, in granting charters, irrevocably to grant away privileges and rights contrary to the public interest and welfare. In an economic sense the decision was of great importance in giving to those who invested money in corporate enterprises assurance that the corporations would be free from legislative interference, and it thus encouraged the expansion of business enterprise in the fields of railroad construction, insurance, commerce, and industry.

About ten days after its decision in the Dartmouth College Case, the Court decided another contract clause case with which the business world was deeply concerned. This was the case of Sturges v. Crowninshield (1819), in which the question was raised of whether the New York bankruptcy act impaired the obligation of contracts. There was at this time no federal bankruptcy law. The Court held that the New York statute impaired the obligation of contracts of debt entered into before the act was passed. But in speaking for the Court, Marshall went beyond this and declared his view that the state law was also invalid as applied to contracts made after its passage, a point not before the Court for decision. This dictum, which caused widespread uncertainty and concern, was rejected in Ogden v. Saunders (1827), the first case in which Marshall dissented on a constitutional law question. The Court held that a state bankruptcy law when applied to future debt contracts did not impair the obligation of those contracts. Marshall argued that the obligation of a contract was to be found in the terms of the agreement between the parties and nowhere else; under no circumstances could that agreement be modified by state law. The majority opinion in Ogden was of far-reaching importance. The validity of the so-called "reservation clauses," by which the states retain certain powers to modify or repeal corporate charters or franchises, rests upon it.

With the replacement of Marshall by Chief Justice Taney, the direction of the Court away from the rigid Dartmouth College rule was made clearer. In Charles River Bridge v. Warren Bridge (1837) the Court laid down the important rule that the terms of a charter contract must be strictly construed, and that no rights or privileges can be held to be granted away by the public by mere implication. The Charles River Bridge Company was privately owned, and under a state franchise operated a toll bridge for profit. During the life of this franchise the state incorporated the Warren Bridge Company, which was authorized to build and operate a toll bridge within a few rods of the Charles River Bridge, but

with the stipulation that within a short time it should become a free bridge and part of the public highway. The charter of the Charles River Bridge Company said nothing about its grant being exclusive, but since its business would be ruined by the opening of a free bridge close by, the company plausibly contended that its charter contract, reasonably construed, implied the grant of a monopoly; and the obligation of the contract was therefore impaired by the chartering of the new bridge. The Court rejected this contention. No grant of monopoly can be "read into" a charter, the words of which make no such grant.

In the years that followed, the scope and power of the contract clause dwindled under the pressure of the rising doctrine of "paramount power." This doctrine holds that certain powers possessed by the state are so vital and indispensable to its existence and its power to govern that they cannot be contracted away. If one legislature does contract them away, a subsequent legislature may rescind the agreement and recover the power. This does not violate the contract clause because the state had no authority to contract away this power permanently in the first place.

This doctrine is evident in West River Bridge Co. v. Dix (1848) which held that a state cannot contract away its power of eminent domain. The Supreme Court held that the state could validly condemn the 100-year franchise of a toll bridge company and convert the bridge into a free public highway. This point was even more sharply made in Pennsylvania Hospital v. Philadelphia (1917). In 1845 the hospital secured an agreement with the state that no streets or alleys should ever be opened through its grounds, and in return the hospital granted some land and paid some money to the state. In 1913 the city, under authority from the state, sought to condemn a street through the hospital grounds in plain violation of the 1845 contract. The Court held that the power of eminent domain overrode the contract and the condemnation was valid.

Nor can the state contract away its police power. A lottery corporation had been chartered by the state of Mississippi in 1867 and in 1869 the state's new constitution forbade lotteries. The state sued to close up the lottery, and in Stone v. Mississippi (1880) the Supreme Court held that the constitutional provision did not violate the contract clause. There was, in fact, no real contract, because the state had no power to "bargain away the police power." "Anyone, therefore, who accepts a lottery charter, does so with the implied understanding that the People, in their sovereign capacity . . . may resume it at any time. . . ." It need hardly be emphasized that if the police power of the state may be exercised to override contracts which the state itself has made, it certainly may limit or destroy contracts between private individuals which come within its reach.

The most devastating blow to the contract clause came in 1934 in Home Building & Loan Ass'n. v. Blaisdell, in which the Court upheld the Minnesota Mortgage Moratorium Law. In an effort to alleviate one of the most *pressing problems of the Great Depression, the state had provided a two-year moratorium on the foreclosure of real-estate mortgages, thus making it impossible for banks to dispossess homeowners and small businessmen.*

In upholding the Act, the Court emphasized that the prohibition of the contract clause "is not an absolute one and is not to be read with literal exactness like a mathematical formula. . . . Not only is the constitutional provision qualified by the measure of control which the State retains over remedial processes, but the State also continues to possess authority to safeguard the vital interests of its people. It does not matter that legislation appropriate to that end 'has the result of modifying or abrogating contracts already in effect.' . . . Not only are existing laws read into contracts in order to fix obligations as between the parties, but the reservation of essential attributes of sovereign power is also read into contracts as a postulate of the legal order. The policy of protecting contracts against impairment presupposes the maintenance of a government by virtue of which contractual relations are worthwhile,—a government which retains adequate authority to secure the peace and good order of society. This principle of harmonizing the constitutional prohibition with the necessary residuum of state power has had progressive recognition in the decisions of this Court."

Mr. Chief Justice **Marshall**, in delivering the opinion of the Court, said in part:

This court can be insensible neither to the magnitude nor delicacy of this question. The validity of a legislative act is to be examined; and the opinion of the highest law tribunal of a state is to be revised: an opinion which carries with it intrinsic evidence of the diligence, of the ability, and the integrity, with which it was formed. On more than one occasion this court has expressed the cautious circumspection with which it approaches the consideration of such questions; and has declared that, in no doubtful case would it pronounce a legislative act to be contrary to the constitution. But the American people have said, in the constitution of the United States, that "no state shall pass any bill of attainder, ex post facto law, or law impairing the obligation of contracts." In the same instrument they have also said, "that the judicial power shall extend to all cases in law and equity arising under the constitution." On the judges of this court, then, is imposed the high and solemn duty of protecting, from even legislative violation, those contracts which the constitution of our country has placed beyond legislative control; and however irksome the task may be, this is a duty from which we dare not shrink. . . .

It can require no argument to prove that the circumstances of this case constitute a contract. An application is made to the crown for a charter to incorporate a religious and literary institution. In the application, it is stated that large contributions have been made for the object, which will be conferred on the corporation as soon as it shall be created. The charter is granted, and on its faith the property is conveyed. Surely in this transaction every ingredient of a complete and legitimate contract is to be found.

The points for consideration are: 1. Is this contract protected by the constitution of the United States? 2. Is it impaired by the acts under which the defendant holds?

1. On the first point it has been argued that the word "contract," in its broadest sense, would comprehend the political relations between the government and its citizens, would extend to offices held within a state for state purposes, and to many of those laws concerning civil institutions, which must change with circumstances, and be modified by ordinary legislation; which deeply concern the public, and which, to preserve good government, the public judgment must control. That even marriage is a contract, and its obligations are affected by the laws respecting divorces. That the clause in the constitution, if construed in its greatest latitude, would prohibit these laws. Taken in its broad unlimited sense, the clause would be an unprofitable and vexatious interference with the internal concerns of a state, would unnecessarily and unwisely embarrass its legislation, and render immutable those civil institutions which are established for purposes of internal government, and which, to subserve those purposes, ought to vary with varying circumstances. That as the framers of the constitution could never have intended to insert in that instrument a provision so unnecessary, so mischievous, and so repugnant to its general spirit, the term "contract" must be understood in a more limited sense. That it must be understood as intended to guard against a power of at least doubtful utility, the abuse of which had been extensively felt; and to restrain the legislature in future from violating the right to property. That anterior to the formation of the constitution, a course of legislation had prevailed in many, if not in all, of the states, which weakened the confidence of man in man, and embarrassed all transactions between individuals, by dispensing with a faithful performance of engagements. To correct this mischief, by restraining the power which produced it, the state legislatures were forbidden "to pass any law impairing the obligation of contracts," that is, of contracts respecting property, under which some individual could claim a right to something beneficial to himself; and that since the clause in the constitution must in construction receive some limitation, it may be confined, and ought to be confined, to cases of this description; to cases within the mischief it was intended to remedy.

The general correctness of these observations cannot be controverted. That the framers of the constitution did not intend to restrain the states in the regulation of their civil institutions, adopted for internal government, and that the instrument they have given us is not to be so construed, may be admitted. The provision of the constitution never has been understood to embrace other contracts than those which respect property or some object of value, and confer rights which may be asserted in a court of justice. It never has been understood to restrict the general right of the legislature to legislate on the subject of divorces. Those acts enable some tribunal, not to impair a marriage contract, but to liberate one of the parties because it has been broken by the other. When any state legislature shall pass an act annulling all marriage contracts, or allowing either party to annul it without the consent of the other, it will be time enough to inquire whether such an act be constitutional.

The parties in this case differ less on general principles, less on the true construction of the constitution in the abstract, than on the application of those principles to this case, and on the true construction of the charter of 1769. This is the point on which the cause essentially depends. If the act of incorporation be a grant of political power, if it create a civil institution to be employed in the administration of the government, or if the funds of the college be public property, or if the state of New Hampshire, as a government, be alone interested in its transactions, the subject is one in which the legislature of the state may act according to its own judgment, unrestrained by any limitation of its power imposed by the constitution of the United States.

But if this be a private eleemosynary institution, endowed with a capacity to take property for objects unconnected with government, whose funds are bestowed by individuals on the faith of the charter; if the donors have stipulated for the future disposition and management of those funds in the manner prescribed by themselves, there may be more difficulty in the case, although neither the persons who have made these stipulations nor those for whose benefit they are made, should be parties to the cause. Those who are no longer interested in the property, may yet retain such an interest in the preservation of their own arrangements as to have a right [to] insist that those arrangements shall be held sacred. Or, if they have themselves disappeared, it becomes a subject of serious and anxious inquiry, whether those whom they have legally empowered to represent them forever may not assert all the rights which they possessed, while in being; whether, if they be without personal representatives who may feel injured by a violation of the compact, the trustees be not so completely their representatives, in the eye of the law, as to stand in their place, not only as respects the government of the college, but also as respects the maintenance of the college charter.

It becomes, then, the duty of the court most seriously to examine this charter, and to ascertain its true character. . . .

[In the course of his comment upon the charitable objects of the donors of Dartmouth College occurs Marshall's classic description of a corporation.]

A corporation is an artificial being, invisible, intangible, and existing only in contemplation of law. Being the mere creature of law, it possesses only those properties which the charter of its creation confers upon it, either expressly or as incidental to its very existence. These are such as are supposed best calculated to effect the object for which it was created. Among the most important are immortality, and, if the expression may be allowed, individuality; properties by which a perpetual succession of many persons are considered as the same, and may act as a single individual. They enable a corporation to manage its own affairs, and to hold property

without the perplexing intricacies, the hazardous and endless necessity, of perpetual conveyances for the purpose of transmitting it from hand to hand. It is chiefly for the purpose of clothing bodies of men, in succession, with these qualities and capacities that corporations were invented and are in use. By these means, a perpetual succession of individuals are capable of acting for the promotion of the particular object, like one immortal being. . . .

From this review of the charter, it appears that Dartmouth College is an eleemosynary institution, incorporated for the purpose of perpetuating the application of the bounty of the donors, to the specified objects of that bounty; that its trustees or governors were originally named by the founder, and invested with the power of perpetuating themselves; that they are not public officers, nor is it a civil institution, participating in the administration of government; but a charity school, or a seminary of education, incorporated for the preservation of its property, and the perpetual application of that property to the objects of its creation. . . .

According to the theory of the British constitution, their parliament is omnipotent. To annul corporate rights might give a shock to public opinion, which that government has chosen to avoid; but its power is not questioned. Had parliament, immediately after the emanation of this charter and the execution of those conveyances which followed it, annulled the instrument, so that the living donors would have witnessed the disappointment of their hopes, the perfidy of the transaction would have been universally acknowledged. Yet then, as now, the donors would have had no interest in the property; then, as now, those who might be students would have had no rights to be violated; then, as now, it might be said, that the trustees, in whom the rights of all were combined, possessed no private, individual, beneficial interest in the property confided to their protection. Yet the contract would at that time have been deemed sacred by all. What has since occurred to strip it of its inviolability? Circumstances have not changed it. In reason, in justice, and in law, it is now what it was in 1769.

This is plainly a contract to which the donors, the trustees, and the crown (to whose rights and obligations New Hampshire succeeds), were the original parties. It is a contract made on a valuable consideration. It is a contract for the security and disposition of property. It is a contract, on the faith of which real and personal estate has been conveyed to the corporation. It is then a contract within the letter of the constitution, and within its spirit also, unless the fact that the property is invested by the donors in trustees for the promotion of religion and education, for the benefit of persons who are perpetually changing, though the objects remain the same, shall create a particular exception, taking this case out of the prohibition contained in the constitution.

It is more than possible that the preservation of rights of this description was not particularly in the view of the framers of the constitution when the clause under consideration was introduced into that instrument. It is probable that interferences of more frequent recurrence, to which the temptation was stronger and of which the mischief was more extensive, constituted the great motive for imposing this restriction on the state legislatures. But although a particular and a rare case may not in itself be of sufficient magnitude to induce a rule, yet it must be governed by the rule, when established unless some plain and strong reason for excluding it can be given. It is not enough to say that this particular case was not in the mind of the convention when the article was framed, nor of the American people when it was adopted. It is necessary to go farther, and to say that, had this particular case been suggested, the language would have been so varied as to exclude it, or it would have been made a special exception. The case being within the words of the rule, must be within its operation likewise, unless there be something in the literal construction so obviously absurd, or mischievous, or repugnant to the general spirit of the instrument, as to justify those who expound the constitution in making it an exception.

On what safe and intelligible ground can this exception stand[?] There is no expression in the constitution, no sentiment delivered by its contemporaneous expounders, which would justify us in making it. In the absence of all authority of this kind, is there, in the nature and reason of the case itself, that which would sustain a construction of the constitution, not warranted by its words? Are contracts of this description of a character to excite so little interest that we must exclude them from the provisions of the constitution, as being unworthy of the attention of those who framed the instrument? Or does public policy so imperiously demand their remaining exposed to legislative alteration, as to compel us, or rather permit us to say that these words, which were introduced to give stability to contracts, and which in their plain import comprehend this contract, must yet be so construed as to exclude it?

Almost all eleemosynary corporations, those which are created for the promotion of religion, of charity, or of education, are of the same character. The law of this case is the law of all. . . .

The opinion of the court, after mature deliberation, is, that this is a contract, the obligation of which cannot be impaired without violating the constitution of the United States. This opinion appears to us to be equally supported by reason, and by the former decisions of this court.

2. We next proceed to the inquiry whether its obligation has been impaired by those acts of the legislature of New Hampshire to which the special verdict refers.

From the review of this charter, which has been taken, it appears that the whole power of governing the college, of appointing and removing tutors, of fixing their salaries, of directing the course of study to be pursued by the students, and of filling up vacancies created in their own body, was vested in the trustees. On the part of the crown it was expressly stipulated that this corporation, thus constituted, should continue forever; and that the number of trustees should forever consist of twelve, and no more. By this contract the crown was bound, and could have made no violent alteration in its essential terms without impairing its obligation.

By the revolution, the duties, as well as the powers, of government devolved on the people of New Hampshire. It is admitted, that among the latter was comprehended the transcendent power of parliament, as well as that of the executive department. It is too clear to require the support of argument that all contracts, and rights, respecting property, remained unchanged by the revolution. The obligations, then, which were created by the charter to Dartmouth College, were the same in the new that they had been in the old government. The power of the government was also the same. A repeal of this charter at any time prior to the adoption of the present constitution of the United States, would have been an extraordinary and unprecedented act of power, but one which could have been contested only by the restrictions upon the legislature, to be found in the constitution of the state. But the constitution of the United States has imposed this additional limitation, that the legislature of a state shall pass no act "impairing the obligation of contracts."

It has been already stated that the act "to amend the charter, and enlarge and improve the corporation of Dartmouth College," increases the number of trustees to twenty-one, gives the appointment of the additional members to the executive of the state, and creates a board of overseers, to consist of twenty-five persons, of whom twenty-one are also appointed by the executive of New Hampshire, who have power to inspect and control the most important acts of the trustees.

On the effect of this law two opinions cannot be entertained. Between acting directly, and acting through the agency of trustees and overseers, no essential difference is perceived. The whole power of governing the college is transformed from trustees appointed according to the will of the founder, expressed in the charter, to the executive of New Hampshire. The management and application of the funds of this eleemosynary institution, which are placed by the donors in the hands of trustees named in the charter, and empowered to perpetuate themselves, are placed by this act under the control of the government of the state. The will of the state is substituted for the will of the donors in every essential operation of the college. This is not an immaterial change. The founders of the college contracted, not merely for the perpetual application of the funds which they gave, to the objects for which those funds were given; they contracted also to secure that application by the constitution of the corporation. They contracted for a system which should, as far as human foresight can provide, retain forever the government of the literary institution they had formed, in the hands of persons approved by themselves. This system is totally changed. The charter of 1769 exists no longer. It is reorganized; and reorganized in such a manner as to convert a literary institution, molded according to the will of its founders, and placed under the control of private literary men, into a machine entirely subservient to the will of government. This may be for the advantage of this college in particular, and may be for the advantage of literature in general, but it is not according to the will of the donors, and is subversive of that contract, on the faith of which their property was given.

In the view which has been taken of this interesting case, the court has confined itself to the right possessed by the trustees, as the assignees and representatives of the donors and founders, for the benefit of religion and literature. Yet it is not clear that the trustees ought to be considered as destitute of such beneficial interest in themselves as the law may respect. In addition to their being the legal owners of the property, and to their having a freehold right in the powers confided to them, the charter itself countenances the idea that trustees may also be tutors with salaries. The first president was one of the original trustees; and the charter provides, that in case of vacancy in that office, "the senior professor or tutor, being one of the trustees, shall exercise the office of president, until the trustees shall make choice of, and appoint a president." According to the tenor of the charter, then, the trustees might, without impropriety, appoint a president and other professors from their own body. This is a power not entirely unconnected with an interest. Even if the proposition of the counsel for the defendant were sustained; if it were admitted that those contracts only are protected by the constitution, a beneficial interest in which is vested in the party, who appears in court to assert that interest; yet it is by no means clear that the trustees of Dartmouth College have no beneficial interest in themselves.

But the court has deemed it unnecessary to investigate this particular point, being of opinion, on general principles, that in these private eleemosynary institutions, the body corporate, as possessing the whole legal and equitable interest, and completely representing the donors, for the purpose of executing the trust, has rights which are protected by the constitution.

It results from this opinion, that the acts of the legislature of New Hampshire, which are stated in the special verdict found in this cause, are repugnant to the constitution of the United States; and that the judgment on this special verdict ought to have been for the plaintiffs. The judgment of the State Court must therefore be reversed.

Mr. Justice **Washington** and Mr. Justice **Story** rendered separate concurring opinions.

Mr. Justice **Duvall** dissented.

2

The Nationalization of the Bill of Rights

EARLY EFFORTS TO EXTEND THE BILL OF RIGHTS TO THE STATES

BARRON v. BALTIMORE

7 Peters 243; 8 L. Ed. 672 (1833)

One of the bitter criticisms of our federal Constitution as it came from the hands of the Convention was that it contained no bill of rights. It was feared that without specific guarantees the civil rights and liberties of the people and the states would be at the mercy of the proposed national government. Ratification was secured, but with a tacit understanding that a bill of rights should promptly be added which should restrict the national government in behalf of individual liberty. That the early statesmen thought of a federal bill of rights only in terms of restrictions on national power is emphasized by Hamilton's ingenious argument in The Federalist (No. 84) that since the proposed central government was one which possessed only the powers delegated to it, it would be not only unnecessary but unwise to prohibit it from doing things which were clearly outside the scope of its delegated authority.

When the First Congress convened, the House of Representatives proposed seventeen amendments in the nature of a bill of rights. One of these, the fourteenth, provided that "no state should infringe the right of trial by jury in criminal cases, nor the rights of conscience,
nor the freedom of speech or of the press." (Emphasis added). This amendment, which was the only one restricting the powers of the states, was rejected by the Senate. The substance of the others was consolidated into twelve amendments, ten of which were finally ratified by the states.

The First Amendment indicates by its own language that it is directed only against the federal government, for it begins, "Congress shall make no law. . . ." The other amendments are couched in terms of general prohibition; and in spite of the perfectly clear historical evidence as to the intention of those who framed them, it came to be argued that these guarantees of civil liberty ought to be construed as restrictions upon state and federal governments alike. Whether this view is correct is the issue involved in Barron v. Baltimore, the last constitutional decision in which Chief Justice Marshall participated.

While paving its streets, the city of Baltimore had diverted from their natural courses certain streams, with the result that sand and gravel were deposited near Barron's wharf. The wharf, which had previously enjoyed the deepest water in the harbor, was rendered practically useless, for the deposits prevented the approach of vessels. A verdict of $4500 for Barron had been reversed by the state court of appeals, and a writ of error was taken to the Supreme Court of the United States. It was alleged by Barron that this action upon the part of the city constituted a violation of that clause of the Fifth Amendment which forbids taking private property for public use without just compensation. He insisted that *this amendment, being a guarantee in behalf of individual liberty, ought to be construed to restrain the states as well as the national government.*

The decision in Barron v. Baltimore has left an indelible impression on the development of civil rights in this country. While today Barron would have brought his case under the due process clause of the Fourteenth Amendment (which does restrict the states), the process of change by which parts of the Bill of Rights have come to be applicable to the states has been slow, uncertain, and confusing. Most rights in the Bill of Rights now do apply to the states, but they do so only because they are essential to due process of law. The ruling in the present case that the Bill of Rights does not apply directly to the states has never been overruled.

Mr. Chief Justice **Marshall** delivered the opinion of the court:

The judgment brought up by this writ of error having been rendered by the court of a State, this tribunal can exercise no jurisdiction over it unless it be shown to come within the provisions of the twenty-fifth section of the Judicial Act.

The plaintiff in error contends that it comes within that clause in the fifth amendment to the Constitution which inhibits the taking of private property for public use without just compensation. He insists that this amendment, being in favor of the liberty of the citizen, ought to be so construed as to restrain the legislative power of a State, as well as that of the United States. If this proposition be untrue, the court can take no jurisdiction of the cause.

The question thus presented is, we think, of great importance, but not of much difficulty.

The Constitution was ordained and established by the people of the United States for themselves, for their own government, and not for the government of the individual States. Each State established a constitution for itself, and in that constitution provided such limitations and restrictions on the powers of its particular government as its judgment dictated. The people of the United States framed such a government for the United States as they supposed best adapted to their situation, and best calculated to promote their interests. The powers they conferred on this government were to be exercised by itself; and the limitations on power, if expressed in general terms, are naturally, and, we think, necessarily applicable to the government created by the instrument. They are limitations of power granted in the instrument itself; not of distinct governments, framed by different persons and for different purposes.

If these propositions be correct, the fifth amendment must be understood as restraining the power of the general government, not as applicable to the States. In their several constitutions they have imposed such restrictions on their respective governments as their own wisdom suggested; such as they deemed most proper for themselves. It is a subject on which they judge exclu-

sively, and with which others interfere no farther than they are supposed to have a common interest.

The counsel for the plaintiff in error insists that the Constitution was intended to secure the people of the several States against the undue exercise of power by their respective State governments; as well as against that which might be attempted by their general government. In support of this argument he relies on the inhibitions contained in the tenth section of the first article.

We think that section affords a strong if not a conclusive argument in support of the opinion already indicated by the court.

The preceding section contains restrictions which are obviously intended for the exclusive purpose of restraining the exercise of power by the departments of the general government. Some of them use language applicable only to Congress; others are expressed in general terms. The third clause, for example, declares that "no bill of attainder or ex post facto law shall be passed." No language can be more general; yet the demonstration is complete that it applies solely to the government of the United States. In addition to the general arguments furnished by the instrument itself, some of which have been already suggested, the succeeding section, the avowed purpose of which is to restrain State legislation, contains in terms the very prohibition. It declares that "no State shall pass any bill of attainder or ex post facto law." This provision, then, of the ninth section, however comprehensive its language, contains no restriction on State legislation.

The ninth section having enumerated, in the nature of a bill of rights, the limitations intended to be imposed on the powers of the general government, the tenth proceeds to enumerate those which were to operate on the State legislatures. These restrictions are brought together in the same section, and are by express words applied to the States. "No State shall enter into any treaty," etc. Perceiving that in a constitution framed by the people of the United States for the government of all, no limitation of the action of government on the people would apply to the State government, unless expressed in terms; the restrictions contained in the tenth section are in direct words so applied to the States.

It is worthy of remark, too, that these inhibitions generally restrain State legislation on subjects intrusted to the general government, or in which the people of all the States feel an interest.

A State is forbidden to enter into any treaty, alliance or confederation. If these compacts are with foreign nations, they interfere with the treaty-making power which is conferred entirely on the general government; if with each other, for political purposes, they can scarcely fail to interfere with the general purpose and intent of the Constitution. To grant letters of marque and reprisal would lead directly to war, the power of declaring which is expressly given to Congress. To coin money is also the exercise of a power conferred on Congress. It would be tedious to recapitulate the several limitations on the powers of the States which are contained in this section. They will be found, generally, to restrain State legislation on subjects intrusted to the government of the Union, in which the citizens of all the States are interested. In these alone were the whole people concerned. The question of their application to States is not left to construction. It is averred in positive words.

If the original Constitution, in the ninth and tenth sections of the first article, draws this plain and marked line of discrimination between the limitations it imposes on the powers of the general government and on those of the States; if in every inhibition intended to act on State power, words are employed which directly express that intent, some strong reason must be assigned for departing from this safe and judicious course in framing the amendments, before that departure can be assumed.

We search in vain for that reason.

Had the people of the several States, or any of them, required changes in their constitutions; had they required additional safeguards to liberty from the apprehended encroachments of their particular governments, the remedy was in their own hands, and would have been applied by themselves. A convention would have been assembled by the discontented State, and the required improvements would have been made by itself. The unwieldy and cumbrous machinery of procuring a recommendation from two-thirds of Congress, and the assent of three-fourths of their sister States, could never have occurred to any human being as a mode of doing that which might be effected by the State itself. Had the framers of these amendments intended them to be limitations on the powers of the State governments they would have imitated the framers of the original Constitution, and have expressed that intention. Had Congress engaged in the extraordinary occupation of improving the constitutions of the several States by affording the people additional protection from the exercise of power by their own governments in matters which concerned themselves alone, they would have declared this purpose in plain and intelligible language.

But it is universally understood, it is a part of the history of the day, that the great revolution which established the Constitution of the United States was not effected without immense opposition. Serious fears were extensively entertained that those powers which the patriot statesmen who then watched over the interests of our country, deemed essential to union, and to the attainment of those invaluable objects for which union was sought, might be exercised in a manner dangerous to liberty. In almost every convention by which the Constitution was adopted, amendments to guard against the abuse of power were recommended. These amendments demanded security against the apprehended encroachments of the general government—not against those of the local governments.

In compliance with a sentiment thus generally expressed, to quiet fears thus extensively entertained, amendments were proposed by the required majority in Congress, and adopted by the States. These amendments contain no expression indicating an intention to apply them to the State governments. This court cannot so apply them.

We are of opinion that the provision in the fifth amendment to the Constitution, declaring that private property shall not be taken for public use without just compensation, is intended solely as a limitation on the exercise of power by the government of the United States, and is not applicable to the legislation of the States. We are therefore of opinion that there is no repugnancy between the several acts of the General Assembly of Maryland, given in evidence by the defendants at the trial of this cause in the court of that State, and the Constitution of the United States.

This court, therefore, has no jurisdiction of the cause, and [it] is dismissed.

SUBSTANTIVE DUE PROCESS AND THE POLICE POWER

MUNN v. ILLINOIS

94 U. S. 133; 24 L. Ed. 77 (1877)

At the time the Fourteenth Amendment was adopted the due process clause of the Fifth Amendment had been in effect against the federal government for three-quarters of a century. During that entire period the Supreme Court had decided only four or five cases interpreting the clause, but from Coke and Blackstone the ancient lineage and narrow meaning of the clause were abundantly clear. The clause traces its beginning to the guarantee embodied in Magna Charta that "no freeman shall be taken or imprisoned or deprived of his freehold or his liberties or free customs, or outlawed or exiled, or in any manner destroyed, nor shall we come upon him or send against him, except by a legal judgment of his peers or by the law of the land." With the reaffirmation of these guarantees in the Statute of Westminster (1354) Ed. III, "per legem terrae" became "due process of the law," although at the time of the adoption of the Bill of Rights the eight state constitutions providing such protection used the term "law of the land." Whichever words were used, the guarantee involved was the same: the government was forbidden to limit in any way the individual's personal or property rights unless it did so through proper procedures. In short, it was a check not on what the government could do, but on the process it had to follow in order to do it.

This "procedural" due process was the only kind of due process there was until after the middle of the nineteenth century, when pressure from important property interests for a "substantive" content to the due process clause began to make itself felt. Among the leading purposes for which the United States Constitution had been framed was the protection of private property from the attacks of the "too-popular" state governments. Hence those with vested property rights looked from the beginning to the judicially enforceable Consti-

tution to protect them from legislation, particularly state legislation. They turned first to the protection against bills of attainder and ex post facto laws, but in Calder v. Bull (1798) the Supreme Court held that the ex post facto clause applied only to criminal legislation. Better luck was had with the contract clause, and in such cases as Fletcher v. Peck (1810) and the Dartmouth College Case (1819) the Court held that a vested right implied a contract not to divest it or interfere with its exercise. But with the passing of Chief Justice Marshall the strength of even this doctrine began to wane. In Charles River Bridge v. Warren Bridge (1837) the Court under Taney made clear that henceforth contracts would be strictly construed in favor of the people and against the vested interests; and much later, in Stone v. Mississippi (1880), the Court held that the police power to legislate in the public interest could not be limited by the contract clause.

So it was natural that pressure should mount to persuade the courts that the guarantee of due process of law should provide constitutional protection to the vested interests. In 1856 in Wynhammer v. New York a state court finally struck down a provision of a state prohibition statute as a denial of due process of law because the law provided for the confiscation of stocks of liquor in possession when the law took effect. The court's basic premise was that liquor was property which could not be transformed into a nuisance merely by the whim of the legislature; hence a statute providing for its confiscation was void, even though the procedures by which the confiscation took place followed "the forms which belong to due process of law." The court said, "The act . . . itself pronounces the sentence of condemnation, and the judicial machinery, such as it is, which it provides are agencies merely to insure the execution of the sentence."

This theory that the substance of a law itself could be held void for want of due process made its way slowly into the Supreme Court. In 1857, Chief Justice Taney in the Dred Scott case, after holding the Missouri Compromise Act void on a number of grounds, added that "an act of Congress which deprives a citizen of the United States of his liberty or property merely because he came himself or brought his property into a particular territory of the United States and who had committed no offense against the laws could hardly be dignified with the name of due process of law." But the Court was not yet ready to receive the doctrine. Justice Miller rejected it in the Slaughter-House Cases (1873); and in 1875 in Loan Association v. Topeka, the Court, instead of relying on the due process clause, held bad the expenditure of public money for a private purpose on the ground that this was a violation of those limits on governmental power "which grow out of the essential nature of all free governments; implied reservations of individual rights, without which the social compact could not exist. . . ." Again in 1878 in Davidson v. New Orleans, the Court made clear its attitude toward due process, going so far as to scold the bar for pressing upon them this new concept of due process. "There is here abundant evidence that there exists some strange misconception of the scope of

this provision as found in the Fourteenth Amendment. In fact, it would seem, from the character of many of the cases before us, and the arguments made in them, that the clause under consideration is looked upon as a means of bringing to the test of the decision of this court the abstract opinions of every unsuccessful litigant in a State court of the justice of the decision against him, and of the merits of the legislation on which such a decision may be founded."

The present case was the first of a famous group of cases known as the "Granger Cases," which brought to the Supreme Court for the first time the important question of the right of a state legislature to regulate private business. The close of the Civil War ushered in a period of rapid railroad expansion. In the East, where industrial development tended to keep pace with the multiplication of transportation facilities, railroad building proved satisfactorily profitable. In the West, however, where new country was being opened up and population was sparse, the railroads had difficulty in paying dividends and frequently yielded to the temptation to indulge in stock-watering, questionable manipulation of credits, and doubtful practices in respect to grants of lands; to rebating and discrimination; and to other objectionable practices. Pitted against the desperate efforts of the railroads to make profits was the Western farmer, who wished to enjoy adequate railroad facilities at reasonable rates in order to facilitate the movement of crops in sparsely settled communities and who resented the unfair or dishonest methods of which some of the roads were known to be guilty. Out of this conflict of interests grew the Granger Movement, an organized effort on the part of the Western farmers which finally culminated in state legislation designed to cure the worst abuses. Starting in Illinois in 1871, the movement spread to other states; and soon railroads and warehousemen in Minnesota, Iowa, and Wisconsin found themselves subject to severe regulation with respect to rates and services. It was these laws which were challenged in the Granger Cases.

The present case involved an Illinois statute requiring the licensing of grain elevators and fixing the prices they could charge for the storage of grain. Munn was one of a group of elevator owners in Chicago who annually got together and fixed the prices to be charged by the elevators in the city during the coming year. The prices set by the law were lower than those set by the owners, and Munn refused to take out a license or submit to the regulation.

Mr. Chief Justice **Waite** delivered the opinion of the Court, saying in part:

Every statute is presumed to be constitutional. The courts ought not to declare one to be unconstitutional, unless it is clearly so. If there is doubt, the expressed will of the Legislature should be sustained.

The Constitution contains no definition of the word "deprive," as used in the 14th Amendment. To determine its signification, therefore, it is necessary to ascertain the effect which usage has given it, when employed in the same or a like connection.

While this provision of the Amendment is new in the Constitution of the United States as a limitation upon the powers of the States, it is old as a principle of civilized government. It is found in Magna Charta, and, in substance if not in form, in nearly or quite all the constitutions that have been from time to time adopted by the several States of the Union. By the 5th Amendment, it was introduced into the Constitution of the United States as a limitation upon the powers of the National Government, and by the 14th, as a guaranty against any encroachment upon an acknowledged right of citizenship by the Legislatures of the States. . . .

When one becomes a member of society, he necessarily parts with some rights or privileges which, as an individual not affected by his relations to others, he might retain. "A body politic," as aptly defined in the preamble of the Constitution of Massachusetts, "is a social compact by which the whole people covenants with each citizen, and each citizen with the whole people, that all shall be governed by certain laws for the common good." This does not confer power upon the whole people to control rights which are purely and exclusively private . . . , but it does authorize the establishment of laws requiring each citizen to so conduct himself, and so use his own property as not unnecessarily to injure another. This is the very essence of government, and has found expression in the maxim, Sic utere tuo ut alienum non laedas. From this source come the police powers, which . . . [a]re nothing more or less than the powers of government inherent in every sovereignty, . . . that is to say, . . . the power to govern men and things." Under these powers the government regulates the conduct of its citizens one towards another, and the manner in which each shall use his own property, when such regulation becomes necessary for the public good. In their exercise it has been customary in England from time immemorial, and in this country from its first colonization, to regulate ferries, common carriers, hackmen, bakers, millers, wharfingers, innkeepers, etc., and in so doing to fix a maximum of charge to be made for services rendered, accommodations furnished, and articles sold. To this day, statutes are to be found in many of the states upon some or all these subjects; and we think it has never yet been successfully contended that such legislation came within any of the constitutional prohibitions against interference with private property. . . .

From this it is apparent that, down to the time of the adoption of the 14th Amendment, it was not supposed that statutes regulating the use, or even the price of the use, of private property necessarily deprived an owner of his property without due process of law. Under some circumstances they may, but not under all. The Amendment does not change the law in this particular; it simply prevents the states from doing that which will operate as such a deprivation.

This brings us to inquire as to the principles upon which this power of regulation rests, in order that we may determine what is within and what without its op-

erative effect. Looking, then, to the common law, from whence came the right which the Constitution protects, we find that when private property is "affected with a public interest, it ceases to be juris privati only." This was said by Lord Chief Justice Hale more than two hundred years ago. . . . Property does become clothed with a public interest when used in a manner to make it of public consequence, and affect the community at large. When, therefore, one devotes his property to a use in which the public has an interest, he, in effect, grants to the public an interest in that use, and must submit to be controlled by the public for the common good, to the extent of the interest he has thus created. He may withdraw his grant by discontinuing the use; but, so long as he maintains the use, he must submit to the control. . . .

And the same has been held as to warehouses and warehousemen. . . .

From the same source comes the power to regulate the charges of common carriers, which was done in England as long ago as the third year of the reign of William and Mary, and continued until within a comparatively recent period. . . .

Common carriers exercise a sort of public office, and have duties to perform in which the public is interested. . . .

Their business is, therefore, "affected with a public interest," within the meaning of the doctrine which Lord Hale has so forcibly stated.

But we need not go further. Enough has already been said to show that, when private property is devoted to a public use, it is subject to public regulation. It remains only to ascertain whether the warehouses of these plaintiffs in error, and the business which is carried on there, come within the operation of this principle.

For this purpose we accept as true the statements of fact contained in the elaborate brief of one of the counsel of the plaintiffs in error. From these it appears that ". . . The quantity (of grain) received in Chicago has made it the greatest grain market in the world. This business has created a demand for means by which the immense quantity of grain can be handled or stored, and these have been found in grain warehouses. . . . In this way the largest traffic between the citizens of the country north and west of Chicago, and the citizens of the country lying on the Atlantic coast north of Washington is in grain which passes through the elevators of Chicago. In this way the trade in grain is carried on by the inhabitants of seven or eight of the great States of the West with four or five of the States lying on the seashore, and forms the largest part of interstate commerce in these States. The grain warehouses or elevators in Chicago are immense structures, holding from 300,000 to 1,000,000 bushels at one time, according to size. . . . It has been found impossible to preserve each owner's grain separate, and this has given rise to a system of inspection and grading, by which the grain of different owners is mixed, and receipts issued for the number of bushels which are negotiable, and redeemable in like kind, upon demand. This mode of conducting the business was inaugurated more than twenty years ago, and has grown to immense proportions. The railways have found it impracticable to own such elevators, and public policy forbids the transaction of such business by the carrier; the ownership has, therefore, been by private individuals, who have embarked their capital and devoted their industry to such business as a private pursuit.''

In this connection it must also be borne in mind that, although in 1874 there were in Chicago fourteen warehouses adapted to this particular business, and owned by about thirty persons, nine business firms controlled them, and that the prices charged and received for storage were such ''as have been from year to year agreed upon and established by the different elevators or warehouses in the city of Chicago, and which rates have been annually published in one or more newspapers printed in said city, in the month of January in each year, as the established rates for the year then next ensuing such publication.'' Thus it is apparent that all the elevating facilities through which these vast productions ''of seven or eight great States of the West'' must pass on the way ''to four or five of the States on the seashore'' may be a ''virtual'' monopoly.

Under such circumstances it is difficult to see why, if the common carrier, or the miller, or the ferryman, or the innkeeper, or the wharfinger, or the baker, or the cartman, or the hackney-coachman, pursues a public employment and exercises ''a sort of public office,'' these plaintiffs in error do not. They stand, to use again the language of their counsel, in the very ''gateway of commerce,'' and take toll from all who pass. Their business most certainly ''tends to a common charge, and is become a thing of public interest and use.'' ... Certainly, if any business can be clothed ''with a public interest, and cease to be juris privati only,'' this has been. It may not be made so by the operation of the Constitution of Illinois or this statute, but it is by the facts.

We also are not permitted to overlook the fact that, for some reason, the people of Illinois, when they revised their Constitution in 1870, saw fit to make it the duty of the general assembly to pass laws ''for the protection of producers, shippers and receivers of grain and produce,'' Art. XIII., sec. 7; and by sec. 5 of the same article, to require all railroad companies receiving and transporting grain in bulk or otherwise to deliver the same at any elevator to which it might be consigned, that could be reached by any track that was or could be used by such company, and that all railroad companies should permit connections to be made with their tracks, so that any public warehouse, etc., might be reached by the cars on their railroads. This indicates very clearly that during the twenty years in which this peculiar business had been assuming its present ''immense proportions,'' something had occurred which led the whole body of the people to suppose that remedies such as are usually employed to prevent abuses by virtual monopolies might not be inappropriate here. For our purposes we must assume that, if a state of facts could exist that would justify such legislation, it actually did exist when the statute now under consideration was passed. For us the question is one of power, not of expediency. If no state of circumstances

could exist to justify such a statute, then we may declare this one void, because in excess of the legislative power of the State. But if it could, we must presume it did. Of the propriety of legislative interference within the scope of legislative power, the Legislature is the exclusive judge.

Neither is it a matter of any moment that no precedent can be found for a statute precisely like this. It is conceded that the business is one of recent origin, that its growth has been rapid, and that it is already of great importance. And it must also be conceded that it is a business in which the whole public has a direct and positive interest. It presents, therefore, a case for the application of a long known and well established principle in social science, and this statute simply extends the law so as to meet this new development of commercial progress. There is no attempt to compel these owners to grant the public an interest in their property, but to declare their obligations, if they use it in this particular manner.

It matters not in this case that these plaintiffs in error had built their warehouses and established their business before the regulations complained of were adopted. What they did was, from the beginning, subject to the power of the body politic to require them to conform to such regulations as might be established by the proper authorities for the common good. They entered upon their business and provided themselves with the means to carry it on subject to this condition. If they did not wish to submit themselves to such interference, they should not have clothed the public with an interest in their concerns. ...

It is insisted, however, that the owner of property is entitled to a reasonable compensation for its use, even though it be clothed with a public interest, and that what is reasonable is a judicial and not a legislative question.

As has already been shown, the practice has been otherwise. In countries where the common law prevails, it has been customary from time immemorial for the Legislature to declare what shall be a reasonable compensation under such circumstances, or, perhaps more properly speaking, to fix a maximum beyond which any charge made would be unreasonable. Undoubtedly, in mere private contracts, relating to matters in which the public has no interest, what is reasonable must be ascertained judicially. But this is because the Legislature has no control over such a contract. So, too, in matters which do affect the public interest, and as to which legislative control may be exercised, if there are no statutory regulations upon the subject, the courts must determine what is reasonable. The controlling fact is the power to regulate at all. If that exists, the right to establish the maximum of charge, as one of the means of regulation, is implied. In fact, the common law rule, which requires the charge to be reasonable, is itself a regulation as to price. Without it the owner could make his rates at will, and compel the public to yield to his terms, or forego the use.

But a mere common law regulation of trade or business may be changed by statute. A person has no property, no vested interest, in any rule of the common law. That is only one of the forms of municipal law, and is no more sacred than any other. Rights of property which have been created by the common law cannot be taken away without due process; but the law itself, as a rule of conduct, may be changed at the will, or even at the whim, of the Legislature, unless prevented by constitutional limitations. Indeed, the great office of statutes is to remedy defects in the common law as they are developed, and to adapt it to the changes of time and circumstances. To limit the rate of charge for services rendered in a public employment, or for the use of property in which the public has an interest, is only changing a regulation which existed before. It establishes no new principle in the law, but only gives a new effect to an old one.

We know that this is a power which may be abused; but that is no argument against its existence. For protection against abuses by Legislatures the people must resort to the polls, not to the courts. . . .

We conclude, therefore, that the statute in question is not repugnant to the Constitution of the United States, and that there is no error in the judgment. . . . Judgment affirmed.

Mr. Justice **Field**, with Mr. Justice **Strong** concurring, dissenting, said in part:

I am compelled to dissent from the decision of the court in this case, and from the reasons upon which that decision is founded. The principle upon which the opinion of the majority proceeds is, in my judgment, subversive of the rights of private property, heretofore believed to be protected by constitutional guaranties against legislative interference, and is in conflict with the authorities cited in its support. . . .

The declaration of the Constitution of 1870, that private buildings used for private purposes shall be deemed public institutions, does not make them so. The receipt and storage of grain in a building erected by private means for that purpose does not constitute the building a public warehouse. There is no magic in the language, though used by a constitutional convention, which can change a private business into a public one, or alter the character of the building in which the business is transacted. . . . One might as well attempt to change the nature of colors, by giving them a new designation. . . .

If this be sound law, if there be no protection, either in the principles upon which our republican government is founded, or in the prohibitions of the Constitution against such invasion of private rights, all property and all business in the State are held at the mercy of a majority of its Legislature. The public has no greater interest in the use of buildings for the storage of grain than it has in the use of buildings for the residences of families, nor, indeed, anything like so great an interest; and, according to the doctrine announced, the Legislature may fix the rent of all tenements used for residences, without reference to the cost of their erection. If the owner does not like the rates prescribed, he may cease renting his houses. . . .

By the term "liberty," as used in the provisions, something more is meant than mere freedom from physical restraint or the bounds of a prison. It means freedom to go where one may choose, and to act in such manner, not inconsistent with the equal rights of others, as his judgment may dictate for the promotion of his happiness, that is, to pursue such callings and avocations as may be most suitable to develop his capacities, and to give them their highest enjoyment.

The same liberal construction which is required for the protection of life and liberty, in all particulars in which life and liberty are of any value, should be applied to the protection of private property. If the Legislature of a State, under pretense of providing for the public good, or for any other reason, can determine, against the consent of the owner, the uses to which private property shall be devoted, or the prices which the owner shall receive for its uses, it can deprive him of the property as completely as by a special Act for its confiscation or destruction. . . .

There is nothing in the character of the business of the defendants as warehousemen which called for the interference complained of in this case. Their buildings are not nuisances; their occupation of receiving and storing grain infringes upon no rights of others, disturbs no neighborhood, infects not the air, and in no respect prevents others from using and enjoying their property as to them may seem best. The legislation in question is nothing less than a bold assertion of absolute power by the State to control, at its discretion, the property and business of the citizen, and fix the compensation he shall receive. The will of the Legislature is made the condition upon which the owner shall receive the fruits of his property and the just reward of his labor, industry and enterprise. "That government," says Story, "can scarcely be deemed to be free where the rights of property are left solely dependent upon the will of a legislative body without any restraint. The fundamental maxims of a free government seem to require that the rights of personal liberty and private property should be held sacred." Wilkinson v. Leland [1829]. The decision of the court in this case gives unrestrained license to legislative will.

NEBBIA v. NEW YORK

291 U. S. 502; 54 S. Ct. 505; 78 L. Ed. 940
(1934)

The acceptance by the Supreme Court of "substantive" due process, in addition to the earlier exclusively "procedural" due process, took place gradually over a period of nearly twenty years as cases involving the validity of state laws came before it. The change came first in the area of rate controls. Within a decade after the Munn case (1877) the Court started to backtrack from Chief Justice Waite's dictum in that case—that the only appeal from an unjust rate was to elect a new legislature to enact a just one. In the Railroad Commission Cases (Stone

v. Farmers' Loan & Trust Co., 1886) the Court, while confirming the legislature's power to regulate rates, added that "this power to regulate is not a power to destroy, and limitation is not the equivalent of confiscation. Under pretense of regulating fares and freights, the State cannot require a railroad corporation to carry persons or property without reward; neither can it do that which in law amounts to taking of private property for public use without just compensation, or without due process of law." Thus the legislature is apparently forbidden by due process to enact a regulatory measure which in substance is unreasonable. For over fifty years following Stone the courts had the last word as to what rates set for regulated industries were fair. Finally, in Federal Power Comm. v. Hope Natural Gas Co., it abandoned its earlier policy of scrutinizing the precise formula by which rates were fixed. Noting that the value of a company depends on the rates it is allowed to charge, the Court indicated that henceforth it would judge the rate in terms of its general effect on the business, and leave to the proper agency the method by which the rate was to be set.

In Munn v. Illinois and the cases which followed it, the Court established the doctrine that the government could regulate prices and control terms of service (within limits) only of businesses which were "affected with a public interest." To impose these regulations upon a business not affected with a public interest was to deprive it of its liberty and property without due process of law. This doctrine seemed fair on its face and comported with the tradition of American individualism. But what is a business "affected with a public interest"? The Court found it difficult to answer this question because as cases involving it arose, it became obvious that there was no single characteristic by which a business so affected with a public interest could invariably be identified. In Wolff Packing Co. v. Industrial Court (1923), holding that a meat-packing establishment is not a business affected with public interest, Chief Justice Taft went on to say that such businesses fall into three categories. These are as follows: "(1) Those which are carried on under the authority of a public grant of privileges which either expressly or impliedly imposes the affirmative duty of rendering a public service demanded by any member of the public. Such are the railroads, other common carriers and public utilities. (2) Certain occupations, regarded as exceptional, the public interest attaching to which, recognized from earliest times, has survived the period of arbitrary laws by Parliament or colonial legislatures for regulating all trades and callings. Such are those of the keepers of inns, cabs, and gristmills. . . . (3) Businesses which, though not public at their inception, may be fairly said to have risen to be such, and have become subject in consequence to some government regulation. They have come to hold such a peculiar relation to the public that this is superimposed upon them. In the language of the cases, the owner by devoting his business to the public use, in effect grants the public an interest in that use, and subjects himself to public regulation to the extent of that interest, although the property continues to belong to its private owner, and to be entitled to protection accordingly." None of this seemed very helpful as a guide for the decision of future cases.

The continued application of so vague a judicial test did not fail to produce criticism, and some of the sharpest of this came from the members of the Court itself. In a powerful dissenting opinion in Ribnik v. McBride (1928), Justice Stone declared: "[Price] . . . regulation is within the state's power whenever any combination of circumstances seriously curtails the regulative force of competition, so that buyers or sellers are placed at such a disadvantage in the bargaining struggle that a legislature might reasonably anticipate serious consequences to the community as a whole." And in his dissenting opinion in New State Ice Co. v. Liebmann (1932), Justice Brandeis struck out boldly with the assertion: "The notion of a distinct category of business 'affected with a public interest' employing property 'devoted to a public use' rests upon historical error. . . . In my opinion, the true principle is that the State's power extends to every regulation of any business reasonably required and appropriate for the public protection. I find in the due process clause no other limitation upon the character or the scope of regulation permissible."

These minority views finally prevailed in the area of rate-making. The Nebbia case printed below abandons entirely the concept of a business affected with a public interest as the constitutional test of price control. The milk business admittedly is not affected with a public interest in the traditional sense. Price control is merely a phase of the police power of the state subject only to the limitations of due process of law upon arbitrary interference with liberty and property.

Mr. Justice **Roberts** delivered the opinion of the Court, saying in part:

The Legislature of New York established a Milk Control Board with power, among other things, to "fix minimum and maximum . . . retail prices to be charged by . . . stores to consumers for consumption off the premises where sold." The Board fixed nine cents as the price to be charged by a store for a quart of milk. Nebbia, the proprietor of a grocery store in Rochester, sold two quarts and a five cent loaf of bread for eighteen cents; and was convicted for violating the Board's order. At his trial he asserted the statute and order contravene the equal protection clause and the due process clause. . . .

The question for decision is whether the Federal Constitution prohibits a state from so fixing the selling price of milk. We first inquire as to the occasion for the legislation and its history.

During 1932 the prices received by farmers for milk were much below the cost of production. The decline in prices during 1931 and 1932 was much greater than that of prices generally. The situation of the families of dairy producers had become desperate and called for state aid similar to that afforded the unemployed, if conditions should not improve.

On March 10, 1932, the senate and assembly resolved "That a joint legislative committee is hereby created . . . to investigate the causes of the decline of the price of milk to producers and the resultant effect of the low prices upon the dairy industry. . . ."

In part those conclusions [of the committee] are:

Milk is an essential item of diet. It cannot long be stored. It is an excellent medium for growth of bacteria. These facts necessitate safeguards in its production and handling for human consumption which greatly increase the cost of the business. Failure of producers to receive a reasonable return for their labor and investment over an extended period threatens a relaxation of vigilance against contamination.

The production and distribution of milk is a paramount industry of the state, and largely affects the health and prosperity of its people. Dairying yields fully one-half of the total income from all farm products. Dairy farm investment amounts to approximately $1,000,000. Curtailment or destruction of the dairy industry would cause a serious economic loss to the people of the state.

In addition to the general price decline, other causes for the low price of milk include a periodic increase in the number of cows and in milk production, the prevalence of unfair and destructive trade practices in the distribution of milk, leading to a demoralization of prices in the metropolitan area and other markets, and the failure of transportation and distribution charges to be reduced in proportion to the reduction in retail prices for milk and cream.

The fluid milk industry is affected by factors of instability peculiar to itself which call for special methods of control. . . . [The Court here analyzes these factors in detail.]

The legislature adopted Chapter 158 [creating a Milk Control Board with power to fix prices] as a method of correcting the evils, which the report of the committee showed could not be expected to right themselves through the ordinary play of the forces of supply and demand, owing to the peculiar and uncontrollable factors affecting the industry. . . .

First. The appellant urges that the order of the Milk Control Board denies him the equal protection of the laws. It is shown that the order requires him, if he purchases his supply from a dealer, to pay eight cents per quart and five cents per pint, and to resell at not less than nine and six, whereas the same dealer may buy his supply from a farmer at lower prices and deliver milk to consumers at ten cents the quart and six cents the pint. We think the contention that the discrimination deprives the appellant of equal protection is not well founded. For aught that appears, the appellant purchased his supply of milk from a farmer as do distributors, or could have procured it from a farmer if he so desired. There is therefore no showing that the order placed him at a disadvantage, or in fact affected him adversely, and this alone is fatal to the claim of denial of equal protection. But if it were shown that the appellant is compelled to buy from a distributor, the difference in the retail price he is required to charge his customers from that prescribed for sales by

distributors is not on its face arbitrary or unreasonable, for there are obvious distinctions between the two sorts of merchants which may well justify a difference of treatment, if the legislature possesses the power to control the prices to be charged for fluid milk. . . .

Second. The more serious question is whether in the light of the conditions disclosed, . . . [the price-regulation] denied the appellant the due process secured to him by the Fourteenth amendment. . . .

Under our form of government the use of property and the making of contracts are normally matters of private and not of public concern. The general rule is that both shall be free of governmental interference. But neither property rights nor contract rights are absolute; for government cannot exist if the citizen may at will use his property to the detriment of his fellows, or exercise his freedom of contract to work them harm. Equally fundamental with the private right is that of the public to regulate it in the common interest. . . .

The milk industry in New York has been the subject of long-standing and drastic regulation in the public interest. The legislative investigation of 1932 was persuasive of the fact that for this and other reasons unrestricted competition aggravated existing evils and the normal law of supply and demand was insufficient to correct maladjustments detrimental to the community. The inquiry disclosed destructive and demoralizing competitive conditions and unfair trade practices which resulted in retail price cutting and reduced the income of the farmer below the cost of production. We do not understand the appellant to deny that in these circumstances the legislature might reasonably consider further regulation and control desirable for protection of the industry and the consuming public. That body believed conditions could be improved by preventing destructive price-cutting by stores which, due to the flood of surplus milk, were able to buy at much lower prices than the larger distributors and to sell without incurring the delivery costs of the latter. In the order of which complaint is made the Milk Control Board fixed a price of ten cents per quart for sales by a distributor to a consumer, and nine cents by a store to a consumer, thus recognizing the lower costs of the store, and endeavoring to establish a differential which would be just to both. In the light of the facts the order appears not to be unreasonable or arbitrary, or without relation to the purpose to prevent ruthless competition from destroying the wholesale price structure on which the farmer depends for his livelihood, and the community for an assured supply of milk.

But we are told that because the law essays to control prices it denies due process. Notwithstanding the admitted power to correct existing economic ills by appropriate regulation of business, even though an indirect result may be a restriction of the freedom of contract or a modification of charges for services or the price of commodities, the appellant urges that direct fixation of prices is a type of regulation absolutely forbidden. His position is that the Fourteenth Amendment requires us to hold the challenged statute void for this reason alone. The argument runs that the public control of rates or prices is per se unreasonable and unconstitutional, save as applied to businesses affected with a public interest; that a business so affected is one in which property is devoted to an enterprise of a sort which the public itself might appropriately undertake, or one whose owner relies on a public grant or franchise for the right to conduct the business, or in which he is bound to serve all who apply; in short, such as is commonly called a public utility; or a business in its nature a monopoly. The milk industry, it is said, possesses none of these characteristics, and, therefore, not being affected with a public interest, its charges may not be controlled by the state. Upon the soundness of this contention the appellant's case against the statute depends.

We may as well say at once that the dairy industry is not, in the accepted sense of the phrase, a public utility. We think the appellant is also right in asserting that there is in this case no suggestion of any monopoly or monopolistic practice. It goes without saying that those engaged in the business are in no way dependent upon public grants or franchises for the privilege of conducting their activities. But if, as must be conceded, the industry is subject to regulation in the public interest, what constitutional principle bars the state from correcting existing maladjustments by legislation touching prices? We think there is no such principle. The due process clause makes no mention of sales or of prices any more than it speaks of business or contracts or buildings or other incidents of property. The thought seems nevertheless to have persisted that there is something peculiarly sacrosanct about the price one may charge for what he makes or sells, and that, however able to regulate other elements of manufacture or trade, with incidental effect upon price, the state is incapable of directly controlling the price itself. This view was negatived many years ago. Munn v. Illinois [1877]. . . . [Here follows an analysis of the Munn case in which it is pointed out that the Court therein regarded the term "affected with a public interest" as the equivalent of "subject to the exercise of the police power."]

It is clear that there is no closed class or category of businesses affected with a public interest, and the function of courts in the application of the Fifth and Fourteenth Amendments is to determine in each case whether circumstances vindicate the challenged regulation as a reasonable exertion of governmental authority or condemn it as arbitrary or discriminatory. . . . The phrase "affected with a public interest" can, in the nature of things, mean no more than that an industry, for adequate reason, is subject to control for the public good. In several of the decisions of this court wherein the expressions "affected with a public interest," and "clothed with a public use," have been brought forward as the criteria of the validity of price control, it has been admitted that they are not susceptible of definition and form an unsatisfactory test of the constitutionality of legislation directed at business practices or prices. These decisions must rest, finally, upon the basis that the requirements of due process were not met because the laws were found arbitrary in their operation and effect. But

there can be no doubt that upon proper occasion and by appropriate measures the state may regulate a business in any of its aspects, including the prices to be charged for the products or commodities it sells.

So far as the requirement of due process is concerned, and in the absence of other constitutional restriction, a state is free to adopt whatever economic policy may reasonably be deemed to promote public welfare, and to enforce that policy by legislation adapted to its purpose. The courts are without authority either to declare such policy, or, when it is declared by the legislature, to override it. . . .

. . . The Constitution does not secure to any one liberty to conduct his business in such fashion as to inflict injury upon the public at large, or upon any substantial group of the people. Price control, like any other form of regulation, is unconstitutional only if arbitrary, discriminatory, or demonstrably irrelevant to the policy the legislature is free to adopt, and hence an unnecessary and unwarranted interference with individual liberty.

Tested by these considerations we find no basis in the due process clause of the Fourteenth Amendment for condemning the provisions of the Agriculture and Markets Law here drawn into question.

The judgment is affirmed.

Mr. Justice **McReynolds** dissented in an opinion concurred in by Justices **Van Devanter, Sutherland** and **Butler,** saying in part:

Regulation to prevent recognized evils in business has long been upheld as permissible legislative action. But fixation of the price at which "A," engaged in an ordinary business, may sell, in order to enable "B," a producer, to improve his condition, has not been regarded as within legislative power. This is not regulation, but management, control, dictation—it amounts to the deprivation of the fundamental right which one has to conduct his own affairs honestly and along customary lines. . . .

The statement by the court below that—"Doubtless the statute before us would be condemned by an earlier generation as a temerarious interference with the rights of property and contract . . . ; with the natural law of supply and demand," is obviously correct. But another, that "statutes . . . aiming to stimulate the production of a vital food product by fixing living standards of prices for the producer, are to be interpreted with that degree of liberality which is essential to the attainment of the end in view," conflicts with views of constitutional rights accepted since the beginning. An end although apparently desirable cannot justify inhibited means. Moreover the challenged act was not designed to stimulate production—there was too much milk for the demand and no prospect of less for several years; also "standards of prices" at which the producer might sell were not prescribed. The Legislature cannot lawfully destroy guaranteed rights of one man with the prime purpose of enriching another, even if for the moment, this may seem advantageous to the public. And the adoption of any "concept of jurisprudence" which permits facile disregard of the Constitution as long interpreted and respected will inevitably lead to its destruction. Then, all rights will be subject to the caprice of the hour; government by stable laws will pass.

LOCHNER v. NEW YORK

198 U. S. 45; 25 S. Ct. 539; 49 L. Ed. 937 (1905)

At the same time that the states were trying to regulate rates, they were also trying to alleviate some of the more abusive labor conditions that had arisen with the industrial revolution. The Court's hostility to these efforts was similar to that shown to rate control in the post-Munn era. What persuaded the Supreme Court to assert a supervisory power over the substance of state legislation which it had so carefully rejected in the Slaughter-House Cases (1873) is not difficult to surmise. During the two decades involved, the entire personnel of the Court, with the exception of Justice Field, had changed; and Field, who had dissented in the Slaughter-House Cases, had always been an apostle of the new faith. The new members coming onto the Court tended to reflect the social and economic pressures of the post-Civil War period: the tremendous expansion of the railroads and industry, the brawling struggle between management and labor with the growth of the trade union movement, and the increasing use of political power by the workingman to secure the enactment of protective labor legislation. Naturally, organized industry looked upon legislative efforts to ameliorate factory conditions and hours of labor as intolerable interferences with the employer's private affairs and a deprivation of his liberty and property. A generation of judges steeped in the individualism of the common law tended to share this view. Due process of law came to seem the completely appropriate and adequate constitutional weapon with which to combat the onward march of the new social control—the new police power.

This individualistic interpretation by the courts of due process of law found finally a definite basis in the development in the state courts during the 1880s of the doctrine of "liberty of contract," which was first introduced into the Supreme Court by Justice Peckham in Allgeyer v. Louisiana (1897), a case involving the right to buy insurance. There he interpreted due process as including "the right of the citizen . . . to live and work where he will; to earn his livelihood by any lawful calling; to pursue any livelihood or avocation, and for that purpose to enter into all contracts which may be proper, necessary, and essential to his carrying out to a successful conclusion the purposes above mentioned."

The concept of "liberty of contract" was both plausible and alluring. It asserted in substance that when two parties, neither of whom was under any legal disability, came together to make a contract which was not contrary to public policy, the legislature had no right to interfere and dictate the terms of the agreement. The application of this doctrine to the problem of protective labor legislation produced, however, some very startling results, due in large measure to the naïve assumption by the courts that the individual employee of a great industrial corporation possessed full liberty of contract and could dicker with an employer upon equal terms. Naturally, as time went on the courts found frequently that this vaunted liberty of contract was infringed by the laws regulating hours of labor, method and time of wage payment, employer's liability, factory conditions, and similar matters.

Sir Henry Maine's statement that "the movement of the progressive societies has hitherto been a movement from status to contract" marked this as a liberal doctrine which emancipated the individual, especially the laborer, from governmental controls and allowed the person to bargain freely about his or her affairs. Hence it was only natural that it should receive a preferred place in the constitutional scheme. The normal presumption that a state statute is constitutional gradually gave way, and the burden of proof was placed upon those who would sustain a law alleged to limit such liberty of contract. The Court's insistence in Mugler v. Kansas (1887) that a state statute purporting to protect the public health, safety, and morals must bear a "real or substantial relation to those objects" meant that the Court had to be shown that such was the case before the act could be upheld.

The difficulty came in persuading the Court that such a relationship did in fact exist. In the Mugler case the Court had taken judicial notice of the evils of drink and had upheld the validity of a state prohibition statute; but the judges themselves had no knowledge of the social and economic conditions which led to the passage of laws regulating the hours of labor and working conditions, and to the extent they had such knowledge their inclination was to protect the right of entrepreneurs to conduct their affairs under the old common-law rules to which they were accustomed—rules which gave them virtually uncontrolled discretion over marketing policies, labor relations and working conditions. Nor was the bar, if it had such knowledge, in a position to transmit such knowledge to the bench, since the traditional method of arguing cases was to cite case precedents and attempt to show by rational analysis how the case at bar was similar. Thus the protagonists of protective labor laws found themselves with a strong presumption against the validity of the laws and no effective way to rebut the presumption.

Most of the court decisions now regarded as more or less reactionary were rendered by the state courts. They had been invalidating state social legislation for nearly twenty years before the Supreme Court followed suit. The case of Lochner v. New York is interesting for two reasons: first, because it is the earliest and one of the most important cases in which the Supreme Court invalidated a state law under the liberty of contract phrase of the due process clause; and second, because it contains Justice Holmes's dissenting opinion upholding the validity of such reform laws. Lochner was convicted of violating a New York statute called the Labor Law, which provided that no employee should be "required or permitted to work in a biscuit, bread or cake bakery or confectionery establishment more than sixty hours in any one week, or more than ten hours in any one day unless for the purpose of making a shorter day on the last day of the week." The legislature had proceeded upon the assumption that the conditions in the baking industry were such as to demand the intervention of the state in behalf of the employees. The majority of the Supreme Court did not agree that such protection was reasonably necessary and accordingly held that there was no adequate justification for this infringement of the private rights of the employer. Four justices dissented on the ground that there was sufficient support for the view of the legislature to make it a debatable question whether the law was arbitrary or not and that when such was the case, the courts should not override the legislative judgment. The dissenting opinion of Justice Holmes has become almost a classic as a statement of the more liberal judicial attitude toward the question of the validity of social and economic legislation under the Fourteenth Amendment. It is interesting to note that in the 1980s, under the rubric of "law and economics," the assumption that individuals and corporations are equal bargaining agents—a basic assumption of Lochner—is undergoing a revival.

Mr. Justice **Peckham** delivered the opinion of the Court, saying in part:

The statute necessarily interferes with the right of contract between the employer and employees, concerning the number of hours in which the latter may labor in the bakery of the employer. The general right to make a contract in relation to his business is part of the liberty of the individual protected by the 14th Amendment of the Federal Constitution. ... Under that provision no state can deprive any person of life, liberty, or property without due process of law. The right to purchase or to sell labor is part of the liberty protected by this amendment, unless there are circumstances which exclude the right. There are, however, certain powers, existing in the sovereignty of each state in the Union, somewhat vaguely termed police powers, the exact description and limitation of which have not been attempted by the courts. Those powers, broadly stated, and without, at present, any attempt at a more specific limitation, relate to the safety, health, morals, and general welfare of the public. Both property and liberty are held on such reasonable conditions as may be imposed by the governing power of the state in the exercise of those powers, and with such conditions the 14th Amendment was not designed to interfere. ...

The state, therefore, has power to prevent the individual from making certain kinds of contracts, and in regard to them the Federal Constitution offers no protection. If the contract be one which the state, in the legitimate exercise of its police power, has the right to prohibit, it is not prevented from prohibiting it by the 14th Amendment. Contracts in violation of a statute, either of the Federal or state government, or a contract to let one's property for immoral purposes, or to do any other unlawful act, could obtain no protection from the Federal Constitution, as coming under the liberty of person or of free contract. Therefore, when the state, by its legislature, in the assumed exercise of its police powers, has passed an act which seriously limits the right to labor or the right of contract in regard to their means of livelihood between persons who are sui juris (both employer and employee), it becomes of great importance to determine which shall prevail,—the right of the individual to labor for such time as he may choose, or the right of the state to prevent the individual from laboring, or from entering into any contract to labor, beyond a certain time prescribed by the state. ...

It must, of course, be conceded that there is a limit to the valid exercise of the police power by the state. There is no dispute concerning this general proposition. Otherwise the 14th Amendment would have no efficacy and the legislatures of the states would have unbounded power, and it would be enough to say that any piece of legislation was enacted to conserve the morals, the health, or the safety of the people; such legislation would be valid, no matter how absolutely without foundation the claim might be. The claim of the police power would be a mere pretext,—become another and delusive name for the supreme sovereignty of the state to be exercised free from constitutional restraint. This is not contended for. In every case that comes before this court, therefore, where legislation of this character is concerned, and where the protection of the Federal Constitution is sought, the question necessarily arises: Is this a fair, reasonable, and appropriate exercise of the police power of the state, or is it an unreasonable, unnecessary, and arbitrary interference with the right of the individual to his personal liberty, or to enter into those contracts in relation to labor which may seem to him appropriate or necessary for the support of himself and his family? Of course the liberty of contract relating to labor includes both parties to it. The one has as much right to purchase as the other to sell labor.

This is not a question of substituting the judgment of the court for that of the legislature. If the act be within the power of the state it is valid, although the judgment of the court might be totally opposed to the enactment of such a law. But the question would still remain: Is it within the police power of the state? and that question must be answered by the court.

The question whether this act is valid as a labor law, pure and simple, may be dismissed in a few words. There is no reasonable ground for interfering with the liberty of person or the right of free contract, by determining the hours of labor, in the occupation of a baker. There is no contention that bakers as a class are not equal in intelligence and capacity to men in other trades or manual occupations, or that they are not able to assert their rights and care for themselves without the protecting arm of the state, interfering with their independence of judgment and of action. They are in no sense wards of the state. Viewed in the light of a purely labor law, with no reference whatever to the question of health, we think that a law like the one before us involves neither the safety, the morals, nor the welfare, of the public, and that the interest of the public is not in the slightest degree affected by such an act. The law must be upheld, if at all, as a law pertaining to the health of the individual engaged in the occupation of a baker. It does not affect any other portion of the public than those who are engaged in that occupation. Clean and wholesome bread does not depend upon whether the baker works but ten hours per day or only sixty hours a week. The limitation of the hours of labor does not come within the police power on that ground.

It is a question of which of two powers or rights shall prevail,—the power of the state to legislate or the right of the individual to liberty of person and freedom of contract. The mere assertion that the subject relates, though but in a remote degree, to the public health, does not necessarily render the enactment valid. The act must have a more direct relation, as a means to an end, and the end itself must be appropriate and legitimate, before an act can be held to be valid which interferes with the general right of an individual to be free in his person and in his power to contract in relation to his own labor. . . .

We think the limit of the police power has been reached and passed in this case. There is, in our judgment, no reasonable foundation for holding this to be necessary or appropriate as a health law to safeguard the public health, or the health of the individuals who are following the trade of a baker. If this statute be valid, and if, therefore, a proper case is made out in which to deny the right of an individual, sui juris, as employer or employee, to make contracts for the labor of the latter under the protection of the provisions of the Federal Constitution, there would seem to be no length to which legislation of this nature might not go. . . .

We think that there can be no fair doubt that the trade of a baker, in and of itself, is not an unhealthy one to that degree which would authorize the legislature to interfere with the right to labor, and with the right of free contract on the part of the individual, either as employer or employee. In looking through statistics regarding all trades and occupations, it may be true that the trade of a baker does not appear to be as healthy as some other trades, and is also vastly more healthy than still others. To the common understanding the trade of a baker has never been regarded as an unhealthy one. Very likely physicians would not recommend the exercise of that or of any other trade as a remedy for ill health. Some occupations are more healthy than others, but we think there are none which might not come under the power of the legislature to supervise and control the hours of working therein, if the mere fact that the occupation is not absolutely and perfectly healthy is to confer that right upon the legislative department of the government. It might be safely affirmed that almost all occupations more or less affect the health. There must be more than the mere fact of the possible existence of some small amount of un-

healthiness to warrant legislative interference with liberty. It is unfortunately true that labor, even in any department, may possibly carry with it the seeds of unhealthiness. But are we all, on that account, at the mercy of legislative majorities? A printer, a tinsmith, a locksmith, a carpenter, a cabinetmaker, a dry goods clerk, a bank's, a lawyer's, or a physician's clerk, or a clerk in almost any kind of business, would all come under the power of the legislature, on this assumption. No trade, no occupation, no mode of earning one's living, could escape this all-pervading power, and the acts of the legislature in limiting the hours of labor in all employments would be valid, although such limitation might seriously cripple the ability of the laborer to support himself and his family. In our large cities there are many buildings into which the sun penetrates for but a short time in each day, and these buildings are occupied by people carrying on the business of bankers, brokers, lawyers, real estate, and many other kinds of business, aided by many clerks, messengers, and other employees. Upon the assumption of the validity of this act under review, it is not possible to say that an act, prohibiting lawyers' or bank clerks, or others, from contracting to labor for their employers more than eight hours a day would be invalid. It might be said that it is unhealthy to work more than that number of hours in an apartment lighted by artificial light during the working hours of the day; that the occupation of the bank clerk, the lawyer's clerk, the real-estate clerk, or the broker's clerk, in such offices is therefore unhealthy, and the legislature, in its paternal wisdom, must, therefore, have the right to legislate on the subject of and to limit, the hours for such labor; and, if it exercises that power, and its validity be questioned, it is sufficient to say, it has reference to the public health; it has reference to the health of the employees condemned to labor day after day in buildings where the sun never shines; it is a health law, and therefore it is valid, and cannot be questioned by the courts.

It is also urged, pursuing the same line of argument, that it is to the interest of the state that its population should be strong and robust, and therefore any legislation which may be said to tend to make people healthy must be valid as health laws, enacted under the police power. If this be a valid argument and a justification for this kind of legislation, it follows that the protection of the Federal Constitution from undue interference with liberty of person and freedom of contract is visionary, wherever the law is sought to be justified as a valid exercise of the police power. Scarcely any law but might find shelter under such assumptions, and conduct, properly so called, as well as contract, would come under the restrictive sway of the legislature. Not only the hours of employees, but the hours of employers, could be regulated, and doctors, lawyers, scientists, all professional men, as well as athletes and artisans, could be forbidden to fatigue their brains and bodies by prolonged hours of exercise, lest the fighting strength of the state be impaired. We mention these extreme cases because the contention is extreme. We do not believe in the soundness of the views which uphold this law. On the contrary, we think that such a law as this, although passed in the assumed exercise of the police power, and as relating to the public health, or the health of the employees named, is not within that power, and is invalid. The act is not, within any fair meaning of the term, a health law, but is an illegal interference with the rights of individuals, both employers and employees, to make contracts regarding labor upon such terms as they may think best, or which they may agree upon with the other parties to such contracts. Statutes of the nature of that under review, limiting the hours in which grown and intelligent men may labor to earn their living, are mere meddlesome interferences with the rights of the individual, and they are not saved from condemnation by the claim that they are passed in the exercise of the police power and upon the subject of the health of the individual whose rights are interfered with, unless there be some fair ground, reasonable in and of itself, to say that there is material danger to the public health, or to the health of the employees, if the hours of labor are not curtailed. . . .

It was further urged on the argument that restricting the hours of labor in the case of bakers was valid because it tended to cleanliness on the part of the workers, as a man was more apt to be cleanly when not overworked, and if cleanly then his "output" was also more likely to be so. . . . The connection, if any exist, is too shadowy and thin to build any argument for the interference of the legislature. If the man works ten hours a day it is all right, but if ten and a half or eleven his health is in danger and his bread may be unhealthy, and, therefore, he shall not be permitted to do it. This, we think, is unreasonable and entirely arbitrary. . . .

. . . It seems to us that the real object and purpose were simply to regulate the hours of labor between the master and his employees (all being men, sui juris), in a private business, not dangerous in any degree to morals, or in any real and substantial degree to the health of the employees. Under such circumstances the freedom of master and employee to contract with each other in relation to their employment, and in defining the same, cannot be prohibited or interfered with, without violating the Federal Constitution.

The judgment . . . must be reversed. . . .

Mr. Justice **Harlan,** with whom Mr. Justice **White** and Mr. Justice **Day** concurred in dissenting, said in part:

. . . I find it impossible, in view of common experience, to say that there is here no real or substantial relation between the means employed by the state and the end sought to be accomplished by its legislation. . . .

We judicially know that the question of the number of hours during which a workman should continuously labor has been, for a long period, and is yet, a subject of serious consideration among civilized peoples, and by those having special knowledge of the laws of health. Suppose the statute prohibited labor in bakery and confectionery establishments in excess of eighteen hours each day. No one, I take it, could dispute the power of the state to enact such a statute. But the statute

before us does not embrace extreme or exceptional cases. It may be said to occupy a middle ground in respect of the hours of labor. What is the true ground for the state to take between legitimate protection, by legislation, of the public health and liberty of contract is not a question easily solved, nor one in respect of which there is or can be absolute certainty. There are very few, if any, questions in political economy about which entire certainty may be predicated. . . .

I do not stop to consider whether any particular view of this economic question presents the sounder theory. What the precise facts are it may be difficult to say. It is enough for the determination of this case, and it is enough for this court to know, that the question is one about which there is room for debate and for an honest difference of opinion. There are many reasons of a weighty, substantial character, based upon the experience of mankind, in support of the theory that, all things considered, more than ten hours steady work each day, from week to week, in a bakery or confectionery establishment, may endanger the health and shorten the lives of the workmen, thereby diminishing their physical and mental capacity to serve the state and to provide for those dependent upon them.

If such reasons exist that ought to be the end of this case, for the state is not amenable to the judiciary, in respect of its legislative enactments, unless such enactments are plainly, palpably, beyond all question, inconsistent with the Constitution of the United States. . . .

Mr. Justice **Holmes** dissenting:

I regret sincerely that I am unable to agree with the judgment in this case, and I think it my duty to express my dissent.

This case is decided upon an economic theory which a large part of the country does not entertain. If it were a question whether I agreed with that theory, I should desire to study it further and long before making up my mind. But I do not conceive that to be my duty, because I strongly believe that my agreement or disagreement has nothing to do with the right of a majority to embody their opinions in law. It is settled by various decisions of this court that state constitutions and state laws may regulate life in many ways which we as legislators might think as injudicious, or if you like as tyrannical, as this, and which equally with this, interfere with the liberty to contract. Sunday laws and usury laws are ancient examples. A more modern one is the prohibition of lotteries. The liberty of the citizen to do as he likes so long as he does not interfere with the liberty of others to do the same, which has been a shibboleth for some well-known writers, is interfered with by school laws, by the Postoffice, by every state or municipal institution which takes his money for purposes thought desirable, whether he likes it or not. The 14th Amendment does not enact Mr. Herbert Spencer's Social Statics. The other day we sustained the Massachusetts vaccination law. Jacobson v. Massachusetts [1905]. United States and state statutes and decisions cutting down the liberty to contract by way of combination are familiar to this court. Northern Securities Co. v. United States [1904]. Two years ago we upheld the prohibition of sales of stock on margins, or for future delivery, in the Constitution of California. . . . The decision sustaining an eight-hour law for miners is still recent. Holden v. Hardy [1898]. Some of these laws embody convictions or prejudices which judges are likely to share. Some may not. But a constitution is not intended to embody a particular economic theory, whether of paternalism and the organic relation of the citizen to the state or of laissez faire. It is made for people of fundamentally differing views, and the accident of our finding certain opinions natural and familiar, or novel, and even shocking, ought not to conclude our judgment upon the question whether statutes embodying them conflict with the Constitution of the United States.

General propositions do not decide concrete cases. The decision will depend on a judgment or intuition more subtle than any articulate major premise. But I think that the proposition just stated, if it is accepted, will carry us far toward the end. Every opinion tends to become a law. I think that the word "liberty," in the 14th Amendment, is perverted when it is held to prevent the natural outcome of a dominant opinion, unless it can be said that a rational and fair man necessarily would admit that the statute proposed would infringe fundamental principles as they have been understood by the traditions of our people and our law. It does not need research to show that no such sweeping condemnation can be passed upon the statute before us. A reasonable man might think it a proper measure on the score of health. Men whom I certainly could not pronounce unreasonable would uphold it as a first instalment of a general regulation of the hours of work. Whether in the latter aspect it would be open to the charge of inequality I think it unnecessary to discuss.

WEST COAST HOTEL CO. v. PARRISH

300 U. S. 379; 57 S. Ct. 578; 81 L. Ed. 703 (1937)

The first break in the doctrine of the Lochner case came three years later in Muller v. Oregon (1908). The case involved the validity of the Oregon ten-hour day for women, which had been challenged on the ground that it bore no reasonable relation to the public health, safety, and morals and therefore denied due process. Louis D. Brandeis, who had been invited to participate by the state of Oregon, undertook to persuade the justices that the law was a valid exercise of the state's police power. He filed with the Court the first of the famous "Brandeis briefs." It contained two pages of legal argument and over 100 pages of sociological facts and statistics showing the evil effect of long working hours upon women. The Court was obviously impressed and paid one of its rare personal tributes to counsel: "It may not be amiss, in the present case, before examining the constitutional question, to notice the course of legislation, as well as expressions of opinion from other than judicial sources. In the brief filed by Mr. Louis D. Brandeis for the defendant in error is a very copious collection of all these matters, an epitome of which is found in the margin." More important, Brandeis had succeeded in getting his information across to the Court. "The legislation and opinions referred to in the margin may not be, technically speaking, authorities, and in them is little or no discussion of the constitutional questions presented to us for determination, yet they are significant of a widespread belief that woman's physical structure, and the functions she performs in consequence thereof, justify special legislation restricting or qualifying the conditions under which she should be permitted to toil. Constitutional questions, it is true, are not settled by even a consensus of present public opinion. . . . At the same time, when a question of fact is debated and debatable, and the extent to which a special constitutional limitation goes is affected by the truth in respect to that fact, a widespread and long continued belief concerning it is worthy of consideration. We take judicial cognizance of all matters of general knowledge." The Court unanimously sustained the act.

A second break in the doctrine of the Lochner case came in 1917 in the case of Bunting v. Oregon, a case involving an Oregon statute providing a ten-hour day for all industrial workers. In a five-to-three decision the Court sustained the act and in doing so made it plain that the burden of proof had shifted to those who attacked its validity. "But we need not cast about for reasons for the legislative judgment. We are not required to be sure of the precise reasons for its exercise, or be convinced of the wisdom of its exercise. . . . It is enough for our decision if the legislation under review was passed in the exercise of an admitted power of government. . . . There is a contention made that the law . . . is not either necessary or useful 'for preservation of the health of employees. . . . ' The record contains no facts to support the contention, and against it is the judgment of the legislature and the supreme court. . . ." The same day the Court divided four to four to sustain the Oregon minimum wage law in Stettler v. O'Hara (1917). Justice Brandeis took no part in the decision of either of these cases. He had been counsel in the cases in the beginning, and with his appointment to the Supreme Court his place on the briefs had been taken by Felix Frankfurter, a professor in the Harvard Law School.

While the Court decided the Bunting case without any mention of the Lochner decision, it was widely assumed that the Lochner doctrine had been permanently abandoned. But in 1922 George Sutherland and Pierce Butler were appointed to the Court, and the following year the minimum wage statute of the District of Columbia was held void as a denial of due process of law. This was the case of Adkins v. Children's Hospital (1923). The Court divided five to three. Again Justice Brandeis did not sit, this time because his daughter was a member of the minimum wage commission. The majority opinion of Justice Sutherland reads like the opinion of the Court in the Lochner case, from which it quotes at length with approval. It held that there is no connection between the wages women receive and their health, morals, or welfare that can be justified by destroying by law the freedom of contract of employers and the women who work for them. Furthermore, the Court said, the act does not guarantee that the minimum wage fixed shall not exceed the fair value of the service for which it is paid. Thus the Court returned to the old presumption of the invalidity of the statute and announced that while the materials in Professor Frankfurter's brief were useful enough to the legislature in passing the law, "they reflect no legitimate light upon the question of its validity." Chief Justice Taft and Justice Holmes wrote dissenting opinions. Justice Sanford concurred with the Chief Justice. In 1925 and in 1927 the Court without opinion ruled that the Adkins case rendered invalid the state minimum wage laws of Arizona and Arkansas respectively.

In 1933 New York passed a minimum wage law for women and children. Its framers sought to escape the ban of the Adkins decision by providing that the wages fixed should be based on the fair value of the labor paid for. The attempt failed. In Morehead v. New York ex rel. Tipaldo (1936) the Supreme Court in a five-to-four decision held the New York statute invalid. In the majority opinion Justice Butler stated that the statute was like the one held void in the Adkins case, but further said in substance that any minimum wage law, regardless of its provisions, would be invalid as a denial of due process of law. In a dissenting opinion Justice Stone observed: "It is difficult to imagine any grounds, other than our own personal economic predilections, for saying that the contract of employment is any the less an appropriate subject of legislation than are scores of others, in dealing with which this court has held that legislatures may curtail individual freedom in the public interest."

Public disenchantment with the Tipaldo decision was almost universal. Even the Republican Party repudiated it as it organized for the 1936 presidential campaign, and President Roosevelt, following his overwhelming reelection that November, immediately began laying plans for an attack on a Supreme Court he was convinced would ultimately strike down his entire New Deal program. On February 5, with his national prestige at an all-time high, he sent to Congress his ill-fated court-packing plan calling for the addition of a new justice to the Court for every justice over the age of seventy (of which there were six). While it presented no technical constitutional problems, since Congress sets the size of the Supreme Court, it aroused almost as much public antagonism as had the Tipaldo decision before it. A public which badly wanted New Deal legislation declared constitutional was clearly unprepared to sacrifice the independence of the Supreme Court to get it.

During all this time Washington's minimum wage law of 1913 had been in force and the case below attacking its validity had been argued in December, shortly after FDR's reelection. In March, with the court-packing battle in full swing, the Court handed down its decision. Two months later the judiciary committee reported the court-packing plan unfavorably and it ultimately failed to pass the Senate.

Mr. Chief Justice **Hughes** delivered the opinion of the Court, saying in part:

This case presents the question of the constitutional validity of the minimum wage law of the State of Washington. [Passed in 1913.]
. . . It provides:
"Section 1. The welfare of the State of Washington demands that women and minors be protected from conditions of labor which have a pernicious effect on their health and morals. The State of Washington, therefore, exercising herein its police and sovereign power declares that inadequate wages and unsanitary conditions of labor exert such pernicious effect.
"Sec. 2. It shall be unlawful to employ women or minors in any industry or occupation within the State of Washington under conditions of labor detrimental to their health or morals; and it shall be unlawful to employ women workers in any industry within the State of Washington at wages which are not adequate for their maintenance.
"Sec. 3. There is hereby created a commission to be known as the 'Industrial Welfare Commission' for the State of Washington, to establish such standards of wages and conditions of labor for women and minors employed within the State of Washington, as shall be held hereunder to be reasonable and not detrimental to health and morals, and which shall be sufficient for the decent maintenance of women." . . .
[Further provisions outlined the procedure to be followed by the commission in fixing minimum wages in various occupations.]
The appellant conducts a hotel. The appellee Elsie Parrish was employed as a chambermaid and (with her husband) brought this suit to recover the difference between the wages paid her and the minimum wage fixed pursuant to the state law. The minimum wage was $14.50 per week of 48 hours. The appellant challenged the act as repugnant to the due process clause of the Fourteenth Amendment of the Constitution of the United States. The Supreme Court of the State, reversing the trial court, sustained the statute and directed judgment for the plaintiffs. . . .
The appellant relies upon the decision of this Court in Adkins v. Children's Hospital [1923] which held invalid the District of Columbia Minimum Wage Act which was attacked under the due process clause of the Fifth Amendment. . . . [Here follows comment upon Morehead v. New York ex rel. Tipaldo (1936), discussed above, and a review of the judicial history of minimum wage legislation.]
The principle which must control our decision is not in doubt. The constitutional provision invoked is the due process clause of the Fourteenth Amendment governing the States, as the due process clause invoked in the Adkins Case governed Congress. In each case the violation alleged by those attacking minimum wage

regulation for women is deprivation of freedom of contract. What is this freedom? The Constitution does not speak of freedom of contract. It speaks of liberty and prohibits the deprivation of liberty without due process of law. In prohibiting that deprivation the Constitution does not recognize an absolute and uncontrollable liberty. Liberty in each of its phases has its history and connotation. But the liberty safeguarded is liberty in a social organization which requires the protection of law against the evils which menace the health, safety, morals and welfare of the people. Liberty under the Constitution is thus necessarily subject to the restraints of due process, and regulation which is reasonable in relation to its subject and is adopted in the interests of the community is due process.

This essential limitation of liberty in general governs freedom of contract in particular. More than twenty-five years ago we set forth the applicable principle in these words, after referring to the cases where the liberty guaranteed by the Fourteenth Amendment had been broadly described:

"But it was recognized in the cases cited, as in many others, that freedom of contract is a qualified and not an absolute right. There is no absolute freedom to do as one wills or to contract as one chooses. The guaranty of liberty does not withdraw from legislative supervision that wide department of activity which consists of the making of contracts, or deny to government the power to provide restrictive safeguards. Liberty implies the absence of arbitrary restraint, not immunity from reasonable regulations and prohibitions imposed in the interests of the community." Chicago, B. & Q. R. Co. v. McGuire [1911].

This power under the Constitution to restrict freedom of contract has had many illustrations. That it may be exercised in the public interest with respect to contracts between employer and employee is undeniable. . . . [The Court lists here numerous cases holding valid under the Fourteenth Amendment various types of protective labor legislation.]

The point that has been strongly stressed that adult employees should be deemed competent to make their own contracts was decisively met nearly forty years ago in Holden v. Hardy [1898], where we pointed out the inequality in the footing of the parties. We said:

"The legislature has also recognized the fact, which the experience of legislators in many States has corroborated, that the proprietors of these establishments and their operatives do not stand upon an equality, and that their interests are, to a certain extent, conflicting. The former naturally desire to obtain as much labor as possible from their employees, while the latter are often induced by the fear of discharge to conform to regulations which their judgment, fairly exercised, would pronounce to be detrimental to their health or strength. In other words, the proprietors lay down the rules and the laborers are practically constrained to obey them. In such cases self-interest is often an unsafe guide, and the legislature may properly interpose its authority."

And we added that the fact "that both parties are of full age and competent to contract does not necessarily deprive the State of the power to interfere where the parties do not stand upon an equality, or where the public health demands that one party to the contract shall be protected against himself." . . .

It is manifest that this established principle is peculiarly applicable in relation to the employment of women in whose protection the State has a special interest. That phase of the subject received elaborate consideration in Muller v. Oregon (1908), where the constitutional authority of the State to limit the working hours of women was sustained. We emphasized the consideration that "woman's physical structure and the performance of maternal functions place her at a disadvantage in the struggle for subsistence" and that her physical well-being "becomes an object of public interest and care in order to preserve the strength and vigor of the race." We emphasized the need of protecting women against oppression despite her possession of contractual rights. We said that "though limitations upon personal and contractual rights may be removed by legislation, there is that in her disposition and habits of life which will operate against a full assertion of those rights. She will still be where some legislation to protect her seems necessary to secure a real equality or right." Hence she was "properly placed in a class by herself, and legislation designed for her protection may be sustained even when like legislation is not necessary for men and could not be sustained." We concluded that the limitations which the statute there in question "placed upon her contractual powers, upon her right to agree with her employer as to the time she shall labor" were "not imposed solely for her benefit, but also largely for the benefit of all." . . .

This array of precedents and the principles they applied were thought by the dissenting justices in the Adkins Case to demand that the minimum wage statute be sustained. The validity of the distinction made by the Court between a minimum wage and a maximum of hours in limiting liberty of contract was especially challenged. That challenge persists and is without any satisfactory answer. As Chief Justice Taft observed: "In absolute freedom of contract the one term is as important as the other, for both enter equally into the consideration given and received; a restriction as to one is not any greater in essence than the other, and is of the same kind. One is the multiplier and the other the multiplicand." And Mr. Justice Holmes, while recognizing that "the distinctions of the law are distinctions of degree," could "perceive no difference in the kind or degree of interference with liberty, the only matter with which we have any concern, between the one case and the other. The bargain is equally affected whichever half you regulate." . . .

The minimum wage to be paid under the Washington statute is fixed after full consideration by representatives of employers, employees and the public. It may be assumed that the minimum wage is fixed in consideration of the services that are performed in the particular occupations under normal conditions. Provision is made for special licenses at less wages in the case of women who are incapable of full service. The statement of Mr. Justice Holmes in the Adkins Case is pertinent: "This statute does not compel anybody to pay anything. It simply forbids employment at rates below those fixed as the minimum requirement of health and right living. It is safe to assume that women will not be employed at even the lowest wages allowed unless they earn them, or unless the employer's business can sustain the burden. In short the law in its character and operation is like hundreds of so-called police laws that have been upheld." And Chief Justice Taft forcibly pointed out the consideration which is basic in a statute of this character: "Legislatures which adopt a requirement of maximum hours or minimum wages may be presumed to believe that when sweating employers are prevented from paying unduly low wages by positive law they will continue their business, abating that part of their profits, which were wrung from the necessities of their employees, and will concede the better terms required by the law; and that while in individual cases hardship may result, the restriction will enure to the benefit of the general class of employees in whose interest the law is passed and so to that of the community at large."

We think that the views thus expressed are sound and that the decision in the Adkins Case was a departure from the true application of the principles governing the regulation by the State of the relation of employer and employed. . . .

With full recognition of the earnestness and vigor which characterize the prevailing opinion of the Adkins Case, we find it impossible to reconcile that ruling with these well-considered declarations. What can be closer to the public interest than the health of women and their protection from unscrupulous and overreaching employers? And if the protection of women is a legitimate end of the exercise of state power, how can it be said that the requirement of the payment of a minimum wage fairly fixed in order to meet the very necessities of the existence is not an admissible means to that end? The legislature of the State was clearly entitled to consider the situation of women in employment, the fact that they are in the class receiving the least pay, that their bargaining power is relatively weak, and that they are the ready victims of those who would take advantage of their necessitous circumstances. The legislature was entitled to adopt measures to reduce the evils of the "sweating system," the exploiting of workers at wages so low as to be insufficient to meet the bare cost of living, thus making their very helplessness the occasion of a most injurious competition. The legislature had the right to consider that its minimum wage requirements would be an important aid in carrying out its policy of protection. The adoption of similar requirements by many States evidences a deep-seated conviction both as to the presence of the evil and as to the means adapted to check it. Legislative response to that conviction cannot be regarded as arbitrary or capricious and that is all we have to decide. Even if the wisdom of the policy be regarded as debatable and its effects uncertain, still the legislature is entitled to its judgment.

There is an additional and compelling consideration which recent economic experience has brought into a strong light. The exploitation of a class of workers who are in an unequal position with respect to bargaining power and are thus relatively defenseless against the denial of a living wage is not only detrimental to their health and well being but casts a direct burden for their support upon the community. What these workers lose in wages the taxpayers are called upon to pay. The bare cost of living must be met. We may take judicial notice of the unparalleled demands for relief which arose during the recent period of depression and still continue to an alarming extent despite the degree of economic recovery which has been achieved. It is unnecessary to cite official statistics to establish what is of common knowledge through the length and breadth of the land. While in the instant case no factual brief has been presented, there is no reason to doubt that the State of Washington has encountered the same social problem that is present else where.The community is not bound to provide what is in effect a subsidy for unconscionable employers. The community may direct its law-making power to correct the abuse which springs from their selfish disregard of the public interest. The argument that the legislation in question constitutes an arbitrary discrimination, because it does not extend to men, is unavailing. This Court has frequently held that the legislative authority, acting within its proper field, is not bound to extend its regulation to all cases which it might possibly reach. The legislature "is free to recognize degrees of harm and it may confine its restrictions to those classes of cases where the need is deemed to be clearest." If "the law presumably hits the evil where it is most felt, it is not to be overthrown because there are other instances to which it might have been applied." There is no "doctrinaire requirement" that the legislation should be couched in all embracing terms. . . .

Our conclusion is that the case of Adkins v. Children's Hospital should be, and it is, overruled. The judgment of the Supreme Court of the State of Washington is affirmed.

Mr. Justice **Sutherland** dissented in an opinion in which Justices **Van Devanter, McReynolds,** and **Butler** concurred.

CRIMINAL PROCEDURE AND THE BILL OF RIGHTS

HURTADO v. CALIFORNIA

110 U. S. 516; 4 S. Ct. 111; 28 L. Ed. 232 (1884)

While the due process clauses of the Fifth and Fourteenth Amendments came to be restrictions by which the validity of the substance of legislation was tested in the courts, it should not be forgotten that originally due process was construed only as a limitation on governmental procedure. Whatever the government did, it had to do in accordance with the "process" which was "due" under the law of the land. But what, concretely, did such process include? To nonprofessionals, thinking in terms of criminal procedure, it undoubtedly included the common-law procedures with which they were familiar—procedures spelled out in detail in the Bill of Rights. The Supreme Court, however, rejected the idea that due process required adherence to a fixed list of prescribed procedures, and in Davidson v. New Orleans (1878) it explained that the meaning of the clause would be determined "by the gradual process of judicial inclusion and exclusion, as the cases presented for decision shall require, with the reasoning on which such decisions may be founded."

The Court had already decided, in the case of Murray's Lessee v. Hoboken Land & Improvement Co. (1856), that "due" process did not always mean "judicial" process; and an administrative agency could employ procedures which had the sanction of long-established custom. In this case an administrative warrant authorizing the seizure of a man's property to satisfy a debt to the government was found to be a well-established procedure and hence due process of law.

But if old established procedures were due process of law, then surely those common-law procedures listed in the Bill of Rights were due process of law. And if this were the case, why were they not guaranteed by the Fourteenth Amendment in state criminal cases? This was the argument of Hurtado in the present case. He had been convicted of murder by the state of California and sentenced to be hanged. He claimed a denial of due process because instead of a grand jury indictment, to which he would have been entitled under the common law, he had been charged by an information prepared by the prosecuting attorney—a form of charge authorized by the state of California, but limited at common law to misdemeanors.

Mr. Justice **Matthews** delivered the opinion of the Court, saying in part:

... The proposition of law we are asked to affirm is, that an indictment or presentment by a grand jury, as known to the common law of England, is essential to that "due process of law," when applied to prosecutions for felonies, which is secured and guaranteed by this provision of the Constitution of the United States, and which accordingly it is forbidden to the States respectively to dispense with in the administration of criminal law.

... It is maintained on behalf of the plaintiff in error that the phrase "due process of law" is equivalent to "law of the land," as found in the [thirty-]ninth chapter of Magna Charta; that, by immemorial usage, it has acquired a fixed, definite and technical meaning; that it refers to and includes, not only the general principles of public liberty and private right, which lie at the founda-

tion of all free government, but the very institutions which, venerable by time and custom, have been tried by experience and found fit and necessary for the preservation of those principles, and which, having been the birthright and inheritance of every English subject, crossed the Atlantic with the colonists and were transplanted and established in the fundamental laws of the State; that, having been originally introduced into the Constitution of the United States as a limitation upon the powers of the government, brought into being by that instrument, it has now been added as an additional security to the individual against oppression by the States themselves; that one of these institutions is that of the grand jury, an indictment or presentment by which against the accused in cases of alleged felonies is an essential part of due process of law, in order that he may not be harassed or destroyed by prosecutions founded only upon private malice or popular fury. . . .

It is urged upon us, however, in argument, that the claim made in behalf of the plaintiff in error is supported by the decision of this court in Murray's Lessee v. Hoboken Land & Improvement Company [1856]. There, Mr. Justice Curtis delivering the opinion of the court, after showing that due process of law must mean something more than the actual existing law of the land, for otherwise it would be no restraint upon legislative power, proceeds as follows: "To what principle, then, are we to resort to ascertain whether this process, enacted by Congress, is due process? To this the answer must be twofold. We must examine the Constitution itself to see whether this process be in conflict with any of its provisions. If not found to be so, we must look to those settled usages and modes of proceeding existing in the common and statute law of England before the emigration of our ancestors, and which are shown not to have been unsuited to their civil and political condition by having been acted on by them after the settlement of this country."

This, it is argued, furnishes an indispensable test of what constitutes "due process of law"; that any proceeding otherwise authorized by law, which is not thus sanctioned by usage, or which supersedes and displaces one that is, cannot be regarded as due process of law.

But this inference is unwarranted. The real syllabus of the passage quoted is, that a process of law, which is not otherwise forbidden, must be taken to be due process of law, if it can show the sanction of settled usage both in England and in this country; but it by no means follows, that nothing else can be due process of law. The point in the case cited arose in reference to a summary proceeding, questioned on that account, as not due process of law. The answer was: however exceptional it may be, as tested by definitions and principles of ordinary procedure, nevertheless, this, in substance, has been immemorially the actual law of the land, and, therefore, is due process of law. But to hold that such a characteristic is essential to due process of law, would be to deny every quality of the law but its age, and to render it incapable of progress or improvement. It would be to stamp upon our jurisprudence the unchangeableness attributed to the laws of the Medes and Persians.

This would be all the more singular and surprising, in this quick and active age, when we consider that, owing to the progressive development of legal ideas and institutions in England, the words of Magna Charta stood for very different things at the time of the separation of the American Colonies from what they represented originally. . . .

The Constitution of the United States was ordained, it is true, by descendants of Englishmen, who inherited the traditions of English law and history; but it was made for an undefined and expanding future, and for a people gathered and to be gathered from many Nations and of many tongues. And while we take just pride in the principles and institutions of the common law, we are not to forget that in lands where other systems of jurisprudence prevail, the ideas and processes of civil justice are also not unknown. Due process of law, in spite of the absolutism of continental governments, is not alien to that Code which survived the Roman Empire as the foundation of modern civilization in Europe, and which has given us that fundamental maxim of distributive justice, *suum cuique tribuere*. There is nothing in Magna Charta, rightly construed as a broad charter of public right and law, which ought to exclude the best ideas of all systems and of every age; and as it was the characteristic principle of the common law to draw its inspiration from every fountain of justice, we are not to assume that the sources of its supply have been exhausted. On the contrary, we should expect that the new and various experiences of our own situation and system will mold and shape it into new and not less useful forms. . . .

We are to construe this phrase in the 14th Amendment by the usus loquendi of the Constitution itself. The same words are contained in the 5th Amendment. That article makes specific and express provision for perpetuating the institution of the grand jury, so far as relates to prosecutions, for the more aggravated crimes under the laws of the United States. It declares that "No person shall be held to answer for a capital or otherwise infamous crime, unless on a presentment or indictment of a grand jury, except in cases arising in the land or naval forces, or in the militia when in actual service in time of war or public danger; nor shall any person be subject for the same offense to be twice put in jeopardy of life or limb; nor shall he be compelled in any criminal case to be a witness against himself." It then immediately adds: "nor be deprived of life, liberty or property, without due process of law." According to a recognized canon interpretation, especially applicable to formal and solemn instruments of constitutional law, we are forbidden to assume, without clear reason to the contrary, that any part of this most important Amendment is superfluous. The natural and obvious inference is, that in the sense of the Constitution, "due process of law" was not meant or intended to include, ex vi termini, the institution and procedure of a grand jury in any case. The conclusion is

equally irresistible, that when the same phrase was employed in the 14th Amendment to restrain the action of the States, it was used in the same sense and with no greater extent; and that if in the adoption of that Amendment it had been part of its purpose to perpetuate the institution of the grand jury in all the States, it would have embodied, as did the 5th Amendment, express declarations to that effect. Due process of law in the latter refers to that law of the land, which derives its authority from the legislative powers conferred upon Congress by the Constitution of the United States, exercised within the limits therein prescribed, and interpreted according to the principles of the common law. In the 14th Amendment, by parity of reason, it refers to that law of the land in each State, which derives its authority from the inherent and reserved powers of the State, exerted within the limits of those fundamental principles of liberty and justice which lie at the base of all our civil and political institutions, and the greatest security for which resides in the right of the people to make their own laws, and alter them at their pleasure. "The 14th Amendment," as was said by Mr. Justice Bradley in Mo. v. Lewis [1880], "does not profess to secure to all persons in the United States the benefit of the same laws and the same remedies. Great diversities in these respects may exist in two States separated only by an imaginary line. On one side of this line there may be a right of trial by jury, and on the other side no such right. Each State prescribes its own modes of judicial proceeding."

But it is not to be supposed that these legislative powers are absolute and despotic, and that the Amendment prescribing due process of law is too vague and indefinite to operate as a practical restraint. It is not every Act, legislative in form, that is law. Law is something more than mere will exerted as an act of power. . . . Arbitrary power, enforcing its edicts to the injury of the persons and property of its subjects, is not law, whether manifested as the decree of a personal monarch or of an impersonal multitude. And the limitations imposed by our constitutional law upon the action of the governments, both state and national, are essential to the preservation of public and private rights, notwithstanding the representative character of our political institutions. . . .

It follows that any legal proceeding enforced by public authority, whether sanctioned by age and custom, or newly devised in the discretion of the legislative power, in furtherance of the general public good, which regards and preserves these principles of liberty and justice, must be held to be due process of law. . . .

Tried by these principles, we are unable to say that the substitution for a presentment or indictment by a grand jury of the proceeding by information, after examination and commitment by a magistrate, certifying to the probable guilt of the defendant, with the right on his part to the aid of counsel, and to the cross-examination of the witnesses produced for the prosecution, is not due process of law. It is, as we have seen, an ancient proceeding at common law, which might include every case of an offense of less grade than a felony, except misprision of treason; and in every circumstance of its administration, as authorized by the Statute of California, it carefully considers and guards the substantial interest of the prisoner. It is merely a preliminary proceeding, and can result in no final judgment, except as the consequence of a regular judicial trial, conducted precisely as in cases of indictments. . . .

For these reasons, finding no error therein, the judgment of the Supreme Court of California is affirmed.

Mr. Justice **Harlan,** dissenting, said in part:

. . . I cannot agree that the State may, consistently with due process of law, require a person to answer for a capital offense, except upon the presentment or indictment of a grand jury. . . .

. . . To what principles are we to resort to ascertain whether this process . . . is due process? To this the answer must be twofold. We must examine the Constitution itself to see whether this process be in conflict with any of its provisions. If not found to be so, we must look *"to those settled usages and modes of proceeding existing in the common and statute law of England before the emigration of our ancestors, and which are shown not to have been unsuited to their civil and political condition by having been acted on by them after the settlement of this country,"* . . .

. . . Let us inquire (and no other inquiry is at all pertinent) whether according to the settled usages and modes of proceeding to which, this court has said, reference must be had, an information for a capital offense was, prior to the adoption of our Constitution, regarded as due process of law. . . . [Justice Harlan here reviews the authorities and finds it was not.]

My brethren concede that there are principles of liberty and justice, lying at the foundation of our civil and political institutions, which no State can violate consistently with that due process of law required by the 14th Amendment in proceedings involving life, liberty or property. Some of these principles are enumerated in the opinion of the court. But, for reasons which do not impress my mind as satisfactory, they exclude from that enumeration the exemption from prosecution, by information, for a public offense involving life. By what authority is that exclusion made? Is it justified by the settled usages and modes of procedure, existing under the common and statute law of England at the emigration of our ancestors or at the foundation of our government? Does not the fact that the people of the original States required an amendment of the National Constitution, securing exemption from prosecution, for a capital offense, except upon the indictment or presentment of a grand jury, prove that, in their judgment, such an exemption was essential to protection against accusation and unfounded prosecution and, therefore, was a fundamental principle in liberty and justice? . . .

But it is said that the framers of the Constitution did not suppose that due process of law necessarily required for a capital offense the institution and procedure of a grand jury, else they would not in the same amendment prohibiting the deprivation of life, liberty or property without due process of law, have made specific and express provision for a grand jury where the crime is capital or otherwise infamous; therefore, it is argued, the requirement by the 14th Amendment, of due process of law in all proceedings involving life, liberty and property, without specific reference to grand juries in any case whatever, was not intended as a restriction upon the power which it is claimed that the States previously had, so far as the express restrictions of the National Constitution are concerned, to dispense altogether with grand juries.

The line of argument, it seems to me, would lead to results which are inconsistent with the vital principles of republican government. If the presence in the 5th Amendment of a specific provision for grand juries in capital cases, alongside the provision for due process of law in proceedings involving life, liberty or property, is held to prove that due process of law did not, in the judgment of the framers of the Constitution, necessarily require a grand jury in capital cases, inexorable logic would require it to be, likewise, held that the right not to be put twice in jeopardy of life and limb for the same offense, nor compelled in a criminal case to testify against one's self (rights and immunities also specifically recognized in the 5th Amendment) were not protected by that due process of law required by the settled usages and proceedings existing under the common and statute law of England at the settlement of this country. More than that, other Amendments of the Constitution proposed at the same time, expressly recognize the right of persons to just compensation for private property taken for public use; their right, when accused of crime, to be informed of the nature and cause of the accusation against them, and to a speedy and public trial, by an impartial jury of the State and district wherein the crime was committed; to be confronted by the witnesses against them; and to have compulsory process for obtaining witnesses in their favor. Will it be claimed that these rights were not secured by the "law of the land" or by "due process of law," as declared and established at the foundation of our government? Are they to be excluded from the enumeration of the fundamental principles of liberty and justice and, therefore, not embraced by "due process of law?" . . .

It seems to me that too much stress is put upon the fact that the framers of the Constitution made express provision for the security of those rights which at common law were protected by the requirement of due process of law and, in addition, declared, generally, that no person shall "be deprived of life, liberty or property without due process of law." The rights, for the security of which these express provisions were made, were of a character so essential to the safety of the people that it was deemed wise to avoid the possibility that Congress, in regulating the processes of law, would impair or destroy them. Hence their specific enumeration in the earlier Amendments of the Constitution. . . .

POWELL v. ALABAMA

287 U. S. 45; 53 S. Ct. 55; 77 L. Ed. 158 (1932)

The Court in the Hurtado case (1884) not only rejected the idea that the protections listed in the Bill of Rights are included in due process, but the reasoning on which the decision was based made logically impossible their inclusion in the future. In 1897, however, following the advent of the concept of substantive due process in Munn v. Illinois (1877), the Court held that due process forbade a state to seize private property without just compensation; see Chicago, B. & Q. R. Co. v. Chicago. Justice Harlan, who had dissented in Hurtado, wrote the opinion of the Court without alluding to that case or calling attention to the fact that the right was one listed in the Bill of Rights. He held, simply, that the right to compensation was a right "founded in natural equity" and "laid down as a principle of universal law. Indeed, in a free government almost all other rights would become worthless if the government possessed an uncontrollable power over the private fortune of every citizen." He emphasized that "in determining what is due process of law regard must be had to substance, not to form," and pointed out that while "the legislature may prescribe a form of procedure to be observed in the taking of private property for public use, . . . it is not due process of law if provision be not made for compensation."

The C. B. & Q. decision had not overruled Hurtado, but since the two cases were in some ways incompatible, it seemed plausible to suppose that some of the Bill of Rights guarantees for persons accused of crime might also be found essential to due process. In Twining v. New Jersey (1908), however, the Court rejected the notion. The right to just compensation, it noted, was part of due process because of its fundamental nature, not because it was listed in the Bill of Rights. Not only was the guarantee against self-incrimination not of this fundamental nature, as Twining claimed, but added that the Court had never held void any state criminal procedure for want of due process of law. "Salutary as the principle [self-incrimination] may seem to the great majority, it cannot be ranked with the right to hearing before condemnation, the immunity from arbitrary power not acting by general laws, and the inviolability of private property." Clearly, the rights protected by due process were property rights—not rights involving criminal procedure. It was not until 1964, in Malloy v. Hogan, that the Court overruled Twining and held the protection against self-incrimination essential to due process.

With the rise of the doctrine of substantive due process it was increasingly urged on the Court that the

"liberty" protected by the due process clause of the Fourteenth Amendment should include, at the very least, the freedom of speech and press mentioned in the First Amendment. The pressure was not only from members of the bar, but from the Court itself. In 1907 Justice Harlan, in a dissenting opinion in Patterson v. Colorado, declared, "I go further and hold that the privileges of free speech and a free press, belonging to every citizen of the United States, constitute essential parts of every man's liberty, and are protected against violation by that clause of the Fourteenth Amendment forbidding a state to deprive any person of his liberty without due process of law." Essentially the same view was expressed by Justice Brandeis in his dissenting opinion in Gilbert v. Minnesota (1920), a case in which the Court assumed for the sake of argument that freedom of speech was "a natural and inherent" right but held that it had not been violated. Although in Prudential Insurance Co. v. Cheek (1922) the Court insisted that "neither the Fourteenth Amendment nor any other provision of the Constitution of the United States imposes upon the states any restrictions about 'freedom of speech,'" the following year it began to show signs of conversion to a broader conception of the term "liberty." In Meyer v. Nebraska (1923) Justice McReynolds, in an opinion holding invalid a Nebraska statute forbidding the teaching of any subject in any language but English in any private, parochial, or public school, defined the "liberty" protected by the due process clause as follows: "Without doubt, it denotes not merely freedom from bodily restraint, but also the right of the individual to contract, to engage in any of the common occupations of life, to acquire useful knowledge, to marry, establish a home and bring up children, to worship God according to the dictates of his own conscience, and, generally, to enjoy those privileges long recognized at common law as essential to the orderly pursuit of happiness by free men."

Two years later, in what was in fact a constitutional revolution, the Court, in Gitlow v. New York (1925), reversed its stand. Gitlow had challenged a state statute as violating his freedom of speech and thereby denying him due process; the Supreme Court took jurisdiction under the due process clause, declaring that "For present purposes we may and do assume that freedom of speech and of the press—which are protected by the First Amendment from abridgment by Congress—are among the fundamental personal rights and 'liberties' protected by the due process clause of the Fourteenth Amendment from impairment by the states." In Gitlow's case the Court held the state statute valid and upheld Gitlow's conviction; but in 1931, in Near v. Minnesota, the Court held a state statute void on the ground that it denied due process by unreasonably restricting freedom of speech and press. With these two cases these important liberties became effectively "nationalized," and the states came under federal judicial scrutiny and discipline in dealing with freedom of speech and press.

The other liberties mentioned in the First Amendment followed in due course. In Hamilton v. Regents of the U. of California (1934) freedom of religion was held to be protected by the Fourteenth Amendment, although the Court held that Hamilton's religious liberty was not abridged by making him take military drill as a condition of attending the state university. In De Jonge v. Oregon (1937) freedom of assembly was added to the list. The assimilation of the First Amendment into the Fourteenth was completed in Everson v. Board of Education (1947). The preceding cases were decided on the theory that the due process clause protects "liberty" and that "liberty" includes freedom of speech, press, religion, and assembly. The Everson case, however, which involved state aid to parochial school pupils, raised no question of "freedom" of religion but the question of whether the state action amounted to an "establishment" of religion. It could be argued that a state-supported religion does not abridge freedom of religion and hence is not an abridgment of "liberty" protected by due process of law, but the Supreme Court in the Everson case did not argue the point; it simply declared that "the First Amendment, as made applicable to the states by the Fourteenth ... commands that a state 'shall make no law respecting an establishment of religion. . . .' "

With the incorporation of First Amendment rights into the due process clause of the Fourteenth, pressure was brought on the Court to reconsider its stand in Hurtado (1884) and Twining (1908) to find other rights in the Bill of Rights to be "essential to due process" and hence applicable to the states. The present case, one of the famous Scottsboro Cases, raises the question of whether the right to counsel, guaranteed against federal infringement by the Sixth Amendment, is applicable to the states through the Fourteenth.

Mr. Justice **Sutherland** delivered the opinion of the Court, saying in part:

The petitioners, hereinafter referred to as defendants, are negroes charged with the crime of rape, committed upon the persons of two white girls. The crime is said to have been committed on March 25, 1931. The indictment was returned in a state court of first instance on March 31, and the record recites that on the same day the defendants were arraigned and entered pleas of not guilty. There is a further recital to the effect that upon the arraignment they were represented by counsel. But no counsel had been employed, and aside from a statement made by the trial judge several days later during a colloquy immediately preceding the trial, the record does not disclose when, or under what circumstances, an appointment of counsel was made, or who was appointed. During the colloquy referred to, the trial judge, in response to a question, said that he had appointed all the members of the bar for the purpose of arraigning the defendants and then of course anticipated that the members of the bar would continue to help the defendants if no counsel appeared. Upon the argument here both sides accepted that as a correct statement of the facts concerning the matter.

There was a severance upon the request of the state, and the defendants were tried in three several groups, as indicated above. As each of the three cases was called for trial, each defendant was arraigned, and, having the indictment read to him, entered a plea of not guilty. Whether the original arraignment and pleas were regarded as ineffective is not shown. Each of the three trials was completed within a single day. Under the Alabama statute the punishment for rape is to be fixed by jury, and in its discretion may be from ten years' imprisonment to death. The juries found defendants guilty and imposed the death penalty upon all. The trial court overruled motions for new trials and sentenced the defendants in accordance with the verdicts. The judgments were affirmed by the state supreme court. Chief Justice Anderson thought the defendants had not been accorded a fair trial and strongly dissented.

In this court the judgments are assailed upon the grounds that the defendants, and each of them, were denied due process of law and the equal protection of the laws, in contravention of the Fourteenth Amendment, specifically as follows: (1) They were not given a fair, impartial and deliberate trial; (2) they were denied the right of counsel, with the accustomed incidents of consultation and opportunity of preparation for trial; and (3) they were tried before juries from which qualified members of their own race were systematically excluded. These questions were properly raised and saved in the courts below.

The only one of the assignments which we shall consider is the second, in respect of the denial of counsel; and it becomes unnecessary to discuss the facts of the case or the circumstances surrounding the prosecution except in so far as they reflect light upon that question.

The record shows that on the day when the offense is said to have been committed, these defendants, together with a number of other negroes, were upon a freight train on its way through Alabama. On the same train were seven white boys and two white girls. A fight took place between the negroes and the white boys, in the course of which the white boys, with the exception of one named Gilley, were thrown off the train. A message was sent ahead, reporting the fight and asking that every negro be gotten off the train. The participants in the fight, and the two girls, were in an open gondola car. The two girls testified that each of them was assaulted by six different negroes in turn, and they identified the seven defendants as having been among the number. None of the white boys was called to testify, with the exception of Gilley, who was called in rebuttal.

Before the train reached Scottsboro, Alabama, a sheriff's posse seized the defendants and two other negroes. Both girls and the negroes then were taken to Scottsboro, the county seat. Word of their coming and of the alleged assault had preceded them, and they were met at Scottsboro by a large crowd. It does not sufficiently appear that the defendants were seriously threatened with, or that they were actually in danger of, mob violence; but it does appear that the attitude of the community was one of great hostility. The sheriff thought it necessary to call for the militia to assist in safeguarding the prisoners. Chief Justice Anderson pointed out in his opinion that every step taken from the arrest and arraignment to the sentence was accompanied by the military. Soldiers took the defendants to Gadsden for safekeeping, brought them back to Scottsboro for arraignment, returned them to Gadsden for safekeeping while awaiting trial, escorted them to Scottsboro for trial a few days later, and guarded the courthouse and grounds at every stage of the proceedings. It is perfectly apparent that the proceedings, from beginning to end, took place in an atmosphere of tense, hostile and excited public sentiment. During the entire time, the defendants were closely confined or were under military guard. The record does not disclose their ages, except that one of them was nineteen; but the record clearly indicates that most, if not all, of them were youthful, and they are constantly referred to as "the boys." They were ignorant and illiterate. All of them were residents of other states, where alone members of their families or friends resided.

However guilty defendants, upon due inquiry might prove to have been, they were, until convicted, presumed to be innocent. It was the duty of the court having their cases in charge to see that they were denied no necessary incident of a fair trial. With any error of the state court involving alleged contravention of the state statutes or constitution we, of course, have nothing to do. The sole inquiry which we are permitted to make is whether the federal Constitution was contravened ... and as to that, we confine ourselves, as already suggested, to the inquiry whether the defendants were in substance denied the right of counsel, and if so, whether such denial infringes the due process clause of the Fourteenth Amendment.

First. The record shows that immediately upon the return of the indictment defendants were arraigned and pleaded not guilty. Apparently they were not asked whether they had, or were able to employ counsel, or wished to have counsel appointed; or whether they had friends or relatives who might assist in that regard if communicated with. That it would not have been an idle ceremony to have given the defendants reasonable opportunity to communicate with their families and endeavor to obtain counsel is demonstrated by the fact that very soon after conviction able counsel appeared in their behalf. ...

It is hardly necessary to say that the right to counsel being conceded, a defendant should be afforded a fair opportunity to secure counsel of his own choice. Not only was that not done here, but such designation of counsel as was attempted was either so indefinite or so close upon the trial as to amount to a denial of effective and substantial aid in that regard. This will be amply demonstrated by a brief review of the record.

April 6, six days after indictment, the trials began. When the first case was called, the court inquired whether the parties were ready for trial. The state's attorney replied that he was ready to proceed. No one answered for the defendants or appeared to represent or defend them. Mr. Roddy, a Tennessee lawyer not a member of the local bar, addressed the court, saying that he had not been employed, but that people who were interested had spoken to him about the case. He was asked by the court whether he intended to appear for the defendants, and answered that he would like to appear along with counsel that the court might appoint. ...

It thus will be seen that until the very morning of the trial no lawyer had been named or definitely designated to represent the defendants. Prior to that time, the trial judge had "appointed all the members of the bar" for the limited "purpose of arraigning the defendants." Whether they would represent the defendants thereafter if no counsel appeared in their behalf, was a matter of speculation only, or, as the judge indicated, of mere anticipation on the part of the court. Such a designation, even if made for all purposes, would, in our opinion, have fallen far short of meeting, in any proper sense, a requirement for the appointment of counsel. How many lawyers were members of the bar does not appear; but, in the very nature of things, whether many or few, they would not, thus collectively named, have been given that clear appreciation of responsibility or impressed with that individual sense of duty which should and naturally would accompany the appointment of a selected member of the bar, specifically named and assigned. ...

... In any event, the circumstance lends emphasis to the conclusion that during perhaps the most critical period of the proceedings against these defendants, that is to say, from the time of their arraignment until the beginning of their trial, when consultation, thorough-going investigation and preparation were vitally important, the defendants did not have the aid of counsel in any real sense, although they were as much entitled to such aid during that period as at the trial itself. ...

Second. The Constitution of Alabama provides that in all criminal prosecutions the accused shall enjoy the right to have the assistance of counsel; and a state statute requires the court in a capital case, where the defendant is unable to employ counsel, to appoint counsel for him. The state supreme court held that these provisions had not been infringed, and with that holding we are powerless to interfere. The question, however, which it is our duty, and within our power, to decide, is whether the denial of the assistance of counsel contravenes the due process clause of the Fourteenth Amendment to the federal Constitution. ...

One test which has been applied to determine whether due process of law has been accorded in given instances is to ascertain what were the settled usages and modes of proceeding under the common and statute law of England before the Declaration of Independence, subject, however, to the qualification that they be shown not to have been unsuited to the civil and political conditions of our ancestors by having been followed in this country after it became a nation. ... Plainly, as appears from the foregoing, this test, as thus qualified, has not been met in the present case.

We do not overlook the case of Hurtado v. California [1884], where this court determined that due process of law does not require an indictment by a grand jury as a prerequisite to prosecution by a state for murder. In support of that conclusion the court referred to the fact that the Fifth Amendment, in addition to containing the due process of law clause, provides in explicit terms that "No person shall be held to answer for a capital, or otherwise infamous crime, unless on a presentment or indictment of a grand jury," and said that since no part of this important amendment could be regarded as superfluous, the obvious inference is that in the sense of the Constitution due process of law was not intended to include, ex vi termini, the institution and procedure of a grand jury in any case; and that the same phrase, employed in the Fourteenth Amendment to restrain the action of the states, was to be interpreted as having been used in the same sense and with no greater extent; and that if it had been the purpose of that Amendment to perpetuate the institution of the grand jury in the states, it would have embodied, as did the Fifth Amendment, an express declaration to that effect.

The Sixth Amendment, in terms, provides that in all criminal prosecutions the accused shall enjoy the right "to have the assistance of counsel for his defense." In the face of the reasoning of the Hurtado Case, if it stood alone, it would be difficult to justify the conclusion that the right to counsel, being thus specifically granted by the Sixth Amendment, was also within the intendment of the due process of law clause. But the Hurtado Case does not stand alone. In the later case of Chicago, B. & Q. R. Co. v. Chicago [1897], this court held that a judgment of a state court, even though authorized by statute, by which private property was taken for public use without just compensation, was in violation of the due process of law required by the Fourteenth Amendment, notwithstanding that the Fifth Amendment explicitly declares that private property shall not be taken for public use without just compensation. . . .

Likewise, this court has considered that freedom of speech and of the press are rights protected by the due process clause of the Fourteenth Amendment, although in the First Amendment, Congress is prohibited in specific terms from abridging the right. Gitlow v. New York [1925]. . . .

These later cases establish that notwithstanding the sweeping character of the language in the Hurtado Case, the rule laid down is not without exceptions. The rule is an aid to construction, and in some instances may be conclusive; but it must yield to more compelling considerations whenever such considerations exist. The fact that the right involved is of such a character that it cannot be denied without violating those "fundamental principles of liberty and justice which lie at the base of all our civil and political institutions" (Hebert v. Louisiana [1926]), is obviously one of those compelling considerations which must prevail in determining whether it is embraced within the due process clause of the Fourteenth Amendment, although it be specifically dealt with in another part of the federal Constitution. Evidently this court, in the later cases enumerated, regarded the rights

there under consideration as of this fundamental character. That some such distinction must be observed is foreshadowed in Twining v. New Jersey [1908], where Mr. Justice Moody, speaking for the court, said that ". . . it is possible that some of the personal rights safeguarded by the first eight Amendments against national action may also be safeguarded against state action, because a denial of them would be a denial of due process of law. Chicago, B. & Q. R. Co. v. Chicago [1897]. If this is so, it is not because those rights are enumerated in the first eight Amendments, but because they are of such a nature that they are included in the conception of due process of law." While the question has never been categorically determined by this court, a consideration of the nature of the right and a review of the expressions of this and other courts, make it clear that the right to the aid of counsel is of this fundamental character.

It never has been doubted by this court, or any other so far as we know, that notice and hearing are preliminary steps essential to the passing of an enforceable judgment, and that they, together with a legally competent tribunal having jurisdiction of the case, constitute basic elements of the constitutional requirement of due process of law. . . .

What, then, does a hearing include? Historically and in practice, in our own country at least, it has always included the right to the aid of counsel when desired and provided by the party asserting the right. The right to be heard would be, in many cases, of little avail if it did not comprehend the right to be heard by counsel. Even the intelligent and educated layman has small and sometimes no skill in the science of law. If charged with crime, he is incapable, generally, of determining for himself whether the indictment is good or bad. He is unfamiliar with the rules of evidence. Left without the aid of counsel he may be put on trial without a proper charge, and convicted upon incompetent evidence, or evidence irrelevant to the issue or otherwise inadmissible. He lacks both the skill and knowledge adequately to prepare his defense, even though he have a perfect one. He requires the guiding hand of counsel at every step in the proceedings against him. Without it, though he be not guilty, he faces the danger of conviction because he does not know how to establish his innocence. If that be true of men of intelligence, how much more true is it of the ignorant and illiterate, or those of feeble intellect. If in any case, civil or criminal, a state or federal court were arbitrarily to refuse to hear a party by counsel, employed by and appearing for him, it reasonably may not be doubted that such a refusal would be a denial of a hearing, and, therefore, of due process in the constitutional sense.

The decisions all point to that conclusion. . . . In Ex parte Chin Loy You (D. C.) 223 Fed. 833 [1915], also a deportation case, the district judge held that under the particular circumstances of the case the prisoner, having reasonably made demand, was entitled to confer with and have the aid of counsel. Pointing to the fact that the right to counsel as secured by the Sixth Amendment relates only to criminal prosecutions, the judge said, "But it is equally true that the provision was inserted in the Constitution because the assistance of counsel was recognized as essential to any fair trial of a case against a prisoner." . . .

In the light of the facts outlined in the forepart of this opinion—the ignorance and illiteracy of the defendants, their youth, the circumstances of public hostility, the imprisonment and the close surveillance of the defendants by the military forces, the fact that their friends and families were all in other states and communication with them necessarily difficult, and above all that they stood in deadly peril of their lives—we think the failure of the trial court to give them reasonable time and opportunity to secure counsel was a clear denial of due process.

But passing that, and assuming their inability, even if opportunity had been given, to employ counsel, as the trial court evidently did assume, we are of opinion that, under the circumstances just stated, the necessity of counsel was so vital and imperative that the failure of the trial court to make an effective appointment of counsel was likewise a denial of due process within the meaning of the Fourteenth Amendment. Whether this would be so in other criminal prosecutions, or under other circumstances, we need not determine. All that it is necessary now to decide, as we do decide, is that in a capital case, where the defendant is unable to employ counsel, and is incapable adequately of making his own defense because of ignorance, feeblemindedness, illiteracy, or the like, it is the duty of the court, whether requested or not, to assign counsel for him as a necessary requisite of due process of law; and that duty is not discharged by an assignment at such a time or under such circumstances as to preclude the giving of effective aid in the preparation and trial of the case. To hold otherwise would be to ignore the fundamental postulate, already adverted to, "that there are certain immutable principles of justice which inhere in the very idea of free government which no member of the Union may disregard." . . . In a case such as this, whatever may be the rule in other cases, the right to have counsel appointed, when necessary, is a logical corollary from the constitutional right to be heard by counsel. . . .

The United States by statute and every state in the Union by express provision of law, or by the determination of its courts, make it the duty of the trial judge, where the accused is unable to employ counsel, to appoint counsel for him. In most states the rule applies broadly to all criminal prosecutions, in others it is limited to the more serious crimes, and in a very limited number, to capital cases. A rule adopted with such unanimous accord reflects, if it does not establish, the inherent right to have counsel appointed at least in cases like the present, and lends convincing support to the conclusion we have reached as to the fundamental nature of that right.

The judgments must be reversed and the causes remanded for further proceedings not inconsistent with this opinion.

Judgments reversed.

Mr. Justice **Butler** wrote a dissenting opinion in which Mr. Justice **McReynolds** concurred.

PALKO v. CONNECTICUT

302 U. S. 319; 58 S. Ct. 149; 82 L. Ed. 288
(1937)

With the decision in Powell v. Alabama (1932) it appeared that the long struggle to nationalize the Bill of Rights might at last be bearing fruit. The Court had acknowledged that it no longer felt bound by the Hurtado reasoning; the application to the states of the Fifth Amendment right to just compensation and the First Amendment rights of free speech, press, religion, and assembly showed that some of the Bill of Rights guarantees could be applied to the states through due process of law. And now, in Powell, the Court for the first time had found one of the rights of persons accused of crime to be essential to due process.

The Palko case, printed below, made clear that the Court was not prepared to abandon earlier decisions such as Hurtado and Twining. Instead, it undertook to explain why some rights, such as the rights to counsel and free speech, are absorbed into due process; and why others, like jury trial and grand jury indictment, are not. It should be emphasized that the cases "absorbing" rights into the Fourteenth Amendment do not overrule Barron v. Baltimore (1833). The provisions of the federal Bill of Rights still limit directly only the federal government; it is the Fourteenth Amendment which limits the states. What the Court has done is to reverse the practical effect of the rule in Barron v. Baltimore with respect to part, but not all, of the Bill of Rights. Some of these rights are still not considered by the Court to be so fundamental as to be required by due process of law. The Court in case after case has been classifying the provisions of the Bill of Rights into those which are essential to due process of law and thus bind the states through the operation of the Fourteenth Amendment, and those which are not essential to due process and by which the states are not bound. In effect, the Court has established an "honor roll" of superior rights which bind both state and national governments. The opinion in the present case is important since it gives an official summary of this classification up to 1937 and states clearly the principles upon which the classification rests.

One question which the Palko case failed to answer satisfactorily was what was meant by "absorption" or "incorporation" of a Bill of Rights guarantee into due process. Did it mean that the right, as listed in the Bill of Rights and interpreted by the Supreme Court in federal cases, was made applicable to the states? Or was the right as applied to the states a more general right, less clearly defined and permitting more leeway and discretion on the part of the states? Clearly, incor-

poration of the First Amendment has meant its application to the states exactly as it is applied to the national government. Justices Brandeis and Holmes, in their dissent in the Gitlow case, suggested that the free speech applicable to the states perhaps "may be accepted with a somewhat larger latitude of interpretation than is allowed to Congress by the sweeping language that governs or ought to govern the laws of the United States." The Court, however, with the exception of whether jury verdicts must be unanimous (see Apodaca v. Oregon, 1972), has never acknowledged such a distinction, and the same rules for deciding such cases are applied to the states and the nation alike.

With the gradual extension of due process to include other rights, an important controversy developed as to how these rights would apply to the states. This problem is discussed in connection with the specific rights in the chapter below.

Mr. Justice **Cardozo** delivered the opinion of the Court, saying in part:

. . . Appellant was indicted . . . for the crime of murder in the first degree. A jury found him guilty of murder in the second degree, and he was sentenced to confinement in the state prison for life. Thereafter the state of Connecticut, with the permission of the judge presiding at the trial, gave notice of appeal to the Supreme Court of Errors. This it did pursuant to an act adopted in 1886 which is printed in the margin.* . . . Upon such appeal, the Supreme Court of Errors reversed the judgment and ordered a new trial. . . . It found that there had been error of law to the prejudice of the state. . . .

. . . [The] defendant was brought to trial again. Before a jury was impaneled and also at later stages of the case he made the objection that the effect of the new trial was to place him twice in jeopardy for the same offense, and in so doing to violate the Fourteenth Amendment of the Constitution of the United States. Upon the overruling of the objection the trial proceeded. The jury returned a verdict of murder in the first degree, and the court sentenced the defendant to the punishment of death. . . . The case is here upon appeal.

1. The execution of the sentence will not deprive appellant of his life without the process of law assured to him by the Fourteenth Amendment of the Federal Constitution.

The argument for appellant is that whatever is forbidden by the Fifth Amendment is forbidden by the Fourteenth also. The Fifth Amendment, which is not directed to the states, but solely to the federal government, creates immunity from double jeopardy. No person shall

---

*"Sec. 6494. *Appeals by the state in criminal cases.* Appeals from the rulings and decisions of the superior court or of any criminal court of common pleas, upon all questions of law arising on the trial of criminal cases, may be taken by the state, with the permission of the presiding judge, to the supreme court of errors, in the same manner and to the same effect as if made by the accused. . . ."

be "subject for the same offense to be twice put in jeopardy of life or limb." The Fourteenth Amendment ordains, "nor shall any state deprive any person of life, liberty, or property, without due process of law." To retry a defendant, though under one indictment and only one, subjects him, it is said, to double jeopardy in violation of the Fifth Amendment, if the prosecution is one on behalf of the United States. From this the consequence is said to follow that there is a denial of life or liberty without due process of law, if the prosecution is one on behalf of the People of a State. . . .

We have said that in appellant's view the Fourteenth Amendment is to be taken as embodying the prohibitions of the Fifth. His thesis is even broader. Whatever would be a violation of the original bill of rights (Amendments 1 to 8) if done by the federal government is now equally unlawful by force of the Fourteenth Amendment if done by a state. There is no such general rule.

The Fifth Amendment provides, among other things, that no person shall be held to answer for a capital or otherwise infamous crime unless on presentment or indictment of a grand jury. This court has held that, in prosecutions by a state, presentment or indictment by a grand jury may give way to informations at the instance of a public officer. Hurtado v. California [1884]. . . . The Fifth Amendment provides also that no person shall be compelled in any criminal case to be a witness against himself. This court has said that, in prosecutions by a state, the exemption will fail if the state elects to end it. Twining v. New Jersey [1908]. . . . The Sixth Amendment calls for a jury trial in criminal cases and the Seventh for a jury trial in civil cases at common law where the value in controversy shall exceed twenty dollars. This court has ruled that consistently with those amendments trial by jury may be modified by a state or abolished altogether. Walker v. Sauvinet [1876]; Maxwell v. Dow [1900]. . . . As to the Fourth Amendment, one should refer to Weeks v. United States [1914] and as to other provisions of the Sixth, to West v. Louisiana [1904].

On the other hand, the due process clause of the Fourteenth Amendment may make it unlawful for a state to abridge by its statutes the freedom of speech which the First Amendment safeguards against encroachment by the Congress (De Jonge v. Oregon [1937]) or the like freedom of the press (Near v. Minnesota [1931]), or the free exercise of religion (Hamilton v. University of California [1934]; . . .), or the right of peaceable assembly, without which speech would be unduly trammeled (De Jonge v. Oregon), or the right of one accused of crime to the benefit of counsel (Powell v. Alabama [1932]). In these and other situations immunities that are valid as against the federal government by force of the specific pledges of particular amendments have been found to be implicit in the concept of ordered liberty, and thus, through the Fourteenth Amendment, become valid as against the states.

The line of division may seem to be wavering and broken if there is a hasty catalogue of the cases on the one side and the other. Reflection and analysis will induce a different view. There emerges the perception of a rationalizing principle which gives to discrete instances a proper order and coherence. The right to trial by jury and the immunity from prosecution except as the result of an indictment may have value and importance. Even so, they are not of the very essence of a scheme of ordered liberty. To abolish them is not to violate a "principle of justice so rooted in the traditions and conscience of our people as to be ranked as fundamental." . . . Few would be so narrow or provincial as to maintain that a fair and enlightened system of justice would be impossible without them. What is true of jury trials and indictments is true also, as the cases show, of the immunity from compulsory self-incrimination. Twining v. New Jersey. This too might be lost, and justice still be done. Indeed, today as in the past there are students of our penal system who look upon the immunity as a mischief rather than a benefit, and who would limit its scope or destroy it altogether. . . . The exclusion of these immunities and privileges from the privileges and immunities protected against the action of the states has not been arbitrary or casual. It has been dictated by a study and appreciation of the meaning, the essential implications, of liberty itself.

We reach a different plane of social and moral values when we pass to the privileges and immunities that have been taken over from the earlier articles of the federal bill of rights and brought within the Fourteenth Amendment by a process of absorption. These in their origin were effective against the federal government alone. If the Fourteenth Amendment has absorbed them, the process of absorption has had its source in the belief that neither liberty nor justice would exist if they were sacrificed. Twining v. New Jersey. This is true, for illustration, of freedom of thought and speech. Of that freedom one may say that it is the matrix, the indispensable condition, of nearly every other form of freedom. With rare aberrations a pervasive recognition of that truth can be traced in our history, political and legal. So it has come about that the domain of liberty, withdrawn by the Fourteenth Amendment from encroachment by the states, has been enlarged by latter-day judgments to include liberty of the mind as well as liberty of action. . . . Fundamental too in the concept of due process, and so in that of liberty, is the thought that condemnation shall be rendered only after trial. . . . The hearing, moreover, must be a real one, not a sham or a pretense. Moore v. Dempsey [1923]. . . . For that reason, ignorant defendants in a capital case were held to have been condemned unlawfully when in truth, though not in form, they were refused the aid of counsel. Powell v. Alabama. The decision did not turn upon the fact that the benefit of counsel would have been guaranteed to the defendants by the provisions of the Sixth Amendment if they had been prosecuted in a federal court. The decision turned upon the fact that in the particular situation laid before us in the evidence the benefit of counsel was essential to the substance of a hearing.

Our survey of the cases serves, we think, to justify the statement that the dividing line between them, if not unfaltering throughout its course, has been true for the most part to a unifying principle. On which side of the line the case made out by the appellant has appropriate location must be the next inquiry and the final one. Is that kind of double jeopardy to which the statute has subjected him a hardship so acute and shocking that our polity will not endure it? Does it violate those "fundamental principles of liberty and justice which lie at the base of all our civil and political institutions?" . . . The answer surely must be "no." What the answer would have to be if the state were permitted after a trial free from error to try the accused over again or to bring another case against him, we have no occasion to consider. We deal with the statute before us and no other. The state is not attempting to wear the accused out by a multitude of cases with accumulated trials. It asks no more than this, that the case against him shall go on until there shall be a trial free from the corrosion of substantial legal error. . . . This is not cruelty at all, nor even vexation in any immoderate degree. If the trial had been infected with error adverse to the accused, there might have been review at his instance, and as often as necessary to purge the vicious taint. A reciprocal privilege, subject at all times to the discretion of the presiding judge . . . , has now been granted to the state. There is here no seismic innovation. The edifice of justice stands, in its symmetry, to many, greater than before.

2. The conviction of appellant is not in derogation of any privileges or immunities that belong to him as a citizen of the United States. . . .

Maxwell v. Dow [1900], gives all the answer that is necessary.

The judgment is affirmed.

Mr. Justice **Butler** dissents.

DUE PROCESS AS FUNDAMENTAL FAIRNESS

BETTS v. BRADY

316 U. S. 455; 62 S. Ct. 1252; 86 L. Ed. 1595
(1942)

The procedural side of due process developed slowly. As late as 1908 the Court in Twining v. New Jersey conceded that no state procedure had ever been held void for want of due process, and in both Hurtado and Twining the Court made clear that due process did not make the procedures of the Bill of Rights applicable to the states. State procedures, as long as they conformed to state law and did not violate the "fundamental principles of liberty and justice which lie at the base of all our civil and political institutions," were due process.

Nor was the Court willing to use the Fifth Amend-

ment's due process clause in the field of criminal procedure. Since the two clauses meant the same thing, the Fifth Amendment protection could not be applied to federal criminal trials without at the same time applying the Fourteenth Amendment to state criminal trials—a step the Court was not prepared to take. So where the Court wished to enforce against the federal government standards of fairness more exacting than those spelled out in the Bill of Rights, it did not invoke the due process clause of the Fifth Amendment; instead it relied on what may be called "quasi-due process" based on its general supervisory power over the administration of justice in the United States courts.

This doctrine was enunciated first in 1943 in *McNabb v. United States:* "Judicial supervision of the administration of criminal justice in the Federal courts implies the duty of establishing and maintaining civilized standards of procedure and evidence. Such standards are not satisfied merely by observance of those minimal historic safeguards for securing trial by reason which are summarized as 'due process of law' and below which we reach what is really trial by force." In this case the Court held inadmissible in a federal court admissions secured from a prisoner who was held by the police without being taken immediately before a committing magistrate as required by statute. It was upon this ground, also, that evidence which federal officers obtain illegally was first held inadmissible in federal courts (see *Nardone v. United States,* 1937) and stricter standards are maintained in the selection of federal juries.

Despite its obvious reluctance to incorporate the specific guarantees of the Bill of Rights, the Court did take increasing interest in state procedures and machinery, and grew more watchful lest they not meet the requirements of fundamental fairness. Such insistence on fundamental fairness, especially for persons accused of crime, was bound to bring before the Court the widest variety of state activities. In 1927, for instance, the Court in *Tumey v. Ohio* reversed the conviction of a bootlegger who had been tried before the mayor of a small town. An ordinance provided that the mayor should retain the court costs as payment for his judicial work, but no costs were paid if the defendant were acquitted. Tumey had been fined one hundred dollars, and the costs involved were twelve dollars. The Supreme Court held it to be a denial of due process to "subject his liberty or property to the judgment of a court, the judge of which has a direct, personal, substantial pecuniary interest in reaching a conclusion against him in his case. ... There are doubtless mayors," the Court conceded, "who would not allow such a consideration as twelve dollar costs in each case to affect their judgment in it, but the requirement of due process of law in judicial procedure is not satisfied by the argument that men of the highest honor and the greatest self-sacrifice could carry it on without danger of injustice. Every procedure which would offer a possible temptation to the average man as a judge to forget the burden of proof required to convict the defendant, or which might lead him not to hold the balance nice, clear and true between the state and the accused

denies the latter due process of law." The doctrine of *Tumey* was reaffirmed as recently as 1977 when the Court in *Connally v. Georgia* held void a search warrant issued by a justice of the peace. The justice received five dollars if he issued the warrant but nothing if he didn't.

Nor are jury members expected to be persons of unrestrained self-sacrifice, and a trial conducted in an atmosphere of mob violence is inherently unfair. In *Moore v. Dempsey* (1923) five blacks were convicted in an Arkansas court of the murder of a white man and sentenced to death. The Court described the trial in these words: "The court and the neighborhood were thronged with an adverse crowd that threatened the most dangerous consequences to any one interfering with the desired result. The counsel did not venture to demand delay or a change of venue, to challenge a juryman, or to ask for separate trials. He had had no preliminary consultation with the accused, called no witnesses for the defense, although they could have been produced, and did not put the defendants on the stand. The trial lasted about three quarters of an hour, and in less than five minutes the jury brought in a verdict of murder in the first degree. According to the allegations and affidavits there never was a chance for the petitioners to be acquitted; no juryman could have voted for an acquittal and continued to live in Phillips County, and if any prisoner, by any chance, had been acquitted by a jury, he could not have escaped the mob." Under these conditions no trial in the true sense was possible and the defendants were denied due process of law.

The Supreme Court has made it clear that due process is denied by an attempt to punish a person for a crime which is not clearly defined. In 1934 New Jersey passed an act punishing by $10,000 or twenty years or both the crime of being "a gangster." A gangster was defined as "any person not engaged in any lawful occupation, known to be a member of any gang consisting of two or more persons, who has been convicted at least three times of being a disorderly person, or who has been convicted of any crime. ..." In *Lanzetta v. New Jersey* (1939) the Court held the statute void, noting that "no one may be required at peril of his life, liberty or property to speculate as to the meaning of penal statues. All are entitled to be informed as to what the State commands or forbids."

In 1972 the Supreme Court struck down a Jacksonville vagrancy ordinance which, in the archaic language of the Elizabethan Poor Law, defines as vagrants (among others) "rogues and vagabonds, or dissolute persons who go about begging, ... common night walkers, ... common railers and brawlers, persons wandering or strolling around from place to place without any lawful purpose or object, habitual loafers, [and] ... persons able to work but habitually living upon the earnings of their wives or minor children. ..." Two white girls and their black dates were arrested on the main thoroughfare in Jacksonville and convicted of "prowling by auto." In *Papachristou v. Jacksonville* (1972) a unanimous Court found the ordinance void for vagueness both in the sense that it "fails to give a person of ordinary intelligence fair notice that his contemplated conduct is forbidden by the statute, . . . and because it encourages arbitrary and erratic arrests and convictions." Not only does it "make criminal activities which by modern standards are normally innocent," but it puts "unfettered discretion in the hands of the Jacksonville police." "Those generally implicated by the imprecise terms of the ordinance—poor people, nonconformists, dissenters, idlers—may be required to comport themselves according to the life-style deemed appropriate by the Jacksonville police and the courts. Where, as here, there are no standards governing the exercise of the discretion granted by the ordinance, the scheme permits and encourages an arbitrary and discriminatory enforcement of the law . . . It results in a regime in which the poor and unpopular are permitted to 'stand on a public sidewalk . . . only at the whim of any police officer.' Shuttlesworth v. Birmingham [1969]." In 1983 the case was reaffirmed in Kolender v. Lawson where the Court struck down a California statute making it a crime to be unable to produce "credible and reliable" identification when asked to do so by a police officer. The statute was violated unless "the officer [is] satisfied that the identification is reliable."

The fairness which due process requires in civil and criminal procedures alike demands that when the law creates a presumption of guilt or misconduct or incapacity, this presumption may not be made irrebuttable. The person who is the subject of the presumption must be given the chance to rebut it if he can. This principle governed the Court's decision in Slochower v. Board of Education (1956). The New York City charter provides that if any city employee pleads self-incrimination to avoid answering questions relating to his or her official conduct, he or she shall be automatically removed from office and ineligible for reappointment. Slochower was an associate professor at Brooklyn College, maintained by the City of New York. In 1953 he refused on grounds of self-incrimination to testify before a subcommittee of the United States Senate concerning alleged Communist activities. He was dismissed from his post. The Board of Education contended that one of two possible inferences flowed from his plea of self-incrimination: "(1) that the answering of the question would tend to prove him guilty of a crime in some way connected with his official conduct; or (2) that in order to avoid answering the question he falsely invoked the privilege by stating that the answer would tend to incriminate him, and thus committed perjury. Either inference, it insists, is sufficient to justify the termination of his employment."

The Supreme Court held that Slochower's dismissal denied him due process of law, since he had been given no opportunity to rebut the presumption of guilt or unfitness based on his plea of self-incrimination. The New York charter made that presumption conclusive. The Court condemned the "practice of imputing a sinister meaning to the exercise of a person's constitutional right under the Fifth Amendment," and emphasized that "the privilege against self-incrimination would be reduced to a hollow mockery if its exercise could be taken

as equivalent either to a confession of guilt or a conclusive presumption of perjury." In 1958, however, the Court held that a Philadelphia schoolteacher could validly be dismissed on grounds of incompetence for the lack of candor shown by refusal to answer questions concerning possible subversive associations at a fairly conducted hearing; see Beilan v. Board of Education. The same result was reached in Lerner v. Casey (1958), in which a New York subway guard who refused to testify was dismissed on grounds of "unreliability."

Among the things a state cannot do is knowingly to permit a conviction to rest upon perjured testimony. In Mooney v. Holohan (1935) the Court held that "depriving a defendant of liberty through a deliberate deception of court and jury by the presentation of testimony known to be perjured . . . is as inconsistent with the rudimentary demands of justice as is the obtaining of a like result by intimidation." The state must also provide "corrective judicial process by which a conviction obtained may be set aside."

Nor can a state through its criminal procedure favor the wealthy over the poor. In order to carry an appeal to the supreme court of Illinois in a criminal case it is necessary to have a stenographic transcript of the trial proceedings. Only an indigent defendant who had been sentenced to death was provided with a free transcript; all other defendants had to buy it. As a result, a poor person convicted of a noncapital crime and therefore not entitled to a free transcript would be deprived of the right to appeal because of poverty—a right easily available to the well-to-do convict. In Griffin v. Illinois, (1956) the Supreme Court held this to be a violation of due process and equal protection of the laws. "In criminal trials," the Court said, "a State can no more discriminate on account of poverty than on account of religion, race, or color. Plainly the ability to pay costs in advance bears no rational relationship to a defendant's guilt or innocence and could not be used as an excuse to deprive a defendant of a fair trial. . . . There is no meaningful distinction between a rule which would deny the poor the right to defend themselves in a trial court and one which effectively denies the poor an adequate appellate review accorded to all who have money enough to pay the costs in advance." In Mayer v. Chicago (1972) the Court extended the rule to include persons charged with a misdemeanor and liable only to a fine. "Griffin," it emphasized, ". . . is a flat protection against pricing indigent defendants out of as effective an appeal as would be available to others able to pay their own way."

It is clear that rights which are not mentioned in the Bill of Rights must be protected, if at all, through that aspect of due process of law that guarantees a person "fundamental fairness" of treatment at the hands of the state. Thus in the Palko case the Court not only declined to "incorporate" the right against double jeopardy into due process, but it found that the state had not, on the facts of his particular case, denied him essentially fair treatment. To use Justice Frankfurter's phrase, while it had not accorded him "civilized" treatment, neither had it dropped to the level of "trial by force." The language *used by the Court to describe these two aspects of due process is often confusing. While it will describe a right listed in the Bill of Rights as sufficiently "fundamental" to be incorporated into due process, it also uses "fundamental" to describe the level of fairness demanded of the states in its exercise of those procedures not so incorporated.*

The decision in Powell v. Alabama (1932) was widely regarded as incorporating the Sixth Amendment right to counsel into due process in the sense that a state would have had to supply counsel in all cases where the Sixth Amendment would have required it. This assumption was bolstered by its inclusion in Palko in the list of rights "that have been taken over from the earlier articles of the federal Bill of Rights and brought within the Fourteenth Amendment by a process of absorption." In a number of other cases, mentioned in the opinion below, the Court appeared to assume that the right to counsel was "fundamental" (in the former sense) and had thus been incorporated into due process. But the Court, in deciding the present case, rejected this interpretation. The right to counsel, like the right against double jeopardy involved in the Palko case, is not in its very nature "fundamental" so as to be required in all cases, i. e., incorporated. It is the right to a fair trial, i.e., fair treatment by the state, and not any specific ingredient thereof, that is fundamental and hence guaranteed by due process.

It was not until two decades later, in Gideon v. Wainwright (1963), that Betts v. Brady was overruled and the right to counsel duly "incorporated."

Mr. Justice **Roberts** delivered the opinion of the Court, saying in part:

The petitioner was indicted for robbery in the Circuit Court of Carroll County, Maryland. Due to lack of funds, he was unable to employ counsel, and so informed the judge at his arraignment. He requested that counsel be appointed for him. The judge advised him that this would not be done as it was not the practice in Carroll County to appoint counsel for indigent defendants save in prosecutions for murder and rape.

Without waiving his asserted right to counsel the petitioner pleaded not guilty and elected to be tried without a jury. At his request witnesses were summoned in his behalf. He cross-examined the State's witnesses and examined his own. The latter gave testimony tending to establish an alibi. Although afforded the opportunity, he did not take the witness stand. The judge found him guilty and imposed a sentence of eight years. . . .

3. Was the petitioner's conviction and sentence a deprivation of his liberty without due process of law, in violation of the Fourteenth Amendment, because of the court's refusal to appoint counsel at his request?

The Sixth Amendment of the national Constitution applies only to trials in federal courts. The due process clause of the Fourteenth Amendment does not incorporate, as such, the specific guarantees found in the Sixth Amendment although a denial by a state of rights or privileges specifically embodied in that and others of the first eight amendments may, in certain circumstances, or in connection with other elements, operate, in a given case, to deprive a litigant of due process of law in violation of the Fourteenth. Due process of law is secured against invasion by the federal Government by the Fifth Amendment and is safeguarded against state action in identical words by the Fourteenth. The phrase formulates a concept less rigid and more fluid than those envisaged in other specific and particular provisions of the Bill of Rights. Its application is less a matter of rule. Asserted denial is to be tested by an appraisal of the totality of facts in a given case. That which may, in one setting, constitute a denial of fundamental fairness, shocking to the universal sense of justice, may, in other circumstances, and in the light of other considerations, fall short of such denial. In the application of such a concept there is always the danger of falling into the habit of formulating the guarantee into a set of hard and fast rules the application of which in a given case may be to ignore the qualifying factors therein disclosed.

The petitioner, in this instance, asks us, in effect, to apply a rule in the enforcement of the due process clause. He says the rule to be deduced from our former decisions is that, in every case, whatever the circumstances, one charged with crime, who is unable to obtain counsel, must be furnished counsel by the state. Expressions in the opinions of this court lend color to the argument,* but, as the petitioner admits, none of our decisions squarely adjudicates the questions now presented.

In Powell v. Alabama [1932] ignorant and friendless negro youths, strangers in the community, without friends or means to obtain counsel, were hurried to trial for a capital offense without effective appointment of counsel on whom the burden of preparation and trial would rest, and without adequate opportunity to consult even the counsel casually appointed to represent them. This occurred in a State whose statute law required the appointment of counsel for indigent defendants prosecuted for the offense charged. Thus the trial was conducted in disregard of every principle of fairness and in disregard of that which was declared by the law of the State a requisite of a fair trial. This court held the resulting convictions were without due process of law. It said that, in the light of all the facts, the failure of the trial court to afford the defendants reasonable time and opportunity to secure counsel was a clear denial of due process. The court stated further that "under the circumstances, the necessity of counsel was so vital and imperative that the failure of the trial court to make an effective appointment of counsel was likewise a denial of due process," but added: "whether this would be so in other criminal prosecutions, or under other circumstances, we need not determine. All that it is necessary now to decide, as we do decide, is that, in a capital case, where the defendant is unable to employ counsel, and is incapable adequately of making his own defense because of igno-

---

*Powell v. Alabama [1932]; Grosjean v. American Press Co. [1936]; Johnson v. Zerbst [1938]; Avery v. Alabama [1940].

rance, feeble-mindedness, illiteracy, or the like, it is the duty of the court, whether requested or not, to assign counsel for him as a necessary requisite of due process of law.'' . . .

Those cases, which are the petitioner's chief reliance, do not rule this. The question we are now to decide is whether due process of law demands that in every criminal case, whatever the circumstances, a state must furnish counsel to an indigent defendant. Is the furnishing of counsel in cases whatever dictated by natural, inherent, and fundamental principles of fairness? The answer to the question may be found in the common understanding of those who have lived under the Anglo-American system of law. By the Sixth Amendment the people ordained that, in all criminal prosecutions, the accused should ''enjoy the right . . . to have the assistance of counsel for his defense.'' We have construed the provision to require appointment of counsel in all cases where a defendant is unable to procure the services of an attorney, and where the right has not been intentionally and competently waived. Though, as we have noted, the amendment lays down no rule for the conduct of the states, the question recurs whether the constraint laid by the amendment upon the national courts expresses a rule so fundamental and essential to a fair trial, and so, to due process of law, that it is made obligatory upon the states by the Fourteenth Amendment. Relevant data on the subject are afforded by constitutional and statutory provisions subsisting in the colonies and the states prior to the inclusion of the Bill of Rights in the national Constitution, and in the constitutional, legislative, and judicial history of the states to the present date. These constitute the most authoritative sources for ascertaining the considered judgment of the citizens of the states upon the question. . . .

In the light of this common law practice, it is evident that the constitutional provisions to the effect that a defendant should be ''allowed'' counsel or should have a right ''to be heard by himself and his counsel,'' or that he might be heard by ''either or both,'' at his election, were intended to do away with the rules which denied representation, in whole or in part, by counsel in criminal prosecutions, but were not aimed to compel the state to provide counsel for a defendant. At the least, such a construction by state courts and legislators can not be said to lack reasonable basis.

The statutes in force in the thirteen original states at the time of the adoption of the Bill of Rights are also illuminating. It is of interest that the matter of appointment of counsel for defendants, if dealt with at all, was dealt with by statute rather than by constitutional provision. The contemporary legislation exhibits great diversity of policy. . . .

This material demonstrates that, in the great majority of the states, it has been the considered judgment of the people, their representatives and their courts that appointment of counsel is not a fundamental right, essential to a fair trial. On the contrary, the matter has generally been deemed one of legislative policy. In the light of this evidence we are unable to say that the concept of due process incorporated in the Fourteenth Amendment obligates the states, whatever may be their own views, to furnish counsel in every such case. Every court has power, if it deems proper, to appoint counsel where that course seems to be required in the interest of fairness.

The practice of the courts of Maryland gives point to the principle that the states should not be strait-jacketed in this respect, by a construction of the Fourteenth Amendment. Judge Bond's opinion states, and counsel at the bar confirmed the fact, that in Maryland the usual practice is for the defendant to waive a trial by jury. This the petitioner did in the present case. Such trials, as Judge Bond remarks, are much more informal than jury trials and it is obvious that the judge can much better control the course of the trial and is in a better position to see impartial justice done than when the formalities of a jury trial are involved.

In this case there was no question of the commission of a robbery. The State's case consisted of evidence identifying the petitioner as the perpetrator. The defense was an alibi. Petitioner called and examined witnesses to prove that he was at another place at the time of the commission of the offense. The simple issue was the veracity of the testimony for the State and that for the defendant. As Judge Bond says, the accused was not helpless, but was a man forty-three years old, of ordinary intelligence and ability to take care of his own interests on the trial of that narrow issue. He had once before been in a criminal court, pleaded guilty to larceny and served a sentence and was not wholly unfamiliar with criminal procedure. It is quite clear that in Maryland, if the situation had been otherwise and it had appeared that the petitioner was, for any reason, at a serious disadvantage by reason of the lack of counsel, a refusal to appoint would have resulted in the reversal of a judgment of conviction. Only recently the Court of Appeals has reversed a conviction because it was convinced on the whole record that an accused tried without counsel had been handicapped by the lack of representation.

To deduce from the due process clause a rule binding upon the states in this matter would be to impose upon them, as Judge Bond points out, a requirement without distinction between criminal charges of different magnitude or in respect of courts of varying jurisdiction. As he says: ''Charges of small crimes tried before justices of the peace and capital charges tried in the higher courts would equally require the appointment of counsel. Presumably it would be argued that trials in the Traffic Court would require it.'' And indeed it was said by petitioner's counsel both below and in this court, that as the Fourteenth Amendment extends the protection of due process to property as well as to life and liberty, if we hold with the petitioner logic would require the furnishing of counsel in civil cases involving property.

As we have said, the Fourteenth Amendment prohibits the conviction and incarceration of one whose trial is offensive to the common and fundamental ideas of fairness and right, and while want of counsel in a particular case may result in a conviction lacking in such fundamental fairness, we cannot say that the amendment embodies an inexorable command that no trial for any offense, or in any court, can be fairly conducted and justice accorded a defendant who is not represented by counsel.

The judgment is affirmed.

Mr. Justice **Black**, dissenting, with whom Mr. Justice **Douglas** and Mr. Justice **Murphy** concur, said in part:

If this case had come to us from a federal court, it is clear we should have to reverse it, because the Sixth Amendment makes the right to counsel in criminal cases inviolable by the federal government. I believe that the Fourteenth Amendment made the Sixth applicable to the states. But this view, although often urged in dissents, has never been accepted by a majority of this Court and is not accepted today. A statement of the grounds supporting it is, therefore, unnecessary at this time. I believe, however, that under the prevailing view of due process, as reflected in the opinion just announced, a view which gives this Court such vast supervisory powers that I am not prepared to accept it without grave doubts, the judgment below should be reversed.

This Court has just declared that due process of law is denied if a trial is conducted in such manner that it is "shocking to the universal sense of justice" or "offensive to the common and fundamental ideas of fairness and right." On other occasion this Court has recognized that whatever is "implicit in the concept of ordered liberty" and "essential to the substance of a hearing" is within the procedural protection afforded by the constitutional guaranty of due process. Palko v. Connecticut [1937].

The right to counsel in a criminal proceeding is "fundamental." Powell v. Alabama. . . .

A practice cannot be reconciled with "common and fundamental ideas of fairness and right," which subjects innocent men to increased dangers of conviction merely because of their poverty. Whether a man is innocent cannot be determined from a trial in which, as here, denial of counsel has made it impossible to conclude, with any satisfactory degree of certainty, that the defendant's case was adequately presented. . . .

ROCHIN v. CALIFORNIA

342 U.S. 165; 72 S. Ct. 205; 96 L. Ed. 183 (1952)

The Supreme Court had held in the case of Wolf v. Colorado (1949) that the right of privacy protected by the search and seizure provision of the Fourth Amendment was essential to due process, but at the same time had refused to hold that evidence gotten by such seizures was inadmissible in court. Thus a state could get evidence against a person in an unconstitutional way and use it against him in court. The Supreme Court, however, took a very different attitude with respect to evidence got by coercion. In Brown v. Mississippi (1936) the conviction of three blacks for murder solely upon the basis of confessions obtained by brutality and physical torture was held to deny them due process of law. The Court explained that merely "because a State may dispense with a jury trial, it does not follow that it may substitute trial by ordeal. The rack and torture chamber may not be substituted for the witness stand. . . . It would be difficult to conceive of methods more revolting to the sense of justice than those taken to procure the confessions of these petitioners, and the use of the confessions thus obtained as the basis for conviction and sentence was a clear denial of due process."

The problem of what constitutes coercion has been a difficult one for the Court. While physical violence clearly amounts to coercion, it is apparent that certain types of psychological pressure may do so, too. In Chambers v. Florida (1940) the Court held a denial of due process the "sunrise confessions" of four blacks which followed five days of interrogation in the absence of "friends, advisors or counselors, and under circumstances calculated to break the strongest nerves and the stoutest resistance." The same result was reached in Ashcraft v. Tennessee (1944), where the prisoner confessed to a murder after thirty-six hours of continuous questioning under powerful electric lights, though he was not subjected to any physical abuse.

In Lisenba v. California (1941), however, the Court upheld the use of a confession despite the fact that the defendant had been subject to two sleepless days and nights of almost continuous questioning by relays of police officers. The confession took place ten days after this questioning, and the Court concluded that he had not "so lost his freedom of action that the statements made were not his but were the result of the deprivation of his free choice to admit, to deny, or to refuse to answer." A similar result was reached in Stein v. New York (1953), the Reader's Digest murder case. Here the judge had left to the jury the question of admissibility, and since the jury had delivered a general verdict of guilty the Court faced two problems: (1) could the jury have constitutionally found the confessions voluntary and used them as the basis of the conviction, and (2) if the jury found the confessions inadmissible, could it convict on the basis of other evidence or did the use of the confessions vitiate the entire trial? The Court held the confessions were "'voluntary,' in the only sense in which confessions to the police by one under arrest and suspicion ever are" and hence were admissible. After prolonged questioning, one defendant had confessed after receiving assurances that his father and brother would not be molested by the police; the second had confessed when confronted with the confession of the first. "Of course, these confessions were not voluntary in the sense that petitioners wanted to make them or that they were completely spontaneous, like a confession to a priest, a lawyer, or a psychiatrist. But in this sense no criminal confession is voluntary." The Court made it clear that "the limits in any case depend upon a weighing of the circumstances of pressure against the power of resistance of the person confessing." Neither man, the Court noted, was "young, soft, ignorant or timid.'' Their will to resist had not been broken by psychological coercion. The Court also found that the jury could convict on other evidence even if it found the confessions to have been coerced.

It is interesting to note that the Court is not entirely consistent in its reasons for excluding evidence obtained by coercion. The common law rule against the admission of forced confessions was not based on any theory of fairness, but was a practical one designed to prevent the admission in court of untrustworthy evidence. A confession was rejected if sufficient force was applied in getting it to cast doubt upon its reliability. In Lisenba v. California, however, the Court made clear what was implied in previous cases, that ''the aim of the requirement of due process is not to exclude presumptively false evidence, but to prevent fundamental unfairness in the use of evidence whether true or false. . . . Such unfairness exists when a coerced confession is used as a means of obtaining a verdict of guilt.'' Without mentioning either the Lisenba or Rochin cases, the Court in the Stein case suggested a return to the common law rationale, noting that forced confessions constitute ''illusory and deceptive evidence,'' while stolen or wire-tap evidence ''often is of the utmost verity.'' In Spano v. New York (1959) it was made clear that only where the Court has not found a confession to be involuntary may a jury convict on the basis of other evidence; a forced confession always voids the conviction. And in Rogers v. Richmond (1961) the Court reaffirmed the rule that the truth or falsity of a confession does not determine its admissibility.

Somewhat different problems are presented when the state undertakes to obtain from a suspect evidence other than oral testimony. This occurs when a person is asked to submit to fingerprinting, blood typing, trying on items of clothing, and the like. In Breithaupt v. Abram (1957) the Court held valid the taking of a blood sample from the unconscious victim of an automobile accident to see if he was intoxicated. It distinguished the Rochin case on the ground that ''there is nothing 'brutal' or 'offensive' in the taking of a sample of blood when done, as in this case, under the protective eye of a physician. . . . Certainly the test as administered here would not be considered offensive by even the most delicate.'' The holding in Breithaupt was reaffirmed in 1966 in Schmerber v. California on a set of facts similar except that the defendant was awake and protested, on the advice of counsel, the taking of the blood sample. In addition, the Court found that the activity violated neither the guarantee against unreasonable searches and seizures nor compulsory self-incrimination—both made applicable to the states since the Breithaupt decision. In 1983 in South Dakota v. Neville the Court extended the Schmerber doctrine to permit the admission as trial evidence the fact a drunken motorist had refused to take a blood test at the time of his arrest on the ground that he was ''too drunk to pass it.'' He was warned that his refusal might cost him his license, but not that it could be used in court against him.

In United States v. Wade (1967) the Court held that a robbery suspect could be forced to take part in a police line up, wear strips of adhesive tapes on his face as the robber allegedly did, and repeat the words ''put the money in the bag'' allegedly spoken by the robber. Gilbert v. California (1967) held that a suspect could be forced to furnish a sample of his handwriting.

Mr. Justice **Frankfurter** delivered the opinion of the Court, saying in part:

Having ''some information that [the petitioner here] was selling narcotics,'' three deputy sheriffs of the County of Los Angeles, on the morning of July 1, 1949, made for the two-story dwelling house in which Rochin lived with his mother, common-law wife, brothers and sisters. Finding the outside door open, they entered and then forced open the door to Rochin's room on the second floor. Inside they found petitioner sitting partly dressed on the side of the bed, upon which his wife was lying. On a ''night stand'' beside the bed the deputies spied two capsules. When asked ''Whose stuff is this?'' Rochin seized the capsules and put them in his mouth. A struggle ensued, in the course of which the three officers ''jumped upon him'' and attempted to extract the capsules. The force they applied proved unavailing against Rochin's resistance. He was handcuffed and taken to a hospital. At the direction of one of the officers a doctor forced an emetic solution through a tube into Rochin's stomach against his will. This ''stomach pumping'' produced vomiting. In the vomited matter were found two capsules which proved to contain morphine.

Rochin was brought to trial before a California Superior Court, sitting without a jury, on the charge of possessing ''a preparation of morphine'' in violation of the California Health and Safety Code. Rochin was convicted and sentenced to sixty days' imprisonment. The chief evidence against him was the two capsules. They were admitted over petitioner's objection, although the means of obtaining them was frankly set forth in the testimony by one of the deputies, substantially as here narrated. . . .

. . . Regard for the requirements of the Due Process Clause ''inescapably imposes upon this Court an exercise of judgment upon the whole course of the proceedings [resulting in a conviction] in order to ascertain whether they offend those canons of decency and fairness which express the notions of justice of English-speaking peoples even toward those charged with the most heinous offenses.'' Malinski v. New York [1945]. These standards of justice are not authoritatively formulated anywhere as though they were specifics. Due process of law is a summarized constitutional guarantee of respect for those personal immunities which, as Mr. Justice Cardozo twice wrote for the Court, are ''so rooted in the traditions and conscience of our people as to be ranked as fundamental,'' Snyder v. Massachusetts [1934], or are ''implicit in the concept of ordered liberty.'' Palko v. Connecticut [1937].

The Court's function in the observance of this settled conception of the Due Process Clause does not leave us without adequate guides in subjecting State criminal procedures to constitutional judgment. In dealing not with the machinery of government but with human rights, the absence of formal exactitude, or want of fixity of meaning, is not an unusual or even regrettable attribute of constitutional provisions. Words being symbols do not speak without a gloss. On the one hand the gloss may be the deposit of history, whereby a term gains technical content. Thus the requirements of the Sixth and Seventh Amendments for trial by jury in the Federal courts have a rigid meaning. No changes or chances can alter the content of the verbal symbol of ''jury''—a body of twelve men who must reach a unanimous conclusion if the verdict is to go against the defendant. On the other hand, the gloss of some of the verbal symbols of the Constitution does not give them a fixed technical content. It exacts a continuing process of application.

When the gloss has thus not been fixed but is a function of the process of judgment, the judgment is bound to fall differently at different times and differently at the same time through different judges. Even more specific provisions, such as the guaranty of freedom of speech and the detailed protection against unreasonable searches and seizures, have inevitably evoked as sharp divisions in this Court as the least specific and most comprehensive protection of liberties, the Due Process Clause.

The vague contours of the Due Process Clause do not leave judges at large. We may not draw on our merely personal and private notions and disregard the limits that bind judges in their judicial function. Even though the concept of due process of law is not final and fixed, these limits are derived from considerations that are fused in the whole nature of our judicial process. See Cardozo, The Nature of the Judicial Process; The Growth of the Law; The Paradoxes of Legal Science. These are considerations deeply rooted in reason and in the compelling traditions of the legal profession. The Due Process Clause places upon this Court the duty of exercising a judgment, within the narrow confines of judicial power in reviewing State convictions, upon interests of society pushing in opposite directions.

Due process of law thus conceived is not to be derided as resort to a revival of ''natural law.'' To believe that this judicial exercise of judgment could be avoided by freezing ''due process of law'' at some fixed stage of time or thought is to suggest that the most important aspect of constitutional adjudication is a function for inanimate machines and not for judges, for whom the independence safeguarded by Article 3 of the Constitution was designed and who are presumably guided by established standards of judicial behavior. Even cybernetics has not yet made that haughty claim. To practice the requisite detachment and to achieve sufficient objectivity no doubt demands of judges the habit of self-discipline and self-criticism, incertitude that one's own views are incontestable and alert tolerance toward views not shared.

But these are precisely the presuppositions of our judicial process. They are precisely the qualities society has a right to expect from those entrusted with ultimate judicial power.

Restraints on our jurisdiction are self-imposed only in the sense that there is from our decisions no immediate appeal short of impeachment or constitutional amendment. But that does not make due process of law a matter of judicial caprice. The faculties of the Due Process Clause may be indefinite and vague, but the mode of their ascertainment is not self-willed. In each case ''due process of law'' requires an evaluation based on a disinterested inquiry pursued in the spirit of science, on a balanced order of facts exactly and fairly stated, on the detached consideration of conflicting claims, . . . on a judgment not ad hoc and episodic but duly mindful of reconciling the needs both of continuity and of change in a progressive society.

Applying these general considerations to the circumstances of the present case, we are compelled to conclude that the proceedings by which this conviction was obtained do more than offend some fastidious squeamishness or private sentimentalism about combatting crime too energetically. This is conduct that shocks the conscience. Illegally breaking into the privacy of the petitioner, the struggle to open his mouth and remove what was there, the forcible extraction of his stomach's contents—this course of proceeding by agents of government to obtain evidence is bound to offend even hardened sensibilities. They are methods too close to the rack and the screw to permit of constitutional differentiation.

It has long since ceased to be true that due process of law is heedless of the means by which otherwise relevant and credible evidence is obtained. This was not true even before the series of recent cases enforced the constitutional principle that the States may not base convictions upon confessions, however much verified, obtained by coercion. These decisions are not arbitrary exceptions to the comprehensive right of States to fashion their own rules of evidence for criminal trials. They are not sports in our constitutional law but applications of a general principle. They are only instances of the general requirement that States in their prosecutions respect certain decencies of civilized conduct. Due process of law, as a historic and generative principle, precludes defining, and thereby confining, these standards of conduct more precisely than to say that convictions cannot be brought about by methods that offend ''a sense of justice.'' See Mr. Chief Justice Hughes, speaking for a unanimous Court in Brown v. Mississippi [1936]. It would be a stultification of the responsibility which the course of constitutional history has cast upon this Court to hold that in order to convict a man the police cannot extract by force what is in his mind but can extract what is in his stomach.

To attempt in this case to distinguish what lawyers call ''real evidence'' from verbal evidence is to ignore the reasons for excluding coerced confessions. Use of involuntary verbal confessions in State criminal trials is constitutionally obnoxious not only because of their un-reliability. They are inadmissible under the Due Process Clause even though statements contained in them may be independently established as true. Coerced confessions offend the community's sense of fair play and decency. So here, to sanction the brutal conduct which naturally enough was condemned by the court whose judgment is before us, would be to afford brutality the cloak of law. Nothing would be more calculated to discredit law and thereby to brutalize the temper of a society. . . .

On the facts of this case the conviction of the petitioner has been obtained by methods that offend the Due Process Clause. The judgment below must be

Reversed.

Mr. Justice **Minton** took no part in the consideration or decision of this case.

Mr. Justice **Black,** concurring, said in part:

Adamson v. California [1947] sets out reasons for my belief that state as well as federal courts and law enforcement officers must obey the Fifth Amendment's command that "No person . . . shall be compelled in any criminal case to be a witness against himself." I think a person is compelled to be a witness against himself not only when he is compelled to testify, but also when as here, incriminating evidence is forcibly taken from him by a contrivance of modern science. . . .

Mr. Justice **Douglas** wrote a concurring opinion.

IRVINE v. CALIFORNIA

347 U. S. 128; 74 S. Ct. 381; 98 L. Ed. 561
(1954)

Certain theoretical and practical difficulties accompany the attempts to enforce the essential fairness doctrine—or the "shock-the-conscience" doctrine, as it came to be known after the Rochin case. What is essentially fair, or shocking, tends to be a matter of individual judgment reflecting the background and personality of the judge. Moreover, the lack of clear guidelines as to what is fair and what is not makes it difficult for police and prosecutors, however well intentioned, to know what conduct on their part is prohibited. While Justice Frankfurter's opinion in the Rochin case is a masterful analysis and defense of the doctrine in its purest form, it does not provide completely satisfactory answers on these two points.

In the present case the California police had broken into the home of a suspected bookmaker and placed microphones in several rooms of the house, including the bedroom. For over a month police officers eavesdropped in this way, and on the basis of information thus obtained Irvine was tried and convicted. Justice Jackson,

speaking for four members of the Court, conceded that "few police measures have come to our attention that more flagrantly, deliberately, and persistently violated the fundamental principle declared by the Fourth Amendment," but the Court refused to declare the evidence inadmissible although two members of the majority urged the Attorney General of the United States to determine whether the state officials might not be prosecuted under § 242 of the Criminal Code for violating rights guaranteed by the Constitution.

Mr. Justice **Jackson** announced the judgment of the Court and an opinion in which The Chief Justice [**Warren**], Mr. Justice **Reed**, and Mr. Justice **Minton** join, saying in part:

. . . The decision in Wolf v. Colorado [1949], for the first time established that "[t]he security of one's privacy against arbitrary intrusion by the police" is embodied in the concept of due process found in the Fourteenth Amendment.

But Wolf, for reasons set forth therein, declined to make the subsidiary procedural and evidentiary doctrines developed by the federal courts limitations on the states. On the contrary, it declared, "We hold, therefore, that in a prosecution in a State court for a State crime the Fourteenth Amendment does not forbid the admission of evidence obtained by an unreasonable search and seizure." . . . That holding would seem to control here.

An effort is made, however, to bring this case under the sway of Rochin v. California [1952]. That case involved, among other things, an illegal search of the defendant's person. But it also presented an element totally lacking here—coercion . . . applied by a physical assault upon his person to compel submission to the use of a stomach pump. This was the feature which led to a result in Rochin contrary to that in Wolf. Although Rochin raised the search-and-seizure question, this Court studiously avoided it and never once mentioned the Wolf Case. Obviously, it thought that illegal search and seizure alone did not call for reversal. However obnoxious are the facts in the case before us, they do not involve coercion, violence or brutality to the person, but rather a trespass to property, plus eavesdropping.

It is suggested, however, that although we affirmed the conviction in Wolf, we should reverse here because this invasion of privacy is more shocking, more offensive, than the one involved there. The opinions in Wolf were written entirely in the abstract and did not disclose the details of the constitutional violation. Actually, the search was offensive to the law in the same respect, if not the same degree, as here. A deputy sheriff and others went to a doctor's office without a warrant and seized his appointment book, searched through it to learn the names of all his patients, looked up and interrogated certain of them, and filed an information against the doctor on the information that the District Attorney had obtained from the books. The books also were introduced in evidence against the doctor at his trial.

We are urged to make inroads upon Wolf by holding that it applies only to searches and seizures which produce on our minds a mild shock, while if the shock is more serious, the states must exclude the evidence or we will reverse the conviction. We think that the Wolf decision should not be overruled, for the reasons so persuasively stated therein. We think, too, that a distinction of the kind urged would leave the rule so indefinite that no state court could know what it should rule in order to keep its processes on solid constitutional ground. . . .

Judgment affirmed.

Mr. Justice **Clark,** concurring.

Had I been here in 1949 when Wolf was decided, I would have applied the doctrine of Weeks v. United States [1914] to the states. But the Court refused to do so then, and it still refuses today. Thus Wolf remains the law and, as such, is entitled to the respect of this Court's membership.

Of course, we could sterilize the rule announced in Wolf by adopting a case-by-case approach to due process in which inchoate notions of propriety concerning local police conduct guide our decisions. But this makes for such uncertainty and unpredictability that it would be impossible to foretell—other than by guesswork—just how brazen the invasion of the intimate privacies of one's home must be in order to shock itself into the protective arms of the Constitution. In truth, the practical result of this ad hoc approach is simply that when five Justices are sufficiently revolted by local police action, a conviction is overturned and a guilty man may go free. Rochin bears witness to this. We may thus vindicate the abstract principle of due process, but we do not shape the conduct of local police one whit; unpredictable reversals on dissimilar fact situations are not likely to curb the zeal of those police and prosecutors who may be intent on racking up a high percentage of successful prosecutions. I do not believe that the extension of such a vacillating course beyond the clear cases of physical coercion and brutality, such as Rochin, would serve a useful purpose.

In light of the "incredible" activity of the police here, it is with great reluctance that I follow Wolf. Perhaps strict adherence to the tenor of that decision may produce needed converts for its extinction. Thus I merely concur in the judgment of affirmance.

Mr. Justice **Black,** with whom Mr. Justice **Douglas** concurs, wrote a dissenting opinion.

Mr. Justice **Frankfurter,** whom Mr. Justice **Burton** joins, dissenting, said in part:

In the Wolf Case, the Court rejected one absolute. In Rochin, it rejected another. . . .

Rochin decided that the Due Process Clause of the Fourteenth Amendment does not leave States free in their prosecutions for crime. The Clause puts limits on the wide discretion of a State in the process of enforcing its criminal law. The holding of the case is that a State cannot resort to methods that offend civilized standards of decency and fairness. The conviction in the Rochin Case was found to offend due process not because evidence had been obtained through an unauthorized search and seizure or was the fruit of compulsory self-incrimination. Neither of these concepts, relevant to federal prosecutions, was invoked by the Court in Rochin, so of course the Wolf Case was not mentioned. While there is in the case before us, as there was in Rochin, an element of unreasonable search and seizure, what is decisive here, as in Rochin, is additional aggravating conduct which the Court find repulsive. . . .

There was lacking here physical violence, even to the restricted extent employed in Rochin. We have here, however, a more powerful and offensive control over the Irvine's life than a single, limited physical trespass. Certainly the conduct of the police here went far beyond a bare search and seizure. The police devised means to hear every word that was said in the Irvine household for more than a month. Those affirming the conviction find that this conduct, in its entirety, is "almost incredible if it were not admitted." Surely the Court does not propose to announce a new absolute, namely, that even the most reprehensible means for securing a conviction will not taint a verdict so long as the body of the accused was not touched by State officials. . . .

Since due process is not a mechanical yardstick, it does not afford mechanical answers. In applying the Due Process Clause judicial judgment is involved in an empiric process in the sense that results are not predetermined or mechanically ascertainable. But that is a very different thing from conceiving the results as ad hoc decisions in the opprobrious sense of ad hoc. Empiricism implies judgment upon variant situations by the wisdom of experience. Ad hocness in adjudication means treating a particular case by itself and not in relation to the meaning of a course of decisions and the guides they serve for the future. There is all the difference in the world between disposing of a case as though it were a discreet instance and recognizing it as part of the process of judgment, taking its place in relation to what went before and further cutting a channel for what is to come.

The effort to imprison due process within tidy categories misconceives its nature and is a futile endeavor to save the judicial function from the pains of judicial judgment. It is pertinent to recall how the Court dealt with this craving for unattainable certainty in the Rochin Case:

"The vague contours of the Due Process Clause do not leave judges at large. We may not draw on our merely personal and private notions and disregard the limits that bind judges in their judicial function. Even though the concept of due process of law is not final and fixed, these limits are derived from considerations that are fused in the whole nature of our judicial process. See Cardozo, The Nature of the Judicial Process; The Growth of the Law; The Paradoxes of Legal Science. These are considerations deeply rooted in reason and in the compelling traditions of the legal profession. The Due Process Clause places upon this Court the duty of exercising a judgment, within the narrow confines of judicial power in reviewing State convictions, upon interests of society pushing in opposite directions." ...

McKEIVER v. PENNSYLVANIA

403 U. S. 528; 91 S. Ct. 1976; 29 L. Ed. 2d 647
(1971)

Since the birth of the common law, society has struggled to provide ways of humanizing it, of increasing its flexibility, and of getting around its insistence on procedure.

From time to time, systems of executive justice are instituted to provide needed reforms; supported by the enthusiasm of the reformers, they work well and produce the desired results. But with the passage of time the interest of the reformers wanes, and among the highly competent idealists who made the system work appear others to whom a job is simply a job. Freedom and discretion, exercised wisely and with a broad social conscience by the idealists, become, in the hands of the latter, tools by which to achieve less lofty goals. Incompetent, selfish, and occasionally venal, these people bring criticism on a system that for the most part does not deserve it. The result is a demand for instituting the very procedural protections that were abandoned when the system was set up. Procedures that might not be necessary if demigods were in control or when an alert and conscientious public is watching seem to be the only way to ensure fairness when public interest flags and mere human beings take over. The reversion, of course, is never complete; and the result is usually a modified version of what went before, with the best of the reform ideas being retained. But the unfettered freedom to be a "philosopher king," to act and decide "in the public interest," ends up hedged about with procedures that centuries of experience have shown are necessary if the rights of individuals are not to be overlooked.

In greater or lesser degree this life-span characterizes the history of that branch of the law known as equity, accounts in part for the writing of our own Constitution, and in recent times colors the development of administrative agencies. It is against this background of what Dean Roscoe Pound calls the "vitality and tenacity" of the common-law tradition that the history of the juvenile court system should be read. The system was born at the turn of the century from the feelings of reformers that it was unconscionable to try children by regular criminal proceedings and sentence them to long terms in the same prisons with hardened adult criminals. If the child was to be saved from a life of crime, the state had to see where that child had gone wrong and what could be done to set him or her back on the right track. The result was that the practice of informal proceedings, presided over by juvenile court judges, was adopted

throughout the country. The judges, acting as parental figures, determined whether the child was delinquent and, if so, what should be done. The constitutional problem raised by the denial of procedural rights was gotten around by insisting that the state was proceeding "in loco parentis," that the proceedings were civil rather than criminal, and that the child was being rehabilitated rather than punished.

However ideally the system might have worked in its heyday, it was in a sad state of deterioration when its processes were finally challenged in the Supreme Court in In re Gault (1967). Gerald Gault, fifteen, was charged with making obscene phone calls, an offense carrying a maximum sentence of two months if committed by an adult. He was given a hearing for which his parents had no adequate notice of charges against him, at which the complaining witness failed to appear, at which he was not represented by counsel or warned of his right to silence, and from which there was no right of appeal. He was sentenced to six years in the State Industrial School. While acknowledging that much desirable informality could be retained, eight members of the Supreme Court agreed that these procedures failed to provide due process of law. Five justices held that as a matter of fundamental fairness he was entitled at least to adequate notice, the right to counsel, the right to confront his accusers, and a warning that he need not incriminate himself.

The hopes of those pushing for more procedural protection for juveniles were raised by the Supreme Court's decision in In re Winship (1970) that a delinquent child could not be imprisoned unless guilt was established beyond a reasonable doubt. Samuel Winship had been committed to a state training school for theft after a hearing at which his guilt was based "on a preponderance of the evidence." Emphasizing that "the reasonable-doubt standard plays a vital role in the American scheme of criminal procedure" since "it is a prime instrument for reducing the risk of convictions resting on factual error," the Court made clear that such a standard was essential to due process of law.

Moreover, "the same considerations that demand extreme caution in factfinding to protect the innocence of adults apply as well to the innocent child." The Court rejected, as it had in Gault, the state's reliance on the "civil label-of-convenience" as a basis for holding the due process clause inapplicable to juvenile proceedings, and its justification that such proceedings were designed "not to punish, but to save the child." "We made clear in [Gault] that civil labels and good intentions do not themselves obviate the need for criminal due process safeguards in juvenile courts, for '[a] proceeding where the issue is whether the child will be found to be "delinquent" and subject to the loss of his liberty for years is comparable in seriousness to a felony prosecution.' "

The present case involved sixteen-year-old Joseph McKeiver, who was charged with robbery, larceny, and receiving stolen goods (felonies under Pennsylvania law), and Barbara Burrus, who, with some forty-five other black children, was arrested with a group of adults for obstructing traffic in connection with a protest in North Carolina against school segregation policies.

Mr. Justice **Blackmun** announced the judgment of the Court and an opinion in which The Chief Justice [**Burger**], Mr. Justice **Stewart**, and Mr. Justice **White** join, saying in part:

These cases present the narrow but precise issue whether the Due Process Clause of the Fourteenth Amendment assures the right to trial by jury in the adjudicative phase of a state juvenile court delinquency proceeding. . . .

IV.

The right to an impartial jury ''[i]n all criminal prosecutions'' under federal law is guaranteed by the Sixth Amendment. Through the Fourteenth Amendment that requirement has now been imposed upon the States ''in all criminal cases which—were they to be tried in a federal court—would come within the Sixth Amendment's guarantee.'' This is because the Court has said it believes ''that trial by jury in criminal cases is fundamental to the American scheme of justice.'' Duncan v. Louisiana [1968]. . . .

This, of course, does not automatically provide the answer to the present jury trial issue, if for no other reason than that the juvenile court proceeding has not yet been held to be a ''criminal prosecution,'' within the meaning and reach of the Sixth Amendment, and also has not yet been regarded as devoid of criminal aspects merely because it usually has been given the civil label. . . .

V.

The Pennsylvania juveniles' basic argument is that they were tried in proceedings ''substantially similar to a criminal trial.'' They say that a delinquency proceeding in their State is initiated by a petition charging a penal code violation in the conclusory language of an indictment; that a juvenile detained prior to trial is held in a building substantially similar to an adult prison; that in Philadelphia juveniles over 16 are, in fact, held in the cells of a prison; that counsel and the prosecution engage in plea bargaining; that motions to suppress are routinely heard and decided; that the usual rules of evidence are applied; that the customary common law defenses are available; that the press is generally admitted in the Philadelphia juvenile courtrooms; that members of the public enter the room; that arrest and prior record may be reported by the press (from police sources, however, rather than from the juvenile court records); that, once adjudged delinquent, a juvenile may be confined until his majority in what amounts to a prison (see In re Bethea, 215 Pa. Super. 75 (1969), describing the state correctional institution at Camp Hill as a ''maximum security prison for adjudged delinquents and youthful

criminal offenders''); and that the stigma attached upon delinquency adjudication approximates that resulting from conviction in an adult criminal proceeding.

The North Carolina juveniles particularly urge that the requirement of a jury trial would not operate to deny the supposed benefits of the juvenile court system; that the system's primary benefits are its discretionary intake procedure permitting disposition short of adjudication, and its flexible sentencing permitting emphasis on rehabilitation; that realization of these benefits does not depend upon dispensing with the jury; that adjudication of factual issues on the one hand and disposition of the case on the other are very different matters with very different purposes; that the purpose of the former is indistinguishable from that of the criminal trial; that the jury trial provides an independent protective factor; that experience has shown that jury trials in juvenile courts are manageable; that no reason exists why protection traditionally accorded in criminal proceedings should be denied young people subject to involuntary incarceration for lengthy periods; and that the juvenile courts deserve healthy public scrutiny.

VI.

All the litigants here agree that the applicable due process standard in juvenile proceedings, as developed by Gault [1967] and Winship [1970], is fundamental fairness. As that standard was applied in those two cases, we have an emphasis on factfinding procedures. The requirements of notice, counsel, confrontation, cross-examination, and standard of proof naturally flowed from this emphasis. But one cannot say that in our legal system the jury is a necessary component of accurate factfinding. There is much to be said for it, to be sure, but we have been content to pursue other ways for determining facts. Juries are not required, and have not been, for example, in equity cases, in workmen's compensation, in probate, or in deportation cases. Neither have they been generally used in military trials. In Duncan the Court stated, ''We would not assert, however, that every criminal trial—or any particular trial—held before a judge alone is unfair or that a defendant may never be as fairly treated by a judge as he would be by a jury.'' In DeStefano [v. Woods, 1968] for this reason and others, the Court refrained from retrospective application of Duncan, an action it surely would have not taken had it felt that the integrity of the result was seriously at issue. And in Williams v. Florida (1970), the Court saw no particular magic in a 12-man jury for a criminal case, thus revealing that even jury concepts themselves are not inflexible.

We must recognize, as the Court has recognized before, that the fond and idealistic hopes of the juvenile court proponents and early reformers of three generations ago have not been realized. The devastating commentary upon the system's failure as a whole, contained in the Task Force Report: Juvenile Delinquency and Youth Crime (President's Commission on Law Enforcement and the Administration of Justice (1967), pp. 7-9), reveals the depth of disappointment in what has been accomplished. Too often the juvenile court judge falls far short of that stalwart, protective and communicating figure the system envisaged.* The community's unwillingness to provide people and facilities and to be concerned, the insufficiency of time devoted, the scarcity of professional help, the inadequacy of dispositional alternatives, and our general lack of knowledge all contribute to dissatisfaction with the experiment.†

The Task Force Report, however, also said, page 7, "To say that juvenile courts have failed to achieve their goals is to say no more than what is true of criminal courts in the United States. But failure is most striking when hopes are highest."

Despite all these disappointments, all these failures, and all these shortcomings, we conclude that trial by jury in the juvenile court's adjudicative stage is not a constitutional requirement. We so conclude for a number of reasons:

1. The Court has refrained, in the cases heretofore decided, from taking the easy way with a flat holding that all rights constitutionally assured for the adult accused are to be imposed upon the state juvenile proceeding. . . .

2. There is a possibility, at least, that the jury trial, if required as a matter of constitutional precept, will remake the juvenile proceeding into a fully adversary process and will put an effective end to what has been the idealistic prospect of an intimate, informal protective proceeding.

3. The Task Force Report, although concededly pre-Gault, is notable for its not making any recommendation that the jury trial be imposed upon the juvenile court system. . . .

5. The imposition of the jury trial on the juvenile court system would not strengthen greatly, if at all, the factfinding function, and would, contrarily, provide an attrition of the juvenile court's assumed ability to function in a unique manner. It would not remedy the defects of the system. Meager as has been the hoped-for advance in the juvenile field, the alternative would be regressive, would lose what has been gained, and would tend once again to place the juvenile squarely in the routine of the criminal process.

6. The juvenile concept held high promise. We are reluctant to say that, despite disappointments of grave dimensions, it still does not hold promise, and we are particularly reluctant to say, as do the Pennsylvania petitioners here, that the system cannot accomplish its rehabilitative goals. So much depends on the availability of resources, on the interest and commitment of the public, on willingness to learn, and on understanding as to cause and effect and cure. In this field, as in so many others, one perhaps learns best by doing. We are reluctant to disallow the States further to experiment and to seek in new and different ways the elusive answers to the problems of the young, and we feel that we would be impeding that experimentation by imposing the jury trial. The States, indeed, must go forward. If, in its wisdom, any State feels the jury trial is desirable in all cases, or in certain kinds, there appears to be no impediment to its installing a system embracing that feature. That, however, is the State's privilege and not its obligation. . . .

10. Since Gault and since Duncan the great majority of States, in addition to Pennsylvania and North Carolina, that have faced the issue have concluded that the considerations that led to the result in those two cases do not compel trial by jury in the juvenile court. . . .

11. Stopping short of proposing the jury trial for juvenile proceedings are the Uniform Juvenile Court Act, § 24(a), approved in July 1968 by the National Conference of Commissioners on Uniform State Laws; the Standard Juvenile Court Act, Article V, § 19, proposed by the National Council on Crime and Delinquency (see W. Sheridan, Standards for Juvenile and Family Courts 73 (1968)); and the Legislative Guide for Drafting Family and Juvenile Court Acts § 29(a) (1969) (issued by the Children's Bureau, Social and Rehabilitation Service, United States Department of H. E. W.).

12. If the jury trial were to be injected into the juvenile court system as a matter of right, it would bring with it into that system the traditional delay, the formality and the clamor of the adversary system and, possibly, the public trial. . . .

13. Finally, the arguments advanced by the juveniles here are, of course, the identical arguments that underlie the demand for the jury trial for criminal proceedings. The arguments necessarily equate the juvenile proceeding—or at least the adjudicative phase of it—with the criminal trial. Whether they should be so equated is our issue. Concern about the inapplicability of exclusionary and other rules of evidence, about the juvenile court judge's possible awareness of the juvenile's prior record and of the contents of the social file; about

---

*"A recent study of juvenile court judges . . . revealed that half had not received undergraduate degrees; a fifth had received no college education at all; a fifth were not members of the bar." Task Force Report, p. 7.

†What emerges, then, is this: In theory the juvenile court was to be helpful and rehabilitative rather than punitive. In fact the distinction often disappears, not only because of the absence of facilities and personnel but also because of the limits of knowledge and technique. In theory the court's action was to affix no stigmatizing label. In fact a delinquent is generally viewed by employers, schools, the armed services—by society generally—as a criminal. In theory the court was to treat children guilty of criminal acts in noncriminal ways. In fact it labels truants and runaways as junior criminals.

"In theory the court's operations could justifiably be informal, its findings and decisions made without observing ordinary procedural safeguards, because it would act only in the best interest of the child.

"In fact it frequently does nothing more nor less than deprive a child of liberty without due process of law—knowing not what else to do and needing, whether admittedly or not, to act in the community's interest even more imperatively than the child's. In theory it was to exercise its protective powers to bring an errant child back into the fold. In fact there is increasing reason to believe that its intervention reinforces the juvenile's unlawful impulses. In theory it was to concentrate on each case the best of current social science learning. In fact it has often become a vested interest in its turn, loathe to cooperate with innovative programs or avail itself of forward-looking methods." Task Force Report, p. 9.

repeated appearances of the same familiar witnesses in the persons of juvenile and probation officers and social workers—all to the effect that this will create the likelihood of prejudgment—chooses to ignore, it seems to us, every aspect of fairness, of concern, of sympathy, and of paternal attention that the juvenile court system contemplates.

If the formalities of the criminal adjudicative process are to be superimposed upon the juvenile court system, there is little need for its separate existence. Perhaps that ultimate disillusionment will come one day, but for the moment we are disinclined to give impetus to it.

Affirmed.

Mr. Justice **White,** concurring, said in part:

The criminal law proceeds on the theory that defendants have a will and are responsible for their actions. A finding of guilt establishes that they have chosen to engage in conduct so reprehensible and injurious to others that they must be punished to deter them and others from crime. Guilty defendants are considered blameworthy; they are branded and treated as such, however much the State also pursues rehabilitative ends in the criminal justice system.

For the most part, the juvenile justice system rests on more deterministic assumptions. Reprehensible acts by juveniles are not deemed the consequence of mature and malevolent choice but of environmental pressures (or lack of them) or of other forces beyond their control. Hence the state legislative judgment not to stigmatize the juvenile delinquent by branding him a criminal; his conduct is not deemed so blameworthy that punishment is required to deter him or others. Coercive measures, where employed, are considered neither retribution nor punishment. Supervision or confinement is aimed at rehabilitation, not at convincing the juvenile of his error simply by imposing pains and penalties. Nor is the purpose to make the juvenile delinquent an object lesson for others, whatever his own merits or demerits may be. A typical disposition in the juvenile court where delinquency is established may authorize confinement until age 21, but it will last no longer and within that period will last only so long as his behavior demonstrates that he remains an unacceptable risk if returned to his family. Nor is authorization for custody until 21 any measure of the seriousness of the particular act which the juvenile has performed.

Against this background and in light of the distinctive purpose of requiring juries in criminal cases, I am satisfied with the Court's holding. To the extent that the jury is a buffer to the corrupt or overzealous prosecutor in the criminal law system, the distinctive intake policies and procedures of the juvenile court system to a great extent obviate this important function of the jury. As for the necessity to guard against judicial bias, a system eschewing blameworthiness and punishment for evil choice is itself an operative force against prejudice and short-tempered justice. Nor where juveniles are involved is there the same opportunity for corruption to the juvenile's detriment or the same temptation to use the courts for political ends.

Mr. Justice **Brennan,** concurring in No. 322 [Pennsylvania] and dissenting in No. 128 [North Carolina], said in part:

I agree with the plurality opinion's conclusion that the proceedings below in these cases were not "criminal prosecutions" within the meaning of the Sixth Amendment. For me, therefore, the question in these cases is whether jury trial is among the "essentials of due process and fair treatment," . . . required during the adjudication of a charge of delinquency based upon acts which would constitute a crime if engaged in by an adult. . . . This does not, however, mean that the interests protected by the Sixth Amendment's guarantee of jury trial in all "criminal prosecutions" are of no importance in the context of these cases. The Sixth Amendment, where applicable, commands that these interests be protected by a particular procedure, that is, trial by jury. The Due Process Clause commands not a particular procedure, but only a result: in my Brother Blackmun's words, "fundamental fairness . . . in factfinding." In the context of these and similar juvenile delinquency proceedings, what this means is that the States are not bound to provide jury trials on demand so long as some other aspect of the process adequately protects the interests that Sixth Amendment jury trials are intended to serve.

In my view, therefore, the due process question cannot be decided upon the basis of general characteristics of juvenile proceedings, but only in terms of the adequacy of a particular state procedure to "protect the [juvenile] from oppression by the Government," . . . and to protect him against "the compliant, biased, or eccentric judge." . . .

Examined in this light, I find no defect in the Pennsylvania cases before us. The availability of trial by jury allows an accused to protect himself against possible oppression by what is in essence an appeal to the community conscience, as embodied in the jury that hears his case. To some extent, however, a similar protection may be obtained when an accused may in essence appeal to the community at large, by focusing public attention upon the facts of his trial, exposing improper judicial behavior to public view, and obtaining if necessary executive redress through the medium of public indignation. . . .

. . . In the Pennsylvania cases before us, there appears to be no statutory ban upon admission of the public to juvenile trials. Appellants themselves, without contradiction, assert that "the press is generally admitted" to juvenile delinquency proceedings in Philadelphia. Most important, the record in these cases is bare of any indication that any person whom appellants sought to have admitted to the courtroom was excluded. In these circumstances, I agree that the judgment in No. 322 must be affirmed.

The North Carolina cases, however, present a different situation. North Carolina law either permits or requires exclusion of the general public from juvenile trials. In the cases before us, the trial judge "ordered the general public excluded from the hearing room and stated that only officers of the court, the juveniles, their parents or guardians, their attorney and witnesses would be present for the hearing," . . . notwithstanding petitioners' repeated demand for a public hearing. The cases themselves, which arise out of a series of demonstrations by black adults and juveniles who believed that the Hyde County, North Carolina, school system unlawfully discriminated against black schoolchildren, present a paradigm of the circumstances in which there may be a substantial "temptation to use the courts for political ends." Opinion of Mr. Justice White, ante, . . .

Mr. Justice **Harlan,** concurring in the judgments, said in part:

If I felt myself constrained to follow Duncan v. Louisiana (1968), which extended the Sixth Amendment right of jury trial to the States, I would have great difficulty, upon the premise seemingly accepted in my Brother Blackmun's opinion, in holding that the jury trial right does not extend to state juvenile proceedings. That premise is that juvenile delinquency proceedings have in practice actually become in many, if not all, respects criminal trials. . . . If that premise be correct, then I do not see why, given Duncan, juveniles as well as adults would not be constitutionally entitled to jury trials, so long as juvenile delinquency systems are not restructured to fit their original purpose. When that time comes I would have no difficulty in agreeing with my Brother Blackmun, and indeed with my Brother White, the author of Duncan, that juvenile delinquency proceedings are beyond the pale of Duncan.

I concur in the judgments in these cases however, on the ground that criminal jury trials are not constitutionally required of the States, either as a matter of Sixth Amendment law or due process. See my dissenting opinion in Duncan and my concurring opinion in Williams v. Florida (1970).

Mr. Justice **Douglas,** with whom Mr. Justice **Black** and Mr. Justice **Marshall** concur, dissenting, said in part:

These cases from Pennsylvania and North Carolina present the issue of the right to a jury trial for offenders charged in juvenile court and facing a possible incarceration until they reach their majority. I believe the guarantees of the Bill of Rights, made applicable to the States by the Fourteenth Amendment, require a jury trial. . . . We had held in In re Gault that "neither the Fourteenth Amendment nor the Bill of Rights is for adults alone." As we noted in that case, the Juvenile Court movement was designed to avoid procedures to ascertain whether the child was "guilty" or "innocent" but to bring to bear on these problems a "clinical" approach. It is of course not our task to determine as a matter of policy whether a "clinical" or "punitive" approach to these

problems should be taken by the States. But where a State uses its juvenile court proceedings to prosecute a juvenile for a criminal act and to order "confinement" until the child reaches 21 years of age or where the child at the threshold of the proceedings faces that prospect, then he is entitled to the same procedural protection as an adult. As Mr. Justice Black said in In re Gault (concurring):

"Where a person, infant or adult, can be seized by the State, charged, and convicted for violating a state criminal law, and then ordered by the State to be confined for six years, I think the Constitution requires that he be tried in accordance with the guarantes of all the provisions of the Bill of Rights made applicable to the States by the Fourteenth Amendment. Undoubtedly this would be true of an adult defendant, and it would be a plain denial of equal protection of the laws—an invidious discrimination—to hold that others subject to heavier punishments could, because they are children, be denied these same constitutional safeguards."

Just as courts have sometimes confused delinquency with crime, so have law enforcement officials treated juveniles not as delinquents but as criminals. . . .

In the present cases imprisonment or confinement up to 10 years was possible for one child and each faced at least a possible five-year incarceration. No adult could be denied a jury trial in those circumstances. Duncan v. Louisiana. The Fourteenth Amendment which makes trial by jury provided in the Sixth Amendment applicable to States speaks of denial of rights to "any person," not denial of rights to "any adult person"; and we have held indeed that where a juvenile is charged with an act that would constitute a crime if committed by an adult, he is entitled to trial by jury with proof beyond a reasonable doubt. . . .

DeSHANEY v. WINNEBAGO SOC. SERV.

489 U. S. 189; 103 L. Ed. 2d 249; 109 S. Ct. 998
(1989)

Probably the major difference between a legislative enactment and a constitutional provision is that the former is designed to regulate the conduct of individuals while the purpose of the latter is to indicate how the government is to be organized and to impose limits upon its powers. So well accepted is this distinction that provisions in the federal Constitution forbidding individuals to hold slaves or (in the Eighteenth Amendment) manufacture liquor are viewed as legislation and hence anomalies in the constitutional scheme. Generally speaking, our constitutions neither restrict the behavior of private individuals nor guarantee affirmative aid from the government. Constitutions merely protect them from certain forms of government interference with their liberty.

When the Framers met in Philadelphia it was generally accepted "that government was best which governs least." Nobody looked to the government to help them in times of trouble. All that was required was a regulated society in which people, especially those with property, could conduct their affairs as they were accustomed to do and be protected from those who wished to interfere with them. To savor the Court's attitude toward the rights of businessmen, see Lochner v. New York (1905).

The twentieth century, however, has seen dramatic and wholly unforseen changes in the relations between the people and their government. Triggered by a demand for protection from unscrupulous business magnates, and later by the desperate need for government help to survive the horrors of the Great Depression, the governments, both state and federal, have become increasingly the beneficent protectors to which the people look for help of all kinds. Private enterprise in such crucial areas as care for the aged, welfare for the poor, fire protection and ambulance service, hospitals, child care centers, to name a few, has given way to a reliance on government.

The failure of government to deal adequately with the increasing incidence of street crime, rioting, battered women, and injury by drunken, unlicensed, or uninsured drivers appears to have generated two answers by the public. One is illustrated by the New York City subway rider who shot a number of attackers and was convicted merely of carrying a gun without a license. The other is an increasing insistence that individuals should have a constitutional right to protection by the government itself against such threats. The Court's implicit rejection of the latter claim in the case below represents a conscious refusal to extend the "fundamental fairness" doctrine to this contentious area.

Chief Justice Rehnquist delivered the opinion of the Court.

Petitioner is a boy who was beaten and permanently injured by his father, with whom he lived. The respondents are social workers and other local officials who received complaints that petitioner was being abused by his father and had reason to believe that this was the case, but nonetheless did not act to remove petitioner from his father's custody. Petitioner sued respondents claiming that their failure to act deprived him of his liberty in violation of the Due Process Clause of the Fourteenth Amendment to the United States Constitution. We hold that it did not.

I.

The facts of this case are undeniably tragic. Petitioner Joshua DeShaney was born in 1979. In 1980, a Wyoming court granted his parents a divorce and awarded custody of Joshua to his father, Randy DeShaney. The father shortly thereafter moved to Neenah, a city located in Winnebago County, Wisconsin, taking the infant Joshua with him. There he entered into a second marriage, which also ended in divorce.

The Winnebago County authorities first learned that Joshua DeShaney might be a victim of child abuse in January 1982, when his father's second wife complained to the police, at the time of their divorce, that he had previously "hit the boy causing marks and [was] a prime case for child abuse." The Winnebago County Department of Social Services (DSS) interviewed the father, but he denied the accusations, and DSS did not pursue them further. In January 1983, Joshua was admitted to a local hospital with multiple bruises and abrasions. The examining physician suspected child abuse and notified DSS, which immediately obtained an order from a Wisconsin juvenile court placing Joshua in the temporary custody of the hospital. Three days later, the county convened an ad hoc "Child Protection Team"—consisting of a pediatrician, a psychologist, a police detective, the county's lawyer, several DSS caseworkers, and various hospital personnel—to consider Joshua's situation. At this meeting, the Team decided that there was insufficient evidence of child abuse to retain Joshua in the custody of the court. The Team did, however, decide to recommend several measures to protect Joshua, including enrolling him in a preschool program, providing his father with certain counselling services, and encouraging his father's girlfriend to move out of the home. Randy DeShaney entered into a voluntary agreement with DSS in which he promised to cooperate with them in accomplishing these goals.

Based on the recommendations of the Child Protection Team, the juvenile court dismissed the child protection case and returned Joshua to the custody of his father. A month later, emergency room personnel called the DSS caseworker handling Joshua's case to report that he had once again been treated for suspicious injuries. The caseworker concluded that there was no basis for action. For the next six months, the caseworker made monthly visits to the DeShaney home, during which she observed a number of suspicious injuries on Joshua's head; she also noticed that he had not been enrolled in school and that the girlfriend had not moved out. The caseworker dutifully recorded these incidents in her files, along with her continuing suspicions that someone in the DeShaney household was physically abusing Joshua, but she did nothing more. In November 1983, the emergency room notified DSS that Joshua had been treated once again for injuries that they believed to be caused by child abuse. On the caseworker's next two visits to the DeShaney home, she was told that Joshua was too ill to see her. Still DSS took no action.

In March 1984, Randy DeShaney beat 4-year-old Joshua so severely that he fell into a life-threatening coma. Emergency brain surgery revealed a series of hemorrhages caused by traumatic injuries to the head inflicted over a long period of time. Joshua did not die, but he suffered brain damage so severe that he is expected to spend the rest of his life confined to an institution for the profoundly retarded. Randy DeShaney was subsequently tried and convicted of child abuse.

Joshua and his mother brought this action under 42 USC § 1983 in the United States District Court for the

Eastern District of Wisconsin against respondents Winnebago County, its Department of Social Services, and various individual employees of the Department. The complaint alleged that respondents had deprived Joshua of his liberty without due process of law, in violation of his rights under the Fourteenth Amendment, by failing to protect him against a risk of violence at his father's hands of which they knew or should have known. The District Court granted summary judgment for respondents.

The Court of Appeals for the Seventh Circuit affirmed . . . .

Because of the inconsistent approaches taken by the lower courts in determining when, if ever, the failure of a state or local governmental entity or its agents to provide an individual with adequate protective services constitutes a violation of the individual's due process rights . . . and the importance of the issue to the administration of state and local governments, we granted certiorari. We now affirm.

II.

The Due Process Clause of the Fourteenth Amendment provides that "[n]o State shall . . . deprive any person of life, liberty, or property, without due process of law." Petitioners contend that the State deprived Joshua of his liberty interest in "free[dom] from . . . unjustified intrusions on person security," . . . by failing to provide him with adequate protection against his father's violence. The claim is one invoking the substantive rather than procedural component of the Due Process Clause; petitioners do not claim that the State denied Joshua protection without according him appropriate procedural safeguards, . . . but that it was categorically obliged to protect him in these circumstances, see Youngberg v. Romeo (1982).

But nothing in the language of the Due Process Clause itself requires the State to protect the life, liberty, and property of its citizens against invasion by private actors. The Clause is phrased as a limitation on the State's power to act, not as a guarantee of certain minimal levels of safety and security. It forbids the State itself to deprive individuals of life, liberty or property without "due process of law," but its language cannot fairly be extended to impose an affirmative obligation on the State to ensure that those interests do not come to harm through other means. Nor does history support such an expansive reading of the constitutional text. Like its counterpart in the Fifth Amendment, the Due Process Clause of the Fourteenth Amendment was intended to prevent government "from abusing [its] power, or employing it as an instrument of oppression." . . . Its purpose was to protect the people of the State, not to ensure that the State protected them from each other. The Framers were content to leave the extent of governmental obligation in the latter area to the democratic political processes.

Consistent with these principles, our cases have recognized that the Due Process Clauses generally confer no affirmative right to governmental aid, even where such aid may be necessary to secure life, liberty or property interest of which the government itself may not deprive the individual. See, e. g., Harris v. McRae (1980) (no obligation to fund abortions or other medical services) (discussing Due Process Clause of Fifth Amendment); Lindsey v. Normet (1972) (no obligation to provide adequate housing) (discussing Due Process Clause of Fourteenth Amendment); see also Youngberg v. Romeo [1982] ("As a general matter, a State is under no constitutional duty to provide substantive services for those within its border."). As we said in Harris v. McRae, "[a]lthough the liberty protected by the Due Process Clause affords protection against unwarranted *government* interference . . . , it does not confer an entitlement to such [governmental aid] as may be necessary to realize all the advantages of that freedom." (emphasis added). If the Due Process Clause does not require the State to provide its citizens with particular protective services, it follows that the State cannot be held liable under the Clause for injuries that could have been averted had it chosen to provide them. As a general matter, then, we conclude that a State's failure to protect an individual against private violence simply does not constitute a violation of the Due Process Clause.

Petitioners contend, however, that even if the Due Process Clause imposes no affirmative obligation on the State to provide the general public with adequate protective services, such a duty may arise out of certain "special relationships" created or assumed by the State with respect to particular individuals. Petitioners argue that such a "special relationship" existed here because the State knew that Joshua faced a special danger of abuse at his father's hands, and specifically proclaimed, by word and by deed, its intention to protect him against that danger. Having actually undertaken to protect Joshua from this danger—which petitioner concedes the State played no part in creating—the State acquired an affirmative "duty," enforceable through the Due Process Clause, to do so in a reasonably competent fashion. Its failure to discharge that duty, so the argument goes, was an abuse of governmental power that so "shocks the conscience," Rochin v. California (1952), as to constitute a substantive due process violation.

We reject this argument. It is true that in certain limited circumstances the Constitution imposes upon the State affirmative duties of care and protection with respect to particular individuals. In Estelle v. Gamble (1976), we recognized that the Eighth Amendment's prohibition against cruel and unusual punishment, made applicable to the States through the Fourteenth Amendment's Due Process Clause, . . . requires the State to provide adequate medical care to incarcerated prisoners. We reasoned that because the prisoner is unable " 'by reason of the deprivation of his liberty [to] care for himself,' " it is only " 'just' " that the State be required to care for him.

In Youngberg v. Romeo (1982), we extended this analysis beyond the Eighth Amendment setting, holding that the substantive component of the Fourteenth Amendment's Due Process Clause requires the State to provide involuntarily committed mental patients with such services as are necessary to ensure their "reasonable safety" from themselves and others. . . . As we explained, "[i]f it is cruel and unusual punishment to hold convicted criminals in unsafe conditions, it must be unconstitutional [under the Due Process Clause] to confine the involuntarily committed—who may not be punished at all—in unsafe conditions." . . .

But these cases afford petitioners no help. Taken together, they stand only for the proposition that when the State takes a person into its custody and holds him there against his will, the Constitution imposes upon it a corresponding duty to assume some responsibility for his safety and general well-being. . . . The rationale for this principle is simple enough: when the State by the affirmative exercise of its power so restrains an individual's liberty that it renders him unable to care for himself, and at the same time fails to provide for his basic human needs—e.g., food, clothing, shelter, medical care, and reasonable safety—it transgresses the substantive limits on state action set by the Eighth Amendment and the Due Process Clause. . . . The affirmative duty to protect arises not from the State's knowledge of the individual's predicament or from its expressions of intent to help him, but from the limitations which it has imposed on his freedom to act on his own behalf. . . . In the substantive due process analysis, it is the State's affirmative act of restraining the individual's freedom to act on his own behalf—through incarceration, institutionalization, or other similar restraint of personal liberty—which is the "deprivation of liberty" triggering the protections of the Due Process Clause, not its failure to act to protect his liberty interests against harms inflicted by other means.

The Estelle-Youngberg analysis simply has no applicability in the present case. Petitioners concede that the harms Joshua suffered did not occur while he was in the State's custody, but while he was in the custody of his natural father, who was in no sense a state actor. While the State may have been aware of the dangers that Joshua faced in the free world, it played no part in their creation, nor did it do anything to render him any more vulnerable to them. That the State once took temporary custody of Joshua does not alter the analysis, for when it returned him to his father's custody, it placed him in no worse position than that in which he would have been had it not acted at all; the State does not become the permanent guarantor of an individual's safety by having once offered him shelter. Under these circumstances, the State had no constitutional duty to protect Joshua. . . . A state may, through its courts and legislatures, impose such affirmative duties of care and protection upon its agents as it wishes. But not "all common-law duties owed by government actors were . . . constitutionalized by the Fourteenth Amendment." Because, as explained above, the State had no constitutional duty to protect

Joshua against his father's violence, its failure to do so—though calamitous in hindsight—simply does not constitute a violation of the Due Process Clause.

Judges and lawyers, like other humans, are moved by natural sympathy in a case like this to find a way for Joshua and his mother to receive adequate compensation for the grievous harm inflicted upon them. But before yielding to that impulse, it is well to remember once again that the harm was inflicted not by the State of Wisconsin, but by Joshua's father. The most that can be said of the state functionaries in this case is that they stood by and did nothing when suspicious circumstances dictated a more active role for them. In defense of them it must also be said that had they moved too soon to take custody of the son away from the father, they would likely have been met with charges of improperly intruding into the parent-child relationship, charges based on the same Due Process Clause that forms the basis for the present charge of failure to provide adequate protection.

The people of Wisconsin may well prefer a system of liability which would place upon the State and its officials the responsibility for failure to act in situations such as the present one. They may create such a system, if they do not have it already, by changing the tort law of the State in accordance with the regular law-making process. But they should not have it thrust upon them by this Court's expansion of the Due Process Clause of the Fourteenth Amendment.

Affirmed.

Justice **Brennan**, with whom Justice **Marshall** and Justice **Blackmun** joined, dissented, saying in part:

"The most that can be said of the state functionaries in this case," the Court today concludes, "is that they stood by and did nothing when suspicious circumstances dictated a more active role for them." Because I believe that this description of respondents' conduct tells only part of the story and that, accordingly, the Constitution itself "dictated a more active role" for respondents in the circumstances presented here, I cannot agree that respondents had no constitutional duty to help Joshua DeShaney. . . .

The Court's baseline is the absence of positive rights in the Constitution and a concomitant suspicion of any claim that seems to depend on such rights. From this perspective, the DeShaney's claim is first and foremost about inaction (the failure, here, of respondents to take steps to protect Joshua), and only tangentially about action (the establishment of a state program specifically designed to help children like Joshua.) And from this perspective, holding these Wisconsin officials liable—where the only difference between this case and one involving a general claim to protective services is Wisconsin's establishment and operation of a program to protect children—would seem to punish an effort that we should seek to promote. . . .

Because of the Court's initial fixation on the general principle that the Constitution does not establish positive rights, it is unable to appreciate our recognition in Estelle and Youngberg that this principle does not hold true in all circumstances. Thus, in the Court's view, Youngberg can be explained (and dismissed) in the following way: "In the substantive due process analysis, it is the State's affirmative act of restraining the individual's freedom to act on his own behalf—through incarceration, institutionalization, or other similar restraint of personal liberty—which is the 'deprivation of liberty' triggering the protection of the Due Process Clause, not its failure to act to protect his liberty interests against harms inflicted by other means." This restatement of Youngberg's holding should come as a surprise when one recalls our explicit observation in that case that Romeo did not challenge his commitment to the hospital, but instead "argue[d] that he had a constitutionally protected liberty interest in safety, freedom of movement, and training within the institution; and that petitioners infringed these rights *by failing to provide* constitutionally required conditions of confinement." (emphasis added). I do not mean to suggest that "the State's affirmative act of restraining the individual's freedom to act on his own behalf" was irrelevant in Youngberg; rather I emphasize that this conduct would have led to no injury, and consequently no cause of action under § 1983, unless the State then had failed to take steps to protect Romeo from himself and from others. In addition, the Court's exclusive attention to State-imposed restraints of "the individual's freedom to act on his own behalf" suggests that it was the State that rendered Romeo unable to care for himself, whereas in fact—with an I. Q. of between 8 and 10, and the mental capacity of an 18-month-old child—he had been quite incapable of taking care of himself long before the State stepped into his life. Thus, the fact of hospitalization was critical in Youngberg not because it rendered Romeo helpless to help himself, but because it separated him from other sources of aid that, we held, the State was obligated to replace. Unlike the Court, therefore, I am unable to see in Youngberg a neat and decisive divide between action and inaction.

Moreover, to the Court, the only fact that seems to count as an "affirmative act of restraining the individual's freedom to act on his own behalf" is direct physical control. . . . I would not, however, give Youngberg and Estelle such a stingy scope. I would recognize, as the Court apparently cannot, that "the State's knowledge of [an] individual's predicament [and] its expression of intent to help him" can amount to a "limitation of his freedom to act on his own behalf" or to obtain help from others. Thus, I would read Youngberg and Estelle to stand for a much more generous proposition that, if a State cuts off private sources of aid and then refuses aid itself, it cannot wash its hands of the harm that results from its inaction. . . .

Wisconsin has established a child-welfare system specifically designed to help children like Joshua. Wisconsin law places upon the local department of social services such as respondent (DSS or Department) a duty to investigate reported instances of child abuse. While other governmental bodies and private persons are largely responsible for the reporting of possible cases of child abuse, Wisconsin law channels all such reports to the local department of social services for evaluation and, if necessary, further action. Even when it is the sheriff's office or police department that receives a report of suspected child abuse, that report is referred to local social services departments for action; the only exception to this occurs when the reporter fears for the child's *immediate* safety. In this way, Wisconsin law invites—indeed, directs—citizens and other governmental entities to depend on local departments of social services such as respondent to protect children from abuse.

The specific facts before us bear out this view of Wisconsin's system of protecting children. Each time someone voiced a suspicion that Joshua was being abused, that information was relayed to the Department for investigation and possible action. When Randy DeShaney's second wife told the police that he had "'hit the boy causing marks and [was] a prime case for child abuse,'" the police referred her complaint to DSS. When, on three separate occasions, emergency room personnel noticed suspicious injuries on Joshua's body, they went to DSS with this information. When neighbors informed the police that they had seen or heard Joshua's father or his father's lover beating or otherwise abusing Joshua, the police brought these reports to the attention of DSS. And when respondent Kemmeter, through these reports and through her own observations in the course of nearly 20 visits to the DeShaney home, compiled growing evidence that Joshua was being abused, that information stayed within the Department—chronicled by the social worker in detail that seems almost eerie in light of her failure to act upon it. (As to the extent of the social worker's involvement in and knowledge of Joshua's predicament, her reaction to the news of Joshua's last and most devastating injuries is illuminating: "I just knew the phone would ring some day and Joshua would be dead.")

Even more telling than these examples is the Department's control over the decision whether to take steps to protect a particular child from suspected abuse. While many different people contributed information and advice to this decision, it was up to the people at DSS to make the ultimate decision (subject to the approval of the local government's Corporation Counsel) whether to disturb the family's current arrangements. When Joshua first appeared at a local hospital with injuries signaling physical abuse, for example, it was DSS that made the decision to take him into temporary custody for the purpose of studying his situation—and it was DSS, acting in conjunction with the Corporation Counsel, that returned him to his father. Unfortunately for Joshua DeShaney, the buck effectively stopped with the Department.

In these circumstances, a private citizen, or even a

person working in a government agency other than DSS, would doubtless feel that her job was done as soon as she had reported her suspicions of child abuse to DSS. Through its child-welfare program, in other words, the State of Wisconsin has relieved ordinary citizens and governmental bodies other than the Department of any sense of obligation to do anything more than report their suspicions of child abuse to DSS. If DSS ignores or dismisses these suspicions, no one will step in to fill the gap. Wisconsin's child-protection program thus effectively confined Joshua DeShaney within the walls of Randy DeShaney's violent home until such time as DSS took action to remove him. Conceivably, then, children like Joshua are made worse off by the existence of this program when the persons and entities charged with carrying it out fail to do their jobs.

It simply belies reality, therefore, to contend that the State "stood by and did nothing" with respect to Joshua. Through its child-protection program, the State actively intervened in Joshua's life and, by virtue of this intervention, acquired ever more certain knowledge that Joshua was in grave danger. These circumstances, in my view, plant this case solidly within the tradition of cases like Youngberg and Estelle.

Justice **Blackmun**, dissenting, said in part:

Today, the Court purports to be the dispassionate oracle of the law, unmoved by "natural sympathy." But, in this pretense, the Court itself retreats into a sterile formalism which prevents it from recognizing either the facts of the case before it or the legal norms that should apply to those facts. As Justice Brennan demonstrates, the facts here involve not merely passivity, but active state intervention in the life of Joshua DeShaney—intervention that triggered a fundamental duty to aid the boy once the State learned of the severe danger to which he was exposed.

The Court fails to recognize this duty because it attempts to draw a sharp and rigid line between action and inaction. But such formalistic reasoning has no place in the interpretation of the broad and stirring clauses of the Fourteenth Amendment. Indeed, I submit that these clauses were designed, at least in part, to undo the formalistic legal reasoning that infected antebellum jurisprudence, which the late Professor Robert Cover analyzed so effectively in his significant work entitled Justice Accused (1975).

Like the antebellum judges who denied relief to fugitive slaves, the Court today claims that its decision, however harsh, is compelled by existing legal doctrine. On the contrary, the question presented by this case is an open one, and our Fourteenth Amendment precedents may be read more broadly or narrowly depending upon how one chooses to read them. Faced with the choice, I would adopt a "sympathetic" reading, one which comports with dictates of fundamental justice and recognizes

that compassion need not be exiled from the province of judging.

SUBSTANTIVE DUE PROCESS REVISITED

GRISWOLD v. CONNECTICUT

381 U. S. 479; 85 S. Ct. 1678; 14 L. Ed. 2d 510
(1965)

While the Constitution prescribes certain limits on governmental power, these limits are in a continual state of change. As the Court engages in the endless process of interpreting the constitutional guarantees, certain protections are withdrawn and others are added. Ordinarily this process occurs so slowly and subtly that only a careful observer can detect that a real change is actually taking place. While apparently applying the same principles to a new set of facts, the Court is in reality altering the principle by an almost indistinguishable increment. Now and again the Court will find this process incapable of producing the results that it wants; a former interpretation or principle no longer fills what the Court sees as the needs of society, so that principle must be rejected and another put in its place. On such occasions the Court will overrule its previous interpretation of the Constitution and substitute another interpretation—usually one which has been long clamoring for acceptance. This is what the Court did when, starting in the early 1960s, under the leadership of Chief Justice Warren, it began in a serious way to incorporate Bill of Rights guarantees into the due process clause of the Fourteenth Amendment.

On very rare occasions, when what seems to the Court to be an important right cannot be brought comfortably under any existing constitutional guarantee, the Court is forced to draw upon what it conceives to be the general or fundamental principles of the Constitution to supply the necessary protection. In the early days little effort was made to tie such protection to specific parts of the document: in Loan Association v. Topeka (1875), for example, the Court forbade spending tax money for private purposes on the ground that it violated limits on governmental power that "grow out of the essential nature of all free governments." With the evolution of the due process clause, this right and the celebrated "liberty of contract" became elements of due process of law. See the note to Lochner v. New York (1905).

In raising the "right of privacy" to the status of an independent right, the Court in the present case draws on a "penumbra" cast by a number of specific constitutional rights, without resting the right squarely on any one of them. Three justices, in addition to endorsing the "penumbra" theory, also invoked the Ninth Amendment and Fourteenth Amendment due process. It is interesting to note that Justice Black, a staunch proponent of incorporating the entire Bill of Rights into due process, here dissents on the ground that due process should be limited to what is in the Bill of Rights, as well as extended to it. He rejects the idea that it should include what he views as a "natural justice" component of either fairness or reasonableness.

A test of the validity of Connecticut's birth-control statute first came to the Supreme Court in Tileston v. Ullman (1943). Tileston, a physician, asked a declaratory judgment that the statute was void because it forbade him recommending contraceptives to three patients whose lives would be endangered by childbearing. The Court dismissed the case on the ground that no threatened injury to Tileston was shown. In 1961 a second challenge to the statute was dismissed for lack of justiciable controversy, the Court finding that despite the notorious and common sale of contraceptives in Connecticut, no one had ever been tried for violating the statute; see Poe v. Ullman. The present case was brought after Connecticut abandoned, following the opening of birth-control clinics, its long-standing policy of nonenforcement. In Eisenstadt v. Baird (1972) the Court held that equal protection required that unmarried women, too, be allowed birth control information and articles.

Mr. Justice **Douglas** delivered the opinion of the Court, saying in part:

Appellant Griswold is Executive Director of the Planned Parenthood League of Connecticut. Appellant Buxton is a licensed physician and a professor at the Yale Medical School who served as Medical Director for the League at its Center in New Haven—a center open and operating from November 1 to November 10, 1961, when appellants were arrested.

They gave information, instruction, and medical advice to *married persons* as to the means of preventing conception. They examined the wife and prescribed the best contraceptive device or material for her use. Fees were usually charged, although some couples were serviced free.

The statutes whose constitutionality is involved in this appeal are §§ 53-32 and 54-196 of the General Statutes of Connecticut (1958 rev.). The former provides:

"Any person who uses any drug, medicinal article or instrument for the purpose of preventing conception shall be fined not less than fifty dollars or imprisoned not less than sixty days nor more than one year or be both fined and imprisoned."

Section 54-196 provides:

"Any person who assists, abets, counsels, causes, hires or commands another to commit any offense may be prosecuted and punished as if he were the principal offender."

The appellants were found guilty as accessories and fined $100 each, against the claim that the accessory statute as so applied violated the Fourteenth Amendment. . . .

We think that appellants have standing to raise the constitutional rights of the married people with whom they had a professional relationship. Tileston v. Ullman [1943] is different, for there the plaintiff seeking to represent others asked for a declaratory judgment. In that situation we thought that the requirements of standing should be strict, lest the standards of "case or controversy" in Article III of the Constitution become blurred. Here those doubts are removed by reason of a criminal conviction for serving married couples in violation of an aiding-and-abetting statute. Certainly the accessory should have standing to assert that the offense which he is charged with assisting is not, or cannot constitutionally be, a crime. . . .

Coming to the merits, we are met with a wide range of questions that implicate the Due Process Clause of the Fourteenth Amendment. Overtones of some arguments suggest that Lochner v. New York [1905] should be our guide. But we decline that invitation as we did in West Coast Hotel Co. v. Parrish [1937]. . . . We do not sit as a super-legislature to determine the wisdom, need, and propriety of laws that touch economic problems, business affairs, or social conditions. This law, however, operates directly on an intimate relation of husband and wife and their physician's role in one aspect of that relation.

The association of people is not mentioned in the Constitution nor in the Bill of Rights. The right to educate a child in a school of the parents' choice—whether public or private or parochial—is also not mentioned. Nor is the right to study any particular subject or any foreign language. Yet the First Amendment has been construed to include certain of those rights.

By Pierce v. Society of Sisters [1925] the right to educate one's children as one chooses is made applicable to the States by the force of the First and Fourteenth Amendments. By Meyer v. Nebraska [1923] the same dignity is given the right to study the German language in a private school. In other words, the State may not, consistently with the spirit of the First Amendment, contract the spectrum of available knowledge. The right of freedom of speech and press includes not only the right to utter or to print, but the right to distribute, the right to receive, the right to read . . . and freedom of inquiry, freedom of thought, and freedom to teach . . . —indeed the freedom of the entire university community. . . . Without those peripheral rights the specific rights would be less secure. And so we reaffirm the principle of the Pierce and the Meyer cases.

In NAACP v. Alabama [1958] we protected the "freedom to associate and privacy in one's association," noting that freedom of association was a peripheral First Amendment right. Disclosure of membership lists of a constitutionally valid association, we held, was invalid "as entailing the likelihood of a substantial restraint upon the exercise by petitioner's members of their right to freedom of association." In other words, the First Amendment has a penumbra where privacy is protected from governmental intrusion. In like context, we have protected forms of "association" that are not political in the customary sense but pertain to the social, legal, and economic benefit of the members. NAACP v. Button [1963]. In Schware v. Board of Bar Examiners [1957] we held it not permissible to bar a lawyer from practice, because he had once been a member of the Communist Party. The man's "association with that Party" was not shown to be "anything more than a political faith in a political party" and was not action of a kind proving bad moral character.

Those cases involved more than the "right of assembly"—a right that extends to all irrespective of their race or ideology. . . . The right of "association" like the right of belief . . . is more than the right to attend a meeting; it includes the right to express one's attitudes or philosophies by membership in a group or by affiliation with it or by other lawful means. Association in that context is a form of expression of opinion; and while it is not expressly included in the First Amendment its existence is necessary in making the express guarantees fully meaningful.

The foregoing cases suggest that specific guarantees in the Bill of Rights have penumbras, formed by emanations from those guarantees that help give them life and substance. . . . Various guarantees create zones of privacy. The right of association contained in the penumbra of the First Amendment is one, as we have seen. The Third Amendment in its prohibition against the quartering of soldiers "in any house" in time of peace without the consent of the owner is another facet of that privacy. The Fourth Amendment explicitly affirms the "right of the people to be secure in their persons, houses, papers, and effects, against unreasonable searches and seizures." The Fifth Amendment in its Self-Incrimination Clause enables the citizen to create a zone of privacy which government may not force him to surrender to his detriment. The Ninth Amendment provides: "The enumeration in the Constitution, of certain rights, shall not be construed to deny or disparage others retained by the people." . . .

The present case, then, concerns a relationship lying within the zone of privacy created by several fundamental constitutional guarantees. And it concerns a law which, in forbidding the *use* of contraceptives rather than regulating their manufacture or sale, seeks to achieve its goals by means having a maximum destructive impact upon that relationship. Such a law cannot stand in light of the familiar principle, so often applied by this Court, that a "governmental purpose to control or prevent activities constitutionally subject to state regulation may not be achieved by means which sweep unnecessarily broadly and thereby invade the area of protected freedoms." NAACP v. Alabama [1964]. Would we allow the police to search the sacred precincts of marital bedrooms for telltale signs of the use of contraceptives? The very idea is repulsive to the notions of privacy surrounding the marriage relationship.

We deal with a right of privacy older than the Bill of Rights—older than our political parties, older than our school system. Marriage is a coming together for better or for worse, hopefully enduring, and intimate to the degree of being sacred. It is an association that promotes a way of life, not causes; a harmony in living, not political faiths; a bilateral loyalty, not commercial or social projects. Yet it is an association for as noble a purpose as any involved in our prior decisions.

Reversed.

Mr. Justice **Goldberg,** whom the Chief Justice [**Warren**] and Mr. Justice **Brennan** join, concurring, said in part:

While this Court has had little occasion to interpret the Ninth Amendment, "[i]t cannot be presumed that any clause in the constitution is intended to be without effect." Marbury v. Madison [1803]. . . . To hold that a right so basic and fundamental and so deep-rooted in our society as the right of privacy in marriage may be infringed because that right is not guaranteed in so many words by the first eight amendments to the Constitution is to ignore the Ninth Amendment and to give it no effect whatsoever. Moreover, a judicial construction that this fundamental right is not protected by the Constitution because it is not mentioned in explicit terms by one of the first eight amendments or elsewhere in the Constitution would violate the Ninth Amendment, which specifically states that "[t]he enumeration in the Constitution, of certain rights, shall not be *construed* to deny or disparage others retained by the people." (Emphasis added.)

. . . I do not take the position of my Brother Black . . . that the entire Bill of Rights is incorporated in the Fourteenth Amendment, and I do not mean to imply that the Ninth Amendment is applied against the States by the Fourteenth. Nor do I mean to state that the Ninth Amendment constitutes an independent source of rights protected from infringement by either the States or the Federal Government. Rather, the Ninth Amendment shows a belief of the Constitution's authors that fundamental rights exist that are not expressly enumerated in the first eight amendments and an intent that the list of rights included there not be deemed exhaustive. . . .

. . . In sum, the Ninth Amendment simply lends strong support to the view that the "liberty" protected by the Fifth and Fourteenth Amendments from infringement by the Federal Government or the States is not restricted to rights specifically mentioned in the first eight amendments. . . .

Mr. Justice **Harlan,** concurring in the judgment, said in part:

. . . What I find implicit in the Court's opinion is that the "incorporation" doctrine may be used to *restrict* the reach of Fourteenth Amendment Due Process. For me this is just as unacceptable constitutional doctrine as is the use of the "incorporation" approach to *impose* upon the States all the requirements of the Bill of Rights as found in the provisions of the first eight amendments and in the decisions of this Court interpreting them. . . .

In my view, the proper constitutional inquiry in this case is whether this Connecticut statute infringes the Due Process Clause of the Fourteenth Amendment because the enactment violates basic values "implicit in the concept of ordered liberty," Palko v. Connecticut [1937]. . . .

Mr. Justice **White** concurred in the judgment.

Mr. Justice **Black,** with whom Mr. Justice **Stewart** joins, dissented, saying in part:

The Court talks about a constitutional "right of privacy" as though there is some constitutional provision or provisions forbidding any law ever to be passed which might abridge the "privacy" of individuals. But there is not. There are, of course, guarantees in certain specific constitutional provisions which are designed in part to protect privacy at certain times and places with respect to certain activities. Such, for example, is the Fourth Amendment's guarantee against "unreasonable searches and seizures." But I think it belittles that Amendment to talk about it as though it protects nothing but "privacy." To treat it that way is to give it a niggardly interpretation, not the kind of liberal reading I think any Bill of Rights provision should be given. The average man would very likely not have his feelings soothed any more by having his property seized openly than by having it seized privately and by stealth. He simply wants his property left alone. And a person can be just as much, if not more, irritated, annoyed and injured by an unceremonious public arrest by a policeman as he is by a seizure in the privacy of his office or home.

One of the most effective ways of diluting or expanding a constitutionally guaranteed right is to substitute for the crucial word or words of a constitutional guarantee another word or words more or less flexible and more or less restricted in meaning. This fact is well illustrated by the use of the term "right of privacy" as a comprehensive substitute for the Fourth Amendment's guarantee against "unreasonable searches and seizures." "Privacy" is a broad, abstract and ambiguous concept which can easily be shrunken in meaning but which can also, on the other hand, easily be interpreted as a constitutional ban against many things other than searches and seizures. I have expressed the view many times that First Amendment freedoms, for example, have suffered from a failure of the courts to stick to the simple language of the First Amendment in construing it, instead of invoking multitudes of words substituted for those the Framers used. . . .

I realize that many good and able men have eloquently spoken and written, sometimes in rhapsodical strains, about the duty of this Court to keep the Constitution in tune with the times. The idea is that the Constitution must be changed from time to time and that this Court is charged with a duty to make those changes. For myself, I must with all deference reject that philosophy.

The Constitution makers knew the need for change and provided for it. Amendments suggested by the people's elected representatives can be submitted to the people or their selected agents for ratification. That method of change was good for our Fathers, and being somewhat old-fashioned I must add it is good enough for me. And so, I cannot rely on the Due Process Clause or the Ninth Amendment or any mysterious and uncertain natural law concept as a reason for striking down this state law. The Due Process Clause with an "arbitrary and capricious" or "shocking to the conscience" formula was liberally used by this Court to strike down economic legislation in the early decades of this century, threatening, many people thought, the tranquility and stability of the Nation. See, e.g., Lochner v. New York [1905]. That formula, based on subjective considerations of "natural justice," is no less dangerous when used to enforce this Court's views about personal rights than those about economic rights. I had thought that we had laid that formula, as a means for striking down state legislation, to rest once and for all in cases like West Coast Hotel Co. v. Parrish [1937].

Mr. Justice **Stewart** wrote a dissenting opinion in which Mr. Justice **Black** joined.

ROE v. WADE

410 U. S. 113; 93 S. Ct. 705; 35 L. Ed. 2d 147 (1973)

"The Court today does not pick out particular human activities, characterize them as 'fundamental,' and give them added protection. . . . To the contrary, the Court simply recognizes, as it must, an established constitutional right, and gives to that right no less protection than the Constitution itself demands."

Although this quotation from Justice Stewart by the Court in San Antonio v. Rodriguez (1973) states the orthodox view of the Court's role, few scholars today would subscribe to it. While in theory all rights in the Constitution are of equal value (the Constitution nowhere suggests that some rights are more important than others), over the years the Court has always cherished certain rights which it considered more important than other rights and hence entitled to greater constitutional protection. The rights so honored have changed from time to time as the Court perceived changes in basic social values. In the early days private property was given special consideration, and later this came to include the rights of businessmen and "liberty of contract." Then in the 1930s and 1940s, while the economic rights fell from grace, the rights listed in the First Amendment rose to favor. In recent years the rights of privacy and the right to vote have joined the ranks of the elite.

Since the ranking of these rights is a matter of value judgment, it has been condemned by those who disapproved the particular ranking as "judicial legisla-

tion," "substituting judicial values for those of the community," a "violation of the democratic process," and a "lack of proper judicial restraint." While such attacks seem to challenge the role of the Court in this area, in fact few justices have rejected philosophically the idea that some rights are better than others. The classic example is Justice Holmes, who condemned the judicial favoritism shown to economic rights (see Lochner v. New York, 1905) while insisting that speech could be curtailed only if it presented a "clear and present danger," (see his dissent in Gitlow v. New York, 1925).

Perhaps the easiest method of giving added protection to a right, once it is identified, is to clothe it in language that nullifies the normal presumption in favor of legislative acts and forces the government to show that its laws are reasonable and necessary. Such language abounds in the areas of the First Amendment: the "clear and present danger" test, the statement that First Amendment rights are in a "preferred position" (see Murdock v. Pennsylvania, 1943) and the rule (since modified) that publications cannot be condemned as obscene unless they are utterly without redeeming social value—all serve to tip the scales in favor of the right and against the government wishing to suppress or regulate it.

In 1960 in Bates v. Little Rock a new phrase made its appearance. The Court held bad the demand of the city of Little Rock for the publication of the membership lists of the NAACP on the ground that it would destroy the group's organizational privacy and impair its operations. "Where there is a significant encroachment upon personal liberty, the State may prevail only upon showing a subordinating interest which is compelling." This "compelling state interest" phrase appeared again in several cases in 1963 (see Gibson v. Florida Investigation Committee), where its impact was to make the state produce evidence that it had a compelling interest which could be met only by infringing a claimed right of association. In none of the cases was sufficient interest shown.

In 1969 the "compelling state interest" doctrine was applied to the equal protection clause. The Court in this area had long granted favored status to certain bases of classification, such as race and religion, holding that legislative distinctions based on them were, if not "invidious," at least "inherently suspect." But with Shapiro v. Thompson and Kramer v. Union Free School Dist. the Court looked not at the bases of classification alone, but at the aims sought to be achieved by these bases. In striking down the requirement of a year's residence to receive welfare and the requirement of taxpayer (or parental) status to vote in school board elections, the Court found that where a classification limits the right to move freely across state lines or the right to vote, it could only be justified by a compelling state interest.

In the case below, the phrase is moved again—this time into the area of privacy protected by the Constitution. Here the Court not only upholds the right of a mother to decide, in consultation with her doctor, whether or not to have an abortion, but spells out the "compelling points" at which the state's "compelling interest" permits it to undertake regulation of abortions.

While the case below in effect holds invalid the statutes of some thirty states which forbid abortions except to save the life of the mother, in Doe v. Bolton, decided the same day, the Court dealt with a Georgia statute patterned after the American Law Institute's Penal Code and followed in about a dozen states. The Georgia statute permitted abortion if it was necessary to the preservation of the health of the mother, if the fetus was likely to be born with a serious defect, or if the pregnancy resulted from rape. Although the Court held that the validity of these provisions was not properly before it, the questions they raise are clearly answered in the Texas case below. In addition, the Georgia law required a number of procedural conditions, such as that the woman's doctor and two other doctors put in writing the judgment that an abortion was needed, that the abortion be performed in a hospital accredited by the nongovernmental Joint Committee on Accreditation of Hospitals, and that the abortion be approved in advance by three members of the hospital's abortion committee. All these requirements were held invalid since they were not required in any surgical procedure other than abortion. Two years later the Court made clear that this language did not forbid a state to apply its anti-abortion statute to punish the performance of an abortion by a non-physician with no medical training; see Connecticut v. Menillo (1975).

The present case involved the efforts of a pregnant, unmarried woman to get an abortion "performed by a competent, licensed physician under safe, clinical conditions." Since Texas law forbade abortions except for "the purpose of saving the life of the mother," she sought a declaratory judgment holding the statute unconstitutional and enjoining its enforcement.

Mr. Justice **Blackmun** delivered the opinion of the Court, saying in part:

V.

The principal thrust of appellant's attack on the Texas statutes is that they improperly invade a right, said to be possessed by the pregnant woman, to choose to terminate her pregnancy. Appellant would discover this right in the concept of personal "liberty" embodied in the Fourteenth Amendment's Due Process Clause; or in personal, marital, familial, and sexual privacy said to be protected by the Bill of Rights or its penumbras, see Griswold v. Connecticut (1965); Eisenstadt v. Baird (1972); (White, J., concurring); or among those rights reserved to the people by the Ninth Amendment, Griswold v. Connecticut (Goldberg, J., concurring). Before addressing this claim, we feel it desirable briefly to survey, in several aspects, the history of abortion, for such insight as that history may afford us, and then to examine the state purposes and interests behind the criminal abortion laws.

VI.

It perhaps is not generally appreciated that the restrictive criminal abortion laws in effect in a majority of States today are of relatively recent vintage. Those laws, generally proscribing abortion or its attempt at any time during pregnancy except when necessary to preserve the pregnant woman's life, are not of ancient or even of common law origin. Instead, they derive from statutory changes effected, for the most part, in the latter half of the 19th century. . . .

[The Court here reviews the history of attitudes toward abortion and abortion laws since ancient times.]

VII.

Three reasons have been advanced to explain historically the enactment of criminal abortion laws in the 19th century and to justify their continued existence.

It has been argued occasionally that these laws were the product of a Victorian social concern to discourage illicit sexual conduct. Texas, however, does not advance this justification in the present case, and it appears that no court or commentator has taken the argument seriously. The appellants and amici contend, moreover, that this is not a proper state purpose at all and suggest that, if it were, the Texas statutes are overbroad in protecting it since the law fails to distinguish between married and unwed mothers.

A second reason is concerned with abortion as a medical procedure. When most criminal abortion laws were first enacted, the procedure was a hazardous one for the woman. This was particularly true prior to the development of antisepsis. Antiseptic techniques, of course, were based on discoveries by Lister, Pasteur, and others first announced in 1867, but were not generally accepted and employed until about the turn of the century. Abortion mortality was high. Even after 1900, and perhaps until as late as the development of antibiotics in the 1940's, standard modern techniques such as dilation and curettage were not nearly so safe as they are today. Thus it has been argued that a State's real concern in enacting a criminal abortion law was to protect the pregnant woman, that is, to restrain her from submitting to a procedure that placed her life in serious jeopardy.

Modern medical techniques have altered this situation. Appellants and various amici refer to medical data indicating that abortion in early pregnancy, that is, prior to the end of first trimester, although not without its risk, is now relatively safe. Mortality rates for women undergoing early abortions, where the procedure is legal, appear to be as low as or lower than the rates for normal childbirth. Consequently, any interest of the State in protecting the woman from an inherently hazardous procedure, except when it would be equally dangerous for her to forego it, has largely disappeared. Of course, important state interests in the area of health and medical standards do remain. The State has a legitimate interest in seeing to it that abortion, like any other medical procedure, is performed under circumstances that insure maximum safety for the patient. This interest obviously extends at least to the performing physician and his staff, to the facilities involved, to the availability of after-care, and to adequate provision for any complication or emergency that might arise. The prevalence of high mortality rates at illegal "abortion mills" strengthens, rather than weakens, the State's interest in regulating the conditions under which abortions are performed. Moreover, the risk to the woman increases as her pregnancy continues. Thus the State retains a definite interest in protecting the woman's own health and safety when an abortion is proposed at a late stage of pregnancy.

The third reason is the State's interest—some phrase it in terms of duty—in protecting prenatal life. Some of the argument for this justification rests on the theory that a new human life is present from the moment of conception. The State's interest and general obligation to protect life then extends, it is argued, to prenatal life. Only when the life of the pregnant mother herself is at stake, balanced against the life she carries within her, should the interest of the embryo or fetus not prevail. Logically, of course, a legitimate State interest in this area need not stand or fall on acceptance of the belief that life begins at conception or at some other point prior to live birth. In assessing the State's interest, recognition may be given to the less rigid claim that as long as at least *potential* life is involved, the State may assert interests beyond the protection of the pregnant woman alone.

Parties challenging state abortion laws have sharply disputed in some courts the contention that a purpose of these laws, when enacted, was to protect prenatal life. . . .

It is with these interests, and the weight to be attached to them, that this case is concerned.

VIII.

The Constitution does not explicitly mention any right of privacy. In a line of decisions, however, going back perhaps as far as Union Pacific R. Co. v. Botsford (1891), the Court has recognized that a right of personal privacy, or a guarantee of certain areas or zones of privacy, does exist under the Constitution. In varying contexts the Court or individual Justices have indeed found at least the roots of that right in the First Amendment, Stanley v. Georgia (1969); in the Fourth and Fifth Amendments, Terry v. Ohio (1968), Katz v. United States (1967) . . . ; in the penumbras of the Bill of Rights, Griswold v. Connecticut (1965); in the Ninth Amendment; or in the concept of liberty guaranteed by the first section of the Fourteenth Amendment, see Meyer v. Nebraska (1923). These decisions make it clear that only personal rights that can be deemed "fundamental" or "implicit in the concept of ordered liberty," Palko v. Connecticut (1937), are included in this guarantee of personal privacy. They also make it clear that the right has some extension to activities relating to marriage, Loving v. Virginia (1967), procreation, Skinner v. Oklahoma (1942), contraception, Eisenstadt v. Baird (1972). . . .

This right of privacy, whether it be founded in the Fourteenth Amendment's concept of personal liberty and restrictions upon state action, as we feel it is, or, as the District Court determined, in the Ninth Amendment's reservation of rights to the people, is broad enough to encompass a woman's decision whether or not to terminate her pregnancy. The detriment that the State would impose upon the pregnant woman by denying this choice altogether is apparent. Specific and direct harm medically diagnosable even in early pregnancy may be involved. Maternity, or additional offspring, may force upon the woman a distressful life and future. Psychological harm may be imminent. Mental and physical health may be taxed by child care. There is also the distress, for all concerned, associated with the unwanted child, and there is the problem of bringing a child into a family already unable, psychologically and otherwise, to care for it. In other cases, as in this one, the additional difficulties and continuing stigma of unwed motherhood may be involved. All these are factors the woman and her responsible physician necessarily will consider in consultation.

On the basis of elements such as these, appellants and some amici argue that the woman's right is absolute and that she is entitled to terminate her pregnancy at whatever time, in whatever way, and for whatever reason she alone chooses. With this we do not agree. Appellants' arguments that Texas either has no valid interest at all in regulating the abortion decision, or no interest strong enough to support any limitation upon the woman's sole determination, is unpersuasive. The Court's decisions recognizing a right of privacy also acknowledge that some state regulation in areas protected by that right is appropriate. As noted above, a State may properly assert important interests in safeguarding health, in maintaining medical standards, and in protecting potential life. At some point in pregnancy, these respective interests become sufficiently compelling to sustain regulation of the factors that govern the abortion decision. The privacy right involved, therefore, cannot be said to be absolute. In fact, it is not clear to us that the claim asserted by some amici that one has an unlimited right to do with one's body as one pleases bears a close relationship to the right of privacy previously articulated in the Court's decisions. The Court has refused to recognize an unlimited right of this kind in the past. Jacobson v. Massachusetts (1905) (vaccination); Buck v. Bell (1927) (sterilization).

We therefore conclude that the right of personal privacy includes the abortion decision, but that this right is not unqualified and must be considered against state interests in regulation.

Where certain "fundamental rights" are involved, the Court has held that regulation limiting these rights may be justified only by a "compelling state interest," Kramer v. Union Free School District (1969), Shapiro v. Thompson (1969), . . . and that legislative enactments must be narrowly drawn to express only the legitimate state interests at stake. Griswold v. Connecticut (1965). . . .

IX.

The District Court held that the appellee failed to meet his burden of demonstrating that the Texas statute's infringement upon Roe's rights was necessary to support a compelling state interest. . . . Appellee argues that the State's determination to recognize and protect prenatal life from and after conception constitutes a compelling state interest. As noted above, we do not agree fully with either formulation.

A. The appellee and certain amici argue that the fetus is a "person" within the language and meaning of the Fourteenth Amendment. In support of this they outline at length and in detail the well-known facts of fetal development. If this suggestion of personhood is established, the appellant's case, of course, collapses, for the fetus' right to life is then guaranteed specifically by the Amendment. The appellant conceded as much on reargument. On the other hand, the appellee conceded on reargument that no case could be cited that holds that a fetus is a person within the meaning of the Fourteenth Amendment.

The Constitution does not define "person" in so many words. Section 1 of the Fourteenth Amendment contains three references to "person." The first, in defining "citizens," speaks of "persons born or naturalized in the United States." The word also appears both in the Due Process Clause and in the Equal Protection Clause. "Person" is used in other places in the Constitution. . . . But in nearly all these instances, the use of the word is such that it has application only postnatally. None indicates, with any assurance, that it has any possible pre-natal application.* All this, together with our observation, that throughout the major portion of the 19th century prevailing legal abortion practices were far freer than they are today, persuades us that the word "person," as used in the Fourteenth Amendment, does not include the unborn. . . .

B. The pregnant woman cannot be isolated in her privacy. She carries an embryo and, later, a fetus, if one accepts the medical definitions of the developing young in the human uterus. . . . The situation therefore is inherently different from marital intimacy, or bedroom possession of obscene material, or marriage, or procreation, or education, with which Eisenstadt, Griswold, Stanley, Loving, Skinner, Pierce, and Meyer were respectively concerned. As we have intimated above, it is reasonable and appropriate for a State to decide that at some point

---

*When Texas urges that a fetus is entitled to Fourteenth Amendment protection as a person, it faces a dilemma. Neither in Texas nor in any other State are all abortions prohibited. Despite broad proscription, an exception always exists. The exception contained in Art. 1196, for an abortion procured or attempted by medical advice for the purpose of saving the life of the mother, is typical. But if the fetus is a person who is not to be deprived of life without due process of law, and if the mother's condition is the sole determinant, does not the Texas exception appear to be out of line with the Amendment's command? . . .

in time another interest, that of health of the mother or that of potential human life, becomes significantly involved. The woman's privacy is no longer sole and any right of privacy she possesses must be measured accordingly.

Texas urges that, apart from the Fourteenth Amendment, life begins at conception and is present throughout pregnancy, and that, therefore, the State has a compelling interest in protecting that life from and after conception. We need not resolve the difficult question of when life begins. When those trained in the respective disciplines of medicine, philosophy, and theology are unable to arrive at any consensus, the judiciary, at this point in the development of man's knowledge, is not in a position to speculate as to the answer.

It should be sufficient to note briefly the wide divergence of thinking on this most sensitive and difficult question. . . .

X.

In view of all this, we do not agree that, by adopting one theory of life, Texas may override the rights of the pregnant woman that are at stake. We repeat, however, that the State does have an important and legitimate interest in preserving and protecting the health of the pregnant woman, whether she be a resident of the State or a nonresident who seeks medical consultation and treatment there, and that it has still *another* important and legitimate interest in protecting the potentiality of human life. These interests are separate and distinct. Each grows in substantiality as the woman approaches term and, at a point during pregnancy, each becomes ''compelling.''

With respect to the State's important and legitimate interest in the health of the mother, the ''compelling'' point, in the light of present medical knowledge, is at approximately the end of the first trimester. This is so because of the now established medical fact, referred to above . . . that until the end of the first trimester mortality in abortion is less than mortality in normal childbirth. It follows that, from and after this point, a State may regulate the abortion procedure to the extent that the regulation reasonably relates to the preservation and protection of maternal health. Examples of permissible state regulation in this area are requirements as to the qualifications of the person who is to perform the abortion; as to the licensure of that person; as to the facility in which the procedure is to be performed, that is, whether it must be a hospital or may be a clinic or some other place of less-than-hospital status; as to the licensing of the facility; and the like.

This means, on the other hand, that, for the period of pregnancy prior to this ''compelling'' point, the attending physician, in consultation with his patient, is free to determine, without regulation by the State, that in his medical judgment the patient's pregnancy should be terminated. If that decision is reached, the judgment may be effectuated by an abortion free of interference by the State.

With respect to the State's important and legitimate interest in potential life, the ''compelling'' point is at viability. This is so because the fetus then presumably has the capability of meaningful life outside the mother's womb. State regulation protective of fetal life after viability thus has both logical and biological justifications. If the State is interested in protecting fetal life after viability, it may go so far as to proscribe abortion during that period except when it is necessary to preserve the life or health of the mother.

Measured against these standards, the Texas Penal Code, in restricting legal abortions to those ''procured or attempted by medical advice for the purpose of saving the life of the mother,'' sweeps too broadly. The statute makes no distinction between abortions performed early in pregnancy and those performed later, and it limits to a single reason, ''saving'' the mother's life, the legal justification for the procedure. The statute, therefore, cannot survive the constitutional attack made upon it here. . . .

XI.

To summarize and to repeat:

1. A state criminal abortion statute of the current Texas type, that excepts from criminality only a *life saving* procedure on behalf of the mother, without regard to pregnancy stage and without recognition of the other interests involved, is violative of the Due Process Clause of the Fourteenth Amendment.

(a) For the stage prior to approximately the end of the first trimester, the abortion decision and its effectuation must be left to the medical judgment of the pregnant woman's attending physician.

(b) For the stage subsequent to approximately the end of the first trimester, the State, in promoting its interest in the health of the mother, may, if it chooses, regulate the abortion procedure in ways that are reasonably related to maternal health.

(c) For the stage subsequent to viability the State, in promoting its interest in the potentiality of human life, may, if it chooses, regulate, and even proscribe, abortion except where it is necessary, in appropriate medical judgment, for the preservation of the life or health of the mother.

2. The State may define the term ''physician,'' as it has been employed in the preceding numbered paragraphs of this Part XI of this opinion, to mean only a physician currently licensed by the State, and may proscribe any abortion by a person who is not a physician as so defined.

In Doe v. Bolton procedural requirements contained in one of the modern abortion statutes are considered. That opinion and this one, of course, are to be read together. . . .

Mr. Chief Justice **Burger** concurred.

Mr. Justice **Douglas** concurred.

Mr. Justice **Stewart,** concurring said in part:

In 1963, this Court, in Ferguson v. Skrupa, purported to sound the death knell for the doctrine of substantive due process, a doctrine under which many state laws had in the past been held to violate the Fourteenth Amendment. As Mr. Justice Black's opinion for the Court in Skrupa put it: "We have returned to the original constitutional proposition that courts do not substitute their social and economic beliefs for the judgment of legislative bodies, who are elected to pass laws."

Barely two years later, in Griswold v. Connecticut, the Court held a Connecticut birth control law unconstitutional. In view of what had been so recently said in Skrupa, the Court's opinion in Griswold understandably did its best to avoid reliance on the Due Process Clause of the Fourteenth Amendment as the ground for decision. Yet, the Connecticut law did not violate any provision of the Bill of Rights, nor any other specific provision of the Constitution. So it was clear to me then, and it is equally clear to me now, that the Griswold decision can be rationally understood only as a holding that the Connecticut statute substantively invaded the "liberty" that is protected by the Due Process Clause of the Fourteenth Amendment. As so understood, Griswold stands as one in a long line of pre-Skrupa cases decided under the doctrine of substantive due process, and I now accept it as such.

"In a Constitution for a free people, there can be no doubt that the meaning of 'liberty' must be broad indeed." . . . The Constitution nowhere mentions a specific right of personal choice in matters of marriage and family life, but the "liberty" protected by the Due Process Clause of the Fourteenth Amendment covers more than those freedoms explicitly named in the Bill of Rights. . . .

Several decisions of this Court make clear that freedom of personal choice in matters of marriage and family life is one of the liberties protected by the Due Process Clause of the Fourteenth Amendment. Loving v. Virginia, Griswold v. Connecticut . . . . That right necessarily includes the right of a woman to decide whether or not to terminate her pregnancy. "Certainly the interests of a woman in giving of her physical and emotional self during pregnancy and the interests that will be affected throughout her life by the birth and raising of a child are of a far greater degree of significance and personal intimacy than the right to send a child to private school protected in Pierce v. Society of Sisters (1925), or the right to teach a foreign language protected in Meyer v. Nebraska (1923)." . . .

Mr. Justice **Rehnquist,** dissenting, said in part:

. . . I have difficulty in concluding, as the Court does, that the right of "privacy" is involved in this case.

Texas by the statute here challenged bars the performance of a medical abortion by a licensed physician on a plaintiff such as Roe. A transaction resulting in an operation such as this is not "private" in the ordinary usage of that word. . . .

If the Court means by the term "privacy" no more than that the claim of a person to be free from unwanted state regulation of consensual transactions may be a form of "liberty" protected by the Fourteenth Amendment, there is no doubt that similar claims have been upheld in our earlier decisions on the basis of that liberty. I agree with the statement of Mr. Justice Stewart in his concurring opinion that the "liberty," against deprivation of which without due process the Fourteenth Amendment protects, embraces more than the rights found in the Bill of Rights. But that liberty is not guaranteed absolutely against deprivation, but only against deprivation without due process of law. The test traditionally applied in the area of social and economic legislation is whether or not a law such as that challenged has a rational relation to a valid state objective. . . . But the Court's sweeping invalidation of any restrictions on abortion during the first trimester is impossible to justify under that standard, and the conscious weighing of competing factors which the Court's opinion apparently substitutes for the established test is far more appropriate to a legislative judgment than to a judicial one.

The Court eschews the history of the Fourteenth Amendment in its reliance on the "compelling state interest" test. . . . But the Court adds a new wrinkle to this test by transposing it from the legal considerations associated with the Equal Protection Clause of the Fourteenth Amendment to this case arising under the Due Process Clause of the Fourteenth Amendment. Unless I misapprehend the consequences of this transplanting of the "compelling state interest test," the Court's opinion will accomplish the seemingly impossible feat of leaving this area of the law more confused than it found it.

While the Court's opinion quotes from the dissent of Mr. Justice Holmes in Lochner v. New York (1905), the result it reaches is more closely attuned to the majority opinion of Mr. Justice Peckham in that case. As in Lochner and similar cases applying substantive due process standards to economic and social welfare legislation, the adoption of the compelling state interest standard will inevitably require this Court to examine the legislative policies and pass on the wisdom of these policies in the very process of deciding whether a particular state interest put forward may or may not be "compelling." . . .

The fact that a majority of the States, reflecting after all the majority sentiment in those States, have had restrictions on abortions for at least a century is a strong indication, it seems to me, that the asserted right to an abortion is not "so rooted in the traditions and conscience of our people as to be ranked as fundamental," Snyder v. Massachusetts (1934). . . .

Mr. Justice **White,** with whom Mr. Justice **Rehnquist** joins, dissented.

BOWERS v. HARDWICK

478 U. S. 186; 92 L. Ed. 2d 140; 106 S. Ct. 2841
(1986)

While the right to sell obscene material enjoys no protection under the First Amendment, the freedom of thought implicitly guaranteed by that provision ensures the right of persons to enjoy such material in the privacy of their own home. Relying on the Court's statement in Roth that "obscenity is not within the area of constitutionally protected speech or press," the state of Georgia made the mere possession of obscene material a crime. In Stanley v. Georgia (1969), the Court held the statute void. It conceded the wording of Roth v. United States (1957), but pointed out that it and other obscenity cases all involved the sale and distribution of obscene materials to others, and should be read in that context. "This right to receive information and ideas, regardless of their social worth, . . . is fundamental to our free society," and "also fundamental is the right to be free, except in very limited circumstances, from unwanted governmental intrusions into one's privacy."

The Court rejected outright the idea that Georgia had a right to "control the moral content of a person's thoughts." "Whatever may be the justification for other statutes regulating obscenity, we do not think they reach into the privacy of one's own home. If the First Amendment means anything, it means that a State has no business telling a man, sitting alone in his own house, what books he may read or what films he may watch. Our whole constitutional heritage rebels at the thought of giving government the power to control men's minds." Nor could Georgia justify its statute on the ground that the possession of pornography led to antisocial conduct. "Given the present state of knowledge, the State may no more prohibit mere possession of obscenity on the ground that it may lead to antisocial conduct than it may prohibit possession of chemistry books on the ground that they may lead to the manufacture of home-made spirits."

While it seems clear that homosexual conduct was condoned if not approved in ancient Greece and Rome, not since the advent of the Judeo-Christian moral code has been publicly accepted in the Western World, and later books of the Bible consider it a sin punishable by death. While social disapproval has made almost impossible any assessment of its prevalence, there is no question that it exists almost everywhere to some extent. In large cities, where greater anonymity exists, homosexuals may form a subculture with its own vernacular, accepted gathering places, and agreed patterns of behavior. Recent years have seen the formation of highly visible "gay rights" organizations campaigning for the abolition of laws and discriminatory rules against their mode of sexual preference.

The present case is the first one to bring to the Court the question whether a state could punish homosexual conduct. At least two lines of precedent were ar-guably relevant. First, the privacy cases from Griswold to Roe, which emphasized the intensely personal nature of consensual sexual behavior among adults (including unmarried adults), and the right to make choices affecting this conduct free of government intrusion. Second, the obscenity cases, which, while also involving privacy concerns, were grounded in the First Amendment and thus provided a minimal protection for conduct as opposed to speech or thought.

The choice between these two lines of precedents is critical: put simply, seeing homosexual conduct as akin to heterosexual conduct suggests one result, while seeing it as akin to obscenity suggests another. In the case below the Court leaned heavily on the obscenity cases, emphasizing that Stanley involved First Amendment materials while here physical activity was involved. In contrast, the dissent drew more heavily on the heterosexual cases and thus did not get entangled in the problems of protecting conduct under the First Amendment. The two approaches result not only in different conclusions; they tell fundamentally different stories about both the nature of homosexual conduct and the appropriate stance of the government and heterosexual individuals toward the gay community. A Newsweek poll taken shortly after the Bowers decision revealed that over half those answering the question disapproved the outcome. But while the trend seems to be in favor of making sodomy legal, the apparent relationship between sodomy and the AIDS epidemic (Acquired Immunity Deficiency Syndrome, a fatal and incurable disease) which first burgeoned in the homosexual community, has added to the difficulties of those pressing for legalization. As of January 1990, 25 states and the District of Columbia still had laws against sodomy.

Justice **White** delivered the opinion of the Court, saying in part:

In August 1982, respondent Hardwick (hereafter respondent) was charged with violating the Georgia statute criminalizing sodomy by committing that act with another adult male in the bedroom of respondent's home. After a preliminary hearing, the District Attorney decided not to present the matter to the grand jury unless further evidence developed.

Respondent then brought suit in the Federal District Court, challenging the constitutionality of the statute insofar as it criminalized consensual sodomy. He asserted that he was a practicing homosexual, that the Georgia sodomy statute, as administered by the defendants, placed him in imminent danger of arrest, and that the statute for several reasons violates the Federal Constitution. . . .

. . . Relying on our decisions in Griswold v. Connecticut (1965), Eisenstadt v. Baird (1972), Stanley v. Georgia (1969), and Roe v. Wade (1973), the [court of appeals held] that the Georgia statute violated respondent's fundamental rights because his homosexual activity is a private and intimate association that is beyond the reach of state regulation by reason of the Ninth Amendment and the Due Process Clause of the Fourteenth Amendment. The case was remanded for trial, at which, to prevail, the State would have to prove that the statute is supported by a compelling interest and is the most narrowly drawn means of achieving that end.

. . . We agree with the petitioner that the Court of Appeals erred, and hence reverse its judgment.

This case does not require a judgment on whether laws against sodomy between consenting adults in general, or between homosexuals in particular, are wise or desirable. It raises no question about the right or propriety of state legislative decisions to repeal their laws that criminalize homosexual sodomy, or of state-court decisions invalidating those laws on state constitutional grounds. The issue presented is whether the Federal Constitution confers a fundamental right upon homosexuals to engage in sodomy and hence invalidates the laws of the many States that still make such conduct illegal and have done so for a very long time. The case also calls for some judgment about the limits of the Court's role in carrying out its constitutional mandate.

We first register our disagreement with the Court of Appeals and with respondent that the Court's prior cases have construed the Constitution to confer a right of privacy that extends to homosexual sodomy and for all intents and purposes have decided this case. [The Court here notes a series of cases dealing with child rearing, procreation, marriage, contraception and abortion.]

Accepting the decisions in these cases and the above description of them, we think it evident that none of the rights announced in those cases bears any resemblance to the claimed constitutional right of homosexuals to engage in acts of sodomy that is asserted in this case. No connection between family, marriage, or procreation on the one hand and homosexual activity on the other has been demonstrated, either by the Court of Appeals or by respondent. Moreover, any claim that these cases nevertheless stand for the proposition that any kind of private sexual conduct between consenting adults is constitutionally insulated from state proscription is unsupportable. . . .

Precedent aside, however, respondent would have us announce, as the Court of Appeals did, a fundamental right to engage in homosexual sodomy. This we are quite unwilling to do. It is true that despite the language of the Due Process Clauses of the Fifth and Fourteenth Amendments, which appears to focus only on the processes by which life, liberty or property is taken, the cases are legion in which those Clauses have been interpreted to have substantive content, subsuming rights that to a great extent are immune from federal or state regulation or proscription. Among such cases are those recognizing rights that have little or no textual support in the constitutional language. . . .

Striving to assure itself and the public that announcing rights not readily identifiable in the Constitution's text involves much more than the imposition of the Justices' own choice of values on the States and the Federal Government, the Court has sought to identify the nature of the rights qualifying for heightened judicial protection. In Palko v. Connecticut (1937) it was said that this category includes those fundamental liberties that are "implicit in the concept of ordered liberty," such that "neither liberty nor justice would exist if [they] were sacrificed." A different description of fundamental liberties appeared in Moore v. East Cleveland (1977) (opinion of Powell, J.), where they are characterized as those liberties that are "deeply rooted in this nation's history and tradition." . . .

It is obvious to us that neither of these formulations would extend a fundamental right to homosexuals to engage in acts of consensual sodomy. Proscriptions against that conduct have ancient roots. Sodomy was a criminal offense at common law and was forbidden by the laws of the original 13 States when they ratified the Bill of Rights. In 1868, when the Fourteenth Amendment was ratified, all but 5 of the 37 States in the Union had criminal sodomy laws. In fact, until 1961, all 50 States outlawed sodomy, and today, 25 States and the District of Columbia continue to provide criminal penalties for sodomy performed in private and between consenting adults. Against this background, to claim that a right to engage in such conduct is "deeply rooted in this nation's history and tradition" or "implicit in the concept of ordered liberty" is, at best, facetious.

Nor are we inclined to take a more expansive view of our authority to discover new fundamental rights imbedded in the Due Process Clause. The Court is most vulnerable and comes nearest to illegitimacy when it deals with judge-made constitutional law having little or no cognizable roots in the language or design of the Constitution. That this is so was painfully demonstrated by the face-off between the Executive and the Court in the 1930's, which resulted in the repudiation of much of the substantive gloss that the Court had placed on the Due Process Clause of the Fifth and Fourteenth Amendments. There should be, therefore, great resistance to expand the substantive reach of those Clauses, particularly if it requires redefining the category of rights deemed to be fundamental. Otherwise, the Judiciary necessarily takes to itself further authority to govern the country without express constitutional authority. The claimed right pressed on us today falls far short of overcoming this resistance.

Respondent, however, asserts that the result should be different where the homosexual conduct occurs in the privacy of the home. He relies on Stanley v. Georgia (1969) where the Court held that the First Amendment prevents conviction for possessing and reading obscene material in the privacy of one's home. "If the First Amendment means anything, it means that a State has no business telling a man, sitting alone in his house, what books he may read or what films he may watch."

Stanley did protect conduct that would not have been protected outside the home, and it partially prevented the enforcement of state obscenity laws; but the decision was firmly grounded in the First Amendment. The right pressed upon us here has no similar support in the text of the Constitution, and it does not qualify for recognition under the prevailing principles for construing the Fourteenth Amendment. Its limits are also difficult to discern. Plainly enough, otherwise illegal conduct is not always immunized whenever it occurs in the home. Victimless crimes, such as the possession and use of illegal drugs do not escape the law where they are committed at home. Stanley itself recognized that its holding offered no protection for the possession in the home of drugs, firearms, or stolen goods. And if respondent's submission is limited to the voluntary sexual conduct between consenting adults, it would be difficult, except by fiat, to limit the claimed right to homosexual conduct while leaving exposed to prosecution adultery, incest, and other sexual crimes even though they are committed in the home. We are unwilling to start down that road. . . .

Chief Justice **Burger**, concurring, said in part:

I join the Court's opinion, but I write separately to underscore my view that in constitutional terms there is no such thing as a fundamental right to commit homosexual sodomy. . . .
This is essentially not a question of personal "preferences" but rather of the legislative authority of the State. I find nothing in the Constitution depriving a State of the power to enact the statute challenged here.

Justice **Powell**, concurring, said in part:

I join the opinion of the Court. . . . This is not to suggest, however, that respondent may not be protected by the Eighth Amendment of the Constitution. The Georgia statute at issue in this case authorizes a court to imprison a person for up to 20 years for a single private, consensual act of sodomy. In my view, a prison sentence for such conduct—certainly a sentence of long duration—would create a serious Eighth Amendment issue. . . .

Justice **Blackmun**, with whom Justice **Brennan**, Justice **Marshall** and Justice **Stevens** join, dissenting, said in part:

This case is no more about "a fundamental right to engage in homosexual sodomy," as the Court purports to declare, than Stanley v. Georgia (1969) was about a fundamental right to watch obscene movies, or Katz v. United States (1967) was about a fundamental right to place interstate bets from a telephone booth. Rather, this case is about "the most comprehensive of rights and the right most valued by civilized men," namely, "the right to be let alone." Olmstead v. United States (1928) (Brandeis, J., dissenting).
The statute at issue denies individuals the right to decide for themselves whether to engage in particular forms of private, consensual sexual activity. The Court concludes that § 16-6-2 is valid essentially because "the laws of . . . many States . . . still make such conduct illegal and have done so for a very long time." But the fact that the moral judgments expressed by statutes like § 16-6-2 may be "natural and familiar . . . ought not to conclude our judgment upon the question whether statutes

embodying them conflict with the Constitution of the United States." Roe v. Wade (1973), quoting Lochner v. New York (1905) (Holmes, J., dissenting). Like Justice Holmes, I believe that "[i]t is revolting to have no better reason for a rule of law than that so it was laid down in the time of Henry IV. It is still more revolting if the grounds upon which it was laid down have vanished long since, and the rule simply persists from blind imitation of the past." . . . I believe we must analyze respondent Hardwick's claim in the light of the values that underlie the constitutional right to privacy. If that right means anything, it means that, before Georgia can prosecute its citizens for making choices about the most intimate aspects of their lives, it must do more than assert that the choice they have made is an " 'abominable crime not fit to be named among Christians.' " Herring v. State, 119 Ga. 709 (1904).

I.

. . . A fair reading of the statute and of the complaint clearly reveals that the majority has distorted the question this case presents.
First, the Court's almost obsessive focus on homosexual activity is particularly hard to justify in light of the broad language Georgia has used. Unlike the Court, the Georgia Legislature has not proceeded on the assumption that homosexuals are so different from other citizens that their lives may be controlled in a way that would not be tolerated if it limited the choices of those other citizens. . . . Michael Hardwick's standing may rest in significant part on Georgia's apparent willingness to enforce against homosexuals a law it seems not to have any desire to enforce against heterosexuals. But his claim that § 16-6-2 involves an unconstitutional intrusion into his privacy and his right of intimate association does not depend in any way on his sexual orientation. . . .

II.

A.

Only the most willful blindness could obscure the fact that sexual intimacy is "a sensitive, key relationship of human existence, central to family life, community welfare, and the development of human personality." Paris Adult Theatre I v. Slaton (1973) . . . . The fact that individuals define themselves in a significant way through their intimate sexual relationships with others suggests, in a Nation as diverse as ours, that there may be many "right" ways of conducting those relationships, and that much of the richness of a relationship will come from the freedom an individual has to *choose* the form and nature of these intensely personal bonds. . . .
In a variety of circumstances we have recognized that a necessary corollary of giving individuals freedom to choose how to conduct their lives is acceptance of the fact that different individuals will make different choices. For example, in holding that the clearly impor-

tant state interest in public education should give way to a competing claim by the Amish to the effect that extended formal schooling threatened their way of life, the Court declared: "There can be no assumption that today's majority is 'right' and the Amish and others like them are 'wrong.' A way of life that is odd or even erratic but interferes with no rights or interests of others is not to be condemned because it is different." Wisconsin v. Yoder (1972). The Court claims that its decision today merely refuses to recognize a fundamental right to engage in homosexual sodomy; what the Court really has refused to recognize is the fundamental interest all individuals have in controlling the nature of their intimate associations with others.

B.

The behavior for which Hardwick faces prosecution occurred in his own home, a place to which the Fourth Amendment attaches special significance. The Court's treatment of this aspect of the case is symptomatic of its overall refusal to consider the broad principles that have informed our treatment of privacy in specific cases. Just as the right to privacy is more than the mere aggregation of a number of entitlements to engage in specific behavior, so too, protecting the physical integrity of the home is more than merely a means of protecting specific activities that often take place there. . . .

The Court's interpretation of the pivotal case of Stanley v. Georgia (1969) is entirely unconvincing. Stanley held that Georgia's undoubted power to punish the public distribution of constitutionally unprotected, obscene material did not permit the State to punish the private possession of such material. According to the majority here, Stanley relied entirely on the First Amendment, and thus, it is claimed, sheds no light on cases not involving printed materials. But that is not what Stanley said. Rather, the Stanley Court anchored its holding in the Fourth Amendment's special protection for the individual in his home: " 'The makers of our Constitution undertook to secure conditions favorable to the pursuit of happiness. They recognized the significance of man's spiritual nature, of his feelings and of his intellect. They knew that only a part of the pain, pleasure and satisfactions of life are to be found in material things. They sought to protect Americans in their beliefs, their thoughts, their emotions and their sensations.' . . .

"These are the rights that appellant is asserting in the cases before us. He is asserting the right to read or observe what he pleases—the right to satisfy his intellectual and emotional needs in the privacy of his own home."(Quoting Olmstead v. United States [1928], Brandeis, J., dissenting).

The central place that Stanley gives Justice Brandeis' dissent in Olmstead, a case raising *no* First Amendment claim, shows that Stanley rested as much on the Court's understanding of the Fourth Amendment as it did on the First. Indeed, in Paris Adult Theatre I v. Sla-

ton (1973), the Court suggested that reliance on the Fourth Amendment not only supported the Court's outcome in Stanley but actually was *necessary* to it: "If obscene material unprotected by the First Amendment in itself carried with it a 'penumbra' of constitutionally protected privacy, this Court would not have found it necessary to decide Stanley on the narrow basis of the 'privacy of the home,' which was hardly more than a reaffirmation that 'a man's home is his castle.' " "The right of the people to be secure in their . . . houses," expressly guaranteed by the Fourth Amendment, is perhaps the most "textual" of the various constitutional provisions that inform our understanding of the right to privacy, and thus I cannot agree with the Court's statement that "[t]he right pressed upon us here has no . . . support in the text of the Constitution." Indeed, the right of an individual to conduct intimate relationships in the intimacy of his or her own home seems to me to be the heart of the Constitution's protection of privacy. . . .

III.

The core of petitioner's defense of § 16-6-2 . . . is that respondent and others who engage in the conduct prohibited by § 16-6-2 interfere with Georgia's exercise of the " 'right of the Nation and of the States to maintain a decent society.' " Paris Adult Theatre I v. Slaton . . . . Essentially, petitioner argues, and the Court agrees, that the fact that the acts described in § 16-6-2 "for hundreds of years, if not thousands, have been uniformly condemned as immoral" is a sufficient reason to permit a State to ban them today. . . .

I cannot agree that either the length of time a majority has held its convictions or the passions with which it defends them can withdraw legislation from this Court's scrutiny. . . . As Justice Jackson wrote so eloquently for the Court in West Virginia Board of Education v. Barnette (1943), ". . . [F]reedom to differ is not limited to things that do not matter much. That would be a mere shadow of freedom. The test of its substance is the right to differ as to things that touch the heart of the existing order." It is precisely because the issue raised by this case touches the heart of what makes individuals what they are that we should be especially sensitive to the rights of those whose choices upset the majority.

The assertion that "traditional Judeo-Christian values proscribe" the conduct involved cannot provide an adequate justification for § 16-6-2. That certain, but by no means all, religious groups condemn the behavior at issue gives the State no license to impose their judgments on the entire citizenry. The legitimacy of secular legislation depends instead on whether the State can advance some justification for its law beyond its conformity to religious doctrine. . . . Thus, far from buttressing his case, petitioner's invocation of Leviticus, Romans, St. Thomas Aquinas, and sodomy's heretical status during the Middle Ages undermines his suggestion that § 16-6-2 represents a legitimate use of secular coercive power.

Justice **Stevens**, with whom Justice **Brennan** and Justice **Marshall** joined, wrote a dissenting opinion.

PLANNED PARENTHOOD v. CASEY

120 L. Ed. 2d 674; 505 U. S. — (1992)

Following the decisions of the Court in Roe and Doe, Missouri enacted an elaborate statute for the regulation of abortions. In Planned Parenthood of Missouri v. Danforth (1976) the Court upheld some of these provisions and struck down others. It could find no quarrel with the definition of viability as "that state of fetal development when the life of the unborn child may be continued indefinitely outside the womb by natural or artificial life support systems." This, the Court found, merely endorsed the flexibility called for in Roe, since "the determination of whether a particular fetus is viable is, and must be, a matter for the judgment of the responsible attending physician." Nor did it find fault with the requirement that the woman give her informed consent to the abortion freely, and in writing, and that the physician keep certain records which the state argued would "advance the sum of medical knowledge." The Court found no constitutional reason why the state could not require written consent for any surgery, and it upheld the record-keeping on the assumption that it would not be allowed to become a burden on the abortion procedure.

In addition to the consent of the pregnant woman, the statute also required the consent of her spouse, and, in the case of an unmarried woman under eighteen, the consent of a parent or guardian. Since the state has no power itself to forbid the termination of the pregnancy, it "does not have the constitutional authority to give a third party an absolute, and possibly arbitrary veto over the decision of the physician and his patient to terminate the patient's pregnancy, regardless of the reason for withholding consent." It was unpersuaded that marital harmony would be promoted by the requirement, and since only the wishes of one could prevail, the interests of the woman bearing the child took precedence. Nor could the Court see how giving parents an absolute veto would "strengthen the family unit" or "enhance parental authority or control where the minor and the non-consenting parent are so fundamentally in conflict and the very existence of the pregnancy already has fractured the family structure. Any independent interest the parent may have in the termination of the minor daughter's pregnancy is no more weighty than the right of privacy of the competent minor mature enough to have become pregnant."

The Court's decision that a state could not forbid abortions triggered a highly emotional nationwide political battle. With the political and financial support of "anti-abortion" and "right to life" groups, efforts were made to overturn or undo the effects of the case by con-

stitutional amendment, by Congressional statutes defining a fetus as a "person" entitled to due process of law, and by various procedural statutes designed to prevent federal courts from enforcing its ruling. While these failed to pass, a substantial victory was achieved when the Court held valid state laws giving financial aid to normal childbirth while withholding it from abortions, since most abortions are sought by those requiring financial aid from the state; see Maher v. Roe (1977). It was hoped that this victory was an indication that the Court was weakening in its enthusiasm for Roe, and should the opportunity arise, it would respond to the efforts in Congress and the intense publicity by overruling it.

The Court, however, seemed remarkably committed to Roe through much of the 1980s. For example, in June 1983 the Court reaffirmed Roe in three separate cases. Justice Powell speaking for the Court in Akron v. Akron Center for Reproductive Health, noted that "the doctrine of stare decisis . . . demands respect in a society governed by the rule of law," and in a footnote added: "There are especially compelling reasons for adhering to stare decisis in applying the principles of Roe v. Wade. That case was considered with special care. It was first argued during the 1971 Term, and reargued—with extensive briefing—the following term. The decision was joined by the Chief Justice and six other Justices. Since Roe was decided in February 1973, the Court repeatedly and consistently has accepted and applied the basic principle that a woman has a fundamental right to make the highly personal choice whether or not to terminate her pregnancy. . . ."

Over the dissents of Justices O'Connor, Rehnquist and White, the Court struck down a number of requirements imposed by the City of Akron. These included a requirement that all second trimester abortions be performed in a full-service hospital (most of which do not perform such abortions) rather than a clinic; that a minor under the age of fifteen must have either parental consent or a court order before an abortion can be performed (regardless of the maturity of the minor); that a woman must be given detailed information regarding the abortion—much of which, the Court noted, "is designed not to inform the woman's consent but rather to persuade her to withhold it altogether"; and that the physician, under threat of criminal penalties, dispose of the fetus in a "humane and sanitary" manner (which the Court found void for vagueness.) The Court made clear that while the mental health of the woman was a legitimate concern of the state, there were limits beyond which it could not reasonably go.

In Planned Parenthood v. Ashcroft the Court conceded that the compelling interest of the state entitled it to ban abortions entirely once the fetus became viable, and Missouri had done so except to preserve the life or health of the mother. Hence it was not unreasonable to require the presence of a second physician to care for the fetus, since the attending physician would be occupied with the care of the mother. Moreover, the statute requiring parental or judicial consent for a minor to have an abortion required the court to deny such request only for "good cause," which sufficiently protected both the interest of the pregnant minor herself and the state's legitimate interest in protecting immature minors generally. And in *Simopoulos v. Virginia* it held that a state could require a license of out-patient clinics performing second trimester abortions as a way of protecting the mother's health and upheld the conviction of an operator of an unlicensed clinic. The dissenting justices, while not directly urging the overruling of *Roe*, argued that the requirement that state regulations not be "unduly burdensome" should be applied throughout the term of the pregnancy, and if it was not unduly burdensome its validity should be judged by whether it "rationally relates to a legitimate state purpose."

The Court's commitment to *Roe* was again manifested in *Thornburgh v. American College of Obstetricians (1986)*. In that case the Court invalidated a Pennsylvania law that required doctors to (1) inform women seeking abortions of the risks of abortion, availability of prenatal care, and agencies willing to assist in pregnancy; (2) report information about women seeking abortion; and (3) use the abortion technique that maximizes the chance that the fetus will survive. It began to seem that the *Maher* victory mentioned above was more a function of the Court's approach to poverty, namely that the Constitution is largely unconcerned with the unfairness resulting from economic hardship, than a reflection of the Court's weak commitment to *Roe*.

The summer of 1989 brought a change. After fifteen years of invalidating laws that strictly limited a woman's right to choose to terminate her pregnancy, the Supreme Court in *Webster v. Reproductive Health Services* upheld Missouri's highly restrictive abortion law. The Missouri law not only prohibited public funding of abortion it prohibited performing privately-paid-for abortions in any facility supported by public funds. Moreover, the Missouri law required doctors to conduct tests to determine whether a fetus was viable before performing any abortion. The preamble to the Missouri law declared; "life ... begins at conception," and stated that unborn children enjoy the same rights as other persons. Although in upholding the challenged provisions of the law the Court did not thereby "uphold" the preamble, sustaining a law that began as the Missouri law did was read by those on both sides of the debate as a significant departure for the Court from past cases.

Was the Court was ready to abandon *Roe*? So badly was the Court divided in *Webster* that one was left to read tea leaves or count votes, predict retirements from the Court and guess at the position of new appointees. Several things were, however, becoming clear: Justice Scalia was clearly ready to overrule *Roe* and at least two other Justices, Rehnquist and White, were ready to go along with him; Justices Blackmun and Marshall, strong adherents to *Roe*, were old and not likely to be on the Court much longer; and Justice O'Connor was prepared to require that abortion statutes meet only a ra-

tional basis test, not a test generally used to judge infringements of "fundamental rights."

The women of Missouri were the most affected by the *Webster* decision, but the next two nominees to the Court, Justices Souter and Thomas, and state legislators across the country felt the effect of the decision as well. Both Justice Souter and Justice Thomas faced stiff opposition from pro-*Roe* groups who suspected that both Justices were at best weakly committed to *Roe*, and Justice Thomas had to sit through repeated questions on his views on abortion posed by members of the Senate Judiciary Committee. Justice Thomas managed to avoid answering these questions, as his predecessor Justice Souter had in his bid for confirmation to the Court, although with considerably less artfulness. At one point, Justice Thomas actually stated that although he was in law school at the time *Roe* was decided he had no recollection of having discussed the case then or at any time in the more than fifteen years since the decision was issued.

In sum, his position was the improbable one that he had never thought about or discussed one of the central constitutional dilemmas of our time, the constitutionality of anti-abortion legislation. Until Professor Anita Hill came forward with her charges that the Supreme Court nominee had sexually harassed her when she worked for him at the Equal Employment Opportunity Commission, Thomas' position on abortion seemed the major threat to his ascension to the Supreme Court. The nominee was able to overcome both obstacles.

The impact of *Webster* was also felt in state legislatures across the country. Anti-*Roe* forces saw *Webster* as an invitation to seek the passage of ever-more restrictive abortion legislation. Since *Webster*, over 600 bills restricting abortion were introduced in 44 state legislatures and the United States territory of Guam. In Guam, Louisiana, Pennsylvania and Utah very restrictive bills of varying degrees of harshness were passed into law. Idaho also passed a highly restrictive bill, but after what the governor described as "considerable soul-searching," he vetoed it. The 130,000 residents of Guam are overwhelmingly Catholic and the Archbishop of the territory threatened to excommunicate any Catholic in the legislature who voted against the law.

The Pennsylvania law at issue in the present case, unlike the laws discussed above which are focused on outlawing abortion with limited exceptions, imposes restrictions on access to abortion services. While doctors are subject to punishment as felons for violating most of the law's provisions, women seeking abortions are not subject to criminal penalties for violating the law's regulations. The specific provisions of the Pennsylvania law are outlined by the Court at the beginning of the opinion printed below.

Between *Webster* and the case printed below, the Court decided one other significant abortion case, *Rust v. Sullivan (1991)*. In that case the Court upheld a regulation issued by the Health and Human Resources Department and championed by then-President Bush. The *regulation prohibited dissemination of information regarding abortion by employees of family planning clinics that receive federal funds. This regulation, known as the "gag rule," effectively prohibited people working at institutions that receive such funds from mentioning the abortion option to women. President Clinton has stated his intention to repeal this regulation, so the specific holding in Rust will likely be moot by the time this note is read. Rust is nonetheless important because it demonstrates lax protection of the right to speak—an attitude the Court may transport out of the abortion context into other areas.*

The abortion debate and the Roe decision have divided the country as few issues before the Supreme Court have. Anti-Roe activists have engaged in creative acts of civil disobedience, such as chaining themselves to abortion clinic doors and furniture, staging "rescues" of fetuses by haranguing women as they enter abortion clinics, including thrusting pictures of dead fetuses in their faces. These activists see the question as the killing of innocent children and are willing to risk imprisonment and to inflict emotional discomfort, if not physical pain, in the name of this important cause.

On the other side, pro-Roe forces are moved by the staggering population growth and the specter of the return to back-alley, coat-hanger abortions by those who can't afford to go to another state or get an illegal abortion in their own state. For these people, the moral imperative is the lives of women, which they argue our society has never fully valued and has all too often treated cheaply in the name of one moral imperative or another.

Query: Should the Supreme Court have stayed out of this debate? Could it have refused to decide Roe's case or the claim raised in the case below with integrity? Is it the Supreme Court's job to decide cases and controversies no matter how hotly disputed the underlying issues are?

Justice **O'Connor,** Justice **Kennedy,** and Justice **Souter** announced the judgment of the Court and delivered the opinion of the Court with respect to Parts I, II, III, V-A, V-C, and VI, an opinion with respect to Part V-E, in which Justice **Stevens** joins, and an opinion with respect to Parts IV, V-B, and V-D, saying in part:

I.

Liberty finds no refuge in a jurisprudence of doubt. Yet 19 years after our holding that the Constitution protects a woman's right to terminate her pregnancy in its early stages, Roe v. Wade (1973), that definition of liberty is still questioned. Joining the respondents as amicus curiae, the United States, as it has done in five other cases in the last decade, again asks us to overrule Roe.

At issue in these cases are five provisions of the Pennsylvania Abortion Control Act of 1982 as amended in 1988 and 1989. The Act requires that a woman seek-

ing an abortion give her informed consent prior to the abortion procedure, and specifies that she be provided with certain information at least 24 hours before the abortion is performed. For a minor to obtain an abortion, the Act requires the informed consent of one of her parents, but provides for a judicial bypass option if the minor does not wish to or cannot obtain a parent's consent. Another provision of the Act requires that, unless certain exceptions apply, a married woman seeking an abortion must sign a statement indicating that she has notified her husband of her intended abortion. The Act exempts compliance with these three requirements in the event of a "medical emergency." . . . In addition . . . the Act imposes certain reporting requirements on facilities that provide abortion services. . . .

After considering the fundamental constitutional questions resolved by Roe, principles of institutional integrity, and the rule of stare decisis, we are led to conclude this: the essential holding of Roe v. Wade should be retained and once again reaffirmed. . . .

II.

Constitutional protection of the woman's decision to terminate her pregnancy derives from the Due Process Clause of the Fourteenth Amendment. It declares that no State shall "deprive any person of life, liberty, or property, without due process of law." The controlling word in the case before us is "liberty." Although a literal reading of the Clause might suggest that it governs only the procedures by which a State may deprive persons of liberty, for at least 105 years, at least since Mugler v. Kansas (1887), the Clause has been understood to contain a substantive component as well, one "barring certain government actions regardless of the fairness of the procedures used to implement them." . . .

It is tempting, as a means of curbing the discretion of federal judges, to suppose that liberty encompasses no more than those rights already guaranteed to the individual against federal interference by the express provisions of the first eight amendments to the Constitution. . . . But of course this Court has never accepted that view.

It is also tempting, for the same reason, to suppose that the Due Process Clause protects only those practices, defined at the most specific level, that were protected against government interference by other rules of law when the Fourteenth Amendment was ratified. . . . But such a view would be inconsistent with our law. It is a promise of the Constitution that there is a realm of personal liberty which the government may not enter. We have vindicated this principle before. Marriage is mentioned nowhere in the Bill of Rights and interracial marriage was illegal in most States in the 19th century, but the Court was no doubt correct in finding it to be an aspect of liberty protected against state interference by the substantive component of the Due Process Clause in Loving v. Virginia (1967) (relying, in an opinion for eight Justices, on the Due Process Clause). . . .

The inescapable fact is that adjudication of substantive due process claims may call upon the Court in interpreting the Constitution to exercise that same capacity which by tradition courts always have exercised: reasoned judgment. Its boundaries are not susceptible of expression as a simple rule. That does not mean we are free to invalidate state policy choices with which we disagree; yet neither does it permit us to shrink from the duties of our office. As Justice Harlan observed: "Due process has not been reduced to any formula; its content cannot be determined by reference to any code. The best that can be said is that through the course of this Court's decisions it has represented the balance which our Nation, built upon postulates of respect for the liberty of the individual, has struck between that liberty and the demands of organized society. . . ."

Our law affords constitutional protection to personal decisions relating to marriage, procreation, contraception, family relationships, child rearing, and education. . . .Our cases recognize "the right of the individual, married or single, to be free from unwarranted governmental intrusion into matters so fundamentally affecting a person as the decision whether to bear or beget a child." Eisenstadt v. Baird (emphasis in original). Our precedents "have respected the private realm of family life which the state cannot enter." Prince v. Massachusetts (1944). These matters, involving the most intimate and personal choices a person may make in a lifetime, choices central to personal dignity and autonomy, are central to the liberty protected by the Fourteenth Amendment. At the heart of liberty is the right to define one's own concept of existence, of meaning, of the universe, and of the mystery of human life. Beliefs about these matters could not define the attributes of personhood were they formed under compulsion of the State.

. . .Though abortion is conduct, it does not follow that the State is entitled to proscribe it in all instances. That is because the liberty of the woman is at stake in a sense unique to the human condition and so unique to the law. The mother who carries a child to full term is subject to anxieties, to physical constraints, to pain that only she must bear. That these sacrifices have from the beginning of the human race been endured by women with a pride that ennobles her in the eyes of others and gives to the infant a bond of love cannot alone be grounds for the State to insist she make the sacrifice. Her suffering is too intimate and personal for the State to insist, without more, upon its own vision of the woman's role, however dominant that vision has been in the course of our history and our culture. . . .

. . . As with abortion, reasonable people will have differences of opinion about these matters. One view is based on such reverence for the wonder of creation that any pregnancy ought to be welcomed and carried to full term no matter how difficult it will be to provide for the child and ensure its well-being. Another is that the inability to provide for the nurture and care of the infant is a cruelty to the child and an anguish to the parent. These are intimate views with infinite variations, and their deep, personal character underlay our decisions in Griswold, Eisenstadt, and Carey. The same concerns are present when the woman confronts the reality that, perhaps despite her attempts to avoid it, she has become pregnant.

It was this dimension of personal liberty that Roe sought to protect, and its holding invoked the reasoning and the tradition of the precedents we have discussed, granting protection to substantive liberties of the person. Roe was, of course, an extension of those cases and, as the decision itself indicated, the separate States could act in some degree to further their own legitimate interests in protecting pre-natal life. The extent to which the legislatures of the States might act to outweigh the interests of the woman in choosing to terminate her pregnancy was a subject of debate both in Roe itself and in decisions following it.

While we appreciate the weight of the arguments made on behalf of the State in the case before us, arguments which in their ultimate formulation conclude that Roe should be overruled, the reservations any of us may have in reaffirming the central holding of Roe are outweighed by the explication of individual liberty we have given combined with the force of stare decisis. We turn now to that doctrine.

III.

A.

The obligation to follow precedent begins with necessity, and a contrary necessity marks its outer limit. With Cardozo, we recognize that no judicial system could do society's work if it eyed each issue afresh in every case that raised it. . . . Indeed, the very concept of the rule of law underlying our own Constitution requires such continuity over time that a respect for precedent is, by definition, indispensable. . . . At the other extreme, a different necessity would make itself felt if a prior judicial ruling should come to be seen so clearly as error that its enforcement was for that very reason doomed. . . .

So in this case we may inquire whether Roe's central rule has been found unworkable; whether the rule's limitation on state power could be removed without serious inequity to those who have relied upon it or significant damage to the stability of the society governed by the rule in question; whether the law's growth in the intervening years has left Roe's central rule a doctrinal anachronism discounted by society; and whether Roe's premises of fact have so far changed in the ensuing two decades as to render its central holding somehow irrelevant or unjustifiable in dealing with the issue it addressed.

1.

Although Roe has engendered opposition, it has in no sense proven "unworkable," . . . representing as it does a simple limitation beyond which a state law is unenforceable. . . .

2.

The inquiry into reliance counts the cost of a rule's repudiation as it would fall on those who have relied reasonably on the rule's continued application. . . .

. . . For two decades of economic and social developments, people have organized intimate relationships and made choices that define their views of themselves and their places in society, in reliance on the availability of abortion in the event that contraception should fail. The ability of women to participate equally in the economic and social life of the Nation has been facilitated by their ability to control their reproductive lives. . . . The Constitution serves human values, and while the effect of reliance on Roe cannot be exactly measured, neither can the certain cost of overruling Roe for people who have ordered their thinking and living around that case be dismissed.

3.

No evolution of legal principle has left Roe's doctrinal footings weaker than they were in 1973. No development of constitutional law since the case was decided has implicitly or explicitly left Roe behind as a mere survivor of obsolete constitutional thinking.

It will be recognized, of course, that Roe stands at an intersection of two lines of decisions, but in whichever doctrinal category one reads the case, the result for present purposes will be the same. The Roe Court itself placed its holding in the succession of cases most prominently exemplified by Griswold v. Connecticut (1965). When it is so seen, Roe is clearly in no jeopardy, since subsequent constitutional developments have neither disturbed, nor do they threaten to diminish, the scope of recognized protection accorded to the liberty relating to intimate relationships, the family, and decisions about whether or not to beget or bear a child. . . .

Roe, however, may be seen not only as an exemplar of Griswold liberty but as a rule (whether or not mistaken) of personal autonomy and bodily integrity, with doctrinal affinity to cases recognizing limits on governmental power to mandate medical treatment or to bar its rejection. If so, our cases since Roe accord with Roe's view that a State's interest in the protection of life falls short of justifying any plenary override of individual liberty claims. . . .

4.

We have seen how time has overtaken some of Roe's factual assumptions: advances in maternal health care allow for abortions safe to the mother later in pregnancy than was true in 1973, . . . and advances in neonatal care have advanced viability to a point somewhat earlier. . . . But these facts go only to the scheme of time limits on the realization of competing interests, and the divergences from the factual premises of 1973 have no bearing on the validity of Roe's central holding, that viability marks the earliest point at which the State's interest in fetal life is constitutionally adequate to justify a legislative ban on nontherapeutic abortions. The soundness or unsoundness of that constitutional judgment in no sense turns on whether viability occurs at approximately 28 weeks, as was usual at the time of Roe, at 23 to 24 weeks, as it sometimes does today, or at some moment even slightly earlier in pregnancy, as it may if fetal respiratory capacity can somehow be enhanced in the future. Whenever it may occur, the attainment of viability may continue to serve as the critical fact, just as it has done since Roe was decided; which is to say that no change in Roe's factual underpinning has left its central holding obsolete, and none supports an argument for overruling it. . . .

B.

In a less significant case, stare decisis analysis could, and would, stop at the point we have reached. But the sustained and widespread debate Roe has provoked calls for some comparison between that case and others of comparable dimension that have responded to national controversies and taken on the impress of the controversies addressed. Only two such decisional lines from the past century present themselves for examination, and in each instance the result reached by the Court accorded with the principles we apply today.

The first example is that line of cases identified with Lochner v. New York (1905), which imposed substantive limitations on legislation limiting economic autonomy in favor of health and welfare regulation, adopting, in Justice Holmes' view, the theory of laissez-faire. The Lochner decisions were exemplified by Adkins v. Children's Hospital of D.C. (1923), in which this Court held it to be an infringement of constitutionally protected liberty of contract to require the employers of adult women to satisfy minimum wage standards. Fourteen years later, West Coast Hotel Co. v. Parrish (1937), signalled the demise of Lochner by overruling Adkins. In the meantime, the Depression had come and, with it, the lesson that seemed unmistakable to most people by 1937, that the interpretation of contractual freedom protected in Adkins rested on fundamentally false factual assumptions about the capacity of a relatively unregulated market to satisfy minimal levels of human welfare. As Justice Jackson wrote of the constitutional crisis of 1937 shortly before he came on the bench, ''The older world of laissez faire was recognized everywhere outside the Court to be dead.'' . . . The facts upon which the earlier case had premised a constitutional resolution of social controversy had proved to be untrue, and history's demonstration of their untruth not only justified but required the new choice of constitutional principle that West Coast Hotel announced. . . .

The second comparison that 20th century history invites is with the cases employing the separate-but-equal rule for applying the Fourteenth Amendment's equal protection guarantee. They began with Plessy v.

Ferguson (1896), holding that legislatively mandated racial segregation in public transportation works no denial of equal protection, rejecting the argument that racial separation enforced by the legal machinery of American society treats the black race as inferior. The Plessy Court considered "the underlying fallacy of the plaintiff's argument to consist in the assumption that the enforced separation of the two races stamps the colored race with a badge of inferiority. If this be so, it is not by reason of anything found in the act, but solely because the colored race chooses to put that construction upon it." . . .

The Court in Brown addressed these facts of life by observing that whatever may have been the understanding in Plessy's time of the power of segregation to stigmatize those who were segregated with a "badge of inferiority," it was clear by 1954 that legally sanctioned segregation had just such an effect, to the point that racially separate public educational facilities were deemed inherently unequal. Society's understanding of the facts upon which a constitutional ruling was sought in 1954 was thus fundamentally different from the basis claimed for the decision in 1896. While we think Plessy was wrong the day it was decided, we must also recognize that the Plessy Court's explanation for its decision was so clearly at odds with the facts apparent to the Court in 1954 that the decision to reexamine Plessy was on this ground alone not only justified but required.

West Coast Hotel and Brown each rested on facts, or an understanding of facts, changed from those which furnished the claimed justifications for the earlier constitutional resolutions. Each case was comprehensible as the Court's response to facts that the country could understand, or had come to understand already, but which the Court of an earlier day, as its own declarations disclosed, had not been able to perceive. As the decisions were thus comprehensible they were also defensible, not merely as the victories of one doctrinal school over another by dint of numbers (victories though they were), but as applications of constitutional principle to facts as they had not been seen by the Court before. In constitutional adjudication as elsewhere in life, changed circumstances may impose new obligations, and the thoughtful part of the Nation could accept each decision to overrule a prior case as a response to the Court's constitutional duty.

Because the case before us presents no such occasion it could be seen as no such response. Because neither the factual underpinnings of Roe's central holding nor our understanding of it has changed (and because no other indication of weakened precedent has been shown) the Court could not pretend to be reexamining the prior law with any justification beyond a present doctrinal disposition to come out differently from the Court of 1973. To overrule prior law for no other reason than that would run counter to the view repeated in our cases, that a decision to overrule should rest on some special reason over and above the belief that a prior case was wrongly decided. . . . ("A basic change in the law upon a ground no firmer than a change in our membership invites the popular misconception that this institution is little different from the two political branches of the Government. No misconception could do more lasting injury to this Court and to the system of law which it is our abiding mission to serve") . . . .

C.

. . . Where, in the performance of its judicial duties, the Court decides a case in such a way as to resolve the sort of intensely divisive controversy reflected in Roe and those rare, comparable cases, its decision has a dimension that the resolution of the normal case does not carry. It is the dimension present whenever the Court's interpretation of the Constitution calls the contending sides of a national controversy to end their national division by accepting a common mandate rooted in the Constitution.

The Court is not asked to do this very often, having thus addressed the Nation only twice in our lifetime, in the decisions of Brown and Roe. But when the Court does act in this way, its decision requires an equally rare precedential force to counter the inevitable efforts to overturn it and to thwart its implementation. Some of those efforts may be mere unprincipled emotional reactions; others may proceed from principles worthy of profound respect. But whatever the premises of opposition may be, only the most convincing justification under accepted standards of precedent could suffice to demonstrate that a later decision overruling the first was anything but a surrender to political pressure, and an unjustified repudiation of the principle on which the Court staked its authority in the first instance. So to overrule under fire in the absence of the most compelling reason to reexamine a watershed decision would subvert the Court's legitimacy beyond any serious question. . . .

The Court's duty in the present case is clear. In 1973, it confronted the already-divisive issue of governmental power to limit personal choice to undergo abortion, for which it provided a new resolution based on the due process guaranteed by the Fourteenth Amendment. Whether or not a new social consensus is developing on that issue, its divisiveness is no less today than in 1973, and pressure to overrule the decision, like pressure to retain it, has grown only more intense. A decision to overrule Roe's essential holding under the existing circumstances would address error, if error there was, at the cost of both profound and unnecessary damage to the Court's legitimacy, and to the Nation's commitment to the rule of law. It is therefore imperative to adhere to the essence of Roe's original decision, and we do so today.

IV.

From what we have said so far it follows that it is a constitutional liberty of the woman to have some freedom to terminate her pregnancy. We conclude that the basic decision in Roe was based on a constitutional analysis which we cannot now repudiate. The woman's liberty is not so unlimited, however, that from the outset the State cannot show its concern for the life of the unborn, and at a later point in fetal development the State's interest in life has sufficient force so that the right of the woman to terminate the pregnancy can be restricted. . . .

We conclude the line should be drawn at viability, so that before that time the woman has a right to choose to terminate her pregnancy. We adhere to this principle for two reasons. First, as we have said, is the doctrine of stare decisis. Any judicial act of line-drawing may seem somewhat arbitrary, but Roe was a reasoned statement, elaborated with great care. We have twice reaffirmed it in the face of great opposition. See Thornburgh v. American College of Obstetricians & Gynecologists [1986], Akron I [Akron v. Akron Center for Reproductive Health Inc. (1983)]. Although we must overrule those parts of Thornburgh and Akron I which, in our view, are inconsistent with Roe's statement that the State has a legitimate interest in promoting the life or potential life of the unborn, the central premise of those cases represents an unbroken commitment by this Court to the essential holding of Roe. It is that premise which we reaffirm today.

The second reason is that the concept of viability, as we noted in Roe, is the time at which there is a realistic possibility of maintaining and nourishing a life outside the womb, so that the independent existence of the second life can in reason and all fairness be the object of state protection that now overrides the rights of the woman. . . .

. . . It must be remembered that Roe v. Wade speaks with clarity in establishing not only the woman's liberty but also the State's "important and legitimate interest in potential life." That portion of the decision in Roe has been given too little acknowledgement and implementation by the Court in its subsequent cases. Those cases decided that any regulation touching upon the abortion decision must survive strict scrutiny, to be sustained only if drawn in narrow terms to further a compelling state interest. Not all of the cases decided under that formulation can be reconciled with the holding in Roe itself that the State has legitimate interests in the health of the woman and in protecting the potential life within her. In resolving this tension, we choose to rely upon Roe, as against the later cases.

Roe established a trimester framework to govern abortion regulations. Under this elaborate but rigid construct, almost no regulation at all is permitted during the first trimester of pregnancy; regulations designed to protect the woman's health, but not to further the State's interest in potential life, are permitted during the second trimester; and during the third trimester, when the fetus is viable, prohibitions are permitted provided the life or health of the mother is not at stake. . . .

The trimester framework no doubt was erected to ensure that the woman's right to choose not become so subordinate to the State's interest in promoting fetal life that her choice exists in theory but not in fact. We do not agree, however, that the trimester approach is necessary to accomplish this objective. A framework of this rigid-ity was unnecessary and in its later interpretation sometimes contradicted the State's permissible exercise of its powers.

Though the woman has a right to choose to terminate or continue her pregnancy before viability, it does not at all follow that the State is prohibited from taking steps to ensure that this choice is thoughtful and informed. Even in the earliest stages of pregnancy, the State may enact rules and regulations designed to encourage her to know that there are philosophic and social arguments of great weight that can be brought to bear in favor of continuing the pregnancy to full term and that there are procedures and institutions to allow adoption of unwanted children as well as a certain degree of state assistance if the mother chooses to raise the child herself. . . . It follows that States are free to enact laws to provide a reasonable framework for a woman to make a decision that has such profound and lasting meaning. This, too, we find consistent with Roe's central premises, and indeed the inevitable consequence of our holding that the State has an interest in protecting the life of the unborn.

We reject the trimester framework, which we do not consider to be part of the essential holding of Roe. . . . The trimester framework suffers from these basic flaws: in its formulation it misconceives the nature of the pregnant woman's interest; and in practice it undervalues the State's interest in potential life, as recognized in Roe.

As our jurisprudence relating to all liberties save perhaps abortion has recognized, not every law which makes a right more difficult to exercise is, ipso facto, an infringement of that right. An example clarifies the point. We have held that not every ballot access limitation amounts to an infringement of the right to vote. Rather, the States are granted substantial flexibility in establishing the framework within which voters choose the candidates for whom they wish to vote. . . .

The abortion right is similar. Numerous forms of state regulation might have the incidental effect of increasing the cost or decreasing the availability of medical care, whether for abortion or any other medical procedure. The fact that a law which serves a valid purpose, one not designed to strike at the right itself, has the incidental effect of making it more difficult or more expensive to procure an abortion cannot be enough to invalidate it. Only where state regulation imposes an undue burden on a woman's ability to make this decision does the power of the State reach into the heart of the liberty protected by the Due Process Clause. . . .

It is so ordered.

Justice **Steven,** concurring in part and dissenting in part, said in part:

I.

The Court is unquestionably correct in concluding that the doctrine of stare decisis has controlling significance in a case of this kind, notwithstanding an individual justice's concerns about the merits.* . . . The societal costs of overruling Roe at this late date would be enormous. Roe is an integral part of a correct understanding of both the concept of liberty and the basic equality of men and women. . . .

I also accept what is implicit in the Court's analysis, namely, a reaffirmation of Roe's explanation of why the State's obligation to protect the life or health of the mother must take precedence over any duty to the unborn. . . .

II.

My disagreement with the joint opinion begins with its understanding of the trimester framework established in Roe. Contrary to the suggestion of the joint opinion, it is not a "contradiction" to recognize that the State may have a legitimate interest in potential human life and, at the same time, to conclude that that interest does not justify the regulation of abortion before viability (although other interests, such as maternal health, may). The fact that the State's interest is legitimate does not tell us when, if ever, that interest outweighs the pregnant woman's interest in personal liberty. It is appropriate, therefore, to consider more carefully the nature of the interests at stake.

First, it is clear that, in order to be legitimate, the State's interest must be secular; consistent with the First Amendment the State may not promote a theological or sectarian interest. . . .

Identifying the State's interests—which the States rarely articulate with any precision—makes clear that the interest in protecting potential life is not grounded in the Constitution. It is, instead, an indirect interest supported by both humanitarian and pragmatic concerns. . . .

Weighing the State's interest in potential life and the woman's liberty interest, I agree with the joint opinion that the State may " 'expres[s] a preference for normal childbirth,' " that the State may take steps to ensure that a woman's choice "is thoughtful and informed," and that "States are free to enact laws to provide a reasonable framework for a woman to make a decision that has such profound and lasting meaning." Serious questions arise, however, when a State attempts to "persuade the woman to choose childbirth over abortion." Decisional autonomy must limit the State's power to inject into a woman's most personal deliberations its own views of what is best. The State may promote its preferences by funding childbirth, by creating and maintaining alternatives to abortion, and by espousing the virtues of family; but it must respect the individual's freedom to make such judgments.

This theme runs throughout our decisions concerning reproductive freedom. In general, Roe's requirement that restrictions on abortions before viability be justified by the State's interest in maternal health has prevented States from interjecting regulations designed to influence a woman's decision. Thus, we have upheld regulations of abortion that are not efforts to sway or direct a woman's choice but rather are efforts to enhance the deliberative quality of that decision or are neutral regulations on the health aspects of her decision. . . . Conversely, we have consistently rejected state efforts to prejudice a woman's choice, either by limiting the information available to her, . . . [or by requiring] a physician or counselor to provide the woman with a range of materials clearly designed to persuade her to choose not to undergo the abortion. While the State is free, pursuant to § 3208 of the Pennsylvania law, to produce and disseminate such material, the State may not inject such information into the woman's deliberations just as she is weighing such an important choice. . . .

III.

The 24-hour waiting period required by the Pennsylvania statute raises even more serious concerns. . . .

Part of the constitutional liberty to choose is the equal dignity to which each of us is entitled. A woman who decides to terminate her pregnancy is entitled to the same respect as a woman who decides to carry the fetus to term. The mandatory waiting period denies women that equal respect.

IV.

In my opinion, a correct application of the "undue burden" standard leads to the same conclusion concerning the constitutionality of these requirements. A state-imposed burden on the exercise of a constitutional right is measured both by its effects and by its character: A burden may be "undue" either because the burden is too severe or because it lacks a legitimate, rational justification.

The 24-hour delay requirement fails both parts of this test. The findings of the District Court establish the severity of the burden that the 24-hour delay imposes on many pregnant women. Yet even in those cases in which the delay is not especially onerous, it is, in my opinion, "undue" because there is no evidence that such a delay serves a useful and legitimate purpose.

Justice **Blackmun,** concurring in part, concurring in the judgment in part, and dissenting in part, said in part:

I join parts I, II, III, V-A, V-C, and VI of the joint opinion of Justices O'Connor, Kennedy, and Souter.

Three years ago, in Webster v. Reproductive Health Serv. (1989), four Members of this Court appeared poised to "cast into darkness the hopes and vi-

---

*It is sometimes useful to view the issue of stare decisis from a historical perspective. In the last nineteen years, fifteen Justices have confronted the basic issue presented in Roe. Of those, eleven have voted as the majority does today: Chief Justice Burger, Justices Douglas, Brennan, Stewart, Marshall, and Powell, and Justices Blackmun, O'Connor, Kennedy, Souter, and myself. Only four—all of whom happen to be on the Court today—have reached the opposite conclusion.

sions of every woman in this country'' who had come to believe that the Constitution guaranteed her the right to reproductive choice. . . .

I do not underestimate the significance of today's joint opinion. Yet I remain steadfast in my belief that the right to reproductive choice is entitled to the full protection afforded by this Court before Webster. And I fear for the darkness as four Justices anxiously await the single vote necessary to extinguish the light.

I.

Make no mistake, the joint opinion of Justices O'Connor, Kennedy, and Souter is an act of personal courage and constitutional principle. In contrast to previous decisions in which Justices O'Connor and Kennedy postponed reconsideration of Roe v. Wade (1973), the authors of the joint opinion today join Justice Stevens and me in concluding that ''the essential holding of Roe should be retained and once again reaffirmed.'' In brief, five Members of this Court today recognize that ''the Constitution protects a woman's right to terminate her pregnancy in its early stages.''

A fervent view of individual liberty and the force of stare decisis have led the Court to this conclusion. Today a majority reaffirms that the Due Process Clause of the Fourteenth Amendment establishes ''a realm of personal liberty which the government may not enter,''—a realm whose outer limits cannot be determined by interpretations of the Constitution that focus only on the specific practices of States at the time the Fourteenth Amendment was adopted. Included within this realm of liberty is '' 'the right of the individual, married or single, to be free from unwarranted governmental intrusion into matters so fundamentally affecting a person as the decision whether to bear or beget a child.' '' Finally, the Court today recognizes that in the case of abortion, ''the liberty of the woman is at stake in a sense unique to the human condition and so unique to the law. The mother who carries a child to full term is subject to anxieties, to physical constraints, to pain that only she must bear.'' . . .

II.

Today, no less than yesterday, the Constitution and decisions of this Court require that a State's abortion restrictions be subjected to the strictest of judicial scrutiny. Our precedents and the joint opinion's principles require us to subject all non-de minimis abortion regulations to strict scrutiny. Under this standard, the Pennsylvania statute's provisions requiring content-based counseling, a 24-hour delay, informed parental consent, and reporting of abortion-related information must be invalidated. . . .

B.

The final, and more genuine, criticism of the trimester framework is that it fails to find the State's interest in potential human life compelling throughout pregnancy. No member of this Court—nor for that matter, the Solicitor General—has ever questioned our holding in Roe that an abortion is not ''the termination of life entitled to Fourteenth Amendment protection.'' Accordingly, a State's interest in protecting fetal life is not grounded in the Constitution. Nor, consistent with our Establishment Clause, can it be a theological or sectarian interest. . . . It is, instead, a legitimate interest grounded in humanitarian or pragmatic concerns.

But while a State has ''legitimate interests from the outset of the pregnancy in protecting the health of the woman and the life of the fetus that may become a child,'' legitimate interests are not enough. To overcome the burden of strict scrutiny, the interests must be compelling. The question then is how best to accommodate the State's interest in potential human life with the constitutional liberties of pregnant women. . . .

III.

At long last, The Chief Justice admits it. Gone are the contentions that the issue need not be (or has not been) considered. There, on the first page, for all to see, is what was expected: ''We believe that Roe was wrongly decided, and that it can and should be overruled consistently with our traditional approach to stare decisis in constitutional cases.'' If there is much reason to applaud the advances made by the joint opinion today, there is far more to fear from The Chief Justice's opinion. The Chief Justice's criticism of Roe follows from his stunted conception of individual liberty. While recognizing that the Due Process Clause protects more than simple physical liberty, he then goes on to construe this Court's personal-liberty cases as establishing only a laundry list of particular rights, rather than a principled account of how these particular rights are grounded in a more general right of privacy. This constricted view is reinforced by The Chief Justice's exclusive reliance on tradition as a source of fundamental rights. He argues that the record in favor of a right to abortion is no stronger than the record in Michael H. v. Gerald D. (1989), where the plurality found no fundamental right to visitation privileges by an adulterous father, or in Bowers v. Hardwick (1986), where the Court found no fundamental right to engage in homosexual sodomy, or in a case involving the ''firing of a gun . . . into another person's body.'' In The Chief Justice's world, a woman considering whether to terminate a pregnancy is entitled to no more protection than adulterers, murderers, and so-called ''sexual deviates.'' Given The Chief Justice's exclusive reliance on tradition, people using contraceptives seem the next likely candidate for his list of outcasts.

Even more shocking than The Chief Justice's cramped notion of individual liberty is his complete omission of any discussion of the effects that compelled childbirth and motherhood have on women's lives. The only expression of concern with women's health is purely instrumental—for The Chief Justice, only women's psychological health is a concern, and only to the extent that he assumes that every woman who decides to have an abortion does so without serious consideration of the moral implications of their decision. In short, The Chief Justice's view of the State's compelling interest in maternal health has less to do with health than it does with compelling women to be maternal. . . .

IV.

In one sense, the Court's approach is worlds apart from that of The Chief Justice and Justice Scalia. And yet, in another sense, the distance between the two approaches is short—the distance is but a single vote.

I am 83 years old. I cannot remain on this Court forever, and when I do step down, the confirmation process for my successor well may focus on the issue before us today. That, I regret, may be exactly where the choice between the two worlds will be made.

Chief Justice **Rehnquist** with whom Justice White, Justice Scalia, and Justice Thomas join, concurring in the judgment in part and dissenting in part, said in part:

The joint opinion, following its newly-minted variation on stare decisis, retains the outer shell of Roe v. Wade (1973), but beats a wholesale retreat from the substance of that case. We believe that Roe was wrongly decided, and that it can and should be overruled consistently with our traditional approach to stare decisis in constitutional cases. We would adopt the approach of the plurality in Webster v. Reproductive Health Services (1989), and uphold the challenged provisions of the Pennsylvania statute in their entirety.

I.

We have held that a liberty interest protected under the Due Process Clause of the Fourteenth Amendment will be deemed fundamental if it is "implicit in the concept of ordered liberty." Palko v. Connecticut (1937). Three years earlier, in Snyder v. Massachusetts (1934), we referred to a "principle of justice so rooted in the traditions and conscience of our people as to be ranked as fundamental." . . . These expressions are admittedly not precise, but our decisions implementing this notion of "fundamental" rights do not afford any more elaborate basis on which to base such a classification.

In construing the phrase "liberty" incorporated in the Due Process Clause of the Fourteenth Amendment, we have recognized that its meaning extends beyond freedom from physical restraint. In Pierce v. Society of Sisters (1925), we held that it included a parent's right to send a child to private school; in Meyer v. Nebraska (1923), we held that it included a right to teach a foreign language in a parochial school. Building on these cases, we have held that the term "liberty" includes a right to marry, Loving v. Virginia (1967); a right to procreate, Skinner v. Oklahoma (1942); and a right to use contra-

ceptives. Griswold v. Connecticut (1965); Eisenstadt v. Baird (1972). But a reading of these opinions makes clear that they do not endorse any all-encompassing "right of privacy."

In Roe v. Wade, the Court recognized a "guarantee of personal privacy" which "is broad enough to encompass a woman's decision whether or not to terminate her pregnancy." We are now of the view that, in terming this right fundamental, the Court in Roe read the earlier opinions upon which it based its decision much too broadly. Unlike marriage, procreation and contraception, abortion "involves the purposeful termination of potential life." Harris v. McRae (1980). The abortion decision must therefore "be recognized as sui generis, different in kind from the others that the Court has protected under the rubric of personal or family privacy and autonomy." . . . One cannot ignore the fact that a woman is not isolated in her pregnancy, and that the decision to abort necessarily involves the destruction of a fetus. . . . (To look "at the act which is assertedly the subject of a liberty interest in isolation from its effect upon other people [is] like inquiring whether there is a liberty interest in firing a gun where the case at hand happens to involve its discharge into another person's body").

Nor do the historical traditions of the American people support the view that the right to terminate one's pregnancy is "fundamental." The common law which we inherited from England made abortion after "quickening" an offense. At the time of the adoption of the Fourteenth Amendment, statutory prohibitions or restrictions on abortion were commonplace; in 1868, at least 28 of the then-37 States and 8 Territories had statutes banning or limiting abortion. . . . By the turn of the century virtually every State had a law prohibiting or restricting abortion on its books. By the middle of the present century, a liberalization trend had set in. But 21 of the restrictive abortion laws in effect in 1868 were still in effect in 1973 when Roe was decided, and an overwhelming majority of the States prohibited abortion unless necessary to preserve the life or health of the mother. On this record, it can scarcely be said that any deeply rooted tradition of relatively unrestricted abortion in our history supported the classification of the right to abortion as "fundamental" under the Due Process Clause of the Fourteenth Amendment.

We think, therefore, both in view of this history and of our decided cases dealing with substantive liberty under the Due Process Clause, that the Court was mistaken in Roe when it classified a woman's decision to terminate her pregnancy as a "fundamental right" that could be abridged only in a manner which withstood "strict scrutiny." In so concluding, we repeat the observation made in Bowers v. Hardwick (1986): "Nor are we inclined to take a more expansive view of our authority to discover new fundamental rights imbedded in the Due Process Clause. The Court is most vulnerable and comes nearest to illegitimacy when it deals with judge-made constitutional law having little or no cognizable roots in the language or design of the Constitution.". . .

II.

The joint opinion of Justices O'Connor, Kennedy, and Souter cannot bring itself to say that Roe was correct as an original matter, but the authors are of the view that "the immediate question is not the soundness of Roe's resolution of the issue, but the precedential force that must be accorded to its holding." Instead of claiming that Roe was correct as a matter of original constitutional interpretation, the opinion therefore contains an elaborate discussion of stare decisis. This discussion of the principle of stare decisis appears to be almost entirely dicta, because the joint opinion does not apply that principle in dealing with Roe. Roe decided that a woman had a fundamental right to an abortion. The joint opinion rejects that view. Roe decided that abortion regulations were to be subjected to "strict scrutiny" and could be justified only in the light of "compelling state interests." The joint opinion rejects that view. Roe analyzed abortion regulation under a rigid trimester framework, a framework which has guided this Court's decisionmaking for 19 years. The joint opinion rejects that framework.

Stare decisis is defined in Black's Law Dictionary as meaning "to abide by, or adhere to, decided cases." Whatever the "central holding" of Roe that is left after the joint opinion finishes dissecting it is surely not the result of that principle. While purporting to adhere to precedent, the joint opinion instead revises it. Roe continues to exist, but only in the way a storefront on a western movie set exists: a mere facade to give the illusion of reality. ...

The joint opinion discusses several stare decisis factors which, it asserts, point toward retaining a portion of Roe. Two of these factors are that the main "factual underpinning" of Roe has remained the same, and that its doctrinal foundation is no weaker now than it was in 1973. Of course, what might be called the basic facts which gave rise to Roe have remained the same—women become pregnant, there is a point somewhere, depending on medical technology, where a fetus becomes viable, and women give birth to children. But this is only to say that the same facts which gave rise to Roe will continue to give rise to similar cases. It is not a reason, in and of itself, why those cases must be decided in the same incorrect manner as was the first case to deal with the question. And surely there is no requirement, in considering whether to depart from stare decisis in a constitutional case, that a decision be more wrong now than it was at the time it was rendered. If that were true, the most outlandish constitutional decision could survive forever, based simply on the fact that it was no more outlandish later than it was when originally rendered.

Nor does the joint opinion faithfully follow this alleged requirement. The opinion frankly concludes that Roe and its progeny were wrong in failing to recognize that the State's interests in maternal health and in the protection of unborn human life exist throughout pregnancy. But there is no indication that these components of Roe are any more incorrect at this juncture than they were at its inception.

The joint opinion also points to the reliance interests involved in this context in its effort to explain why precedent must be followed for precedent's sake. ... But, as the joint opinion apparently agrees, any traditional notion of reliance is not applicable here. The Court today cuts back on the protection afforded by Roe, and no one claims that this action defeats any reliance interest in the disavowed trimester framework. Similarly, reliance interests would not be diminished were the Court to go further and acknowledge the full error of Roe, as "reproductive planning could take virtually immediate account of" this action.

The joint opinion thus turns to what can only be described as an unconventional—and unconvincing—notion of reliance, a view based on the surmise that the availability of abortion since Roe has led to "two decades of economic and social developments" that would be undercut if the error of Roe were recognized. The joint opinion's assertion of this fact is undeveloped and totally conclusory. In fact, one can not be sure to what economic and social developments the opinion is referring. Surely it is dubious to suggest that women have reached their "places in society" in reliance upon Roe, rather than as a result of their determination to obtain higher education and compete with men in the job market, and of society's increasing recognition of their ability to fill positions that were previously thought to be reserved only for men. In the end, having failed to put forth any evidence to prove any true reliance, the joint opinion's argument is based solely on generalized assertions about the national psyche, on a belief that the people of this country have grown accustomed to the Roe decision over the last 19 years and have "ordered their thinking and living around" it. ... The "separate but equal" doctrine lasted 58 years after Plessy, and Lochner's protection of contractual freedom lasted 32 years. However, the simple fact that a generation or more had grown used to these major decisions did not prevent the Court from correcting its errors in those cases, nor should it prevent us from correctly interpreting the Constitution here. ...

Taking the joint opinion on its own terms, we doubt that its distinction between Roe, on the one hand, and Plessy and Lochner, on the other, withstands analysis. The joint opinion acknowledges that the Court improved its stature by overruling Plessy in Brown on a deeply divisive issue. And our decision in West Coast Hotel, which overruled Adkins v. Children's Hospital and Lochner, was rendered at a time when Congress was considering President Franklin Roosevelt's proposal to "reorganize" this Court and enable him to name six additional Justices in the event that any member of the Court over the age of 70 did not elect to retire. It is difficult to imagine a situation in which the Court would face more intense opposition to a prior ruling than it did at that time, and, under the general principle proclaimed in the joint opinion, the Court seemingly should have responded to this opposition by stubbornly refusing to reexamine the Lochner rationale, lest it lose legitimacy by appearing to "overrule under fire."

The joint opinion agrees that the Court's stature would have been seriously damaged if in Brown and West Coast Hotel it had dug in its heels and refused to apply normal principles of stare decisis to the earlier decisions. But the opinion contends that the Court was entitled to overrule Plessy and Lochner in those cases, despite the existence of opposition to the original decisions, only because both the Nation and the Court had learned new lessons in the interim. This is at best a feebly supported, post hoc rationalization for those decisions.

For example, the opinion asserts that the Court could justifiably overrule its decision in Lochner only because the Depression had convinced "most people" that constitutional protection of contractual freedom contributed to an economy that failed to protect the welfare of all. Surely the joint opinion does not mean to suggest that people saw this Court's failure to uphold minimum wage statutes as the cause of the Great Depression! In any event, the Lochner Court did not base its rule upon the policy judgment that an unregulated market was fundamental to a stable economy; it simply believed, erroneously, that "liberty" under the Due Process Clause protected the "right to make a contract." . . .

The joint opinion also agrees that the Court acted properly in rejecting the doctrine of "separate but equal" in Brown. In fact, the opinion lauds Brown in comparing it to Roe. This is strange, in that under the opinion's "legitimacy" principle the Court would seemingly have been forced to adhere to its erroneous decision in Plessy because of its "intensely divisive" character. To us, adherence to Roe today under the guise of "legitimacy" would seem to resemble more closely adherence to Plessy on the same ground. Fortunately, the Court did not choose that option in Brown, and instead frankly repudiated Plessy. The joint opinion concludes that such repudiation was justified only because of newly discovered evidence that segregation had the effect of treating one race as inferior to another. But it can hardly be argued that this was not urged upon those who decided Plessy, as Justice Harlan observed in his dissent that the law at issue "puts the brand of servitude and degradation upon a large class of our fellow-citizens, our equals before the law." Plessy v. Ferguson, (Harlan, J., dissenting). . . .

The end result of the joint opinion's paeans of praise for legitimacy is the enunciation of a brand new standard for evaluating state regulation of a woman's right to abortion—the "undue burden" standard. As indicated above, Roe v. Wade adopted a "fundamental right" standard under which state regulations could survive only if they met the requirement of "strict scrutiny." While we disagree with that standard, it at least had a recognized basis in constitutional law at the time Roe was decided. The same cannot be said for the "undue burden" standard, which is created largely out of whole cloth by the authors of the joint opinion. It is a standard which even today does not command the support of a majority of this Court. And it will not, we believe, result in the sort of "simple limitation," easily applied, which the joint opinion anticipates. In sum, it is a standard which is not built to last. . . .

The sum of the joint opinion's labors in the name of stare decisis and "legitimacy" is this: Roe v. Wade stands as a sort of judicial Potemkin Village, which may be pointed out to passers by as a monument to the importance of adhering to precedent. But behind the facade, an entirely new method of analysis, without any roots in constitutional law, is imported to decide the constitutionality of state laws regulating abortion. Neither stare decisis nor "legitimacy" are truly served by such an effort. . . .

Justice **Scalia,** with whom The Chief Justice, Justice **White,** and Justice **Thomas** join, concurring in the judgment in part and dissenting in part, said in part:

My views on this matter are unchanged from those I set forth in my separate opinions in Webster v. Reproductive Health Services (1989). . . The States may, if they wish, permit abortion-on-demand, but the Constitution does not require them to do so. The permissibility of abortion, and the limitations upon it, are to be resolved like most important questions in our democracy: by citizens trying to persuade one another and then voting. As the Court acknowledges, "where reasonable people disagree the government can adopt one position or the other." The Court is correct in adding the qualification that this "assumes a state of affairs in which the choice does not intrude upon a protected liberty,"—but the crucial part of that qualification is the penultimate word. A State's choice between two positions on which reasonable people can disagree is constitutional even when (as is often the case) it intrudes upon a "liberty" in the absolute sense. Laws against bigamy, for example—which entire societies of reasonable people disagree with—intrude upon men and women's liberty to marry and live with one another. But bigamy happens not to be a liberty specially "protected" by the Constitution.

That is, quite simply, the issue in this case: not whether the power of a woman to abort her unborn child is a "liberty" in the absolute sense; or even whether it is a liberty of great importance to many women. Of course it is both. The issue is whether it is a liberty protected by the Constitution of the United States. I am sure it is not. I reach that conclusion not because of anything so exalted as my views concerning the "concept of existence, of meaning, of the universe, and of the mystery of human life." Rather, I reach it for the same reason I reach the conclusion that bigamy is not constitutionally protected—because of two simple facts: (1) the Constitution says absolutely nothing about it, and (2) the longstanding traditions of American society have permitted it to be legally proscribed. . . .

Beyond that brief summary of the essence of my position, I will not swell the United States Reports with repetition of what I have said before; and applying the rational basis test, I would uphold the Pennsylvania statute in its entirety. I must, however, respond to a few of the more outrageous arguments in today's opinion, which it is beyond human nature to leave unanswered. I shall discuss each of them under a quotation from the Court's opinion to which they pertain.

"The inescapable fact is that adjudication of substantive due process claims may call upon the Court in interpreting the Constitution to exercise that same capacity which by tradition courts always have exercised: reasoned judgment."

Assuming that the question before us is to be resolved at such a level of philosophical abstraction, in such isolation from the traditions of American society, as by simply applying "reasoned judgment," I do not see how that could possibly have produced the answer the Court arrived at in Roe v. Wade (1973). Today's opinion describes the methodology of Roe, quite accurately, as weighing against the woman's interest the State's " 'important and legitimate interest in protecting the potentiality of human life.' " But "reasoned judgment" does not begin by begging the question, as Roe and subsequent cases unquestionably did by assuming that what the State is protecting is the mere "potentiality of human life." ... The whole argument of abortion opponents is that what the Court calls the fetus and what others call the unborn child is a human life. Thus, whatever answer Roe came up with after conducting its "balancing" is bound to be wrong, unless it is correct that the human fetus is in some critical sense merely potentially human. There is of course no way to determine that as a legal matter; it is in fact a value judgment. Some societies have considered newborn children not yet human, or the incompetent elderly no longer so. ...

The emptiness of the "reasoned judgment" that produced Roe is displayed in plain view by the fact that, after more than 19 years of effort by some of the brightest (and most determined) legal minds in the country, after more than 10 cases upholding abortion rights in this Court, and after dozens upon dozens of amicus briefs submitted in this and other cases, the best the Court can do to explain how it is that the word "liberty" must be thought to include the right to destroy human fetuses is to rattle off a collection of adjectives that simply decorate a value judgment and conceal a political choice. The right to abort, we are told, inheres in "liberty" because it is among "a person's most basic decisions"; it involves a "most intimate and personal choice"; it is "central to personal dignity and autonomy"; it "originates within the zone of conscience and belief"; it is "too intimate and personal" for state interference; it reflects "intimate views" of a "deep, personal character"; it involves "intimate relationships," and notions of "personal autonomy and bodily integrity"; and it concerns a particularly " 'important decision.' " But it is obvious to anyone applying "reasoned judgment" that the same adjectives can be applied to many forms of conduct that this Court (including one of the Justices in today's majority, see Bowers v. Hardwick (1986)) has held are not entitled to constitutional protection—be-

cause, like abortion, they are forms of conduct that have long been criminalized in American society. Those adjectives might be applied, for example, to homosexual sodomy, polygamy, adult incest, and suicide, all of which are equally "intimate" and "deeply personal" decisions involving "personal autonomy and bodily integrity," and all of which can constitutionally be proscribed because it is our unquestionable constitutional tradition that they are proscribable. It is not reasoned judgment that supports the Court's decision; only personal predilection. ...

"Liberty finds no refuge in a jurisprudence of doubt."

One might have feared to encounter this august and sonorous phrase in an opinion defending the real Roe v. Wade, rather than the revised version fabricated today by the authors of the joint opinion. The shortcomings of Roe did not include lack of clarity: Virtually all regulation of abortion before the third trimester was invalid. But to come across this phrase in the joint opinion—which calls upon federal district judges to apply an "undue burden" standard as doubtful in application as it is unprincipled in origin—is really more than one should have to bear. ...

The ultimately standardless nature of the "undue burden" inquiry is a reflection of the underlying fact that the concept has no principled or coherent legal basis. As The Chief Justice points out, Roe's strict-scrutiny standard "at least had a recognized basis in constitutional law at the time Roe was decided," while "the same cannot be said for the 'undue burden' standard, which is created largely out of whole cloth by the authors of the joint opinion." ...

"While we appreciate the weight of the arguments ... that Roe should be overruled, the reservations any of us may have in reaffirming the central holding of Roe are outweighed by the explication of individual liberty we have given combined with the force of stare decisis."

The Court's reliance upon stare decisis can best be described as contrived. It insists upon the necessity of adhering not to all of Roe, but only to what it calls the "central holding." It seems to me that stare decisis ought to be applied even to the doctrine of stare decisis, and I confess never to have heard of this new, keep-what-you-want-and-throw-away-the-rest version. I wonder whether, as applied to Marbury v. Madison (1803), for example, the new version of stare decisis would be satisfied if we allowed courts to review the constitutionality of only those statutes that (like the one in Marbury) pertain to the jurisdiction of the courts.

I am certainly not in a good position to dispute that the Court has saved the "central holding" of Roe, since to do that effectively I would have to know what the Court has saved, which in turn would require me to understand (as I do not) what the "undue burden" test means. I must confess, however, that I have always thought, and I think a lot of other people have always thought, that the arbitrary trimester framework, which the Court today discards, was quite as central to Roe as the arbitrary viability test, which the Court today retains. It seems particularly ungrateful to carve the trimester framework out of the core of Roe, since its very rigidity (in sharp contrast to the utter indeterminability of the "undue burden" test) is probably the only reason the Court is able to say, in urging stare decisis, that Roe "has in no sense proven 'unworkable.'" . . .

"Where, in the performance of its judicial duties, the Court decides a case in such a way as to resolve the sort of intensely divisive controversy reflected in Roe . . . , its decision has a dimension that the resolution of the normal case does not carry. It is the dimension present whenever the Court's interpretation of the Constitution calls the contending sides of a national controversy to end their national division by accepting a common mandate rooted in the Constitution."

The Court's description of the place of Roe in the social history of the United States is unrecognizable. Not only did Roe not, as the Court suggests, resolve the deeply divisive issue of abortion; it did more than anything else to nourish it, by elevating it to the national level where it is infinitely more difficult to resolve. National politics were not plagued by abortion protests, national abortion lobbying, or abortion marches on Congress, before Roe v. Wade was decided. Profound disagreement existed among our citizens over the issue—as it does over other issues, such as the death penalty—but that disagreement was being worked out at the state level. As with many other issues, the division of sentiment within each State was not as closely balanced as it was among the population of the Nation as a whole, meaning not only that more people would be satisfied with the results of state-by-state resolution, but also that those results would be more stable. Pre-Roe, moreover, political compromise was possible.

Roe's mandate for abortion-on-demand destroyed the compromises of the past, rendered compromise impossible for the future, and required the entire issue to be resolved uniformly, at the national level. At the same time, Roe created a vast new class of abortion consumers and abortion proponents by eliminating the moral opprobrium that had attached to the act. ("If the Constitution *guarantees* abortion, how can it be bad?"—not an accurate line of thought, but a natural one.) Many favor all of those developments, and it is not for me to say that they are wrong. But to portray Roe as the statesmanlike "settlement" of a divisive issue, a jurisprudential Peace of Westphalia that is worth preserving, is nothing less than Orwellian. Roe fanned into life an issue that has inflamed our national politics in general, and has obscured with its smoke the selection of Justices to this Court in particular, ever since. And by keeping us in the abortion-umpiring business, it is the perpetuation of that disruption, rather than of any pax Roeana, that the Court's new majority decrees. . . .

What makes all this relevant to the bothersome application of "political pressure" against the Court are the twin facts that the American people love democracy and the American people are not fools. As long as this Court thought (and the people thought) that we Justices were doing essentially lawyers' work up here—reading text and discerning our society's traditional understanding of that text—the public pretty much left us alone. Texts and traditions are facts to study, not convictions to demonstrate about. But if in reality our process of constitutional adjudication consists primarily of making value judgments; if we can ignore a long and clear tradition clarifying an ambiguous text, as we did, for example, five days ago in declaring unconstitutional invocations and benedictions at public-high-school graduation ceremonies. Lee v. Weisman (1992); if, as I say, our pronouncement of constitutional law rests primarily on value judgments, then a free and intelligent people's attitude towards us can be expected to be (*ought* to be) quite different. The people know that their value judgments are quite as good as those taught in any law school—maybe better. If, indeed, the "liberties" protected by the Constitution are, as the Court says, undefined and unbounded, then the people should demonstrate, to protest that we do not implement their values instead of ours. Not only that, but confirmation hearings for new Justices should deteriorate into question-and-answer sessions in which Senators go through a list of their constituents' most favored and most disfavored alleged constitutional rights, and seek the nominee's commitment to support or oppose them. Value judgments, after all, should be voted on, not dictated; and if our Constitution has somehow accidently committed them to the Supreme Court, at least we can have a sort of plebiscite each time a new nominee to that body is put forward. Justice Blackmun not only regards this prospect with equanimity, he solicits it.

There is a poignant aspect to today's opinion. Its length, and what might be called its epic tone, suggest that its authors believe they are bringing to an end a troublesome era in the history of our Nation and of our Court. "It is the dimension" of authority, they say, to "call the contending sides of national controversy to end their national division by accepting a common mandate rooted in the Constitution."

There comes vividly to mind a portrait by Emanuel Leutze that hangs in the Harvard Law School: Roger Brooke Taney, painted in 1859, the 82d year of his life, the 24th of his Chief Justiceship, the second after his opinion in Dred Scott. He is all in black, sitting in a shadowed red armchair, left hand resting upon a pad of paper in his lap, right hand hanging limply, almost lifelessly, beside the inner arm of the chair. He sits facing the viewer, and staring straight out. There seems to be on his face, and in his deep-set eyes, an expression of profound sadness and disillusionment. Perhaps he always looked that way, even when dwelling upon the happiest of thoughts. But those of us who know how the lustre of his great Chief Justiceship came to be eclipsed by Dred Scott cannot help believing that he had that case—its already apparent consequences for the Court, and its soon-to-be-played-out consequences for the Nation—burning on his mind. I expect that two years earlier he, too, had thought himself "calling the contending sides of national controversy to end their national division by accepting a common mandate rooted in the Constitution."

It is no more realistic for us in this case, than it was for him in that, to think that an issue of the sort they both involved—an issue involving life and death, freedom and subjugation—can be "speedily and finally settled" by the Supreme Court, as President James Buchanan in his inaugural address said the issue of slavery in the territories would be. Quite to the contrary, by foreclosing all democratic outlet for the deep passions this issue arouses, by banishing the issue from the political forum that gives all participants, even the losers, the satisfaction of a fair hearing and an honest fight, by continuing the imposition of a rigid national rule instead of allowing for regional differences, the Court merely prolongs and intensifies the anguish.

We should get out of this area, where we have no right to be, and where we do neither ourselves nor the country any good by remaining.

3

Rights of Persons Accused of Crime

THE EXCLUSION OF UNCONSTITUTIONAL EVIDENCE

WEEKS v. UNITED STATES

232 U. S. 383; 34 S. Ct. 341; 58 L. Ed. 652
(1914)

At common law the admission of evidence in court had nothing to do with any illegal action by the police in securing the evidence. A lawyer could argue that certain evidence was incompetent, irrelevant, and immaterial; but if the court found it wasn't, it was admissible. The court was not concerned with the legality of the methods used to obtain it. If it had been stolen, either by a private person or by a police officer, the common law provided for prosecution of the thief or a civil action for trespass and the return of the property.

With the growth of professional police forces and the burgeoning of personal rights against searches and seizures and compulsory self-incrimination, it became clear that these approaches were not effective restraints on enthusiastic police investigation. Not only were juries, who as individuals depended on these same police for the protection of themselves and their homes, reluctant to convict an officer who had turned up evidence of crime or induced a confession, but such financial awards as were made were normally not large enough to serve as a serious deterrent. It was long argued, therefore, that

evidence illegally obtained should not be admitted in court, because refusal to admit it provided the only effective deterrent to the illegal conduct. This argument was slow to find favor, and for years most of the states continued to follow the common-law rule. The Supreme Court itself apparently adhered to it until the decision in the present case. See Adams v. New York (1904).

In Silverthorne Lumber Co. v. United States (1920) the Court made it clear that the "Weeks" rule requiring the exclusion of illegal evidence was not merely the formal requirement that things stolen from an accused must be returned. Here the government had seized all the company's books without warrant and made photographic copies of them. The trial court ordered the return of the originals but impounded the photographs and issued a subpoena for the production of the originals. Justice Holmes, speaking for the Court, rejected the claim that "the protection of the Constitution covers the physical possession, but not any advantages that the government can gain over the object of its pursuit by doing the forbidden act. Weeks v. United States . . . is taken to mean only that two steps are required instead of one. In our opinion such is not the law. It reduces the Fourth Amendment to a form of words. The essence of a provision forbidding the acquisition of evidence in a certain way is that not merely evidence so acquired shall not be used before the court, but that it shall not be used at all."

Despite the undisputed acceptance of the Weeks "exclusion of evidence" doctrine in the federal system, two problems have plagued the Supreme Court: (1) how, as a rational matter, can the rule be justified, and (2) is it really a Constitutional requirement or is it just a convenient rule of evidence promulgated by the Court. One justification for the rule, characterized as the "imperative of judicial integrity," was expressed in two classic dissents in Olmstead v. United States (1928). In the words of Justice Holmes, "We have to choose, and for my part I think it a less evil that some criminals should escape than that the government should play an ignoble part." Or, as Justice Brandeis put it, "Decency, security, and liberty alike demand that government officials shall be subjected to the same rules of conduct that are commands to the citizen. In a government of laws, existence of the government will be imperiled if it fails to observe the law scrupulously. Our government is the potent, the omnipresent, teacher. For good or for ill, it teaches the whole people by its example. Crime is contagious. If the government becomes a law-breaker, it breeds contempt for the law; it invites every man to become a law unto himself; it invites anarchy. To declare that in the administration of the criminal law the end justifies the means—to declare that the government may commit crimes in order to secure the conviction of a private criminal—would bring terrible retribution. Against that pernicious doctrine this court should resolutely set its face." The underlying assumption that makes these two classic statements relevant here is that a court which makes use of illegally or unconstitutionally gotten evidence, like a fence who receives stolen goods, shares in the criminality of the original theft.

The "deterrent effect" argument is the one on which the Court has clearly placed its reliance. Since it is apparent that the traditional common-law actions against a police officer by the victim of an unreasonable search are totally ineffective in preventing such searches, the Court has concluded that only by making it unrewarding to search illegally will the practice be abandoned. Although persuasive in theory, the technique has not proven as effective as it might be in practice. In the first place many investigative goals, such as the location and identification of witnesses, conspirators, and investigative leads, are furthered by illegal searches even though the results cannot be used in court. In the second place, the Court has not set the kind of comprehensive ban on the use of unconstitutional searches that would produce a really deterrent effect. Clearly it has not been designed to deter stealing evidence in general, as shown both by the fact the Court admits evidence stolen by private individuals and by the Weeks case itself, in which evidence stolen by the state police was held admissible. This "silver platter" doctrine was later abandoned as to evidence stolen by state officials; see Benanti v. United States (1957) and Elkins v. United States (1960).

Nor has the Court held inadmissible evidence gotten unconstitutionally, even by federal officers, where it was not used directly against the victim of the search. In Goldstein v. United States (1942) the telephones of Goldstein's accomplices had been illegally tapped, and, when they were confronted with the transcript of their conversation, they agreed to testify against Goldstein. The Court upheld the use of the testimony on the ground that the protection against unconstitutional search and seizure, like that against self-incrimination, was a purely personal right.

There are, in addition, purposes for which illegally gotten evidence may be used even against the victim himself. Thus, in Walder v. United States (1954) the Court held that narcotics which had been unreasonably seized from the defendant could be used to impeach his credibility at a later (and unrelated) trial at which he had testified broadly that he had never possessed narcotics before. The Court distinguished between using the evidence to convict him and using it to make him out a liar. In 1971 in Harris v. New York, the Court reaffirmed the Walder doctrine and permitted statements taken from the accused without the warnings required by Miranda v. Arizona (1966) to be used to impeach his credibility. In both cases the accused had taken the stand in his own defense, but unlike Walder, the statements introduced in Harris contradicted his protestations of innocence. The jury had been instructed to use the statement only to assess the defendant's credibility and not as evidence of guilt, and there was no denial that the statements made were voluntary. "The shield provided by Miranda," said Chief Justice Burger, "cannot be perverted into a license to use perjury by way of a defense, free from the risk of confrontation with prior inconsistent utterances."

In the case which follows, Weeks was arrested by a city police officer at his place of business and indicted in a federal court on a charge of sending lottery tickets through the mails. The police also searched his house and turned over to a United States marshal papers and articles found there. Thereupon the marshal himself, accompanied by police officers, searched Week's room and carried away other documents and letters. No warrants had been obtained either for the arrest or for the search by the police or marshal. Before the trial Weeks petitioned the federal district court to return all the papers and articles seized by the various officers. The district court, however, allowed the papers to be used against Weeks at the trial.

Mr. Justice **Day** delivered the opinion of the Court, saying in part:

The defendant assigns error, among other things, in the court's refusal to grant his petition for the return of his property, and in permitting the papers to be used at the trial. . . .

. . . The tendency of those who execute the criminal laws of the country to obtain conviction by means of unlawful seizures and enforced confessions, the latter often obtained after subjecting accused persons to unwarranted practices destructive of rights secured by the federal Constitution, should find no sanction in the judgments of the courts, which are charged at all times with the support of the Constitution, and to which people of all conditions have a right to appeal for the maintenance of such fundamental rights. . . .

. . . If letters and private documents can thus be seized and held and used in evidence against a citizen accused of an offense, the protection of the 4th Amendment, declaring his right to be secure against such searches and seizures, is of no value, and, so far as those thus placed are concerned, might as well be stricken from the Constitution. The efforts of the courts and their officials to bring the guilty to punishment, praiseworthy as they are, are not to be aided by the sacrifice of those great principles established by years of endeavor and suffering which have resulted in their embodiment in the fundamental law of the land. . . .

. . . While there is no opinion in the case, the court in this proceeding doubtless relied upon what is now contended by the government to be the correct rule of law under such circumstances, that the letters having come into the control of the court, it would not inquire into the manner in which they were obtained, but, if competent, would keep them and permit their use in evidence. . . .

The right of the court to deal with papers and documents in the possession of the district attorney and other officers of the court, and subject to its authority, was recognized in Wise v. Henkel [1911]. That papers wrongfully seized should be turned over to the accused has been frequently recognized in the early as well as later decisions of the courts.

We therefore reach the conclusion that the letters in question were taken from the house of the accused by an official of the United States, acting under color of his office in direct violation of the constitutional rights of the defendant; that having made a seasonable application for their return, which was heard and passed upon by the court, there was involved in the order refusing the application a denial of the constitutional rights of the accused, and that the court should have restored these letters to the accused. In holding them and permitting their use upon the trial, we think prejudicial error was committed. As to the papers and property seized by the policemen, it does not appear that they acted under any claim of federal authority such as would make the amendment applicable to such unauthorized seizures. The record shows that what they did by way of arrest and search and seizure was done before the finding of the indictment in the Federal court; under what supposed right or authority does not appear. What remedies the defendant may have against them we need not inquire, as the 4th Amendment is not directed to individual misconduct of such officials. Its limitations reach the Federal government and its agencies. . . .

Reversed.

WOLF v. COLORADO

338 U. S. 25; 69 S. Ct. 1359; 93 L. Ed. 1782
(1949)

The question whether the "exclusionary rule" was required by the Fourth Amendment or was merely a rule of evidence did not reach the Court as a problem until the present case, and it did so here as an aspect of the "incorporation" doctrine. Justice Frankfurter's reference to the "security of one's privacy against arbitrary intrusion by the police—which is at the core of the Fourth Amendment . . ." appeared to incorporate the search and seizure provision of the Fourth Amendment; the four dissenting justices clearly assumed this, dissenting only from the Court's failure to exclude the evidence. The Court in Elkins v. United States (1960) assumed that incorporation had taken place in Wolf, while Justice Frankfurter, in his dissent in Mapp v. Ohio (1961), denied that this was so.

For twelve years following the Wolf decision the Court continued to hold the Weeks rule regarding the exclusion of evidence not applicable to state search and seizure cases, regardless of how offensive to the sense of fairness the search had been. In Stefanelli v. Minard (1951) the Supreme Court refused to exercise its equity jurisdiction to suppress unconstitutionally gotten evidence, although in Rea v. United States (1956) the Court did forbid a federal officer to turn over evidence which he had illegally gotten to a state for use as evidence, and in Monroe v. Pape (1961) it held that the victim of an unreasonable search (in which no evidence had been turned up) could sue the Chicago police under the Civil Rights Act.

In the present case a deputy sheriff went to a doctor's office and, without a warrant, seized his appointment book, obtaining from it the names of patients who were then interrogated; and on evidence contained in the book the district attorney filed an information. The books were introduced against Wolf at his trial.

Mr. Justice **Frankfurter** delivered the opinion of the Court, saying in part:

The precise question for consideration is this: Does a conviction by a State court for a State offense deny the "due process of law" required by the Fourteenth Amendment, solely because evidence that was admitted at the trial was obtained under circumstances which would have rendered it inadmissible in a prosecution for violation of a federal law in a court of the United States because there deemed to be an infraction of the Fourth Amendment as applied in Weeks v. United States [1914]? . . .

Unlike the specific requirements and restrictions placed by the Bill of Rights (Amendments I to VIII) upon the administration of criminal justice by federal authority, the Fourteenth Amendment did not subject criminal justice in the States to specific limitations. The notion that the "due process of law" guaranteed by the Fourteenth Amendment is shorthand for the first eight amendments of the Constitution and thereby incorporates them has been rejected by this Court again and again, after impressive consideration. . . . Only the other day the Court reaffirmed this rejection after thorough reexamination of the scope and function of the Due Process Clause of the Fourteenth Amendment. Adamson v. California [1947]. The issue is closed.

For purposes of ascertaining the restriction which the Due Process Clause imposed upon the States in the enforcement of their criminal law, we adhere to the views expressed in Palko v. Connecticut [1937]. That decision speaks to us with the great weight of the authority, particularly in matters of civil liberty, of a court that included Mr. Chief Justice Hughes, Mr. Justice Brandeis, Mr. Justice Stone and Mr. Justice Cardozo, to name only the dead. In rejecting the suggestion that the Due Process Clause incorporated the original Bill of Rights, Mr. Justice Cardozo reaffirmed on behalf of that Court a different but deeper and more pervasive conception of the due process clause. This Clause exacts from the States for the lowliest and most outcast all that is "implicit in the concept of ordered liberty."

Due process of law thus conveys neither formal nor fixed nor narrow requirements. It is the compendious expression for all those rights which the courts must enforce because they are basic to our free society. But basic rights do not become petrified as of any one time, even though, as a matter of human experience, some may not too rhetorically be called eternal verities. It is of the very nature of a free society to advance in its standards of what is deemed reasonable and right. Representing as it does a living principle, due process is not confined within a permanent catalogue of what may at a given time be deemed the limits or the essentials of fundamental rights.

To rely on a tidy formula for the easy determination of what is a fundamental right for purposes of legal enforcement may satisfy a longing for certainty but ignores the movements of a free society. It belittles the scale of the conception of due process. The real clue to the problem confronting the judiciary in the application of the Due Process Clause is not to ask where the line is once and for all to be drawn but to recognize that it is for the Court to draw it by the gradual and empiric process of "inclusion and exclusion." . . .

The security of one's privacy against arbitrary intrusion by the police—which is at the core of the Fourth Amendment—is basic to a free society. It is therefore implicit in "the concept of ordered liberty" and as such enforceable against the States through the Due Process Clause. The knock at the door, whether by day or by night, as a prelude to a search, without authority of law but solely on the authority of the police, did not need the commentary of recent history to be condemned as inconsistent with the conception of human rights enshrined in the history and the basic constitutional documents of English-speaking peoples.

Accordingly, we have no hesitation in saying that were a State affirmatively to sanction such police incursion into privacy it would run counter to the guaranty of the Fourteenth Amendment. But the ways of enforcing such a basic right raise questions of a different order. How such arbitrary conduct should be checked, what remedies against it should be afforded, the means by which the right should be made effective, are all questions that are not to be so dogmatically answered as to preclude the varying solutions which spring from an al-lowable range of judgment on issues not susceptible of quantitative solution.

In Weeks v. United States, this Court held that in a federal prosecution the Fourth Amendment barred the use of evidence secured through an illegal search and seizure. This ruling was made for the first time in 1914. It was not derived from the explicit requirements of the Fourth Amendment; it was not based on legislation expressing Congressional policy in the enforcement of the Constitution. The decision was a matter of judicial implication. Since then it has been frequently applied and we stoutly adhere to it. But the immediate question is whether the basic right to protection against arbitrary intrusion by the police demands the exclusion of logically relevant evidence obtained by an unreasonable search and seizure because, in a federal prosecution for a federal crime, it would be excluded. As a matter of inherent reason, one would suppose this to be an issue as to which men with complete devotion to the protection of the right of privacy might give different answers. When we find that in fact most of the English-speaking world does not regard as vital to such protection the exclusion of evidence thus obtained, we must hesitate to treat this remedy as an essential ingredient of the right. The contrariety of views of the States is particularly impressive in view of the careful reconsideration which they have given the problem in the light of the Weeks decision.

I. Before the Weeks decision 27 States had passed on the admissibility of evidence obtained by unlawful search and seizure.
 A. Of these, 26 States opposed the Weeks doctrine.
 B. Of these, 1 State anticipated the Weeks doctrine.
II. Since the Weeks decision 47 States all told have passed on the Weeks doctrine.
 A. Of these, 20 passed on it for the first time.
  1. Of the foregoing States, 6 followed the Weeks doctrine.
  2. Of the foregoing States, 14 rejected the Weeks doctrine.
 B. Of these, 26 States reviewed prior decisions contrary to the Weeks doctrine.
  1. Of these, 10 States have followed Weeks, overruling or distinguishing their prior decisions.
  2. Of these, 16 States adhered to their prior decisions against Weeks.
 C. Of these, 1 State adhered to its prior formulation of the Weeks doctrine.
III. As of today 30 States reject the Weeks doctrine, 17 States are in agreement with it.
IV. Of 10 jurisdictions with the United Kingdom and the British Commonwealth of Nations which have passed on the question, none has held evidence obtained by illegal search and seizure inadmissible.

[An appendix to the opinion lists the states and countries which comprise the categories just listed.]

The jurisdictions which have rejected the Weeks doctrine have not left the right to privacy without other means of protection. Indeed, the exclusion of evidence is a remedy which directly serves only to protect those upon whose person or premises something incriminating has been found. We cannot, therefore, regard it as a departure from basic standards to remand such persons, together with those who emerge scatheless from a search, to the remedies of private action and such protection as the internal discipline of the police, under the eyes of an alert public opinion, may afford. Granting that in practice the exclusion of evidence may be an effective way of deterring unreasonable searches, it is not for this Court to condemn as falling below the minimal standards assured by the Due Process Clause a State's reliance upon other methods which, if consistently enforced, would be equally effective. Weighty testimony against such an insistence on our own view is furnished by the opinion of Mr. Justice (then Judge) Cardozo in People v. Defore, 242 N. Y. 13 [1926]. We cannot brush aside the experience of States which deem the incidence of such conduct by the police too slight to call for a deterrent remedy not by way of disciplinary measures but by overriding the relevant rules of evidence. There are, moreover, reasons for excluding evidence unreasonably obtained by the federal police which are less compelling in the case of police under State or local authority. The public opinion of a community can far more effectively be exerted against oppressive conduct on the part of police directly responsible to the community itself than can local opinion, sporadically aroused, be brought to bear upon remote authority pervasively exerted throughout the country.

We hold, therefore, that in a prosecution in a State court for a State crime the Fourteenth Amendment does not forbid the admission of evidence obtained by an unreasonable search and seizure. And though we have interpreted the Fourth Amendment to forbid the admission of such evidence, a different question would be presented if Congress under its legislative powers were to pass a statute purporting to negate the Weeks doctrine. We would then be faced with the problem of the respect to be accorded the legislative judgment on an issue as to which, in default of that judgment, we have been forced to depend upon our own. Problems of a converse character, also not before us, would be presented should Congress under § 5 of the Fourteenth Amendment undertake to enforce the rights there guaranteed by attempting to make the Weeks doctrine binding upon the States.

Affirmed.

Mr. Justice **Black** concurred.

Justices **Douglas, Murphy,** and **Rutledge** dissented.

MAPP v. OHIO

367 U. S. 643; 81 S. Ct. 1684; 6 L. Ed. 2d 1081 (1961)

The Supreme Court was very slow to add to the list of Bill of Rights guarantees which had been assimilated, or incorporated, into the due process clause of the Four-

teenth Amendment. There was no serious doubt that the First Amendment rights had been incorporated, but Betts v. Brady (1942) made it clear that the right to counsel, at least as the Sixth Amendment applied it to the federal government, had not been. A lack of agreement as to what incorporation really meant made it difficult to determine whether or not it had taken place in a given case. An example is the early attempt to incorporate the Eighth Amendment protection against cruel and unusual punishments. In 1946 one Willie Francis was to be electrocuted for murder and through some failure of the equipment did not receive enough electric current to kill him. Before the state could make a second attempt he obtained a writ of habeas corpus on the ground that such an attempt would subject him to cruel and unusual punishment in violation of the due process clause of the Fourteenth Amendment. The Supreme Court rejected his contentions in Louisiana ex rel. Francis v. Resweber (1947). Four members of the majority declared that "the Fourteenth [Amendment] would prohibit by its due process clause execution by a state in a cruel manner," but they did not say whether or not they considered this an "incorporation" of the provisions of the Eighth Amendment into the Fourteenth. Justice Frankfurter concurred in a separate opinion in order to state that in his view "the penological policy of a State is not to be tested by the scope of the Eighth Amendment. . . ." In 1962, however, the Court held that a California law providing a jail sentence for being addicted to narcotics amounted to a cruel and unusual punishment "in violation of the Eighth and Fourteenth Amendments," and cited Resweber as the case in which the right had been incorporated. See Robinson v. California (1962). And in Ker v. California (1963) eight justices made clear the effect of the Mapp decision by holding that state officers were subject to federal standards in searches and seizures.

> Query: *What is the significance of Justice Black's separate concurring opinion in the present case in view of the fact the Court had not yet incorporated the Fifth Amendment into the due process clause? Does the case incorporate the exclusionary rule?*

Mr. Justice **Clark** delivered the opinion of the Court [sic], saying in part:

Appellant stands convicted of knowingly having had in her possession and under her control certain lewd and lascivious books, pictures, and photographs in violation of § 2905.34 of Ohio's Revised Code. . . . The Supreme Court of Ohio found that her conviction was valid though "based primarily upon the introduction in evidence of lewd and lascivious books and pictures unlawfully seized during an unlawful search of defendant's home. . . ."

On May 23, 1957, three Cleveland police officers arrived at appellant's residence in that city pursuant to information that "a person [was] hiding out in the home, who was wanted for questioning in connection with a recent bombing, and that there was a large amount of policy paraphernalia being hidden in the home.'' . . . Upon their arrival at that house, the officers knocked on the door and demanded entrance but appellant, after telephoning her attorney, refused to admit them without a search warrant. They advised their headquarters of the situation and undertook a surveillance of the house.

The officers again sought entrance some three hours later when four or more additional officers arrived on the scene. When Miss Mapp did not come to the door immediately, at least one of the several doors to the house was forcibly opened and the policemen gained admittance. Meanwhile Miss Mapp's attorney arrived, but the officers, having secured their own entry, and continuing in their defiance of the law, would permit him neither to see Miss Mapp nor to enter the house. It appears that Miss Mapp was halfway down the stairs from the upper floor to the front door when the officers, in this highhanded manner, broke into the hall. She demanded to see the search warrant. A paper, claimed to be a warrant, was held up by one of the officers. She grabbed the ''warrant'' and placed it in her bosom. A struggle ensued in which the officers recovered the piece of paper and as a result of which they handcuffed appellant because she had been ''belligerent'' in resisting their official rescue of the ''warrant'' from her person. Running roughshod over appellant, a policeman ''grabbed'' her, ''twisted [her] hand,'' and she ''yelled [and] pleaded with him'' because ''it was hurting.'' Appellant, in handcuffs, was then forcibly taken upstairs to her bedroom where the officers searched a dresser, a chest of drawers, a closet and some suitcases. They also looked into a photo album and through personal papers belonging to the appellant. The search spread to the rest of the second floor including . . . the living room, the kitchen and a dinette. The basement of the building and a trunk found therein were also searched. The obscene materials for possession of which she was ultimately convicted were discovered in the course of that widespread search.

At the trial no search warrant was produced by the prosecution, nor was the failure to produce one explained or accounted for. At best, ''There is, in the record, considerable doubt as to whether there ever was any warrant for the search of defendant's home.'' . . .

The State says that even if the search were made without authority, or otherwise unreasonably, it is not prevented from using the unconstitutionally seized evidence at trial, citing Wolf v. Colorado [1949], in which this Court did indeed hold ''that in a prosecution in a State court for a State crime the Fourteenth Amendment does not forbid the admission of evidence obtained by an unreasonable search and seizure.'' On this appeal . . . it is urged once again that we review that holding. . . .

[The Court here discusses the appearance of the exclusion doctrine in Boyd v. United States (1886) and Weeks v. United States (1914).]

There are in the cases of this Court some passing references to the Weeks rule as being one of evidence.

But the plain and unequivocal language of Weeks—and its later paraphrase in Wolf—to the effect that the Weeks rule is of constitutional origin, remains entirely undisturbed. . . . The Court, in Olmstead v. United States [1928] in unmistakable language restated the Weeks rule:

''The striking outcome of the Weeks case and those which followed it was the sweeping declaration that the Fourth Amendment, although not referring to or limiting the use of evidence in courts, really forbade its introduction if obtained by government officers through a violation of the Amendment.'' . . .

In 1949, 35 years after Weeks was announced, this Court, in Wolf v. Colorado, again for the first time, discussed the effect of the Fourth Amendment upon the States through the operation of the Due Process Clause of the Fourteenth Amendment. . . .

Nevertheless, after declaring that the ''security of one's privacy against arbitrary intrusion by the police'' is ''implicit in 'the concept of ordered liberty' and as such enforceable against the States through the Due Process Clause,'' . . . the Court decided that the Weeks exclusionary rule would not then be imposed upon the States as ''an essential ingredient of the right.'' The Court's reasons . . . were bottomed on factual considerations. . . .

[The Court here notes that at the time Wolf was decided almost two-thirds of the states rejected the Weeks doctrine, but that this situation has changed. Moreover, the futility of other means of protection and remedies to prevent police lawlessness has become apparent since Wolf.]

It, therefore, plainly appears that the factual considerations supporting the failure of the Wolf Court to include the Weeks exclusionary rule when it recognized the enforceability of the right to privacy against the States in 1949, while not basically relevant to the constitutional consideration, could not, in any analysis, now be deemed controlling. . . .

. . . Today we once again examine Wolf's constitutional documentation of the right to privacy free from unreasonable state intrusion, and, after its dozen years on our books, are led by it to close the only courtroom door remaining open to evidence secured by official lawlessness in flagrant abuse of that basic right, reserved to all persons as a specific guarantee against that very same unlawful conduct. We hold that all evidence obtained by searches and seizures in violation of the Constitution is, by that same authority, inadmissible in a state court.

Since the Fourth Amendment's right of privacy has been declared enforceable against the States through the Due Process Clause of the Fourteenth, it is enforceable against them by the same sanction of exclusion as is used against the Federal Government. Were it otherwise, then just as without the Weeks rule the assurance against unreasonable federal searches and seizures would be ''a form of words,'' valueless and undeserving of mention in a perpetual charter of inestimable human liberties, so too, without that rule the freedom from state invasions of privacy would be so ephemeral and so neatly severed from its conceptual nexus with the freedom from all brutish means of coercing evidence as not to merit this Court's high regard as a freedom "implicit in the concept of ordered liberty." At the time that the Court held in Wolf that the Amendment was applicable to the States through the Due Process Clause, the cases of this Court, as we have seen, had steadfastly held that as to federal officers the Fourth Amendment included the exclusion of the evidence seized in violation of its provisions. Even Wolf "stoutly adhered" to that proposition. The right to privacy, when conceded operatively enforceable against the States, was not susceptible of destruction by avulsion of the sanction upon which its protection and enjoyment had always been deemed dependent under the Boyd, Weeks and Silverthorne cases. Therefore, in extending the substantive protections of due process to all constitutionally unreasonable searches—state or federal—it was logically and constitutionally necessary that the exclusion doctrine—an essential part of the right to privacy—be also insisted upon as an essential ingredient of the right newly recognized by the Wolf Case. In short, the admission of the new constitutional right by Wolf could not consistently tolerate denial of its most important constitutional privilege, namely, the exclusion of the evidence which an accused had been forced to give by reason of the unlawful seizure. To hold otherwise is to grant the right but in reality to withhold its privilege and enjoyment. Only last year the Court itself recognized that the purpose of the exclusionary rule "is to deter—to compel respect for the constitutional guaranty in the only effectively available way—by removing the incentive to disregard it." Elkins v. United States [1960].

Indeed, we are aware of no restraint, similar to that rejected today, conditioning the enforcement of any other basic constitutional right. The right to privacy, no less important than any other right carefully and particularly reserved to the people, would stand in marked contrast to all other rights declared as "basic to a free society." Wolf v. Colorado. This Court has not hesitated to enforce as strictly against the States as it does against the Federal Government the rights of free speech and of a free press, the rights to notice and to a fair, public trial, including, as it does, the right not to be convicted by use of a coerced confession, however logically relevant it be, and without regard to its reliability. . . . And nothing could be more certain than that when a coerced confession is involved, "the relevant rules of evidence" are overridden without regard to "the incidence of such conduct by the police," slight or frequent. Why should not the same rule apply to what is tantamount to coerced testimony by way of unconstitutional seizure of goods, papers, effects, documents, etc.? We find that, as to the Federal Government, the Fourth and Fifth Amendments and, as to the States, the freedom from unconscionable invasions of privacy and the freedom from convictions based upon coerced confessions do enjoy an "intimate relation" in their perpetuation of "principles of humanity and civil liberty [secured] . . . only after years of struggle," Bram v. United States (1897). . . .

Moreover, our holding that the exclusionary rule is an essential part of both the Fourth and Fourteenth Amendments is not only the logical dictate of prior cases, but it also makes very good sense. There is no war between the Constitution and common sense. Presently, a federal prosecutor may make no use of evidence illegally seized, but a State's attorney across the street may, although he supposedly is operating under the enforceable prohibitions of the same Amendment. Thus the State, by admitting evidence unlawfully seized, serves to encourage disobedience to the Federal Constitution which it is bound to uphold. Moreover, as was said in Elkins, "[t]he very essence of a healthy federalism depends upon the avoidance of needless conflict between state and federal courts." . . . Yet the double standard recognized until today hardly put such a thesis into practice. In nonexclusionary States, federal officers, being human, were by it invited to and did, as our cases indicate, step across the street to the State's attorney with their unconstitutionally seized evidence. Prosecution on the basis of that evidence was then had in a state court in utter disregard of the enforceable Fourth Amendment. If the fruits of an unconstitutional search had been inadmissible in both state and federal courts, this inducement to evasion would have been sooner eliminated. . . .

Federal-state cooperation in the solution of crime under constitutional standards will be promoted, if only by recognition of their now mutual obligation to respect the same fundamental criteria in their approaches. "However much in a particular case insistence upon such rules may appear as a technicality that inures to the benefit of a guilty person, the history of the criminal law proves that tolerance of shortcut methods in law enforcement impairs its enduring effectiveness." . . . Denying shortcuts to only one of two cooperating law enforcement agencies tends naturally to breed legitimate suspicion of "working arrangements" whose results are equally tainted. . . .

There are those who say, as did Justice (then Judge) Cardozo, that under our constitutional exclusionary doctrine "[t]he criminal is to go free because the constable has blundered." People v. Defore, 242 N. Y., at page 21 [1926]. In some cases this will undoubtedly be the result. But, as was said in Elkins, "there is another consideration—the imperative of judicial integrity." The criminal goes free, if he must, but it is the law that sets him free. Nothing can destroy a government more quickly than its failure to observe its own laws, or worse, its disregard of the charter of its own existence. . . .

The ignoble shortcut to conviction left open to the State tends to destroy the entire system of constitutional restraints on which the liberties of the people rest. Having once recognized that the right to privacy embodied in the Fourth Amendment is enforceable against the

States, and that the right to be secure against rude invasions of privacy by state officers is, therefore, constitutional in origin, we can no longer permit that right to remain an empty promise. Because it is enforceable in the same manner and to like effect as other basic rights secured by the Due Process Clause, we can no longer permit it to be revocable at the whim of any police officer who, in the name of law enforcement itself, chooses to suspend its enjoyment. Our decision, founded on reason and truth, gives to the individual no more than that which the Constitution guarantees him, to the police officer no less than that to which honest law enforcement is entitled, and, to the courts, that judicial integrity so necessary in the true administration of justice.

The judgment of the Supreme Court of Ohio is reversed and the cause remanded for further proceedings not inconsistent with this opinion.

Reversed and remanded.

Mr. Justice **Black,** concurring, said in part:

I am still not persuaded that the Fourth Amendment, standing alone, would be enough to bar the introduction into evidence against an accused of papers and effects seized from him in violation of its commands. For the Fourth Amendment does not itself contain any provision expressly precluding the use of such evidence, and I am extremely doubtful that such a provision could properly be inferred from nothing more than the basic command against unreasonable searches and seizures. Reflection on the problem, however, in the light of cases coming before the Court since Wolf, has led me to conclude that when the Fourth Amendment's ban against unreasonable searches and seizures is considered together with the Fifth Amendment's ban against compelled self-incrimination, a constitutional basis emerges which not only justifies but actually requires the exclusionary rule.

The close interrelationship between the Fourth and Fifth Amendments, as they apply to this problem, has long been recognized and, indeed, was expressly made the ground for this Court's holding in Boyd v. United States. There the Court fully discussed this relationship and declared itself "unable to perceive that the seizure of a man's private books and papers to be used in evidence against him is substantially different from compelling him to be a witness against himself." . . . And, although I rejected the argument at that time, its force has, for me at least, become compelling with the more thorough understanding of the problem brought on by recent cases. In the final analysis, it seems to me that the Boyd doctrine, though perhaps not required by the express language of the Constitution strictly construed, is amply justified from an historical standpoint, soundly based in reason, and entirely consistent with what I regard to be the proper approach to interpretation of our Bill of Rights. . . . [After discussing cases involving the "shock

the conscience" standard, Mr. Justice Black goes on to say:]

. . . As I understand the Court's opinion in this case, we again reject the confusing "shock-the-conscience" standard of the Wolf and Rochin cases and, instead, set aside this state conviction in reliance upon the precise, intelligible and more predictable constitutional doctrine enunciated in the Boyd Case. . . . The Court's opinion, in my judgment, dissipates the doubt and uncertainty in this field of constitutional law and I am persuaded, for this and other reasons stated, to depart from my prior views, to accept the Boyd doctrine as controlling in this state case and to join the Court's judgment and opinion which are in accordance with that constitutional doctrine.

Mr. Justice **Douglas,** concurring, said in part:

Though I have joined the opinion of the Court, I add a few words. This criminal proceeding started with a lawless search and seizure. The police entered a home forcefully, and seized documents that were later used to convict the occupant of a crime. . . .

We held in Wolf v. Colorado that the Fourth Amendment was applicable to the States by reason of the Due Process Clause of the Fourteenth Amendment. But a majority held that the exclusionary rule of the Weeks Case was not required of the States, that they could apply such sanctions as they chose. That position had the necessary votes to carry the day. But with all respect it was not the voice of reason or principle.

As stated in the Weeks Case, if evidence seized in violation of the Fourth Amendment can be used against an accused, "his right to be secure against such searches and seizures is of no value, and . . . might as well be stricken from the Constitution."

When we allowed States to give constitutional sanction to the "shabby business" of unlawful entry into a home (to use an expression of Mr. Justice Murphy, Wolf v. Colorado), we did indeed rob the Fourth Amendment of much meaningful force. . . .

Wolf v. Colorado was decided in 1949. The immediate result was a storm of constitutional controversy which only today finds its end. I believe that this is an appropriate case in which to put an end to the asymmetry which Wolf imported into the law. . . .

Mr. Justice **Harlan,** with whom Mr. Justice **Frankfurter** and Mr. Justice **Whittaker** join, dissenting, said in part:

In overruling the Wolf Case the Court, in my opinion, has forgotten the sense of judicial restraint which, with due regard for stare decisis, is one element that should enter into deciding whether a past decision of this Court should be overruled. Apart from that I also believe that the Wolf rule represents sounder Constitutional doctrine than the new rule which now replaces it.

I.

From the Court's statement of the case one would gather that the central, if not controlling, issue on this appeal is whether illegally state seized evidence is Constitutionally admissible in a state prosecution, an issue which would of course face us with the need for reexamining Wolf. However, such is not the situation. For, although that question was indeed raised here and below among appellant's subordinate points, the new and pivotal issue brought to the Court by this appeal is whether § 2905.34 of the Ohio Revised Code making criminal the *mere* knowing possession or control of obscene material, and under which appellant has been convicted, is consistent with rights of free thought and expression assured against state action by the Fourteenth Amendment. That was the principal issue which was decided by the Ohio Supreme Court, . . . and which was briefed and argued in this Court.

In this posture of things, I think it fair to say that five members of this Court have simply "reached out" to overrule Wolf. With all respect for the views of the majority, and recognizing that stare decisis carries different weight in Constitutional adjudication than it does in nonconstitutional decision, I can perceive no justification for regarding this case as an appropriate occasion for reexamining Wolf. . . .

II.

Essential to the majority's argument against Wolf is the proposition that the rule of Weeks v. United States excluding in federal criminal trials the use of evidence obtained in violation of the Fourth Amendment, derives not from the "supervisory power" of this Court over the federal judicial system, but from Constitutional requirement. This is so because no one, I suppose, would suggest that this Court possesses any general supervisory power over the state courts. Although I entertain considerable doubt as to the soundness of this foundational proposition of the majority, . . . I shall assume, for present purposes, that the Weeks rule "is of constitutional origin."

At the heart of the majority's opinion in this case is the following syllogism: (1) the rule excluding in federal criminal trials evidence which is the product of an illegal search and seizure is "part and parcel" of the Fourth Amendment; (2) Wolf held that the "privacy" assured against federal action by the Fourth Amendment is also protected against state action by the Fourteenth Amendment; and (3) it is therefore "logically and constitutionally necessary" that the Weeks exclusionary rule should also be enforced against the States.

This reasoning ultimately rests on the unsound premise that because Wolf carried into the States, as part of "the concept of ordered liberty" embodied in the Fourteenth Amendment, the principle of "privacy" underlying the Fourth Amendment, it must follow that whatever configurations of the Fourth Amendment have been developed in the particularizing federal precedents are likewise to be deemed a part of "ordered liberty," and as such are enforceable against the States. For me, this does not follow at all.

It cannot be too much emphasized that what was recognized in Wolf was not that the Fourth Amendment *as such* is enforceable against the States as a facet of due process, a view of the Fourteenth Amendment which, as Wolf itself pointed out, has long since been discredited, but the principle of privacy "which is at the core of the Fourth Amendment." . . .

. . . Here we are reviewing not a determination that what the state police did was Constitutionally permissible (since the state court quite evidently assumed that it was not), but a determination that appellant was properly found guilty of conduct which, for present purposes, it is to be assumed the State could Constitutionally punish. Since there is not the slightest suggestion that Ohio's policy is "affirmatively to sanction . . . police incursion into privacy," . . . what the Court is now doing is to impose upon the States not only federal substantive standards of "search and seizure" but also the basic federal remedy for violation of those standards. For I think it entirely clear that the Weeks exclusionary rule is but a remedy which, by penalizing past official misconduct, is aimed at deterring such conduct in the future.

I would not impose upon the States this federal exclusionary remedy. The reasons given by the majority for now suddenly turning its back on Wolf seem to me notably unconvincing.

First, it is said that "the factual grounds upon which Wolf was based" have since changed, in that more States now follow the Weeks exclusionary rule than was so at the time Wolf was decided. While that is true, a recent survey indicates that at present one-half of the States still adhere to the common-law non-exclusionary rule, and one, Maryland, retains the rule as to felonies. . . . But in any case surely all this is beside the point, as the majority itself indeed seems to recognize. . . .

Further, we are told that imposition of the Weeks rule on the States makes "very good sense," in that it will promote recognition by state and federal officials of their "mutual obligation to respect the same fundamental criteria" in their approach to law enforcement, and will avoid "needless conflict between state and federal courts." . . .

An approach which regards the issue as one of achieving procedural symmetry or of serving administrative convenience surely disfigures the boundaries of this Court's functions in relation to the state and federal courts. . . . I do not believe that the Fourteenth Amendment empowers this Court to mould state remedies effectuating the right to freedom from "arbitrary intrusion by the police" to suit its own notions of how things should be done . . . .

. . . I do not see how it can be said that a trial becomes unfair simply because a State determines that evidence may be considered by the trier of fact, regardless of how it was obtained, if it is relevant to the one issue with which the trial is concerned, the guilt or innocence of the accused. Of course, a court may use its procedures as an incidental means of pursuing other ends than the correct resolution of the controversies before it. Such indeed is the Weeks rule, but if a State does not choose to use its courts in this way, I do not believe that this Court is empowered to impose this much-debated procedure on local courts, however efficacious we may consider the Weeks rule to be as a means of securing Constitutional rights.

Finally, it is said that the overruling of Wolf is supported by the established doctrine that the admission in evidence of an involuntary confession renders a state conviction Constitutionally invalid. Since such a confession may often be entirely reliable, and therefore of the greatest relevance to the issue of the trial, the argument continues, this doctrine is ample warrant in precedent that the way evidence was obtained, and not just its relevance, is Constitutionally significant to the fairness of a trial. I believe this analogy is not a true one. The "coerced confession" rule is certainly not a rule that any illegally obtained statements may not be used in evidence. . . .

The point, then, must be that in requiring exclusion of an involuntary statement of an accused, we are concerned not with an appropriate remedy for what the police have done, but with something which is regarded as going to the heart of our concepts of fairness in judicial procedure. . . . The pressures brought to bear against an accused leading to a confession, unlike an unconstitutional violation of privacy, do not, apart from the use of the confession at trial, necessarily involve independent Constitutional violations. What is crucial is that the trial defense to which an accused is entitled should not be rendered an empty formality by reason of statements wrung from him, for then "a prisoner . . . [has been] made the deluded instrument of his own conviction." . . . That this is a *procedural right*, and that its violation occurs at the time his improperly obtained statement is admitted at trial, is manifest. For without this right all the careful safeguards erected around the giving of testimony, whether by an accused or any other witness, would become empty formalities in a procedure where the most compelling possible evidence of guilt, a confession, would have already been obtained at the unsupervised pleasure of the police.

This, and not the disciplining of the police, as with illegally seized evidence, is surely the true basis for excluding a statement of the accused which was unconstitutionally obtained. In sum, I think the coerced confession analogy works strongly *against* what the Court does today. . . .

Memorandum of Mr. Justice **Stewart**.

Agreeing fully with Part I of Mr. Justice Harlan's dissenting opinion, I express no view as to the merits of the constitutional issue which the Court today decides. I would, however, reverse the judgment in this case, because I am persuaded that the provision of § 2905.34 of the Ohio Revised Code, upon which the petitioner's conviction was based, is, in the words of Mr. Justice Harlan, not "consistent with the rights of free thought and expression assured against state action by the Fourteenth Amendment."

EXCLUSION IN ACTION: SELF-INCRIMINATION

MIRANDA v. ARIZONA

384 U. S. 436; 86 S. Ct. 1602; 16 L. Ed. 2d 694 (1966)

The privilege against compulsory self-incrimination grew up in England as a revolt against procedures, especially those in the ecclesiastical courts and the Court of Star Chamber, whereby persons were questioned by the judges in order both to get evidence on which to accuse them and to secure a confession from them after they were accused. Immunity from such questioning gradually became established in the common law, and it was this immunity that was written into the Fifth Amendment of the Constitution. Over the years it has been one of the most controversial guarantees in the Bill of Rights. At the time the first colonists came to America it was still not universally accepted in England, and important deviations occurred during the colonial period, notably in the Salem "witch trials." Throughout much of its history the desirability of the protection has been questioned by various bodies of opinion on two grounds: First, it is considered no longer a necessary protection; modern courts would prevent any attempt to get evidence from an accused by means of torture or intimidation. The second ground is that the protection is a shield only to the guilty, since only guilty persons can legitimately refuse to give evidence on the ground that their testimony would tend to incriminate them. This position is bolstered by the historical fact that prominent among those who brought about the adoption of the protection in England were the early Puritans, who were obviously guilty of heresy but who objected to being forced to provide the only testimony upon which they could be convicted in the ecclesiastical courts and the Court of Star Chamber.

Despite these attacks, the protection against compulsory self-incrimination continues to command strong support. There is a strong moral sense which regards it as uncivilized to put a person, whether innocent or guilty, through the degrading process of having to give the evidence upon which he may be convicted of crime. The protection is also felt to promote sound police meth-

ods by preventing the lazy prosecutor from relying upon evidence he can secure by the relatively easy method of torturing his suspects. Sir James Fitzjames Stephens illustrates this point by quoting an Indian policeman who said, "It is far pleasanter to sit comfortably in the shade rubbing red pepper into a poor devil's eyes than to go about in the sun hunting up evidence." Wigmore, the great authority on evidence, while criticizing many aspects of the guarantee, supported it on the ground that it protected innocent and guilty alike from the overzealousness of prosecuting officials who are forced by public opinion to maintain a high conviction record if they are to continue to hold their offices.

Unlike the protection against unreasonable searches and seizures, the protection against self-incrimination contains what amounts to a built-in exclusionary rule. Evidence that is coerced cannot be used in court to convict a person. Thus, although the Court in Mapp v. Ohio held that the exclusionary rule of the Weeks case (1914) was incorporated into the Fourteenth Amendment, the five-man majority could not agree on which constitutional clause actually embodied the rule. Four members held it to be an aspect of the Fourth Amendment, while Justice Black held it was required by the self-incrimination provision of the Fifth Amendment. At the time Mapp was decided, self-incrimination had not been incorporated and when the Court finally did incorporate the doctrine in Malloy v. Hogan (1964), Justice Clark, who had joined the majority in Mapp, agreed with the dissenting opinion of Justice Harlan that in neither Mapp nor Gideon did "incorporation," as such, take place. So, while the results of Mapp were to make the exclusionary rule applicable to the states, it is not possible to point to a constitutional clause that dictates this result, let alone be sure that such clause was "incorporated," since only four members of the Court appeared to agree with either of these propositions.

The Hogan case made the question academic and with both searches and seizures and self-incrimination made applicable to the states, which clause actually does the work ceases to be of crucial importance. With the decision in Ker v. California (1963) that federal standards applied in state search and seizure cases, even Justice Harlan conceded that incorporation of this clause had taken place.

The Court had always made clear that the right not to be a witness against one's self was not limited to being excused from taking the witness stand at one's criminal trial. Any statement coerced from a person by the government, wherever the coercion took place, constituted self-incrimination and in addition any information gotten by the government as a result of such coerced statements were excluded from court as "fruit of the poisoned tree." Since statements could be gotten from a person under an almost unlimited range of circumstances, the Court was continually faced with the question whether they were voluntary or coerced. As a result of the slow convergence of two very different doctrines the Court finally arrived at what it hoped would be a solution to its problem. Have a lawyer on hand when the person makes a statement!

In 1963, in the celebrated case of Gideon v. Wainwright, the Supreme Court held applicable to trials in state courts the Sixth Amendment right to counsel and in the years following it decided a series of cases, some of them highly controversial, extending that right to points both earlier and later in the criminal process. In Hamilton v. Alabama (1961) it held that an accused was entitled to counsel (at state expense, if necessary) at the time of his arraignment, since certain defenses such as insanity had to be plead at that time or completely forfeited. In White v. Maryland (1963) it was pushed back to the preliminary hearing stage, because a guilty plea made at that stage became a permanent part of the record; and in Douglas v. California (1963) it was moved forward to cover the first appeal from a criminal conviction which is normally given by the state as a matter of right. The rationale behind all these cases was that these were "critical stages" in the criminal process. It was at these points that a person might do or fail to do, or say or fail to say, something that could irrevocably prejudice his chances of acquittal. It was at these points that the "guiding hand of counsel" was vital if his rights were to receive full protection. In United States v. Wade (1967) and Gilbert v. California (1967) the Court extended the right of counsel to include that point where an accused is identified as a wanted suspect by being picked out of a police line-up by an eyewitness, although it did hold in Gilbert that taking a handwriting sample from a man before he saw his lawyer did not violate his rights. Here, too, the suspect's right to an unprejudiced identification may easily be jeopardized by an excess of police enthusiasm.

While these changes were going on the Court was also struggling with the somewhat unrelated problem of coerced confessions; see the note to Rochin v. California. Although it had held in Brown v. Mississippi (1936) that a confession based on coercion—in this case physical torture—was void, it was continually plagued by the problem of what constituted coercion. It conceded that coercion could be psychological as well as physical, but it was haunted by the fact so clearly stated in Stein v. New York (1953), that "no criminal confession is voluntary" in the "sense that petitioners wanted to make them." A definition of "voluntary" that meant some pressure could be used, but not too much, raised endless difficulties for the Court. Since most confessions are secured before a person is formally charged with crime, the Court had managed to solve much of the problem in the federal courts by requiring that an accused be taken immediately before a committing magistrate. But this ruling rested on the supervisory authority of the Court over the administration of federal justice and so could not be extended to the states. Consequently the Court had to trace a guideline for the states as cases came before it, and as the Court noted in Spano v. New York (1959), as "the methods used to extract confessions become more sophisticated, our duty . . . only becomes more difficult because of the more delicate judgments to be made." In the Spano case the defendant was persuaded to confess by fatigue and the false sympathy aroused by a boyhood friend on the police force, while in subsequent cases the techniques used included threatening to bring the defendant's wife in for questioning (Rogers v. Richmond, 1961), threatening to take her infant children from her and give them to strangers (Lynumn v. Illinois, 1963), injecting "truth serum" into his veins (Townsend v. Sain, 1963), and refusing to let him call his wife or lawyer until he had confessed (Haynes v. Washington, 1963). While in some of these cases the police disputed the defendant's version, in all of them the defendants were denied access to counsel who might have given them moral support and perhaps furnished a dispassionate version of the proceedings. Claims that the right to counsel was being denied were noted by the Court but not reached because the confessions were held to be coerced. Clearly the amount of "pressure" a state could use to invoke a confession was getting less and less.

Then in 1964 the Court moved sharply to merge these two lines of development, extending the right to counsel, but in such a way that would serve also as a protection against forced confessions. In Massiah v. United States (1964) the government was forbidden to question an accused, who was under indictment, in the absence of his lawyer, and in Escobedo v. Illinois (1964) it held that where "the investigation is no longer a general inquiry into an unsolved crime but has begun to focus on a particular suspect, the suspect has been taken into police custody, the police carry out a process of interrogations that lends itself to eliciting incriminating statements, the suspect has requested and been denied an opportunity to consult with his lawyer, and the police have not effectively warned him of his absolute constitutional right to remain silent, the accused has been denied 'the Assistance of Counsel' in violation of the Sixth Amendment to the Constitution as 'made obligatory upon the States by the Fourteenth Amendment.'"

The two years following the Escobedo decision (1964) witnessed a nationwide debate on the implications and wisdom of what the Court had done. The case itself had involved only the denial of Danny Escobedo's request to see his attorney and reaffirmed his absolute right to remain silent. But did it imply, in effect, an adoption of the English "Judge's Rule" that a suspect must be warned of his right to silence and cautioned that anything he said could be used against him? Did it require that he be told of his right to counsel? That he be furnished counsel at state expense? Did it, perhaps, outlaw all confessions? All police interrogation?

The Court itself was bitterly attacked for what was considered a gratuitous hamstringing of the police in their efforts to protect society against criminals. It was asserted that between 75 and 80 percent of the convictions in major crimes were dependent upon confessions; and police officers and prosecutors across the country, together with some courts, echoed the conviction of New York City's police commissioner, Michael J. Murphy,

that "if suspects are told of their rights they will not confess." Certainly a competent lawyer would tell them not to confess, and then this effective method of solving crimes would come to an end.

Meanwhile, public confidence in the reliability of confessions as a substitute for investigatory evidence was badly shaken in early 1965 when George Whitmore, Jr., was conceded to be innocent of the sensational murder of career girls Janice Wylie and Emily Hoffert in their New York apartment. Whitmore had been arrested a year and a half after the murders and during twenty-eight hours of questioning had given a sixty-one-page confession filled with details "which only he, as the killer, could have known." Although Whitmore repudiated his confession to this and two other major crimes, the police contended it had been freely given, and his indictment was not dismissed until eight months later when incontrovertible evidence of his innocence was presented—evidence which the police could have obtained at once had they checked into the truth of his alibi.

Not until 1971 in Harris v. New York did the Court move to reduce the impact of Miranda by permitting the use in court of evidence gotten in violation of the rule. Harris, on trial for a narcotics violation, took the stand and testified that a bag of powder he had sold to an undercover agent was baking powder rather than heroin. He was asked on cross-examination if this did not contradict statements made to the police at the time of his arrest and without the Miranda warnings and the statements were then read to him. The jury was instructed that they could not be used to determine his guilt, but only his credibility. In a five-to-four decision the Court held this use of the statements valid. Conceding that "some comments in the Miranda opinion can indeed be read as indicating a bar to use of any uncounseled statement for any purpose," they were only dicta and "it does not follow from Miranda that evidence inadmissible against an accused in the prosecution's case in chief is barred for all purposes, provided of course that the trustworthiness of the evidence satisfies legal standards." The Court reaffirmed Walder v. United States (1954) in which a similar decision had been reached with regard to illegally seized evidence (see the note to Weeks v. United States, 1914) and added, "the shield provided by Miranda cannot be perverted into a license to use perjury by way of a defense, free from the risk of confrontation with prior inconsistent utterances."

In Oregon v. Hass (1975) the Court not only reaffirmed Harris but extended it to a defendant who had been given the Miranda warnings and had his request for an attorney ignored. "One might concede that when proper Miranda warnings have been given, and the officer then continues his interrogation after the suspect asks for an attorney, the officer may be said to have little to lose and perhaps something to gain by way of possibly uncovering impeachment material. . . . In any event, the balance was struck in Harris, and we are not disposed to change it now."

Where the testimony is used to convict, however, the Court has adhered firmly to Miranda. In Edwards v.

Arizona (1981) Edwards' request for a lawyer was ignored and a resumption of questioning produced a confession. The Court made clear that a suspect who has "expressed his desire to deal with the police only through counsel is not subject to further interrogation by the authorities until counsel has been made available to him, unless the accused himself initiates further communication, exchanges, or conversations with the police." In Arizona v. Roberson (1988) the court extended the Edwards reasoning to a case in which the accused was interrogated about an offense unrelated to the one for which he was being held.

The purpose of the Miranda warnings is to inform suspects that they need not aid the police in making a case against them and that they are entitled to legal counsel as to what they should say and not say. But suppose a person is arrested without probable cause, given the Miranda warnings, and voluntarily confesses. Does the invalidity of the arrest make the confession inadmissible even though it was voluntarily made? In Brown v. Illinois (1975) Justice Blackmun, speaking for six members of a unanimous court, held that it did. Here Brown had been illegally seized by the police (a Fourth Amendment violation) and voluntarily confessed after Miranda warnings which assured there was no Fifth Amendment violation. The Court pointed out that despite the intimate relationship between the two amendments the exclusionary rule did not serve the same purpose with regard to each. When used with the Fourth Amendment it excluded all statements or evidence—not just those which were self-incriminating. Not only do the Miranda warnings not inform the suspect about the right not to be illegally detained, but they do nothing to deter other Fourth Amendment violations. "If Miranda warnings, by themselves, were held to attenuate the taint of an unconstitutional arrest, regardless of how wanton and purposeful the Fourth Amendment violation, the effect of the exclusionary rule would be substantially diluted. . . . Arrests made without warrant or without probable cause, for questioning or 'investigation,' would be encouraged by the knowledge that evidence derived therefrom hopefully could well be made admissible at trial by the simple expedient of giving Miranda warnings. Any incentive to avoid the Fourth Amendment violations would be eviscerated by making the warnings, in effect, a 'cure-all' and the constitutional guarantee against unlawful searches and seizures could be said to be reduced to a 'form of words.' " Of course it is possible for a person to confess voluntarily even though subjected to an unreasonable search and seizure, but the Court made clear that in passing on the validity of such confessions "the temporal proximity of the arrest and the confession, the presence of intervening circumstances, . . . and, particularly, the purpose and flagrancy of the official misconduct are all relevant." The decision was reaffirmed in Taylor v. Alabama (1982).

The case below is a combination of four cases, all raising questions of the admissibility of confessions. Miranda was convicted of kidnapping and rape on the basis of a confession obtained after two hours of questioning in which he was not told of his right to counsel or silence.

Mr. Chief Justice **Warren** delivered the opinion of the Court, saying in part:

The cases before us raise questions which go to the roots of our concepts of American criminal jurisprudence: the restraints society must observe consistent with the Federal Constitution in prosecuting individuals for crime. More specifically, we deal with the admissibility of statements obtained from an individual who is subjected to custodial police interrogation and the necessity for procedures which assure that the individual is accorded his privilege under the Fifth Amendment to the Constitution not to be compelled to incriminate himself. . . .

Our holding will be spelled out with some specificity in the pages which follow but briefly stated it is this: the prosecution may not use statements, whether exculpatory or inculpatory, stemming from custodial interrogation of the defendant unless it demonstrates the use of procedural safeguards effective to secure the privilege against self-incrimination. By custodial interrogation, we mean questioning initiated by law enforcement officers after a person has been taken into custody or otherwise deprived of his freedom of action in any significant way. As for the procedural safeguards to be employed, unless other fully effective means are devised to inform accused persons of their right of silence and to assure a continuous opportunity to exercise it, the following measures are required. Prior to any questioning, the person must be warned that he has a right to remain silent, that any statement he does make may be used as evidence against him, and that he has a right to the presence of an attorney, either retained or appointed. The defendant may waive effectuation of these rights, provided the waiver is made voluntarily, knowingly and intelligently. If, however, he indicates in any manner and at any stage of the process that he wishes to consult with an attorney before speaking there can be no questioning. Likewise, if the individual is alone and indicates in any manner that he does not wish to be interrogated, the police may not question him. The mere fact that he may have answered some questions or volunteered some statements on his own does not deprive him of the right to refrain from answering any further inquiries until he has consulted with an attorney and thereafter consents to be questioned.

I.

The constitutional issue we decide in each of these cases is the admissibility of statements obtained from a defendant questioned while in custody or otherwise deprived of his freedom of action in any significant way. In each, the defendant was questioned by police officers, detectives, or a prosecuting attorney in a room in which he was cut off from the outside world. In none of these cases was the defendant given a full and effective warning of his rights at the outset of the interrogation process. In all the cases, the questioning elicited oral admissions, and in three of them, signed statements as well which were admitted at their trials. They all thus share salient features—incommunicado interrogation of individuals in a police-dominated atmosphere, resulting in self-incriminating statements without full warnings of constitutional rights.

. . . The use of physical brutality and violence is not, unfortunately, relegated to the past. . . .

. . . Unless a proper limitation upon custodial interrogation is achieved—such as these decisions will advance—there can be no assurance that practices of this nature will be eradicated in the foreseeable future. . . .

Again we stress that the modern practice of in-custody interrogation is psychologically rather than physically oriented. As we have stated before, "Since Chambers v. Florida [1940] this Court has recognized that coercion can be mental as well as physical, and that the blood of the accused is not the only hallmark of an unconstitutional inquisition." Blackburn v. Alabama (1960). Interrogation still takes place in privacy. Privacy results in secrecy and this in turn results in a gap in our knowledge as to what in fact goes on in the interrogation rooms. A valuable source of information about present police practices, however, may be found in various police manuals and texts which document procedures employed with success in the past, and which recommend various other effective tactics. These texts are used by law enforcement agencies themselves as guides. It should be noted that these texts professedly present the most enlightened and effective means presently used to obtain statements through custodial interrogation. By considering these texts and other data, it is possible to describe procedures observed and noted around the country. . . . [The Court here quotes at length from a number of books on criminal investigation.]

From these representative samples of interrogation techniques, the setting prescribed by the manuals and observed in practice becomes clear. In essence, it is this: To be alone with the subject is essential to prevent distraction and to deprive him of any outside support. The aura of confidence in his guilt undermines his will to resist. He merely confirms the preconceived story the police seek to have him describe. Patience and persistence, at times relentless questioning are employed. To obtain a confession, the interrogator must "patiently maneuver himself or his quarry into a position from which the desired objective may be obtained." When normal procedures fail to produce the needed result, the police may resort to deceptive stratagems such as giving false legal advice. It is important to keep the subject off balance, for example, by trading on his insecurity about himself or his surroundings. The police then persuade, trick, or cajole him out of exercising his constitutional rights.

Even without employing brutality, the "third degree" or the specific stratagems described above, the very fact of custodial interrogation exacts a heavy toll on individual liberty and trades on the weakness of individuals. This fact may be illustrated simply by referring to three confession cases decided by this Court in the Term immediately preceding our Escobedo decision. In Townsend v. Sain (1963), the defendant was a 19 year-old heroin addict, described as a "near mental defective." The defendant in Lynumn v. Illinois (1963), was a woman who confessed to the arresting officer after being importuned to "cooperate" in order to prevent her children from being taken by relief authorities. This Court as in those cases reversed the conviction of a defendant in Haynes v. Washington (1963), whose persistent request during his interrogation was to phone his wife or attorney. In other settings, these individuals might have exercised their constitutional rights. In the incommunicado police-dominated atmosphere, they succumbed.

[The Court here discusses the facts of the cases before it, noting that in each the questioning in an "incommunicado police-dominated atmosphere" had resulted in a confession.]

In these cases, we might not find the defendant's statements to have been involuntary in traditional terms. Our concern for adequate safeguards to protect precious Fifth Amendment rights is, of course, not lessened in the slightest. In each of the cases, the defendant was thrust into an unfamiliar atmosphere and run through menacing police interrogation procedures. The potentiality for compulsion is forcefully apparent, for example, in Miranda, where the indigent Mexican defendant was a seriously disturbed individual with pronounced sexual fantasies, and in Stewart, in which the defendant was an indigent Los Angeles Negro who had dropped out of school in the sixth grade. To be sure, the records do not evince overt physical coercion or patent psychological ploys. The fact remains that in none of these cases did the officers undertake to afford appropriate safeguards at the outset of the interrogation to insure that the statements were truly the product of free choice.

It is obvious that such an interrogation environment is created for no purpose other than to subjugate the individual to the will of his examiner. This atmosphere carries its own badge of intimidation. To be sure, this is not physical intimidation, but it is equally destructive of human dignity. The current practice of incommunicado interrogation is at odds with one of our Nation's most cherished principles—that the individual may not be compelled to incriminate himself. Unless adequate protective devices are employed to dispel the compulsion inherent in custodial surroundings, no statement obtained from the defendant can truly be the product of his free choice.

From the foregoing, we can readily perceive an intimate connection between the privilege against self-incrimination and police custodial questioning. . . .

II.

. . . We have recently noted that the privilege against self-incrimination—the essential mainstay of our adversary system—is founded on a complex of values. . . . All these policies point to one overriding thought: the constitutional foundation underlying the privilege is the respect a government—state or federal—must accord to the dignity and integrity of its citizens. To maintain a "fair state-individual balance," to require the government "to shoulder the entire load," . . . to respect the inviolability of the human personality, our accusatory system of criminal justice demands that the government seeking to punish an individual produce the evidence against him by its own independent labors, rather than by the cruel, simple expedient of compelling it from his own mouth. . . . In sum, the privilege is fulfilled only when the person is guaranteed the right "to remain silent unless he chooses to speak in the unfettered exercise of his will." . . .

The question in these cases is whether the privilege is fully applicable during a period of custodial interrogation. . . . We are satisfied that all the principles embodied in the privilege apply to informal compulsion exerted by law-enforcement officials during in-custody questioning. An individual swept from familiar surroundings into police custody, surrounded by antagonistic forces, and subjected to the techniques of persuasion described above cannot be otherwise than under compulsion to speak. As a practical matter, the compulsion to speak in the isolated setting of the police station may well be greater than in courts or other official investigations, where there are often impartial observers to guard against intimidation or trickery.

This question, in fact, could have been taken as settled in federal courts almost 70 years ago, when, in Bram v. United States (1897), this Court held:

"In criminal trials, in the courts of the United States, wherever a question arises whether a confession is incompetent because not voluntary, the issue is controlled by that portion of the Fifth Amendment . . . commanding that no person 'shall be compelled in any criminal case to be a witness against himself.' " . . .

III.

It is impossible for us to foresee the potential alternatives for protecting the privilege which might be devised by Congress or the States in the exercise of their creative rule-making capacities. Therefore we cannot say that the Constitution necessarily requires adherence to any particular solution for the inherent compulsions of the interrogation process as it is presently conducted. Our decision in no way creates a constitutional straitjacket which will handicap sound efforts at reform, nor is it intended to have this effect. We encourage Congress and the States to continue their laudable search for increasingly effective ways of protecting the rights of the individual while promoting efficient enforcement of our criminal laws. However, unless we are shown other procedures which are at least as effective in apprising accused persons of their right of silence and in assuring a continuous opportunity to exercise it, the following safeguards must be observed. . . .

[The Court here elaborates on and justifies the requirements summarized at the beginning of the opinion.]

If the interrogation continues without the presence of an attorney and a statement is taken, a heavy burden rests on the government to demonstrate that the defendant knowingly and intelligently waived his privilege against self-incrimination and his right to retained or appointed counsel. . . . This Court has always set high standards of proof for the waiver of constitutional rights, Johnson v. Zerbst (1938), and we reassert these standards as applied to in-custody interrogation. Since the State is responsible for establishing the isolated circumstances under which the interrogation takes place and has the only means of making available corroborated evidence of warnings given during incommunicado interrogation, the burden is rightly on its shoulders. . . .

The warnings required and the waiver necessary in accordance with our opinion today are, in the absence of a fully effective equivalent, pre-requisites to the admissibility of any statement made by a defendant. No distinction can be drawn between statements which are direct confessions and statements which amount to "admissions" of part or all of an offense. The privilege against self-incrimination protects the individual from being compelled to incriminate himself in any manner; it does not distinguish degrees of incrimination. Similarly for precisely the same reason, no distinction may be drawn between inculpatory statements and statements alleged to be merely "exculpatory." If a statement made were in fact truly exculpatory it would, of course, never be used by the prosecution. In fact, statements merely intended to be exculpatory by the defendant are often used to impeach his testimony at trial or to demonstrate untruths in the statement given under interrogation and thus to prove guilt by implication. These statements are incriminating in any meaningful sense of the word and may not be used without the full warnings and effective waiver required for any other statements. In Escobedo itself, the defendant fully intended his accusation of another as the slayer to be exculpatory as to himself.

The principles announced today deal with the protection which must be given to the privilege against self-incrimination when the individual is first subjected to police interrogation while in custody at the station or otherwise deprived of his freedom of action in any significant way. It is at this point that our adversary system of criminal proceedings commences, distinguishing itself at the outset from the inquisitorial system recognized in some countries. Under the system of warnings we delineate today or under any other system which may be devised and found effective, the safeguards to be erected about the privilege must come into play at this point. . . .

In dealing with statements obtained through interrogation, we do not purport to find all confessions inadmissible. Confessions remain a proper element in law enforcement. Any statement given freely and voluntarily without any compelling influences is, of course, admissible in evidence. The fundamental import of the privilege while an individual is in custody is not whether he is allowed to talk to the police without the benefit of warnings and counsel, but whether he can be interrogated. There is no requirement that police stop a person who enters a police station and states that he wishes to confess to a crime, or a person who calls the police to offer a confession or any other statement he desires to make. Volunteered statements of any kind are not barred by the Fifth Amendment and their admissibility is not affected by our holding today. . . .

IV.

A recurrent argument made in these cases is that society's need for interrogation outweighs the privilege. This argument is not unfamiliar to this Court. . . . The whole thrust of our foregoing discussion demonstrates that the Constitution has prescribed the rights of the individual when confronted with the power of government when it provided in the Fifth Amendment that an individual cannot be compelled to be a witness against himself. That right cannot be abridged. As Mr. Justice Brandeis once observed:

"Decency, security and liberty alike demand that government officials shall be subjected to the same rules of conduct that are commands to the citizen. In a government of laws, existence of the government will be imperilled if it fails to observe the law scrupulously. Our Government is the potent, the omnipresent teacher. For good or for ill, it teaches the whole people by its example.

Crime is contagious. If the Government becomes a lawbreaker, it breeds contempt for law; it invites every man to become a law unto himself; it invites anarchy. To declare that in the administration of the criminal law the end justifies the means . . . would bring terrible retribution. Against that pernicious doctrine this Court should resolutely set its face." Olmstead v. United States [1928] (dissenting opinion). . . .

V.

Because of the nature of the problem and because of its recurrent significance in numerous cases, we have to this point discussed the relationship of the Fifth Amendment privilege to police interrogation without specific concentration on the facts of the cases before us. We turn now to these facts to consider the application to these cases of the constitutional principles discussed above. In each instance, we have concluded that statements were obtained from the defendant under circumstances that did not meet constitutional standards for protection of the privilege.

[The Court here reviews in detail the facts of the four cases and concludes either that the defendant did not waive his right to silence, or was not informed that he had a right to silence or to counsel.]

Mr. Justice **Clark** dissented in part.

Mr. Justice **Harlan,** whom Mr. Justice **Stewart** and Mr. Justice **White** joined, dissented, saying in part:

I believe the decision of the Court represents poor constitutional law and entails harmful consequences for the country at large. How serious these consequences may prove to be only time can tell. But the basic flaws in the Court's justification seem to me readily apparent now once all sides of the problem are considered. . . .

While the fine points of this scheme are far less clear than the Court admits, the tenor is quite apparent. The new rules are not designed to guard against police brutality or other unmistakably banned forms of coercion. Those who use third-degree tactics and deny them in court are equally able and destined to lie as skillfully about warnings and waivers. Rather, the thrust of the new rules is to negate all pressures, to reinforce the nervous or ignorant suspect, and ultimately to discourage any confession at all. The aim in short is toward "voluntariness" in a utopian sense, or to view it from a different angle, voluntariness with a vengeance. . . .

What the Court largely ignores is that its rules impair, if they will not eventually serve wholly to frustrate, an instrument of law enforcement that has long and quite reasonably been thought worth the price paid for it. There can be little doubt that the Court's new code would markedly decrease the number of confessions. To warn the suspect that he may remain silent and remind him that his confession may be used in court are minor obstructions. To require also an express waiver by the suspect and an end to questioning whenever he demurs must heavily handicap questioning. And to suggest or provide counsel for the suspect simply invites the end of the interrogation.

How much harm this decision will inflict on law enforcement cannot fairly be predicted with accuracy. Evidence on the role of confessions is notoriously incomplete, . . . and little is added by the Court's reference to the FBI experience and the resources believed wasted in interrogation. . . . We do know that some crimes cannot be solved without confessions, that ample expert testimony attests to their importance in crime control, and that the Court is taking a real risk with society's welfare in imposing its new regime on the country. The social costs of crime are too great to call the new rules anything but a hazardous experimentation.

While passing over the costs and risks of its experiment, the Court portrays the evils of normal police questioning in terms which I think are exaggerated. Albeit stringently confined by the due process standards interrogation is no doubt often inconvenient and unpleasant for the suspect. However, it is not less so for a man to be arrested and jailed, to have his house searched, or to stand trial in court, yet all this may properly happen to the most innocent given probable cause, a warrant, or an indictment. Society has always paid a stiff price for law and order, and peaceful interrogation is not one of the dark moments of the law. . . .

Mr. Justice **White,** with whom Mr. Justice **Harlan** and Mr. Justice **Stewart** joined, dissented, saying in part:

The proposition that the privilege against self-incrimination forbids in-custody interrogation without the warnings specified in the majority opinion and without a clear waiver of counsel has no significant support in the history of the privilege or in the language of the Fifth Amendment. As for the English authorities and the common-law history, the privilege, firmly established in the second half of the seventeenth century, was never applied except to prohibit compelled judicial interrogations. The rule excluding coerced confessions matured about 100 years later, "[b]ut there is nothing in the reports to suggest that the theory has its roots in the privilege against self-incrimination. And so far as the cases reveal, the privilege, as such, seems to have been given effect only in judicial proceedings, including the preliminary examinations by authorized magistrates." . . .

DUCKWORTH v. EAGAN

492 U.S. 195; 109 S. Ct. 2875; 106 L. Ed. 2d 166 (1989)

Miranda v. Arizona was decided in 1966 by a Court headed by Chief Justice Earl Warren. Its purpose was to ensure that the underprivileged, uneasy in the presence of the police and unfamiliar with their rights under the law, would be told of their right to legal counsel and assured that they did not need to answer questions until such counsel was provided. Police and prosecutors alike viewed this class of people as providing the bulk of the "criminal element" and were concerned that providing them with lawyers would make it exceedingly difficult if not impossible to get them to confess to their crimes and would thus reduce the number of convictions. The political pressure provided by the law enforcement agencies, abetted by those who viewed themselves as possible victims of crime, has resulted over the years in a watering down of the protections afforded by the Miranda rule. (See the note to the Miranda case.)

In New York v. Quarles (1984) the Court held the Miranda warnings unnecessary in cases in which the public safety was at stake. The police had cornered a suspected criminal in a supermarket at about 12:30 A.M., handcuffed him and frisked him and found an empty shoulder holster under his arm. They asked him where the gun was and he nodded in the direction of some empty cartons and said, "The gun is over there." The police retrieved the gun and then read the defendant his Miranda rights. He waived right to counsel, answered the questions asked, and was convicted with the use of the statements given both before and after the Miranda warnings were given.

In holding valid the use of the statements the Court announced and justified what it called a "public safety"

exception to the Miranda rule. "In such a situation, if the police are required to recite the familiar Miranda warnings before asking the whereabouts of the gun, suspects in Quarles' position might well be deterred from responding. Procedural safeguards that deter a suspect from responding were deemed acceptable in Miranda in order to protect the Fifth Amendment privilege; when the primary social cost of those added protections is the possibility of fewer convictions, the Miranda majority was willing to bear that cost. Here, had Miranda warnings deterred Quarles from responding . . . the cost would have been something more than merely the failure to obtain evidence. . . . Officer Kraft needed an answer to his question not simply to make his case against Quarles but to ensure that additional danger to the public did not result from the concealment of the gun in a public area. We conclude that the need for answers to questions in a situation posing a threat to the public safety outweighs the need for the prophylactic rule protecting the Fifth Amendment's privilege against self-incrimination."

In Oregon v. Elstad (1985) the Court refused to hold that a confession given without Miranda warnings made invalid later confessions made after Miranda warnings. When an 18-year old boy was asked by police about his involvement in a burglary and admitted his involvement, the Court rejected his contention that this made inadmissible later statements made after Miranda warnings. "Respondent's contention that his confession was tainted by the earlier failure of the police to provide Miranda warnings and must be excluded as 'fruit of the poisonous tree' assumes the existence of a constitutional violation."

A rigid, technical approach to the Miranda rule is another way in which the purpose of the rule to provide legal help for a defendant can be defeated. There is no better illustration of this than the case of Moran v. Burbine (1986). Burbine had been picked up by the Cranston, Rhode Island, police for breaking and entering, and while he was in their custody they learned that he might be implicated in a recent murder in Providence. The Providence police immediately sent over three men to question him. About two hours later Burbine's sister, not knowing anything about the murder charge, obtained a public defender to represent him in the breaking and entering inquiry. The public defender phoned the Cranston police and notified them that she would represent Burbine if the police intended to put him in a lineup or question him. The police informed her that he would not be questioned until the next day. Burbine was not notified that his sister had obtained counsel or the substance of the phone conversation.

Less than an hour later the police began a series of interrogations, following properly administered Miranda warnings, which ultimately produced three signed confessions admitting the murder. The trial court ruled that the constitutional right to request a lawyer was personal to the defendant and could not be exercised by the lawyer. Since Burbine had never requested a lawyer, the phone call was irrelevant.

Justice O'Connor, joined by Justices Burger, White, Blackmun, Powell and Rehnquist, upheld Burbine's conviction. They concluded that whatever the motives or conduct of the police, the freely signed confessions following valid Miranda warnings made the conviction constitutional. "Events occurring outside of the presence of the suspect and entirely unknown to him surely can have no bearing on the capacity to comprehend and knowingly relinquish a constitutional right. Under the analysis of the Court of Appeals, the same defendant, armed with the same information and confronted with precisely the same police conduct, would have knowingly waived his Miranda rights had a lawyer not telephoned the police station to inquire about his status. Nothing in any of our waiver decisions or in our understanding of the essential components of a valid waiver requires so incongruous a result. No doubt the additional information would have been useful to respondent; perhaps even it might have affected his decision to confess. But we have never read the Constitution to require that the police supply a suspect with a flow of information to help him calibrate his self-interest in deciding whether to speak or stand by his rights."

Justices Stevens, Brennan and Marshall addressed the moral aspects of the case in their dissent. "The Court concludes that the police may deceive an attorney by giving her false information about whether her client will be questioned, and that the police may deceive a suspect by failing to inform him of his attorney's communications and efforts to represent him. For the majority, this conclusion, though 'distaste[ful],' is not even debatable. The deception of the attorney is irrelevant because the attorney has no right to information, accuracy, honesty, or fairness in the police response to her questions about her client. The deception of the client is acceptable, because, although the information would affect the client's assertion of his rights, the client's actions in ignorance of the availability of his attorney are voluntary, knowing, and intelligent; additionally, society's interest in apprehending, prosecuting, and punishing criminals outweighs the suspect's interest in information regarding his attorney's efforts to communicate with him. Finally, even mendacious police interference in the communications between a suspect and his lawyer does not violate any notion of fundamental fairness because it does not shock the conscience of the majority."

While the Court has shown no willingness to overrule Miranda, the invocation of technical legal procedures to attenuate its effectiveness continues. In the present case Justices O'Connor and Scalia would withdraw "the suppression remedy" now available to those seeking federal habeas corpus review when a state court has held their Miranda rights had not been violated. And in Arizona v. Fulminante (1991) the protection against the use of forced confessions was further attenuated by holding that such confessions might constitute a harmless error—an error the presence of which would not have changed the outcome of the trial. This issue has traditionally been exempt from "harmless error" review.

Chief Justice **Rehnquist** delivered the opinion of the Court, saying in part.

Late on May 16, 1982, respondent contacted a Chicago police officer he knew to report that he had seen the naked body of a dead woman lying on a Lake Michigan beach. Respondent denied any involvement in criminal activity. He then took several Chicago police officers to the beach, where the woman was crying for help. When she saw respondent, the woman exclaimed: "Why did you stab me? Why did you stab me?" Respondent told the officers that he had been with the woman earlier that night, but that they had been attacked by several men who abducted the woman in a van.

The next morning, after realizing that the crime had been committed in Indiana, the Chicago police turned the investigation over to the Hammond, Indiana, Police Department. Respondent repeated to the Hammond police officers his story that he had been attacked on the lakefront, and that the woman had been abducted by several men. After he filled out a battery complaint at a local police station, respondent agreed to go to the Hammond police headquarters for further questioning.

At about 11 a.m., the Hammond police questioned respondent. Before doing so, the police read to respondent a waiver form, entitled "Voluntary Appearance; Advice of Rights," and they asked him to sign it. The form provided: "Before we ask you any questions, you must understand your rights. You have the right to remain silent. Anything you say can be used against you in court. *You have a right to talk to a lawyer for advice before we ask you any questions, and to have him with you during questioning.* You have this right to the advice and presence of a lawyer even if you cannot afford to hire one. *We have no way of giving you a lawyer, but one will be appointed for you, if you wish, if and when you go to court.* If you wish to answer questions now without a lawyer present, you have the right to stop answering questions at any time. You also have the right to stop answering at any time until you've talked to a lawyer." (emphasis added).

Respondent signed the form and repeated his exculpatory explanation for his activities of the previous evening.

Respondent was then placed in the "lockup" at the Hammond police headquarters. Some 29 hours later, at about 4 p.m. on May 18, the police again interviewed respondent. Before this questioning, one of the officers read the following waiver form to respondent: "1. Before making this statement, I was advised that I have the right to remain silent and that anything I might say may or will be used against me in a court of law.

"1. That I have the right to consult with an attorney of my own choice before saying anything, and that an attorney may be present while I am making any statement or throughout the course of any conversation with any police officer if I so choose.

"2. That I can stop and request an attorney at any

time during the course of the taking of any statement or during the course of any such conversation.

"3. That in the course of any conversation I can refuse to answer any further questions and remain silent, thereby terminating the conversation.

"4. That if I do not hire an attorney, one will be provided for me."

Respondent read the form back to the officers and signed it. He proceeded to confess to stabbing the woman. The next morning, respondent led the officers to the Lake Michigan beach where they recovered the knife he had used in the stabbing and several items of clothing.

At trial, over respondent's objection, the state court admitted his confession, his first statement denying any involvement in the crime, the knife, and the clothing. The jury found respondent guilty of attempted murder, but acquitted him of rape. He was sentenced to 35 years' imprisonment. The conviction was upheld on appeal. . . .

In Miranda v. Arizona (1966), the Court established certain procedural safeguards that require police to advise criminal suspects of their rights under the Fifth and Fourteenth Amendments before commencing custodial interrogation. In now-familiar words, the Court said that the suspect must be told that "he has the right to remain silent, that anything he says can be used against him in a court of law, that he has the right to the presence of an attorney, and that if he cannot afford an attorney one will be appointed for him prior to any questioning if he so desires." The Court in Miranda "presumed that interrogation in certain custodial circumstances is inherently coercive and . . . that statements made under those circumstances are inadmissible unless the suspect is specifically warned of his Miranda rights and freely decides to forgo those rights." . . .

We have never insisted that Miranda warnings be given in the exact form described in that decision. In Miranda itself, the Court said that "the warnings required and the waiver necessary in accordance with our opinion today are, *in the absence of a fully effective equivalent*, prerequisites to the admissibility of any statement made by a defendant." . . . In California v. Prysock (1981) (per curiam), we stated that "the 'rigidity' of Miranda [does not] extend to the precise formulation of the warnings given a criminal defendant," and that "no talismanic incantation [is] required to satisfy its strictures." . . .

. . .The prophylactic Miranda warnings are "not themselves rights protected by the Constitution but [are] instead measures to insure that the right against compulsory self-incrimination [is] protected." . . . Reviewing courts therefore need not examine Miranda warnings as if construing a will or defining the terms of an easement. The inquiry is simply whether the warnings reasonably "convey to [a suspect] his rights as required by Miranda."

We think the initial warnings given to respondent touched all of the bases required by Miranda. The police told respondent that he had the right to remain silent, that anything he said could be used against him in court, that

he had the right to speak to an attorney before and during questioning, that he had "this right to the advice and presence of a lawyer even if [he could] not afford to hire one," and that he had the "right to stop answering at any time until [he] talked to a lawyer." As noted, the police also added that they could not provide respondent with a lawyer, but that one would be appointed "if and when you go to court." The Court of Appeals thought this "if and when you go to court" language suggested that "only those accused who can afford an attorney have the right to have one present before answering any questions," and "implie[d] that if the accused does not 'go to court,' i. e.[,] the government does not file charges, the accused is not entitled to [counsel] at all."

In our view, the Court of Appeals misapprehended the effect of the inclusion of "if and when you go to court" language in Miranda warnings. First, this instruction accurately described the procedure for the appointment of counsel in Indiana. Under Indiana law, counsel is appointed at the defendant's initial appearance in court, and formal charges must be filed at or before that hearing. We think it must be relatively commonplace for a suspect, after receiving Miranda warnings, to ask when he will obtain counsel. The "if and when you go to court" advice simply anticipates that question. Second, Miranda does not require that attorneys be producible on call, but only that the suspect be informed, as here, that he has the right to an attorney before and during questioning, and that an attorney would be appointed for him if he could not afford one. The Court in Miranda emphasized that it was not suggesting that "each police station must have a 'station house lawyer' present at all times to advise prisoners." If the police cannot provide appointed counsel, Miranda requires only that the police not question a suspect unless he waives his right to counsel. Here, respondent did just that. . . .

Justice **O'Connor,** with whom Justice **Scalia** joins, concurred on the ground that the suppression remedy should not be available to the defendant.

Justice **Marshall,** with whom Justice **Brennan** joins, and with whom Justice **Blackmun** and Justice **Stevens** join as to Part I, dissenting, said in part.

The majority holds today that a police warning advising a suspect that he is entitled to an appointed lawyer only "if and when he goes to court" satisfies the requirements of Miranda v. Arizona (1966). The majority reaches this result by seriously mischaracterizing that decision. Under Miranda, a police warning must *"clearly infor[m]"* a suspect taken into custody "that if he cannot afford an attorney one will be appointed for him prior to any questioning if he so desires." (emphasis added). A warning qualified by an "if and when you go to court" caveat does nothing of the kind; instead, it leads the suspect to believe that a lawyer will not be provided until some indeterminate time in the future after questioning. I refuse to acquiesce in the continuing debasement of this historic precedent . . . and therefore dissent. I also write to express my disagreement with Justice O'Connor's uninvited suggestion that the rationale of Stone v. Powell (1976), should be extended to bar federal habeas review of Miranda claims.

I.

In Miranda, the Court held that law enforcement officers who take a suspect into custody must inform the suspect of, among other things, his right to have counsel appointed to represent him before and during interrogation:

"In order fully to apprise a person interrogated of the extent of his rights . . . , it is necessary to warn him not only that he has the right to consult with an attorney, but also that if he is indigent a lawyer will be appointed to represent him. Without this additional warning, the admonition of the right to consult with counsel would often be understood as meaning only that he can consult with a lawyer if he has one or has the funds to obtain one. The warning of a right to counsel would be hollow if not couched in terms that would convey to the indigent—the person most often subjected to interrogation—the knowledge that he too has a right to have counsel present. As with the warning of the right to remain silent and of the general right to counsel, only by effective and express explanation to the indigent of this right can there be assurance that he was truly in a position to exercise it." Miranda mandated no specific verbal formulation that police must use, but the Court, speaking through Chief Justice Warren, emphasized repeatedly that the offer of appointed counsel must be "effective and express." . . . A clear and unequivocal offer to provide appointed counsel prior to questioning is, in short, an "absolute prerequisite to interrogation."

In concluding that the first warning given to respondent Eagan satisfies the dictates of Miranda, the majority makes a mockery of that decision. Eagan was initially advised that he had the right to the presence of counsel before and during questioning. But in the very next breath, the police informed Eagan that, if he could not afford a lawyer, one would be appointed to represent him only "if and when" he went to court. As the Court of Appeals found, Eagan could easily have concluded from the "if and when" caveat that only "those accused who can afford an attorney have the right to have one present before answering any questions; those who are not so fortunate must wait." . . . Eagan was, after all, never told that questioning would be delayed until a lawyer was appointed "if and when" Eagan did, in fact, go to court. Thus, the "if and when" caveat may well have had the effect of negating the initial promise that counsel could be present. At best, a suspect like Eagan "would not know . . . whether or not he had a right to the services of a lawyer." . . .

In lawyerlike fashion, The Chief Justice parses the initial warnings given Eagan and finds that the most plausible interpretation is that Eagan would not be questioned until a lawyer was appointed when he later appeared in court. What goes wholly overlooked in The Chief Justice's analysis is that the recipients of police warnings are often frightened suspects unlettered in the law, not lawyers or judges or others schooled in interpreting legal or semantic nuance. Such suspects can hardly be expected to interpret, in as facile a manner as The Chief Justice, "the pretzel-like warnings here—intertwining, contradictory, and ambiguous as they are." . . . The majority thus refuses to recognize that "the warning of a right to counsel would be hollow if not couched in terms that would convey to the indigent—the person most often subjected to interrogation—the knowledge that he too has the right to have counsel present."

Even if the typical suspect could draw the inference the majority does—that questioning will not commence until a lawyer is provided at a later court appearance—a warning qualified by an "if and when" caveat still fails to give a suspect any indication of when he will be taken to court. Upon hearing the warnings given in this case, a suspect would likely conclude that no lawyer would be provided until trial. In common parlance, "going to court" is synonymous with "going to trial." Furthermore, the negative implication of the caveat is that, if the suspect is never taken to court, he "is not entitled to an attorney at all." An unwitting suspect harboring uncertainty on this score is precisely the sort of person who may feel compelled to talk "voluntarily" to the police, without the presence of counsel, in an effort to extricate himself from his predicament . . . . That the warning given to Eagan "accurately described the procedure for the appointment of counsel in Indiana," does nothing to mitigate the possibility that he would feel coerced into talking to the police. Miranda, it is true, does not require the police to have a "station house lawyer" ready at all times to counsel suspects taken into custody. But if a suspect does not understand that a lawyer will be made available within a reasonable period of time after he has been taken into custody and advised of his rights, the suspect may decide to talk to the police for that reason alone. The threat of an indefinite deferral of interrogation, in a system like Indiana's, thus constitutes an effective means by which the police can pressure a suspect to speak without the presence of counsel. Sanctioning such police practices simply because the warnings given do not misrepresent state law does nothing more than let the state-law tail wag the federal constitutional dog.

The majority's misreading of Miranda—stating that police warnings need only "touch all of the bases required by Miranda," that Miranda warnings need only be "reasonably 'conveyed'" to a suspect, and that Miranda warnings are to be measured not point by point but "in their totality,"—is exacerbated by its interpretation of California v. Prysock (1981) (per curiam), a decision that squarely supports Eagan's claim in this case. The juvenile suspect in Prysock was initially told that he had the right to have a lawyer present before and during questioning. He then was told that he had the right to have his parents present as well. At this point the suspect was informed that a lawyer would be appointed to represent him at no cost if he could not afford one. The California Court of Appeal ruled these warnings insufficient because the suspect was not expressly told of his right to an appointed attorney before and during questioning. This Court reversed, finding that "nothing in the warnings given respondent suggested any limitation on the right to the presence of appointed counsel."

In reaching this result, the Prysock Court pointedly distinguished a series of lower court decisions that had found inadequate warnings in which "the reference to the right to appointed counsel was linked with some future point in time." . . . These lower courts had correctly found these warnings defective, the Prysock Court explained, because "in both instances the reference to appointed counsel was linked to a future point in time after police interrogation," and therefore did not clearly advise the suspect of his right to appointed counsel before such interrogation. The initial, conditional warning given Eagan suffers from precisely the same fatal defect. It is highly disingenuous for the majority to ignore this fact, characterizing Prysock as involving only the question whether a particular warning "apprise[d] the accused of his right to have an attorney present if he chose to answer questions."

II.

Not content with disemboweling Miranda directly, Justice O'Connor seeks to do so indirectly as well, urging that federal courts be barred from considering Miranda claims on habeas corpus review. In Stone v. Powell (1976) the Court held that a state prisoner may not seek federal habeas corpus relief on the ground that evidence was obtained in violation of his Fourth Amendment rights if the state courts had provided a full and fair opportunity for litigation of that claim. I joined Justice Brennan's dissenting opinion in that case, in which he warned that the majority's rationale "portends substantial evisceration of federal habeas corpus jurisdiction." Justice Powell, writing for the Stone majority, dismissed as "misdirected" the "hyperbole of the dissenting opinion," insisting that his opinion was based on considerations unique to the exclusionary rule. Today, however, Justice O'Connor seeks to extend Stone beyond the Fourth Amendment even though this issue was not raised by petitioner Duckworth below or in his petition for certiorari. Her concurring opinion evinces such a palpable distaste for collateral review of state-court judgments that it can only be viewed as a harbinger of future assaults on federal habeas corpus.

Stone was wrong when it was decided and it is wrong today. I have read and reread the federal habeas corpus statute, but I am unable to find any statement to the effect that certain federal claims are unworthy of collateral protection, or that certain federal claims are more worthy of collateral protection than others. Congress did not delineate "second class" claims when it created federal habeas jurisdiction. On the contrary, Congress

deemed all federal claims worthy of collateral protection when it extended the writ to any person "in custody pursuant to the judgment of a State Court . . . in violation of the Constitution or laws or treaties of the United States." At a time when plain language is supposed to count for something, Justice O'Connor's suggestion that the Court carve out an exception that has no rooting in the text of the habeas statute is difficult to justify. . . .

EXCLUSION IN ACTION: SEARCHES AND SEIZURES

TERRY v. OHIO

392 U. S. 1; 88 S. Ct. 1868; 20 L. Ed. 2d 889
(1968)

One of the areas in which the Supreme Court has had the most difficulty agreeing on a consistent philosophy is that of unreasonable searches and seizures. In part this is merely a reflection of the conflicting values in the country as a whole, but it is also the result of the methods by which the guarantee is enforced. Individual rights can be divided into two types. Those like free speech and religion have intrinsic value to the individual and are thought of as "substantive" rights, while those like the right to counsel and a jury trial are termed "procedural" because their purpose is to ensure that one will only be convicted of crime on the basis of true evidence fairly presented and impartially appraised. Appellate courts will normally enforce the substantive rights by ordering the government either to stop interfering with their exercise or to grant those which are being withheld. The procedural rights, on the other hand, are usually policed by ordering a new, untainted trial to take the place of the unfair one.

The guarantee against unreasonable searches and seizures, like the protection against compulsory self-incrimination, is in the anomalous position of being a substantive right, of value to the individual for its own sake, but enforceable by the courts only through the procedural technique of ordering excluded at a new trial the evidence gotten by its violation. The result in those cases where the tainted evidence was essential to conviction is the release of a person who has been found guilty on the basis of probative evidence fairly appraised, not because the person might be innocent, but because the police have violated his or her rights. In Justice Cardozo's famous phrase, "the criminal is to go free because the constable has blundered." People v. Defore, 242 N. Y. 13 (1926). While Supreme Court justices are not supposed to be influenced in constitutional judgments by the apparent guilt or innocence of a particular defendant, it is hard to escape the conclusion that a more consistent concern for the rights of the accused might emerge if the price were not the freeing of so many obviously guilty defendants.

The flexibility needed by the Court to provide reasoned arguments to go with its ever-changing views on searches and seizures has been provided by what has become known as the "talismanic" approach. Essentially this involves taking a constitutional theory, giving it a shorthand name, then using that name until it comes to have an entity of its own quite unrelated to the theory from which it sprang. When using the talisman the Court does not look back to the original theory, but interprets the talisman as though it were the true statement of the rule. This has the advantage of freeing it from the restraints of the rule without apparently abandoning the rule itself.

For example, the basic constitutional theory underlying the Fourth Amendment is that a magistrate, not a police officer, should decide when a person's privacy should yield to a search, and a search without a magistrate's warrant is "unreasonable" unless it can be justified by some "exigent circumstance" that makes getting a warrant impractical. Two such exceptions discussed in the cases below are the warrantless search of an automobile before it can escape and the warrantless search of a person by an arresting officer to protect both the officer and the evidence of the crime. However, since probable cause is necessary to get a search warrant, there must be probable cause to search without a warrant; and the arresting officer must be prepared to satisfy the court that the probable cause existed before the search was made.

The talismans that have evolved from these two exceptions to the warrant requirement are the "Carroll" and the "search incident" doctrines. Carroll v. United States (1925) involved stopping and searching without a warrant a bootlegger's car. The Supreme Court upheld the search, but emphasized that "where the securing of a warrant is reasonably practicable it must be used. . . . In cases where seizure is impossible except without a warrant, the seizing officer acts unlawfully and at his peril unless he can show the court probable cause." In its talismanic form these last requirements are dropped and the Carroll doctrine becomes the right to search a car without a warrant.

The common law authorized a police officer to conduct a limited search, or "frisk," at the time of a lawful arrest. The obvious justification was that an arrested person might then be carrying either a weapon with which the person could effect an escape, or evidence which he or she might find an opportunity to destroy. On this theory the extent of a search, both in time and space, is limited to what is necessary to protect the arresting officer or the evidence. But "search incident," once it had been given a name, took on a life of its own and in its talismanic form became an automatic right to search any arrested person. While the original theory had built-in limits stemming from the need that gave rise to it, the talismanic form knew no limits at all.

In the past half-century the Supreme Court has wandered back and forth between the theory and the talisman like a restless ghost. In Agnello v. United States (1925) it said that a search incident could extend "to the place where the arrest is made," but held it could not extend to another house several blocks away, and in Harris v. United States (1947) it upheld the search of Harris' four-room apartment because it was "under his immediate control." A year later, in Trupiano v. United States (1948), the talismanic approach was abandoned. Revenue agents had watched an illegal still being constructed and put into operation for a period of several weeks, during which they could have obtained both search and arrest warrants. When they finally closed in, one man was engaged in running the still and the Court sustained his arrest. But returning to the basic theory, it held that the "fortuitous circumstance" that he was in the building rather than out in the yard did not justify seizing the still without a warrant as incident to lawful arrest, since there had been plenty of time to get one. In McDonald v. United States (1948), after a two-month surveillance of McDonald in connection with a numbers racket investigation, the police broke into McDonald's room, arrested him, and seized an adding machine and other lottery paraphernalia. Without discussing the question of lawful arrest, the Court held the search unreasonable. "Where, as here, officers are not responding to an emergency, there must be compelling reasons to justify the absence of a search warrant. A search without a warrant demands exceptional circumstances. . . ."

Two years later in United States v. Rabinowitz (1950) the Court abruptly overruled Trupiano and held valid a widespread search of the defendant's property on the strength of his lawful arrest alone. Noting that the Constitution required only that a search be reasonable, not that it be made with a warrant if practicable, the Court found that, considering all the circumstances, this search was reasonable. The impact of this holding was to make possible a much broader search in conjunction with lawful arrest than could be made under a search warrant—as long as the arrest took place on the premises to be searched—since there were no limits as in the case of search warrants, as to "places to be searched" or "things to be seized." This was so much easier that in some communities the traditional search warrant became virtually extinct.

After nearly twenty years of this approach the Supreme Court overruled Harris and Rabinowitz and returned to the restrictive doctrines of Trupiano. Although in Chimel v. California (1969), the police had, as incident to arrest, searched an entire house including a garage and workshop, the Court declined to draw distinguishing lines between this search and that of the single room involved in Rabinowitz or the four rooms in Harris. "The only reasoned distinction is one between a search of the person arrested and the area within his reach on the one hand, and more extensive searches on the other." Furthermore, the theory justifying the search incident to arrest, the Court explained, itself marks its proper extent. "When an arrest is made, it is reasonable for the arresting officer to search the person arrested in order to remove any weapons that the latter might seek to use in order to resist arrest or effect his escape. Otherwise, the officer's safety might well be endangered, and the arrest itself frustrated. In addition, it is entirely reasonable for the arresting officer to search and seize any evidence on the arrestee's person in order to prevent its concealment or destruction. And the area into which an arrestee might reach in order to grab a weapon or evidentiary items must, of course, be governed by a like rule. A gun on a table or in a drawer in front of one who is arrested can be as dangerous to the arresting officer as one concealed in the clothing of the person arrested. There is ample justification, therefore, for a search of the arrestee's person and the area "within his immediate control"—construing that phrase to mean the area from within which he might gain possession of a weapon or destructible evidence.

"There is no comparable justification, however, for routinely searching rooms other than that in which an arrest occurs—or, for that matter, for searching through all the desk drawers or other closed or concealed areas in that room itself. Such searches, in the absence of well-recognized exceptions, may be made only under the authority of a search warrant. The 'adherence to judicial processes' mandated by the Fourth Amendment requires no less."

Any idea that the Court had abandoned the talismanic approach to the search incident doctrine was destined to be short-lived. While it had been rejected in 1971 in Coolidge v. New Hampshire, by 1974 it was back in full force in United States v. Edwards. There the defendant had been arrested for burglarizing a United States post office by jimmying a window—an operation which had chipped the paint on the window sill. The next day the police came to his cell, gave him new clothes, and without a warrant took his clothes and searched them for evidence of paint chips (which they found). In upholding the validity of the search, the Court, dividing five to four, argued that the mere fact of a full "custodial" arrest justified a complete warrantless search of his clothing, and since they could have searched him that night, it was not unreasonable to wait until the next morning when substitute clothes could be made available. Referring with approval to a case decided two years prior to Chimel, the Court noted that "it was no answer [in that case] to say that the police could have obtained a search warrant, for the Court held the test to be not whether it was reasonable to procure a search warrant, but whether the search itself was reasonable, which it was." Four dissenting justices pointed out that this language had been expressly rejected in Chimel and that, in view of the time-lapse, "the considerations that typically justify a warrantless search incident to a lawful arrest were wholly absent here . . . The police had ample time to seek a warrant, and no exigent circumstances were present to excuse their failure to do so."

The persistent attractiveness of the talismanic approach is exemplified by New York v. Belton (1981). There four men were stopped for speeding and when the police smelled burned marijuana in the car they ordered them out of the car, arrested them for possession and separated them from one another along the Thruway. They then searched the car and found heroin in the pocket of a jacket left on the back seat. The Court converted the Chimel doctrine into a "workable rule" by holding that "when a policeman has made a lawful custodial arrest of the occupant of an automobile, he may, as a contemporaneous incident of that arrest, search the passenger compartment of that automobile." He may, "also examine the contents of any containers found within the passenger compartment, for if the passenger compartment is within reach of the arrestee, so also will containers in it be within his reach."

The right of the police to arrest a person, like any other "seizure," has to be made on probable cause. If the arrest is to be made by warrant the magistrate who is to issue it must be told the facts so he can decide if there is probable cause. This does not necessarily mean sufficient evidence to obtain a conviction. It is enough that it reflect the "practical considerations of everyday life on which reasonable and prudent men, not legal technicians, act"; see Brinegar v. United States (1949). Where a police officer actually sees a felony being committed, or where the officer knows a felony has been committed and has probable cause to believe the suspect committed it, the officer may arrest the person without a warrant. These situations, however, involve the actual commission of a felony and it is this that is involved when the search incident doctrine speaks of a search incident to a "valid arrest." The policeman in the case below was not witnessing the commission of a crime, nor even overt preparations for the commission of a crime. There was nothing he could have taken to a magistrate to obtain either a search or arrest warrant based upon probable cause.

The Court, in holding valid the "frisk" in this case, opened up an entirely new dimension to the law of search and seizure. Never before had there been a valid way in which an officer could stop persons against their will and conduct a quick, superficial check to see if they passed some elementary test. Thus in United States v. Brignoni-Ponce (1975) the Court applied Terry in upholding the brief stop of a car near the Mexican border to check the citizenship of its occupants, while in United States v. Place (1983) it made clear that a ninety-minute detention at an airport while a suspect's luggage was subjected to a "sniff" test by narcotic-hunting dogs was well beyond the limits in both time and personal inconvenience permitted by Terry.

In United States v. Robinson (1973) the police stopped Robinson with probable cause to believe he was driving a car after the revocation of his license. He was *placed under arrest and given a full-scale search which turned up a crumpled cigarette package containing capsules of heroin, for whose possession he was later convicted. The Court rejected the claim that since Robinson was being stopped for a license violation, and no search, however thorough, would turn up further evidence on that score, that the police should be limited to a Terry-type search which would determine whether or not Robinson was armed. The search incident to arrest could be a full-scale search, whatever the charge.*

Perhaps the most complex set of facts involving the sufficiency of "reasonable suspicion" to search without a warrant arose in United States v. Sokolow (1989). Andrew Sokolow (together with a Janet Norian) flew from Honolulu to Miami and back, and upon his return was stopped by Drug Enforcement Administration agents. The agents found 1,063 grams of cocaine in his carry-on luggage.

Evidence leading to the decision to stop him included the fact that prior to departing Hawaii he paid $2,100 for two round-trip tickets from a roll of $20 bills containing nearly twice that amount; he travelled under a name that did not match his telephone listing; that he flew to Miami, a "source city" for illicit drugs, and returned within 48 hours, despite the fact the flight took 20 hours each way. In addition he appeared nervous, wore a black jumpsuit and gold jewelry, appeared about 25 years old and checked none of his luggage. Some of these characteristics matched a "drug courier profile" used by DEA agents to identify possible smugglers. In a seven-to-two decision the Court upheld the search. "Any one of these factors is not by itself proof of any illegal conduct and is quite consistent with innocent travel. But we think taken together they amount to reasonable suspicion." Justice Marshall and Brennan dissented, emphasizing that the Fourth Amendment was designed to protect innocent persons from overbearing or harassing police conduct carried out solely on the basis of imprecise stereotypes of what criminals look like, or on the basis of irrelevant personal characteristics such as race. They condemned the use of "profiles" by the DEA on the ground that they "can only dull the officer's ability and determination to make sensitive and fact-specific inferences 'in light of his experience,' ... a risk enhanced by the profile's 'chameleon-like way of adapting to any particular set of observations.' "

Mr. Chief Justice **Warren** delivered the opinion of the Court, saying in part:

This case presents serious questions concerning the role of the Fourth Amendment in the confrontation on the street between the citizen and the policeman investigating suspicious circumstances.

Petitioner Terry was convicted of carrying a concealed weapon and sentenced to the statutorily prescribed term of one to three years in the penitentiary. Following the denial of a pretrial motion to suppress, the prosecution introduced in evidence two revolvers and a number of bullets seized from Terry and a co-defendant, Richard Chilton, by Cleveland Police Detective Martin McFadden. At the hearing on the motion to suppress this evidence, Officer McFadden testified that while he was patrolling in plain clothes in downtown Cleveland at approximately 2:30 in the afternoon of October 31, 1963, his attention was attracted by two men, Chilton and Terry, standing on the corner of Huron Road and Euclid Avenue. He had never seen the two men before, and he was unable to say precisely what first drew his eye to them. However, he testified that he had been a policeman for 39 years and a detective for 35 and that he had been assigned to patrol this vicinity of downtown Cleveland for shoplifters and pickpockets for 30 years. He explained that he had developed routine habits of observation over the years and that he would "stand and watch people or walk and watch people at many intervals of the day." He added: "Now, in this case when I looked over they didn't look right to me at the time."

His interest aroused, Officer McFadden took up a post of observation in the entrance to a store 300 to 400 feet away from the two men. "I got more purpose to watch them when I seen their movements," he testified. He saw one of the men leave the other one and walk southwest on Huron Road, past some stores. The man paused for a moment and looked in a store window, then walked on a short distance, turned around and walked back toward the corner, pausing once again to look in the same store window. He rejoined his companion at the corner, and the two conferred briefly. Then the second man went through the same series of motions, strolling down Huron Road, looking in the same window, walking on a short distance, turning back, peering in the store window again, and returning to confer with the first man at the corner. The two men repeated this ritual alternately between five and six times apiece—in all, roughly a dozen trips. At one point, while the two were standing together on the corner, a third man approached them and engaged them briefly in conversation. This man then left the two others and walked west on Euclid Avenue. Chilton and Terry resumed their measured pacing, peering, and conferring. After this had gone on for 10 to 12 minutes, the two men walked off together, heading west on Euclid Avenue, following the path taken earlier by the third man.

By this time Officer McFadden had become thoroughly suspicious. He testified that after observing their elaborately casual and oft-repeated reconnaissance of the store window on Huron Road, he suspected the two men of "casing a job, a stick-up," and that he considered it his duty as a police officer to investigate further. He added that he feared "they may have a gun." Thus, Officer McFadden followed Chilton and Terry and saw them stop in front of Zucker's store to talk to the same man who had conferred with them earlier on the street corner. Deciding that the situation was ripe for direct action, Officer McFadden approached the three men, identified himself as a police officer and asked for their names. At this point his knowledge was confined to what he had observed. He was not acquainted with any of the three men by name or by sight, and he had received no information concerning them from any other source. When the men "mumbled something" in response to his inquiries, Officer McFadden grabbed petitioner Terry, spun him around so that they were facing the other two, with Terry between McFadden and the others, and patted down the outside of his clothing. In the left breast pocket of Terry's overcoat Officer McFadden felt a pistol. He reached inside the overcoat pocket, but was unable to remove the gun. At this point, keeping Terry between himself and the others, the officer ordered all three men to enter Zucker's store. As they went in, he removed Terry's overcoat completely, retrieved a .38 caliber revolver from the pocket and ordered all three men to face the wall with their hands raised. Officer McFadden proceeded to pat down the outer clothing of Chilton and the third man, Katz. He discovered another revolver in the outer pocket of Chilton's overcoat, but no weapons were found on Katz. The officer testified that he only patted the men down to see whether they had weapons, and that he did not put his hands beneath the outer garments of either Terry or Chilton until he felt their guns. So far as appears from the record, he never placed his hands beneath Katz's outer garments. Officer McFadden seized Chilton's gun, asked the proprietor of the store to call a police wagon, and took all three men to the station, where Chilton and Terry were formally charged with carrying concealed weapons.

On the motion to suppress the guns the prosecution took the position that they had been seized following a search incident to a lawful arrest. The trial court rejected this theory, stating that it "would be stretching the facts beyond reasonable comprehension" to find that Officer McFadden had had probable cause to arrest the men before he patted them down for weapons. However, the court denied the defendant's motion on the ground that Officer McFadden, on the basis of his experience, "had reasonable cause to believe . . . that the defendants were conducting themselves suspiciously, and some interrogation should be made of their action." Purely for his own protection, the court held, the officer had the right to pat down the outer clothing of these men, whom he had reasonable cause to believe might be armed. The court distinguished between an investigatory "stop" and an arrest, and between a "frisk" of the outer clothing for weapons and a full-blown search for evidence of crime. The frisk, it held, was essential to the proper performance of the officer's investigatory duties, for without it "the answer to the police officer may be a bullet, and a loaded pistol discovered during the frisk is admissible."

After the court denied their motion to suppress, Chilton and Terry waived jury trial and pleaded not guilty. The court adjudged them guilty. . . . We granted certiorari (1967) to determine whether the admission of the revolvers in evidence violated petitioner's rights under the Fourth Amendment, made applicable to the States by the Fourteenth. Mapp v. Ohio (1961). We affirm the conviction. . . .

II.

Our first task is to establish at what point in this encounter the Fourth Amendment becomes relevant. That is, we must decide whether and when Officer McFadden "seized" Terry and whether and when he conducted a "search." There is some suggestion in the use of such terms as "stop" and "frisk" that such police conduct is outside the purview of the Fourth Amendment because neither action rises to the level of a "search" or "seizure" within the meaning of the Constitution. We emphatically reject this notion. It is quite plain that the Fourth Amendment governs "seizures" of the person which do not eventuate in a trip to the station house and prosecution for crime—"arrests" in traditional terminology. It must be recognized that whenever a police officer accosts an individual and restrains his freedom to walk away, he has "seized" that person. And it is nothing less than sheer torture of the English language to suggest that a careful exploration of the outer surfaces of a person's clothing all over his or her body in an attempt to find weapons is not a "search." Moreover, it is simply fantastic to urge that such a procedure performed in public by a policeman while the citizen stands helpless, perhaps facing a wall with his hands raised, is a "petty indignity." It is a serious intrusion upon the sanctity of the person, which may inflict great indignity and arouse strong resentment, and it is not to be undertaken lightly.

The danger in the logic which proceeds upon distinctions between a "stop" and an "arrest," or "seizure" of the person, and between a "frisk" and a "search" is twofold. It seeks to isolate from constitutional scrutiny the initial stages of the contact between the policeman and the citizen. And by suggesting a rigid all-or-nothing model of justification and regulation under the Amendment, it obscures the utility of limitations upon the scope, as well as the initiation, of police action as a means of constitutional regulation. This Court has held in the past that a search which is reasonable at its inception may violate the Fourth Amendment by virtue of its intolerable intensity and scope. . . . The scope of the search must be "strictly tied to and justified by" the circumstances which rendered its initiation permissible. Warden v. Hayden (1967) (Mr. Justice Fortas, concurring). . . .

The distinctions of classical "stop-and-frisk" theory thus serve to divert attention from the central inquiry under the Fourth Amendment—the reasonableness in all the circumstances of the particular governmental invasion of a citizen's personal security. "Search" and "seizure" are not talismans. We therefore reject the notions that the Fourth Amendment does not come into play at all as a limitation upon police conduct if the officers stop short of something called "technical arrest" or a "full-blown search."

In this case there can be no question, then, that Officer McFadden "seized" petitioner and subjected him to a "search" when he took hold of him and patted down the outer surfaces of his clothing. We must decide whether at that point it was reasonable for Officer McFadden to have interfered with petitioner's personal security as he did.* And in determining whether the seizure and search were "unreasonable" our inquiry is a dual one—whether the officer's action was justified at its inception, and whether it was reasonably related in scope to the circumstances which justified the interference in the first place.

III.

If this case involved police conduct subject to the Warrant Clause of the Fourth Amendment, we would have to ascertain whether "probable cause" existed to justify the search and seizure which took place. However, that is not the case. We do not retreat from our holdings that the police must, whenever practicable, obtain advance judicial approval of searches and seizures through the warrant procedure, see, e. g., Katz v. United States (1967); Beck v. Ohio (1964); Chapman v. United States (1961), or that in most instances failure to comply with the warrant requirement can only be excused by exigent circumstances, see, e. g., Warden v. Hayden (1967) (hot pursuit); cf. Preston v. United States (1964). But we deal here with an entire rubric of police conduct—necessarily swift action predicated upon the on-the-spot observations of the officer on the beat—which historically has not been, and as a practical matter could not be, subjected to the warrant procedure. Instead, the conduct involved in this case must be tested by the Fourth Amendment's general proscription against unreasonable searches and seizures.

Nonetheless, the notions which underlie both the warrant procedure and the requirement of probable cause remain fully relevant in this context. In order to assess the reasonableness of Officer McFadden's conduct as a general proposition, it is necessary "first to focus upon the governmental interest which allegedly justifies official intrusion upon the constitutionally protected interests of the private citizen," for there is "no ready test for determining reasonableness other than by balancing the need to search [or seize] against the invasion which the search [or seizure] entails." Camara v. Municipal Court (1967). And in justifying the particular intrusion the police officer must be able to point to specific and articulate facts which, taken together with rational inferences from those facts reasonably warrant that intrusion. . . .

Applying these principles to this case, we consider first the nature and extent of the governmental interests involved. One general interest is of course that of effective crime prevention and detection; it is this interest which underlies the recognition that a police officer may in appropriate circumstances and in an appropriate manner approach a person for purposes of investigating possibly criminal behavior even though there is no probable cause to make an arrest. It was this legitimate investigative function Officer McFadden was discharging when he decided to approach petitioner and his companions. He had observed Terry, Chilton, and Katz go through a series of acts, each of them perhaps innocent in itself, but which taken together warranted further investigation . . .

The crux of this case, however, is not the propriety of Officer McFadden's taking steps to investigate petitioner's suspicious behavior, but rather, whether there was justification for McFadden's invasion of Terry's personal security by searching him for weapons in the course of that investigation. . . .

Petitioner does not argue that a police officer should refrain from making any investigation of suspicious circumstances until such time as he has probable cause to make an arrest; nor does he deny that police officers in properly discharging their investigative function may find themselves confronting persons who might well be armed and dangerous. Moreover, he does not say that an officer is always unjustified in searching a suspect to discover weapons. Rather, he says it is unreasonable for the policeman to take that step until such time as the situation evolves to a point where there is probable cause to make an arrest. When that point has been reached, petitioner would concede the officer's right to conduct a search of the suspect for weapons, fruits or instrumentalities of the crime, or "mere" evidence, incident to the arrest.

There are two weaknesses in this line of reasoning, however. First, it fails to take account of traditional limitations upon the scope of searches, and thus recognizes no distinction in purpose, character, and extent between a search incident to an arrest and a limited search for weapons. The former, although justified in part by the acknowledged necessity to protect the arresting officer from assault with a concealed weapon . . . , is also justified on other grounds and can therefore involve a relatively extensive exploration of the person. A search for weapons in the absence of probable cause to arrest, however, must, like any other search, be strictly circumscribed by the exigencies which justify its initiation. . . . Thus it must be limited to that which is necessary for the discovery of weapons which might be used to harm the officer or others nearby, and may realistically be characterized as something less than a "full" search, even though it remains a serious intrusion.

A second, and related, objection to petitioner's argument is that it assumes that the law of arrest has al-

---

*We thus decide nothing today concerning the constitutional propriety of an investigative "seizure" upon less than probable cause for purposes of "detention" and/or interrogation. Obviously, not all personal intercourse between policemen and citizens involves "seizures" of persons. Only when the officer, by means of physical force or show of authority, has in some way restrained the liberty of a citizen may we conclude that a "seizure" has occurred. We cannot tell with any certainty upon this record whether any such "seizure" took place here prior to Officer McFadden's initiation of physical contact for purposes of searching Terry for weapons, and we thus may assume that up to that point no intrusion upon constitutionally protected rights had occurred.

ready worked out the balance between the particular interests involved here—the neutralization of danger to the policeman in the investigative circumstance and the sanctity of the individual. But this is not so. An arrest is a wholly different kind of intrusion upon individual freedom from a limited search for weapons, and the interests each is designed to serve are likewise quite different. An arrest is the initial stage of a criminal prosecution. It is intended to vindicate society's interest in having its laws obeyed, and it is inevitably accompanied by future interference with the individual's freedom of movement, whether or not trial or conviction ultimately follows. The protective search for weapons, on the other hand, constitutes a brief, though far from inconsiderable, intrusion upon the sanctity of the person. It does not follow that because an officer may lawfully arrest a person only when he is apprised of facts sufficient to warrant a belief that the person has committed or is committing a crime, the officer is equally unjustified, absent that kind of evidence, in making any intrusions short of an arrest. Moreover, a perfectly reasonable apprehension of danger may arise long before the officer is possessed of adequate information to justify taking a person into custody for the purpose of prosecuting him for a crime. Petitioner's reliance on cases which have worked out standards of reasonableness with regard to "seizures" constituting arrests and searches incident thereto is thus misplaced. It assumes that the interests sought to be vindicated and the invasions of personal security may be equated in the two cases, and thereby ignores a vital aspect of the analysis of the reasonableness of particular types of conduct under the Fourth Amendment. . . .

Our evaluation of the proper balance that has to be struck in this type of case leads us to conclude that there must be a narrowly drawn authority to permit a reasonable search for weapons for the protection of the police officer, where he has reason to believe that he is dealing with an armed and dangerous individual, regardless of whether he has probable cause to arrest the individual for a crime. The officer need not be absolutely certain that the individual is armed; the issue is whether a reasonably prudent man in the circumstances would be warranted in the belief that his safety or that of others was in danger. . . . And in determining whether the officer acted reasonably in such circumstances, due weight must be given, not to his inchoate and unparticularized suspicion or "hunch," but to the specific reasonable inferences which he is entitled to draw from the facts in light of his experience. . . .

IV.

We must now examine the conduct of Officer McFadden in this case to determine whether his search and seizure of petitioner were reasonable, both at their inception and as conducted. He had observed Terry, together with Chilton and another man, acting in a manner he took to be preface to a "stick-up." We think on the facts and circumstances Officer McFadden detailed before the trial judge a reasonably prudent man would have been warranted in believing petitioner was armed and thus presented a threat to the officer's safety while he was investigating his suspicious behavior. . . .

The scope of the search in this case presents no serious problem in light of these standards. Officer McFadden patted down the outer clothing of petitioner and his two companions. He did not place his hands in their pockets or under the outer surface of their garments until he had felt weapons, and then he merely reached for and removed the guns. He never did invade Katz's person beyond the outer surfaces of his clothes, since he discovered nothing in his pat down which might have been a weapon. Officer McFadden confined his search strictly to what was minimally necessary to learn whether the men were armed and to disarm them once he discovered the weapons. He did not conduct a general exploratory search for whatever evidence of criminal activity he might find.

V.

We conclude that the revolver seized from Terry was properly admitted in evidence against him. At the time he seized petitioner and searched him for weapons, Officer McFadden had reasonable grounds to believe that petitioner was armed and dangerous, and it was necessary for the protection of himself and others to take swift measures to discover the true facts and neutralize the threat of harm if it materialized. The policeman carefully restricted his search to what was appropriate to the discovery of the particular items which he sought. Each case of this sort will, of course, have to be decided on its own facts. We merely hold today that where a police officer observes unusual conduct which leads him reasonably to conclude in light of his experience that criminal activity may be afoot and that the persons with whom he is dealing may be armed and presently dangerous; where in the course of investigating this behavior he identifies himself as a policeman and makes reasonable inquiries; and where nothing in the initial stages of the encounter serves to dispel his reasonable fear for his own or others' safety, he is entitled for the protection of himself and others in the area to conduct a carefully limited search of the outer clothing of such persons in an attempt to discover weapons which might be used to assault him. Such a search is reasonable search under the Fourth Amendment, and any weapons seized may properly be introduced in evidence against the person from whom they were taken.

Affirmed.

Mr. Justice **Black** concurs in the judgment and the opinion except where the opinion quotes from and relies upon this Court's opinion in Katz v. United States and the concurring opinion in Warden v. Hayden.

Justices **Harlan** and **White** wrote concurring opinions.

Mr. Justice **Douglas,** dissenting, said in part:

I agree that petitioner was "seized" within the meaning of the Fourth Amendment. I also agree that frisking petitioner and his companions for guns was a "search." But it is a mystery how that "search" and that "seizure" can be constitutional by Fourth Amendment standards, unless there was "probable cause" to believe that (1) a crime had been committed or (2) a crime was in the process of being committed or (3) a crime was about to be committed.

The opinion of the Court disclaims the existence of "probable cause." If loitering were an issue and that was the offense charged, there would be "probable cause" shown. But the crime here is carrying concealed weapons; and there is no basis for concluding that the officer had "probable cause" for believing that crime was being committed. Had a warrant been sought, a magistrate would, therefore, have been unauthorized to issue one, for he can act only if there is a showing of "probable cause." We hold today that the police have greater authority to make a "seizure" and conduct a "search" than a judge has to authorize such action. We have said precisely the opposite over and over again.

KATZ v. UNITED STATES

389 U. S. 347; 88 S. Ct. 507, 19 L. Ed. 2d 576
(1967)

The common law set narrow limits to the things that could be seized under a search warrant. A warrant would issue only to seize smuggled goods, the fruits and instruments of crime, and contraband articles. The Court in the Boyd v. United States (1886) stressed this rule, explaining that only "stolen or forfeited goods or goods liable to duties and concealed to avoid the payment thereof" were subject to seizure because only there did the government have a property interest. "In the case of stolen goods, the owner . . . is entitled to their possession; and in the case of excisable or dutiable articles, the Government has an interest in them for the payment of duties thereon, and until such duties are paid has a right to keep them under observation, or to pursue and drag them from concealment. . . ."

This decision was reaffirmed in 1921 in Gouled v. United States. There an officer, "pretending to make a friendly call upon the defendant, gained admission to his office, and, in his absence, without warrant of any character, seized and carried away several documents . . . [one of which was] 'of evidential value only.' " . . . Later, certain papers and documents tending to show mail fraud were seized under a search warrant. The Court not only found that the fraudulent entrance violated the Fourth Amendment, but held that none of the seized documents could be admitted as evidence. "Although search warrants have . . . been used in many cases ever since the adoption of the Constitution, and although their use has been extended from time to time to meet new cases within the old rules, nevertheless it is clear that, at common law and as the result of the Boyd and Weeks [Weeks v. United States, 1914] Cases, they may not be used as a means of gaining access to a person's house or office and papers solely for the purpose of making search to secure evidence to be used against him in a criminal or penal proceeding, but that they may be resorted to only when a primary right to such search and seizure may be found in the interest which the public or the complainant may have in the property to be seized, or in the right to the possession of it, or when a valid exercise of the police power renders possession of the property by the accused unlawful, and provides that it may be taken. . . ."

In the years following the Gouled decision the Court paid lip-service to its holding in several dicta, but no further evidence was actually held inadmissible on the ground that it was "mere evidence." Federal statutes authorized search warrants for those limited kinds of evidence only, and in the lower courts there was a tendency to find nearly all things remotely connected with a crime to be "instruments," since the crime could not have been committed without them.

Finally, in Warden v. Hayden (1967), the pretense was abandoned and the Gouled case overruled. The Court pointed out that over the years it had "recognized that the principal object of the Fourth Amendment is the protection of privacy rather than property, and [had] increasingly discarded fictional and procedural barriers rest[ing] on property concepts." That being the case, the "mere evidence" rule served no useful purpose, since "the requirements of the Fourth Amendment can secure the same protection of privacy whether the search is for 'mere evidence' or for fruits, instrumentalities or contraband. There must, of course, be a nexus—automatically provided in the case of fruits, instrumentalities or contraband—between the item to be seized and criminal behavior. Thus in the case of 'mere evidence,' probable cause must be examined in terms of cause to believe that the evidence sought will aid in a particular apprehension or conviction. In so doing, consideration of police purposes will be required. . . . But no such problem is presented in this case. The clothes found in the washing machine matched the description of those worn by the robber and the police therefore could reasonably believe that the items would aid in the identification of the culprit."

While the protection against unreasonable searches and seizures has come to protect individual privacy, it was originally, as its wording suggests, a protection only against the physical invasion of persons or their houses and the seizure of tangible things belonging to them. What could be heard by the eavesdropper under the window or seen by peeping at the keyhole was not being seized, and the search of a defendant's open field which resulted in the finding of a whiskey bottle was held to be neither a search nor a seizure. See Hester v. United States (1924).

The protection of the Fourth Amendment had been

extended in *Ex parte Jackson* (1878) to sealed letters in the United States mails, and the Court in *Olmstead v. United States* (1928) faced for the first time the question whether such protection should be extended to other forms of communication, in this case the telephone. Olmstead was the ringleader of a gigantic conspiracy of rum-runners and bootleggers operating mainly from Seattle, involving two seagoing vessels and several coastwise craft, underground storage caches, and elaborate offices. The yearly income from the business was over two million dollars. Federal prohibition officers tapped the telephone wires in the basement of Olmstead's office building and the transcribed record was introduced in court to prove the conspiracy. The question was whether either the Fourth or Fifth Amendment forbade wiretapping.

The decision of the Court that neither amendment was violated rested first on the proposition that since Olmstead had not been compelled to talk, there was no room for a claim that he had been forced to incriminate himself unless he had been the victim of an unreasonable search or seizure in violation of the Fourth. That he had not been was evident from a number of facts. In the first place, the wire tap had not taken place on Olmstead's property—there had been no trespass. "The language of the Amendment can not be extended and expanded to include telephone wires reaching to the whole world from the defendant's house or office. The intervening wires are not part of his house or office, any more than are the highways along which they are stretched. . . ."

In the second place, Olmstead had not intended to limit his conversations to those in the room with him. "The reasonable view is that one who installs in his house a telephone instrument with connecting wires intends to project his voice to those quite outside, and that the wires beyond his house and messages while passing over them are not within the protection of the Fourth Amendment." And third, since the Fourth Amendment speaks only of "things" to be seized, it clearly was not intended to cover merely verbal material. "The Amendment does not forbid what was done here. There was no searching. There was no seizure. The evidence was secured by the use of the sense of hearing and that only."

In deciding that wiretapping did not violate the Fourth Amendment, the Court rejected the warning of four justices that electronic inventions would ultimately make physical search and seizure unnecessary and completely destroy privacy. Time has not blunted the argument of Justice Brandeis that the Fourth Amendment should keep pace with discoveries and inventions which have "made it possible for the Government by means far more effective than stretching upon the rack, to obtain disclosure in court of what is whispered in the closet."

After the decision in the Olmstead case several bills were introduced in Congress to forbid wiretapping by federal officers. None of these passed, but in the Federal Communications Act of 1934 Congress provided that "no person not being authorized by the sender shall intercept any communication and divulge or publish the existence, contents, substance . . . of such intercepted communication to any person." This act, applying to individuals and government agents alike, remained law until 1968 when Congress passed the Omnibus Crime Control and Safe Streets Act which set up rules by which state and federal law enforcement officials could tap telephone wires under court order and use the results in the prosecution of a wide variety of crimes.

When the Supreme Court decided in *Olmstead v. United States* (1928) that wire tapping did not constitute an unreasonable search and seizure in violation of the Fourth Amendment, it did so on three grounds. First, there was no physical trespass. Second, Olmstead had intended "to project his voice to those quite outside." And third, what had been seized from Olmstead was his spoken word. Nothing tangible had been taken that would make applicable the constitutional injunction requiring a warrant describing "things to be seized."

The last of these grounds was the first to go. In *Goldman v. United States* (1942) the Court held that eavesdropping by means of a detectophone, a sensitive device which could pick up conversations in an adjoining room, was not an unreasonable search and seizure; and in 1952 the rule was reaffirmed in *On Lee v. United States*, in which an undercover narcotics agent with a hidden pocket transmitter engaged a shopkeeper in conversation and transmitted damaging admissions to an agent in a car outside. In both these cases the Court relied on the absence of trespass to sustain the use of the evidence rather than upon the fact that nothing tangible was being seized. Finally, in *Silverman v. United States* (1961) the Court held void a search for intangibles where there was trespass. A "spike-mike" had been driven into a hot-air duct in a building wall so that police could overhear conversations within the building. While probably not amounting to trespass under local law, it was considered by the Court to be a "physical intrusion into a constitutionally protected area." The Court emphasized that physical trespass distinguished the case from Olmstead, but simply ignored Olmstead's limitation of the amendment to "things" that were tangible.

While breaking into a home or office, or an obvious physical intrusion however slight (like a spike-mike), could clearly be viewed as trespass, what was the status of the traditional undercover agent who posed as a member of the "gang" in order to gain evidence of crime? In 1921 the Court in *Gouled v. United States* had held unanimously that "whether entrance to the home or office of a person suspected of crime be obtained by a representative of . . . the government . . . by stealth or through social acquaintance, or in the guise of a business call, and whether the owner be present or not when he enters, any search and seizure subsequently and secretly made in his absence falls within the scope of the Fourth Amendment." Does this mean that planting an informer in a criminal conspiracy violates the Fourth Amendment right of the conspirators? In *Hoffa v. United States* (1966), the Court held that it did not. Partin, a local teamster official, acted as a paid informer to bring federal officials reports on Hoffa's efforts to bribe the jury in a federal trial in which Hoffa was involved. The

Court conceded that a hotel room can be an area protected by the Fourth Amendment, that the amendment can be violated by guile as well as by forceful entry, and that its protection is not limited to tangibles. But Hoffa had no protection in this instance because "what the Fourth Amendment protects is the security a man relies upon when he places himself or his property within a constitutionally protected area." In this case Hoffa "was not relying on the security of the hotel room; he was relying upon his misplaced confidence that Partin would not reveal his wrongdoing." A similar result was reached in Lewis v. United States (1966) where a narcotics pusher had invited a federal agent to his home and sold him narcotics, not knowing what he was. By converting his home into a "commercial center to which outsiders are invited for purposes of transacting unlawful business" the pusher forfeited its sanctity under the Fourth Amendment.

Mr. Justice **Stewart** delivered the opinion of the Court, saying in part:

The petitioner was convicted in the District Court for the Southern District of California under an eight-count indictment charging him with transmitting wagering information by telephone from Los Angeles to Miami and Boston, in violation of a federal statute. At the trial the Government was permitted, over the petitioner's objection, to introduce evidence of the petitioner's end of telephone conversations, overheard by FBI agents who had attached an electronic listening and recording device to the outside of the public telephone booth from which he had placed his calls. In affirming his conviction, the Court of Appeals rejected the contention that the recordings had been obtained in violation of the Fourth Amendment, because "[t]here was no physical entrance into the area occupied by [the petitioner]." We granted certiorari in order to consider the constitutional questions thus presented.

The petitioner has phrased those questions as follows:

"A. Whether a public telephone booth is a constitutionally protected area so that evidence obtained by attaching an electronic listening recording device to the top of such a booth is obtained in violation of the right to privacy of the user of the booth.

"B. Whether physical penetration of a constitutionally protected area is necessary before a search and seizure can be said to be violative of the Fourth Amendment to the United States Constitution."

We decline to adopt this formulation of the issues. In the first place, the correct solution of Fourth Amendment problems is not necessarily promoted by incantation of the phrase "constitutionally protected area." Secondly, the Fourth Amendment cannot be translated into a general constitutional "right to privacy." That Amendment protects individual privacy against certain kinds of governmental intrusion, but its protections go further, and often have nothing to do with privacy at all. Other provisions of the Constitution protect personal privacy from other forms of governmental invasion. But the protection of a person's *general* right to privacy—his right to be let alone by other people—is, like the protection of his property and of his life, left largely to the law of the individual states.

Because of the misleading way the issues have been formulated, the parties have attached great significance to the characterization of the telephone booth from which the petitioner placed his calls. The petitioner has strenuously argued that the booth was a "constitutionally protected area." The Government has maintained with equal vigor that it was not. But this effort to decide whether or not a given "area," viewed in the abstract, is "constitutionally protected" deflects attention from the problem presented by this case.* For the Fourth Amendment protects people, not places. What a person knowingly exposes to the public, even in his own home or office, is not a subject of Fourth Amendment protection. . . . But what he seeks to preserve as private, even in an area accessible to the public, may be constitutionally protected. See . . . Ex parte Jackson [1878].

The Government stresses the fact that the telephone booth from which the petitioner made his calls was constructed partly of glass, so that he was as visible after he entered it as he would have been if he had remained outside. But what he sought to exclude when he entered the booth was not the intruding eye—it was the uninvited ear. He did not shed his right to do so simply because he made his calls from a place where he might be seen. No less than an individual in a business office, in a friend's apartment, or in a taxicab, a person in a telephone booth may rely upon the protection of the Fourth Amendment. One who occupies it, shuts the door behind him, and pays the toll that permits him to place a call, is surely entitled to assume that the words he utters into the mouthpiece will not be broadcast to the world. To read the Constitution more narrowly is to ignore the vital role that the public telephone has come to play in private communication.

The Government contends, however, that the activities of its agents in this case should not be tested by Fourth Amendment requirements, for the surveillance technique they employed involved no physical penetration of the telephone booth from which the petitioner placed his calls. It is true that the absence of such penetration was at one time thought to foreclose further Fourth Amendment inquiry, Olmstead v. United States [1928]; Goldman v. United States [1942], for that Amendment was thought to limit only searches and seizures of tangible property. But "[t]he premise that property interests control the right of the Government to search and seize has been discredited." Warden v. Hayden [1967]. Thus, although a closely divided Court supposed in Olmstead that surveillance without any trespass

---

*It is true that this Court has occasionally described its conclusions in terms of "constitutionally protected areas," see, e.g., Silverman v. United States [1961]; Lopez v. United States [1963]; Berger v. New York [1967], but we have never suggested that this concept can serve as a talismanic solution to every Fourth Amendment problem.

and without the seizure of any material object fell out-side the ambit of the Constitution, we have since departed from the narrow view on which that decision rested. Indeed, we have expressly held that the Fourth Amendment governs not only the seizure of tangible items, but extends as well to the recording of oral statements, overheard without any "technical trespass under . . . local property law." Silverman v. United States [1961]. Once this much is acknowledged, and once it is recognized that the Fourth Amendment protects people—and not simply "areas"—against unreasonable searches and seizures, it becomes clear that the reach of that Amendment cannot turn upon the presence or absence of a physical intrusion into any given enclosure. We conclude that the underpinnings of Olmstead and Goldman have been so eroded by our subsequent decisions that the "trespass" doctrine there enunciated can no longer be regarded as controlling. The Government's activities in electronically listening to and recording the petitioner's words violated the privacy upon which he justifiably relied while using the telephone booth and thus constituted a "search and seizure" within the meaning of the Fourth Amendment. The fact that the electronic device employed to achieve that end did not happen to penetrate the wall of the booth can have no constitutional significance.

The question remaining for decision, then, is whether the search and seizure conducted in this case complied with constitutional standards. In that regard, the Government's position is that its agents acted in an entirely defensible manner: They did not begin their electronic surveillance until investigation of the petitioner's activities had established a strong probability that he was using the telephone in question to transmit gambling information to persons in other States, in violation of federal law. Moreover, the surveillance was limited, both in scope and in duration, to the specific purpose of establishing the contents of the petitioner's unlawful telephonic communications. The agents confined their surveillance to the brief periods during which he used the telephone booth, and they took great care to overhear only the conversations of the petitioner himself.

Accepting this account of the Government's actions as accurate, it is clear that this surveillance was so narrowly circumscribed that a duly authorized magistrate, properly notified of the need for such investigation, specifically informed of the basis on which it was to proceed, and clearly apprised of the precise intrusion it would entail, could constitutionally have authorized, with appropriate safeguards, the very limited search and seizure that the Government asserts in fact took place. . . .

The Government urges that, because its agents relied upon the decisions in Olmstead and Goldman, and because they did no more here than they might properly have done with prior judicial sanction, we should retroactively validate their conduct. That we cannot do. It is apparent that the agents in this case acted with restraint. Yet the inescapable fact is that this restraint was imposed by the agents themselves, not by a judicial officer. They were not required, before commencing the search, to pre-sent their estimate of probable cause for detached scrutiny by a neutral magistrate. They were not compelled, during the conduct of the search itself, to observe precise limits established in advance by a specific court order. Nor were they directed, after the search had been completed, to notify the authorizing magistrate in detail of all that had been seized. In the absence of such safeguards, this Court has never sustained a search upon the sole ground that officers reasonably expected to find evidence of a particular crime and voluntarily confined their activities to the least intrusive means consistent with that end. Searches conducted without warrants have been held unlawful "notwithstanding facts unquestionably showing probable cause," Agnello v. United States [1925], for the Constitution requires "that the deliberate, impartial judgment of a judicial officer . . . be interposed between the citizen and the police. . . ." Wong Sun v. United States [1963] . . . —subject only to a few specifically established and well-delineated exceptions.

It is difficult to imagine how many of those exceptions could ever apply to the sort of search and seizure involved in this case. Even electronic surveillance substantially contemporaneous with an individual's arrest could hardly be deemed an "incident" of that arrest. Nor could the use of electronic surveillance without prior authorization be justified on grounds of "hot pursuit." And, of course, the very nature of electronic surveillance precludes its use pursuant to the suspect's consent.

The Government does not question these basic principles. Rather, it urges the creation of a new exception to cover this case.* It argues that surveillance of a telephone booth should be exempted from the usual requirement of advance authorization by a magistrate upon a showing of probable cause. We cannot agree. Omission of such authorization "bypasses the safeguards provided by an objective predetermination of probable cause, and substitutes instead the far less reliable procedure of an after-the-event justification for the . . . search, too likely to be subtly influenced by the familiar shortcomings of hindsight judgment." . . .

And bypassing a neutral predetermination of the *scope* of a search leaves individuals secure from Fourth Amendment violations "only in the discretion of the police." . . .

These considerations do not vanish when the search in question is transferred from the setting of a home, an office, or a hotel room, to that of a telephone booth. Wherever a man may be, he is entitled to know that he will remain free from unreasonable searches and seizures. The government agents here ignore "the procedure of antecedent justification . . . that is central to the Fourth Amendment, a procedure that we hold to be a constitutional precondition of the kind of electronic surveillance involved in this case. Because the surveillance here failed to meet that condition, and because it led to

---

*Whether safeguards other than prior authorization by a magistrate would satisfy the Fourth Amendment in a situation involving the national security is a question not presented by this case.

the petitioner's conviction, the judgment must be reversed.

It is so ordered.

Mr. Justice **Marshall** took no part in the consideration or decision of this case.

Mr. Justice **Douglas,** with whom Mr. Justice **Brennan** joins, concurring, said in part:

While I join the opinion of the Court, I feel compelled to reply to the separate concurring opinion of my Brother White, which I view as a wholly unwarranted green light for the Executive Branch to resort to electronic eavesdropping without a warrant in cases which the Executive Branch itself labels "national security" matters.

Neither the President nor the Attorney General is a magistrate. In matters where they believe national security may be involved they are not detached, disinterested, and neutral as a court or magistrate must be. . . . They may even be the intended victims of subversive action. Since spies and saboteurs are as entitled to the protection of the Fourth Amendment as suspected gamblers like petitioner, I cannot agree that where spies and saboteurs are involved adequate protection of Fourth Amendment rights is assured when the President and Attorney General assume both the position of adversary-and-prosecutor and disinterested, neutral magistrate.

Mr. Justice **Harlan,** concurring, said in part:

I join the opinion of the Court, which I read to hold only (a) that an enclosed telephone booth is an area where, like a home, Weeks v. United States [1914], and unlike a field, Hester v. United States [1924], a person has a constitutionally protected reasonable expectation of privacy; (b) that electronic as well as physical intrusion into a place that is in this sense private may constitute a violation of the Fourth Amendment; and (c) that the invasion of a constitutionally protected area by federal authorities is, as the Court has long held, presumptively unreasonable in the absence of a warrant.

As the Court's opinion states, "The Fourth Amendment protects people, not places." The question, however, is what protection it affords to those people. Generally, as here, the answer to that question requires reference to a "place." . . . Thus a man's home is, for most purposes, a place where he expects privacy, but objects, activities, or statements that he exposes to the "plain view" of outsiders are not "protected" because no intention to keep them to himself has been exhibited. On the other hand, conversations in the open would not be protected against being overheard, for the expectation of privacy under the circumstances would be unreasonable. Hester v. United States. . . .

Mr. Justice **White,** concurring, said in part:

In joining the Court's opinion, I note the Court's acknowledgment that there are circumstances in which it is reasonable to search without a warrant. In this connection the Court points out that today's decision does not reach national security cases. Wiretapping to protect the security of the Nation has been authorized by successive Presidents. The present Administration would apparently save national security cases from restrictions against wiretapping. . . . We should not require the warrant procedure and the magistrate's judgment if the President of the United States or his chief legal officer, the Attorney General, has considered the requirements of national security and authorized electronic surveillance as reasonable.

Mr. Justice **Black,** dissenting, said in part:

If I could agree with the Court that eavesdropping carried on by electronic means (equivalent to wiretapping) constitutes a "search" or "seizure," I would be happy to join the Court's opinion. . . .

My basic objection is twofold: (1) I do not believe that the words of the Amendment will bear the meaning given them by today's decision, and (2) I do not believe that it is the proper role of this Court to rewrite the Amendment in order "to bring it into harmony with the times" and thus reach a result that many people believe to be desirable.

MICHIGAN STATE POLICE v. SITZ

496 U. S. 444; 110 S. Ct. 248; 110 L. Ed. 2d 412
(1990)

While the "search incident" exception to the warrant requirement is of ancient origin, the "Carroll" doctrine exempting automobiles from the requirement stems from the Court's decision in Carroll v. United States decided in 1925. Carroll, a known bootlegger, was recognized and stopped by federal prohibition agents without a warrant and his car searched. The agents had ample cause to believe Carroll would be carrying contraband and since there was no time in which to get a warrant the Supreme Court held the search valid. In reaching its decision it made clear that "where the securing of a warrant is reasonably practicable it must be used. . . . In cases where seizure is impossible except without a warrant, the seizing officer acts unlawfully and at his peril unless he can show the court probable cause."

Like the search incident doctrine, the Carroll doctrine has become a talisman or shorthand for the right to search an automobile without a warrant, and a number of justices have argued that it should be independent of whether or not there was time to get a warrant. The Court in Coolidge v. New Hampshire (1971) rejected the argument of the state that "the police may make a warrantless search of an automobile whenever they have probable cause to do so" and also Justice White's suggestion that "for Fourth Amendment purposes the differ-

ence between a moving and movable vehicle is tenuous at best." "The word 'automobile'," said the Court, "is not a talisman in whose presence the Fourth Amendment fades away and disappears."

The Carroll case left unanswered two problems that have since come before the Court. The first of these, the question of timing, was answered in *Chambers v. Maroney (1970)* in which the Court extended the Carroll doctrine to justify a search later in time than the arrest. There the police had been given a description of a car, its occupants, and the clothing they wore, seen near the scene of a nighttime holdup. Within an hour a car answering the description, and containing the described occupants and clothing was stopped. The occupants were arrested and the car driven to the police station where it was searched and incriminating evidence discovered.

The Court agreed unanimously that the evidence was properly admitted. Speaking for seven members of the Court, Justice White conceded that the "search incident" doctrine could not apply because the search was not made at the time and place of arrest. But while the right to search incident to lawful arrest expired when the car was moved, the right to search under the Carroll doctrine did not. In view of the facts, the police had probable cause to search the car for guns and loot before it escaped their jurisdiction. Since it was impractical to follow it around, either they had to search it on the spot without a warrant, or they had to seize it without a warrant and detain it until a search warrant could be obtained. Conceding that arguably the search was the greater infringement and should only be made with a warrant, the Court held that where there was probable cause to search, either course was reasonable under the Fourth Amendment.

Cardwell v. Lewis (1974) involved the warrantless seizure of the defendant's car from a public parking lot after he was in police custody. The car was impounded by the police and tire imprints and paint scrapings were taken to compare with information found at the scene of a murder. Justice Blackmun, writing for himself and Justices Burger, White and Rehnquist, argued that a search of the outside of the car was not really a breach of privacy and that in any event, cars were not entitled to as "stringent warrant requirements" as other places. Not only were they mobile, but "one has a lesser expectation of privacy in a motor vehicle because its function is transportation and it seldom serves as one's residence or as the repository of personal effects. A car has little capacity for escaping public scrutiny. It travels public thoroughfares where both its occupants and its contents are in plain view." Repeating the Court's statement in *Katz v. United States (1976)* that "what a person knowingly exposes to the public, even in his own home or office, is not a subject of Fourth Amendment protection," he added, "this is not to say that no part of the interior of an automobile has Fourth Amendment protection; the exercise of a desire to be mobile does not, of course, waive one's right to be free of unreasonable government intrusion. But insofar as Fourth Amendment protection

extends to a motor vehicle, it is the right to privacy that is the touchstone of our inquiry." Justice Powell concurred on the ground that such questions, if fairly litigated in the state courts, should not be subject to federal court review. Justices Stewart, Douglas, Brennan and Marshall dissented, pointing out that the Carroll doctrine did not apply since the car was immobilized, and while "the plurality opinion suggests that other 'exigent circumstances' might have excused the failure of the police to procure a warrant, . . . the opinion nowhere states what these mystical exigencies might have been, and counsel for the petitioner has not been so inventive as to suggest any."

The second question left unanswered by Carroll was the status of a sealed container found within an automobile which was itself subject to search without warrant. Since the very existence of such a container suggests the owner's desire for privacy and since the container can be immobilized until a search warrant can be obtained, what is the exigency that permits opening it without such a warrant? Encouraged by the language of the Cardwell case, the government in *United States v. Chadwick (1977)* argued that "the Fourth Amendment warrant clause protects only interests traditionally identified with the home." It had been tipped off that a suspicious-looking footlocker was arriving in Boston by rail, and a number of agents were on hand to witness its arrival. They watched while the owners claimed it and a specially trained police dog signaled secretly that it contained drugs. After it was loaded into the trunk of their car and before the engine was started, the agents arrested the defendants and took them and the footlocker to the federal building where, over an hour later, they opened and searched it without a warrant. It contained some 200 pounds of marijuana.

In a seven-to-two decision the Court held the search unconstitutional. It rejected the government's interpretation, noting that "a fundamental purpose of the Fourth Amendment is to safeguard individuals from unreasonable government invasions of legitimate privacy interests, and not simply those interests found inside the four walls of the home. . . . By placing personal effects inside a double-locked footlocker, respondents manifested an expectation that the contents would remain free from public examination. No less than one who locks the doors of his home against intruders, one who safeguards his personal possessions in this manner is due the protection of the Fourth Amendment Warrant Clause."

Nor was "luggage analogous to motor vehicles for Fourth Amendment purposes," as the government argued. While the Court reaffirmed the language in Cardwell that there was a diminished expectation of privacy surrounding an automobile, it pointed out that the same factors did not apply here. "Unlike an automobile, whose primary function is transportation, luggage is intended as a repository of personal effects. In sum, a person's expectations of privacy in personal luggage are substantially greater than in an automobile.

"Nor does the footlocker's mobility justify dispensing with the added protections of the Warrant

Clause. Once the federal agents had seized it at the railroad station and had safely transferred it to the Boston federal building under their exclusive control, there was not the slightest danger that the footlocker or its contents could have been removed before a valid search warrant could be obtained."

But if Chadwick had settled the status of formal luggage, what of things like paper bags, cigarette packages, plastic baggies, and the like that might contain drugs? In the years that followed the police and lower courts disagreed on the immunity of such items from search and it wasn't until 1982 in United States v. Ross that the Court finally answered the question. Following a tip by a reliable informant that Ross was selling narcotics out of the trunk of his car, Ross was identified by the District of Columbia police, ordered to pull his car over to the curb and get out. The police searched the car and found a bullet on the seat, a gun in the glove compartment, and a closed paper bag in the trunk which contained a number of glassine bags containing white powder. The car was driven to police headquarters where a further search turned up a zippered leather pouch containing $3,200 in cash. The powder in the bags turned out to be heroin. The district court denied a motion to suppress the evidence and Ross was convicted of possession with intent to distribute.

Stating that the the police "may conduct a search of the vehicle that is as thorough as a magistrate could authorize in a warrant 'particularly describing the place to be searched,'" the Court held the search valid. It pointed out that "an individual's expectation of privacy in a vehicle and its contents may not survive if probable cause is given to believe that the vehicle is transporting contraband. Certainly the privacy interests in a car's trunk or glove compartment may be no less than those in a movable container. An individual undoubtedly has a significant interest that the upholstery of his automobile will not be ripped or a hidden compartment within it opened. These interests must yield to the authority of a search, however, which—in light of Carroll—does not itself require the prior approval of a magistrate. The scope of a warrantless search based on probable cause is no narrower—and no broader—than the scope of a search authorized by a warrant supported by probable cause. Only the prior approval of the magistrate is waived; the search otherwise is as the magistrate could authorize.

The scope of a warrantless search of an automobile thus is not defined by the nature of the container in which the contraband is secreted. Rather, it is defined by the object of the search and the places in which there is probable cause to believe that it may be found."

The background of the present case lies in a series of cases arising out of the efforts of the federal government to prevent illegal immigrants from crossing the Mexican border into the United States. To ease the enforcement problem, Congress authorized the search without warrant of all vehicles "within a reasonable distance from any external boundary," and administrative regulations have interpreted this as "100 air miles," a distance which includes such cities as San Diego and El Paso.

In Almeida-Sanchez v. United States (1973), the Court held the Fourth Amendment violated by the stopping and searching of a vehicle 25 miles from the border without either a warrant or probable cause, but in United States v. Brignoni-Ponce (1975), the Court, while reaffirming Almeida-Sanchez, held that where the roving border patrol merely stopped a car to question its occupants for "usually no more than a minute" it needed only the kind of suspicion held adequate for the "pat down" in Terry v. Ohio (1968). As in Terry, the intrusion was "modest," and while in Terry the officers' need for self-protection justified a properly limited search, here it was "the importance of the governmental interest at stake, the minimal intrusion of a grief stop, and the absence of practical alternatives for policing the border . . . . Except at the border and its functional equivalents, officers on roving patrol may stop vehicles only if they are aware of specific articulable facts, that reasonably warrant suspicion that the vehicles contain aliens who may be illegally in the country."

While in United States v. Martinez-Fuerte (1976) the doctrine of Brignoni-Ponce was extended to cover a permanent routine border check stop, in United States v. Place (1983) the Court held void as unreasonably long a 90-minute detention at an airport while a suspect's luggage was subjected to a "sniff" test by narcotic-hunting dogs.

Rehnquist, C. J., delivered the opinion of the Court, saying in part:

This case poses the question whether a State's use of highway sobriety checkpoints violates the Fourth and Fourteenth Amendments to the United States Constitution. We hold that it does not and therefore reverse the contrary holding of the Court of Appeals of Michigan. . . .

Under the [established] guidelines, checkpoints would be set up at selected sites along state roads. All vehicles passing through a checkpoint would be stopped and their drivers briefly examined for signs of intoxication. In cases where a checkpoint officer detected signs of intoxication, the motorist would be directed to a location out of the traffic flow where an officer would check the motorist's driver's license and car registration and, if warranted, conduct further sobriety tests. Should the field tests and the officer's observations suggest that the driver was intoxicated, an arrest would be made. All other drivers would be permitted to resume their journey immediately.

The first—and to date the only—sobriety checkpoint operated under the program was conducted in Saginaw County with the assistance of the Saginaw County Sheriff's Department. During the hour-and-fifteen-minute duration of the checkpoint's operation, 126 vehicles passed through the checkpoint. The average delay for each vehicle was approximately 25 seconds. Two drivers were detained for field sobriety testing, and one of the two was arrested for driving under the influence of alcohol. A third driver who drove through without stopping was pulled over by an officer in an observation vehicle and arrested for driving under the influence.

On the day before the operation of the Saginaw County checkpoint, respondents filed a complaint in the Circuit Court of Wayne County seeking declaratory and injunctive relief from potential subjection to the checkpoints. . . .

To decide this case the trial court performed a balancing test derived from our opinion in Brown v. Texas (1979). As described by the Court of Appeals, the test involved "balancing the state's interest in preventing accidents caused by drunk drivers, the effectiveness of sobriety checkpoints in achieving that goal, and the level of intrusion on an individual's privacy caused by the checkpoints." The Court of Appeals agreed that "the Brown three-prong balancing test was the correct test to be used to determine the constitutionality of the sobriety checkpoint plan."

As characterized by the Court of Appeals, the trial court's findings with respect to the balancing factors were that the State has "a grave and legitimate" interest in curbing drunken driving; that sobriety checkpoint programs are generally "ineffective" and, therefore, do not significantly further that interest; and that the checkpoints' "subjective intrusion" on individual liberties is substantial. . . .

In this Court respondents seek to defend the judgment in their favor by insisting that the balancing test derived from Brown v. Texas was not the proper method of analysis. Respondents maintain that the analysis must proceed from a basis of probable cause or reasonable suspicion and rely for support on language from our decision last Term in Treasury Employees v. Von Raab (1989). We said in Von Raab: "Where a Fourth Amendment intrusion serves special governmental needs, beyond the normal need for law enforcement, it is necessary to balance the individual's privacy expectations against the Government's interests to determine whether it is impractical to require a warrant or some level of individualized suspicion in the particular context." Respondents argue that there must be a showing of some special governmental need "beyond the normal need" for criminal law enforcement before a balancing analysis is appropriate, and that petitioners have demonstrated no such special need.

But it is perfectly plain from a reading of Von Raab, which cited and discussed with approval our earlier decision in United States v. Martinez-Fuerte (1976), that it was in no way designed to repudiate our prior cases dealing with police stops of motorists on public highways. Martinez-Fuerte, which utilized a balancing analysis in approving highway checkpoints for detecting illegal aliens, and Brown v. Texas, are the relevant authorities here. . . .

It is important to recognize what our inquiry is not about. No allegations are before us of unreasonable treatment of any person after an actual detention at a particular checkpoint. . . . As pursued in the lower courts, the instant action challenges only the use of sobriety check-

points generally. We address only the initial stop of each motorist passing through a checkpoint and the associated preliminary questioning and observation by checkpoint officers. Detention of particular motorists for more extensive field sobriety testing may require satisfaction of an individualized suspicion standard.

No one can seriously dispute the magnitude of the drunken driving problem or the States' interest in eradicating it. Media reports of alcohol-related death and mutilation on the Nation's roads are legion. The anecdotal is confirmed by the statistical. "Drunk drivers cause an annual death toll of over 25,000 and in the same time span cause nearly one million personal injuries and more than five billion dollars in property damage." . . .

Conversely, the weight bearing on the other scale—the measure of the intrusion on motorists stopped briefly at sobriety checkpoints—is slight. We reached a similar conclusion as to the intrusion on motorists subjected to a brief stop at a highway checkpoint for detecting illegal aliens. . . . We see virtually no difference between the levels of intrusion on law-abiding motorists from the brief stops necessary to the effectuation of these two types of checkpoints, which to the average motorist would seem identical save for the nature of the questions the checkpoint officers might ask. The trial court and the Court of Appeals, thus, accurately gauged the "objective" intrusion, measured by the duration of the seizure and the intensity of the investigation, as minimal.

With respect to what it perceived to be the "subjective" intrusion on motorists, however, the Court of Appeals found such intrusion substantial. The court first affirmed the trial court's finding that the guidelines governing checkpoint operation minimize the discretion of the officers on the scene. But the court also agreed with the trial court's conclusion that the checkpoints have the potential to generate fear and surprise in motorists. This was so because the record failed to demonstrate that approaching motorists would be aware of their option to make U-turns or turnoffs to avoid the checkpoints. On that basis, the court deemed the subjective intrusion from the checkpoints unreasonable.

We believe the Michigan courts misread our cases concerning the degree of "subjective intrusion" and the potential for generating fear and surprise. The "fear and surprise" to be considered are not the natural fear of one who has been drinking over the prospect of being stopped at a sobriety checkpoint but, rather, the fear and surprise engendered in law abiding motorists by the nature of the stop. This was made clear in Martinez-Fuerte. Comparing checkpoint stops to roving patrol stops considered in prior cases, we said, "we view checkpoint stops in a different light because the subjective intrusion—the generating of concern or even fright on the part of lawful travelers—is appreciably less in the case of a checkpoint stop. In [United States v.] Ortiz (1975),] we noted: " '[T]he circumstances surrounding a checkpoint stop and search are far less intrusive than those attending a roving-patrol stop. Roving patrols often operate at night on seldom-traveled roads, and their approach may frighten motorists. At traffic checkpoints the motorist can see that other vehicles are being stopped, he can see visible signs of the officers' authority, and he is much less likely to be frightened or annoyed by the intrusion.' '' Martinez-Fuerte. Here, checkpoints are selected pursuant to the guidelines, and uniformed police officers stop every approaching vehicle. The intrusion resulting from the brief stop at the sobriety checkpoint is for constitutional purposes indistinguishable from the checkpoint stops we upheld in Martinez-Fuerte.

The Court of Appeals went on to consider as part of the balancing analysis the "effectiveness" of the proposed checkpoint program. Based on extensive testimony in the trial record, the court concluded that the checkpoint program failed the "effectiveness" part of the test, and that this failure materially discounted petitioners' strong interest in implementing the program. We think the Court of Appeals was wrong on this point as well. . . .

Experts in police science might disagree over which of several methods of apprehending drunken drivers is preferrable as an ideal. But for purposes of Fourth Amendment analysis, the choice among such reasonable alternatives remains with the governmental officials who have a unique understanding of, and a responsibility for, limited public resources, including a finite number of police officers. . . .

During the operation of the Saginaw County checkpoint, the detention of each of the 126 vehicles that entered the checkpoint resulted in the arrest of two drunken drivers. Stated as a percentage, approximately 1.5 percent of the drivers passing through the checkpoint were arrested for alcohol impairment. In addition, an expert witness testified at the trial that experience in other States demonstrated that, on the whole, sobriety checkpoints resulted in drunken driving arrests of around 1 percent of all motorists stopped. By way of comparison, the record from one of the consolidated cases in Martinez-Fuerte, showed that in the associated checkpoint, illegal aliens were found in only 0.12 percent of the vehicles passing through the checkpoint. The ratio of illegal aliens detected to vehicles stopped (considering that on occasion two or more illegal aliens were found in a single vehicle) was approximately 0.5 percent. We concluded that this "record . . . provides a rather complete picture of the effectiveness of the San Clemente checkpoint'', and we sustained its constitutionality. We see no justification for a different conclusion here.

Reversed.

Justice **Blackmun,** concurring in the judgment, wrote a brief opinion.

Justice **Brennan,** with whom Justice **Marshall** joins, dissenting said in part:

Today, the Court rejects a Fourth Amendment challenge to a sobriety checkpoint policy in which police stop all cars and inspect all drivers for signs of intoxication without any individualized suspicion that a specific driver is intoxicated. The Court does so by balancing "the State's interest in preventing drunken driving, the extent to which this system can reasonably be said to advance that interest, and the degree of intrusion upon individual motorists who are briefly stopped.'' For the reasons stated by Justice Stevens in Parts I and II of his dissenting opinion, I agree that the Court misapplies that test by undervaluing the nature of the intrusion and exaggerating the law enforcement need to use the roadblocks to prevent drunken driving. . . . I write separately to express a few additional points. . . .

I do not dispute the immense social cost caused by drunken drivers, nor do I slight the government's efforts to prevent such tragic losses. Indeed, I would hazard a guess that today's opinion will be received favorably by a majority of our society, who would willingly suffer the minimal intrusion of a sobriety checkpoint stop in order to prevent drunken driving. But consensus that a particular law enforcement technique serves a laudable purpose has never been the touchstone of constitutional analysis.

"The Fourth Amendment was designed not merely to protect against official intrusions whose social utility was less as measured by some 'balancing test' than its intrusion on individual privacy; it was designed in addition to grant the individual a zone of privacy whose protections could be breached only where the 'reasonable' requirements of the probable cause standard were met. Moved by whatever momentary evil has aroused their fears, officials—perhaps even supported by a majority of citizens—may be tempted to conduct searches that sacrifice the liberty of each citizen to assuage the perceived evil. But the Fourth Amendment rests on the principle that a true balance between the individual and society depends on the recognition of 'the right to be let alone—the most comprehensive of rights and the right most valued by civilized men.' Olmstead v. United States (1928).

Justice **Stevens,** with whom Justice **Brennan** and Justice **Marshall** join as to Parts I and II, dissenting, said in part:

A sobriety checkpoint is usually operated at night at an unannounced location. Surprise is crucial to its method. The test operation conducted by the Michigan State Police and the Saginaw County Sheriff's Department began shortly after midnight and lasted until about 1 a.m. During that period, the 19 officers participating in the operation made two arrests and stopped and questioned 125 other unsuspecting and innocent drivers. It is, of course, not known how many arrests would have been made during that period if those officers had been engaged in normal patrol activities. However, the findings of the trial court, based on an extensive record and affirmed by the Michigan Court of Appeals, indicate that the net effect of sobriety checkpoints on traffic safety is infinitesimal and possibly negative.

Indeed, the record in this case makes clear that a decision holding these suspicionless seizures unconstitutional would not impede the law enforcement community's remarkable progress in reducing the death toll on our highways. Because the Michigan program was patterned after an older program in Maryland, the trial judge gave special attention to that State's experience. Over a period of several years, Maryland operated 125 checkpoints; of the 41,000 motorists passing through those checkpoints, only 143 persons (0.3%) were arrested. The number of man hours devoted to these operations is not in the record, but it seems inconceivable that a higher arrest rate could not have been achieved by more conventional means. Yet, even if the 143 checkpoint arrests were assumed to involve a net increase in the number of drunk driving arrests per year, the figure would still be insignificant by comparison to the 71,000 such arrests made by Michigan State Police without checkpoints in 1984 alone.

Any relationship between sobriety checkpoints and an actual reduction in highway fatalities is even less substantial than the minimal impact on arrest rates. As the Michigan Court of Appeals pointed out, "Maryland had conducted a study comparing traffic statistics between a county using checkpoints and a control county. The results of the study showed that alcohol-related accidents in the checkpoint county decreased by ten percent, whereas the control county saw an eleven percent decrease; and while fatal accidents in the control county fell from sixteen to three, fatal accidents in the checkpoint county actually doubled from the prior year."

In light of these considerations, it seems evident that the Court today misapplies the balancing test announced in Brown v. Texas (1979). The Court overvalues the law enforcement interest in using sobriety checkpoints, undervalues the citizen's interest in freedom from random, unannounced investigatory seizures, and mistakenly assumes that there is "virtually no difference" between a routine stop at a permanent, fixed checkpoint and a surprise stop at a sobriety checkpoint. . . .

I.

There is a critical difference between a seizure that is preceded by fair notice and one that is effected by surprise. . . . That is one reason why a border search, or indeed any search at a permanent and fixed checkpoint, is much less intrusive than a random stop. A motorist with advance notice of the location of a permanent checkpoint has an opportunity to avoid the search entirely, or at least to prepare for, and limit, the intrusion on her privacy.

No such opportunity is available in the case of a random stop or a temporary checkpoint, which both depend for their effectiveness on the element of surprise. A driver who discovers an unexpected checkpoint on a familiar local road will be startled and distressed. She may infer, correctly, that the checkpoint is not simply "business as usual," and may likewise infer, again correctly, that the police have made a discretionary decision to focus their law enforcement efforts upon her and others who pass the chosen point.

These fears are not, as the Court would have it, solely the lot of the guilty. To be law abiding is not necessarily to be spotless, and even the most virtuous can be unlucky. Unwanted attention from the local police need

not be less discomforting simply because one's secrets are not the stuff of criminal prosecutions. Moreover, those who have found—by reason of prejudice or misfortune—that encounters with the police may become adversarial or unpleasant without good cause will have grounds for worrying at any stop designed to elicit signs of suspicious behavior. Being stopped by the police is distressing even when it should not be terrifying, and what begins mildly may by happenstance turn severe.

For all these reasons, I do not believe that this case is analogous to Martinez-Fuerte. In my opinion, the sobriety checkpoints are instead similar to—and in some respects more intrusive than—the random investigative stops that the Court held unconstitutional in Brignone-Ponce . . . .

II.

The Court, unable to draw any persuasive analogy to Martinez-Fuerte, rests its decision today on application of a more general balancing test taken from Brown v. Texas (1979). In that case the appellant, a pedestrian, had been stopped for questioning in an area of El Paso, Texas, that had "a high incidence of drug traffic" because he "looked suspicious." He was then arrested and convicted for refusing to identify himself to police officers. We set aside his conviction because the officers stopped him when they lacked any reasonable suspicion that he was engaged in criminal activity. In our opinion, we stated: "Consideration of the constitutionality of such seizures involves a weighing of the gravity of the public concerns served by the seizure, the degree to which the seizure advances the public interest, and the severity of the interference with individual liberty."

The gravity of the public concern with highway safety that is implicated by this case is, of course, undisputed. Yet . . . I do not understand the Court to have placed any lesser value on the importance of the drug problem implicated in Texas v. Brown, or on the need to control the illegal border crossings that were at stake in Almeida-Sanchez and its progeny. A different result in this case must be justified by the other two factors in the Brown formulation.

As I have already explained, I believe the Court is quite wrong in blithely asserting that a sobriety checkpoint is no more intrusive than a permanent checkpoint. In my opinion, unannounced investigatory seizures are, particularly when they take place at night, the hallmark of regimes far different from ours; the surprise intrusion upon individual liberty is not minimal. On that issue, my difference with the Court may amount to nothing less than a difference in our respective evaluations of the importance of individual liberty, a serious albeit inevitable source of constitutional disagreement. On the degree to which the sobriety checkpoint seizures advance the public interest, however, the Court's position is wholly indefensible.

The Court's analysis of this issue resembles a business decision that measures profits by counting gross receipts and ignoring expenses. The evidence in this case indicates that sobriety checkpoints result in the arrest of a fraction of one percent of the drivers who are stopped, but there is absolutely no evidence that this figure represents an increase over the number of arrests that would have been made by using the same law enforcement resources in conventional patrols. Thus, although the gross number of arrests is more than zero, there is a complete failure of proof on the question whether the wholesale seizures have produced any net advance in the public interest in arresting intoxicated drivers.

Indeed, the position adopted today by the Court is not one endorsed by any of the law enforcement authorities to whom the Court purports to defer. The Michigan police do not rely, as the Court does, on the arrest rate at sobriety checkpoints to justify the stops made there. Colonel Hough, the commander of the Michigan State Police and a leading proponent of the checkpoints, admitted at trial that the arrest rate at the checkpoints was "very low." Instead, Colonel Hough and the State have maintained that the mere threat of such arrests is sufficient to deter drunk driving and so to reduce the accident rate. The Maryland police officer who testified at trial took the same position with respect to his State's program. There is, obviously, nothing wrong with a law enforcement technique that reduces crime by pure deterrence without punishing anybody; on the contrary, such an approach is highly commendable. One cannot, however, prove its efficacy by counting the arrests that were made. One must instead measure the number of crimes that were avoided. Perhaps because the record is wanting, the Court simply ignores this point. . . .

I respectfully dissent.

UNITED STATES v. LEON

468 U. S. 897; 104 S. Ct. 3424; 82 L. Ed. 2d 677 (1984)

Over the years in a wide variety of decisions the Court had manifested a basic discontent with the exclusionary rule of Weeks v. United States. The Court seemed to agree that blatant violations of the right of personal privacy could only be discouraged by the use of the doctrine, yet it balked at having to exclude from court unimpeachable evidence of a person's guilt simply because of some legal flaw in the way it was obtained. It had vacillated in its application of the Carroll and "search incident" doctrines and in Terry v. Ohio it had eased dramatically the restrictions on warrantless searches. But it had still failed to find a doctrine that would let it ban illegal evidence gotten in ways it found objectionable, while admitting equally illegal evidence whose admission seemed to promote the cause of justice.

Curiously enough, it was in the context of the retroactivity question that the Court finally devised a theory that it hoped would provide this flexibility. The abrupt reversal of many long-standing constitutional

rules in the years of the Warren Court brought to the fore a new kind of problem: To what extent were the new interpretations of the Constitution to be made retroactive so as to free prisoners held under the old interpretations. The traditional rule had always been to apply any new interpretation retroactively, but faced with the specter of thousands of retrials, the Court reexamined this doctrine and in Linkletter v. Walker (1965) set a precedent for limiting the retroactivity of certain rights. Whether a holding is to be applied retroactively depends on the nature of the right and the purposes it is designed to serve. In its decision in United States v. Calandra (1974) the Court had leaned heavily on the "deterrent effect" of the exclusionary rule and concluded that if, in fact, excluding the evidence would not have deterred the police conduct, there was no point in excluding the evidence through a retroactive application of the rule.

A year later in United States v. Peltier (1975) the Court refined the doctrine into what has become known as the "good faith" exception to the exclusion rule. Bluntly stated, if the purpose of the exclusion of evidence is to deter the police from making illegal searches, there is no point in excluding the evidence if the police did not know the search was illegal. Why punish a police officer? If the police are acting "in good faith," then the evidence should be admissible.

The Peltier case arose out of the enforcement of legislation regulating our border patrols and again involved the questions of the retroactivity of a newly announced interpretation of the law. The Court found that the guards along the Mexican border were relying on what they believed to be valid rules regarding the stopping and searching of vehicles near the border and there was no point in "punishing" them by refusing to admit their evidence simply because the rules had been changed.

Four years later, in Michigan v. DeFillippo (1979), the Court extended the "good faith" doctrine of Peltier beyond the confines of the retroactivity question to hold admissible evidence gotten by a search incident to an unconstitutional arrest. DeFillippo was stopped by the police in a Detroit alley under suspicious circumstances and asked to identify himself. When he refused he was arrested under a city ordinance that made it a crime to refuse such identification, was searched incident to the arrest, and marijuana was found in his pocket. He was charged with possession but the Michigan court, holding the identification ordinance void for vagueness and hence the arrest invalid, held the evidence inadmissible as the product of an invalid search.

The Supreme Court reversed. A police officer, it held, has a duty to enforce a law until it is held void unless it is "so grossly and flagrantly unconstitutional that any person of reasonable prudence would be bound to see its flaws." Such was not the case here, and since the refusal to give his name was a crime being committed in the presence of the officer, the arrest and incident search were valid. The unconstitutionality of the ordinance under which DeFillippo had been arrested was stressed in a companion case holding void on its face an

El Paso ordinance making it a crime for a person to refuse to identify himself to a police officer; see Brown v. Texas (1979).

California v. Hodari D. (1991) arose under a similar set of facts. Hodari, who was standing around a parked car, fled when the police appeared. Suspicious, the police pursued him, and just before an officer tackled him he discarded what appeared to be a rock. The rock, which turned out to be crack cocaine, was admitted in evidence against him on the ground that he had not been "seized" until the officer actually tackled him, and therefore the search for the crack was not the product of an unreasonable seizure.

Originally limited to evidence gotten by an unreasonable search and seizure, the "good faith" doctrine moved within a year into the area of evidence obtained by questioning suspects. After giving a murder suspect Miranda warnings, three police officers were taking him to the police station for questioning. During the ride, two of them discussed the danger posed to the community by the fact that the murder gun was still missing. A school for handicapped children was nearby "and God forbid one of them might find a weapon with shells and might hurt themselves." The suspect interrupted and asked the officers to return to the scene of the crime. There he produced the hidden weapon because " 'he wanted to get the gun out of the way because of the kids in the area in the school.' " The Court upheld the admission of the gun and the defendant's statements pointing out that the officers, acting in good faith, had not intended their conversation as interrogation and they could not have known of the defendant's sensitivity where handicapped children were concerned. See Rhode Island v. Innis (1980).

In the present case a confidential informant of unproven reliability tipped off the police of Burbank, Calif., that Leon and others were selling cocaine and methaqualone from their home and other places. The police watched the comings and goings of the five or six persons involved, some of whom were known to have been involved in the drug traffic, and concluded that they were engaged in a drug smuggling operation. Several district attorneys reviewed the evidence collected by the police, and at their request a state judge issued a warrant to search a number of residences and vehicles. The defendants were indicted on drug charges. They filed a motion to suppress the evidence seized under the warrant and the district court granted the motion on the ground that the reliability and credibility of the informant had not been established. "I just cannot find this warrant sufficient for a showing of probable cause" for the issuance of a search warrant.

Justice **White** delivered the opinion of the Court, saying in part:

This case presents the question whether the Fourth Amendment exclusionary rule should be modified so as not to bar the use in the prosecutions's case-in-chief of evidence obtained by officers acting in reasonable reliance on a search warrant issued by a detached and neutral magistrate but ultimately found to be unsupported by probable cause. To resolve this question, we must consider once again the tension between the sometimes competing goals of, on the one hand, deterring official misconduct and removing inducements to unreasonable invasions of privacy and, on the other, establishing procedures under which criminal defendants are "acquitted or convicted on the basis of all the evidence which exposes the truth." . . .

I.

We have concluded that, in the Fourth Amendment context, the exclusionary rule can be modified somewhat without jeopardizing its ability to perform its intended functions. . . .

II.

A.

The Fourth Amendment contains no provision expressly precluding the use of evidence obtained in violation of its commands, and an examination of its origin and purposes makes clear that the use of fruits of a past unlawful search or seizure "work[s] no new Fourth Amendment wrong." United States v. Calandra (1974). The wrong condemned by the Amendment is "fully accomplished" by the unlawful search or seizure itself, and the exclusionary rule is neither intended nor able to "cure the invasion of the defendant's rights which he has already suffered." . . . The rule thus operates as "a judicially created remedy designed to safeguard Fourth Amendment rights generally through its deterrent effect, rather than a personal constitutional right of the person aggrieved." . . .

Whether the exclusionary sanction is appropriately imposed in a particular case, our decisions make clear, is "an issue separate from the question whether the Fourth Amendment rights of the party seeking to invoke the rule were violated by police conduct." Illinois v. Gates [1983]. Only the former question is currently before us, and it must be resolved by weighing the costs and benefits of preventing the use in the prosecution's case-in-chief of inherently trustworthy tangible evidence obtained in reliance on a search warrant issued by a detached and neutral magistrate that ultimately is found to be defective.

The substantial social costs exacted by the exclusionary rule for the vindication of Fourth Amendment rights have long been a source of concern. "Our cases have consistently recognized that unbending application of the exclusionary sanction to enforce ideals of government rectitude would impede unacceptably the truth-finding functions of judge and jury." . . . An objectionable collateral consequence of this interference with the criminal justice system's truth-finding function is that some guilty defendants may go free or receive reduced sentences as a result of favorable plea bargains. Particularly when law enforcement officers have acted in objective good faith or their transgressions have been minor, the magnitude of the benefit conferred on such guilty defendants offends basic concepts of the criminal justice system. . . . Indiscriminate application of the exclusionary rule, therefore, may well "generat[e] disrespect for the law and the administration of justice." . . .

B.

. . . The Court has, to be sure, not seriously questioned, "in the absence of a more efficacious sanction, the continued application of the rule to suppress evidence from the [prosecution's] case where a Fourth Amendment violation has been substantial and deliberate. . . ." Nevertheless, the balancing approach that has evolved in various contexts—including criminal trials—"forcefully suggest[s] that the exclusionary rule be more generally modified to permit the introduction of evidence obtained in the reasonable good-faith belief that a search or seizure was in accord with the Fourth Amendment." . . .

[The Court here reviews the past cases and the exceptions to the exclusionary rule.]

As yet, we have not recognized any form of good-faith exception to the Fourth Amendment exclusionary rule. But the balancing approach that has evolved during the years of experience with the rule provides strong support for the modification currently urged upon us. As we discuss below, our evaluation of the costs and benefits of suppressing reliable physical evidence seized by officers reasonably relying on a warrant issued by a detached and neutral magistrate leads to the conclusion that such evidence should be admissible in the prosecution's case-in-chief.

III.

A.

Because a search warrant "provides the detached scrutiny of a neutral magistrate, which is a more reliable safeguard against improper searches than the hurried judgment of a law enforcement officer 'engaged in the often competitive enterprise of ferreting out crime,'" . . . we have expressed a strong preference for warrants and declared that "in a doubtful or marginal case a search under a warrant may be sustainable where without one it would fail." . . . Reasonable minds frequently may differ on the question whether a particular affidavit establishes probable cause, and we have thus concluded that the preference for warrants is most appropriately effectuated by according "great deference" to a magistrate's determination. . . .

Deference to the magistrate, however, is not boundless. It is clear, first, that the deference accorded to a magistrate's finding of probable cause does not preclude inquiry into the knowing or reckless falsity of the affidavit on which that determination was based. . . . Second, the courts must also insist that the magistrate purport to "perform his 'neutral and detached' function and not serve merely as a rubber stamp for the police." . . . A magistrate failing to "manifest that neutrality and detachment demanded of a judicial officer when presented with a warrant application" and who acts instead as "an adjunct law enforcement officer" cannot provide valid authorization for an otherwise unconstitutional search. . . .

Third, reviewing courts will not defer to a warrant based on an affidavit that does not "provide the magistrate with a substantial basis for determining the existence of probable cause." Illinois v. Gates. "Sufficient information must be presented to the magistrate to allow that official to determine probable cause; his action cannot be a mere ratification of the bare conclusions of others." . . . Even if the warrant application was supported by more than a "bare bones" affidavit, a reviewing court may properly conclude that, notwithstanding the deference that magistrates deserve, the warrant was invalid because the magistrate's probable-cause determination reflected an improper analysis of the totality of the circumstances . . . or because the form of the warrant was improper in some respect.

Only in the first of these three situations, however, has the Court set forth a rationale for suppressing evidence obtained pursuant to a search warrant; in the other areas, it has simply excluded such evidence without considering whether Fourth Amendment interests will be advanced. To the extent that proponents of exclusion rely on its behavioral effects on judges and magistrates in these areas, their reliance is misplaced. First, the exclusionary rule is designed to deter police misconduct rather than to punish the errors of judges and magistrates. Second, there exists no evidence suggesting that judges and magistrates are inclined to ignore or subvert the Fourth Amendment or that lawlessness among these actors requires application of the extreme sanction of exclusion.

Third, and most important, we discern no basis, and are offered none, for believing that exclusion of evidence seized pursuant to a warrant will have a significant deterrent effect on the issuing judge or magistrate. Many of the factors that indicate that the exclusionary rule cannot provide an effective "special" or "general" deterrent for individual offending law enforcement officers apply as well to judges or magistrates. And, to the extent that the rule is thought to operate as a "systemic" deterrent on a wider audience, it clearly can have no such effect on individuals empowered to issue search warrants. Judges and magistrates are not adjuncts to the law enforcement team; as neutral judicial officers, they have no stake in the outcome of particular criminal prosecutions. The threat of exclusion thus cannot be expected significantly to deter them. Imposition of the exclusionary sanction is not necessary meaningfully to inform judicial officers of their errors, and we cannot conclude that admitting evidence obtained pursuant to a warrant while at the same time declaring that the warrant was somehow defective will in any way reduce judicial officers' professional incentives to comply with the Fourth Amendment, encourage them to repeat their mistakes, or lead to the granting of all colorable warrant requests.

B.

If exclusion of evidence obtained pursuant to a subsequently invalidated warrant is to have any deterrent effect, therefore, it must alter the behavior of individual law enforcement officers or the policies of their departments. One could argue that applying the exclusionary rule in cases where the police failed to demonstrate probable cause in the warrant application deters future inadequate presentations or ''magistrate shopping'' and thus promotes the ends of the Fourth Amendment. Suppressing evidence obtained pursuant to a technically defective warrant supported by probable cause also might encourage officers to scrutinize more closely the form of the warrant and to point out suspected judicial errors. We find such arguments speculative and conclude that suppression of evidence obtained pursuant to a warrant should be ordered only on a case-by-case basis and only in those unusual cases in which exclusion will further the purposes of the exclusionary rule.

We have frequently questioned whether the exclusionary rule can have any deterrent effect when the offending officers acted in the objectively reasonable belief that their conduct did not violate the Fourth Amendment. ''No empirical researcher, proponent or opponent of the rule, has yet been able to establish with any assurance whether the rule has a deterrent effect. . . .'' . . . But even assuming that the rule effectively deters some police misconduct and provides incentives for the law enforcement profession as a whole to conduct itself in accord with the Fourth Amendment, it cannot be expected, and should not be applied, to deter objectively reasonable law enforcement activity. . . .

This is particularly true, we believe, when an officer acting with objective good faith has obtained a search warrant from a judge or magistrate and acted within its scope. In most such cases, there is no police illegality and thus nothing to deter. It is the magistrate's responsibility to determine whether the officer's allegations establish probable cause and, if so, to issue a warrant comporting in form with the requirements of the Fourth Amendment. In the ordinary case, an officer cannot be expected to question the magistrate's probable-cause determination or his judgment that the form of the warrant is technically sufficient. . . . Penalizing the officer for the magistrate's error, rather than his own, cannot logically contribute to the deterrence of Fourth Amendment violations.

C.

We conclude that the marginal or nonexistent benefits produced by suppressing evidence obtained in objectively reasonable reliance on a subsequently invalidated search warrant cannot justify the substantial costs of exclusion. We do not suggest, however, that exclusion is always inappropriate in cases where an officer has obtained a warrant and abided by its terms. . . .

Suppression . . . remains an appropriate remedy if the magistrate or judge in issuing a warrant was misled by information in an affidavit that the affiant knew was false or would have known was false except for his reckless disregard of the truth. . . . The exception we recognize today will also not apply in cases where the issuing magistrate wholly abandoned his judicial role . . . ; in such circumstances, no reasonably well-trained officer should rely on the warrant. Nor would an officer manifest objective good faith in relying on a warrant based on an affidavit ''so lacking in indicia of probable cause as to render official belief in its existence entirely unreasonable.'' . . . Finally, depending on the circumstances of the particular case, a warrant may be so facially deficient—i.e., in failing to particularize the place to be searched or the things to be seized—that the executing officers cannot reasonably presume it to be valid. . . .

Justice **Blackmun,** concurring, said in part:

. . . I write separately . . . to underscore what I regard as the unavoidably provisional nature of today's decisions. . . .

What must be stressed . . . is that any empirical judgment about the effect of the exclusionary rule in a particular class of cases necessarily is a provisional one. By their very nature, the assumptions on which we proceed today cannot be cast in stone. To the contrary, they now will be tested in the real world of state and federal law enforcement, and this Court will attend to the results. If it should emerge from experience that, contrary to our expectations, the good faith exception to the exclusionary rule results in a material change in police compliance with the Fourth Amendment, we shall have to reconsider what we have undertaken here. The logic of a decision that rests on untested predictions about police conduct demands no less.

Justice **Brennan,** with whom Justice **Marshall** joins, dissenting said in part:

I.

A.

. . . Because seizures are executed principally to secure evidence, and because such evidence generally has utility in our legal system only in the context of a trial supervised by a judge, it is apparent that the admission of illegally obtained evidence implicates the same constitutional concerns as the initial seizure of that evidence. Indeed, by admitting unlawfully seized evidence, the judiciary becomes a part of what is in fact a single governmental action prohibited by the terms of the Amendment. . . .

It is difficult to give any meaning at all to the limitations imposed by the Amendment if they are read to proscribe only certain conduct by the police but to allow other agents of the same government to take advantage of evidence secured by the police in violation of its requirements. The Amendment therefore must be read to condemn not only the initial unconstitutional invasion of privacy—which is done, after all, for the purpose of securing evidence—but also the subsequent use of any evidence so obtained.

The Court evades this principle by drawing an artificial line between the constitutional rights and responsibilities that are engaged by actions of the police and those that are engaged when a defendant appears before the courts. According to the Court, the substantive protections of the Fourth Amendment are wholly exhausted at the moment when police unlawfully invade an individual's privacy and thus no substantive force remains to those protections at the time of trial when the government seeks to use evidence obtained by the police.

I submit that such a crabbed reading of the Fourth Amendment casts aside the teaching of those Justices who first formulated the exclusionary rule, and rests ultimately on an impoverished understanding of judicial responsibility in our constitutional scheme. For my part, "[t]he right of the people to be secure in their persons, houses, papers and effects, against unreasonable searches and seizures" comprises a personal right to exclude all evidence secured by means of unreasonable searches and seizures. The right to be free from the initial invasion of privacy and the right of exclusion are coordinate components of the central embracing right to be free from unreasonable searches and seizures. . . .

B.

. . . The Court since Calandra has gradually pressed the deterrence rationale for the rule back to center stage. . . . The various arguments advanced by the Court in this campaign have only strengthened my conviction that the deterrence theory is both misguided and unworkable. First, the Court has frequently bewailed the "cost" of excluding reliable evidence. In large part, this criticism rests upon a refusal to acknowledge the function of the Fourth Amendment itself. If nothing else, the Amendment plainly operates to disable the government from gathering information and securing evidence in certain ways. In practical terms, of course, this restriction of official power means that some incriminating evidence inevitably will go undetected if the government obeys these constitutional restraints. It is the loss of that evidence that is the "price" our society pays for enjoying the freedom and privacy safeguarded by the Fourth Amendment. Thus, some criminals will go free *not*, in Justice (then Judge) Cardozo's misleading epigram, "because the constable has blundered," People v. Defore, 242 N. Y. 13 (1926), but rather because official compliance with Fourth Amendment requirements makes it more difficult to catch criminals. Understood in this way, the Amendment directly contemplates that some reliable

and incriminating evidence will be lost to the government; therefore, it is not the exclusionary rule, but the Amendment itself that has imposed this cost.

In addition, the Court's decisions over the past decade have made plain that the entire enterprise of attempting to assess the benefits and costs of the exclusionary rule in various contexts is a virtually impossible task for the judiciary to perform honestly or accurately. Although the Court's language in those cases suggests that some specific empirical basis may support its analyses, the reality is that the Court's opinions represent inherently unstable compounds of intuition, hunches, and occasional pieces of partial and often inconclusive data. In Calandra, for example, the Court, in considering whether the exclusionary rule should apply in grand jury proceedings, had before it no concrete evidence whatever concerning the impact that application of the rule in such proceedings would have either in terms of the long-term costs or the expected benefits. To the extent empirical data is available regarding the general costs and benefits of the exclusionary rule, it has shown, on the one hand, as the Court acknowledges today, that the costs are not as substantial as critics have asserted in the past, and, on the other hand, that while the exclusionary rule may well have certain deterrent effects, it is extremely difficult to determine with any degree of precision whether the incidence of unlawful conduct by police is now lower than it was prior to Mapp. . . . The Court has sought to turn this uncertainty to its advantage by casting the burden of proof upon proponents of the rule. . . . "Obviously," however, "the assignment of the burden of proof on an issue where evidence does not exist and cannot be obtained is outcome determinative. [The] assignment of the burden is merely a way of announcing a predetermined conclusion."* By remaining within its redoubt of empiricism and by basing the rule solely on the deterrence rationale, the Court has robbed the rule of legitimacy. A doctrine that is explained as if it were an empirical proposition but for which there is only limited empirical support is both inherently unstable and an easy mark for critics. The extent of this Court's fidelity to Fourth Amendment requirements, however, should not turn on such statistical uncertainties. . . .

III.

Even if I were to accept the Court's general approach to the exclusionary rule, I could not agree with today's result. There is no question that in the hands of the present Court the deterrence rationale has proved to be a powerful tool for confining the scope of the rule. In Calandra, for example, the Court concluded that the "speculative and undoubtedly minimal advance in the deterrence of police misconduct," was insufficient to

---

*Dworkin, Fact Style Adjudication and the Fourth Amendment: The Limits of Lawyering, 48 Ind. L. J. 329, 332-333 (1973). . . .

outweigh the "expense of substantially impeding the grand jury." In Stone v. Powell [1976], the Court found that "the additional contribution, if any, of the consideration of search-and-seizure claims of state prisoners on collateral review is small in relation to the costs. In United States v. Janis (1976), the Court concluded that "exclusion from federal civil proceedings of evidence unlawfully seized by a state criminal enforcement officer has not been shown to have a sufficient likelihood of deterring the conduct of the state police so that it outweighs the societal costs imposed by the exclusion." And in an opinion handed down today, the Court finds that the "balance between costs and benefits comes out against applying the exclusionary rule in civil deportation hearings held by the Immigration and Naturalization Service." INS v. Lopez-Mendoza [1984]. . . .

At the outset, the Court suggests that society has been asked to pay a high price—in terms either of setting guilty persons free or of impeding the proper functioning of trials—as a result of excluding relevant physical evidence in cases where the police, in conducting searches and seizing evidence, have made only an "objectively reasonable" mistake concerning the constitutionality of their actions. But what evidence is there to support such a claim?

Significantly, the Court points to none, and, indeed, as the Court acknowledges, recent studies have demonstrated that the "costs" of the exclusionary rule—calculated in terms of dropped prosecutions and lost convictions—are quite low. Contrary to the claims of the rule's critics that exclusion leads to "the release of countless guilty criminals," . . . these studies have demonstrated that federal and state prosecutors very rarely drop cases because of potential search and seizure problems. For example, a 1979 study prepared at the request of Congress by the General Accounting Office reported that only 0.4% of all cases actually declined for prosecution by federal prosecutors were declined primarily because of illegal search problems. . . .

What then supports the Court's insistence that this evidence be admitted? Apparently, the Court's only answer is that even though the costs of exclusion are not very substantial, the potential deterrent effect in these circumstances is so marginal that exclusion cannot be justified. . . .

. . . But what the Court overlooks is that the deterrence rationale for the rule is not designed to be, nor should it be thought of as, a form of "punishment" of individual police officers for their failures to obey the restraints imposed by the Fourth Amendment. . . . Instead, the chief deterrent function of the rule is its tendency to promote institutional compliance with Fourth Amendment requirements on the part of law enforcement agencies generally. Thus, as the Court has previously recognized, "over the long term, [the] demonstration [provided by the exclusionary rule] that our society attaches serious consequences to violations of constitutional rights is thought to encourage those who formulate law enforcement policies, and the officers who implement them, to incorporate Fourth Amendment ideals into their value system." . . . It is only through such an institution-wide mechanism that information concerning the Fourth Amendment standards can be effectively communicated to rank and file officers. . . .

After today's decision, however, that institutional incentive will be lost. Indeed, the Court's "reasonable mistake" exception to the exclusionary rule will tend to put a premium on police ignorance of the law. . . .

. . . A chief consequence of today's decision will be to convey a clear and unambiguous message to magistrates that their decisions to issue warrants are now insulated from subsequent judicial review. Creation of this new exception for good faith reliance upon a warrant implicitly tells magistrates that they need not take much care in reviewing warrant applications, since their mistakes will from now on have virtually no consequences: If their decision to issue a warrant was correct, the evidence will be admitted; if their decision was incorrect but the police relied in good faith on the warrant, the evidence will also be admitted. Inevitably, the care and attention devoted to such an inconsequential chore will dwindle.

THE RIGHT OF COUNSEL

GIDEON v. WAINWRIGHT

372 U.S. 335; 83 S. Ct. 792; 9 L. Ed. 2d 799
(1963)

The right of a person being tried for a crime to be represented by counsel trained in the law has been recognized in this country since earliest times. It rests on an appreciation of the fact that trial procedure is complex and confusing, that its rules are highly technical, and that a nonprofessional's ignorance of them may cause a mistrial, may cause the loss of valuable procedural rights, and may hopelessly frustrate efforts to get the accused's story into the record. There is much truth in the aphorism that one who defends oneself has a fool for a lawyer.

The Sixth Amendment expressly guarantees that in "all criminal prosecutions the accused shall . . . have the assistance of counsel for his defense." Designed originally to ensure to the accused the presence of his or her own counsel, it has long since come to include the right to court-appointed counsel if one cannot afford an attorney. The importance attached by the Supreme Court to the right to counsel in a federal court is shown by two rules which the Court has laid down. One is that if the right to counsel is not accorded to a defendant in a federal court, the court loses its jurisdiction to proceed with the case. The other rule is that while the right to counsel, like some other constitutional rights, may be waived by an accused person, such waiver must be both clear and intelligently made. The right is not waived merely by failure to claim it, nor is the waiver valid unless the accused understands adequately the consequences of waiving the right.

Both of the rules were set out clearly in the landmark case of Johnson v. Zerbst (1938). Here a young marine on leave had been arraigned, tried for forgery, convicted, and sentenced to four years in prison, all in one afternoon. He informed the district court on arraignment that he had no counsel, but was ready for trial. He conducted his own defense, and failed, through ignorance of the law, to make timely application for an appeal. The Supreme Court held that he had not "intelligently" waived his right to counsel, and it also stated that "if this requirement of the Sixth Amendment is not complied with, the court no longer has jurisdiction to proceed." The Court emphasized that "the Sixth Amendment withholds from Federal Courts, in all criminal proceedings, the power and authority to deprive an accused of his life or liberty unless he has or waives the assistance of Counsel . . . [and the] 'courts indulge every reasonable presumption against waiver'. . . ." Moreover, "the constitutional right of an accused to be represented by Counsel invokes, of itself, the protection of a trial court, in which the accused—whose life or liberty is at stake—is without Counsel. This protecting duty imposes the serious and weighty responsibility upon the trial judge of determining whether there is an intelligent and competent waiver by the accused. While an accused may waive the right to Counsel, whether there is a proper waiver should be clearly determined by the trial court; and it would be fitting and appropriate for that determination to appear upon the record."

This doctrine was reaffirmed in Von Moltke v. Gillies (1948), where the signing of a formal waiver of the right to counsel even by an "intelligent, mentally acute woman" was not, in the circumstances, the kind of "intelligent" waiver which could deprive her of her Sixth Amendment right. The Court said: "To be valid such waiver must be made with an apprehension of the nature of the charges, the statutory offenses included within them, the range of allowable punishments thereunder, possible defenses to the charges and circumstances in mitigation thereof, and all other facts essential to a broad understanding of the whole matter. A judge can make certain that an accused's professed waiver of counsel is understandingly and wisely made only from a penetrating and comprehensive examination of all the circumstances under which such a plea is tendered." Mrs. Von Moltke had pleaded guilty without the aid of counsel to espionage charges under which she could have been sentenced to death or thirty years in prison.

The right to counsel includes the right to consult a lawyer without the conversation being monitored by the government, as in wiretapping, or relayed to the government through a government informer planted in the same cell block where the defendant was awaiting trial in the hope that the defendant would volunteer incriminating statements in the absence of counsel. Here the informer, also an inmate, was paid on a contingency fee basis and testified against the defendant at trial. United States v. Henry (1980).

By the language of the Sixth Amendment the right to counsel is guaranteed "in all criminal prosecutions." It is not guaranteed in noncriminal proceedings. Thus a congressional investigating committee, which conducts a civil—not criminal—proceeding, may do as it pleases about allowing witnesses called before it to be represented by counsel. In recent years committees have usually allowed witnesses this privilege, though the role played by the attorney is very narrowly limited.

In the years following Betts v. Brady (1942) the Supreme Court continued to deal with state right-to-counsel cases under the due process rule requiring essential fairness, the cases turning on the question whether the defendant was capable of conducting his or her own defense. The Court clearly assumed, however, that the right to counsel in a capital case was absolute, and since 1950, even in noncapital cases, no one had been found capable enough to be tried without counsel. In 1954 in Chandler v. Fretag the defendant had been denied a chance to obtain counsel at his own expense, and the Supreme Court held that he had been denied due process. "Regardless of whether petitioner would have been entitled to the appointment of counsel, his right to be heard through his own counsel was unqualified. See Palko v. Connecticut [1937] . . . Powell v. Alabama [1932]. . . ."

Following the reversal of his conviction in the present case, Gideon was retried by the state of Florida in the same courtroom, before the same judge, with the same witnesses, but with a lawyer appointed by the court at Gideon's request. This time he was acquitted.

Mr. Justice **Black** delivered the opinion of the Court, saying in part:

Petitioner was charged in a Florida state court with having broken and entered a poolroom with intent to commit a misdemeanor. This offense is a felony under Florida law. Appearing in court without funds and without a lawyer, petitioner asked the court to appoint counsel for him, whereupon the following colloquy took place:

"The Court: Mr. Gideon, I am sorry, but I cannot appoint Counsel to represent you in this case. Under the laws of the State of Florida, the only time the Court can appoint Counsel to represent a Defendant is when that person is charged with a capital offense. I am sorry, but I will have to deny your request to appoint Counsel to defend you in this case.

"The Defendant: The United States Supreme Court says I am entitled to be represented by Counsel."

Put to trial before a jury, Gideon conducted his defense about as well as could be expected from a layman. He made an opening statement to the jury, cross-examined the State's witnesses, presented witnesses in his own defense, declined to testify himself, and made a short argument "emphasizing his innocence to the

charge contained in the Information filed in this case.''
The jury returned a verdict of guilty, and petitioner was
sentenced to serve five years in the state prison. . . .
Since 1942, when Betts v. Brady was decided by a divided Court, the problem of a defendant's federal constitutional right to counsel in a state court has been a continuing source of controversy and litigation in both state
and federal courts. To give this problem another review
here, we granted certiorari. Since Gideon was proceeding in forma pauperis, we appointed counsel to represent
him and requested both sides to discuss in their briefs
and oral arguments the following: ''Should this Court's
holding in Betts v. Brady be reconsidered?''

I.

The facts upon which Betts claimed that he had
been unconstitutionally denied the right to have counsel
appointed to assist him are strikingly like the facts upon
which Gideon here bases his federal constitutional claim.
Betts was indicted for robbery in a Maryland state court.
On arraignment, he told the trial judge of his lack of
funds to hire a lawyer and asked the court to appoint one
for him. Betts was advised that it was not the practice in
that county to appoint counsel for indigent defendants
except in murder and rape cases. He then pleaded not
guilty, had witnesses summoned, cross-examined the
State's witnesses, examined his own, and chose not to
testify himself. He was found guilty by the judge, sitting
without a jury, and sentenced to eight years in prison.
Like Gideon, Betts sought release by habeas corpus, alleging that he had been denied the right to assistance of
counsel in violation of the Fourteenth Amendment. Betts
was denied any relief, and on review this Court affirmed.
It was held that a refusal to appoint counsel for an indigent defendant charged with a felony did not necessarily
violate the Due Process Clause of the Fourteenth
Amendment, which for reasons given the Court deemed
to be the only applicable federal constitutional provision.
The Court said:

''Asserted denial [of due process] is to be tested by
an appraisal of the totality of facts in a given case. That
which may, in one setting, constitute a denial of fundamental fairness, shocking to the universal sense of justice, may, in other circumstances, and in the light of
other considerations, fall short of such denial.''

Treating due process as ''a concept less rigid and
more fluid than those envisaged in other specific and
particular provisions of the Bill of Rights,'' the Court
held that refusal to appoint counsel under the particular
facts and circumstances in the Betts Case was not so
''offensive to the common and fundamental ideas of fairness'' as to amount to a denial of due process. Since the
facts and circumstances of the two cases are so nearly
indistinguishable, we think the Betts v. Brady holding if
left standing would require us to reject Gideon's claim
that the Constitution guarantees him the assistance of
counsel. Upon full reconsideration we conclude that
Betts v. Brady should be overruled.

II.

The Sixth Amendment provides, ''In all criminal
prosecutions, the accused shall enjoy the right . . . to
have the Assistance of Counsel for his defence.'' We
have construed this to mean that in federal courts counsel must be provided for defendants unable to employ
counsel unless the right is competently and intelligently
waived. Betts argued that this right is extended to indigent defendants in state courts by the Fourteenth Amendment. In response the Court stated that, while the Sixth
Amendment laid down ''no rule for the conduct of the
States, the question recurs whether the constraint laid by
the Amendment upon the national courts expresses a rule
so fundamental and essential to a fair trial, and so, to due
process of law, that it is made obligatory upon the States
by the Fourteenth Amendment.'' In order to decide
whether the Sixth Amendment's guarantee of counsel is
of this fundamental nature, the Court in Betts set out and
considered ''[r]elevant data on the subject . . . afforded
by constitutional and statutory provisions subsisting in
the colonies and the States prior to the inclusion of the
Bill of Rights in the national Constitution, and in the
constitutional, legislative, and judicial history of the
States to the present date.'' On the basis of this historical
data the Court concluded that ''appointment of counsel
is not a fundamental right, essential to a fair trial.'' It
was for this reason the Betts Court refused to accept the
contention that the Sixth Amendment's guarantee of
counsel for indigent federal defendants was extended to
or, in the words of that Court, ''made obligatory upon
the States by the Fourteenth Amendment.'' Plainly, had
the Court concluded that appointment of counsel for indigent criminal defendant was ''a fundamental right, essential to a fair trial,'' it would have held that the Fourteenth Amendment requires appointment of counsel in a
state court, just as the Sixth Amendment requires in a
federal court.

We think the Court in Betts had ample precedent
for acknowledging that those guarantees of the Bill of
Rights which are fundamental safeguards of liberty immune from federal abridgment are equally protected
against state invasion by the Due Process Clause of the
Fourteenth Amendment. This same principle was recognized, explained and applied in Powell v. Alabama
(1932), a case upholding the right of counsel, where the
Court held that despite sweeping language to the contrary in Hurtado v. California (1884), the Fourteenth
Amendment ''embraced'' those ''fundamental principles
of liberty and justice which lie at the base of all our civil
and political institutions,'' even though they had been
''specifically dealt with in another part of the federal
Constitution.'' In many cases other than Powell and
Betts, this Court has looked to the fundamental nature of
original Bill of Rights guarantees to decide whether the
Fourteenth Amendment makes them obligatory on the
States. Explicitly recognized to be of this ''fundamental
nature'' and therefore made immune from state invasion
by the Fourteenth, or some part of it, are the First

Amendment's freedoms of speech, press, religion, assembly, association, and petition for redress of grievances. For the same reason, though not always in precisely the same terminology, the Court has made obligatory on the States the Fifth Amendment's command that private property shall not be taken for public use without just compensation, the Fourth Amendment's prohibition of unreasonable searches and seizures, and the Eighth's ban on cruel and unusual punishment. On the other hand, this Court in Palko v. Connecticut (1937), refused to hold that the Fourteenth Amendment made the double jeopardy provision of the Fifth Amendment obligatory on the States. In so refusing, however, the Court, speaking through Mr. Justice Cardozo, was careful to emphasize that "immunities that are valid as against the federal government by force of the specific pledges of particular amendments have been found to be implicit in the concept of ordered liberty, and thus, through the Fourteenth Amendment, become valid as against the states" and that guarantees "in their origin . . . effective against the federal government alone" had by prior cases "been taken over from the earlier articles of the federal bill of rights and brought within the Fourteenth Amendment by a process of absorption."

We accept Betts v. Brady's assumption, based as it was on our prior cases, that a provision of the Bill of Rights which is "fundamental and essential to a fair trial" is made obligatory upon the States by the Fourteenth Amendment. We think the Court in Betts was wrong, however, in concluding that the Sixth Amendment's guarantee of counsel is not one of these fundamental rights. Ten years before Betts v. Brady, this Court, after full consideration of all the historical data examined in Betts, had unequivocally declared that "the right to the aid of counsel is of this fundamental character." . . . While the Court at the close of its Powell opinion did by its language, as this Court frequently does, limit its holding to the particular facts and circumstances of that case, its conclusions about the fundamental nature of the right to counsel are unmistakable. Several years later, in 1936, the Court reemphasized what it had said about the fundamental nature of the right to counsel in this language:

"We concluded that certain fundamental rights, safeguarded by the first eight amendments against federal action, were also safeguarded against state action by the due process of law clause of the Fourteenth Amendment, and among them the fundamental right of the accused to the aid of counsel in a criminal prosecution." Grosjean v. American Press Co. (1936).

And again in 1938 this Court said:

"[The assistance of counsel] is one of the safeguards of the Sixth Amendment deemed necessary to insure fundamental human rights of life and liberty. . . . The Sixth Amendment stands as a constant admonition that if the constitutional safeguards it provides be lost, justice will not 'still be done,'" Johnson v. Zerbst (1938). . . .

In light of these many other prior decisions of this Court, it is not surprising that the Betts Court, when faced with the contention that "one charged with crime, who is unable to obtain counsel, must be furnished counsel by the State," conceded that "[e]xpressions in the opinions of this court lend color to the argument. . . ." The fact is that in deciding as it did—that "appointment of counsel is not a fundamental right, essential to a fair trial"—the Court in Betts v. Brady made an abrupt break with its own well-considered precedents. In returning to these old precedents, sounder we believe than the new, we but restore constitutional principles established to achieve a fair system of justice. Not only these precedents but also reason and reflection require us to recognize that in our adversary system of criminal justice, any person haled into court, who is too poor to hire a lawyer, cannot be assured a fair trial unless counsel is provided for him. This seems to us to be an obvious truth. Governments, both state and federal, quite properly spend vast sums of money to establish machinery to try defendants accused of crime. Lawyers to prosecute are everywhere deemed essential to protect the public's interest in an orderly society. Similarly, there are few defendants charged with crime, few indeed, who fail to hire the best lawyers they can get to prepare and present their defenses. That government hires lawyers to prosecute and defendants who have the money hire lawyers to defend are the strongest indications of the widespread belief that lawyers in criminal courts are necessities, not luxuries. The right of one charged with crime to counsel may not be deemed fundamental and essential for fair trials in some countries, but it is in ours. From the very beginning, our state and national constitutions and laws have laid great emphasis on procedural and substantive safeguards designed to assure fair trials before impartial tribunals in which every defendant stands equal before the law. This noble ideal cannot be realized if the poor man charged with crime has to face his accusers without a lawyer to assist him. A defendant's need for a lawyer is nowhere better stated than in the moving words of Mr. Justice Sutherland in Powell v. Alabama:

"The right to be heard would be, in many cases, of little avail if it did not comprehend the right to be heard by counsel. Even the intelligent and educated layman has small and sometimes no skill in the science of law. If charged with crime, he is incapable, generally, of determining for himself whether the indictment is good or bad. He is unfamiliar with the rules of evidence. Left without the aid of counsel he may be put on trial without a proper charge, and convicted upon incompetent evidence, or evidence irrelevant to the issue or otherwise inadmissible. He lacks both the skill and knowledge adequately to prepare his defense, even though he have a perfect one. He requires the guiding hand of counsel at every step in the proceedings against him. Without it, though he be not guilty, he faces the danger of conviction because he does not know how to establish his innocence."

The Court in Betts v. Brady departed from the sound wisdom upon which the Court's holding in Powell v. Alabama rested. Florida, supported by two other States, has asked that Betts v. Brady be left intact.

Twenty-two States, as friends of the Court, argue that Betts was "an anachronism when handed down" and that it should now be overruled. We agree.

The judgment is reversed and the cause is remanded to the Supreme Court of Florida for further action not inconsistent with this opinion.

Reversed.

Mr. Justice **Douglas,** while joining the opinion of the Court, wrote a separate opinion, saying in part:

My Brother Harlan is of the view that a guarantee of the Bill of Rights that is made applicable to the States by reason of the Fourteenth Amendment is a lesser version of that same guarantee as applied to the Federal Government. Mr. Justice Jackson shared the view. But that view has not prevailed and rights protected against state invasion by the Due Process Clause of the Fourteenth Amendment are not watered-down versions of what the Bill of Rights guarantees.

Mr. Justice **Clark,** concurring in the result, wrote a separate opinion.

Mr. Justice **Harlan,** concurring, said in part:

I agree that Betts v. Brady should be overruled, but consider it entitled to a more respectful burial than has been accorded, at least on the part of those of us who were not on the Court when that case was decided.

I cannot subscribe to the view that Betts v. Brady represented "an abrupt break with its own well considered precedents." In 1932, in Powell v. Alabama, a capital case, this Court declared that under the particular facts there presented—"the ignorance and illiteracy of the defendants, their youth, the circumstances of public hostility . . . and above all that they stood in deadly peril of their lives"—the state court had a duty to assign counsel for the trial as a necessary requisite of due process of law. It is evident that these limiting facts were not added to the opinion as an afterthought; they were repeatedly emphasized, and were clearly regarded as important to the result.

Thus when this Court, a decade later, decided Betts v. Brady, it did no more than to admit of the possible existence of special circumstances in noncapital as well as capital trials, while at the same time insisting that such circumstances be shown in order to establish a denial of due process. The right to appointed counsel had been recognized as being considerably broader in federal prosecutions, see Johnson v. Zerbst, but to have imposed these requirements on the States would indeed have been "an abrupt break" with the almost immediate past. The declaration that the right to appointed counsel in state prosecutions, as established in Powell v. Alabama, was not limited to capital cases was in truth not a departure from, but an extension of, existing precedent. . . .

[Mr. Justice Harlan here notes the "troubled journey" of the Powell and Betts doctrines and concedes that since 1950 no "special circumstances" have been found to justify the absence of counsel.]

. . . The Court has come to recognize, in other words, that the mere existence of a serious criminal charge constituted in itself special circumstances requiring the services of counsel at trial. In truth the Betts v. Brady rule is no longer a reality.

This evaluation, however, appears not to have been fully recognized by many state courts, in this instance charged with the front-line responsibility for the enforcement of constitutional rights. To continue a rule which is honored by this Court only with lip service is not a healthy thing and in the long run will do disservice to the federal system. . . .

In agreeing with the Court that the right to counsel in a case such as this should now be expressly recognized as a fundamental right embraced in the Fourteenth Amendment, I wish to make a further observation. When we hold a right or immunity, valid against the Federal Government, to be "implicit in the concept of ordered liberty" and thus valid against the States, I do not read our past decisions to suggest that by so holding, we automatically carry over an entire body of federal law and apply it in full sweep to the States. Any such concept would disregard the frequently wide disparity between the legitimate interests of the States and of the Federal Government, the divergent problems that they face, and the significantly different consequences of their actions. . . . In what is done today I do not understand the Court to depart from the principles laid down in Palko v. Connecticut, or to embrace the concept that the Fourteenth Amendment "incorporates" the Sixth Amendment as such.

On these premises I join in the judgment of the Court.

CRUEL AND UNUSUAL PUNISHMENTS

GREGG v. GEORGIA

428 U. S. 153; 96 St. Ct. 2909; 49 L. Ed. 2d 859
(1976)

The Eighth Amendment prohibits the infliction of cruel and unusual punishment, but makes no effort to define such punishment. In early England most felonies were punished by hanging, and for certain serious crimes, such as treason, a person could be drawn and quartered. In colonial America the pillory and stocks were a feature of nearly every town square, and flogging was common for many offenses. At the time the Constitution was adopted both branding and piercing the nostrils were accepted punishments in some jurisdictions. Many, if not all, of these forms of punishment would be considered uncivilized today, and have long since been abolished. In 1963 the supreme court of Delaware, the last state to permit flogging (except for infraction of prison rules), upheld the sentence of twenty lashes for breaking parole in a car theft case; but the state pardons board freed the man and the sentence was not carried out. In *Louisiana ex rel. Francis v. Resweber* (1947) the Supreme Court, assuming capital punishment to be valid, rejected the contention that the state's failure to electrocute the defendant on the first try made subsequent tries cruel and unusual. In *Wilkerson v. Utah* (1879) the Court had held shooting was not cruel and unusual, but suggested the ban would include both drawing and quartering and burning alive.

The idea that punishment could be cruel and unusual not in the abstract, but because it did not "fit the crime" to which it was attached, was argued as early as 1892 by Justice Field in his dissent in *O'Neil v. Vermont*, a case in which a New Yorker selling liquor illegally in Vermont stood to serve 19,914 days in jail for 307 separate illegal sales. The Court found that since the Eighth Amendment did not limit the states, no federal question was involved. In reviewing a case arising under the Philippine constitution, whose cruel and unusual punishment clause was identical to the Eighth Amendment's, the Court struck down as cruel and unusual a twelve-year sentence at hard labor in irons for knowingly making a false statement in a public document; see *Weems v. United States* (1910). The Court, however, appeared to reject this approach in the 1980s. It upheld a sentence of life imprisonment for violating Texas' recidivist statute despite the fact that none of the three felonies involved the theft of more than a \$120.75; see *Rummel v. Estelle* (1980). And in *Hutto v. Davis* (1982) it held that a person with nine ounces of marijuana could be sentenced to two consecutive twenty-year terms in prison and a \$20,000 fine for the two crimes of possession and possession with intent to distribute.

Then in 1983, with Justice Blackmun switching over, it again held that the punishment should fit the crime. In *Solem v. Holm*, it held void as disproportionately cruel a life sentence for a series of crimes virtually indistinguishable from those of *Rummel*. It did not overrule *Rummel*, but noted that while Rummel would become eligible for parole in twelve years, Solem would spend his life in prison unless his sentence were commuted by the governor.

In 1991, in *Harmelin v. Michigan*, the Court returned to the *Rummel* approach and upheld a mandatory life sentence without possibility of parole for possession of 672 grams of cocaine. Conceding that "severe, mandatory penalties may be cruel, but they are not unusual in the constitutional sense," the court virtually limited the Eighth Amendment protections to the death penalty. Two members of the Court urged overruling *Solem*.

The Court did hold it cruel and unusual to punish a person for being sick or having some affliction over which he has no control. In *Robinson v. California* (1962) the Court struck down a state statute making it a misdemeanor "to be addicted to the use of narcotics." While the state was free to punish the use of narcotics or prescribe a mandatory program of treatment for addicts,

such addiction was an "illness which may be contracted innocently or involuntarily. We hold that a state law which imprisons a person thus afflicted as a criminal, even though he has never touched any narcotic drug within the State or been guilty of any irregular behavior there, inflicts cruel and unusual punishment in violation of the Fourteenth Amendment. To be sure, imprisonment for ninety days is not, in the abstract, a punishment which is either cruel or unusual. But the question cannot be considered in the abstract. Even one day in prison would be a cruel and unusual punishment for the 'crime' of having a common cold."

Following the *Robinson* case, a sixty-year-old bootblack with over one hundred convictions for public drunkenness argued that alcoholism, like drug addiction, was a disease and could not be punished. Five members of the Court agreed that his conviction for public drunkenness was not a cruel and unusual punishment. While they were unable to agree on an opinion regarding alcoholism, they did agree that Powell was not being punished for alcoholism, but for being in public while drunk. Four members of the Court dissented on the ground that his affliction was such that he could not resist being drunk in public. See *Powell v. Texas* (1968).

Unlike most constitutional developments, which take place gradually with the Court hinting broadly at the path it plans to follow, the inclusion of the death penalty in the Eighth Amendment came with startling suddenness. In nearly every case involving cruel and unusual punishment, the Court had discussed the death penalty, and while none of these cases had raised the Eighth Amendment question directly, in each of them the Court had left no doubt that the penalty, as such, was valid. As late as 1958, four members of the majority (Justice Brennan concurred on other grounds) said in *Trop v. Dulles* that while expatriation was a cruel and unusual punishment, the death penalty "cannot be said to violate the constitutional concept of cruelty."

Then in the 1960s an all-out legal attack was launched against the penalty, underwritten largely by the American Civil Liberties Union and the NAACP Legal Defense Fund, which had evidence that most of those executed since 1930 were black. The penalty was challenged on a variety of grounds, and on June 3, 1967, the execution of more than 500 condemned prisoners throughout the country came to a halt while courts and governors waited to see what the Supreme Court would do.

The first of these challenges reached the Supreme Court in *Witherspoon v. Illinois* (1968), and for the first time the Court gave an indication that the death penalty was in trouble. Illinois permitted a verdict of guilty and a sentence of death to be handed down by a jury from which the state had deliberately excluded all persons with scruples against capital punishment. The Court declined to reverse the verdict of guilty, since the jury would not be necessarily prone to convict, but it held that no jury so constituted could hand down a sentence of death since such a jury "fell woefully short of that impartiality to which the petitioner was entitled under the Sixth and Fourteenth Amendments." "A jury that must choose between life imprisonment and capital punishment can do little more—and must do nothing less—than express the conscience of the community on the ultimate question of life or death. Yet, in a nation less than half of whose people believe in the death penalty, a jury composed exclusively of such people cannot speak for the community. Culled of all who harbor doubts about the wisdom of capital punishment—of all who would be reluctant to pronounce the extreme penalty—such a jury can speak only for a distinct and dwindling minority." Justice Black, dissenting with Justices Harlan and White, pointed up the majority's underlying motives. "If this Court is to hold capital punishment unconstitutional, I think it should do so forthrightly, not by making it impossible for States to get juries that will enforce the death penalty."

The hopes of opponents of the death penalty that it had been abolished by the Witherspoon case proved unduly optimistic, but the moratorium on executions remained in effect while other challenges were readied for Supreme Court review. One such challenge involved the question of whether a jury could constitutionally impose the death penalty without any governing standards, and in McGautha v. California (1971) the Court held that it could. Justice Harlan, writing for a six-man majority, traced the efforts of the states to reduce the rigors of mandatory death sentences, first by introducing "degrees" of murder, and, when juries still took the law into their own hands, finally giving way to reality and providing for complete jury discretion to hang or not to hang.

On the basis of this history the Court concluded that "to identify before the fact those characteristics of criminal homicides and their perpetrators which call for the death penalty, and to express these characteristics in language which can be fairly understood and applied by the sentencing authority, appear to be tasks which are beyond present human ability." It cited the efforts of a British Royal Commission to solve the same problem and its conclusion that "no simple formula can take account of the innumerable degrees of culpability, and no formula which fails to do so can claim to satisfy public opinion." The list of "aggravating and mitigating circumstances" provided in the Model Penal Code for jury consideration, the Court said, "bear witness to the intractable nature of the problem of 'standards'. . . . [and] caution against this Court's undertaking to establish such standards itself." . . .

The Court concluded that "in the light of history, experience, and the present limitations of human knowledge, we find it quite impossible to say that committing to the untrammeled discretion of the jury the power to pronounce life or death in capital cases is offensive to anything in the Constitution." At the same time it held that the Ohio system of having the jury decide both guilt and punishment together did not deny due process merely because a defendant who wanted to argue for clemency could hardly do so without incriminating himself. "The criminal process, like the rest of the legal system, is replete with situations requiring 'the making of difficult judgments' as to which course to follow."

In a long and carefully reasoned dissent Justice Brennan, joined by Justices Douglas and Marshall, attacked the discretion of the sentencing jury to kill or not to kill as it wished as amounting to "nothing more than government by whim"—a form totally at odds with the "government of laws" protected by the due process clause. "We are not presented with the slightest attempt to bring the power of reason to bear on the considerations relevant to capital sentencing. We are faced with nothing more than stark legislative abdication. Not once in the history of this Court, until today, have we sustained against a due process challenge such an unguided, unbridled, unreviewable exercise of naked power. Almost a century ago, we found an almost identical California procedure constitutionally inadequate to license a laundry. Yick Wo v. Hopkins (1886). Today we hold it adequate to license life."

The decision in McGautha was widely viewed as the Supreme Court's final word on the death penalty. No more cases involving it were pending before the Court, and with the right of juries to act arbitrarily firmly guaranteed, there seemed little likelihood that an Eighth Amendment argument would prevail. As states made preparations to start executing the now almost 700 prisoners on death row, the Court announced it would hear a group of cases involving the Eighth Amendment. In June 1972, in Furman v. Georgia, it held the death penalty void.

None of the five members of the majority could agree on an opinion. Justices Marshall and Brennan agreed that all capital punishment was cruel and unusual, with the latter reasoning that "a punishment may not be so severe as to be degrading to the dignity of human beings," and no punishment met this test which was inflicted arbitrarily, which was unacceptable to contemporary society, and which was excessive in view of the purpose to be achieved. In view of its waning popularity and erratic application, the death penalty failed on all counts. Justice Douglas argued that since it was applied disproportionately to the underprivileged, it was therefore "not compatible with the idea of equal protection of the laws that is implicit in the ban on 'cruel and unusual' punishments." Justice Marshall agreed about the discrimination, but stressed that it was ineffective as a deterrent of the crimes for which it was inflicted and would be rejected by a public that was truly "informed" about its operation and impact. Justices Stewart and White, without arguing that the death penalty was cruel per se, noted that the cruelty of the provisions currently in use lay in the results they produced—that the infliction of the penalty was so infrequent and unpredictable that it served neither the goal of deterrence nor of retribution.

The dissenting justices argued that since the Fifth Amendment alluded to capital offenses, it was clear that the framers of the Eighth did not consider death cruel and unusual; that the Court had said uniformly over the years and as recently as Trop v. Dulles in 1958 that it *was not cruel; and that the evidence did not show "that capital punishment offends the conscience of society to such a degree that our traditional deference to legislative judgment must be abandoned."*

The effect of Furman was to invalidate every death penalty statute in the country, and legislatures studied the case in the hope of discerning from the multitude of opinions what sort of statute might pass constitutional muster. Since the fault of previous statutes seemed to lie in the erratic use of the penalty, two answers suggested themselves. Either the discretion of the sentencing authority could be taken away altogether in an effort to have the penalty inflicted in all cases, or it could be carefully guided to produce more consistent results.

The first of these approaches came to the Court in the cases of Stanislaus Roberts v. Louisiana and Woodson v. North Carolina. There, Justices Stewart, Powell and Stevens joined Justices Brennan and Marshall to hold the statutes void. Insistence that the death penalty always be applied, the Court found, would merely perpetuate the pre-Furman pattern in which juries would simply refuse to convict if they felt the death penalty inappropriate for a particular case. A similar result was reached in Sumner v. Shuman (1987) where a mandatory death penalty for murder for a life-sentence prison inmate was held void as not allowing for mitigating circumstances.

Mr. Justice **Stewart**, Mr. Justice **Powell**, and Mr. Justice **Stevens** announced the judgment of the Court and filed an opinion delivered by Mr. Justice **Stewart**, saying in part:

The issue in this case is whether the imposition of the sentence of death for the crime of murder under the law of Georgia violates the Eight and Fourteenth Amendments.

I.

The petitioner, Troy Gregg, was charged with committing armed robbery and murder. In accordance with Georgia procedure in capital cases, the trial was in two stages, a guilt stage and a sentencing stage. The evidence at the guilt trial established that on November 21, 1973, the petitioner and a traveling companion, Floyd Allen, while hitchhiking north in Florida were picked up by Fred Simmons and Bob Moore. Their car broke down, but they continued north after Simmons purchased another vehicle with some of the cash he was carrying. While still in Florida, they picked up another hitchhiker, Denis Weaver, who rode with them to Atlanta, where he was let out about 11 p.m. A short time later the four men interrupted their journey for a rest stop along the highway. The next morning the bodies of Simmons and Moore were discovered in a ditch nearby.

On November 23, after reading about the shootings in an Atlanta newspaper, Weaver communicated with the Gwinnett County police and related information concerning the journey with the victims, including a description of the car. The next afternoon, the petitioner and Allen, while in Simmons' car, were arrested in Asheville, N. C. In the search incident to the arrest a .25-caliber pistol, later shown to be that used to kill Simmons and Moore, was found in the petitioner's pocket. After receiving the warnings required by Miranda v. Arizona (1966), and signing a written waiver of his rights, the petitioner signed a statement in which he admitted shooting, then robbing Simmons and Moore. He justified the slayings on grounds of self-defense. The next day, while being transferred to Lawrenceville, Ga., the petitioner and Allen were taken to the scene of the shootings. Upon arriving there, Allen recounted the events leading to the slayings. His version of these events was as follows: After Simmons and Moore left the car, the petitioner stated that he intended to rob them. The petitioner then took his pistol in hand and positioned himself on the car to improve his aim. As Simmons and Moore came up an embankment toward the car, the petitioner fired three shots and the two men fell near a ditch. The petitioner, at close range, then fired a shot into the head of each. He robbed them of valuables and drove away with Allen. . . .

The trial judge submitted the murder charges to the jury on both felony-murder and nonfelony-murder theories. He also instructed on the issue of self-defense but declined to instruct on manslaughter. He submitted the robbery case to the jury on both an armed-robbery theory and on the lesser included offense of robbery by intimidation. The jury found the petitioner guilty of two counts of armed robbery and two counts of murder.

At the penalty stage, which took place before the same jury, neither the prosecutor nor the petitioner's lawyer offered any additional evidence. Both counsel, however, made lengthy arguments dealing generally with the propriety of capital punishment under the circumstances and with the weight of the evidence of guilt. The trial judge instructed the jury that it could recommend either a death sentence or a life prison sentence on each count. The judge further charged the jury that in determining what sentence was appropriate the jury was free to consider the facts and circumstances, if any, presented by the parties in mitigation or aggravation.

Finally, the judge instructed the jury that it "would not be authorized to consider [imposing] the penalty of death" unless it first found beyond a reasonable doubt one of these aggravating circumstances:

"One—That the offense of murder was committed while the offender was engaged in the commission of two other capital felonies, to-wit the armed robbery of [Simmons and Moore].

"Two—That the offender committed the offense of murder for the purpose of receiving money and the automobile described in the indictment.

"Three—The offense of murder was outrageously and wantonly vile, horrible and inhuman, in that they [sic] involved the depravity of [the] mind of the defendant."

Finding the first and second of these circumstances, the jury returned verdicts of death on each count.

The Supreme court of Georgia affirmed the convictions and the imposition of the death sentences for murder. After reviewing the trial transcript and the record, including the evidence, and comparing the evidence and sentence in similar cases in accordance with the requirements of Georgia law, the court concluded that, considering the nature of the crime and the defendant, the sentences of death had not resulted from prejudices or any other arbitrary factor and were not excessive or disproportionate to the penalty applied in similar cases. The death sentences imposed for armed robbery, however, were vacated on the grounds that the death penalty had rarely been imposed in Georgia for that offense and that the jury improperly considered the murders as aggravating circumstances for the robberies after having considered the armed robberies as aggravating circumstances for the murders. . . .

II.

Before considering the issues presented it is necessary to understand the Georgia statutory scheme for the imposition of the death penalty. The Georgia statute, as amended after our decision in Furman v. Georgia (1972), retains the death penalty for six categories of crime: murder, kidnapping for ransom or where the victim is harmed, armed robbery, rape, treason, and aircraft hijacking. The capital defendant's guilt or innocence is determined in the traditional manner, either by a trial judge or a jury, in the first stage of a bifurcated trial.

If trial is by jury, the trial judge is required to charge lesser included offenses when they are supported by any view of the evidence. . . . After a verdict, finding, or plea of guilty to a capital crime, a presentence hearing is conducted before whoever made the determination of guilt. the sentencing procedures are essentially the same in both bench and jury trials. At the hearing: "[T]he judge [or jury] shall hear additional evidence in extenuation, mitigation, and aggravation of punishment, including the record of any prior criminal convictions and pleas of guilty or pleas of nolo contendere of the defendant, or the absence of any prior conviction and pleas: Provided, however, that only such evidence in aggravation as the State has made known to the defendant prior to his trial shall be admissible. The judge [or jury] shall also hear argument by the defendant or his counsel and the prosecuting attorney . . . regarding the punishment to be imposed." . . .

III.

[The Court here review previous cases dealing with the death penalty.]

It is clear from the foregoing precedents that the Eighth Amendment has not been regarded as a static concept. As Mr. Chief Justice Warren said, in an oft-quoted phrase, "[t]he Amendment must draw its meaning from the evolving standards of decency that mark the progress of a maturing society." Trop v. Dulles [1958]. . . . Thus, an assessment of contemporary values concerning the infliction of a challenged sanction is relevant to the application of the Eighth Amendment. As we develop below more fully, this assessment does not call for a subjective judgment. It requires, rather, that we look to objective indicia that reflect the public attitude toward a given sanction.

But our cases also make clear that public perceptions of standards of decency with respect to criminal sanctions are not conclusive. A penalty also must accord with "the dignity of man," which is the "basic concept underlying the Eighth Amendment." Trop v. Dulles. This means, at least, that the punishment not be "excessive." When a form of punishment in the abstract (in this case, whether capital punishment may ever be imposed as a sanction for murder) rather than in the particular (the propriety of death as a penalty to be applied to a specific defendant for a specific crime) is under consideration, the inquiry into "excessiveness" has two aspects. First, the punishment must not involve the unnecessary and wanton infliction of pain. Furman v. Georgia (Burger, C.J., dissenting). . . . Second, the punishment must not be grossly out of proportion to the severity of the crime. Trop v. Dulles. . . .

C.

. . . We now consider specifically whether the sentence of death for the crime of murder is a per se violation of the Eighth and Fourteenth Amendments to the Constitution. We note first that history and precedent strongly support a negative answer to this question.

The imposition of the death penalty for the crime of murder has a long history of acceptance both in the United States and in England. The common-law rule imposed a mandatory death sentence on all convicted murderers. McGautha v. California (1971). . . .

It is apparent from the text of the Constitution itself that the existence of capital punishment was accepted by the Framers. At the time the Eighth Amendment was ratified, capital punishment was a common sanction in every State. Indeed, the First Congress of the United States enacted legislation providing death as the penalty for specified crimes. The Fifth Amendment, adopted at the same time as the Eighth, contemplated the continued existence of the capital sanction by imposing certain limits on the prosecution of capital cases. . . . And the Fourteenth Amendment, adopted over three-quarters of a century later, similarly contemplates the existence of the capital sanction in providing that no State shall deprive any person of "life, liberty, or property" without due process of law.

For nearly two centuries, this Court, repeatedly and often expressly, has recognized that capital punishment is not invalid per se. . . .

Four years ago, the petitioners in Furman and its

companion cases predicated their argument primarily upon the asserted proposition that standards of decency had evolved to the point where capital punishment no longer could be tolerated. The petitioners in those cases said, in effect, that the evolutionary process had come to an end, and that standards of decency required that the Eighth Amendment be construed finally as prohibiting capital punishment for any crime regardless of its depravity and impact on society. This view was accepted by two Justices. Three other justices were unwilling to go so far; focusing on the procedures by which convicted defendants were selected for the death penalty rather than on the actual punishment inflicted, they joined in the conclusion that the statutes before the Court were constitutionally invalid.

The petitioners in the capital cases before the Court today renew the "standards of decency" argument, but developments during the four years since Furman have undercut substantially the assumptions upon which their argument rested. Despite the continuing debate, dating back to the 19th century, over the morality and utility of capital punishment, it is now evident that a large proportion of American society continues to regard it as an appropriate and necessary criminal sanction.

The most marked indication of society's endorsement of the death penalty of murder is the legislative response to Furman. The legislatures of at least 35 States have enacted new statutes that provide for the death penalty for at least some crimes that result in the death of another person. And the Congress of the United States, in 1974, enacted a statute providing the death penalty for aircraft conspiracy that results in death. These recently adopted statutes have attempted to address the concerns expressed by the Court in Furman primarily (i) by specifying the factors to be weighed and the procedures to be followed in deciding when to impose a capital sentence, or (ii) by making the death penalty mandatory for specified crimes. But all of the post-Furman statutes make clear that capital punishment itself has not been rejected by the elected representatives of the people.

In the only statewide referendum occurring since Furman and brought to our attention, the people of California adopted a constitutional amendment that authorized capital punishment, in effect negating a prior ruling by the Supreme Court of California ... that the death penalty violated the California Constitution. ...

As we have seen, however, the Eighth Amendments demands more than that a challenged punishment be acceptable to contemporary society. The Court also must ask whether it comports with the basic concept of human dignity at the core of the Amendment. ...

The death penalty is said to serve two principal social purposes: retribution and deterrence of capital crimes by prospective offenders.

In part, capital punishment is an expression of society's moral outrage at particularly offensive conduct. This function may be unappealing to many, but it is essential in an ordered society that asks its citizens to rely on legal processes rather than self-help to vindicate their wrongs. "The instinct for retribution is part of the nature of man, and channeling that instinct in the administration of criminal justice serves an important purpose in promoting the stability of a society governed by law. When people begin to believe that organized society is unwilling or unable to impose upon criminal offenders the punishment they 'deserve,' then there are sown the seeds of anarchy—of self-help, vigilante justice, and lynch law." Furman v. Georgia (Stewart, J., concurring). ...

Statistical attempts to evaluate the worth of the death penalty as a deterrent to crimes by potential offenders have occasioned a great deal of debate. The results simply have been inconclusive. As one opponent of capital punishment has said: "[A]fter all possible inquiry, including the probing of all possible methods of inquiry, we do not know, and for systematic and easily visible reasons cannot know, what the truth about this 'deterrent' effect may be . . . ."

In sum, we cannot say that the judgment of the Georgia legislature that capital punishment may be necessary in some cases is clearly wrong. Considerations of federalism, as well as respect for the ability of a legislature to evaluate, in terms of its particular state the moral consensus concerning the death penalty and its social utility as a sanction, require us to conclude, in the absence of more convincing evidence, that the infliction of death as a punishment for murder is not without justification and thus is not unconstitutionally severe.

Finally, we must consider whether the punishment of death is disproportionate in relation to the crime for which it is imposed. There is no question that death as a punishment is unique in its severity and irrevocability. Furman v. Georgia, (Stewart, J., concurring). When a defendant's life is at stake, the Court has been particularly sensitive to insure that every safeguard is observed. ... But we are concerned here only with the imposition of capital punishment for the crime of murder, and when a life has been taken deliberately by the offender, we cannot say that the punishment is invariably disproportionate to the crime. It is an extreme sanction, suitable to the most extreme of crimes.

We hold that the death penalty is not a form of punishment that may never be imposed, regardless of the circumstances of the offense, regardless of the character of the offender, and regardless of the procedure followed in reaching the decision to impose it.

IV.

We now consider whether Georgia may impose the death penalty on the petitioner in this case.

A.

Furman mandates that where discretion is afforded a sentencing body on a matter so grave as the determination of whether a human life should be taken or spared, that discretion must be suitably directed and limited so as to minimize the risk of wholly arbitrary and capricious action.

It is certainly not a novel proposition that discretion in the area of sentencing be exercised in an informed manner. We have long recognized that "[f]or the determination of sentences, justice generally requires . . . that there be taken into account the circumstances of the offense together with the character and propensities of the offender." . . .

Jury sentencing has been considered desirable in capital cases in order "to maintain a link between contemporary community values and the penal system—a link without which the determination of punishment could hardly reflect 'the evolving standards of decency that mark the progress of a maturing society.' But it creates special problems. Much of the information that is relevant to the sentencing decision may have no relevance to the question of guilt, or may even be extremely prejudicial to a fair determination of that question. This problem, however, is scarcely insurmountable. Those who have studied the question suggest that a bifurcated procedure—one in which the question of sentence is not considered until the determination of guilt has been made—is the best answer. . . .

. . . When a human life is at stake and when the jury must have information prejudicial to the question of guilt but relevant to the question of penalty in order to impose a rational sentence, a bifurcated system is more likely to ensure elimination of the constitutional deficiencies identified in Furman. . . .

The idea that a jury should be given guidance in its decision making is also hardly a novel proposition. Juries are invariably given careful instruction on the law and how to apply it before they are authorized to decide the merits of a lawsuit. It would be virtually unthinkable to follow any other course in a legal system that has traditionally operated by following prior precedents and fixed rules of law. . . .

While some have suggested that standards to guide a capital jury's sentencing deliberations are impossible to formulate, the fact is that such standards have been developed. When the drafters of the Model Penal Code faced this problem, they concluded "that it is within the realm of possibility to point to the main circumstances of aggravation and of mitigation that should be weighted, *and weighed against each other*, when they are presented in a concrete case." . . .

B.

We now turn to consideration of the constitutionality of Georgia's capital-sentencing procedures. In the wake of Furman, Georgia amended its capital punishment statute, but chose not to narrow the scope of its murder provisions. Thus, now as before Furman, in Georgia "[a] person commits murder when he unlawfully and with malice aforethought, either express or im-

plied, causes the death of another human being." All persons convicted of murder "shall be punished by death or by imprisonment for life."

Georgia did act, however, to narrow the class of murderers subject to capital punishment by specifying 10 statutory aggravating circumstances, one of which must be found by the jury to exist beyond a reasonable doubt before a death sentence can ever be imposed. In addition, the jury is authorized to consider any other appropriate aggravating or mitigating circumstances. The jury is not required to find any mitigating circumstance in order to make a recommendation of mercy that is binding on the trial court, but it must find a *statutory* aggravating circumstance before recommending a sentence of death.

These procedures require the jury to consider the circumstances of the crime and the criminal before it recommends sentence. No longer can a Georgia jury do as Furman's jury did: reach a finding of the defendant's guilt, and then, without guidance or direction, decide whether he should live or die. Instead, the jury's attention is directed to the specific circumstances of the crime: Was it committed in the course of another capital felony? Was it committed for money? Was it committed upon a peace officer or judicial officer? Was it committed in a particularly heinous way or in a manner that endangered the lives of many persons? In addition, the jury's attention is focused on the characteristics of the person who committed the crime: Does he have a record of prior convictions for capital offenses? Are there any special acts about this defendant that mitigate against imposing capital punishment (e.g., his youth, the extent of his cooperation with the police, his emotional state at the time of the crime). As a result, while some jury discretion still exists, "the discretion to be exercised is controlled by clear and objective standards so as to produce non-discriminatory application." . . .

3.

Finally, the Georgia statute has an additional provision designed to assure that the death penalty will not be imposed on a capriciously selected group of convicted defendants. The new sentencing procedures require that the state supreme court review every death sentence to determine whether it was imposed under the influence of passion, prejudice, or any other arbitrary factor, whether the evidence supports the findings of a statutory aggravating circumstance, and "[w]hether the sentence of death is excessive or disproportionate to the penalty imposed in similar cases, considering both the crime and the defendant." In performing its sentence-review function, the Georgia court has held that "if the death penalty is only rarely imposed for an act or it is substantially out of line with sentences imposed for other acts it will be set aside as excessive." . . . The court on another occasion stated that "we view it to be our duty under the similarity standard to assure that no death sentence is affirmed unless in similar cases throughout the state the death penalty has been imposed generally. . . .''

It is apparent that the Supreme Court of Georgia has taken its review responsibilities seriously. . . . Although armed robbery is a capital offense under Georgia law, the Georgia court concluded that the death sentences imposed in this case for that crime were ''unusual in that they are rarely imposed for [armed robbery]. Thus, under the test provided by statute, . . . they must be considered to be excessive or disproportionate to the penalties imposed in similar cases.'' The Court therefore vacated Gregg's death sentences for armed robbery and has followed a similar course in every other armed robbery death penalty case to come before it. . . .

The provision for appellate review in the Georgia capital-sentencing system serves as a check against the random or arbitrary imposition of the death penalty. In particular, the proportionality review substantially eliminates the possibility that a person will be sentenced to die by the action of an aberrant jury. If a time comes when juries generally do not impose the death sentence in a certain kind of murder case, the appellate review procedures assures that no defendant convicted under such circumstances will suffer a sentence of death.

V.

. . . For the reasons expressed in this opinion, we hold that the statutory system under which Gregg was sentenced to death does not violate the Constitution. Accordingly, the judgment of the Georgia Supreme Court is affirmed.

It is so ordered.

Mr. Justice **White,** with whom **The Chief Justice** and Mr. Justice **Rehnquist** join, concurring in the judgment, said in part:

III.

. . . The Georgia Legislature has made an effort to identify those aggravating factors which it considers necessary and relevant to the question whether a defendant convicted of capital murder should be sentenced to death. The jury which imposes sentences is instructed on all statutory aggravating factors which are supported by the evidence, and is told that it may not impose the death penalty unless it unanimously finds at least one of those factors to have been established beyond a reasonable doubt. The Georgia Legislature has plainly made an effort to guide the jury in the exercise of its discretion, while at the same time permitting the jury to dispense mercy on the basis of factors too intangible to write into a statute, and I cannot except the naked assertion that the effort is bound to fail. As the types of murders of which the death penalty may be imposed become more narrowly defined and are limited to those which are particularly serious or for which the death penalty is peculiarly

appropriate as they are in Georgia by reason of the aggravating-circumstance requirement, it becomes reasonable to expect that juries—even given discretion not to impose the death penalty—will impose the death penalty in a substantial portion of the cases so defined. If they do, it can no longer be said that the penalty is being imposed wantonly and freakishly or so infrequently that it loses its usefulness as a sentencing device. There is, therefore, reason to expect that Georgia's current system would escape the infirmities which invalidated its previous system under Furman. However, the Georgia Legislature was not satisfied with a system which might, but also might not turn out in practice to result in death sentences being imposed with reasonable consistence for certain serious murders. Instead, it gave the Georgia Supreme Court the power and the obligation to perform precisely the task which three Justices of this Court, whose opinions were necessary to the result, performed in Furman: namely, the task of deciding whether *in fact* the death penalty was being administered for any given class of crime in a discriminatory, standardless, or rare fashion. . . .

Statement of **The Chief Justice** and Mr. Justice **Rehnquist:**

We concur in the judgment and join the opinion of Mr. Justice White, agreeing with its analysis that Georgia's system of capital punishment comports with the Court's holding in Furman v. Georgia.

Mr. Justice **Blackmun,** concurring in the judgment.

I concur in the judgment. See Furman v. Georgia, (1972) (Blackmun, J., dissenting).

Mr. Justice **Brennan,** dissenting, said in part:

The Cruel and Unusual Punishments Clause ''must draw its meaning from the evolving standards of decency that mark the progress of a maturing society.'' The opinions of Mr. Justice Stewart, Mr. Justice Powell, and Mr. Justice Stevens today hold that ''evolving standards of decency'' require focus not on the essence of the death penalty itself but primarily upon the procedures employed by the State to single out persons to suffer the penalty of death. Those opinions hold further that, so viewed, the Clause invalidates the mandatory infliction of the death penalty but not its infliction under sentencing procedures that Mr. Justice Stewart, Mr. Justice Powell, and Mr. Justice Stevens conclude adequately safeguard against the risk that the death penalty was imposed in an arbitrary and capricious manner.

In Furman v. Georgia (1972), I read ''evolving standards of decency'' as requiring focus upon the essence of the death penalty itself and not primarily or solely upon the procedures under which the determination to inflict the penalty upon a particular person was made. . . .

This Court inescapably has the duty, as the ultimate arbiter of the meaning of our Constitution, to say whether, when individuals condemned to death stand before our Bar, "moral concepts" require us to hold that the law has progressed to the point where we should declare that the punishment of death, like punishments on the rack, the screw, and the wheel, is no longer morally tolerable in our civilized society. My opinion in Furman v. Georgia concluded that our civilization and the law had progressed to this point and that therefore the punishment of death, for whatever crime and under all circumstances, is "cruel and unusual" in violation of the Eighth and Fourteenth Amendments of the Constitution. . . .

The fatal constitutional infirmity in the punishment of death is that it treats "members of the human race as nonhumans, as objects to be toyed with and discarded. [It is] thus inconsistent with the fundamental premise of the Clause, that even the vilest criminal remains a human being possessed of common human dignity." As such it is a penalty that "subjects the individual to a fate forbidden by the principle of civilized treatment guaranteed by the [Clause]." I therefore would hold, on that ground alone, that death is today a cruel and unusual punishment prohibited by the Clause. "Justice of this kind is obviously no less shocking than the crime itself, and the new 'official' murder, far from offering redress for the offense committed against society, adds instead a second defilement to the first."

Mr. Justice **Marshall**, dissenting, said in part:

In Furman I concluded that the death penalty is constitutionally invalid for two reasons. First, the death penalty is excessive. And second, the American people, fully informed as to the purposes of the death penalty and its liabilities, would in my view reject it as morally unacceptable.

Since the decision in Furman, the legislatures of 35 States have enacted new statutes authorizing the imposition of the death sentence for certain crimes, and Congress has enacted a law providing the death penalty for air piracy resulting in death. I would be less than candid if I did not acknowledge that these developments have a significant bearing on a realistic assessment of the moral acceptability of the death penalty to the American people. But if the constitutionality of the death penalty turns, as I have urged, on the opinion of an *informed* citizenry, then even the enactment of new death statutes cannot be viewed as conclusive. In Furman, I observed that the American people are largely unaware of the information critical to a judgment on the morality of the death penalty, and concluded that if they were better informed they would consider it shocking, unjust, and unacceptable. A recent study, conducted after the enactment of the post-Furman statutes, has confirmed that the American people know little about the death penalty, and that the opinions of an informed public unaware of the consequences and efforts of the death penalty.

Once the Court decided that execution did not constitute a cruel and unusual punishment, two kinds of problems arose to plague it. One involved the culpability of persons who had conspired to commit the murder but had not actually done the killing. In 1978 in Lockett v. Ohio the Court had held that the death penalty could not be inflicted on the driver of a get-away car where the victim of an attempted robbery had been shot. In 1982 in Ennmund v. Florida, a case almost identical in facts to the Lockett case, the Court in a five-to-four decision reaffirmed its holding in Lockett. Noting that only eight states allow the death penalty to be imposed "solely because the defendant somehow participated in a robbery in the course of which a murder was committed" and a survey showed "only 6 cases out of 362 where a nontriggerman felony murderer was executed," the Court concluded that society had rejected "the death penalty for accomplice liability in felony murders." Relying on its conclusion that "cruel and unusual" is to be judged in terms of present standards, the Court held that "the Eighth Amendment [forbids] imposition of the death penalty on one . . . who aids and abets a felony in the course of which a murder is committed by others but who does not himself kill, attempt to kill, or intend that a killing will take place or that lethal force will be employed." In Tison v. Arizona (1987), however, the fact the non-shooter played a major role in the felony leading to the murder and showed reckless indifference regarding human life justified the death penalty.

Another facet of the problem arose in Cabana v. Bullock (1986), where the accused had held the victim's head while the murderer had hit him first with a whisky bottle and then with a cement block. The issue was which court should decide if the test of Ennmund had been met, and Justices White, Burger, Powell, Rehnquist and O'Connor concluded that the Mississippi state courts should make the initial determination, rather than a federal court on a writ of habeas corpus.

A more difficult problem involved the question whether a particular crime was offensive enough to merit the death penalty. A year after the Gregg decision the Court in Coker v. Georgia (1977) held the same statute invalid as applied to the crime of rape of an adult woman. Here the Court, with only Justices Burger and Rehnquist dissenting, found that in the absence of gross brutality in the act itself, death "is a disproportionate punishment for rape." Not only was Georgia the only state to punish the rape of an adult woman by death, but in 90 percent of the rape convictions under the new law the jury had not imposed the death sentence. In Godfrey v. Georgia (1980) the Court held the limiting aggravating circumstance provided in the statute that the murder be "outrageously and wantonly vile" was unconstitu-

tionally vague and without force as a standard where it was clear a jury could find every murder outrageously and wantonly vile. Here the defendant had simply shot his wife and mother-in-law instantly to death.

In Gregg the Court upheld the death penalty because the Georgia legislature had devised a method of limiting jury discretion. It narrowed the "class of murderers subject to capital punishment by specifying 10 statutory aggravating circumstances, one of which must be found by the jury to exist beyond a reasonable doubt before a death sentence can ever be imposed." The Court was satisfied that the jury could no longer "reach a finding of the defendant's guilt, and then, without guidance or direction, decide whether he should live or die."

However, Georgia law does not require that the jury give any special weight to the aggravating circumstance which it finds; this was attacked in Zant v. Stephens (1983) on the ground that once a murderer was found to belong in a class which made him eligible for the death penalty, the sentencing jury was free from all restriction. The Supreme Court rejected this argument. "Respondent argues that the mandate of Furman is violated by a scheme that permits the jury to exercise unbridled discretion in determining whether the death penalty should be imposed after it has found that the defendant is a member of the class made eligible for that penalty by statute. But that argument could not be accepted without overruling our specific holding in Gregg." There was no suggestion that Gregg should be reconsidered.

In Thompson v. Oklahoma (1988), the Court held the death penalty "cruel and unusual punishment" when applied to a fifteen-year-old boy, despite the finding that he was an incorrigible for whom there was virtually no reasonable prospect of rehabilitation within the juvenile system which resulted in his being tried and convicted as an adult. The Court, in a plurality opinion, took account of the fact that of the 1,393 persons sentenced to death in the previous four years, only five of them, including Thompson, were under sixteen. "Statistics of this kind can, of course, be interpreted in different ways, but they do suggest that these five young offenders have received sentences that are 'cruel and unusual in the same way that being struck by lightning is cruel and unusual.' Furman v. Georgia (Stewart, J., concurring). . . . The death penalty is said to serve two principal social purposes: retribution and deterrence of capital crimes by prospective offenders. . . . In Gregg we concluded that as 'an expression of society's moral outrage at particularly offensive conduct,' retribution was not 'inconsistent with our respect for the dignity of men.' Given the lesser culpability of the juvenile offender, the teenager's capacity for growth, and society's fiduciary obligations to its children, this conclusion is simply inapplicable to the execution of a 15-year-old offender.

"For such a young offender, the deterrence rationale is equally unacceptable. The Department of Justice statistics indicate that about 98 percent of the arrests for willful homicide involved persons who were over 16 at the time of the offense. Thus, excluding younger persons from the class that is eligible for the death penalty will not diminish the deterrent value of capital punishment for the vast majority of potential offenders."

In Payne v. Tennessee (1991) the Court overruled two cases decided within the previous four years and held that "victim impact" evidence was admissible in deciding whether or not to impose the death penalty. In Booth v. Maryland (1987) and South Carolina v. Gathers (1989) the Court had held that only evidence regarding the defendant's attitude and behavior was relevant to his degree of culpability. Following the retirement of Justice Brennan and his replacement by Justice Souter, the Court invited the reargument of Booth and Gathers and overruled both. Noting that the criminal law has long been concerned with the effect of a crime in determining both its definition and its punishment, the Court saw no reason why the emotional impact on the victim's survivors was less important than the character of the defendant in deciding upon the death penalty.

Justice Marshall, in what is believed to be his last written opinion, condemned the majority's feeling "to discard any principle or constitutional liberty which was recognized or reaffirmed over the dissenting votes of four Justices and with which five or more Justices now disagree." "Cast aside today are those condemned to face society's ultimate penalty. Tomorrow's victims may be minorities, women, or the indigent. Inevitably, this campaign to resurrect yesterday's 'spirited dissents' will squander the authority and the legitimacy of this Court as a protector of the powerless."

Justice **Powell** delivered the opinion of the Court, saying in part.

This case presents the question whether a complex statistical study that indicates a risk that racial considerations enter into capital sentencing determinations proves that petitioner McCleskey's capital sentence is unconstitutional under the Eighth or Fourteenth Amendment.

I.

McCleskey, a black man, was convicted of two counts of armed robbery and one count of murder in the Superior Court of Fulton County, Georgia, on October 12, 1978. McCleskey's convictions arose out of the robbery of a furniture store and the killing of a white police officer during the course of the robbery. . . .

The jury convicted McCleskey of murder. At the penalty hearing, the jury heard arguments as to the appropriate sentence. Under Georgia law, the jury could not consider imposing the death penalty unless it found beyond a reasonable doubt that the murder was accompanied by one of the statutory aggravating circumstances. The jury in this case found two aggravating circumstances to exist beyond a reasonable doubt: the murder was committed during the course of an armed robbery; and the murder was committed upon a peace officer engaged in the performance of his duties. In making its decision whether to impose the death sentence, the jury considered the mitigating and aggravating circumstances of McCleskey's conduct. McCleskey offered no mitigating evidence. The jury recommended that he be sentenced to death on the murder charge and to consecutive life sentences on the armed robbery charges. The court followed the jury's recommendation and sentenced McCleskey to death. . . .

McCleskey . . . filed a petition for a writ of habeas corpus in the Federal District Court for the Northern District of Georgia. His petition raised 18 claims, one of which was that the Georgia capital sentencing process is administered in a racially discriminatory manner in violation of the Eighth and Fourteenth Amendments to the United States Constitution. In support of his claim, McCleskey proffered a statistical study performed by Professors David C. Baldus, Charles Pulaski, and George Woodworth (the Baldus study) that purports to show a disparity in the imposition of the death sentence in Georgia based on the race of the murder victim and, to a lesser extent, the race of the defendant. The Baldus study is actually two sophisticated statistical studies that examine over 2,000 murder cases that occurred in Georgia during the 1970's. The raw numbers collected by Professor Baldus indicate that defendants charged with killing white persons received the death penalty in 11% of the cases, but defendants charged with killing blacks received the death penalty in only 1% of the cases. The raw numbers also indicate a reverse racial disparity according to the race of the defendant: 4% of the black defendants received the death penalty, as opposed to 7% of the white defendants.

Baldus also divided the cases according to the combination of the race of the defendant and the race of the victim. He found that the death penalty was assessed in 22% of the cases involving black defendants and white victims; 8% of the cases involving white defendants and white victims; 1% of the cases involving black defendants and black victims; and 3% of the cases involving white defendants and black victims. Similarly, Baldus found that prosecutors sought the death penalty in 70% of the cases involving black defendants and white victims; 32% of the cases involving white defendants and white victims; 15% of the cases involving black defendants and black victims; and 19% of the cases involving white defendants and black victims.

Baldus subjected his data to an extensive analysis, taking account of 230 variables that could have explained the disparities on nonracial grounds. One of his models concludes that, even after taking account of 39 nonracial variables, defendants charged with killing white victims were 4.3 times as likely to receive a death sentence as defendants charged with killing blacks. According to this model, black defendants were 1.1 times as likely to receive a death sentence as other defendants. Thus, the Baldus study indicates that black defendants, such as McCleskey, who kill white victims have the greatest likelihood of receiving the death penalty.

The District Court . . . considered the Baldus study with care. It concluded that McCleskey's "statistics do not demonstrate a prima facie case in support of the contention that the death penalty was imposed upon him because of his race, because of the race of the victim, or because of any Eighth Amendment concern." . . . As to McCleskey's Fourteenth Amendment claim, the court found that the methodology of the Baldus study was flawed in several respects. Because of these defects, the court held that the Baldus study "fail[ed] to contribute anything of value" to McCleskey's claim. Accordingly, the court denied the petition insofar as it was based upon the Baldus study.

The Court of Appeals for the Eleventh Circuit, sitting en banc, carefully reviewed the District Court's decision on McCleskey's claim. It assumed the validity of the study itself and addressed the merits of McCleskey's Eighth and Fourteenth Amendment claims. That is, the court assumed that the study "showed that systematic and substantial disparities existed in the penalties imposed upon homicide defendants in Georgia based on race of the homicide victim, that the disparities existed at a less substantial rate in death sentencing based on race of defendants, and that the factors of race of the victim and defendant were at work in Fulton County." . . .

The Court of Appeals affirmed the denial by the District Court of McCleskey's petition for a writ of habeas corpus insofar as the petition was based upon the Baldus study, with three judges dissenting as to McCleskey's claims based on the Baldus study. We granted certiorari and now affirm.

II.

McCleskey's first claim is that the Georgia capital punishment statute violates the Equal Protection Clause of the Fourteenth Amendment. He argues that race has infected the administration of Georgia's statute in two ways: persons who murder whites are more likely to be sentenced to death than persons who murder blacks, and black murderers are more likely to be sentenced to death than white murderers. As a black defendant who killed a white victim, McCleskey claims that the Baldus study demonstrates that he was discriminated against because of his race and because of the race of his victim. In its broadest form, McCleskey's claim of discrimination extends to every actor in the Georgia capital sentencing process, from the prosecutor who sought the death penalty and the jury that imposed the sentence, to the State itself that enacted the capital punishment statute and allows it to remain in effect despite its allegedly discriminatory application. We agree with the Court of Appeals, and every other court that has considered such a challenge, that this claim must fail.

Our analysis begins with the basic principle that a defendant who alleges an equal protection violation has the burden of proving "the existence of purposeful discrimination." . . . A corollary to this principle is that a criminal defendant must prove that the purposeful discrimination "had a discriminatory effect" on him. . . . Thus, to prevail under the Equal Protection Clause, McCleskey must prove that the decisionmakers in his case acted with discriminatory purpose. He offers no evidence specific to his own case that would support an inference that racial considerations played a part in his sentence. Instead, he relies solely on the Baldus study. McCleskey argues that the Baldus study compels an inference that his sentence rests on purposeful discrimination. McCleskey's claim that these statistics are sufficient proof of discrimination, without regard to the facts of a particular case, would extend to all capital cases in Georgia, at least where the victim was white and the defendant is black.

The Court has accepted statistics as proof of intent to discriminate in certain limited contexts. First, this Court has accepted statistical disparities as proof of an equal protection violation in the selection of the jury venire in a particular district. Although statistical proof normally must present a "stark" pattern to be accepted as the sole proof of discriminatory intent under the Constitution, . . . "because of the nature of the jury-selection task, . . . we have permitted a finding of constitutional violation even when the statistical pattern does not approach [such] extremes." Second, this Court has accepted statistics in the form of multiple-regression analysis to prove statutory violations under Title VII of the Civil Rights Act of 1964. . . .

But the nature of the capital sentencing decision, and the relationship of the statistics to that decision, are fundamentally different from the corresponding elements in the venire-selection or Title VII cases. Most importantly, each particular decision to impose the death penalty is made by a petit jury selected from a properly constituted venire. Each jury is unique in its composition, and the Constitution requires that its decision rest on consideration of innumerable factors that vary according to the characteristics of the individual defendant and the facts of the particular capital offense. . . . Thus, the application of an inference drawn from the general statistics to a specific decision in a trial and sentencing simply is not comparable to the application of an inference drawn from general statistics to a specific venire-selection or Title VII case. In those cases, the statistics relate to fewer entities, and fewer variables are relevant to the challenged decisions.

Another important difference between the cases in which we have accepted statistics as proof of discriminatory intent and this case is that, in the venire-selection and Title VII contexts, the decisionmaker has an opportunity to explain the statistical disparity. . . . Here, the State has no practical opportunity to rebut the Baldus study. "Controlling considerations of . . . public policy," . . . dictate that jurors "cannot be called . . . to testify to the motives and influences that led to their verdict." . . . Similarly, the policy considerations behind a prosecutor's traditionally "wide discretion" suggest the impropriety of our requiring prosecutors to defend their decisions to seek death penalties, "often years after they were made." . . . Moreover, absent far stronger proof, it is unnecessary to seek such a rebuttal, because a legitimate and unchallenged explanation for the decision is apparent from the record: McCleskey committed an act for which the United States Constitution and Georgia laws permit imposition of the death penalty.

Finally, McCleskey's statistical proffer must be viewed in the context of his challenge. McCleskey challenges decisions at the heart of the State's criminal justice system. "One of society's most basic tasks is that of protecting the lives of its citizens and one of the most basic ways in which it achieves the task is through criminal laws against murder." . . . Implementation of these laws necessarily requires discretionary judgments. Because discretion is essential to the criminal justice process, we would demand exceptionally clear proof before we would infer that the discretion has been abused. The unique nature of the decisions at issue in this case also counsels against adopting such an inference from the disparities indicated by the Baldus study. Accordingly, we hold that the Baldus study is clearly insufficient to support an inference that any of the decisionmakers in McCleskey's case acted with discriminatory purpose.

B.

McCleskey also suggests that the Baldus study proves that the State as a whole has acted with a discriminatory purpose. He appears to argue that the State has violated the Equal Protection Clause by adopting the capital punishment statute and allowing it to remain in force despite its allegedly discriminatory application. But " 'discriminatory purpose' . . . implies more than intent as volition or intent as awareness of consequences. It implies that the decisionmaker, in this case a state legislature, selected or reaffirmed a particular course of action at least in part 'because of,' not merely 'in spite of,' its adverse effects upon an identifiable group." . . . For this claim to prevail, McCleskey would have to prove that the Georgia Legislature enacted or maintained the death penalty statute because of an anticipated racially discriminatory effect. In Gregg v. Georgia this Court found that the Georgia capital sentencing system could operate in a fair and neutral manner. There was no evidence then, and there is none now, that the Georgia Legislature enacted the capital punishment statute to further a racially discriminatory purpose.

Nor has McCleskey demonstrated that the legislature maintains the capital punishment statute because of the racially disproportionate impact suggested by the Baldus study. As legislatures necessarily have wide discretion in the choice of criminal laws and penalties, and as there were legitimate reasons for the Georgia Legislature to adopt and maintain capital punishment, . . . we will not infer a discriminatory purpose on the part of the State of Georgia. Accordingly, we reject McCleskey's equal protection claims.

III.

McCleskey also argues that the Baldus study demonstrates that the Georgia capital sentencing system violates the Eighth Amendment. We begin our analysis of this claim by reviewing the restrictions on death sentences established by our prior decisions under that Amendment.

[The Court here reviews the cases interpreting the Eighth Amendment.]

D.

In sum, our decisions since Furman have identified a constitutionally permissible range of discretion in imposing the death penalty. First, there is a required threshold below which the death penalty cannot be imposed. In this context, the State must establish rational criteria that narrow the decisionmaker's judgment as to whether the circumstances of a particular defendant's case meet the threshold. Moreover, a societal consensus that the death penalty is disproportionate to a particular offense prevents a State from imposing the death penalty for that offense. Second, States cannot limit the sentencer's consideration of any relevant circumstance that could cause it to decline to impose the penalty. In this respect, the State cannot channel the sentencer's discretion, but must allow it to consider any relevant information offered by the defendant.

IV.

A.

In light of our precedents under the Eighth Amendment, McCleskey cannot argue successfully that his sentence is "disproportionate to the crime in the traditional sense." ... He does not deny that he committed a murder in the course of a planned robbery, a crime for which this Court has determined that the death penalty constitutionally may be imposed. ... His disproportionality claim "is of a different sort." ... McCleskey argues that the sentence in his case is disproportionate to the sentences in other murder cases.

On the one hand, he cannot base a constitutional claim on an argument that his case differs from other cases in which defendants did receive the death penalty. On automatic appeal, the Georgia Supreme Court found that McCleskey's death sentence was not disproportionate to other death sentences imposed in the State. ... The court supported this conclusion with an appendix containing citations to 13 cases involving generally similar murders. ...

On the other hand, absent a showing that the Georgia capital punishment system operates in an arbitrary and capricious manner, McCleskey cannot prove a constitutional violation by demonstrating that other defendants who may be similarly situated did not receive the death penalty. In Gregg, the Court confronted the argument that "the opportunities for discretionary action that are inherent in the processing of any murder case under Georgia law," specifically the opportunities for discretionary leniency, rendered the capital sentences imposed arbitrary and capricious. We rejected this contention , , , ,

Because McCleskey's sentence was imposed under Georgia sentencing procedures that focus discretion "on the particularized nature of the crime and the particularized characteristics of the individual defendant," we lawfully may presume that McCleskey's death sentence was not "wantonly and freakishly" imposed, and thus that the sentence is not disproportionate within any recognized meaning under the Eighth Amendment. ...

VI.

Accordingly, we affirm the judgment of the Court of Appeals for the Eleventh Circuit.

It is so ordered.

Justice **Brennan,** with whom Justice **Marshall** joins, and with whom Justice **Blackmun** and Justice **Stevens** join in all but Part I, dissenting, said in part:

I.

Adhering to my view that the death penalty is in all circumstances cruel and unusual punishment forbidden by the Eighth and Fourteenth Amendments, I would vacate the decision below insofar as it left undisturbed the death sentence imposed in this case. ...

Even if I did not hold this position, however, I would reverse the Court of Appeals, for petitioner McCleskey has clearly demonstrated that his death sentence was imposed in violation of the Eighth and Fourteenth Amendments. While I join Parts I through IV-A of Justice Blackmun's dissenting opinion discussing petitioner's Fourteenth Amendment claim, I write separately to emphasize how conclusively McCleskey has also demonstrated precisely the type of risk of irrationality in sentencing that we have consistently condemned in our Eighth Amendment jurisprudence.

II.

At some point in this case, Warren McCleskey doubtless asked his lawyer whether a jury was likely to sentence him to die. A candid reply to this question would have been disturbing. First, counsel would have to tell McCleskey that few of the details of the crime or of McCleskey's past criminal conduct were more important than the fact that his victim was white. Furthermore, counsel would feel bound to tell McCleskey that defendants charged with killing white victims in Georgia are 4.3 times as likely to be sentenced to death as defendants charged with killing blacks. In addition, frankness would compel the disclosure that it was more likely than not that the race of McCleskey's victim would determine whether he received a death sentence: 6 of every 11 defendants convicted of killing a white person would not have received the death penalty if their victims had been black, while, among defendants with aggravating and mitigating factors comparable to McCleskey's, 20 of every 34 would not have been sentenced to die if their victims had been black. Finally, the assessment would not be complete without the information that cases involving black defendants and white victims are more likely to result in a death sentence than cases featuring any other racial combination of defendant and victim. The story could be told in a variety of ways, but McCleskey could not fail to grasp its essential narrative line: there was a significant chance that race would play a prominent role in determining if he lived or died.

The Court today holds that Warren McCleskey's sentence was constitutionally imposed. It finds no fault in a system in which lawyers must tell their clients that race casts a large shadow on the capital sentencing process. The Court arrives at this conclusion by stating that the Baldus study cannot ''prove that race enters into any capital sentencing decisions or that race was a factor in McCleskey's particular case.'' Since, according to Professor Baldus, we cannot say ''to a moral certainty'' that race influenced a decision, we can identify only ''a likelihood that a particular factor entered into some decisions,'' and ''a discrepancy that appears to correlate with race.'' This ''likelihood'' and ''discrepancy,'' holds the Court, is insufficient to establish a constitutional violation. . . .

III.

A.

It is important to emphasize at the outset that the Court's observation that McCleskey cannot prove the influence of race on any particular sentencing decision is irrelevant in evaluating his Eighth Amendment claim. Since Furman v. Georgia (1972), the Court has been concerned with the *risk* of the imposition of an arbitrary sentence, rather than the proven fact of one. Furman held that the death penalty ''may not be imposed under sentencing procedures that create a substantial risk that the punishment will be inflicted in an arbitrary and capricious manner.'' . . . This emphasis on risk acknowledges the difficulty of divining the jury's motivation in an individual case. In addition, it reflects the fact that concern for arbitrariness focuses on the rationality of the system as a whole, and that a system that features a significant probability that sentencing decisions are influenced by impermissible considerations cannot be regarded as rational. As we said in Gregg v. Georgia, ''the petitioner looks to the sentencing system as a whole (as the Court did in Furman and we do today)'': a constitutional violation is established if a plaintiff demonstrates a ''pattern of arbitrary and capricious sentencing.'' . . .

Defendants challenging their death sentences thus never have had to prove that impermissible considerations have actually infected sentencing decisions. We have required instead that they establish that the system under which they were sentenced posed a significant risk of such an occurrence. McCleskey's claim does differ, however, in one respect from these earlier cases: it is the first to base a challenge not on speculation about how a system might operate, but on empirical documentation of how it does operate. . . .

C.

Evaluation of McCleskey's evidence cannot rest solely on the numbers themselves. We must also ask whether the conclusion suggested by those numbers is consonant with our understanding of history and human experience. Georgia's legacy of a race-conscious criminal justice system, as well as this Court's own recognition of the persistent danger that racial attitudes may affect criminal proceedings, indicates that McCleskey's claim is not a fanciful product of mere statistical artifice.

For many years, Georgia operated openly and formally precisely the type of dual system the evidence shows is still effectively in place. The criminal law expressly differentiated between crimes committed by and against blacks and whites, distinctions whose lineage traced back to the time of slavery. During the colonial period, black slaves who killed whites in Georgia, regardless of whether in self-defense or in defense of another, were automatically executed. . . .

By the time of the Civil War, a dual system of crime and punishment was well established in Georgia. The state criminal code contained separate sections for ''Slaves and Free Persons of Color,'' and for all other persons. The code provided, for instance, for an automatic death sentence for murder committed by blacks, but declared that anyone else convicted of murder might receive life imprisonment if the conviction were founded solely on circumstantial testimony or simply if the jury so recommended. The code established that the rape of a free white female by a black ''shall be'' punishable by death. However, rape by anyone else of a free white female was punishable by a prison term not less than 2 nor more than 20 years. The rape of blacks was punishable ''by fine and imprisonment, at the discretion of the court.'' . . .

In more recent times, some 40 years ago, Gunnar Myrdal's epochal study of American race relations produced findings mirroring McCleskey's evidence:

''As long as only Negroes are concerned and no whites are disturbed, great leniency will be shown in most cases . . . . The sentences for even major crimes are ordinarily reduced when the victim is another Negro.

''For offenses which involve any actual or potential danger to whites, however, Negroes are punished more severely than whites.

''On the other hand, it is quite common for a white criminal to be set free if his crime was against a Negro.''

G. Myrdal, An American Dilemma 551-553 (1944). . . .

This historical review of Georgia criminal law is not intended as a bill of indictment calling the State to account for past transgressions. Citation of past practices does not justify the automatic condemnation of current ones. But it would be unrealistic to ignore the influence of history in assessing the plausible implications of McCleskey's evidence. "Americans share a historical experience that has resulted in individuals within the culture ubiquitously attaching a significance to race that is irrational and often outside their awareness." . . .

The majority thus misreads our Eighth Amendment jurisprudence in concluding that McCleskey has not demonstrated a degree of risk sufficient to raise constitutional concern. The determination of the significance of his evidence is at its core an exercise in human moral judgment, not a mechanical statistical analysis. It must first and foremost be informed by awareness of the fact that death is irrevocable, and that as a result "the qualitative difference of death from all other punishments requires a greater degree of scrutiny of the capital sentencing determination." . . . For this reason, we have demanded a uniquely high degree of rationality in imposing the death penalty. A capital sentencing system in which race more likely than not plays a role does not meet this standard. . . .

In more recent times, we have sought to free ourselves from the burden of this history. Yet it has been scarcely a generation since this Court's first decision striking down racial segregation, and barely two decades since the legislative prohibition of racial discrimination in major domains of national life. These have been honorable steps, but we cannot pretend that in three decades we have completely escaped the grip of a historical legacy spanning centuries. Warren McCleskey's evidence confronts us with the subtle and persistent influence of the past. His message is a disturbing one to a society that has formally repudiated racism, and a frustrating one to a Nation accustomed to regarding its destiny as the product of its own will. Nonetheless, we ignore him at our peril, for we remain imprisoned by the past as long as we deny its influence in the present.

Justice **Blackmun,** with whom Justice **Marshall** and Justice **Stevens** join, and with whom Justice Brennan joins in all but Part IV-B, dissenting, said in part:

The Court today sanctions the execution of a man despite his presentation of evidence that establishes a constitutionally intolerable level of racially based discrimination leading to the imposition of his death sentence. I am disappointed with the Court's action not only because of its denial of constitutional guarantees to petitioner McCleskey individually, but also because of its departure from what seems to me to be well-developed constitutional jurisprudence.

Justice Brennan has thoroughly demonstrated that, if one assumes that the statistical evidence presented by petitioner McCleskey is valid, as we must in light of the Court of Appeals' assumption, there exists in the Georgia capital sentencing scheme a risk of racially based discrimination that is so acute that it violates the Eighth Amendment. His analysis of McCleskey's case in terms of the Eighth Amendment is consistent with this Court's recognition that because capital cases involve the State's imposition of a punishment that is unique both in kind and degree, the decision in such cases must reflect a heightened degree of reliability under the Amendment's prohibition of the infliction of cruel and unusual punishments. . . . I therefore join Parts II through V of Justice Brennan's dissenting opinion.

I.

A.

The Court today seems to give a new meaning to our recognition that death is different. Rather than requiring "a correspondingly greater degree of scrutiny of the capital sentencing determination," . . . the Court relies on the very fact that this is a case involving capital punishment to apply a lesser standard of scrutiny under the Equal Protection Clause. The Court concludes that "legitimate" explanations outweigh McCleskey's claim that his death sentence reflected a constitutionally impermissible risk of racial discrimination. The Court explains that McCleskey's evidence is too weak to require rebuttal "because a legitimate and unchallenged explanation for the decision is apparent from the record: McCleskey committed an act for which the United States Constitution and Georgia laws permit imposition of the death penalty." The Court states that it will not infer a discriminatory purpose on the part of the state legislature because "there were legitimate reasons for the Georgia Legislature to adopt and maintain capital punishment."

The Court's assertion that the fact of McCleskey's conviction undermines his constitutional claim is inconsistent with a long and unbroken line of this Court's case law. The Court on numerous occasions during the past century has recognized that an otherwise legitimate basis for a conviction does not outweigh an equal protection violation. In cases where racial discrimination in the administration of the criminal justice system is established, it has held that setting aside the conviction is the appropriate remedy. . . .

B.

In analyzing an equal protection claim, a court must first determine the nature of the claim and the responsibilities of the state actors involved to determine what showing is required for the establishment of a prima facie case. . . . The Court correctly points out: "In its broadest form, McCleskey's claim of discrimination extends to every actor in the Georgia capital sentencing process, from the prosecutor who sought the death penalty and the jury that imposed the sentence, to the State itself that enacted the capital punishment statute and allows it to remain in effect despite its allegedly discriminatory application.'' Having recognized the complexity of McCleskey's claim, however, the Court proceeds to ignore a significant element of that claim. The Court treats the case as if it is limited to challenges to the actions of two specific decisionmaking bodies—the petit jury and the state legislature. This self-imposed restriction enables the Court to distinguish this case from the venire-selection cases and cases under Title VII of the Civil Rights Act of 1964 in which it long has accepted statistical evidence and has provided an easily applicable framework for review. ... Considering McCleskey's claim in its entirety, however, reveals that the claim fits easily within that same framework. A significant aspect of his claim is that racial factors impermissibly affected numerous steps in the Georgia capital sentencing scheme between his indictment and the jury's vote to sentence him to death. ...

II.

B.

I agree with the Court's observation as to the difficulty of examining the jury's decisiomaking process. There perhaps is an inherent tension between the discretion accorded capital sentencing juries and the guidance for use of that discretion that is constitutionally required. In his dissenting opinion, Justice Brennan demonstrates that the Eighth Amendment analysis is well suited to address that aspect of the case. The Court's refusal to require that the prosecutor provide an explanation for his actions, however, is completely inconsistent with this Court's longstanding precedents. ... Prosecutors undoubtedly need adequate discretion to allocate the resources of their offices and to fulfill their responsibilities to the public in deciding how best to enforce the law, but this does not place them beyond the constraints imposed on state action under the Fourteenth Amendment. Cf. Ex parte Virginia (1880) (upholding validity of conviction of state judge for discriminating on the basis of race in his selection of jurors). ...

IV.

A.

One of the final concerns discussed by the Court may be the most disturbing aspect of its opinion. Granting relief to McCleskey in this case, it is said, could lead to further constitutional challenges. That, of course, is no reason to deny McCleskey his rights under the Equal Protection Clause. If a grant of relief to him were to lead to a closer examination of the effects of racial considerations throughout the criminal justice system, the system, and hence society, might benefit. Where no such factors come into play, the integrity of the system is enhanced. Where such considerations are shown to be significant, efforts can be made to eradicate their imper-

missible influence and to ensure an evenhanded application of criminal sanctions. ...

Justice **Stevens,** with whom Justice **Blackmun** joins, dissenting, said in part:

The Court's decision appears to be based on a fear that the acceptance of McCleskey's claim would sound the death knell for capital punishment in Georgia. If society were indeed forced to choose between a racially discriminatory death penalty (one that provides heightened protection against murder "for whites only'') and no death penalty at all, the choice mandated by the Constitution would be plain. ... But the Court's fear is unfounded. One of the lessons of the Baldus study is that there exist certain categories of extremely serious crimes for which prosecutors consistently seek, and juries consistently impose, the death penalty without regard to the race of the victim or the race of the offender. If Georgia were to narrow the class of death-eligible defendants to those categories, the danger of arbitrary and discriminatory imposition of the death penalty would be significantly decreased, if not eradicated. As Justice Brennan has demonstrated in his dissenting opinion, such a restructuring of the sentencing scheme is surely not too high a price to pay.

TRIAL BY JURY

DUNCAN v. LOUISIANA

391 U. S. 145; 88 S. Ct. 1444; 20 L. Ed. 2d 491
(1968)

The present century has seen the increasing erosion of one of the most venerable procedures of the common law—the jury trial. In England, its birthplace, it has been virtually abandoned in civil cases and in all but the most important criminal cases. Increasingly in the United States it is waived by the contending parties, and some states have moved to streamline their jury systems by reducing the number of jurors or providing for less than a unanimous verdict. Such changes were held in Maxwell v. Dow (1900) not to deny the accused due process of law. But the framers of the Constitution clearly intended that the right of jury trial be maintained; both in Article III of the original document and in the Sixth Amendment the right of jury trial in criminal cases is ensured, and the Seventh Amendment guarantees it in all civil cases involving over $20.

In Patton v. United States (1930) the Court made clear that this meant the traditional common-law jury trial—a presiding judge and twelve jurors rendering a unanimous verdict. The agreement of the defendant in that case to go on with eleven jurors after one got sick was as much a waiver of a jury as if he had elected to be tried by the judge alone. Such waiver requires the consent of both the government and the trial court, and the defendant has no constitutional right to be tried by a judge alone in the absence of such consent; see Singer v. United States (1965). To reduce the likelihood of a mistrial because of a sick juror, especially in long trials, the federal rules of procedure now provide for the selection of alternate jurors who meet all the qualifications and hear all the evidence, but who do not retire with the jury to consider the verdict unless a regular juror has had to be replaced.

In the guarantee of jury trial in the Sixth it is stated that the jury shall be "impartial," a requirement normally met through a system of challenges. Each prospective juror is examined under oath (voir dire) and may be challenged by either party for "cause." If found by the presiding judge to be prejudiced or to have an interest in the case, the potential juror is disqualified for service in that trial. Each side is also allowed a certain number of "peremptory challenges," which may be exercised without any assignment of cause. In cases involving sensational crimes which have received widespread local publicity it is sometimes impossible to impanel an impartial jury. Lurid or inflammatory crime reporting by press, radio, or television may create a climate of opinion in which a fair trial is impossible, and in which to conduct a trial denies the defendant due process of law. There is no easy solution to this conflict between the two major civil liberties, freedom of the press and the right to a fair trial. In such cases the defendant, even though only charged with a misdemeanor, may request a change of venue so the trial may be held in another community; see Groppi v. Wisconsin (1971).

In 1962 a national scandal broke involving Texas millionaire Billie Sol Estes, accused of influence and fraud in grain-storage and cotton-acreage dealings. Against a backdrop of a dead Department of Agriculture official, two congressional inquiries, and four fraud indictments, Estes was convicted before a national TV audience of swindling a farmer. In Estes v. Texas (1965) the Court reversed for lack of due process. Noting that "we start with the proposition that it is a 'public trial' that the Sixth Amendment guarantees to the 'accused,'" it concluded that a day in court is not a day in a "stadium . . . or nationwide arena."

In Walker v. Sauvinet (1876) and Maxwell v. Dow (1900) the Supreme Court held that trial by jury was not required of the states by either the privileges and immunities or the due process clauses of the Fourteenth Amendment, but as the Court said in Brown v. Mississippi (1936), "because a State may dispense with a jury trial, it does not follow that it may substitute trial by ordeal." The trial must meet the test of essential fairness, and the Court incorporated some of the specifics of the Sixth Amendment designed to ensure such fairness. In Pointer v. Texas (1965) the right of the accused "to be confronted with the witnesses against him" was held applicable to the states; in Parker v. Gladden (1966) the right to a trial "by an impartial jury" was added, apparently to cover such jury trials as the state actually provided; and in Klopfer v. North Carolina (1967) the Court incorporated the "right to a speedy . . . trial." In Washington v. Texas (1967) the Court held applicable to the states the right of an accused "to have compulsory process for obtaining witnesses in his favor."

There are well-established exceptions to the general rule requiring trial by jury in criminal cases. Even at common law, petty offenses were tried without a jury, and punishment for contempt of court has always been imposed summarily by the presiding judge. One of the most tangible distinctions between "law" and "equity" is the absence of a jury in equity cases, although these normally do not involve criminal matters.

A jury trial problem of recent origin involved the right of Congress to subject civilian citizens to the jurisdiction of a military court. Article I of the Constitution authorizes Congress "to make rules for the government and regulation of the land and naval forces," and under this authority the first Congress adopted from the British the Articles of War to be administered by a system of courts-martial. This body of military law not only includes the common-law crimes but in addition covers purely military offenses the punishment of which is necessary to the discipline of the armed forces. Courts-martial are an essential part of this system of discipline, and differ in many ways from civilian courts of justice.

They are specifically exempt by the Fifth Amendment from the requirement of grand jury indictment, and by implication they are also exempt from the jury trial provisions of the Sixth. While the federal courts can review court-martial convictions on habeas corpus, their review is largely limited to ensuring the jurisdiction of the military court. Legal errors are subject to review only within the executive branch of the government, and in Hiatt v. Brown (1950) a United States district court was held in error "in extending its review, for the purpose of determining compliance with the due process clause, to such matters as the propositions of law set forth . . . , the sufficiency of the evidence . . . , the adequacy of the pretrial investigation, and the competence of the law member and defense counsel."

In 1950 Congress adopted the Uniform Code of Military Justice, which provided for all the armed forces a system of military justice more in harmony with the concept of due process of law as it has developed in civilian courts. In two controversial sections the new code undertook to extend court-martial jurisdiction to civilians. One of these (Art. 3a) provided that a person who had been discharged from the armed forces could thereafter still be tried by court-martial for certain offenses committed while in the service. In United States ex rel. Toth v. Quarles (1955) the Supreme Court held this section of the act void. Toth had been discharged from the Air Force and returned to his civilian job. Five months later he was arrested by the military police and returned to Korea to stand trial for murder. Relying on Ex parte Milligan (1866), the Court rejected the theory that the "commander-in-chief" clause provided such power; nor could it, except by "an extremely broad construction," be brought under the power of Congress to make rules for governing the armed forces, whose natural meaning clearly limited it to persons actually in military service. "There is a compelling reason for construing the clause this way; any expansion of court-martial jurisdiction like that in the 1950 Act necessarily encroaches on the jurisdiction of federal courts set up under Article III of the Constitution where persons on trial are surrounded with more constitutional safeguards than in military tribunals. . . . We find nothing in the history or constitutional treatment of military tribunals which entitles them to rank along with Article III courts as adjudicators of the guilt or innocence of people charged with offenses for which they can be deprived of their life, liberty or property."

The post-World War II policy of the United States has resulted, for the first time in our history, in the stationing abroad of American military personnel on a more or less permanent basis. Such troops normally serve a three-year tour of duty overseas, and Congress has wisely made it possible for them to be accompanied by their families. These troops are, in a sense, the guests of the country in which they are stationed, and would normally be subject to the penal laws of that country in the same way as would a civilian tourist. But, by the Status of Forces Agreements concluded with the NATO countries and Japan, the United States has jurisdiction to try criminal cases involving its military personnel by its own courts-martial, provided the host country agrees to waive its jurisdiction. The host country normally does waive jurisdiction, and there is no question of the right of the United States to subject military personnel to trial by court-martial. An awkward question arises, however, in cases involving the civilian dependents of these troops. On the rare occasions when they commit crimes, can they be tried, as those actually in the armed forces would be, by an army court-martial?

After the Status of Forces Agreements went into effect Mrs. Dorothy Krueger Smith and Mrs. Clarice B. Covert were accused of murdering their soldier-husbands on foreign military bases. The countries where the crimes were committed waived jurisdiction, and they were tried and convicted by Army courts-martial under the provision of the Status of Forces Agreements.

Although the Supreme Court at first upheld their convictions, the decision was apparently hastily reached and at the opening of the following term of Court the case was reheard and the decision reversed. Although there was no majority opinion, four members of the Court relied on the Toth case, and the Court clearly agreed that, at least in capital cases, civilians could not be denied their right to a jury trial by an agreement to try them by court-martial. See Reid v. Covert (1957).

In 1960 three cases came to the Court involving the scope of the Reid holding. In Kinsella v. United States ex rel. Singleton (civilian dependent in a noncapital case); Grisham v. Hagan (American civilian employee in a capital case); and McElroy v. United States ex rel. Guagliardo (American civilian employee in a noncapital case) the Court held void trial by court-martial. To the criticism that in these cases persons accused

of serious crimes escaped trial, the Court replied that Congress has power to establish civilian courts in which the constitutional rights of such persons, including jury trial, will be guaranteed.

In 1969, in O'Callahan v. Parker, the Supreme Court again reaffirmed its faith in the common-law judicial process by ruling that the armed forces could not court-martial a soldier for a non-service-connected crime—in this case an attempted rape that took place while the soldier was away on leave. Quoting at length from United States ex rel. Toth v. Quarles (1955), the Court emphasized the command influence in military trials and the resultant shortcomings from the standpoint of judicial impartiality. The Court found that the Fifth Amendment's guarantee of grand jury indictment "except in cases arising in the land or naval forces, or in the militia, when in actual service in time of war or public danger," did not entitle Congress to authorize the trial by court-martial of soldiers for purely civilian crimes. The absence of especially persuasive logical or historical reasoning to back its decision, together with a failure to tell the military what crimes they could and could not try, prompted a strong dissent from Justices Harlan, Stewart, and White. "Absolutely nothing," they concluded, "in the language, history, or logic of the Constitution justifies this uneasy state of affairs which the Court has today created." In Relford v. Commandant (1971) the situation was eased somewhat when the Court agreed unanimously that the rape by a serviceman, on a military base, of members of another serviceman's family was a "service connected crime" within the meaning of O'Callahan.

While recent years have seen most of the rights of criminal defendants listed in the Bill of Rights incorporated into due process, jury trial and grand jury indictment remained conspicuously absent from the list. Both rights have been subject to a good deal of professional criticism that raised serious questions as to whether or not they should be considered fundamental and hence required of the states. Many states have substituted the "information," a charge signed by the prosecutor alone, for the grand jury indictment, and the argument is made that it is a fairer, more efficient procedure. The grand jury, it is contended, is usually under the thumb of the prosecutor anyway, yet lets the prosecutor escape the onus of bringing to trial someone who is later found to be innocent.

Serious question was raised, too, about the competence of trial juries, especially in complex civil cases, to understand the facts of a case and apply the law to it properly. Public concern for the concept of jury secrecy has made the gathering of information on the subject extremely difficult, so the charges have gone largely unrefuted.

Mr. Justice **White** delivered the opinion of the Court, saying in part:

Appellant, Gary Duncan, was convicted of simple battery in the Twenty-fifth Judicial District Court of

Louisiana. Under Louisiana law simple battery is a misdemeanor, punishable by two years' imprisonment and a $300 fine. Appellant sought trial by jury, but because the Louisiana Constitution grants jury trials only in cases in which capital punishment or imprisonment at hard labor may be imposed, the trial judge denied the request. Appellant was convicted and sentenced to serve 60 days in the parish prison and pay a fine of $150. Appellant sought review in the Supreme Court of Louisiana, asserting that the denial of jury trial violated rights guaranteed to him by the United States Constitution. The Supreme Court, finding "no error of law in the ruling complained of," denied appellant a writ of certiorari. . . . Appellant sought review in this Court, alleging that the Sixth and Fourteenth Amendments to the United States Constitution secure the right to jury trial in state criminal prosecutions where a sentence as long as two years may be imposed. . . .

I.

The Fourteenth Amendment denies the States the power to "deprive any person of life, liberty, or property, without due process of law." In resolving conflicting claims concerning the meaning of this spacious language, the Court has looked increasingly to the Bill of Rights for guidance; many of the rights guaranteed by the first eight Amendments to the Constitution have been held to be protected against state action by the Due Process Clause of the Fourteenth Amendment. That clause now protects the right to compensation for property taken by the State, the rights of speech, press, and religion covered by the First Amendment; the Fourth Amendment rights to be free from unreasonable searches and seizures and to have excluded from criminal trials any evidence illegally seized, the right guaranteed by the Fifth Amendment to be free of compelled self-incrimination; and the Sixth Amendment rights to counsel, to a speedy and public trial, to confrontation of opposing witnesses, and to compulsory process for obtaining witnesses.

The test for determining whether a right extended by the Fifth and Sixth Amendments with respect to federal criminal proceedings is also protected against state action by the Fourteenth Amendment has been phrased in a variety of ways in the opinions of this Court. The question has been asked whether a right is among those " 'fundamental principles of liberty and justice which lie at the base of all our civil and political institutions,' " Powell v. Alabama, (1932); whether it is "basic in our system of jurisprudence," In re Oliver (1948); and whether it is "a fundamental right, essential to a fair trial," Gideon v. Wainwright (1963). . . . The claim before us is that the right to trial by jury guaranteed by the Sixth Amendment meets these tests. The position of Louisiana, on the other hand, is that the Constitution imposes upon the States no duty to give a jury trial in any criminal case, regardless of the seriousness of the crime or the size of the punishment which may be imposed.

Because we believe that trial by jury in criminal cases is fundamental to the American scheme of justice, we hold that the Fourteenth Amendment guarantees a right of jury trial in all criminal cases which—were they to be tried in a federal court—would come within the Sixth Amendment's guarantee.* Since we consider the appeal before us to be such a case, we hold that the Constitution was violated when appellant's demand for jury trial was refused.

The history of trial by jury in criminal cases has been frequently told. It is sufficient for present purposes to say that by the time our Constitution was written, jury trial in criminal cases had been in existence in England for several centuries and carried impressive credentials traced by many to Magna Carta. Its preservation and proper operation as a protection against arbitrary rule were among the major objectives of the revolutionary settlement which was expressed in the Declaration and Bill of Rights of 1689. In the 18th century Blackstone could write:

"Our law has therefore wisely placed this strong and two-fold barrier, of a presentment and a trial by jury, between the liberties of the people and the prerogative of

---

*In one sense recent cases applying provisions of the first eight amendments to the States represent a new approach to the "incorporation" debate. Earlier the Court can be seen as having asked, when inquiring into whether some particular procedural safeguard was required of a State, if a civilized system could be imagined that would not accord the particular protection. For example, Palko v. Connecticut (1937) stated: "The right to trial by jury and the immunity from prosecution except as the result of an indictment may have value and importance. Even so, they are not of the very essence of a scheme of ordered liberty. . . . Few would be so narrow or provincial as to maintain that a fair and enlightened system of justice would be impossible without them." The recent cases, on the other hand, have proceeded upon the valid assumption that state criminal processes are not imaginary and theoretical schemes but actual systems bearing virtually every characteristic of the common-law system that has been developing contemporaneously in England and in this country. The question thus is whether given this kind of system a particular procedure is fundamental—whether, that is, a procedure is necessary to an Anglo-American regime of ordered liberty. . . . Of immediate relevance for this case are the Court's holdings that the States must comply with certain provisions of the Sixth Amendment, specifically that the States may not refuse a speedy trial, confrontation of witnesses, and the assistance, at state expense if necessary, of counsel. Of each of these determinations that a constitutional provision originally written to bind the Federal Government should bind the States as well it might be said that the limitation in question is not necessarily fundamental to fairness in every criminal system that might be imagined but is fundamental in the context of the criminal process maintained by the American States.

When the inquiry is approached in this way the question whether the States can impose criminal punishment without granting a jury trial appears quite different from the way it appeared in the older cases opining that States might abolish jury trial. See, e. g., Maxwell v. Dow (1900). A criminal process which was fair and equitable but used no juries is easy to imagine. It would make use of alternative guarantees and protections which would serve the purposes that the jury serves in the English and American systems. Yet no American State has undertaken to construct such a system. Instead, every American State, including Louisiana, uses the jury extensively, and imposes very serious punishments only after a trial at which the defendant has a right to a jury's verdict. In every State, including Louisiana, the structure and style of the criminal process—the supporting framework and the subsidiary procedures—are of the sort that naturally complement jury trial, and have developed in connection with and in reliance upon jury trial.

the crown. It was necessary, for preserving the admirable balance of our constitution, to vest the executive power of the laws in the prince: and yet this power might be dangerous and destructive to that very constitution, if exerted without check or control, by justices of oyer and terminer occasionally named by the crown; who might then, as in France or Turkey, imprison, dispatch, or exile any man that was obnoxious to the government, by an instant declaration that such is their will and pleasure. But the founders of the English law have, with excellent forecast, contrived that . . . the truth of every accusation, whether preferred in the shape of indictment, information, or appeal, should afterwards be confirmed by the unanimous suffrage of twelve of his equals and neighbors, indifferently chosen and superior to all suspicion.''

Jury trial came to America with English colonists, and received strong support from them. Royal interference with the jury trial was deeply resented. Among the resolutions adopted by the First Congress of the American Colonies (the Stamp Act Congress) on October 19, 1765—resolutions deemed by their authors to state ''the most essential rights and liberties of the colonists''—was the declaration: ''That trial by jury is the inherent and invaluable right of every British subject in these colonies.'' . . . The Declaration of Independence stated solemn objections to the King making ''judges dependent on his will alone, for the tenure of their offices, and the amount and payment of their salaries,'' to his ''depriving us, in many cases, of the benefits of trial by jury,'' and to his ''transporting us beyond the seas to be tried for pretended offenses.'' The Constitution itself, in Art. III, § 2, commanded:

''The Trial of all Crimes, except in cases of Impeachment, shall be by Jury; and such Trial shall be held in the State where the said Crimes shall have been committed.''

Objections to the Constitution because of the absence of a bill of rights were met by the immediate submission and adoption of the Bill of Rights. Included was the Sixth Amendment which, among other things, provided:

''In all criminal prosecutions, the accused shall enjoy the right to a speedy and public trial, by an impartial jury of the State and district wherein the crime shall have been committed.''

The constitutions adopted by the original States guaranteed jury trial. Also, the constitution of every State entering the Union thereafter in one form or another protected the right to jury trial in criminal cases.

Even such skeletal history is impressive support for considering the right to jury trial in criminal cases to be fundamental to our system of justice, an importance frequently recognized in the opinions of this Court. . . .

Jury trial continues to receive strong support. The laws of every State guarantee a right to jury trial in serious criminal cases; no State has dispensed with it; nor are there significant movements underway to do so. Indeed, the three most recent state constitutional revisions, in Maryland, Michigan, and New York, carefully preserved the right of the accused to have the judgment of a jury when tried for a serious crime.

We are aware of prior cases in this Court in which the prevailing opinion contains statements contrary to our holding today that the right to jury trial in serious criminal cases is a fundamental right and hence must be recognized by the States as part of their obligation to extend due process of law to all persons within their jurisdiction. Louisiana relies especially on Maxwell v. Dow (1900); Palko v. Connecticut (1937); and Snyder v. Massachusetts (1934). None of these cases, however, dealt with a State which had purported to dispense entirely with a jury trial in serious criminal cases. Maxwell held that no provision of the Bill of Rights applied to the States—a position long since repudiated—and that the Due Process Clause of the Fourteenth Amendment did not prevent a State from trying a defendant for a non-capital offense with fewer than 12 men on the jury. It did not deal with a case in which no jury at all had been provided. In neither Palko nor Snyder was jury trial actually at issue, although both cases contain important dicta asserting that the right to jury trial is not essential to ordered liberty and may be dispensed with by the States regardless of the Sixth and Fourteenth Amendments. These observations, though weighty and respectable, are nevertheless dicta, unsupported by holdings in this Court that a State may refuse a defendant's demand for a jury trial when he is charged with a serious crime. . . .

The guarantees of jury trial in the Federal and State Constitutions reflect a profound judgment about the way in which law should be enforced and justice administered. A right to jury trial is granted to criminal defendants in order to prevent oppression by the Government. Those who wrote our constitutions knew from history and experience that it was necessary to protect against unfounded criminal charges brought to eliminate enemies and against judges too responsive to the voice of higher authority. The framers of the constitutions strove to create an independent judiciary but insisted upon further protection against arbitrary action. Providing an accused with the right to be tried by a jury of his peers gave him an inestimable safeguard against the corrupt or overzealous prosecutor and against the compliant, biased, or eccentric judge. If the defendant preferred the common-sense judgment of a jury to the more tutored but perhaps less sympathetic reaction of the single judge, he was to have it. Beyond this, the jury trial provisions in the Federal and State Constitutions reflect a fundamental decision about the exercise of official power—a reluctance to entrust plenary powers over the life and liberty of the citizen to one judge or to a group of judges. Fear of unchecked power, so typical of our State and Federal Governments in other respects, found expression in the criminal law in this insistence upon community participation in the determination of guilt or innocence. The deep commitment of the Nation to the right of jury trial in serious criminal cases as a defense against arbitrary law enforcement qualifies for protection under the

Due Process Clause of the Fourteenth Amendment, and must therefore be respected by the States.

Of course jury trial has "its weaknesses and the potential for misuse." ... We are aware of the long debate, especially in this century, among those who write about the administration of justice, as to the wisdom of permitting untrained laymen to determine the facts in civil and criminal proceedings. Although the debate has been intense, with powerful voices on either side, most of the controversy has centered on the jury in civil cases. Indeed, some of the severest critics of civil juries acknowledge that the arguments for criminal juries are much stronger. In addition, at the heart of the dispute have been express or implicit assertions that juries are incapable of adequately understanding evidence or determining issues of fact, and that they are unpredictable, quixotic, and little better than a roll of dice. Yet, the most recent and exhaustive study of the jury in criminal cases concluded that juries do understand the evidence and come to sound conclusions in most of the cases presented to them and that when juries differ with the result at which the judge would have arrived, it is usually because they are serving some of the very purposes for which they were created and for which they are now employed.

The State of Louisiana urges that holding that the Fourteenth Amendment assures a right to jury trial will cast doubt on the integrity of every trial conducted without a jury. ... We would not assert, however, that every criminal trial—or any particular trial—held before a judge alone is unfair or that a defendant may never be as fairly treated by a judge as he would be by a jury. Thus we hold no constitutional doubts about the practices, common in both federal and state courts, of accepting waivers of jury trial and prosecuting petty crimes without extending a right to jury trial. However, the fact is that in most places more trials for serious crimes are to juries than to a court alone; a great many defendants prefer the judgment of a jury to that of a court. Even where defendants are satisfied with bench trials, the right to a jury trial very likely serves its intended purpose of making judicial or prosecutorial unfairness less likely.*

II.

Louisiana's final contention is that even if it must grant jury trials in serious criminal cases, the conviction before us is valid and constitutional because here the petitioner was tried for simple battery and was sentenced to only 60 days in the parish prison. We are not persuaded. It is doubtless true that there is a category of petty crimes or offenses which is not subject to the Sixth Amendment jury trial provision and should not be subject to the Fourteenth Amendment jury trial requirement here applied to the States. Crimes carrying possible penalties up to six months do not require a jury trial if they otherwise qualify as petty offenses, Cheff v. Schnackenberg (1966). But the penalty authorized for a particular crime is of major relevance in determining whether it is serious or not and may in itself, if severe enough, subject the trial to the mandates of the Sixth Amendment. ... In the case before us the Legislature of Louisiana has made simple battery a criminal offense punishable by imprisonment for two years and a fine. The question, then, is whether a crime carrying such a penalty is an offense which Louisiana may insist on trying without a jury.

We think not. So-called petty offenses were tried without juries both in England and in the Colonies and have always been held to be exempt from the otherwise comprehensive language of the Sixth Amendment's jury trial provisions. ... Of course the boundaries of the petty offense category have always been ill defined, if not ambulatory. In the absence of an explicit constitutional provision, the definitional task necessarily falls on the courts, which must either pass upon the validity of legislative attempts to identify those petty offenses which are exempt from jury trial or, where the legislature has not addressed itself to the problem, themselves face the question in the first instance. In either case it is necessary to draw a line in the spectrum of crime, separating petty from serious infractions. This process, although essential, cannot be wholly satisfactory, for it requires attaching different consequences to events which, when they lie near the line, actually differ very little. ...

... We need not, however, settle in this case the exact location of the line between petty offenses and serious crimes. It is sufficient for our purposes to hold that a crime punishable by two years in prison is, based on past and contemporary standards in this country, a serious crime and not a petty offense. Consequently, appellant was entitled to a jury trial and it was error to deny it.

The judgment below is reversed and the case is remanded for proceedings not inconsistent with this opinion.

Mr. Justice **Fortas** joined the judgment and opinion of the Court in a concurring opinion.

---

*... Louisiana objects to application of the decisions of this Court interpreting the Sixth Amendment as guaranteeing a 12-man jury in serious criminal cases, Thompson v. Utah (1898); as requiring a unanimous verdict before guilt can be found, Maxwell v. Dow (1900); and as barring procedures by which crimes subject to the Sixth Amendment jury trial provision are tried in the first instance without a jury but at the first appellate stage by de novo trial with a jury, Callan v. Wilson (1888). It seems very unlikely to us that our decision today will require widespread changes in state criminal processes. First, our decisions interpreting the Sixth Amendment are always subject to reconsideration, a fact amply demonstrated by the instant decision. In addition, most of the States have provisions for jury trials equal in breadth to the Sixth Amendment, if that amendment is construed, as it has been, to permit the trial of petty crimes and offenses without a jury. Indeed, there appear to be only four States in which juries of fewer than 12 can be used without the defendant's consent for offenses carrying a maximum penalty of greater than one year. Only in Oregon and Louisiana can a less-than-unanimous jury convict for an offense with a maximum penalty greater than one year. However 10 States authorize first-stage trials without juries for crimes carrying lengthy penalties; these States give a convicted defendant the right to a de novo trial before a jury in a different court. ...

Mr. Justice **Black,** with whom Mr. Justice **Douglas** concurred, wrote a concurring opinion.

Mr. Justice **Harlan,** with whom Mr. Justice **Stewart** joined, wrote a dissenting opinion.

WILLIAMS v. FLORIDA

399 U. S. 78; 90 S. Ct. 1893; 26 L. Ed. 2d 446
(1970)

Two important questions were raised by the Court's decision in Duncan v. Louisiana (1968). First, would it mean that all states now had to go back to the old common-law jury of 12 persons, since the Sixth Amendment had consistently been held to require that kind of jury in the federal courts? Second, to what kind of cases would the jury requirement apply? Traditionally, petty offenses were tried before a judge rather than a jury, and in the Duncan case the Court held that the rule applied to the states as well as to the federal government—the severity of the crime to be determined not by the sentence actually imposed, but by the maximum sentence provided by law. In Baldwin v. New York (1970), decided the same day as Williams v. Florida, the Court struck down a conviction for ''jostling'' handed down by the New York City Criminal Court, which by law operated without a jury. The misdemeanor of jostling carried a maximum sentence of one year in jail, and Justices White, Brennan, and Marshall agreed that ''no offense can be deemed 'petty' for purposes of the right to trial by jury where imprisonment for more than six months is authorized.'' In this case the defendant had been given the maximum sentence of one year in jail. Justices Black and Douglas concurred on the ground that all crimes should be tried by jury regardless of seriousness.

In McKeiver v. Pennsylvania (1971) the Court, without agreeing upon an opinion, held that a state was not required to provide a jury trial in juvenile court adjudications. Four members of the Court stressed there that ''if the jury trial were to be injected into the juvenile court system as a matter of right, it would bring with it into that system the traditional delay, the formality and the clamor of the adversary system and, possibly, the public trial.''

In a number of cases, the most notable being the conspiracy trial of the ''Chicago Seven'' before district Judge Julius J. Hoffman, a systematic attempt had been made to disrupt the orderly trial process as a way either of showing contempt for that process or of preventing the trial proceeding to a conviction. In two important cases the Court has laid down rules regarding the power of judges to deal with such disruption. In Illinois v. Allen (1970) the defendant, an accused robber whose mental stability was dubious, had so disrupted his trial that the judge had removed him from the courtroom. The Supreme Court held that while it was within the authority of the judge to bind and gag him or fine him for con-

tempt, the Sixth Amendment guarantee of confrontation did forbid removing him from the courtroom if he refused to behave. Following this decision, New York state made plans to resume, with the aid of closed circuit TV so the defendants could follow the trial, the disrupted trial of thirteen Black Panthers accused of plotting to bomb public places. Although there were further disruptions, the plans were never put into effect.

While the court clearly has what power it needs to prevent disruption of a trial, it cannot tolerate the disruptive conduct and then, at the end of the trial, accumulate the contempts into one summary contempt sentence. In Mayberry v. Pennsylvania (1971) a prisoner on trial for jail break insulted and provoked the judge on eleven occasions. Before the judge pronounced sentence on his conviction, he pronounced him guilty of contempt and sentenced him to one to two years for each contempt. The Supreme Court, while sympathizing with the judge and praising his patience, held that ''no one so cruelly slandered is likely to maintain that calm detachment necessary for fair adjudication,'' and that the question of contempt should be returned for trial before another judge.

In the present case the defendant was tried for robbery before a six-man jury provided by Florida law in all but capital cases. His request for a twelve-man jury was denied and he was sentenced to life imprisonment.

Mr. Justice **White** delivered the opinion of the Court, saying in part:

III

In Duncan v. Louisiana (1968), we held that the Fourteenth Amendment guarantees a right to trial by jury in all criminal cases which—were they to be tried in a federal court—would come within the Sixth Amendment's guarantee. . . .

The question in this case then is whether the constitutional guarantee of a trial by ''jury'' necessarily requires trial by exactly 12 persons, rather than some lesser number—in this case six. We hold that the 12-man panel is not a necessary ingredient of ''trial by jury,'' and that respondent's refusal to impanel more than the six members provided for by Florida law did not violate petitioner's Sixth Amendment rights as applied to the States through the Fourteenth.

We had occasion in Duncan v. Louisiana to review briefly the oft-told history of the development of trial by jury in criminal cases. That history revealed a long tradition attaching great importance to the concept of relying on a body of one's peers to determine guilt or innocence as a safeguard against arbitrary law enforcement. That same history, however, affords little insight into the considerations which gradually led the size of that body to be generally fixed at 12. Some have suggested that the number 12 was fixed upon simply because that was the number of the presentment jury from the hundred, from which the petty jury developed. Other, less circular but more fanciful reasons for the number 12 have been given, "but they were all brought forward after the number was fixed," and rest on little more than mystical or superstitious insights into the significance of "12." Lord Coke's explanation that the "number of twelve is much respected in holy writ, as 12 apostles, 12 stones, 12 tribes, etc." is typical. In short, while sometime in the 14th century the size of the jury at common law came to be fixed generally at 12, that particular feature of the jury system appears to have been an historical accident, unrelated to the great purposes which gave rise to the jury in the first place. The question before us is whether this accidental feature of the jury has been immutably codified into our Constitution.

This Court's earlier decisions have assumed an affirmative answer to this question. The leading case so construing the Sixth Amendment if Thompson v. Utah (1898). There the defendant had been tried and convicted by a 12-man jury for a crime committed in the Territory of Utah. A new trial was granted, but by that time Utah had been admitted as a State. The defendant's new trial proceeded under Utah's Constitution, providing for a jury of only eight members. This Court reversed the resulting conviction, holding that Utah's constitutional provision was an ex post facto law as applied to the defendant. In reaching its conclusion, the Court announced that the Sixth Amendment was applicable to the defendant's trial when Utah was a territory, and that the jury referred to in the Amendment was a jury "constituted, as it was at common law, of twelve persons, neither more nor less." Arguably unnecessary for the result,* this announcement was supported simply by referring to the Magna Carta, and by quoting passages from treatises which noted—what has already been seen—that at common law the jury did indeed consist of 12. Noticeably absent was any discussion of the essential step in the argument: namely, that every feature of the jury as it existed at common law—whether incidental or essential to that institution—was necessarily included in the Constitution wherever that document referred to a "jury." Subsequent decisions have reaffirmed the announcement in Thompson, often in dictum[†] and usually by relying—where there was any discussion of the issue at all—solely on the fact that the common law jury consisted of

12. See Patton v. United States (1930);[‡] Rassmussen v. United States (1905); Maxwell v. Dow (1900).

While "the intent of the Framers" is often an elusive quarry, the relevant constitutional history casts considerable doubt on the easy assumption in our past decisions that if a given feature existed in a jury at common law in 1789, then it was necessarily preserved in the Constitution. Provisions for jury trial were first placed in the Constitution in Article III's provision that "[t]he Trial of all Crimes . . . shall be by jury; and such Trial shall be held in the State where the said Crimes shall have been committed." The "very scanty history [on this provision] in the records of the Constitutional Convention" sheds little light either way on the intended correlation between Article III's "jury" and the features of the jury at common law. . . .

[The Court here reviews in detail the unsuccessful efforts to write a Sixth Amendment explicitly calling for the "accustomed requisites" of the common law and concludes that Congress at the very least showed no interest in being specific about the matter.]

We do not pretend to be able to divine precisely what the word "jury" imported to the Framers, the First Congress, or the States in 1789. It may well be that the usual expectation was that the jury would consist of 12, and that hence, the most likely conclusion to be drawn is simply that little thought was actually given to the specific question we face today. But there is absolutely no indication in "the intent of the Framers" of an explicit decision to equate the constitutional and common law characteristics of the jury. Nothing in this history suggests, then, that we do violence to the letter of the Constitution by turning to other than purely historical considerations to determine which features of the jury system, as it existed at common law, were preserved in the Constitution. The relevant inquiry, as we see it, must be the function which the particular feature performs and its relation to the purposes of the jury trial. Measured by this standard, the 12-man requirement cannot be regarded as an indispensable component of the Sixth Amendment.

The purpose of the jury trial, as we noted in Duncan, is to prevent oppression by the Government. "Providing an accused with the right to be tried by a jury of his peers gave him an inestimable safeguard against the corrupt or overzealous prosecutor and against the compliant, biased, or eccentric judge." Duncan v. Louisiana. Given this purpose, the essential feature of a jury obviously lies in the interposition between the accused and his accuser of the common-sense judgment of a group of laymen, and in the community participation and shared responsibility which results from that group's determination of guilt or innocence. The performance of this role

---

*At the time of the crime and at the first trial the statutes of the Territory of Utah—wholly apart from the Sixth Amendment—ensured Thompson a 12-man jury. The court found the ex post facto question easy to solve, once it was assumed that Utah's subsequent constitutional provision deprived Thompson of a right previously guaranteed him by the United States Constitution; the possibility that the same result might have been reached solely on the basis of the rights formerly accorded Thompson under the territorial statute was hinted at, but was not explicitly considered.

[†]A ruling that the Sixth Amendment refers to a common law jury was essential to the holding in Rassmussen v. United States (1905), where the Court held invalid a conviction by a six-man jury in Alaska. The ruling was accepted at the Government's concession without discussion or citation. . . .

[‡]The Patton opinion furnishes an interesting illustration of the Court's willingness to re-examine earlier assertions about the nature of "jury trial" in almost every respect except the 12-man jury requirement. Patton reaffirmed the 12-man requirement with a simple citation to Thompson v. Utah, while at the same time discarding as "dictum" the equally dogmatic assertion in Thompson that the requirement could not be waived.

is not a function of the particular number of the body which makes up the jury. To be sure, the number should probably be large enough to promote group deliberation, free from outside attempts at intimidation, and to provide a fair possibility for obtaining a representative cross section of the community. But we find little reason to think that these goals are in any meaningful sense less likely to be achieved when the jury numbers six, than when it numbers 12—particularly if the requirement of unanimity is retained.* And, certainly the reliability of the jury as a factfinder hardly seems likely to be a function of its size.

It might be suggested that the 12-man jury gives a defendant a greater advantage since he has more "chances" of finding a juror who will insist on acquittal and thus prevent conviction. But the advantage might just as easily belong to the State, which also needs only one juror out of twelve insisting on guilt to prevent acquittal. What few experiments have occurred—usually in the civil area—indicate that there is no discernible difference between the results reached by the two different-sized juries. In short, neither currently available evidence nor theory suggests that the 12-man jury is necessarily more advantageous to the defendant than a jury composed of fewer members.

Similarly, while in theory the number of viewpoints represented on a randomly selected jury ought to increase as the size of the jury increases, in practice the difference between the 12-man and the six-man jury in terms of the cross section of the community represented seems likely to be negligible. Even the 12-man jury cannot insure representation of every distinct voice in the community, particularly given the use of the peremptory challenge. As long as arbitrary exclusions of a particular class from the jury rolls are forbidden, . . . the concern that the cross section will be significantly diminished if the jury is decreased in size from 12 to six seems an unrealistic one.

We conclude, in short, as we began: the fact that the jury at common law was composed of precisely 12 is an historical accident, unnecessary to effect the purposes of the jury system and wholly without significance "except to mystics." . . . To read the Sixth Amendment as forever codifying a feature so incidental to the real purpose of the Amendment is to ascribe a blind formalism to the Framers which would require considerably more evidence than we have been able to discover in the history and language of the Constitution or in the reasoning of our past decisions. . . . We conclude that petitioner's Sixth Amendment rights, as applied to the States through the Fourteenth Amendment, were not violated by Florida's decision to provide a six-man rather than a 12-man jury. The judgment of the Florida District Court of Appeal is

Affirmed.

Mr. Justice **Blackmun** took no part in the consideration or decision of this case.

Mr. Chief Justice **Burger** joined the opinion of the Court and wrote a brief concurring opinion dealing with Part I.

Mr. Justice **Harlan,** dissenting in [Baldwin v. New York], and concurring in [Williams v. Florida] said in part:

In Duncan v. Louisiana (1968), the Court held, over my dissent and that of Mr. Justice Stewart, that a state criminal defendant is entitled to a jury trial in any case which, if brought in a federal court, would require a jury under the Sixth Amendment. Today the Court holds, in Baldwin v. New York, that New York cannot constitutionally provide that misdemeanors carrying sentences up to one year shall be tried in New York City without a jury. At the same time the Court holds in Williams v. Florida that Florida's six-member jury statute satisfies the Sixth Amendment as carried to the States by the Duncan holding. The necessary consequence of this decision is that 12-member juries are not *constitutionally* required in *federal* criminal trials either.

The historical argument by which the Court undertakes to justify its view that the Sixth Amendment does not require 12-member juries is, in my opinion, much too thin to mask the true thrust of this decision. The decision evinces, I think, a recognition that the "incorporationist" view of the Due Process Clause of the Fourteenth Amendment, which underlay Duncan and is now carried forward into Baldwin, must be tempered to allow the States more elbow room in ordering their own criminal systems. With that much I agree. But to accomplish this by diluting constitutional protections within the federal system itself is something to which I cannot possibly subscribe. Tempering the rigor of Duncan should be done forthrightly, by facing up to the fact that at least in this area the "incorporation" doctrine does not fit well with our federal structure, and by the same token that Duncan was wrongly decided. . . .

Mr. Justice **Stewart,** dissenting in [Baldwin v. New York], and concurring in [Williams v. Florida], said in part:

I substantially agree with the separate opinion Mr. Justice Harlan has filed in these cases—an opinion that fully demonstrates some of the basic errors in a mechanistic "incorporation" approach to the Fourteenth Amendment. I cannot subscribe to his opinion in its entirety, however, if only for the reason that it relies in part upon certain dissenting and concurring opinions in previous cases in which I did not join. . . .

---

*We intimate no view whether or not the requirement of unanimity is an indispensable element of the Sixth Amendment jury trial. While much of the above historical discussion applies as well to the unanimity as to the 12-man requirement, the former, unlike the latter, may well serve an important role in the jury function, for example, as a device for insuring that the Government bear the heavier burden of proof.

Mr. Justice **Black,** with whom Mr. Justice **Douglas** joins, concurring in part and dissenting in part, said in part:

The Court today holds that a State can, consistently with the Sixth Amendment to the United States Constitution, try a defendant in a criminal case with a jury of six members. I agree with that decision for substantially the same reasons given by the Court. . . .

Mr. Justice **Marshall,** dissenting in part, said in part:

. . . Since I believe that the Fourteenth Amendment guaranteed Williams a jury of 12 to pass upon the question of his guilt or innocence before he could be sent to prison for the rest of his life, I dissent from the affirmance of his conviction. . . .

APODACA v. OREGON

406 U. S. 404; 92 S. Ct. 1628; 32 L. Ed. 2d 184 (1972)

If, as the Court held in Williams v. Florida (1970), the old common-law jury is not the measure of the jury required by the Constitution, what kind of jury is required? Two cases decided in 1972 added a new and unexpected dimension to this problem. Both cases raised the question of non-unanimous jury verdicts, but because one was started before Duncan v. Louisiana (1968) and the other after it, the first raised only a fundamental fairness question under the due process clause while the second involved the applicability to the states of the Sixth Amendment.

In Johnson v. Louisiana (1972) the Court upheld the conviction of a man who was tried for robbery before a twelve-member jury and convicted by a nine-to-three verdict, in accordance with Louisiana law. Two years before in In re Winship (1970), a case involving the rights of juveniles to a fair trial, the Court had held explicitly "that the Due Process Clause protects the accused against conviction except upon proof beyond a reasonable doubt . . ." and the question was whether a less-than-unanimous verdict met such a standard. Justice White, joined by the recent appointees to the Court, stressed that "want of jury unanimity is not to be equated with the existence of a reasonable doubt. . . ." If this were not the case, the failure of the common-law jury required by the federal law to reach a unanimous verdict in any case would call for a directed verdict of acquittal rather than a mistrial and there would be no such thing as a hung jury. "Of course, the State's proof could perhaps be regarded as more certain if it had convinced all twelve jurors instead of only nine; it would have been more compelling if it had been required to convince and had, in fact, convinced twenty-four or thirty-six jurors. But the fact remains that nine jurors—a substantial majority of the jury—were convinced by the

evidence. . . . That rational men disagree is not in itself equivalent to a failure of proof by the state, nor does it indicate infidelity to the reasonable doubt standard." Justice Blackmun joined the Court's opinion but noted that use of a seven-to-five standard rather than nine-to-three minimum would afford him "great difficulty."

Justice Stewart, joined by Justices Brennan and Marshall, pointed out in dissent that the effect of the decision was to undermine the principle that a jury had to be an indiscriminate cross-section of the community. "The clear purpose of these decisions has been to ensure universal participation of the citizenry in the administration of criminal justice. Yet today's judgment approves the elimination of the one rule that can ensure that such participation will be meaningful. . . . Under today's judgment, nine jurors can simply ignore the views of their fellow panel members of a different race or class."

When the Court decided Williams v. Florida, it expressly left unanswered the question of whether the ruling applied to federal trials under the Seventh Amendment which provides that "in suits at common law . . . the right of trial by jury shall be preserved," and the agreement of five justices in the case below that the Sixth Amendment requires a unanimous verdict in federal trials suggested that it might not. In Colegrove v. Battin (1973), with Justice Brennan switching sides and writing the opinion, the Court held on the basis of an historical argument that seems to answer the unanimity question as well, that a six-member jury met the Seventh Amendment requirement. "We can only conclude, therefore, that by referring to the 'common law,' the Framers of the Seventh Amendment were concerned with preserving the right of trial by jury in civil cases where it existed at common law, rather than the various incidents of trial by jury. In short, what was said in Williams with respect to the criminal jury is equally applicable here: constitutional history reveals no intention on the part of the Framers 'to equate the constitutional and common-law characteristics of the Jury.' " Two of the four dissenters did not reach the constitutional question, arguing only that Congress had not intended to permit federal courts to use a six-member jury.

Mr. Justice **White** announced the judgment of the Court and an opinion in which The Chief Justice [**Burger**], Mr. Justice **Blackmun,** and Mr. Justice **Rehnquist** joined, and said in part:

Robert Apodaca, Henry Morgan Cooper, Jr., and James Arnold Madden were convicted respectively of assault with a deadly weapon, burglary in a dwelling, and grand larceny before separate Oregon juries, all of which returned less than unanimous verdicts. The vote in the cases of Apodaca and Madden was 11–1 while the vote in the case of Cooper was 10–2, the minimum requisite vote under Oregon law for sustaining a conviction. After their convictions had been affirmed by the Oregon Court of Appeals and review had been denied by the Supreme Court of Oregon, all three sought review in this

Court upon a claim that conviction of crime by a less than unanimous jury violates the right to trial by jury in criminal cases specified by the Sixth Amendment and made applicable to the States by the Fourteenth. See Duncan v. Louisiana (1968). We granted certiorari to consider this claim, which we now find to be without merit.

In Williams v. Florida (1970), we had occasion to consider a related issue: whether the Sixth Amendment's right to trial by jury requires that all juries consist of 12 men. After considering the history of the 12-man requirement and the functions it performs in contemporary society, we concluded that it was not of constitutional stature. We reach the same conclusion today with regard to the requirement of unanimity.

I.

Like the requirement that juries consist of 12 men, the requirement of unanimity arose during the middle ages and had become an accepted feature of the common-law jury by the 18th century. But, as we observed in Williams, "the relevant constitutional history casts considerable doubt on the easy assumption . . . that if a given feature existed in a jury at common law in 1789, then it was necessarily preserved in the Constitution." . . .

As in Williams, we must accordingly consider what is meant by the concept "jury" and determine whether a feature commonly associated with it is constitutionally required. And, as in Williams, our inability to divine "the intent of the Framers" when they eliminated references to the "accustomed requisites" requires that in determining what is meant by a jury we must turn to other than purely historical considerations.

II.

Our inquiry must focus upon the function served by the jury in contemporary society. . . . As we said in Duncan the purpose of trial by jury is to prevent oppression by the Government by providing a "safeguard against the corrupt or overzealous prosecutor and against the compliant, biased, or eccentric judge." . . . "Given this purpose, the essential feature of a jury obviously lies in the interposition between the accused and his accuser of the commonsense judgment of a group of laymen. . . ." Williams v. Florida. A requirement of unanimity, however, does not materially contribute to the exercise of this commonsense judgment. As we said in Williams, a jury will come to such a judgment as long as it consists of a group of laymen representative of a cross section of the community who have the duty and the opportunity to deliberate, free from outside attempts at intimidation, on the question of a defendant's guilt. In terms of this function we perceive no difference between juries required to act unanimously and those permitted to convict or acquit by votes of 10 to two or 11 to one. Requiring unanimity would obviously produce hung juries in some situations where nonunanimous juries will convict or acquit. But in either case, the interest of the defendant in having the judgment of his peers interposed between himself and the officers of the State who prosecute and judge him is equally well served.

III.

Petitioners nevertheless argue that unanimity serves other purposes constitutionally essential to the continued operation of the jury system. Their principal contention is that a Sixth Amendment "jury trial" made mandatory on the States by virtue of the Due Process Clause of the Fourteenth Amendment . . . should be held to require a unanimous jury verdict in order to give substance to the reasonable doubt standard otherwise mandated by the Due Process Clause. See In re Winship (1970).

We are quite sure, however, that the Sixth Amendment itself has never been held to require proof beyond a reasonable doubt in criminal cases. The reasonable doubt standard developed separately from both the jury trial and the unanimous verdict. As the Court noted in the Winship case, the rule requiring proof of crime beyond a reasonable doubt did not crystallize in this country until after the Constitution was adopted. And in that case, which held such a burden of proof to be constitutionally required, the Court purported to draw no support from the Sixth Amendment.

Petitioners' argument that the Sixth Amendment requires jury unanimity in order to give effect to the reasonable doubt standard thus founders on the fact that the Sixth Amendment does not require proof beyond a reasonable doubt at all. The reasonable doubt argument is rooted, in effect, in due process and has been rejected in Johnson v. Louisiana [1972].

IV.

Petitioners also cite quite accurately a long line of decisions of this Court upholding the principle that the Fourteenth Amendment requires jury panels to reflect a cross section of the community. . . . They then contend that unanimity is a necessary precondition for effective application of the cross section requirement, because a rule permitting less than unanimous verdicts will make it possible for convictions to occur without the acquiescence of minority elements within the community.

There are two flaws in this argument. One is petitioners' assumption that every distinct voice in the community has a right to be represented on every jury and a right to prevent conviction of a defendant in any case. All that the Constitution forbids, however, is systematic exclusion of identifiable segments of the community from jury panels and from the juries ultimately drawn from those panels; a defendant may not, for example, challenge the makeup of a jury merely because no members of his race are on the jury, but must prove that his race has been systematically excluded. . . . No group, in short, has the right to block convictions; it has only the right to participate in the overall legal processes by which criminal guilt and innocence are determined.

We also cannot accept petitioners' second assumption—that minority groups, even when they are represented on a jury, will not adequately represent the viewpoint of those groups simply because they may be outvoted in the final result. They will be present during all deliberations, and their views will be heard. We cannot assume that the majority of the jury will refuse to weigh the evidence and reach a decision upon rational grounds, just as it must now do in order to obtain unanimous verdicts, or that a majority will deprive a man of his liberty on the basis of prejudice when a minority is presenting a reasonable argument in favor of acquittal. We simply find no proof for the notion that a majority will disregard its instructions and cast its votes for guilt or innocence based on prejudice rather than the evidence.

We accordingly affirm the judgment of the Court of Appeals of Oregon.

It is so ordered.

Mr. Justice **Blackmun,** concurring, said in part:

I do not hesitate to say that a system employing a 7–5 standard, rather than a 9–3 or 75% minimum, would afford me great difficulty. As Mr. Justice White points out [in Johnson], "a substantial majority of the jury" are to be convinced. That is all that is before us in each of these cases.

Mr. Justice **Powell** concurring in the judgment said in part:

II.

... I concur in the plurality opinion in this case insofar as it concludes that a defendant in a state court may constitutionally be convicted by less than a unanimous verdict, but I am not in accord with a major premise upon which that judgment is based. Its premise is that the concept of jury trial, as applicable to the States under the Fourteenth Amendment, must be identical in every detail to the concept required in federal courts by the Sixth Amendment. I do not think that all of the elements of jury trial within the meaning of the Sixth Amendment are necessarily embodied in or incorporated into the Due Process Clause of the Fourteenth Amendment. As Mr. Justice Fortas, concurring in Duncan v. Louisiana said: "Neither logic nor history nor the intent of the draftsmen of the Fourteenth Amendment can possibly be said to require that the Sixth Amendment or its jury trial provision be applied to the States together with the total gloss that the Court's decisions have supplied."

In an unbroken line of cases reaching back into the late 1800's, the Justices of this Court have recognized, virtually without dissent, that unanimity is one of the indispensable features of *federal* jury trial. Andres v.

United States (1948); Patton v. United States (1930); Hawaii v. Mankichi, (1903) (see also Mr. Justice Harlan's dissenting opinion); Maxwell v. Dow, (1900) (see also Mr. Justice Harlan's dissenting opinion); Thompson v. Utah, (1898). In these cases, the Court has presumed that unanimous verdicts are essential in federal jury trials, not because unanimity is necessarily fundamental to the function performed by the jury, but because that result is mandated by history.* The reasoning which revision runs throughout this Court's Sixth Amendment precedents is that, in amending the Constitution to guarantee the right to jury trial, the Framers desired to preserve the jury safeguard as it was known to them at common law. At the time the Bill of Rights was adopted, unanimity had long been established as one of the attributes of a jury conviction at common law. It therefore seems to me, in accord both with history and precedent, that the Sixth Amendment requires a unanimous jury verdict to convict in a federal criminal trial.

But it is the Fourteenth Amendment, rather than the Sixth, which imposes upon the States the requirement that they provide jury trials to those accused of serious crimes. This Court has said, in cases decided when the intendment of that Amendment was not as clouded by the passage of time, that due process does not require that the States apply the federal jury trial right with all its gloss. In Maxwell v. Dow, Mr. Justice Peckham, speaking for eight of the nine members of the Court, so stated: "[W]hen providing in their constitution and legislation for the manner in which civil or criminal actions shall be tried, it is in entire conformity with the character of the Federal Government that [the States] should have the right to decide for themselves what shall be the form and character of the procedure in such trials, . . . whether there shall be a jury of twelve or a lesser number, and whether the verdict must be unanimous or not. . . ." Again, in Jordan v. Massachusetts (1912), the Court concluded that "[i]n criminal cases due process of law is not denied by a state law which dispenses with . . . the necessity of a jury of twelve, or unanimity in the verdict." . . .

The question, therefore, which should be addressed in this case is whether unanimity is in fact so fundamental to the essentials of jury trial that this particular requirement of the Sixth Amendment is necessarily binding on the States under the Due Process Clause of the Fourteenth Amendment. An affirmative answer, ignoring the strong views previously expressed to the contrary by this Court in Maxwell and Jordan, would give unwarranted and unwise scope to the incorporation doctrine as it applies to the due process right of state criminal defendants to trial by jury. . . .

Viewing the unanimity controversy as one requiring a fresh look at the question of what is fundamental

---

*. . . No reason, other than the conference committee's revision of the House draft of the Sixth Amendment, has been offered to justify departure from this Court's prior precedents. The admitted ambiguity of that piece of legislative history is not sufficient, in my view, to override the unambiguous history of the common law right. Williams v. Florida.

in jury trial, I see no constitutional infirmity in the provision adopted by the people of Oregon. It is the product of a constitutional amendment, approved by a vote of the people in the State, and appears to be patterned on a provision of the American Law Institute's Code of Criminal Procedure. A similar decision has been echoed more recently in England where the unanimity requirement was abandoned by statutory enactment. Less than unanimous verdict provisions also have been viewed with approval by the American Bar Association's Criminal Justice Project. Those who have studied the jury mechanism and recommended deviation from the historic rule of unanimity have found a number of considerations to be significant. Removal of the unanimity requirement could well minimize the potential for hung juries occasioned either by bribery or juror irrationality. Furthermore, the rule that juries must speak with a single voice often leads, not to full agreement among the 12 but to agreement by none and compromise by all, despite the frequent absence of a rational basis for such compromise. Quite apart from whether Justices sitting on this Court would have deemed advisable the adoption of any particular less than unanimous jury provision, I think that considerations of this kind reflect a legitimate basis for experimentation and deviation from the federal blueprint.

Mr. Justice **Douglas,** with whom Mr. Justice **Brennan** and Mr. Justice **Marshall** concur, dissenting, said in part:

II.

The plurality approves a procedure which diminishes the reliability of jury. First, it eliminates the circumstances in which a minority of jurors (a) could have rationally persuaded the entire jury to acquit, or (b) while unable to persuade the majority to acquit, nonetheless could have convinced them to convict only on a lesser-included offense. Second, it permits prosecutors in Oregon and Louisiana to enjoy a conviction-acquittal ratio substantially greater than that ordinarily returned by unanimous juries.

The diminution of verdict reliability flows from the fact that nonunanimous juries need not debate and deliberate as fully as must unanimous juries. As soon as the requisite majority is attained, further consideration is not required either by Oregon or by Louisiana even though the dissident jurors might, if given the chance, be able to convince the majority. Such persuasion does in fact occasionally occur in States where the unanimous requirement applies: "In roughly one case in ten, the minority eventually succeeds in reversing an initial majority, and these may be cases of special importance."* One explanation for this phenomenon is that because jurors are often not permitted to take notes and because they

---

*Kalven & Zeisel, The American Jury 490 (1966). . . .

have imperfect memories, the forensic process of forcing jurors to defend their conflicting recollections and conclusions flushes out many nuances which otherwise would go overlooked. This collective effort to piece together the puzzle of historical truth, however, is cut short as soon as the requisite majority is reached in Oregon and Louisiana. Indeed, if a necessary majority is immediately obtained, then no deliberation at all is required in these States. (There is a suggestion that this may have happened in the 10–2 verdict rendered in only 41 minutes in Apodaca's case.) To be sure, in jurisdictions other than these two States, initial majorities normally prevail in the end, but about a tenth of the time the rough and tumble of the juryroom operates to reverse completely their preliminary perception of guilt or innocence. The Court now extracts from the juryroom this automatic check against hasty fact-finding by relieving jurors of the duty to hear out fully the dissenters.

It is said that there is no evidence that majority jurors will refuse to listen to dissenters whose votes are unneeded for conviction. Yet human experience teaches that polite and academic conversation is no substitute for the earnest and robust argument necessary to reach unanimity. As mentioned earlier, in Apodaca's case, whatever courtesy dialogue transpired could not have lasted more than 41 minutes. I fail to understand why the Court should lift from the States the burden of justifying so radical a departure from an accepted and applauded tradition and instead demand that these defendants document with empirical evidence what has always been thought to be too obvious for further study.

To be sure in Williams v. Florida, we held that a State could provide a jury less than 12 in number in criminal trial. We said "What few experiments have occurred—usually in the civil area—indicate that there is no discernible difference between the results reached by the two different-sized juries. In short, neither currently available evidence nor theory suggests that the 12-man jury is necessarily more advantageous to the defendant than a jury composed of fewer members."

That rationale of Williams can have no application here. Williams requires that the change be neither more nor less advantageous to either the State or the defendant. It is said that such a showing is satisfied here since a 3:9 (Louisiana) or 2:10 (Oregon) verdict will result in acquittal. Yet experience shows that the less than unanimous jury overwhelmingly favors the States.

Moreover, even where an initial majority wins the dissent over to its side, the ultimate result in unanimous jury States may nonetheless reflect the reservations of uncertain jurors. I refer to many compromise verdicts on lesser-included offenses and lesser sentences. Thus, even though a minority may not be forceful enough to carry the day, their doubts may nonetheless cause a majority to exercise caution. Obviously, however, in Oregon and Louisiana, dissident jurors will not have the opportunity through full deliberation to temper the opposing faction's degree of certainty of guilt.

The new rule also has an impact on cases in which a unanimous jury would have neither voted to acquit nor to convict, but would have deadlocked. In unanimous jury States, this occurs about 5.6 percent of the time. Of these deadlocked juries, Kalven and Zeisel say that 56% contain either one, two, or three dissenters. In these latter cases, the majorities favor the prosecution 44% (of the 56%) but the defendant only 12% (of the 56%). Thus, by eliminating these deadlocks, Louisiana wins 44 cases for every 12 that it loses, obtaining in this band of outcomes a substantially more favorable conviction ratio (3.67) than the unanimous jury ratio of slightly less than two guilty verdicts for every acquittal. . . . By eliminating the one and two dissenting juror cases, Oregon does even better, gaining 4.25 convictions for every acquittal. While the statutes on their face deceptively appear to be neutral, the use of the nonunanimous jury stacks the truth-determining process against the accused. Thus, we take one step more away from the accusatorial system that has been our proud boast.

Mr. Justice **Brennan,** with whom Mr. Justice **Marshall** joins, dissenting, said in part:

. . . When verdicts must be unanimous, no member of the jury may be ignored by the others. When less than unanimity is sufficient, consideration of minority views may become nothing more than a matter of majority grace. In my opinion, the right of all groups in this Nation to participate in the criminal process means the right to have their voices heard. A unanimous verdict vindicates that right. Majority verdicts could destroy it.

Mr. Justice **Stewart,** with whom Mr. Justice **Brennan** and Mr. Justice **Marshall** join, dissenting, said in part:

In Duncan v. Louisiana, the court squarely held that the Sixth Amendment right to trial by jury in a federal criminal case is made wholly applicable to state criminal trials by the Fourteenth Amendment. Unless Duncan is to be overruled, therefore, the only relevant question here is whether the Sixth Amendment's guarantee of trial by jury embraces a guarantee that the verdict of the jury must be unanimous. The answer to that question is clearly ''yes,'' as my Brother Powell has cogently demonstrated in that part of his concurring opinion that reviews almost a century of Sixth Amendment adjudication.

Until today, it has been universally understood that a unanimous verdict is an essential element of a Sixth Amendment jury trial. . . .

I would follow these settled Sixth Amendment precedents and reverse the judgment before us.

Mr. Justice **Marshall,** with whom Mr. Justice **Brennan** joins, dissenting, said in part:

Today the Court cuts the heart out of two of the most important and inseparable safeguards the Bill of Rights offers a criminal defendant: the right to submit his case to a jury, and the right to proof beyond a reasonable doubt. Together, these safeguards occupy a fundamental place in our constitutional scheme, protecting the individual defendant from the awesome power of the State. After today, the skeleton of these safeguards remains, but the Court strips them of life and of meaning. I cannot refrain from adding my protest to that of my Brothers Douglas, Brennan, and Stewart, whom I join.

In Apodaca v. Oregon, the question is too frighteningly simple to bear much discussion. We are asked to decide what is the nature of the ''jury'' that is guaranteed by the Sixth Amendment. I would have thought that history provided the appropriate guide, and as Mr. Justice Powell has demonstrated so convincingly, history compels the decision that unanimity is an essential feature of that jury. But the majority has embarked on a ''functional'' analysis of the jury that allows it to strip away, one by one, virtually all the characteristic features of the jury as we know it. Two years ago, over my dissent, the Court discarded as an essential feature the traditional size of the jury. Williams v. Florida (1970). Today the Court discards, at least in state trials, the traditional requirement of unanimity. It seems utterly and ominously clear that so long as the tribunal bears the label ''jury,'' it will meet Sixth Amendment requirements as they are presently viewed by this Court. The Court seems to require only that jurors be laymen, drawn from the community without systematic exclusion of any group, who exercise common sense judgment.

More distressing still than the Court's treatment of the right to jury trial is the cavalier treatment the Court gives to proof beyond a reasonable doubt. The Court asserts that when a jury votes nine to three for conviction, the doubts of the three do not impeach the verdict of the nine. The argument seems to be that since, under Williams, nine jurors are enough to convict, the three dissenters are mere surplusage. But there is all the difference in the world between three jurors who aren't there, and three jurors who entertain doubts after hearing all the evidence. In the first case we can never know, and it is senseless to ask, whether the prosecutor might have persuaded additional jurors had they been present. But in the second case we know what has happened: the prosecutor has tried and failed to persuade those jurors of the defendant's guilt. In such circumstances, it does violence to language and to logic to say that the government has proved the defendant's guilt beyond a reasonable doubt.

It is said that this argument is fallacious because a deadlocked jury does not, under our law, bring about an acquittal or bar a retrial. The argument seems to be that if the doubt of a dissenting juror were the ''reasonable doubt'' that constitutionally bars conviction, then it would necessarily result in an acquittal and bar retrial. But that argument rests on a complete non sequitur. The reasonable doubt rule, properly viewed, simply establishes that, as a prerequisite to obtaining a valid conviction, the prosecutor must overcome all of the jury's reasonable doubts; it does not, of itself, determine what shall happen if he fails to do so. That is a question to be answered with reference to a wholly different constitutional provision, the Fifth Amendment ban on double jeopardy, made applicable to the States through the Due

Process Clause of the Fourteenth Amendment in Benton v. Maryland (1969).

Under prevailing notions of double jeopardy, if a jury has tried and failed to reach a unanimous verdict, a new trial may be held. United States v. Perez (1824). The State is free, consistent with the ban on double jeopardy, to treat the verdict of a nonunanimous jury as a nullity rather than as an acquittal. On retrial, the prosecutor may be given the opportunity to make a stronger case if he can: new evidence may be available, old evidence may have disappeared, and even the same evidence may appear in a different light if, for example, the demeanor of witnesses is different. Because the second trial may vary substantially from the first, the doubts of the dissenting jurors at the first trial do not necessarily impeach the verdict of a new jury on retrial. But that conclusion is wholly consistent with the view that the doubts of dissenting jurors create a constitutional bar to conviction at the trial which produced those doubts. Until today, I had thought that was the law.

THE BARGAINING AWAY OF CONSTITUTIONAL RIGHTS

WYMAN v. JAMES

400 U. S. 309; 91 S. Ct. 381; 27 L. Ed. 2d 408 (1971)

When Justice Holmes was still serving on the Supreme Judicial Court of Massachusetts he said, in the course of upholding the dismissal of a policeman for political activities, he "may have a constitutional right to talk politics, but he has no constitutional right to be a policeman"; McAuliffe v. Mayor of New Bedford, 155 Mass. 216 (1892). While the matter would not be handled in this offhand manner today, the problem is symbolic of a relationship between the public and the government that because of its nature bears careful and constant scrutiny. On the one hand stands an individual with certain guaranteed rights against the powers of government; on the other stands that government with almost unlimited resources with which to buy those rights from the individual. What is to prevent a state offering to educate its children free and feed them a free lunch on condition that the child's parents, should they be accused under the criminal law, agree to waive their right to a court trial and accept the decision of the prosecuting attorney as to guilt and appropriate punishment? The parents are free to reject the offer if they are prepared to pay the expenses of educating their children. They are not coerced out of their rights, they are merely tempted out of them. Given the enormous variety of rights and benefits involved, it is scarcely surprising that the courts have not come up with a single rule for all cases.

In an earlier period the courts eased the problem somewhat by drawing a distinction between "rights" and "privileges." Privileges, since they were a gift of the state, could be withdrawn at will, while rights could only be withdrawn for cause and after a full hearing to see that such cause existed. Historically, a license to operate a pool hall or a saloon was granted as a privilege and could be revoked summarily, while the license to practice law or medicine was a right which could only be revoked for cause and after notice and hearing. The courts, over time, have blunted this distinction and now nearly any advantage offered by statute is held by those eligible as a matter of right.

Although, as W. S. Gilbert put it, there are times when a "policeman's lot is not a happy one" he or she does not have to forfeit political rights, including the right to express the hope the President may be assassinated, in order to hold his or her his job; see Rankin v. McPherson (1987). On the other hand, an assistant district attorney is not free to circulate a critical questionnaire within the office raising questions of office procedure which are not matters of public concern; see Connick v. Myers (1983).

The Supreme Court early recognized the dangers latent in the exaction of "unconstitutional conditions" and in Terral v. Burke Construction Co. (1922) held void a state law that required any out-of-state corporation, as a condition of doing business in the state, to waive its right to sue in the federal courts. And in Frost v. Railroad Commission (1926) it struck down as unconstitutional a stipulation that all truckers, as a condition of using the highways of the state, convert themselves into common carriers for hire. In both cases the conditions were being used to favor one economic group over another.

The area in which the Court has been the most unyielding in this matter is where the person applying for state benefits is asked to forfeit some First Amendment right. In Speiser v. Randall (1958) and First Unitarian Church v. Los Angeles (1958) the Court struck down California laws denying tax exemption to anyone who refused to take a loyalty oath so structured as to place on them the burden of proving their innocence, and in Sherbert v. Verner (1936) it held bad a rule whereby unemployment compensation was withheld from a woman who would not accept "suitable employment" involving Saturday work in violation of her religious beliefs.

As the quotation from Justice Holmes would suggest, the group most vulnerable to the temptation to accept unconstitutional conditions is that of public servants, especially security forces, and it is from this group that the legislature is most apt to exact such conditions as the price of employment. During the Cold War era of the 1950s states and municipalities began demanding loyalty oaths of their employees, especially teachers. The Court struggled with the problem in a substantial group of cases, but the general result was that the employee's right to protest was protected while the right to try to *overthrow the government by force and violence was forbidden. See Cole v. Richardson (1972). Nor has the Court permitted the state to require of a police officer as a condition of employment a waiver of the right against self-incrimination; see Garrity v. New Jersey (1967) and Gardner v. Broderick (1968). The Court did say in the latter case, however, that while the officer could not be deprived of immunity from prosecution, if the testimony he or she gave justified dismissal the officer could be dismissed.*

The present case involves another group that is peculiarly susceptible to the temptation to waive their right, and that is the group that receives public assistance in one form or another. It is an enormous group, ranging from cotton farmers and airlines to all recipients of Social Security benefits. With the exception of the situation below, the government has refrained from demanding as a price of these benefits the waiver of constitutional rights.

Mr. Justice **Blackmun** delivered the opinion of the Court, saying in part:

III

When a case involves a home and some type of official intrusion into that home, as this case appears to do, an immediate and natural reaction is one of concern about Fourth Amendment rights and the protection which that Amendment is intended to afford. Its emphasis indeed is upon one of the most precious aspects of personal security in the home. "The right of the people to be secure in their persons, houses, papers, and effects. . . ." This Court has characterized that right as "basic to our free society." Wolf v. Colorado (1949); Camara v. Municipal Court (1967). And over the years the Court consistently has been most protective of the privacy of the dwelling. See, for example, Boyd v. United States (1886); Mapp v. Ohio (1961). . . . In Camara Mr. Justice White, after noting that the "translation of the abstract prohibition against 'unreasonable searches and seizures' into workable guidelines for the decision of particular cases is a difficult task," went on to observe, "Nevertheless, one governing principle, justified by history and by current experience, has consistently been followed: except in certain carefully defined classes of cases, a search of private property without proper consent is 'unreasonable' unless it has been authorized by a valid search warrant." He pointed out, too, that one's Fourth Amendment protection subsists apart from his being suspected of criminal behavior.

IV.

This natural and quite proper protective attitude, however, is not a factor in this case, for the seemingly obvious and simple reason that we are not concerned here with any search by the New York social service

agency in the Fourth Amendment meaning of that term. It is true that the governing statute and regulations appear to make mandatory the initial home visit and the subsequent periodic "contacts" (which may include home visits) for the inception and continuance of aid. It is also true that the caseworker's posture in the home visit is perhaps, in a sense, both rehabilitative and investigative. But this latter aspect, we think, is given too broad a character and far more emphasis than it deserves if it is equated with a search in the traditional criminal law context. We note, too, that the visitation in itself is not forced or compelled, and that the beneficiary's denial of permission is not a criminal act. If consent to the visitation is withheld, no visitation takes place. The aid then never begins or merely ceases, as the case may be. There is no entry of the home and there is no search.

V.

If however, we were to assume that a caseworker's home visit, before or subsequent to the beneficiary's initial qualification for benefits, somehow (perhaps because the average beneficiary might feel she is in no position to refuse consent to the visit), and despite its interview nature, does possess some of the characteristics of a search in the traditional sense, we nevertheless conclude that the visit not fall within the Fourth Amendment's proscription. This is because it does not descend to the level of unreasonableness. It is unreasonableness which is the Fourth Amendment's standard. Terry v. Ohio (1968). . . .

There are a number of factors which compel us to conclude that the home visit proposed for Mrs. James is not unreasonable:

1. The public's interest in this particular segment of the area of assistance to the unfortunate is protection and aid for the dependent child whose family requires such aid for that child. The focus is on the *child* and, further, it is on the child who is *dependent*. There is no more worthy object of the public's concern. The dependent child's needs are paramount, and only with hesitancy would we relegate those needs, in the scale of comparative values, to a position secondary to what the mother claims as her rights.

2. The agency, with tax funds provided from federal as well as from state sources, is fulfilling a public trust. The State, working through its qualified welfare agency, has appropriate and paramount interest and concern in seeing and assuring that the intended and proper objects of that tax-produced assistance are the ones who benefit from the aid it dispenses. Surely it is not unreasonable, in the Fourth Amendment sense or in any other sense of that term, that the State have at its command a gentle means, of limited extent and of practical and considerate application, of achieving that assurance.

3. One who dispenses purely private charity naturally has an interest in and expects to know how his charitable funds are utilized and put to work. The public,

when it is the provider, rightly expects the same. It might well expect more, because of the trust aspect of public funds, and the recipient, as well as the caseworker, has not only an interest but an obligation.

4. The emphasis of the New York statutes and regulations is upon the home, upon "close (contact)" with the beneficiary, upon restoring the aid recipient "to a condition of self-support," and upon the relief of his distress. The federal emphasis is no different. ... And it is concerned about any possible exploitation of the child. ...

7. Mrs. James, in fact, on this record presents no specific complaint of any unreasonable intrusion of her home and nothing which supports an inference that the desired home visit had as its purpose the obtaining of information as to criminal activity. She complains of no proposed visitation at an awkward or retirement hour. She suggests no forcible entry. She refers to no snooping. She describes no impolite or reprehensible conduct of any kind. She alleges only, in general and nonspecific terms, that on previous visits and, on information and belief, on visitation at the home of other aid recipients, "questions concerning personal relationships, beliefs and behavior are raised and pressed which are unnecessary for a determination of continuing eligibility." Paradoxically, this same complaint could be made of a conference held elsewhere than in the home, and yet this is what is sought by Mrs. James. The same complaint could be made of the census taker's questions. ... What Mrs. James appears to want from the agency which provides her and her infant son with the necessities for life is the right to receive those necessities upon her own informational terms, to utilize the Fourth Amendment as a wedge for imposing those terms and to avoid questions of any kind.*

8. We are not persuaded, as Mrs. James would have us be, that all information pertinent to the issue of eligibility can be obtained by the agency through an interview at a place other than the home, or, as the District Court majority suggested, by examining a lease or a birth certificate, or by periodic medical examinations, or by interviews with school personnel. Although these secondary sources might be helpful, they would not always assure verification of actual residence or of actual physical presence in the home, which are requisites for AFDC benefits, or of impending medical needs. And, of course, little children, such as Maurice James, are not yet registered in school.

9. The visit is not one by police or uniformed authority. It is made by a caseworker of some training† whose primary objective is, or should be, the welfare, not the prosecution, of the aid recipient for whom the worker has profound responsibility. As has already been stressed, the program concerns dependent children and the needy families of those children. It does not deal with crime or with the actual or suspected perpetrators of crime. The caseworker is not a sleuth but rather, we trust, is a friend in need.

10. The home visit is not a criminal investigation, does not equate with a criminal investigation, and despite the announced fears of Mrs. James and those who would join her, is not in aid of any criminal proceeding. If the visitation serves to discourage misrepresentation or fraud, such a byproduct of that visit does not impress upon the visit itself a dominant criminal investigative aspect. And if the visit should, by chance, lead to the discovery of fraud and a criminal prosecution should follow, then, even assuming that the evidence discovered upon the home visitation is admissible, an issue upon which we express no opinion, that is a routine and expected fact of life and a consequence no greater than that which necessarily ensues upon any other discovery by a citizen of criminal conduct. ...

It seems to us that the situation is akin to that where an Internal Revenue Service agent, in making a routine civil audit of a taxpayer's income tax return, asks that the taxpayer produce for the agent's review some proof of a deduction the taxpayer has asserted to his benefit in the computation of his tax. If the taxpayer refuses, there is, absent fraud, only a disallowance of the claimed deduction and a consequent additional tax. The taxpayer is fully within his "rights" in refusing to produce the proof, but in maintaining and asserting those rights a tax detriment results and it is a detriment of the taxpayer's own making. So here Mrs. James has the "right" to refuse the home visit, but a consequence in the form of cessation of aid, similar to the taxpayer's resultant additional tax, flows from that refusal. The choice is entirely hers, and nothing of constitutional magnitude is involved.

VI.

Camara v. Municipal Court (1967) and its companion case, See v. City of Seattle (1967), both by a divided Court, are not inconsistent with our result here. Those cases concerned, respectively, a refusal of entry to

---

*We have examined Mrs. James' case record with the New York City Department of Social Services, which, as an exhibit, accompanied defendant Wyman's answer. It discloses numerous interviews from the time of the initial one on April 27, 1967, until the attempted closing in June 1969. The record is revealing as to Mrs. James' failure ever really to satisfy the requirements for eligibility; as to constant and repeated demands; as to attitude toward the caseworker; as to reluctance to cooperate; as to evasiveness; and as to occasional belligerency. There are indications that all was not always well with the infant Maurice (skull fracture, a dent in the head, a possible rat bite). The picture is a sad and unhappy one.

†The amicus brief submitted on behalf of the Social Services Employees Union Local 371, AFSCME, AFL\-CIO, the bargaining representative for the social service staff employed in the New York City Department of Social Services, recites that "caseworkers are either badly trained or untrained" and that "[g]enerally, a caseworker is not only poorly trained, but also young and inexperienced. ..." Despite this astonishing description by the union of the lack of qualification of its own members for the work they are employed to do, we must assume that the caseworker possesses at least some qualifications and some dedication to duty.

city housing inspectors checking for a violation of a building's occupancy permit, and a refusal of entry to a fire department representative interested in compliance with a city's fire code. In each case a majority of this Court held that the Fourth Amendment barred prosecution for refusal to permit the desired warrantless inspection. Frank v. Maryland (1959), a case which reached an opposing result and which concerned a request by a health officer for entry in order to check the source of a rat infestation, was pro tanto overruled. Both Frank and Camara involved dwelling quarters. See had to do with a commercial warehouse.

But the facts of the three cases are significantly different from those before us. Each concerned a true search for violations. Frank was a criminal prosecution for the owner's refusal to permit entry. So, too, was See. Camara had to do with a writ of prohibition sought to prevent an already pending criminal prosecution. The community welfare aspects, of course, were highly important, but each case arose in a criminal context where a genuine search was denied and prosecution followed.

In contrast, Mrs. James is not being prosecuted for her refusal to permit the home visit and is not about to be so prosecuted. Her wishes in that respect are fully honored. We have not been told, and have not found, that her refusal is made a criminal act by any applicable New York or federal statute. The only consequence of her refusal is that the payment of benefits ceases. Important and serious as this is, the situation is no different than if she had exercised a similar negative choice initially and refrained from applying for AFDC benefits. If a statute made her refusal a criminal offense, and if this case were one concerning her prosecution under that statute, Camara and See would have conceivable pertinency. . . .

Mr. Justice **White** concurs in the judgment and joins the opinion of the Court with the exception of Part IV thereof.

Mr. Justice **Douglas,** dissenting, said in part:

In 1969 roughly 126 billion dollars were spent by the federal, state, and local governments on "social welfare." To farmers alone, over four billion dollars was paid, in part for not growing certain crops. Almost 129,000 farmers received $5,000 or more, their total benefit exceeding $1,450,000,000. Those payments were in some instances very large, a few running a million or more a year. But the majority were payments under $5,000 each.

Yet almost every beneficiary whether rich or poor, rural or urban, has a "house"—one of the places protected by the Fourth Amendment against "unreasonable searches and seizures." The question in this case is whether receipt of largesse from the government makes the *home* of the beneficiary subject to access by an inspector of the agency of oversight, even though the beneficiary objects to the intrusion and even though the Fourth Amendment's procedure for access to one's

house or *home* is not followed. The penalty here is not, of course, invasion of the privacy of Barbara James, only her loss of federal or state largesse. That, however, is merely rephrasing the problem. Whatever the semantics, the central question is whether the government by force of its largesse has the power to "buy up" rights guaranteed by the Constitution. But for the assertion of her constitution right, Barbara James in this case would have received the welfare benefit.

[Justice Douglas here discusses Speiser v. Randall (1958), Hannegan v. Esquire (1946) and Sherbert v. Verner (1963), in which state benefits were conditioned on the forfeiture of First Amendment rights.]

These cases are in the tradition of United States v. Chicago M. St. P. & P. R. Co. [1931], where Mr. Justice Sutherland, writing for the Court said: "... the rule is that the right to continue the exercise of a privilege granted by the state cannot be made to depend upon the grantee's submission to a condition prescribed by the state which is hostile to the provisions of the federal Constitution."

What we said in those cases is as applicable to Fourth Amendment rights as to those of the First. The Fourth, of course, speaks of "unreasonable" searches and seizures, while the First is written in absolute terms. But the right of privacy which the Fourth protects is perhaps as vivid in our lives as the right of expression sponsored by the First. Griswold v. Connecticut [1965]. If the regime under which Barbara James lives were enterprise capitalism as, for example, if she ran a small factory geared into the Pentagon's procurement program, she certainly would have a right to deny inspectors access to her *home* unless they came with a warrant. . . .

. . . It is a strange jurisprudence indeed which safeguards the businessman at his place of work from warrantless searches but will not do the same for a mother in her *home*.

Is a search of her home without a warrant made "reasonable" merely because she is dependent on government largesse? . . .

If the welfare recipient was not Barbara James but a prominent, affluent cotton or wheat farmer receiving benefit payments for not growing crops, would not the approach be different? Welfare in aid of dependent children, like social security and unemployment benefits, has an aura of suspicion. There doubtless are frauds in every sector of public welfare whether the recipient be a Barbara James or someone who is prominent or influential. But constitutional rights—here the privacy of the *home*—are obviously not dependent on the poverty or on the affluence of the beneficiary. It is the precincts of the *home* that the Fourth Amendment protects; and their privacy is as important to the lowly as to the mighty. . . .

I would place the same restrictions on inspectors entering the *homes* of welfare beneficiaries as are on inspectors entering the *homes* of those on the payroll of government, or the *homes* of those who contract with the government, or the *homes* of those who work for those having government contracts. . . .

Mr. Justice **Marshall**, whom Mr. Justice **Brennan** joins, dissenting, said in part:

Although I substantially agree with its initial statement of the issue in this case, the Court's opinion goes on to imply that the appellee has refused to provide information germane to a determination of her eligibility for AFDC benefits. The record plainly shows, however, that Mrs. James offered to furnish any information that the appellants desired and to be interviewed at any place other than her home. Appellants rejected her offers and terminated her benefits solely on the ground that she refused to permit a home visit. In addition, appellants make no contention that any sort of probable cause exists to suspect appellee of welfare fraud or child abuse.

Simply stated, the issue in this case is whether a state welfare agency can require all recipients of AFDC benefits to submit to warrantless "visitations" of their homes. In answering that question, the majority dodges between constitutional issues to reach a result clearly inconsistent with the decisions of this Court. We are told that there is no search involved in this case; that even if there were a search, it would not be unreasonable; and that even if this were an unreasonable search, a welfare recipient waives her right to object by accepting benefits. I emphatically disagree with all three conclusions. Furthermore, I believe that binding regulations of the Department of Health, Education, and Welfare prohibit appellants from requiring the home visit.

I.

The Court's assertion that this case concerns no search "in the Fourth Amendment meaning of the term" is neither "obvious" nor "simple." I should have thought that the Fourth Amendment governs all intrusions by agents of the public upon personal security, Terry v. Ohio (1968). . . .

Even if the Fourth Amendment does not apply to each and every governmental entry into the home, the welfare visit is not some sort of purely benevolent inspection. No one questions the motives of the dedicated welfare caseworker. Of course, caseworkers seek to be friends, but the point is that they are also required to be sleuths. The majority concedes that the "visitation" is partially investigative, but claims that this investigative aspect has been given "too much emphasis." Emphasis has indeed been given. Time and again, in briefs and at oral argument, appellants emphasized the need to enter AFDC homes to guard against welfare fraud and child abuse, both of which are felonies. The New York statutes provide emphasis by requiring all caseworkers to report any evidence of fraud which a home visit uncovers. . . . And appellants have strenuously emphasized the importance of the visit to provide evidence leading to civil forfeitures including elimination of benefits and loss of child custody.

Actually, the home visit is precisely the type of inspection proscribed by Camara and its companion case, See v. City of Seattle (1967), except that the welfare visit is a more severe intrusion upon privacy and family dignity. . . .

The Court attempts to distinguish See and Camara by telling us that those cases involved "true" and "genuine" searches. The only concrete distinction offered is that See and Camara concerned criminal prosecutions for refusal to permit the search. The Camara opinion did observe that one could be prosecuted for a refusal to allow that search; but, apart from the issue of consent, there is neither logic in, nor precedent for, the view that the ambit of the Fourth Amendment depends not on the character of the governmental intrusion but on the size of the club that the State wields against a resisting citizen. Even if the magnitude of the penalty were relevant, which sanction for resisting the search is more severe? For protecting the privacy of her home, Mrs. James lost the sole means of support for herself and her infant son. For protecting the privacy of his commercial warehouse, Mr. See received a $100 suspended fine.

Conceding for the sake of argument that someone might view the "visitation" as a search, the majority nonetheless concludes that such a search is not unreasonable. However, their mode of reaching that conclusion departs from the entire history of Fourth Amendment case law. Of course, the Fourth Amendment test is reasonableness, but in determining whether a search is reasonable, this Court is not free merely to balance, in a totally ad hoc fashion, any number of subjective factors. An unbroken line of cases holds that, subject to a few narrowly drawn exceptions, any search without a warrant is constitutionally unreasonable. . . . In this case, no suggestion that evidence will disappear, that a criminal will escape, or that an officer will be injured, justifies the failure to obtain a warrant. Instead, the majority asserts what amounts to three state interests which allegedly render this search reasonable. None of these interests is sufficient to carve out a new exception to the warrant requirement.

First, it is argued that the home visit is justified to protect dependent children from "abuse" and "exploitation." These are heinous crimes, but they are not confined to indigent households. Would the majority sanction, in the absence of probable cause, compulsory visits to all American homes for the purpose of discovering child abuse? Or is this Court prepared to hold as a matter of constitutional law that a mother, merely because she is poor, is substantially more likely to injure or exploit her children? Such a categorical approach to an entire class of citizens would be dangerously at odds with the tenets of our democracy.

Second, the Court contends that caseworkers must enter the homes of AFDC beneficiaries to determine eligibility. Interestingly, federal regulations do not require the home visit. In fact, the regulations specify the recipient himself as the primary source of eligibility information thereby rendering an inspection of the home only one of several alternative secondary sources. The majority's implication that a biannual home visit somehow assures the verification of actual residence or actual physical presence in the home strains credulity in the context of urban poverty. Despite the caseworker's responsibility for dependent children, he is not even required to see the children as a part of the home visit. Appellants offer scant explanation for their refusal even to attempt to utilize public records, expenditure receipts, documents such as leases, non-home interviews, personal financial records, sworn declarations, etc.—all sources which governmental agencies regularly accept as adequate to establish eligibility for other public benefits. In this setting, it ill behooves appellants to refuse to utilize informational sources less drastic than an invasion of the privacy of the home.

We are told that the plight of Mrs. James is no different from that of a taxpayer who is required to document his right to a tax deduction, but this analogy is seriously flawed. The record shows that Mrs. James has offered to be interviewed anywhere other than her home, to answer any questions and to provide any documentation which the welfare agency desires. The agency curtly refused all these offers and insisted on its "right" to pry into appellee's home. Tax exemptions are also governmental "bounty." A true analogy would be an Internal Revenue Service requirement that in order to claim a dependency exemption, a taxpayer *must* allow a specially trained IRS agent to invade the home for the purpose of questioning the occupants and looking for evidence that the exemption is being properly utilized for the benefit of the dependent. If such a system were even proposed, the cries of constitutional outrage would be unanimous.

Appellants offer a third state interest which the Court seems to accept as partial justification for this search. We are told that the visit is designed to rehabilitate, to provide aid. This is strange doctrine indeed. A paternalistic notion that a complaining citizen's constitutional rights can be violated so long as the State is somehow helping him is alien to our Nation's philosophy. More than 40 years ago, Mr. Justice Brandeis warned: ". . . experience should teach us to be most on our guard to protect liberty when the government's purposes are beneficent." Olmstead v. United States (1928) (dissenting opinion). . . .

Although the Court does not agree with my conclusion that the home visit is an unreasonable search, its opinion suggests that even if the visit were unreasonable, appellee has somehow waived her right to object. Surely the majority cannot believe that valid Fourth Amendment consent can be given under the threat of the loss of one's sole means of support. Nor has Mrs. James waived her rights. Had the Court squarely faced the question of whether the State can condition welfare payments on the waiver of clear constitutional rights, the answer would be plain. The decisions of this Court do not support the notion that a State can use welfare benefits as a wedge to coerce "waiver" of Fourth Amendment rights. . . . In Sherbert v. Verner this Court did not say, "Aid merely ceases. There is no abridgement of religious freedom." Nor did the Court say in Speiser v. Randall, "The tax is simply increased. No one is compelled to relinquish First Amendment rights." As my Brother Douglas points out,

the majority's statement that Mrs. James' "choice (to be searched or to lose her benefits) is entirely hers and nothing of constitutional magnitude is involved" merely restates the issue. To Mr. Justice Douglas' eloquent discussion of the law of unconstitutional conditions, I would add only that this Court last Term reaffirmed Sherbert and Speiser as applicable to the law of public welfare:

"Relevant constitutional restraints apply as much to the withdrawal of public assistance benefits as to the disqualification for unemployment compensation . . . denial of tax exemptions . . . or discharge from public employment." Goldberg v. Kelly (1970).

BORDENKIRCHER v. HAYES

434 U. S. 357; 98 S.Ct. 663; 54 L. Ed.2d 604
(1978)

In a simpler era when communities were less congested and the crime rate lower, it was expected that someone charged with crime would be duly examined before a magistrate, held for a grand jury if the crime were serious enough, and if the grand jury returned an indictment he or she would be tried by a court. Now, with the crime rate soaring and the number of judges dwindling, another technique has developed to take the place of the criminal trial. This is the negotiated guilty plea, or "plea bargain." The exact routine varies, but in essence an accused person is presented by the prosecuting attorney with the evidence against him or her, told what the sentence might be if he or she went to trial and were found guilty, and given the option of pleading guilty to a lesser offense carrying a smaller sentence. While a prosecutor is not authorized by law to guarantee what sentence will result from this guilty plea, in practice criminal judges, recognizing that the system is vital to the efficient operation of their court, accept the prosecutor's recommendation. In 1964, of the criminal convictions recorded in New York and California, 95.5 percent in the first and 74 percent in the second were the result of guilty pleas. It is safe to assume that these percentages have not diminished in the intervening years.

The plea bargain has much to offer both parties. It saves the state enormous sums in trial costs, saves the prosecutor from having to present his case and saves the time involved in empaneling a jury and trying the case. The defendant is given a chance to serve a far lighter sentence than might otherwise be the case and he or she can get about the business of serving the sentence without having to languish in jail for an extended period waiting for the case to come to trial.

The drawbacks to the system are less obvious and their implications less well-understood. However it is viewed, the accused person is clearly bargaining away the right to a court trial. If he or she is really getting a bargain, then the public, which has an interest in having criminals punished according to their deserts, is being cheated. If, on the other hand, the accused is not guilty of any crime, but the crime for which the prosecutor threatens to prosecute him or her carries an intolerable sentence, the person accused dares not take the chance on acquittal and is thus pressured into jail even though innocent. A simple example is a case of mistaken identity where an entirely innocent person is identified as a murderer by several witnesses. The accused is offered a bargain of a maximum of thirty years for a lesser degree of homicide if he or she pleads guilty, or a possible death sentence if he or she goes to trial and is convicted. In some measure the voluntariness of the guilty plea, which is an essential ingredient of the plea, has been cast in doubt. Clearly the system of justice has been fundamentally altered.

In Santabello v. New York (1971) the Supreme Court gave its first official approval to the practice of plea bargaining, at the same time laying down the rule that the prosecution had to live up to its side of the bargain. Here the defendant, with the aid of his attorney, worked out a plea which was accepted by the judge. A date was set for sentencing but when, after a delay of two months, the moment came for sentencing a different judge and different prosecutor were in the courtroom and there was no record of the original bargain. The Court scolded the New York City attorney's office for its inadequate communications and record keeping and remanded the case to the New York court.

Mr. Justice **Stewart** delivered the opinion of the Court, saying in part:

The question in this case is whether the Due Process Clause of the Fourteenth Amendment is violated when a state prosecutor carries out a threat made during plea negotiations to reindict the accused on more serious charges if he does not plead guilty to the offense with which he was originally charged.

I.

. . . Paul Lewis Hayes was indicted by a Fayette County, Ky., grand jury on a charge of uttering a forged instrument in the amount of $88.30, an offense then punishable by a term of 2 to 10 years in prison. After arraignment, Hayes, his retained counsel, and the Commonwealth's Attorney met in the presence of the Clerk of the Court to discuss a possible plea agreement. During these conferences the prosecutor offered to recommend a sentence of five years in prison if Hayes would plead guilty to the indictment. He also said that if Hayes did not plead guilty and "save the court the inconvenience and necessity of a trial," he would return to the grand jury to seek an indictment under the Kentucky Habitual Criminal Act,* which would subject Hayes to a mandatory sentence of life imprisonment by reason of his two prior felony convictions. Hayes chose not to plead guilty, and the prosecutor did obtain an indictment charging him under the Habitual Criminal Act. It is not disputed that the recidivist charge was fully justified by the evi-

dence, that the prosecutor was in possession of this evidence at the time of the original indictment, and that Hayes' refusal to plead guilty to the original charge was what led to his indictment under the habitual criminal statute.

A jury found Hayes guilty on the principal charge of uttering a forged instrument, and, in a separate proceeding, further found that he had twice before been convicted of felonies. As required by the habitual offender statute, he was sentenced to a life term in the penitentiary. . . .

II.

It may be helpful to clarify at the outset the nature of the issue in this case. While the prosecutor did not actually obtain the recidivist indictment until after the plea conferences had ended, his intention to do so was clearly expressed at the outset of the plea negotiations. Hayes was thus fully informed of the true terms of the offer when he made his decision to plead not guilty. This is not a situation, therefore, where the prosecutor brought an additional and more serious charge after plea negotiations relating only to the original indictment had ended with the defendant's insistence on pleading not guilty. As a practical matter, in short, this case would be no different if the grand jury had indicted Hayes as a recidivist from the outset, and the prosecutor had offered to drop that charge as part of the plea bargain.

The Court of Appeals nonetheless drew a distinction between "concessions relating to prosecution under an existing indictment," and threats to bring more severe charges not contained in the original indictment—a line it thought necessary in order to establish a prophylactic rule to guard against the evil of prosecutorial vindictiveness.[†] Quite apart from this chronological distinction, however, the Court of Appeals found that the prosecutor had acted vindictively in the present case since he had conceded that the indictment was influenced by his desire to induce a guilty plea.[‡] The ultimate conclusion of the Court of Appeals thus seems to have been that a

---

*While cross-examining Hayes during the subsequent trial proceedings the prosecutor described the plea offer in the following language: "Isn't it a fact that I told you at that time [the initial bargaining session] if you did not intend to plead guilty to five years for this charge and . . . save the court the inconvenience and necessity of a trial and taking up this time that I intended to return to the grand jury and ask them to indict you based upon these prior felony convictions?"

†"Although a prosecutor may in the course of plea negotiations offer a defendant concessions relating to prosecution under an existing indictment . . . he may not threaten a defendant with the consequence that more severe charges may be brought if he insists on going to trial. When a prosecutor obtains an indictment less severe than the facts known to him at the time might permit, he makes a discretionary determination that the interests of the state are served by not seeking more serious charges. . . . Accordingly, if after plea negotiations fail, he then procures an indictment charging a more serious crime, a strong inference is created that the only reason for the more serious charge is vindictiveness. Under these circumstances, the prosecutor should be required to justify his action."

‡"In this case, a vindictive motive need not be inferred. The prosecutor has admitted it."

prosecutor acts vindictively and in violation of due process of law whenever his charging decision is influenced by what he hopes to gain in the course of plea bargaining negotiations.

III.

We have recently had occasion to observe that "[w]hatever might be the situation in an ideal world, the fact is that the guilty plea and the often concomitant plea bargain are important components of this country's criminal justice system. Properly administered, they can benefit all concerned. . . . The open acknowledgement of this previously clandestine practice has led this Court to recognize the importance of counsel during plea negotiations, . . . the need for a public record indicating that a plea was knowingly and voluntarily made, . . . and the requirement that a prosecutor's plea bargaining promise must be kept. . . . The decision of the Court of Appeals in the present case, however, did not deal with considerations such as these, but held that the substance of the plea offer itself violated the limitations imposed by the Due Process Cause of the Fourteenth Amendment. For these reasons, we have concluded that the Court of Appeals was mistaken in so ruling.

IV.

This Court held in North Carolina v. Pearce [1969], that the Due Process Clause of the Fourteenth Amendment "requires that vindictiveness against a defendant for having successfully attacked his first conviction must play no part in the sentence he receives after a new trial." The same principle was later applied to prohibit a prosecutor from reindicting a convicted misdemeanant on a felony charge after the defendant had invoked an appellate remedy, since in this situation there was also a "realistic likelihood of 'vindictiveness.'" Blackledge v. Perry [1974].

In those cases, the Court was dealing with the State's unilateral imposition of a penalty upon a defendant who had chosen to exercise a legal right to attack his original conviction—a situation "very different from the give-and-take negotiation common in plea bargaining between the prosecution and defense, which arguably possess relatively equal bargaining power." . . . The Court has emphasized that the due process violation in cases such as Pearce and Perry lay not in the possibility that a defendant might be deterred from the exercise of a legal right . . . but rather in the danger that the State might be retaliating against the accused for lawfully attacking his conviction. . . .

To punish a person because he has done what the law plainly allows him to do is a due process violation of the most basic sort, . . . and for an agent of the State to pursue a course of action whose objective is to penalize a person's reliance on his legal rights is "patently unconstitutional." . . . But in the "give-and-take" of plea bargaining, there is no such element of punishment

or retaliation so long as the accused is free to accept or reject the prosecution's offer.

Plea bargaining flows from "the mutuality of advantage" to defendants and prosecutors, each with his own reasons for wanting to avoid trial. . . . Defendants advised by competent counsel and protected by other procedural safeguards are presumptively capable of intelligent choice in response to prosecutorial persuasion, and unlikely to be driven to false self-condemnation. Indeed, acceptance of the basic legitimacy of plea bargaining necessarily implies rejection of any notion that a guilty plea is involuntary in a constitutional sense simply because it is the end result of the bargaining process. By hypothesis, the plea may have been induced by promises of a recommendation of a lenient sentence or a reduction of charges, and thus by fear of the possibility of a greater penalty upon conviction after a trial. . . .

While confronting a defendant with the risk of more severe punishment clearly may have a "discouraging effect on the defendant's assertion of his trial rights, the imposition of these difficult choices [is] an inevitable"—and permissible—"attribute of any legitimate system which tolerates and encourages the negotiation of pleas." . . . It follows that, by tolerating and encouraging the negotiation of pleas, this Court has necessarily accepted as constitutionally legitimate the simple reality that the prosecutor's interest at the bargaining table is to persuade the defendant to forgo his right to plead not guilty.

It is not disputed here that Hayes was properly chargeable under the recidivist statute, since he had in fact been convicted of two previous felonies. In our system, so long as the prosecutor has probable cause to believe that the accused committed an offense defined by statute, the decision whether or not to prosecute, and what charge to file or bring before a grand jury, generally rests entirely in his discretion.* Within the limits set by the legislatures constitutionally valid definition of chargeable offenses, "the conscious exercise of some selectivity in enforcement is not in itself a federal constitutional violation" so long as "the selection was [not] deliberately based upon an unjustifiable standard such as race, religion, or other arbitrary classification." . . . To hold that the prosecutor's desire to induce a guilty plea is an "unjustifiable standard," which, like race or religion, may play no part in his charging decision, would contradict the very premises that underlie the concept of plea bargaining itself. Moreover, a rigid constitutional rule that would prohibit a prosecutor from acting forthrightly in his dealings with the defense could only invite unhealthy subterfuge that would drive the practice of plea bargaining back into the shadows from which it has so recently emerged.

There is no doubt that the breadth of discretion that

---

*This case does not involve the constitutional implications of a prosecutor's offer during plea bargaining of adverse or lenient treatment for some person *other* than the accused . . . which might pose a greater danger of inducing a false guilty plea by skewing the assessment of the risks a defendant must consider. . . .

our country's legal system vests in prosecuting attorneys carries with it the potential for both individual and institutional abuse. And broad though that discretion may be, there are undoubtedly constitutional limits upon its exercise. We hold only that the course of conduct engaged in by the prosecutor in this case, which no more than openly presented the defendant with the unpleasant alternatives of forgoing trial or facing charges on which he was plainly subject to prosecution, did not violate the Due Process Clause of the Fourteenth Amendment.

Accordingly, the judgment of the Court of Appeals is reversed.

Mr. Justice **Blackmun,** with whom Mr. Justice **Brennan** and Mr. Justice **Marshall** join, dissenting, said in part:

I feel that the Court, although purporting to rule narrowly (that is, on "the course of conduct engaged in by the prosecutor in this case,") is departing from, or at least restricting, the principles established in North Carolina v. Pearce (1969), and in Blackledge v. Perry (1974). If those decisions are sound and if those principles are salutary, as I must assume they are, they require, in my view, an affirmance, not a reversal, of the judgment of the Court of Appeals in the present Case.

In Pearce, as indeed the Court notes, it was held that "vindictiveness against a defendant for having successfully attacked his first conviction must play no part in the sentence he receives after a new trial." Accordingly, if, on the new trial, the sentence the defendant receives from the court is greater than that imposed after the first trial, it must be explained by reasons "based upon objective information concerning identifiable conduct on the part of the defendant occurring after the time of the original sentencing proceeding," other than his having pursued the appeal or collateral remedy. On the other hand, if the sentence is imposed by the jury and not by the court, if the jury is not aware of the original sentence, and if the second sentence is not otherwise shown to be a product of vindictiveness, Pearce has no application.

Then later, in Perry, the Court applied the same principle to prosecutorial conduct where there was a "realistic likelihood of 'vindictiveness.'" It held that the requirement of Fourteenth Amendment due process prevented a prosecutor's reindictment of a convicted misdemeanant on a felony charge after the defendant had exercised his right to appeal the misdemeanor conviction and thus to obtain a trial de novo. It noted the prosecution's "considerable stake" in discouraging the appeal.

The Court now says, however, that this concern with vindictiveness is of no import in the present case, despite the difference between five years in prison and a life sentence, because we are here concerned with plea bargaining where there is give-and-take negotiation, and where, it is said, "there is no such element of punishment or retaliation so long as the accused is free to accept or reject the prosecution's offer." Yet in this case vindictiveness is present to the same extent as it was

thought to be in Pearce and in Perry; the prosecutor here admitted that the sole reason for the new indictment was to discourage the respondent from exercising his right to a trial. Even had such an admission not been made, when plea negotiations, conducted in the face of the less serious charge under the first indictment, fail, charging by a second indictment a more serious crime for the same conduct creates "a strong inference" of vindictiveness. As then Judge McCree aptly observed, in writing for a unanimous panel of the Sixth Circuit, the prosecutor initially "makes a discretionary determination that the interests of the state are served by not seeking more serious charges." I therefore do not understand why, as in Pearce, due process does not require that the prosecution justify its action on some basis other than discouraging respondent from the exercise of his right to a trial.

Prosecutorial vindictiveness, it seems to me, in the present narrow context, is the fact against which the Due Process Clause ought to protect. I perceive little difference between vindictiveness after what the Court describes as the exercise of a "legal right to attack his original conviction," and vindictiveness in the "'give-and-take negotiation common in plea bargaining.'" Prosecutorial vindictiveness in any context is still prosecutorial vindictiveness. The Due Process Clause should protect an accused against it, however it asserts itself. The Court of Appeals so held, and I would affirm the judgment.

It might be argued that it really makes little difference how this case, now that it is here, is decided. The Court's holding gives plea bargaining full sway despite vindictiveness. A contrary result, however, merely would prompt the aggressive prosecutor to bring the greater charge initially in every case, and only thereafter to bargain. The consequences to the accused would still be adverse, for then he would bargain against a greater charge, face the likelihood of increased bail, and run the risk that the court would be less inclined to accept a bargained plea. Nonetheless, it is far preferable to hold the prosecution to the charge it was originally content to bring and to justify it in the eyes of its public.*

Mr. Justice **Powell,** dissenting, said in part:

Although I agree with much of the Court's opinion, I am not satisfied that the result in this case is just or that the conduct of plea bargaining met the requirements of due process. . . .

The prosecutor's initial assessment of respondent's case led him to forgo an indictment under the habitual

---

*That prosecutors, without saying so, may sometimes bring charges more serious than they think appropriate for the ultimate disposition of a case, in order to gain bargaining leverage with a defendant, does not add support to today's decision, for this Court, in its approval of the advantages to be gained from plea negotiations has never openly sanctioned such deliberate overcharging or taken such a cynical view of the bargaining process. . . . Normally, of course, it is impossible to show that this is what the prosecutor is doing, and the courts necessarily have deferred to the prosecutor's exercise of discretion in initial charging decisions. . . .

criminal statute. The circumstances of respondent's prior convictions are relevant to this assessment and to my view of the case. Respondent was 17 years old when he committed his first offense. He was charged with rape but pleaded guilty to the lesser included offense of "detaining a female." One of the other participants in the incident was sentenced to life imprisonment. Respondent was sent not to prison but to a reformatory where he served five years. Respondent's second offense was robbery. This time he was found guilty by a jury and was sentenced to five years in prison, but he was placed on probation and served no time. Although respondent's prior convictions brought him within the terms of the Habitual Criminal Act, the offenses themselves did not result in imprisonment; yet the addition of a conviction on a charge involving $88.30 subjected respondent to a mandatory sentence of imprisonment for life. Persons convicted of rape and murder often are not punished so severely.

No explanation appears in the record for the prosecutor's decision to escalate the charge against respondent other than respondent's refusal to plead guilty. The prosecutor has conceded that his purpose was to discourage respondent's assertion of constitutional rights, and the majority accepts this characterization of events.

It seems to me that the question to be asked under the circumstances is whether the prosecutor reasonably might have charged respondent under the Habitual Criminal Act in the first place. The deference that courts properly accord the exercise of a prosecutor's discretion perhaps would foreclose judicial criticism if the prosecu-

tor originally had sought an indictment under that Act, as unreasonable as it would have seemed.* But here the prosecutor evidently made a reasonable, responsible judgment not to subject an individual to a mandatory life sentence when his only new offense had societal implications as limited as those accompanying the uttering of a single $88 forged check and when the circumstances of his prior convictions confirmed the inappropriateness of applying the habitual criminal statute. I think it may be inferred that the prosecutor himself deemed it unreasonable and not in the public interest to put this defendant in jeopardy of a sentence of life imprisonment.

There may be situations in which a prosecutor would be fully justified in seeking a fresh indictment for a more serious offense. . . .

But this is not such a case. Here, any inquiry into the prosecutor's purpose is made unnecessary by his candid acknowledgement that he threatened to procure and in fact procured the habitual criminal indictment because of respondent's insistence on exercising his constitutional rights. We have stated in unequivocal terms . . . ". . . if the only objective of a state practice is to discourage the assertion of constitutional rights it is 'patently unconstitutional' " . . .

. . . In this case, the prosecutor's actions denied respondent due process because their admitted purpose was to discourage and then to penalize with unique severity his exercise of constitutional rights. Implementation of a strategy calculated solely to deter the exercise of constitutional rights is not a constitutionally permissible exercise of discretion. . . .

---

*The majority suggests that this case cannot be distinguished from the case where the prosecutor initially obtains an indictment under an enhancement statute and later agrees to drop the enhancement charge in exchange for a guilty plea. I would agree that these two situations would be alike *only if* it were assumed that the hypothetical prosecutor's decision to charge under the enhancement statute was occasioned not by consideration of the public interest but by a strategy to discourage the defendant from exercising his constitutional rights. In theory, I would condemn both practices. In practice, the hypothetical situation is largely unreviewable. The majority's view confuses the propriety of a particular exercise of prosecutorial discretion with its unreviewability. In the instant case, however, we have no problem of proof.

4

First Amendment Rights

FREE SPEECH AND SECURITY

SCHENCK v. UNITED STATES

249 U. S. 47; 39 S. Ct. 247; 63 L. Ed. 470 (1919)

Freedom of speech and press are not absolute rights and were never intended to be so. They are relative, in the sense that they are limited by the coexisting rights of others (as in the matter of libel) and by the demands of national security and public decency. As Justice Holmes put it (below), "The most stringent protection of free speech would not protect a man in falsely shouting fire in a theatre and causing a panic." Free-speech and free-press cases present to the courts difficult questions of degree: questions involved in drawing the line that separates the speech and publication which government must suppress in order to be safe and decent from that which it must allow and protect in order to be free and democratic.

Perhaps the most conspicuous and interesting instance in our history of interference with freedom of expression never came before the Supreme Court of the United States. The Sedition Act of 1798 provided among other things for the severe punishment of false, scandalous, and malicious writings against the government, either house of Congress, or the President if published with intent to defame any of them, or to excite against them the hatred of the people, or to stir up sedition. It was limited in operation to two years. Ten persons were convicted under it, and many others were indicted but not tried. Its enactment and enforcement called forth great popular indignation, and President Jefferson upon assuming office pardoned all persons still imprisoned under its provisions. Many years later Congress refunded with interest the fines which had been imposed.

The relative character of the right of free speech and press becomes particularly obvious in time of war. Where is the line to be drawn between legitimate and salutary freedom of discussion and utterances which, by reason of their disloyal or seditious character, must be deemed incompatible with the public safety? This is a delicate and important question. During the Civil War such interferences with freedom of speech and press as occurred were perpetrated by military officers under the sanction of martial law, and no question of the validity of these acts of repression ever came squarely before the Supreme Court. World War I brought forth a large grist of restrictive legislation, both state and federal, and numerous judicial questions arose as to the validity of these acts and their application to specific cases. Most conspicuous of these laws were the Espionage Act of 1917—which penalized any circulation of false statements made with intent to interfere with military success, as well as any attempt to cause disloyalty in the Army or Navy or to obstruct recruiting—and the Sedition Act of 1918—which made it a crime to say or do anything which could obstruct the sale of government bonds, or to utter or publish words intended to bring into contempt or disrepute the form of government of the United States, the Constitution, flag, uniform, etc., or to incite resistance to the government or promote the cause of its enemies. Nearly a thousand persons were convicted under these two acts. Their validity was sustained in six cases coming to the Supreme Court after the close of the war. *Schenck v. United States,* printed below, was the first of these cases; and in it Justice Holmes announced the now famous "clear and present danger" test. A week later the Court decided two more cases, *Frohwerk v. United States* (1919), involving a pro-German newspaper man, and *Debs v. United States* (1919), involving the famous Socialist leader. Holmes wrote the opinions sustaining the convictions of the two men on the grounds that their writings and speeches met the test of clear and present danger. Nine months later the Supreme Court decided *Abrams v. United States* (1919), upholding the conviction under the Sedition Act of 1918 of a group of so-called Bolshevists who were urging strikes in ammunition plants to prevent American military interference with the Russian Revolution. Without mentioning the clear and present danger doctrine the Court found that the defendants had intended to "urge, incite, and advocate" curtailment of production necessary to the war. "It will not do," the Court reasoned, "to say, as is now argued, that the only intent of these defendants was to prevent injury to the Russian cause. Men must be held to have intended, and to be accountable for, the effects which their acts were likely to produce." Holmes, with whom Brandeis concurred, dissented: "I do not doubt for a moment that by the same reasoning that would justify punishing persuasion to murder, the United States constitutionally may punish speech that produces or is intended to produce a clear and imminent danger that it will bring about forthwith certain substantive evils that the United States constitutionally may seek to prevent. . . . It is only the present danger of immediate evil or an intent to bring it about that warrants Congress in setting a limit to the expression of opinion where private rights are not concerned." As for there being such danger here, "nobody can suppose that the surreptitious publishing of a silly leaflet by an unknown man, without more, would present any immediate danger that its opinions would hinder the success of the government. . . ." Nor was there the "intent" required to constitute a violation of the statute, since the intent of the defendants had been to protect Russia, not Germany, with whom we were at war.

In *Schaefer v. United States* (1920) and *Pierce v. United States* (1920) the Court sustained convictions under the Espionage Act of 1917 on the ground that the defendants willfully published "false reports and statements with intent to interfere with the operation or success of military or naval forces of the United States or to promote the success of its enemies." The Court applied to the utterances in the Schaefer case

what is called the "bad tendency" test of validity (see *Gitlow v. New York,* 1925): "Their effect on the persons affected could not be shown, nor was it necessary. The tendency of the articles and their efficacy were enough for offense. . . ." It is in Brandeis's dissent in the Schaefer case that he makes his well-known comment about the test of clear and present danger. He said: "This is a rule of reason. Correctly applied, it will preserve the right of free speech both from suppression by tyrannous, well-meaning majorities, and from abuse by irresponsible, fanatical minorities."

Only one case, *Hartzel v. United States* (1944), came to the Supreme Court under the Espionage Act of 1917 during or after World War II. (In 1921 Congress had repealed the Sedition Act of 1918.) Hartzel was prosecuted for publishing and mailing "scurrilous and vitriolic attacks on the English, the Jews and the President of the United States" to those on a carefully selected mailing list. These facts, similar in their essentials to those in Schenck, the Court found insufficient to constitute a crime under the statute. The Court emphasized that "two major elements are necessary to constitute an offense under these clauses. The first element is a subjective one, consisting of a specific intent . . . to cause insubordination or disloyalty in the armed forces. . . . This . . . springs from the statutory use of the word 'willfully.' . . . The second element is an objective one, consisting of a clear and present danger that the activities in question will bring about the substantive evils which Congress has a right to prevent. . . . Both elements must be proved by the Government beyond a reasonable doubt." The Court failed to find the requisite intent. Four justices dissented, agreeing with Justice Holmes's earlier comment that "of course the document would not have been sent unless it had been intended to have some effect. . . ."

Mr. Justice **Holmes** delivered the opinion of the Court, saying in part:

[Schenck was convicted in a federal district court of violation of the Espionage Act of 1917, by causing and attempting to cause insubordination in the armed forces of the United States when the United States was at war with Germany. Schenck had circulated among men called and accepted for military service a document alleged to be intended to cause insubordination and obstruction of the draft. He claimed that the statute abridged his freedom of speech and press in violation of the First Amendment.]

. . . The document in question upon its first printed side recited the 1st section of the 13th Amendment, said that the idea embodied in it was violated by the Conscription Act, and that a conscript is little better than a convict. In impassioned language it intimated that conscription was despotism in its worst form and a monstrous wrong against humanity, in the interest of Wall Street's chosen few. It said: "Do not submit to intimidation;" but in form at least confined itself to peaceful measures, such as a petition for the repeal of the act. The other and later printed side of the sheet was headed "Assert Your Rights." It stated reasons for alleging that any one violated the Constitution when he refused to recognize "your right to assert your opposition to the draft," and went on: "If you do not assert and support your rights, you are helping to deny or disparage rights which it is the solemn duty of all citizens and residents of the United States to retain." It described the arguments on the other side as coming from cunning politicians and a mercenary capitalist press, and even silent consent to the Conscription Law as helping to support an infamous conspiracy. It denied the power to send our citizens away to foreign shores to shoot up the people of other lands, and added that words could not express the condemnation such cold-blooded ruthlessness deserves, etc., etc., winding up, "You must do your share to maintain, support and uphold the rights of the people of this country." Of course the document would not have been sent unless it had been intended to have some effect, and we do not see what effect it could be expected to have upon persons subject to the draft except to influence them to obstruct the carrying of it out. The defendants do not deny that the jury might find against them on this point.

But it is said, suppose that that was the tendency of this circular, it is protected by the 1st Amendment to the Constitution. Two of the strongest expressions are said to be quoted respectively from well-known public men. It well may be that the prohibition of laws abridging the freedom of speech is not confined to previous restraints, although to prevent them may have been the main purpose, as intimated in Patterson v. Colorado [1907]. We admit that in many places and in ordinary times the defendants, in saying all that was said in the circular, would have been within their constitutional rights. But the character of every act depends upon the circumstances in which it is done. The most stringent protection of free speech would not protect a man in falsely shouting fire in a theatre, and causing a panic. It does not even protect a man from an injunction against uttering words that may have all the effect of force. Gompers v. Buck's Stove & Range Co. [1911]. The question in every case is whether the words used are used in such circumstances and are of such a nature as to create a clear and present danger that they will bring about the substantive evils that Congress has a right to prevent. It is a question of proximity and degree. When a nation is at war many things that might be said in time of peace are such a hindrance to its effort that their utterance will not be endured so long as men fight, and that no court could regard them as protected by any constitutional right. It seems to be admitted that if an actual obstruction of the recruiting service were proved, liability for words that produced that effect might be enforced. The statute of 1917, in § 4, punishes conspiracies to obstruct as well as actual obstruction. If the act (speaking, or circulating a paper), its tendency and the intent with which it is done, are the same, we perceive no ground for saying that success alone warrants making the act a crime. . . .

Judgments affirmed.

GITLOW v. NEW YORK

268 U. S. 652; 45 S. Ct. 625; 69 L. Ed. 1138 (1925)

The Espionage Act of 1917 forbade certain kinds of action, such as causing or attempting to cause insubordination or obstructing the draft. It did not expressly limit freedom of speech; it limited it only when speech amounted to the kind of action forbidden by the statute. In order to determine when a particular speech became "action" and thus punishable under the statute, the Court resorted to two tests, the "bad tendency" test and the "clear and present danger" test.

The "bad tendency" test was designed, as Professor Chafee put it, "to kill the serpent in the egg" by preventing all speech which had a tendency, however remote, to bring about acts in violation of the law. It had its roots in the doctrine of constructive treason, so infamous in English history, under which criticism of the government was construed as an attempt to accomplish the overthrow of that government and was punished as treason. The "clear and present danger" test, devised by Justice Holmes in the Schenck case (1919), held that speech becomes punishable as action only when there is a danger, clear and present, that it will bring the action about. If there is no clear and present danger the speech does not amount to action, and the statute forbidding the action has not been violated. Holmes's doctrine was not intended as a test of the validity of the statute itself, since presumably the "action" which the statute forbids is, like obstructing the draft, something Congress could legitimately prohibit.

The clear and present danger test is not simple to apply. It is, for instance, difficult to apply to a statute which by its language forbids certain kinds of speech. If a person makes the kind of speech thus forbidden, then he has violated the statute; in other words, once the legislature has decided for itself what kind of speech is dangerous and forbidden it, the courts can hold the statute unconstitutional but they cannot say it has not been violated. Holmes and Brandeis apparently felt that statutes of this kind could not constitutionally be applied to cases in which there was no clear and present danger of serious substantive evil. See Whitney v. California (1927).

In the present case Benjamin Gitlow was prosecuted under the New York Criminal Anarchy Act of 1902 for distributing a document similar to the Communist Manifesto of Marx and Engels (1848). This statute, which formed the model for the federal Smith Act, pun-

ishes certain kinds of speech and publication regardless of the intent of the speaker or publisher.

Not until 1965 was the New York act again invoked successfully, when William Epton was convicted of criminal anarchy for conspiring to instigate and inflame the Harlem race riots that followed the killing by a policeman of a fifteen-year-old Negro boy.

Mr. Justice **Sanford** delivered the opinion of the Court, saying in part:

Benjamin Gitlow was indicted in the supreme court of New York, with three others, for the statutory crime of criminal anarchy. . . .

The contention here is that the statute, by its terms and as applied in this case, is repugnant to the due process clause of the 14th Amendment. Its material provisions are:

"§ 160. Criminal anarchy defined.—Criminal anarchy is the doctrine that organized government should be overthrown by force or violence, or by assassination of the executive head or of any of the executive officials of government, or by any unlawful means. The advocacy of such doctrine either by word of mouth or writing is a felony.

"§ 161. Advocacy of criminal anarchy.—Any person who:

"1. By word of mouth or writing advocates, advises or teaches the duty, necessity or propriety of overthrowing or overturning organized government by force or violence, or by assassination of the executive head or of any of the executive officials of government, or by any unlawful means; or

"2. Prints, publishes, edits, issues or knowingly circulates, sells, distributes or publicly displays any book, paper, document, or written or printed matter in any form, containing or advocating, advising or teaching the doctrine that organized government should be overthrown by force, violence or any unlawful means . . . ,

"Is guilty of a felony and punishable" by imprisonment or fine, or both.

The indictment was in two counts. The first charged that the defendants had advocated, advised, and taught the duty, necessity, and propriety of overthrowing and overturning organized government by force, violence, and unlawful means, by certain writings therein set forth, entitled, "The Left Wing Manifesto"; the second, that he had printed, published, and knowingly circulated and distributed a certain paper called "The Revolutionary Age," containing the writings set forth in the first count, advocating, advising, and teaching the doctrine that organized government should be overthrown by force, violence, and unlawful means.

. . . It was admitted that the defendant signed a card subscribing to the Manifesto and Program of the Left Wing, which all applicants were required to sign before being admitted to membership; that he went to different parts of the state to speak to branches of the Socialist party about the principles of the Left Wing, and advocated their adoption; and that he was responsible [as business manager] for the Manifesto as it appeared, that "he knew of the publication, in a general way, and he knew of its publication afterwards, and is responsible for its circulation."

There was no evidence of any effect resulting from the publication and circulation of the Manifesto.

No witnesses were offered in behalf of the defendant.

Extracts from the Manifesto are set forth in the margin. Coupled with a review of the rise of Socialism, it condemned the dominant "moderate Socialism" for its recognition of the necessity of the democratic parliamentary state; repudiated its policy of introducing Socialism by legislative measures; and advocated, in plain and unequivocal language, the necessity of accomplishing the "Communist Revolution" by a militant and "revolutionary Socialism," based on "the class struggle" and mobilizing the "power of the proletariat in action," through mass industrial revolts developing into mass political strikes and "revolutionary mass action" for the purpose of conquering and destroying the parliamentary state and establishing in its place, through a "revolutionary dictatorship of the proletariat," the system of Communist Socialism. The then recent strikes in Seattle and Winnipeg were cited as instances of a development already verging on revolutionary action and suggestive of proletarian dictatorship, in which the strike workers were "trying to usurp the functions of municipal government"; and Revolutionary Socialism, it was urged, must use these mass industrial revolts to broaden the strike, make it general and militant, and develop it into mass political strikes and revolutionary mass action for the annihilation of the parliamentary state.

. . . The sole contention here is, essentially, that, as there was no evidence of any concrete result flowing from the publication of the Manifesto, or of circumstances showing the likelihood of such result, the statute as construed and applied by the trial court penalizes the mere utterance, as such, of "doctrine" having no quality of incitement, without regard either to the circumstances of its utterance or to the likelihood of unlawful sequences; and that, as the exercise of the right of free expression with relation to government is only punishable "in circumstances involving likelihood of substantive evil," the statute contravenes the due process clause of the Fourteenth Amendment. The argument in support of this contention rests primarily upon the following propositions: 1st, that the "liberty" protected by the 14th Amendment includes the liberty of speech and of the press; and 2nd, that while liberty of expression "is not absolute," it may be restrained "only in circumstances where its exercise bears a causal relation with some substantive evil, consummated, attempted, or likely"; and as the statute "takes no account of circumstances," it unduly restrains this liberty, and is therefore unconstitutional.

The precise question presented, and the only question which we can consider under this writ of error, then, is whether the statute, as construed and applied in this case by the state courts, deprived the defendant of his liberty of expression, in violation of the due process clause of the 14th Amendment.

The statute does not penalize the utterance or publication of abstract "doctrine" or academic discussion having no quality of incitement to any concrete action. It is not aimed against mere historical or philosophical essays. It does not restrain the advocacy of changes in the form of government by constitutional and lawful means. What it prohibits is language advocating, advising, or teaching the overthrow of organized government by unlawful means. These words imply urging to action. Advocacy is defined in the Century Dictionary as: "1. The act of pleading for, supporting, or recommending; active espousal." It is not the abstract "doctrine" of overthrowing organized government by unlawful means which is denounced by the statute, but the advocacy of action for the accomplishment of that purpose. . . .

The Manifesto, plainly, is neither the statement of abstract doctrine nor, as suggested by counsel, mere prediction that industrial disturbances and revolutionary mass strikes will result spontaneously in an inevitable process of evolution in the economic system. It advocates and urges in fervent language mass action which shall progressively foment industrial disturbances, and, through political mass strikes and revolutionary mass action, overthrow and destroy organized parliamentary government. It concludes with a call to action in these words: "The proletariat revolution and the Communist reconstruction of society—*the struggle for these*—is now indispensable. . . . The Communist International calls the proletariat of the world to the final struggle!" This is not the expression of philosophical abstraction, the mere prediction of future events: it is the language of direct incitement.

The means advocated for bringing about the destruction of organized parliamentary government, namely, mass industrial revolts usurping the functions of municipal government, political mass strikes directed against the parliamentary state, and revolutionary mass action for its final destruction, necessarily imply the use of force and violence, and in their essential nature are inherently unlawful in a constitutional government of law and order. That the jury were warranted in finding that the Manifesto advocated not merely the abstract doctrine of overwhelming organized government by force, violence, and unlawful means, but action to that end, is clear.

For present purposes we may and do assume that freedom of speech and of the press—which are protected by the 1st Amendment from abridgment by Congress— are among the fundamental personal rights and "liberties" protected by the due process clause of the 14th Amendment from impairment by the states. . . .

It is a fundamental principle, long established, that freedom of speech and of the press which is secured by the Constitution does not confer an absolute right to speak or publish, without responsibility, whatever one may choose, or an unrestricted and unbridled license that gives immunity for every possible use of language, and prevents the punishment of those who abuse this free-

dom. 2 Story, Const. 5th ed. § 1580, p. 634. . . . Reasonably limited, it was said by Story in the passage cited, this freedom is an inestimable privilege in a free government; without such limitation, it might become the scourge of the Republic.

That a state, in the exercise of its police power, may punish those who abuse this freedom by utterances inimical to the public welfare, tending to corrupt public morals, incite to crime, or disturb the public peace, is not open to question. . . . Thus it was held by this court in the Fox Case [Fox v. Washington, 1915], that a state may punish publications advocating and encouraging a breach of its criminal laws; and, in the Gilbert Case [Gilbert v. Minnesota, 1920], that a state may punish utterances teaching or advocating that its citizens should not assist the United States in prosecuting or carrying on war with its public enemies.

And, for yet more imperative reasons, a state may punish utterances endangering the foundations of organized government and threatening its overthrow by unlawful means. These imperil its own existence as a constitutional state. Freedom of speech and press, said Story (supra), does not protect disturbances of the public peace or the attempt to subvert the government. It does not protect publications or teachings which tend to subvert or imperil the government, or to impede or hinder it in the performance of its governmental duties. . . . It does not protect publications prompting the overthrow of government by force; the punishment of those who publish articles which tend to destroy organized society being essential to the security of freedom and the stability of the state. . . . And a state may penalize utterances which openly advocate the overthrow of the representative and constitutional form of government of the United States and the several states, by violence or other unlawful means. . . . In short, this freedom does not deprive a state of the primary and essential right of self-preservation, which, so long as human governments endure, they cannot be denied. . . .

By enacting the present statute the state has determined, through its legislative body, that utterances advocating the overthrow of organized government by force, violence, and unlawful means, are so inimical to the general welfare, and involve such danger of substantive evil, that they may be penalized in the exercise of its police power. That determination must be given great weight. Every presumption is to be indulged in favor of the validity of the statute. . . . That utterances inciting to the overthrow of organized government by unlawful means present a sufficient danger of substantive evil to bring their punishment within the range of legislative discretion is clear. Such utterances, by their very nature, involve danger to the public peace and to the security of the state. They threaten breaches of the peace and ultimate revolution. And the immediate danger is none the less real and substantial because the effect of a given utterance cannot be accurately foreseen. The state cannot reasonably be required to measure the danger from every such utterance in the nice balance of a jeweler's scale. A single revolutionary spark may kindle a fire that, smoldering for a time, may burst into a sweeping and destructive conflagration. It cannot be said that the state is acting arbitrarily or unreasonably when, in the exercise of its judgment as to the measures necessary to protect the public peace and safety, it seeks to extinguish the spark without waiting until it has enkindled the flame or blazed into the conflagration. It cannot reasonably be required to defer the adoption of measures for its own peace and safety until the revolutionary utterances lead to actual disturbances of the public peace or imminent and immediate danger of its own destruction; but it may, in the exercise of its judgment, suppress the threatened danger in its incipiency. . . .

We cannot hold that the present statute is an arbitrary or unreasonable exercise of the police power of the state, unwarrantably infringing the freedom of speech or press; and we must and do sustain its constitutionality.

This being so it may be applied to every utterance—not too trivial to be beneath the notice of the law—which is of such a character and used with such intent and purpose as to bring it within the prohibition of the statute. . . . In other words, when the legislative body has determined generally, in the constitutional exercise of its discretion, that utterances of a certain kind involve such danger of substantive evil that they may be punished, the question whether any specific utterance coming within the prohibited class is likely, in and of itself, to bring about the substantive evil, is not open to consideration. It is sufficient that the statute itself be constitutional, and that the use of the language comes within its prohibition.

It is clear that the question in such cases is entirely different from that involved in those cases where the statute merely prohibits certain acts involving the danger of substantive evil, without any reference to language itself, and it is sought to apply its provisions to language used by the defendant for the purpose of bringing about prohibited results. There, if it be contended that the statute cannot be applied to the language used by the defendant because of its protection by the freedom of speech or press, it must necessarily be found, as an original question, without any previous determination by the legislative body, whether the specific language used involved such likelihood of bringing about the substantive evil as to deprive it of the constitutional protection. In such cases it has been held that the general provisions of the statute may be constitutionally applied to the specific utterance of the defendant if its natural tendency and probable effect were to bring about the substantive evil which the legislative body might prevent. Schenck v. United States [1919]; Debs v. United States [1919]. And the general statement in the Schenck Case that the "question in every case is whether the words are used in such circumstances and are of such a nature as to create a clear and present danger that they will bring about the substantive evils,"—upon which great reliance is placed in the defendant's argument,—was manifestly intended, as shown by the context, to apply only in cases of this class, and has no application to those like the present, where the legislative body itself has previously determined the danger of substantive evil arising from utterances of a specified character. . . .

And finding, for the reasons stated, that the statute is not in itself unconstitutional, and that it has not been applied in the present case in derogation of any constitutional right, the judgment of the Court of Appeals is affirmed.

Mr. Justice **Holmes** dissented:

Mr. Justice Brandeis and I are of the opinion that this judgment should be reversed. The general principle of free speech, it seems to me, must be taken to be included in the 14th Amendment, in view of the scope that has been given to the word "liberty" as there used, although perhaps it may be accepted with a somewhat larger latitude of interpretation than is allowed to Congress by the sweeping language that governs, or ought to govern, the laws of the United States. If I am right, then I think that the criterion sanctioned by the full court in Schenck v. United States, applies: "The question in every case is whether the words used are used in such circumstances and are of such a nature as to create a clear and present danger that they will bring about the substantive evils that [the state] has a right to prevent." It is true that in my opinion this criterion was departed from in Abrams v. United States [1919] but the convictions that I expressed in that case are too deep for it to be possible for me as yet to believe that it and Schaefer v. United States [1920] have settled the law. If what I think the correct test is applied, it is manifest that there was no present danger of an attempt to overthrow the government by force on the part of the admittedly small minority who shared the defendant's views. It is said that this Manifesto was more than a theory, that it was an incitement. Every idea is an incitement. It offers itself for belief, and, if believed, it is acted on unless some other belief outweighs it, or some failure of energy stifles the movement at its birth. The only difference between the expression of an opinion and an incitement in the narrower sense is the speaker's enthusiasm for the result. Eloquence may set fire to reason. But whatever may be thought of the redundant discourse before us, it had no chance of starting a present conflagration. If, in the long run, the beliefs expressed in proletarian dictatorship are destined to be accepted by the dominant forces of the community, the only meaning of free speech is that they should be given their chance and have their way.

If the publication of this document had been laid as an attempt to induce an uprising against government at once, and not at some indefinite time in the future, it would have presented a different question. The object would have been one with which the law might deal, subject to the doubt whether there was any danger that the publication could produce any result; or, in other words, whether it was not futile and too remote from possible consequences. But the indictment alleges the publication and nothing more.

DENNIS v. UNITED STATES

341 U. S. 494; 71 S. Ct. 857; 95 L. Ed. 1137
(1951)

The Smith Act of 1940, which in 1948 became § 2385 of Title 18 of the United States Code, directs a five-pronged attack against subversion. First, it punishes anyone who "knowingly or willfully advocates . . . or teaches the duty . . . or propriety of overthrowing . . . the government of the United States . . . by force or violence. . . ." Second, it punishes the dissemination of literature advocating such overthrow "with intent to cause such overthrow." Third, it punishes anyone who "organizes . . . any society, group or assembly of persons to teach, advocate or encourage" such overthrow. Fourth, it punishes anyone who "becomes or is a member of . . . any such society, group or assembly . . . knowing the purposes thereof." Finally, it makes it a separate offense to conspire to do any of the above things.

The validity of the act was considered by the Supreme Court for the first time in the Dennis case below. In 1948, the eleven top leaders of the American Communist party were indicted under the act for willfully and knowingly conspiring to teach and advocate the overthrow of government by force and violence, and to organize the Communist party for the purpose of so doing. The trial in District Judge Medina's court in New York ran from January 20 to September 23, 1949, and resulted in conviction. Judge Medina's charge to the jury included two important interpretations of the law. First, he ruled out the possibility that "teaching" or "conspiring to teach" alone would violate the statute. "You must be satisfied from the evidence beyond a reasonable doubt that the defendants had an intent to cause the overthrow or destruction of the Government of the United States by force and violence, and that it was with this intent and for the purpose of furthering that objective that they conspired both (1) to organize the Communist Party . . . and (2) to teach and advocate. . . ." Second, should the jury find that the statute as so construed had been violated, it was their duty to find the defendants guilty. "I find as a matter of law that there is sufficient danger of a substantive evil that the Congress has a right to prevent to justify the application of the statute under the First Amendment. . . ."

Both the conviction and this charge to the jury were upheld by the court of appeals in an opinion by Judge Learned Hand. The Supreme Court limited the scope of its review to the constitutional questions raised, chief of which was the First Amendment question of free speech. It did not review the sufficiency of the evidence to support the verdict.

In the five opinions written in the Dennis case, there are four interpretations of the clear and present danger test. Chief Justice Vinson, speaking for four members of the Court, paid allegiance to Holmes's statement and application of the test, but in reality adopted in its place Judge Hand's test of "clear and probable

danger." The danger need not be imminent; it is enough that there is a group willing to attempt the overthrow of government if and when possible. The Chief Justice read the time element out of clear and present danger.

Justice Frankfurter had always rejected the idea that a law which on its face invades free speech must be presumed to be unconstitutional, or that the First Amendment occupies any "preferred position." See Thomas v. Collins (1945). He felt that free-speech cases call for the weighing of competing interests, and that the legislative judgment embodied in the Smith Act, that the Communist threat to the security of the country justifies punitive action, is amply supported by evidence.

In an incisive concurring opinion Justice Jackson bluntly declared that the test of clear and present danger has no applicability to a criminal conspiracy such as that carried on by the Communist Party. It was never intended to be applied in a case like this, and should be reserved for cases involving restrictions upon speeches and publications.

Justices Black and Douglas, dissenting, felt that the clear and present danger test had been destroyed. Justice Douglas emphasized that the defendants were charged with no overt acts, only with speeches and publications. He also felt that the question of clear and present danger should be decided by the jury and not by the court.

The decision in the Dennis case provided for the first time a legal basis for the idea that the Communist Party is a criminal conspiracy dedicated to overthrowing the government of the United States by force and violence. It therefore seemed logical to suppose that any official of the party, and probably any member who was familiar with the aims of the party, could be convicted for taking part in the conspiracy. Acting upon this assumption the government moved against fourteen second-string Communist leaders, and in Yates v. United States (1957) the Supreme Court reversed their convictions, acquitting five of them outright and remanding the other nine for retrial. The District Court, it explained, had failed to charge the jury that in order to convict it must find the defendants guilty of advocating "action" in the "language of incitement." "The essence of the Dennis holding," the Court said, "was that indoctrination of a group in preparation for future violent action, as well as exhortation to immediate action, by advocacy found to be directed to 'action for the accomplishment' of forcible overthrow, to violence 'as a rule or principle of action,' and employing 'language of incitement,' is not constitutionally protected when the group is of sufficient size and cohesiveness, is sufficiently oriented towards action, and other circumstances are such as reasonably to justify apprehension that action will occur. This is quite a different thing from the view of the District Court here that mere doctrinal justification of forcible overthrow, if engaged in with the intent to accomplish overthrow, is punishable per se under the Smith Act. That sort of advocacy, even though uttered with the hope that it may ultimately lead to violent revolution, is too remote from concrete action to be regarded as the kind of indoctrination preparatory to action which was condemned in Dennis.''

Although Justice Harlan stresses that he is merely applying the doctrine of the Dennis case, it seems apparent that in insisting in Yates that advocacy amount to incitement to action, he is, without actually using the well-known phrase, moving back toward the clear and present danger rule of Holmes and Brandeis. The Dennis case was widely believed to have modified and weakened that rule.

Four years after Yates, in Scales v. United States (1961), the Supreme Court passed on the validity of the membership section for the first time, and in a five-to-four decision held it valid as applied to Scales. It stated that this was not mere "guilt by association." The guilt was personal and punishable under the act if it was "active membership in an organization [in this case the Communist party] engaged in illegal advocacy by one having guilty knowledge and intent." Scales had been convicted first in 1955, and after a second trial and two full arguments before the Court his case was finally heard and considered in conjunction with Communist Party v. Subversive Activities Control Board (1961). Scales argued that the membership section of the Smith Act had been repealed by the section of the Subversive Activities Control Act of 1950 (requiring registration of Communists), which provides that : "Neither the holding of office nor membership in any Communist organization by any person shall constitute per se a violation of subsection (a) or subsection (c) of this section or any other criminal statute." Justice Harlan's opinion for the majority held that the section quoted from the act of 1950 clarified, rather than repealed, the membership section of the Smith Act; and he emphasized the difference between punishing someone for membership per se and punishing the person for membership with guilty knowledge and with intent to aid in the violent overthrow of government. In the dissenting opinions it was urged that the act of 1950 had repealed the Smith Act provision and that the membership section violated the First Amendment.

In Brandenburg v. Ohio (1969), the Supreme Court held void Ohio's criminal syndicalism act—an act passed in the 1920s and patterned after that of California which had been held valid in Whitney v. California (1927). Without actually using the words "clear and present danger," the Court held the act void as forbidding mere advocacy of violence or sabotage, whether or not it would incite the hearers to lawless action. The Court overruled Whitney v. California.

In Meese v. Keene (1987) a member of the California senate wanted to show three films dealing with acid rain and the effects of nuclear war, and when he imported them from Canada the Justice Department designated them political propaganda. The Court refused to find the statute or the designation a violation of free speech. It argued that Keene was not forbidden to show the films, that the term "propaganda" was not pejorative and thus inhibiting to free expression, and that while Keene had to say that the films were listed as propaganda, he was free to say anything else about them he wished by way of explanation.

Mr. Chief Justice **Vinson** announced the judgment of the Court and an opinion in which Mr. Justice **Reed**, Mr. Justice **Burton**, and Mr. Justice **Minton** join, saying in part:

I.

It will be helpful in clarifying the issues to treat next the contention that the trial judge improperly interpreted the statute by charging that the statute required an unlawful intent before the jury could convict. . . .

. . . The structure and purpose of the statute demand the inclusion of intent as an element of the crime. Congress was concerned with those who advocate and organize for the overthrow of the Government. Certainly those who recruit and combine for the purpose of advocating overthrow intend to bring about that overthrow. We hold that the statute required as an essential element of the crime proof of the intent of those who are charged with its violation to overthrow the Government by force and violence. . . .

II.

The obvious purpose of the statute is to protect existing Government, not from change by peaceable, lawful and constitutional means, but from change by violence, revolution and terrorism. That it is within the power of the Congress to protect the Government of the United States from armed rebellion is a proposition which requires little discussion. Whatever theoretical merit there may be to the argument that there is a "right" to rebellion against dictatorial governments is without force where the existing structure of the government provides for peaceful and orderly change. We reject any principle of governmental helplessness in the face of preparation for revolution, which principle, carried to its logical conclusion, must lead to anarchy. No one could conceive that it is not within the power of Congress to prohibit acts intended to overthrow the Government by force and violence. The question with which we are concerned here is not whether Congress has such power, but whether the means which it has employed conflict with the First and Fifth Amendments to the Constitution.

One of the bases for the contention that the means which Congress has employed are invalid takes the form of an attack on the face of the statute on the grounds that by its terms it prohibits academic discussion of the merits of Marxism-Leninism, that it stifles ideas and is contrary to all concepts of a free speech and a free press. Although we do not agree that the language itself has that significance, we must bear in mind that it is the duty of the federal courts to interpret federal legislation in a manner not inconsistent with the demands of the Constitution. . . . This is a federal statute which we must interpret as well as judge. . . .

The very language of the Smith Act negates the interpretation which petitioners would have us impose on the Act. It is directed at advocacy, not discussion. Thus, the trial judge properly charged the jury that they could not convict if they found that petitioners did "no more than pursue peaceful studies and discussions or teaching and advocacy in the realm of ideas." He further charged that it was not unlawful "to conduct in an American college and university a course explaining the philosophical theories set forth in the books which have been placed in evidence." Such a charge is in strict accord with the statutory language, and illustrates the meaning to be placed on those words. Congress did not intend to eradicate the free discussion of political theories, to destroy the traditional rights of Americans to discuss and evaluate ideas without fear of governmental sanction. Rather Congress was concerned with the very kind of activity in which the evidence showed these petitioners engaged.

III.

But although the statute is not directed at the hypothetical cases which petitioners have conjured, its application in this case has resulted in convictions for the teaching and advocacy of the overthrow of the Government by force and violence, which, even though coupled with the intent to accomplish that overthrow, contains an element of speech. For this reason, we must pay special heed to the demands of the First Amendment marking out the boundaries of speech.

We pointed out in [American Communications Ass'n v. Douds, 1950] that the basis of the First Amendment is the hypothesis that speech can rebut speech, propaganda will answer propaganda, free debate of ideas will result in the wisest governmental policies. It is for this reason that this Court has recognized the inherent value of free discourse. An analysis of the leading cases in this Court which have involved direct limitations on speech, however, will demonstrate that both the majority of the Court and the dissenters in particular cases have recognized that this is not an unlimited, unqualified right, but that the societal value of speech must, on occasion, be subordinated to other values and considerations.

No important case involving free speech was decided by this Court prior to Schenck v. United States (1919). . . . Writing for a unanimous Court, Justice Holmes states that the "question in every case is whether the words used are used in such circumstances and are of such a nature as to create a clear and present danger that they will bring about the substantive evils that Congress has a right to prevent." . . . The fact is inescapable, too, that the phrase bore no connotation that the danger was to be any threat to the safety of the Republic. The charge was causing and attempting to cause insubordination in the military forces and obstruct recruiting. The objec-

tionable document denounced conscription and its most inciting sentence was, "You must do your share to maintain, support and uphold the rights of the people of this country." Fifteen thousand copies were printed and some circulated. This insubstantial gesture toward insubordination in 1917 during war was held to be a clear and present danger of bringing about the evil of military insubordination.

In several later cases involving convictions under the Criminal Espionage Act, the nub of the evidence the Court held sufficient to meet the "clear and present danger" test enunciated in Schenck was as follows: [Five cases, 1919–1920, are here discussed.] . . .

The rule we deduce from these cases is that where an offense is specified by a statute in nonspeech or nonpress terms, a conviction relying upon speech or press as evidence of violation may be sustained only when the speech or publication created a "clear and present danger" of attempting or accomplishing the prohibited crime, e. g., interference with enlistment. The dissents, we repeat, in emphasizing the value of speech, were addressed to the argument of the sufficiency of the evidence.

The next important case before the Court in which free speech was the crux of the conflict was Gitlow v. New York [1925]. There New York had made it a crime to "advocate . . . the necessity or propriety of overthrowing . . . the government by force. . . ." The evidence of violation of the statute was that the defendant had published a Manifesto attacking the Government and capitalism. The convictions were sustained, Justices Holmes and Brandeis dissenting. The majority refused to apply the "clear and present danger" test to the specific utterance. Its reasoning was as follows: The "clear and present danger" test was applied to the utterance itself in Schenck because the question was merely one of sufficiency of evidence under an admittedly constitutional statute. Gitlow, however, presented a different question. There a legislature had found that a certain kind of speech was, itself, harmful and unlawful. The constitutionality of such a state statute had to be adjudged by this Court just as it determined the constitutionality of any state statute, namely, whether the statute was "reasonable." Since it was entirely reasonable for a state to attempt to protect itself from violent overthrow, the statute was perforce reasonable. The only question remaining in the case became whether there was evidence to support the conviction, a question which gave the majority no difficulty. Justices Holmes and Brandeis refused to accept this approach, but insisted that wherever speech was the evidence of the violation, it was necessary to show that the speech created the "clear and present danger" of the substantive evil which the legislature had the right to prevent. Justices Holmes and Brandeis, then, made no distinction between a federal statute which made certain acts unlawful, the evidence to support the conviction being speech, and a statute which made speech itself the crime. This approach was emphasized in Whitney v. California [1927], where the Court was confronted with a conviction under the California Criminal Syndicalist statute. The Court sustained the conviction, Justices Brandeis and Holmes concurring in the result. In their concurrence they repeated that even though the legislature had designated certain speech as criminal, this could not prevent the defendant from showing that there was no danger that the substantive evil would be brought about.

Although no case subsequent to Whitney and Gitlow has expressly overruled the majority opinions in those cases, there is little doubt that subsequent opinions have inclined toward the Holmes-Brandeis rationale. And in American Communications Ass'n v. Douds ... we pointed out that Congress did not intend to punish belief, but rather intended to regulate the conduct of union affairs. We therefore held that any indirect sanction on speech which might arise from the oath requirement did not present a proper case for the "clear and present danger" test, for the regulation was aimed at conduct rather than speech. In discussing the proper measure of evaluation of this kind of legislation, we suggested that the Holmes-Brandeis philosophy insisted that where there was a direct restriction upon speech, a "clear and present danger" that the substantive evil would be caused was necessary before the statute in question could be constitutionally applied. And we stated, "[The First] Amendment requires that one be permitted to believe what he will. It requires that one be permitted to advocate what he will unless there is a clear and present danger that a substantial public evil will result therefrom." But we further suggested that neither Justice Holmes nor Justice Brandeis ever envisioned that a shorthand phrase should be crystallized into a rigid rule to be applied inflexibly without regard to the circumstances of each case. Speech is not an absolute, above and beyond control by the legislature when its judgment, subject to review here, is that certain kinds of speech are so undesirable as to warrant criminal sanction. Nothing is more certain in modern society than the principle that there are no absolutes, that a name, a phrase, a standard has meaning only when associated with the considerations which gave birth to the nomenclature. ... To those who would paralyze our Government in the face of impending threat by encasing it in a semantic straitjacket we must reply that all concepts are relative.

In this case we are squarely presented with the application of the "clear and present danger" test, and must decide what that phrase imports. We first note that many of the cases in which this Court has reversed convictions by use of this or similar tests have been based on the fact that the interest which the State was attempting to protect was itself too insubstantial to warrant restriction of speech. ... Overthrow of the Government by force and violence is certainly a substantial enough interest for the Government to limit speech. Indeed, this is the ultimate value of any society, for if a society cannot protect its very structure from armed internal attack, it must follow that no subordinate value can be protected. If, then, this interest may be protected, the literal problem which is presented is what has been meant by the use of the phrase "clear and present danger" of the utterances

bringing about the evil within the power of Congress to punish.

Obviously, the words cannot mean that before the Government may act, it must wait until the *putsch* is about to be executed, the plans have been laid and the signal is awaited. If Government is aware that a group aiming at its overthrow is attempting to indoctrinate its members and to commit them to a course whereby they will strike when the leaders feel the circumstances permit, action by the Government is required. The argument that there is no need for Government to concern itself, for Government is strong, it possesses ample powers to put down a rebellion, it may defeat the revolution with ease needs no answer. For that is not the question. Certainly an attempt to overthrow the Government by force, even though doomed from the outset because of inadequate numbers or power of the revolutionists, is a sufficient evil for Congress to prevent. The damage which such attempts create both physically and politically to a nation makes it impossible to measure the validity in terms of the probability of success, or the immediacy of a successful attempt. In the instant case the trial judge charged the jury that they could not convict unless they found that petitioners intended to overthrow the Government "as speedily as circumstances would permit." This does not mean, and could not properly mean, that they would not strike until there was certainty of success. What was meant was that the revolutionists would strike when they thought the time was ripe. We must therefore reject the contention that success or probability of success is the criterion.

The situation with which Justices Holmes and Brandeis were concerned in Gitlow was a comparatively isolated event, bearing little relation in their minds to any substantial threat to the safety of the community. ... They were not confronted with any situation comparable to the instant one—the development of an apparatus designed and dedicated to the overthrow of the Government, in the context of world crisis after crisis.

Chief Judge Learned Hand, writing for the majority below, interpreted the phrase as follows: "In each case [courts] must ask whether the gravity of the 'evil,' discounted by its improbability, justifies such invasion of free speech as is necessary to avoid the danger." We adopt this statement of the rule. As articulated by Chief Judge Hand, it is as succinct and inclusive as any other we might devise at this time. It takes into consideration those factors which we deem relevant, and relates their significances. More we cannot expect from words.

Likewise, we are in accord with the court below, which affirmed the trial court's finding that the requisite danger existed. The mere fact that from the period 1945 to 1948 petitioners' activities did not result in an attempt to overthrow the Government by force and violence is of course no answer to the fact that there was a group that was ready to make the attempt. The formation by petitioners of such a highly organized conspiracy, with rigidly disciplined members subject to call when the leaders, these petitioners, felt that the time had come for action, coupled with the inflammable nature of world conditions, similar uprisings in other countries, and the touch-and-go nature of our relations with countries with whom petitioners were in the very least ideologically attuned, convince us that their convictions were justified on this score. And this analysis disposes of the contention that a conspiracy to advocate, as distinguished from the advocacy itself, cannot be constitutionally restrained, because it comprises only the preparation. It is the existence of the conspiracy which creates the danger. ... If the ingredients of the reaction are present, we cannot bind the Government to wait until the catalyst is added.

IV.

[The Court here considers whether the trial court was correct in not submitting to the jury the question of the existence of clear and present danger.]

... The argument that the action of the trial court is erroneous, in declaring as a matter of law that such violation shows sufficient danger to justify the punishment despite the First Amendment, rests on the theory that a jury must decide a question of the application of the First Amendment. We do not agree.

When facts are found that establish the violation of a statute, the protection against conviction afforded by the First Amendment is a matter of law. The doctrine that there must be a clear and present danger of a substantive evil that Congress has a right to prevent is a judicial rule to be applied as a matter of law by the courts. The guilt is established by proof of facts. Whether the First Amendment protects the activity which constitutes the violation of the statute must depend upon a judicial determination of the scope of the First Amendment applied to the circumstances of the case. ...

V.

There remains to be discussed the question of vagueness—whether the statute as we have interpreted it is too vague, not sufficiently advising those who would speak of the limitations upon their activity. ...

We hold that §§ 2(a) (1), (2)(a) (3) and 3 of the Smith Act, do not inherently, or as construed or applied in the instant case, violate the First Amendment and other provisions of the Bill of Rights, or the First and Fifth Amendments because of indefiniteness. Petitioners intended to overthrow the Government of the United States as speedily as the circumstances would permit. Their conspiracy to organize the Communist Party and to teach and advocate the overthrow of the Government of the United States by force and violence created a "clear and present danger" of an attempt to overthrow the Government by force and violence. They were properly and constitutionally convicted for violation of the Smith Act. The judgments of conviction are

Affirmed.

Mr. Justice **Clark** took no part in this case.

Mr. Justice **Frankfurter** wrote a concurring opinion.

Mr. Justice **Jackson** wrote a concurring opinion.

Mr. Justice **Black** wrote a dissenting opinion.

Mr. Justice **Douglas** wrote a dissenting opinion.

FREE ASSEMBLY AND PUBLIC ORDER

ADDERLEY v. FLORIDA

385 U. S. 39; 87 S. Ct. 242; 17 L. Ed. 2d 149
(1966)

During the late 1950s and early 1960s Southern blacks, led by such people as Martin Luther King, Jr., undertook to bring an end to segregation by nonviolent means. This was to be done by attracting public attention to segregation policies in the hope that the public conscience would be aroused and demand their abolition.

Against these efforts the Southern communities rolled out a battery of legal field pieces, some of them dating back to the early days of the common law. One of these was a prosecution for criminal trespass. Among the techniques employed to publicize segregation was the "sit-in" demonstration, in which blacks, sometimes accompanied by sympathetic whites, would enter a restaurant or lunch counter with a **WHITE ONLY** *sign in the window and ask to be served. When service was denied, they refused to leave, and the police would be called to arrest them for trespass.*

In five cases decided in 1964 the Supreme Court reversed on nonconstitutional grounds convictions for sit-in demonstrations. Although the Court carefully avoided the issue of whether state enforcement of trespass laws to effect private discrimination made the state a party to the discrimination, six justices in separate opinions indicated their stand on this issue. Justices Black, Harlan, and White argued that in the absence of a statute forbidding such discrimination, the impartial enforcement of trespass statutes does not make the state a party to the discrimination and hence does not deny equal protection, while Justices Warren, Goldberg, and Douglas argued that the framers of the Fourteenth Amendment had assumed the continued existence of the right of all citizens to enter places of public accommodation, and the refusal of the state to enforce that right as to blacks denies them the equal protection of the law. See Bell v. Maryland, Bouie v. Columbia, Griffin v. Maryland, Robinson v. Florida, and Barr v. Columbia.

The final chapter in the sit-in cases was written in Hamm v. Rock Hill (1964), decided the same day as Heart of Atlanta Motel v. United States. Again the Court failed to reach the constitutional issue but concluded that the Civil Rights Act of 1964, by making sit-ins no longer a crime, had abated sit-in prosecutions then in progress, since the states no longer had a policy to be served by such prosecutions. Federal statutes would decree this result as far as federal crimes were concerned, and the supremacy clause dictated the same result for state crimes. The effect of the decision was to stop the prosecution of some three thousand sit-in demonstrators.

A second technique relied upon by the Southern communities was the well-established right of any organized community to protect itself from a breach of the peace. Such a breach is "a substantive evil which the state can prevent" through the exercise of its police power; therefore a speech which presents a "clear and present danger" of causing a breach of the peace is punishable. Although the use of such statutes against demonstrations and "marches" presented some novel features, the general rules regarding them had been laid down years before. The Supreme Court, in reviewing cases which allege a violation of freedom of speech on this ground must determine (1) that the statute, as interpreted by the state court or by the judge in his charge to the jury, really defines a breach of the peace, and (2) that a clear and present danger of such breach actually exists.

In Chaplinsky v. New Hampshire (1942) a Jehovah's Witness called a police officer "a God damned racketeer" and "a damned Fascist," in violation of state statute whose purpose, the state court said, was to forbid words "such as have a direct tendency to cause acts of violence by the persons to whom, individually, the remark is addressed." The Court agreed that such speech could constitutionally be punished: "There are certain well-defined and narrowly limited classes of speech, the prevention and punishment of which have never been thought to raise any constitutional problem. These include the lewd and obscene, the profane, the libelous, and the insulting or 'fighting' words—those which by their very utterance inflict injury or tend to incite an immediate breach of the peace. ... 'Resort to epithets or personal abuse is not in any proper sense communication of information or opinion safeguarded by the Constitution. ...' " There was, moreover, a clear and present danger: "... the appellations 'damned racketeer' and 'damned Fascist' are epithets likely to provoke the average person to retaliation, and thereby cause a breach of the peace."

Another case in which the making of a speech was punished by the city as a breach of the peace was Terminiello v. Chicago (1949), a case which remains bitterly controversial. Terminiello (who denied he was a Fascist) was introduced by Gerald L. K. Smith and spoke in an auditorium in Chicago to a crowd of about eight hundred persons, under the sponsorship of the Christian Veterans of America. Outside, a protesting crowd of over a thousand (who denied they were Communist-led) milled about, yelling and throwing stones at the windows. Inside Terminiello spoke despite the tumult, linking Democrats, Jews, and Communists together in a speech filled with race hatred. A cordon of police assigned to the meeting was unable to prevent several outbreaks of violence, including the smashing of doors and windows.

Terminiello was found guilty of inciting a breach of the peace and fined $100. The trial court charged the jury that " 'breach of the peace' consists of any 'misbehavior which violates the public peace and decorum'; and that the 'misbehavior may constitute a breach of the peace if it stirs the public to anger, invites dispute, brings about a condition of unrest, or creates a disturbance. ...' " The Supreme Court never reached the question whether the speech itself might be punishable, because it found that the statute as interpreted by the trial judge permitted the punishment of speech that was protected by the Constitution: "... A function of free speech under our system of government is to invite dispute. It may indeed best serve its high purpose when it induces a condition of unrest, creates dissatisfaction with conditions as they are, or even stirs people to anger. Speech is often provocative and challenging. It may strike at prejudices and preconceptions and have profound unsettling effects as it presses for acceptance of an idea. ... The ordinance as construed by the trial court seriously invaded this province."

In contrast to the Terminiello decision, the Court in Feiner v. New York (1951) upheld the disorderly conduct conviction of a Syracuse University student for a street-corner speech in which he was apparently "endeavoring to arouse the Negro people against the whites, urging that they rise up in arms and fight for equal rights." The two policemen present later testified that the mixed crowd of seventy-five to eighty persons "was restless and there was some pushing, shoving, and milling around." Fearful that they could not control the crowd if violence erupted, they asked Feiner to stop speaking and arrested him when he refused. The Court held the trial court justified in finding a clear and present danger of causing a riot.

In 1963 in Edwards v. South Carolina the Court upheld the right to demonstrate on public property. A group of black students had gathered on the statehouse lawn to protest state segregation policies. The pickets listened to a religious harangue, sang, stamped their feet, and clapped. They refused to disperse when ordered and were arrested for a breach of the peace. The Court held that "the Fourteenth Amendment does not permit a State to make criminal the peaceful expression of unpopular views ..." and the breach of the peace statute was so vague as to "permit punishment of the fair use of this opportunity." In this case "there was no violence or threat of violence on their part, or on the part of any member of the crowd watching them. Police protection was ample. ... And the record is barren of any evidence of 'fighting words.' "

Two years later, in Cox v. Louisiana (1965), a civil rights leader was arrested when a group of some two thousand students assembled across the street from the courthouse, with police permission, to protest the arrest of twenty-three of their fellows for picketing segregated lunch counters. As in the Edwards case they began to sing and clap, and upon their refusal to disperse when ordered were arrested for breach of the peace. The Court found the facts and the statute almost identical to those in Edwards, and void for the same reasons. The Court also rejected the claim that the pickets had been illegally obstructing the sidewalk. It denied that physical demonstrations enjoyed the same freedom as mere speech, but noted that the city police customarily permitted the obstruction of sidewalks for some purposes "in their completely uncontrolled discretion." In a companion case by the same name and involving the same facts, the Court reversed Cox's conviction for picketing near a courthouse. Conceding that a state could legitimately protect its "judicial system from the pressures which picketing near a courthouse might create" the Court held that Cox had police permission to picket where he did and was not arrested until ordered (invalidly) to move on. (In April 1983 the Court, in United States v. Grace, held void on its face a federal statute forbidding picketing or the display of banners or signs on the grounds of the Supreme Court building itself. One sign carried the text of the First Amendment.)

The courageous efforts of the Southern black to achieve racial equality through nonviolent means won widespread admiration and support from the liberal white community and strong encouragement was given the National Association for the Advancement of Colored People (NAACP) in its efforts to win recognition for black rights in the courts. Since the average victim of race discrimination was ill-equipped to fight for legal rights, the NAACP shouldered the financial burden and provided those victimized with legal assistance, with the result that a number of Southern states made serious efforts to oust or cripple the organization. The result was a series of Supreme Court holdings that the organization need not divulge its membership lists either as a condition of doing business in the state (NAACP v. Alabama, 1958), or to a legislative committee investigating Communism in civil rights organizations (Gibson v. Florida Investigation Committee, 1963). Nor was its bringing of test cases punishable as barratry (NAACP v. Button, 1963), and it could not be forbidden to do business in the state (NAACP v. Alabama, 1964). All these decisions rested on a freedom of association held to be protected by the First Amendment and made applicable to the states by the Fourteenth.

With the outbreak of racial violence in Northern cities in the summer of 1965 and with the breach between the conservative, law-oriented NAACP on the one hand and the more militant Congress of Racial Equality (CORE) and Student Nonviolent Coordinating Committee (SNCC) on the other, Northern white support for the civil rights movement fell off sharply. The 1966 civil rights bill with provisions against anti-civil rights terrorism and an open housing provision failed to pass Congress, and in the fall elections of that year a number of congressional candidates and advocates of referendum measures exploited the fear of "black power" and looked, in some cases successfully, to a "white backlash" for support.

In the present case the Supreme Court for the first time held valid a state criminal trespass statute against black demonstrators. A group of some two hundred students from Florida A&M had marched to the jail in Tallahassee to protest the arrest of some of their body for trying to integrate public theaters, as well as against segregation policies generally. Over one hundred remained after being ordered to leave, and were arrested for trespass.

Mr. Justice **Black** delivered the opinion of the Court, saying in part:

Petitioners, Harriett Louise Adderley and 31 other persons, were convicted by a jury in a joint trial in the County Judge's Court of Leon County, Florida, on a charge of "trespass with a malicious and mischievous intent" upon the premises of the county jail contrary to § 821.18 of the Florida statutes. . . . Petitioners, apparently all students of the Florida A. & M. University in Tallahassee, had gone from the school to the jail about a mile away, along with many other students, to "demonstrate" at the jail their protests because of arrests of other protesting students the day before, and perhaps to protest more generally against state and local policies and practices of racial segregation, including segregation of the jail. The county sheriff, legal custodian of the jail and jail grounds, tried to persuade the students to leave the jail grounds. When this did not work, he notified them that they must leave, that if they did not leave he would arrest them for trespassing, and that if they resisted he would charge them with that as well. Some of the students left but others, including petitioners, remained and they were arrested. . . .

I.

Petitioners have insisted from the beginning of this case that they are controlled and must be reversed because of our prior cases of Edwards v. South Carolina [1963] and Cox v. Louisiana [1965]. We cannot agree.

The Edwards case, like this one, did come up when a number of persons demonstrated on public property against their State's segregation policies. They also sang hymns and danced, as did the demonstrators in this case. But here the analogies to this case end. In Edwards, the demonstrators went to the South Carolina State Capitol grounds to protest. In this case they went to the jail. Traditionally, state capitol grounds are open to the public. Jails, built for security purposes, are not. The demonstrators at the South Carolina Capitol went in through a public driveway and as they entered they were told by state officials there that they had a right as citizens to go through the State House grounds as long as they were peaceful. Here the demonstrators entered the jail grounds through a driveway used only for jail purposes and without warning to or permission from the sheriff. More importantly, South Carolina sought to prosecute its State Capitol demonstrators by charging them with the common-law crime of breach of the peace. This Court in Edwards took pains to point out at length the indefinite, loose, and broad nature of this charge; indeed, this Court pointed out . . . that the South Carolina Supreme Court had itself declared that the ''breach of the peace'' charge is ''not susceptible of exact definition.'' South Carolina's power to prosecute, it was emphasized . . . , would have been different had the State proceeded under a ''precise and narrowly drawn regulatory statute evincing a legislative judgment that certain specific conduct be limited or proscribed'' such as, for example, ''limiting the periods during which the State House grounds were open to the public. . . .'' The South Carolina breach-of-the-peace statute was thus struck down as being so broad and all-embracing as to jeopardize speech, press, assembly and petition, under the constitutional doctrine enunciated in Cantwell v. Connecticut [1940], and followed in many subsequent cases. And it was on this same ground of vagueness that in Cox v. Louisiana the Louisiana breach-of-the-peace law used to prosecute Cox was invalidated.

The Florida trespass statute under which these petitioners were charged cannot be challenged on this ground. It is aimed at conduct of one limited kind, that is for one person or persons to trespass upon the property of another with a malicious and mischievous intent. There is no lack of notice in this law, nothing to entrap or fool the unwary.

Petitioners seem to argue that the Florida trespass law is void for vagueness because it requires a trespass to be ''with a malicious and mischievous intent. . . .'' But these words do not broaden the scope of trespass so as to make it cover a multitude of types of conduct as does the common-law breach-of-the-peace charge. On the contrary, these words narrow the scope of the offense. The trial court charged the jury as to their meaning and petitioners have not argued that this definition . . . is not a reasonable and clear definition of the terms. The use of these terms in the statute, instead of contributing to uncertainty and misunderstanding, actually makes its meaning more understandable and clear.

II.

Petitioners in this Court invoke the doctrine of abatement announced by this Court in Hamm v. Rock Hill [1964]. But that holding was that the Civil Rights Act of 1964, which made it unlawful for places of public accommodation to deny service to any person because of race, effected an abatement of prosecutions of persons for seeking such services that arose prior to the passage of the Act. But this case in no way involves prosecution of petitioners for seeking service in establishments covered by the Act. It involves only an alleged trespass on jail grounds—a trespass which can be prosecuted regardless of the fact that it is the means of protesting segregation of establishments covered by the Act.

III.

Petitioners next argue that ''petty criminal statues may not be used to violate minorities' consitutional rights.'' This of course is true but this abstract proposition gets us nowhere in deciding this case.

IV.

Petitioners here contend that ''Petitioners' convictions are based on a total lack of relevant evidence.'' If true, this would be a denial of due process. . . . Petitioners' summary of facts as well as that of the Circuit Court show an abundance of facts to support the jury's verdict of guilty in this case.

In summary both these statements show testimony ample to prove this: Disturbed and upset by the arrest of their schoolmates the day before, a large number of Florida A. & M. students assembled on the school grounds and decided to march down to the county jail. Some apparently wanted to be put in jail too, along with the students already there. A group of around 200 marched from the school and arrived at the jail singing and clapping. They went directly to the jail-door entrance where they were met by a deputy sheriff, evidently surprised by their arrival. He asked them to move back, claiming they were blocking the entrance to the jail and fearing that they might attempt to enter the jail. They moved back part of the way, where they stood or sat, singing, clapping, and dancing, on the jail driveway and on an adjacent grassy area upon the jail premises. This particular jail entrance and driveway were not normally used by the public, but by the sheriff's department for transporting prisoners to and from the courts several blocks away and by commercial concerns for servicing the jail. Even after their partial retreat, the demonstrators continued to block vehicular passage over this driveway up to the entrance of the jail.* Someone called the sheriff who was at the moment apparently conferring with one of the state court judges about incidents connected with prior arrests for demonstrations. When the sheriff returned to the jail, he immediately inquired if all was safe inside the jail and was told it was. He then engaged in a conversation with two of the leaders. He told them they were trespassing upon jail property and that he would give them 10 minutes to leave or he would arrest them. Neither of the leaders did anything to disperse the crowd, and one of them told the sheriff that they wanted to get arrested. A local minister talked with some of the demonstrators

---

*Although some of the petitioners testified that they had no intention of interfering with vehicular traffic to and from the jail entrance and that they noticed no vehicle trying to enter or leave the driveway, the deputy sheriff testified that it would have been impossible for automobiles to drive up to the jail entrance and that one serviceman, finished with his business in the jail, waited inside because the demonstrators were sitting around and leaning against his truck parked outside. The sheriff testified that the time the demonstrators were there, between 9:30 and 10 Monday morning, was generally a very busy time for using the jail entrance to transport weekend inmates to the courts and for tradesmen to make service calls at the jail.

and told them not to enter the jail, because they could not arrest themselves, but just to remain where they were. After about 10 minutes, the sheriff, in a voice loud enough to be heard by all, told the demonstrators that he was the legal custodian of the jail and its premises, that they were trespassing on county property in violation of the law, that they should all leave forthwith or he would arrest them, and that if they attempted to resist arrest, he would charge them with that as a separate offense. Some of the group then left. Others, including all petitioners, did not leave. Some of them sat down. In a few minutes, realizing that the remaining demonstrators had no intention of leaving, the sheriff ordered his deputies to surround those remaining on jail premises and place them, 107 demonstrators, under arrest. The sheriff unequivocally testified that he did not arrest any persons other than those who were on the jail premises. Of the three petitioners testifying, two insisted that they were arrested before they had a chance to leave, had they wanted to, and one testified that she did not intend to leave. The sheriff again explicitly testified that he did not arrest any person who was attempting to leave.

Under the foregoing testimony the jury was authorized to find that the State had proven every essential element of the crime, as it was defined by the state court. That interpretation is, of course, binding on us, leaving only the question of whether conviction of the state offense, thus defined, unconstitutionally deprives petitioners of their rights to freedom of speech, press, assembly or petition. We hold it does not. The sheriff, as jail custodian, had power, as the state courts have here held, to direct that this large crowd of people get off the grounds. There is not a shred of evidence in this record that this power was exercised, or that its exercise was sanctioned by the lower courts, because the sheriff objected to what was being sung or said by the demonstrators or because he disagreed with the objectives of their protest. The record reveals that he objected only to their presence on that part of the jail grounds reserved for jail uses. There is no evidence at all that on any other occasion had similarly large groups of the public been permitted to gather on this portion of the jail grounds for any purpose. Nothing in the Constitution of the United States prevents Florida from even-handed enforcement of its general trespass statute against those refusing to obey the sheriff's order to remove themselves from what amounted to the curtilage of the jailhouse. The State, no less than a private owner of property, has power to preserve the property under its control for the use to which it is lawfully dedicated. For this reason there is no merit to the petitioners' argument that they had a constitutional right to stay on the property, over the jail custodian's objections, because this "area chosen for the peaceful civil rights demonstration was not only 'reasonable' but also particularly appropriate. . . ." Such an argument has as its major unarticulated premise the assumption that people who want to propagandize protests or views have a constitutional right to do so whenever and however and wherever they please. That concept of constitutional law was vigorously and forthrightfully rejected in two of the cases petitioners rely on, Cox v. Louisiana, at 554-555 and 563-564. We reject it again. The United States Constitution does not forbid a State to control the use of its own property for its own lawful nondiscriminatory purpose.

These judgments are
Affirmed.

Mr. Justice **Douglas,** with whom the Chief Justice **[Warren],** Mr. Justice **Brennan,** and Mr. Justice **Fortas** concur, dissenting, said in part:

The First Amendment, applicable to the States by reason of the Fourteenth . . . , provides that "Congress shall make no law abridging . . . the right of the people peaceably to assemble, and to petition the Government for a redress of grievances." These rights, along with religion, speech, and press, are preferred rights of the Constitution, made so by reason of that explicit guarantee and what Edmond Cahn in Confronting Injustice (1966) referred to as "The Firstness of the First Amendment." With all respect, therefore, the Court errs in treating the case as if it were an ordinary trespass case or an ordinary picketing case.

The jailhouse, like an executive mansion, a legislative chamber, a courthouse, or the statehouse itself (Edwards v. South Carolina) is one of the seats of government whether it be the Tower of London, the Bastille, or a small county jail. And when it houses political prisoners or those whom many think are unjustly held, it is an obvious center for protest. The right to petition for the redress of grievances has an ancient history and is not limited to writing a letter or sending a telegram to a congressman; it is not confined to appearing before the local city council, or writing letters to the President or Governor or Mayor. . . . Conventional methods of petitioning may be, and often have been, shut off to large groups of our citizens. Legislators may turn deaf ears; formal complaints may be routed endlessly through a bureaucratic maze; courts may let the wheels of justice grind very slowly. Those who do not control television and radio, those who cannot afford to advertise in newspapers or circulate elaborate pamphlets may have only a more limited type of access to public officials. Their methods should not be condemned as tactics of obstruction and harassment as long as the assembly and petition are peaceable, as these were.

There is no question that petitioners had as their purpose a protest against the arrest of Florida A. & M. students for trying to integrate public theatres. The sheriff's testimony indicates that he well understood the purpose of the rally. The petitioners who testified unequivocally stated that the group was protesting the arrests, and state and local policies of segregation, including segregation of the jail. This testimony was not contradicted or even questioned. The fact that no one gave a formal speech, that no elaborate handbills were distributed, and that the group was not laden with signs would seem to be immaterial. Such methods are not the sine qua non of petitioning for the redress grievances. The group did sing "freedom" songs. And history shows that a song can be a powerful tool of protest. . . . There was no violence; no threat of violence; no attempted jail break; no storming of a prison; no plan or plot to do anything but protest. The evidence is uncontradicted that the petitioners' conduct did not upset the jailhouse routine; things went on as they normally would. None of the group entered the jail. Indeed, they moved back from the entrance as they were instructed. There was no shoving, no pushing, no disorder or threat of riot. It is said that some of the group blocked part of the driveway leading to the jail entrance. The chief jailer, to be sure, testified that vehicles would not have been able to use the driveway. Never did the students locate themselves so as to cause interference with persons or vehicles going to or coming from the jail. Indeed, it is undisputed that the sheriff and deputy sheriff, in separate cars, were able to drive up the driveway to the parking places near the entrance and that no one obstructed their path. Further, it is undisputed that the entrance to the jail was not blocked. And whenever the students were requested to move they did so. If there was congestion, the solution was a further request to move to lawns or parking areas, not complete ejection and arrest. The claim is made that a tradesman waited inside the jail because some of the protestants were sitting around and leaning on his truck. The only evidence supporting such a conclusion is the testimony of a deputy sheriff that the tradesman "came to the door . . . and then did not leave." His remaining is just as consistent with a desire to satisfy his curiosity as it is with a restraint. Finally, the fact that some of the protestants may have felt their cause so just that they were willing to be arrested for making their protest outside the jail seems wholly irrelevant. A petition is nonetheless a petition, though its futility may make martyrdom attractive.

We do violence to the First Amendment when we permit this "petition for redress of grievances" to be turned into a trespass action. It does not help to analogize this problem to the problem of picketing. Picketing is a form of protest usually directed against private interests. I do not see how rules governing picketing in general are relevant to this express constitutional right to assemble and to petition for redress of grievances. In the first place the jailhouse grounds were not marked with "NO TRESPASSING!" signs, nor does respondent claim that the public was generally excluded from the grounds. Only the sheriff's fiat transformed lawful conduct into an unlawful trespass. To say that a private owner could have done the same if the rally had taken place on private property is to speak of a different case, as an assembly and a petition for redress of grievances run to government, not to private proprietors.

. . . When we allow Florida to construe her "malicious trespass" statute to bar a person from going on property knowing it is not his own and to apply that prohibition to public property, we discard Cox and Edwards. Would the case be any different if, as is common, the demonstration took place outside a building which housed both the jail and the legislative body? I think not.

There may be some public places which are so clearly committed to other purposes that their use for the airing of grievances is anomalous. There may be some instances in which assemblies and petitions for redress of grievances are not consistent with other necessary purposes of public property. A noisy meeting may be out of keeping with the serenity of the statehouse or the quiet of the courthouse. No one, for example, would suggest that the Senate gallery is the proper place for a vociferous protest rally. And in other cases it may be necessary to adjust the right to petition for redress of grievances to the other interests inhering in the uses to which the public property is normally put. . . . But this is quite different than saying that all public places are off limits to people with grievances. . . . And it is farther yet from saying that the "custodian" of the public property in his discretion can decide when public places shall be used for the communication of ideas, especially the constitutional right to assemble and petition for redress of grievances. . . . For to place such discretion in any public official, be he the "custodian" of the public property or the local police commissioner . . . is to place those who assert their First Amendment rights at his mercy. It gives him the awesome power to decide whose ideas may be expressed and who shall be denied a place to air their claims and petition their government. Such power is out of step with all our decisions prior to today where we have insisted that before a First Amendment right may be curtailed under the guise of a criminal law, any evil that may be collateral to the exercise of the right, must be isolated and defined in a "narrowly drawn" statute . . . lest the power to control excesses of conduct be used to suppress the constitutional right itself. . . .

That tragic consequence happens today when a trespass law is used to bludgeon those who peacefully exercise a First Amendment right to protest to government against one of the most grievous of all modern oppressions which some of our States are inflicting on our citizens. . . .

Today a trespass law is used to penalize people for exercising a constitutional right. Tomorrow a disorderly conduct statute, a breach-of-the-peace statute, a vagrancy statute will be put to the same end. It is said that the sheriff did not make the arrests because of the views which petitioners espoused. That excuse is usually given, as we know from the many cases involving arrests of minority groups for breaches of the peace, unlawful assemblies, and parading without a permit. The charge against William Penn, who preached a nonconformist doctrine in a street in London, was that he caused "a great concourse and tumult of people" in contempt of the King and "to the great disturbance of his peace." That was in 1670. In modern times also such arrests are usually sought to be justified by some legitimate function of government. Yet by allowing these orderly and civilized protests against injustice to be suppressed, we only increase the forces of frustration which the conditions of second-class citizenship are generating amongst us.

R. A. V. v. ST. PAUL

505 U. S. . . .; 112 S. Ct. 2538; 120 L. Ed. 2d
305 (1992)

A great many groups in American society rely heavily upon symbols to personify or embody the organization. While the organization itself, with its political structure, its rules and its procedures is difficult for people to feel close to, a symbol representing the organization can evoke tremendous emotional involvement and loyalty. Since prehistoric times, mankind has used idols as symbols to denote its deities and many churches today rely on physical representations to epitomize the spiritual essence of their beliefs. In this way the difficulty of relating to a complex and often contradictory set of beliefs is avoided. The symbol supports the group or community by keeping alive the myth and promise of a known and shared normative vision.

Few problems would exist were these symbols merely the property of private groups, limited in use to the members of those groups. The meaning of an icon used by a secret society does not concern the public at large. When a symbol, such as a flag, is used to represent a nation, however, a very different situation exists. What the adopted symbol represents, among the varied and diverse beliefs present in the nation, can become a very serious question indeed. To what is one subscribing when he pays homage to the flag of a country? Which of the many beliefs in a country is one showing loyalty to when he salutes the British flag? The flag of the Confederate States?

The first major constitutional challenge to saluting the American flag involved, not the beliefs for which the flag stood, but whether one could be required to give homage to any symbol. In the 1940s in a small town in West Virginia the Jehovah's Witnesses challenged the requirement that their children salute the flag on the ground that this constituted bowing down to a graven image contrary to the Second Commandment. In West Virginia State Board of Education v. Barnette (1943) the Court held the children involved could not be compelled to salute the flag. Conceding the right of the government to try to foster a spirit of national unity, the Court clearly forbade the use of force to achieve it.

"There is no mysticism in the American concept of the State or of the nature or origin of its authority. We set up government by consent of the governed, and the Bill of Rights denies those in power any legal opportunity to coerce that consent. . . . The case is made difficult not because the principles of its decision are obscure but because the flag involved is our own."

The use of the American flag by a number of conservative organizations to symbolize their beliefs has re-sulted in the unfortunate conclusion by others that that is what the flag does stand for. In Texas v. Johnson (1989) a group of demonstrators burned an American flag to "protest the policies of the Reagan administration and certain Dallas-based corporations." Johnson, who actually did the burning, was convicted of desecrating a flag in violation of Texas law. In a five-to-four decision the Court found the burning to be an "expression of dissatisfaction with the policies of this country" and therefore protected by the First and Fourteenth Amendments.

Following this decision Congress passed the Flag Protection Act of 1989 which forbade the burning of the United States flag. While the government conceded that the flag burning constituted expressive conduct, it urged that it be denied First Amendment protection, like obscenity or "fighting words." In its attempt to distinguish the case from Texas v. Johnson it urged that "the Flag Protection Act is constitutional because, unlike the statute addressed in Johnson, the Act does not target expressive conduct on the basis of the content of its message. The Government asserts an interest in 'protect[ing] the physical integrity of the flag under all circumstances' in order to safeguard the flag's identity "'as the unique and unalloyed symbol of the Nation.'" The Act proscribes conduct (other than disposal) that damages or mistreats a flag, without regard to the actor's motive, his intended message, or the likely effects of his conduct on onlookers. By contrast, the Texas statute expressly prohibited only those acts of physical flag desecration 'that the actor knows will seriously offend' onlookers . . . ."

In a five-to-four decision, the Court found that "although the Flag Protection Act contains no explicit content-based limitation on the scope of prohibited conduct, it is nevertheless clear that the Government's asserted interest is 'related "to the suppression of free expression,"' and concerned with the content of such expression." "Although Congress cast the Flag Protection Act in somewhat broader terms than the Texas statute at issue in Johnson, the Act still suffers from the same fundamental flaw: it suppresses expression out of concern for its likely communicative impact. Despite the Act's wider scope, its restriction on expression cannot be 'justified without reference to the content of the regulated speech.' The Act therefore must be subjected to 'the most exacting scrutiny' and for the reasons stated in Johnson the Government's interest cannot justify its infringement on First Amendment rights."

The case below involved, not the attack on a symbol, but rather the use of symbols as instruments of attack. While the Court found in both cases that such symbols were modes of expression protected the First Amendment, the majority in R. A. V. invoked an innovative interpretation of that amendment as the basis for its opinion.

Justice **Scalia** delivered the opinion of the Court, saying in part:

In the predawn hours of June 21, 1990, petitioner and several other teenagers allegedly assembled a crudely-made cross by taping together broken chair legs. They then allegedly burned the cross inside the fenced yard of a black family that lived across the street from the house where petitioner was staying. Although this conduct could have been punished under any of a number of laws, one of the two provisions under which respondent city of St. Paul chose to charge petitioner (then a juvenile) was the St. Paul Bias-Motivated Crime Ordinance which provides:

"Whoever places on public or private property a symbol, object, appellation, characterization or graffiti, including, but not limited to, a burning cross or Nazi swastika, which one knows or has reasonable grounds to know arouses anger, alarm or resentment in others on the basis of race, color, creed, religion or gender commits disorderly conduct and shall be guilty of a misdemeanor."

Petitioner moved to dismiss this count on the ground that the St. Paul ordinance was substantially overbroad and impermissibly content-based and therefore facially invalid under the First Amendment. The trial court granted this motion, but the Minnesota Supreme Court reversed. That court rejected petitioner's overbreadth claim because, as construed in prior Minnesota cases the modifying phrase "arouses anger, alarm or resentment in others" limited the reach of the ordinance to conduct that amounts to "fighting words," i.e., "conduct that itself inflicts injury or tends to incite immediate violence . . .," and therefore the ordinance reached only expression "that the first amendment does not protect." The court also concluded that the ordinance was not impermissibly content-based because, in its view, "the ordinance is a narrowly tailored means toward accomplishing the compelling governmental interest in protecting the community against bias-motivated threats to public safety and order."

I.

In construing the St. Paul ordinance, we are bound by the construction given to it by the Minnesota court. . . . Accordingly, we accept the Minnesota Supreme Court's authoritative statement that the ordinance reaches only those expressions that constitute "fighting words" within the meaning of Chaplinsky. Petitioner and his amici urge us to modify the scope of the Chaplinsky formulation, thereby invalidating the ordinance as "substantially overbroad," . . . We find it unnecessary to consider this issue. Assuming, arguendo, that all of the expression reached by the ordinance is proscribable under the "fighting words" doctrine, we nonetheless conclude that the ordinance is facially unconstitutional in that it prohibits otherwise permitted speech solely on the basis of the subjects the speech addresses.

The First Amendment generally prevents government from proscribing speech . . . or even expressive conduct, . . . because of disapproval of the ideas expressed. Content-based regulations are presumptively invalid. Simon & Schuster, Inc. v. Members of N. Y. State Crime Victims Bd. (1991). . . . From 1791 to the present, however, our society, like other free but civilized societies, has permitted restrictions upon the content of speech in a few limited areas, which are "of such slight social value as a step to truth that any benefit that may be derived from them is clearly outweighed by the social interest in order and morality." Chaplinsky. . . .

We have sometimes said that these categories of expression are "not within the area of constitutionally protected speech," Roth [v. United States (1957)] . . . or that the "protection of the First Amendment does not extend" to them . . . . Such statements must be taken in context, however, and are no more literally true than is the occasionally repeated shorthand characterizing obscenity "as not being speech at all." . . . What they mean is that these areas of speech can, consistently with the First Amendment, be regulated *because of their constitutionally proscribable content* (obscenity, defamation, etc.)—not that they are categories of speech entirely invisible to the Constitution, so that they may be made the vehicles for content discrimination unrelated to their distinctively proscribable content. Thus, the government may proscribe libel; but it may not make the further content discrimination of proscribing *only* libel critical of the government. . . .

Our cases surely do not establish the proposition that the First Amendment imposes no obstacle whatsoever to regulation of particular instances of such proscribable expression, so that the government "may regulate [them] freely." That would mean that a city council could enact an ordinance prohibiting only those legally obscene works that contain criticism of the city government or, indeed, that do not include endorsement of the city government. Such a simplistic, all-or-nothing-at-all approach to First Amendment protection is at odds with common sense and with our jurisprudence as well. It is not true that "fighting words" have at most a "de minimis" expressive content, or that their content is in all respects "worthless and undeserving of constitutional protection"; sometimes they are quite expressive indeed. We have not said that they constitute "no part of the expression of ideas," but only that they constitute "no *essential* part of any exposition of ideas." Chaplinsky (emphasis added).

The proposition that a particular instance of speech can be proscribable on the basis of one feature (e.g., obscenity) but not on the basis of another (e.g., opposition to the city government) is commonplace, and has found application in many contexts. We have long held, for example, that nonverbal expressive activity can be banned because of the action it entails, but not because of the ideas it expresses—so that burning a flag in violation of an ordinance against outdoor fires could be punishable, whereas burning a flag in violation of an ordinance against dishonoring the flag is not. . . . Similarly, we have upheld reasonable "time, place, or manner" restrictions, but only if they are "justified without reference to the content of the regulated speech." . . . And just as the power to proscribe particular speech on the basis of a noncontent element (e.g., noise) does not entail the power to proscribe the same speech on the basis of a content element; so also, the power to proscribe it on the basis of one content element (e.g., obscenity) does not entail the power to proscribe it on the basis of other content elements.

In other words, the exclusion of "fighting words" from the scope of the First Amendment simply means that, for purposes of that Amendment, the unprotected features of the words are, despite their verbal character, essentially a "nonspeech" element of communication. Fighting words are thus analogous to a noisy sound truck . . . ; both can be used to convey an idea; but neither has, in and of itself, a claim upon the First Amendment. As with the sound truck, however, so also with fighting words: The government may not regulate use based on hostility—or favoritism—towards the underlying message expressed. . . .

The concurrences describe us as setting forth a new First Amendment principle that prohibition of constitutionally proscribable speech cannot be "underinclusiv[e]." . . . That easy target is of the concurrences' own invention. In our view, the First Amendment imposes not an "underinclusiveness" limitation but a "content discrimination" limitation upon a State's prohibition of proscribable speech. There is no problem whatever, for example, with a State's prohibiting obscenity (and other forms of proscribable expression) only in certain media or markets, for although that prohibition would be "underinclusive," it would not discriminate on the basis of content. . . .

Even the prohibition against content discrimination that we assert the First Amendment requires is not absolute. It applies differently in the context of proscribable speech than in the area of fully protected speech. The rationale of the general prohibition, after all, is that content discrimination "raises the specter that the Government may effectively drive certain ideas or viewpoints from the marketplace," . . . But content discrimination among various instances of a class of proscribable speech often does not pose this threat.

When the basis for the content discrimination consists entirely of the very reason the entire class of speech at issue is proscribable, no significant danger of idea or viewpoint discrimination exists. Such a reason, having been adjudged neutral enough to support exclusion of the entire class of speech from First Amendment protection, is also neutral enough to form the basis of distinction within the class. To illustrate: A State might choose to prohibit only that obscenity which is the most patently offensive in its prurience—i.e., that which involves the most lascivious displays of sexual activity. But it may not prohibit, for example, only that obscenity which includes offensive political messages. . . . And the Federal Government can criminalize only those threats of violence that are directed against the President—since the reasons why threats of violence are outside the First Amendment (protecting individuals from the fear of violence, from the disruption that fear engenders, and from the possibility that the threatened violence will occur) have special force when applied to the person of the President. . . . But the Federal Government may not criminalize only those threats against the President that mention his policy on aid to inner cities. And to take a final example (one mentioned by Justice Stevens) a State may choose to regulate price advertising in one industry but not in others, because the risk of fraud (one of the characteristics of commercial speech that justifies depriving it of full First Amendment protection . . .) is in its view greater there. . . . But a State may not prohibit only that commercial advertising that depicts men in a demeaning fashion . . . .

Another valid basis for according differential treatment to even a content-defined subclass of proscribable speech is that the subclass happens to be associated with particular "secondary effects" of the speech, so that the regulation is "justified without reference to the content of the . . . speech," . . . A State could, for example, permit all obscene live performances except those involving minors. Moreover, since words can in some circumstances violate laws directed not against speech but against conduct (a law against treason, for example, is violated by telling the enemy the nation's defense secrets), a particular content-based subcategory of a proscribable class of speech can be swept up incidentally within the reach of a statute directed at conduct rather than speech. . . . Thus, for example, sexually derogatory "fighting words," among other words, may produce a violation of Title VII's general prohibition against sexual discrimination in employment practices . . . . Where the government does not target conduct on the basis of its expressive content, acts are not shielded from regulation merely because they express a discriminatory idea or philosophy. . . .

II.

Applying these principles to the St. Paul ordinance, we conclude that, even as narrowly construed by the Minnesota Supreme Court, the ordinance is facially unconstitutional. Although the phrase in the ordinance, "arouses anger, alarm or resentment in others," has been limited by the Minnesota Supreme Court's construction to reach only those symbols or displays that amount to "fighting words," the remaining, unmodified terms make clear that the ordinance applies only to "fighting words" that insult, or provoke violence, "on the basis of race, color, creed, religion or gender." Displays containing abusive invective, no matter how vicious or severe, are permissible unless they are addressed to one of the specified disfavored topics. Those who wish to use "fighting words" in connection with other ideas—to express hostility, for example, on the basis of political affiliation, union membership, or homosexuality—are not covered. The First Amendment does not permit St. Paul to impose special prohibitions on those speakers who express views on disfavored subjects. . . .

In its practical operation, moreover, the ordinance goes even beyond mere content discrimination, to actual viewpoint discrimination. Displays containing some words—odious racial epithets, for example—would be prohibited to proponents of all views. But "fighting words" that do not themselves invoke race, color, creed, religion, or gender—aspersions upon a person's mother, for example—would seemingly be usable ad libitum in the placards of those arguing in favor of racial, color, etc. tolerance and equality, but could not be used by that speaker's opponents. One could hold up a sign saying, for example, that all "anti-Catholic bigots" are misbegotten; but not that all "papists" are, for that would insult and provoke violence "on the basis of religion." St. Paul has no such authority to license one side of a debate to fight freestyle, while requiring the other to follow Marquis of Queensbury Rules.

What we have here, it must be emphasized, is not a prohibition of fighting words that are directed at certain persons or groups (which would be facially valid if it met the requirements of the Equal Protection Clause); but rather, a prohibition of fighting words that contain (as the Minnesota Supreme Court repeatedly emphasized) messages of "bias-motivated" hatred and in particular, as applied to this case, messages "based on virulent notions of racial supremacy." One must wholeheartedly agree with the Minnesota Supreme Court that "it is the responsibility, even the obligation, of diverse communities to confront such notions in whatever form they appear," but the manner of that confrontation cannot consist of selective limitations upon speech. . . .

Finally, St. Paul and its amici defend the conclusion of the Minnesota Supreme Court that, even if the ordinance regulates expression based on hostility towards its protected ideological content, this discrimination is nonetheless justified because it is narrowly tailored to serve compelling state interests. Specifically, they assert that the ordinance helps to ensure the basic human rights of members of groups that have historically been subjected to discrimination, including the right of such group members to live in peace where they wish. We do not doubt that these interests are compelling, and that the ordinance can be said to promote them. But the "danger of censorship" presented by a facially content-based statute . . . requires that that weapon be employed only where it is "necessary to serve the asserted [compelling] interest," . . . The existence of adequate content-neutral alternatives thus "undercuts significantly" any defense of such a statute, casting considerable doubt on the government's protestations that "the asserted justification is in fact an accurate description of the purpose and effect of the law." . . . The dispositive question in this case, therefore, is whether content discrimination is reasonably necessary to achieve St. Paul's compelling interests; it plainly is not. An ordinance not limited to the favored topics, for example, would have precisely the same beneficial effect. In fact the only interest distinctively served by the content limitation is that of displaying the city council's special hostility towards the particular biases thus singled out. That is precisely what the First Amendment forbids. The politicians of St. Paul are entitled to express that hostility—but not through the means of imposing unique limitations upon speakers who (however benightedly) disagree.

* * *

Let there be no mistake about our belief that burning a cross in someone's front yard is reprehensible. But St. Paul has sufficient means at its disposal to prevent such behavior without adding the First Amendment to the fire.

The judgment of the Minnesota Supreme Court is reversed, and the case is remanded for proceedings not inconsistent with this opinion.

It is so ordered.

Justice **White,** with whom Justice **Blackmun** and Justice **O'Connor** join, and with whom Justice **Stevens** joins except as to Part I(A), concurring in the judgment, said in part:

I agree with the majority that the judgment of the Minnesota Supreme Court should be reversed. However, our agreement ends there.

This case could easily be decided within the contours of established First Amendment law by holding, as petitioner argues, that the St. Paul ordinance is fatally overbroad because it criminalizes not only unprotected expression but expression protected by the First Amendment. Instead, "finding it unnecessary" to consider the questions upon which we granted review, the Court holds the ordinance facially unconstitutional on a ground that was never presented to the Minnesota Supreme Court, a ground that has not been briefed by the parties before this Court, a ground that requires serious departures from the teaching of prior cases . . . .

This Court ordinarily is not so eager to abandon its precedents. Twice within the past month, the Court has declined to overturn longstanding but controversial decisions on questions of constitutional law. . . . In each case, we had the benefit of full briefing on the critical issue, so that the parties and amici had the opportunity to apprise us of the impact of a change in the law. And in each case, the Court declined to abandon its precedents, invoking the principle of stare decisis. . . .

But in the present case, the majority casts aside long-established First Amendment doctrine without the benefit of briefing and adopts an untried theory. This is hardly a judicious way of proceeding, and the Court's reasoning in reaching its result is transparently wrong.

I.

A.

This Court's decisions have plainly stated that expression falling within certain limited categories so lacks the values the First Amendment was designed to protect that the Constitution affords no protection to that expression. Chaplinsky v. New Hampshire (1942), made the point in the clearest possible terms: "There are certain well-defined and narrowly limited classes of speech, the prevention and punishment of which have never been thought to raise any Constitutional problem. . . . It has been well observed that such utterances are no essential part of any exposition of ideas, and are of such slight social value as a step to truth that any benefit that may be derived from them is clearly outweighed by the social interest in order and morality." . . .

Thus, as the majority concedes, this Court has long held certain discrete categories of expression to be proscribable on the basis of their content. For instance, the Court has held that the individual who falsely shouts "fire" in a crowded theatre may not claim the protection of the First Amendment. Schenck v. United States (1919). The Court has concluded that neither child pornography, nor obscenity, is protected by the First Amendment. . . . Miller v. California (1973); Roth v. United States (1957). And the Court has observed that, "leaving aside the special considerations when public officials [and public figures] are the target, a libelous publication is not protected by the Constitution." . . .

All of these categories are content based. But the Court has held that First Amendment does not apply to them because their expressive content is worthless or of de minimis value to society. We have not departed from this principle, emphasizing repeatedly that, "within the confines of [these] given classifications, the evil to be restricted so overwhelmingly outweighs the expressive interests, if any, at stake, that no process of case-by-case adjudication is required." . . . This categorical approach has provided a principled and narrowly focused means for distinguishing between expression that the government may regulate freely and that which it may regulate on the basis of content only upon a showing of compelling need.

Today, however, the Court announces that earlier Courts did not mean their repeated statements that certain categories of expression are "not within the area of constitutionally protected speech." The present Court submits that such clear statements "must be taken in context" and are not "literally true."

To the contrary, those statements meant precisely what they said: The categorical approach is a firmly entrenched part of our First Amendment jurisprudence. Indeed, the Court in Roth reviewed the guarantees of freedom of expression in effect at the time of the ratification of the Constitution and concluded, "in light of this history, it is apparent that the unconditional phrasing of the First Amendment was not intended to protect every utterance."

In its decision today, the Court points to "nothing . . . in this Court's precedents warranting disregard of this longstanding tradition." Nevertheless, the majority holds that the First Amendment protects those narrow categories of expression long held to be undeserving of First Amendment protection—at least to the extent that lawmakers may not regulate some fighting words more

strictly than others because of their content. The Court announces that such content-based distinctions violate the First Amendment because "the government may not regulate use based on hostility—or favoritism—towards the underlying message expressed." Should the government want to criminalize certain fighting words, the Court now requires it to criminalize all fighting words.

The majority's observation that fighting words are "quite expressive indeed," is no answer. Fighting words are not a means of exchanging views, rallying supporters, or registering a protest; they are directed against individuals to provoke violence or to inflict injury. Therefore, the Court's insistence on inventing its brand of First Amendment underinclusiveness puzzles me. The overbreadth doctrine has the redeeming virtue of attempting to avoid the chilling of protected expression, . . . but the Court's new "underbreadth" creation serves no desirable function. Instead, it permits, indeed invites, the continuation of expressive conduct that in this case is evil and worthless in First Amendment terms until the city of St. Paul cures the underbreadth by adding to its ordinance a catch-all phrase such as "and all other fighting words that may constitutionally be subject to this ordinance."

Any contribution of this holding to First Amendment jurisprudence is surely a negative one, since it necessarily signals that expressions of violence, such as the message of intimidation and racial hatred conveyed by burning a cross on someone's lawn, are of sufficient value to outweigh the social interest in order and morality that has traditionally placed such fighting words outside the First Amendment. Indeed, by characterizing fighting words as a form of "debate," the majority legitimates hate speech as a form of public discussion.

Furthermore, the Court obscures the line between speech that could be regulated freely on the basis of content (i.e., the narrow categories of expression falling outside the First Amendment) and that which could be regulated on the basis of content only upon a showing of a compelling state interest (i.e., all remaining expression). By placing fighting words, which the Court has long held to be valueless, on at least equal constitutional footing with political discourse and other forms of speech that we have deemed to have the greatest social value, the majority devalues the latter category. . . .

B.

In a second break with precedent, the Court refuses to sustain the ordinance even though it would survive under the strict scrutiny applicable to other protected expression. Assuming, arguendo, that the St. Paul ordinance is a content-based regulation of protected expression, it nevertheless would pass First Amendment review under settled law upon a showing that the regulation " 'is necessary to serve a compelling state interest and is narrowly drawn to achieve that end.' " . . . St. Paul has urged that its ordinance, in the words of the majority, "helps to ensure the basic human rights of members of groups that have historically been subjected to discrimination . . . ." The Court expressly concedes that this interest is compelling and is promoted by the ordinance. Nevertheless, the Court treats strict scrutiny analysis as irrelevant to the constitutionality of the legislation: "The dispositive question . . . is whether content discrimination is reasonably necessary in order to achieve St. Paul's compelling interests; it plainly is not. An ordinance not limited to the favored topics would have precisely the same beneficial effect."

Under the majority's view, a narrowly drawn, content-based ordinance could never pass constitutional muster if the object of that legislation could be accomplished by banning a wider category of speech. This appears to be a general renunciation of strict scrutiny review, a fundamental tool of First Amendment analysis. . . .

As with its rejection of the Court's categorical analysis, the majority offers no reasoned basis for discarding our firmly established strict scrutiny analysis at this time. The majority appears to believe that its doctrinal revisionism is necessary to prevent our elected lawmakers from prohibiting libel against members of one political party but not another and from enacting similarly preposterous laws. The majority is misguided.

Although the First Amendment does not apply to categories of unprotected speech, such as fighting words, the Equal Protection Clause requires that the regulation of unprotected speech be rationally related to a legitimate government interest. A defamation statute that drew distinctions on the basis of political affiliation or "an ordinance prohibiting only those legally obscene works that contain criticism of the city government," would unquestionably fail rational basis review. . . .

As I see it, the Court's theory does not work and will do nothing more than confuse the law. Its selection of this case to rewrite First Amendment law is particularly inexplicable, because the whole problem could have been avoided by deciding this case under settled First Amendment principles.

II.

Although I disagree with the Court's analysis, I do agree with its conclusion: The St. Paul ordinance is unconstitutional. However, I would decide the case on overbreadth grounds.

We have emphasized time and again that overbreadth doctrine is an exception to the established principle that "a person to whom a statute may constitutionally be applied will not be heard to challenge that statute on the ground that it may conceivably be applied unconstitutionally to others, in other situations not before the Court." . . . A defendant being prosecuted for speech or expressive conduct may challenge the law on its face if it reaches protected expression, even when that person's activities are not protected by the First Amendment. This is because "the possible harm to society in permitting some unprotected speech to go unpunished is out-

weighed by the possibility that protected speech of others may be muted." . . .

I agree with petitioner that the ordinance is invalid on its face. Although the ordinance as construed reaches categories of speech that are constitutionally unprotected, it also criminalizes a substantial amount of expression that—however repugnant—is shielded by the First Amendment. . . .

In construing the St. Paul ordinance, the Minnesota Supreme Court drew upon the definition of fighting words that appears in Chaplinsky—words "which by their very utterance inflict injury or tend to incite an immediate breach of the peace." However, the Minnesota court was far from clear in identifying the "injuries" inflicted by the expression that St. Paul sought to regulate. Indeed, the Minnesota court emphasized (tracking the language of the ordinance) that "the ordinance censors only those displays that one knows or should know will create anger, alarm or resentment based on racial, ethnic, gender or religious bias." I therefore understand the court to have ruled that St. Paul may constitutionally prohibit expression that "by its very utterance" causes "anger, alarm or resentment."

Our fighting words cases have made clear, however, that such generalized reactions are not sufficient to strip expression of its constitutional protection. The mere fact that expressive activity causes hurt feelings, offense, or resentment does not render the expression unprotected. . . .

III.

Today, the Court has disregarded two established principles of First Amendment law without providing a coherent replacement theory. Its decision is an arid, doctrinaire interpretation, driven by the frequently irresistible impulse of judges to tinker with the First Amendment. The decision is mischievous at best and will surely confuse the lower courts. I join the judgment, but not the folly of the opinion.

Justice **Blackmun**, concurring in the judgment, said in part:

I regret what the Court has done in this case. The majority opinion signals one of two possibilities: it will serve as precedent for future cases, or it will not. Either result is disheartening.

In the first instance, by deciding that a State cannot regulate speech that causes great harm unless it also regulates speech that does not (setting law and logic on their heads), the Court seems to abandon the categorical approach, and inevitably to relax the level of scrutiny applicable to content-based laws. As Justice White points out, this weakens the traditional protections of speech. If all expressive activity must be accorded the same protection, that protection will be scant. . . .

I concur in the judgment, however, because I agree with Justice White that this particular ordinance reaches beyond fighting words to speech protected by the First Amendment.

Justice **Stevens,** with whom Justice **White** and Justice **Blackmun** join as to Part I, concurring in the judgment, said in part:

I.

As an initial matter, the Court's revision of the categorical approach seems to me something of an adventure in a doctrinal wonderland, for the concept of "obscene antigovernment" speech is fantastical. The category of the obscene is very narrow; to be obscene, expression must be found by the trier of fact to "appeal to the prurient interest, . . . depict or describe, in a patently offensive way, sexual conduct, [and] taken as a whole, *lac[k] serious literary, artistic, political or scientific value.*" Miller v. California (1973) (emphasis added). "Obscene antigovernment" speech, then, is a contradiction in terms: If expression is antigovernment, it does not "lack serious . . . political . . . value" and cannot be obscene.

The Court attempts to bolster its argument by likening its novel analysis to that applied to restrictions on the time, place, or manner of expression or on expressive conduct. It is true that loud speech in favor of the Republican Party can be regulated because it is loud, but not because it is pro-Republican; and it is true that the public burning of the American flag can be regulated because it involves public burning and not because it involves the flag. But these analogies are inapposite. In each of these examples, the two elements (e.g., loudness and pro-Republican orientation) can coexist; in the case of "obscene antigovernment" speech, however, the presence of one element ("obscenity") by definition means the absence of the other. To my mind, it is unwise and unsound to craft a new doctrine based on such highly speculative hypotheticals.

I am, however, even more troubled by the second step of the Court's analysis—namely, its conclusion that the St. Paul ordinance is an unconstitutional content-based regulation of speech. Drawing on broadly worded dicta, the Court establishes a near-absolute ban on content-based regulations of expression and holds that the First Amendment prohibits the regulation of fighting words by subject matter. Thus, while the Court rejects the "all-or-nothing-at-all" nature of the categorical approach, it promptly embraces an absolutism of its own: within a particular "proscribable" category of expression, the Court holds, a government must either proscribe *all* speech or no speech at all. This aspect of the Court's ruling fundamentally misunderstands the role and constitutional status of content-based regulations on speech, conflicts with the very nature of First Amendment jurisprudence, and disrupts well-settled principles of First Amendment law. . . .

This is true at every level of First Amendment law. In broadest terms, our entire First Amendment jurisprudence creates a regime based on the content of speech. The scope of the First Amendment is determined by the content of expressive activity: Although the First Amendment broadly protects "speech," it does not protect the right to "fix prices, breach contracts, make false warranties, place bets with bookies, threaten, [or] extort." Whether an agreement among competitors is a violation of the Sherman Act or protected activity under the Noerr-Pennington doctrine hinges upon the content of the agreement. Similarly, "the line between permissible advocacy and impermissible incitation to crime or violence depends, not merely on the setting in which the speech occurs, but also on exactly what the speaker had to say." . . .

Likewise, whether speech falls within one of the categories of "unprotected" or "proscribable" expression is determined, in part, by its content. Whether a magazine is obscene, a gesture a fighting word, or a photograph child pornography is determined, in part, by its content. Even within categories of protected expression, the First Amendment status of speech is fixed by its content. New York Times Co. v. Sullivan (1964) . . . establish[es] that the level of protection given to speech depends upon its subject matter: speech about public officials or matters of public concern receives greater protection than speech about other topics. It can, therefore, scarcely be said that the regulation of expressive activity cannot be predicated on its content: much of our First Amendment jurisprudence is premised on the assumption that content makes a difference. . . .

All of these cases involved the selective regulation of speech based on content—precisely the sort of regulation the Court invalidates today. Such selective regulations are unavoidably content based, but they are not, in my opinion, "presumptively invalid." . . .

Our First Amendment decisions have created a rough hierarchy in the constitutional protection of speech. Core political speech occupies the highest, most protected position; commercial speech and nonobscene, sexually explicit speech are regarded as a sort of second-class expression; obscenity and fighting words receive the least protection of all. Assuming that the Court is correct that this last class of speech is not wholly "unprotected," it certainly does not follow that fighting words and obscenity receive the same sort of protection afforded core political speech. Yet in ruling that proscribable speech cannot be regulated based on subject matter, the Court does just that. Perversely, this gives fighting words greater protection than is afforded commercial speech. If Congress can prohibit false advertising directed at airline passengers without also prohibiting false advertising directed at bus passengers and if a city can prohibit political advertisements in its buses while allowing other advertisements, it is ironic to hold that a city cannot regulate fighting words based on "race, color, creed, religion or gender" while leaving unregulated fighting words based on "union membership or homosexuality." The Court today turns First Amendment law on its head: Communication that was once entirely unprotected (and that still can be wholly proscribed) is now entitled to greater protection than commercial speech—and possibly greater protection than core political speech. . . .

III.

As the foregoing suggests, I disagree with both the Court's and part of Justice White's analysis of the constitutionality of the St. Paul ordinance. Unlike the Court, I do not believe that all content-based regulations are equally infirm and presumptively invalid; unlike Justice White, I do not believe that fighting words are wholly unprotected by the First Amendment. To the contrary, I believe our decisions establish a more complex and subtle analysis, one that considers the content and context of the regulated speech, and the nature and scope of the restriction on speech. . . .

WALKER v. BIRMINGHAM

388 U. S. 307; 87 S. Ct. 1824; 18 L. Ed. 2d 1210 (1967)

The difficulties that confront a state in imposing those ''reasonable'' limits on free speech which the Constitution allows are illustrated by cases involving the suppression of public nuisances. The Supreme Court held that a statute which forbade entirely the distribution of literature was unconstitutional. In Jamison v. Texas (1943) an ordinance forbade the distribution of handbills on the streets of Dallas. Mrs. Jamison, a member of Jehovah's Witnesses, was convicted of violating the ordinance and fined five dollars. The Court held that ''one who is rightfully on a street which the state has left open to the public carries with him there as elsewhere the constitutional right to express his views in an orderly fashion. . . . The right to distribute handbills concerning religious subjects on the streets may not be prohibited at all times, at all places, and under all circumstances.''

The state may, on the other hand, place freedom of speech under reasonable police regulations for the protection of the recognized social interests of the community. In Kovacs v. Cooper (1949) the Court upheld a Trenton, New Jersey, ordinance which forbade the use on the streets of a sound-truck which emitted ''loud and raucous noises.'' The Court found that ''loud and raucous'' was a sufficiently clear definition of the crime, since it has ''through daily use acquired a content that conveys to any interested person a sufficiently accurate concept of what is forbidden.'' Moreover, the restriction was a reasonable one, since ''the unwilling listener is not like the passer-by who may be offered a pamphlet in the street but cannot be made to take it. In his home or on the street he is practically helpless to escape this interference with his privacy by loud speakers except through the protection of the municipality.'' Here the Court was striking a balance between the right to quiet and privacy and the right to free speech.

What a state may not limit directly by statute, it *may not permit a policeman or other officer to limit under a grant of administrative discretion which amounts to censorship. Many municipalities have used the device of requiring a license for all public modes of expression, and making it a crime to violate the license requirement. The Supreme Court has almost uniformly held these ordinances to be unconstitutional limitations on freedom of speech and press. If the licensing officer has authority to pass on the desirability of the intended speech, or has authority broad enough to forbid a speech protected by the First Amendment, the ordinance is void on its face because it establishes previous censorship, condemned by the Court in Near v. Minnesota (1931). Thus in Lovell v. Griffin (1938) the Court held void a municipal ordinance which punished as a nuisance the distribution of any literature on the streets without a license from the city manager. The Court emphasized that ''the ordinance is not limited to 'literature' that is obscene or offensive to public morals or that advocates unlawful conduct. . . . There is . . . no restriction in its application with respect to time or place. It is not limited to ways which might be regarded as inconsistent with the maintenance of public order. . . .'' In Largent v. Texas (1943) an ordinance was held void which forbade soliciting orders or selling books without a license which the mayor had power to issue if he deemed it ''proper or advisable.'' In Saia v. New York (1948) the Court held void an ordinance which forbade the use of a sound-truck on the streets without the permission of the chief of police: ''There are no standards prescribed for the exercise of his discretion. The statute is not narrowly drawn to regulate the hours or places of use of loud-speakers, or the volume of sound. . . .'' And in Kunz v. New York (1951) the Court reversed the conviction of an itinerant preacher for preaching without a license after his application had been disapproved with no reason given. ''It is noteworthy that there is no mention in the ordinance of reasons for which such a permit application can be refused. This interpretation allows the police commissioner, an administrative official, to exercise discretion in denying subsequent permit applications on the basis of his interpretation, at that time, of what is deemed to be conduct condemned by the ordinance. We have here, then, an ordinance which gives an administrative official discretionary power to control in advance the right of citizens to speak on religious matters on the streets of New York. As such, the ordinance is clearly invalid as a prior restraint on the exercise of First Amendment rights.'' The Court was unimpressed with the fact that Kunz had had a previous license revoked for ridiculing and denouncing other religions.*

What the state may do directly by statute it may also do through the device of administrative discretion provided the discretion is so narrow that the administrator may not censor speech or press. In Cox v. New Hampshire (1941) the Court sustained an ordinance that required a permit from a license board in order to parade in the streets. A group of Jehovah's Witnesses staged an ''information march'' without applying for a permit and were convicted of violating the ordinance;

the state court held that any other form of expression was open to them, and "the defendants, separately, or collectively in groups not constituting a parade or procession" were "under no contemplation of the Act." Furthermore, the discretion of the license board had to be exercised with "uniformity of method of treatment upon the facts of each application, free from improper or inappropriate considerations and from unfair discrimination." The statutory mandate was held to be a "systematic consistent and just order of treatment, with reference to the convenience of public use of the highways." This, the Supreme Court found, was a valid use of the authority to "control the use of its public streets for parades or processions."

But if a state may not deny a person a license to speak, may it, nevertheless, enjoin a person from speaking and then punish that person when the injunction is lifted? This problem first arose in the case of Thomas v. Collins (1945). A Texas statute required every labor union organizer operating in the state to secure from the secretary of state an organizer's card before soliciting any members for a union. In order to get the card organizers had to give their name and union affiliations and show their credentials. The secretary of state had no discretion to refuse to register such organizers if these requirements were met. When registered, they were given cards which they were required to carry with them and show to any person they solicited for membership. R. J. Thomas, president of the United Automobile Workers, went to Texas after the passage of this act for the express purpose of contesting its validity. He announced his intention to address a labor union meeting, and this plan was widely advertised in advance. He did not apply for registration as a labor organizer as required by the statute. He addressed a meeting of union men and he specifically invited any nonunion person present to join the union. Prior to the meeting, a restraining order was served on Thomas, forbidding him to address the meeting in the capacity of an organizer since he had not registered; and he was later cited for contempt for a deliberate and willful violation of the order.

The Court held the statute void on two grounds. First, the statute was so broad as to make possible the punishment of legitimate speech. It forbade soliciting members, and "how," the Court said, "one might 'laud unionism,' as the State and the State Supreme Court conceded Thomas was free to do, yet in these circumstances not imply an invitation, is hard to conceive. . . . The restriction's effect, as applied, in a very practical sense was to prohibit Thomas not only to solicit members and memberships, but also to speak in advocacy of the cause of trade unionism. . . ." In the second place, there was not a clear and present danger of bringing about a sufficiently substantial injury to the public to justify the restriction: "We cannot say that 'solicit' in this setting is such a dangerous word. So far as free speech alone is concerned, there can be no ban or restriction or burden placed on the use of such a word except on showing of exceptional circumstances where the public safety, morality or health is involved or some other substantial in-

terest of the community is at stake. . . . A restriction so destructive of the right of public discussion, without greater or more imminent danger to the public interest than existed in this case, is incompatible with the freedoms secured by the First Amendment. . . . If the exercise of the rights of free speech and free assembly cannot be made a crime, we do not think this can be accomplished by the device of requiring previous registration as a condition for exercising them and making such a condition the foundation for restraining in advance their exercise and for imposing a penalty for violating such a restraining order."

A similar problem was presented in Poulos v. New Hampshire (1953), which arose under an ordinance like the one involved in the Cox case. Poulos, a Jehovah's Witness, applied for a permit to speak in Goodwin Park in Portsmouth on a particular Sunday and was refused; Poulos spoke without the permit and was arrested. The state court interpreted the statute as it had in the Cox case, as requiring uniformity and impartiality of treatment. It found that Poulos had not received such treatment, and that the denial of the license had been arbitrary and unreasonable. It held, however, that Poulos was properly convicted; he had no right to violate the ordinance, but should have brought a civil suit in the courts to compel the issuance of a license.

The Supreme Court sustained the conviction on the ground that the ordinance was valid and the state could validly require that arbitrary administrative action be corrected by orderly court procedure: "It must be admitted that judicial correction of arbitrary refusal by administrators to perform official duties under valid laws is exulcerating and costly. But to allow applicants to proceed without the required permits to run businesses, erect structures, purchase firearms, transport or store explosives or inflammatory products, hold public meetings without prior safety arrangements or take other unauthorized action is apt to cause breaches of the peace or create public dangers. The valid requirements of license are for the good of the applicants and the public. It would be unreal to say that such official failures to act in accordance with state law, redressable by state judicial procedures, are state acts violative of the Federal Constitution. Delay is unfortunate, but the expense and annoyance of litigation is a price citizens must pay for life in an orderly society where the rights of the First Amendment have a real and abiding meaning. Nor can we say that a state's requirement that redress must be sought through appropriate judicial procedure violates due process." The Court distinguished this case from Thomas v. Collins, holding that there the statute was void on its face. "The statutes were as though they did not exist. Therefore there were no offenses in violation of a valid law. In the present prosecution there was a valid ordinance, an unlawful refusal of a license, with the remedial state procedure for the correction of the error. . . . Our Constitution does not require that we approve the violation of a reasonable requirement for a license to speak in public parks because an official error occurred in refusing a proper application."

While *Thomas v. Collins* suggests that a person is free to ignore a judicial restraining order if the statute under which it is issued is void on its face, the case printed below cast serious doubt upon the vitality of this holding. In April of 1963, Martin Luther King, Jr., together with two other ministers, Wyatt T. Walker and Fred L. Shuttlesworth, announced plans for a "march" on Good Friday. They requested, and were denied, a permit for the march under § 1159 of the Birmingham city code which provided that the city commission "shall grant a written permit for such parade, procession or other public demonstration, prescribing the streets or other public ways which may be used therefor, unless in its judgment the public welfare, peace, safety, health, decency, good order, morals or convenience require that it be refused."

Apparently fearing the march would take place without a permit, city officials applied the Wednesday before Good Friday for an injunction against "participating in or encouraging mass street parades or mass processions without a permit." The injunction was served the following day, and that night a meeting was held at which one of the petitioners announced that "injunction or no injunction we are going to march tomorrow." No attempt was made to seek judicial review of the injunction, and the petitioners marched both on Good Friday and again on Easter Sunday, leading a group of fifty to sixty followers each time.

The petitioners were convicted both of disobeying the injunction and of marching without a license, receiving sentences of five days in jail and a $50 fine for the first and ninety days at hard labor (plus forty-eight days at hard labor in default of payment of a $75 fine and $24 costs) for the second.

Because of their different rates of movement through the judicial labyrinth, the two cases reached the Supreme Court almost two years apart. When *Shuttlesworth v. Birmingham* (1969) reached the Court it found the parade ordinance void on its face. "There can be no doubt that the Birmingham ordinance, as it was written, conferred upon the City Commission virtually unbridled and absolute power to prohibit any "parade," "procession," or "demonstration" on the city's streets or public ways. For in deciding whether or not to withhold a permit, the members of the Commission were to be guided only by their own ideas of "public welfare, peace, safety, health, decency, good order, morals or convenience." When the ordinance finally reached the Alabama supreme court it was given a very restrictive interpretation which the Supreme Court was prepared to assume made it valid. But "it would have taken extraordinary clairvoyance for anyone to perceive that this language meant what the Supreme Court of Alabama was destined to find that it meant more than four years later" and "we would hesitate long before assuming that either the members of the Commission or the petitioner possessed any such clairvoyance at the time of the Good Friday march." The Court also noted that success of Alabama's attempt to validate the ordinance "would depend upon, among other things, the availability of expeditious judicial review of the Commission's refusal of a permit. ... *Freedman v. Maryland [1965]*." It is interesting to speculate what the outcomes might have been had Shuttlesworth been decided before Walker, rather than the other way around.

Mr. Justice **Stewart** delivered the opinion of the Court, saying in part:

... On Easter Sunday, April 14, a crowd of between 1,500 and 2,000 people congregated in the midafternoon in the vicinity of Seventh Avenue and Eleventh Street North in Birmingham. One of the petitioners was seen organizing members of the crowd in formation. A group of about 50, headed by three other petitioners, started down the sidewalk two abreast. At least one other petitioner was among the marchers. Some 300 or 400 people from among the onlookers followed in a crowd that occupied the entire width of the street and overflowed onto the sidewalks. Violence occurred. Members of the crowd threw rocks that injured a newspaperman and damaged a police motorcycle.

The next day the city officials who had requested the injunction applied to the state circuit court for an order to show cause why the petitioners should not be held in contempt for violating it. At the ensuing hearing the petitioners sought to attack the constitutionality of the injunction on the ground that it was vague and overbroad, and restrained free speech. They also sought to attack the Birmingham parade ordinance upon similar grounds, and upon the further ground that the ordinance had previously been administered in an arbitrary and discriminatory manner.

The circuit judge refused to consider any of these contentions, pointing out that there had been neither a motion to dissolve the injunction, nor an effort to comply with it by applying for a permit from the city commission before engaging in the Good Friday and Easter Sunday parades. Consequently, the court held that the only issues before it were whether it had jurisdiction to issue the temporary injunction, and whether thereafter the petitioners had knowingly violated it. Upon these issues the court found against the petitioners, and imposed upon each of them a sentence of five days in jail and a $50 fine, in accord with an Alabama statute.

The Supreme Court of Alabama affirmed. ...

Howat v. Kansas [1922] was decided by this Court almost 50 years ago. That was a case in which people had been punished by a Kansas trial court for refusing to obey an anti-strike injunction issued under the state industrial relations act. They had claimed a right to disobey the court's order upon the ground that the state statute and the injunction based upon it were invalid under the Federal Constitution. The Supreme Court of Kansas had affirmed the judgment, holding that the trial court "had general power to issue injunctions in equity and that, even if its exercise of the power was erroneous, the injunction was not void, and the defendants were precluded from attacking it in this collateral proceeding . . . that, if the injunction was erroneous, jurisdiction was not thereby forfeited, that the error was subject to correction only by the ordinary method of appeal, and disobedience to the order constituted contempt.''

This Court, in dismissing the writ of error, not only unanimously accepted but fully approved the validity of the rule of state law upon which the judgment of the Kansas court was grounded:

"An injunction duly issuing out of a court of general jurisdiction with equity powers upon pleadings properly invoking its action, and served upon persons made parties therein and within the jurisdiction, must be obeyed by them however erroneous the action of the court may be, even if the error be in the assumption of the validity of a seeming but void law going to the merits of the case. It is for the court of first instance to determine the question of the validity of the law, and until its decision is reversed for error by orderly review, either by itself or by a higher court, its orders based on its decision are to be respected, and disobedience of them is contempt of its lawful authority, to be punished.''

The rule of state law accepted and approved in Howat v. Kansas is consistent with the rule of law followed by the federal courts.

In the present case, however, we are asked to hold that this rule of law, upon which the Alabama courts relied, was constitutionally impermissible. We are asked to say that the Constitution compelled Alabama to allow the petitioners to violate this injunction, to organize and engage in these mass street parades and demonstrations, without any previous effort on their part to have the injunction dissolved or modified, or any attempt to secure a parade permit in accordance with its terms. Whatever the limits of Howat v. Kansas, we cannot accept the petitioners' contentions in the circumstances of this case.

Without question the state court that issued the injunction had, as a court of equity, jurisdiction over the petitioners and over the subject matter of the controversy. And this is not a case where the injunction was transparently invalid or had only a frivolous pretense to validity. We have consistently recognized the strong interest of state and local governments in regulating the use of their streets and other public places. Cox v. New Hampshire [1941]; Kovacs v. Cooper [1949]; Poulos v. New Hampshire [1953]; Adderley v. Florida [1966]. When protest takes the form of mass demonstrations, parades, or picketing on public streets and sidewalks, the free passage of traffic and the prevention of public disorder and violence become important objects of legitimate state concern. As the Court stated, in Cox v. Louisiana, "We emphatically reject the notion . . . that the First and Fourteenth Amendments afford the same kind of freedom to those who would communicate ideas by conduct such as patrolling, marching, and picketing on streets and highways, as these amendments afford to those who communicate ideas by pure speech.'' . . .

. . . The generality of the language contained in the Birmingham parade ordinance upon which the injunction was based would unquestionably raise substantial constitutional issues concerning some of its provisions. . . . The petitioners, however, did not even attempt to apply to the Alabama courts for an authoritative construction of the ordinance. Had they done so, those courts might have given the licensing authority granted in the ordinance a narrow and precise scope, as did the New Hampshire courts in Cox v. New Hampshire and Poulos v. New Hampshire. . . . Here, just as in Cox and Poulos, it could not be assumed that this ordinance was void on its face.

The breadth and vagueness of the injunction itself would also unquestionably be subject to substantial constitutional question. But the way to raise that question was to apply to the Alabama courts to have the injunction modified or dissolved. The injunction in all events clearly prohibited mass parading without a permit, and the evidence shows that the petitioners fully understood that prohibition when they violated it.

. . . The petitioners also claim that they were free to disobey the injunction because the parade ordinance on which it was based had been administered in the past in an arbitrary and discriminatory fashion. In support of this claim they sought to introduce evidence that, a few days before the injunction issued, requests for permits to picket had been made to a member of the city commission. One request had been rudely rebuffed, and this same official had later made clear that he was without power to grant the permit alone, since the issuance of such permits was the responsibility of the entire city commission. Assuming the truth of this proffered evidence, it does not follow that the parade ordinance was void on its face. The petitioners, moreover, did not apply for a permit either to the commission itself or to any commissioner after the injunction issued. Had they done so, and had the permit been refused, it is clear that their claim of arbitrary or discriminatory administration of the ordinance would have been considered by the state circuit court upon a motion to dissolve the injunction.

This case would arise in quite a different constitutional posture if the petitioners, before disobeying the injunction, had challenged it in the Alabama courts, and had been met with delay or frustration of their constitutional claims. But there is no showing that such would have been the fate of a timely motion to modify or dissolve the injunction. There was an interim of two days between the issuance of the injunction and the Good Friday march. The petitioners give absolutely no explanation of why they did not make some application to the state court during that period. The injunction had issued ex parte; if the court had been presented with the petitioners' contentions, it might well have dissolved or at least modified its order in some respects. If it had not done so, Alabama procedure would have provided for an expedited process of appellate review. It cannot be presumed that the Alabama courts would have ignored the petitioners' constitutional claims. Indeed, these contentions were accepted in another case by an Alabama appellate court that struck down on direct review the conviction under this very ordinance of one of these same petitioners. . . .

The rule of law that Alabama followed in this case reflects a belief that in the fair administration of justice no man can be judge in his own case, however exalted his station, however righteous his motives, and irrespective of his race, color, politics, or religion. This Court cannot hold that the petitioners were constitutionally free to ignore all the procedures of the law and carry their battle to the streets. One may sympathize with the petitioners' impatient commitment to their cause. But respect for judicial process is a small price to pay for the civilizing hand of law, which alone can give abiding meaning to constitutional freedom.

Affirmed.

Mr. Chief Justice **Warren,** whom Mr. Justice **Brennan** and Mr. Justice **Fortas** join, dissenting, said in part:

Petitioners in this case contend that they were convicted under an ordinance that is unconstitutional on its face because it submits their First and Fourteenth Amendment rights to free speech and peaceful assembly to the unfettered discretion of local officials. They further contend that the ordinance was unconstitutionally applied to them because the local officials used their discretion to prohibit peaceful demonstrations by a group whose political viewpoint the officials opposed. The Court does not dispute these contentions, but holds that petitioners may nonetheless be convicted and sent to jail because the patently unconstitutional ordinance was copied into an injunction—issued ex parte without prior notice or hearing on the request of the Commissioner of Public Safety—forbidding all persons having notice of the injunction to violate the ordinance without any limitation of time. I dissent because I do not believe that the fundamental protections of the Constitution were meant to be so easily evaded, or that "the civilizing hand of law" would be hampered in the slightest by enforcing the First Amendment in this case. . . .

The salient facts can be stated very briefly. Petitioners are Negro ministers who sought to express their concern about racial discrimination in Birmingham, Alabama, by holding peaceful protest demonstrations in that city on Good Friday and Easter Sunday, 1963. For obvious reasons, it was important for the significance of the demonstrations that they be held on those particular dates. A representative of petitioners' organization went to the City Hall and asked "to see the person or persons in charge to issue permits, permits for parading, picketing, and demonstrating." She was directed to Public Safety Commissioner Connor, who denied her request for a permit in terms that left no doubt that petitioners were not going to be issued a permit under any circumstances. "He said, 'No, you will not get a permit in Birmingham, Alabama to picket. I will picket you over to the City Jail,' and he repeated that twice." A second, telegraphic request was also summarily denied, in a telegram signed by "Eugene 'Bull' Connor," with the added information that permits could be issued only by the full City Commission, a three-man body consisting of Commissioner Connor and two others.* According to petitioners' offer of proof, the truth of which is assumed for purposes of this case, parade permits had uniformly been issued for all other groups by the city clerk on the request of the traffic bureau of the police department, which was under Commissioner Connor's direction. The requirement that the approval of the full Commission be obtained was applied only to this one group.

Understandably convinced that the City of Birmingham was not going to authorize their demonstrations under any circumstances, petitioners proceeded with their plans despite Commissioner Connor's orders. On Wednesday, April 10, at 9 in the evening, the city filed in a state circuit court a bill of complaint seeking an ex parte injunction. . . .

. . . The Circuit Court issued the injunction in the form requested, and in effect ordered petitioners and all other persons having notice of the order to refrain for an unlimited time from carrying on any demonstrations without a permit. A permit, of course, was clearly unobtainable; the city would not have sought this injunction if it had any intention of issuing one.

Petitioners were served with copies of the injunction at various times on Thursday and on Good Friday. Unable to believe that such a blatant and broadly drawn prior restraint on their First Amendment rights could be valid, they announced their intention to defy it and went ahead with the planned peaceful demonstrations on Easter weekend. On the following Monday, when they promptly filed a motion to dissolve the injunction, the court found them in contempt, holding that they had waived all their First Amendment rights by disobeying the court order.

These facts lend no support to the court's charges that petitioners were presuming to act as judges in their own case, or that they had a disregard for the judicial process. They did not flee the jurisdiction or refuse to appear in the Alabama courts. Having violated the injunction, they promptly submitted themselves to the courts to test the constitutionality of the injunction and the ordinance it parroted. They were in essentially the same position as persons who challenge the constitutionality of a statute by violating it, and then defend the en-

---

*. . . The attitude of the city administration in general and of its Public Safety Commissioner in particular are a matter of public record, of course, and are familiar to this Court from previous litigation. See Shuttlesworth v. City of Birmingham (1965); Shuttlesworth v. City of Birmingham (1964); Shuttlesworth v. City of Birmingham (1963); Gober v. City of Birmingham (1963); In Re Shuttlesworth (1962). The United States Commission on Civil Rights found continuing abuse of civil rights protestors by the Birmingham police, including use of dogs, clubs, and firehoses. . . . Commissioner Eugene "Bull" Connor, a self-proclaimed white supremacist, . . . made no secret of his personal attitude toward the rights of Negroes and the decisions of this Court. He vowed that racial integration would never come to Birmingham, and wore a button inscribed "Never" to advertise that vow. Yet the Court indulges in speculation that these civil rights protesters might have obtained a permit from this city and this man had they made enough repeated applications.

suing criminal prosecution on constitutional grounds. It has never been thought that violation of a statute indicated such a disrespect for the legislature that the violator always must be punished even if the statute was unconstitutional. . . .

I do not believe that giving this Court's seal of approval to such a gross misuse of the judicial process is likely to lead to greater respect for the law any more than it is likely to lead to greater protection for First Amendment freedoms. The ex parte temporary injunction has a long and odious history in this country, and its susceptibility to misuse is all too apparent from the facts of the case. As a weapon against strikes, it proved so effective in the hands of judges friendly to employers that Congress was forced to take the drastic step of removing from federal district courts the jurisdiction to issue injunctions in labor disputes. The labor injunction fell into disrepute largely because it was abused in precisely the same way that the injunctive power was abused in this case. Judges who were not sympathetic to the union cause commonly issued, without notice or hearing, broad restraining orders addressed to large numbers of persons and forbidding them to engage in acts that were either legally permissible or, if illegal, that could better have been left to the regular course of criminal prosecution. The injunctions might later be dissolved, but in the meantime strikes would be crippled because the occasion on which concerted activity might have been effective had passed. Such injunctions, so long discredited as weapons against concerted labor activities, have now been given new life by this Court as weapons against the exercise of First Amendment freedoms. Respect for the courts and for judicial process was not increased by the history of the labor injunction. . . .

. . . The majority opinion in this case rests essentially on a single precedent, and that a case the authority of which has clearly been undermined by subsequent decisions. Howat v. Kansas (1922), was decided in the days when the labor injunction was in fashion. . . .

It is not necessary to question the continuing validity of the holding in Howat v. Kansas, however, to demonstrate that neither it nor the Mine Workers [United States v. United Mine Workers (1947)] case supports the holding of the majority in this case. In Howat the subpoena and injunction were issued to enable the Kansas Court of Industrial Relations to determine an underlying labor dispute. In the Mine Workers case, the District Court issued a temporary anti-strike injunction to preserve existing conditions during the time it took to decide whether it had authority to grant the Government relief in a complex and difficult action of enormous importance to the national economy. In both cases the orders were of questionable legality, but in both cases they were reasonably necessary to enable the court or administrative tribunal to decide an underlying controversy of considerable importance before it at the time. This case involves an entirely different situation. The Alabama Circuit Court did not issue this temporary injunction to preserve existing conditions while it proceeded to decide some underlying dispute. There was no underlying dispute before it, and the court in practical effect merely added a judicial signature to a pre-existing criminal ordinance. Just as the court had no need to issue the injunction to preserve its ability to decide some underlying dispute, the city had no need of an injunction to impose a criminal penalty for demonstrating on the streets without a permit. The ordinance already accomplished that. In point of fact, there is only one apparent reason why the city sought this injunction and why the court issued it: to make it possible to punish petitioners for contempt rather than for violating the ordinance, and thus to immunize the unconstitutional statute and its unconstitutional application from any attack. I regret that this strategy has been so successful. . . .

Mr. Justice **Douglas,** with whom **The Chief Justice,** Mr. Justice **Brennan,** and Mr. Justice **Fortas** concur, dissenting, said in part:

The right to defy an unconstitutional statute is basic in our scheme. Even when an ordinance requires a permit to make a speech, to deliver a sermon, to picket, to parade, or to assemble, it need not be honored when it is invalid on its face. Lovell v. Griffin [1938] . . . Thomas v. Collins [1945]. . . .

Mr. Justice **Brennan,** with whom **The Chief Justice,** Mr. Justice **Douglas,** and Mr. Justice **Fortas** joined, wrote a dissenting opinion.

CENSORSHIP AND THE RIGHT TO PUBLISH

NEAR v. MINNESOTA

283 U. S. 697; 51 S. Ct. 625; 75 L. Ed. 1357
(1931)

The struggle to achieve freedom of the press has been long and difficult. Once the invention of the printing press made possible the dissemination of information to the people generally, it became painfully clear to the monarchs of Europe that here lay a serious threat to their absolute powers. Their first reaction was to outlaw and destroy this new engine of seditious propaganda. Failing in this, they resorted to a system of licensing under which all publications, before being released to the public, had to be submitted to the King's Licenser. Serious penalties were meted out to those whose publications did not bear the official "imprimatur." Obviously no criticism of the sovereign or government, whether just or unjust, could be published under such a system; and the long fight against the official licenser was a major part of the fight to establish democratic institutions.

It is against this background that the case of Near v. Minnesota must be read. The law involved had been dubbed the "Minnesota gag law." It provided for the "padlocking," by injunctive process, of a newspaper for printing matter which was scandalous, malicious, defamatory, or obscene. Such a "padlock" injunction, enforceable by the customary process of summary punishment for contempt of court, could be lifted only by convincing the judge who issued it that the publication would, in the future, be unobjectionable. This, in the judgment of the majority of the Court, amounted to previous censorship of publication and a violation of long-established canons of free speech and press.

The present case represents the climax of a striking evolution in our constitutional law whereby freedom of speech and press was at last effectively "nationalized" or confided to the protection of the federal courts against both national and state impairment. The steps in that evolution are traced in the note to Powell v. Alabama (1932). The case of Near v. Minnesota was the first case in which a state law was held unconstitutional as violating that freedom of press protected by the due process clause of the Fourteenth Amendment.

Mr. Chief Justice **Hughes** delivered the opinion of the Court, saying in part:

Chapter 285 of the Session Laws of Minnesota for the year 1925 provides for the abatement, as a public nuisance, of a "malicious, scandalous and defamatory newspaper, magazine or other periodical." Section one of the act is as follows:

"Section 1: Any person who, as an individual, or as a member or employee of a firm, or association or organization, or as an officer, director, member or employee of a corporation, shall be engaged in the business of regularly or customarily producing, publishing or circulating, having in possession, selling or giving away,

(a) an obscene, lewd and lascivious newspaper, magazine, or other periodical, or

(b) a malicious, scandalous and defamatory newspaper, magazine or other periodical, is guilty of a nuisance, and all persons guilty of such nuisance may be enjoined, as hereinafter provided.

"Participation in such business shall constitute a commission of such nuisance and render the participant liable and subject to the proceedings, orders and judgments provided for in this act. Ownership, in whole or in part, directly or indirectly, of any such periodical, or of any stock or interest in any corporation or organization which owns the same in whole or in part, or which publishes the same, shall constitute such participation." . . .

Section two provides that whenever any such nuisance is committed or exists, the county attorney of any county where any such periodical is published or circulated, or, in case of his failure or refusal to proceed upon written request in good faith of a reputable citizen, the attorney general, or upon like failure or refusal of the latter, any citizen of the county, may maintain an action in the district court of the county in the name of the state to enjoin perpetually the persons committing or maintaining any such nuisance from further committing or maintaining it. Upon such evidence as the court shall deem sufficient, a temporary injunction may be granted. The defendants have the right to plead by demurrer or answer, and the plaintiff may demur or reply as in other cases.

The action, by section three, is to be "governed by the practice and procedure applicable to civil actions for injunctions," and after trial the court may enter judgment permanently enjoining the defendants found guilty of violating the act from continuing the violation and, "in and by such judgment, such nuisance may be wholly abated." The court is empowered, as in other cases of contempt, to punish disobedience to a temporary or permanent injunction by fine of not more than $1000 or by imprisonment in the county jail for not more than twelve months.

Under this statute, (section one, clause (b)), the county attorney of Hennepin county brought this action to enjoin the publication of what was described as a "malicious, scandalous and defamatory newspaper, magazine and periodical," known as "The Saturday Press," published by the defendants in the city of Minneapolis. . . .

Without attempting to summarize the contents of the voluminous exhibits attached to the complaint, we deem it sufficient to say that the articles charged in substance that a Jewish gangster was in control of gambling, bootlegging and racketeering in Minneapolis, and that law enforcing officers and agencies were not energetically performing their duties. Most of the charges were directed against the chief of police; he was charged with gross neglect of duty, illicit relations with gangsters, and with participation in graft. The county attorney was charged with knowing the existing conditions and with failure to take adequate measures to remedy them. The mayor was accused of inefficiency and dereliction. One member of the grand jury was stated to be in sympathy with the gangsters. A special grand jury and a special prosecutor were demanded to deal with the situation in general, and, in particular, to investigate an attempt to assassinate one Guilford, one of the original defendants, who, it appears from the articles, was shot by gangsters after the first issue of the periodical had been published. There is no question but that the articles made serious accusations against the public officers named and others in connection with the prevalence of crimes and the failure to expose and punish them. . . .

[Upon complaint the state court ordered Near to show cause why a temporary injunction should not be issued and forbade, meanwhile, further publication of the periodical. Near demurred on constitutional grounds. The district court certified the question of the constitutionality of the statute to the state supreme court, which held it valid. Near then answered the complaint but presented no evidence, and a permanent injunction was issued.]

From the judgment as thus affirmed, the defendant Near appeals to this court.

This statute, for the suppression as a public nuisance of a newspaper or periodical, is unusual, if not unique, and raises questions of grave importance transcending the local interests involved in the particular action. It is no longer open to doubt that the liberty of the press, and of speech, is within the liberty safeguarded by the due process clause of the 14th Amendment from invasion by state action. . . . In maintaining this guaranty, the authority of the State to enact laws to promote the health, safety, morals and general welfare of its people is necessarily admitted. The limits of this sovereign power must always be determined with appropriate regard to the particular subject of its exercise. . . . Liberty of speech and of the press is also not an absolute right, and the state may punish its abuse. . . . Liberty, in each of its phases, has its history and connotation and, in the present instance, the inquiry is as to the historic conception of the liberty of the press and whether the statute under review violates the essential attributes of that liberty. . . .

With respect to these contentions it is enough to say that in passing upon constitutional questions the court has regard to substance and not to mere matters of form, and that, in accordance with familiar principles, the statute must be tested by its operation and effect. . . . That operation and effect we think are clearly shown by the record in this case. We are not concerned with mere errors of the trial court, if there be such, in going beyond the direction of the statute as construed by the supreme court of the state. It is thus important to note precisely the purpose and effect of the statute as the state court has construed it.

First. The statute is not aimed at the redress of individual or private wrongs. Remedies for libel remain available and unaffected. The statute, said the state court, "is not directed at threatened libel but at an existing business which, generally speaking, involves more than libel." It is aimed at the distribution of scandalous matter as "detrimental to public morals and to the general welfare," tending "to disturb the peace of the community" and "to provoke assaults and the commission of crime." In order to obtain an injunction to suppress the future publication of the newspaper or periodical, it is not necessary to prove the falsity of the charges that have been made in the publication condemned. In the present action there was no allegation that the matter published was not true. It is alleged, and the statute requires the allegation, that the publication was "malicious." But, as in prosecutions for libel, there is no requirement of proof by the state of malice in fact as distinguished from malice inferred from the mere publication of the defamatory matter. The judgment in this case proceeded upon the mere proof of publication. The statute permits the defense, not of the truth alone, but only that the truth was published with good motives and for justifiable ends. It is apparent that under the statute the publication is to be regarded as defamatory if it injures reputation, and that it is scandalous if it circulates charges of reprehensible conduct, whether criminal or otherwise, and the publication is thus deemed to invite public reprobation and to constitute a public scandal. The court sharply defined the purpose of the statute, bringing out the precise point, in these words: "There is no constitutional right to publish a fact merely because it is true. It is a matter of common knowledge that prosecutions under the criminal libel statutes do not result in efficient repression or suppression of the evils of scandal. Men who are the victims of such assaults seldom resort to the courts. This is especially true if their sins are exposed and the only question relates to whether it was done with good motives and for justifiable ends. This law is not for the protection of the person attacked nor to punish the wrongdoer. It is for the protection of the public welfare."

Second. The statute is directed not simply at the circulation of scandalous and defamatory statements with regard to private citizens, but at the continued publication by newspapers and periodicals of charges against public officers of corruption, malfeasance in office, or serious neglect of duty. Such charges by their very nature create a public scandal. They are scandalous and defamatory within the meaning of the statute, which has its normal operation in relation to publications dealing prominently and chiefly with the alleged derelictions of public officers.

Third. The object of the statute is not punishment, in the ordinary sense, but suppression of the offending newspaper or periodical. The reason for the enactment, as the state court has said, is that prosecutions to enforce penal statutes for libel do not result in "efficient repression or suppression of the evils of scandal." Describing the business of publication as a public nuisance, does not obscure the substance of the proceeding which the statute authorizes. It is the continued publication of scandalous and defamatory matter that constitutes the business and the declared nuisance. In the case of public officers, it is the reiteration of charges of official misconduct, and the fact that the newspaper or periodical is principally devoted to that purpose, that exposes it to suppression. In the present instance, the proof was that nine editions of the newspaper or periodical in question were published on successive dates, and that they were chiefly devoted to charges against public officers and in relation to the prevalence and protection of crime. In such a case, these officers are not left to their ordinary remedy in a suit for libel, or the authorities to a prosecution for criminal libel. Under this statute, a publisher of a newspaper or periodical, undertaking to conduct a campaign to expose and to censure official derelictions, and devoting his publication principally to that purpose, must face not simply the possibility of a verdict against him in a suit or prosecution for libel, but a determination that his newspaper or periodical is a public nuisance to be abated, and that this abatement and suppression will follow unless he is prepared with legal evidence to prove the truth of the charges and also to satisfy the court that, in addition to being true, the matter was published with good motives and for justifiable ends.

This suppression is accomplished by enjoining publications and that restraint is the object and effect of the statute.

Fourth. The statute not only operates to suppress the offending newspaper or periodical but to put the publisher under an effective censorship. When a newspaper or periodical is found to be "malicious, scandalous and defamatory," and is suppressed as such, resumption of publication is punishable as a contempt of court by fine or imprisonment. Thus, where a newspaper or periodical has been suppressed because of the circulation of charges against public officers of official misconduct, it would seem to be clear that the renewal of the publication of such charges would constitute a contempt and that the judgment would lay a permanent restraint upon the publisher, to escape which he must satisfy the court as to the character of a new publication. Whether he would be permitted again to publish matter deemed to be derogatory to the same or other public officers would depend upon the court's ruling. In the present instance the judgment restrained the defendants from "publishing, circulating, having in their possession, selling or giving away any publication whatsoever which is a malicious, scandalous or defamatory newspaper, as defined by law." The law gives no definition except that covered by the words "scandalous and defamatory," and publications charging official misconduct are of that class. While the court, answering the objection that the judgment was too broad, saw no reason for construing it as restraining the defendants "from operating a newspaper in harmony with the public welfare to which all must yield," and said that the defendants had not indicated "any desire to conduct their business in the usual and legitimate manner," the manifest inference is that, at least with respect to a new publication directed against official misconduct, the defendant would be held, under penalty of punishment for contempt as provided in the statute, to a manner of publication which the court considered to be "usual and legitimate" and consistent with the public welfare.

If we cut through mere details of procedure, the operation and effect of the statute in substance is that public authorities may bring the owner or publisher of a newspaper or periodical before a judge upon a charge of conducting a business of publishing scandalous and defamatory matter—in particular that the matter consists of charges against public officers of official dereliction—and unless the owner or publisher is able and disposed to bring competent evidence to satisfy the judge that the charges are true and are published with good motives and for justifiable ends, his newspaper or periodical is suppressed and further publication is made punishable as a contempt. This is of the essence of censorship.

The question is whether a statute authorizing such proceedings in restraint of publication is consistent with the conception of the liberty of the press as historically conceived and guaranteed. In determining the extent of the constitutional protection, it has been generally, if not universally, considered that it is the chief purpose of the guaranty to prevent previous restraints upon publication. The struggle in England, directed against the legislative power of the licenser, resulted in renunciation of the censorship of the press. The liberty deemed to be established was thus described by Blackstone: "The liberty of the press is indeed essential to the nature of a free state; but this consists in laying no *previous* restraints upon publications, and not in freedom from censure for criminal matter when published. Every freeman has an undoubted right to lay what sentiments he pleases before the public; to forbid this, is to destroy the freedom of the press; but if he publishes what is improper, mischievous or illegal, he must take the consequence of his own temerity." . . .

The criticism upon Blackstone's statement has not been because immunity from previous restraint upon publication has not been regarded as deserving of special emphasis, but chiefly because that immunity cannot be deemed to exhaust the conception of the liberty guaranteed by state and Federal constitutions. The point of criticism has been "that the mere exemption from previous restraints cannot be all that is secured by the constitutional provisions;" and that "the liberty of the press might be rendered a mockery and a delusion, and the phrase itself a by-word, if, while every man was at liberty to publish what he pleased, the public authorities might nevertheless punish him for harmless publications." . . . But it is recognized that punishment for the abuse of the liberty accorded to the press is essential to the protection of the public, and that the common law rules that subject the libeler to responsibility for the public offense, as well as for the private injury, are not abolished by the protection extended in our constitutions. . . . In the present case, we have no occasion to inquire as to the permissible scope of subsequent punishment: For whatever wrong the appellant has committed or may commit, by his publications, the state appropriately affords both public and private redress by its libel laws. As has been noted, the statute in question does not deal with punishments; it provides for no punishment, except in case of contempt for violation of the court's order, but for suppression and injunction, that is, for restraint upon publication.

The objection has also been made that the principle as to immunity from previous restraint is stated too broadly, if every such restraint is deemed to be prohibited. That is undoubtedly true; the protection even as to previous restraint is not absolutely unlimited. But the limitation has been recognized only in exceptional cases. "When a nation is at war many things that might be said in time of peace are such a hindrance to its effort that their utterance will not be endured so long as men fight and that no court could regard them as protected by any constitutional right." Schenck v. United States [1919]. No one would question but that a government might prevent actual obstruction to its recruiting service or the publication of the sailing dates of transports or the number and location of troops. On similar grounds, the primary requirements of decency may be enforced against obscene publications. The security of the community life may be protected against incitements to acts of violence and the overthrow by force of orderly government. The constitutional guaranty of free speech does not "protect a man from an injunction against uttering words that may have all the effect of force. . . ."

The exceptional nature of its limitations places in a strong light the general conception that liberty of the press, historically considered and taken up by the Federal Constitution, has meant, principally although not exclusively, immunity from previous restraints or censorship. The conception of the liberty of the press in this country had broadened with the exigencies of the colonial period and with the efforts to secure freedom from oppressive administration. That liberty was especially cherished for the immunity it afforded from previous restraint of the publication of censure of public officers and charges of official misconduct. . . .

The importance of this immunity has not lessened. While reckless assaults upon public men, and efforts to bring obloquy upon those who are endeavoring faithfully to discharge official duties, exert a baleful influence and deserve the severest condemnation in public opinion, it cannot be said that this abuse is greater, and it is believed to be less, than that which characterized the period in which our institutions took shape. Meanwhile, the administration of government has become more complex, the opportunities for malfeasance and corruption have multiplied, crime has grown to most serious proportions, and the danger of its protection by unfaithful officials and of the impairment of the fundamental security of life and property by criminal alliances and official neglect, emphasizes the primary need of a vigilant and courageous press, especially in great cities. The fact that the liberty of the press may be abused by miscreant purveyors of scandal does not make any the less necessary the immunity of the press from previous restraint in dealing with official misconduct. Subsequent punishment for such abuses as may exist is the appropriate remedy, consistent with constitutional privilege. . . .

The statute in question cannot be justified by reason of the fact that the publisher is permitted to show, before injunction issues, that the matter published is true and is published with good motives and for justifiable ends. If such a statute, authorizing suppression and injunction on such a basis, is constitutionally valid, it would be equally permissible for the legislature to provide that at any time the publisher of any newspaper could be brought before a court, or even an administrative officer (as the constitutional protection may not be regarded as resting on mere procedural details) and required to produce proof of the truth of his publication, or of what he intended to publish, and of his motives, or stand enjoined. If this can be done, the legislature may provide machinery for determining in the complete exercise of its discretion what are justifiable ends and restrain publication accordingly. And it would be but a step to a complete system of censorship. The recognition of authority to impose previous restraint upon publication in order to protect the community against the circulation of charges of misconduct, and especially of official misconduct, necessarily would carry with it the admission of the authority of the censor against which the constitutional barrier was erected. The preliminary freedom, by virtue of the very reason for its existence, does not depend, as this court has said, on proof of truth. . . .

Equally unavailing is the insistence that the statute is designed to prevent the circulation of scandal which tends to disturb the public peace and to provoke assaults and the commission of crime. Charges of reprehensible conduct, and in particular of official malfeasance, unquestionably create a public scandal, but the theory of the constitutional guaranty is that even a more serious public evil would be caused by authority to prevent publication. . . . There is nothing new in the fact that charges of reprehensible conduct may create resentment and the disposition to resort to violent means of redress, but this well-understood tendency did not alter the determination to protect the press against censorship and restraint upon publication. . . . The danger of violent reactions becomes greater with effective organization of defiant groups resenting exposure, and if this consideration warranted legislative interference with the initial freedom of publication, the constitutional protection would be reduced to a mere form of words.

For these reasons we hold the statute, so far as it authorized the proceedings in this action under clause (b) of section one, to be an infringement of the liberty of the press guaranteed by the 14th Amendment. We should add that this decision rests upon the operation and effect of the statute, without regard to the question of the truth of the charges contained in the particular periodical. The fact that the public officers named in this case, and those associated with the charges of official dereliction, may be deemed to be impeccable, cannot affect the conclusion that the statute imposes an unconstitutional restraint upon publication.

Judgment reversed.

Mr. Justice **Butler** dissented in an opinion in which Justices **Van Devanter, McReynolds,** and **Sutherland** concurred.

KINGSLEY BOOKS v. BROWN

354 U. S. 436; 77 S. Ct. 1325; 1 L. Ed. 2d 1469
(1957)

Justice Holmes's wise rule that only those utterances should be suppressed that present a clear and present danger of bringing about some substantive evil probably expresses the ideal of free speech in a democracy. It is, in essence, a reflection of the doctrine that that government is best which governs least. But few people live easily with such a rule when it involves expressions of which they disapprove. There is as natural tendency in most of us to feel that the First Amendment should protect the right to say those things we want to say or hear, while permitting the government to suppress those expressions which we find offensive. Thus, those who are repelled by attacks on their religious beliefs see no merit in having "that sort of thing" protected by the First Amendment; at the same time they feel their own beliefs and practices should be immune from governmental interference. Those who find what they consider disloyal or subversive utterances a threat to their way of life see no reason why they should not be suppressed—as long as their own right to complain about the government and agitate for change is not restricted.

One aspect of the broad problem of censorship is that presented by the publication of obscene materials. Although a state may not resort to prior censorship of the press, it does have authority to punish the publication of matter offensive to public morals and decency. While it had long been assumed that clearly obscene publications could validly be punished, the question was never squarely decided by the Supreme Court until 1957 in the case of Roth v. United States. On historical grounds the Court decided that the First Amendment was not intended to protect obscenity, and therefore the question of whether an obscene publication presented a clear and present danger of "antisocial conduct" was entirely irrelevant.

Although the Court had insisted as early as Near v. Minnesota (1931) that "the protection even as to previous restraint is not absolutely unlimited," no scheme of previous censorship had ever been found valid and the Court had never undertaken to explain just what this dictum meant. It had spoken of "exceptional" circumstances that might justify such censorship, but it had defined them, not in terms of when or how the state could censor, but in terms of the kinds of ideas that could be suppressed. But how, without resorting to a general scheme of censorship and licensing, were these suppressible ideas to be located? How was a state to identify and suppress "utterances creating a hindrance to the . . . war effort," or which offended "the primary requirements of decency," without examining all utterances before they were published? Since it was this very "examining" before publication that the Court had held void in the Near case, the theory underlying the dictum seemed incompatible with the holding of the case.

The Court's greatest challenge came with the censorship of movies. In early years movies were not considered part of the press of the country, and were therefore not eligible for whatever protection was available at that time; see Mutual Film Corp. v. Industrial Commission of Ohio (1915). Then, in an antitrust case in 1948 (United States v. Paramount Pictures, Inc.), the Court observed by way of dictum: "We have no doubt that moving pictures, like newspapers and radio, are included in the press whose freedom is guaranteed by the First Amendment." It was thus only a matter of time before a movie censorship case came to the Court, and the first one involved a highly controversial Italian film called The Miracle. The picture was built up around the birth of a child to a poor, simple-minded girl who, while tending goats on a mountainside, is seduced by a bearded stranger. The girl, in her religious ecstasy, believes the man to be her favorite saint. The film was licensed and shown in New York City. Bitter attacks upon it immediately ensued. The Vatican had considered the film profane, and Catholic prelates in this country denounced it as blasphemous and sacrilegious. It had, however, important and respected defenders. The New

York Board of Regents, who had the authority to censor motion pictures, reconsidered the film and withdrew its license on the ground that it was "sacrilegious" within the meaning of the New York censorship statute. The New York courts held that the statute was valid and that the Regents had acted within the proper range of their discretion under it.

In Burstyn v. Wilson (1952) the Supreme Court reversed. Without holding void all movie censorship, it pointed out that "in seeking to apply the broad and all-inclusive definition of 'sacrilegious' given by the New York courts, the censor is set adrift upon a boundless sea amid a myriad of conflicting currents of religious views with no charts but those provided by the most vocal and powerful orthodoxies. New York cannot vest such unlimited restraining control over motion pictures in a censor." Moreover, while such censorship raised serious questions of religious freedom, "from the standpoint of freedom of speech and the press, it is enough to point out that the state has no legitimate interest in protecting any or all religions from views distasteful to them which is sufficient to justify prior restraint upon the expression of those views. It is not the business of government in our nation to suppress real or imagined attacks upon a particular religious doctrine, whether they appear in publications, speeches, or motion pictures."

While the Court in post-Burstyn cases had held bad all movie censorship, it had always confined itself to the particular censorship under review and had carefully avoided saying whether all censorship was void per se. The problem of the right to censor finally reached the Court in Times Film Corp. v. Chicago (1961). The Times Film Corporation undertook to show in Chicago a picture entitled Don Juan based upon Mozart's opera Don Giovanni. It had paid the license fees required by the city, but had refused to submit the picture for censorship. Thus the validity of whatever standards the censors might have applied were not an issue—the only question was whether the picture could be shown without being submitted to the censors at all. In a five-to-four decision the Court upheld movie censorship. Stressing that "obscenity is not within the area of constitutionally protected speech or press," it conceded Chicago's right to find out if a movie was obscene and suggested that movies might have a "capacity for evil" that was greater than that of other forms of publication.

Four years later, in Freedman v. Maryland (1965), the Court acted to bring the business of movie censorship into line with the Kingsley Books doctrine, announcing strict standards which a censorship plan must meet in order to be valid. While it did not actually overrule Times Film, all the censorship plans then in use, including that in Chicago, failed to meet the constitutional test and had to be rewritten to comply with the procedural requirements.

In the present case New York had provided by law that the legal officer in any town who learns that someone is about to sell obscene matter may go to the state supreme court and request an injunction against such sale. The question whether the injunction should be is-

sued had to be tried within one day after the defendant had been properly notified and the court had to render its decision within two days of the trial. If the materials are found to be obscene the judge was to order the sheriff to seize and destroy them. Books kept for sale by Kingsley Books were found on trial to be "dirt for dirt's sake," their distribution enjoined and they were ordered destroyed. The sale of future issues was not enjoined since this would constitute a prior restraint.

Mr. Justice **Frankfurter** delivered the opinion of the Court, saying in part:

Neither in the New York Court of Appeals, nor here, did appellants assail the legislation insofar as it outlaws obscenity. The claim they make lies within a very narrow compass. Their attack is upon the power of New York to employ the remedial scheme of § 22-a. Authorization of an injunction pendente lite, as part of this scheme, during the period within which the issue of obscenity must be promptly tried and adjudicated in an adversary proceeding for which "[a]dequate notice, judicial hearing, [and] fair determination" are assured, is a safeguard against frustration of the public interest in effectuating judicial condemnation of obscene matter. It is a brake on the temptation to exploit a filthy business offered by the limited hazards of piecemeal prosecutions, sale by sale, of a publication already condemned as obscene. New York enacted this procedure on the basis of study by a joint legislative committee. Resort to this injunctive remedy, it is claimed, is beyond the constitutional power of New York in that it amounts to a prior censorship of literary product and as such is violative of that "freedom of thought, and speech" which has been "withdrawn by the Fourteenth Amendment from encroachment by the states." Palko v. Connecticut [1937]. Reliance is particularly placed upon Near v. Minnesota [1931].

In an unbroken series of cases extending over a long stretch of this Court's history, it has been accepted as a postulate that "the primary requirements of decency may be enforced against obscene publications." And so our starting point is that New York can constitutionally convict appellants of keeping for sale the booklets incontestably found to be obscene. Alberts v. California, decided this day. The immediate problem then is whether New York can adopt as an auxiliary means of dealing with such obscene merchandising the procedure of § 22-a.

We need not linger over the suggestion that something can be drawn out of the Due Process Clause of the Fourteenth Amendment that restricts New York to the criminal process in seeking to protect its people against the dissemination of pornography. It is not for this Court thus to limit the State in resorting to various weapons in the armory of the law. Whether proscribed conduct is to be visited by a criminal prosecution or by a qui tam action or by an injunction or by some or all of these remedies in combination, is a matter within the legislature's range of choice. . . . If New York chooses to subject persons who disseminate obscene "literature" to criminal prosecution and also to deal with such books as deodands of old, or both, with due regard, of course, to appropriate opportunities for the trial of the underlying issue, it is not for us to gainsay its selection of remedies. Just as Near v. Minnesota, one of the landmark opinions in shaping the constitutional protection of freedom of speech and of the press, left no doubts that "Liberty of speech, and of the press, is also not an absolute right," it likewise made clear that "the protection even as to previous restraint is not absolutely unlimited." To be sure, the limitation is the exception; it is to be closely confined so as to preclude what may fairly be deemed licensing or censorship.

The judicial angle of vision in testing the validity of a statute like § 22-a is "the operation and effect of the statute in substance." The phrase "prior restraint" is not a self-wielding sword. Nor can it serve as a talismanic test. The duty of closer analysis and critical judgment in applying the thought behind the phrase has thus been authoritatively put by one who brings weighty learning to his support of constitutionally protected liberties: "What is needed," writes Professor Paul Freund, "is a pragmatic assessment of its operation in the particular circumstances. The generalization that prior restraint is particularly obnoxious in civil liberties cases must yield to more particularistic analysis." . . .

Wherein does § 22-a differ in its effective operation from the type of statute upheld in Alberts? Section 311 of California's Penal Code provides that "Every person who wilfully and lewdly . . . keeps for sale . . . any obscene . . . book . . . is guilty of a misdemeanor. . . ." Section 1141 of New York's Penal Law is similar. One would be bold to assert that the in terrorem effect of such statutes less restrains booksellers in the period before the law strikes than does § 22-a. Instead of requiring the bookseller to dread that the offer for sale of a book may without prior warning subject him to a criminal prosecution with the hazard of imprisonment, the civil procedure assures him that such consequences cannot follow unless he ignores a court order specifically directed to him for a prompt and carefully circumscribed determination of the issue of obscenity. Until then, he may keep the book for sale and sell it on his own judgment rather than "steer nervously among the treacherous shoals." . . .

Criminal enforcement and the proceeding under § 22-a interfere with a book's solicitation of the public precisely at the same stage. In each situation the law moves after publication; the book need not in either case have yet passed into the hands of the public. The Alberts record does not show that the matter there found to be obscene had reached the public at the time that the criminal charge of keeping such matter for sale was lodged, while here as a matter of fact copies of the booklets whose distribution was enjoined had been on sale for several weeks when process was served. In each case the bookseller is put on notice by the complaint that sale of the publication charged with obscenity in the period before trial may subject him to penal consequences. In the one case he may suffer fine and imprisonment for violation of the criminal statute, in the other, for disobedience of the temporary injunction. The bookseller may of course stand his ground and confidently believe that in any judicial proceeding the book could not be condemned as obscene, but both modes of procedure provide an effective deterrent against distribution prior to adjudication of the book's content—the threat of subsequent penalization. . . .

Nor are the consequences of a judicial condemnation for obscenity under § 22-a more restrictive of freedom of expression than the result of conviction for a misdemeanor. In Alberts, the defendant was fined $500, sentenced to sixty days in prison, and put on probation for two years on condition that he not violate the obscenity statute. Not only was he completely separated from society for two months but he was also seriously restrained from trafficking in all obscene publications for a considerable time. Appellants, on the other hand, were enjoined from displaying for sale or distributing only the particular booklets theretofore published and adjudged to be obscene. Thus, the restraint upon appellants as merchants in obscenity was narrower than that imposed on Alberts.

Section 22-a's provision for the seizure and destruction of the instruments of ascertained wrongdoing expresses resort to a legal remedy sanctioned by the long history of Anglo-American law. . . . It is worth noting that although the Alberts record does not reveal whether the publications found to be obscene were destroyed, provision is made for that by §§ 313 and 314 of the California Penal Code. Similarly, § 1144 of New York's Penal Law provides for destruction of obscene matter following conviction for its dissemination.

It only remains to say that the difference between Near v. Minnesota and this case is glaring in fact. The two cases are no less glaringly different when judged by the appropriate criteria of constitutional law. Minnesota empowered its courts to enjoin the dissemination of future issues of a publication because its past issues had been found offensive. In the language of Mr. Chief Justice Hughes, "This is of the essence of censorship." As such, it was found unconstitutional. This was enough to condemn that statute wholly apart from the fact that the proceeding in Near involved not obscenity but matters deemed to be derogatory to a public officer. Unlike Near, § 22-a is concerned solely with obscenity and, as authoritatively construed, it studiously withholds restraint upon matters not already published and not yet found to be offensive.

The judgment is
Affirmed.

Mr. Chief Justice **Warren,** dissenting.

My views on the rights of a State to protect its people against the purveyance of obscenity were expressed in Alberts v. California, also decided today. Here we have an entirely different situation.

This is not a criminal obscenity case. Nor is it a case ordering the destruction of materials disseminated by a person who has been convicted of an offense for doing so, as would be authorized under provisions in the laws of New York and other States. It is a case wherein the New York police, under a different state statute, located books which, in their opinion, were unfit for public use because of obscenity and then obtained a court order for their condemnation and destruction.

The majority opinion sanctions this proceeding. I would not. Unlike the criminal cases decided today, this New York law places the book on trial. There is totally lacking any standard in the statute for judging the book in context. The personal element basic to the criminal laws is entirely absent. In my judgment, the same object may have wholly different impact depending upon the setting in which it is placed. Under this statute, the setting is irrelevant.

It is the manner of use that should determine obscenity. It is the conduct of the individual that should be judged, not the quality of art or literature. To do otherwise is to impose a prior restraint and hence to violate the Constitution. Certainly in the absence of a prior judicial determination of illegal use, books, pictures and other objects of expression should not be destroyed. It savors too much of book burning.

I would reverse.

Mr. Justice **Douglas,** with whom Mr. Justice **Black** concurs, dissenting, said in part:

There are two reasons why I think this restraining order should be dissolved.

First, the provision for an injunction pendente lite gives the State the paralyzing power of a censor. A decree can issue ex parte—without a hearing and without any ruling or finding on the issue of obscenity. This provision is defended on the ground that it is only a little encroachment, that a hearing must be promptly given and finding of obscenity promptly made. But every publisher knows what awful effect a decree issued in secret can have. We tread here on First Amendment grounds. And nothing is more devastating to the rights that it guarantees than the power to restrain publication before even a hearing is held. This is prior restraint and censorship at its worst.

Second, the procedure for restraining by equity decree the distribution of all the condemned literature does violence to the First Amendment. The judge or jury which finds the publisher guilty in New York City acts on evidence that may be quite different from evidence before the judge or jury that finds the publisher not guilty in Rochester. . . . Yet the present statute makes one criminal conviction conclusive and authorizes a statewide decree that subjects the distributor to the contempt power. I think every publication is a separate offense which entitles the accused to a separate trial. . . .

Mr. Justice **Brennan,** dissenting, said in part:

I believe the absence in this New York obscenity statute of a right to jury trial is a fatal defect. . . .

The jury represents a cross-section of the community and has a special aptitude for reflecting the view of the average person. Jury trial of obscenity therefore provides a peculiarly competent application of the standard for judging obscenity which, by its definition, calls for an appraisal of material according to the average person's application of contemporary community standards. A statute which does not afford the defendant, of right, a jury determination of obscenity falls short, in my view, of giving proper effect to the standard fashioned as the necessary safeguard demanded by the freedoms of speech and press for material which is not obscene. . . .

MILLER v. CALIFORNIA

413 U. S. 15; 93 S. Ct. 2067; 37 L. Ed. 2d 419
(1973)

The states have experienced great difficulty in drafting legislation under which the publication of objectionable material can validly be punished. In the first place, the problem of finding a sufficiently clear definition of crime in this area has proved to be an extremely challenging one. The state may, of course, properly forbid the publication of "lewd, lascivious, salacious, obscene and filthy" matter. These are words with which the courts are familiar; and despite the diverse results obtained in their interpretations, for historical reasons they constitute valid definitions of crime. But these words are not adequate to handle a problem which has aroused public concern— the problem of "horror comic books." Some of these cheap pulp-paper publications contain stories of crime and bloodshed, lust and depravity, and are believed by many to contribute directly to delinquency. In Winters v. New York (1948) a statute designed to deal with this problem was held void for vagueness.

In the second place, such machinery as the state provides for enforcement must be so designed that publications which are protected by the First Amendment are not suppressed along with those that enjoy no such protection. In Butler v. Michigan (1957) the Supreme Court held unconstitutional a Michigan statute which forbade "any person" to sell or give away anything "containing obscene, immoral, lewd or lascivious language . . . tending to incite minors to violent or depraved or immoral acts, manifestly tending to the corruption of the morals of youth. . . ." The Court set aside the conviction of an adult who sold such a book to another adult, in this case a policeman, on the ground that the state could not, under its police power, quarantine "the general reading public against books not too rugged for grown men and women in order to shield juvenile innocence. . . ." This, the Court decided, was "legislation not reasonably restricted to the evil with which it is said to deal. The incidence of this enactment is to reduce the adult population of Michigan to reading only what is fit

for children. It thereby arbitrarily curtails one of those liberties of the individual, now enshrined in the Due Process Clause. . . ." The Court noted that Michigan had a statute which forbade selling or giving such books to children.

In Roth v. United States (1947), the five members of the Court had agreed that obscene material was that "which deals with sex in a manner appealing to prurient interest." In applying this definition, the Court rejected the so-called Hicklin rule, which judged isolated excerpts of writings by their likely effect on the most susceptible persons, and affirmed, instead, the test "whether to the average person, applying contemporary community standards, the dominant theme of the material taken as a whole appeals to prurient interest." Such material, it was emphasized, does not enjoy constitutional protection because it is "utterly without social importance." The Court in Roth found that the jury had been properly instructed on the standard, so the conviction was valid.

In Jacobellis v. Ohio (1964) the Court again applied the Roth rule and reversed the Ohio court decision that the movie The Lovers was obscene. The Court divided badly on the reasoning for its decision, no more than two justices agreeing on the test to be applied. Justices Brennan and Goldberg reaffirmed the Roth test, but added that "community standards" meant national, not local, standards; and the question whether something was obscene could not be left solely to a jury, but must ultimately be decided by the Supreme Court itself. They also relied on the "redeeming social importance" of any publication, however erotic its contents, to justify First Amendment protection. Justices Black and Douglas joined in the judgment on the ground that punishing any publication was unconstitutional, and Justice Stewart held that the First Amendment forbids only hard-core pornography." I shall not today attempt further to define the kinds of material I understand to be embraced within that shorthand description; and perhaps I could never succeed in intelligibly doing so. But I know it when I see it, and the motion picture involved in this case is not that." Justices Warren and Clark, on the other hand, supported the Roth rule, but dissented on the ground that "community standards" meant local standards, such as those applied by the jury in this case; and obscenity, moreover, was as much a question of the conduct of the purveyors and the purposes to which the material was put, as of the character of the material itself. Justice Harlan dissented on the ground that the First and Fourteenth Amendments apply differently, and the state should be allowed to outlaw obscenity as it sees fit.

In Memoirs v. Massachusetts (1966) six members of the Court joined in overruling a Massachusetts court decision that Fanny Hill was obscene—still without agreeing on a definition of obscenity. In an opinion written by Justice Brennan, the Court held that "a book can not be proscribed unless it is found to be utterly without redeeming social value. This is so even though the book is found to possess the requisite prurient appeal and to be patently offensive." Justice Harlan dissented for the reasons given in *Jacobellis*, while Justice White dissented because he felt a lack of redeeming social value was a characteristic of all patently offensive material and should not be used as an independent test.

In the still controversial case of *Ginzburg v. United States* (1966), decided the same day as *Memoirs*, the Court upheld the conviction of Ralph Ginzburg for sending through the mails copies of Eros, an American Heritage-*style magazine of erotica, and* The Housewife's Handbook of Selective Promiscuity. *Abandoning the approach of its previous cases, the Court conceded that the publications were not in themselves obscene, but that they took their obscenity from the fact that Ginzburg was in "the sordid business of pandering—'the business of purveying textual or graphic matter openly advertised to appeal to the erotic interest of their customers.'" Moreover, the "leer of the sensualist" permeated his advertising. "The deliberate representation of petitioners' publications as erotically arousing, for example, stimulated the reader to accept them as prurient; he looks for titillation, not for saving intellectual content." Three of the four dissenting justices attacked the Court's jailing of Ginzburg for "pandering" and "titillating," things which Congress had not made illegal and which the Court had not previously declared to be a crime.*

While the right to sell obscene material enjoys no protection under the First Amendment, the freedom of thought implicitly guaranteed by that provision ensures one's right to enjoy such material in the privacy of one's own home. Relying on the Court's statement in Roth that "obscenity is not within the area of constitutionally protected speech or press," the state of Georgia forbade the mere possession of obscene material. In Stanley v. Georgia (1969), the Court held the statute void. It conceded the wording of Roth, but pointed out that it and other obscenity cases all involved the sale and distribution of obscene materials to others, and should be read in that context. "This right to receive information and ideas, regardless of their social worth, . . . is fundamental to our free society," and "also fundamental is the right to be free, except in very limited circumstances, from unwanted governmental intrusions into one's privacy." The Court rejected outright the idea that Georgia had a right to "control the moral content of a person's thoughts." "Whatever may be the justification for other statutes regulating obscenity, we do not think they reach into the privacy of one's own home. If the First Amendment means anything, it means that a State has no business telling a man, sitting alone in his own house, what books he may read or what films he may watch. Our whole constitutional heritage rebels at the thought of giving government the power to control men's minds." Nor could Georgia justify its statute on the ground that the possession of pornography led to antisocial conduct. "Given the present state of knowledge, the State may no more prohibit mere possession of obscenity on the ground that it may lead to antisocial conduct than it may prohibit possession of chemistry books on the ground that they may lead to the manufacture of home-made spirits."

In Paris Adult Theater I, decided five-to-four the same day as Miller, the Court rejected Justice Brennan's contention that "consenting adults" should be able to see "dirty movies" if they wish. Here the city of Atlanta, Georgia, had moved, under procedures that met the test of Freedman v. Maryland (1965), to suppress two "adult" movies shown only to adults in a theater devoid of offensive advertising. The trial court agreed the movies were obscene but refused to enjoin their exhibition. The Georgia Supreme Court reversed. Although Justice Brennan had written the opinions in both Roth and Ginzburg, in his dissent in the Paris Adult Theater case (1973) he abandoned his approach in Roth of describing how offensive matter must be in order to be banned, and argued that the right to publish should be protected where no one is injured by such publication. "After 15 years of experimentation and debate I am reluctantly forced to the conclusion that none of the available formulas, including the one announced today, can reduce the vagueness to a tolerable level . . ."

A majority of the Court, however, agreeing for the first time since Roth on language to describe obscenity, suggests in the Miller case below that it is prepared to let obscenity decisions be made by local juries on the basis of local standards of good taste—although apparently only as long as they ban only "hard core" pornography.

The following year, in Jenkins v. Georgia (1974), a unanimous Court made clear that despite Miller, the last word on questions of obscenity still rested with it. There a theater operator had shown "Carnal Knowledge," a movie dealing with sex, although not in an explicit way. A jury, properly charged to apply local community standards, had found him guilty of showing an obscene film. "Even though questions of appeal to the 'prurient interest' or of patent offensiveness are 'essentially questions of fact,' it would be a serious misreading of Miller to conclude that juries have unbridled discretion in determining what is 'patently offensive.' . . . Our own view of the film satisfies us that 'Carnal Knowledge' could not be found under the Miller standard to depict sexual conduct in a patently offensive way."

Mr. Chief Justice **Burger** delivered the opinion of the Court, saying in part:

This is one of a group of "obscenity-pornography" cases being reviewed by the Court in a re-examination of standards enunciated in earlier cases involving what Mr. Justice Harlan called "the intractable obscenity problem."

Appellant conducted a mass mailing campaign to advertise the sale of illustrated books, euphemistically called "adult" material. After a jury trial, he was convicted of violating California Penal Code § 311.2(a), a misdemeanor, by knowingly distributing obscene matter. . . . Appellant's conviction was specifically based on his conduct in causing five unsolicited advertising brochures to be sent through the mail in an envelope addressed to a restaurant in Newport Beach, California. The envelope was opened by the manager of the restaurant and his mother. They had not requested the brochures; they complained to the police.

The brochures advertise four books entitled "Intercourse," "Man-Woman," "Sex Orgies Illustrated," and "An Illustrated History of Pornography," and a film entitled "Marital Intercourse." While the brochures contain some descriptive printed material, primarily they consist of pictures and drawings very explicitly depicting men and women in groups of two or more engaging in a variety of sexual activities, with genitals often prominently displayed.

I.

This case involves the application of a state's criminal obscenity statute to a situation in which sexually explicit materials have been thrust by aggressive sales action upon unwilling recipients who had in no way indicated any desire to receive such materials. This Court has recognized that the States have a legitimate interest in prohibiting dissemination or exhibition of obscene material when the mode of dissemination carries with it a significant danger of offending the sensibilities of unwilling recipients or of exposure to juveniles. Stanley v. Georgia (1969). Ginsberg v. New York (1968). Interstate Circuit, Inc. v. Dallas (1968). Redrup v. New York (1967). Jacobellis v. Ohio (1964). . . . It is in this context that we are called on to define the standards which must be used to identify obscene material that a State may regulate without infringing the First Amendment as applicable to the States through the Fourteenth Amendment.

The dissent of Mr. Justice Brennan reviews the background of the obscenity problem, but since the Court now undertakes to formulate standards more concrete than those in the past, it is useful for us to focus on two of the landmark cases in the somewhat tortured history of the Court's obscenity decisions. In Roth v. United States (1957), the Court sustained a conviction under a federal statute punishing the mailing of "obscene, lewd, lascivious or filthy . . ." materials. The key to that holding was the Court's rejection of the claim that obscene materials were protected by the First Amendment. Five Justices joined in the opinion stating:

"All ideas having even the slightest redeeming social importance—unorthodox ideas, controversial ideas, even ideas hateful to the prevailing climate of opinion— have full protection of the [First Amendment] guaranties, unless excludable because they encroach upon the limited area of more important interests. But implicit in the history of the First Amendment is the rejection of obscenity as utterly without redeeming social importance. . . . This is the same judgment expressed by this Court in Chaplinsky v. New Hampshire [1942].

" ' . . . There are certain well-defined and narrowly limited classes of speech, the prevention and punishment of which have never been thought to raise any Constitutional problem. *These include the lewd and obscene . . . .*

It has been well observed that such utterances are no essential part of any exposition of ideas, and are of such slight social value as a step to truth that any benefit that may be derived from them is clearly outweighed by the social interest in order and morality. . . .' " [Emphasis by Court in Roth opinion.]

We hold that obscenity is not within the area of constitutionally protected speech or press."

Nine years later in Memoirs v. Massachusetts (1966), the Court veered sharply away from the Roth concept and, with only three Justices in the plurality opinion, articulated a new test of obscenity. The plurality held that under the Roth definition: ". . . as elaborated in subsequent cases, three elements must coalesce: it must be established that (a) the dominant theme of the material taken as a whole appeals to a prurient interest in sex; (b) the material is patently offensive because it affronts contemporary community standards relating to the description or representation of sexual matters; and (c) the material is utterly without redeeming social value." The sharpness of the break with Roth, represented by the third element of the Memoirs test and emphasized by Mr. Justice White's dissent, was further underscored when the Memoirs plurality went on to state: "The Supreme Judicial Court erred in holding that a book need not be 'unqualifiedly worthless before it can be deemed obscene.' A book cannot be proscribed unless it is found to be *utterly* without redeeming social value." (Emphasis in original.)

While Roth presumed "obscenity" to be "utterly without redeeming social value," Memoirs required that to prove obscenity it must be affirmatively established that the material is "*utterly* without redeeming social value." Thus, even as they repeated the words of Roth, the Memoirs plurality produced a drastically altered test that called on the prosecution to prove a negative, i.e., that the material was "*utterly* without redeeming social value"—a burden virtually impossible to discharge under our criminal standards of proof. Such considerations caused Mr. Justice Harlan to wonder if the *utterly* without redeeming social value" test had any meaning at all. . . .

Apart from the initial formulation in the Roth case, no majority of the Court has at any given time been able to agree on a standard to determine what constitutes obscene, pornographic material subject to regulation under the States' police power. . . . We have seen "a variety of views among the members of the Court unmatched in any other course of constitutional adjudication [footnote omitted]." Interstate Circuit, Inc. v. Dallas (Harlan, J., concurring and dissenting). This is not remarkable, for in the area of freedom of speech and press the courts must always remain sensitive to any infringement on genuinely serious literary, artistic, political, or scientific expression. This is an area in which there are few eternal verities.

The case we now review was tried on the theory that the California Penal Code § 311 approximately incorporates the three-stage Memoirs test. But now the Memoirs test has been abandoned as unworkable by its author and no member of the Court today supports the Memoirs formulation.

II.

This much has been categorically settled by the Court, that obscene material is unprotected by the First Amendment. . . . We acknowledge, however, the inherent dangers of undertaking to regulate any form of expression. State statutes designed to regulate obscene materials must be carefully limited. . . . As a result, we now confine the permissible scope of such regulation to works which depict or describe sexual conduct. That conduct must be specifically defined by the applicable state law, as written or authoritatively construed. A state offense must also be limited to works which, taken as a whole, appeal to the prurient interest in sex, which portray sexual conduct in a patently offensive way, and which, taken as a whole, do not have serious literary, artistic, political, or scientific value.

The basic guidelines for the trier of fact must be: (a) whether "the average person, applying contemporary community standards" would find that the work, taken as a whole, appeals to the prurient interest. . . . (b) whether the work depicts or describes, in a patently offensive way, sexual conduct specifically defined by the applicable state law, and (c) whether the work, taken as a whole, lacks serious literary, artistic, political, or scientific value. We do not adopt as a constitutional standard the "*utterly* without redeeming social value" test of Memoirs v. Massachusetts; that concept has never commanded the adherence of more than three Justices at one time. If a state law that regulates obscene material is thus limited, as written or construed, the First Amendment values applicable to the States through the Fourteenth Amendment are adequately protected by the ultimate power of appellate courts to conduct an independent review of constitutional claims when necessary. . . .

We emphasize that it is not our function to propose regulatory schemes for the States. That must await their concrete legislative efforts. It is possible, however, to give a few plain examples of what a state statute could define for regulation under the second part (b) of the standard announced in this opinion, supra:

(a) Patently offensive representations or descriptions of ultimate sexual acts, normal or perverted, actual or simulated.

(b) Patently offensive representations or descriptions of masturbation, excretory functions, and lewd exhibition of the genitals.

Sex and nudity may not be exploited without limit by films or pictures exhibited or sold in places of public accommodation any more than live sex and nudity can be exhibited or sold without limit in such public places. At a minimum, prurient, patently offensive depiction or description of sexual conduct must have serious literary, artistic, political, or scientific value to merit First Amendment protection. . . . For example, medical books for the education of physicians and related personnel necessarily use graphic illustrations and descriptions of human anatomy. In resolving the inevitably sensitive questions of fact and law, we must continue to rely on the jury system, accompanied by the safeguards that judges, rules of evidence, presumption of innocence, and other protective features provide, as we do with rape, murder, and a host of other offenses against society and its individual members.*

Mr. Justice Brennan, author of the opinions of the Court, or the plurality opinions, in Roth v. United States, Jacobellis v. Ohio, Ginzburg v. United States (1966), Mishkin v. New York (1966), and Memoirs v. Massachusetts, has abandoned his former positions and now maintains that no formulation of this Court, the Congress, or the States can adequately distinguish obscene material unprotected by the First Amendment from protected expression, Paris Adult Theatre v. Slaton (1973) (Brennan, J., dissenting). Paradoxically, Mr. Justice Brennan indicates that suppression of unprotected obscene material is permissible to avoid exposure to unconsenting adults, as in this case, and to juveniles, although he gives no indication of how the division between protected and nonprotected materials may be drawn with greater precision for these purposes than for regulation of commercial exposure to consenting adults only. Nor does he indicate where in the Constitution he finds the authority to distinguish between a willing "adult" one month past the state law age of majority and a willing "juvenile" one month younger.

Under the holdings announced today, no one will be subject to prosecution for the sale or exposure of obscene materials unless these materials depict or describe patently offensive "hard core" sexual conduct specifically defined by the regulating state law, as written or construed. We are satisfied that these specific prerequisites will provide fair notice to a dealer in such materials that his public and commercial activities may bring prosecution. . . . If the inability to define regulated materials with ultimate, godlike precision altogether removes the power of the States or the Congress to regulate, then "hard core" pornography may be exposed without limit to the juvenile, the passerby, and the consenting adult alike, as, indeed, Mr. Justice Douglas contends. . . . In this belief, however, Mr. Justice Douglas now stands alone.

Mr. Justice Brennan also emphasizes "institutional stress" in justification of his change of view. Noting that "the number of obscenity cases on our docket gives ample testimony to the burden that has been placed upon this Court," he quite rightly remarks that the examination of contested materials "is hardly a source of edification to members of this Court." Paris Adult Theatre v. Slaton (Brennan, J., dissenting). He also notes, and we agree, that "uncertainty of the standards creates a con-

---

*The mere fact juries may reach different conclusions as to the same material does not mean that constitutional rights are abridged. As this Court observed in Roth v. United States, "It is common experience that different juries may reach different results under any criminal statute. That is one of the consequences we accept under our jury system."

tinuing source of tension between state and federal courts. ...'' ''The problem is ... that one cannot say with certainty that material is obscene until at least five members of this Court, applying inevitably obscure standards, have pronounced it so.''

It is certainly true that the absence, since Roth, of a single majority view of this Court as to proper standards for testing obscenity has placed a strain on both state and federal courts. But today, for the first time since Roth was decided in 1957, a majority of this Court has agreed on concrete guidelines to isolate ''hard core'' pornography from expression protected by the First Amendment. Now we may abandon the casual practice of Redrup v. New York and attempt to provide positive guidance to the federal and state courts alike.

This may not be an easy road, free from difficulty. But no amount of ''fatigue'' should lead us to adopt a convenient ''institutional'' rationale—an absolutist, ''anything goes'' view of the First Amendment—because it will lighten our burdens. ''Such an abnegation of judicial supervision in this field would be inconsistent with our duty to uphold the constitutional guarantees.'' ... Nor should we remedy ''tension between state and federal courts'' by arbitrarily depriving the States of a power reserved to them under the Constitution, a power which they have enjoyed and exercised continuously from before the adoption of the First Amendment to this day. ... ''Our duty admits of no 'substitute for facing up to the tough individual problems of constitutional judgment involved in every obscenity case.' ...''

III.

Under a national Constitution, fundamental First Amendment limitations on the powers of the States do not vary from community to community, but this does not mean that there are, or should or can be, fixed, uniform national standards of precisely what appeals to the ''prurient interest'' or is ''patently offensive.'' These are essentially questions of fact, and our nation is simply too big and too diverse for this Court to reasonably expect that such standards could be articulated for all 50 States in a single formulation, even assuming the prerequisite consensus exists. When triers of fact are asked to decide whether ''the average person, applying contemporary community standards'' would consider certain materials ''prurient,'' it would be unrealistic to require that the answer be based on some abstract formulation. The adversary system, with lay jurors as the usual ultimate factfinders in criminal prosecutions, has historically permitted triers-of-fact to draw on the standards of their community, guided always by limiting instructions on the law. To require a State to structure obscenity proceedings around evidence of a *national* ''community standard'' would be an exercise in futility. ...

It is neither realistic nor constitutionally sound to read the First Amendment as requiring that the people of Maine or Mississippi accept public depiction of conduct found tolerable in Las Vegas, or New York City. ...

People in different States vary in their tastes and attitudes, and this diversity is not to be strangled by the absolutism of imposed uniformity. As the Court made clear in Mishkin v. New York (1966), the primary concern with requiring a jury to apply the standard of ''the average person, applying contemporary community standards'' is to be certain that, so far as material is not aimed at a deviant group, it will be judged by its impact on an average person, rather than a particularly susceptible or sensitive person—or indeed a totally insensitive one. ... We hold the requirement that the jury evaluate the materials with reference to ''contemporary standards of the State of California'' serves this protective purpose and is constitutionally adequate.

IV.

The dissenting justices sound the alarm of repression. But, in our view, to equate the free and robust exchange of ideas and political debate with commercial exploitation of obscene material demeans the grand conception of the First Amendment and its high purposes in the historic struggle for freedom. It is a ''misuse of the great guarantees of free speech and free press. ...'' ...

The First Amendment protects works which, taken as a whole, have serious literary, artistic, political, or scientific value, regardless of whether the government or a majority of the people approve of the ideas these works represent. ''The protection given speech and press was fashioned to assure unfettered interchange of *ideas* for the bringing about of political and social changes desired by the people.'' ... But the public portrayal of hard core sexual conduct for its own sake, and for the ensuing commercial gain, is a different matter.*

There is no evidence, empirical or historical, that the stern nineteenth century American censorship of public distribution and display of material relating to sex, ... in any way limited or affected expression of serious literary, artistic, political, or scientific ideas. On the contrary, it is beyond any question that the era following Thomas Jefferson to Theodore Roosevelt was an ''extraordinarily vigorous period'' not just in economics and politics, but in *belles lettres* and in ''the outlying fields of social and political philosophies.''[†] We do not see the harsh hand of censorship of ideas—good or bad, sound or unsound—and ''repression'' of political liberty lurking in every state regulation of commercial exploitation of human interest in sex.

Mr. Justice Brennan finds ''it is hard to see how state ordered regimentation of our minds can ever be forestalled.'' Paris Adult Theatre I v. Slaton. These doleful anticipations assume that courts cannot distinguish

---

*In the apt words of Mr. Chief Justice Warren, the petitioner in this case was ''plainly engaged in the commercial exploitation of the morbid and shameful craving for materials with prurient effect. I believe that the State and Federal Governments can constitutionally punish such conduct. That is all that these cases present to us, and that is all that we need to decide.'' Roth v. United States (1957) (concurring opinion).

[†]See Parrington, *Main Currents in American Thought*, Vol. 2.

commerce in ideas, protected by the First Amendment, from commercial exploitation of obscene material. Moreover, state regulation of hard core pornography so as to make it unavailable to nonadults, a regulation which Mr. Justice Brennan finds constitutionally permissible, has all the elements of "censorship" for adults; indeed even more rigid enforcement techniques may be called for with such dichotomy of regulation. . . . One can concede that the "sexual revolution" of recent years may have had useful byproducts in striking layers of prudery from a subject long irrationally kept from needed ventilation. But it does not follow that no regulation of patently offensive "hard core" materials is needed or permissible; civilized people do not allow unregulated access to heroin because it is a derivative of medicinal morphine.

In sum we (a) reaffirm the Roth holding that obscene material is not protected by the First Amendment, (b) hold that such material can be regulated by the States, subject to the specific safeguards enunciated above, without a showing that the materials is "*utterly* without redeeming social value," and (c) hold that obscenity is to be determined by applying "contemporary community standards," . . . not "national standards." . . .

NEW YORK TIMES CO. v. UNITED STATES

403 U. S. 713; 91 S. Ct. 2140; 29 L. Ed. 2d 820 (1971)

On Sunday Morning, June 13, 1971, The New York Times *ran on its front page a modest headline spanning columns five, six, and seven:*

Vietnam Archive: Pentagon Study Traces
3 Decades of Growing U. S. Involvement

A small box underneath said, "Three pages of documentary material from the Pentagon study begin on page 35."

In this unobtrusive way, the reading public was introduced to what was to become one of the most dramatic and sensational cases ever to reach the Supreme Court. The study, tracing the deliberate involvement of the United States in Vietnam during the administrations of four presidents, was based on a 7000-page top secret study made by the Pentagon and was turned over to the Times *by Daniel Ellsberg, a Pentagon employee, as an act of conscience.*

The following Monday night, just as the third in the series was about to appear, the Justice Department called the Times *and asked them to desist from further publication on the ground that publication violated the Espionage Act. The* Times *refused, and Tuesday afternoon the Attorney General filed a motion for an injunction in the district court in New York. That afternoon District Judge Gurfein, who just that day had started work as a federal judge, issued the first federal injunc-*

tion against a newspaper publication in the history of the nation.

Three days later the district court in Washington refused to enjoin the publication of the "Pentagon Papers" by the Washington Post, *and the following day Judge Gurfein abolished his restraining order. Both orders freeing the newspapers were set aside by courts of appeal within hours and on Wednesday of the following week the* Boston Globe *was added to the list.*

Following the decision in the present case, Ellsberg, and his assistant, Anthony Russo, were indicted by a federal grand jury for stealing and releasing the papers. The trial jury had been no more than sworn in the case when Justice Douglas, sitting as a circuit justice, stayed the trial pending a determination of whether the defendants were entitled to hear the tapes of unwarranted government eavesdropping involving one of the defense attorneys. The case ultimately resumed, only to be plagued by the disclosures that the FBI had tapped Ellsberg's telephone in 1969 and 1970 (before the Pentagon Papers were published), that investigators under the direction of White House staff members broke into the office of Ellsberg's psychiatrist, and that the presiding judge, W. Matthew Byrne, Jr., had twice been offered the directorship of the FBI by presidential aide John Ehrlichman while the trial was in progress. In mid-May 1973, clearly angered by the government's overzealous behavior, Judge Byrne dismissed all charges against Ellsberg and Russo and ordered that they not be brought to trial again.

While it is perhaps true, as Justice Holmes said, that great cases make bad law, the importance of the Supreme Court's decision in the present case would be hard to overstate. Over the past forty years, the growing complexity and pervasiveness of government have resulted in a steady increase in presidential power at the expense of congressional power. Nowhere is this more apparent than in the areas of foreign affairs and national defense, in which the President has special constitutional authority, and it is widely assumed that constitutional limitations on presidential prerogatives in these areas should bow to presidential determinations of what the national security requires. The Supreme Court has apparently agreed, and not since Ex parte Milligan (1866), except for the Steel Seizure Case in 1952, has the Supreme Court said "no" to the President on matters of this kind. It thus came as a shock to those who approve such presidential authority that the Court should refuse to prevent the publication of material which the government deemed harmful to the national interest despite the refusal of Congress to provide such a remedy.

While Justice Black was probably right in saying that the First Amendment was drafted to prevent just such assumptions of governmental power over the press, his contention that the Amendment should be applied absolutely literally was so at odds with its judicial development that it attracted few adherents. Far more impressive were the votes of Justices Stewart and White, who felt that the publication was certainly wrong and might even be a crime, but refused to enjoin it because the "heavy burden" borne by the government under the First Amendment had not been met.

In a far less spectacular case decided some six weeks before the Pentagon Papers case the Court also held void an injunction against publication—in this case the distribution of pamphlets in the home neighborhood of an Illinois realtor accused of "block-busting." The leaflets were designed to let "his neighbors know what he was doing to us" in the hope he would agree to stop such tactics. Rejecting the argument that the purpose of the leaflets was to "force" rather than "inform" and that the injunction was a valid protection for the realtor's right of privacy, the Court held it void as a previous restraint on speech and publication. "The claim that the expressions were intended to exercise a coercive impact on respondent does not remove them from the reach of the First Amendment. Petitioners plainly intended to influence respondent's conduct by their activities; this is not fundamentally different from the function of a newspaper. . . . But so long as the means are peaceful, the communication need not meet standards of acceptability." See Organization for a Better Austin v. Keefe (1971).

On similar grounds the Court reviewed the conviction of a young man wearing a jacket bearing the words FUCK THE DRAFT. "The only 'conduct' which the State sought to punish," said the Court, "is the fact of communication. Thus, we deal here with a conviction resting solely upon 'speech'. . . ." Since these were not "fighting words" in the sense of Chaplinsky v. New Hampshire (1942) and were not obscene in the sense of being erotic, they could not be banned merely because some persons objected to them." The ability of government, consonant with the Constitution, to shut off discourse solely to protect others from hearing it is, in other words, dependent upon a showing that substantial privacy interests are being invaded in an essentially intolerable manner. Any broader view of this authority would effectively empower a majority to silence dissidents simply as a matter of personal predilections." See Cohen v. California (1971). And in Schacht v. United States (1970) the Court held void a statute forbidding an actor to wear a United States military uniform unless the actor's portrayal was favorable to the service. While the law could have banned all civilian use of uniforms, forbidding an actor wearing a uniform to say things critical of the service denied him freedom of speech.

In Branzburg v. Hayes (1972) the Supreme Court refused to create a constitutional privilege under the First Amendment for newsmen to withhold confidential sources of information from a grand jury investigating crime. The case involved newspaper reporters who had won the confidence of drug users and of the Black Panther Party and had written behind-the-scenes stories about them. Grand juries investigating these matters subpoenaed the reporters to testify and they refused on the ground that to do so would dry up their news sources and obstruct the free flow of news protected by the First Amendment. A five-man majority rejected their claim, holding that "the First Amendment does not guarantee the press a constitutional right of special access to information not available to the public generally." Nor was there any evidence that there would be "a significant constriction of the flow of news to the public" if reporters had to testify like anyone else, and it was clear that the state's interest in "extirpating the traffic in illegal drugs, in forestalling assassination attempts on the President, and in preventing the community from being disrupted" were "compelling" enough to justify this indirect burden on the press. Justice Stewart, speaking for three of the four dissenters, argues that the Court has now shifted the burden to those trying to defend their First Amendment rights, and notes that the victory of the grand jury is a Pyrrhic one at best. "The sad paradox of the Court's position is that when a grand jury may exercise an unbridled subpoena power, and sources involved in sensitive matters become fearful of disclosing information, the newsman will not only cease to be a useful grand jury witness; he will cease to investigate and publish information about issues of public import."

The success of felons who commit highly publicized crimes in marketing books about their exploits prompted New York, in 1977, to enact what is popularly known as "the Son of Sam" law to prevent a notorious serial killer from profiting from his notoriety. The law required persons contracting to publish reenactments of the crime, or the criminal's "thoughts, feelings, opinions, or emotions regarding such crime," to pay the proceeds from the sale to the state Crime Victim Board to compensate the victims of such crime for their losses. A unanimous Court held the statute void, noting that it was a "content-based statute" which "singles out income derived from expressive activity for a burden the State places on no other income, and is directed at works with a specified content." Conceding the compelling interest the state has in ensuring that criminals do not profit from their crimes, "the Board cannot explain why the State should have any greater interest in compensating victims from the proceeds of such 'storytelling' than from any of the criminal's other assets. Nor can the Board offer any justification for a distinction between this expressive activity and any other activity in connection with its interest in transferring the fruits of crime from criminals to their victims."

Per Curiam.

We granted certiorari in these cases in which the United States seeks to enjoin the New York Times and the Washington Post from publishing the contents of a classified study entitled "History of U. S. Decision-Making Process on Viet Nam Policy."

"Any system of prior restraints of expression comes to this Court bearing a heavy presumption against its constitutional validity." Bantam Books, Inc. v. Sullivan (1963); see also Near v. Minnesota (1931). The Government "thus carries a heavy burden of showing justification for the imposition of such a restraint." Organization for a Better Austin v. Keefe (1971). The District Court for the Southern District of New York in the

New York Times case and the District Court for the District of Columbia and the Court of Appeals for the District of Columbia Circuit in the Washington Post case held that the Government had not met that burden. We agree.

The judgment of the Court of Appeals for the District of Columbia Circuit is therefore affirmed. The order of the Court of Appeals for the Second Circuit is reversed and the case is remanded with directions to enter a judgment affirming the judgment of the District Court for the Southern District of New York. The stays entered June 25, 1971, by the Court are vacated. The judgments shall issue forthwith.

So ordered.

Mr. Justice **Black,** with whom Mr. Justice **Douglas** joins, concurring, said in part:

. . . I agree completely that we must affirm the judgment of the Court of Appeals for the District of Columbia and reverse the judgment of the Court of Appeals for the Second Circuit for the reasons stated by my Brothers Douglas and Brennan. In my view it is unfortunate that some of my Brethren are apparently willing to hold that the publication of news may sometimes be enjoined. Such a holding would make a shambles of the First Amendment. . . .

In seeking injunctions against these newspapers and its presentation to the Court, the Executive Branch seems to have forgotten the essential purpose and history of the First Amendment. When the Constitution was adopted, many people strongly opposed it because the document contained no Bill of Rights to safeguard certain basic freedoms. They especially feared that the new powers granted to a central government might be interpreted to permit the government to curtail freedom of religion, press, assembly, and speech. In response to an overwhelming public clamor, James Madison offered a series of amendments to satisfy citizens that these great liberties would remain safe and beyond the power of government to abridge. . . . The amendments were offered to *curtail* and *restrict* the general powers granted to the Executive, Legislative, and Judicial Branches two years before in the original Constitution. The Bill of Rights changed the original Constitution into a new charter under which no branch of government could abridge the people's freedoms of press, speech, religion, and assembly. Yet the Solicitor General argues and some members of the Court appear to agree that the general powers of the Government adopted in the original Constitution should be interpreted to limit and restrict the specific and emphatic guarantees of the Bill of Rights adopted later. I can imagine no greater perversion of history. Madison and the other Framers of the First Amendment, able men that they were, wrote in language they earnestly believed could never be misunderstood: "Congress shall make no law . . . abridging the freedom of the press. . . ." Both the history and language of the First Amendment support the view that the press must be left free to publish news, whatever the source, without censorship, injunctions, or prior restraints.

In the First Amendment the Founding Fathers gave the free press the protection it must have to fulfill its essential role in our democracy. The press was to serve the governed, not the governors. The Government's power to censor the press was abolished so that the press would remain forever free to censure the Government. The press was protected so that it could bare the secrets of government and inform the people. Only a free and unrestrained press can effectively expose deception in government. And paramount among the responsibilities of a free press is the duty to prevent any part of the government from deceiving the people and sending them off to distant lands to die of foreign fevers and foreign shot and shell. In my view, far from deserving condemnation for their courageous reporting, the New York Times, the Washington Post, and other newspapers should be commended for serving the purpose that the Founding Fathers saw so clearly. In revealing the workings of government that led to the Viet Nam war, the newspapers nobly did precisely that which the Founders hoped and trusted they would do.

The Government's case here is based on premises entirely different from those that guided the Framers of the First Amendment. . . . And the Government argues in its brief that in spite of the First Amendment, "[t]he authority of the Executive Department to protect the nation against publication of information whose disclosure would endanger the national security stems from two interrelated sources: the constitutional power of the President over the conduct of foreign affairs and his authority as Commander-in-Chief."

. . . To find that the President has "inherent power" to halt the publication of news by resort to the courts would wipe out the First Amendment and destroy the fundamental liberty and security of the very people the Government hopes to make "secure." No one can read the history of the adoption of the First Amendment without being convinced beyond any doubt that it was injunctions like those sought here that Madison and his collaborators intended to outlaw in this Nation for all time.

The word "security" is a broad, vague generality whose contours should not be invoked to abrogate the fundamental law embodied in the First Amendment. The guarding of military and diplomatic secrets at the expense of informed representative government provides no real security for our Republic. The Framers of the First Amendment, fully aware of both the need to defend a new nation and the abuses of the English and Colonial governments, sought to give this new society strength and security by providing that freedom of speech, press, religion, and assembly should not be abridged. This thought was eloquently expressed in 1937 by Mr. Chief Justice Hughes—great man and great Chief Justice that he was—when the Court held a man could not be punished for attending a meeting run by Communists.

"The greater the importance of safeguarding the community from incitements to the overthrow of our institutions by force and violence, the more imperative is the need to preserve inviolate the constitutional rights of free speech, free press and free assembly in order to maintain the opportunity for free political discussion, to the end that government may be responsive to the will of the people and that changes, if desired, may be obtained by peaceful means. Therein lies the security of the Republic, the very foundation of constitutional government'' [De Jonge v. Oregon, 1937].

Mr. Justice **Douglas,** with whom Mr. Justice **Black** joins, concurring, said in part:

While I join the opinion of the Court I believe it necessary to express my views more fully.

It should be noted at the outset that the First Amendment provides that ''Congress shall make no law . . . abridging the freedom of speech or of the press.'' That leaves, in my view, no room for governmental restraint on the press.

There is, moreover, no statute barring the publication by the press of the material which the Times and Post seek to use. . . .

[Justice Douglas reviewed the wording of the Espionage Act and argued that Congress, in prohibiting ''communication'' of defense information, deliberately rejected a prohibition on ''publication.'']

Judge Gurfein's holding in the Times case that this Act does not apply to this case was therefore pre-eminently sound. Moreover, the Act of September 23, 1950, in amending 18 USC § 793 states in § 1 (b) that: ''Nothing in this Act shall be construed to authorize, require, or establish military or civilian censorship or in any way to limit or infringe upon freedom of the press or of speech as guaranteed by the Constitution of the United States and no regulation shall be promulgated hereunder having that effect.'' Thus Congress had been faithful to the command of the First Amendment in this area.

So any power that the Government possesses must come from its ''inherent power.'' . . .

The Government says that it has inherent powers to go into court and obtain an injunction to protect that national interest, which in this case is alleged to be national security.

Near v. Minnesota [1931] repudiated that expansive doctrine in no uncertain terms.

The dominant purpose of the First Amendment was to prohibit the widespread practice of governmental suppression of embarrassing information. It is common knowledge that the First Amendment was adopted against the widespread use of the common law of seditious libel to punish the dissemination of material that is embarrassing to the powers-that-be. . . . The present cases will, I think, go down in history as the most dramatic illustration of that principle. A debate of large proportions goes on in the Nation over our posture in Vietnam. That debate antedated the disclosure of the contents of the present documents. The latter are highly relevant to the debate in progress.

Secrecy in government is fundamentally anti-democratic, perpetuating bureaucratic errors. Open debate and discussion of public issues are vital to our national health. On public questions there should be ''open and robust debate.'' New York Times, Inc. v. Sullivan [1964].

I would affirm the judgment of the Court of Appeals in the Post case, vacate the stay of the Court of Appeals in the Times case and direct that it affirm the District Court. . . .

Mr. Justice **Brennan,** concurring, said in part:

I write separately in these cases only to emphasize what should be apparent: that our judgment in the present cases may not be taken to indicate the propriety, in the future, of issuing temporary stays and restraining orders to block the publication of material sought to be suppressed by the Government. So far as I can determine, never before has the United States sought to enjoin a newspaper from publishing information in its possession. . . .

II.

The error which has pervaded these cases from the outset was the granting of any injunctive relief whatsoever, interim or otherwise. The entire thrust of the Government's claim throughout these cases has been that publication of the material sought to be enjoined ''could,'' or ''might,'' or ''may'' prejudice the national interest in various ways. But the First Amendment tolerates absolutely no prior judicial restraints of the press predicated upon surmise or conjecture that untoward consequences may result. . . . Our cases, it is true, have indicated that there is a single, extremely narrow class of cases in which the First Amendment's ban on prior judicial restraint may be overridden. Our cases have thus far indicated that such cases may arise only when the Nation ''is at war,'' Schenck v. United States (1919), during which times ''no one would question but that a Government might prevent actual obstruction to its recruiting service or the publication of the sailing dates of transports or the number and location of troops.'' Near v. Minnesota (1931). Even if the present world situation were assumed to be tantamount to a time of war, or if the power of presently available armaments would justify even in peacetime the suppression of information that would set in motion a nuclear holocaust, in neither of these actions has the Government presented or even alleged that publication of items from or based upon the material at issue would cause the happening of an event of that nature. ''The chief purpose of [the First Amendment's] guarantee [is] to prevent previous restraints upon publication.'' Near v. Minnesota. Thus, only governmental allegation and proof that publication must inevitably, directly and immediately cause the occurrence of an event kindred to imperiling the safety of a transport already at sea can support even the issuance of an interim restraining order. In no event may mere conclusions be sufficient: for if the Executive Branch seeks judicial aid in preventing the publication, it must inevitably submit the basis upon which that aid is sought to scrutiny by the judiciary. And therefore, every restraint issued in this case, whatever its form, has violated the First Amendment—and none the less so because that restraint was justified as necessary to afford the court an opportunity to examine the claim more thoroughly. Unless and until the Government has clearly made out its case, the First Amendment commands that no injunction may issue.

Mr. Justice **Stewart,** with whom Mr. Justice **White** joins, concurring, said in part:

In the absence of the governmental checks and balances present in other areas of our national life, the only effective restraint upon executive policy and power in the areas of national defense and international affairs may lie in an enlightened citizenry—in an informed and critical public opinion which alone can here protect the values of democratic government. For this reason, it is perhaps here that a press that is alert, aware, and free most vitally serves the basic purpose of the First Amendment. For without an informed and free press there cannot be an enlightened people.

Yet it is elementary that the successful conduct of international diplomacy and the maintenance of an effective national defense require both confidentiality and secrecy. Other nations can hardly deal with this Nation in an atmosphere of mutual trust unless they can be assured that their confidences will be kept. And within our own executive departments, the development of considered and intelligent international policies would be impossible if those charged with their formulation could not communicate with each other freely, frankly, and in confidence. In the area of basic national defense the frequent need for absolute secrecy is, of course, self-evident.

I think there can be but one answer to this dilemma, if dilemma it be. The responsibility must be where the power is. If the Constitution gives the Executive a large degree of unshared power in the conduct of foreign affairs and the maintenance of our national defense, then under the Constitution the Executive must have the largely unshared duty to determine and preserve the degree of internal security necessary to exercise that power successfully. It is an awesome responsibility, requiring judgment and wisdom of a high order. I should suppose that moral, political, and practical considerations would dictate that a very first principle of that wisdom would be an insistence upon avoiding secrecy for its own sake. For when everything is classified, then nothing is classified, and the system becomes one to be disregarded by the cynical or the careless, and to be manipulated by those intent on self-protection or self-promotion. I should suppose, in short, that the hallmark of a truly effective internal security system would be the maximum possible disclosure, recognizing that secrecy can best be preserved only when credibility is truly maintained. But be that as it may, it is clear to me that it is the constitutional duty of the Executive—as a matter of sovereign prerogative and not as a matter of law as the courts know law—through the promulgation and enforcement of executive regulations, to protect the confidentiality necessary to carry out its responsibilities in the fields of international relations and national defense.

This is not to say that Congress and the courts have no role to play. Undoubtedly Congress has the power to enact specific and appropriate criminal laws to protect government property and preserve government secrets. Congress has passed such laws, and several of them are of very colorable relevance to the apparent circumstances of these cases. And if a criminal prosecution is instituted, it will be the responsibility of the courts to decide the applicability of the criminal law under which the charge is brought. Moreover, if Congress should pass a specific law authorizing civil proceedings in this field, the courts would likewise have the duty to decide the constitutionality of such a law as well as its applicability to the facts proved.

But in the cases before us we are asked neither to construe specific regulations nor to apply specific laws. We are asked, instead, to perform a function that the Constitution gave to the Executive, not the Judiciary. We are asked, quite simply, to prevent the publication by two newspapers of material that the Executive Branch insists should not, in the national interest, be published. I am convinced that the Executive is correct with respect to some of the documents involved. But I cannot say that disclosure of any of them will surely result in direct, immediate, and irreparable damage to our Nation or its people. That being so, there can under the First Amendment be but one judicial resolution of the issues before us. I join the judgments of the Court.

Mr. Justice **White,** with whom Mr. Justice **Stewart** joins, concurring, said in part:

I concur in today's judgments, but only because of the concededly extraordinary protection against prior restraints enjoyed by the press under our constitutional system. I do not say that in no circumstances would the First Amendment permit an injunction against publishing information about government plans or operations. Nor, after examining the materials the Government characterizes as the most sensitive and destructive, can I deny that revelation of these documents will do substantial damage to public interests. Indeed, I am confident that their disclosure will have that result. But I nevertheless agree that the United States has not satisfied the very heavy burden which it must meet to warrant an injunction against publication in these cases, at least in the absence of express and appropriately limited congressional authorization for prior restraints in circumstances such as these.

The Government's position is simply stated: The responsibility of the Executive for the conduct of the foreign affairs and for the security of the Nation is so basic that the President is entitled to an injunction against publication of a newspaper story whenever he can convince a court that the information to be revealed threatens "grave and irreparable" injury to the public interest; and the injunction should issue whether or not the material to be published is classified, whether or not publication would be lawful under relevant criminal statutes enacted by Congress and regardless of the circumstances by which the newspaper came into possession of the information.

At least in the absence of legislation by Congress, based on its own investigations and findings, I am quite unable to agree that the inherent powers of the Executive and the courts reach so far as to authorize remedies having such sweeping potential for inhibiting publications by the press. . . .

What is more, terminating the ban on publication of the relatively few sensitive documents the Government now seeks to suppress does not mean that the law either requires or invites newspapers or others to publish them or that they would be immune from criminal action if they do. Prior restraints require an unusually heavy justification under the First Amendment; but failure by the Government to justify prior restraints does not measure its constitutional entitlement to a conviction for criminal publication. That the Government mistakenly chose to proceed by injunction does not mean that it could not successfully proceed in another way.

When the Espionage Act was under consideration in 1917, Congress eliminated from the bill a provision that would have given the President broad powers in time of war to proscribe, under threat of criminal penalty, the publication of various categories of information related to the national defense. Congress at that time was unwilling to clothe the President with such far-reaching powers to monitor the press, and those opposed to this part of the legislation assumed that a necessary concomitant of such power was the power to "filter out the news to the people through some man." . . . However, these same members of Congress appeared to have little doubt that newspapers would be subject to criminal prosecution if they insisted on publishing information of the type Congress had itself determined should not be revealed. . . .

. . . If any of the material here at issue is of this nature, the newspapers are presumably now on full notice of the position of the United States and must face the consequences if they publish. I would have no difficulty in sustaining convictions under these sections on facts that would not justify the intervention of equity and the imposition of a prior restraint. . . .

It is thus clear that Congress has addressed itself to the problems of protecting the security of the country and the national defense from unauthorized disclosure of potentially damaging information. . . . It has not, however, authorized the injunctive remedy against threatened publication. It has apparently been satisfied to rely on criminal sanctions and their deterrent effect on the responsible as well as the irresponsible press. I am not, of course, saying that either of these newspapers has yet committed a crime or that either would commit a crime if they published all the material now in their possession. That matter must await resolution in the context of a criminal proceeding if one is instituted by the United States. In that event, the issue of guilt or innocence would be determined by procedures and standards quite different from those that have purported to govern these injunctive proceedings.

Mr. Justice **Marshall,** concurring, said in part:

It would, however, be utterly inconsistent with the concept of separation of power for this Court to use its power of contempt to prevent behavior that Congress has specifically declined to prohibit. There would be a similar damage to the basic concept of these coequal branches of Government if when the Executive has adequate authority granted by Congress to protect "national security" it can choose instead to invoke the contempt power of a court to enjoin the threatened conduct. The Constitution provides that Congress shall make laws, the President execute laws, and courts interpret law. . . . It did not provide for government by injunction in which the courts and the Executive can "make law" without regard to the action of Congress. It may be more convenient for the Executive if it need only convince a judge to prohibit conduct rather than to ask the Congress to pass a law and it may be more convenient to enforce a contempt order than seek a criminal conviction in a jury trial. Moreover, it may be considered politically wise to get a court to share the responsibility for arresting those who the Executive has probable cause to believe are violating the law. But convenience and political considerations of the moment do not justify a basic departure from the principles of our system of government. . . .

Even if it is determined that the Government could not in good faith bring criminal prosecutions against the New York Times and the Washington Post, it is clear that Congress has specifically rejected passing legislation that would have clearly given the President the power he seeks here and made the current activity of the newspapers unlawful. When Congress specifically declines to make conduct unlawful it is not for this Court to redecide those issues—to overrule Congress. . . .

Mr. Chief Justice **Burger,** dissenting.

So clear are the constitutional limitations on prior restraint against expression, that from the time of Near v. Minnesota (1931) until recently in Organization for a Better Austin v. Keefe (1971), we have had little occasion to be concerned with cases involving prior restraints against news reporting on matters of public interest. There is, therefore, little variation among the members of the Court in terms of resistance to prior restraints against publication. Adherence to this basic constitutional principle, however, does not make this case a simple one. In this case, the imperative of a free and unfettered press comes into collision with another imperative, the effective functioning of a complex modern government and specifically the effective exercise of certain constitutional powers of the Executive. Only those who view the First Amendment as an absolute in all circumstances—a view I respect, but reject—can find such a case as this to be simple or easy.

This case is not simple for another and more immediate reason. We do not know the facts of the case. No District Judge knew all the facts. No Court of Appeals judge knew all the facts. No member of this Court knows all the facts.

Why are we in this posture, in which only those judges to whom the First Amendment is absolute and permits of no restraint in any circumstances or for any reason, are really in a position to act?

I suggest we are in this posture because these cases have been conducted in unseemly haste. Mr. Justice Harlan covers the chronology of events demonstrating the hectic pressures under which these cases have been processed and I need not restate them. The prompt setting of these cases reflects our universal abhorrence of prior restraint. But prompt judicial actions does not mean unjudicial haste.

Here, moreover, the frenetic haste is due in large part to the manner in which the Times proceeded from the date it obtained the purloined documents. It seems reasonably clear now that the haste precluded reasonable and deliberate judicial treatment of these cases and was not warranted. The precipitous action of this Court aborting a trial not yet completed is not the kind of judicial conduct which ought to attend the disposition of a great issue.

The newspapers make a derivative claim under the First Amendment; they denominate this right as the public right-to-know; by implication, the Times asserts a sole trusteeship of that right by virtue of its journalistic "scoop." The right is asserted as an absolute. Of course, the First Amendment right itself is not an absolute, as Justice Holmes so long ago pointed out in his aphorism concerning the right to shout fire in a crowded theater. There are other exceptions, some of which Chief Justice Hughes mentioned by way of example in Near v. Minnesota. There are no doubt other exceptions no one has had the occasion to describe or discuss. Conceivably such exceptions may be lurking in these cases and would have been flushed had they been properly considered in the trial courts, free from unwarranted deadlines and frenetic pressures. A great issue of this kind should be tried in a judicial atmosphere conducive to thoughtful, reflective deliberation, especially when haste, in terms of hours, is unwarranted in light of the long period the Times, by its own choice, deferred publication.

It is not disputed that the Times has had unauthorized possession of the documents for three to four months, during which it has had its expert analysts studying them, presumably digesting them and preparing the material for publication. During all of this time, the Times, presumably in its capacity as trustee of the public's "right to know," has held up publication for purposes it considered proper and thus public knowledge was delayed. No doubt this was for a good reason; the

analysis of 7,000 pages of complex material drawn from a vastly greater volume of material would inevitably take time and the writing of good news stories takes time. But why should the United States Government, from whom this information was illegally acquired by someone, along with all the counsel, trial judges, and appellate judges be placed under needless pressure? After these months of deferral, the alleged right-to-know has somehow and suddenly become a right that must be vindicated instanter.

Would it have been unreasonable, since the newspaper could anticipate the government's objections to release of secret material, to give the government an opportunity to review the entire collection and determine whether agreement could be reached on publication? Stolen or not, if security was not in fact jeopardized, much of the material could no doubt have been declassified, since it spans a period ending in 1968. With such an approach—one that great newspapers have in the past practiced and stated editorially to be the duty of an honorable press—the newspapers and government might well have narrowed the area of disagreement as to what was and was not publishable, leaving the remainder to be resolved in orderly litigation if necessary. To me it is hardly believable that a newspaper long regarded as a great institution in American life would fail to perform one of the basic and simple duties of every citizen with respect to the discovery or possession of stolen property or secret government documents. That duty, I had thought—perhaps naively—was to report forthwith, to responsible public officers. This duty rests on taxi drivers, Justices and the New York Times. The course followed by the Times, whether so calculated or not, removed any possibility of orderly litigation of the issues. If the action of the judges up to now has been correct, that result is sheer happenstance.*

Our grant of the writ before final judgment in the Times case aborted the trial in the District Court before it had made a complete record pursuant to the mandate of the Court of Appeals, Second Circuit.

The consequence of all this melancholy series of events is that we literally do not know what we are acting on. As I see it we have been forced to deal with litigation concerning rights of great magnitude without an adequate record, and surely without time for adequate treatment either in the prior proceedings or in this Court. It is interesting to note that counsel in oral argument before this Court were frequently unable to respond to questions on factual points. Not surprisingly they pointed out that they had been working literally "around the clock" and simply were unable to review the documents that give rise to these cases and were not familiar with them. This Court is in no better posture. I agree with Mr.

---

*Interestingly the Times explained its refusal to allow the government to examine its own purloined documents by saying in substance this might compromise *their* sources and informants! The Times thus asserts a right to guard the secrecy of its sources while denying that the Government of the United States has that power.

Justice Harlan and Mr. Justice Blackmun but I am not prepared to reach the merits.*

I would affirm the Court of Appeals for the Second Circuit and allow the District Court to complete the trial aborted by our grant of certiorari meanwhile preserving the status quo in the Post case. I would direct that the District Court on remand give priority to the Times case to the exclusion of all other business of that court but I would not set arbitrary deadlines.

I should add that I am in general agreement with much of what Mr. Justice White has expressed with respect to penal sanctions concerning communication or retention of documents or information relating to the national defense.

We all crave speedier judicial processes but when judges are pressured as in these cases the result is a parody of the judicial process.

Mr. Justice **Harlan**, with whom **the Chief Justice** and Mr. Justice **Blackmun** join, dissenting, said in part:

These cases forcefully call to mind the wise admonition of Mr. Justice Holmes, dissenting in Northern Securities Co. v. United States (1904):

"Great cases like hard cases make bad law. For great cases are called great, not by reason of their real importance in shaping the law of the future, but because of some accident of immediate overwhelming interest which appeals to the feelings and distorts the judgment. These immediate interests exercise a kind of hydraulic pressure which makes what previously was clear seem doubtful, and before which even well settled principles of law will bend."

With all respect, I consider that the Court has been almost irresponsibly feverish in dealing with these cases. . . .

Forced as I am to reach the merits of these cases, I dissent from the opinion and judgments of the Court. Within the severe limitations imposed by the time constraints under which I have been required to operate, I can only state my reasons in telescoped form. . . .

It is a sufficient basis for affirming the Court of Appeals for the Second Circuit in the Times litigation to observe that its order must rest on the conclusion that because of the time elements the Government had not been given an adequate opportunity to present its case to the District Court. At least this conclusion was not an abuse of discretion.

In the Post litigation the Government had more time to prepare; this was apparently the basis for the refusal of the Court of Appeals for the District of Colum-

bia Circuit on rehearing to conform its judgment to that of the Second Circuit. But I think there is another and more fundamental reason why this judgment cannot stand—a reason which also furnishes an additional ground for not reinstating the judgment of the District Court in the Times litigation, set aside by the Court of Appeals. It is plain to me that the scope of the judicial function in passing upon the activities of the Executive Branch of the Government in the field of foreign affairs is very narrowly restricted. This view is, I think, dictated by the concept of separation of powers upon which our constitutional system rests.

In a speech on the floor of the House of Representatives, Chief Justice John Marshall, then a member of that body, stated: "The President is the sole organ of the nation in its external relations, and its sole representative with foreign nations." . . .

From that time, shortly after the founding of the Nation, to this, there has been no substantial challenge to this description of the scope of executive power. See United States v. Curtiss-Wright Export Corp. (1936), collecting authorities. . . .

The power to evaluate the "pernicious influence" of premature disclosure is not, however, lodged in the Executive alone. I agree that, in performance of its duty to protect the values of the First Amendment against political pressures, the judiciary must review the initial Executive determination to the point of satisfying itself that the subject matter of the dispute does lie within the proper compass of the President's foreign relations power. Constitutional considerations forbid "a complete abandonment of judicial control." Moreover, the judiciary may properly insist that the determination that disclosure of the subject matter would irreparably impair the national security be made by the head of the Executive Department concerned—here the Secretary of State or the Secretary of Defense—after actual personal consideration by that officer. This safeguard is required in the analogous area of executive claims of privilege for secrets of state. See United States v. Reynolds [1953]. . . . But in my judgment the judiciary may not properly go beyond these two inquiries and redetermine for itself the probable impact of disclosure on the national security. "[T]he very nature of executive decisions as to foreign policy is political, not judicial. Such decisions are wholly confided by our Constitution to the political departments of the government, Executive and Legislative. They are delicate, complex, and involve large elements of prophecy. They are and should be undertaken only by those directly responsible to the people whose welfare they advance or imperil. They are decisions of a kind for which the Judiciary has neither aptitude, facilities nor responsibility and which has long been held to belong in the domain of political power not subject to judicial intrusion or inquiry." Chicago & Southern Air Lines v. Waterman Steamship Corp. (1948) (Jackson, J.). . . . Pending further hearings in each case conducted under the appropriate ground rules, I would continue the restraints on publication. I cannot believe that the doctrine prohibiting prior restraints reaches to the point of pre-

---

*With respect to the question of inherent power of the Executive to classify papers, records and documents as secret, or otherwise unavailable for public exposure, and to secure aid of the courts for enforcement, there may be an analogy with respect to this Court. No statute gives this Court express power to establish and enforce the utmost security measures for the secrecy of our deliberations and records. Yet I have little doubt as to the inherent power of the Court to protect the confidentiality of its internal operations by whatever judicial measures may be required.

venting courts from maintaining the status quo long enough to act responsibly in matters of such national importance as those involved here.

Mr. Justice **Blackmun**, said in part:

I join Mr. Justice Harlan in his dissent. I also am in substantial accord with much that Mr. Justice White says, by way of admonition, in the latter part of his opinion. . . .

Two federal district courts, two United States courts of appeals, and this Court—within a period of less than three weeks from inception until today—have been pressed into hurried decision of profound constitutional issues on inadequately developed and largely assumed facts without the careful deliberation that, hopefully, should characterize the American judicial process. There has been much writing about the law and little knowledge and less digestion of the facts. In the New York case the judges, both trial and appellate, had not yet examined the basic material when the case was brought here. In the District of Columbia case, little more was done, and what was accomplished in this respect was only on required remand, with the Washington Post, on the excuse that it was trying to protect its source of information, initially refusing to reveal what material it actually possessed, and with the district court forced to make assumptions as to that possession.

With such respect as may be due to the contrary view, this, in my opinion, is not the way to try a lawsuit of this magnitude and asserted importance. It is not the way for federal courts to adjudicate, and to be required to adjudicate, issues that allegedly concern the Nation's vital welfare. The country would be none the worse off were the cases tried quickly, to be sure, but in the customary and properly deliberative manner. The most recent of the material, it is said, dates no later than 1968, already about three years ago, and the Times itself took three months to formulate its plan of procedure and, thus, deprived its public for that period.

The First Amendment, after all, is only one part of an entire Constitution. Article II of the great document vests in the Executive Branch primary power over the conduct of foreign affairs and places in that branch the responsibility for the Nation's safety. Each provision of the Constitution is important, and I cannot subscribe to a doctrine of unlimited absolutism for the First Amendment at the cost of downgrading other provisions. First Amendment absolutism has never commanded a majority of this Court. . . .

RUST v. SULLIVAN

114 L. Ed2d 233 (1991)

As the federal government plays an increasingly active role in the functioning of the welfare state its ability to grant or withhold vital benefits and spend almost unlim-

ited sums of money to buy compliance with its wishes, poses a growing threat to the civil rights of individuals.

The use of this power has taken a variety of forms. In Wyman v. James (1971) it was used to force a recipient of welfare to permit an unwanted invasion of her home; in Maher v. Roe (1977) it was used to persuade a woman to carry an unwanted child to term rather than undergo an abortion; in Bordenkircher v. Hayes (1978) it was used to persuade a person to plead guilty to a crime; in Lyng v. Automobile Workers (1988), by withholding food stamps from the families of striking workers, it was used to discourage strikes.

Rarely has the power been used to attack directly rights under the First Amendment. In Sherbert v. Verner (1936) the Court refused to permit the withholding of unemployment compensation from a woman who would not accept work which violated her religious scruples. The present case, however, raises the right of the government to use its power to buy the silence of a doctor on the subject of abortion in a conversation with one of his pregnant patients.

Chief Justice **Rehnquist** delivered the opinion of the Court, saying in part:

These cases concern a facial challenge to Department of Health and Human Services (HHS) regulations which limit the ability of Title X fund recipients to engage in abortion-related activities. . . .

I.

A.

In 1970, Congress enacted Title X of the Public Health Service Act (Act) which provides federal funding for family-planning services. The Act authorizes the Secretary to "make grants to and enter into contracts with public or nonprofit private entities to assist in the establishment and operation of voluntary family planning projects which shall offer a broad range of acceptable and effective family planning methods and services." Grants and contracts under Title X must "be made in accordance with such regulations as the Secretary may promulgate." Section 1008 of the Act, however, provides that "[n]one of the funds appropriated under this subchapter shall be used in programs where abortion is a method of family planning. That restriction was intended to ensure that Title X funds would "be used only to support preventive family planning services, population research, infertility services, and other related medical, informational, and educational activities."

In 1988, the Secretary promulgated new regulations designed to provide " 'clear and operational guidance' to grantees about how to preserve the distinction between Title X programs and abortion as a method of family planning." The regulations clarify, through the definition of the term "family planning," that Congress intended Title X funds "to be used only to support preventive family planning services." Accordingly, Title X services are limited to "preconceptual counseling, education, and general reproductive health care," and expressly exclude "pregnancy care (including obstetric or prenatal care)." The regulations "focus the emphasis of the Title X program on its traditional mission: The provision of preventive family planning services specifically designed to enable individuals to determine the number and spacing or their children, while clarifying that pregnant women must be referred to appropriate prenatal care services."

The regulations attach three principal conditions on the grant of federal funds for Title X projects. First, the regulations specify that a "Title X project may not provide counseling concerning the use of abortion as a method of family planning or provide referral for abortion as a method of family planning." . . . The Title X project is expressly prohibited from referring a pregnant woman to an abortion provider, even upon specific request. One permissible response to such an inquiry is that "the project does not consider abortion an appropriate method of family planning and therefore does not counsel or refer for abortion." . . .

B.

Petitioners are Title X grantees and doctors who supervise Title X funds suing on behalf of themselves and their patients. Respondent is the Secretary of the Department of Health and Human Services. After the regulations had been promulgated, but before they had been applied, petitioners filed two separate actions, later consolidated, challenging the facial validity of the regulations and seeking declaratory and injunctive relief to prevent implementation of the regulations. Petitioners challenged the regulations on the grounds that they were not authorized by Title X and that they violate the First and Fifth Amendment rights of Title X clients and the First Amendment rights of Title X health providers. . . .

II.

A.

We need not dwell on the plain language of the statute because we agree with every court to have addressed the issue that the language is ambiguous. The language of § 1008—that "[n]one of the funds appropriated under this subchapter shall be used in programs where abortion is a method of family planning"—does not speak directly to the issues of counseling, referral, advocacy, or program integrity. If a statute is "silent or ambiguous with respect to the specific issue, the question for the court is whether the agency's answer is based on a permissible construction of the statute." . . .

The broad language of Title X plainly allows the Secretary's construction of the statute. By its own terms, § 1008 prohibits the use of Title X funds "in programs where abortion is a method of family planning." Title X does not define the term "method of family planning," nor does it enumerate what types of medical and counseling services are entitled to Title X funding. Based on the broad directives provided by Congress in Title X in general and § 1008 in particular, we are unable to say that the Secretary's construction of the prohibition in § 1008 to require a ban on counseling, referral, and advocacy within the Title X project, is impermissible. . . .

III.

Petitioners contend that the regulations violate the First Amendment by impermissibly discriminating based on viewpoint because they prohibit "all discussion about abortion as a lawful option—including counseling, referral, and the provision of neutral and accurate information about ending a pregnancy—while compelling the clinic or counselor to provide information that promotes continuing a pregnancy to term." They assert that the regulations violate the "free speech rights of private health care organizations that receive Title X funds, of their staff and of their patients" by impermissibly imposing "viewpoint-discriminatory conditions on government subsidies" and thus "penaliz[e] speech funded with non-Title X monies." Because "Title X continues to fund speech ancillary to pregnancy testing in a manner that is not evenhanded with respect to views and information about abortion, it invidiously discriminates on the basis of view-point."

There is no question but that the statutory prohibition contained in § 1008 is constitutional. In Maher v. Roe (1977) we upheld a state welfare regulation under which Medicaid recipients received payments for services related to childbirth, but not for nontherapeutic abortions. The Court rejected the claim that this unequal subsidization worked a violation of the Constitution. We held that the government may "make a value judgment favoring childbirth over abortion, and . . . implement that judgment by the allocation of public funds." Here the Government is exercising the authority it possesses under Maher and Harris v. McRae (1980) to subsidize family planning services which will lead to conception and child birth, and declining to "promote or encourage abortion." The Government can, without violating the Constitution, selectively fund a program to encourage certain activities it believes to be in the public interest, without at the same time funding an alternate program which seeks to deal with the problem in another way. In so doing, the Government has not discriminated on the basis of viewpoint; it has merely chosen to fund one activity to the exclusion of the other. "[A] legislature's decision not to subsidize the exercise of a fundamental right does not infringe the right." . . . See also, Buckley v. Valeo (1978) . . . . "A refusal to fund protected activity, without more, cannot be equated with the imposition of a 'penalty' on that activity." . . . "There is a basic difference between direct state interference with a protected activity and state encouragement of an alternative activity consonant with legislative policy." *Maher v. Roe* (1977).

The challenged regulations implement the statutory prohibition by prohibiting counseling, referral, and the provision of information regarding abortion as a method of family planning. They are designed to ensure that: the limits of the federal program are observed. The Title X program is designed not for prenatal care, but to encourage family planning. A doctor who wished to offer prenatal care to a project patient who became pregnant could properly be prohibited from doing so because such service is outside the scope of the federally funded program. The regulations prohibiting abortion counseling and referral are of the same ilk; "no funds appropriated for the project may be used in programs where abortion is a method of family planning," and a doctor employed by the project may be prohibited in the course of his project duties from counseling abortion or referring for abortion. This is not a case of the Government "suppressing a dangerous idea," but of a prohibition on a project grantee or its employees from engaging in activities outside of its scope.

To hold that the Government unconstitutionally discriminates on the basis of viewpoint when it chooses to fund a program dedicated to advance certain permissible goals, because the program in advancing those goals necessarily discourages alternate goals, would render numerous government programs constitutionally suspect. When Congress established a National Endowment for Democracy to encourage other countries to adopt democratic principles, it was not constitutionally required to fund a program to encourage competing lines of political philosophy such as Communism and Fascism. Petitioners' assertions ultimately boil down to the position that if the government chooses to subsidize one protected right, it must subsidize analogous counterpart rights, but the Court has soundly rejected that proposition. . . .

Petitioners also contend that the restrictions on the subsidization of abortion-related speech contained in the regulations are impermissible because they condition the receipt of a benefit, in this case Title X funding, on the relinquishment of a constitutional right, the right to engage in abortion advocacy and counseling. Relying on *Perry v. Sindermann* (1972), and *FCC v. League of Women Voters of Cal.* (1984), petitioners argue that "even though the government may deny a benefit for any number of reasons, there are some reasons upon which the government may not rely. It may not deny a benefit to a person on a basis that infringes his constitutionally protected interests—especially, his interest in freedom of speech."

Petitioners' reliance on these cases is unavailing, however, because here the government is not denying a benefit to anyone, but is instead simply insisting that public funds be spent for the purposes for which they were authorized. The Secretary's regulations do not force the Title X grantee to give up abortion related speech; they merely require that the grantee keep such activities separate and distinct from Title X activities. Ti-

tle X expressly distinguishes between a Title X *grantee* and a Title X *project*. The grantee, which normally is a health care organization, may receive funds from a variety of sources for a variety of purposes. The grantee receives Title X funds, however, for the specific and limited purpose of establishing and operating a Title X project. The regulations govern the scope of the Title X *project's* activities, and leave the grantee unfettered in its other activities. The Title X grantee can continue to perform abortions, provide abortion-related services, and engage in abortion advocacy; it simply is required to conduct those activities through programs that are separate and independent from the project that receives Title X funds.

In contrast, our "unconstitutional conditions" cases involve situations in which the government has placed a condition on the recipient of the subsidy rather than on a particular program or service, thus effectively prohibiting the recipient from engaging in the protected conduct outside the scope of the federally funded program. In *FCC v. League of Women Voters of Cal.*, we invalidated a federal law providing that noncommercial television and radio stations that receive federal grants may not "engage in editorializing." Under that law, a recipient of federal funds was "barred absolutely from all editorializing" because it "is not able to segregate its activities according to the source of its funding" and thus "has no way of limiting the use of its federal funds to all noneditorializing activities." The effect of the law was that "a noncommercial educational station that receives only 1% of its overall income from [federal] grants is barred absolutely from all editorializing" and "barred from using even wholly private funds to finance its editorial activity." We expressly recognized, however, that were Congress to permit the recipient stations to "establish 'affiliate' organizations which could then use the station's facilities to editorialize with nonfederal funds, such a statutory mechanism would plainly be valid." Such a scheme would permit the station "to make known its views on matter's of public importance through its nonfederally funded, editorializing affiliate without losing federal grants for its noneditorializing broadcast activities." . . .

The same principles apply to petitioners' claim that the regulations abridge the free speech rights of the grantee's staff: individuals who are voluntarily employed for a Title X project must perform their duties in accordance with the regulation's restrictions on abortion counseling and referral. The employees remain free, however, to pursue abortion-related activities when they are not acting under the auspices of the Title X project. The regulations, which govern solely the scope of the Title X project's activities, do not in any way restrict the activities of those persons acting as private individuals. The employees' freedom of expression is limited during the time that they actually work for the project: but this limitation is a consequence of their decision to accept employment in a project, the scope of which is permissibly restricted by the funding authority.

. . . Similarly, we have recognized that the univer-

sity is a traditional sphere of free expression so fundamental to the functioning of our society that the Government's ability to control speech within that sphere by
means of conditions attached to the expenditure of Government funds is restricted by the vagueness and overbreadth doctrines of the First Amendment. *Keyishian v.
Board of Regents* (1967). It could be argued by analogy
that traditional relationships such as that between doctor
and patient should enjoy protection under the First
Amendment from government regulation, even when
subsidized by the Government. We need not resolve that
question here, however, because the Title X program
regulations do not significantly impinge upon the doctor-
patient relationship. Nothing in them requires a doctor to
represent as his own any opinion that he does not in fact
hold. Nor is the doctor-patient relationship established
by the Title X program sufficiently all-encompassing so
as to justify an expectation on the part of the patient of
comprehensive medical advice. The program does not
provide post-conception medical care, and therefore a
doctor's silence with regard to abortion cannot reasonably be thought to mislead a client into thinking that the
doctor does not consider abortion an appropriate option
for her. The doctor is always free to make clear that advice regarding abortion is simply beyond the scope of
the program. In these circumstances, the general rule that
the Government may choose not to subsidize speech applies with full force. . . .

IV.

Petitioners contend, however, that most Title X clients are effectively precluded by indigence and poverty
from seeing a health care provider who will provide
abortion-related services. But once again, even these Title X clients are in no worse position than if Congress
had never enacted Title X. "The financial constraints
that restrict an indigent woman's ability to enjoy the full
range of constitutionally protected freedom of choice are
the product not of governmental restrictions on access to
abortion, but rather of her indigence." . . .

Justice **Blackmun,** with whom Justice **Marshall** joins,
with whom Justice **Stevens** joins as to Parts II and III,
and with whom Justice **O'Connor** joins as to Part I,
dissenting.

Casting aside established principles of statutory
construction and administrative jurisprudence, the majority in these cases today unnecessarily passes upon important questions of constitutional law. In so doing, the
Court, for the first time, upholds viewpoint-based suppression of speech solely because it is imposed on those
dependent upon the Government for economic support.
Under essentially the same rationale, the majority upholds direct regulation of dialogue between a pregnant
woman and her physician when that regulation has both
the purpose and the effect of manipulating her decision as
to the continuance of her pregnancy. I conclude that the
Secretary's regulation of referral, advocacy, and counsel-

ing activities exceeds his statutory authority, and, also,
that the Regulation violates the First and Fifth Amendments of our Constitution. Accordingly, I dissent . . . .

I.

The majority does not dispute that "[f]ederal statutes are to be so construed as to avoid serious doubt of
their constitutionality. . . ." Nor does the majority deny
that this principle is fully applicable to cases such as the
instant one, in which a plausible but constitutionally suspect statutory interpretation is embodied in an administrative regulation. . . . Rather, in its zeal to address the
constitutional issues, the majority sidesteps this established canon of construction with the feeble excuse that
the challenged Regulations "do not raise the sort of
'grave and doubtful constitutional questions,' . . . that
would lead us to assume Congress did not intend to
authorize their issuance." . . .

This facile response to the intractable problem the
Court addresses today is disingenuous at best. Whether
or not one believes that these regulations are valid, it
avoids reality to contend that they do not give rise to
serious constitutional questions. The canon is applicable
to this case not because "it was likely that [the Regula-
tions] . . . would be challenged on constitutional
grounds," but because the question squarely presented
by the Regulations—the extent to which the Government
may attach an otherwise unconstitutional condition to the
receipt of a public benefit—implicates a troubled area of
our jurisprudence in which a court ought not to entangle
itself unnecessarily. . . .

As is discussed in Parts II and III, *infra,* the Regulations impose viewpoint-based restrictions upon protected speech and are aimed at a woman's decision
whether to continue or terminate her pregnancy. In both
respects, they implicate core constitutional values. This
verity is evidenced by the fact that two of the three
Courts of Appeals that have entertained challenges to the
Regulations have invalidated them on constitutional
grounds. . . .

. . . That a bare majority of this Court today
reaches a different result does not change the fact that
the constitutional questions raised by the Regulations are
both grave and doubtful.

Nor is this a case in which the statutory language
itself requires us to address a constitutional question.
Section 1008 of the Public Health Service Act provides
simply: "None of the funds appropriated under this title
shall be used in programs where abortion is a method of
family planning." The majority concedes that this language "does not speak directly to the issues of counseling, referral, advocacy, or program integrity," and that
"the legislative history is ambiguous" in this respect.
Consequently, the language of § 1008 easily sustains a
constitutionally trouble-free interpretation. . . .

Because I conclude that a plainly constitutional
construction of § 1008 "is not only 'fairly possible' but
entirely reasonable," I would reverse the judgment of

the Court of Appeals on this ground without deciding the constitutionality of the Secretary's Regulations.

II.

I also strongly disagree with the majority's disposition of petitioners' constitutional claims, and because I feel that a response thereto is indicated, I move on to that issue.

A.

Until today, the Court never has upheld viewpoint-based suppression of speech simply because that suppression was a condition upon the acceptance of public funds. Whatever may be the Government's power to condition the receipt of its largess upon the relinquishment of constitutional rights, it surely does not extend to a condition that suppresses the recipient's cherished freedom of speech based solely upon the content or viewpoint of that speech. Speiser v. Randall (1958) ("To deny an exemption to claimants who engage in certain forms of speech is in effect to penalize them for such speech . . . The denial is 'frankly aimed at the suppression of dangerous ideas,' " quoting American Communications Assn. v. Douds (1950)). . . . This rule is a sound one, for, as the Court often has noted: " 'A regulation of speech that is motivated by nothing more than a desire to curtail expression of a particular point of view on controversial issues of general interest is the purest example of a "law . . . abridging the freedom of speech, or of the press." ' " . . . "[A]bove all else, the First Amendment means that government has no power to restrict expression because of its message, its ideas, its subject matter, or its content." . . .

It cannot seriously be disputed that the counseling and referral provisions at issue in the present cases constitute content-based regulation of speech. Title X grantees may provide counseling and referral regarding any of a wide range of family planning and other topics, save abortion. . . .

The Regulations are also clearly viewpoint-based. While suppressing speech favorable to abortion with one hand, the Secretary compels anti-abortion speech with the other. For example, the Department of Health and Human Services' own description of the Regulations makes plain that "Title X projects are *required* to facilitate access to prenatal care and social services, including adoption services, that might be needed by the pregnant client to promote her well-being and that of her child, while making it abundantly clear that the project is not permitted to promote abortion by facilitating access to abortion through the referral process." (emphasis added).

Moreover, the regulations command that a project refer for prenatal care each woman diagnosed as pregnant, irrespective of the woman's expressed desire to continue or terminate her pregnancy. If a client asks directly about abortion, a Title X physician or counselor is required to say, in essence, that the project does not consider abortion to be an appropriate method of family planning. Both requirements are antithetical to the First Amendment. . . .

The Regulations pertaining to "advocacy" are even more explicitly viewpoint-based. These provide: "A Title X project may not *encourage promote or advocate* abortion as a method of family planning." (emphasis added). They explain: "This requirement prohibits sections to *assist* women to obtain abortions or *increase* the availability or accessibility of abortion for family planing purposes." (emphasis added). The Regulations do not, however, proscribe or even regulate antiabortion advocacy. These are clearly restrictions aimed at the suppression of "dangerous ideas."

Remarkably, the majority concludes that "the Government has not discriminated on the basis of viewpoint; it has merely chosen to fund one activity to the exclusion of the other." But the majority's claim that the Regulations merely limit a Title X project's speech to preventive or preconceptional services rings hollow in light of the broad range of non-preventive services that the Regulations authorize Title X projects to provide. By refusing to fund those family-planning projects that advocate abortion because they advocate abortion, the Government plainly has targeted a particular viewpoint. . . . The majority's reliance on the fact that the Regulations pertain solely to funding decisions simply begs the question. Clearly, there are some bases upon which government may not rest its decision to fund or not to fund. For example, the Members of the majority surely would agree that government may not base its decision to support an activity upon considerations of race. See, e.g., Yick Wo v. Hopkins, (1886). As demonstrated above, our cases make clear that ideological viewpoint is a similarly repugnant ground upon which to base funding decisions. . . .

B.

The Court concludes that the challenged Regulations do not violate the First Amendment rights of Title X staff members because any limitation of the employees' freedom of expression is simply a consequence of their decision to accept employment at a federally funded project. But it has never been sufficient to justify an otherwise unconstitutional condition upon public employment that the employee may escape the condition by relinquishing his or her job. It is beyond question "that a government may not require an individual to relinquish rights guaranteed him by the First Amendment as a condition of public employment." . . . Nearly two decades ago, it was said:

"For at least a quarter-century, this Court has made clear that even though a person has no 'right' to a valuable governmental benefit and even though the government may deny him the benefit for any number of reasons, there are some reasons upon which the government may not rely. It may not deny a benefit to a person on a basis that infringes his constitutionally protected interest—especially, his interest in freedom of speech. For if the government could deny a benefit to a person because of his constitutionally protected speech or associations, his exercise of those freedoms would in effect be penalized and inhibited. This would allow the government to 'produce a result which [it] could not command directly.'" Perry v. Sindermann [1972] quoting Speiser v. Randall (1958).

The majority attempts to circumvent this principle by emphasizing that Title X physicians and counselors "remain free . . . to pursue abortion-related activities when they are not acting under the auspices of the Title X project." "The regulations," the majority explains, "do not in any way restrict the activities of those persons acting as private individuals." Under the majority's reasoning, the First Amendment could be read to tolerate any governmental restriction upon an employee's speech so long as that restriction is limited to the funded workplace. This is a dangerous proposition, and one the Court has rightly rejected in the past. . . .

In the cases at bar, the speaker's interest in the communication is both clear and vital. In addressing the family-planning needs of their clients, the physicians and counselors who staff Title X projects seek to provide them with the full range of information and options regarding their health and reproductive freedom. Indeed, the legitimate expectations of the patient and the ethical responsibilities of the medical profession demand no less. "The patient's right of self-decision can be effectively exercised only if the patient possesses enough information to enable an intelligent choice. . . . The physician has an ethical obligation to help the patient make choices from among the therapeutic alternatives consistent with good medical practice." . . . When a client becomes pregnant, the full range of therapeutic alternatives includes the abortion option, and Title X counselors' interest in providing this information is compelling. . . .

C.

Finally, it is of no small significance that the speech the Secretary would suppress is truthful information regarding constitutionally protected conduct of vital importance to the listener. One can imagine no legitimate governmental interest that might be served by suppressing such information. Concededly, the abortion debate is among the most divisive and contentious issues that our Nation has faced in recent years. "But freedom to differ is not limited to things that do not matter much. That would be a mere shadow of freedom. The test of its substance is the right to differ as to things that touch the heart of the existing order." West Virginia Board of Education v. Barnette (1943).

III. . . .

In view of the inevitable effect of the Regulations, the majority's conclusion that "[t]he difficulty that a woman encounters when a Title X project does not provide abortion counseling or referral leaves her in no different position than she would have been if the government had not enacted Title X" is insensitive and contrary to common human experience. Both the purpose and result of the challenged Regulations is to deny women the ability voluntarily to decide their procreative destiny. For these women, the Government will have obliterated the freedom to choose as surely as if it had banned abortions outright. The denial of this freedom is not a consequence of poverty but of the Government's ill-intentioned distortion of information it has chosen to provide.

The substantial obstacles to bodily self-determination that the Regulations impose are doubly offensive because they are effected by manipulating the very words spoken by physicians and counselors to their patients. In our society, the doctor/patient dialogue embodies a unique relationship of trust. The specialized nature of medical science and the emotional distress often attendant to health-related decisions requires that patients place their complete confidence, and often their very lives, in the hands of medical professionals. One seeks a physician's aid not only for medication or diagnosis, but also for guidance, professional judgment, and vital emotional support. Accordingly, each of us attaches profound importance and authority to the words of advice spoken by the physician.

It is for this reason that we have guarded so jealously the doctor/patient dialogue from governmental intrusion. "[I]n Roe and subsequent cases we have 'stressed repeatedly the central role of the physician, both in consulting with the woman about whether or not to have an abortion, and in determining how any abortion was to be carried out.'" . . . The majority's approval of the Secretary's Regulations flies in the face of our repeated warnings that regulations tending to "confine the attending physician in an undesired and uncomfortable straitjacket in the practice of his profession," cannot endure. . . .

Justice **Stevens**, dissenting, said in part:

Because I am convinced that the 1970 Act did not authorize the Secretary to censor the speech of grant recipients or their employees, I would hold the challenged regulations invalid and reverse the judgment of the Court of Appeals.

Even if I thought the statute were ambiguous, however, I would reach the same result for the reasons stated in Justice O'Connor's dissenting opinion. . . .

Justice **O'Connor**, dissenting, said in part:

"[W]here an otherwise acceptable construction of a statute would raise serious constitutional problems, the Court will construe the statute to avoid such problems unless such construction is plainly contrary to the intent of Congress." . . . Justice Blackmun has explained well why this long-standing canon of statutory construction applies in this case, and I join Part I of his dissent. . . .

FREE PRESS - FAIR TRIAL

RICHMOND NEWSPAPERS, INC. v. VIRGINIA

488 U. S. 555; 100 S. Ct. 2814; 65 L. Ed. 2d 973
(1980)

Although it has always been assumed that libelous utterances were beyond constitutional protection, it was not until 1952, in Beauharnais v. Illinois, that the Court first passed on the validity of a state libel law. There it upheld Beauharnais' conviction under a so-called "group libel" statute, a criminal libel law designed to punish defamation of racial or religious groups, for publishing a bitterly anti-Negro leaflet in Chicago. The Court found the adoption of this law was justified by the "tendency [of such statements] to cause a breach of the peace"; and since libelous utterances themselves were beyond First Amendment protection, there was no need to show they created a clear and present danger of actually bringing about such a breach of the peace.

In a landmark case in 1964, however, the Court sharply restricted the power of a state to punish libels directed at public officials. A full-page advertisement in The New York Times *accused the police of Montgomery, Alabama, of abuse of power in connection with Negro demonstrations; and some of the statements in the ad were conceded to be false. Sullivan, the commissioner of police, claimed that the charges were directed at him and sued the* Times *for a half million dollars. The judge instructed the jury that under the law the statements were libelous, and hence falsity, malice, and injury could all be inferred from the fact of publication if they were found to apply to Sullivan. The jury awarded the full amount of damages claimed, and in New York Times v. Sullivan (1964) the Supreme Court reversed the judgment. Affirming a "profound national commitment to the principle that debate on public issues should be uninhibited, robust, and wide-open," the Court ruled that in order to be exempt from First Amendment protection, a statement about public officials must be made with " 'actual malice'—that is, with knowledge that it was false or with reckless disregard of whether it was false or not." Any rule requiring a critic of official conduct to guarantee the truth of his statements "on pain of libel judgments virtually unlimited in amount" would result in self-censorship and dampen the vigor of public debate by deterring criticism "even though it is believed to be true and even though it is in fact true, because of the doubt whether it can be proved in court."*

In Garrison v. Louisiana (1964) the Court used the new test to reverse the criminal contempt conviction of a New Orleans district attorney who publicly charged lo-

cal judges with "inefficiency, laziness, and excessive vacations," and with hampering his efforts to enforce the vice laws. The Supreme Court emphasized that the New York Times rule gave absolute protection to truthful criticism of public officials, regardless of motive, and even protected false criticism not made with "actual malice."

In two cases in 1971 the Court extended the rule to cover candidates for public office in regard to any matter bearing on their fitness for office (Monitor Patriot Co. v. Roy), but in Gertz v. Welch in 1974 it made clear that it did not extend to persons who were neither public officials nor public persons. In the latter case Gertz was an attorney who was falsely accused in a John Birch Society publication of being a Communist.

The cardinal value which we attach to freedom of speech and press in a democratic society sometimes tends to obscure the fact that the use of these freedoms may jeopardize other civil liberties of the individual. One of these is the right of a litigant in a court of law to have the case tried by an impartial judge or jury. The conflict arises when unrestrained newspaper comment on a pending or current trial threatens the impartiality of any jury which could be drawn, or brings pressure upon judge or jury to reach a particular decision. An essential phase of judicial power has always been the power of a judge to protect the administration of justice in court by punishing for contempt those who would interfere with it. In England, this power has always been very sternly used, and as recently as 1949 the Lord Chief Justice fined the London Daily Mirror *£10,000 and sentenced the editor to three months in jail for the paper's lurid comments on the crimes of the so-called "English Bluebeard" who was then on trial for murder.*

In dealing with this conflict, courts in the United States have been far more lenient to questionable newspaper comment than have courts in England. While a motion for a new trial was pending in a case involving a dispute between an AF of L union and a CIO union of which Harry Bridges was an officer, Bridges sent to the Secretary of Labor, and also released to the press, a telegram which described the judge's decision as "outrageous," and further stated: "Attempted enforcement of . . . decision will tie up port of Los Angeles and involve entire Pacific Coast. . . . [CIO union] does not intend to allow state courts to override the majority vote of members in choosing its officers and representatives and to override the National Labor Relations Board." Bridges was cited for contempt of court on the ground that this telegram was an attempt to interfere by threats with the fair and orderly administration of justice. The Court reversed the contempt in Bridges v. California (1941), holding there was no clear and present danger of influencing the court, since the telegram told the judge nothing he did not already know.

Two important cases which followed the Bridges case make it clear that to spell out contempt of court there must be a clear and present danger of subverting justice, and this danger must be proved by solid evidence and not by mere conjectures or worries. In Pennekamp v. Florida (1946) the publisher of the Miami Herald *was fined for contempt for publishing a cartoon and editorials charging that a local trial judge was playing into the hands of criminal elements and thwarting the efforts of the district attorney to enforce the law. In setting aside the conviction, the Supreme Court conceded that some of the comment was directed at cases then pending in court, and that some of it was not truthful. Nevertheless, "in the borderline instances where it is difficult to say upon which side the alleged offense falls, we think the specific freedom of public comment should weigh heavily against a possible tendency to influence pending cases. Freedom of discussion should be given the widest range compatible with the essential requirement of the fair and orderly administration of justice."*

Craig v. Harney (1947) involved an intemperate and inaccurate newspaper attack on a lay judge who had directed a verdict in a civil suit. Three times the jury ignored the judge's direction, and finally capitulated with the announcement that it had acted under coercion of the court and against its conscience. The newspaper characterized the judge's order as "arbitrary action" and a "gross miscarriage of justice," and reported public demands for a new trial. The publisher was convicted in a criminal trial of contempt of court for attempting to force the judge to alter his decision. The Supreme Court, in reversing the contempt conviction, admitted that the "news articles were by any standard an unfair report of what transpired," but added that "it takes more imagination than we possess to find in this rather sketchy and one-sided report of a case any imminent or serious threat to a judge of reasonable fortitude. . . . The vehemence of the language used is not alone the measure of the power to punish for contempt. The fires which it kindles must constitute an imminent, not merely a likely, threat to the administration of justice. The danger must not be remote or even probable; it must immediately imperil. . . . A judge who is part of such a dramatic episode can hardly help but know that his decision is apt to be unpopular. But the law of contempt is not made for the protection of judges who may be sensitive to the winds of public opinion. Judges are supposed to be men of fortitude, able to thrive in a hardy climate. . . . Nor can we assume that the trial judge was not a man of fortitude."

The balance struck by the Supreme Court between free speech and fair trial has not gone unchallenged by members of the Court itself. In Shepherd v. Florida (1951) the Court reversed the conviction of four Negroes because discrimination had been practiced in the selection of the grand jury. Justices Frankfurter and Jackson, who with Chief Justice Vinson had dissented in Craig v. Harney, emphasized that inflammatory newspaper comment made a fair trial in the community impossible. And in 1949 a trial court in Maryland punished for contempt a broadcasting company which had allowed on the air extremely prejudicial comment upon a pending murder trial. The broadcast stated that the man charged with the murder had confessed, had a long criminal record, and upon being taken to the scene of the crime, had reenacted it. The Maryland court of appeals reversed the

contempt conviction on the basis of Bridges, Pennekamp, and Craig. While the Supreme Court of the United States denied certiorari, Justice Frankfurter felt called upon to explain at length that this did not necessarily signify approval of the lower court decision. See Maryland v. Baltimore Radio Show (1950).

While the Court has been unwilling to permit the punishment of newspapers for trying to influence the course of justice, it has not hesitated to reverse the conviction of persons whose trials were clearly so influenced. In Irvin v. Dowd (1961) the police issued a press release stating that Irvin had confessed to six murders. The one change of venue allowed by the state law merely took him into the next county—a county so blanketed by the adverse publicity that nearly 90 percent of the prospective jurors, and eight of the twelve members of the actual jury, believed the defendant was guilty before the trial even started. And in Rideau v. Louisiana (1963) police permitted the filming of a twenty-minute interview between Rideau and the sheriff, in which Rideau confessed to robbery, kidnapping, and murder. He was denied a change of venue despite the fact that three television broadcasts had carried the "interview," and three members of the jury had seen it. The Supreme Court reversed both convictions. In Beck v. Washington (1962), however, the Court (voting four to three) found that despite adverse publicity Teamster president David Beck had been indicted by an impartial grand jury and convicted by an impartial petit jury on charges of embezzling union funds. "A study of the voir dire indicates clearly that each juror's qualifications as to impartiality far exceeded the minimum standards this Court established in its earlier cases as well as in Irvin v. Dowd, on which petitioner depends."

The cooperation between police and the news media following President Kennedy's assassination, which culminated in the murder of Lee Harvey Oswald before a nationwide television audience, brought public demand for reform even before the Sheppard case. In 1964 the New Jersey supreme court ordered a ban on pretrial statements to newsmen by prosecutors, police, and defense attorneys, while the Judicial Conference of the United States recommended to Congress the passage of a bill prohibiting the release of information to the press which had not previously been filed with the trial court. And in 1966 a committee of the American Bar Association recommended strong limits on pretrial reporting by both prosecutors and defense attorneys. While official moves of this kind met considerable opposition from the organized press, informal codes of conduct, such as those adopted in Nebraska in the case below, have been worked out in conference among the industry, the bar associations, and the courts.

Strong impetus was given the reform movement by the decision in Sheppard v. Maxwell (1966) overturning the conviction of Dr. Sam Sheppard for the murder of his wife. "Doctor Sam," a prominent Cleveland physician, was tried in a suburban court in what the Supreme Court described as a "carnival atmosphere." The press, convinced of his guilt, demanded his conviction and inun-

dated the community with highly inflammatory, prejudicial statements which the judge, who refused to sequester the jury or grant a change of venue, was unable to keep from reaching the jury. The Court noted that "every court that has considered this case, save the court that tried it, has deplored the manner in which the news media inflamed and prejudiced the public." As for the trial itself, "the fact is that bedlam reigned at the courthouse during the trial, and newsmen took over practically the entire courtroom hounding most of the participants in the trial, especially Sheppard." After a careful review of the authority of a trial court to control the conduct of the trials before it, the Court concluded that they were adequate to protect the fairness of the trial. Strict rules of press behavior were enforced when Dr. Sheppard was retried by Ohio in 1966. An unspectacular trial resulted in his acquittal.

The result of the efforts at reform has been to shift the constitutional battle between the courts and the press to new ground as courts have tried to devise ways of preventing the publication of prejudicial news comments. In 1975, Erwin Simants was arrested and prosecuted for the brutal murder of six members of the Henry Kellie family in their home in Sutherland, Nebraska, a town of about 850 people. The crime attracted nationwide attention, and both Simant's attorney and the county attorney, fearing the "reasonable likelihood of prejudicial news which would make difficult, if not impossible, the impaneling of an impartial jury and tend to prevent a fair trial," obtained from the county court an order restricting press coverage. The news media asked the United States district court to vacate the order, but that court issued an order of its own prohibiting reporting on five subjects: "(1) the existence or contents of a confession Simants had made to law enforcement officers, which had been introduced in open court at arraignment; (2) the fact or nature of statements Simants had made to other persons; (3) the contents of a note he had written the night of the crime; (4) certain aspects of the medical testimony at the preliminary hearing; (5) the identity of the victims of the alleged sexual assault and the nature of the assault."

In Nebraska Press Asso. v. Stuart (1976), the Supreme Court unanimously held the court's order void. While conceding that the trial judge was justified in concluding there would be intense pretrial publicity, it found no evidence that the restraining order, on its face a serious limit on freedom of the press, was the only or even an effective way of guaranteeing an impartial jury. Not only did the trial court not explore other alternatives open to it, but in a town of 850 there was no reason to suppose the press accounts would be any more damaging than the rumors that were bound to circulate. As far as the material that had been introduced in open court, the Court reiterated its statement in Sheppard v. Maxwell (1966) that "there is nothing that proscribes the press from reporting events that transpire in the courtroom." In 1979, this latter point was reaffirmed and extended to information obtained by normal reporting techniques—in this case the name of a juvenile killer ob-

tained by merely querying witnesses. The Court held the state's interest in protecting the privacy of juveniles insufficient to justify punishing the paper for publishing the name, especially since the law did not apply to either radio or television. See Smith v. Daily Mail Publishing Co. (1979).

To what extent does the news media, as the eyes and ears of a public that can rarely if ever witness events and conditions first hand, have a right of access to information not available to the public at large? In Branzburg v. Hayes (1972) the Supreme Court refused to create a constitutional privilege under the First Amendment for journalists to withhold confidential sources of information from a grand jury investigating crime. The case involved newspaper reporters who had won the confidence of drug users and of the Black Panther Party and had written behind-the-scenes stories about them. Grand juries investigating these matters subpoenaed the reporters to testify and they refused on the ground that to do so would dry up their news sources and obstruct the free flow of news protected by the First Amendment. A five-man majority rejected their claim, holding that "the First Amendment does not guarantee the press a constitutional right of special access to information not available to the public generally."

In a series of cases the Supreme Court used this statement to justify forbidding the press access to prison facilities not available to the public at large. In Pell v. Procunier (1974), it upheld rules adopted by a California prison forbidding interviews with selected inmates on the ground that the inmates so selected became celebrities and posed a disciplinary problem. The Court noted that the rules reflected no intention to conceal conditions within the prison and that the press was free to visit the prison and speak with prisoners they happened to meet. In Saxbe v. Washington Post Co. (1974), the Court extended the same rule to federal prisons, and in Houchins v. KQED, Inc. (1978), in a four-to-three decision, it extended it to a California jail where it seemed apparent that the authorities were trying to conceal conditions within the jail from public scrutiny.

The first suggestion that the Court might be rethinking the question of access came in Gannett Co. v. DePasquale (1979). Following the apparent murder of an upstate New York man, three suspects were apprehended in Michigan with the victim's pickup truck and gun. They were returned to New York for trial, and following their arraignment asked for a pretrial hearing to argue the inadmissibility in evidence of the gun and certain statements made to the Michigan police that they claimed were involuntary. Arguing that the "unabated buildup of adverse publicity had jeopardized the ability of the defendants to receive a fair trial," they moved that the hearings be closed to the public and the press. Without objection from the press the hearing was closed but the trial judge later held a full hearing on whether or not the transcript of the hearing should be released. The trial judge presumed a constitutional right of access on the part of the press but after finding on the record that an open suppression hearing would pose a "reasonable *probability of prejudice to these defendants," he refused to release the transcript.*

In a five-to-four decision, the Court upheld the trial judge. Justice Stewart's opinion reviewed the commentaries and precedents and concluded that the Sixth Amendment guarantee of a public trial was for the benefit of the accused, not the public. While he conceded the importance of open trials to the public, he made clear that "recognition of an independent public interest in the enforcement of Sixth Amendment guarantees is a far cry . . . from the creation of a constitutional right on the part of the public." Furthermore, while "there is no question that the Sixth Amendment permits and even assumes open trials as a norm," historically the public had no right to attend pretrial proceedings. In addition, even assuming a constitutional right of access on the part of the press, it had not been violated in this case because the trial court had properly "balanced the 'constitutional rights of the press and public' against the 'defendant's right to a fair trial.' " In 1965 in Estes v. Texas the Court had held that televising a sensational trial had denied the defendant due process of law, noting that the "public trial" guaranteed by the Sixth Amendment was not the equivalent of a day in a "stadium . . . or nationwide arena." In 1981, however, the Court in Chandler v. Florida construed Estes as not banning all television coverage, although a defendant clearly had a right (which had not been exercised in this case) to try to show that media coverage had an adverse affect upon the fairness of his trial.

In the present case, the state's prosecution of the defendant for murder had resulted in three mistrials, at least one of which was apparently the result of a prospective juror reading about inadmissible evidence. At the start of the fourth trial, the defendant asked that the trial be closed. A hearing was held from which the press was excluded and the judge ruled that the press and public be excluded from the trial.

Mr. Chief Justice **Burger** announced the judgment of the Court and delivered an opinion in which Mr. Justice **White** and Mr. Justice **Stevens** joined, saying in part:

II.

We begin consideration of this case by noting that the precise issue presented here has not previously been before this Court for decision. In Gannett Co., Inc. v. DePasquale (1979), the Court was not required to decide whether a right of access to *trials,* as distinguished from hearings on *pre*trial motions, was constitutionally guaranteed. The Court held that the Sixth Amendment's guarantee to the accused of a public trial gave neither the public nor the press an enforceable right of access to a *pre*trial suppression hearing. One concurring opinion specifically emphasized that "a hearing on a motion before trial to suppress evidence is not a *trial.* . . ." (Burger, C.J., concurring). Moreover, the Court did not de-

cide whether the First and Fourteenth Amendments guarantee a right of the public to attend trials: nor did the dissenting opinion reach this issue.

In prior cases the Court has treated questions involving conflicts between publicity and a defendant's right to a fair trial; as we observed in Nebraska Press Assn. v. Stuart (1976), "[t]he problems presented by this [conflict] are almost as old as the Republic." . . . But here for the first time the Court is asked to decide whether a criminal trial itself may be closed to the public upon the unopposed request of a defendant, without any demonstration that closure is required to protect the defendant's superior right to a fair trial, or that some other overriding consideration requires closure.

A.

The origins of the proceeding which has become the modern criminal trial in Anglo-American justice can be traced back beyond reliable historical records. We need not here review all details of its development, but a summary of that history is instructive. What is significant for present purposes is that throughout its evolution, the trial has been open to all who cared to observe. . . .

[The Court here traced the development of the English court system from the days before the Norman Conquest down to the sixteenth century, noting the uniform openness of the criminal trial.] Three centuries later, Sir Frederic Pollock was able to state of the "rule of publicity" that, "[h]ere we have one tradition, at any rate, which has persisted through all changes." . . . See also E. Jenks, The Book of English Law 73–74 (6th ed. 1967): "[O]ne of the most conspicuous features of English justice, that all judicial trials are held in open court, to which the public have free access, . . . appears to have been the rule in England from time immemorial."

We have found nothing to suggest that the presumptive openness of the trial, which English courts were later to call "one of the essential qualities of a court of justice," . . . was not also an attribute of the judicial systems of colonial America. In Virginia, for example, such records as there are of early criminal trials indicate that they were open, and nothing to the contrary has been cited. . . . Indeed, when in the mid-1600's the Virginia Assembly felt that the respect due the courts was "by the clamorous unmannerlyness of the people lost, and order, gravity and decoram which should manifest the authority of a court in the court it selfe neglicted," the response was not to restrict the openness of the trials to the public, but instead to prescribe rules for the conduct of those attending them. . . .

In some instances, the openness of trials was explicitly recognized as part of the fundamental law of the colony. . . .

B.

As we have shown, and as was shown in both the Court's opinion and the dissent in Gannett, the historical evidence demonstrates conclusively that at the time when our organic laws were adopted, criminal trials both here and in England had long been presumptively open. This is no quirk of history; rather, it has long been recognized as an indispensible attribute of an Anglo-American trial. Both Hale in the 17th century and Blackstone in the 18th saw the importance of openness to the proper functioning of a trial; it gave assurance that the proceedings were conducted fairly to all concerned, and it discouraged perjury, the misconduct of participants, and decisions based on secret bias or partiality. . . . The nexus between openness, fairness, and the perception of fairness was not lost on [foreign observers]: "[T]he judge, the counsel, and the jury, are constantly exposed to public animadversion; and this greatly tends to augment the extraordinary confidence, which the English repose in the administration of justice."

This observation raises the important point that "[t]he publicity of a judicial proceeding is a requirement of much broader bearing than its mere effect on the quality of testimony." . . . The early history of open trials in part reflects the widespread acknowledgement, long before there were behavioral scientists, that public trials had significant community therapeutic value. Even without such experts to frame the concept in words, people sensed from experience and observation that, especially in the administration of criminal justice, the means used to achieve justice must have the support derived from public acceptance of both the process and its results.

When a shocking crime occurs, a community reaction of outrage and public protest often follows. . . . Thereafter the open processes of justice serve an important prophylactic purpose, providing an outlet for community concern, hostility, and emotion. Without an awareness that society's responses to criminal conduct are underway, natural human reactions of outrage and protest are frustrated and may manifest themselves in some form of vengeful "self-help," as indeed they did regularly in the activities of vigilante "committees" on our frontiers. . . .

Civilized societies withdraw both from the victim and the vigilante the enforcement of criminal laws, but they cannot erase from people's consciousness the fundamental, natural yearning to see justice done—or even the urge for retribution. The crucial prophylactic aspects of the administration of justice cannot function in the dark; no community catharsis can occur if justice is "done in a corner [or] in any covert manner." It is not enough to say that results alone will satiate the natural community desire for "satisfaction." A result considered untoward may undermine public confidence, and where the trial has been concealed from public view an unexpected outcome can cause a reaction that the system at best has failed and at worst has been corrupted. To work effectively, it is important that society's criminal process "satisfy the appearance of justice," . . . and the appearance of justice can best be provided by allowing people to observe it.

Looking back, we see that when the ancient "town meeting" form of trial became too cumbersome, twelve members of the community were delegated to act as its surrogates, but the community did not surrender its right to observe the conduct of trials. The people retained a "right of visitation" which enabled them to satisfy themselves that justice was in fact being done. . . .

In earlier times, both in England and America, attendance at court was a common mode of "passing the time." . . . With the press, cinema, and electronic media now supplying the representations or reality of the real life drama once available only in the courtroom, attendance at court is no longer a widespread pastime. Yet "[i]t is not unrealistic even in this day to believe that public inclusion affords citizens a form of legal education and hopefully promotes confidence in the fair administration of justice." . . . Instead of acquiring information about trials by firsthand observation or by word of mouth from those who attended, people now acquire it chiefly through the print and electronic media. In a sense, this validates the media claim of functioning as surrogates for the public. While media representatives enjoy the same right of access as the public, they often are provided special seating and priority of entry so that they may report what people in attendance have seen and heard. This "contributes[s] to public understanding of the rule of law and to comprehension of the functioning of the entire criminal justice system. . . ." Nebraska Press Assn. v. Stuart (Brennan, J., concurring).

C.

From this unbroken, uncontradicted history, supported by reasons as valid today as in centuries past, we are bound to conclude that a presumption of openness inheres in the very nature of a criminal trial under our system of justice. This conclusion is hardly novel; without a direct holding on the issue, the Court has voiced its recognition of it in a variety of contexts over the years. . . . Recently in Gannett Co. Inc. v. DePasquale (1979), both the majority and dissenting opinions agreed that open trials were part of the common law tradition.

Despite the history of criminal trials being presumptively open since long before the Constitution, the State presses its contention that neither the Constitution nor the Bill of Rights contains any provision which by its terms guarantees to the public the right to attend criminal trials. Standing alone, this is correct, but there remains the question whether, absent an explicit provision, the Constitution affords protection against exclusion of the public from criminal trials.

III.

A.

The First Amendment, in conjunction with the Fourteenth, prohibits governments from "abridging the freedom of speech, or of the press; or the right of the people peaceably to assemble, and to Petition the Government for a redress of grievances." These expressly guaranteed freedoms share a common core purpose of assuring freedom of communication on matters relating to the functioning of government. Plainly it would be difficult to single out any aspect of government of higher concern and importance to the people than the manner in which criminal trials are conducted; as we have shown, recognition of this pervades the centuries-old history of open trials and the opinions of this Court.

The Bill of Rights was enacted against the backdrop of the long history of trials being presumptively open. Public access to trials was then regarded as an important aspect of the process itself; the conduct of trials "before as many of the people as chuse to attend" was regarded as one of "the inestimable advantages of a free English constitution of government." . . . In guaranteeing freedoms such as those of speech and press, the First Amendment can be read as protecting the right of everyone to attend trials so as to give meaning to those explicit guarantees. "[T]he First Amendment goes beyond protection of the press and the self-expression of individuals to prohibit government from limiting the stock of information from which members of the public may draw." First National Bank of Boston v. Bellotti (1978). Free speech carries with it some freedom to listen. "In a variety of contexts this Court has referred to a First Amendment right to 'receive information and ideas.'" Kleindienst v. Mandel (1972). What this means in the context of trials is that the First Amendment guarantees of speech and press, standing alone, prohibit government from summarily closing courtroom doors which had long been open to the public at the time that amendment was adopted. "For the First Amendment does not speak equivocally. . . . It must be taken as a command of the broadest scope that explicit language, read in the context of a liberty-loving society, will allow." Bridges v. California (1941).

It is not crucial whether we describe this right to attend criminal trials to hear, see, and communicate observations concerning them as a "right of access," cf. Gannett (Powell, J., concurring); Saxbe v. Washington Post Co. (1974); Pell v. Procunier (1974)* or a "right to gather information," for we have recognized that "without some protection for seeking out the news, freedom of the press could be eviscerated." Branzburg v. Hayes (1972). The explicit, guaranteed rights to speak and to publish concerning what takes place at a trial would lose much meaning if access to observe the trial could, as it was here, be foreclosed arbitrarily.

B.

The right of access to places traditionally open to the public, as criminal trials have long been, may be seen as assured by the amalgam of the First Amendment guarantees of speech and press; and their affinity to the right

of assembly is not without relevance. From the outset, the right of assembly was regarded not only as an independent right but also as a catalyst to augment the free exercise of the other First Amendment rights with which it was deliberately linked by the draftsmen. "The right of peaceable assembly is a right cognate to those of free speech and free press and is equally fundamental." De Jonge v. Oregon (1937). People assemble in public places not only to speak or to take action, but also to listen, observe, and learn; indeed, they may "assembl[e] for any lawful purpose," Hague v. C.I.O. (1939) (opinion of Stone, J.). Subject to the traditional time, place and manner restrictions, . . . streets, sidewalks, and parks are places traditionally open, where First Amendment rights may be exercised . . . ; a trial courtroom also is a public place where the people generally—and representatives of the media—have a right to be present, and where their presence historically has been thought to enhance the integrity and quality of what takes place.

C.

The State argues that the Constitution nowhere spells out a guarantee for the right of the public to attend trials, and that accordingly no such right is protected. The possibility that such a contention could be made did not escape the notice of the Constitution's draftsmen; they were concerned that some important rights might be thought disparaged because not specifically guaranteed. . . .

But arguments such as the State makes have not precluded recognition of important rights not enumerated. Notwithstanding the appropriate caution against reading into the Constitution rights not explicitly defined, the Court has acknowledged that certain unarticulated rights are implicit in enumerated guarantees. For example, the rights of association and of privacy, the right to be presumed innocent and the right to be judged by a standard of proof beyond a reasonable doubt in a criminal trial, as well as the right to travel, appear nowhere in the Constitution or Bill of Rights. Yet these important, but unarticulated rights have nonetheless been found to share constitutional protection in common with explicit guarantees. The concerns expressed by Madison and others have thus been resolved; fundamental rights, even though not expressly guaranteed, have been recognized by the Court as indispensable to the enjoyment of rights explicitly defined.

We hold that the right to attend criminal trials is implicit in the guarantees of the First Amendment; without the freedom to attend such trials, which people have exercised for centuries, important aspects of freedom of speech and "of the press could be eviscerated." . . .

D.

. . . Despite the fact that this was the fourth trial of the accused, the trial judge made no findings to support closure; no inquiry was made as to whether alternative

---

*Procunier and Saxbe, supra, are distinguishable in the sense that they were concerned with penal institutions which, by definition, are not "open" or public places. Penal institutions do not share the long tradition of openness. . . .

solutions would have met the need to ensure fairness; there was no recognition of any right under the Constitution for the public or press to attend the trial. In contrast to the proceeding dealt with in Gannett, there exist in the context of the trial itself various tested alternatives to satisfy the constitutional demands of fairness. See, e.g., Nebraska Press Association v. Stuart, Sheppard v. Maxwell. There was no suggestion that any problems with witnesses could not have been dealt with by their exclusion from the courtroom or their sequestration during the trial. Nor is there anything to indicate that sequestration of the jurors would not have guarded against their being subjected to any improper information. All of the alternatives admittedly present difficulties for trial courts, but none of the factors relied on here was beyond the realm of the manageable. Absent an overriding interest articulated in findings, the trial of a criminal case must be open to the public. Accordingly, the judgment under review is reversed.

Reversed.

Mr. Justice **Powell** took no part in the consideration or decision of this case.

Mr. Justice **White** wrote a short concurring opinion.

Mr. Justice **Stevens,** concurring, said in part:

This is a watershed case. Until today the Court has accorded virtually absolute protection to the dissemination of ideas, but never before has it squarely held that the acquisition of newsworthy matter is entitled to any constitutional protection whatsoever. An additional word of emphasis is therefore appropriate. . . .

. . . In Houchins v. KQED, Inc. [1978], I explained at length why Mr. Justice Brennan, Mr. Justice Powell, and I were convinced that ''[a]n official prison policy of concealing . . . knowledge from the public by arbitrarily cutting off the flow of information at its source abridges the freedom of speech and of the press protected by the First and Fourteenth Amendments to the Constitution.'' . . .

It is somewhat ironic that the Court should find more reason to recognize a right of access today than it did in Houchins. For Houchins involved the plight of a segment of society least able to protect itself, an attack on a longstanding policy of concealment, and an absence of any legitimate justification for abridging public access to information about how government operates. In this case we are protecting the interests of the most powerful voices in the community, we are concerned with an almost unique exception to an established tradition of openness in the conduct of criminal trials, and it is likely that the closure order was motivated by the judge's desire to protect the individual defendant from the burden of a fourth criminal trial.

Mr. Justice **Brennan,** with whom Mr. Justice **Marshall** joins, concurring in the judgment, said in part:

Gannett Co. v. DePasquale (1979), held that the Sixth Amendment right to a public trial was personal to the accused, conferring no right of access to pretrial proceedings that is separately enforceable by the public or the press. The instant case raises the question whether the First Amendment, of its own force and as applied to the States through the Fourteenth Amendment, secures the public an independent right of access to trial proceedings. Because I believe that the First Amendment—of itself and as applied to the States through the Fourteenth Amendment—secures such a public right of access, I agree with those of my Brethren who hold that, without more agreement of the trial judge and the parties cannot constitutionally close a trial to the public.

Mr. Justice **Blackmun,** concurring in the judgment, said in part:

II.

The Court's ultimate ruling in Gannett, with such clarification as is provided by the opinions in this case today, apparently is now to the effect that there is no *Sixth* Amendment right on the part of the public—or the press—to an open hearing on a motion to suppress. I, of course, continue to believe that Gannett was in error, both in its interpretation of the Sixth Amendment generally, and in its application to the suppression hearing, for I remain convinced that the right to a public trial is to be found where the constitution explicitly placed it—in the Sixth Amendment.

The Court, however, has eschewed the Sixth Amendment route. The plurality turns to other possible constitutional sources and invokes a veritable potpourri of them—the speech clause of the First Amendment, the press clause, the assembly clause, the Ninth Amendment, and a cluster of penumbral guarantees recognized in past decisions. This course is troublesome, but it is the route that has been selected, and, at least for now, we must live with it. . . .

Having said all this, and with the Sixth Amendment set to one side in this case, I am driven to conclude, as a secondary position, that the First Amendment must provide some measure of protection for public access to the trial. The opinion in partial dissent in Gannett explained that the public has an intense need and a deserved right to know about the administration of justice in general; about the prosecution of local crimes in particular; about the conduct of the judge, the prosecutor, defense counsel, police officers, other public servants, and all the actors in the judicial arena; and about the trial itself. . . . It is clear and obvious to me, on the approach the Court has chosen to take, that, by closing this criminal trial, the trial judge abridged these First Amendment interests of the public.

I also would reverse, and I join the judgment of the Court.

Mr. Justice **Rehnquist,** dissenting, said in part:

For the reasons stated in my separate concurrence in Gannett Co., Inc. v. DePasquale, I do not believe that either the First or Sixth Amendments as made applicable to the States by the Fourteenth, require that a State's reasons for denying public access to a trial, where both the prosecuting attorney and the defendant have consented to an order of closure approved by the judge, are subject to any additional constitutional review at our hands. And I most certainly do not believe that the Ninth Amendment confers upon us any such power to review orders of state trial judges closing trials in such situations. . . .

The proper administration of justice in any nation is bound to be a matter of the highest concern to all thinking citizens. But to gradually rein in, as this Court has done over the past generation, all of the ultimate decision-making power over how justice shall be administered, not merely in the federal system but in each of the 50 States, is a task that no Court consisting of nine persons, however gifted, is equal to. Nor is it desirable that such authority be exercised by such a tiny numerical fragment of the 220 million people who compose the population of this country.

FREEDOM OF RELIGION

MURDOCK v. PENNSYLVANIA

319 U. S. 105; 63 S. Ct. 870; 87 L. Ed. 1292
(1943)

In its first 150 years the Supreme Court decided but one important case which dealt with freedom of religion. In 1879 the case of Reynolds v. United States reached the conclusion that the religious liberty protected by the First Amendment does not include the right to commit immoral or criminal acts, even though these are sanctioned by religious doctrine. Thus Reynolds, a Mormon in the Territory of Utah, was held properly convicted of the crime of polygamy in spite of the fact that the Mormon religion held polygamy to be proper and desirable. In Cleveland v. United States (1946) Cleveland, a polygamist, had transported his plural wife across state lines; he was convicted of violating the Mann Act, which forbids the interstate transportation of "any woman or girl for the purpose of prostitution or debauchery, or for any other immoral purpose." Supreme Court cases involving religious liberty were rare because the First Amendment, which protects freedom of religion, applies only to Congress and not to the states; see Barron v. Baltimore (1833). Congress had little opportunity and less inclination to violate the First Amendment, and what the states did by way of dealing with religious matters was their own business so far as the federal Constitution was concerned.

By the 1930s this situation had begun to change. As we have seen in Near v. Minnesota (1931), the Court had by this time held that certain of the civil liberties (freedom of speech and press) which are protected by the First Amendment against invasion by the federal government are also part of the liberty which the due process clause of the Fourteenth Amendment forbids the states to abridge. This suggested that state action dealing with religious matters could also be attacked on constitutional grounds in the Supreme Court. Thus in 1934 the Court passed upon the question whether a student who had religious scruples against bearing arms could be compelled, under penalty of expulsion, to take military drill in the University of California. It held in Hamilton v. Regents of University of California (1934) that while the religious beliefs of Hamilton were protected by due process of law, he was not being compelled to attend the university and could assert no constitutional right to do so without complying with the state's requirement of military training.

In the early 1930s a religious group called Jehovah's Witnesses began a militant nationwide campaign to spread their religious doctrines. In this enterprise all Witnesses regard themselves as ministers of the gospel. The doctrines themselves are grounded on calculations as to the second coming of Christ and the battle of Armageddon, but they also include virulent condemnation of all organized religion and churches, especially the Roman Catholic Church. These are denounced as the works of Satan. The Jehovah's Witnesses spread their teachings by personal appeals, by the sale or free distribution of literature, and by canvassing house to house asking permission to play phonograph records, one of which, called "Enemies," is a bitter attack on religious organizations. Community resentment against the Witnesses and their methods was often intense; it expressed itself at first in a good deal of mob violence, and later in resort to a variety of legal measures designed to discourage the Witnesses and curb their more unpopular activities. With fanatical zeal the Witnesses fought every legal attempt to restrict their freedom of action. As a result they have brought to the Supreme Court since 1938 some thirty major cases involving religious liberty issues. In a majority of these they have been successful. These decisions have done much to clarify our constitutional law relating to freedom of religion.

The first of these cases was Lovell v. Griffin (1938), which held that a municipal ordinance forbidding the distribution within the city of all literature, including circular and handbills, without the written consent of the city manager established "a censorship of the press" and was therefore a denial of due process of law. "Liberty of the press is not confined to newspapers and periodicals. . . . [It] comprehends every sort of publication which affords a vehicle of information and opinion." This constitutional right to distribute literature without prior permission was held to exist in a company-owned town (see Marsh v. Alabama, 1946), and also in a town established by a federal housing authority (see Tucker v. Texas, 1946.) In Martin v. Struthers (1943) the Court decided that freedom of speech and press was violated by a city ordinance which made it unlawful to knock on doors or ring doorbells to summon the occupant of a residence in order to give him handbills, circulars, or other literature. In Cantwell v. Connecticut (1940) a state statute was held void which made it a crime for any person to solicit or canvass from house to house for any religious, charitable, or philanthropic cause without securing the prior approval of the secretary of the public welfare council, who was authorized to determine whether the cause was a religious one, was bona fide, and conformed to reasonable standards of efficiency and integrity. The Court found that, as applied to Jehovah's Witnesses or other religious groups, this requirement constituted a "censorship of religion as a means of determining its right to survive" and denied due process of law. The same case held that Cantwell could not be punished for a breach of the peace for playing phonograph records on the street, even though they were offensive to those who heard them. The right to do so is part of the religious liberty protected by the Constitution.

The most serious threat to the Jehovah's Witnesses was the widespread attempt of towns and cities to collect from them the usual license taxes or fees imposed on those who peddle, sell, or canvass. There was no discrimination against those religious pamphlets or books; the tax was the same regardless of what was sold. Some of the taxes were, however, substantial; and since in many parts of the country the Jehovah's Witnesses traveled from town to town in their religious crusade, the sum total of the taxes collected in all the towns visited might well be prohibitive. The Supreme Court found great difficulty in deciding whether such taxes could validly be collected on the sale of religious literature. In Jones v. Opelika (1942) it held, by a five-to-four vote, that since the taxes were nondiscriminatory and placed no special burdens on those who sold religious literature, they did not invalidly restrict freedom of religion. In the following year the Court, in Murdock v. Pennsylvania, printed below, reversed the Opelika decision, again by a vote of five to four. The new majority on the Court declared that the activities of the Witnesses in selling their literature constitute an exercise of religion, not a commercial enterprise. It is not enough that religious activities are not taxed higher than other activities. They may not be taxed at all. This complete immunity from taxation was later sustained in Follett v. McCormick (1944), in which a Jehovah's Witness was shown to make his entire living from the sale of religious literature.

The opinion in the Murdock case strongly indicates that religious speech and press enjoy a protection against restraint and regulation which may be denied to secular or commercial speech and press. This doctrine finds support in Breard v. Alexandria (1951), in which the Supreme Court held valid a city ordinance which forbade door-to-door solicitations (without the prior consent of those solicited) as applied to subscriptions to nationally known magazines. The Court distinguished this from Martin v. Struthers (1943) on the ground that in the earlier case "no element of the commercial entered into

this free solicitation and the opinion was narrowly limited to the precise fact of the free distribution of an invitation to religious services. ..." Secular books enjoy a broad range of freedom of the press; but it is not as broad as that enjoyed by religious literature.

Mr. Justice **Douglas** delivered the opinion of the Court, saying in part:

The City of Jeanette, Pennsylvania, has an ordinance, some forty years old, which provides in part:

"That all persons canvassing for or soliciting within said Borough, orders for goods, paintings, pictures, wares, or merchandise of any kind, or persons delivering such articles under orders so obtained or solicited, shall be required to procure from the Burgess a license to transact said business and shall pay to the Treasurer of said Borough therefore the following sums according to the time for which said license shall be granted.

"For one day $1.50, for one week seven dollars ($7.00), for two weeks twelve dollars ($12.00), for three weeks twenty dollars ($20.00), provided that the provisions of this ordinance shall not apply to persons selling by sample to manufacturers or licensed merchants or dealers doing business in said Borough of Jeanette."

Petitioners are "Jehovah's Witnesses." They went about from door to door in the City of Jeanette distributing literature and soliciting people to "purchase" certain religious books and pamphlets, all published by the Watch Tower Bible & Tract Society. The "price" of the books was twenty-five cents each, the "price" of the pamphlets five cents each. In connection with these activities petitioners used a phonograph on which they played a record expounding certain of their views on religion. None of them obtained a license under the ordinance. Before they were arrested each had made "sales" of books. There was evidence that it was their practice in making these solicitations to request a "contribution" of twenty-five cents each for the books and five cents each for the pamphlets but to accept lesser sums or even to donate the volumes in case an interested person was without funds. In the present case some donations of pamphlets were made when books were purchased. Petitioners were convicted and fined for violation of the ordinance. ...

The First Amendment, which the Fourteenth makes applicable to the states, declares that "Congress shall make no law respecting an establishment of religion, or prohibiting the free exercise thereof; or abridging the freedom of speech, or of the press. ..." It could hardly be denied that a tax laid specifically on the exercise of those freedoms would be unconstitutional. Yet the license tax imposed by this ordinance is in substance just that.

Petitioners spread their interpretations of the Bible and their religious beliefs largely through the hand distribution of literature by full or part time workers. They claim to follow the example of Paul, teaching "pubickly, and from house to house." Acts 20:20. They take literally the mandate of the Scriptures, "Go ye into all the world, and preach the gospel to every creature." Mark 16:15. In doing so they believe that they are obeying a commandment of God.

The hand distribution of religious tracts is an age-old form of missionary evangelism—as old as the history of printing presses. It has been a potent force in various religious movements down through the years. This form of evangelism is utilized today on a large scale by various religious sects whose colporteurs carry the Gospel to thousands upon thousands of homes and seek through personal visitations to win adherents to their faith. It is more than preaching; it is more than distribution of religious literature. It is a combination of both. Its purpose is as evangelical as the revival meeting. This form of religious activity occupies the same high estate under the First Amendment as do worship in the churches and preaching from the pulpits. It has the same claim to protection as the more orthodox and conventional exercises of religion. It also has the same claim as the others to the guarantees of freedom of speech and freedom of the press.

The integrity of this conduct or behavior as a religious practice has not been challenged. Nor do we have presented any question as to the sincerity of petitioners in their religious beliefs and practices, however misguided they may be thought to be. Moreover, we do not intimate or suggest in respecting their sincerity that any conduct can be made a religious rite and by the zeal of the practitioners swept into the First Amendment. Reynolds v. United States [1879] denied any such claim to the practice of polygamy and bigamy. Other claims may well arise which deserve the same fate. We only hold that spreading one's religious beliefs or preaching the Gospel through distribution of religious literature and through personal visitations is an age-old type of evangelism with as high a claim to constitutional protection as the more orthodox types. The manner in which it is practiced at times gives rise to special problems with which the police power of the states is competent to deal. See for example Cox v. New Hampshire [1941] and Chaplinsky v. New Hampshire [1942]. But that merely illustrates that the rights with which we are dealing are not absolutes. . . . We are concerned, however, in these cases merely with one narrow issue. There is presented for decision no question whatsoever concerning punishment for any alleged unlawful acts during the solicitation. Nor is there involved here any question as to the validity of a registration system for colporteurs and other solicitors. The cases present a single issue—the constitutionality of an ordinance which as construed and applied requires religious colporteurs to pay a license tax as a condition to the pursuit of their activities.

The alleged justification for the exaction of this license tax is the fact that the religious literature is distributed with a solicitation of funds. Thus it was stated in Jones v. Opelika [1942] that when a religious sect uses "ordinary commercial methods of sales of articles to raise propaganda funds," it is proper for the state to charge "reasonable fees for the privilege of canvassing." . . . But the mere fact that the religious literature is "sold" by itinerant preachers rather than "donated" does not transform evangelism into a commercial enterprise. If it did, then the passing of the collection plate in church would make the church service a commercial project. The constitutional rights of those spreading their religious beliefs through the spoken and printed word are not to be gauged by standards governing retailers or wholesalers of books. The right to use the press for expressing one's views is not to be measured by the protection afforded commercial handbills. It should be remembered that the pamphlets of Thomas Paine were not distributed free of charge. It is plain that a religious organization needs funds to remain a going concern. But an itinerant evangelist however misguided or intolerant he may be, does not become a mere book agent by selling the Bible or religious tracts to help defray his expenses or to sustain him. Freedom of speech, freedom of the press, freedom of religion are available to all, not merely to those who can pay their own way. As we have said, the problem of drawing the line between a purely commercial activity and a religious one will at times be difficult. On this record it plainly cannot be said that petitioners were engaged in a commercial rather than a religious venture. It is a distortion of the facts of record to describe their activities as the occupation of selling books and pamphlets. . . .

We do not mean to say that religious groups and the press are free from all financial burdens of government. . . . We have here something quite different, for example, from a tax on the income of one who engages in religious activities or a tax on property used or employed in connection with those activities. It is one thing to impose a tax on the income or property of a preacher. It is quite another thing to exact a tax from him for the privilege of delivering a sermon. . . . Those who can tax the exercise of this religious practice can make its exercise so costly as to deprive it of the resources necessary for its maintenance. Those who can tax the privilege of engaging in this form of missionary evangelism can close its doors to all those who do not have a full purse. Spreading religious beliefs in this ancient and honorable manner would thus be denied the needy. Those who can deprive religious groups of their colporteurs can take from them a part of the vital power of the press which has survived from the Reformation.

It is contended, however, that the fact that the license tax can suppress or control this activity is unimportant if it does not do so. But that is to disregard the nature of this tax. It is a license tax—a flat tax imposed on the exercise of a privilege granted by the Bill of Rights. A state may not impose a charge for the enjoyment of a right granted by the federal constitution. Thus, it may not exact a license tax for the privilege of carrying on interstate commerce. . . . A license tax applied to activities guaranteed by the First Amendment would have the same destructive effect. It is true that the First Amendment, like the commerce clause, draws no distinction between license taxes, fixed sum taxes, and other kinds of taxes. But that is no reason why we should shut our eyes to the nature of the tax and its destructive influence. The power to impose a license tax on the exercise of these freedoms is indeed as potent as the power of censorship which this Court has repeatedly struck down. . . . In all of these cases the issuance of the permit or license is dependent on the payment of a license tax. And the license tax is fixed in amount and unrelated to the scope of the activities of petitioners or to their realized revenues.

It is not a nominal fee imposed as a regulatory measure to defray the expenses of policing the activities in question. . . .

The taxes imposed by this ordinance can hardly help but be as severe and telling in their impact on the freedom of the press and religion as the ''taxes on knowledge'' at which the First Amendment was partly aimed. . . . They may indeed operate even more subtly. Itinerant evangelists moving throughout a state or from state to state would feel immediately the cumulative effect of such ordinances as they become fashionable. The way of the religious dissenter has long been hard. But if the formula of this type of ordinance is approved, a new device for the suppression of religious minorities will have been found. This method of disseminating religious beliefs can be crushed and closed out by the sheer weight of the toll or tribute which is exacted town by town, village by village. The spread of religious ideas through personal visitations by the literature ministry of numerous religious groups would be stopped.

The fact that the ordinance is ''nondiscriminatory'' is immaterial. The protection afforded by the First Amendment is not so restricted. A license tax certainly does not acquire constitutional validity because it classifies the privileges protected by the First Amendment along with the wares and merchandise of hucksters and peddlers and treats them all alike. Such equality in treatment does not save the ordinance. Freedom of press, freedom of speech, freedom of religion are in a preferred position.

It is claimed, however, that the ultimate question in determining the constitutionality of this license tax is whether the state has given something for which it can ask a return. That principle has wide applicability. . . . But it is quite irrelevant here. This tax is not a charge for the enjoyment of a privilege or benefit bestowed by the state. The privilege in question exists apart from state authority. It is guaranteed the people by the Federal constitution.

Considerable emphasis is placed on the kind of literature which petitioners were distributing—its provocative, abusive, and ill-mannered character and the assault which it makes on our established churches and the cherished faiths of many of us. . . . But those considerations are no justification for the license tax which the ordinance imposes. Plainly a community may not suppress, or the state tax, the dissemination of views because they are unpopular, annoying or distasteful. If that device were ever sanctioned, there would have been forged a ready instrument for the suppression of the faith which any minority cherishes but which does not happen to be

in favor. That would be a complete repudiation of the philosophy of the Bill of Rights.

Jehovah's Witnesses are not ''above the law.'' But the present ordinance is not directed to the problems with which the police power of the state is free to deal. It does not cover, and petitioners are not charged with breaches of the peace. They are pursuing their solicitations peacefully and quietly. . . .

The judgment in Jones v. Opelika has this day been vacated. Freed from that controlling precedent, we can restore to their high, constitutional position the liberties of itinerant evangelists who disseminate their religious beliefs and the tenets of their faith through distribution of literature. The judgments are reversed and the causes are remanded to the Pennsylvania Superior Court for proceedings not inconsistent with this opinion.

Reversed.

Mr. Justice **Reed** dissented and Justices **Roberts, Frankfurter,** and **Jackson** concurred.

Mr. Justice **Frankfurter** also wrote a dissenting opinion.

WEST VIRGINIA STATE BOARD OF EDUCATION v. BARNETTE

319 U. S. 624; 63 S. Ct. 1178; 87 L. Ed. 1628 (1943)

The most spectacular issue of religious liberty to be raised by the Jehovah's Witnesses was that of the compulsory flag salute. The Witnesses refuse to salute the flag or permit their children to do so, because they believe that this violates the First Commandment. This refusal caused bitter resentment, and some seventeen states passed statutes requiring all school children to salute the flag and providing for the expulsion of those who refused. The question of whether these acts unconstitutionally restricted freedom of religion came to the Court in Minersville School District v. Gobitis (1940). With one judge dissenting, the Court held that it did not. In an opinion by Justice Frankfurter it was stated that freedom of religion is not absolute, and that some compromises may be necessary in order to secure the national unity, which is the basis of national security. The flag salute contributes to that national unity, or at least the question of whether it does or not is ''an issue of educational policy for which the courtroom is not the proper arena.'' For the Court to hold the requirement void as abridging religious liberty ''would amount to no less than the pronouncement of a pedagogical and psychological dogma in a field where courts possess no marked and certainly no controlling competence.'' The Court seemed content to assume that the Minersville school board was more competent to settle the flag salute issue than the Supreme Court, and it allowed the board's judgment to prevail. Justice Stone wrote a powerful dissenting opinion. The decision came as a shock and was widely and sharply criticized. Members of the Court who had participated in it began to have misgivings. When Jones v. Opelika was decided in 1942, Justices Black, Douglas, and Murphy dissented, and went further to state that they had become convinced that the Gobitis case was "wrongly decided." With Justice Stone, this made four members of the Court who no longer supported the Gobitis decision. When, in February, 1943, Justice Rutledge replaced Justice Byrnes on the bench, he joined with these four to overrule the Gobitis case by the decision in the case below.

These cases suggest that the Supreme Court, in dealing with questions of religious freedom, seeks to find a sound balance between the competing interests of the individual and of the society in which he or she lives. Society's interest is upheld where the disadvantage to the religious interest of the individual is relatively slight. Thus Cox v. New Hampshire (1941) held that a reasonable, nondiscriminatory fee, suitable to cover the cost of extra police service, may be charged for the privilege of holding public parades or processions, even though they be for religious purposes. And Prince v. Massachusetts (1944) held that a state child labor law may be validly enforced against those who allow young children under their care to sell religious literature on the streets.

In Sherbert v. Verner (1963), however, the free exercise clause was held violated where unemployment compensation was denied a Seventh Day Adventist who refused "suitable" work which required her to work on Saturday. Such a rule, the Court held, "forces her to choose between following the precepts of her religion and forfeiting benefits, on the one hand, and abandoning one of the precepts of her religion in order to accept work on the other hand. Governmental imposition of such a choice puts the same kind of burden upon the free exercise of religion as would a fine imposed against appellant for her Saturday worship." The holding was reaffirmed in Thomas v. Review Board (1981) where a Jehovah's Witness was held entitled to unemployment insurance after quitting for religious reasons a job which involved making weapons. The steel company for which he worked had closed the roll foundry where he worked and transferred him to a department making gun turrets.

In contrast, the Court in Employment Division v. Smith (1990) upheld the denial of unemployment compensation to two members of the Native American Church who were fired for using peyote in their religious ceremonies. Oregon law forbade the use of peyote, and five members of the Court, quoting Justice Frankfurter in the Gobitis case, agreed that "Conscientious scruples have not, in the course of the long struggle for religious toleration, relieved the individual from obedience to a general law not aimed at the promotion or restriction of religious beliefs. The mere possession of religious convictions which contradict the relevant concerns of a political society does not relieve the citizen from the discharge of political responsibilities."

In two cases the Court dealt with the unusual demands of the Old Order Amish, a plain people who lead a simple, rural farm life in cohesive, self-supporting re-ligious communities, stressing "a life of 'goodness,' rather than a life of intellect; wisdom, rather than technical knowledge; community welfare rather than competition; and separation from, rather than integration with, contemporary worldly society." They dress plainly, do not use machinery or electricity and their transportation consists of horse-drawn wagons and buggies lighted at night with a lantern. In Wisconsin v. Yoder (1972) they resisted the efforts of the state to make their children attend school past the eighth grade. They argued that by sending their children to high school "they would not only expose themselves to the danger of the censure of the church community, but . . . endanger their own salvation and that of their children." The Court held that in view of the kind of life for which the Amish children were being trained and the unquestioned success of the Amish society, the state did not have sufficiently compelling interest in the additional years of schooling to warrant interfering with the free exercise of their religion. In United States v. Lee (1982), however, the Court held that Amish employers and employees had to pay into the social security system despite the self-sufficiency of the Amish and the fact "that both payment and receipt of social security benefits is forbidden by the Amish faith." The Court found mandatory participation essential to the fiscal vitality of the system and noted the lack of difference in principle between this and the payment of income taxes which any number of religious groups might object to paying through religious objection to the purposes for which the money was spent.

Bob Jones University v. United States (1983) brought to the Court the unusual issue whether the IRS could validly withhold the normally available tax exemption from a private educational institution simply because it discriminated against blacks. The case, which turned primarily on the intent of Congress in adopting the statute, was given a bizarre twist when President Reagan ordered the government to change sides after certiorari had been granted. The case was kept from becoming moot when the court of appeals enjoined the government's grant of tax immunity, and since the Attorney General was now on the side of Bob Jones, the Court appointed outside counsel to defend the government's position. It found the IRS interpretation to be correct and held that it did not violate Bob Jones' religious freedom. It noted that freedom of religion was not an absolute but had to yield to "an overriding, governmental interest" and here "the Government has a fundamental, overriding interest in eradicating racial discrimination in education—discrimination that prevailed, with official approval, for the first 165 years of this Nation's history."

Mr. Justice **Jackson** delivered the opinion of the Court, saying in part:

Following the decision by this Court on June 3, 1940, in Minersville School Dist. v. Gobitis the West Virginia legislature amended its statutes to require all schools therein to conduct courses of instruction in history, civics, and in the Constitutions of the United States and of the State "for the purpose of teaching, fostering and perpetuating the ideals, principles and spirit of Americanism, and increasing the knowledge of the organization and machinery of the government." . . .

The Board of Education on January 9, 1942, adopted a resolution containing recitals taken largely from the Court's Gobitis opinion and ordering that the salute to the flag become "a regular part of the program of activities in the public schools," that all teachers and pupils "shall be required to participate in the salute honoring the Nation represented by the Flag; provided, however, that refusal to salute the Flag be regarded as an Act of insubordination, and shall be dealt with accordingly."

The resolution originally required the "commonly accepted salute to the Flag" which it defined. Objections to the salute as "being too much like Hitler's" were raised by the Parent and Teachers Association, the Boy and Girl Scouts, the Red Cross, and the Federation of Women's Clubs. Some modification appears to have been made in deference to these objections, but no concession was made to Jehovah's Witnesses. What is now required is the "stiff-arm" salute, the saluter to keep the right hand raised with palm turned up while the following is repeated: "I pledge allegiance to the Flag of the United States of America and to the Republic for which it stands; one Nation, indivisible, with liberty and justice for all."

Failure to conform is "insubordination" dealt with by expulsion. Readmission is denied by statute until compliance. Meanwhile the expelled child is "unlawfully absent" and may be proceeded against as a delinquent. His parents or guardians are liable to prosecution, and if convicted are subject to fine not exceeding $50 and jail terms not exceeding thirty days.

Appellees, citizens of the United States and of West Virginia, brought suit in the United States District Court for themselves and others similarly situated asking its injunction to restrain enforcement of these laws and regulations against Jehovah's Witnesses. The Witnesses are an unincorporated body teaching that the obligation imposed by law of God is superior to that of laws enacted by temporal government. Their religious beliefs include a literal version of Exodus, Chapter 20, verses 4 and 5, which says: "Thou shalt not make unto thee any graven image, or any likeness of anything that is in heaven above, or that is in the earth beneath or that is in the water under the earth; thou shalt not bow down thyself to them, nor serve them." They consider that the flag is an "image" within this command. For this reason they refuse to salute it.

Children of this faith have been expelled from school and are threatened with exclusion for no other cause. Officials threaten to send them to reformatories maintained for criminally inclined juveniles. Parents of such children have been prosecuted and are threatened with prosecutions for causing delinquency. . . .

This case calls upon us to reconsider a precedent decision, as the Court throughout its history often has been required to do. Before turning to the Gobitis Case,

however, it is desirable to notice certain characteristics by which this controversy is distinguished.

The freedom asserted by these appellees does not bring them into collision with rights asserted by any other individual. It is such conflicts which most frequently require intervention of the State to determine where the rights of one end and those of another begin. But the refusal of these persons to participate in the ceremony does not interfere with or deny rights of others to do so. Nor is there any question in this case that their behavior is peaceable and orderly. The sole conflict is between authority and rights of the individual. The State asserts power to condition access to public education on making a prescribed sign and profession and at the same time to coerce attendance by punishing both parent and child. The latter stand on a right of self-determination in matters that touch individual opinion and personal attitude.

As the present Chief Justice said in dissent in the Gobitis Case, the State may "require teaching by instruction and study of all in our history and in the structure and organization of our government, including the guaranties of civil liberty, which tend to inspire patriotism and love of country." Here, however, we are dealing with a compulsion of students to declare a belief. They are not merely made acquainted with the flag salute so that they may be informed as to what it is or even what it means. The issue here is whether this slow and easily neglected route to aroused loyalties constitutionally may be short-cut by substituting a compulsory salute and slogan. . . .

There is no doubt that, in connection with the pledges, the flag salute is a form of utterance. Symbolism is a primitive but effective way of communicating ideas. The use of an emblem or flag to symbolize some system, idea, institution, or personality, is a short cut from mind to mind. Causes and nations, political parties, lodges and ecclesiastical groups seek to knit the loyalty of their followings to a flag or banner, a color or design. The State announces rank, function, and authority through crowns and maces, uniforms and black robes; the church speaks through the Cross, the Crucifix, the altar and shrine, and clerical raiment. Symbols of State often convey political ideas just as religious symbols come to convey theological ones. Associated with many of these symbols are appropriate gestures of acceptance or respect: a salute, a bowed or bared head, a bended knee. A person gets from a symbol the meaning he puts into it, and what is one man's comfort and inspiration is another's jest and scorn.

Over a decade ago Chief Justice Hughes led this Court in holding that the display of a red flag as a symbol of opposition by peaceful and legal means to organized government was protected by the free speech guaranties of the Constitution. Stromberg v. California [1931]. Here it is the State that employs a flag as a symbol of adherence to government as presently organized. It requires the individual to communicate by word and sign his acceptance of the political ideas it thus bespeaks.

Objection to this form of communication when coerced is an old one, well known to the framers of the Bill of Rights.

It is also to be noted that the compulsory flag salute and pledge requires affirmation of a belief and an attitude of mind. It is not clear whether the regulation contemplates that pupils forego any contrary convictions of their own and become unwilling converts to the prescribed ceremony or whether it will be acceptable if they simulate assent by words without belief and by a gesture barren of meaning. It is now a commonplace that censorship or suppression of expression of opinion is tolerated by our Constitution only when the expression presents a clear and present danger of action of a kind the State is empowered to prevent and punish. It would seem that involuntary affirmation could be commanded only on even more immediate and urgent grounds than silence. But here the power of compulsion is invoked without any allegation that remaining passive during a flag salute ritual creates a clear and present danger that would justify an effort even to muffle expression. To sustain the compulsory flag salute we are required to say that a Bill of Rights which guards the individual's right to speak his own mind, left it open to public authorities to compel him to utter what is not in his mind.

Whether the First Amendment to the Constitution will permit officials to order observance of ritual of this nature does not depend upon whether as a voluntary exercise we would think it to be good, bad or merely innocuous. Any credo of nationalism is likely to include what some disapprove or to omit what others think essential, and to give off different overtones as it takes on different accents or interpretations. If official power exists to coerce acceptance of any patriotic creed, what it shall contain cannot be decided by courts, but must be largely discretionary with the ordaining authority, whose power to prescribe would no doubt include power to amend. Hence validity of the asserted power to force an American citizen publicly to profess any statement of belief or to engage in any ceremony of assent to one, presents questions of power that must be considered independently of any idea we may have as to the utility of the ceremony in question.

Nor does the issue as we see it turn on one's possession of particular religious views or the sincerity with which they are held. While religion supplies appellees' motive for enduring the discomforts of making the issue in this case, many citizens who do not share these religious views hold such a compulsory rite to infringe constitutional liberty of the individual. It is not necessary to inquire whether non-conformist beliefs will exempt from the duty to salute unless we first find power to make the salute a legal duty.

The Gobitis decision, however, *assumed,* as did the argument in that case and in this, that power exists in the State to impose the flag salute discipline upon school children in general. The Court only examined and rejected a claim based on religious beliefs of immunity from an unquestioned general rule. The question which underlies the flag salute controversy is whether such a ceremony so touching matters of opinion and political attitude may be imposed upon the individual by official authority under powers committed to any political organization under our Constitution. We examine rather than assume existence of this power and, against this broader definition of issues in this case, re-examine specific grounds assigned for the Gobitis decision.

1. It was said that the flag-salute controversy confronted the Court with "the problem which Lincoln cast in memorable dilemma: 'Must a government of necessity be too *strong* for the liberties of its people, or too *weak* to maintain its own existence?'" and that the answer must be in favor of strength. Minersville School District v. Gobitis.

We think these issues may be examined free of pressure or restraint growing out of such considerations.

It may be doubted whether Mr. Lincoln would have thought that the strength of government to maintain itself would be impressively vindicated by our confirming power of the state to expel a handful of children from school. Such oversimplification, so handy in political debate, often lacks the precision necessary to postulates of judicial reasoning. If validly applied to this problem, the utterance cited would resolve every issue of power in favor of those in authority and would require us to override every liberty thought to weaken or delay execution of their policies.

Government of limited power need not be anemic government. Assurance that rights are secure tends to diminish fear and jealousy of strong government, and by making us feel safe to live under it makes for its better support. Without promise of a limiting Bill of Rights it is doubtful if our Constitution could have mustered enough strength to enable its ratification. To enforce those rights today is not to choose weak government over strong government. It is only to adhere as a means of strength to individual freedom of mind in preference to officially disciplined uniformity for which history indicates a disappointing and disastrous end.

The subject now before us exemplifies this principle. Free public education, if faithful to the ideal of secular instruction and political neutrality, will not be partisan or enemy of any class, creed, party, or faction. If it is to impose any ideological discipline, however, each party or denomination must seek to control, or failing that, to weaken the influence of the educational system. Observance of the limitations of the Constitution will not weaken government in the field appropriate for its exercise.

2. It was also considered in the Gobitis Case that functions of educational officers in states, counties and school districts were such that to interfere with their authority "would in effect make us the school board for the country."

The Fourteenth Amendment, as now applied to the States, protects the citizen against the State itself and all of its creatures—Boards of Education not excepted. These have, of course, important, delicate, and highly discretionary functions, but none that they may not perform within the limits of the Bill of Rights. That they are educating the young for citizenship is reason for scrupulous protection of Constitutional freedoms of the individual, if we are not to strangle the free mind at its source and teach youth to discount important principles of our government as mere platitudes.

Such Boards are numerous and their territorial jurisdiction often small. But small and local authority may feel less sense of responsibility to the Constitution, and agencies of publicity may be less vigilant in calling it to account. The action of Congress in making flag observance voluntary and respecting the conscience of the objector in a matter so vital as raising the Army contrasts sharply with these local regulations in matters relatively trivial to the welfare of the nation. There are village tyrants as well as village Hampdens, but none who acts under color of law is beyond reach of the Constitution.

3. The Gobitis opinion reasoned that this is a field "where courts possess no marked and certainly no controlling competence," that it is committed to the legislatures as well as the courts to guard cherished liberties and that it is constitutionally appropriate to "fight out the wise use of legislative authority in the forum of public opinion and before legislative assemblies rather than to transfer such a contest to the judicial arena," since all the "effective means of inducing political changes are left free."

The very purpose of a Bill of Rights was to withdraw certain subjects from the vicissitudes of political controversy, to place them beyond the reach of majorities and officials and to establish them as legal principles to be applied by the courts. One's rights to life, liberty, and property, to free speech, a free press, freedom of worship and assembly, and other fundamental rights may not be submitted to vote; they depend on the outcome of no elections.

In weighing arguments of the parties it is important to distinguish between the due process clause of the Fourteenth Amendment as an instrument for transmitting the principles of the First Amendment and those cases in which it is applied for its own sake. The test of legislation which collides with the Fourteenth Amendment, because it also collides with the principles of the First, is much more definite than the test when only the Fourteenth is involved. Much of the vagueness of the due process clause disappears when the specific prohibitions of the First become its standard. The right of a State to regulate, for example, a public utility may well include, so far as the due process test is concerned, power to impose all of the restrictions which a legislature may have a "rational basis" for adopting. But freedoms of speech and of press, of assembly, and of worship may not be infringed on such slender grounds. They are susceptible of restriction only to prevent grave and immediate danger to interests which the state may lawfully protect. It is important to note that while it is the Fourteenth Amendment which bears directly upon the State it is the more specific limiting principles of the First Amendment that finally govern this case.

Nor does our duty to apply the Bill of Rights to assertions of official authority depend upon our possession of marked competence in the field where the invasion of rights occurs. True, the task of translating the majestic generalities of the Bill of Rights, conceived as part of the pattern of liberal government in the eighteenth century, into concrete restraints on officials dealing with the problems of the twentieth century, is one to disturb self-confidence. These principles grew in soil which also produced a philosophy that the individual was the center of society, that his liberty was attainable through mere absence of governmental restraints, and that government should be entrusted with few controls and only the mildest supervision over men's affairs. We must transplant these rights to a soil in which the laissez-faire concept or principle of non-interference has withered at least as to economic affairs, and social advancements are increasingly sought through closer integration of society and through expanded and strengthened governmental controls. These changed conditions often deprive precedents of reliability and cast us more than we would choose upon our own judgment. But we act in these matters not by authority of our competence but by force of our commissions. We cannot, because of modest estimates of our competence in such specialities as public education, withhold the judgment that history authenticates as the function of this Court when liberty is infringed.

4. Lastly, and this is the very heart of the Gobitis opinion, it reasons that "national unity is the basis of national security," that the authorities have "the right to select appropriate means for its attainment," and hence reaches the conclusion that such compulsory measures toward "national unity" are constitutional. Upon the verity of this assumption depends our answer in this case.

National unity as an end which officials may foster by persuasion and example is not in question. The problem is whether under our Constitution compulsion as here employed is a permissible means for its achievement.

Struggles to coerce uniformity of sentiment in support of some end thought essential to their time and country have been waged by many good as well as by evil men. Nationalism is a relatively recent phenomenon but at other times and places the ends have been racial or territorial security, support of a dynasty or regime, and particular plans for saving souls. As first and moderate methods to attain unity have failed, those bent on its accomplishment must resort to an ever increasing severity. As governmental pressure toward unity becomes greater, so strife becomes more bitter as to whose unity it shall be. Probably no deeper division of our people could proceed from any provocation than from finding it necessary to choose what doctrine and whose program public educational officials shall compel youth to unite in embracing. Ultimate futility of such attempts to compel coherence is the lesson of every such effort from the Roman drive to stamp out Christianity as a disturber to its pagan unity, the Inquisition, as a means to religious and dynastic unity, the Siberian exiles as a means to Russian unity, down to the fast-failing efforts of our present totalitarian enemies. Those who begin coercive elimination of dissent soon find themselves exterminating dissenters. Compulsory unification of opinion achieves only the unanimity of the graveyard.

It seems trite but necessary to say that the First Amendment to our Constitution was designed to avoid these ends by avoiding these beginnings. There is no mysticism in the American concept of the State or of the nature or origin of its authority. We set up government by consent of the governed, and the Bill of Rights denies those in power any legal opportunity to coerce that consent. Authority here is to be controlled by public opinion, not public opinion by authority.

The case is made difficult not because the principles of its decision are obscure but because the flag involved is our own. Nevertheless, we apply the limitations of the Constitution with no fear that freedom to be intellectually and spiritually diverse or even contrary will disintegrate the social organization. To believe that patriotism will not flourish if patriotic ceremonies are voluntary and spontaneous instead of a compulsory routine is to make an unflattering estimate of the appeal of our institutions to free minds. We can have intellectual individualism and the rich cultural diversities that we owe to exceptional minds only at the price of occasional eccentricity and abnormal attitudes. When they are so harmless to others or to the State as those we deal with here, the price is not too great. But freedom to differ is not limited to things that do not matter much. That would be a mere shadow of freedom. The test of its substance is the right to differ as to things that touch the heart of the existing order.

If there is any fixed star in our constitutional constellation, it is that no official, high or petty, can prescribe what shall be orthodox in politics, nationalism, religion, or other matters of opinion or force citizens to confess by word or act their faith therein. If there are any circumstances which permit an exception, they do not now occur to us.

We think the action of the local authorities in compelling the flag salute and pledge transcends constitutional limitations on their power and invades the sphere of intellect and spirit which it is the purpose of the First Amendment to our Constitution to reserve from all official control.

The decision of this Court in Minersville School District v. Gobitis . . . [is] overruled, and the judgment enjoining enforcement of the West Virginia Regulation is affirmed.

Justices **Black** and **Douglas** joined in a concurring opinion.

Mr. Justice **Murphy** wrote a concurring opinion.

Justices **Roberts** and **Reed** dissented.

Mr. Justice **Frankfurter,** in dissenting, said in part:

. . . As a member of this Court I am not justified in writing my private notions of policy into the Constitution, no matter how deeply I may cherish them or how mischievous I may deem their disregard. The duty of a judge who must decide which of two claims before the Court shall prevail, that of a State to enact and enforce laws within its general competence or that of an individual to refuse obedience because of the demands of his conscience, is not that of the ordinary person. It can never be emphasized too much that one's own opinion about the wisdom or evil of a law should be excluded altogether when one is doing one's duty on the bench. The only opinion of our own even looking in that direction that is material is our opinion whether legislators could in reason have enacted such a law. In the light of all the circumstances, including the history of this question in this Court, it would require more daring than I possess to deny that reasonable legislators could have taken the action which is before us for review. Most unwillingly, therefore, I must differ from my brethren with regard to legislation like this, I cannot bring my mind to believe that the 'liberty' secured by the Due Process Clause gives this Court authority to deny to the State of West Virginia the attainment of that which we all recognize as a legitimate legislative end, namely, the promotion of good citizenship, by employment of the means here chosen. . . .

ESTABLISHMENT OF RELIGION

ZORACH v. CLAUSON

343 U. S. 306; 72 S. Ct. 679; 96 L. Ed. 954
(1952)

In the Jehovah's Witnesses cases just presented the Supreme Court had to decide whether the government had violated the freedom of religion protected by the First and Fourteenth Amendments. The cases concerned directly a small militant group. In the cases below the Court faced highly complex problems affecting the interests of all citizens: namely, the problems of public aid to religion in connection with our nationwide system of compulsory education.

Early education in America was religious education, supported by the civil government in the Bible-commonwealth of Massachusetts, and by the various church groups in the middle and southern colonies. In the early nineteenth century the demand for free public education resulted in a system of public schools free from religious control and largely free from sectarian influence, a situation wholly satisfactory to an overwhelmingly Protestant nation. Waves of Catholic immigration injected a new element into the picture. The Catholic Church regards the teaching of religion as a primary function of education. Unwilling to send their children to the public schools, which they regarded as either devoid of all religious influence or tainted with Protestantism, the Catholics felt obliged to build and maintain a system of parochial schools at their own expense. When these parochial schools met the state's educational standards they were accredited as schools in which the requirements of the compulsory education laws could be satisfied. In 1922 the state of Oregon passed a law requiring all parents to send their children to the public schools of the state. The Supreme Court, in *Pierce v. Society of Sisters* (1925), held that the statute denied due process of law by taking from parents their freedom to "direct the upbringing and education" of their children by sending them either to parochial or to private nonsectarian schools of approved educational standards.

It is not surprising that Catholic citizens, who paid taxes to support public schools which they did not use, should try to secure some public aid for the parochial schools; and they exerted a good deal of pressure to bring this about. Opposition to this was, however, bitter and widespread; and by the end of the nineteenth century practically every state had adopted some kind of prohibition against the use of state funds for the support of religious education. In numerous cases the state courts held void attempts to extend direct or indirect aid to parochial schools.

Since the 1930s new and varied services and benefits have been offered by the states to pupils in the public schools. These include free textbooks, free bus transportation, free lunches, and free medical service. Can the state, if it desires, also give these benefits to children attending parochial or private schools? It was argued on the one hand that to do so would not only violate the constitutional clauses which forbid the use of public money in aid of religion or religious education, but would violate also the clause of the First Amendment which forbids "an establishment of religion," a clause now carried over into the Fourteenth Amendment as a limitation on the states. It was argued on the other side that in providing these services and benefits the state was aiding the child and not the school. Most state courts accepted this latter reasoning, which came to be known as the "child benefit theory"; and the Supreme Court, in *Cochran v. Louisiana State Board of Education* (1930), held valid a state law authorizing the use of public funds to supply "school books to the school children of the state," including children in parochial and private nonsectarian schools. The Court agreed that "the school children and the state alone are beneficiaries" of these appropriations, and not the schools which the children attend. The Supreme Court again applied the theory in *Everson v. Board of Education* (1947) to hold valid the provision of free bus transportation to children attending parochial schools.

Unfortunately, the child benefit theory, while giving a plausible explanation for the results reached, does not provide any real test for reaching those results in the first place. If the fact that a child is benefited makes an expenditure valid, it is hard to see why the state cannot build and support religious schools. On the other hand,

if anything that aids religion is forbidden by the First Amendment, why are not fire and police protection for churches unconstitutional? What the Constitution demands is state neutrality toward religion, but what constitutes neutrality in a society where governmental aid and supervision are almost ubiquitous? How is the line to be drawn between neutrality and impermissible state aid to religion?

While the Everson case held valid certain kinds of aid to children attending religious schools (discussed further in the note to *Mueller v. Allen* (1983), below) it did not answer the needs of parents whose children were getting what was viewed as a "Godless" education in the public schools. Two lines of attack were used in an effort to solve this problem. One was a series of efforts to introduce religious materials directly into the public schools; see the note to *Edwards v. Aguillard* (1987). The other, discussed below, was the use of what came to be known as "released time."

Churches, whose success in competing for the time and interest of children has never been outstanding, and parents who wanted their children to have religious training but could no longer get them to go to Sunday School finally devised a scheme whereby children could get such religious training during their "working day" rather than after school or on weekends. One such program was set up in Champaign, Illinois. Public school pupils whose parents signed "request cards" attended religious-instruction classes conducted during regular school hours in the school building, but taught by outside teachers (chosen by a religious council representing the various faiths) who were subject to the approval and supervision of the superintendent of schools. These teachers were not paid from public funds. Records of attendance at these classes were kept and reported to the school authorities, and pupils who did not attend them spent their time on their ordinary studies. The Supreme Court held the plan void in *Illinois ex rel. McCollum v. Board of Education* (1948). The facts stated, the Court said, "show the use of tax-supported property for religious instruction and the close cooperation between the school authorities and the religious council in promoting religious education. The operation of the State's compulsory education system thus assists and is integrated with the program of religious instruction carried on by separate religious sects. Pupils compelled by law to go to school for secular education are released in part from their legal duty upon the condition that they attend the religious classes. This is beyond all question a utilization of the tax-established and tax-supported public school system to aid religious groups to spread their faith." The Court reaffirmed its statement in Everson that the First Amendment sets up a complete separation of church and state, and any government aid to religion violates this principle.

Although the justices in both Everson and McCollum agreed unanimously that the First Amendment set up a complete separation of church and state, they differed sharply in each case on whether aid to religion was in fact shown. They did not question that if it had been, it would have been bad. Religious leaders, both Catholic and Protestant, together with some lay critics, have challenged the basic rule which the Court has announced. They urge that the framers did not intend by the First Amendment to forbid completely all government aid to religion, but only such aid as favors one religion over another.

They argue, first, that there is no really persuasive historical ground for holding that the framers had in mind an absolute separation of church and state; the "establishment" clause was intended merely to prevent the establishment of a state church, such as the Church of England. Second, the historical material mustered by Justice Black in the Everson case to show that what the framers intended was, in Jefferson's phrase, a wall of separation between church and state has been sharply criticized by a number of historical scholars as presenting an incomplete and distorted picture. Third, the Supreme Court had itself recognized some aid to religion. In Bradfield v. Roberts (1899) it had held valid federal aid to a Roman Catholic hospital, although on the technical ground that the hospital corporation was a secular body which served patients without regard to denomination. Also, weight has been attached to the fact that in 1844 in the Girard will case, Vidal v. Girard's Executors, Justice Story had announced (though by way of dictum) that the "Christian religion is part of the common law."

In Widmar v. Vincent (1981) the problems of McCollum and Zorach came back to haunt the Court in a different form. Here a group of students at the University of Missouri at Kansas City wanted to use for a meeting of "evangelical Christian students" one of the rooms assigned for the use of the one-hundred-odd student organizations on the campus. The University denied the request on the ground that it would constitute aid to religion while the students argued that their freedom of speech was being abridged on account of its content. The Supreme Court upheld the students. It agreed that two of the three tests for establishment were easily met. A nondiscriminatory open-forum policy, including nondiscrimination against religious speech, would have a secular purpose and would avoid entanglement with religion. Nor was it persuaded that "the primary effect of the public forum, open to all forms of discourse, would be to advance religion. . . . This Court has explained that a religious organization's enjoyment of merely "incidental" benefits does not violate the prohibition against the "primary advancement" of religion. Here, any religious benefits would be "incidental."

One of the main difficulties encountered in challenging alleged aid to religious schools has been a rule of the Supreme Court dating back to 1923 that a person could not contest in federal court the expenditure of tax money solely on the ground that he was a taxpayer and had an interest in how the money was spent. See Frothingham v. Mellon (1923). Not only was the share of the interested taxpayer in the money too small to deserve judicial notice, but the Court clearly viewed with concern the specter of millions of taxpayers in a position to challenge in the courts every expenditure of federal funds. The result of this ruling was to make virtually impregnable to judicial attack any distribution of federal funds to religious groups. With the passage of Titles I and II of the Elementary and Secondary Education Act of 1965, under which funds could be used to finance secular education in religious schools, the attack on the "no taxpayer suits" rule was reopened. In Flast v. Cohen (1968) the Court eased the rule as applied to challenges brought under the establishment clause of the First Amendment. The Court held that "the taxpayer must show that the challenged enactment exceeds specific constitutional limitations imposed upon the exercise of the congressional taxing and spending power and not simply that the enactment is generally beyond the powers delegated to Congress by Art. I, § 8." Since one of the reasons for adopting the establishment clause was to prevent using the tax power to aid religion, this clause was such a "specific limitation." In Valley Forge Christian College v. Americans United (1982), however, the Court made clear that this restriction applied only to the taxing power. There the government had given to a religious school the land and buildings of a former veterans hospital valued at about $3 million. Since no money had changed hands no taxpayer had standing, as a taxpayer, to bring suit to contest the misuse of tax moneys.

Mr. Justice **Douglas** delivered the opinion of the Court, saying in part:

New York City has a program which permits its public schools to release students during the school day so that they may leave the school buildings and school grounds and go to religious centers for religious instruction or devotional exercises. A student is released on written request of his parents. Those not released stay in the classrooms. The churches make weekly reports to the schools, sending a list of children who have been released from public school but who have not reported for religious instruction.

This "released time" program involves neither religious instruction in public school classrooms nor the expenditure of public funds. All costs, including the application blanks, are paid by the religious organizations. The case is therefore unlike McCollum v. Board of Education [1948] which involved a "released time" program from Illinois. In that case the classrooms were turned over to religious instructors. We accordingly held that the program violated the First Amendment which (by reason of the Fourteenth Amendment) prohibits the states from establishing religion or prohibiting its free exercise.

Appellants, who are taxpayers and residents of New York City and whose children attend its public schools, challenge the present law, contending it is in essence not different from the one involved in the McCollum Case. Their argument, stated elaborately in various ways, reduces itself to this: the weight and influence of the school is put behind a program for religious instruction; public school teachers police it, keeping tab on students who are released; the classroom activities come to a halt while the students who are released for religious instruction are on leave; the school is a crutch on which the churches are leaning for support in their religious training; without the cooperation of the schools this "released time" program, like the one in the McCollum Case, would be futile and ineffective. The New York Court of Appeals sustained the law against this claim of unconstitutionality. . . . The case is here on appeal. . . .

It takes obtuse reasoning to inject any issue of the "free exercise" of religion into the present case. No one is forced to go to the religious classroom and no religious exercise or instruction is brought to the classrooms of the public schools. A student need not take religious instruction. He is left to his own desires as to the manner or time of his religious devotions, if any.

There is a suggestion that the system involves the use of coercion to get public school students into religious classrooms. There is no evidence in the record before us that supports that conclusion. The present record indeed tells us that the school authorities are neutral in this regard and do no more than release students whose parents so request. If in fact coercion were used, if it were established that any one or more teachers were using their office to persuade or force students to take the religious instruction, a wholly different case would be presented. Hence we put aside that claim of coercion both as respects the "free exercise" of religion and "an establishment of religion" within the meaning of the First Amendment.

Moreover, apart from that claim of coercion, we do not see how New York by this type of "released time" program has made a law respecting an establishment of religion within the meaning of the First Amendment. There is much talk of the separation of Church and State in the history of the Bill of Rights and in the decisions clustering around the First Amendment. See Everson v. Board of Education [1947]; McCollum v. Board of Education. There cannot be the slightest doubt that the First Amendment reflects the philosophy that Church and State should be separated. And so far as interference with the "free exercise" of religion and an "establishment" of religion are concerned, the separation must be complete and unequivocal. The First Amendment within the scope of its coverage permits no exception; the prohibition is absolute. The First Amendment, however, does not say that in every and all respects there shall be a separation of Church and State. Rather, it studiously defines the manner, the specific ways, in which there shall be no concert or union or dependency one on the other. That is the common sense of the matter. Otherwise, the state and religion would be aliens to each other—hostile, suspicious, and even unfriendly. Churches could not be required to pay even property taxes. Municipalities would not be permitted to render police or fire protection to religious groups. Policemen who helped parishioners into their places of worship would violate the Constitution. Prayers in our legislative halls; the appeals to the Almighty in the mes-sages of the Chief Executive; the proclamations making Thanksgiving Day a holiday; "so help me God" in our courtroom oaths—these and all other references to the Almighty that run through our laws, our public rituals, our ceremonies would be flouting the First Amendment. A fastidious atheist or agnostic could even object to the supplication with which the Court opens each session: "God save the United States and this Honorable Court."

We would have to press the concept of separation of Church and State to these extremes to condemn the present law on constitutional grounds. The nullification of this law would have wide and profound effects. A Catholic student applies to his teacher for permission to leave the school during hours on a Holy Day of Obligation to attend a mass. A Jewish student asks his teacher for permission to be excused for Yom Kippur. A Protestant wants the afternoon off for a family baptismal ceremony. In each case the teacher requires parental consent in writing. In each case the teacher, in order to make sure the student is not a truant, goes further and requires a report from the priest, the rabbi, or the minister. The teacher in other words cooperates in a religious program to the extent of making it possible for her students to participate in it. Whether she does it occasionally for a few students, regularly for one, or pursuant to a systematized program designed to further the religious needs of all the students does not alter the character of the act.

We are a religious people whose institutions presuppose a Supreme Being. We guarantee the freedom to worship as one chooses. We make room for as wide a variety of beliefs and creeds as the spiritual needs of man deem necessary. We sponsor an attitude on the part of government that shows no partiality to any one group and that lets each flourish according to the zeal of its adherents and the appeal of its dogma. When the state encourages religious instruction or cooperates with religious authorities by adjusting the schedule of public events to sectarian needs, it follows the best of our traditions. For it then respects the religious nature of our people and accommodates the public service to their spiritual needs. To hold that it may not would be to find in the Constitution a requirement that the government show a callous indifference to religious groups. That would be preferring those who believe in no religion over those who do believe. Government may not finance religious groups nor undertake religious instruction nor blend secular and sectarian education nor use secular institutions to force one or some religion on any person. But we find no constitutional requirement which makes it necessary for government to be hostile to religion and to throw its weight against efforts to widen the effective scope of religious influence. The government must be neutral when it comes to competition between sects. It may not thrust any sect on any person. It may not make a religious observance compulsory. It may not coerce anyone to attend church, to observe a religious holiday, or to take religious instruction. But it can close its doors or suspend its operations as to those who want to repair to their religious sanctuary for worship or instruction. No more than that is undertaken here. . . .

In the McCollum case the classrooms were used for religious instruction and the force of the public school was used to promote that instruction. Here, as we have said, the public schools do no more than accommodate their schedules to a program of outside religious instruction. We follow the McCollum case. But we cannot expand it to cover the present released time program unless separation of Church and State means that public institutions can make no adjustments of their schedules to accommodate the religious needs of the people. We cannot read into the Bill of Rights such a philosophy of hostility to religion.

Affirmed.

Justices **Black** and **Frankfurter** wrote dissenting opinions.

Mr. Justice **Jackson,** dissenting, said in part:

This released time program is founded upon a use of the State's power of coercion, which, for me, determines its unconstitutionality. Stripped to its essentials, the plan has two stages, first, that the State compel each student to yield a large part of his time for public secular education and, second, that some of it be "released" to him on condition that he devote it to sectarian religious purposes.

No one suggests that the Constitution would permit the State directly to require this "released" time to be spent "under the control of a duly constituted religious body." This program accomplishes that forbidden result by indirection. If public education were taking so much of the pupils' time as to injure the public or the students' welfare by encroaching upon their religious opportunity, simply shortening everyone's school day would facilitate voluntary and optional attendance at Church classes. But that suggestion is rejected upon the ground that if they are made free many students will not go to the Church. Hence, they must be deprived of freedom for this period, with Church attendance put to them as one of the two permissible ways of using it.

The greater effectiveness of this system over voluntary attendance after school hours is due to the truant officer who, if the youngster fails to go to the Church school, dogs him back to the public schoolroom. Here schooling is more or less suspended during the "released time" so the nonreligious attendants will not forge ahead of the churchgoing absentees. But it serves as a temporary jail for a pupil who will not go to Church. It takes more subtlety of mind than I possess to deny that this is governmental constraint in support of religion. It is as unconstitutional, in my view, when exerted by indirection as when exercised forthrightly.

As one whose children, as a matter of free choice, have been sent to privately supported Church schools, I may challenge the Court's suggestion that opposition to this plan can only be antireligious, atheistic, or agnostic. My evangelistic brethren confuse an objection to compulsion with an objection to religion. It is possible to hold a faith with enough confidence to believe that what

should be rendered to God does not need to be decided and collected by Caesar.

The day that this country ceases to be free from irreligion it will cease to be free for religion—except for the sect that can win political power. The same epithetical jurisprudence used by the Court today to beat down those who oppose pressuring children into some religion can devise as good epithets tomorrow against those who object to pressuring them into a favored religion. And, after all, if we concede to the State power and wisdom to single out "duly constituted religious" bodies as exclusive alternatives for compulsory secular instruction, it would be logical to also uphold the power and wisdom to choose the true faith among those "duly constituted." We start down a rough road when we begin to mix compulsory public education with compulsory godliness.

A number of Justices just short of a majority of the majority that promulgates today's passionate dialectics joined in answering them in Illinois ex rel. McCollum v. Board of Education. The distinction attempted between that case and this is trivial, almost to the point of cynicism, magnifying its nonessential details and disparaging compulsion which was the underlying reason for invalidity. A reading of the Court's opinion in that case along with its opinion in this case will show such difference of overtones and undertones as to make clear that the McCollum case has passed like a storm in a teacup. The wall which the Court was professing to erect between Church and State has become even more warped and twisted than I expected. Today's judgment will be more interesting to students of psychology and of the judicial processes than to students of constitutional law.

MUELLER v. ALLEN

463 U. S. 388; 103 S. Ct. 3062; 77 L. Ed. 2d (1983)

"Well, in our country," said Alice, still panting a little, "You'd generally get to somewhere else—if you ran very fast for a long time as we've been doing."

"A slow sort of country!" said the Queen. "Now, here, you see, it takes all the running you can do, to keep in the same place."

—Lewis Carroll, Through the Looking Glass

This sums up the plight of religious education in the United States. Born in an era when school teachers were poorly paid, school facilities simple and inexpensive, and extracurricular activities virtually nonexistent, the religious school had little difficulty keeping up with its public counterpart. But time has seen marked changes in the public schools. The curriculum, once limited to the three "R's," now includes a wide and sophisticated group of "cultural" subjects; organized athletics has replaced the simple playground games; pupils are transported to school, fed lunch in school, and transported home again; expensive electronic teaching de-

vices have replaced or supplemented the traditional classroom teacher, and even that teacher comes to the job more completely and expensively educated, asking and receiving more money. The religious school must compete with all this if it is to "keep in the same place." An additional difficulty for the Roman Catholic Church, which operates most religious schools, is the falling enrollment in those religious orders whose members were called to teaching and who received no personal compensation.

In *Board of Education v. Allen* (1968) the Court held valid the provision by the state of New York of secular textbooks to religious schools. Noting the "significant and valuable role" played by private education in this country, it found that both the "purpose and primary effect" of providing such aid was to advance secular education and hence was not a violation of the establishment clause. In the years that followed, other states provided such aid as buses, textbooks, health services, and school lunches. But helpful as such services were they did not solve the problem of the rising cost of labor, and a number of states undertook to provide direct financial help for the secular segment of the religious school curriculum by paying part of the teachers' salaries.

In *Lemon v. Kurtzman* (1971) the plans adopted by Pennsylvania and Rhode Island were held void. In addition to the tests devised in Allen regarding purpose and primary effect, the Court added a test adopted in *Walz v. Tax Commission* (1970) holding that a statute must not foster "an excessive entanglement with religion." It was the last of these tests which the Court found to be violated by the teacher payment plans. Since the money was to be used to pay only for secular teaching, "a comprehensive, discriminating, and continuing state surveillance will inevitably be required to ensure that these restrictions are obeyed and the First Amendment otherwise respected. Unlike a book, a teacher cannot be inspected once so as to determine the extent and intent of his or her personal beliefs and subjective acceptance of the limitations imposed by the First Amendment. These prophylactic contacts will involve excessive and enduring entanglement between state and church. . . ." In Pennsylvania the entanglement was increased by a system of post-audit of school records "to determine which expenditures are religious and which are secular."

The Court found an even "broader base of entanglement . . . presented by the divisive political potential of these state programs." "Political division along religious lines was one of the principal evils against which the First Amendment was intended to protect," and in this case the inevitable religious divisiveness would be aggravated by "the need for continuing annual appropriations and the likelihood of larger and larger demands as costs and populations grow."

In the wake of the Lemon decision the states turned their efforts to finding ways of aiding religious schools that did not involve such entanglement. The revised New York law made a three-pronged attack on the problem. First, lump-sum payments to nonpublic schools on a per-pupil basis were given to reimburse the school for the cost of carrying out state-mandated functions, such as the maintenance and recording of pupil enrollment, health records, and the "administration, grading and the compiling and reporting of the results of tests and examinations." Second, the state provided as a safety measure grants to nonpublic schools serving low-income areas for the "maintenance and repair" of school facilities. Third, the parents of children in nonpublic schools were given financial help—those in low income brackets getting tuition reimbursement and those in higher brackets getting a tax credit.

In *Levitt v. Committee for Public Education* (1973) and *Committee for Public Education v. Nyquist* (1973) the Court held void all these plans and in *Sloan v. Lemon* (1973) it held void a Pennsylvania tuition plan similar to New York's, but passed after the Lemon decision. In this latter case a nonreligious private school argued that the aid statute was valid as to it, and a Catholic parochial school contended that if that were the case, then it was entitled to aid under the equal protection clause. The Court found the aid statute void in its entirety but noted that even if the state had decided to aid only nonreligious private schools, the equal protection clause could still not be invoked to get similar (but otherwise unconstitutional) aid for religious schools. It was not until the decision in the case below that the Court found valid a state plan which provided financial assistance to the parents of children attending religious elementary and secondary schools.

In 1963, in response to a demand for federal help for higher education, Congress passed the Higher Education Facilities Act, which provided building grants and loans to colleges and universities. The act expressly excluded "any facility used or to be used for sectarian instructions or as a place of worship . . ." or "any part of the program of a school or department of divinity," but did not otherwise rule out denominational schools. The interest of the government was to last only twenty years, after which the school was allowed to do what it pleased with the buildings.

In *Tilton v. Richardson* (1971), decided the same day as the Lemon case, the Court upheld the validity of the grants to religious colleges, except that the interest of the United States could not end at the end of twenty years. Chief Justice Burger, speaking for himself and Justices Harlan, Stewart, and Blackmun, found that the purpose of the act was to aid education, not religion; that the schools in this case had apparently quite separable secular and religious activities, and the buildings were devoted solely to the former. He refused to deal with the case in terms of a "composite profile" of sectarian institutions, which "imposes religious restrictions on admissions, requires attendance at religious activities, compels obedience to the doctrines and dogmas of the faith . . . and does everything it can to propagate a particular religion." He noted that a number of institutions had been denied aid, and at least one had had its funds withdrawn. "Individual projects can be properly evaluated if and when challenges arise with respect to particular recipients and some evidence is then presented to show that the institution does in fact possess these characteristics. We cannot, however, strike down an Act of Congress on the basis of a hypothetical profile." He agreed, however, that unless the restriction on the use of the buildings were maintained, the grant might become an aid to religion and hence violate the First Amendment.

The four justices found that the Tilton case did not violate the "excessive entanglement" test under which the aid in Lemon had been stricken down. First, it was not the dominant purpose of these colleges, as it was the secondary schools, to inculcate religious values in their students "to assure future adherents to a particular faith." Not only were the courses taught with the normal internal self-discipline and academic freedom, but "the skepticism of the college student is not an inconsiderable barrier to any attempt or tendency to subvert the congressional objectives and limitations." In addition, both the one-shot nature of the aid and the fact it was in the form of buildings rather than teachers tended to reduce the entanglement.

Mr. Justice White, the fifth member of the majority, concurred with the Chief Justice on the theory that since the purpose of all the aid was secular, the fact it aided religion did not make it unconstitutional.

Justices Douglas, Black, and Marshall agreed that the twenty-year limit to federal interest was void, but dissented from the rest on the ground that the "entanglement" was as great here as in the state case ("How can the Government know what is taught in the federally financed building without a continuous auditing of classroom instruction?") and that it is aid to religion ("Money saved from one item in the budget is free to be used elsewhere. By conducting religious services in another building, the school has—rent free—a building for nonsectarian use.")

The precedents the Supreme Court sets in solving one set of problems occasionally rise up to haunt it in wholly unforeseen circumstances, and the conflicts between justice and the demands of logical consistency pose some of the Court's stickiest legal wickets. In Board of Education v. Allen (1968) the Court had held that providing free textbooks to all pupils in the state did not constitute aid to the schools the pupils attended, so that a child attending a religious school could receive such books without its being an unconstitutional aid to the religious school. In Norwood v. Harrison (1973), the Court confronted a Mississippi law under which free textbooks were being given to pupils attending racially segregated schools. The Court held that such textbooks were an aid to the school and could not constitutionally be given to private schools which discriminated on the basis of race.

"This Court has consistently affirmed decisions enjoining state tuition grants to students attending racially discriminatory private schools. A textbook lending program is not legally distinguishable from the forms of state assistance foreclosed by the prior cases. Free textbooks, like tuition grants directed to private school students, are a form of financial assistance inuring to the benefit of the private schools themselves." In a footnote it distinguished the Allen case; "Plainly, religion benefits indirectly from governmental aid to parents and children; nevertheless, 'that religion may indirectly benefit from governmental aid . . . does not convert that aid into an impermissible establishment of religion.' . . . The leeway for indirect aid to sectarian schools has no place in defining the permissible scope of state aid to private racially discriminatory schools." In Bob Jones University v. United States (1983) the Court upheld the refusal of the IRS to grant tax exemption to segregated private schools.

While the preceding cases were not particularly encouraging to those who sought aid to religious schools, the fact that some kinds of aid were held permissible encouraged increasing experimentation on the part of the states. Each case involved a broad spectrum of aid, and in general the Court upheld those features that closely resembled such things as secular textbooks which could not be put to religious use, but held void those which either could be so used, or where the policing necessary to ensure proper use resulted in undue "entanglement."

Thus in Meek v. Pittenger (1975) the Court struck down the loan of instructional material made to the school and not the pupil, and a provision for professional personnel was held bad because it involved both an "entangling" degree of supervision and a potential for political entanglement and divisiveness. A similar result was reached in Wolman v. Walter (1977) in which items like tape recorders and projectors and the cost of field trips was involved, since all were susceptible of conversion to religious use. In Committee for Public Education v. Regan (1980), however, the Court in a five-to-four decision held that a revised New York law providing for state reimbursement to cover the costs of administering standardized tests and keeping attendance and other required records did not "foster an excessive government entanglement with religion." Meanwhile efforts to find a formula that would permit tuition aid to private school pupils persisted, and it is Minnesota's statue, passed in 1982, that is involved in the case below.

Justice **Rehnquist** delivered the opinion of the Court, saying in part:

Minnesota allows taxpayers, in computing their state income tax, to deduct certain expenses incurred in providing for the education of their children. . . .

Minnesota, like every other state, provides its citizens with free elementary and secondary schooling. It seems to be agreed that about 820,000 students attended this school system in the most recent school year. During the same year, approximately 91,000 elementary and secondary students attended some 500 privately supported schools located in Minnesota, and about 95% of these students attended schools considering themselves to be sectarian.

Minnesota, by a law originally enacted in 1955

and revised in 1976 and again in 1978, permits state tax-payers to claim a deduction from gross income for certain expenses incurred in educating their children. The deduction is limited to actual expenses incurred for the "tuition, textbooks and transportation" of dependents attending elementary or secondary schools. A deduction may not exceed $500 per dependent in grades K through six and $700 per dependent in grades seven through twelve. . . .

Today's case is no exception to our oft-repeated statement that the Establishment Clause presents especially difficult questions of interpretation and application. It is easy enough to quote the few words comprising that clause—"Congress shall make no law respecting an establishment of religion." It is not at all easy, however, to apply this Court's various decisions construing the Clause to governmental programs of financial assistance to sectarian schools and the parents of children attending those schools. Indeed, in many of these decisions "we have expressly or implicitly acknowledged that 'we can only dimly perceive the lines of demarcation in this extraordinarily sensitive area of constitutional law.'" Lemon v. Kurtzman (1971), quoted with approval in Nyquist.

One fixed principle in this field is our consistent rejection of the argument that "any program which in some manner aids an institution with a religious affiliation" violates the Establishment Clause. . . . For example, it is now well-established that a state may reimburse parents for expenses incurred in transporting their children to school, Everson v. Board of Education (1947), and that it may loan secular textbooks to all schoolchildren within the state, Board of Education v. Allen (1968).

Notwithstanding the repeated approval given programs such as those in Allen and Everson, our decisions also have struck down arrangements resembling, in many respects, these forms of assistance. . . . In this case we are asked to decide whether Minnesota's tax deduction bears greater resemblance to those types of assistance to parochial schools we have approved, or to those we have struck down. Petitioners place particular reliance on our decision in Committee for Public Education v. Nyquist where we held invalid a New York statute providing public funds for the maintenance and repair of the physical facilities of private schools and granting thinly disguised "tax benefits," actually amounting to tuition grants, to the parents of children attending private schools. As explained below, we conclude that § 290.09(22) bears less resemblance to the arrangement struck down in Nyquist than it does to assistance programs upheld in our prior decisions and those discussed with approval in Nyquist.

The general nature of our inquiry in this area has been guided, since the decision in Lemon v. Kurtzman (1971), by the "three-part" test laid down in that case: "First, the statute must have a secular legislative purpose; second, its principle or primary effect must be one that neither advances nor inhibits religion . . . ; finally,

the statute must not foster 'an excessive government entanglement with religion.' " . . .

Little time need be spent on the question of whether the Minnesota tax deduction has a secular purpose. Under our prior decisions, governmental assistance programs have consistently survived this inquiry even when they have run afoul of other aspects of the Lemon framework. . . . This reflects, at least in part, our reluctance to attribute unconstitutional motives to the states, particularly when a plausible secular purpose for the state's program may be discerned from the face of the statute.

A state's decision to defray the cost of educational expenses incurred by parents—regardless of the type of schools their children attend—evidences a purpose that is both secular and understandable. An educated populace is essential to the political and economic health of any community, and a state's efforts to assist parents in meeting the rising cost of educational expenses plainly serves this secular purpose of ensuring that the state's citizenry is well-educated. Similarly, Minnesota, like other states, could conclude that there is a strong public interest in assuring the continued financial health of private schools, both sectarian and non-sectarian. By educating a substantial number of students such schools relieve public schools of a correspondingly great burden—to the benefit of all taxpayers. In addition, private schools may serve as a benchmark for public schools, in a manner analogous to the "TVA yardstick" for private power companies. . . . All these justifications are readily available to support § 290.09(22), and each is sufficient to satisfy the secular purpose inquiry of Lemon.

We turn therefore to the more difficult but related question whether the Minnesota statute has "the primary effect of advancing the sectarian aims of the nonpublic schools." . . . In concluding that it does not, we find several features of the Minnesota tax deduction particularly significant. . . . Under our prior decisions, the Minnesota legislature's judgment that a deduction for educational expenses fairly equalizes the tax burden of its citizens and encourages desirable expenditures for educational purposes is entitled to substantial deference.

Other characteristics of § 290.09(22) argue equally strongly for the provision's constitutionality. Most importantly, the deduction is available for educational expenses incurred by *all* parents, including those whose children attend non-sectarian private schools or sectarian private schools. Just as in Widmar v. Vincent (1981) where we concluded that the state's provision of a forum neutrally "open to a broad class of nonreligious as well as religious speakers" does not "confer any imprimatur of State approval," so here: "the provision of benefits to so broad a spectrum of groups is an important index of secular effect."

In this respect, as well as others, this case is vitally different from the scheme struck down in Nyquist. There, public assistance amounting to tuition grants, was provided only to parents of children in *nonpublic* schools. This fact had considerable bearing on our decision striking down the New York statute at issue; we explicitly distinguished both Allen and Everson on the grounds that "In both cases the class of beneficiaries included *all* schoolchildren, those in public as well as those in private schools." . . . We think the tax deduction adopted by Minnesota is more similar to this latter type of program than it is to the arrangement struck down in Nyquist. Unlike the assistance at issue in Nyquist, § 290.09(22) permits *all* parents—whether their children attend public school or private—to deduct their children's educational expenses. As Widmar and our other decisions indicate, a program, like § 290.09(22), that neutrally provides state assistance to a broad spectrum of citizens is not readily subject to challenge under the Establishment Clause. . . .

We find it useful, in the light of the foregoing characteristics of § 290.09(22), to compare the attenuated financial benefits flowing to parochial schools from the section to the evils against which the Establishment Clause was designed to protect. These dangers are well-described by our statement that "what is at stake as a matter of policy [in Establishment Clause cases] is preventing that kind and degree of government involvement in religious life that, as history teaches us, is apt to lead to strife and frequently strain a political system to the breaking point." . . . The Establishment Clause of course extends beyond prohibition of a state church or payment of state funds to one or more churches. We do not think, however, that its prohibition extends to the type of tax deduction established by Minnesota. The historic purposes of the clause simply do not encompass the sort of attenuated financial benefit, ultimately controlled by the private choices of individual parents, that eventually flows to parochial schools from the neutrally available tax benefit at issue in this case.

Petitioners argue that, notwithstanding the facial neutrality of § 290.09(22), in application the statute primarily benefits religious institutions. Petitioners rely, as they did below, on a statistical analysis of the type of persons claiming the tax deduction. They contend that most parents of public school children incur no tuition expenses and that other expenses deductible under § 290.09(22) are negligible in value; moreover, they claim that 96% of the children in private schools in 1978-79 attended religiously-affiliated institutions. Because of all this, they reason, the bulk of deductions taken under § 290.09(22) will be claimed by parents of children in sectarian schools. Respondents reply that petitioners have failed to consider the impact of deductions for items such as transportation, summer school tuition, tuition paid by parents whose children attended schools outside the school districts in which they resided, rental or purchase costs for a variety of equipment, and tuition for certain types of instruction not ordinarily provided in public schools.

We need not consider these contentions in detail. We would be loath to adopt a rule grounding the constitutionality of a facially neutral law on annual reports re-

citing the extent to which various classes of private citizens claimed benefits under the law. Such an approach would scarcely provide the certainty that this field stands in need of, nor can we perceive principled standards by which such statistical evidence might be evaluated. Moreover, the fact that private persons fail in a particular year to claim the tax relief to which they are entitled—under a facially neutral statute—should be of little importance in determining the constitutionality of the statute permitting such relief.

Finally, private educational institutions, and parents paying for their children to attend these schools, make special contributions to the areas in which they operate. "Parochial schools, quite apart from their sectarian purpose, have provided an educational alternative for millions of young Americans; they often afford wholesome competition with our public schools; and in some States they relieve substantially the tax burden incident to the operation of public schools." Wolman (Powell, J., concurring and dissenting). If parents of children in private schools choose to take especial advantage of the relief provided by § 290.09(22), it is no doubt due to the fact that they bear a particularly great financial burden in educating their children. More fundamentally, whatever unequal effect may be attributed to the statutory classification can fairly be regarded as a rough return for the benefits, discussed above, provided to the state and all taxpayers by parents sending their children to parochial schools. In the light of all this, we believe it wiser to decline to engage in the type of empirical inquiry into those persons benefited by state law which petitioners urge.

Thus, we hold that the Minnesota tax deduction for educational expenses satisfies the primary effect inquiry of our Establishment Clause cases.

Turning to the third part of the Lemon inquiry, we have no difficulty in concluding that the Minnesota statute does not "excessively entangle" the state in religion. The only plausible source of the "comprehensive, discriminating, and continuing state surveillance" necessary to run afoul of this standard would lie in the fact that state officials must determine whether particular textbooks qualify for a deduction. In making this decision, state officials must disallow deductions taken from "instructional books and materials used in the teaching of religious tenets, doctrines or worship, the purpose of which is to inculcate such tenets, doctrines or worship" Minn. Stat. § 290.09(22). Making decisions such as this does not differ substantially from making the types of decisions approved in earlier opinions of this Court. In Board of Education v. Allen (1968), for example, the Court upheld the loan of secular textbooks to parents or children attending nonpublic schools; though state officials were required to determine whether particular books were or were not secular, the system was held not to violate the Establishment Clause. . . . The same result follows in this case.

Justice **Marshall,** with whom Justice **Brennan,** Justice

Blackmun and Justice Stevens join, dissenting, said in part:

The Establishment Clause of the First Amendment prohibits a State from subsidizing religious education, whether it does so directly or indirectly. In my view, this principle of neutrality forbids not only the tax benefits struck down in Committee for Public Education v. Nyquist (1973), but any tax benefit, including the tax deduction at issue here, which subsidizes tuition payments to sectarian schools. I also believe that the Establishment Clause prohibits the tax deductions that Minnesota authorizes for the cost of books and other instructional materials used for sectarian purposes.

I.

The majority today does not question the continuing vitality of this Court's decision in Nyquist. That decision established that a State may not support religious education either through direct grants to parochial schools or through financial aid to parents of parochial school students. Nyquist also established that financial aid to parents of students attending parochial schools is no more permissible if it is provided in the form of a tax credit than if provided in the form of cash payments. Notwithstanding these accepted principles, the Court today upholds a statute that provides a tax deduction for the tuition charged by religious schools. The Court concludes that the Minnesota statute is "vitally different" from the New York statute at issue in Nyquist. As demonstrated below, there is no significant difference between the two schemes. The Minnesota tax statute violates the Establishment Clause for precisely the same reason as the statute struck down in Nyquist: it has a direct and immediate effect of advancing religion. . . .

B.

The majority attempts to distinguish Nyquist by pointing to two differences between the Minnesota tuition-assistance program and the program struck down in Nyquist. Neither of these distinctions can withstand scrutiny.

1.

The majority first attempts to distinguish Nyquist on the ground that Minnesota makes all parents eligible to deduct up to $500 or $700 for each dependent, whereas the New York law allowed a deduction only for parents whose children attended nonpublic schools. Although Minnesota taxpayers who send their children to local public schools may not deduct tuition expenses because they incur none, they may deduct other expenses, such as the cost of gym clothes, pencils, and notebooks, which are shared by all parents of school-age children. This, in the majority's view, distinguishes the Minnesota scheme from the law at issue in Nyquist.

That the Minnesota statute makes some small benefit available to all parents cannot alter the fact that the most substantial benefit provided by the statute is available only to those parents who send their children to schools that charge tuition. It is simply undeniable that the single largest expense that may be deducted under the Minnesota statute is tuition. The statute is little more than a subsidy of tuition masquerading as a subsidy of general educational expenses. The other deductible expenses are de minimis in comparison to tuition expenses.

Contrary to the majority's suggestion, the bulk of the tax benefits afforded by the Minnesota scheme are enjoyed by parents of parochial school children not because parents of public school children fail to claim deductions to which they are entitled, but because the latter are simply *unable* to claim the largest tax deduction that Minnesota authorizes. Fewer than 100 of more than 900,000 school-age children in Minnesota attend public schools that charge a general tuition. Of the total number of taxpayers who are eligible for the tuition deduction, approximately 96% send their children to religious schools. Parents who send their children to free public schools are simply ineligible to obtain the full benefit of the deduction except in the unlikely event that they buy $700 worth of pencils, notebooks, and bus rides for their school-age children. Yet parents who pay at least $700 in tuition to nonpublic, sectarian schools can claim the full deduction even if they incur no other educational expenses.

That this deduction has a primary effect of promoting religion can easily be determined without resort to the type of "statistical evidence" that the majority fears would lead to constitutional uncertainty. The only factual inquiry necessary is the same as that employed in Nyquist and Sloan v. Lemon (1973): whether the deduction permitted for tuition expenses primarily benefits those who send their children to religious schools. In Nyquist we unequivocally rejected any suggestion that, in determining the effect of a tax statute, this Court should look exclusively to what the statute on its face purports to do and ignore the actual operation of the challenged provision. In determining the effect of the New York statute, we emphasized that "virtually all" of the schools receiving direct grants for maintenance and repair were Roman Catholic schools, that reimbursements were given to parents "who send their children to nonpublic schools, the bulk of which is concededly sectarian in orientation," that "it is precisely the function of New York's law to provide assistance to private schools, the great majority of which are sectarian," and that "tax reductions authorized by this law flow primarily to the parents of children attending sectarian, nonpublic schools." . . .

In this case, it is undisputed that well over 90% of the children attending tuition-charging schools in Minnesota are enrolled in sectarian schools. History and experience likewise instruct us that any generally available financial assistance for elementary and secondary school tuition expenses mainly will further religious education because the majority of the schools which charge tuition are sectarian. . . . Because Minnesota, like every other State, is committed to providing free public education, tax assistance for tuition payments inevitably redounds to the benefit of nonpublic, sectarian schools and parents who send their children to those schools. . . .

C.

The majority incorrectly asserts that Minnesota's tax deduction for tuition expenses "bears less resemblance to the arrangement struck down in Nyquist than it does to assistance programs upheld in our prior decisions and discussed with approval in Nyquist." One might as well say that a tangerine bears less resemblance to an orange than to an apple. The two cases relied on by the majority, Board of Education v. Allen (1968) and Everson v. Board of Education (1947), are inapposite today for precisely the same reasons that they were inapposite in Nyquist.

We distinguished these cases in Nyquist and again in Sloan v. Lemon. Financial assistance for tuition payments has a consequence that "is quite unlike the sort of 'indirect' and 'incidental' benefits that flowed to sectarian schools from programs aiding *all* parents by supplying bus transportation and secular textbooks for their children. *Such benefits were carefully restricted to the purely secular side of church-affiliated institutions* and provided no special aid for those who had chosen to support religious schools. Yet such aid approached the 'verge' of the constitutionally impermissible." Sloan v. Lemon (emphasis added in part.) As previously noted, the Minnesota tuition tax deduction is not available to *all* parents, but only to parents whose children attend schools that charge tuition, which are comprised almost entirely of sectarian schools. More importantly, the assistance that flows to parochial schools as a result of the tax benefit is not restricted, and cannot be restricted, to the secular functions of those schools.

EDWARDS v. AGUILLARD

482 U. S. 578; 107 S. Ct. 2573; 96 L. Ed. 2d 510 (1987)

Those who felt that the public schools were becoming "Godless," and for whom released time was not an available or desirable solution, undertook a campaign to retain some religion in the public schools. In most public schools it was long the custom to begin the day with a short religious exercise. This usually consisted of reading excerpts from the Protestant Bible and sometimes of singing hymns and repeating the Lord's Prayer. Usually those children whose parents objected were excused from these exercises, although this was not always the case. State court decisions on the validity of these exercises were in sharp conflict, and this specific question never reached the Supreme Court.

In 1962 in Engel v. Vitale, the Supreme Court held
void the following prayer composed by the New York Board of Regents for use in the public schools. "Almighty God, we acknowledge our dependence upon Thee, and we beg Thy blessings upon us, our parents, our teachers and our Country." The Court conceded that no issue of religious freedom was involved, since no one was forced to hear or say the prayer. It emphasized, however, that under the establishment clause, "government in this country, be it state or federal, is without power to prescribe by law any particular form of prayer which is to be used as an official prayer in carrying on any program of governmentally sponsored religious activity."

The decision aroused a storm of protest. Members in both Houses of Congress began work on a constitutional amendment which would nullify the decision, while school boards throughout the country sought ways of avoiding the impact of the decision. Some required students to recite stanzas of "America" and "The Star Spangled Banner" in which there is reference to God; while others, evidently assuming that it was official participation that made the Regents' Prayer bad, merely authorized children to bring prayers to school and take turns reciting them "voluntarily." One common solution was the adoption of a "moment of silence," which a student could use for silent prayer or not, as he wished.

By 1965 the storm had largely abated. The proposed constitutional amendment had been opposed by most religious groups and was conceded to be dead; legal attempts to reverse New York's prohibition on "voluntary" prayers and the singing of the fourth stanza of "America" as a devotional (rather than a patriotic) exercise had failed; Chief Justice Warren had successfully opposed a House proposal to inscribe "In God We Trust" above the Supreme Court bench. On the other hand, a legal attack on the inclusion of "under God" in the pledge of allegiance had also failed, and the Supreme Court continued to open its sessions with the marshal asking that "God save the United States and this honorable Court."

In Abington School District v. Schempp (1963) the Court for the first time held the use of the Bible in morning devotionals to be in violation of the First Amendment. The state of Pennsylvania required by law that "at least ten verses from the Holy Bible shall be read, without comment, at the opening of each public school on each school day. Any child shall be excused from such Bible reading . . . upon the written request of his parent or guardian." The Schempps were Unitarians who objected to some doctrines purveyed by a literal reading of the Bible, but who declined to ask that their children be excused because they would not only have to stand out in the hall during the exercise but would probably miss the school announcements which followed immediately after. A three-judge federal district court held the practice void on the basis of the Vitale case, and enjoined its continuance. In 1980 the doctrine was applied to hold void a Kentucky law requiring the posting in every classroom of a copy of the Ten Commandments. The Court found the document had "no secular legislative purpose." See Stone v. Graham.

Many religious leaders, together with some lay critics, have challenged the basic rule which the Court has announced. They urge that the framers did not intend by the First Amendment to forbid all government aid to religion, but only such aid as favors one religion over another. They argue, first, that there is no really persuasive historical ground for holding that the framers had in mind an absolute separation of church and state; the "establishment" clause was intended merely to prevent the establishment of a state church, such as the Church of England. Second, the historical material mustered by Justice Black in the Everson case to show that what the framers intended was, in Jefferson's phrase, a wall of separation between church and state has been sharply criticized by a number of historical scholars as presenting an incomplete and distorted picture. Third, the Supreme Court had itself recognized some aid to religion. In Bradfield v. Roberts (1899) it had held valid federal aid to a Roman Catholic hospital, although on the technical ground that the hospital corporation was a secular body which served patients without regard to denomination. Also, some cite Justice Storey in the Girard will case, Vidal v. Girard's Executors (1844), where he said the "Christian religion is part of the common law."

In Wallace v. Jaffree (1985) the state of Alabama had sequentially adopted three statutes apparently designed to get as much prayer in the public schools as possible. The first statute, passed in 1978, merely authorized a one-minute period of silence in all public schools "for meditation." The second, passed in 1981, authorized a period of silence "for meditation or voluntary prayer," while the third, passed the following year, authorized teachers to lead "willing students" in a prescribed prayer to "Almighty God . . . the Creator and Supreme Judge of the world."

At trial the district judge found all three statutes valid. Relying on what he perceived to be newly discovered historical evidence, he held that, in his opinion, "Alabama has the power to establish a state religion if it chooses to do so." The court of appeals rejected this approach and the Supreme Court found it "unnecessary to comment at length on the District Court's remarkable conclusion that the Federal Constitution imposes no obstacle to Alabama's establishment of a state religion." The court of appeals also found the last two statutes void under the establishment clause, but no argument was made that the statute merely requiring "meditation" was in any way invalid.

A number of religions rely upon a literal interpretation of the Bible as the word of God. In their view the Darwinian theory that humans, like the earth and all forms of life upon it, have evolved over hundreds of thousands of years, is a contradiction of the Book of Genesis which states that God created the world and all its creatures in six days in the forms in which they appear today.

The year after the decision of the Tennessee courts upholding that state's so-called "monkey law" which banned the teaching of evolution (see Scopes v. State, 154 Tenn. 105 (1927)), members of these religious groups secured the enactment of a similar law in Arkansas. In Epperson v. Arkansas (1968) the Supreme Court struck down the Arkansas statute as an establishment of religion. "There can be no doubt that Arkansas has sought to prevent its teachers from discussing the theory of evolution because it is contrary to the belief of some that the Book of Genesis must be the exclusive source of doctrine as to the origin of man. No suggestion has been made that Arkansas' law may be justified by considerations of state policy other than the religious views of some of its citizens. It is clear that fundamentalist sectarian conviction was and is the law's reason for existence. Its antecedent, Tennessee's 'monkey law,' candidly stated its purpose: to make it unlawful 'to teach any theory that denies the story of the Divine Creation of man as taught in the Bible, and to teach instead that man has descended from a lower order of animals.' Perhaps the sensational publicity attendant upon the Scopes trial induced Arkansas to adopt less explicit language. It eliminated Tennessee's reference to 'the story of the Divine Creation of man' as taught in the Bible, but there is no doubt that the motivation for the law was the same: to suppress the teaching of a theory which, it was thought, 'denied' the divine creation of man."

Justice **Brennan** delivered the opinion of the Court, saying in part:

The question for decision is whether Louisiana's "Balanced Treatment for Creation-Science and Evolution-Science in Public School Instruction" Act (Creationism Act), is facially invalid as violative of the Establishment Clause of the First Amendment.

I.

The Creationism Act forbids the teaching of the theory of evolution in public schools unless accompanied by instruction in "creation science." No school is required to teach evolution or creation science. If either is taught, however, the other must also be taught. The theories of evolution and creation science are statutorily defined as "the scientific evidences for [creation or evolution] and inferences from those scientific evidences.

Appellees, who include parents of children attending Louisiana public schools, Louisiana teachers, and religious leaders, challenged the constitutionality of the Act in District Court, seeking an injunction and declaratory relief. Appellants, Louisiana officials charged with implementing the Act, defended on the ground that the purpose of the Act is to protect a legitimate secular interest, namely, academic freedom. Appellees attacked the Act as facially invalid because it violated the Establishment Clause and made a motion for summary judgment. . . .

II.

The Establishment Clause forbids the enactment of any law "respecting an establishment of religion." The

Court has applied a three-pronged test to determine whether legislation comports with the Establishment Clause. First, the legislature must have adopted the law with a secular purpose. Second, the statute's principal or primary effect must be one that neither advances nor inhibits religion. Third, the statute must not result in an excessive entanglement of government with religion. Lemon v. Kurtzman [1971]. State action violates the Establishment Clause if it fails to satisfy any of these prongs. . . .

The Court has been particularly vigilant in monitoring compliance with the Establishment Clause in elementary and secondary schools. Families entrust public schools with the education of their children, but condition their trust on the understanding that the classroom will not purposely be used to advance religious views that may conflict with the private beliefs of the student and his or her family. Students in such institutions are impressionable and their attendance is involuntary. . . . The State exerts great authority and coercive power through mandatory attendance requirements, and because of the students' emulation of teachers as role models and the children's susceptibility to peer pressure. . . .

Therefore, in employing the three-pronged Lemon test, we must do so mindful of the particular concerns that arise in the context of public elementary and secondary schools. We now turn to the evaluation of the Act under the Lemon test.

III.

Lemon's first prong focuses on the purpose that animated adoption of the Act. "The purpose prong of the Lemon test asks whether government's actual purpose is to endorse or disapprove of religion." Lynch v. Donnelly [1984] (O'Connor, J., concurring.) A governmental intention to promote religion is clear when the State enacts a law to serve a religious purpose. This intention may be evidenced by promotion of religion in general, see Wallace v. Jaffree [1985] (Establishment Clause protects individual freedom of conscience "to select any religious faith or none at all"), or by advancement of a particular religious belief. e.g., Stone v. Graham [1980] (invalidating requirement to post Ten Commandments, which are "undeniably a sacred text in the Jewish and Christian faiths"); Epperson v. Arkansas [1968] (holding that banning the teaching of evolution in public schools violates the First Amendment since "teaching and learning" must not be tailored to the principles or prohibitions of any religious sect or dogma.") If the law was enacted for the purpose of endorsing religion, "no consideration of the second or third criteria [of Lemon] is necessary. . . . In this case, the petitioners have identified no clear secular purpose for the Louisiana Act.

True, the Act's stated purpose is to protect academic freedom. This phrase might, in common parlance, be understood as referring to enhancing the freedom of teachers to teach what they will. The Court of Appeals, however, correctly concluded that the Act was not designed to further that goal. We find no merit in the State's argument that the "legislature may not [have] use[d] the terms 'academic freedom' in the correct legal sense. They might have [had] in mind, instead, a basic concept of fairness; teaching all of the evidence." Even if "academic freedom" is read to mean "teaching all of the evidence" with respect to the origin of human beings, the Act does not further this purpose. The goal of providing a more comprehensive science curriculum is not furthered either by outlawing the teaching of evolution or by requiring the teaching of creation science.

A.

While the Court is normally deferential to a State's articulation of a secular purpose, it is required that the statement of such purpose be sincere and not a sham. . . . As Justice O'Connor stated in Wallace: It is not a trivial mater, however, to require that the legislature manifest a secular purpose and omit all sectarian endorsements from its laws. That requirement is precisely tailored to the Establishment Clause's purpose of assuring that Government not intentionally endorse religion or a religious practice."

It is clear from the legislative history that the purpose of the legislative sponsor, Senator Bill Keith, was to narrow the science curriculum. During the legislative hearings, Senator Keith stated: "My preference would be that neither [creationism nor evolution] be taught." Such a ban on teaching does not promote—indeed, it undermines—the provision of a comprehensive scientific education.

It is equally clear that requiring schools to teach creation science with evolution does not advance academic freedom. The Act does not grant teachers a flexibility that they did not already possess to supplant the present science curriculum with the presentation of theories, besides evolution, about the origin of life. Indeed, the Court of Appeals found that no law prohibited Louisiana public schoolteachers from teaching any scientific theory. As the president of the Louisiana Science Teachers Association testified, "[a]ny scientific concept that's based on established fact can be included in our curriculum already and no legislation allowing this is necessary." The Act provides Louisiana schoolteachers with no new authority. Thus the stated purpose is not furthered by it.

The Alabama statute held unconstitutional in Wallace v. Jaffree [1985] is analogous. In Wallace, the State characterized its new law as one designed to provide a one-minute period for meditation. We rejected that stated purpose as insufficient, because a previously adopted Alabama law already provided for such a one-minute period. Thus, in this case, as in Wallace, "[a]ppellants have not identified any secular purpose that was not fully served by [existing state law] before the enactment of [the statute in question]."

Furthermore, the goal of basic "fairness" is hardly furthered by the Act's discriminatory preference for the teaching of creation science and against the teaching of evolution. While requiring that curriculum guides be developed for creation science, the Act says nothing of comparable guides for evolution. Similarly, research services are supplied for creation science but not for evolution. Only "creation scientists" can serve on the panel that supplies the resource services. The Act forbids school boards to discriminate against anyone who "chooses to be a creation-scientist" or to teach "creationism," but fails to protect those who choose to teach evolution or any other non-creation science theory, or refuse to teach creation science.

If the Louisiana legislature's purpose was solely to maximize the comprehensiveness and effectiveness of science instruction, it would have encouraged the teaching of all scientific theories about the origins of humankind. But under the Act's requirements, teachers who were once free to teach any and all facts of this subject are now unable to do so. Moreover, the Act fails even to ensure that creation science will be taught, but instead requires the teaching of this theory only when the theory of evolution is taught. Thus we agree with the Court of Appeals' conclusion that the Act does not serve to protect academic freedom, but has the distinctly different purpose of discrediting "evolution by counterbalancing its teaching at every turn with the teaching of creation science. . . ."

B.

Stone v. Graham invalidated the State's requirement that the Ten Commandments be posted in public classrooms. "The Ten Commandments are undeniably a sacred text in the Jewish and Christian faiths, and no legislative recitation of a supposed secular purpose can blind us to that fact." As a result, the contention that the law was designed to provide instruction on a "fundamental legal code" was "not sufficient to avoid conflict with the First Amendment." Similarly Abington School District v. Schempp [1963] held unconstitutional a statute "requiring the selection and reading at the opening of the school day of verses from the Holy Bible and the recitation of the Lord's Prayer by the students in unison," despite the proffer of such secular purposes as the "promotion of moral values, the contradiction to the materialistic trends of our times, the perpetuation of our institutions and the teaching of literature."

As in Stone and Abington, we need not be blind in this case to the legislature's preeminent religious purpose in enacting this statute. There is a historic and contemporaneous link between the teachings of certain religious denominations and the teaching of evolution. It was this link that concerned the court in Epperson v. Arkansas which also involved a facial challenge to a statute regulating the teaching of evolution. In that case, the Court reviewed an Arkansas statute that made it unlawful for an instructor to teach evolution or to use a textbook that referred to this scientific theory. Although the Arkansas anti-evolution law did not explicitly state its predominate religious purpose, the Court could not ignore that "[t]he statute was a product of the upsurge of 'fundamentalist' religious fervor" that has long viewed this particular scientific theory as contradicting the literal interpretation of the Bible. After reviewing the history of anti-evolution statutes, the Court determined that "there can be no doubt that the motivation for the [Arkansas] law was the same [as other anti-evolution statutes]: to suppress the teaching of a theory which, it was thought, 'denied' the divine creation of man." The Court found that there can be no legitimate state interest in protecting particular religions from scientific views "distasteful to them," and concluded "that the First Amendment does not permit the State to require that teaching and learning must be tailored to the principles or prohibitions of any religious sect or dogma."

These same historic and contemporaneous antagonisms between the teachings of certain religious denominations and the teaching of evolution are present in this case. The preeminent purpose of the Louisiana legislature was clearly to advance the religious viewpoint that a supernatural being created humankind.

Furthermore, it is not happenstance that the legislature required the teaching of a theory that coincided with religious view. The legislative history documents that the Act's primary purpose was to change the science curriculum of public schools in order to provide persuasive advantage to a particular religious doctrine that rejects the factual basis of evolution in its entirety. The sponsor of the Creationism Act, Senator Keith, explained during the legislative hearings that his disdain for the theory of evolution resulted from the support that evolution supplied to views contrary to his own religious beliefs. According to Senator Keith, the theory of evolution was consonant with the "cardinal principle[s] of religious humanism, secular humanism, theological liberalism, aetheistism [sic]." The state senator repeatedly stated that scientific evidence supporting his religious views should be included in the public school curriculum to redress the fact that the theory of evolution incidentally coincided with what he characterized as religious beliefs antithetical to his own. The legislation therefore sought to alter the science curriculum to reflect endorsement of a religious view that is antagonistic to the theory of evolution.

In this case, the purpose of the Creationism Act was to restructure the science curriculum to conform with a particular religious viewpoint. Out of many possible science subjects taught in the public schools, the legislature chose to affect the teaching of the one scientific theory that historically has been opposed by certain religious sects. As in Epperson, the legislature passed the Act to give preference to those religious groups which have as one of their tenets the creation of humankind by a divine creator. The "overriding fact" that confronted the Court in Epperson was "that Arkansas' law selects from the body of knowledge a particular segment which it proscribes for the sole reason that it is deemed to conflict with ... a particular interpretation of the Book of Genesis by a particular religious group.'' Similarly, the Creationism Act is designed *either* to promote the theory of creation science which embodies a particular religious tenet by requiring that creation science be taught whenever evolution is taught *or* to prohibit the teaching of a scientific theory disfavored by certain religious sects by forbidding the teaching of evolution when creation science is not also taught. The Establishment Clause, however, ''forbids *alike* the preference of a religious doctrine *or* the prohibition of a theory which is deemed antagonistic to a particular dogma.'' (Emphasis added). Because the primary purpose of the Creationism Act is to advance a particular religious belief, the Act endorses religion in violation of the First Amendment. ...

V.

The Louisiana Creationism Act advances a religious doctrine by requiring either the banishment of the theory of evolution from public school classrooms or the presentation of a religious viewpoint that rejects evolution in its entirety. The Act violates the Establishment Clause of the First Amendment because it seeks to employ the symbolic and financial support of government to achieve a religious purpose. The judgment of the Court of Appeals therefore is

Affirmed.

Justice **Powell,** with whom Justice **O'Connor** joins, concurring, said in part:

I write separately to note certain aspects of the legislative history, and to emphasize that nothing in the Court's opinion diminishes the traditionally broad discretion accorded state and local school officials in the selection of the public school curriculum. ...

B.

In June 1980, Senator Bill Keith introduced Senate Bill 956 in the Louisiana legislature. The stated purpose of the bill was to ''assure academic freedom by requiring the teaching of the theory of creation ex nihilo in all public schools where the theory of evolution is taught.'' The bill defined the ''theory of creation ex nihilo'' as ''the belief that the origin of the elements, the galaxy, the solar system, of life, of all the species of plants and animals, the origin of man, and the origin of all things and their processes and relationships were created ex nihilo and fixed by God.'' This theory was referred to by Senator Keith as ''scientific creationism.''

While a Senate committee was studying scientific creationism, Senator Keith introduced a second draft of the bill, requiring balanced treatment of ''evolution-science'' and ''creation-science.'' Although the Keith bill prohibited ''instruction in any religious doctrine or ma-

terials,'' it defined ''creation-science'' to include ''the scientific evidences and related inferences that indicate (a) sudden creation of the universe, energy, and life from nothing; (b) the insufficiency of mutation and natural selection in bringing about development of all living kinds from a single organism; (c) changes only within fixed limits or originally created kinds of plants and animals; (d) separate ancestry for man and apes; (e) explanation of the earth's geology by catastrophism, including the occurrence of a worldwide flood; and (f) a relatively recent inception of the earth and living kinds.''

Significantly, the model act on which the Keith bill relied was also the basis for a similar statute in Arkansas. See McLean v. Arkansas Board of Education, 529 F. Supp. 1255 (1982). The District Court in McLean carefully examined this model act, particularly the section defining creation-science, and concluded that ''[b]oth [its] concepts and wording ... convey an inescapable religiosity.'' The court found that ''[t]he ideas of [this section] are not merely similar to the literal interpretation of Genesis; they are identical and parallel to no other story of creation.''

The complaint in McLean was filed on May 27, 1981. On May 28, the Louisiana Senate committee amended the Keith bill to delete the illustrative list of scientific evidences. According to the legislator who proposed the amendment, it was ''not intended to try to gut [the bill] in any way, or defeat the purpose [for] which Senator Keith introduced [it],'' and was not viewed as working ''any violence to the bill.'' Instead, the concern was ''whether this should be an all inclusive list.''

The legislature then held hearings on the amended bill, that became the Balanced Treatment Act under review. The principal creation-scientist to testify in support of the Act was Dr. Edward Boudreaux. He did not elaborate on the nature of creation-science except to indicate that the ''scientific evidences'' of the theory are ''the objective information of science [that] point[s] to conditions of a creator.'' He further testified that the recognized creation-scientists in the United States, who ''numbe[r] something like a thousand [and] who hold doctorate and masters degrees in all areas of science,'' are affiliated with either or both the Institute for Creation Research and the Creation Research Society. Information on both these organizations is part of the legislative history, and a review of their goals and activities sheds light on the nature of creation-science as it was presented to, and understood by, the Louisiana legislature.

The Institute for Creation Research is an affiliate of the Christian Heritage College in San Diego, California. The Institute was established to address the ''urgent need for our nation to return to belief in a personal, omnipotent Creator, who has a purpose for His creation and to whom all people must eventually give account.'' A goal of the Institute is ''a revival of belief in special creation as the true explanation of the origin of the world.'' Therefore, the Institute currently is working on the ''development of new methods for teaching scientific creationism in public schools." The Creation Research Society (CRS) is located in Ann Arbor, Michigan. A member must subscribe to the following statement of belief: "The Bible is the written word of God, and because it is inspired throughout, all of its assertions are historically and scientifically true." To study creation-science at the CRS, a member must accept "that the account of origins in Genesis is a factual presentation of simple historical truth."

C.

When, as here, "both courts below are unable to discern an arguably valid secular purpose, this Court normally should hesitate to find one. . . . My examination of the language and the legislative history of the Balanced Treatment Act confirms that the intent of the Louisiana legislature was to promote a particular religious belief. . . .

Justice **White,** concurring in the judgment, said in part:

As it comes to us, this is not a difficult case. Based on the historical setting and plain language of the act both courts construed the statutory words "creation-science" to refer to a religious belief, which the act required to be taught if evolution was taught. In other words, the teaching of evolution was conditioned on the teaching of a religious belief. Both courts concluded that the state legislature's primary purpose was to advance religion and that the statute was therefore unconstitutional under the Establishment Clause.

. . . Unless . . . we are to reconsider the Court's decisions interpreting the Establishment Clause, I agree that the judgment of the Court of Appeals must be affirmed.

Justice **Scalia,** with whom Chief Justice **Rehnquist** joined, dissented, saying in part:

Even if I agreed with the questionable premise that legislation can be invalidated under the Establishment Clause on the basis of its motivation alone, without regard to its effects, I would still find no justification for today's decision. The Louisiana legislators who passed the "Balanced Treatment for Creation-Science and Evolution-Science Act," each of whom had sworn to support the Constitution, were well aware of the potential Establishment Clause problems and considered that aspect of the legislation with great care. After seven hearings and several months of study, resulting in substantial revision of the original proposal, they approved the Act overwhelmingly and specifically articulated the secular purpose they meant it to serve. Although the records contains abundant evidence of the sincerity of that purpose (the only issue pertinent to this case), the Court today holds, essentially on the basis of "its visceral knowledge regarding what *must* have motivated the legislators" that the members of the Louisiana Legislature

knowingly violated their oaths and then lied about it. I dissent. . . .

I.

. . . The only evidence in the record of the "received meaning and acceptation" of "creation science" is found in five affidavits filed by appellants. In those affidavits, two scientists, a philosopher, a theologian, and an educator, all of whom claim extensive knowledge of creation science, swear that it is essentially a collection of scientific data supporting the theory that the physical universe and life within it appeared suddenly and have not changed substantially since appearing. These experts insist that creation science is a strictly scientific concept that can be presented without religious references. At this point, then, we must assume that the Balanced Treatment Act does *not* require the presentation of religious doctrine.

Nothing in today's opinion is plainly to the contrary, but what the statute means and what it requires are of rather little concern to the Court. Like the Court of Appeals, the Court finds it necessary to consider only the motives of the legislators who supported the Balanced Treatment Act. After examining the statute, its legislative history, and its historical and social context, the Court holds that the Louisiana Legislature acted without "a secular legislative purpose" and that the Act therefore fails the "purpose" prong of the three-part test set forth in Lemon v. Kurtzman (1971). As I explain below, I doubt whether that "purpose" requirement of Lemon is a proper interpretation of the Constitution; but even if it were, I could not agree with the Court's assessment that the requirement was not satisfied here.

This Court has said little about the first component of the Lemon test. Almost invariably, we have effortlessly discovered a secular purpose for measures challenged under the Establishment Clause. . . . [Justice Scalia here lists a dozen cases, most of which turned on the "entanglement" prong of Lemon.] In fact, only once before deciding Lemon, and twice since, have we invalidated a law for lack of a secular purpose. See Wallace v. Jaffree (1985); Stone v. Graham (1980) (per curiam); Epperson v. Arkansas (1968).

Nevertheless, a few principles have emerged from our cases, principles which should, but to an unfortunately large extent do not, guide the Court's application of Lemon today. It is clear, first of all, that regardless of what "legislative purpose" may mean in other contexts, for the purpose of the Lemon test it means the "actual" motives of those responsible for the challenged action. . . . Thus, if those legislators who supported the Balanced Treatment Act *in fact* acted with a "sincere" secular purpose, the Act survives the first component of the Lemon test, regardless of whether that purpose is likely to be achieved by the provisions they enacted.

Our cases have also confirmed that when the Lemon Court referred to "a secular . . . purpose," it meant "*a* secular purpose." The author of Lemon, writing for the Court, has said that invalidation under the purpose prong is appropriate when "there [is] *no question* that the statute or activity was motivated *wholly* by religious considerations." Lynch v. Donnelly (1984) (Burger, C.J.) (emphasis added); see also Wallace v. Jaffree ("the First Amendment requires that a statute must be invalidated if it is *entirely* motivated by a purpose to advance religion") (emphasis added). In all three cases in which we struck down laws under the Establishment Clause for lack of a secular purpose, we found that the legislature's sole motive was to promote religion. . . . Thus, the majority's invalidation of the Balanced Treatment Act is defensible only if the record indicates that the Louisiana Legislature had *no* secular purpose.

It is important to stress that the purpose forbidden by Lemon is the purpose of "advance religion." . . . Our cases in no way imply that the Establishment Clause forbids legislators merely to act upon their religious convictions. We surely would not strike down a law providing money to feed the hungry or shelter the homeless if it could be demonstrated that, but for the religious beliefs of the legislators, the funds would not have been approved. Also, political activism by the religiously motivated is part of our heritage. Notwithstanding the majority's implication to the contrary, we do not presume that the sole purpose of a law is to advance religion merely because it was supported strongly by organized religions or by adherents of particular faiths. . . . To do so would deprive religious men and women of their right to participate in the political process. Today's religious activism may give us the Balanced Treatment Act, but yesterday's resulted in the abolition of slavery, and tomorrow's may bring relief for famine victims.

Similarly, we will not presume that a law's purpose is to advance religion merely because it " 'happens to coincide or harmonize with the tenets of some or all religions,' " . . . or because it benefits religion, even substantially. We have, for example, turned back Establishment Clause challenges to restrictions on abortion funding, Harris v. McRae [1980], and to Sunday closing laws, McGowan v. Maryland [1961], despite the fact that both "agre[e] with the dictates of [some] Judaeo-Christian religions." "In many instances, the Congress or state legislatures conclude that the general welfare of society, wholly apart from any religious considerations, demands such regulation." Ibid. On many occasions we have had no difficulty finding a secular purpose for governmental action far more likely to advance religion than the Balanced Treatment Act. See, e.g., Mueller v. Allen [1983]. . . . Thus, the fact that creation science coincides with the beliefs of certain religions, a fact upon which the majority relies heavily, does not itself justify invalidation of the Act.

Finally, our cases indicate that even certain kinds of governmental actions undertaken with the specific intention of improving the position of religion do not "advance religion" as that term is used in Lemon. Rather, we have said that in at least two circumstances government *must* act to advance religion, and that in a third it *may* do so.

First, since we have consistently described the Establishment Clause as forbidding not only state action motivated by the desire to *advance* religion, but also intended to "disapprove," "inhibit," or evince "hostility" toward religion, . . . and since we have said that governmental "neutrality" toward religion is the preeminent goal of the First Amendment, . . . a State which discovers that its employees are inhibiting religion must take steps to prevent them from doing so, even though its purpose would clearly be to advance religion. . . . Thus, if the Louisiana Legislature sincerely believed that the State's science teachers were being hostile to religion, our cases indicate that it could act to eliminate that hostility without running afoul of Lemon's purpose test.

Second, we have held that intentional governmental advancement of religion is sometimes required by the Free Exercise Clause. For example, in . . . Wisconsin v. Yoder (1972) . . . we held that in some circumstances States must accommodate the beliefs of religious citizens by exempting them from generally applicable regulations. We have not yet come close to reconciling Lemon and our Free Exercise cases, and typically we do not really try. . . . It is clear, however, that members of the Louisiana Legislature were not impermissibly motivated for purpose of the Lemon test if they believed that approval of the Balanced Treatment Act was *required* by the Free Exercise Clause.

We have also held that in some circumstances government may act to accommodate religion, even if that action is not required by the First Amendment. . . . We have implied that voluntary governmental accommodation of religion is not only permissible, but desirable. Thus, few would contend that Title VII of the Civil Rights Act of 1964, which both forbids religious discrimination by private-sector employers and requires them reasonably to accommodate the religious practices of their employees, violates the Establishment Clause, even though its "purpose" is, of course, to advance religion, and even though it is almost certainly not required by the Free Exercise Clause. . . . It is possible, then, that even if the sole motive of those voting for the Balanced Treatment Act was to advance religion, and its passage was not actually required, or even believed to be required, by either the Free Exercise or Establishment Clauses, the Act would nonetheless survive scrutiny under Lemon's purpose test.

One final observation about the application of that test: Although the Court's opinion gives no hint of it, in the past we have repeatedly affirmed "our reluctance to attribute unconstitutional motives to the States." . . . Whenever we are called upon to judge the constitutionality of an act of a state legislature, "we must have 'due regard to the fact that this Court is not exercising a primary judgment but is sitting in judgment upon those who also have taken the oath to observe the Constitution and who have the responsibility for carrying on government.' " . . . This is particularly true, we have said, where the legislature has specifically considered the question of a law's constitutionality.

With the foregoing in mind, I now turn to the purposes underlying adoption of the Balanced Treatment Act.

II.

A.

We have relatively little information upon which to judge the motives of those who supported the Act. About the only direct evidence is the statute itself and transcripts of the seven committee hearings at which it was considered. . . . Nevertheless, there is ample evidence that the majority is wrong in holding that the Balanced Treatment Act is without secular purpose. . . .

. . . The Act had its genesis (so to speak) in legislation introduced by Senator Bill Keith in June 1980. . . .

Before summarizing the testimony of Senator Keith and his supporters, I wish to make clear that I by no means intended to endorse its accuracy. But my views (and the views of this Court) about creation science and evolution are (or should be) beside the point. Our task is not to judge the debate about teaching the origins of life, but to ascertain what the members of the Louisiana Legislature believed. The vast majority of them voted to approve a bill which explicitly stated a secular purpose; what is crucial is not their *wisdom* in believing that purpose would be achieved by the bill, but their *sincerity* in believing it would be.

Most of the testimony in support of Senator Keith's bill came from the Senator himself and from scientists and educators he presented, many of whom enjoyed academic credentials that may have been regarded as quite impressive by members of the Louisiana Legislature. To a substantial extent, their testimony was devoted to lengthy, and, to the layman, seemingly expert scientific expositions on the origin of life. . . . These scientific lectures touched upon, inter alia, biology, paleontology, genetics, astronomy, astrophysics, probability analysis, and biochemistry. The witnesses repeatedly assured committee members that "hundreds and hundreds" of highly respected, internationally renowned scientists believed in creation science and would support their testimony. . . .

Senator Keith and his witnesses testified essentially as set forth in the following numbered paragraphs:

(1) There are two and only two scientific explanations for the beginning of life—evolution and creation science. . . . Evolution posits that life arose out of inanimate chemical compounds and has gradually evolved over millions of years. Creation science posits that all life forms now on earth appeared suddenly and relatively recently and have changed little. . . .

(2) The body of scientific evidence supporting creation science is as strong as that supporting evolution. In fact, it may be *stronger*. . . . The evidence for evolution is far less compelling than we have been led to believe. Evolution is not a scientific "fact," since it cannot actually be observed in a laboratory. Rather, evolution is merely a scientific theory or "guess." . . .

(3) Creation science is educationally valuable. Students exposed to it better understand the current state of scientific evidence about the origin of life. . . . Those students even have a better understanding of evolution. . . .

(4) Although creation science is educationally valuable and strictly scientific, it is now being censored from or misrepresented in the public schools. . . . Teachers have been brainwashed by an entrenched scientific establishment composed almost exclusively of scientists to whom evolution is like a "religion." These scientists discriminate against creation scientists so as to prevent evolution's weaknesses from being exposed. . . .

(5) The censorship of creation science has at least two harmful effects. First, it deprives students of knowledge of one of the two scientific explanations for the origin of life and leads them to believe that evolution is a proven fact; thus, their education suffers and they are wrongly taught that science has proven their religious beliefs false. Second, it violates the Establishment Clause. The United States Supreme Court has held that secular humanism is a religion. [Sen. Keith, referring to Torcaso v. Watkins (1961)]. . . . Belief in evolution is a central tenet of that religion. . . . Thus, by censoring creation science and instructing students that evolution is fact, public school teachers are *now* advancing religion in violation of the Establishment Clause. . . .

We have no way of knowing, of course, how many legislators believed the testimony of Senator Keith and his witnesses. But the absence of evidence to the contrary, we have to assume that many of them did. Given that assumption, the Court today plainly errs in holding that the Louisiana Legislature passed the Balanced Treatment Act for exclusively religious purposes.

B.

. . . Even if the legislative history were silent or ambiguous about the existence of a secular purpose—and here it is not—the statute should survive Lemon's purpose test. But even more validation than mere legislative history is present here. The Louisiana Legislature explicitly set forth its secular purpose ("protecting academic freedom") in the very test of the Act. . . .

The Court seeks to evade the force of this expression of purpose by stubbornly misinterpreting it, and then finding that the provisions of the Act do not advance that misinterpreted purpose, thereby showing it to be a sham. The Court first surmises that "academic freedom" means "enhancing the freedom of teachers to teach what they will," even though "academic freedom" in that sense has little scope in the structured elementary and secondary curriculums with which the Act is concerned. Alternatively, the Court suggests that it might mean "maximiz[ing] the comprehensiveness and effectiveness of science instruction," though that is an exceedingly strange interpretation of the words, and one that is refuted on the very face of the statute. Had the

Court devoted to this central question of the meaning of the legislatively expressed purpose a small fraction of the research into legislative history that produced its quotations of religiously motivated statements by individual legislators, it would have discerned quite readily what "academic freedom" meant: *students'* freedom from *indoctrination*. The legislature wanted to ensure that students would be free to decide for themselves how life began, based upon a fair and balanced presentation of the scientific evidence—that is, to protect "the right of each [student] voluntarily to determine what to believe (and what not to believe) free of any coercive pressures from the State." . . .

It is undoubtedly true that what prompted the Legislature to direct its attention to the misrepresentation of evolution in the schools (rather than the inaccurate presentation of other topics) was its awareness of the tension between evolution and the religious beliefs of many children. But even appellees concede that a valid secular purpose is not rendered impermissible simply because its pursuits prompted by concern for religious sensitivities. If a history teacher falsely told her students that the bones of Jesus Christ had been discovered, or a physics teacher that the Shroud of Turin had been conclusively established to be inexplicable on the basis of natural causes, I cannot believe (despite the majority's implication to the contrary) that legislators or school board members would be constitutionally prohibited from taking corrective action, simply because that action was prompted by concern for the religious beliefs of the misinstructed students.

In sum, even if one concedes, for the sake of argument, that a majority of the Louisiana Legislature voted for the Balanced Treatment Act partly in order to foster (rather than merely eliminate discrimination against) Christian fundamentalist beliefs, our cases establish that that alone would not suffice to invalidate the Act, so long as there was a genuine secular purpose as well. We have, moreover, no adequate basis for disbelieving the secular purpose set forth in the Act itself, or for concluding that it is a sham enacted to conceal the legislators' violation of their oaths of office. I am astonished by the Court's unprecedented readiness to reach such a conclusion, which I can only attribute to an intellectual predisposition created by the facts and the legend of Scopes v. State, 154 Tenn. 105 (1927)—an instinctive reaction that any governmentally imposed requirements bearing upon the teaching of evolution must be a manifestation of Christian fundamentalist repression. In this case, however, it seems to me the Court's position is the repressive one. The people of Louisiana, including those who are Christian fundamentalists, are quite entitled, as a secular matter, to have whatever scientific evidence there may be against evolution presented in their schools, just as Mr. Scopes was entitled to present whatever scientific evidence there was for it. Perhaps what the Louisiana Legislature has done is unconstitutional because there *is* no such evidence, and the scheme they have established will amount to no more than a presentation of the Book of Genesis. But we cannot say that on the evidence before using this summary judgment context, which includes ample uncontradicted testimony that "creation science" is a body of scientific knowledge rather than revealed belief. *Infinitely less* can we say (or should we say) that the scientific evidence for evolution is so conclusive that no one could be gullible enough to believe that there is any real scientific evidence to the contrary, so that the legislation's stated purpose must be a lie. Yet that illiberal judgment, that Scopes-in-reverse, is ultimately the basis on which the Court's facile rejection of the Louisiana Legislature's purpose must rest. . . .

III.

I have to this point assumed the validity of the Lemon "purpose" test. In fact, however, I think the pessimistic evaluation that the Chief Justice [Rehnquist] made of the totality of Lemon is particularly applicable to the "purpose" prong: it is "a constitutional theory [that] has no basis in the history of the amendment it seeks to interpret, is difficult to apply and yields unprincipled results." Wallace v. Jaffree (Rehnquist, J., dissenting). . . .

Given the many hazards involved in assessing the subjective intent of governmental decisionmakers, the first prong of Lemon is defensible, I think, only if the text of the Establishment Clause demands it. That is surely not the case. . . .

LYNCH v. DONNELLY

465 U. S. 668; 104 S. Ct. 1355; 79 L. Ed. 2d 604
(1984)

It seems apparent that while the early governments in this country tended to let the individual fend for himself as far as his economic welfare went, they did not take any such hands-off policy with regard to his spiritual welfare. Even those that did not have established religions tended to encourage religion, usually a Protestant Christianity. Among the most common forms of such encouragement were the so-called Sunday Blue Laws, or Sunday Closing Laws, adopted to advance "the true and sincere worship of God according to his holy will" (New York) or "to the end that the Sabbath may be celebrated in a religious manner" (Massachusetts Bay Colony). Such laws, now present in every state but Alaska, forbid to a greater or lesser extent various forms of physical or economic activity on Sunday. Some merely forbid the selling of liquor, while others forbid all economic activity and then set up elaborate exceptions to the rule. In four cases in 1961 the Court held valid the Sunday closing laws of Maryland and Pennsylvania. In two of the cases the defendants did not allege that their religious freedom was involved, but merely that they were denied equal protection and that the laws constituted an establishment of religion. The Court rejected both these contentions. It held that the laws did not deny equal protec-

tion by the varied exceptions they permitted, since these were not shown to be completely irrational and unjustifiable. Nor did they constitute an establishment of religion. Conceding that the origin of such laws was undoubtedly religious and that the day chosen favored the dominant Christian sects, the Court pointed out that such laws had long since ceased to be religiously inspired and were merely an exercise of the police power of the state to provide the community a day of rest, amusement, and family togetherness. The state, the Court held, could reasonably decide that everyone should rest on the same day (rather than let each individual choose his own day) and it was not an establishment of religion to pick the day that most people thought of as a "day off," even though it had a religious origin. See *McGowan v. Maryland* (1961) and *Two Guys from Harrison-Allentown, Inc. v. McGinley* (1961). In two of the cases the Court faced the additional question of the free exercise of religion. *Gallagher v. Crown Kosher Super Market* (1961) and *Braunfeld v. Brown* (1961) involved Orthodox Jews who closed their businesses on Saturday, the Jewish Sabbath, and claimed that forcing them to close on Sunday, too, was in effect to place an economic burden upon them because of their religion. Although the six members of the majority could not agree on an opinion, they did agree that since the laws were valid under the police power and were not intended to discriminate against persons on religious grounds, the indirect economic disadvantage visited on persons because of their religious beliefs did not render the law a violation of their religious liberties. In illustration they pointed to the validity of laws against polygamy, held valid in *Reynolds v. United States* (1879). In 1964 New York City replaced its Sunday closing law with a Fair Sabbath Law, which permitted family-run businesses to stay open on Sunday if they were closed on Saturday.

In 1977 Connecticut amended its Sunday-closing law to provide that "no person who states that a particular day of the week is observed as his Sabbath may be required by his employer to work on such day. An employee's refusal to work on his Sabbath shall not constitute grounds for dismissal." In *Thornton v. Caldor* (1985) the Court held the statute a violation of the establishment clause because it had no secular purpose. "The State . . . commands that Sabbath religious concerns automatically control over all secular interests at the work place; the statute takes no account of the convenience or interests of the employer or those of other employees who do not observe a Sabbath. . . . There is no exception under the statute for special circumstances, such as the Friday Sabbath observer employed in an occupation with a Monday through Friday schedule—a school teacher, for example. . . . This unyielding weighting in favor of Sabbath observers over all other interests contravenes a fundamental principle of the Religion Clauses. . . ."

While Article VI of the Constitution contains the provision that "no religious test shall ever be required

as a qualification to any office or public trust under the United States," most of the early state constitutions did require such tests and some of those have survived. The constitution of Maryland provides that no religious test for public office shall be required "other than a declaration of belief in the existence of God." Torcaso was appointed to the office of notary public in Maryland but was refused his commission to the office because he would not declare his belief in God. In a unanimous decision the Court held that "this Maryland religious test for public office unconstitutionally invades the appellant's freedom of belief and religion and therefore cannot be enforced against him." The Court expressly rejected any suggestion that *Zorach v. Clauson* (1952) had weakened the holding of the Everson case (1947). "We repeat and again reaffirm that neither a State nor the Federal Government can constitutionally force a person 'to profess a belief or disbelief in any religion.' Neither can constitutionally pass laws or impose requirements which aid all religions as against non-believers, and neither can aid those religions based on a belief in the existence of God as against those religions founded on different beliefs." See *Torcaso v. Watkins* (1961).

The free exercise and no establishment clauses of the First Amendment were the framers' answer to the place of religion in the highly pluralistic social structures of the time. Religion was to be a private affair; the heavy thumb of the government was to be used neither to aid nor hinder, lest man's freedom to worship as he chose and the right to support only the church of his choice be jeopardized. But even as the framers wrote, many of the practices of the time made clear that the "separation of church and state" would not entail the government ignoring the existence of religion. Both houses of the Congress employed a chaplain; "In God We Trust" was embossed on our coins; and the help and understanding of God were exhorted on all public occasions. In general the people thought of themselves as religious, mostly Christian, and a government recognition of that fact did not seem in any way inconsistent with the doctrines of the First Amendment.

With the gradual diversification of religious beliefs many well-accepted religious practices and manifestations were challenged in the courts, and with the application to the states of the religion clauses of the First Amendment, these challenges raised potential federal questions.

The Supreme Court has shown considerable reluctance to review many activities that have been part of our historical heritage. In November 1964, it left untouched a New York decision upholding the words "under God" in the pledge of allegiance; in 1966 (*Murray v. Goldstein*) it declined to review a Maryland case upholding the validity of tax exemption for church buildings, and as recently as 1971 it let stand the rejection by a district court of an effort to stop the astronauts from praying over television on their way to the moon (*O'Hair v. Paine*, 1971).

But the issue of tax exemption for churches could

*not stay buried forever, and in Walz v. Tax Commission
the Supreme Court took a case involving a Staten Island
resident who owned a 22 x 29 foot piece of land on
which he owed the state $5.24 in property taxes. He re-
fused to pay on the ground he was being forced to support churches and synagogues, which pay no taxes. The
Court recognized its past struggles to "find a neutral
course between the two Religion Clauses, both of which
are cast in absolute terms, and either of which, if expanded to a logical extreme, would tend to clash with the
other." It concluded that "no perfect or absolute separation is really possible," that both had to coexist, and
the real function of the Court was to prevent "excessive
entanglement" between the two. Since tax exemption for
churches had been in existence since the formation of the
Union, it posed no real threat to the separation of
church and state. "The exemption creates only a minimal and remote involvement between church and state
and far less than the taxation of churches. It restricts the
fiscal relationship between church and state, and tends
to complement and reinforce the desired separation in-
sulating each from the other."*

*In Marsh v. Chambers (1983) the Court held valid
the employment of a chaplain for the state legislature
noting that the framers had employed one for Congress
at the same time they were proposing the First Amendment, and "the practice of opening legislative sessions
with prayer has become part of the fabric of our society."*

*The present case involves a challenge to the inclu-
sion of a crèche in a city-owned Christmas display on
the ground that "the erection of the crèche has the real
and substantial effect of affiliating the City with the
Christian beliefs that the crèche represents."*

Chief Justice **Burger** delivered the opinion of the
Court, saying in part:

We granted certiorari to decide whether the Establishment Clause of the First Amendment prohibits a municipality from including a crèche, or Nativity scene, in
its annual Christmas display.

I.

Each year, in cooperation with the downtown retail
merchants' association, the city of Pawtucket, R. I.,
erects a Christmas display as part of its observance of the
Christmas holiday season. The display is situated in a
park owned by a nonprofit organization and located in
the heart of the shopping district. The display is essentially like those to be found in hundreds of towns or cities across the Nation—often on public grounds—during
the Christmas season. The Pawtucket display comprises
many of the figures and decorations traditionally associated with Christmas, including, among other things, a
Santa Claus house, reindeer pulling Santa's sleigh,
candy-striped poles, a Christmas tree, carolers, cutout
figures representing such characters as a clown, an ele-

phant, and a teddy bear, hundreds of colored lights, a
large banner that reads "SEASONS GREETINGS," and
the crèche at issue here. All components of this display
are owned by the city.

The crèche, which has been included in the display
for 40 or more years, consists of the traditional figures,
including the Infant Jesus, Mary and Joseph, angels,
shepherds, kings, and animals, all ranging in height from
5″ to 5′. In 1973, when the present crèche was acquired,
it cost the city $1365; it now is valued at $200. The erection and dismantling of the crèche costs the city about
$20 per year; nominal expenses are incurred in lighting
the crèche. No money has been expended on its maintenance for the past 10 years. . . .

II.

A.

This Court has explained that the purpose of the
Establishment and Free Exercise Clauses of the First
Amendment is "to prevent, as far as possible, the intrusion of either [the church or the state] into the precincts
of the other." Lemon v. Kurtzman (1971). At the same
time, however, the Court has recognized that "total
separation is not possible in an absolute sense. Some relationship between government and religious organizations is inevitable." In every Establishment Clause case,
we must reconcile the inescapable tension between the
objective of preventing unnecessary intrusion of either
the church or the state upon the other, and the reality
that, as the Court has so often noted, total separation of
the two is not possible.

The Court has sometimes described the Religion
Clauses as erecting a "wall" between church and state,
see, e.g., Everson v. Board of Education (1947). The
concept of a "wall" of separation is a useful figure of
speech probably deriving from views of Thomas Jefferson. The metaphor has served as a reminder that the Establishment Clause forbids an established church or anything approaching it. But the metaphor itself is not a
wholly accurate description of the practical aspects of
the relationship that in fact exists between church and
state.

No significant segment of our society and no institution within it can exist in a vacuum or in total or absolute isolation from all the other parts, much less from
government. "It has never been thought either possible
or desirable to enforce a regime of total separation. . . ."
. . . Nor does the Constitution require complete separation of church and state; it affirmatively mandates accommodation, not merely tolerance, of all religions, and
forbids hostility toward any. . . . Anything less would require the "callous indifference" we have said was never
intended by the Establishment Clause. Zorach [v.
Clauson (1952)]. Indeed, we have observed, such hostility would bring us into "war with our national tradition

as embodied in the First Amendment's guaranty of the free exercise of religion." . . .

B.

The Court's interpretation of the Establishment Clause has comported with what history reveals was the contemporaneous understanding of its guarantees. A significant example of the contemporaneous understanding of that Clause is found in the events of the first week of the First Session of the First Congress in 1789. In the very week that Congress approved the Establishment Clause as part of the Bill of Rights for submission to the states, it enacted legislation providing for paid chaplains for the House and Senate. . . .

The interpretation of the Establishment Clause by Congress in 1789 takes on special significance in light of the Court's emphasis that the First Congress "was a Congress whose constitutional decisions have always been regarded, as they should be regarded, as of the greatest weight in the interpretation of that fundamental instrument," Myers v. United States (1926).

It is clear that neither the 17 draftsmen of the Constitution who were Members of the First Congress, nor the Congress of 1789, saw any establishment problem in the employment of congressional Chaplains to offer daily prayers in the Congress, a practice that has continued for nearly two centuries. It would be difficult to identify a more striking example of the accommodation of religious belief intended by the Framers.

C. . . .

Other examples of reference to our religious heritage are found in the statutorily prescribed national motto "In God We Trust," which Congress and the President mandated for our currency, and in the language "One nation under God," as part of the Pledge of Allegiance to the American flag. That pledge is recited by many thousands of public school children—and adults—every year.

Art galleries supported by public revenues display religious paintings of the 15th and 16th centuries, predominantly inspired by one religious faith. . . . The very chamber in which oral arguments on this case were heard is decorated with a notable and permanent—not seasonal—symbol of religion: Moses with the Ten Commandments. Congress has long provided chapels in the Capitol for religious worship and meditation. . . .

III.

This history may help explain why the Court consistently has declined to take a rigid, absolutist view of the Establishment Clause. We have refused "to construe the Religion Clauses with a literalness that would undermine the ultimate constitutional objective *as illuminated by history*." Walz v. Tax Commission (1970) (Emphasis

added). In our modern, complex society, whose traditions and constitutional underpinnings rest on and encourage diversity and pluralism in all areas, an absolutist approach in applying the Establishment Clause is simplistic and has been uniformly rejected by the Court.

Rather than mechanically invalidating all governmental conduct or statutes that confer benefits or give special recognition to religion in general or to one faith—as an absolutist approach would dictate—the Court has scrutinized challenged legislation or official conduct to determine whether, in reality, it establishes a religion or religious faith, or tends to do so. . . .

In the line-drawing process we have often found it useful to inquire whether the challenged law or conduct has a secular purpose, whether its principal or primary effect is to advance or inhibit religion, and whether it creates an excessive entanglement of government with religion. But, we have repeatedly emphasized our unwillingness to be confined to any single test or criterion in this sensitive area. . . .

In this case, the focus of our inquiry must be on the crèche in the context of the Christmas season. . . . Focus exclusively on the religious component of any activity would inevitably lead to its invalidation under the Establishment Clause.

The Court has invalidated legislation or governmental action on the ground that a secular purpose was lacking, but only when it has concluded there was no question that the statute or activity was motivated wholly by religious considerations. . . .

The District Court inferred from the religious nature of the crèche that the city has no secular purpose for the display. In so doing, it rejected the city's claim that its reasons for including the crèche are essentially the same as its reasons for sponsoring the display as a whole. . . . The city, like the Congresses and Presidents, . . . has principally taken note of a significant historical religious event long celebrated in the Western World. The crèche in the display depicts the historical origins of this traditional event long recognized as a National Holiday. . . .

The narrow question is whether there is a secular purpose for Pawtucket's display of the crèche. The display is sponsored by the city to celebrate the Holiday and to depict the origins of that Holiday. These are legitimate secular purposes. The District Court's inference, drawn from the religious nature of the crèche, that the city has no secular purpose was, on this record, clearly erroneous. . . .

The dissent asserts some observers may perceive that the city has aligned itself with the Christian faith by including a Christian symbol in its display and that this serves to advance religion. We can assume, arguendo, that the display advances religion in a sense; but our precedents plainly contemplate that on occasion some advancement of religion will result from governmental action. The Court has made it abundantly clear, however, that "not every law that confers an 'indirect,' 'remote,' or 'incidental' benefit upon [religion] is, for that reason alone, constitutionally invalid." [Committee for Public Education v.] Nyquist [1973]. . . .

The District Court found that there had been no administrative entanglement between religion and state resulting from the city's ownership and use of the crèche. But it went on to hold that some political divisiveness was engendered by this litigation. Coupled with its finding of an impermissible sectarian purpose and effect, this persuaded the court that there was "excessive entanglement." . . .

The Court of Appeals correctly observed that this Court has not held that political divisiveness alone can serve to invalidate otherwise permissible conduct. And we decline to so hold today. . . . In any event, apart from this litigation there is no evidence of political friction or divisiveness over the crèche in the 40-year history of Pawtucket's Christmas celebration. . . . A litigant cannot, by the very act of commencing a lawsuit . . . create the appearance of divisiveness and then exploit it as evidence of entanglement.

We are satisfied that the city has a secular purpose for including the crèche, that the city has not impermissibly advanced religion, and that including the crèche does not create excessive entanglement between religion and government. . . .

Justice **O'Connor,** concurring, said in part:

I concur in the opinion of the Court. I write separately to suggest a clarification of our Establishment Clause doctrine. . . .

I.

The Establishment Clause prohibits government from making adherence to a religion relevant in any way to a person's standing in the political community. Government can run afoul of that prohibition in two principal ways. One is excessive entanglement with religious institutions, which may interfere with the independence of the institutions, give the institutions access to government or governmental powers not fully shared by nonadherents of the religion, and foster the creation of political constituencies defined along religious lines. . . . The second and more direct infringement is government endorsement or disapproval of religion. Endorsement sends a message to nonadherents that they are outsiders, not full members of the political community, and an accompanying message to adherents that they are insiders, favored members of the political community. Disapproval sends the opposite message. . . .

III. . . .

B. . . .

Pawtucket's display of its crèche, I believe, does not communicate a message that the government intends to endorse the Christian beliefs represented by the crèche. Although the religious and indeed sectarian significance of the crèche, as the district court found, is not neutralized by the setting, the overall holiday setting changes what viewers may fairly understand to be the purpose of the display—as a typical museum setting, though not neutralizing the religious content of a religious painting, negates any message of endorsement of that content. The display celebrates a public holiday, and no one contends that declaration of that holiday is understood to be an endorsement of religion. . . .

Justice **Brennan,** with whom Justice **Marshall,** Justice **Blackmun** and Justice **Stevens** join, dissenting, said in part:

The principles announced in the compact phrases of the Religion Clauses have, as the Court today reminds us, proved difficult to apply. Faced with that uncertainty, the Court properly looks for guidance to the settled test announced in Lemon v. Kurtzman (1971). . . .

I. . . .

A. . . .

This well-defined three-part test expresses the essential concerns animating the Establishment Clause. Thus, the test is designed to ensure that the organs of government remain strictly separate and apart from religious affairs, for "a union of government and religion tends to destroy government and degrade religion." . . .

Applying the three-part test to Pawtucket's crèche, I am persuaded that the city's inclusion of the crèche in its Christmas display simply does not reflect a "clearly . . . secular purpose." . . . Here we have no explicit statement of purpose by Pawtucket's municipal government accompanying its decision to purchase, display, and maintain the crèche. Governmental purpose may nevertheless be inferred. . . . In the present case, the city claims that its purposes were exclusively secular. Pawtucket sought, according to this view, only to participate in the celebration of a national holiday and to attract people to the downtown area in order to promote pre-Christmas retail sales and to help engender the spirit of goodwill and neighborliness commonly associated with the Christmas season.

Despite these assertions, two compelling aspects of this case indicate that our generally prudent "reluctance to attribute unconstitutional motives" to a governmental body . . . should be overcome. First, . . . all of Pawtucket's "valid secular objectives can be readily accomplished by other means." Plainly, the city's interest in celebrating the holiday and in promoting both retail sales and goodwill are fully served by the elaborate display of Santa Claus, reindeer, and wishing wells that are already a part of Pawtucket's annual Christmas display. More importantly, the nativity scene, unlike every other element of the Hodgson Park display, reflects a sectarian exclusivity that the avowed purposes of celebrating the holiday season and promoting retail commerce simply do not encompass. To be found constitutional, Pawtucket's seasonal celebration must at least be nondenominational and not serve to promote religion. The inclusion of a distinctively religious element like the crèche, however, demonstrates that a narrower sectarian purpose lay behind the decision to include a nativity scene. That the crèche retained this religious character for the people and municipal government of Pawtucket is suggested by the Mayor's testimony at trial in which he stated that for him, as well as others in the city, the effort to eliminate the nativity scene from Pawtucket's Christmas celebration "is a step towards establishing another religion, non-religion that it may be." Plainly, the city and its leaders understood that the inclusion of the crèche in its display would serve the wholly religious purpose of "keep[ing] 'Christ in Christmas.' " From this record, therefore, it is impossible to say with the kind of confidence that was possible in *McGowan v. Maryland* (1961) that a wholly secular goal predominates.

The "primary effect" of including a nativity scene in the city's display is, as the District Court found, to place the government's imprimatur of approval on the particular religious beliefs exemplified by the crèche. Those who believe in the message of the nativity receive the unique and exclusive benefit of public recognition and approval of their views. For many, the city's decision to include the crèche as part of its extensive and costly efforts to celebrate Christmas can only mean that the prestige of the government has been conferred on the beliefs associated with the crèche, thereby providing "a significant symbolic benefit to religion. . . ." . . . The effect on minority religious groups, as well as on those who may reject all religion, is to convey the message that their views are not similarly worthy of public recognition nor entitled to public support. It was precisely this sort of religious chauvinism that the Establishment Clause was intended forever to prohibit. . . .

Finally, it is evident that Pawtucket's inclusion of a crèche as part of its annual Christmas display does pose a significant threat of fostering "excessive entanglement." . . . It is worth noting that after today's decision, administrative entanglements may well develop. Jews and other non-Christian groups, prompted perhaps by the Mayor's remark that he will include a Menorah in future displays, can be expected to press government for inclusion of their symbols, and faced with such requests, government will have to become involved in accommodating the various demands. . . . More importantly, although no political divisiveness was apparent in Pawtucket prior to the filing of respondents' lawsuit, that act, as the District Court found, unleashed powerful emotional reactions which divided the city along religious lines. The fact that calm had prevailed prior to this suit does not immediately suggest the absence of any division on the point for, as the District Court observed, the quiescence of those opposed to the crèche may have reflected nothing more than their sense of futility in opposing the majority. Of course, the Court is correct to note that we have never held that the potential for divisiveness alone is sufficient to invalidate a challenged governmental practice; we have, nevertheless, repeatedly emphasized that "too close a proximity" between religious and civil authorities . . . may represent a "warning signal" that the values embodied in the Establishment Clause are at risk. . . .

B. . . .

. . . I refuse to accept the notion implicit in today's decision that non-Christians would find that the religious content of the crèche is eliminated by the fact that it appears as part of the city's otherwise secular celebration of the Christmas holiday. The nativity scene is clearly distinct in its purpose and effect from the rest of the Hodgson Park display for the simple reason that it is the only one rooted in a biblical account of Christ's birth. It is the chief symbol of the characteristically Christian belief that a divine Savior was brought into the world and that the purpose of this miraculous birth was to illuminate a path toward salvation and redemption. For Christians, that path is exclusive, precious, and holy. But for those who do not share these beliefs, the symbolic reenactment of the birth of a divine being who has been miraculously incarnated as a man stands as a dramatic reminder of their differences with Christian faith. When government appears to sponsor such religiously inspired views, we cannot say that the practice is " 'so separate and so indisputably marked off from the religious function,' . . . that [it] may fairly be viewed as reflect[ing] a neutral posture toward religious institutions." . . . To be so excluded on religious grounds by one's elected government is an insult and an injury that, until today, could not be countenanced by the Establishment Clause.

Second. . . . The Court apparently believes that once it finds that the designation of Christmas as a public holiday is constitutionally acceptable, it is then free to conclude that virtually every form of governmental association with the celebration of the holiday is also constitutional. The vice of this dangerously superficial argument is that it overlooks the fact that the Christmas holiday in our national culture contains both secular and sectarian elements. To say that government may recognize the holiday's traditional, secular elements of giftgiving, public festivities, and community spirit, does not mean that government may indiscriminately embrace the distinctively sectarian aspects of the holiday. Indeed, in its eagerness to approve the crèche, the Court has advanced a rationale so simplistic that it would appear to allow the Mayor of Pawtucket to participate in the celebration of a Christmas Mass, since this would be just another unobjectionable way for the city to "celebrate the holiday." As is demonstrated below, the Court's logic is fundamentally flawed both because it obscures the reason why public designation of Christmas Day as a holiday is constitutionally acceptable, and blurs the distinction between the secular aspects of Christmas and its distinctively religious character, as exemplified by the crèche. . . .

III.

The American historical experience concerning the public celebration of Christmas, if carefully examined, provides no support for the Court's decision. The opening sections of the Court's opinion, while seeking to rely on historical evidence, do no more than recognize the obvious: because of the strong religious currents that run through our history, an inflexible or absolutistic enforcement of the Establishment Clause would be both imprudent and impossible. This observation is at once uncontroversial and unilluminating. Simply enumerating the various ways in which the Federal Government has recognized the vital role religion plays in our society does nothing to help decide the question presented in *this* case.

Indeed, the Court's approach suggests a fundamental misapprehension of the proper uses of history in constitutional interpretation. Certainly, our decisions reflect the fact that an awareness of historical practice often can provide a useful guide in interpreting the abstract language of the Establishment Clause. . . . But historical acceptance of a particular practice alone is never sufficient to justify a challenged governmental action, since, as the Court has rightly observed, "no one acquires a vested or protected right in violation of the Constitution by long use, even when that span of time covers our entire national existence and indeed predates it." . . .

In McGowan, for instance, the Court carefully canvassed the entire history of Sunday Closing Laws from the colonial period up to modern times. On the basis of this analysis, we concluded that while such laws were rooted in religious motivations, the current purpose was to serve the wholly secular goal of providing a uniform day of rest for all citizens. Our inquiry in Walz was similarly confined to the special history of the practice under review. There the Court found a pattern of "undeviating acceptance" over the entire course of the Nation's history of according property-tax exemptions to religious organizations, a pattern which supported our finding that the practice did not violate the Religion Clauses. Finally, where direct inquiry into the Framer's intent reveals that the First Amendment was not understood to prohibit a particular practice, we have found such an understanding compelling. Thus, in Marsh v. Chambers, after marshaling the historical evidence which indicated that the First Congress had authorized the appointment of paid chaplains for its own proceedings only three days before it reached agreement on the final wording of the Bill of Rights, the Court concluded on the basis of this "unique history" that the modern-day practice of opening legislative sessions with prayer was constitutional.

Although invoking these decisions in support of its result, the Court wholly fails to discuss the history of the public celebration of Christmas or the use of publicly displayed nativity scenes. The Court, instead, simply asserts, without any historical analysis or support whatsoever, that the now familiar celebration of Christmas springs from an unbroken history of acknowledgement "by the people, by the Executive Branch, by the Congress, and the courts for two centuries. . . ." The Court's complete failure to offer any explanation of its assertion is perhaps understandable, however, because the historical record points in precisely the opposite direction. Two features of this history are worth noting. First, at the time of the adoption of the Constitution and the Bill of Rights, there was no settled pattern of celebrating Christmas, either as a purely religious holiday or as a public event. Second, the historical evidence, such as it is, offers no uniform pattern of widespread acceptance of the holiday and indeed suggests that the development of Christmas as a public holiday is a comparatively recent phenomenon.* . . .

Furthermore, unlike the religious tax exemptions upheld in Walz, the public display of nativity scenes as part of governmental celebrations of Christmas does not come to us supported by an unbroken history of widespread acceptance. It was not until 1836 that a State first granted legal recognition to Christmas as a public holiday. This was followed in the period between 1845 and 1865, by 28 jurisdictions which included Christmas Day as a legal holiday. Congress did not follow the States' lead until 1870 when it established December 25th, along with the Fourth of July, New Year's Day, and Thanksgiving, as a legal holiday in the District of Columbia. This pattern of legal recognition tells us only that public acceptance of the holiday was gradual and that the practice—in stark contrast to the record presented in either Walz or Marsh—did not take on the character of a widely recognized holiday until the middle of the nineteenth century. . . .

In sum, there is no evidence whatsoever that the Framers would have expressly approved a federal celebration of the Christmas holiday including public displays of a nativity scene; accordingly, the Court's repeated invocation of the decision in Marsh is not only baffling, it is utterly irrelevant. Nor is there any suggestion that publicly financed and supported displays of Christmas crèche are supported by a record of widespread, undeviating acceptance that extends throughout our history. Therefore, our prior decisions which relied upon concrete, specific historical evidence to support a particular practice simply have no bearing on the question presented in this case. Contrary to today's careless decision, those prior cases have all recognized that the "illumination" provided by history must always be focused on the particular practice at issue in a given case. Without that guiding principle and the intellectual discipline it imposes, the Court is at sea, free to select random elements of America's varied history solely to suit the views of five Members of this Court.

Justice **Blackmun,** with whom Justice **Stevens** joins, dissenting, said in part:

---

*The Court's insistence upon pursuing this vague historical analysis is especially baffling since even the petitioners and their supporting amici concede that no historical evidence equivalent to that relied upon in Marsh, McGowan, or Walz supports publicly sponsored Christmas displays. . . .

Not only does the Court's resolution of this controversy make light of our precedents, but also, ironically, the majority does an injustice to the crèche and the message it manifests. While certain persons, including the Mayor of Pawtucket, undertook a crusade to "keep 'Christ' in Christmas," the Court today has declared that presence virtually irrelevant. The majority urges that the display, "with or without a crèche," "recall[s] the religious nature of the Holiday," and "engenders a friendly community spirit of good will in keeping with the season." Before the District Court, an expert witness for the city made a similar, though perhaps more candid, point, stating that Pawtucket's display invites people "to participate in the Christmas spirit, brotherhood, peace, and let loose with their money." The crèche has been relegated to the role of a neutral harbinger of the holiday season, useful for commercial purposes, but devoid of any inherent meaning and incapable of enhancing the religious tenor of a display of which it is an integral part. The city has its victory—but it is a Pyrrhic one indeed.

5

Equal Protection of the Laws

HOW EQUAL IS EQUAL? THE TRADITIONAL TEST

GOESAERT v. CLEARY

335 U. S. 464; 69 S. Ct. 198; 93 L. Ed. 163
(1948)

At the time the Fourteenth Amendment was being considered, it was obvious that the Southern states, left to their own devices, would subject newly freed blacks to numerous and drastic discriminatory laws and regulations designed to prevent them from achieving anything like a status of legal equality with the white citizens of the Southern states. Accordingly the Fourteenth Amendment contains the explicit statement that no state shall "deny to any person within its jurisdiction the equal protection of the law," a clause much clearer in its meaning than its companion clauses in the amendment relating to "due process of law" and "the privileges and immunities of citizens of the United States." The equal protection clause does not mention race, but when it first came before the Supreme Court for interpretation in the Slaughter-House Cases, in 1873, Justice Miller, with contemporary history and conditions in mind, observed: "We doubt very much whether any action of a state not directed by way of discrimination against the negroes as a class, or on account of their race, will ever be held to come within the purview of this provision." Justice

Miller's appraisal of current history may have been correct, but his prophecy as to the limited use of the equal protection clause was very bad. Over the years equal protection of the law has come to afford broad and general relief against all forms of arbitrary classification and discrimination, regardless of the persons affected or the character of the rights involved. In fact, blacks would probably constitute a minority of those who have invoked the equal protection clause against discriminatory treatment.

The equal protection clause does not, of course, forbid all legal classification. Classification in the law is not only constitutional but desirable and necessary; it is almost impossible to conceive of a law which does not in some way employ it. But however necessary such classification and grouping is, it is a function which lends itself to abuse; and it is this abuse which the equal protection clause seeks to prevent.

When does classification become discrimination? How equal is equal? Over the years the Court's approach to these questions has evolved from a laissez-faire attitude that upheld almost all legislative classifications to a more searching review that barred almost all use of certain classifications. But like the natural evolution of any organism, the evolution of the equal protection clause has been a gradual one. Just as in nature where the older systems survive alongside more recent adaptations, so in equal protection the first test used by the Court to determine the legitimacy of legislative classification still exists to judge certain classifications while newer tests have evolved to judge others.

The first, or traditional test, is often referred to as the "rational basis" test. It requires that the government have a rational basis for treating people or activities differently [and] that that basis must be related to a constitutionally permissible objective. Thus it is rational to demand of automobile drivers that they be able to meet certain standards of vision, and the highway safety it promotes is a constitutional goal. On the other hand, if the government were seeking to oppress blacks it would be perfectly rational to forbid them to go to school. But the oppression of people is not a constitutionally permissible goal and the government's action would not survive even the traditional test. Nevertheless, "mere rationality," as the Court sometimes calls it, is an easy standard to meet because governments can usually find a plausible constitutional objective to put forth no matter how constitutionally questionable the real objective may be.

The first appearance of the rational basis test in F. S. Royster Guano Co. v. Virginia (1920) suggested a good deal more rigorous requirement of equality than in fact developed. "The classification must be reasonable, not arbitrary, and must rest upon some ground of difference having a fair and substantial relation to the object of the legislation, so that all persons similarly circumstanced shall be treated alike." The words "fair and substantial" defining the relationship between the classification and the government's objective suggest that the Court would examine the fit between means and ends with considerable care. This did not happen, and today when the Court invokes the rational basis test it first asks whether the government's objective is constitutional. If it is, it then asks merely if there is some connection between that objective and the classification that divides people or things into categories for differential treatment. The Court does not concern itself with how tight a fit exists between the means and the end; the merits of the classification, or whether there ought to be any classification at all, are simply not considered. The right to treat people differently is simply assumed.

The words "fair and substantial" and the ideas they suggest have long ago been dropped from the formula. For example, in McGowan v. Maryland (1961), the Court stated that under this test the equal protection clause is "offended only if the classification rests on grounds wholly irrelevant to the achievement of the State's objective," and in Dandridge v. Williams (1970) the Court said that "a State does not violate the Equal Protection Clause merely because the classifications are imperfect. If the classification has some 'reasonable basis,' it does not offend the Constitution simply because the classification 'is not made with mathematical nicety or because in practice it results in some inequality.' " Thus, where the law undertakes to classify on a numerical basis, as with regard to money earned, hours worked, workers employed, etc., the choice by the legislature of a maximum or minimum number will not be considered arbitrary merely because those who are just over the line do not differ much from those who are not. To apply the original Social Security Act solely to those who employed eight or more persons was held not to discriminate invalidly despite the fact that those employing seven persons were not significantly different.

In addition, the Court has repeatedly held that in enacting remedial legislation the state is under no constitutional obligation to cure all evils merely because it undertakes to cure some of them. Thus a law forbidding the sale of obscene pictures is not invalid because it does not also apply to obscene phonograph records. As Justice Holmes expressed it in Keokee Consolidated Coke Co. v. Taylor (1914), "it is established by repeated decisions that a statute aimed at what is deemed an evil, and hitting it presumably where experience shows it to be most felt, is not to be upset by thinking up and enumerating other instances to which it might have been applied equally well, so far as the Court can see." (It should be noted that the requirement of a fair and substantial relationship between the classification and the objective has resurfaced as part of the new "intermediate" test—proof that it had long ceased to be part of the traditional test.)

The rational basis test assumes that the legislature had a valid, nondiscriminatory reason for passing the law and anyone challenging its validity bears the burden of proving the legislature's irrationality. This has proved to be an almost impossible burden to meet. Currently the rational basis test is most often used in challenges to laws regulating economic activities, but whenever it is invoked the result is almost certain to be a holding that the law is constitutional. In the past the rational basis test was used to uphold many laws that would be struck down today because a more demanding test would be used. This is particularly true of laws that discriminate on the basis of sex, such as the law at issue in the case below. See Mississippi v. Hogan (1983).

In Goesaert v. Cleary a Michigan law prohibited women from working as bartenders, with an exception for women who were married to, or the daughters of, men who owned bars. The law was challenged as unconstitutional under the Equal Protection Clause. Note the difference in the Court's justification of Michigan's right to prohibit all women to tend bar and its right to draw the distinction used here.

Mr. Justice **Frankfurter** delivered the opinion of the court:

. . . Beguiling as the subject is, it need not detain us long. To ask whether or not the Equal Protection of the Laws Clause of the Fourteenth Amendment barred Michigan from making the classification the State has made between wives and daughters of owners of liquor places and wives and daughters of non-owners, is one of those rare instances where to state the question is in effect to answer it.

We are, to be sure, dealing with a historic calling. We meet the ale-wife sprightly and ribald, in Shakespeare, but centuries before him she played a role in the social life of England. . . . The Fourteenth Amendment did not tear history up by the roots, and the regulation of the liquor traffic is one of the oldest and most untrammeled of legislative powers. Michigan could, beyond question, forbid all women from working behind a bar. This is so despite the vast changes in the social and legal position of women. The fact that women may now have achieved the virtues that men have long claimed as their prerogatives and now indulge in vices that men have long practiced, does not preclude the States from drawing a sharp line between the sexes, certainly in such matters as the regulation of the liquor traffic. . . . The Constitution does not require legislatures to reflect sociological insight, or shifting social standards, any more than it requires them to keep abreast of the latest scientific standards.

While Michigan may deny to all women opportunities for bartending, Michigan cannot play favorites among women without rhyme or reason. The Constitution in enjoining the equal protection of the laws upon States precludes irrational discrimination as between persons or groups of persons in the incidence of a law. But the Constitution does not require situations "which are different in fact or opinion to be treated in law as though they were the same." . . . Since bartending by women may, in the allowable legislative judgment, give rise to moral and social problems against which it may devise preventive measures, the legislature need not go to the full length of prohibition if it believes that as to a defined group of females other factors are operating which either eliminate or reduce the moral and social problems otherwise calling for prohibition. Michigan evidently believes that the oversight assured through ownership of a bar by a barmaid's husband or father minimizes hazards that may confront a barmaid without such protecting oversight. This Court is certainly not in a position to gainsay such a belief by the Michigan legislature. If it is entertainable, as we think it is, Michigan has not violated its duty to afford equal protection of its laws. We cannot cross-examine either actually or argumentatively the mind of Michigan legislators nor question their motives. Since the line they have drawn is not without a basis in reason, we cannot give ear to the suggestion that the real impulse behind this legislation was an unchivalrous desire of male bartenders to try to monopolize the calling. . . .

Nor is it unconstitutional for Michigan to withdraw from women the occupation of bartending because it allows women to serve as waitresses where liquor is dispensed. The District Court has sufficiently indicated the reasons that may have influenced the legislature in allowing women to be waitresses in a liquor establishment over which a man's ownership provides control. Nothing need be added to what was said below as to the other grounds on which the Michigan law was assailed.

Judgment affirmed.

Mr. Justice **Rutledge,** with whom Mr. Justice **Douglas** and Mr. Justice **Murphy** join, dissenting.

While the equal protection clause does not require a legislature to achieve "abstract symmetry" or to classify with "mathematical nicety," that clause does require lawmakers to refrain from invidious distinctions of the sort drawn by the statute challenged in this case.

The statute arbitrarily discriminates between male and female owners of liquor establishments. A male owner, although he himself is always absent from his bar, may employ his wife and daughter as barmaids. A female owner may neither work as a barmaid herself nor employ her daughter in that position, even if a man is always present in the establishment to keep order. This inevitable result of the classification belies the assumption that the statute was motivated by a legislative solicitude for the moral well-being of women who, but for the law, would be employed as barmaids. Since there could be no other conceivable justification for such discrimination against women owners of liquor establishments, the statute should be held invalid as a denial of equal protection.

STRICT SCRUTINY

KOREMATSU v. UNITED STATES

323 U. S. 214; 65 S. Ct. 193; 89 L. Ed. 194
(1944)

While the Fourteenth Amendment does not mention race, the Court has always recognized that racial discrimination against blacks was the primary concern of its framers and has therefore examined racial classifications with particular care. In 1880 in Strauder v. West Virginia the Court held that a black man had a right to be tried by a jury on which blacks had been eligible to sit. Laws that discriminate against other racial minorities were similarly treated. In Yick Wo v. Hopkins (1886) the Court struck down a San Francisco ordinance that prohibited anyone from operating a laundry in a wooden building without a permit issued by the Board of Supervisors. The Court found that the law as administered discriminated against Chinese applicants; non-Chinese applicants were routinely granted permits while almost all Chinese applications were denied.

As a greater variety of laws began to be challenged under the equal protection clause and the rational basis test began to take on its present form, it became clear that that test was an insufficient guard against racial discrimination. Allowing a state to discriminate on the basis of race any time it could show a rational relationship to a legitimate governmental purpose would provide too little protection for racial minorities. There was little question that states were being held to a higher standard when they attempted to treat people differently based on their race; decisions as early as Yick Wo in (1886) demonstrated that. The higher standard was, however, not spelled out until the decision in the present case in which the Court identifies race as a "suspect" classification for the first time. Justice

Black, writing for the majority, states that because it is a suspect classification it must be subjected to the "most rigid scrutiny." Herein lies the genesis of what is usually called the "strict scrutiny" test.

Unlike the rational basis test, the strict scrutiny test assumes that the law is unconstitutional when it includes a suspect classification. Those defending the law bear the burden of proving that the government's objectives are not only legitimate but are compelling. Even more difficult, the law's defenders must show that the suspect classification is necessary to accomplish the government's purpose—that it cannot be accomplished in any other way. The fit between the suspect classification and the compelling government objective must be nearly perfect.

The strict scrutiny test is used whenever a law employs a suspect classification. In addition to race, the prime examples of this are religion and national origin. A classification is more apt to be treated as suspect if its characteristics are immutable, so that a person born into it can never escape it. Generally, a suspect classification is also one that has been used historically to oppress a particular group, and one that discriminates against a "discrete and insular" minority—a phrase taken from Justice Stone's now famous footnote 4 in United States v. Carolene Products Co. (1938) in which he suggested that prejudice against such groups might tend "seriously to curtail the operation of those political processes ordinarily to be relied upon to protect minorities, and which may call for a correspondingly more searching judicial inquiry." See University of California v. Bakke (1978).

The rational basis test and the strict scrutiny test are functional opposites: Laws usually pass the rational basis test while they almost always fail the strict scrutiny test. It is therefore ironic that the strict scrutiny test was first articulated in one of the only cases to uphold the use of a racial classification.

The present case involved perhaps the most alarming use of executive military authority in our nation's history. Following the bombing of Pearl Harbor in December, 1941, the anti-Japanese sentiment on the West Coast brought the residents of that area to a state of near hysteria; and in February, 1942, President Roosevelt issued an executive order authorizing the creation of military areas from which any or all persons might be excluded as the military authorities might decide. On March 2, the entire West Coast to a depth of about forty miles was designated by the commanding general as Military Area No. 1, and he thereupon proclaimed a curfew in that area for all persons of Japanese ancestry. Later he ordered the compulsory evacuation from the area of all persons of Japanese ancestry, and by the middle of the summer most of these people had been moved inland to "war relocation centers," the American equivalent of concentration camps. Congress subsequently made it a crime to violate these military orders. Of the 112,000 persons of Japanese ancestry involved, about seventy thousand were native-born American citizens, none of whom had been specifically accused of disloyalty. Three cases were brought to the Supreme Court challenging the right of the government to override in this manner the customary civil rights of these citizens. In Hirabayashi v. United States (1943) the Court upheld the curfew regulations as a valid military measure to prevent espionage and sabotage. "Whatever views we may entertain regarding the loyalty to this country of the citizens of Japanese ancestry, we cannot reject as unfounded the judgment of the military authorities and of Congress that there were disloyal members of that population, whose number and strength could not be precisely and quickly ascertained. We cannot say that the war-making branches of the Government did not have ground for believing that in a critical hour such persons could not readily be isolated and separately dealt with, and constituted a menace to the national defense and safety. . . ." While emphasizing that distinctions based on ancestry were "by their very nature odious to a free people" the Court nonetheless felt "that in time of war residents having ethnic affiliations with an invading enemy may be a greater source of danger than those of a different ancestry."

While the Court, in the present case, held valid the discriminatory mass evacuation of all persons of Japanese descent, it also held in Ex parte Endo (1944), that an American citizen of Japanese ancestry whose loyalty to this country had been established could not constitutionally be held in a war relocation center but must be unconditionally released. The government had allowed persons to leave the relocation centers under conditions and restrictions which aimed to guarantee that there should not be "a dangerously disorderly migration of unwanted people to unprepared communities." Permission to leave was granted only if the applicant had the assurance of a job and a place to live, and wanted to go to a place "approved" by the War Relocation Authority. The Court held that the sole purpose of the evacuation and detention program was to protect the war effort against sabotage and espionage. "A person who is concededly loyal presents no problem of espionage or sabotage . . . He who is loyal is by definition not a spy or a saboteur." It therefore follows that the authority to detain a citizen of Japanese ancestry ends when loyalty is established. To hold otherwise would be to justify a person's detention not on grounds of military necessity but purely on grounds of race. Although no case reached the Court squarely challenging the right of the government to incarcerate citizens of Japanese ancestry pending a determination of their loyalty, the tenor of the opinions leaves little doubt that such action would have been sustained. The present case involved only the right of the military to evacuate such persons from the West Coast.

In the years following World War II evidence accumulated suggesting that the demand for the evacuation was either the result of racism, encouraged by the local press, or the result of the deliberate efforts of persons who stood to gain financially if the Japanese had to abandon their property on short notice. A congressional commission set up in 1980 reported after a two-year study that the only responsible intelligence report, made by Naval Intelligence, rejected outright the justifications *for incarceration advanced by the military. The existence of these reports was deliberately withheld by the Justice Department when it argued both Hirabayashi and Korematsu. See Hohri v. United States, 782 F. 2d 227 (1986). While Congress ultimately authorized a payment as restitution to each Japanese-American who was held in a relocation center, a number of damage suits were later filed. The government, while admitting in oral argument withholding evidence in the cases, argued that the statute of limitations against further suits should have started running with the decision in Korematsu. See United States v. Hohri (1987).*

An unusual tourist attraction is a bronze plaque, installed by the government of the state on the main entry gate of the Manzanar camp located in the desert near Bishop, California. The text is as follows:

* MANZANAR *

IN THE EARLY PART OF WORLD WAR II 110,000 PERSONS OF JAPANESE ANCESTRY WERE INTERNED IN RELOCATION CENTERS BY EXECUTIVE ORDER NO. 9066, ISSUED ON FEBRUARY 19, 1942.

MANZANAR, THE FIRST OF TEN SUCH CONCENTRATION CAMPS, WAS BOUNDED BY BARBED WIRE AND GUARD TOWERS, CONFINING 10,000 PERSONS, THE MAJORITY BEING AMERICAN CITIZENS.

MAY THE INJUSTICE AND HUMILIATION SUFFERED HERE AS A RESULT OF HYSTERIA, RACISM AND ECONOMIC EXPLOITATION NEVER EMERGE AGAIN.

CALIFORNIA REGISTERED HISTORICAL LANDMARK NO. 850

Mr. Justice **Black** delivered the opinion of the Court, saying in part:

The petitioner, an American citizen of Japanese descent, was convicted in a federal district court for remaining in San Leandro, California, a "Military Area," contrary to Civilian Exclusion Order No. 34 of the Commanding General of the Western Command, U. S. Army, which directed that after May 9, 1942, all persons of Japanese ancestry should be excluded from that area. No question was raised as to petitioner's loyalty to the United States. The Circuit Court of Appeals affirmed, and the importance of the constitutional question involved caused us to grant certiorari.

It should be noted, to begin with, that all legal restrictions which curtail the civil rights of a single racial group are immediately suspect. That is not to say that all such restrictions are unconstitutional. It is to say that courts must subject them to the most rigid scrutiny. Pressing public necessity may sometimes justify the existence of such restrictions; racial antagonism never can.

In the instant case prosecution of the petitioner was begun by information charging violation of an Act of Congress, of March 21, 1942, which provides that "... whoever shall enter, remain in, leave, or commit any act in any military area or military zone prescribed, under the authority of an Executive order of the President, by the Secretary of War, or by any military commander designated by the Secretary of War, contrary to the restrictions applicable to any such area or zone or contrary to the order of the Secretary of War or any such military commander, shall, if it appears that he knew or should have known of the existence and extent of the restrictions or order and that his act was in violation thereof, be guilty of a misdemeanor and upon conviction shall be liable to a fine of not to exceed $5,000 or to imprisonment for not more than one year, or both, for each offense."

Exclusion Order No. 34, which the petitioner knowingly and admittedly violated was one of a number of military orders and proclamations, all of which were substantially based upon Executive Order No. 9066. That order, issued after we were at war with Japan, declared that "the successful prosecution of the war requires every possible protection against espionage and against sabotage to national-defense material, national-defense premises, and national-defense utilities. ...."

One of the series of orders and proclamations, a curfew order, which like the exclusion order here was promulgated pursuant to Executive Order 9066, subjected all persons of Japanese ancestry in prescribed West Coast military areas to remain in their residences from 8 p.m. to 6 a.m. As is the case with the exclusion order here, that prior curfew order was designed as a "protection against espionage and against sabotage." In Kiyoshi Hirabayashi v. United States [1943], we sustained a conviction obtained for violation of the curfew order. The Hirabayashi conviction and this one thus rest on the same 1942 Congressional Act and the same basic executive and military orders, all of which orders were aimed at the twin dangers of espionage and sabotage.

The 1942 Act was attacked in the Hirabayashi case as an unconstitutional delegation of power; it was contended that the curfew order and other orders on which it rested were beyond the war powers of the Congress, the military authorities and of the President, as Commander in Chief of the Army; and finally that to apply the order against none but citizens of Japanese ancestry amounted to a constitutionally prohibited discrimination solely on account of race. To these questions, we gave the serious consideration which their importance justified. We upheld the curfew order as an exercise of the power of the government to take steps necessary to prevent espionage and sabotage in an area threatened by Japanese attack.

In the light of the principles we announced in the Hirabayashi case, we are unable to conclude that it was beyond the war power of Congress and the Executive to exclude those of Japanese ancestry from the West Coast war area at the time they did. True, exclusion from the area in which one's home is located is a far greater deprivation than constant confinement to the home from 8 p.m. to 6 a.m. Nothing short of apprehension by the proper military authorities of the gravest imminent danger to the public safety can constitutionally justify either.

But exclusion from a threatened area, no less than curfew, has a definite and close relationship to the prevention of espionage and sabotage. The military authorities, charged with the primary responsibility of defending our shores, concluded that curfew provided inadequate protection and ordered exclusion. They did so, as pointed out in our Hirabayashi opinion, in accordance with Congressional authority to the military to say who should, and who should not, remain in the threatened areas.

In this case the petitioner challenges the assumptions upon which we rested our conclusions in the Hirabayashi case. He also urges that by May 1942, when Order No. 34 was promulgated, all danger of Japanese invasion of the West Coast had disappeared. After careful consideration of these contentions we are compelled to reject them.

Here, as in the Hirabayashi case, ''. . . we cannot reject as unfounded the judgment of the military authorities and of Congress that there were disloyal members of that population, whose number and strength could not be precisely and quickly ascertained. We cannot say that the war-making branches of the Government did not have ground for believing that in a critical hour such persons could not readily be isolated and separately dealt with, and constituted a menace to the national defense and safety, which demanded that prompt and adequate measures be taken to guard against it.''

Like curfew, exclusion of those of Japanese origin was deemed necessary because of the presence of an unascertained number of disloyal members of the group, most of whom we have no doubt were loyal to this country. It was because we could not reject the finding of the military authorities that it was impossible to bring about an immediate segregation of the disloyal from the loyal that we sustained the validity of the curfew order as applying to the whole group. In the instant case, temporary exclusion of the entire group was rested by the military on the same ground. The judgment that exclusion of the whole group was for the same reason a military imperative answers the contention that the exclusion was in the nature of group punishment based on antagonism to those of Japanese origin. That there were members of the group who retained loyalties to Japan has been confirmed by investigations made subsequent to the exclusion. Approximately five thousand American citizens of Japanese ancestry refused to swear unqualified allegiance to the United States and to renounce allegiance to the Japanese Emperor, and several thousand evacuees requested repatriation to Japan.

We uphold the exclusion order as of the time it was made and when the petitioner violated it. . . . In doing so, we are not unmindful of the hardships imposed by it upon a large group of American citizens. . . . But hardships are part of war, and war is an aggregation of hardships. All citizens alike, both in and out of uniform, feel the impact of war in greater or lesser measure. Citizenship has its responsibilities as well as its privileges, and in time of war the burden is always heavier. Compulsory exclusion of large groups of citizens from their homes, except under circumstances of direst emergency and peril, is inconsistent with our basic governmental institution. But when under conditions of modern warfare our shores are threatened by hostile forces, the power to protect must be commensurate with the threatened danger. . . .

[The Court dealt at some length with a technical complication which arose in the case. On May 30, the date on which Korematsu was charged with remaining unlawfully in the prohibited area, there were two conflicting military orders outstanding, one forbidding him to remain in the area, the other forbidding him to leave but ordering him to report to an assembly center. Thus, he alleged, he was punished for doing what it was made a crime to fail to do. The Court held the orders not to be contradictory, since the requirement to report to the assembly center was merely a step in an orderly program of compulsory evacuation from the area.]

It is said that we are dealing here with the case of imprisonment of a citizen in a concentration camp solely because of his ancestry, without evidence or inquiry concerning his loyalty and good disposition towards the United States. Our task would be simple, our duty clear, were this a case involving the imprisonment of a loyal citizen in a concentration camp because of racial prejudice. Regardless of the true nature of the assembly and relocation centers—and we deem it unjustifiable to call them concentration camps with all the ugly connotations that term implies—we are dealing specifically with nothing but an exclusion order. To cast this case into outlines of racial prejudice, without reference to the real military dangers which were presented, merely confuses the issue. Korematsu was not excluded from the Military Area because of hostility to him or his race. He was excluded because we are at war with the Japanese Empire, because the properly constituted military authorities feared an invasion of our West Coast and felt constrained to take proper security measures, because they decided that the military urgency of the situation demanded that all citizens of Japanese ancestry be segregated from the West Coast temporarily, and finally, because Congress, reposing its confidence in this time of war in our military leaders—as inevitably it must—determined that they should have the power to do just this. There was evidence of disloyalty on the part of some, the military authorities considered that the need for action was great, and time was short. We cannot—by availing ourselves of the calm perspective of hindsight—now say that at that time these actions were unjustified.

Affirmed.

Mr. Justice **Frankfurter** wrote a concurring opinion.

Mr. Justice **Roberts,** dissenting, said in part:

I dissent, because I think the indisputable facts exhibit a clear violation of Constitutional rights.

This is not a case of keeping people off the streets at night as was Hirabayashi v. United States (1943), nor a case of temporary exclusion of a citizen from an area for his own safety or that of the community, nor a case of offering him an opportunity to go temporarily out of an area where his presence might cause danger to himself or to his fellows. On the contrary, it is the case of convicting a citizen as a punishment for not submitting to imprisonment in a concentration camp, based on his ancestry, and solely because of his ancestry, without evidence or inquiry concerning his loyalty and good disposition towards the United States. If this be a correct statement of the facts disclosed by this record, and facts of which we take judicial notice, I need hardly labor the conclusion that constitutional rights have been violated.

Mr. Justice **Murphy,** dissenting, said in part:

This exclusion of "all persons of Japanese ancestry, both alien and non-alien," from the Pacific Coast area on a plea of military necessity in the absence of martial law ought not to be approved. Such exclusion goes over "the very brink of constitutional power" and falls into the ugly abyss of racism.

In dealing with matters relating to the prosecution and progress of a war, we must accord great respect and consideration to the judgments of the military authorities who are on the scene and who have full knowledge of the military facts. The scope of their discretion must, as a matter of necessity and common sense, be wide. And their judgments ought not to be overruled lightly by those whose training and duties ill-equip them to deal intelligently with matters so vital to the physical security of the nation.

At the same time, however, it is essential that there be definite limits to military discretion especially where martial law has not been declared. Individuals must not be left impoverished of their constitutional rights on a plea of military necessity that has neither substance nor support. Thus, like other claims conflicting with the asserted constitutional rights of the individual, the military claim must subject itself to the judicial process of having its reasonableness determined and its conflicts with other interests reconciled. . . .

. . . Being an obvious racial discrimination, the order deprives all those within its scope of the equal protection of the laws as guaranteed by the Fifth Amendment. It further deprives these individuals of their constitutional rights to live and work where they will, to establish a home where they choose and to move about freely. In excommunicating them without benefit of hearings, this order also deprives them of all their constitutional rights to procedural due process. Yet no reasonable relation to an "immediate, imminent, and impending" public danger is evident to support this racial restriction which is one of the most sweeping and complete deprivations of constitutional rights in the history of this nation in the absence of martial law.

It must be conceded that the military and naval situation in the spring of 1942 was such as to generate a very real fear of invasion of the Pacific Coast, accompanied by fears of sabotage and espionage in that area. The military command was therefore justified in adopting all reasonable means necessary to combat these dangers. In adjudging the military action taken in light of the then apparent dangers, we must not erect too high or too meticulous standards; it is necessary only that the action have some reasonable relation to the removal of the dangers of invasion, sabotage and espionage. But the exclusion, either temporarily or permanently, of all persons with Japanese blood in their veins has no such reasonable relation. And that relation is lacking because the exclusion order necessarily must rely for its reasonableness upon the assumption that *all* persons of Japanese ancestry may have a dangerous tendency to commit sabotage and espionage and to aid our Japanese enemy in other ways. It is difficult to believe that reason, logic or experience could be marshalled in support of such an assumption.

That this forced exclusion was the result in good measure of this erroneous assumption of racial guilt rather than bona fide military necessity is evidenced by the Commanding General's Final Report on the evacuation from the Pacific Coast area. In it he refers to all individuals of Japanese descent as "subversive," as belonging to "an enemy race" whose "racial strains are undiluted," and as constituting "over 112,000 potential enemies . . . at large today" along the Pacific Coast. In support of this blanket condemnation of all persons of Japanese descent, however, no reliable evidence is cited to show that such individuals were generally disloyal, or had generally so conducted themselves in this area as to constitute a special menace to defense installations or war industries, or had otherwise by their behavior furnished reasonable ground for their exclusion as a group.

Justification for the exclusion is sought, instead, mainly upon questionable racial and sociological grounds not ordinarily within the realm of expert military judgment. . . . [Justice Murphy here reviews and refutes the sociological evidence.]

The main reasons relied upon by those responsible for the forced evacuation, therefore, do not prove a reasonable relation between the group characteristics of Japanese Americans and the dangers of invasion, sabotage and espionage. The reasons appear, instead, to be largely an accumulation of much of the misinformation, half-truths and insinuations that for years have been directed against Japanese Americans by people with racial and economic prejudices—the same people who have been among the foremost advocates of the evacuation. A military judgment based upon such racial and sociological considerations is not entitled to the great weight ordinarily given the judgments based upon strictly military considerations. Especially is this so when every charge relative to race, religion, culture, geographical location, and legal and economic status has been substantially discredited by independent studies made by experts in these matters.

The military necessity which is essential to the validity of the evacuation order thus resolves itself into a few intimations that certain individuals actively aided the enemy, from which it is inferred that the entire group of Japanese Americans could not be trusted to be or remain loyal to the United States. No one denies, of course, that there were some disloyal persons of Japanese descent on the Pacific Coast who did all in their power to aid their ancestral land. Similar disloyal activities have been engaged in by many persons of German, Italian and even more pioneer stock in our country. But to infer that examples of individual disloyalty prove group disloyalty and justify discriminatory action against the entire group is to deny that under our system of law individual guilt is the sole basis for deprivation of rights. Moreover, this inference, which is at the very heart of the evacuation orders, has been used in support of the abhorrent and despicable treatment of minority groups by the dictatorial tyrannies which this nation is now pledged to destroy. To give constitutional sanction to that inference in this case, however well-intentioned may have been the military command on the Pacific Coast, is to adopt one of the cruelest of the rationales used by our enemies to destroy the dignity of the individual and to encourage and open the door to discriminatory actions against other minority groups in the passions of tomorrow.

No adequate reason is given for the failure to treat these Japanese Americans on an individual basis by holding investigations and hearings to separate the loyal from the disloyal, as was done in the case of persons of German and Italian ancestry. . . . It is asserted merely that the loyalties of this group ''were unknown and time was of the essence.'' Yet nearly four months elapsed after Pearl Harbor before the first exclusion order was issued; nearly eight months went by until the last order was issued; and the last of these ''subversive'' persons was not actually removed until almost eleven months had elapsed. Leisure and deliberation seem to have been more of the essence than speed. And the fact that conditions were not such as to warrant a declaration of martial law adds strength to the belief that the factors of time and military necessity were not as urgent as they have been represented to be.

Mr. Justice **Jackson**, dissenting, said in part:

It would be impracticable and dangerous idealism to expect or insist that each specific military command in an area of probable operations will conform to conventional tests of constitutionality. When an area is so beset that it must be put under military control at all, the paramount consideration is that its measures be successful, rather than legal. The armed services must protect a society, not merely its Constitution. . . .

But if we cannot confine military expedients by the Constitution, neither would I distort the Constitution to approve all that the military may deem expedient. That is what the Court appears to be doing, whether consciously or not. I cannot say, from any evidence before me, that the orders of General DeWitt were not reasonably expedient military precautions, nor could I say that they were. But even if they were permissible military procedures, I deny that it follows that they are constitutional. If, as the Court holds, it does follow, then we may

as well say that any military order will be constitutional and have done with it. . . .

Much is said of the danger to liberty from the Army program for deporting and detaining these citizens of Japanese extraction. But a judicial construction of the due process clause that will sustain this order is a far more subtle blow to liberty than the promulgation of the order itself. A military order, however unconstitutional, is not apt to last longer than the military emergency. Even during that period a succeeding commander may revoke it all. But once a judicial opinion rationalizes such an order to show that it conforms to the Constitution, or rather rationalizes the Constitution to show that the Constitution sanctions such an order, the Court for all time has validated the principle of racial discrimination in criminal procedure and of transplanting American citizens. The principle then lies about like a loaded weapon ready for the hand of any authority that can bring forward a plausible claim of an urgent need. . . .

My duties as a justice as I see them do not require me to make a military judgment as to whether General DeWitt's evacuation and detention program was a reasonable military necessity. I do not suggest that the courts should have attempted to interfere with the Army in carrying out its task. But I do not think they may be asked to execute a military expedient that has no place in law under the Constitution. I would reverse the judgment and discharge the prisoner.

KRAMER v. UNION FREE SCHOOL DIST.

393 U. S. 818; 89 S. Ct. 1886; 23 L. Ed. 2d 583 (1969)

The strict scrutiny test developed in Korematsu to deal with suspect classification has been applied to another category of cases brought under the equal protection clause. This second category includes cases challenging laws that affect ''fundamental rights or interests.'' There are at least two different concepts underlying the fundamental interest branch of strict scrutiny. The first involves rights, such as the right to appeal a conviction, that are so basic that even though there is no absolute right to them, once a state chooses to grant them it must allocate them equally—unless the state can show a compelling state interest for doing otherwise. Administrative convenience or added expense to the state do not rank as ''compelling'' in this context.

The second concept is that there are some fundamental rights implicit in the Constitution, such as the right to travel interstate, the exercise of which cannot be made the basis of differential treatment without a compelling governmental interest that cannot be satisfied in some other way. While this latter concept has been attacked on the ground that it should not require an equal protection clause to protect a right already guaranteed in the Constitution, it is apparent that equal protection does serve to prevent actions which may discourage the exercise of a such a right but which do not rise to the level of a violation of the right itself. Thus, while it is clear a state could not directly forbid a person to travel interstate, only the equal protection clause might prevent laws against limiting access to welfare benefits or jobs which would have a discouraging effect on such travel. Criticism of the use of the strict scrutiny test in this area as judicial law-making has perhaps been influential in keeping the list a short one: voting, access to the judicial process and interstate travel.

Some of the criticism of the fundamental interest branch of the strict scrutiny test may be due to the nature of the test itself. Whether it is applied to suspect classifications or fundamental interests, the strict scrutiny test is an exception to the rule of constitutional interpretation that presumes that laws and acts of government are constitutional, and in this sense the rational basis test reflects the Court's traditional approach. From earliest times the Court has regularly expressed the greatest respect for the constitutional interpretations necessarily made by Congress in the passing of legislation. While making clear that it is "the duty of the Court to say what the law is," it recognizes Congress as a coequal branch whose members "take the same oath as we do to uphold the Constitution." While the Court is probably right in attributing considered wisdom to a coequal branch, it is enlightening to consider that in 1981 Senator Moynihan of New York felt called upon to introduce a resolution prohibiting the Senate from voting on any bill unless a specified number of Senators could attest to the fact that they had read it.

The difference between the strict scrutiny test and the rational basis test is no more strikingly illustrated than by contrasting the Kramer case, printed below, with McDonald v. Board of Election (1969). McDonald was an inmate of the Cook County jail who was being held for trial without bail on a charge of murder. At election time he made timely request for an absentee ballot, backed by an affidavit from the warden that he was unable to attend the polls. Such ballots were available to those who were medically incapacitated, absent from the county, attending a religious holiday that precluded their voting, or who were serving as poll watchers in a precinct other than their own. Since McDonald did not fit any of these categories, the absentee ballot was refused.

McDonald argued that, since voting rights were involved, the burden lay on the state to produce a "compelling state interest" to justify its denial of the ballot. The Supreme Court rejected his argument. "Such an exacting approach is not necessary here, however, for two readily apparent reasons. First, the distinctions made by Illinois' absentee provisions are not drawn on the basis of wealth or race [classifications which are highly suspect]. Secondly, there is nothing in the record to indicate that the Illinois statutory scheme has an impact on appellants' ability to exercise the fundamental right to vote. It is thus not the right to vote that is at stake here but a claimed right to receive absentee ballots. Despite appellants' claim to the contrary, the absentee statutes, which are designed to make voting more available to some groups who cannot easily get to the polls, do not themselves deny appellants the exercise of the franchise; nor, indeed, does Illinois' Election Code so operate as a whole, for the State's statutes specifically disenfranchise only those who have been convicted and sentenced, and not those similarly situated to appellants. Faced as we are with a constitutional question, we cannot lightly assume, with nothing in the record to support such an assumption, that Illinois has in fact precluded appellants from voting. We are then left with the more traditional standards for evaluating appellant's equal protection claims." Under these traditional standards the Court found that Illinois' absentee ballot law was among the most liberal, and the state was not required to solve all problems because it had attempted to solve some of them, so long as the distinctions were not arbitrary—which these were not.

Mr. Chief Justice **Warren** delivered the opinion of the Court, saying in part:

In this case we are called on to determine whether § 2012 of the New York Education Law is constitutional. The legislation provides that in certain New York school districts residents who are otherwise eligible to vote in state and federal elections may vote in the school district election only if they (1) own (or lease) taxable real property within the district, or (2) are parents (or have custody of) children enrolled in the local public schools. Appellant, a bachelor who neither owns nor leases taxable real property, filed suit in federal court claiming that § 2012 denied him equal protection of the law in violation of the Fourteenth Amendment. With one judge dissenting, a three-judge District Court dismissed appellant's complaint. Finding that § 2012 does violate the Equal Protection Clause of the Fourteenth Amendment, we reverse.

I.

New York law provides basically three methods of school board selection. In some large city districts, the school board is appointed by the mayor or city council. ... On the other hand, in some cities, primarily those with less than 125,000 residents, the school board is elected at general or municipal elections in which all qualified city voters may participate. ... Finally, in other districts such as the one involved in this case, which are primarily rural and suburban, the school board is elected at an annual meeting of qualified school district voters.

The challenged statute is applicable only in districts which hold annual meetings. To be eligible to vote at an annual district meeting, an otherwise qualified district resident must either (1) be the owner or lessee of taxable real property located in the district, (2) be the spouse of one who owns or leases qualifying property, or (3) be the parent or guardian of a child enrolled for a specified time during the preceding year in a local district school.

Although the New York State Department of Education has substantial responsibility for education in the State, the local school districts maintain significant control over the administration of local school district affairs. Generally, the board of education has the basic responsibility for local school operation, including prescribing the courses of study, determining the textbooks to be used, and even altering and equipping a former schoolhouse for use as a public library. . . . Additionally, in districts selecting members of the board of education at annual meetings, the local voters also pass directly on other district matters. For example, they must approve the school budget submitted by the school board. . . . Moreover, once the budget is approved, the governing body of the villages within the school district must raise the money which has been declared "necessary for teachers' salaries and the ordinary contingent expenses [of the schools]." . . . The voters also may "authorize such acts and vote such taxes as they shall deem expedient . . . for . . . equipping for library use any former schoolhouse, . . . [and] for the purchase of land and buildings for agricultural, athletic, playground or social center purposes . . . ."

Appellant is a 31-year-old college-educated stockbroker who lives in his parents' home in the Union Free School District No. 15, a district to which § 2012 applies. He is a citizen of the United States and has voted in federal and state elections since 1959. However, since he has no children and neither owns nor leases taxable real property, appellant's attempts to register for and vote in the local school district elections have been unsuccessful. After the school district rejected his 1965 application, appellant instituted the present class action challenging the constitutionality of the voter eligibility requirements.

II.

At the outset, it is important to note what is *not* at issue in this case. The requirements of § 2012 that school district voters must (1) be citizens of the United States, (2) be bona fide residents of the school district, and (3) be at least 21 years of age are not challenged. Appellant agrees that the States have the power to impose reasonable citizenship, age and residency requirements on the availability of the ballot. . . . The sole issue in this case is whether the *additional* requirements of § 2012—requirements which prohibit some district residents who are otherwise qualified by age and citizenship from participating in district meetings and school board elections—violate the Fourteenth Amendment's command that no State shall deny persons equal protection of the laws.

"In determining whether or not a state law violates the Equal Protection Clause, we must consider the facts and circumstances of the law, the interests which the State claims to be protecting, and the interests of those who are disadvantaged by the classification." Williams

v. Rhodes (1968). And, in this case, we must give the statute a close and exacting examination. "[S]ince the right to exercise the franchise in a free and unimpaired manner is preservative of other basic civil and political rights, any alleged infringement of the right of citizens to vote must be carefully and meticulously scrutinized." Reynolds v. Sims (1964). . . . This careful examination is necessary because statutes distributing the franchise constitute the foundation of our representative society. Any unjustified discrimination in determining who may participate in political affairs or in the selection of public officials undermines the legitimacy of representative government.

Thus, state apportionment statutes, which may *dilute* the effectiveness of some citizens' votes, receive close scrutiny from this Court. Reynolds v. Sims. . . . No less rigid an examination is applicable to statutes *denying* the franchise to citizens who are otherwise qualified by residence and age.* Statutes granting the franchise to residents on a selective basis always pose the danger of denying some citizens any effective voice in the governmental affairs which substantially affect their lives. Therefore, if a challenged state statute grants the right to vote to some bona fide residents of requisite age and citizenship and denies the franchise to others, the Court must determine whether the exclusions are necessary to promote a compelling state interest. . . .

And, for these reasons, the deference usually given to the judgment of legislators does not extend to decisions concerning which resident citizens may participate in the election of legislators and other public officials. Those decisions must be carefully scrutinized by the Court to determine whether each resident citizen has, as far as is possible, an equal voice in the selections. Accordingly, when we are reviewing statutes which deny some residents the right to vote, the general presumption of constitutionality afforded state statutes and the traditional approval given state classifications if the Court can conceive of a "rational basis" for the distinctions made are not applicable. . . . The presumption of constitutionality and the approval given "rational" classifications in other types of enactments† are based on an assumption that the institutions of state government are structured so as to represent fairly all the people. However, when the challenge to the statute is in effect a challenge of this basic assumption, the assumption can no longer serve as the basis for presuming constitutionality. And, the assumption is no less under attack because the

---

*This case presents an issue different from the one we faced in McDonald v. Board of Election Comm'rs of Chicago (1969). The present appeal involves an absolute denial of the franchise. In McDonald, on the other hand, we were reviewing a statute which made casting a ballot easier for some who were unable to come to the polls. As we noted, there was no evidence that the statute absolutely prohibited anyone from exercising the franchise; at issue was not a claimed right to vote but a claimed right to an absentee ballot.

†Of course, we have long held that if the basis of classification is inherently suspect, such as race, the statute must be subjected to an exacting scrutiny, regardless of the subject matter of the legislation. . . .

legislature which decides who may participate at the various levels of political choice is fairly elected. Legislation which delegates decision-making to bodies elected by only a portion of those eligible to vote for the legislature can cause unfair representation. Such legislation can exclude a minority of voters from any voice in the decisions just as effectively as if the decisions were made by legislators the minority had no voice in selecting.

The need for exacting judicial scrutiny of statutes distributing the franchise is undiminished simply because, under a different statutory scheme, the offices subject to election might have been filled through appointment. States do have latitude in determining whether certain public officials shall be selected by election or chosen by appointment and whether various questions shall be submitted to the voters. In fact, we have held that where a county school board is an administrative, not legislative, body, its members need not be elected. Sailors v. Kent Bd. of Education (1967). However, "once the franchise is granted to the electorate, lines may not be drawn which are inconsistent with the Equal Protection Clause of the Fourteenth Amendment." Harper v. Virginia Bd. of Elections [1966].

Nor is the need for close judicial examination affected because the district meetings and the school board do not have "general" legislative powers. Our exacting examination is necessitated not by the subject of the election; rather, it is required because some resident citizens are permitted to participate and some are not. For example, a city charter might well provide that the elected city council appoint a mayor who would have broad administrative powers. Assuming the council were elected consistent with the commands of the Equal Protection Clause, the delegation of power to the mayor would not call for this Court's exacting review. On the other hand, if the city charter made the office of mayor subject to an election in which only some resident citizens were entitled to vote, there would be presented a situation calling for our close review.

III.

Besides appellant and others who similarly live in their parents' homes, the statute also disenfranchises the following persons (unless they are parents or guardians of children enrolled in the district public school): senior citizens and others living with children or relatives; clergy, military personnel and others who live on tax-exempt property; boarders and lodgers; parents who neither own nor lease qualifying property and whose children are too young to attend school; parents who neither own nor lease qualifying property and whose children attend private schools.

Appellant asserts that excluding him from participation in the district elections denies him equal protection of the law. He contends that he and others of his class are substantially interested in and significantly af-

fected by the school meeting decisions. All members of the community have an interest in the quality and structure of public education, appellant says, and he urges that "the decisions taken by local boards . . . may have grave consequences to the entire population." Appellant also argues that the level of property taxation affects him, even though he does not own property, as property tax levels affect the price of goods and services in the community.

We turn therefore to question whether the exclusion is necessary to promote a compelling state interest. First, appellees argue that the State has a legitimate interest in limiting the franchise in school district elections to "members of the community of interest"—those "primarily interested in such elections." Second, appellees urge that the State may reasonably and permissibly conclude that "property taxpayers" (including lessees of taxable property who share the tax burden through rent payments) and parents of the children enrolled in the district's schools are those "primarily interested" in school affairs.

We do not understand appellees to argue that the State is attempting to limit the franchise to those "subjectively concerned" about school matters. Rather, they appear to argue that the State's legitimate interest is in restricting a voice in school matters to those "directly affected" by such decisions. The State apparently reasons that since the schools are financed in part by local property taxes, persons whose out-of-pocket expenses are "directly" affected by property tax changes should be allowed to vote. Similarly, parents of children in school are thought to have a "direct" stake in school affairs and are given a vote.

Appellees argue that it is necessary to limit the franchise to those "primarily interested" in school affairs because "the very increasing complexity of the many interacting phases of the school system and structure make it extremely difficult for the electorate fully to understand the whys and wherefores of the detailed operations of the school system." Appellees say that many communications of school boards and school administrations are sent home to the parents through the district pupils and are "not broadcast to the general public"; thus, nonparents will be less informed than parents. Further, appellees argue, those who are assessed for local property taxes (either directly or indirectly through rent) will have enough of an interest "through the burden on their pocket books to acquire such information as they may need."

We need express no opinion as to whether the State in some circumstances might limit the exercise of the franchise to those "primarily interested" or "primarily affected." Of course, we therefore do not reach the issue of whether these particular elections are of the type in which the franchise may be so limited. For, assuming arguendo that New York legitimately might limit the franchise in these school district elections to those "primarily interested in school affairs," close scrutiny of the § 2012 classifications demonstrates that they do not accomplish this purpose with sufficient precision to justify denying appellant the franchise.

Whether classifications allegedly limiting the franchise to those resident citizens "primarily interested" deny those excluded equal protection of the law depends, inter alia, on whether all those excluded are in fact substantially less interested or affected than those the statute includes. In other words, the classifications must be tailored so that the exclusion of appellant and members of his class is necessary to achieve the articulated state goal.* Section 2012 does not meet the exacting standard of precision we require of statutes which selectively distribute the franchise. The classifications in § 2012 permit inclusion of many persons who have, at best, a remote and indirect interest in school affairs and on the other hand, exclude others who have a distinct and direct interest in the school meeting decisions.†

Nor do appellees offer any justification for the exclusion of seemingly interested and informed residents—other than to argue that the § 2012 classifications include those "whom the State could understandably deem to be the most intimately interested in actions taken by the school board," and urge that "the task of . . . balancing the interest of the community in the maintenance of orderly school district elections against the interest of any individual in voting in such elections should clearly remain with the legislature." But the issue is not whether the legislative judgments are rational. A more exacting standard obtains. The issue is whether the § 2012 requirements do in fact sufficiently further a compelling state interest to justify denying the franchise to appellant and members of his class. The requirements of § 2012 are not sufficiently tailored to limiting the franchise to those "primarily interested" in school affairs to justify the denial of the franchise to appellant and members of his class.

The judgment of the United States District Court for the Eastern District of New York is therefore reversed. The case is remanded for further proceedings consistent with this opinion.

It is so ordered.

Mr. Justice **Stewart,** with whom Mr. Justice **Black** and Mr. Justice **Harlan** join, dissenting, said in part:

In Lassiter v. Northampton Election Bd. [1959], this Court upheld against constitutional attack a literacy requirement, applicable to voters in all state and federal elections, imposed by the State of North Carolina. Writing for a unanimous Court, Mr. Justice Douglas said:

"The States have long been held to have broad powers to determine the conditions under which the right of suffrage may be exercised, . . . absent of course the discrimination which the Constitution condemns." Believing that the appellant in this case is not the victim of any "discrimination which the Constitution condemns," I would affirm the judgment of the District Court. . . .

Although at times variously phrased, the traditional test of a statute's validity under the equal protection clause is a familiar one: a legislative classification is invalid only "if it rest[s] on grounds wholly irrelevant to achievement of the regulation's objectives." Kotch v. Board of River Port Pilot Comm'rs [1947]. It was under just such a test that the literacy requirement involved in Lassiter was upheld. The premise of our decision in that case was that a State may constitutionally impose upon its citizens voting requirements reasonably "designed to promote intelligent use of the ballot." A similar premise underlies the proposition, consistently endorsed by this Court, that a State may exclude nonresidents from participation in its elections. Such residence requirements, designed to help ensure that voters have a substantial stake in the outcome of elections and an opportunity to become familiar with the candidates and issues voted upon, are entirely permissible exercises of state authority. Indeed, the appellant explicitly concedes, as he must, the validity of voting requirements relating to residence, literacy, and age. Yet he argues—and the Court accepts the argument—that the voting qualifications involved here somehow have a different constitutional status. I am unable to see the distinction.

Clearly a State may reasonably assume that its residents have a greater stake in the outcome of elections held within its boundaries than do other persons. Likewise, it is entirely rational for a state legislature to suppose that residents, being generally better informed regarding state affairs than are nonresidents, will be more likely than nonresidents to vote responsibly. And the same may be said of legislative assumptions regarding the electoral competence of adults and literate persons on the one hand, and of minors and illiterates on the other. It is clear, of course, that lines thus drawn cannot infallibly perform their intended legislative function. Just as "[i]lliterate people may be intelligent voters," nonresidents or minors might also in some instances be interested, informed, and intelligent participants in the electoral process. Persons who commute across a state line to work may well have a great stake in the affairs of the State in which they are employed; some college students under 21 may be both better informed and more passionately interested in political affairs than many adults. But such discrepancies are the inevitable concomitant of the line-drawing that is essential to lawmaking. So long as the classification is rationally related to a permissible legislative end, therefore—as are residence, literacy, and age requirements imposed with respect to voting—there is no denial of equal protection.

---

*Of course, if the exclusions are necessary to promote the articulated state interest, we must then determine whether the interest promoted by limiting the franchise constitutes a compelling state interest. We do not reach that issue in this case.

†For example, appellant resides with his parents in the school district, pays state and federal taxes and is interested in and affected by school board decisions; however, he has no vote. On the other hand, an uninterested unemployed young man who pays no state or federal taxes, but who rents an apartment in the district, can participate in the election.

Thus judged, the statutory classification involved here seems to me clearly to be valid. New York has made the judgment that local educational policy is best left to those persons who have certain direct and definable interests in that policy: those who are either immediately involved as parents of school children or who, as owners or lessees of taxable property, are burdened with the local cost of funding school district operations. True, persons outside those classes may be genuinely interested in the conduct of a school district's business—just as commuters from New Jersey may be genuinely interested in the outcome of a New York City election. But unless this Court is to claim a monopoly of wisdom regarding the sound operation of school systems in the 50 States, I see no way to justify the conclusion that the legislative classification involved here is not rationally related to a legitimate legislative purpose. "There is no group more interested in the operation and management of the public schools than the taxpayers who support them and the parents whose children attend them." Doremus v. Board of Educ. [1952] (Douglas, J., dissenting).

With good reason, the Court does not really argue the contrary. Instead, it strikes down New York's statute by asserting that the traditional equal protection standard is inapt in this case, and that a considerably stricter standard—under which classifications relating to "the franchise" are to be subjected to "exacting judicial scrutiny"—should be applied. But the asserted justification for applying such a standard cannot withstand analysis.

The Court is quite explicit in explaining why it believes this statute should be given "close scrutiny":

"The presumption of constitutionality and the approval given 'rational' classifications in other types of enactments are based on an assumption that the institutions of state government are structured so as to represent fairly all the people. However, when the challenge to the statute is in effect a challenge of this basic assumption, the assumption can no longer serve as the basis for presuming constitutionality." (Footnote omitted.)

I am at a loss to understand how such reasoning is at all relevant to the present case. The voting qualifications at issue have been promulgated not by Union Free School District No. 15, but by the New York State Legislature, and the appellant is of course fully able to participate in the election of representatives in that body. There is simply no claim whatever here that the state government is not "structured so as to represent fairly all the people," including the appellant.

Nor is there any other justification for imposing the Court's "exacting" equal protection test. This case does not involve racial classifications, which in light of the genesis of the Fourteenth Amendment have traditionally been viewed as inherently "suspect." And this statute is not one that impinges upon a constitutionally protected right, and that consequently can be justified only by a "compelling" state interest. For "the Constitution of the United States does not confer the right of suffrage upon any one. . . ." Minor v. Happersett [1875]. . . .

INTERMEDIATE TEST

SAN ANTONIO v. RODRIGUEZ

411 U. S. 1; 93 S. Ct. 1278; 36 L. Ed. 2d 16
(1973)

With two tests for judging cases brought under the equal protection clause, the Court entered the 1970s and found itself facing an increasing number of equal protection claims. The proliferation of government benefits, collectively referred to as the "welfare state" and the growing awareness of the disadvantages of the poor and of women generated new and complex equality questions for which the two tests seemed scarcely adequate. Nevertheless, as the Court took up each of these new questions it recited the formula for one of its two tests and proceeded to decide accordingly. It ultimately became apparent even to the Court, however, that the two-tiered approach was straining at the seams. The case below is an example. It raises the question of whether the equal protection clause requires the state to equalize the amounts spent on education throughout the districts of the state. The importance of the question to public education would be difficult to overestimate.

The city of San Antonio, Texas, finances its schools with a combination of state aid and local property taxes, the latter being divided between an amount which a district is required to raise and which is roughly proportional to its taxing power, and an additional amount which it may raise if it wishes to do so. Two districts are contrasted in this litigation. The first, the Edgewood Independent School District, which is 96 percent Mexican-American and black, with an average property value of $5,960 (the lowest in the metropolitan area) and a tax rate of $1.05 per $100 (the highest in the metropolitan area), contributed $26 per pupil above its legal requirements. In contrast, Alamo Heights District is 81 percent white and has about 5,000 pupils. Its assessed property value is $49,000 per pupil, and with a local tax rate of $.85 per $100 it raised $333 per pupil above the required minimum. In the 1970-1971 school year the state made marked increases in the state aid given to the poorer schools.

Mr. Justice **Powell** delivered the opinion of the Court, saying in part:

Despite these recent increases, substantial interdistrict disparities in school expenditures found by the District Court to prevail in San Antonio and in varying degrees throughout the State still exist. And it was these disparities, largely attributable to differences in the amounts of money collected through local property taxation, that led the District Court to conclude that Texas' dual system of public school finance violated the Equal Protection Clause. The District Court held that the Texas system discriminates on the basis of wealth in the manner in which education is provided for its people. Finding that wealth is a "suspect" classification and that education is a "fundamental" interest, the District Court held that the Texas system could be sustained only if the State could show that it was premised upon some compelling state interest. On this issue the court concluded that "[n]ot only are defendants unable to demonstrate compelling state interests . . . they fail even to establish a reasonable basis for these classifications."

This, then, establishes the framework for our analysis. We must decide, first, whether the Texas system of financing public education operates to the disadvantage of some suspect class or impinges upon a fundamental right explicitly or implicitly protected by the Constitution, thereby requiring strict judicial scrutiny. If so, the judgment of the District Court should be affirmed. If not, the Texas scheme must still be examined to determine whether it rationally furthers some legitimate, articulated state purpose and therefore does not constitute an invidious discrimination in violation of the Equal Protection Clause of the Fourteenth Amendment.

II. . . .

A.

The wealth discrimination discovered by the District Court in this case, and by several other courts that have recently struck down school financing laws in other States, is quite unlike any of the forms of wealth discrimination heretofore reviewed by this Court. Rather than focusing on the unique features of the alleged discrimination, the courts in these cases have virtually assumed their findings of a suspect classification through a simplistic process of analysis: since, under the traditional systems of financing public schools, some poorer people receive less expensive educations than other more affluent people, these systems discriminate on the basis of wealth. This approach largely ignores the hard threshold questions, including whether it makes a difference for purposes of consideration under the Constitution that the class of disadvantaged "poor" cannot be identified or defined in customary equal protection terms, and whether the relative—rather than absolute—nature of the asserted deprivation is of significant consequence. Before a State's laws and the justifications for the classifications they create are subjected to strict judicial scrutiny, we think these threshold considerations must be analyzed more closely than they were in the court below.

The case comes to us with no definitive description of the classifying facts or delineation of the disfavored class. Examination of the District Court's opinion and of appellees' complaint, briefs, and contentions at oral argument suggests, however, at least three ways in which the discrimination claimed here might be described. The Texas system of school finance might be regarded as discriminating (1) against "poor" persons whose incomes fall below some identifiable level of poverty or who might be characterized as functionally "indigent," or (2) against those who are relatively poorer than others, or (3) against all those who, irrespective of their personal incomes, happen to reside in relatively poorer school districts. Our task must be to ascertain whether, in fact, the Texas system has been shown to discriminate on any of these possible bases and, if so, whether the resulting classification may be regarded as suspect.

The precedents of this Court provide the proper starting point. The individuals or groups of individuals who constituted the class discriminated against in our prior cases shared two distinguishing characteristics: because of their impecunity they were completely unable to pay for some desired benefit, and as a consequence, they sustained an absolute deprivation of a meaningful opportunity to enjoy that benefit. In Griffin v. Illinois (1956) and its progeny, the Court invalidated state laws that prevented an indigent criminal defendant from acquiring a transcript, or an adequate substitute for a transcript, for use at several stages of the trial and appeal process. The payment requirements in each case were found to occasion de facto discrimination against those who, because of their indigency, were totally unable to pay for transcripts. . . .

Likewise, in Douglas v. California (1963), a decision establishing an indigent defendant's right to court-appointed counsel on direct appeal, the Court dealt only with defendants who could not pay for counsel from their own resources and who had no other way of gaining representation. . . .

Williams v. Illinois (1970) struck down criminal penalties that subjected indigents to incarceration simply because of their inability to pay a fine. Again, the disadvantaged class was composed only of persons who were totally unable to pay the demanded sum. . . .

Finally, in Bullock v. Carter (1972), the Court invalidated the Texas filing fee requirement for primary elections. Both of the relevant classifying facts found in the previous cases were present there. The size of the fee, often running into thousands of dollars and, in at least one case, as high as $8,900, effectively barred all potential candidates who were unable to pay the required fee. As the system provided "no reasonable alternative means of access to the ballot" inability to pay occasioned an absolute denial of a position on the primary ballot.

Only appellees' first possible basis for describing the class disadvantaged by the Texas school finance system—discrimination against a class of definably "poor" persons—might arguably meet the criteria established in these prior cases. Even a cursory examination, however, demonstrates that neither of the two distinguishing characteristics of wealth classifications can be found here. First, in support of their charge that the system discriminates against the "poor," appellees have made no effort to demonstrate that it operates to the peculiar disadvantage of any class fairly definable as indigent, or as composed of persons whose incomes are beneath any designated poverty level. Indeed, there is no reason to believe that the poorest families are not necessarily clustered in the poorest property districts. A recent and exhaustive study of school districts in Connecticut concluded that "[i]t is clearly incorrect . . . to contend that the 'poor' live in 'poor' districts. . . . Thus, the major factual assumption — that the educational finance system discriminates against the 'poor'—is simply false in Connecticut." Defining "poor" families as those below the Bureau of the Census "poverty level," the Connecticut study found, not surprisingly, that the poor were clustered around commercial and industrial areas—those same areas that provide the most attractive sources of property tax income for school districts. Whether a similar pattern would be discovered in Texas is not known, but there is no basis on the record in this case for assuming that the poorest people—defined by reference to any level of absolute impecunity—are concentrated in the poorest districts.

Second, neither appellees nor the District Court addressed the fact that, unlike each of the foregoing cases, lack of personal resources has not occasioned an absolute deprivation of the desired benefit. The argument here is not that the children in districts having relatively low assessable property values are receiving no public education; rather, it is that they are receiving a poorer quality education than that available to children in districts having more assessable wealth. Apart from the unsettled and disputed question whether the quality of education may be determined by the amount of money expended for it,* a sufficient answer to appellees' argument is that at least where wealth is involved the Equal Protection Clause does not require absolute equality of precisely equal advantages. . . . The State repeatedly asserted in its briefs in this Court that . . . it now assures "every child in every school district an adequate education." No proof was offered at trial persuasively discrediting or refuting the State's assertion.

For these two reasons—the absence of any evidence that the financing system discriminates against any definable category of "poor" people or that it results in the absolute deprivation of education—the disadvantaged class is not susceptible to identification in traditional terms. . . .

[The Court here reviews the evidence and rejects the argument that there is a direct correlation between the family income in a district and the amount it spends for education.]

This brings us, then, to the third way in which the classification scheme might be defined—*district* wealth discrimination. Since the only correlation indicated by the evidence is between district property wealth and expenditures, it may be argued that discrimination might be found without regard to the individual income characteristics of district residents. Assuming a perfect correla-

_____

*Each of appellees' possible theories of wealth discrimination is founded on the assumption that the quality of education varies directly with the amount of funds expended on it and that, therefore, the difference in quality between two schools can be determined simplistically by looking at the difference in per pupil expenditures. This is a matter of considerable dispute among educators and commentators.

tion between district property wealth and expenditures from top to bottom, the disadvantaged class might be viewed as encompassing every child in every district except the district that has the most assessable wealth and spends the most on education. . . .

However described, it is clear that appellees' suit asks this Court to extend its most exacting scrutiny to review a system that allegedly discriminates against a large, diverse, and amorphous class, unified only by the common factor of residence in districts that happen to have less taxable wealth than other districts. The system of alleged discrimination and the class it defines have none of the traditional indicia of suspectness: the class is not saddled with such disabilities, or subjected to such history of purposeful unequal treatment, or relegated to such a position of political powerlessness as to command extraordinary protection from the majoritarian political process.

We thus conclude that the Texas system does not operate to the peculiar disadvantage of any suspect class. But in recognition of the fact that this Court has never heretofore held that wealth discrimination alone provides an adequate basis for invoking strict scrutiny, appellees have not relied solely on this contention. They also assert that the State's system impermissibly interferes with the exercise of a "fundamental" right and that accordingly the prior decisions of this Court require the application of the strict standard of judicial review. It is this question— whether education is a fundamental right, in the sense that it is among the rights and liberties protected by the Constitution—which has so consumed the attention of courts and commentators in recent years.

B.

Nothing this Court holds today in any way detracts from our historic dedication to public education. We are in complete agreement with the conclusion of the three-judge panel below that "the grave significance of education both to the individual and to our society" cannot be doubted. But the importance of a service performed by the State does not determine whether it must be regarded as fundamental for purposes of examination under the Equal Protection Clause. Mr. Justice Harlan, dissenting from the Court's application of strict scrutiny to a law impinging upon the right of interstate travel, admonished that "[v]irtually every state statute affects important rights." Shapiro v. Thompson (1969). In his view, if the degree of judicial scrutiny of state legislation fluctuated depending on a majority's view of the importance of the interest affected, we would have gone "far toward making this Court a 'super-legislature.' " We would indeed then be assuming a legislative role and one for which the Court lacks both authority and competence. But Mr. Justice Stewart's response in Shapiro to Mr. Justice Harlan's concern correctly articulates the limits of the fundamental rights rationale employed in the Court's equal protection decisions:

"The Court today does *not* 'pick out particular human activities, characterize them as "fundamental," and give them added protection. ...' To the contrary, the Court simply recognizes, as it must, an established constitutional right, and gives to that right no less protection than the Constitution itself demands.'' (Emphasis from original.)

Mr. Justice Stewart's statement serves to underline what the opinion of the Court in Shapiro makes clear. ... The right to interstate travel had long been recognized as a right of constitutional significance, and the Court's decision therefore did not require an ad hoc determination as to the social or economic importance of that right.

Lindsey v. Normet (1972) decided only last Term, firmly reiterates that social importance is not the critical determinant for subjecting state legislation to strict scrutiny. ... Mr. Justice White's analysis, in his opinion for the Court, is instructive:

"We do not denigrate the importance of decent, safe, and sanitary housing. But the Constitution does not provide judicial remedies for every social and economic ill. We are unable to perceive in that document any constitutional guarantee of access to dwellings of a particular quality or any recognition of the right of a tenant to occupy the real property of his landlord beyond the term of his lease, without the payment of rent. ... *Absent constitutional mandate,* the assurance of adequate housing and the definition of landlord-tenant relationships are legislative, not judicial, functions.'' ...

The lesson of these cases in addressing the question now before the Court is plain. It is not the province of this Court to create substantive constitutional rights in the name of guaranteeing equal protection of the laws. Thus the key to discovering whether education is "fundamental" is not to be found in comparisons of the relative societal significance of education as opposed to subsistence or housing. Nor is it to be found by weighing whether education is as important as the right to travel. Rather, the answer lies in assessing whether there is a right to education explicitly or implicitly guaranteed by the Constitution. ...

Education, of course, is not among the rights afforded explicit protection under our Federal Constitution. Nor do we find any basis for saying it is implicitly so protected. It is appellees' contention, however, that education ... is itself a fundamental personal right because it is essential to the effective exercise of First Amendment freedoms and to intelligent utilization of the right to vote. ...

We need not dispute any of these propositions. The Court has long afforded zealous protection against unjustifiable governmental interference with the individual's rights to speak and to vote. Yet we have never presumed to possess either the ability or the authority to guarantee to the citizenry the most *effective* speech or the most *informed* electoral choice. ...

Even if it were conceded that some identifiable quantum of education is a constitutionally protected prerequisite to the meaningful exercise of either right, we have no indication that the present levels of educational expenditure in Texas provide an education that falls short. ...

We have carefully considered each of the arguments supportive of the District Court's finding that education is a fundamental right or liberty and have found those arguments unpersuasive. In one further respect we find this a particularly inappropriate case in which to subject state action to strict judicial scrutiny. The present case, in another basic sense, is significantly different from any of the cases in which the Court has applied strict scrutiny to state or federal legislation touching upon constitutionally protected rights. Each of our prior cases involved legislation which "deprived," "infringed," or "interfered" with the free exercise of some such fundamental personal right or liberty. ... A critical distinction between those cases and the one now before us lies in what Texas is endeavoring to do with respect to education. Every step leading to the establishment of the system Texas utilizes today—including the decisions permitting localities to tax and expand locally, and creating and continuously expanding state aid—was implemented in an effort to *extend* public education and to improve its quality. Of course, every reform that benefits some more than others may be criticized for what it fails to accomplish. But we think it plain that, in substance, the thrust of the Texas system is affirmative and reformatory and, therefore, should be scrutinized under judicial principles sensitive to the nature of the State's efforts and to the rights reserved to the States under the Constitution.

C.

It should be clear, for the reasons stated above and in accord with the prior decisions of this Court, that this is not a case in which the challenged state action must be subjected to the searching judicial scrutiny reserved for laws that created suspect classification or impinge upon constitutionally protected rights.

We need not rest our decision, however, solely on the inappropriateness of the strict scrutiny test. A century of Supreme Court adjudication under the Equal Protection Clause affirmatively supports the application of the traditional standard of review, which requires only that the State's system be shown to bear some rational relationship to legitimate state purposes. This case represents far more than a challenge to the manner in which Texas provides for the education of its children. We have here nothing less than a direct attack on the way in which Texas has chosen to raise and disburse state and local tax revenues. ...

[The Court here defends the appropriateness of the traditional standards in the field of taxation.]

The foregoing considerations buttress our conclusion that Texas' system of public school finance is an inappropriate candidate for strict judicial scrutiny. These same considerations are relevant to the determination whether that system, with its conceded imperfections, nevertheless bears some rational relationship to a legitimate state purpose. It is to this question that we next turn our attention. ...

The Texas system of school finance is responsive

to these two forces. While assuring a basic education for every child in the State, it permits and encourages a large measure of participation in and control of each district's schools at the local level. In an era that has witnessed a consistent trend toward centralization of the functions of government, local sharing of responsibility for public education has survived. . . .

The persistence of attachment to government at the lowest level where education is concerned reflects the depth of commitment of its supporters. In part, local control means . . . the freedom to devote more money to the education of one's children. Equally important, however, is the opportunity it offers for participation in the decision-making process that determines how those local tax dollars will be spent. Each locality is free to tailor local programs to local needs. Pluralism also affords some opportunity for experimentation, innovation, and a healthy competition for educational excellence. An analogy to the Nation-State relationship in our federal system seems uniquely appropriate. Mr. Justice Brandeis identified as one of the peculiar strengths of our form of government each State's freedom to "serve as a laboratory . . . and try novel social and economic experiments." No area of social concern stands to profit more from a multiplicity of viewpoints and from a diversity of approaches than does public education. . . .

. . . Appellees suggest that local control could be preserved and promoted under other financing systems that resulted in more equality in educational expenditures. While it is no doubt true that reliance on local property taxation for school revenues provides less freedom of choice with respect to expenditures for some districts than for others, the existence of "some inequality" in the manner in which the State's rationale is achieved is not alone a sufficient basis for striking down the entire system. . . . Only where state action impinges on the exercise of fundamental constitutional rights or liberties must it be found to have chosen the least restrictive alternative. . . . It is also well to remember that even those districts that have reduced ability to make free decisions with respect to how much they spend on education still retain under the present system a large measure of authority as to how available funds will be allocated. They further enjoy the power to make numerous other decisions with respect to the operation of the schools. The people of Texas may be justified in believing that other systems of school finance, which place more of the financial responsibility in the hands of the State, will result in a comparable lessening of desired local autonomy. That is, they may believe that along with increased control of the purse strings at the state level will go increased control over local policies. . . .

. . . One also must remember that the system here challenged is not peculiar to Texas or to any other State. In its essential characteristics the Texas plan for financing public education reflects what many educators for a half century have thought was an enlightened approach to a problem for which there is no perfect solution. We are unwilling to assume for ourselves a level of wisdom superior to that of legislators, scholars, and educational authorities in 49 States, especially where the alternatives proposed are only recently conceived and nowhere yet tested. The constitutional standard under the Equal Protection Clause is whether the challenged state action rationally furthers a legitimate state purpose or interest. . . . We hold that the Texas plan abundantly satisfies this standard.

Mr. Justice **Brennan,** dissenting, said in part:

Although I agree with my Brother White that the Texas statutory scheme is devoid of any rational basis, and for that reason is violative of the Equal Protection Clause, I also record my disagreement with the Court's rather distressing assertion that a right may be deemed "fundamental" for the purposes of equal protection analysis only if it is "explicitly or implicitly guaranteed by the Constitution." As my Brother Marshall convincingly demonstrates, our prior cases stand for the proposition that "fundamentality" is, in large measure, a function of the right's importance in terms of the effectuation of those rights which are in fact constitutionally guaranteed. Thus, "[a]s the nexus between the specific constitutional guarantee and the nonconstitutional interest draws closer, the nonconstitutional interest becomes more fundamental and the degree of judicial scrutiny applied when the interest is infringed on a discriminatory basis must be adjusted accordingly."

Here, there can be no doubt that education is inextricably linked to the right to participate in the electoral process and to the rights of free speech and association guaranteed by the First Amendment. This being so, any classification affecting education must be subjected to strict judicial scrutiny, and since even the State concedes that the statutory scheme now before us cannot pass constitutional muster under this stricter standard of review, I can only conclude that the Texas school financing scheme is constitutionally invalid.

Mr. Justice **White,** with whom Mr. Justice **Douglas** and Mr. Justice **Brennan** join, dissenting, said in part:

The Texas public schools are financed through a combination of state funding, local property tax revenue, and some federal funds. Concededly, the system yields wide disparity in per-pupil revenue among the various districts. In a typical year, for example, the Alamo Heights district had total revenues of $594 per pupil, while the Edgewood district had only $356 per student. The majority and the State concede, as they must, the existence of major disparities in spendable funds. But the State contends that the disparities do not invidiously discriminate against children and families in districts such as Edgewood, because the Texas scheme is designed "to provide an adequate education for all, with local autonomy to go beyond that as individual school districts desire and are able. . . . It leaves to the people of each district the choice whether to go beyond the minimum and, if so, by how much." The majority advances this rationalization: "While assuring a basic education for every child in the State, it permits and encourages a large measure of participation and control of each district's schools at the local level.''

I cannot disagree with the proposition that local control and local decision making play an important part in our democratic system of government. . . .

The difficulty with the Texas system, however, is that it provides a meaningful option to Alamo Heights and like school districts but almost none to Edgewood and those other districts with a low per-pupil real estate tax base. In these latter districts, no matter how desirous parents are of supporting their schools with greater revenues, it is impossible to do so through the use of the real estate property tax. In these districts the Texas system utterly fails to extend a realistic choice to parents, because the property tax, which is the only revenue-raising mechanism extended to school districts, is practically and legally unavailable. That this is a situation may be readily demonstrated. . . .

In order to equal the highest yield in any other Bexar County district, Alamo Heights would be required to tax at the rate of 68¢ per $100 of assessed valuation. Edgewood would be required to tax at the prohibitive rate of $5.76 per $100. But state law places a $1.50 per $100 ceiling on the maintenance tax rate, a limit that would surely be reached long before Edgewood attained an equal yield. Edgewood is thus precluded in law, as well as in fact, from achieving a yield even close to that of some other districts.

The Equal Protection Clause permits discriminations between classes but requires that the classification bear some rational relationship to a permissible object sought to be attained by the statute. It is not enough that the Texas system before us seeks to achieve the valid, rational purpose of maximizing local initiative; the means chosen by the State must also be rationally related to the end sought to be achieved. . . .

Neither Texas nor the majority heeds this rule. If the State aims at maximizing local initiative and local choice, by permitting schools to resort to the real property tax if they choose to do so, it utterly fails in achieving its purpose in districts with property tax bases so low that there is little if any opportunity for interested parents, rich or poor, to augment school district revenues. Requiring the State to establish only that unequal treatment is in furtherance of a permissible goal, without also requiring the State to show that the means chosen to effectuate that goal are rationally related to its achievement, makes equal protection analysis no more than an empty gesture. In my view, the parents and children in Edgewood, and in like districts, suffer from an invidious discrimination violative of the Equal Protection Clause. . . .

There is no difficulty in identifying the class that is subject to the alleged discrimination and that is entitled to the benefits of the Equal Protection Clause. I need go no farther than the parents and children in the Edgewood district, who are plaintiffs here and who assert that they are entitled to the same choice as Alamo Heights to augment local expenditures for schools but are denied that choice by state law. This group constitutes a class

sufficiently definite to invoke the protection of the Constitution. They are as entitled to the protection of the Equal Protection Clause as were the voters in allegedly unrepresented counties in the reapportionment cases. See, e. g., Baker v. Carr (1962). And in Bullock v. Carter (1972), where a challenge to the Texas candidate filing fee on equal protection grounds was upheld, we noted that the victims of alleged discrimination wrought by the filing fee ''cannot be described by reference to discrete and precisely defined segments of the community as is typical of inequities challenged under the Equal Protection Clause,'' but concluded that ''we would ignore reality were we not to recognize that this system falls with unequal weight on voters, as well as candidates, according to economic status.'' Similarly, in the present case we would blink reality to ignore the fact that school districts, and students in the end, are differentially affected by the Texas school financing scheme with respect to their capability to supplement the Minimum Foundation School Program. At the very least, the law discriminates against those children and their parents who live in districts where the per-pupil tax base is sufficiently low to make impossible the provision of comparable school revenues by resort to the real property tax which is the only device the State extends for this purpose.

Mr. Justice **Marshall,** with whom Mr. Justice **Douglas** concurs, dissenting, said in part:

I. . . .

B.

The appellants do not deny the disparities in educational funding caused by variations in taxable district property wealth. They do contend, however, that whatever the differences in per pupil spending among Texas districts, there are no discriminatory consequences for the children of the disadvantaged districts. They recognize that what is at stake in this case is the quality of the public education provided Texas children in the districts in which they live. But appellants reject the suggestion that the quality of education in any particular district is determined by money—beyond some minimal level of funding which they believe to be assured every Texas district by the Minimum Foundation School Program. In their view, there is simply no denial of equal educational opportunity to any Texas school children as a result of the widely varying per pupil spending power provided districts under the current financing scheme.

In my view, though, even an unadorned restatement of this contention is sufficient to reveal its absurdity. Authorities concerned with educational quality no doubt disagree as to the significance of variations in per pupil spending. Indeed, conflicting expert testimony was presented to the District Court in this case concerning the effect of spending variations on educational achievement. We sit, however, not to resolve disputes over educational theory but to enforce our Constitution. It is an inescapable fact that if one district has more funds available per pupil than another district, the former will have greater choice in educational planning than will the latter. In this regard, I believe the question of discrimination in educational quality must be deemed to be an objective one that looks to what the State provides its children, not to what the children are able to do with what they receive. That a child is forced to attend an underfunded school with poorer physical facilities, less experienced teachers, larger classes, and a narrower range of courses than a school with substantially more funds—and thus with greater choice in educational planning—may nevertheless excel is to the credit of the child, not the State, cf. Missouri ex rel. Gaines v. Canada (1938). Indeed, who can ever measure for such a child the opportunities lost and the talents wasted for want of a broader, more enriched education? Discrimination in the opportunity to learn that is afforded a child must be our standard. . . .

II.

To avoid having the Texas financing scheme struck down because of the interdistrict variations in taxable property wealth, the District Court determined that it was insufficient for appellants to show merely that the State's scheme was rationally related to some legitimate state purpose; rather, the discrimination inherent in the scheme had to be shown necessary to promote a "compelling state interest" in order to withstand constitutional scrutiny. The basis for this determination was twofold: first, the financing scheme divides citizens on a wealth basis, a classification which the District Court viewed as highly suspect; and second, the discriminatory scheme directly affects what it considered to be a "fundamental interest," namely, education.

This Court has repeatedly held that state discrimination which either adversely affects a "fundamental interest," see, e.g., Dunn v. Blumstein, (1972); Shapiro v. Thompson, (1969), or is based on a distinction of a suspect character, . . . must be carefully scrutinized to ensure that the scheme is necessary to promote a substantial legitimate state interest. . . . The majority today concludes, however, that the Texas scheme is not subject to such a strict standard of review under the Equal Protection Clause. Instead, in its view, the Texas scheme must be tested by nothing more than that lenient standard of rationality which we have traditionally applied to discriminatory state action in the context of economic and commercial matters. . . . By so doing the Court avoids the telling task of searching for a substantial state interest which the Texas financing scheme, with its variations in taxable district property wealth, is necessary to further. I cannot accept such an emasculation of the Equal Protection Clause in the context of this case.

A.

To begin, I must once more voice my disagreement with the Court's rigidified approach to equal protection analysis. . . . The Court apparently seeks to establish today that equal protection cases fall into one of two neat categories which dictate the appropriate standard of review—strict scrutiny or mere rationality. But this Court's decisions in the field of equal protection defy such easy categorization. A principled reading of what this Court has done reveals that it has applied a spectrum of standards in reviewing discrimination allegedly violative of the Equal Protection Clause. This spectrum clearly comprehends variations in the degree of care with which the Court will scrutinize particular classifications, depending, I believe, on the constitutional and societal importance of the interest adversely affected and the recognized invidiousness of the basis upon which the particular classification is drawn. I find in fact that many of the Court's recent decisions embody the very sort of reasoned approach to equal protection analysis for which I previously argued—that is, an approach in which "concentration [is] placed upon the character of the classification in question, the relative importance to individuals in the class discriminated against of the governmental benefits that they do not receive, and the asserted state interests in support of the classification." Dandridge v. Williams (1970)

[Marshall here summarizes a long series of equal protection cases weighing the fundamentalness of the right and the "invidiousness" of the classification in each.]

In summary, it seems to me inescapably clear that this Court has consistently adjusted the care with which it will review state discrimination in light of the constitutional significance of the interests affected and the invidiousness of the particular classification. In the context of economic interests, we find that discriminatory state action is almost always sustained, for such interests are generally far removed from constitutional guarantees. Moreover, "[t]he extremes to which the Court has gone in dreaming up rational bases for state regulation in that area may in many instances be ascribed to a healthy revulsion from the Court's earlier excesses in using the Constitution to protect interests that have more than enough power to protect themselves in the legislative halls." Dandridge v. Williams. But the situation differs markedly when discrimination against important individual interests with constitutional implications and against particularly disadvantaged or powerless classes is involved. The majority suggests, however, that a variable standard of review would give this Court the appearance of a "super-legislature." Such an approach seems to me a part of the guarantees of our Constitution and of the historic experiences with oppression of and discrimination against discrete, powerless minorities which underlie that document. In truth, the Court itself will be open to the criticism raised by the majority so long as it continues on its present course of effectively selecting in private which cases will be afforded special consideration without acknowledging the true basis of its action. . . .

Nevertheless, the majority today attempts to force this case into the same category for purposes of equal protection analysis as decisions involving discrimination affecting commercial interests. By so doing, the majority singles this case out for analytic treatment at odds with what seems to me to be the clear trend of recent decisions in this Court, and thereby ignores the constitutional importance of the interests at stake and the invidiousness of the particular classification, factors that call for far more than the lenient scrutiny of the Texas financing scheme which the majority pursues. Yet if the discrimination inherent in the Texas scheme is scrutinized with the care demanded by the interest and classification present in this case, the unconstitutionality of that scheme is unmistakable. . . .

D.

The nature of our inquiry into the justifications for state discrimination is essentially the same in all equal protection cases: We must consider the substantiality of the state interests sought to be served, and we must scrutinize the reasonableness of the means by which the State has sought to advance its interests. . . . Differences in the application of this test are, in my view, a function of the constitutional importance of the interests at stake and the invidiousness of the particular classification. In terms of the asserted state interests, the Court has indicated that it will require, for instance, a "compelling," Shapiro v. Thompson, [1969], or a "substantial" or "important", Dunn v. Blumstein, [1972], state interest to justify discrimination affecting individual interests of constitutional significance. Whatever the differences, if any, in these descriptions of the character of the state interest necessary to sustain such discrimination, basic to each is, I believe, a concern with the legitimacy and the reality of the asserted state interests. Thus, when interests of constitutional importance are at stake, the Court does not stand ready to credit the State's classification with any conceivable legitimate purpose, but demands a clear showing that there are legitimate state interests which the classification was in fact intended to serve. Beyond the question of the adequacy of the State's purpose for the classification, the Court traditionally has become increasingly sensitive to the means by which a State chooses to act as its action affects more directly interests of constitutional significance. . . . Thus, by now, "less restrictive alternatives" analysis is firmly established in equal protection jurisprudence. See Dunn v. Blumstein, [1972]; Kramer v. Union School District [1969]. It seems to me that the range of choice we are willing to accord the State in selecting the means by which it will act, and the care with which we scrutinize the effectiveness of the means which the State selects, also must reflect the constitutional importance of the interest affected and the invidiousness of the particular classification. Here both the nature of the interest and the classification dictate close judicial scrutiny of the purposes which Texas seeks to serve with its present educational financing scheme and of the means it has selected to serve that purpose.

The only justification offered by appellants to sustain the discrimination in educational opportunity caused by the Texas financing scheme is local educational control. Presented with this justification, the District Court concluded that "[n]ot only are defendants unable to demonstrate compelling state interests for their classifications based upon wealth, they fail even to establish a reasonable basis for these classifications." I must agree with this conclusion.

PLYLER v. DOE

457 U. S. 202; 102 S. Ct. 2382; 72 L. Ed. 2d 786
(1982)

In his dissent in Rodriguez, Justice Marshall argued that two tests for equal protection cases were not enough. The tests had become not tests, but answers: under the strict scrutiny test, the law is struck down; under the rational basis test the law is upheld. Justice Marshall not only criticized the two-tiered approach, he asserted that the Court had abandoned it and had, in its stead, been applying a "spectrum of standards" to analyze equal protection claims. He urged the Court to give up the pretense of two tests and begin articulating the real underpinnings of its more sophisticated equal protection analysis.

To decide what standard to apply under the equal protection clause, Justice Marshall said the Court was asking two questions. First, how important is the interest that is being adversely affected by the alleged discrimination. Second, how invidious is the classification that is being used. According to Justice Marshall, the answer to these questions determines the level of scrutiny to be applied.

The difference between this approach and the two-tiered approach is demonstrated by Rodriguez and the case below. In Rodriguez, the two-tiered approach can be outlined as follows: education is not a fundamental right, and wealth is not a suspect classification; strict scrutiny cannot therefore be applied; thus the rational basis test must be used. Justice Marshall's approach would be that education, even if not fundamental, is important; wealth, even if not a suspect classification, is questionable. Strict scrutiny does not apply, but neither is the rational basis test appropriate here: an intermediate test should be applied.

Gradually, the Court has come to accept the need for such an intermediate test and has formulated one. Under this test, the challenged classification must serve "important governmental objectives and the discriminatory means employed" must be " substantially related to the achievement of those objectives;" see Mississippi v. Hogan (1982). This test is often referred to as the "substantial interest test" because an alternate and simple formulation of it is that the classification must serve a substantial governmental interest.

The intermediate test originated in sex discrimination cases. In Craig v. Boren (1976) the Court held void a law that set the legal age for drinking at a different point for men than for women. The test used to determine whether this law violated the equal protection test was the long formulation of the substantial interest test given above and was described by the Court in *Craig* as a midlevel test. *Craig* was one of the first explicit instances of the Court's use of this intermediate test and is often cited by the Court as the precedent for using the test.

Sex discrimination cases were fertile ground for the development of the new test for a number of reasons. The sheer number of sex discrimination cases in the 1970s, the growing women's rights movement, the political debate over the Equal Rights Amendment and the greater statutory protection afforded women by the Civil Rights Act and other laws, all contributed to the Court's reluctance to continue its casual scrutiny under the rational basis test. On the other hand, the Court was even less inclined to raise sex to the level of a suspect classification because that would, in effect, outlaw almost all use of sex as a legislative classification.

The heated political debate over the Equal Rights Amendment, with opponents raising the specter of unisex bathrooms and women fighting wars on the front lines, provided no inducement for the Court to preempt the political process by declaring sex a suspect classification. The answer was an intermediate test by which the Court could legitimately consider the invidious nature of sexual discrimination without outlawing all use of sexual classifications.

At the same time that the Court was struggling with an increased number of sex discrimination cases, the existence of the welfare state raised a number of other recurring equal protection problems. Specifically, the Court found itself confronted with equal protection claims alleging discrimination against the poor and discrimination affecting access to education. Some argued that the poor, like blacks, were historically the subjects of the most invidious discrimination and that wealth, therefore, should be treated as a suspect classification. While it is true that the poor have been subjected to some of the cruelest discrimination, wealth, unlike race, is not an immutable characteristic and more important, a capitalist society is one that assumes differential treatment based on wealth as a reward for ability and an incentive to greater productivity. The Court is not on the verge of restructuring the economic basis of the nation.

Nevertheless, when discrimination against the poor, or another group not treated as a suspect class such as aliens, is combined with an adverse effect on an important, although not fundamental right such as education, the Court has apparently abandoned the casual scrutiny of the rational basis test and opted instead for the intermediate test used in the case below.

Plyler v. Doe was a suit brought on behalf of all school-age children of Mexican origin residing in Texas as illegal aliens. The suit challenged a provision of the Texas Education Code that denied free public education to illegal alien children. One year after the decision in Plyler the Court considered a challenge to another provision of the Texas education law in *Martinez v. Bynum (1983). The provision challenged in Martinez denied free public education to any minor, living apart from his natural parents or legal guardian, who resided in the school district for the primary purpose of attending school. It was argued that the law was intended to and did discriminate against children of Mexican heritage. If an illegal alien gives birth to a child while in this country, that child is an American citizen. Some of these illegal aliens later return to Mexico but send their American children to live with friends or relatives in the United States so they may receive a free public education. These Mexican-American children, living apart from their parents, were denied a free education by the Texas law.*

With only Justice Marshall dissenting, the Court in Martinez held that this Texas law was constitutional because it was a bona fide residence requirement designed to further the "substantial state interest in assuring that services provided for its residents are enjoyed only by residents." While the Court did not discuss the standard it was applying, the use of the word "substantial" suggests that the intermediate test was used just as it had been in Plyler—although with a different result. The majority in Martinez also held that the law did not unconstitutionally impede the right to travel interstate. Justice Marshall dissented on a number of grounds, including his continuing belief that education is a fundamental right, which requires the Court to exercise strict scrutiny, striking down any law that is not necessary to further a compelling governmental interest.

Justice **Brennan** delivered the opinion of the Court, saying in part:

The question presented by these cases is whether, consistent with the Equal Protection Clause of the Fourteenth Amendment, Texas may deny to undocumented school-age children the free public education that it provides to children who are citizens of the United States or legally admitted aliens.

I.

Since the late nineteenth century, the United States has restricted immigration into this country. Unsanctioned entry into the United States is a crime, and those who have entered unlawfully are subject to deportation. But despite the existence of these legal restrictions, a substantial number of persons have succeeded in unlawfully entering the United States, and now live within various States, including the State of Texas.

In May 1975, the Texas legislature revised its education laws to withhold from local school districts any state funds for the education of children who were not "legally admitted" into the United States. The 1975 revision also authorized local school districts to deny enrollment in their public schools to children not "legally admitted" to the country. These cases involve constitutional challenges to those provisions. . . .

III.

The Equal Protection Clause directs that "all persons similarly circumstanced shall be treated alike." F. S. Royster Guano Co. v. Virginia (1920). But so too, "[t]he Constitution does not require things which are different in fact or opinion to be treated in law as though they were the same." . . . The initial discretion to determine what is "different" and what is "the same" resides in the legislatures of the States. A legislature must have substantial latitude to establish classifications that roughly approximate the nature of the problem perceived, that accommodate competing concerns both public and private, and that account for limitations on the practical ability of the State to remedy every ill. In applying the Equal Protection Clause to most forms of state action, we thus seek only the assurance that the classification at issue bears some fair relationship to a legitimate public purpose.

But we would not be faithful to our obligations under the Fourteenth Amendment if we applied so deferential a standard to every classification. The Equal Protection Clause was intended as a restriction on state legislative action inconsistent with elemental constitutional premises. Thus we have treated as presumptively invidious those classifications that disadvantage a "suspect class,"* or that impinge upon the exercise of a "fundamental right."† With respect to such classifications, it is appropriate to enforce the mandate of equal protection by requiring the State to demonstrate that its classification has been precisely tailored to serve a compelling governmental interest. In addition, we have recognized that certain forms of legislative classification, while not facially invidious, nonetheless give rise to recurring constitutional difficulties; in these limited circumstances we have sought the assurance that the classification reflects a reasoned judgment consistent with the ideal of equal protection by inquiring whether it may fairly be viewed as furthering a substantial interest of the State. We turn to a consideration of the standard appropriate for the evaluation of § 21.031.

A.

Sheer incapability or lax enforcement of the laws barring entry into this country, coupled with the failure to establish an effective bar to the employment of undocumented aliens has resulted in the creation of a substantial "shadow population" of illegal migrants—numbering in the millions—within our borders. This situation raises the specter of a permanent caste of undocumented resident aliens, encouraged by some to remain here as a source of cheap labor, but nevertheless denied the benefits that our society makes available to citizens and lawful residents. The existence of such an underclass presents most difficult problems for a Nation that prides itself on adherence to principles of equality under law.

The children who are plaintiffs in these cases are special members of this underclass. Persuasive arguments support the view that a State may withhold its beneficence from those whose very presence within the United States is the product of their own unlawful conduct. These arguments do not apply with the same force to classifications imposing disabilities on the minor *children* of such illegal entrants. At the least, those who enter our territory by stealth and in violation of our law should be prepared to bear the consequences, including, but not limited to deportation. But the children of those illegal entrants are not comparably situated. Their "parents have the ability to conform their conduct to societal norms," and presumably the ability to remove themselves from the State's jurisdiction; but the children who are plaintiffs in these cases "can affect neither their parents' conduct nor their own status." . . . Even if the State found it expedient to control the conduct of adults by acting against their children, legislation directing the onus of a parent's misconduct against his children does not comport with fundamental conceptions of justice. . . .

Of course, undocumented status is not irrelevant to any proper legislative goal. Nor is undocumented status an absolutely immutable characteristic since it is the product of conscious, indeed unlawful, action. But § 21.031 is directed against children, and imposes its discriminatory burden on the basis of a legal characteristic over which children can have little control. It is thus difficult to conceive of a rational justification for penalizing these children for their presence within the United States. Yet that appears to be precisely the effect of § 21.031.

Public education is not a "right" granted to individuals by the Constitution. . . . But neither is it merely some governmental "benefit" indistinguishable from other forms of social welfare legislation. Both the importance of education in maintaining our basic institutions,

---

*Several formulations might explain our treatment of certain classifications as "suspect." Some classifications are more likely than others to reflect deep-seated prejudice rather than legislative rationality in pursuit of some legitimate objective. Legislation predicted on such prejudice is easily recognized as incompatible with the constitutional understanding that each person is to be judged individually and is entitled to equal justice under the law. Classifications treated as suspect tend to be irrelevant to any proper legislative goal. . . . Finally, certain groups, indeed largely the same groups, have historically been "relegated to such a position of political powerlessness as to command extraordinary protection from the majoritarian political process." . . . The experience of our Nation has shown that prejudice may manifest itself in the treatment of some groups. Our response to that experience is reflected in the Equal Protection Clause of the Fourteenth Amendment. Legislation imposing special disabilities upon groups disfavored by virtue of circumstances beyond their control suggests the kind of "class or caste" treatment that the Fourteenth Amendment was designed to abolish.

†In determining whether a class-based denial of a particular right is deserving of strict scrutiny under the Equal Protection Clause, we look to the Constitution to see if the right infringed has its source, explicitly or implicitly, therein. But we have also recognized the fundamentality of participation in state "elections on an equal basis with other citizens in the jurisdiction," Dunn v. Blumstein [1972], even though "the right to vote, per se, is not a constitutionally protected right." San Antonio [v. Rodriguez, 1973]. . . . With respect to suffrage, we have explained the need for strict scrutiny as arising from the significance of the franchise as the guardian of all other rights. . . .

and the lasting impact of its deprivation on the life of the child, mark the distinction. The "American people have always regarded education [and] the acquisition of knowledge as matters of supreme importance." ... We have recognized "the public schools as a most vital civic institution for the preservation of a democratic system of government," Abington School District v. Schempp (1963), and as the primary vehicle for transmitting "the values on which our society rests." ... [A]s ... pointed out early in our history, "some degree of education is necessary to prepare citizens to participate effectively and intelligently in our open political system if we are to preserve freedom and independence." Wisconsin v. Yoder (1972). And these historic "perceptions of the public schools as inculcating fundamental values necessary to the maintenance of a democratic political system have been confirmed by the observations of social scientists." ... In addition, education provides the basic tools by which individuals might lead economically productive lives to the benefit of us all. In sum, education has a fundamental role in maintaining the fabric of our society. We cannot ignore the significant social costs borne by our Nation when select groups are denied the means to absorb the values and skills upon which our social order rests.

In addition to the pivotal role of education in sustaining our political and cultural heritage, denial of education to some isolated group of children poses an affront to one of the goals of the Equal Protection Clause: the abolition of governmental barriers presenting unreasonable obstacles to advancement on the basis of individual merit. Paradoxically, by depriving the children of any disfavored group of an education, we foreclose the means by which that group might raise the level of esteem in which it is held by the majority. But more directly, "education prepares individuals to be self-reliant and self-sufficient participants in society." ... Illiteracy is an enduring disability. The inability to read and write will handicap the individual deprived of a basic education each and every day of his life. The inestimable toll of that deprivation on the social, economic, intellectual and psychological well-being of the individual, and the obstacle it poses to individual achievement, make it most difficult to reconcile the cost or the principle of a status-based denial of basic education with the framework of equality embodied in the Equal Protection Clause. ...

B.

These well-settled principles allow us to determine the proper level of deference to be afforded § 21.031. Undocumented aliens cannot be treated as a suspect class because their presence in this country in violation of federal law is not a "constitutional irrelevancy." Nor is education a fundamental right; a State need not justify by compelling necessity every variation in the manner in which education is provided to its population. ... But more is involved in these cases than the abstract question whether § 21.031 discriminates against a suspect class,

or whether education is a fundamental right. Section 21.031 imposes a lifetime hardship on a discrete class of children not accountable for their disabling status. The stigma of illiteracy will mark them for the rest of their lives. By denying these children a basic education, we deny them the ability to live within the structure of our civic institutions, and foreclose any realistic possibility that they will contribute in even the smallest way to the progress of our Nation. In determining the rationality of § 21.031, we may appropriately take into account its costs to the Nation and to the innocent children who are its victims. In light of these countervailing costs, the discrimination contained in § 21.031 can hardly be considered rational unless it furthers some substantial goal of the State.

IV.

It is the State's principal argument, and apparently the view of the dissenting Justices, that the undocumented status of these children vel non establishes a sufficient rational basis for denying them benefits that a State might choose to afford other residents. The State notes that while other aliens are admitted "on an equality of legal privileges with all citizens under non-discriminatory laws," Takahashi v. Fish & Game Comm'n (1948), the asserted right of these children to an education can claim no implicit imprimatur. Indeed, in the State's view, Congress' apparent disapproval of the presence of these children within the United States, and the evasion of the federal regulatory program that is the mark of undocumented status, provides authority for its decision to impose upon them special disabilities. Faced with an equal protection challenge respecting the treatment of aliens, we agree that the courts must be attentive to congressional policy; the exercise of congressional power might well affect the State's prerogatives to afford differential treatment to a particular class of aliens. But we are unable to find in the congressional immigration scheme any statement of policy that might weigh significantly in arriving at an equal protection balance concerning the State's authority to deprive these children of an education. ...

As we recognized in De Canas v. Bica (1976), the States do have some authority to act with respect to illegal aliens, at least where such action mirrors federal objectives and furthers a legitimate state goal. In De Canas, the State's program reflected Congress' intention to bar from employment all aliens except those possessing a grant of permission to work in this country. In contrast, there is no indication that the disability imposed by § 21.031 corresponds to any identifiable congressional policy. The State does not claim that the conservation of state educational resources was ever a congressional concern in restricting immigration. More importantly, the classification reflected in § 21.031 does not operate harmoniously within the federal program.

To be sure, like all persons who have entered the United States unlawfully, these children are subject to deportation. But there is no assurance that a child subject to deportation will ever be deported. An illegal entrant might be granted federal permission to continue to reside in this country, or even to become a citizen. In light of the discretionary federal power to grant relief from deportation, a State cannot realistically determine that any particular undocumented child will in fact be deported until after deportation proceedings have been completed. It would of course be most difficult for the State to justify a denial of education to a child enjoying an inchoate federal permission to remain.

We are reluctant to impute to Congress the intention to withhold from these children, for so long as they are present in this country through no fault of their own, access to a basic education. . . . The State may borrow the federal classification. But to justify its use as a criterion for its own discriminatory policy, the State must demonstrate that the classification is reasonably adapted to *"the purposes for which the state desires to use it."* Oyama v. California (1948) (Murphy, J., concurring) (emphasis added). We therefore turn to the state objectives that are said to support § 21.031.

V.

Appellants argue that the classification at issue furthers an interest in the "preservation of the state's limited resources for the education of its lawful residents." Of course, a concern for the preservation of resources standing alone can hardly justify the classification used in allocating those resources. . . . The State must do more than justify its classification with a concise expression of an intention to discriminate. . . . Apart from the asserted state prerogative to act against undocumented children solely on the basis of their undocumented status—an asserted prerogative that carries only minimal force in the circumstances of these cases—we discern three colorable state interests that might support § 21.031.

First, appellants appear to suggest that the State may seek to protect itself from an influx of illegal immigrants. While a State might have an interest in mitigating the potentially harsh economic effects of sudden shifts in population, § 21.031 hardly offers an effective method of dealing with an urgent demographic or economic problem. There is no evidence in the record suggesting that illegal entrants impose any significant burden on the State's economy. To the contrary, the available evidence suggests that illegal aliens underutilize public services, while contributing their labor to the local economy and tax money to the state. The dominant incentive for illegal entry into the State of Texas is the availability of employment; few if any illegal immigrants come to this country, or presumably to the State of Texas, in order to avail themselves of a free education. Thus, even making the doubtful assumption that the net impact of illegal aliens on the economy is negative, we think it clear that "[c]harging tuition to undocumented children constitutes a ludicrously ineffectual attempt to stem the tide of ille-

gal immigration," at least when compared with the alternative of prohibiting the employment of illegal aliens.

Second, while it is apparent that a State may "not . . . reduce expenditures for education by barring [some arbitrarily chosen class of] children from its schools," Shapiro v. Thompson (1969), appellants suggest that undocumented children are appropriately singled out for exclusion because of the special burdens they impose on the State's ability to provide high quality public education. But the record in no way supports the claim that exclusion of undocumented children is likely to improve the overall quality of education in the State. . . . And, after reviewing the State's school financing mechanism, the District Court concluded that barring undocumented children from local schools would not necessarily improve the quality of education provided in those schools. Of course, even if improvement in the quality of education were a likely result of barring some *number* of children from the schools of the State, the State must support its selection of *this* group as the appropriate target for exclusion. In terms of educational cost and need, however, undocumented children are "basically indistinguishable" from legally resident alien children.

Finally, appellants suggest that undocumented children are appropriately singled out because their unlawful presence within the United States renders them less likely than other children to remain within the boundaries of the State, and to put their education to productive social or political use within the State. Even assuming that such an interest is legitimate, it is an interest that is most difficult to quantify. The State has no assurance that any child, citizen or not, will employ the education provided by the State within the confines of the State's borders. . . . It is difficult to understand precisely what the State hopes to achieve by promoting the creation and perpetuation of a subclass of illiterates within our boundaries, surely adding to the problems and costs of unemployment, welfare, and crime. It is thus clear that whatever savings might be achieved by denying these children an education, they are wholly insubstantial in light of the costs involved to those children, the State, and the Nation.

VI.

If the State is to deny a discrete group of innocent children the free public education that it offers to other children residing within its borders, that denial must be justified by a showing that it furthers some substantial state interest. No such showing was made here. . . .

Justice **Marshall,** concurring.

While I join the Court opinion, I do so without in any way retreating from my opinion in San Antonio Independent School District v. Rodriguez (1973) (dissenting opinion). I continue to believe that an individual's interest in education is fundamental, and that this view is amply supported "by the unique status accorded public education by our society, and by the close relationship between education and some of our most basic constitutional values." Furthermore, I believe that the facts of these cases demonstrate the wisdom of rejecting a rigidified approach to equal protection analysis, and of employing an approach that allows for varying levels of scrutiny depending upon "the constitutional and societal importance of the interest adversely affected and the recognized invidiousness of the basis upon which the particular classification is drawn." See also Dandridge v. Williams (1970) (Marshall, J., dissenting). It continues to be my view that a class-based denial of public education is utterly incompatible with the Equal Protection Clause of the Fourteenth Amendment.

Justice **Blackmun**, concurring, said in part:

I join the opinion and judgment of the Court. . . .

The "fundamental rights" aspect of the Court's equal protection analysis—the now-familiar concept that governmental classifications bearing on certain interests must be closely scrutinized—has been the subject of some controversy. Justice Harlan, for example, warned that "[v]irtually every state statute affects important rights. . . . [T]o extend the 'compelling interest' rule to all cases in which such rights are affected would go far toward making this Court a 'super-legislature.'" Shapiro v. Thompson (1969) (dissenting opinion). . . . Still others have suggested that fundamental rights are not properly a part of equal protection analysis at all, because they are unrelated to any defined principle of equality.

These considerations, combined with doubts about the judiciary's ability to make fine distinctions in assessing the effects of complex social policies, led the Court in Rodriguez to articulate a firm rule: fundamental rights are those that "explicitly or implicitly [are] guaranteed by the Constitution." It therefore squarely rejected the notion that "an ad hoc determination as to the social or economic importance" of a given interest is relevant to the level of scrutiny accorded classifications involving that interest, and made clear that "[i]t is not the province of the Court to create substantive constitutional rights in the name of guaranteeing equal protection of the laws."

I joined Justice Powell's opinion for the Court in Rodriguez, and I continue to believe that it provides the appropriate model for resolving most equal protection disputes. . . .

With all this said, however, I believe the Court's experience has demonstrated that the Rodriguez formulation does not settle every issue of "fundamental rights" arising under the Equal Protection Clause. Only a pedant would insist that there are no meaningful distinctions among the multitude of social and political interests regulated by the States, and Rodriguez does not stand for quite so absolute a proposition. To the contrary, Rodriguez implicitly acknowledged that certain interests, though not constitutionally guaranteed, must be accorded a special place in equal protection analysis. Thus, the Court's decisions long have accorded strict scrutiny to

classifications bearing on the right to vote in state elections, and Rodriguez confirmed the "constitutional underpinnings of the right to equal treatment in the voting process." Yet "the right to vote, per se, is not a constitutionally protected right." . . . Instead, regulation of the electoral process receives unusual scrutiny because "the right to exercise the franchise in a free and unimpaired manner is preservative of other basic civil and political rights." . . .

In my view, when the State provides an education to some and denies it to others, it immediately and inevitably creates class distinctions of a type fundamentally inconsistent with those purposes, mentioned above, of the Equal Protection Clause. Children denied an education are placed at a permanent and insurmountable competitive disadvantage, for an uneducated child is denied even the opportunity to achieve. And when those children are members of an identifiable group, that group—through the State's action—will have been converted into a discrete underclass. . . . In a sense, then, denial of an education is the analogue of denial of the right to vote: the former relegates the individual to second-class social status; the latter places him at a permanent political disadvantage.

This conclusion is fully consistent with Rodriguez. The Court there reserved judgment on the constitutionality of a state system that "occasioned an absolute denial of educational opportunities to any of its children," noting that "no charge fairly could be made that the system [at issue in Rodriguez] fails to provide each child with an opportunity to acquire . . . basic minimal skills." . . . Similarly, it is undeniable that education is not a "fundamental right" in the sense that it is constitutionally guaranteed. Here, however, the State has undertaken to provide an education to most of the children residing within its borders. And, in contrast to the situation in Rodriguez, it does not take an advanced degree to predict the effects of a complete denial of education upon those children targeted by the State's classification. In such circumstances, the voting decisions suggest that the State must offer something more than a rational basis for its classification. . . .

Justice **Powell**, concurring, said in part:

I join the opinion of the Court, and write separately to emphasize the unique character of the cases before us. . . .

Although the analogy is not perfect, our holding today does find support in decisions of this Court with respect to the status of illegitimates. In Weber v. Aetna Casualty & Surety Co. (1972) we said: "[V]isiting . . . condemnation on the head of an infant" for the misdeeds of the parents is illogical, unjust, and "contrary to the basic concept of our system that legal burdens should bear some relationship to individual responsibility or wrongdoing." . . .

In my view, the State's denial of education to these children bears no substantial relation to any substantial state interest. Both of the District Courts found that an uncertain but significant percentage of illegal alien children will remain in Texas as residents and many eventually will become citizens. The discussion by the Court of the State's purported interests demonstrates that they are poorly served by the educational exclusion. Indeed, the interests relied upon by the State would seem to be insubstantial in view of the consequences to the State itself of wholly uneducated persons living indefinitely within its borders. . . .

Chief Justice **Burger,** with whom Justice **White,** Justice **Rehnquist,** and Justice **O'Connor** join, dissenting, said in part:

The Court makes no attempt to disguise that it is acting to make up for Congress' lack of "effective leadership" in dealing with the serious national problems caused by the influx of uncountable millions of illegal aliens across our borders. . . .

The Court's holding today manifests the justly criticized judicial tendency to attempt speedy and wholesale formulation of "remedies" for the failures—or simply the laggard pace—of the political process of our system of government. The Court employs, and in my view abuses, the Fourteenth Amendment in an effort to become an omnipotent and omniscient problem solver. That the motives for doing so are noble and compassionate does not alter the fact that the Court distorts our constitutional function to make amends for the defaults of others.

I. . . .

A.

The Court acknowledges that, except in those cases when state classifications disadvantage a "suspect class" or impinge upon a "fundamental right," the Equal Protection Clause permits a state "substantial latitude" in distinguishing between different groups of persons. Moreover, the Court expressly—and correctly—rejects any suggestion that illegal aliens are a suspect class, or that education is a fundamental right. Yet by patching together bits and pieces of what might be termed quasi-suspect-class and quasi-fundamental-rights analysis, the Court spins out a theory custom-tailored to the facts of these cases.

In the end, we are told little more than that the level of scrutiny employed to strike down the Texas law applies only when illegal alien children are deprived of a public education. If ever a court was guilty of an unabashedly result-oriented approach, this case is a prime example. . . .

B.

Once it is conceded—as the Court does—that illegal aliens are not a suspect class, and that education is not a fundamental right, our inquiry should focus on and

be limited to whether the legislative classification at issue bears a rational relationship to a legitimate state purpose. . . .

The State contends primarily that § 21.031 serves to prevent undue depletion of its limited revenues available for education, and to preserve the fiscal integrity of the State's school-financing system against an ever-increasing flood of illegal aliens—aliens over whose entry or continued presence it has no control. Of course such fiscal concerns alone could not justify discrimination against a suspect class or an arbitrary and irrational denial of benefits to a particular group of persons. Yet I assume no Member of this Court would argue that prudent conservation of finite state revenues is per se an illegitimate goal. Indeed, the numerous classifications this Court has sustained in social welfare legislation were invariably related to the limited amount of revenues available to spend on any given program or set of programs. . . . The significant question here is whether the requirement of tuition from illegal aliens who attend the public schools—as well as from residents of other states, for example—is a rational and reasonable means of furthering the State's legitimate fiscal ends. . . .

RACE DISCRIMINATION

BATSON v. KENTUCKY

476 U.S. 79; 106 S. Ct. 1712; 90 L Ed. 2d 69
(1986)

Despite a strong tendency to water down the guarantees of the Fourteenth Amendment in order to preserve the pre-Civil War balance between nation and state, evidenced by the Slaughter-House Cases (1873) and similar decisions, the Supreme Court did, in the same period, give meaning to the equal protection clause, particularly in the area of the administration of justice. Ex parte Virginia (1880) upheld the conviction of a county court judge for excluding blacks, because of their race, from jury lists made out by him, in violation of a federal statute forbidding such racial discrimination in the selection of jurors. The statute was held valid. In the same year, the Court held that a black was entitled to be tried by a jury from which blacks had not been excluded because of their race, Strauder v. West Virginia (1880). At the same time, however, it was decided that the black is not entitled to have any blacks on the jury; see Virginia v. Rives (1880). The Southern states adjusted themselves to these two judicial rules by the simple process of avoiding any open discrimination against blacks in the calling of grand or petit juries; and yet no names of blacks found their way on to the jury lists and no black was ever called for jury service.

This situation was tacitly acquiesced in until the famous Scottsboro cases—Powell v. Alabama (1932) and Norris v. Alabama—were brought to the Supreme Court. In Norris the Court examined with care the procedure by which the juries which had indicted and tried the blacks had been chosen, found that blacks had been excluded from them because of their race, and held that their rights under the Fourteenth Amendment had been violated. Since it is so difficult to prove either that a particular act of discrimination did occur or that it did not occur, the party who bears the burden of proof in this matter is at a marked disadvantage. In Hill v. Texas (1942) the Supreme Court made it clear that this burden of proof is not borne by the black defendant who alleges discrimination in the matter of jury service. In this case no black had served on a grand jury in the county for at least sixteen years, although there were hundreds of blacks presumably qualified to serve as grand jurors. This, the Court held, amounted to a prima facie case of discrimination which the state must rebut if it could. But such rebuttal was not made merely by showing that the jury commissioners had chosen as jurors personal acquaintances whom they knew to be qualified and that they did not happen to know any qualified blacks; they were constitutionally obligated to acquaint themselves with the qualifications of potential black jurors.

In Avery v. Georgia (1953) the Court set aside the conviction of a black by a petit jury selected from a panel on which no blacks were present. The jury panel was selected as follows: names of prospective jurors were chosen from the tax rolls and printed on tickets, the names of white persons being printed on white tickets and the names of blacks on yellow tickets. These tickets were placed in a box. They were drawn out by a judge, handed to the sheriff, who in turn entrusted them to the clerk who typed up the final list. The Supreme Court held that equal protection had been denied. "Even if the white and yellow tickets were drawn from the jury box without discrimination, opportunity was available to resort to it at other stages in the selection process. And, in view of the case before us, where not a single black was selected to serve on a panel of sixty—though many were available—we think that petitioner has certainly established a prima facie case of discrimination. . . . When a prima facie case of discrimination is presented, the burden falls, forthwith, upon the state to overcome it. The State has failed to meet this test." In Hernandez v. Texas (1954) the Court applied the rule to another racial group. They reversed the conviction of Hernandez by a jury where it was shown that no person with a Mexican or Latin-American name had served on a jury in that county for twenty-five years.

In 1965 a new problem in jury discrimination was presented to the Court. Alabama, instead of using the common-law system of peremptory challenges of individual jurors, employs what is called the "struck jury" system. In a capital case about 100 prospective jurors are assembled and after excusals and removals for cause about seventy-five remain. The prosecutor then strikes one and the defense two, taking turns, until only the necessary twelve remain as the jury. In a trial of a black for rape there had been six blacks in the original venire, but

the prosecutor had struck all of them. The Supreme Court, voting five to four in Swain v. Alabama (1965), held that the resulting jury trial did not deny equal protection of the laws, despite the fact there had never been a black on a jury in this particular county. The Court held that the system of peremptory challenges was designed to produce a fair jury, and the motives of a particular prosecutor in striking a particular venireman could not be questioned without destroying that system. It did concede that a long, uninterrupted, and systematic pattern of the state striking blacks would raise a presumption that equal protection was being denied, but there was no evidence in the record of this case that the all-white juries of the past were not, at least in part, attributable to the defendants.

In cases where blacks actually do appear on the grand or petit jury in a case, it is considerably more difficult to make out a prima facie case of discrimination. In Akins v. Texas (1944) a black was indicted and tried by juries on each of which only one black served. Each jury commissioner testified, "I did not have any intention of placing more than one black on the panel." The Court said that no race or group is entitled to proportional representation on juries, and the presence of only one black did not deny equal protection of the laws. In Cassell v. Texas (1950), however, the Court held there had been discrimination despite the appearance of blacks on the jury lists. As in Hill v. Texas, the commissioners chose jurors from personal acquaintances, and had failed to acquaint themselves with the qualifications of prospective black jurors. However, where the names of jurors are selected from the tax rolls and those with the most property are chosen first, no racial discrimination is shown by the fact that more whites than blacks appear on the jury lists; see Brown v. Allen (1953).

In Peters v. Kiff (1972) the Supreme Court for the first time heard and upheld the complaint of a white man that he had been denied a fair trial because blacks were excluded from the grand jury that indicted him and the petit jury that tried him. Justice Marshall, speaking for Justices Douglas and Stewart, argued that a segregated jury, illegal in itself, failed to provide a cross section of the community and could injure a defendant, regardless of his race, by excluding "from the jury room qualities of human nature and varieties of human experience, the range of which is unknown and perhaps unknowable." Justices White, Brennan, and Powell agreed with the result on the ground that the "majestic generalities of the Fourteenth Amendment" had been given meaning by the federal statute forbidding race discrimination in the selection of juries, while Justices Burger, Blackmun and Rehnquist dissented because there was no showing of jury prejudice.

Justice **Powell** delivered the opinion of the Court, saying in part:

This case requires us to reexamine that portion of Swain v. Alabama (1965) concerning the evidentiary burden placed on a criminal defendant who claims that he has been denied equal protection through the State's use of peremptory challenges to exclude members of his race from the petit jury.

III.

The principles announced in Strauder [v. West Virginia (1880)] never have been questioned in any subsequent decision of this Court. Rather, the Court has been called upon repeatedly to review the application of those principles to particular facts. A recurring question in these cases, as in any case alleging a violation of the Equal Protection Clause, was whether the defendant had met his burden of proving purposeful discrimination on the part of the State. ... That question also was at the heart of the portion of Swain v. Alabama we reexamine today.

A.

Swain required the Court to decide, among other issues, whether a black defendant was denied equal protection by the State's exercise of peremptory challenges to exclude members of his own race from the petit jury. ... The record in Swain showed that the prosecutor had used the State's peremptory challenges to strike the six black persons included on the petit jury venire. While rejecting the defendant's claim for failure to prove purposeful discrimination, the Court nonetheless indicated that the Equal Protection Clause placed some limits on the State's exercise of peremptory challenges.

The Court sought to accommodate the prosecutor's historical privilege of peremptory challenge free of judicial control and the constitutional prohibition on exclusion of persons from jury service on account of race. While the Constitution does not confer a right to peremptory challenges ..., those challenges traditionally have been viewed as one means of assuring the selection of a qualified and unbiased jury. To preserve the peremptory nature of the prosecutor's challenge, the Court in Swain declined to scrutinize his actions in a particular case by relying on a presumption that he properly exercised the State's challenges.

The Court went on to observe, however, that a state may not exercise its challenges in contravention of the Equal Protection Clause. It was impermissible for a prosecutor to use his challenges to exclude blacks from the jury "for reasons wholly unrelated to the outcome of the particular case on trial" or to deny to blacks "the same right and opportunity to participate in the administration of justice enjoyed by the white population." Accordingly, a black defendant could make out a prima facie case of purposeful discrimination on proof that the peremptory challenge system was "being perverted" in that manner. For example, an inference of purposeful discrimination would be raised on evidence that a prosecutor, "in case after case, whatever the circumstances, whatever the crime and whoever the defendant or the victim may be, is responsible for the removal of Negroes

who have been selected as qualified jurors by the jury commissioners and who have survived challenges for cause, with the result that no Negroes ever serve on petit juries." Evidence offered by the defendant in Swain did not meet that standard. While the defendant showed that prosecutors in the jurisdiction had exercised their strikes to exclude blacks from the jury, he offered no proof of the circumstances under which prosecutors were responsible for striking black jurors beyond the facts of his own case. ...

B.

Since the decision in Swain, we have explained that our cases concerning selection of the venire reflect the general equal protection principle that the "invidious quality" of governmental action claimed to be racially discriminatory "must ultimately be traced to a racially discriminatory purpose." Washington v. Davis (1976). As in any equal protection case, the "burden is, of course," on the defendant who alleges discriminatory selection of the venire "to prove the existence of purposeful discrimination." Whitus v. Georgia [1967]. ... In deciding if the defendant has carried his burden of persuasion, a court must undertake "a sensitive inquiry into such circumstantial and direct evidence of intent as may be available." ... Circumstantial evidence of invidious intent may include proof of disproportionate impact. ... We have observed that under some circumstances proof of discriminatory impact "may for all practical purposes demonstrate unconstitutionality because in various circumstances the discrimination is very difficult to explain on nonracial grounds." For example, "total or seriously disproportionate exclusion of Negroes from jury venires," ... "is itself such an 'unequal application of the law ... as to show intentional discrimination,' " ...

Moreover, since Swain, we have recognized that a black defendant alleging that members of his race have been impermissibly excluded from the venire may make out a prima facie case of purposeful discrimination by showing that the totality of the relevant facts gives rise to an inference of discrimination. Washington v. Davis. Once the defendant makes the requisite showing, the burden shifts to the State to explain adequately the racial exclusion. ... The State cannot meet this burden on mere general assertions that its officials did not discriminate or that they properly performed their official duties. ... Rather, the State must demonstrate that "permissible racially neutral selection criteria and procedures have produced the monochromatic result." ...

The showing necessary to establish a prima facie case of purposeful discrimination in selection of the venire may be discerned in this Court's decisions. ... The defendant initially must show that he is a member of a racial group capable of being singled out for differential treatment. ... In combination with the evidence, a defendant may then make a prima facie case by proving that in the particular jurisdiction members of his race have not been summoned for jury service over an extended period of time. Proof of systematic exclusion from the venire raises an inference of purposeful discrimination because the "result bespeaks discrimination." . . .

Since the ultimate issue is whether the State has discriminated in selecting the defendant's venire, however, the defendant may establish a prima facie case "in other ways than by evidence of long-continued unexplained absence" of members of his race "from many panels." . . . In cases involving the venire, this Court has found a prima facie case on proof that members of the defendant's race were substantially underrepresented on the venire from which his jury was drawn, and that the venire was selected under a practice providing "the opportunity for discrimination." Whitus v. Georgia. . . . This combination of factors raises the necessary inference of purposeful discrimination because the Court has declined to attribute to chance the absence of black citizens on a particular jury array where the selection mechanism is subject to abuse. When circumstances suggest the need, the trial court must undertake a "factual inquiry" that "takes into account all possible explanatory factors" in the particular case. . . .

Thus, since the decision in Swain, this Court has recognized that a defendant may make a prima facie showing of purposeful racial discrimination in selection of the venire by relying solely on the facts concerning its selection in *his* case. These decisions are in accordance with the proposition . . . that "a consistent pattern of official racial discrimination" is not "a necessary predicate to a violation of the Equal Protection Clause. A single invidiously discriminatory governmental act" is not "immunized by the absence of such discrimination in the making of other comparable decisions." . . .

C.

The standards for assessing a prima facie case in the context of discriminatory selection of the venire have been fully articulated since Swain. . . . These principles support our conclusion that a defendant may establish a prima facie case of purposeful discrimination in selection of the petit jury solely on evidence concerning the prosecutor's exercise of peremptory challenges at the defendant's trial. To establish such a case, the defendant must first show that he is a member of a cognizable racial group . . . and that the prosecutor has exercised peremptory challenges to remove from the venire members of the defendant's race. Second, the defendant is entitled to rely on the fact, as to which there can be no dispute, that peremptory challenges constitute a jury selection practice that permits "those to discriminate who are of a mind to discriminate." Avery v. Georgia. Finally, the defendant must show that these facts and any other relevant circumstances raise an inference that the prosecutor used that practice to exclude the veniremen from the petit jury on account of their race. This combination of factors in the empaneling of the petit jury, as in the se-

lection of the venire, raises the necessary inference of purposeful discrimination.

SHELLEY v. KRAEMER

334 U. S. 1; 68 S. Ct. 836; 92 L. Ed. 1161 (1948)

The Bill of Rights forbids the federal government to invade the civil liberties of the citizen; the Fourteenth Amendment forbids the state governments to do so. A private citizen cannot violate either the Bill of Rights or the Fourteenth Amendment, because neither forbids him to do anything. This fact has particular significance for the black American. In the Civil Rights Cases (1883) the Supreme Court held that the Fourteenth Amendment does not protect the black against racial discrimination practiced by private individuals. Much later this rule was sharply emphasized in decisions holding that private landowners may lawfully agree with one another not to sell or lease their land to blacks. Such agreements, known as restrictive covenants, became increasingly important after the Supreme Court in Buchanan v. Warley (1917) held that an ordinance of Louisville, Kentucky, establishing exclusive residential zones for whites and blacks violated the due process clause of the Fourteenth Amendment. What the city had tried unsuccessfully to do by law could still be done on a limited scale by private contract. In thousands of communities land in residential areas was sold by deeds which contained "covenants running with the land," by which the successive purchasers bound themselves not to sell or lease the property to blacks. The validity of such a covenant was challenged in the Supreme Court in 1926 in Corrigan v. Buckley. Here thirty white persons, owning twenty-five parcels of land in the District of Columbia, had entered into a mutually restrictive covenant barring the sale or use of the land by blacks for a period of twenty-one years. Buckley, one of the owners, sought to enjoin Corrigan, another owner, from breaching the covenant by selling one of the parcels of land to a black. It was argued that the covenant violated the due process clause of the Fifth Amendment since it discriminated against blacks. (Had the case arisen in a state, the argument would have been grounded on the Fourteenth Amendment.) The Court unanimously held the covenant valid. In a brief opinion it declared: "The Fifth Amendment is a limitation only upon the powers of the general government, and is not directed against the action of individuals."

The Court in the opinion printed below did not deny that a contract between private parties to discriminate against blacks is entirely valid, as Corrigan v. Buckley had held. What was argued, and what the Court decided, was that the judicial enforcement of such a contract by the state courts makes the government a guilty partner in the racial discrimination and thereby violates the Fourteenth Amendment. The companion case of Hurd v. Hodge (1948) held that the enforcement by the federal courts of restrictive covenants in the District of Columbia was a denial of due process of law guaranteed by the Fifth Amendment.

If a state cannot discriminate on the basis of race in its property ownership and housing policies, neither can the people, by using their law-making power, undo government efforts to abolish private discrimination. In the general election of 1964 the voters of California, by a two-to-one vote, approved a constitutional amendment forbidding either state or local governments to "limit or abridge, directly or indirectly, the right of any person, who is willing or desires to sell, lease or rent any part or all of his real property, to decline to sell, lease or rent such property to such person or persons as he, in his absolute discretion, chooses." The amendment, sponsored by the real estate interests of California, had the effect of nullifying the open-housing provisions of the Unruh Act of 1959 and the Rumford Fair Housing Act of 1963 and prohibiting the enactment of such provisions in the future. The supreme court of California held the amendment void as a violation of the Fourteenth Amendment, and in Reitman v. Mulkey (1967) the Supreme Court affirmed. Although the Court did not deny the right of California to repeal its open housing laws, it agreed with the finding of the California court that the amendment "would encourage and significantly involve the State in private racial discrimination contrary to the Fourteenth Amendment. . . . The right to discriminate, including the right to discriminate on racial grounds, was now embodied in the State's basic charter, immune from legislative, executive, or judicial regulation at any level of the state government. Those practicing racial discriminations need no longer rely solely on their personal choice. They could now invoke express constitutional authority, free from censure or interference of any kind from official sources." Justices Harlan, Black, Clark, and Stewart dissented on the ground that the amendment merely left the state as "neutral" with respect to private discrimination as it would have been had it not passed the open housing law in the first place.

In Hunter v. Erickson (1969), involving a very similar situation, the Court held void an amendment to the Akron, Ohio, city charter requiring all fair housing laws (including the one already in existence) to be submitted to a popular referendum at a city election. The Court held the amendment void, pointing out that (1) "only laws to end housing discrimination based on 'race, color, religion, national origin or ancestry' " had to run this difficult gauntlet, (2) "racial classification" bore a " 'far heavier burden of justification' than other classifications," and (3) they were "unimpressed with any of the State's justifications for its discrimination." A similar result was reached when a Seattle, Washington, school district passed by initiative and referendum a prohibition against busing students for purposes of desegregating the schools, while permitting busing for other purposes; see Washington v. Seattle School Dist. No. 1 (1982). The Court did hold valid, however, an amendment to the California constitution forbidding the state courts to order busing unless the federal courts would do so to remedy violations of the Fourteenth Amendment; see Crawford v. Los Angeles Board of Education (1982).

Where, however, discrimination is not based on race a different standard applies, and in James v. Valtierra (1971) the Court upheld, voting five to three, a California constitutional requirement that "low-rent" housing projects be submitted to the voters in the community for approval, while those designed for other groups, including middle-income groups, need pass no such hurdle. The Court stressed that the "distinctions" were not "based on race," and observed that "provisions for referendums demonstrate devotion to democracy, not to bias, discrimination, or prejudice."

The Court has been slow to lay down guides as to how much state participation was necessary to convert clearly discriminatory private action into "state" action under the equal protection clause. While the Court in the present case answered the question with regard to court enforcement, in none of the "sit-in" cases of the 1960s did the Court say whether state enforcement of its trespass laws to back up private discrimination amounted to such action or not.

In Moose Lodge No. 107 v. Irvis (1972) the Court held that the mere granting of a liquor license to a private club that discriminated against blacks did not normally involve the state in discrimination. To hold that any state aid, such as fire or police protection, made a private club an agent of the state would be to destroy entirely the distinction between state and private action. "The State must have 'significantly involved itself with invidious discriminations,' Reitman v. Mulkey (1967), in order for the discriminatory action to fall within the ambit of the constitutional prohibition." In this case, however, state regulations required the club to adhere to its bylaws, and to the extent that these required discrimination, the regulations were unconstitutional since this "would be to invoke the sanctions of the State to enforce a concededly discriminatory private rule."

Mr. Chief Justice **Vinson** delivered the opinion of the Court, saying in part:

These cases present for our consideration questions relating to the validity of court enforcement of private agreements, generally described as restrictive covenants, which have as their purpose the exclusion of persons of designated race or color from the ownership or occupancy of real property. Basic constitutional issues of obvious importance have been raised.

The first of these cases comes to this Court on certiorari to the Supreme Court of Missouri. On February 16, 1911, thirty out of a total of thirty-nine owners of property fronting both sides of Labadie Avenue between Taylor Avenue and Cora Avenue in the city of St. Louis, signed an agreement, which was subsequently recorded, providing in part:

". . . The said property is hereby restricted to the use and occupancy for the term of Fifty (50) years from this date, so that it shall be a condition all the time and whether recited and referred to as [*sic*] not in subsequent conveyances and shall attach to the land, as a condition precedent to the sale of the same, that hereafter no part of said property or any portion thereof shall be, for said term of Fifty years, occupied by any person not of the Caucasian race, it being intended hereby to restrict the use of said property for said period of time against the occupancy as owners or tenants of any portion of said property for resident or other purpose by people of the Negro or Mongolian Race.'' . . .

On August 11, 1945, pursuant to a contract of sale, petitioners Shelley, who are Negroes, for valuable consideration received from one Fitzgerald a warranty deed to the parcel in question. The trial court found that petitioners had no actual knowledge of the restrictive agreement at the time of the purchase.

On October 9, 1945, respondents, as owners of other property subject to the terms of the restrictive covenant, brought suit in the Circuit Court of the city of St. Louis praying that petitioners Shelley be restrained from taking possession of the property and that judgment be entered divesting title out of petitioners Shelley and revesting title in the immediate grantor or in such other person as the court should direct. The trial court denied the requested relief on the ground that the restrictive agreement, upon which respondents based their action, had never become final and complete because it was the intention of the parties to that agreement that it was not to become effective until signed by all property owners in the district, and signatures of all the owners had never been obtained.

The Supreme Court of Missouri sitting en banc reversed and directed the trial court to grant the relief for which respondents had prayed. That court held the agreement effective and concluded that enforcement of its provisions violated no rights guaranteed to petitioners by the Federal Constitution. At the time the court rendered its decision, petitioners were occupying the property in question. . . .

Petitioners have placed primary reliance on their contentions, first raised in the state courts, that judicial enforcement of the restrictive agreements in these cases has violated rights guaranteed to petitioners by the Fourteenth Amendment of the Federal Constitution and Acts of Congress passed pursuant to that Amendment. Specifically, petitioners urge that they have been denied the equal protection of the laws, deprived of property without due process of law, and have been denied privileges and immunities of citizens of the United States. We pass to a consideration of those issues.

I.

Whether the equal protection clause of the Fourteenth Amendment inhibits judicial enforcement by state courts of restrictive covenants based on race or color is a question which this Court has not heretofore been called upon to consider. . . .

It is well, at the outset, to scrutinize the terms of the restrictive agreements involved in these cases. In the Missouri case, the covenant declares that no part of the affected property shall be ''occupied by any person not of the Caucasian race, it being intended hereby to restrict the use of said property . . . against the occupancy as owners or tenants of any portion of said property for resident or other purpose by people of the Negro or Mongolian Race.'' Not only does the restriction seek to proscribe use and occupancy of the affected properties by members of the excluded class, but as construed by the Missouri courts, the agreement requires that title of any person who uses his property in violation of the restriction shall be divested. . . .

It cannot be doubted that among the civil rights intended to be protected from discriminatory state action by the Fourteenth Amendment are the rights to acquire, enjoy, own and dispose of property. Equality in the enjoyment of property rights was regarded by the framers of that Amendment as an essential pre-condition to the realization of other basic civil rights and liberties which the Amendment was intended to guarantee. Thus, § 1978 of the Revised Statutes, derived from § 1 of the Civil Rights Act of 1866 which was enacted by Congress while the Fourteenth Amendment was also under consideration provides:

''All citizens of the United States shall have the same right, in every State and Territory, as is enjoyed by white citizens thereof to inherit, purchase, lease, sell, hold, and convey real and personal property.'' This Court has given specific recognition to the same principle. Buchanan v. Warley (1917).

It is likewise clear that restrictions on the right of occupancy of the sort sought to be created by the private agreements in these cases could not be squared with the requirements of the Fourteenth Amendment if imposed by state statute or local ordinance. . . .

But the present cases, unlike those just discussed, do not involve action by state legislatures or city councils. Here the particular patterns of discrimination and the areas in which the restrictions are to operate, are determined, in the first instance, by the terms of agreements among private individuals. Participation of the State consists in the enforcement of the restrictions so defined. The crucial issue with which we are here confronted is whether this distinction removes these cases from the operation of the prohibitory provisions of the Fourteenth Amendment.

Since the decision of this Court in the Civil Rights Cases (1883) the principle has become firmly embedded in our constitutional law that the action inhibited by the first section of the Fourteenth Amendment is only such action as may fairly be said to be that of the States. That Amendment erects no shield against merely private conduct, however discriminatory or wrongful.

We conclude, therefore, that the restrictive agreements standing alone cannot be regarded as violative of any rights guaranteed to petitioners by the Fourteenth Amendment. So long as the purposes of those agreements are effectuated by voluntary adherence to their terms, it would appear clear that there has been no action by the State and the provisions of the Amendment have not been violated. Cf. Corrigan v. Buckley.

But here there was more. These are cases in which the purposes of the agreements were secured only by judicial enforcement by state courts of the restrictive terms of the agreements. The respondents urge that judicial enforcement of private agreements does not amount to state action; or, in any event, the participation of the States is so attenuated in character as not to amount to state action within the meaning of the Fourteenth Amendment. Finally, it is suggested, even if the States in these cases may be deemed to have acted in the constitutional sense, their action did not deprive petitioners of rights guaranteed by the Fourteenth Amendment. We move to a consideration of these matters.

II.

That the action of state courts and of judicial officers in their official capacities is to be regarded as action of the State within the meaning of the Fourteenth Amendment, is a proposition which has long been established by decisions of this Court. That principle was given expression in the earliest cases involving the construction of the terms of the Fourteenth Amendment. . . . [The Court here discusses several cases in which state judicial action was held to be discriminatory and therefore a violation of the Fourteenth Amendment.]

But the examples of state judicial action which have been held by this Court to violate the Amendment's commands are not restricted to situations in which the judicial proceedings were found in some manner to be procedurally unfair. It has been recognized that the action of state courts in enforcing a substantive common-law rule formulated by those courts, may result in the denial of rights guaranteed by the Fourteenth Amendment, even though the judicial proceedings in such cases may have been in complete accord with the most rigorous conceptions of procedural due process. . . .

The short of the matter is that from the time of the adoption of the Fourteenth Amendment until the present, it has been the consistent ruling of this Court that the action of the States to which the Amendment has reference, includes action of state courts and state judicial officials. Although, in construing the terms of the Fourteenth Amendment, differences have from time to time been expressed as to whether particular types of state action may be said to offend the Amendment's prohibitory provisions, it has never been suggested that state court action is immunized from the operation of those provisions simply because the act is that of the judicial branch of the state government.

III.

Against this background of judicial construction, extending over a period of some three-quarters of a century, we are called upon to consider whether enforcement by state courts of the restrictive agreements in these cases may be deemed to be the acts of those States; and, if so, whether that action has denied these petitioners the equal protection of the laws which the Amendment was intended to insure.

We have no doubt that there has been state action in these cases in the full and complete sense of the phrase. The undisputed facts disclose that petitioners were willing purchasers of properties upon which they desired to establish homes. The owners of the properties were willing sellers; and contracts of sale were accordingly consummated. It is clear that but for the active intervention of the state courts, supported by the full panoply of state power, petitioners would have been free to occupy the properties in question without restraint.

These are not cases, as has been suggested, in which the States have merely abstained from action, leaving private individuals free to impose such discriminations as they see fit. Rather, these are cases in which the States have made available to such individuals the full coercive power of government to deny to petitioners, on the grounds of race or color, the enjoyment of property rights in premises which petitioners are willing and financially able to acquire and which the grantors are willing to sell. The difference between judicial enforcement and non-enforcement of the restrictive covenants is the difference to petitioners between being denied rights of property available to other members of the community and being accorded full enjoyment of those rights on an equal footing. . . .

We hold that in granting judicial enforcement of the restrictive agreements in these cases, the States have denied petitioners the equal protection of the laws and that, therefore, the action of the state courts cannot stand. We have noted that freedom from discrimination by the States in the enjoyment of property rights was among the basic objectives sought to be effectuated by the framers of the Fourteenth Amendment. That such discrimination has occurred in these cases is clear. Because of the race or color of these petitioners they have been denied rights of ownership or occupancy enjoyed as a matter of course by other citizens of different race or color. . . .

Respondents urge, however, that since the state courts stand ready to enforce restrictive covenants excluding white persons from the ownership or occupancy of property covered by such agreements, enforcement of covenants excluding colored persons may not be deemed a denial of equal protection of the laws to the colored persons who are thereby affected. This contention does not bear scrutiny. The parties have directed our attention to no case in which a court, state or federal, has been called upon to enforce a covenant excluding members of the white majority from ownership or occupancy of real property on grounds of race or color. But there are more fundamental considerations. The rights created by the first section of the Fourteenth Amendment are, by its terms, guaranteed to the individual. The rights established are personal rights. It is, therefore, no answer to these petitioners to say that the courts may also be induced to deny white persons rights of ownership and occupancy on grounds of race or color. Equal protection of the laws is not achieved through indiscriminate imposition of inequalities. . . .

The historical context in which the Fourteenth Amendment became a part of the Constitution should not be forgotten. Whatever else the framers sought to achieve, it is clear that the matter of primary concern was the establishment of equality in the enjoyment of basic civil and political rights and the preservation of those rights from discriminatory action on the part of the States based on considerations of race or color. Seventy-five years ago this Court announced that the provisions of the Amendment are to be construed with this fundamental purpose in mind. Upon full consideration, we have concluded that in these cases the States have acted to deny petitioners the equal protection of the laws guaranteed by the Fourteenth Amendment. Having so decided, we find it unnecessary to consider whether petitioners have also been deprived of property without due process of law or denied privileges and immunities of citizens of the United States. . . .

Reversed.

Justices **Reed, Jackson,** and **Rutledge** took no part in the consideration or decision of these cases.

PLESSY v. FERGUSON

163 U. S. 537; 16 S. Ct. 1138; 41 L. Ed. 256
(1896)

With the passing of the Reconstruction era and the return of "white man's government" to the Southern states, state laws were again adopted reminiscent of the "Black Codes" which had been passed right after the Civil War to "keep the Negro in his place." These laws established, and enforced by criminal penalties, a system of racial segregation under which members of the black and white races were required to be separated in the enjoyment of public and semi-public facilities. Separate schools, parks, waiting rooms, bus and railroad accommodations were required by law to be furnished each race; and where completely separate facilities later on proved to be not feasible, as in a dining car, a curtained partition served to separate the races.

Where racial segregation was effected by private action, as in the case of stores or clubs, no constitutional issue could be raised after the decision in the Civil Rights Cases in 1883. Where the segregation was required by law, however, the question arose whether it violated the rights guaranteed to the newly freed black by the Fourteenth Amendment. This problem came to the Court for the first time in the present case, twenty-eight years after the Amendment had been adopted. The legislature of Louisiana had passed in 1890 a statute providing "that all railway companies carrying passengers in their coaches in this state shall provide equal but separate accommodations for the white and colored races, by providing two or more passenger coaches for each pas-

senger train, or by dividing the passenger coaches by a partition so as to secure separate accommodations. . . ." A fine of $25 or twenty days in jail was the penalty for sitting in the wrong compartment. Plessy, a person who was one-eighth black, refused to vacate a seat in the white compartment of a railway car and was arrested for violating the statute.

The Plessy case made lawful for nearly sixty years the doctrine that blacks are not denied the equal protection of the laws by compelling them to accept "separate but equal" accommodations. There is a bit of irony in the fact that the majority opinion in the Plessy case was written by Justice Brown, a Yale man from the state of Michigan, while the eloquent protest against racial discrimination is found in the dissenting opinion of Justice Harlan, a Southerner from Kentucky.

Query: *Does it raise an equal protection question that the Court accepted the state's determination that Plessy, who was seven-eighths white, was black? What would have been the impact of a ruling that permitted segregation but held that a person was to be considered white if he were more than 50 percent white, and black if he were more than 50 percent black?*

Mr. Justice **Brown** delivered the opinion of the Court, saying in part:

The object of the [Fourteenth] amendment was undoubtedly to enforce the absolute equality of the two races before the law, but in the nature of things it could not have been intended to abolish distinctions based upon color, or to enforce social, as distinguished from political, equality, or a commingling of the two races upon terms unsatisfactory to either. Laws permitting, and even requiring their separation in places where they are liable to be brought into contact do not necessarily imply the inferiority of either race to the other, and have been generally, if not universally, recognized as within the competency of the state legislatures in the exercise of their police power. The most common instance of this is connected with the establishment of separate schools for white and colored children, which [has] been held to be a valid exercise of the legislative power even by courts of states where the political rights of the colored race have been longest and most earnestly enforced.

One of the earliest of these cases is that of Roberts v. Boston, 5 Cush. (Mass.) 198 [1849] in which the supreme judicial court of Massachusetts held that the general school committee of Boston had power to make provision for the instruction of colored children in separate schools established exclusively for them, and to prohibit their attendance upon the other schools. . . . Similar laws have been enacted by Congress under its general power of legislation over the District of Columbia, as well as by the legislatures of many of the states, and have been generally, if not uniformly, sustained by the courts. . . .

Laws forbidding the intermarriage of the two races may be said in a technical sense to interfere with the freedom of contract, and yet have been universally recognized as within the police power of the state. . . .

The distinction between laws interfering with the political equality of the negro and those requiring the separation of the two races in schools, theatres, and railway carriages, has been frequently drawn by this court. . . .

In this connection, it is also suggested by the learned counsel for the plaintiff in error that the same argument that will justify the state legislature in requiring railways to provide separate accommodations for the two races will also authorize them to require separate cars to be provided for people whose hair is of a certain color, or who are aliens, or who belong to certain nationalities, or to enact laws requiring colored people to walk upon one side of the street, and white people upon the other, or requiring white men's houses to be painted white, and colored men's black, or their vehicles or business signs to be of different colors, upon the theory that one side of the street is as good as the other, or that a house or vehicle of one color is as good as one of another color. The reply to all this is that every exercise of the police power must be reasonable, and extend only to such laws as are enacted in good faith for the promotion of the public good, and not for the annoyance or oppression of a particular class. . . .

So far, then, as a conflict with the 14th Amendment is concerned, the case reduces itself to the question whether the statute of Louisiana is a reasonable regulation, and with respect to this there must necessarily be a large discretion on the part of the legislature. In determining the question of reasonableness it is at liberty to act with reference to the established usages, customs, and traditions of the people, and with a view to the promotion of their comfort, and the preservation of the public peace and good order. Gauged by this standard, we cannot say that a law which authorizes or even requires the separation of the two races in public conveyances is unreasonable, or more obnoxious to the 14th Amendment than the acts of Congress requiring separate schools for colored children in the District of Columbia, the constitutionality of which does not seem to have been questioned, or the corresponding acts of state legislatures.

We consider the underlying fallacy of the plaintiff's argument to consist in the assumption that the enforced separation of the two races stamps the colored race with a badge of inferiority. If this be so, it is not by reason of anything found in the act, but solely because the colored race chooses to put that construction upon it. The argument necessarily assumes that if, as has been more than once the case, and is not unlikely to be so again, the colored race should become the dominant power in the state legislature, and should enact a law in precisely similar terms, it would thereby relegate the white race to an inferior position. We imagine that the white race, at least, would not acquiesce in this assumption. The argument also assumes that social prejudices may be overcome by legislation, and that equal rights cannot be secured to the negro except by an enforced commingling of the two races. We cannot accept this proposition. If the two races are to meet on terms of social equality, it must be the result of natural affinities, a mutual appreciation of each other's merits and a voluntary consent of individuals. . . . Legislation is powerless to eradicate racial instincts or to abolish distinctions based upon physical differences, and the attempt to do so can only result in accentuating the difficulties of the present situation. If the civil and political rights of both races be equal, one cannot be inferior to the other civilly or politically. If one race be inferior to the other socially, the Constitution of the United States cannot put them upon the same plane. . . .

The judgment of the court below is therefore affirmed.

Mr. Justice **Brewer** took no part in the decision of this case.

Mr. Justice **Harlan** wrote a dissenting opinion, saying in part:

While there may be in Louisiana persons of different races who are not citizens of the United States, the words in the act, ''white and colored races,'' necessarily include all citizens of the United States of both races residing in that state. So that we have before us a state enactment that compels, under penalties, the separation of the two races in railroad passenger coaches, and makes it a crime for a citizen of either race to enter a coach that has been assigned to citizens of the other race.

Thus the state regulates the use of a public highway by citizens of the United States solely upon the basis of race.

However apparent the injustice of such legislation may be, we have only to consider whether it is consistent with the Constitution of the United States. . . .

In respect of civil rights, common to all citizens, the Constitution of the United States does not, I think, permit any public authority to know the race of those entitled to be protected in the enjoyment of such rights. Every true man has pride of race, and under appropriate circumstances, when the rights of others, his equals before the law, are not to be affected, it is his privilege to express such pride and to take such action based upon it as to him seems proper. But I deny that any legislative body or judicial tribunal may have regard to the race of citizens when the civil rights of those citizens are involved. Indeed such legislation as that here in question is inconsistent, not only with that equality of rights which pertains to citizenship, national and state, but with the personal liberty enjoyed by every one within the United States. . . .

The white race deems itself to be the dominant race in this country. And so it is, in prestige, in achievements, in education, in wealth and in power. So, I doubt not that it will continue to be for all time, if it remains true to its great heritage and holds fast to the principles of constitutional liberty. But in view of the Constitution, in the eye of the law, there is in this country no superior, dominant, ruling class of citizens. There is no caste here. Our Constitution is color-blind, and neither knows nor tolerates classes among citizens. In respect of civil rights, all citizens are equal before the law. The humblest is the peer of the most powerful. The law regards man as man, and takes no account of his surroundings or of his color when his civil rights as guaranteed by the supreme law of the land are involved. It is therefore to be regretted that this high tribunal, the final expositor of the fundamental law of the land, has reached the conclusion that it is competent for a state to regulate the enjoyment by citizens of their civil rights solely upon the basis of race.

In my opinion, the judgment this day rendered will, in time, prove to be quite as pernicious as the decision made by this tribunal in the Dred Scott Case. It was adjudged in that case that the descendants of Africans who were imported into this country and sold as slaves were not included nor intended to be included under the word "citizens" in the Constitution, and could not claim any of the rights and privileges which that instrument provided for and secured to citizens of the United States; that at the time of the adoption of the Constitution they were "considered as a subordinate and inferior class of beings, who had been subjugated by the dominant race, and, whether emancipated or not, yet remained subject to their authority, and had no rights or privileges but such as those who held the power and the government might choose to grant them." The recent amendments of the Constitution, it was supposed, had eradicated these principles from our institutions. But it seems that we have yet, in some of the states, a dominant race, a superior class of citizens, which assumes to regulate the enjoyment of civil rights, common to all citizens, upon the basis of race. The present decision, it may well be apprehended, will not [only] stimulate aggressions, more or less brutal and irritating, upon the admitted rights of colored citizens, but will encourage the belief that it is possible, by means of state enactments, to defeat the beneficent purposes which the people of the United States had in view when they adopted the recent amendments of the Constitution, by one of which the blacks of this country were made citizens of the United States and of the states in which they respectively reside and whose privileges and immunities, as citizens, the states are forbidden to abridge. Sixty millions of whites are in no danger from the presence here of eight millions of blacks. The destinies of the two races in this country are indissolubly linked together, and the interests of both require that the common government of all shall not permit the seeds of race hate to be planted under the sanction of law. What can more certainly arouse race hate, what more certainly create and perpetuate a feeling of distrust between these races, than State enactments which in fact proceed on the ground that colored citizens are so inferior and degraded that they cannot be allowed to sit in public coaches occupied by white citizens? That, as all will admit, is the real meaning of such legislation as was enacted in Louisiana.

The sure guarantee of the peace and security of each race is the clear, distinct, unconditional recognition by our governments, national and state, of every right that inheres in civil freedom, and of the equality before the law of all citizens of the United States without regard to race. State enactments, regulating the enjoyment of civil rights, upon the basis of race, and cunningly devised to defeat legitimate results of the war, under the pretense of recognizing equality of rights, can have no other result than to render permanent peace impossible and to keep alive a conflict of races, the continuance of which must do harm to all concerned. This question is not met by the suggestion that social equality cannot exist between the white and black races in this country. That argument, if it can be properly regarded as one, is scarcely worthy of consideration, for social equality no more exists between two races when travelling in a passenger coach or a public highway than when members of the same races sit by each other in a street car or in the jury box, or stand or sit with each other in a political assembly, or when they use in common the streets of a city or town, or when they are in the same room for the purpose of having their names placed on the registry of voters, or when they approach the ballot-box in order to exercise the high privilege of voting. . . .

The arbitrary separation of citizens, on the basis of race, while they are on a public highway, is a badge of servitude wholly inconsistent with the civil freedom and the equality before the law established by the Constitution. It cannot be justified upon any legal grounds.

If evils will result from the commingling of the two races upon public highways established for the benefit of all, they will be infinitely less than those that will surely come from state legislation regulating the enjoyment of civil rights upon the basis of race. We boast of the freedom enjoyed by our people above all other peoples. But it is difficult to reconcile that boast with a state of the law which, practically, puts the brand of servitude and degradation upon a large class of our fellow citizens, our equals before the law. The thin disguise of "equal" accommodations for passengers in railroad coaches will not mislead any one, or atone for the wrong this day done. . . .

I am of opinion that the statute of Louisiana is inconsistent with the personal liberty of citizens, white and black, in that state, and hostile to both the spirit and letter of the Constitution of the United States. If laws of like character should be enacted in the several states of the Union, the effect would be in the highest degree mischievous. Slavery as an institution tolerated by law would, it is true, have disappeared from our country, but there would remain a power in the states, by sinister legislation, to interfere with the full enjoyment of the blessings of freedom; to regulate civil rights, common to all citizens, upon the basis of race; and to place in a condition of legal inferiority a large body of American citizens, now constituting a part of the political community, called the people of the United States, for whom and by whom, through representatives, our government is administered. Such a system is inconsistent with the guarantee given by the Constitution to each state of a republican form of government, and may be stricken down by congressional action, or by the courts in the discharge of their solemn duty to maintain the supreme law of the land, anything in the Constitution or laws of any state to the contrary notwithstanding.

For the reasons stated, I am constrained to withhold my assent from the opinion and judgment of the majority.

SWEATT v. PAINTER

339 U. S. 629; 70 S. Ct. 848; 94 L. Ed. 1114 (1950)

Although Plessy v. Ferguson (1896) involved segregation only in the use of railroad facilities, there was no reason to doubt that the Court would uphold segregation in other areas as well, especially education. This became clear when the Court, in Berea College v. Kentucky (1908), held that the state could validly forbid a college, even though a private institution, to teach whites and blacks at the same time and place. This left no doubt of the validity of the Southern laws requiring the education of white and black children in separate tax-supported schools.

While the segregation of whites and blacks was valid, it was valid only on the theory that the facilities offered were equal, since it is the ''equal'' protection of the laws that is guaranteed by the Fourteenth Amendment. In common usage there are no degrees of equality; things or conditions are either equal or they are not equal. But the Supreme Court has not taken this view. It has held, rather, that equality in accommodations means not exact or mathematical equality, but only ''substantial'' equality. In earlier cases the Court was extremely lenient in construing what ''equality'' required in the segregated school systems of the South. In Cumming v. County Board of Education (1899) it found no denial of equal protection of the laws in the failure of a Southern county to provide a high school for sixty black children, although it maintained a high school for white children. The Court seemed satisfied with the county's defense that it could not afford to build a high school for black children. In Gong Lum v. Rice (1927) the Court held that a Chinese girl could validly be required to attend a school for black children in a neighboring school district, rather than be allowed to attend the nearby school for white children.

In 1914 the Supreme Court began to show signs of requiring a much closer approach to equality under segregation. In McCabe v. Atchison, T. & S. F. Ry. Co. (1914) an Oklahoma law was held not to accord equal accommodations to blacks and whites when it allowed railroads to haul sleeping, dining, and chair cars for the exclusive use of whites without providing such cars on demand for the use of blacks.

The tougher attitude of the Court toward what equality under segregation means was made abundantly clear in 1938 in the leading case of Missouri ex rel.

Gaines v. Canada. Gaines, a black graduate of Lincoln University and a citizen of Missouri, applied for admission to the University of Missouri law school. He was refused solely upon the ground that he was black, but the state agreed to pay his tuition in the law school of any adjacent state which would accept him, pending such time as Missouri should itself build a black law school. Kansas, Nebraska, Iowa, and Illinois had law schools which admitted nonresident blacks. The Supreme Court found that Gaines had been denied equal protection of the laws, and ruled that ''. . . petitioner was entitled to be admitted to the law school of the State University in the absence of other and proper provision for his legal training within the State.'' The Court said, ''The basic consideration is not as to what sort of opportunities other States provide, or whether they are as good as those in Missouri, but as to what opportunities Missouri itself furnishes to white students and denies to negroes solely upon the ground of color. . . . Manifestly, the obligation of the State to give the protection of equal laws can be performed only where its laws operate, that is, within its own jurisdiction.''

In 1948 a case almost identical with the Gaines case came to the Court from Oklahoma. A young black woman applied for admission to the law school of the University of Oklahoma and was refused. In Sipuel v. University of Oklahoma (1948) the Court in a one-page opinion reaffirmed the ruling in the Gaines case. It said: ''The petitioner is entitled to secure legal education afforded by a state institution. To this time it has been denied her although during the same period many white applicants have been afforded legal education by the State. The State must provide it for her in conformity with the equal protection clause of the Fourteenth Amendment and provide it as soon as it does for applicants of any other group.''

A black graduate student was admitted to the University of Oklahoma, but was required to sit in a row in the classroom specified for black students, at a designated table in the library, and at a special table in the cafeteria. In McLaurin v. Oklahoma State Regents (1950) the Supreme Court held that under the equal protection clause the black student must be given the same treatment by the state as students of other races.

While Congress has full power to regulate interstate commerce, it had never abolished racial segregation on interstate trains. All it had done was to forbid any interstate common carrier to give any person or group any ''unreasonable preference or advantage,'' or subject them to ''any undue or unreasonable prejudice or disadvantage.'' In practice these restrictions had been interpreted in the light of the ''separate but equal'' doctrine of Plessy v. Ferguson. The Southern Railway Company segregated blacks in dining cars by reserving ten tables exclusively for white passengers, and one table exclusively for blacks. A curtain or partition cut the black table off from the others. In Henderson v. United States (1950) the Court held that such segregation subjected black passengers to undue prejudice and disadvantage, and in 1961 the Interstate Commerce Commis-

sion issued a regulation forbidding interstate motor carriers of passengers to discriminate on grounds of race, color, creed, or national origin in the seating of such passengers, or in the terminal facilities provided for them, such as "waiting room, restroom, eating, drinking, and ticket sales facilities," or to display signs indicating such discrimination.

In Allston v. School Board (1940) the circuit court of appeals held that in the segregated school system of Norfolk, Virginia, black teachers must be paid the same salaries as white teachers if they did the same work. The Supreme Court refused to review the case on certiorari, thereby affirming the decision of the lower court. The small salaries paid to black teachers had contributed directly to the low standard of black education in the South.

Mr. Chief Justice **Vinson** delivered the opinion of the Court:

This case and McLaurin v. Oklahoma State Regents [1950] present different aspects of this general question: To what extent does the Equal Protection Clause of the Fourteenth Amendment limit the power of a state to distinguish between students of different races in professional and graduate education in a state university? Broader issues have been urged for our consideration, but we adhere to the principle of deciding constitutional questions only in the context of the particular case before the Court. We have frequently reiterated that this Court will decide constitutional questions only when necessary to the disposition of the case at hand, and that such decisions will be drawn as narrowly as possible. . . . Because of this traditional reluctance to extend constitutional interpretations to situations or facts which are not before the Court, much of the excellent research and detailed argument presented in these cases is unnecessary to their disposition.

In the instant case, petitioner filed an application for admission to the University of Texas Law School for the February, 1946 term. His application was rejected solely because he is a Negro. Petitioner thereupon brought this suit for mandamus against the appropriate school officials, respondents here, to compel his admission. At that time, there was no law school in Texas which admitted Negroes.

The state trial court recognized that the action of the State in denying petitioner the opportunity to gain a legal education while granting it to others deprived him of the equal protection of the laws guaranteed by the Fourteenth Amendment. The court did not grant the relief requested, however, but continued the case for six months to allow the State to supply substantially equal facilities. At the expiration of the six months, in December, 1946, the court denied the writ on the showing that the authorized university officials had adopted an order calling for the opening of a law school for Negroes the following February. While petitioner's appeal was pending, such a school was made available, but petitioner refused to register therein. The Texas Court of Civil Appeals set aside the trial court's judgment and ordered the cause "remanded generally to the trial court for further proceedings without prejudice to the rights of any party to this suit."

On remand, a hearing was held on the issue of the equality of the educational facilities at the newly established school as compared with the University of Texas Law School. Finding that the new school offered petitioner "privileges, advantages, and opportunities for the study of law substantially equivalent to those offered by the State to white students at the University of Texas," the trial court denied mandamus. The Court of Civil Appeals affirmed. . . . Petitioner's application for a writ of error was denied by the Texas Supreme Court. We granted certiorari because of the manifest importance of the constitutional issues involved.

The University of Texas Law School, from which petitioner was excluded, was staffed by a faculty of sixteen full-time and three part-time professors, some of whom are nationally recognized authorities in their field. Its student body numbered 850. The library contained over 65,000 volumes. Among the other facilities available to the students were a law review, moot court facilities, scholarship funds, and Order of the Coif affiliation. The school's alumni occupy the most distinguished positions in the private practice of the law and in the public life of the State. It may properly be considered one of the nation's ranking law schools.

The law school for Negroes which was to have opened in February, 1947, would have had no independent faculty or library. The teaching was to be carried on by four members of the University of Texas Law School faculty, who were to maintain their offices at the University of Texas while teaching at both institutions. Few of the 10,000 volumes ordered for the library had arrived; nor was there any full-time librarian. The school lacked accreditation.

Since the trial of this case, respondents report the opening of a law school at the Texas State University for Negroes. It is apparently on the road to full accreditation. It has a faculty of five full-time professors; a student body of 23; a library of some 16,500 volumes serviced by a full-time staff; a practice court and legal aid association; and one alumnus who has become a member of the Texas Bar.

Whether the University of Texas Law School is compared with the original or the new law school for Negroes, we cannot find substantial equality in the educational opportunities offered white and Negro law students by the State. In terms of number of the faculty, variety of courses and opportunity for specialization, size of the student body, scope of the library, availability of law review and similar activities, the University of Texas Law School is superior. What is more important, the University of Texas Law School possesses to a far greater degree those qualities which are incapable of objective measurement but which make for greatness in a law school. Such qualities, to name but a few, include reputation of the faculty, experience of the administration, position and influence of the alumni, standing in the community, traditions and prestige. It is difficult to believe that one who had a free choice between these law schools would consider the question close.

Moreover, although the law is a highly learned profession, we are well aware that it is an intensely practical one. The law school, the proving ground for legal learning and practice, cannot be effective in isolation from the individuals and institutions with which the law interacts. Few students and no one who has practiced law would choose to study in an academic vacuum, removed from the interplay of ideas and the exchange of views with which the law is concerned. The law school to which Texas is willing to admit petitioner excludes from its student body members of the racial groups which number 85% of the population of the State and include most of the lawyers, witnesses, jurors, judges and other officials with whom petitioner will inevitably be dealing when he becomes a member of the Texas Bar. With such a substantial and significant segment of society excluded, we cannot conclude that the education offered petitioner is substantially equal to that which he would receive if admitted to the University of Texas Law School.

It may be argued that excluding petitioner from that school is no different from excluding white students from the new law school. This contention overlooks realities. It is unlikely that a member of a group so decisively in the majority, attending a school with rich traditions and prestige which only a history of consistently maintained excellence could command, would claim that the opportunities afforded him for legal education were unequal to those held open to petitioner. That such a claim, if made, would be dishonored by the State, is no answer. "Equal protection of the laws is not achieved through indiscriminate imposition of inequalities." . . .

It is fundamental that these cases concern rights which are personal and present. This Court has stated unanimously that "The State must provide [legal education] for [petitioner] in conformity with the equal protection clause of the Fourteenth Amendment and provide it as soon as it does for applicants of any other group." Sipuel v. Board of Regents (1948). That case "did not present the issue whether a state might not satisfy the equal protection clause of the Fourteenth Amendment by establishing a separate law school for Negroes." Fisher v. Hurst (1948). In Missouri ex rel. Gaines v. Canada (1938), the Court, speaking through Chief Justice Hughes, declared that "petitioner's right was a personal one. It was as an individual that he was entitled to the equal protection of the laws, and the State was bound to furnish him within its borders facilities for legal education substantially equal to those which the State there afforded for persons of the white race, whether or not other negroes sought the same opportunity." These are the only cases in this Court which present the issue of the constitutional validity of race distinctions in state-supported graduate and professional education.

In accordance with these cases, petitioner may claim his full constitutional right: legal education equivalent to that offered by the State to students of other races. Such education is not available to him in a separate law school as offered by the State. We cannot, therefore, agree with respondents that the doctrine of Plessy v. Ferguson (1896) requires affirmance of the judgment below. Nor need we reach petitioner's contention that Plessy v. Ferguson should be reexamined in the light of contemporary knowledge respecting the purposes of the Fourteenth Amendment and the effects of racial segregation.

We hold that the Equal Protection Clause of the Fourteenth Amendment requires that petitioner be admitted to the University of Texas Law School. The judgment is reversed and the cause is remanded for proceedings not inconsistent with this opinion.

Reversed.

BROWN v. BOARD OF EDUCATION OF TOPEKA

347 U. S. 483; 74 S. Ct. 686; 98 L. Ed. 873 (1954)

In the cases dealing with black segregation which reached the Supreme Court after Plessy v. Ferguson (1896) the doctrine of that case was followed and never reexamined. The Court seemed content with the "separate but equal" rule of that case, which, as someone aptly put it, guaranteed to the black "the equal, but different, protection of the laws." During the forty-year period beginning with the McCabe case in 1914, the Court, applying ever more rigid standards of equality under segregation, found that black plaintiffs in each case had in fact been denied equality of treatment; and so the Court, following the rule that it will not decide constitutional issues if it can avoid doing so, continued to grant relief to blacks not because they were segregated but because they were unequally treated under segregation. While in the Texas Law School case and the dining car case the Court virtually stated that there were circumstances in which segregation in itself resulted in inequality of treatment, the rule of Plessy v. Ferguson remained intact.

In the fall of 1952, however, the Supreme Court had on its docket cases from four states (Kansas, South Carolina, Virginia, and Delaware), and from the District of Columbia, challenging the constitutionality of racial segregation in public schools. In all these cases the facts showed that "the Negro and white schools involved have been equalized, or are being equalized, with respect to buildings, curricula, qualifications and salaries of teachers, and other 'tangible' factors." After nearly sixty years the Court again had squarely before it the question of the constitutionality of segregation per se— the question of whether the doctrine of Plessy v. Ferguson should be affirmed or reversed.

The five cases were argued together in December, 1952, and the country waited with tense interest for the Court's decision. On June 8, 1953, the Court restored the cases to the docket for reargument in the fall and issued a list of questions upon which it wished that argument to turn. The Court asked for enlightenment on two main points. First, is there historical evidence which shows the intentions of those who framed and ratified the Fourteenth Amendment with respect to the impact of that amendment upon racial segregation in the public school? Second, if the Court finds racial segregation violates the Fourteenth Amendment, what kind of decree could and should be issued to bring about an end of segregation?

The cases were reargued in December 1953. Elaborate briefs set forth in great detail the background of the Fourteenth Amendment and the intentions of its framers and ratifiers. The negative result of this historical research is commented on in the opinion below. Some of the briefs, including the one filed by the Attorney General, presented suggestions on the form of the court decree by which segregation might best be ended should the Court hold it to be invalid. Counsel for the National Association for the Advancement of Colored People, which had played a major part in the instigation of these cases, declined to deal with this point. In their counsel's view, segregation, if held invalid, should be abolished completely and without delay.

Again the Court moved with deliberation, and its decision was not handed down until May 17, 1954. It is doubtful if the Supreme Court in its entire history has rendered a decision of greater social and ideological significance than this one. Three things in the present case indicate the high sense of responsibility felt by the justices of the Supreme Court in deciding a case of such vital national importance. First, the Court was unanimous. Second, one opinion was written, and not half a dozen. Third, the Court set for argument in the fall of 1954 the problem of the nature of the decree by which its decision that segregation is invalid might best be given effect. Disagreement in the Court on the decision, or disagreement on the reasons for the decision, would have aided those who resented the Court's ruling and have sought to thwart it. There was wisdom in announcing the constitutional ruling and then allowing a breathing spell during which ways and means of implementing the decision might be carefully and deliberately studied.

Because the Supreme Court wanted a full bench to hear argument on the nature of the decrees necessary to implement its May 17 decision and the Senate marked time on the confirmation of John Marshall Harlan to succeed Justice Robert Jackson on the Court, the argument set for the fall of 1954 was postponed until the spring of 1955. The Court allowed an almost unprecedented fourteen hours of oral argument. On May 31, the Court handed down its decision remanding the cases back to the lower courts, which were directed to fashion decrees in accordance with "equitable principles." While recognizing that to abolish segregation "may call for the elimination of a variety of obstacles in making the transition," the Court declared that the district "courts will require that the defendants make a prompt and rea-

sonable start toward full compliance with our May 17, 1954, ruling. Once such a start has been made, the courts may find that additional time is necessary to carry out the ruling in an effective manner. The burden rests upon the defendants to establish that such time is necessary in the public interest and is consistent with good faith compliance at the earliest practicable date. . . . The cases are remanded to the District Courts to take such proceedings and enter such orders and decrees consistent with this opinion as are necessary and proper to admit to public schools on a racially nondiscriminatory basis with all deliberate speed the parties to these cases."

The only persons directly bound by the decision in Brown v. Topeka were the five school boards actually parties to the suit, and the only laws specifically held unconstitutional were those involved in those cases. Normally, and in less controversial cases, a rule of constitutional law announced by the Court in a particular case will be accepted and complied with by all those across the country to whom the rule clearly applies. But this compliance is technically voluntary, since only the parties to the case are immediately bound by the Court's decree. It follows, therefore, that obstinate school boards can be compelled to desegregate their schools only as cases are brought against them in the courts and those courts apply to them the rule of the Brown case.

Thus the progress of desegregation has been and will continue to be uneven throughout the country. While in some areas it came quickly and easily, in others it is still coming with painful slowness which reflects community hostility to any program of racial integration in the schools. For example, one of the five districts ordered to desegregate its public schools "with all deliberate speed" was Prince Edward County, Virginia. The response of the Virginia legislature was a program of "massive resistance," which included closing integrated schools, cutting off their funds, paying tuition grants to students in private, nonsectarian schools, and providing state and local financial aid (including teacher retirement benefits) for such schools. In 1959 the supreme court of Virginia held the program void under the Virginia constitution, so the legislature repealed it and enacted instead a program under which school attendance was a matter of local option.

Faced with the desegregation order, Prince Edward County closed its public schools and provided various kinds of financial support for privately operated segregated schools. In Griffin v. School Board of Prince Edward County (1964) the Court held that the plan denied equal protection of the law. Noting that "the case has been delayed since 1951 by resistance at the state and county level, by legislation, and by law suits," it emphasized that "there has been entirely too much deliberation and not enough speed." The Court conceded to the state a "wide discretion" in deciding whether state laws should operate statewide or only in some counties, "but the record in the present case could not be clearer that Prince Edward's public schools were closed and private schools operated in their place with state and county assistance, for one reason, and one reason only: to ensure, through measures taken by the county and the State, that white and colored children in Prince Edward County would not, under any circumstances, go to the same school. Whatever nonracial grounds might support a State's allowing a county to abandon public schools, the object must be a constitutional one, and grounds of race and opposition to desegregation do not qualify as constitutional." The district court was told to "enter a decree which will guarantee that these petitioners will get the kind of education that is given in the State's public schools" even if it had to order the Board of Supervisors to levy taxes to do it. After trying in vain to discover what the penalties for refusal would be, the supervisors finally decided to obey, and in the fall of 1964 Prince Edward County reopened its schools on an integrated basis.

The county did not, however, abandon its aid to private segregated schools, and in what Negroes termed "a midnight raid on the treasury," the Board of Supervisors hurriedly paid out $180,000 in tuition grants to white pupils while the issue of the constitutionality of such payments was still being litigated in the United States court of appeals. That court subsequently barred such tuition grants as long as the schools remained segregated, and in 1966, it found the Board in contempt and ordered it to repay the grants. The Supreme Court refused to upset this contempt ruling, and in the summer of 1967 the Board finally returned the money to the county treasury.

Meanwhile the political branches of government had taken a hand in speeding integration, and threats by the Department of Health, Education and Welfare (HEW) to withhold federal aid to segregated schools under the Civil Rights Act of 1964 resulted in widespread token compliance, largely by offering blacks "freedom of choice" among schools. Yet with the start of the 1965-66 school year fewer than 10 percent of the South's blacks were attending desegregated schools. In March of 1966 HEW announced new guidelines designed to desegregate all twelve grades by the fall of 1967; and in December 1966 the United States Court of Appeals for the Fifth Circuit ordered the six states within its jurisdiction—Alabama, Florida, Georgia, Louisiana, Mississippi, and Texas—to desegregate according to the HEW timetable. In April 1967 the Supreme Court refused to delay the effect of the court of appeals order to establish "no Negro schools, and no white schools—just schools." Finally, in May 1968 the Court rejected as inadequate a "freedom of choice" plan under which no desegregation had actually taken place. "The burden on a school board today is to come forward with a plan that promises realistically to work, and promises realistically to work now." See Green v. County School Board (1968). That December the United States court of appeals in a Georgia case ordered that all schools in the states of the fifth circuit—Alabama, Florida, Louisiana, Mississippi, and Texas—be integrated by the fall of 1969 or abandoned.

In July 1969 it became apparent that some thirty

schools in Mississippi would not be ready for integration with the opening of the fall term, and the government suddenly announced that it would no longer try to hold the South to "arbitrary" deadlines for desegregation. At the same time the United States Court of Appeals for the Fifth Circuit reaffirmed its policy and ordered full integration, by September, and the justice department replied by asking for a delay until December 1.

The announced change in policy came as a shock to the lawyers of the NAACP Legal Defense Fund who, after working for many years in partnership with government attorneys for full integration suddenly found themselves carrying on the fight alone. Even the government attorneys themselves had trouble accepting the sudden switch, and a large number of them signed a statement of protest against the new policy. In spite of this the court of appeals granted the requested delay, and the Legal Defense Fund appealed to the Supreme Court. In a brief per curiam opinion, one of the first in which Chief Justice Burger participated, the Court unanimously rejected the government's request for a delay. The "continued operation of segregated schools under a standard of allowing 'all deliberate speed' for desegregation" said the Court, "is no longer constitutionally permissible. Under explicit holdings of this Court the obligation of every school district is to terminate dual school systems at once and to operate now and hereafter only unitary schools." See Alexander v. Holmes County Board of Education (1969).

The extension of the Brown doctrine to other areas of segregation was done by the Court largely through the technique of affirming lower court decisions without opinion. In Baltimore v. Dawson (1955) the desegregation ruling was held applicable to public beaches, and in Holmes v. Atlanta (1955), to public golf courses. In 1963, in deciding Watson v. Memphis, the Court held that recreation facilities, like universities, must be desegregated at once. On the strength of this rule, the city of Jackson, Mississippi, desegregated its parks and golf links but decided instead to close its five swimming pools. In Palmer v. Thompson (1971) the Court upheld the move, noting that a statute could not be held void because of the motivations of the legislature which adopted it, and there was no evidence that the city was "now covertly aiding the maintenance and operation of pools which are private in name only. It shows no state action affecting blacks differently from whites." Three of the four dissenting justices argued that the city action was a public stand against desegregating public facilities and the forbidding of blacks to swim because of their color—both denials of equal protection.

A separate opinion was necessary to invalidate segregation in the schools of the District of Columbia, which is under congressional authority. In Bolling v. Sharpe, the Court held that the due process clause of the Fifth Amendment forbade racial segregation by the federal government.

Mr. Chief Justice **Warren**, delivering the opinion of the Court in the Brown case, said in part:

These cases come to us from the States of Kansas, South Carolina, Virginia, and Delaware. They are premised on different facts and different local conditions, but a common legal question justifies their consideration together in this consolidated opinion.

In each of the cases, minors of the Negro race, through their legal representatives, seek the aid of the courts in obtaining admission to the public schools of their community on a nonsegregated basis. In each instance, they had been denied admission to schools attended by white children under laws requiring or permitting segregation according to race. This segregation was alleged to deprive the plaintiffs of the equal protection of the laws under the Fourteenth Amendment. . . .

The plaintiffs contend that segregated public schools are not "equal" and cannot be made "equal," and that hence they are deprived of the equal protection of the laws. Because of the obvious importance of the question presented, the Court took jurisdiction. Argument was heard in the 1952 Term, and reargument was heard this Term on certain questions propounded by the Court.

Reargument was largely devoted to the circumstances surrounding the adoption of the Fourteenth Amendment in 1868. It covered exhaustively consideration of the Amendment in Congress, ratification by the states, then existing practices in racial segregation, and the views of proponents and opponents of the Amendment. This discussion and our own investigation convince us that, although these sources cast some light, it is not enough to resolve the problem with which we are faced. At best, they are inconclusive. The most avid proponents of the post-War Amendments undoubtedly intended them to remove all legal distinctions among "all persons born or naturalized in the United States." Their opponents, just as certainly, were antagonistic to both the letter and the spirit of the Amendments and wished them to have the most limited effect. What others in Congress and the state legislatures had in mind cannot be determined with any degree of certainty.

An additional reason for the inconclusive nature of the Amendment's history, with respect to segregated schools, is the status of public education at that time. In the South, the movement toward free common schools, supported by general taxation, had not yet taken hold. Education of white children was largely in the hands of private groups. Education of Negroes was almost nonexistent, and practically all of the race were illiterate. In fact, any education of Negroes was forbidden by law in some states. Today, in contrast, many Negroes have achieved outstanding success in the arts and sciences as well as in the business and professional world. It is true that public school education at the time of the Amendment had advanced further in the North, but the effect of the Amendment on Northern States was generally ignored in the congressional debates. Even in the North, the conditions of public education did not approximate those existing today. The curriculum was usually rudimentary; ungraded schools were common in rural areas; the school term was but three months a year in many

states; and compulsory school attendance was virtually unknown. As a consequence, it is not surprising that there should be so little in the history of the Fourteenth Amendment relating to its intended effect on public education.

In the first cases in this Court construing the Fourteenth Amendment, decided shortly after its adoption the Court interpreted it as proscribing all state-imposed discriminations against the Negro race. The doctrine of "separate but equal" did not make its appearance in this Court until 1896 in the case of Plessy v. Ferguson, involving not education but transportation. American courts have since labored with the doctrine for over half a century. In this Court, there have been six cases involving the "separate but equal" doctrine in the field of public education. In Cumming v. Board of Education of Richmond County [1899] and Gong Lum v. Rice [1927] the validity of the doctrine itself was not challenged. In more recent cases, all on the graduate school level, inequality was found in that specific benefits enjoyed by white students were denied to Negro students of the same educational qualifications. State of Missouri ex rel. Gaines v. Canada [1938], Sipuel v. Board of Regents of University of Oklahoma [1948], Sweatt v. Painter [1950], McLaurin v. Oklahoma State Regents [1950]. In none of these cases was it necessary to reexamine the doctrine to grant relief to the Negro plaintiff. And in Sweatt v. Painter the Court expressly reserved decision on the question whether Plessy v. Ferguson should be held inapplicable to public education.

In the instant cases, that question is directly presented. Here, unlike Sweatt v. Painter, there are findings below that the Negro and white schools involved have been equalized, or are being equalized, with respect to buildings, curricula, qualifications and salaries of teachers, and other "tangible" factors. Our decision, therefore, cannot turn on merely a comparison of these tangible factors in the Negro and white schools involved in each of the cases. We must look instead to the effect of segregation itself on public education.

In approaching this problem, we cannot turn the clock back to 1868 when the Amendment was adopted, or even to 1896 when Plessy v. Ferguson was written. We must consider public education in the light of its full development and its present place in American life throughout the Nation. Only in this way can it be determined if segregation in public schools deprives these plaintiffs of the equal protection of the laws.

Today, education is perhaps the most important function of state and local governments. Compulsory school attendance laws and the great expenditures for education both demonstrate our recognition of the importance of education to our democratic society. It is required in the performance of our most basic public responsibilities, even service in the armed forces. It is the very foundation of good citizenship. Today it is a principal instrument in awakening the child to cultural values, in preparing him for later professional training, and in helping him to adjust normally to his environment. In these days, it is doubtful that any child may reasonably be expected to succeed in life if he is denied the opportunity of an education. Such an opportunity, where the state has undertaken to provide it, is a right which must be made available to all on equal terms.

We come then to the question presented: Does segregation of children in public schools solely on the basis of race, even though the physical facilities and other "tangible" factors may be equal, deprive the children of the minority group of equal educational opportunities? We believe that it does.

In Sweatt v. Painter, in finding that a segregated law school for Negroes could not provide them equal educational opportunities, this Court relied in large part on "those qualities which are incapable of objective measurement but which make for greatness in a law school." In McLaurin v. Oklahoma State Regents, the Court, in requiring that a Negro admitted to a white graduate school be treated like all other students, again resorted to intangible considerations: ". . . his ability to study, to engage in discussions and exchange views with other students, and, in general, to learn his profession." Such considerations apply with added force to children in grade and high schools. To separate them from others of similar age and qualifications solely because of their race generates a feeling of inferiority as to their status in the community that may effect their hearts and minds in a way unlikely ever to be undone. The effect of this separation on their educational opportunities was well stated by a finding in the Kansas case by a court which nevertheless felt compelled to rule against the Negro plaintiffs:

"Segregation of white and colored children in public schools has a detrimental effect upon the colored children. The impact is greater when it has the sanction of the law; for the policy of separating the races is usually interpreted as denoting the inferiority of the Negro group. A sense of inferiority affects the motivation of a child to learn. Segregation with the sanction of law, therefore, has a tendency to [retard] the educational and mental development of Negro children and to deprive them of some of the benefits they would receive in a racial[ly] integrated school system." Whatever may have been the extent of psychological knowledge at the time of Plessy v. Ferguson, this finding is amply supported by modern authority.* Any language in Plessy v. Ferguson contrary to this finding is rejected.

We conclude that in the field of public education the doctrine of "separate but equal" has no place. Separate educational facilities are inherently unequal. There-fore, we hold that the plaintiffs and others similarly situated for whom the actions have been brought are, by reason of the segregation complained of, deprived of the equal protection of the laws guaranteed by the Fourteenth Amendment. This disposition makes unnecessary any discussion whether such segregation also violates the Due Process Clause of the Fourteenth Amendment.

Because these are class actions, because of the wide applicability of this decision, and because of the great variety of local conditions, the formulation of decrees in these cases presents problems of considerable complexity. On reargument, the consideration of appropriate relief was necessarily subordinated to the primary question—the constitutionality of segregation in public education. We have now announced that such segregation is a denial of the equal protection of the laws. In order that we may have the full assistance of the parties in formulating decrees, the cases will be restored to the docket, and the parties are requested to present further argument on Questions 4 and 5 previously propounded by the Court for the reargument this Term.† The Attorney General of the United States is again invited to participate. The Attorneys General of the states requiring or permitting segregation in public education will also be permitted to appear as amici curiae upon request to do so by September 15, 1954, and submission of briefs by October 1, 1954.

It is so ordered.

SWANN v. CHARLOTTE-MECKLENBURG BOARD OF EDUCATION

402 U. S. 1; 9 S. Ct. 1267; 28 L. Ed. 2d 554
(1971)

With the refusal of the Supreme Court to delay integration in thirty Mississippi school districts (see Alexander v. Holmes County Board of Education, 1968), the Justice

---

*K. B. Clark, Effect of Prejudice and Discrimination on Personality Development (Midcentury White House Conference on Children and Youth, 1950); Witmer and Kotinsky, Personality in the Making (1952), ch VI; Deutscher and Chein, The Psychological Effects of Enforced Segregation: A Survey of Social Science Opinion, 26 J Psychol 259 (1948); Chein, What are the Psychological Effects of Segregation Under Conditions of Equal Facilities?, 3 Int J Opinion and Attitude Res 229 (1949); Brameld, Educational Costs, in Discrimination and National Welfare (MacIver, ed, 1949), 44–48; Frazier, The Negro in the United States (1949), 674–681. And see generally Myrdal, An American Dilemma (1944).

---

†"4. Assuming it is decided that segregation in public schools violates the Fourteenth Amendment

"(a) would a decree necessarily follow providing that, within the limits set by normal geographic school districting, Negro children should forthwith be admitted to schools of their choice, or

"(b) may this Court, in the exercise of its equity powers, permit an effective gradual adjustment to be brought about from existing segregated systems to a system not based on color distinctions?

"5. On the assumption on which questions 4(a) and (b) are based, and assuming further that this Court will exercise its equity powers to the end described in question 4(b),

"(a) should this Court formulate detailed decrees in these cases;

"(b) if so, what specific issues should the decrees reach;

"(c) should this Court appoint a special master to hear evidence with a view to recommending specific terms for such decrees;

"(d) should this Court remand to the courts of first instance with directions to frame decrees in these cases, and if so, what general directions should the decrees of this Court include and what procedures should the courts of first instance follow in arriving at the specific terms of more detailed decrees?"

Department promptly announced that it would no longer push for more rapid desegregation in over 100 schools in the Deep South. It did not matter much because the Department of Health, Education, and Welfare (HEW) with its authority to withhold funds from schools that were not desegregating effectively had become the principle administrative support for the courts' orders. The Mississippi school districts did integrate, but many whites in heavily black areas transferred to hastily created all white "private academies." HEW promptly urged the Internal Revenue Service (IRS) to withhold tax exemption from such schools, and in July 1970 the IRS complied.

While apparently most rural and small town school districts moved rapidly and peacefully toward integration in 1970, in big cities a new cry was heard. To desegregate urban schools located in the center of black or white neighborhoods, it was necessary to transport students out of their home neighborhoods by school bus. As district courts prepared plans calling for busing between pairs of black and white schools, community voices rose in defense of their "neighborhood schools." In Florida, Governor Claude Kirk seized physically the Bradenton schools to prevent busing and relinquished them only when faced with a $10,000-a-day fine. In both the House and Senate, amendments passed to prevent HEW guidelines from requiring busing, only to have them fail when the act finally passed.

And in Charlotte-Mecklenburg, the country's forty-third largest school district, an "antibusing" school board was elected. The district court rejected a plan devised by the Board as not producing sufficient integration at the elementary level and accepted in its place a plan prepared by an outside expert which called for the pairing and grouping of elementary schools and the busing of pupils between them. In upholding the validity of the district court's plan, the Supreme Court in the present case and in the companion case of Davis v. Board of Commissioners (1971) spelled out the lengths to which district courts can go to achieve an integrated school system. In Nyquist v. Lee (1971) the Court held void without opinion New York's 1969 antibusing statute upon which most of the Southern antibusing statutes had been based.

Mr. Chief Justice **Burger** delivered the opinion of the Court, saying in part:

V.

The central issue in this case is that of student assignment, and there are essentially four problem areas: (1) to what extent racial balance or racial quotas may be used as an implement in a remedial order to correct a previously segregated system; (2) whether every all-Negro and all-white school must be eliminated as an indispensable part of a remedial process of desegregation; (3) what are the limits, if any, on the rearrangement of school districts and attendance zones, as a remedial

measure; and (4) what are the limits, if any, on the use of transportation facilities to correct state-enforced racial school segregation.

(1) *Racial Balances or Racial Quotas.*

The constant theme and thrust of every holding from Brown I [1954] to date is that state-enforced separation of races in public schools is discrimination that violates the Equal Protection Clause. The remedy commanded was to dismantle dual school systems.

We are concerned in these cases with the elimination of the discrimination inherent in the dual school systems, not with myriad factors of human existence which can cause discrimination in a multitude of ways on racial, religious, or ethnic grounds. The target of the cases from Brown I to the present was the dual school system. The elimination of racial discrimination in public schools is a large task and one that should not be retarded by efforts to achieve broader purposes lying beyond the jurisdiction of school authorities. One vehicle can carry only a limited amount of baggage. . . .

Our objective in dealing with the issues presented by these cases is to see that school authorities exclude no pupil of a racial minority from any school, directly or indirectly, on account of race; it does not and cannot embrace all the problems of racial prejudice, even when those problems contribute to disproportionate racial concentrations in some schools.

In this case it is urged that the District Court has imposed a racial balance requirement of 71%–29% on individual schools. . . . If we were to read the holding of the District Court to require, as a matter of substantive constitutional right, any particular degree of racial balance or mixing, that approach would be disapproved and we would be obliged to reverse. The constitutional command to desegregate schools does not mean that every school in every community must always reflect the racial composition of the school system as a whole. . . .

. . . The use made of mathematical ratios was no more than a starting point in the process of shaping a remedy, rather than an inflexible requirement. From that starting point the District Court proceeded to frame a decree that was within its discretionary powers, an equitable remedy for the particular circumstances. As we said in Green [v. County School Board, 1968], a school authority's remedial plan or a district court's remedial decree is to be judged by its effectiveness. Awareness of the racial composition of the whole school system is likely to be a useful starting point in shaping a remedy to correct past constitutional violations. In sum, the very limited use made of mathematical ratios was within the equitable remedial discretion of the District Court.

(2) *One-Race Schools.*

The record in this case reveals the familiar phenomenon that in metropolitan areas minority groups are often found concentrated in one part of the city. In some circumstances certain schools may remain all or largely of one race until new schools can be provided or neighborhood patterns change. Schools all or predominately of one race in a district of mixed population will require close scrutiny to determine that school assignments are not part of state-enforced segregation.

In light of the above, it should be clear that the existence of some small number of one-race, or virtually one-race, schools within a district is not in and of itself the mark of a system which still practices segregation by a law. ... Where the school authority's proposed plan for conversion from a dual to a unitary system contemplates the continued existence of some schools that are all or predominately of one race, they have the burden of showing that such school assignments are genuinely nondiscriminatory. The court should scrutinize such schools, and the burden upon the school authorities will be to satisfy the court that their racial composition is not the result of present or past discriminatory action on their part.

An optional majority-to-minority transfer provision has long been recognized as a useful part of every desegregation plan. Provision for optional transfer of those in the majority racial group of a particular school to other schools where they will be in the minority is an indispensable remedy for those students willing to transfer to other schools in order to lessen the impact on them of the state-imposed stigma of segregation. In order to be effective, such a transfer arrangement must grant the transferring student free transportation and space must be made available in the school to which he desires to move. ... The court orders in this and the companion Davis case now provide such an option.

(3) *Remedial Altering of Attendance Zones.*

The maps submitted in these cases graphically demonstrate that one of the principal tools employed by school planners and by courts to break up the dual school system has been a frank—and sometimes drastic—gerrymandering of school districts and attendance zones. An additional step was pairing, "clustering," or "grouping" of schools with attendance assignments made deliberately to accomplish the transfer of Negro students out of formerly segregated Negro schools and transfer of white students to formerly all-Negro schools. More often than not, these zones are neither compact nor contiguous; indeed they may be on opposite ends of the city. As an interim corrective measure, this cannot be said to be beyond the broad remedial powers of a court.

Absent a constitutional violation there would be no basis for judicially ordering assignment of students on a racial basis. All things being equal, with no history of discrimination, it might well be desirable to assign pupils to schools nearest their homes. But all things are not equal in a system that has been deliberately constructed and maintained to enforce racial segregation. ...

No fixed or even substantially fixed guidelines can be established as to how far a court can go, but it must be recognized that there are limits. The objective is to dismantle the dual school system. "Racially neutral" as-

signment plans proposed by school authorities to a district court may be inadequate; such plans may fail to counteract the continuing effects of past school segregation resulting from discriminatory location of school sites or distortion of school size in order to achieve or maintain an artificial racial separation. When school authorities present a district court with a "loaded game board," affirmative action in the form of remedial altering of attendance zones is proper to achieve truly nondiscriminatory assignments. In short, an assignment plan is not acceptable simply because it appears to be neutral. ...

We hold that the pairing and grouping of noncontiguous school zones is a permissible tool and such action is to be considered in light of the objectives sought. ...

(4) *Transportation of Students.*

The scope of permissible transportation of students as an implement of a remedial decree has never been defined by this Court and by the very nature of the problem it cannot be defined with precision. ...

The importance of bus transportation as a normal and accepted tool of educational policy is readily discernible in this and the companion case. The Charlotte school authorities did not purport to assign students on the basis of geographically drawn zones until 1965 and then they allowed almost unlimited transfer privileges. The District Court's conclusion that assignment of children to the school nearest their home serving their grade would not produce an effective dismantling of the dual system is supported by the record.

Thus the remedial techniques used in the District Court's order were within that court's power to provide equitable relief; implementation of the decree is well within the capacity of the school authority.

The decree provided that the buses used to implement the plan would operate on direct routes. Students would be picked up at schools near their homes and transported to the schools they were to attend. The trips for elementary school pupils average about seven miles and the District Court found that they would take "not over 35 minutes at the most." This system compares favorably with the transportation plan previously operated in Charlotte under which each day 23,600 students on all grade levels were transported an average of 15 miles one way for an average trip requiring over an hour. In these circumstances, we find no basis for holding that the local school authorities may not be required to employ bus transportation as one tool of school desegregation. Desegregation plans cannot be limited to the walk-in school. ...

VI.

... At some point, these school authorities and others like them should have achieved full compliance with this Court's decision in Brown I. The systems will then be "unitary" in the sense required by our decisions in Green and Alexander [v. Holmes County Board of Education, 1968].

It does not follow that the communities served by such systems will remain demographically stable, for in a growing, mobile society, few will do so. Neither school authorities nor district courts are constitutionally required to make year-by-year adjustments of the racial composition of student bodies once the affirmative duty to desegregate has been accomplished and racial discrimination through official action is eliminated from the system. This does not mean that federal courts are without power to deal with future problems; but in the absence of a showing that either the school authorities or some other agency of the State has deliberately attempted to fix or alter demographic patterns to affect the racial composition of the schools, further intervention by a district court should not be necessary. . . .

It is so ordered.

MILLIKEN v. BRADLEY

418 U. S. 717; 94 S. Ct. 3112; 41 L. Ed. 2d 1069
(1974)

As the long fight to integrate Southern schools achieved increasing success, attention was turned to Northern cities in which segregation was as complete in many cases as it had ever been in the South. While segregation in the South had its genesis in laws providing separate facilities for the two races (de jure), in the big cities of the North an equally effective segregation (de facto) came about as a by-product of the development of single-race neighborhoods. The creation of these neighborhoods, while in part probably the result of personal preferences, has been fostered by both a tacit unwillingness of whites to sell to blacks and a system of economic zoning that puts the cost of homes in middle-class white communities beyond the financial reach of blacks whose economic opportunities are in turn restricted by both the inferior "ghetto" education afforded them and the hiring policies of business which reserves the best-paid jobs for whites. Thus, while in Charlotte-Mecklenburg only two-thirds of the black pupils were in schools that were 99 percent black and a quarter of them attended schools more than half white, in Chicago three-quarters of the black children went to all-black schools and only three percent went to schools that were mostly white.

Even systematic desegregation, however, does not always provide a permanent solution to the segregation problem. Experience has shown that the migration that tends to follow desegregation orders in big cities merely converts de jure patterns into de facto ones. The most striking illustration is the District of Columbia school system, which integrated in 1956; in subsequent years so many whites with school-age children left the District that only 3.6 percent of the pupils in the system are white [as of 1988].

This situation faced the cities of Detroit, Michigan, and Richmond, Virginia. The school districts in those cities had such a high concentration of blacks that no amount of line-drawing or busing could change their racial composition. In contrast, the school districts in the surrounding suburban counties were almost entirely white. Despite the fact that the segregated schools were not the product of school board action, the district courts in both cases ordered the black inner-city districts merged with the white suburban districts and pupils bused across county lines to produce integrated schools in both communities. On appeal, the Justice Department sided with the white counties and the court of appeals for the Fourth Circuit, in June 1972, reversed the district court in the Richmond case, while the court of appeals for the Sixth Circuit upheld the district court in the Detroit case. In Richmond School Board v. Virginia Board of Education (1973) the decision of the court of appeals was affirmed by an equally divided Court. Justice Powell, who had been a member of both boards involved in the suit, disqualified himself. Meanwhile the Detroit case was delayed in its efforts to reach the Supreme Court, and in July 1973, a district judge in Indianapolis ordered inter-county transportation of pupils to achieve desegregation.

In contrast to the Detroit and Richmond cases, a number of communities were found to be supporting segregated schools by their deliberate actions and inactions, despite the absence of state laws requiring such segregation. In Pontiac, Michigan, and Denver, Colorado, for instance, district courts found that the school boards, by their power to locate new schools and draw attendance lines, had encouraged segregation. In dealing with this problem in Keyes v. School District (1973), the Court held that such conduct constituted de jure segregative action, and the fact that the board had acted to segregate the Park Hill section of the city created a presumption that heavily segregated parts of the core city were also the product of board action, rather than merely of community social patterns. Justice Powell, in a powerful concurrence, had attacked the de facto-de jure distinction and urged its abolition, pointing out that in the large metropolitan districts, both north and south, the causes of segregation were largely unrelated to government policy, that a pupil has a right not to be compelled by the state to attend a segregated school, and the state has an obligation to operate only integrated schools. Was he, the only southerner on the Court, suggesting the state responsibility for providing desegregated schools made school district lines no more sacred than attendance zones?

In the present case, unlike the Richmond case, both the district court and the court of appeals had found that local school board action in the core city and state action both there and to a limited extent in the suburbs, had contributed to segregation and ordered a plan worked out which would involve both the core city and fifty-three suburban school districts. That the suburban districts as such might not be engaged in segregation was found immaterial. "[T]he State," said the Court, "has committed de jure acts of segregation and . . . the State controls the instrumentalities whose action is necessary to remedy the harmful effects of the State acts." The decision in the present case raises interesting questions regarding state responsibility for desegregation, as opposed to school board responsibility. If a state's obligation to stop segregating can be compartmentalized by district lines, what are its obligations when it decides to alter the size or shape of a district?

Following the remand of the present case the district court, after extensive hearings, ordered the school board to establish a remedial education program designed "to restore the victims of discriminatory conduct to the position they would have occupied in the absence of such conduct." The program was to include remedial reading, special in-service teacher training, the construction of bias-free testing procedures, and improved career guidance and counseling. The cost was to be shared equally by the district and the state. In Milliken v. Bradley (1977) (Milliken II) the Supreme Court unanimously held the plan valid.

Mr. Chief Justice **Burger** delivered the opinion of the Court, saying in part:

II.

Ever since Brown v. Board of Education (1954), judicial consideration of school desegregation cases has begun with the standard: "[I]n the field of public education the doctrine of 'separate but equal' has no place. Separate educational facilities are inherently unequal." This has been reaffirmed time and again as the meaning of the Constitution and the controlling rule of law.

The target of the Brown holding was clear and forthright: the elimination of state-mandated or deliberately maintained dual school systems with certain schools for Negro pupils and others for white pupils. This duality and racial segregation were held to violate the Constitution in the cases subsequent to 1954, including particularly Green v. County School Board of New Kent County (1968); . . . Swann v. Charlotte-Mecklenburg Board of Education (1971). . . .

The Swann case, of course, dealt "with the problem of defining in more precise terms than heretofore the scope of the duty of school authorities and district courts in implementing Brown I and the mandate to eliminate dual systems and establish unitary systems at once." In Brown v. Board of Education (1955) (Brown II), the Court's first encounter with the problem of remedies in school desegregation cases, the Court noted:

"In fashioning and effectuating the decrees, the courts will be guided by equitable principles. Traditionally, equity has been characterized by a practical flexibility in shaping its remedies and by a facility for adjusting and reconciling public and private needs." Brown v. Board of Education. In further refining the remedial process, Swann held, the task is to correct, by balancing of the individual and collective interests, "the condition that offends the Constitution." A federal remedial power may be exercised "only on the basis of a constitutional violation" and, "[a]s with any equity case, the nature of the violation determines the scope of the remedy."

Proceeding from these basic principles, we first note that in the District Court the complainants sought a remedy aimed at the *condition* alleged to offend the Constitution—the segregation within the Detroit City School District. The court acted on this theory of the case and in its initial ruling on the "Desegregation Area" stated:

"The task before this court, therefore, is now, and . . . has always been, how to desegregate the Detroit public schools." Thereafter, however, the District Court abruptly rejected the proposed Detroit-only plans on the ground that "while [they] would provide a racial mix more in keeping with the Black-White proportions of the student population [they] would accentuate the racial identifiability of the [Detroit] district as a Black school system, and would not accomplish desegregation." "[T]he racial composition of the student body is such," said the court, "that the plan's implementation would clearly make the entire Detroit public school system racially identifiable." "leav[ing] many of its schools 75 to 90 percent Black." Consequently, the court reasoned, it was imperative to "look beyond the limits of the Detroit school district for a solution to the problem of segregation in the Detroit public schools . . ." since "[s]chool district lines are simply matters of political convenience and may not be used to deny constitutional rights." Accordingly, the District Court proceeded to redefine the relevant area to include areas of predominantly white pupil population in order to ensure that "upon implementation, no school, grade or classroom [would be] substantially disproportionate to the overall pupil racial composition" of the entire metropolitan area.

While specifically acknowledging that the District Court's findings of a condition of segregation were limited to Detroit, the Court of Appeals approved the use of a metropolitan remedy largely on the grounds that it is "impossible to declare 'clearly erroneous' the District Judge's conclusion that any Detroit only segregation plan will lead directly to a single segregated Detroit school district overwhelmingly black in all of its schools, surrounded by a ring of suburbs and suburban school districts overwhelmingly white in composition in a State in which the racial composition is 87 percent white and 13 percent black."

Viewing the record as a whole, it seems clear that the District Court and the Court of Appeals shifted the primary focus from a Detroit remedy to the metropolitan area only because of their conclusion that total desegregation of Detroit would not produce the racial balance which they perceived as desirable. Both courts proceeded on an assumption that the Detroit schools could not be truly desegregated—in their view of what constituted desegregation—unless the racial composition of the student body of each school substantially reflected the racial composition of the population of the metropolitan area as a whole. The metropolitan area was then defined as Detroit plus 53 of the outlying school districts. . . .

In Swann, which arose in the context of a single independent school district, the Court held: "If we were to read the holding of the District Court to require, as a matter of substantive constitutional right, any particular degree of racial balance or mixing, that approach would be disapproved and we would be obliged to reverse." The clear import of this language from Swann is that desegregation, in the sense of dismantling a dual school system, does not require any particular racial balance in each "school, grade or classroom." . . .

Here the District Court's approach to what constituted "actual desegregation" raises the fundamental question, not presented in Swann, as to the circumstances in which a federal court may order desegregation relief that embraces more than a single school district. The court's analytical starting point was its conclusion that school district lines are no more than arbitrary lines on a map drawn "for political convenience." Boundary lines may be bridged where there has been a constitutional violation calling for interdistrict relief, but the notion that school district lines may be casually ignored or treated as a mere administrative convenience is contrary to the history of public education in our country. No single tradition in public education is more deeply rooted than local control over the operation of schools; local autonomy has long been thought essential both to the maintenance of community concern and support for public schools and to the quality of the educational process. . . .

Of course, no state law is above the Constitution. School district lines and the present laws with respect to local control, are not sacrosanct and if they conflict with the Fourteenth Amendment federal courts have a duty to prescribe appropriate remedies. . . . But our prior holdings have been confined to violations and remedies within a single school district. We therefore turn to address, for the first time, the validity of a remedy mandating cross-district or interdistrict consolidation to remedy a condition of segregation found to exist in only one district.

The controlling principle consistently expounded in our holdings is that the scope of the remedy is determined by the nature and extent of the constitutional violation. Swann. Before the boundaries of separate and autonomous school districts may be set aside by consolidating the separate units for remedial purposes or by imposing a cross-district remedy, it must first be shown that there has been a constitutional violation within one district that produces a significant segregative effect in another district. Specifically, it must be shown that racially discriminatory acts of the state or local school districts, or of a single school district have been a substantial cause of interdistrict segregation. Thus an interdistrict remedy might be in order where the racially discriminatory acts of one or more school districts caused racial segregation in an adjacent district, or where district lines have been deliberately drawn on the basis of race. In

such circumstances an interdistrict remedy would be appropriate to eliminate the interdistrict segregation directly caused by the constitutional violation. Conversely, without an interdistrict violation and interdistrict effect, there is no constitutional wrong calling for an interdistrict remedy. . . .

. . . With no showing of significant violation by the 53 outlying school districts and no evidence of any interdistrict violation or effect, the court went beyond the original theory of the case as framed by the pleadings and mandated a metropolitan area remedy. To approve the remedy ordered by the court would impose on the outlying districts, not shown to have committed any constitutional violation, a wholly impermissible remedy based on a standard not hinted at in Brown I and II or any holding of this Court. . . .

III.

We recognize that the six-volume record presently under consideration contains language and some specific incidental findings thought by the District Court to afford a basis for interdistrict relief. However, these comparatively isolated findings and brief comments concern only one possible interdistrict violation and are found in the context of a proceeding that, as the District Court conceded, included no proof of segregation practiced by any of the 85 suburban school districts surrounding Detroit. . . .

According to the Court of Appeals, the arrangement during the late 1950's which allowed Carver students to be educated within the Detroit District was dependent upon the "tacit or express" approval of the State Board of Education and was the result of the refusal of the white suburban districts to accept the Carver students. Although there is nothing in the record supporting the Court of Appeals' supposition that suburban white schools refused to accept the Carver students, it appears that this situation, whether with or without the State's consent, may have had a segregative effect on the school populations of the two districts involved. However, since "the nature of the violation determines the scope of the remedy" this isolated instance affecting two of the school districts would not justify the broad metropolitan-wide remedy contemplated by the District Court, particularly since it embraced potentially 52 districts having no responsibility for the arrangement and involved 503,000 pupils in addition to Detroit's 276,000 students. . . .

Mr. Justice **Stewart,** concurring, said in part:

The opinion of the Court convincingly demonstrates, that traditions of local control of schools, together with the difficulty of a judicially supervised restructuring of local administration of schools, render improper and inequitable such an interdistrict response to a constitutional violation found to have occurred only within a single school district.

This is not to say, however, that an interdistrict remedy of the sort approved by the Court of Appeals would not be proper, or even necessary, in other factual situations. Were it to be shown, for example, that state officials had contributed to the separation of the races by drawing or redrawing school district lines . . . by transfer of school units between districts, . . . or by purposeful, racially discriminatory use of state housing or zoning laws, then a decree calling for transfer of pupils across district lines or for restructuring of district lines might well be appropriate. . . .

Mr. Justice **Douglas,** dissenting, said in part:

When we rule against the metropolitan area remedy we take a step that will likely put the problem of the blacks and our society back to the period that antedated the "separate but equal" regime of Plessy v. Ferguson [1896]. The reason is simple.

The inner core of Detroit is now rather solidly black; and the blacks, we know, in many instances are likely to be poorer, just as were the Chicanos in San Antonio School District v. Rodriguez [1973]. By that decision the poorer school districts must pay their own way. It is therefore a foregone conclusion that we have now given the States a formula whereby the poor must pay their own way.

Today's decision, given Rodriguez, means that there is no violation of the Equal Protection Clause though the schools are segregated by race and though the black schools are not only "separate" but "inferior."

So far as equal protection is concerned we are now in a dramatic retreat from the 7-to-1 decision in 1896 that blacks could be segregated in public facilities, provided they received equal treatment.

. . . Given the State's control over the educational system in Michigan, the fact that the black schools are in one district and the white schools are in another is not controlling—either constitutionally or equitably. No specific plan has yet been adopted. We are still at an interlocutory stage of a long drawn-out judicial effort at school desegregation. It is conceivable that ghettos develop on their own without any hint of state action. But since Michigan by one device or another has over the years created black school districts and white school districts, the task of equity is to provide a unitary system for the affected area where, as here, the State washes its hands of its own creations.

Mr. Justice **White,** with whom Mr. Justice **Douglas,** Mr. Justice **Brennan,** and Mr. Justice **Marshall** join, dissenting, said in part:

The District Court and the Court of Appeals found that over a long period of years those in charge of the Michigan public schools engaged in various practices calculated to effect the segregation of the Detroit school system. The Court does not question these findings, nor could it reasonably do so. Neither does it question the obligation of the federal courts to devise a feasible and effective remedy. But it promptly cripples the ability of the judiciary to perform this task, which is of fundamental importance to our constitutional system, by fashioning a strict rule that remedies in school cases must stop at the school district line unless certain other conditions are met. As applied here, the remedy for unquestioned violations of the equal protection rights of Detroit's Negroes by the Detroit School Board and the State of Michigan must be totally confined to the limits of the school district and may not reach into adjoining or surrounding districts unless and until it is proved there has been some sort of "interdistrict violation"—unless unconstitutional actions of the Detroit School Board have had segregative impact on other districts, or unless the segregated condition of the Detroit schools has itself been influenced by segregative practices in those surrounding districts into which it is proposed to extend the remedy. . . .

. . . The result is that the State of Michigan, the entity at which the Fourteenth Amendment is directed, has successfully insulated itself from its duty to provide effective desegregation remedies by vesting sufficient power over its public schools in its local school districts. If this is the case in Michigan, it will be the case in most States.

There are undoubted practical as well as legal limits to the remedial powers of federal courts in school desegregation cases. The Court has made it clear that the achievement of any particular degree of racial balance in the school system is not required by the Constitution; nor may it be the primary focus of a court in devising an acceptable remedy for de jure segregation. A variety of procedures and techniques are available to a district court engrossed in fashioning remedies in a case such as this; but the courts must keep in mind that they are dealing with the process of *educating* the young, including the very young. The task is not to devise a system of pains and penalties to punish constitutional violations brought to light. Rather, it is to desegregate an *educational* system in which the races have been kept apart, without, at the same time, losing sight of the central *educational* function of the schools.

Viewed in this light, remedies calling for school zoning, pairing, and pupil assignments, become more and more suspect as they require that school children spend more and more time in buses going to and from school and that more and more educational dollars be diverted to transportation systems. . . .

Despite the fact that a metropolitan remedy, if the findings of the District Court accepted by the Court of Appeals are to be credited, would more effectively desegregate the Detroit schools, would prevent resegregation, and would be easier and more feasible from many standpoints, the Court fashions out of whole cloth an arbitrary rule that remedies for constitutional violations occurring in a single Michigan school district must stop at the school district line. Apparently, no matter how much less burdensome or more effective and efficient in many respects, such as transportation, the metropolitan plan might be, the school district line may not be crossed.

Otherwise, it seems, there would be too much disruption of the Michigan scheme for managing its educational system, too much confusion, and too much administrative burden. . . .

I am surprised that the Court, sitting at this distance from the State of Michigan, claims better insight than the Court of Appeals and the District Court as to whether an inter-district remedy for equal protection violations practiced by the State of Michigan would involve undue difficulties for the State in the management of its public schools. . . .

I am even more mystified as to how the Court can ignore the legal reality that the constitutional violations, even if occurring locally, were committed by governmental entities for which the State is responsible and that it is the State that must respond to the command of the Fourteenth Amendment. An inter-district remedy for the infringements that occurred in this case is well within the confines and powers of the State, which is the governmental entity ultimately responsible for desegregating its schools. . . .

It is unnecessary to catalogue at length the various public misdeeds found by the District Court and the Court of Appeals to have contributed to the present segregation of the Detroit public schools. The legislature contributed directly by enacting a statute overriding a partial high school desegregation plan voluntarily adopted by the Detroit Board of Education. Indirectly, the trial court found the State was accountable for the thinly disguised, pervasive acts of segregation committed by the Detroit Board, for Detroit's school construction plans that would promote segregation, and for the Detroit school district's not having funds for pupil transportation within the district. The State was also chargeable with responsibility for the transportation of Negro high school students in the late 1950's from the suburban Ferndale School District, past closer suburban and Detroit high schools with predominantly white student bodies, to a predominantly Negro high school within Detroit. . . .

The unwavering decisions of this Court over the past 20 years support the assumption of the Court of Appeals that the District Court's remedial power does not cease at the school district line. The Court's first formulation of the remedial principles to be followed in disestablishing racially discriminatory school systems recognized the variety of problems arising from different local school conditions and the necessity for that "practical flexibility" traditionally associated with courts of equity. . . . Indeed, the district courts to which the Brown cases were remanded for the formulation of remedial decrees were specifically instructed that they might consider, inter alia, "revision of school districts and attendance areas into compact units to achieve a system of determining admission to the public schools on a nonracial basis. . . ." The malady addressed in Brown II was the state-wide policy of requiring or permitting school segregation on the basis of race, while the record here concerns segregated schools only in the city of Detroit. The obligation to rectify the unlawful condition nevertheless rests on the State. The permissible revision of school districts contemplated in Brown II rested on the State's responsibility for desegregating its unlawfully segregated schools, not on any segregative effect which the condition of segregation in one school district might have had on the schools of a neighboring district. The same situation obtains here and the same remedial power is available to the District court. . . .

. . . There are indeed limitations on the equity powers of the federal judiciary, but until now the Court has not accepted the proposition that effective enforcement of the Fourteenth Amendment could be limited by political or administrative boundary lines demarcated by the very State responsible for the constitutional violation and for the disestablishment of the dual system. . . .

Mr. Justice **Marshall**, with whom Mr. Justice **Douglas**, Mr. Justice **Brennan**, and Mr. Justice **White** join, dissenting, said in part:

After 20 years of small, often difficult steps toward that great end, the Court today takes a giant step backwards. Notwithstanding a record showing widespread and pervasive racial segregation in the educational system provided by the State of Michigan for children in Detroit, this Court holds that the District Court was powerless to require the State to remedy its constitutional violation in any meaningful fashion. Ironically purporting to base its result on the principle that the scope of the remedy in a desegregation case should be determined by the nature and the extent of the constitutional violation, the Court's answer is to provide no remedy at all for the violation proved in this case, thereby guaranteeing that Negro children in Detroit will receive the same separate and inherently unequal education in the future as they have been unconstitutionally afforded in the past.

I cannot subscribe to this emasculation of our constitutional guarantee of equal protection of the laws and must respectively dissent. Our precedents, in my view, firmly establish that where, as here, state-imposed segregation has been demonstrated, it becomes the duty of the State to eliminate root and branch all vestiges of racial discrimination and to achieve the greatest possible degree of actual desegregation. . . .

II. . . .

Under a Detroit-only decree, Detroit's schools will clearly remain racially identifiable in comparison with neighboring schools in the metropolitan community. Schools with 65% and more Negro students will stand in sharp and obvious contrast to schools in neighboring districts with less than 2% Negro enrollment. Negro students will continue to perceive their schools as segregated educational facilities and this perception will only be increased when whites react to a Detroit-only decree by fleeing to the suburbs to avoid integration. School district lines, however innocently drawn, will surely be perceived as fences to separate the races when under a

Detroit-only decree, white parents withdraw their children from the Detroit city schools and move to the suburbs in order to continue them in all-white schools. The message of this action will not escape the Negro children in the city of Detroit. . . . It will be of scant significance to Negro children who have for years been confined by de jure acts of segregation to a growing core of all-Negro schools surrounded by a ring of all-white schools that the new dividing line between the races is the school district boundary. . . .

RICHMOND v. CROSON

488 U. S. 469; 109 S. Ct. 706; 102 L. Ed. 2d 854
(1989)

A major factor in maintaining the intellectual and cultural disadvantage of blacks has been an almost universal discrimination against them economically. White small businesses and professionals simply did not hire blacks, however well qualified. Large employers hired some, but they were systematically left in the servile or menial positions represented by Pullman porters in the railroad industry and the janitorial staff of industry generally. Labor unions of skilled workers ordinarily discriminated against blacks. Even where whites and blacks could compete for the same jobs, whites were better paid for the same work and their chances for promotion were better. And when technological advances displaced workers, it was the unskilled black workers who most often were out of jobs.

During most of our constitutional history Congress and the Court have left this problem to the states, and only a handful of states forbade discrimination in private employment. During World War II the President's Fair Employment Practices Committee achieved significant results, but with the return to a peace-time economy and the abolition of the Committee, much of the progress was lost. It was not until the Civil Rights Act of 1964, held valid in Heart of Atlanta Motel v. United States (1964), that a systematic national attack on the problem was made. Title VII of the act forbade race discrimination in hiring and the classification of employees in such a way as to "adversely affect" their status because of their race, color, sex, religion, or national origin.

Although the act permitted the use of professionally constructed ability tests provided they were not used to discriminate, in Griggs v. Duke Power Co. (1971) the Court found that the company had violated the act by using a high school diploma and an intelligence test to qualify workers for all but manual labor jobs. The Court noted that the tests bore no demonstrable relationship to the jobs for which they were required, and since blacks had long received an inferior education, the tests could be presumed to, and did in fact, discriminate against them. Speaking for a unanimous Court, Chief Justice Burger emphasized that "Congress has not commanded that the less qualified be preferred over the better quali-

fied simply because of minority origins. Far from disparaging job qualifications as such, Congress had made such qualifications the controlling factor, so that race, religion, nationality and sex become irrelevant."

In Washington v. Davis (1976), however, the Court increased substantially the difficulty of showing that an employer's job qualification tests were discriminatory. It conceded that under Title VII, a job test or other qualification could be invalid even though it was not adopted with the intent to discriminate. Merely showing that a test had a discriminatory effect was enough to switch the burden to the employer to show that the test was valid under Title VII. However, the court made it relatively easy for the employer to meet this burden. Under the statute a test was valid if it were "job-related," but the Court said "job related" did not mean mere ability to perform the job. It could also include the ability to enter a required training program, even though some of that program was unrelated to the job. Washington v. Davis itself, however, involved a test required by the government and thus raised constitutional issues. In this situation, what the Court described as the "more rigorous standard" for tests under Title VII was one which the Court was "not disposed to adopt . . . for the purposes of applying the Fifth and Fourteenth Amendments. . . .

The case involved two blacks who had failed to pass a verbal ability test required as a condition of admission to the Washington, D.C., police department. There was neither evidence nor claim of purposeful discrimination, and the Court declined to hold the test void despite the fact that four times as many blacks as whites failed it. Noting that in both jury cases and in de jure school segregation cases there had been purposeful discrimination, the Court said: "As an initial matter, we have difficulty understanding how a law establishing a racially neutral qualification for employment is nevertheless racially discriminatory and denies 'any person . . . equal protection of the law' simply because a greater proportion of Negroes fail to qualify than members of other racial or ethnic groups. . . . Test 21, which is administered generally to prospective Government employees, concededly seeks to ascertain whether those who take it have acquired a particular level of verbal skill; and it is untenable that the Constitution prevents the Government from seeking modestly to upgrade the communicative abilities of its employees rather than to be satisfied with some lower level of competence, particularly where the job requires special ability to communicate orally and in writing. Respondents, as Negroes, could no more successfully claim that the test denied them equal protection than could white applicants who also failed."

Where both the Constitution and the law look to a policy of nondiscrimination and desegregation, what steps may be taken to bring about the desired result? Can blacks be identified and considered as blacks? And if so, for what purposes? May an employer who has always hired whites now consider only black applicants until the balance is redressed? If he may not, and due to educational background white applicants are better qualified, how is the balance ever to be redressed? If he may, is he not illegally discriminating in favor of blacks over whites? The question is the difficult one of defining equality of racial treatment in the context of a society in which nearly every institution is structured to favor whites.

In *University of California v. Bakke* (1978) the University of California Medical School at Davis had set aside sixteen of its 100 entering seats for minority and disadvantaged applicants. The medical school was created in 1968, had no history of purposeful discrimination and adopted this minority program to increase the number of minority students attending the school. Allan Bakke, a 37-year-old white engineer was denied admission and brought suit against the University claiming he was better qualified than some of the sixteen minority students and was being discriminated against because of his race.

In a five-to-four decision with six opinions the Court held void the Davis set-aside program but refused to hold that race could not be a legitimate consideration in admitting students. Justices Burger, Stewart, Rehnquist and Stevens held that Title VI of the Civil Rights Act of 1964 flatly forbade any discrimination whatsoever based on race. Justice Powell, the swing vote, argued that if race were merely one of a number of considerations used to determine admission, as it was at Harvard, it would not violate the equal protection clause. But to establish a fixed quota to aid "persons perceived as members of relatively victimized groups at the expense of other innocent individuals in the absence of judicial, legislative, or administrative findings of constitutional or statutory violations" would be such a denial.

Justices Brennan, White, Marshall and Blackmun joined Justice Powell on the use of race, holding that as a classification it could be used for benign purposes. "Unquestionably we have held that a government practice or statute which restricts 'fundamental rights' or which contains 'suspect classifications' is to be subjected to 'strict scrutiny' and can be justified only if it furthers a compelling government purpose and, even then, only if no less restrictive alternative is available. . . . But no fundamental right is involved here. . . . Nor do whites as a class have any of the 'traditional indicia of suspectness: the class is not saddled with such disabilities, or subjected to such a history of purposeful unequal treatment, or relegated to such a position of political powerlessness as to command extraordinary protection from the majoritarian political process.' "

In the years following the Bakke decision a divided Court whose membership was changing struggled with interpretations both of the Constitution and of §§ 703 (a) and (d) of Title VII of the Civil Rights Act of 1964, all of which, to some ill-defined extent, forbade race discrimination in employment. The question raised by the cases was the extent to which various employers, public and private, could undertake "affirmative action" or "reverse discrimination" to bring more minority personnel into what were largely all-white or all-male work forces.

While the mixture of constitutional and statutory issues and the wide variations among the facts of the cases make generalization virtually impossible, the cases appear to fall into three roughly defined categories:

First, where the group, whether public or private, had a long established record of discrimination and had defied court orders to desegregate, the Court held valid the court-ordered affirmative action. In *Sheet Metal Workers v. EEOC* (1976) a labor union with a long record of deliberate race discrimination was ordered to mend its ways and fined for contempt when it failed to do so. And in *United States v. Paradise* (1987) the Court found that Alabama state troopers had ignored for over a dozen years court orders to appoint or promote blacks to the force and upheld a court-devised affirmative action plan. With Justices O'Connor, White, Rehnquist and Burger dissenting, Justice Powell cast the deciding vote.

A second pair of cases involved firefighting organizations in two cities. In both cases, to avoid going to trial and risking a court order requiring the adoption of an affirmative action plan, the city fire departments settled by means of a "consent decree"—an official settlement whose terms are approved by the court. In *Firefighters v. Stotts* (1984), the city of Memphis agreed in the consent decree to hire more blacks, but denied having engaged in discrimination. Since there was no showing of deliberate discrimination, and since the consent decree made no mention of a union contract providing "first on, last off" in case of layoffs, the majority upheld the laying off of the last hired, most of whom were black. On the other hand, in *Firefighters v. Cleveland* (1986), the city admitted to a long and serious record of race discrimination and in a six-to-three decision the Court upheld the consent decree, which provided a quota of minority promotions. The court further held that the decree was not a court "order" and hence not limited by the sections of Title VII limiting certain race-conscious relief after trial.

In the third category are four cases in which affirmative action was taken voluntarily, rather than as a result of a court finding of discrimination or a consent decree agreed to in order to avoid a finding of such discrimination. Two of these case involved public agencies, and both held the affirmative action void. The first, of course, was the Bakke decision printed below. The second was *Wygant v. Jackson Board of Education* (1986) in which a Union-School Board agreement gave probationary blacks preference over tenured whites at lay-off time in order to maintain a black quota. The presence of a state agency brought the equal protection clause into play and a four-member plurality applied the "strict scrutiny" test. "Societal discrimination, without more, is too amorphous a basis for imposing a racially classified remedy. The role model theory announced by the District Court and the resultant holding typify this indefiniteness."

Also in the third category are two cases involving voluntary affirmative action plans that the court considered solely under Title VII, not the equal protection clause. In both of these the Court upheld the affirmative action. The language of § 703 (a) made it illegal "to fail or refuse to hire or to discharge any individual, or otherwise to discriminate against any individual with respect to his compensation, terms, conditions, or privileges of employment, because of such individual's race, color, religion, sex, or national origin. . . ." In Steelworkers v. Weber (1979) a majority of the Court found that the intent of Title VII was to improve the lot of blacks and "we cannot agree with respondent that Congress intended to prohibit the private sector from taking effective steps to accomplish the goal that Congress designed Title VII to achieve."

It reached the same result in Johnson v. Transportation Agency (1987). Diane Joyce was appointed to the position of road dispatcher despite the fact a man had scored slightly higher on one of the tests. Prior to her appointment, none of the 238 Skilled Craft Worker positions in the Agency was held by a woman, although the Court conceded that this was a result of societal discrimination and not the deliberate policy of the Agency and that in promoting qualified applicants sex was only one of the factors to be considered. The dissenting justices in both cases argued that the language of . . . 703 forbade discriminating in favor of minorities as well as against them. [While one party in the Johnson case was a government agency, no constitutional issue was raised or considered.]

In Fullilove v. Klutznick (1980), a case raising a different constitutional issue, a badly divided Court held valid a Congressional statute requiring that ten percent of money granted to the states for public works be set aside for minority contractors. Justices White, Burger, and Powell agreed that the law's purpose was to prevent the perpetuation of discriminatory practices, and that Congress could act both under its spending power and under Section 5 of the Fourteenth Amendment, while Justice Powell, speaking for himself, argued that because an appropriate governmental authority had identified the need for such affirmative action the law met the strict scrutiny test he had relied on in Bakke.

The present case arose when Richmond, Virginia, a city with a 50 percent black population with no record of discrimination against minority contractors, undertook to offset (so far as it could within its jurisdiction) the effect of such discrimination in the construction industry. Evidence revealed that only 0.67 percent of the city's construction contracts went to minority-owned business enterprises (MBEs), that only 4.7 percent of the construction firms throughout the country were minority owned, and of these 41 percent were located in California, New York, Illinois, Florida and Hawaii. Testimony indicated that "the general conduct of the construction industry in this area, in the State, and around the nation, is one in which race discrimination and exclusion on the basis of race is widespread." The city adopted a "remedial" plan providing that henceforth 30 percent of the money for such contracts should go to MBEs.

In 1983 the city went out on bid for toilet fixtures for the jail and Croson, a local contractor, found that under the terms of the law the fixtures would have to be supplied by an MBE. One local MBE appeared the day before the bids were due and asked to be considered as a subcontractor. The difficulty he faced getting credit both delayed and raised the amount of the bid. Since Croson was the only bidder, the city decided to rebid the contract and Croson sued on the ground that the set-aside plan was unconstitutional.

It has long been the policy of the Federal Communications Commission to promote minority ownership of radio and television stations, but as recently as 1986 they owned less than 2.1 percent of these facilities. In 1978, with the explicit approval of Congress, the FCC began considering minority ownership among the factors to be considered in the awarding of licenses. It also announced a plan under which the reassignment of an existing license was easier if the new owner were a member of a minority group.

In Metro Broadcasting v. FCC (1990) the Supreme Court upheld the validity of these policies against the challenge that they violated the equal protection component of the Fifth Amendment. It reaffirmed its decision in Fullilove v. Klutznick (1980), noting that that case did not apply "strict scrutiny" to race-based classifications. "We apply [the Klutznick] standard today. We hold that benign race-conscious measures mandated by Congress—even if those measures are not 'remedial' in the sense of being designed to compensate victims of past governmental or societal discrimination—are constitutionally permissible to the extent that they serve important governmental objectives within the power of Congress and are substantially related to achievement of those objectives." It held the goal of broadcast diversity was "an important governmental objective," and the plans were substantially related to achieving that goal. Justices O'Connor, Rehnquist, Scalia and Kennedy dissented, arguing that "strict scrutiny" should be applied to all race classifications.

Justice O'Connor announced the judgment of the Court and delivered an opinion concurred in as indicated below, saying in part:

In this case, we confront once again the tension between the Fourteenth Amendment's guarantee of equal treatment to all citizens, and the use of race-based measures to ameliorate the effects of past discrimination on the opportunities enjoyed by members of minority groups in our society. In Fullilove v. Klutznick (1980) we held that a congressional program requiring that 10% of certain federal construction grants be awarded to minority contractors did not violate the equal protection principles embodied in the Due Process Clause of the Fifth Amendment. Relying largely on our decision in Fullilove, some lower federal courts have applied a similar standard of review in assessing the constitutionality of state and local minority set-aside provisions under the Equal Protection Clause of the Fourteenth Amendment. . . . Since our decision two Terms ago in Wygant v. Jackson Board of Education (1986) the lower federal courts have attempted to apply its standards in evaluating the constitutionality of state and local programs which allocate a portion of public contracting opportunities exclusively to minority-owned businesses. . . . We noted probable jurisdiction in this case to consider the applicability of our decision in Wygant to a minority set-aside program adopted by the city of Richmond, Virginia.

II. [Joined by Justices Rehnquist and White]

The parties and their supporting amici fight an initial battle over the scope of the city's power to adopt legislation designed to address the effects of past discrimination. Relying on our decision in Wygant, appellee argues that the city must limit any race-based remedial efforts to eradicating the effects of its own prior discrimination. This is essentially the position taken by the Court of Appeals below. Appellant argues that our decision in Fullilove is controlling, and that as a result the city of Richmond enjoys sweeping legislative power to define and attack the effects of prior discrimination in its local construction industry. We find that neither of these two rather stark alternatives can withstand analysis.

In Fullilove, we upheld the minority set-aside contained in § 103(f)(2) of the Public Works Employment Act of 1977 against a challenge based on the equal protection component of the Due Process Clause. The Act authorized a four billion [dollar] appropriation for federal grants to state and local governments for use in public works projects. The primary purpose of the Act was to give the national economy a quick boost in a recessionary period; funds had to be committed to state or local grantees by September 30, 1977. The Act also contained the following requirement: " 'Except to the extent the Secretary determines otherwise, no grant shall be made under this Act . . . unless the applicant gives satisfactory assurance to the Secretary that at least 10 per centum of the amount of each grant shall be expended for minority business enterprises.' " Fullilove. . . .

The principal opinion in Fullilove, written by Chief Justice Burger, did not employ "strict scrutiny" or any other traditional standard of equal protection review. The Chief Justice noted at the outset that although racial classifications call for close examination, the Court was at the same time, "bound to approach [its] task with appropriate deference to the Congress, a co-equal branch charged by the Constitution with the power to 'provide for the . . . general Welfare of the United States' and 'to enforce by appropriate legislation,' the equal protection guarantees of the Fourteenth Amendment." The principal opinion asked two questions: First, were the objectives of the legislation within the powers of Congress? Second, was the limited use of racial and ethnic criteria a permissible means for Congress to carry out its objectives within the constraints of the Due Process Clause?

On the issue of congressional power, the Chief Justice found that Congress' commerce power was sufficiently broad to allow it to reach the practices of prime contractors on federally funded local construction projects. Congress could mandate state and local government compliance with the set-aside program under its § 5 power to enforce the Fourteenth Amendment.

The Chief Justice next turned to the constraints on Congress' power to employ race-conscious remedial relief. His opinion stressed two factors in upholding the MBE set-aside. First was the unique remedial powers [sic] of Congress under § 5 of the Fourteenth Amendment: "Here we deal . . . not with the limited remedial powers of a federal court, for example, but with the broad remedial powers of Congress. It is fundamental that *in no organ of government, state or federal, does there repose a more comprehensive remedial power than in the Congress,* expressly charged by the Constitution with competence and authority to enforce equal protection guarantees." (plurality opinion)(emphasis added).

Because of these unique powers, the Chief Justice concluded that "Congress not only may induce voluntary action to assure compliance with existing federal statutory or constitutional antidiscrimination provisions, but also, where Congress has authority to *declare certain conduct unlawful,* it may, as here, authorize and induce state action to avoid such conduct." (emphasis added).

In reviewing the legislative history behind the Act, the principal opinion focused on the evidence before Congress that a nationwide history of past discrimination had reduced minority participation in federal construction grants. . . . The Chief Justice concluded that "Congress had abundant historical basis from which it could conclude that traditional procurement practices, when applied to minority businesses, could perpetuate the effects of prior discrimination."

The second factor emphasized by the principal opinion in Fullilove was the flexible nature of the 10% set-aside. Two "congressional assumptions" underlay the MBE program: first, that the effects of past discrimination had impaired the competitive position of minority businesses, and second, that "adjustment for the effects of past discrimination" would assure that at least 10% of the funds from the federal grant program would flow to minority businesses. The Chief Justice noted that both of these "assumptions" could be "rebutted" by a grantee seeking a waiver of the 10% requirement. Thus a waiver could be sought where minority businesses were not available to fill the 10% requirement or, more importantly, where an MBE attempted "to exploit the remedial aspects of the program by charging an unreasonable price, i.e., a price not attributable to the present effects of prior discrimination." The Chief Justice indicated that without this fine tuning to remedial purpose, the statute would not have "pass[ed] muster." . . .

Appellant and its supporting amici rely heavily on Fullilove for the proposition that a city council, like Congress, need not make specific findings of discrimination to engage in race-conscious relief. Thus, appellant argues "[i]t would be a perversion of federalism to hold that the federal government has a compelling interest in remedying the effects of racial discrimination in its own public works program, but a city government does not."

What appellant ignores is that the Congress, unlike any State or political subdivision, has a specific constitutional mandate to enforce the dictates of the Fourteenth Amendment. The power to "enforce" may at times also include the power to define situations which *Congress* determines threaten principles of equality and to adopt prophylactic rules to deal with those situations. ("Correctly viewed, § 5 is a positive grant of legislative power authorizing Congress to exercise its discretion in determining whether and what legislation is needed to secure the guarantees of the Fourteenth Amendment"). . . .

That Congress may identify and redress the effects of society-wide discrimination does not mean that, a fortiori, the States and their political subdivisions are free to decide that such remedies are appropriate. Section 1 of the Fourteenth Amendment is an explicit *constraint* on state power, and the States must undertake any remedial efforts in accordance with that provision. To hold otherwise would be to cede control over the content of the Equal Protection Clause to the 50 state legislatures and their myriad political subdivisions. The mere recitation of a benign or compensatory purpose for the use of a racial classification would essentially entitle the States to exercise the full power of Congress under § 5 of the Fourteenth Amendment and insulate any racial classification from judicial scrutiny under § 1. We believe that such a result would be contrary to the intentions of the Framers of the Fourteenth Amendment, who desired to place clear limits on the States' use of race as a criterion for legislative action, and to have the federal courts enforce those limitations. . . .

It would seem equally clear, however, that a state or local subdivision (if delegated the authority from the State) has the authority to eradicate the effects of private discrimination within its own legislative jurisdiction. This authority must, of course, be exercised within the constraints of § 1 of the Fourteenth Amendment. Our decision in Wygant is not to the contrary. Wygant addressed the constitutionality of the use of racial quotas by local school authorities pursuant to an agreement reached with the local teachers' union. It was in the context of addressing the school board's power to adopt a race-based layoff program affecting its own work force that the Wygant plurality indicated that the Equal Protection Clause required "some showing of prior discrimination by the governmental unit involved." Wygant. As a matter of state law, the city of Richmond has legislative authority over its procurement policies, and can use its spending powers to remedy private discrimination, if it identifies that discrimination with the particularity required by the Fourteenth Amendment. To this extent, on the question of the city's competence, the Court of Appeals erred in following Wygant by rote in a case involving a state entity which has state-law authority to address discriminatory practices within local commerce under its jurisdiction.

Thus, if the city could show that it had essentially become a "passive participant" in a system of racial exclusion practiced by elements of the local construction industry, we think it clear that the city could take affirmative steps to dismantle such a system. It is beyond dispute that any public entity, state or federal, has a compelling interest in assuring that public dollars, drawn from the tax contributions of all citizens, do not serve to finance the evil of private prejudice. . . .

III.

A. [Joined by Justices Rehnquist, White, Stevens and Kennedy.]

The Equal Protection Clause of the Fourteenth Amendment provides that "[N]o State shall . . . deny to *any person* within its jurisdiction the equal protection of the laws" (emphasis added). As this Court has noted in the past, the "rights created by the first section of the Fourteenth Amendment are, by its terms, guaranteed to the individual. The rights established are personal rights." Shelley v. Kraemer (1948). The Richmond Plan denies certain citizens the opportunity to compete for a fixed percentage of public contracts based solely upon their race. To whatever racial group these citizens belong, their "personal rights" to be treated with equal dignity and respect are implicated by a rigid rule erecting race as the sole criterion in an aspect of public decision-making.

Absent searching judicial inquiry into the justification for such race-based measures, there is simply no way of determining what classifications are "benign" or "remedial" and what classifications are in fact motivated by illegitimate notions of racial inferiority or simple racial politics. Indeed, the purpose of strict scrutiny is to "smoke out" illegitimate uses of race by assuring that the legislative body is pursuing a goal important enough to warrant use of a highly suspect tool. The test also ensures that the means chosen "fit" this compelling goal so closely that there is little or no possibility that the motive for the classification was illegitimate racial prejudice or stereotype.

Classifications based on race carry a danger of stigmatic harm. Unless they are strictly reserved for remedial settings, they may in fact promote notions of racial inferiority and lead to a politics of racial hostility. See University of California Regents v. Bakke ([1978] (opinion of Powell, J.). ("[P]referential programs may only reinforce common stereotypes holding that certain groups are unable to achieve success without special protection based on a factor having no relation to individual worth"). We thus reaffirm the view expressed by the plurality in Wygant that the standard of review under the Equal Protection Clause is not dependent on the race of those burdened or benefited by a particular classification. . . .

Our continued adherence to the standard of review employed in Wygant, does not, as Justice Marshall's dissent suggests, indicate that we view "racial discrimination as largely a phenomenon of the past" or that "government bodies need no longer preoccupy themselves with rectifying racial injustice." As we indicate, States and their local subdivisions have many legislative weapons at their disposal both to punish and prevent present discrimination and to remove arbitrary barriers to minority advancement. Rather, our interpretation of § 1 stems from our agreement with the view expressed by Justice Powell in Bakke, that "[t]he guarantee of equal protection cannot mean one thing when applied to one individual and something else when applied to a person of another color."

... See Weinberger v. Wiesenfeld (1975) ("[T]he mere recitation of a benign, compensatory purpose is not an automatic shield which protects against any inquiry into the actual purposes underlying a statutory scheme"). The dissent's watered-down version of equal protection review effectively assures that race will always be relevant in American life, and that the "ultimate goal" of "eliminat[ing] entirely from governmental decisionmaking such irrelevant factors as a human being's race," Wygant, (Stevens, J., dissenting) will never be achieved.

Even were we to accept a reading of the guarantee of equal protection under which the level of scrutiny varies according to the ability of different groups to defend their interests in the representative process, heightened scrutiny would still be appropriate in the circumstances of this case. One of the central arguments for applying a less exacting standard to "benign" racial classifications is that such measures essentially involve a choice made by dominant racial groups to disadvantage themselves. If one aspect of the judiciary's role under the Equal Protection Clause is to protect "discrete and insular minorities" from majoritarian prejudice or indifference, see United States v. Carolene Products Co. (1938), some maintain that these concerns are not implicated when the "white majority" places burdens upon itself.

In this case, blacks comprise approximately 50% of the population of the city of Richmond. Five of the nine seats on the City Council are held by blacks. The concern that a political majority will more easily act to the disadvantage of a minority based on unwarranted assumptions or incomplete facts would seem to militate for, not against, the application of heightened judicial scrutiny in this case. ("Of course it works both ways: a law that favors Blacks over Whites would be suspect if it were enacted by a predominantly Black legislature").

In Bakke the Court confronted a racial quota employed by the University of California at Davis Medical School. . . .

Justice Powell's opinion applied heightened scrutiny under the Equal Protection Clause to the racial classification at issue. His opinion decisively rejected the first justification for the racially segregated admissions plan. The desire to have more black medical students or doctors, standing alone, was not merely insufficiently compelling to justify a racial classification, it was "discrimination for its own sake," forbidden by the Constitution. Nor could the second concern, the history of discrimination in society at large, justify a racial quota in medical school admissions. Justice Powell contrasted the "focused" goal of remedying "wrongs worked by specific instances of racial discrimination" with "the remedying of the effects of 'societal discrimination,' an amorphous concept of injury that may be ageless in its reach into the past." He indicated that for the governmental interest in remedying past discrimination to be triggered "judicial, legislative, or administrative findings of constitutional or statutory violations" must be made. Only then does the Government have a compelling interest in favoring one race over another.

In Wygant (1986), four Members of the Court applied heightened scrutiny to a race-based system of employee layoffs. Justice Powell, writing for the plurality, again drew the distinction between "societal discrimination" which is an inadequate basis for race-conscious classifications, and the type of identified discrimination that can support and define the scope of race-based relief. The challenged classification in that case tied the layoff of minority teachers to the percentage of minority students enrolled in the school district. The lower courts had upheld the scheme, based on the theory that minority students were in need of "role models" to alleviate the effects of prior discrimination in society. This Court reversed, with a plurality of four Justices reiterating the view expressed by Justice Powell in Bakke that "[s]ocietal discrimination, without more, is too amorphous a basis for imposing a racially classified remedy." Wygant (plurality opinion).

The role model theory employed by the lower courts failed for two reasons. First, the statistical disparity between students and teachers had no probative value in demonstrating the kind of prior discrimination in hiring or promotion that would justify race-based relief. (O'Connor, J., concurring in part and concurring in judgment) ("The disparity between the percentage of minorities on the teaching staff and the percentage of minorities in the student body is not probative of employment discrimination"). Second, because the role model theory had no relation to some basis for believing a constitutional or statutory violation had occurred, it could be used to "justify" race-based decisionmaking essentially limitless in scope and duration. ("In the absence of particularized findings, a court could uphold remedies that are ageless in their reach into the past, and timeless in their ability to affect the future").

B. [Joined by Justices Rehnquist, White, Stevens, Scalia and Kennedy.]

We think it clear that the factual predicate offered in support of the Richmond Plan suffers from the same two defects identified as fatal in Wygant. The District Court found the city council's "findings sufficient to ensure that, in adopting the Plan, it was remedying the present effects of past discrimination in the *construction industry*." (emphasis added). Like the "role model" theory employed in Wygant, a generalized assertion that there has been past discrimination in an entire industry provides no guidance for a legislative body to determine the precise scope of the injury it seeks to remedy. It "has no logical stopping point." Wygant (plurality opinion). "Relief" for such an ill-defined wrong could extend until the percentage of public contracts awarded to MBEs in Richmond mirrored the percentage of minorities in the population as a whole.

Appellant argues that it is attempting to remedy various forms of past discrimination that are alleged to be responsible for the small number of minority businesses in the local contracting industry. Among these the city cites the exclusion of blacks from skilled construction trade unions and training programs. This past discrimination has prevented them "from following the traditional path from laborer to entrepreneur." . . .

While there is no doubt that the sorry history of both private and public discrimination in this country has contributed to a lack of opportunities for black entrepreneurs, this observation, standing alone, cannot justify a rigid racial quota in the awarding of public contracts in Richmond, Virginia. . . .

It is sheer speculation how many minority firms there would be in Richmond absent past societal discrimination, just as it was sheer speculation how many minority medical students would have been admitted to the medical school at Davis absent past discrimination in educational opportunities. Defining these sorts of injuries as "identified discrimination" would give local governments license to create a patchwork of racial preferences based on statistical generalizations about any particular field of endeavor.

These defects are readily apparent in this case. The 30% quota cannot in any realistic sense be tied to any injury suffered by anyone. . . .

The District Court accorded great weight to the fact that the city council designated the Plan as "remedial." But the mere recitation of a "benign" or legitimate purpose for a racial classification is entitled to little or no weight. . . .

. . . The history of racial classifications in this country suggests that blind judicial deference to legislative or executive pronouncements of necessity has no place in equal protection analysis. See Korematsu v. United States (1944) (Murphy, J., dissenting.)

. . . There is no doubt that "[w]here gross statistical disparities can be shown, they alone in a proper case may constitute prima facie proof of a pattern or practice of discrimination" under Title VII. Hazelwood School Dist. v. United States (1977). But it is equally clear that "[w]hen special qualifications are required to fill particular jobs, comparisons to the general population (rather than to the smaller group of individuals who possess the necessary qualifications) may have little probative value." . . .

In this case, the city does not even know how many MBE's in the relevant market are qualified to undertake prime or subcontracting work in public construction projects. . . . Nor does the city know what percentage of total city construction dollars minority firms now receive as subcontractors on prime contracts let by the city.

To a large extent, the set-aside of subcontracting dollars seems to rest on the unsupported assumption that white prime contractors simply will not hire minority firms. See Associated General Contractors of Cal. v. San Francisco ("There is no finding—and we decline to assume—that male caucasian constructors will award contracts only to other male caucasians"). . . . Without any information on minority participation in subcontracting, it is quite simply impossible to evaluate overall minority representation in the city's construction expenditures. . . .

Justice Marshall apparently views the requirement that Richmond identify the discrimination it seeks to remedy in its own jurisdiction as a mere administrative headache, an "onerous documentary obligatio[n]." We cannot agree. In this regard, we are in accord with Justice Stevens' observation in Fullilove, that "[b]ecause racial characteristics so seldom provide a relevant basis for disparate treatment, and because classifications based on race are potentially so harmful to the entire body politic, it is especially important that the reasons for any such classification be clearly identified and unquestionably legitimate." Fullilove (dissenting opinion). The "evidence" relied upon by the dissent, the history of school desegregation in the Richmond and numerous congressional reports, does little to define the scope of any injury to minority contractors in Richmond or the necessary remedy. The factors relied upon by the dissent could justify a preference of any size or duration. . . .

In sum, none of the evidence presented by the city points to any identified discrimination in Richmond construction industry. We, therefore, hold that the city has failed to demonstrate a compelling interest in apportioning public contracting opportunities on the basis of race. . . .

IV. [Joined by Justices Rehnquist, White, Stevens, Scalia and Kennedy.]

As noted by the court below, it is almost impossible to assess whether the Richmond Plan is narrowly tailored to remedy prior discrimination since it is not linked to identified discrimination in any way. We limit ourselves to two observations in this regard.

First, there does not appear to have been any consideration of the use of race-neutral means to increase minority business participation in city contracting. . . . Many of the barriers to minority participation in the construction industry relied upon by the city to justify a racial classification appear to be race neutral. If MBE's disproportionately lack capital or cannot meet bonding requirements, a race-neutral program of city financing for small firms would, a fortiori, lead to greater minority participation. The principal opinion in Fullilove found that Congress had carefully examined and rejected race-neutral alternatives before enacting the MBE set-aside. . . . There is no evidence in this record that Richmond City Council has considered any alternatives to a race-based quota.

Second, the 30% quota cannot be said to be narrowly tailored to any goal, except perhaps outright racial balancing. It rests upon the "completely unrealistic" assumption that minorities will choose a particular trade in lockstep proportion to their representation in the local population. . . .

Given the existence of an individualized procedure, the city's only interest in maintaining a quota system rather than investigating the need for remedial action in particular cases would seem to be simple administrative convenience. But the interest in avoiding the bureaucratic effort necessary to tailor remedial relief to those who truly have suffered the effects of prior discrimination cannot justify a rigid line drawn on the basis of a suspect classification. . . . Under Richmond's scheme, a successful black, Hispanic, or Oriental entrepreneur from anywhere in the country enjoys an absolute preference over other citizens based solely on their race. We think it obvious that such a program is not narrowly tailored to remedy the effects of prior discrimination.

V. . . . [Joined by Justices Rehnquist, White, and Kennedy.]

[The Court here assures cities the right to deal with "identified" discrimination and points out nondiscriminatory ways in which small contractors could legitimately be aided.]
. . . Accordingly, the judgment of the Court of Appeals for the Fourth Circuit is affirmed.

Justice **Stevens**, concurring in part and concurring in the judgment, said in part:

A central purpose of the Fourteenth Amendment is to further the national goal of equal opportunity for all our citizens. In order to achieve that goal we must learn from our past mistakes, but I believe the Constitution requires us to evaluate our policy decisions—including those that govern the relationships among different racial and ethnic groups—primarily by studying their probable impact on the future. I therefore do not agree with the premise that seems to underlie today's decision, as well as the decision in Wygant v. Jackson Board of Education (1986), that a governmental decision that rests on a racial classification is never permissible except as a remedy for a past wrong. I do, however, agree with the Court's explanation of why the Richmond ordinance cannot be justified as a remedy for past discrimination, and therefore join Parts I, III-B, and IV of its opinion. I write separately to emphasize three aspects of the case that are of special importance to me. . . .

Justice **Kennedy**, concurring in part and concurring in the judgment, said in part:
I join all but Part II of Justice O'Connor's opinion and give this further explanation.
Part II examines our case law upholding Congressional power to grant preferences based on overt and explicit classification by race. See Fullilove v. Klutznick (1980). With the acknowledgment that the summary in Part II is both precise and fair, I must decline to join it. The process by which a law that is an equal protection violation when enacted by a State becomes transformed to an equal protection guarantee when enacted by Congress poses a difficult proposition for me; but as it is not before us, any reconsideration of that issue must await some further case. For purposes of the ordinance challenged here, it suffices to say that the State has the power to eradicate racial discrimination and its effects in both the public and private sectors, and the absolute duty to do so where those wrongs were caused intentionally by the State itself. The Fourteenth Amendment ought not to be interpreted to reduce a State's authority in this regard, unless, of course, there is a conflict with federal law or a state remedy is itself a violation of equal protection. The latter is the case presented here.

Justice **Scalia**, concurring in the judgment, said in part:

I agree with much of the Court's opinion, and, in particular, with Justice O'Connor's conclusion that strict scrutiny must be applied to all governmental classification by race, whether or not its asserted purpose is "remedial" or "benign." I do not agree, however, with Justice O'Connor's dictum suggesting that, despite the Fourteenth Amendment, state and local governments may in some circumstances discriminate on the basis of race in order (in a broad sense) "to ameliorate the effects of past discrimination." The benign purpose of compensating for social disadvantages, whether they have been acquired by reason of prior discrimination or otherwise, can no more be pursued by the illegitimate means of racial discrimination than can other assertedly benign purposes we have repeatedly rejected.

Justice **Marshall**, with whom Justice **Brennan** and Justice **Blackmun** join, dissenting, said in part:

It is a welcome symbol of racial progress when the former capital of the Confederacy acts forthrightly to confront the effects of racial discrimination in its midst. In my view, nothing in the Constitution can be construed to prevent Richmond, Virginia, from allocating a portion of its contracting dollars for businesses owned or controlled by members of minority groups. Indeed, Richmond's set-aside program is indistinguishable in all meaningful respects from—and in fact was patterned upon—the federal set-aside plan which this Court upheld in Fullilove v. Klutznick (1980).

A majority of this Court holds today, however, that the Equal Protection Clause of the Fourteenth Amendment blocks Richmond's initiative. The essence of the majority's position* is that Richmond has failed to catalogue adequate findings to prove that past discrimination has impeded minorities from joining or participating fully in Richmond's construction contracting industry. I find deep irony in second-guessing Richmond's judgment on this point. As much as any municipality in the

---

*In the interests of convenience I refer to the opinion in this case authored by Justice O'Connor as "the majority", recognizing that certain portions of that opinion have been joined by only a plurality of the Court.

United States, Richmond knows what racial discrimination is; a century of decisions by this and other federal courts has richly documented the city's disgraceful history of public and private racial discrimination. In any event, the Richmond City Council *has* supported its determination that minorities have been wrongly excluded from local construction contracting. Its proof includes statistics showing that minority-owned businesses have received virtually no city contracting dollars and rarely if ever belonged to area trade associations; testimony by municipal officials that discrimination has been widespread in the local construction industry; and the same exhaustive and widely publicized federal studies relied on in Fullilove, studies which showed that pervasive discrimination in the Nation's tight-knit construction industry had operated to exclude minorities from public contracting. These are precisely the types of statistical and testimonial evidence which, until today, this Court had credited in cases approving of race-conscious measures designed to remedy past discrimination.

More fundamentally, today's decision marks a deliberate and giant step backward in this Court's affirmative-action jurisprudence. Cynical of one municipality's attempt to redress the effects of past racial discrimination in a particular industry, the majority launches a grapeshot attack on race-conscious remedies in general. The majority's unnecessary pronouncements will inevitably discourage or prevent governmental entities, particularly States and localities, from acting to rectify the scourge of past discrimination. This is the harsh reality of the majority's decision, but it is not the Constitution's command.

I.

As an initial matter, the majority takes an exceedingly myopic view of the factual predicate on which the Richmond city council relied when it passed the Minority Business Utilization Plan. The majority analyzes Richmond's initiative as if it were based solely upon the facts about local construction and contracting practices adduced during the City Council session at which the measure was enacted. In so doing, the majority downplays the fact that the City Council had before it a rich trove of evidence that discrimination in the Nation's construction industry had seriously impaired the competitive position of businesses owned or controlled by members of minority groups. It is only against this backdrop of documented national discrimination, however, that the local evidence adduced by Richmond can be properly understood. The majority's refusal to recognize that Richmond has proved itself no exception to the dismaying pattern of national exclusion which Congress so painstakingly identified infects its entire analysis of this case. . . .

. . . "The effects of past inequities stemming from racial prejudice have not remained in the past. The Congress has recognized the reality that past discriminatory practices have, to some degree, adversely affected our present economic system.

"While minority persons comprise about 16 percent of the Nation's population, of the 13 million businesses in the United States, only 382,000, or approximately 3.0 percent, are owned by minority individuals. The most recent data from the Department of Commerce also indicates that the gross receipts of all businesses in this country totals about $2,540.8 billion, and of this amount only $16.6 billion, or about 0.65 percent was realized by minority business concerns.

"These statistics are not the result of random chance. *The presumption must be made that past discriminatory systems have resulted in present economic inequities.*'" (quoted in Fullilove) (opinion of Burger, C.J.) (emphasis deleted and added). A 1977 Report by the same [congressional] Committee concluded: "[O]ver the years, there has developed a business system which has traditionally excluded measurable minority participation. In the past more than the present, this system of conducting business transactions overtly precluded minority input. Currently, we more often encounter a business system which is racially neutral on its face, but because of past overt social and economic discrimination is presently operating, in effect, to perpetuate these past inequities. Minorities, until recently, have not participated to any measurable extent, in our total business system generally, or in the construction industry in particular." (quoted in Fullilove). . . .

II.

"Agreement upon a means for applying the Equal Protection Clause to an affirmative-action program has eluded this Court every time the issue has come before us." Wygant v. Jackson Bd. of Education (1986) (Marshall, J., dissenting). My view has long been that race-conscious classifications designed to further remedial goals "must serve important governmental objectives and must be substantially related to achievement of those objectives" in order to withstand constitutional scrutiny. University of California Regents v. Bakke (1978) . . . .

A.

1.

Turning first to the governmental interest inquiry, Richmond has two powerful interests in setting aside a portion of public contracting funds for minority-owned enterprises. The first is the city's interest in eradicating the effects of past racial discrimination. It is far too late in the day to doubt that remedying such discrimination is a compelling, let alone an important, interest. In Fullilove, six Members of this Court deemed this interest sufficient to support a race-conscious set-aside program governing federal contract procurement. The decision, in holding that the federal set-aside provision satisfied the Equal Protection Clause under any level of scrutiny, recognized that the measure sought to remove "barriers to competitive access which had their roots in racial and ethnic discrimination, and which continue today, even absent any intentional discrimination or unlawful conduct." . . .

Richmond has a second compelling interest in setting aside, where possible, a portion of its contracting dollars. That interest is the prospective one of preventing the city's own spending decisions from reinforcing and perpetuating the exclusionary effects of past discrimination. . . .

The majority pays only lip service to this additional governmental interest. But our decisions have often emphasized the danger of the government tacitly adopting, encouraging, or furthering racial discrimination even by its own routine operations. In Shelley v. Kraemer (1948), this Court recognized this interest as a constitutional command, holding unanimously that the Equal Protection Clause forbids courts to enforce racially restrictive covenants even where such covenants satisfied all requirements of state law and where the State harbored no discriminatory intent. . . .

The majority is wrong to trivialize the continuing impact of government acceptance or use of private institutions or structures once wrought by discrimination. When government channels all its contracting funds to a white-dominated community of established contractors whose racial homogeneity is the product of private discrimination, it does more than place its imprimatur on the practices which forged and which continue to define that community. It also provides a measurable boost to those economic entities that have thrived within it, while denying important economic benefits to those entities which, but for prior discrimination, might well be better qualified to receive valuable government contracts. In my view, the interest in ensuring that the government does not reflect and reinforce prior private discrimination in dispensing public contracts is every bit as strong as the interest in eliminating private discrimination—an interest which this Court has repeatedly deemed compelling. . . . The more government bestows its rewards on those persons or businesses that were positioned to thrive during a period of private racial discrimination, the tighter the dead-hand grip of prior discrimination becomes on the present and future. Cities like Richmond may not be constitutionally required to adopt set-aside plans. . . . But there can be no doubt that when Richmond acted affirmatively to stem the perpetuation of patterns of discrimination through its own decisionmaking, it served an interest of the highest order. . . .

III.

I would ordinarily end my analysis at this point and conclude that Richmond's ordinance satisfies both the governmental interest and substantial relationship prongs of our Equal Protection Clause analysis. However, I am compelled to add more, for the majority has gone beyond the facts of this case to announce a set of principles which unnecessarily restricts the power of governmental entities to take race-conscious measures to redress the effects of prior discrimination.

A.

Today, for the first time, a majority of this Court has adopted strict scrutiny as its standard of Equal Protection Clause review of race-conscious remedial measures. This is an unwelcome development. A profound difference separates governmental actions that themselves are racist, and governmental actions that seek to remedy the effects of prior racism or to prevent neutral governmental activity from perpetuating the effects of such racism. . . .

Racial classifications "drawn on the presumption that one race is inferior to another or because they put the weight of government behind racial hatred and separatism" warrant the strictest judicial scrutiny because of the very irrelevance of these rationales. By contrast, racial classifications drawn for the purpose of remedying the effects of discrimination that itself was race based have a highly pertinent basis: the tragic and indelible fact that discrimination against blacks and other racial minorities in this Nation has pervaded our Nation's history and continues to scar our society. As I stated in Fullilove: "Because the consideration of race is relevant to remedying the continuing effects of past racial discrimination, and because governmental programs employing racial classifications for remedial purposes can be crafted to avoid stigmatization, . . . such programs should not be subjected to conventional 'strict scrutiny'—scrutiny that is strict in theory, but fatal in fact." Fullilove.

In concluding that remedial classifications warrant no different standard of review under the Constitution than the most brutal and repugnant forms of state-sponsored racism, a majority of this Court signals that it regards racial discrimination as largely a phenomenon of the past, and that government bodies need no longer preoccupy themselves with rectifying racial injustice. I, however, do not believe this Nation is anywhere close to eradicating racial discrimination or its vestiges. In constitutionalizing its wishful thinking, the majority today does a grave disservice not only to those victims of past and present racial discrimination in this Nation whom government has sought to assist, but also to this Court's long tradition of approaching issues of race with the utmost sensitivity. . . .

C.

Today's decision, finally, is particularly noteworthy for the daunting standard it imposes upon States and localities contemplating the use of race-conscious measures to eradicate the present effects of prior discrimination and prevent its perpetuation. The majority restricts the use of such measures to situations in which a State or locality can put forth "a prima facie case of a constitutional or statutory violation.'' In so doing, the majority calls into question the validity of the business set-asides which dozens of municipalities across this Nation have adopted on the authority of Fullilove.

Nothing in the Constitution or in the prior decisions of this Court supports limiting state authority to confront the effects of past discrimination to those situations in which a prima facie case of a constitutional or statutory violation can be made out. By its very terms, the majority's standard effectively cedes control of a large component of the content of that constitutional provision to Congress and to state legislatures. If an antecedent Virginia or Richmond law had defined as unlawful the award to nonminorities of an overwhelming share of a city's contracting dollars, for example, Richmond's subsequent set-aside initiative would then satisfy the majority's standard. But without such a law, the initiative might not withstand constitutional scrutiny. The meaning of ''equal protection of the laws'' thus turns on the happenstance of whether a state or local body has previously defined illegal discrimination. Indeed, given that racially discriminatory cities may be the ones least likely to have tough antidiscrimination laws on their books, the majority's constitutional incorporation of state and local statutes has the perverse effect of inhibiting those States or localities with the worst records of official racism from taking remedial action.

Similar flaws would inhere in the majority's standard even if it incorporated only federal anti-discrimination statutes. If Congress tomorrow dramatically expanded Title VII of the Civil Rights Act of 1964—or alternatively, if it repealed that legislation altogether—the meaning of equal protection would change precipitously along with it. Whatever the Framers of the Fourteenth Amendment had in mind in 1868, it certainly was not that the content of their Amendment would turn on the amendments to or the evolving interpretations of a federal statute passed nearly a century later.

To the degree that this parsimonious standard is grounded on a view that either § 1 or § 5 of the Fourteenth Amendment substantially disempowered States and localities from remedying past racial discrimination, the majority is seriously mistaken. With respect, first, to § 5, our precedents have never suggested that this provision—or, for that matter, its companion federal-empowerment provisions in the Thirteenth and Fifteenth Amendments—was meant to pre-empt or limit state police power to undertake race- conscious remedial measures. To the contrary, in Katzenbach v. Morgan (1966), we held that § 5 ''is a *positive* grant of legislative power authorizing Congress to exercise its discretion in determining whether and what legislation is needed to secure the guarantees of the Fourteenth Amendment.'' (emphasis added) . . . . Indeed, we have held that Congress has this authority even where no constitutional violation has been found. See Katzenbach (upholding Voting Rights Act provision nullifying state English literacy requirement we had previously upheld against Equal Protection Clause challenge). . . .

As for § 1, it is too late in the day to assert seri-

ously that the Equal Protection Clause prohibits States—or for that matter, the Federal Government, to whom the equal protection guarantee has largely been applied, see Bolling v. Sharpe (1954)—from enacting race-conscious remedies. Our cases in the areas of school desegregation, voting rights, and affirmative action have demonstrated time and again that race is constitutionally germane, precisely because race remains dismayingly relevant in American life. . . .

The fact is that Congress' concern in passing the Reconstruction Amendments, and particularly their congressional authorization provisions, was that States would *not* adequately respond to racial violence or discrimination against newly freed slaves. To interpret any aspect of these Amendments as proscribing state remedial responses to these very problems turns the Amendments on their heads. As four Justices, of whom I was one, stated in University of California Regents v. Bakke: ''[There is] no reason to conclude that the States cannot voluntarily accomplish under § 1 of the Fourteenth Amendment what Congress under § 5 of the Fourteenth Amendment validly may authorize or compel either the States or private persons to do. A contrary position would conflict with the traditional understanding recognizing the competence of the States to initiate measures consistent with federal policy in the absence of congressional pre- emption of the subject matter. *Nothing whatever in the legislative history of either the Fourteenth Amendment the Civil Rights Acts even remotely suggests that the States are foreclosed from furthering the fundamental purpose of equal opportunity to which the Amendment and those Acts are addressed.* Indeed, voluntary initiatives by the States to achieve the national goal of equal opportunity have been recognized to be essential to its attainment. . . .

Justice **Blackmun**, with whom Justice **Brennan** joins, dissenting.

I join Justice Marshall's perceptive and incisive opinion revealing great sensitivity toward those who have suffered the pains of economic discrimination in the construction trades for so long.

I never thought that I would live to see the day when the city of Richmond, Virginia, the cradle of the Old Confederacy, sought on its own, within a narrow confine, to lessen the stark impact of persistent discrimination. But Richmond, to its great credit, acted. Yet this Court, the supposed bastion of equality, strikes down Richmond's efforts as though discrimination had never existed or was not demonstrated in this particular litigation. Justice Marshall convincingly discloses the fallacy and the shallowness of that approach. History is irrefutable, even though one might sympathize with those who—though possibly innocent in themselves—benefit from the wrongs of past decades.

So the Court today regresses. I am confident, however, that, given time, it one day again will do its best to fulfill the great promises of the Constitution's Preamble and of the guarantees embodied in the Bill of Rights—a fulfillment that would make this Nation very special.

DISCRIMINATION AGAINST WOMEN

GEDULDIG v. AIELLO

417 U. S. 484; 94 S. Ct. 2485; 41 L. Ed. 2d 256 (1974)

Probably no group in the country is subject to a more pervasive, firmly established and staunchly defended system of discrimination than are women. Relying on such varied arguments as biblical authority, the woman's lack of muscular strength, her child-bearing function with its attendant incapacities, and the natural capacity for motherhood, male members of society have undertaken to protect "their women" from having to compete against men by assuring them, insofar as possible, a role of their own in society. States have, at one time or another, forbidden women to work at certain jobs, to engage publicly in certain sports, to work while pregnant or to collect unemployment benefits when on maternity leave. Until 1968, a Connecticut statute provided that a woman serve a three-year indeterminant sentence at the "State Farm" for a crime for which a man could be sentenced to only eighteen months in jail, and until 1982 a state could still establish a one-sex school, while one-race schools were held to deny equal protection of the laws. Even greater is the private discrimination against women. As with blacks, some employers simply refuse to hire women, hire them only for secretarial or clerical jobs, or pay them only about 60 percent of what they would pay a man for comparable work. Section 703(a) of the Civil Rights Act of 1964 provided the first nationwide prohibition against discriminatory hiring practices affecting women and in Phillips v. Marietta Corp. (1971) the Supreme Court held that the act forbade the corporation to refuse to hire a woman with pre-school-age children when it hired men with such children.

On the few occasions when the Court dealt with the rights of women under the equal protection clause, it treated sex as a legitimate basis of classification and as early as 1904 it held, in Cronin v. Adams, that a state could by law not only prevent women from working in saloons, but could even prevent their entering as customers. See the note to Goesaert v. Cleary. Nor was there any constitutional objection to treating men and women differently in regard to jury service. In Strauder v. West Virginia (1880) the Court suggested that a state could "confine the selection to males," and in Hoyt v. Florida (1961) it refused to review the "continuing validity of this dictum . . . which has gone unquestioned for more than eighty years in the decisions of this Court." The Court upheld a state law exempting women from jury

service, noting that "despite the enlightened emancipation of women from the restrictions and protections of bygone years, and their entry into many parts of community life formerly considered to be reserved to men, woman is still regarded as the center of home and family life."

With the woman's rights amendment (ERA) a few votes short of ratification, the attitude of the Supreme Court began to reflect the changed status of women in society. When, in Taylor v. Louisiana (1975), it effectively overruled the Hoyt case, it acknowledged that "if at one time it could be held that Sixth Amendment juries must be drawn from a fair cross section of the community but that this requirement permitted the almost total exclusion of women, this is not the case today. Communities differ at different times and places. What is a fair cross section at one time or place is not necessarily a fair cross section at another time or a different place." The Court noted that 53 percent of the community were women, and added that the fact that 54 percent of all women between eighteen and sixty-four were part of the labor force "certainly put to rest the suggestion that all women should be exempt from jury service based solely on their sex and the presumed role in the home."

But while the Court seemed prepared to accept the new role of women and viewed state laws treating them differently from men more critically than equal protection standards traditionally required, it was apparently not so convinced of their equality as to consider sex, like race, a "suspect" or "invidious" classification which can be used by the state only to achieve some compelling state interest which it cannot achieve in any other way. See the note to Plyler v. Doe.

In deciding Reed v. Reed in 1971, the first case ever to hold void a state classification based on sex, the Court held that women were as entitled as men to serve as administrators of estates. While it conceded that "the objective of reducing the work load on probate courts by eliminating one class of contests is not without some legitimacy," it found that preferring one sex over another "merely to accomplish the elimination of hearings on the merits, is to make the very kind of arbitrary legislative choice forbidden by the Equal Protection Clause."

Although Reed was unanimous, it gave no clue as to the philosophy of the justices, and it was not until 1973 with the decision in Frontiero v. Richardson that their attitudes began to emerge. A divided Court held that a female member of the armed forces could claim her spouse as a dependent in the same way a male member could claim his, without having to prove actual dependency. In a plurality opinion, Justices Brennan, Douglas, White, and Marshall reasoned that "classifications based on sex, like classifications based upon race, alienage, or national origin, are inherently suspect, and must therefore be subjected to strict judicial scrutiny." Applying these standards, the four justices, quoting from Reed, found that "any statutory scheme which draws a sharp line between the sexes, solely for the purpose of achieving administrative convenience, necessarily commands 'dissimilar treatment for men and women who are

... similarly situated,' and therefore involves the 'very kind of arbitrary legislative choice forbidden by the [Constitution].' '' While Justice Rehnquist dissented and Justice Stewart concurred on the basis of Reed, Justices Powell, Burger, and Blackmun expressly rejected the idea ''that all classifications based upon sex'' are inherently suspect.

Despite this division on the nature of woman's equality, where the Court has been able to view a law favoring women as an affirmative action program to offset the economic disadvantages to which women are subjected, it has found there was no denial of equal protection or due process of law. Thus, in 1974 in Kahn v. Shevin, the Court upheld a Florida property tax exemption for widows but not widowers on the ground that ''the financial difficulties confronting the lone woman in Florida or in another State exceed those facing the man. Whether from overt discrimination or from the socialization process or a male-dominated culture, the job market is inhospitable to the woman seeking any but the lowest paid jobs.'' Noting that this was a tax statute, Justice Douglas for a six-man majority applied the traditional rules regarding classification. ''A state tax law is not arbitrary although it 'discriminates in favor of a certain class . . . if the discrimination is founded upon a reasonable distinction, or difference in state policy,' not in conflict with the Federal Constitution.'' And in Schlesinger v. Ballard (1975) a regulation allowing women to stay thirteen years in the Navy although twice passed over for promotion did not discriminate against men who could only stay nine years since the opportunity for promotion among men was greater than among women.

In contrast, in Weinberger v. Wiesenfeld (1975) the Court struck down a provision of the Social Security Act providing that a widow with minor children was entitled to benefit from the earnings of her husband, while a widower with minor children was not entitled to benefit from the earnings of his wife. The government argued that, like Kahn v. Shevin, the scheme was designed to ''offset the adverse economic situation of women,'' but the Court found the legislative purpose was to enable the surviving parent to stay home with the child and, as in Reed, this was not a purpose which justified discrimination on the basis of sex.

While a majority of the Court refused to hold that classifications based on sex were ''invidious'' in the same way as those based on race, it was clearly tightening the reins on the ''rational basis'' test where the challenged classification was sex. In Stanton v. Stanton (1975) it held void a Utah law setting different ages at which males and females became legal adults, and in Craig v. Boren (1976) it struck down an Oklahoma law setting the age for drinking 3.2 beer at eighteen for females and twenty-one for males. In neither case was the Court willing to accept the state's argument that a legitimate state interest was being advanced, and in the latter case it rejected as unpersuasive the state's statistical evidence purporting to justify the law.

In General Electric v. Gilbert (1976) the Court extended the reasoning of the present case to cases arising under Title VII of the Civil Rights Act of 1964 forbidding sex discrimination by private employers. Noting the similarity of language used in the act with that appearing in equal protection decisions, the Court concluded that its decision in Geduldig was ''quite relevant in determining whether or not the pregnancy exclusion did discriminate on the basis of sex.'' Justice Brennan's dissent pointed out that G.E. had a long history of discrimination against women and that its medical coverage included voluntary male-only disabilities such as prostatectomies, vasectomies, and circumcisions. ''Pregnancy affords the only disability, sex-specific or otherwise, that is excluded from coverage.'' In 1978 Congress passed the Pregnancy Discrimination Act to nullify this interpretation.

Two cases in the 1980s broke the sex barrier of two of the nations largest businessmen's organizations, the Junior Chamber of Commerce and Rotary International. In both cases a state law forbade the organizations to discriminate against women and both argued their First Amendment right of ''intimate'' and ''private'' association was being abridged. In neither case were women excluded from meetings, membership in the associations offered important professional contacts and economic advantages and in both cases the organizations size and structure tended to refute the ''intimacy'' claim. See Roberts v. United States Jaycees (1984) and Board of Rotary International v. Rotary Club (1987).

Mr. Justice **Stewart** delivered the opinion of the Court, saying in part:

For almost 30 years California has administered a disability insurance system that pays benefits to persons in private employment who are temporarily unable to work because of disability not covered by workmen's compensation. The appellees brought this action to challenge the constitutionality of a provision of the California program that, in defining ''disability,'' excludes from coverage certain disabilities resulting from pregnancy. Because the appellees sought to enjoin the enforcement of this state statute, a three-judge court was convened. . . . On the appellees' motion for summary judgment, the District Court, by a divided vote, held that this provision of the disability insurance program violates the Equal Protection Clause of the Fourteenth Amendment, and therefore enjoined its continued enforcement. . . .

I.

California's disability insurance system is funded entirely from contributions deducted from the wages of participating employees. Participation in the program is mandatory unless the employees are protected by a voluntary private plan approved by the State. Each employee is required to contribute one percent of his salary, up to an annual maximum of $85. These contributions are placed in the Unemployment Compensation Disability Fund, which is established and administered as a special trust fund within the state treasury. . . .

In return for his one-percent contribution to the Disability Fund, the individual employee is insured against the risk of disability stemming from a substantial number of "mental or physical illness[es] and mental or physical injur[ies]." It is not every disabling condition, however, that triggers the obligation to pay benefits under the program. . . .

At all times relevant to this case, § 2626 of the Unemployment Insurance Code provided:

" 'Disability' or 'disabled' includes both mental or physical illness and mental or physical injury. An individual shall be deemed disabled in any day in which, because of mental or physical condition, he is unable to perform his regular or customary work. *In no case shall the term 'disability' or 'disabled' include any injury or illness caused by or arising in connection with pregnancy up to the termination of such pregnancy and for a period of 28 days thereafter.*" (Emphasis added.) . . .

. . . The state court construed the statute to preclude only the payment of benefits for disability accompanying normal pregnancy. The appellant acquiesced in this construction and issued administrative guidelines that exclude only the payment of "maternity benefits"—i.e., hospitalization and disability benefits for normal delivery and recuperation. . . .

. . . Thus, the issue before the Court on this appeal is whether the California disability insurance program invidiously discriminates against [Aiello] and others similarly situated by not paying insurance benefits for disability that accompanies normal pregnancy and childbirth.

II.

It is clear that California intended to establish this benefit system as an insurance program that was to function essentially in accordance with insurance concepts. Since the program was instituted in 1946, it has been totally self-supporting, never drawing on general state revenues to finance disability or hospital benefits. The Disability Fund is wholly supported by the one percent of wages annually contributed by participating employees. At oral argument, counsel for the appellant informed us that in recent years between 90% and 103% of the revenue to the Disability Fund has been paid out in disability and hospital benefits. This history strongly suggests that the one-percent contribution rate, in addition to being easily computable, bears a close and substantial relationship to the level of benefits payable and to the disability risks insured under the program.

Over the years California has demonstrated a strong commitment not to increase the contribution rate above the one-percent level. The State has sought to provide the broadest possible disability protection that would be affordable by all employees, including those with very low incomes. Because any larger percentage or any flat dollar-amount rate of contribution would impose an increasingly regressive levy bearing most heavily upon those with the lowest incomes, the State has resisted any attempt to change the required contribution from the one-percent level. The program is thus structured, in terms of the level of benefits and the risks insured, to maintain the solvency of the Disability Fund at a one-percent annual level of contribution.

In ordering the State to pay benefits for disability accompanying normal pregnancy and delivery, the District Court acknowledged the State's contention "that coverage of these disabilities is so extraordinarily expensive that it would be impossible to maintain a program supported by employee contributions if these disabilities are included." There is considerable disagreement between the parties with respect to how great the increased costs would actually be, but they would clearly be substantial. For purposes of analysis the District Court accepted the State's estimate, which was in excess of $100 million annually, and stated that "it is clear that including these disabilities would not destroy the program. The increased costs could be accommodated quite easily by making reasonable changes in the contribution rate, the maximum benefits allowable, and the other variables affecting the solvency of the program."

Each of these "variables"—the benefit level deemed appropriate to compensate employee disability, the risks selected to be insured under the program, and the contribution rate chosen to maintain the solvency of the program and at the same time to permit low-income employees to participate with minimal personal sacrifice—represents a policy determination by the State. The essential issue in this case is whether the Equal Protection Clause requires such policies to be sacrificed or compromised in order to finance the payment of benefits to those whose disability is attributable to normal pregnancy and delivery.

We cannot agree that the exclusion of this disability from coverage amounts to invidious discrimination under the Equal Protection Clause. California does not discriminate with respect to the persons or groups which are eligible for disability insurance protection under the program. The classification challenged in this case relates to the asserted underinclusiveness of the set of risks that the State has selected to insure. Although California has created a program to insure most risks of employment disability, it has not chosen to insure all such risks, and this decision is reflected in the level of annual contributions exacted from participating employees. This Court has held that, consistently with the Equal Protection Clause, a State "may take one step at a time, addressing itself to the phase of the problem which seems most acute to the legislative mind. . . . The legislature may select one phase of one field and apply a remedy there, neglecting the others. . . ." . . . Particularly with respect to social welfare programs, so long as the line drawn by the State is rationally supportable, the courts will not interpose their judgment as to the appropriate stopping point. "[T]he Equal Protection Clause does not require a State must choose between attacking every aspect of a problem or not attacking the problem at all." . . .

The State has a legitimate interest in maintaining the self-supporting nature of its insurance program. Similarly, it has an interest in distributing the available resources in such a way as to keep benefit payments at an adequate level for disabilities that are covered, rather than to cover all disabilities inadequately. Finally, California has a legitimate concern in maintaining the contribution rate at a level that will not unduly burden participating employees, particularly low-income employees who may be most in need of the disability insurance.

These policies provide an objective and wholly noninvidious basis for the State's decision not to create a more comprehensive insurance program than it has. There is no evidence in the record that the selection of the risks insured by the program worked to discriminate against any definable group or class in terms of the aggregate risk protection derived by that group or class from the program.* There is no risk from which men are protected and women are not. Likewise, there is no risk from which women are protected and men are not.

The appellee simply contends that, although she has received insurance protection equivalent to that provided all other participating employees, she has suffered discrimination because she encountered a risk that was outside the program's protection. For the reasons we have stated, we hold that this contention is not a valid one under the Equal Protection Clause of the Fourteenth Amendment.

Mr. Justice **Brennan,** with whom Mr. Justice **Douglas** and Mr. Justice **Marshall** join, dissenting, said in part:

. . . The Court today rejects appellees' equal protection claim and upholds the exclusion of normal pregnancy-related disabilities from coverage under California's disability insurance program on the ground that the legislative classification rationally promotes the State's

---

*The dissenting opinion to the contrary, this case is thus a far cry from cases like Reed v. Reed (1971) and Frontiero v. Richardson (1973) involving discrimination based upon gender as such. The California insurance program does not exclude anyone from benefit eligibility because of gender but merely removes one physical condition—pregnancy—from the list of compensable disabilities. While it is true that only women can become pregnant, it does not follow that every legislative classification concerning pregnancy is a sex-based classification like those considered in Reed and Frontiero. Normal pregnancy is an objectively identifiable physical condition with unique characteristics. Absent a showing that distinctions involving pregnancy are mere pretexts designed to effect an invidious discrimination against the members of one sex or the other, lawmakers are constitutionally free to include or exclude pregnancy from the coverage of legislation such as this on any reasonable basis, just as with respect to any other physical condition.

The lack of identity between the excluded disability and gender as such under this insurance program becomes clear upon the most cursory analysis. The program divides potential recipients into two groups—pregnant women and non-pregnant persons. While the first group is exclusively female, the second includes members of both sexes. The fiscal and actuarial benefits of the program thus accrue to members of both sexes.

legitimate cost-saving interests in "maintaining the self-supporting nature of its insurance program[,] . . . distributing the available resources in such a way as to keep benefit payments at an adequate level for disabilities that are covered, . . . [and]maintaining the contribution rate at a level that will not unduly burden participating employees. . . ." Because I believe that Reed v. Reed (1971) and Frontiero v. Richardson (1973) mandate a stricter standard of scrutiny which the State's classification fails to satisfy, I respectfully dissent. . . .

Despite the Act's broad goals and scope of coverage, compensation is denied for disabilities suffered in connection with a "normal" pregnancy—disabilities suffered only by women. Disabilities caused by pregnancy, however, like other physically disabling conditions covered by the Act, require medical care, often include hospitalization, anesthesia and surgical procedures, and may involve genuine risk to life. Moreover, the economic effects caused by pregnancy-related disabilities are functionally indistinguishable from the effects caused by any other disability: wages are lost due to a physical inability to work, and medical expenses are incurred for the delivery of the child and for postpartum care. In my view, by singling out for less favorable treatment a gender-linked disability peculiar to women, the State has created a double standard for disability compensation: a limitation is imposed upon the disabilities for which women workers may recover, while men receive full compensation for all disabilities suffered, including those that effect only or primarily their sex, such as prostatectomies, circumcision, hemophilia, and gout. In effect, one set of rules is applied to females and another to males. Such dissimilar treatment of men and women, on the basis of physical characteristics inextricably linked to one sex, inevitably constitutes sex discrimination. . . .

In the past, when a legislative classification has turned on gender, the Court has justifiably applied a standard of judicial scrutiny more strict than that generally accorded economic or social welfare programs. . . . Yet, by its decision today, the Court appears willing to abandon that higher standard of review without satisfactorily explaining what differentiates the gender-based classification employed in this case from those found unconstitutional in Reed and Frontiero. The Court's decision threatens to return men and women to a time when "traditional" equal protection analysis sustained legislative classifications that treated differently members of a particular sex solely because of their sex. See, e.g., Muller v. Oregon; Goesaert v. Cleary; Hoyt v. Florida (1961).

I cannot join the Court's apparent retreat. I continue to adhere to my view that "classifications based upon sex, like classifications based upon race, alienage, or national origin, are inherently suspect, and must therefore be subjected to strict judicial scrutiny." Frontiero v. Richardson. When, as in this case, the State employs a legislative classification that distinguishes between beneficiaries solely by reference to gender-linked disability risks, "[t]he Court is not ... free to sustain the statute on the ground that it rationally promotes legitimate governmental interests; rather, such suspect classifications can be sustained only when the State bears the burden of demonstrating that the challenged legislation serves overriding or compelling interests that cannot be achieved either by a more carefully tailored legislative classification or by the use of feasible, less drastic means." Kahn v. Shevin (1974) (Brennan, J., dissenting).

MISSISSIPPI UNIVERSITY FOR WOMEN v. HOGAN

458 U. S. 718; 102 S. Ct. 3331; 73 L.Ed. 2d 1090 (1982)

While the failure of the Equal Rights Amendment (ERA) to achieve ratification was a blow to its supporters there are perhaps a number of lessons to be learned from the struggle itself. In the first place, the very fact of the struggle publicized the legitimate and long overlooked claims of women to a status of legal and professional equality. Never again will it be easy to get laws passed denying a wife the right to own property or to enter the business or professional world. In the second place, it became apparent that some women identified with the role they were used to playing, and they both resented and were made to feel insecure by what they viewed as a threat to this role. They saw no reason for shame if they wanted to be housewives and mothers and felt threatened by a movement that seemed to make it hard for them to pursue that role with pride. Third, and this is the point that is most often overlooked, if the ERA had passed there is little assurance that much if any change would have accompanied it. The amending power is touted as the way to make the Constitution say what the people want it to say, but in the long run it is the Supreme Court that decides what the amendments themselves actually mean. One need only view the complete destruction of the "privileges and immunities" clause of the Fourteenth Amendment at the hands of the Court in the Slaughter-House Cases (1873), or the limitations on the right of Congress to tax following the adoption of the Income Tax Amendment to realize that the ERA would have granted women only those rights which the Court was prepared to see them have.

The difficulties of defining an "intermediate" test and knowing when to apply it are illustrated in Michael M. v. Sonoma County (1981). Five members of the Court upheld a state statutory rape law against the challenge that it punished the male participant to a consensual sex act (in this case a minor) but not his minor female partner. The Court gave "great deference" to California's assertion that the purpose of the law was to prevent teenage pregnancies and agreed that this was certainly a legitimate state purpose. Moreover, punishing just the male was sufficiently related to the purpose of the law because the female was already sufficiently deterred from the act by the fear of pregnancy, and were she to become pregnant and have to deal with the consequences she would be further punished while the male would not.

Justices Brennan, White and Marshall dissented, arguing that while ostensibly applying the same test, the majority had failed to carry the burden of showing that a sex-neutral law punishing both parties to the act would not be as effective a deterrent in preventing pregnancy as one punishing only the male. Justice Stevens dissented separately, pointing out that it was "totally irrational to exempt from punishment the one most likely to be injured by the dangerous act. In contrast to the Michael M. case, the Court in Kirchberg v. Feenstra (1981) found no important governmental interest was served by a Louisiana law allowing a husband to mortgage without his wife's consent their jointly owned home.

The Military Selective Service Act authorizes the President, by proclamation, to require the registration of "every male citizen" and male resident alien between the ages of eighteen and twenty-six. The purpose of the act, of course, is to provide a manpower pool should conscription become necessary, although Congress by statute in 1973 forbade any actual conscription under the act. At the time of the Soviet invasion of Afghanistan President Carter invoked the provisions of the act and asked Congress to allocate the necessary funds and to amend the MSSA to permit the registration of women. After prolonged debate Congress declined to amend the act and allocated only sufficient funds to register males.

In Rostker v. Goldberg (1981) the Supreme Court upheld the registration of males against the claim that by failing to register both sexes the act denied a male registrant the equal protection of the laws. Applying the test of Craig v. Boren (1976), the Court agreed that raising and supporting armies was "an important governmental interest," and that these were circumstances under which judicial deference to the congressional judgment was at its highest. It noted the extensive debates on the issue and found that Congress, in reaching its decision, had not acted "unthinkingly" or "reflexively and not for any considered reason," which might have suggested a mere response to prejudices about women in the armed forces. "The fact that Congress and the Executive have decided that women should not serve in combat fully justifies Congress in not authorizing their registration, since the purpose of registration is to develop a pool of potential combat troops. ... The Constitution requires that Congress treat similarly situated persons similarly, not that it engage in gestures of superficial equality."

Justice **O'Connor** delivered the opinion of the Court, saying in part:

This case presents the narrow issue of whether a state statute that excludes males from enrolling in a state-supported professional nursing school violates the Equal Protection Clause of the Fourteenth Amendment.

I.

The facts are not in dispute. In 1884, the Mississippi legislature created the Mississippi Industrial Institute and College for the Education of White Girls of the State of Mississippi, now the oldest state-supported all-female college in the United States. The school, known today as Mississippi University (MUW), has from its inception limited its enrollment to women.

In 1971, MUW established a School of Nursing, initially offering a two-year associate degree. Three years later, the school instituted a four-year baccalaureate program in nursing and today also offers a graduate program. The School of Nursing has its own faculty and administers it own criteria for admission.

Respondent, Joe Hogan, is a registered nurse but does not hold a baccalaureate degree in nursing. Since 1974, he has worked as a nursing supervisor in a medical center in Columbus, the city in which MUW is located. In 1979, Hogan applied for admission to the MUW School of Nursing's baccalaureate program. Although he was otherwise qualified, he was denied admission solely because of his sex. School officials informed him that he could audit the courses in which he was interested, but could not enroll for credit. . . .

II.

We begin our analysis aided by several firmly-established principles. Because the challenged policy expressly discriminates among applicants on the basis of gender, it is subject to scrutiny under the Equal Protection Clause. . . . That this statute discriminates against males rather than against females does not exempt it from scrutiny or reduce the standard of review,* . . . Our decisions also establish that the party seeking to uphold a statute that classifies individuals on the basis of their gender must carry the burden of showing an "exceedingly persuasive justification" for the classification. Kirchberg v. Feenstra (1981). . . . The burden is met only by showing at least that the classification serves "important governmental objectives and that the discriminatory means employed" are "substantially related to the achievement of those objectives." . . .[†]

Although the test for determining the validity of a gender-based classification is straightforward, it must be applied free of fixed notions concerning the roles and abilities of males and females. Care must be taken in ascertaining whether the statutory objective itself reflects archaic and stereotypic notions. Thus, if the statutory objective is to exclude or "protect" members of one gender because they are presumed to suffer from an inherent handicap or to be innately inferior, the objective itself is illegitimate. See Frontiero v. Richardson (1973) (plurality opinion).[‡]

If the State's objective is legitimate and important, we next determine whether the requisite direct, substantial relationship between objective and means is present. The purpose of requiring that close relationship is to assure that the validity of a classification is determined through reasoned analysis rather than through the mechanical application of traditional, often inaccurate, assumptions about the proper roles of men and women. The need for the requirement is amply revealed by reference to the broad range of statutes already invalidated by this Court, statutes that relied upon the simplistic, outdated assumption that gender could be used as a "proxy for other, more germane bases of classification," Craig v. Boren (1976), to establish a link between objective and classification.

Applying this framework, we now analyze the arguments advanced by the State to justify its refusal to allow males to enroll for credit in MUW's School of Nursing.

---

*Without question, MUW's admission policy worked to Hogan's disadvantage. Although Hogan could have attended classes and received credit in one of Mississippi's state-supported coeducational nursing programs, none of which was located in Columbus, he could attend only by driving a considerable distance from his home. A similarly situated female would not have been required to choose between foregoing credit and bearing that inconvenience. Moreover, since many students enrolled in the School of Nursing hold full-time jobs, Hogan's female colleagues had available an opportunity, not open to Hogan, to obtain credit for additional training. The policy of denying males the right to obtain credit toward a baccalaureate degree thus imposed upon Hogan "a burden he would not bear were he female." Orr v. Orr (1979).

[†] . . . Our past decisions establish, however, that when a classification expressly discriminates on the basis of gender, the analysis and level of scrutiny applied to determine the validity of the classification do not vary simply because the objective appears acceptable to individual members of the Court. While the validity and importance of the objective may affect the outcome of the analysis, the analysis itself does not change.

Thus, we apply the test previously relied upon by the Court to measure the constitutionality of gender-based discrimination. Because we conclude that the challenged statutory classification is not substantially related to an important objective, we need not decide whether classifications based upon gender are inherently suspect. . . .

[‡] History provides numerous examples of legislative attempts to exclude women from particular areas simply because legislators believed women were less able than men to perform a particular function. In 1872, this Court remained unmoved by Myra Bradwell's argument that the Fourteenth Amendment prohibited a State from classifying her as unfit to practice law simply because she was female. Bradwell v. Illinois (1872). In his concurring opinion, Justice Brady described the reasons underlying the State's decision to determine which positions only men could fill: "It is the prerogative of the legislator to prescribe regulations founded on nature, reason, and experience for the due admission of qualified persons to professions and callings demanding special skill and confidence. This fairly belongs to the police power of the State; and, in my opinion, in view of the peculiar characteristics, destiny, and mission of woman, it is within the province of the legislature to ordain what offices, positions, and callings shall be filled and discharged by men, and shall receive the benefit of those energies and responsibilities, and that decision and firmness which are presumed to predominate in the sterner sex." . . .

III.

A.

The State's primary justification for maintaining the single-sex admissions policy of MUW's School of Nursing is that it compensates for discrimination against women and, therefore, constitutes educational affirmative action. As applied to the School of Nursing, we find the State's argument unpersuasive.

It is readily apparent that a State can evoke a compensatory purpose to justify an otherwise discriminatory classification only if members of the gender benefited by the classification actually suffer a disadvantage related to the classification. . . .

. . . Mississippi has made no showing that women lacked opportunities to obtain training in the field of nursing or to attain positions of leadership in that field when the MUW School of Nursing opened its doors or that women currently are deprived of such opportunities. In fact, in 1970, the year before the School of Nursing's first class enrolled, women earned 94 percent of the nursing baccalaureate degrees conferred in Mississippi and 98.6 percent of the degrees earned nationwide. . . . That year was not an aberration; one decade earlier, women had earned all the nursing degrees conferred in Mississippi and 98.9 percent of the degrees earned nationwide. . . .

Rather than compensate for discriminatory barriers faced by women, MUW's policy of excluding males from admission to the School of Nursing tends to perpetuate the stereotyped view of nursing as an exclusively woman's job. By assuring that Mississippi allots more openings in its state-supported nursing schools to women than it does to men, MUW's admissions policy lends credibility to the old view that women, not men, should become nurses, and makes the assumption that nursing is a field for women a self-fulfilling prophecy. . . .

The policy is invalid also because it fails the second part of the equal protection test, for the State has made no showing that the gender-based classification is substantially and directly related to its proposed compensatory objective. To the contrary, MUW's policy of permitting men to attend classes as auditors fatally undermines its claim that women, at least those in the School of Nursing, are adversely affected by the presence of men.

. . . The uncontroverted record reveals that admitting men to nursing classes does not affect teaching style, that the presence of men in the classroom would not affect the performance of the female nursing students, and that men in coeducational nursing schools do not dominate the classroom. In sum, the record in this case is flatly inconsistent with the claim that excluding men from the School of Nursing is necessary to reach any of MUW's educational goals.

Thus, considering both the asserted interest and the relationship between the interest and the methods used by the State, we conclude that the State has fallen far short of establishing the "exceedingly persuasive justification" needed to sustain the gender-based classification. Accordingly, we hold that MUW's policy of denying males the right to enroll for credit in its School of Nursing violates the Equal Protection Clause of the Fourteenth Amendment.*

B.

In an additional attempt to justify its exclusion of men from MUW's School of Nursing, the State contends that MUW is the direct beneficiary "of specific congressional legislation which, on its face, permits the institution to exist as it has in the past." The argument is based upon the language of § 901(a) in Title IX of the Education Amendments of 1972, 20 USC § 1681(a) [20 USCS § 1681(a)]. Although § 901(a) prohibits gender discrimination in education programs that receive federal financial assistance, subsection 5 exempts the admissions policies of undergraduate institutions "that traditionally and continually from [their] establishment [have] had a policy of admitting only students of one sex" from the general prohibition. Arguing that Congress enacted Title IX in furtherance of its power to enforce the Fourteenth Amendment, a power granted by § 5 of that Amendment, the State would have us conclude that § 1681(a)(5) is but "a congressional limitation upon the broad prohibitions of the Equal Protection Clause of the Fourteenth Amendment."

The argument requires little comment. Initially, it is far from clear that Congress intended, through § 1681(a)(5), to exempt MUW from any constitutional obligation. Rather, Congress apparently intended, at most, to exempt MUW from the requirements of Title IX.

Even if Congress envisioned a constitutional exemption, the State's argument would fail. Section 5 of the Fourteenth Amendment gives Congress broad power indeed to enforce the command of the Amendment and "to secure to all persons the enjoyment of perfect equality of civil rights and the equal protection of the laws against State denial or invasion. . . ." Ex parte Virginia (1879). Congress' power under § 5 grants Congress no power to restrict, abrogate, or dilute these guarantees." Katzenbach v. Morgan (1966). Although we give deference to congressional decisions and classifications, neither Congress nor a State can validate a law that denies the rights guaranteed by the Fourteenth Amendment. . . .

Chief Justice **Burger,** dissenting.

I agree generally with Justice Powell's dissenting

---

*Justice Powell's dissent suggests that a second objective is served by the gender-based classification in that Mississippi has elected to provide women a choice of educational environments. Since any gender-based classification provides one class a benefit or choice not available to the other class, however, that argument begs the question. The issue is not whether the benefited class profits from the classification, but whether the State's decision to confer a benefit only upon one class by means of a discriminatory classification is substantially related to achieving a legitimate and substantial goal.

opinion. I write separately, however, to emphasize that the Court's holding today is limited to the context of a professional nursing school. Since the Court's opinion relies heavily on its finding that women have traditionally dominated the nursing profession, it suggests that a State might well be justified in maintaining, for example, the option of an all-women's business school or liberal arts program.

Justice **Blackmun** wrote a short dissenting opinion.

Justice **Powell,** with whom Justice **Rehnquist** joins, dissenting, said in part:

The Court's opinion bows deeply to conformity. Left without honor—indeed, held unconstitutional—is an element of diversity that has characterized much of American education and enriched much of American life. The Court in effect holds today that no State now may provide even a single institution of higher learning open only to women students. It gives no heed to the efforts of the State of Mississippi to provide abundant opportunities for young men and young women to attend coeducational institutions, and none to the preferences of the more than 40,000 young women who over the years have evidenced their approval of an all-women's college by choosing Mississippi University for Women (MUW) over seven coeducational universities within the State. The Court decides today that the Equal Protection Clause makes it unlawful for the State to provide women with a traditionally popular and respected choice of educational environment. It does so in a case instituted by one man, who represents no class, and whose primary concern is personal convenience.

. . . His constitutional complaint is based upon a single asserted harm: that he must *travel* to attend the state-supported nursing schools that concededly are available to him. The Court characterizes this injury as one of "inconvenience." This description is fair and accurate, though somewhat embarrassed by the fact that there is, of course, no constitutional right to attend a state-supported university in one's home town. . . .

I.

Coeducation, historically, is a novel educational theory. From grade school through high school, college, and graduate and professional training, much of the nation's population during much of our history has been educated in sexually segregated classrooms. At the college level, for instance, until recently some of the most prestigious colleges and universities—including most of the Ivy League—had long histories of single-sex education. As Harvard, Yale, and Princeton remained all-male colleges well into the second half of this century, the "Seven Sister" institutions established a parallel standard of excellence for women's colleges. Of the Seven Sisters, Mount Holyoke opened as a female seminary in 1837 and was chartered as a college in 1888. Vassar was

founded in 1865, Smith and Wellesley in 1875, Radcliffe in 1879, Bryn Mawr in 1885, and Barnard in 1889. Mount Holyoke, Smith, and Wellesley recently have made considered decisions to remain essentially single-sex institutions. . . .

The sexual segregation of students has been a reflection of, rather than an imposition upon, the preference of those subject to the policy. It cannot be disputed, for example, that the highly qualified women attending the leading women's colleges could have earned admission to virtually any college of their choice. Women attending such colleges have chosen to be there, usually expressing a preference for the special benefits of single-sex institutions. Similar decisions were made by the colleges that elected to remain open to women only.

The arguable benefits of single-sex colleges also continue to be recognized by students of higher education. The Carnegie Commission on Higher Education has reported that it "favor[s] the continuation of colleges for women. They provide an element of diversity . . . and [an environment in which women] generally . . . speak up more in their classes, . . . hold more positions of leadership on campus, . . . and have more role models and mentors among women teachers and administrators."* . . .

Despite the continuing expressions that single-sex institutions may offer singular advantages to their students, there is no doubt that coeducational institutions are far more numerous. But their numerical predominance does not establish—in any sense properly cognizable by a court—that individual preferences for single-sex education are misguided or illegitimate, or that a State may not provide its citizens with a choice.

II.

The issue in this case is whether a State transgresses the Constitution when—within the context of a public system that offers a diverse range of campuses, curricula, and educational alternatives—it seeks to accommodate the legitimate personal preferences of those desiring the advantages of an all-women's college. In my view, the Court errs seriously by assuming—without argument or discussion—that the equal protection standard generally applicable to sex discrimination is appropriate

---

*In this Court the benefits of single-sex education have been asserted by the students and alumnae of MUW. One would expect the Court to regard their views as directly relevant to this case: "[I]n the aspect of life known as courtship or mate-pairing, the American female remains in the old role of the pursued sex, expected to adorn and groom herself to attract the male. Without comment on the equities of this social arrangement, it remains a sociological fact."An institution of collegiate higher learning maintained exclusively for women is uniquely able to provide the education atmosphere in which some, but not all, women can best attain maximum learning potential. It can serve to overcome the historic repression of the past and can orient a woman to function and achieve in the still male-dominated economy. It can free its students of the burden of playing the mating game while attending classes, thus giving academic rather than sexual emphasis. Consequently, many such institutions flourish and their graduates make significant contributions to the arts, professions and business." Brief for Mississippi University for Women Alumnae Assn. as Amicus Curiae.

here. That standard was designed to free women from "archaic and overbroad generalizations. . . ." Schlesinger v. Ballard, (1975). In no previous case have we applied it to invalidate state efforts to *expand* women's choices. Nor are there prior sex discrimination decisions by this Court in which a male plaintiff, as in this case, had the choice of an equal benefit.

The cases cited by the Court therefore do not control the issue now before us. In most of them women were given no opportunity for the same benefit as men. Cases involving male plaintiffs are equally inapplicable. In Craig v. Boren, (1976), a male under 21 was not permitted to buy beer anywhere in the State, and women were afforded no choice as to whether they would accept the "statistically measured but loose-fitting generalities concerning the drinking tendencies of aggregate groups." . . .

By applying heightened equal protection analysis to this case, the Court frustrates the liberating spirit of the Equal Protection Clause. It forbids the States from providing women with an opportunity to choose the type of university they prefer. And yet it is these women whom the Court regards as the *victims* of an illegal, stereotyped perception of the role of women in our society. The Court reasons this way in a case in which no woman has complained, and the only complainant is a man who advances no claims on behalf of anyone else. His claim, it should be recalled, is not that he is being denied a substantive educational opportunity, or even the right to attend an all-male or a coeducational college. It is *only* that the colleges open to him are located at inconvenient distances.

III.

The Court views this case as presenting a serious equal protection claim of sex discrimination. I do not and I would sustain Mississippi's right to continue MUW on a rational basis analysis. But I need not apply this "lowest tier" of scrutiny. I can accept for present purposes the standard applied by the Court: that there is a gender-based distinction that must serve an important governmental objective by means that are substantially related to its achievement. E.g., Wengler v. Druggists Mutual Ins. Co. (1980). The record in this case reflects that MUW has a historic position in the State's educational system dating back to 1884. More than 2,000 women presently evidence their preference for MUW by having enrolled there. The choice is one that discriminates invidiously against no one. And the State's purpose in preserving that choice is legitimate and substantial. Generations of our finest minds, both among educators and students, have believed that single-sex college-level institutions afford distinctive benefits. There are many persons, of course, who have different views. But simply because there are these differences is no reason— certainly none of constitutional dimension—to conclude that no substantial state interest is served when such a choice is made available.

In arguing to the contrary, the Court suggests that the MUW is so operated as to "perpetuate the stereotyped view of nursing as an exclusively women's job." But as the Court itself acknowledges, MUW's School of Nursing was not created until 1971—about 90 years after the single-sex campus itself was founded. This hardly supports a link between nursing as a woman's profession and MUW's single-sex admission policy. Indeed, MUW's School of Nursing was not instituted until more than a decade *after* a separate School of Nursing was established at the coeducational University of Mississippi at Jackson. The School of Nursing makes up only one part—a relatively small part—of MUW's diverse modern university campus and curriculum. The other departments on the MUW campus offer a typical range of degrees and a typical range of subjects. There is no indication that women suffer fewer opportunities at other Mississippi state campuses because of MUW's admission policy.

In sum, the practice of voluntarily chosen single-sex education is an honored tradition in our country, even if it now rarely exists in state colleges and universities. Mississippi's accommodation of such student choices is legitimate because it is completely consensual and is important because it permits students to decide for themselves the type of college education they think will benefit them most. Finally, Mississippi's policy is substantially related to its long-respected objective. . . .

DISCRIMINATION AGAINST THE POOR

MAHER v. ROE

432 U. S. 464; 97 S. Ct. 2376; 53 L. Ed. 2d 484 (1977)

One of the clearest ideological hallmarks of a capitalist society is its general acceptance of wide differences in wealth among its members. Most people assume wealth results from personal earning power, which in turn is a result of natural talents and hard work. The fact that nearly everyone can point to as many exceptions as examples does not shake their belief that poor people are poor because they are lazy—that if they would just get out and work, they would not be poor. Over the years our constitutional doctrines have reflected these attitudes. In 1837 in New York v. Miln the Supreme Court had characterized paupers as a "moral pestilence," and this attitude largely prevailed throughout the nineteenth century.

It was not until the devastating impact of the Great Depression of the 1930s struck rich and poor alike that this view began to change and the first recognition was given to the idea that the poor, the unemployed, the aged, and the handicapped were a national responsibility. Out of this came the Social Security Act and other assistance programs. In Edwards v. California (1941) the Court rejected the characterization of the Miln case and struck down a law designed to keep destitute dustbowl farmers out of California. "Whatever may have been the notion then prevailing, we do not think that it will now be seriously contended that because a person is without employment and without funds he constitutes a 'moral pestilence.' Poverty and immorality are not synonymous."

But the idea dies hard that it is somehow wrong that the money of the "hard-working" taxpayer should be spent to support those who are "too lazy to work." To some persons public welfare is "charity" or "the dole" and should be only sufficient to let the donor feel virtuous and keep the recipient alive without encouraging him in his slothful ways. Others view welfare as the just claim of the recipient to a decent living from a society which has favored some people far more than others and which has failed to provide him with a useful or productive role. It is the eternal conflict between the "survival of the fittest" and the "brotherhood of man."

This conflict in philosophy was highlighted by the Court in Wyman v. James (1971), which held valid the unwarranted inspection of a welfare recipient's home as a condition of receiving aid for her child. The Court justified the intrusion in part on the ground that the taxpayer, like "one who dispenses purely private charity naturally has an interest in and expects to know how his charitable funds are utilized." Justice Douglas in dissent argued that Mrs. James was being discriminated against because she was poor and that no such breach of privacy would be tolerated were the welfare recipient "a prominent, affluent cotton or wheat farmer receiving benefit payments for not growing crops."

Most private institutions and many public ones continue to favor those who can pay their way over those who cannot, but perhaps the most anomalous institutionalized discrimination against the poor lies in the administration of justice. Justice is expensive. In civil litigation every paper filed with a court, every paper written, form filled out, or action taken by a lawyer costs money. A person wishing to enjoin someone's injuring him or her illegally may have to post a bond in case the injury turns out not to be illegal. Even in a criminal case defendants must post bail unless they wish to languish in jail until they can establish their innocence, must hire a lawyer to defend themselves, and if they lose at trial, each level to which they take an appeal multiplies their expenses. Those wishing to protest the procedure of a traffic court that has fined them $10 may be out of pocket thousands of dollars before they reach the Supreme Court. Such costs have traditionally been borne by litigants and have been defended both on the ground that those who use the judicial system should pay for its upkeep, and that making the system easily accessible to all persons would result in its being overburdened to the point of complete collapse. No claim was made that it really was equally available to rich and poor alike.

It was during the Depression that the Supreme Court took the first halting steps to do away with the worst results of this discrimination, and it did it not through any desire to equalize the status of rich and poor before the courts but because the handicap of being poor in some cases was so great that the resulting trial was unfair. In Powell v. Alabama (1932) the Court held that illiterate blacks being tried for a capital offense were entitled to a lawyer at state expense if they could not afford to hire one. While it was made clear in Betts v. Brady (1942) that this was available only to a person whom the Court felt really needed a lawyer, in 1963 in Gideon v. Wainwright it finally conceded that all persons need a lawyer in a felony trial. The same day it assured a lawyer to a convicted indigent so he could bring that "first appeal, granted as a matter of right to rich and poor alike"; see Douglas v. California (1963). And in Argersinger v. Hamlin (1972) the right to appointed trial counsel was extended to all persons, misdemeanants as well as felons, who are faced with the possibility of a jail sentence.

In 1956 in Griffin v. Illinois the Supreme Court made its first attack on the costs imposed by the state to defray the expenses of its judicial system, holding that an indigent could not be denied a right to appeal a noncapital felony conviction merely because he could not afford to purchase a transcript. In his plurality opinion Justice Black noted that both "the Due Process and Equal Protection Clauses protect persons like petitioners from invidious discrimination" and added "there can be no equal justice where the kind of trial a man gets depends on the amount of money he has. Destitute defendants must be afforded as adequate appellate review as defendants who have money enough to buy transcripts."

In 1971 the essence of this protection was extended to indigent misdemeanants; see Mayer v. Chicago.

In Williams v. Illinois (1970) the Court held void a state statute under which an indigent prisoner who could not pay the "fine" part of his sentence had to stay in jail and work it off at the rate of $5 a day. Despite the fact that the practice went back to medieval England and was in use in nearly every state, the Court held it a denial of equal protection of the laws. Chief Justice Burger, speaking for seven members of the Court, cited the progress made since Griffin in mitigating the "disparate treatment of indigents in the criminal process," and concluded that "the Equal Protection Clause of the Fourteenth Amendment requires that the statutory ceiling placed on imprisonment for any substantive offense be the same for all defendants irrespective of their economic status." The holding was reaffirmed in Tate v. Short (1971), in which the Court struck down a Texas statute under which an indigent who could not pay a traffic fine went to jail instead. Nor can a state automatically revoke a convict's probation and commit the person to jail for failing to come up with a sum agreed upon as a condition of probation. Here the probationer had made some payments but had lost his job and had been unsuccessful in his good-faith effort to find another. In Bearden v. Georgia (1983) a unanimous Court held it *unfair to send him to jail without considering alternative methods of punishment that might meet the state's interest in punishment and deterrence.*

The Supreme Court decision in Roe v. Wade (1973) that a state could not forbid abortions triggered a highly emotional nationwide political battle. Efforts were made to overturn the case by constitutional amendment, and when these failed, legislation was introduced at both state and national levels to limit as much as possible the availability of the new freedom. While direct limitations were generally unavailing (see the note to Roe v. Wade) an approach which struck at the public financing of such abortions was successful. In Beal v. Doe (1977), the Court held the Medicaid provisions of the Social Security Act did not require the financing of nontherapeutic abortions, although a state was free to provide such funding under Medicaid if it wished. And in Poelker v. Doe (1977), it held that a city hospital had no constitutional obligation to provide nontherapeutic abortions. "We merely hold, for the reasons stated in Maher, that the Constitution does not forbid a State or city, pursuant to democratic processes, from expressing a preference for normal childbirth as St. Louis has done."

So successful was the technique of withholding funding in the actual limitation of abortions that in 1976 Representative Hyde of Illinois introduced the first of the so-called "Hyde Amendments" to the appropriation acts providing funding for Medicaid, a scheme by which the federal government provides financial help to states that volunteer to provide to the needy certain medically necessary professional services. The 1980 version of the amendment forbids the use of federal funds to perform abortions except "where the life of the mother would be endangered if the fetus were carried to term" or the pregnancy was the result of rape or incest promptly reported to the proper authorities. The result was to forbid the financing of abortions even where these were deemed "medically necessary." In Harris v. McRae (1980) the Court held that the state's obligation to provide necessary medical services "does not require a participating State to pay for those medically necessary abortions for which federal reimbursement is unavailable under the Hyde Amendment." The Court held the law valid. Quoting with approval from the case below, the Court again stressed that "although Congress has opted to subsidize medically necessary services generally, but not certain medically necessary abortions, the fact remains that the Hyde Amendment leaves an indigent woman with at least the same range of choice in deciding whether to obtain a medically necessary abortion as she would have had if Congress had chosen to subsidize no health care costs at all."

Connecticut law limits medicaid benefits for first-trimester abortions to those that are medically necessary, and in the present case two indigent women sought nontherapeutic abortions. One, a sixteen-year-old high school junior, obtained an abortion and the hospital had been denied reimbursement. The other, the unwed mother of three children, was unable to obtain an abor-tion because her physician refused to certify that it was medically necessary.

Mr. Justice **Powell** delivered the opinion of the Court, saying in part:

In Beal v. Doe, we hold today that Title XIX of the Social Security Act does not require the funding of nontherapeutic abortions as a condition of participation in the joint federal-state medicaid program established by that statute. In this case, as a result of our decision in Beal, we must decide whether the Constitution requires a participating State to pay for nontherapeutic abortions when it pays for childbirth. . . .

II.

The Constitution imposes no obligation on the States to pay the pregnancy-related medical expenses of indigent women, or indeed to pay any of the medical expenses of indigents. But when a State decides to alleviate some of the hardships of poverty by providing medical care, the manner in which it dispenses benefits is subject to constitutional limitations. Appellees' claim is that Connecticut must accord equal treatment to both abortion and childbirth, and may not evidence a policy preference by funding only the medical expenses incident to childbirth. This challenge to the classifications established by the Connecticut regulation presents a question arising under the Equal Protection Clause of the Fourteenth Amendment. The basic framework of analysis of such a claim is well-settled: "We must decide, first, whether [state legislation] operates to the disadvantage of some suspect class or impinges upon a fundamental right explicitly or implicitly protected by the Constitution, thereby requiring strict judicial scrutiny. . . . If not, the [legislative] scheme must still be examined to determine whether it rationally furthers some legitimate, articulated state purpose and therefore does not constitute an invidious discrimination. . . ." San Antonio School District v. Rodriguez (1973). . . .

A.

This case involves no discrimination against a suspect class. An indigent woman desiring an abortion does not come within the limited category of disadvantaged classes so recognized by our cases. Nor does the fact that the impact of the regulation falls upon those who cannot pay lead to a different conclusion. In a sense, every denial of welfare to an indigent creates a wealth classification as compared to nonindigents who are able to pay for the desired goods or services. But this Court has never held that financial need alone identifies a suspect class for purposes of equal protection analysis. . . . Accordingly, the central question in this case is whether the regulation "impinges upon a fundamental right explicitly or implicitly protected by the Constitution." The District Court read our decisions in Roe v. Wade, (1973), and the subsequent cases applying it, as establishing a fundamental right to abortion and therefore concluded that nothing less than a compelling state interest would justify Connecticut's different treatment of abortion and childbirth. We think the District Court misconceived the nature and scope of the fundamental right recognized in Roe. . . .

B.

The Texas law in Roe was a stark example of impermissible interference with the pregnant woman's decision to terminate her pregnancy. In subsequent cases, we have invalidated other types of restrictions, different in form but similar in effect, on the woman's freedom of choice. Thus, in Planned Parenthood of Central Missouri v. Danforth, (1976), we held that Missouri's requirement of spousal consent was unconstitutional because it "granted [the husband] the right to prevent unilaterally, and for whatever reason, the effectuation of his wife's and her physician's decision to terminate her pregnancy." Missouri had interposed an "*absolute obstacle* to a woman's decision that Roe held to be constitutionally protected from such interference." (Emphasis added.) . . .

. . . Roe did not declare an unqualified "constitutional right to an abortion," as the District Court seemed to think. Rather, the right protects the woman from unduly burdensome interference with her freedom to decide whether to terminate her pregnancy. It implies no limitation on the authority of a State to make a value judgment favoring childbirth over abortion, and to implement that judgment by the allocation of public funds.

The Connecticut regulation before us is different in kind from the laws invalidated in our previous abortion decisions. The Connecticut regulation places no obstacles—absolute or otherwise—in the pregnant woman's path to an abortion. An indigent woman who desires an abortion suffers no disadvantage as a consequence of Connecticut's decision to fund childbirth; she continues as before to be dependent on private sources for the service she desires. The State may have made childbirth a more attractive alternative, thereby influencing the woman's decision, but it has imposed no restriction on access to abortions that was not already there. The indigency that may make it difficult—and in some cases, perhaps, impossible—for some women to have abortions is neither created nor in any way affected by the Connecticut regulation. We conclude that the Connecticut regulation does not impinge upon the fundamental right recognized in Roe.

C.

Our conclusion signals no retreat from Roe or the cases applying it. There is a basic difference between direct state interference with a protected activity and state encouragement of an alternative activity consonant with legislative policy. Constitutional concerns are greatest when the State attempts to impose its will by force of law; the State's power to encourage actions deemed to be in the public interest is necessarily far broader.

The distinction is implicit in two cases cited in Roe in support of the pregnant woman's right under the Fourteenth Amendment. Meyer v. Nebraska (1923), involved a Nebraska law making it criminal to teach foreign languages to children who had not passed the eighth grade. Nebraska's imposition of a criminal sanction on the providers of desired services makes Meyer closely analogous to Roe. In sustaining the constitutional challenge brought by a teacher convicted under the law, the Court held that the teacher's "right thus to teach and the right of parents to engage him so to instruct their children" were "within the liberty of the Amendment." In Pierce v. Society of Sisters (1925), the Court relied on Meyer to invalidate an Oregon criminal law requiring the parent or guardian of a child to send him to a public school, thus precluding the choice of a private school. Reasoning that the Fourteenth Amendment's concept of liberty "excludes any general power of the State to standardize its children by forcing them to accept instruction from public teachers only," the Court held that the law "unreasonably interfere[d] with the liberty of parents and guardians to direct the upbringing and education of children under their control."

Both cases invalidated substantial restrictions on constitutionally protected liberty interests: in Meyer, the parent's right to have his child taught a particular foreign language; in Pierce, the parent's right to choose private rather than public school education. But either case denied to a State the policy choice of encouraging the preferred course of action. Indeed, in Meyer the Court was careful to state that the power of the State "to prescribe a curriculum" that included English and excluded German in its free public schools "is not questioned." Similarly, Pierce casts no shadow over a State's power to favor public education by funding it—a policy choice pursued in some States for more than a century. . . . Yet, were we to accept appellees' argument, an indigent parent could challenge the state policy of favoring public rather than private schools, or of preferring instruction in English rather than German, on grounds identical in principle to those advanced here. We think it abundantly clear that a State is not required to show a compelling interest for its policy choice to favor normal childbirth any more than a State must so justify its election to fund public but not private education.

D.

The question remains whether Connecticut's regulation can be sustained under the less demanding test of rationality that applies in the absence of a suspect classification or the impingement of a fundamental right. This test requires that the distinction drawn between childbirth and nontherapeutic abortion by the regulation be "rationally related" to a "constitutionally permissible" purpose. . . . We hold that the Connecticut funding scheme satisfies this standard.

Roe itself explicitly acknowledged the State's strong interest in protecting the potential life of the fetus. That interest exists throughout the pregnancy, "grow[ing] in substantiality as the woman approaches term." Because the pregnant woman carries a potential human being, she "cannot be isolated in her privacy. . . . [Her] privacy is no longer sole and any right of privacy she possesses must be measured accordingly." The State unquestionably has a "strong and legitimate interest in encouraging normal childbirth." Beal v. Doe, an interest honored over the centuries. Nor can there be any question that the Connecticut regulation rationally furthers that interest. The medical costs associated with childbirth are substantial, and have increased significantly in recent years. As recognized by the District Court in this case, such costs are significantly greater than those normally associated with elective abortions during the first trimester. The subsidizing of costs incident to childbirth is a rational means of encouraging childbirth.

We certainly are not unsympathetic to the plight of an indigent woman who desires an abortion, but "the Constitution does not provide judicial remedies for every social and economic ill." . . .

The decision whether to expend state funds for nontherapeutic abortion is fraught with judgments of policy and value over which opinions are sharply divided. Our conclusion that the Connecticut regulation is constitutional is not based on a weighing of its wisdom or social desirability, for this Court does not strike down state laws "because they be unwise, improvident, or out of harmony with a particular school of thought." . . . Indeed, when an issue involves policy choices as sensitive as those implicated by public funding of nontherapeutic abortions, the appropriate forum for their resolution in a democracy is the legislature. We should not forget that "legislatures are ultimate guardians of the liberties and welfare of the people in quite as great a degree as the Courts." . . .

In conclusion, we emphasize that our decision today does not proscribe government funding of nontherapeutic abortions. It is open to Congress to require provision of Medicaid benefits for such abortions as a condition of state participation in the Medicaid program. Also, under Title XIX as construed in Beal v. Doe, Connecticut is free—through normal democratic processes—to decide that such benefits should be provided. We hold only that the Constitution does not require a judicially imposed resolution of these difficult issues. . . .

Mr. Justice **Brennan,** with whom Mr. Justice **Marshall** and Mr. Justice **Blackmun** join, dissenting, said in part:

The District Court held: "When Connecticut refuses to fund elective abortions while funding therapeutic abortions and prenatal and postnatal care, it weights the choice of the pregnant mother against choosing to exercise her constitutionally protected right to an elective abortion. . . . Her choice is affected not simply by the absence of payment for the abortion, but by the availability of public funds for childbirth if she chooses not to have the abortion. When the state thus infringes upon a fundamental interest, it must assert a compelling state interest." This Court reverses on the ground that "the District Court misconceived the nature and scope of the fundamental right recognized in Roe [v. Wade (1973)]," and therefore that Connecticut was not required to meet the "compelling interest test to justify its discrimination against elective abortion but only "the less demanding test of rationality that applies in the absence of . . . the impingement of a fundamental right." This holding, the Court insists "places no obstacles—absolute or otherwise—in the pregnant woman's path to an abortion"; she is still at liberty to finance the abortion from "private sources." . . .

But a distressing insensitivity to the plight of impoverished pregnant women is inherent in the Court's analysis. The stark reality for too many, not just "some," indigent pregnant women is that indigency makes access to competent licensed physicians not merely "difficult" but "impossible." As a practical matter, many indigent women will feel they have no choice but to carry their pregnancies to term because the State will pay for the associated medical services, even though they would have chosen to have abortions if the State had also provided funds for that procedure, or indeed if the State had provided funds for neither procedure. This disparity in funding by the State clearly operates to coerce indigent pregnant women to bear children they would not otherwise choose to have, and just as clearly, this coercion can only operate upon the poor, who are uniquely the victims of this form of financial pressure. . . .

None can take seriously the Court's assurance that its "conclusion signals no retreat from Roe [v. Wade] or the cases applying it." That statement must occasion great surprise among the Courts of Appeals and District Courts that, relying upon Roe v. Wade and Doe v. Bolton (1973), have held that States are constitutionally required to fund elective abortions if they fund pregnancies carried to term. . . . Indeed, it cannot be gainsaid that today's decision seriously erodes the principles that Roe and Doe announced to guide the determination of what constitutes an unconstitutional infringement of the fundamental right of pregnant women to be free to decide whether to have an abortion. . . .

Finally, cases involving other fundamental rights also make clear that the Court's concept of what constitutes an impermissible infringement upon the fundamental rights of a pregnant woman to choose to have an abortion makes new law. We have repeatedly found that infringements of fundamental rights are not limited to outright denials of those rights. First Amendment decisions have consistently held in a wide variety of contexts that the compelling-state-interest test has been applied in voting cases, even where only relatively small infringements upon voting power, such as dilution of voting strength caused by malapportionment, have been involved. See, e.g., Reynolds v. Sims (1964). . . .

Until today, I had not thought the nature of the fundamental right established in Roe was open to question, let alone susceptible to the interpretation advanced by the Court. The fact that the Connecticut scheme may not operate as an absolute bar preventing all indigent women from having abortions is not critical. What is critical is that the State has inhibited their fundamental right to make that choice free from state interference.

Nor does the manner in which Connecticut has burdened the right freely to choose to have an abortion save its Medicaid program. The Connecticut scheme cannot be distinguished from other grants and withholdings of financial benefits that we have held unconstitutionally burdened a fundamental right. Sherbert v. Verner, struck down a South Carolina statute that denied unemployment compensation to a woman who for religious reasons could not work on Saturday, but that would have provided such compensation if her unemployment had stemmed from a number of other nonreligious causes. Even though there was no proof of indigency in that case, Sherbert held that "the pressure upon her to forgo [her religious] practice [was] unmistakable," and therefore held the effect was the same as a fine imposed for Saturday worship. Here, though the burden is upon the right to privacy derived from the Due Process Clause and not upon freedom of religion under the Free Exercise Clause of the First Amendment, the governing principle is the same, for Connecticut grants and withholds financial benefits in a manner that discourages significantly the exercise of a fundamental constitutional right. Indeed, the case for application of the principle actually is stronger than in Verner since appellees are all indigents and therefore even more vulnerable to the financial pressures imposed by the Connecticut regulations.

Bellotti v. Baird (1976), held, and the Court today agrees, that a state requirement is unconstitutional if it "unduly burdens the right to seek an abortion." Connecticut has "unduly" burdened the fundamental right of pregnant women to be free to choose to have an abortion because the State has advanced no compelling state interest to justify its interference in that choice.

Although appellant does not argue it as justification, the Court concludes that the State's interest "in protecting the potential life of the fetus" suffices. Since only the first trimester of pregnancy is involved in this case, that justification is totally foreclosed if the Court is not overruling the holding of Roe v. Wade that "[w]ith respect to the State's important and legitimate interest in potential life, the 'compelling' point is at viability," occurring at about the end of the second trimester. The appellant also argues a further justification not relied upon by the Court, namely, that the State needs "to control the amount of its limited public funds which will be allocated to its public welfare budget." The District Court correctly held, however, that the asserted interest was "wholly chimerical" because the "state's assertion that it saves money when it declines to pay the cost of a welfare mother's abortion is simply contrary to undisputed facts."

Mr. Justice **Blackmun,** with whom Mr. Justice **Brennan** and Mr. Justice **Marshall** join, dissenting.

The Court today by its decisions in these cases, allows the States, and such municipalities as chose to do so, to accomplish indirectly what the court in Roe v. Wade (1973), and Doe v. Bolton (1973)—by a substantial majority and with some emphasis, I had thought—said they could not do so directly. The Court concedes the existence of a constitutional right but denies the realization and enjoyment of that right on the ground that existence and realization are separate and distinct. For the individual woman concerned, indigent and financially helpless, as the Court's opinions in the three cases concede her to be, the result is punitive and tragic. Implicit in the Court's holdings is the condescension that she may go elsewhere for her abortion. I find that disingenuous and alarming, almost reminiscent of "let them eat cake."

The result the Court reaches is particularly distressing in Poelker v. Doe, where a presumed majority, in electing as mayor one whom the record shows campaigned on the issue of closing public hospitals to nontherapeutic abortions, punitively impresses upon a needy minority its own concepts of the socially desirable, the publicly acceptable and the morally sound, with a touch of the devil-take-the-hindmost. This is not the kind of thing for which our Constitution stands.

The Court's financial argument, of course, is specious. To be sure, welfare funds are limited and welfare must be spread perhaps as best meets the community's concept of its needs. But the cost of a nontherapeutic abortion is far less than the cost of maternity care and delivery, and holds no comparison whatsoever with the welfare costs that will burden the State for the new indigents and their support in the long, long years ahead.

Neither is it an acceptable answer, as the Court well knows, to say that the Congress and the States are free to authorize the use of funds for nontherapeutic abortions. Why should any politician incur the demonstrated wrath and noise of the abortion opponents when mere silence and nonactivity accomplish the results the opponents want?

There is another world "out there," the existence of which the Court, I suspect, either chooses to ignore or fears to recognize. And so the cancer of poverty will continue to grow. This is a sad day for those who regard the Constitution as a force that would serve justice to all evenhandedly and, in so doing, would better the lot of the poorest among us.

Mr. Justice **Marshall,** dissenting, said in part:

It is all too obvious that the governmental actions in these cases, ostensibly taken to "encourage" women to carry pregnancies to term, are in reality intended to impose a moral viewpoint that no State may constitutionally enforce. . . . I am appalled at the ethical bankruptcy of those who preach a "right to life" that means, under present social policies, a bare existence in utter misery for so many poor women and their children.

I.

The Court's insensitivity to the human dimension of these decisions is particularly obvious in its cursory discussion of appellees' equal protection claims in Maher v. Roe. That case points up once again the need for this Court to repudiate its outdated and intellectually disingenuous "two-tier" equal protection analysis. . . . As I have suggested before, this "model's two fixed modes of analysis, strict scrutiny and mere rationality, simply do not describe the inquiry the Court has undertaken—or should undertake—in equal protection cases." In the present case, in its evident desire to avoid strict scrutiny—or indeed any meaningful scrutiny—of the challenged legislation, which would almost surely result in its invalidation, the Court pulls from thin air a distinction between laws that absolutely prevent exercise of the fundamental right to abortion and those that "merely" make its exercise difficult for some people. . . . Mr. Justice Brennan demonstrates that our cases support no such distinction, and I have argued above that the challenged regulations are little different from a total prohibition from the viewpoint of the poor. But the Court's legal legerdemain has produced the desired result: A fundamental right is no longer at stake and mere rationality becomes the appropriate mode of analysis. To no one's surprise, application of that test—combined with misreading of Roe v. Wade to generate a "strong" state interest in "potential life" during the first trimester of pregnancy, "leaves little doubt about the outcome; the challenged legislation is [as] always, upheld." . . .

As I have argued before, an equal protection analysis far more in keeping with the actions rather than the words of the Court, carefully weighs three factors—"the importance of the governmental benefits denied, the character of the class, and the asserted state interests." Application of this standard would invalidate the challenged regulations.

The governmental benefits at issue here, while perhaps not representing large amounts of money for any individual, are nevertheless of absolutely vital importance in the lives of the recipients. . . .

It is no less disturbing that the effect of the challenged regulations will fall with great disparity upon women of minority races. Nonwhite women now obtain abortions at nearly twice the rate of whites, and it appears that almost 40 percent of minority women—more than five times the proportion of whites—are dependent upon Medicaid for their health care. Even if this strongly disparate racial impact does not alone violate the Equal Protection Clause, . . . "at some point a showing that state action has a devastating impact on the lives of minority racial groups must be relevant."

Against the brutal effect that the challenged laws will have must be weighed the asserted state interest. The Court describes this as a "strong interest in protecting the potential life of the fetus." Yet in Doe v. Bolton, the Court expressly held that any state interest during the first trimester of pregnancy, when 86 percent of all abortions occur, was wholly insufficient to justify state interference with the right to abortion. If a State's interest in potential human life before the point of viability is insufficient to justify requiring several physicians' concurrence for an abortion, I cannot comprehend how it magically becomes adequate to allow the present infringement on rights of disfavored classes. If there is any state interest in potential life before the point of viability, it certainly does not outweigh the deprivation or serious discouragement of a vital constitutional right of especial importance to poor and minority women.

Mr. Chief Justice **Burger** wrote a concurring opinion.

6

The Power to Protect Individuals

THE CIVIL RIGHTS CASES

109 U.S. 3; 3 S. Ct. 18; 27 L. Ed. 835 (1883)

In the closing days of the Reconstruction, with the white race rapidly resuming control of Southern state governments, Congress passed the Civil Rights Act of 1875 to ensure continued federal power to prevent racial discrimination in the South. This act made it both a crime and a civil wrong for any person to deny to any other person "the full and equal enjoyment of any of the accommodations, advantages, facilities and privileges of inns, public conveyances on land or water, theaters and other places of public amusement; subject only to the conditions and limitations established by law, and applicable alike to citizens of every race and color. . . ." In the Civil Rights Cases, printed below, the Supreme Court held the act unconstitutional. It held that the Thirteenth Amendment was not applicable, since racial discrimination is not involuntary servitude, and the Fourteenth Amendment gave Congress no authority to prevent racial discrimination by private individuals. The Court rested its decision upon the explicit language of the Fourteenth Amendment, which is that "no state" shall deny equal protection of the laws or due process of law; it does not say that "no person" shall do these things; and Congress, in passing laws to enforce the amendment, may not make it a crime to do what the amendment does not forbid. Thus the Civil Rights Cases prevented Congress from exercising disciplinary control over private racial discrimination. For protection against such discrimination the citizen had to look to his state government, not to the federal government.

In a forceful forty-page dissenting opinion Justice Harlan directed a many-pronged attack at the Court's decision, most of which, with the passage of time, is no longer relevant. One of his points, however, deserves mention. He argued persuasively that common carriers and those who operate inns and places of amusement are not "private persons." On the contrary, they carry on businesses under state authority subject to public controls, and are in a very real sense agents of the state. This association with and dependence on the state brings them within the prohibiting language of the due process and equal protection clauses.

Mr. Justice **Bradley** delivered the opinion of the Court, saying in part:

These cases are all founded on the 1st and 2nd sections of the Act of Congress, known as the Civil Rights Act, passed March 1, 1875. . . . Two of the cases, those against Stanley and Nichols, are indictments for denying to persons of color the accommodations and privileges of an inn or hotel; two of them, those against Ryan and Singleton, are, one an information, the other an indictment, for denying to individuals the privileges and accommodations of a theatre, the information against Ryan being for refusing a colored person a seat in the dress circle of Maguire's theater in San Francisco; and the indictment against Singleton being for denying to another person, whose color is not stated, the full enjoyment of the accommodations of the theater known as the Grand Opera House in New York. ... The case of Robinson and wife against the Memphis and Charleston R. R. Company was ... the refusal by the conductor of the Railroad Company to allow the wife to ride in the ladies' car, for the reason ... that she was a person of African descent. ...

It is obvious that the primary and important question in all the cases, is the constitutionality of the law; for if the law is unconstitutional, none of the prosecutions can stand. ...

[The Court here reviews the provisions of the law in detail.]

Has Congress constitutional power to make such a law? Of course, no one will contend that the power to pass it was contained in the Constitution before the adoption of the last three Amendments. The power is sought, first, in the 14th Amendment, and the views and arguments of distinguished Senators, advanced whilst the law was under consideration, claiming authority to pass it by virtue of that Amendment, are the principal arguments adduced in favor of the power. ...

The 1st section of the 14th Amendment, which is the one relied on, after declaring who shall be citizens of the United States, and of the several States, is prohibitory in its character, and prohibitory upon the States. It declares that ''No State shall make or enforce any law which shall abridge the privileges or immunities of citizens of the United States; nor shall any State deprive any person of life, liberty, or property without due process of law; nor deny to any person within its jurisdiction the equal protection of the laws.'' It is state action of a particular character that is prohibited. Individual invasion of individual rights is not the subject-matter of the Amendment. It has a deeper and broader scope. It nullifies and makes void all state legislation, and state action of every kind, which impairs the privileges and immunities of citizens of the United States, or which injures them in life, liberty or property without due process of law, or which denies to any of them the equal protection of the laws. It not only does this, but, in order that the national will, thus declared, may not be a mere brutum fulmen, the last section of the Amendment invests Congress with power to enforce it by appropriate legislation. To enforce what? To enforce the prohibition. To adopt appropriate legislation for correcting the effects of such prohibited state laws and state Acts, and thus to render them effectually null, void and innocuous. This is the legislative power conferred upon Congress, and this is the whole of it. It does not invest Congress with power to legislate upon subjects which are within the domain of state legislation; but to provide modes of relief against state legislation or state action, of the kind referred to. It does not authorize Congress to create a code of municipal law for the regulation of private rights; but to provide modes of redress against the operation of state laws, and the action of state officers executive or judicial, when these are

subversive of the fundamental rights specified in the Amendment. Positive rights and privileges are undoubtedly secured by the 14th Amendment; but they are secured by way of prohibition against state laws and state proceedings affecting those rights and privileges, and by power given to Congress to legislate for the purpose of carrying such prohibition into effect; and such legislation must, necessarily, be predicated upon such supposed state laws or state proceedings, and be directed to the correction of their operation and effect. ...

An apt illustration of this distinction may be found in some of the provisions of the original Constitution. Take the subject of contracts, for example; the Constitution prohibited the States from passing any law impairing the obligation of contracts. This did not give to Congress power to provide laws for the general enforcement of contracts; nor power to invest the courts of the United States with jurisdiction over contracts, so as to enable parties to sue upon them in those courts. It did, however, give the power to provide remedies by which the impairment of contracts by state legislation might be counteracted and corrected; and this power was exercised. The remedy which Congress actually provided was that contained in the 25th section of the Judiciary Act of 1789, giving to the Supreme Court of the United States jurisdiction by writ of error to review the final decisions of state courts whenever they should sustain the validity of a state statute or authority alleged to be repugnant to the Constitution or laws of the United States. By this means, if a state law was passed impairing the obligation of a contract, and the state tribunals sustained the validity of the law, the mischief could be corrected in this court. The legislation of Congress, and the proceedings provided for under it, were corrective in their character. No attempt was made to draw into the United States courts the litigation of contracts generally; and no such attempt would have been sustained. ...

And so in the present case, until some state law has been passed or some state action through its officers or agents has been taken, adverse to the rights of citizens sought to be protected by the 14th Amendment, no legislation of the United States under said Amendment, nor any proceeding under such legislation, can be called into activity; for the prohibitions of the Amendment are against state laws and acts done under state authority. Of course, legislation may and should be provided in advance to meet the exigency when it arises; but it should be adapted to the mischief and wrong which the Amendment was intended to provide against; and that is, state laws, or state action of some kind, adverse to the rights of the citizen secured by the Amendment. Such legislation cannot properly cover the whole domain of rights appertaining to life, liberty and property, defining them and providing for their vindication. That would be to establish a code of municipal law regulative of all private rights between man and man in society. It would be to make Congress take the place of the State Legislatures and to supersede them. It is absurd to affirm that, because the rights of life, liberty and property, which include all civil rights that men have, are, by the Amendment, sought to be protected against invasion on the part of the State without due process of law, Congress may, therefore, provide due process of law for their vindication in every case; and that, because the denial by a State to any persons, of the equal protection of the laws, is prohibited by the Amendment, therefore Congress may establish laws for their equal protection. In fine, the legislation which Congress is authorized to adopt in this behalf is not general legislation upon the rights of the citizen, but corrective legislation, that is, such as may be necessary and proper for counteracting such laws as the States may adopt or enforce, and which, by the Amendment, they are prohibited from making or enforcing, or such acts and proceedings as the States may commit or take, and which, by the Amendment, they are prohibited from committing or taking. It is not necessary for us to state, if we could, what legislation would be proper for Congress to adopt. It is sufficient for us to examine whether the law in question is of that character.

An inspection of the law shows that it makes no reference whatever to any supposed or apprehended violation of the 14th Amendment on the part of the States. It is not predicated on any such view. It proceeds ex directo to declare that certain acts committed by individuals shall be deemed offenses, and shall be prosecuted and punished by proceedings in the courts of the United States. It does not profess to be corrective of any constitutional wrong committed by the States; it does not make its operation to depend upon any such wrong committed. It applies only to cases arising in States which have the justest laws respecting the personal rights of citizens, and whose authorities are ever ready to enforce such laws, as to those which arise in States that may have violated the prohibition of the Amendment. In other words, it steps into the domain of local jurisprudence, and lays down rules for the conduct of individuals in society towards each other, and imposes sanctions for the enforcement of those rules, without referring in any manner to any supposed action of the State or its authorities.

If this legislation is appropriate for enforcing the prohibitions of the Amendment, it is difficult to see where it is to stop. Why may not Congress with equal show of authority enact a code of laws for the enforcement and vindication of all rights of life, liberty and property? If it is supposable that the States may deprive persons of life, liberty and property without due process of law, and the Amendment itself does not suppose this, why should not Congress proceed at once to prescribe due process of law for the protection of every one of these fundamental rights, in every possible case, as well as to prescribe equal privileges in inns, public conveyances and theatres? The truth is, that the implication of a power to legislate in this manner is based upon the assumption that if the States are forbidden to legislate or act in a particular way on a particular subject, and power is conferred upon Congress to enforce the prohibition, this gives Congress power to legislate generally upon that subject, and not merely power to provide modes of redress against such state legislation or action. The assumption is certainly unsound. It is repugnant to the 10th Amendment of the Constitution, which declares that powers not delegated to the United States by the Constitution, nor prohibited by it to the States, are reserved to the States respectively or to the people. . . .

In this connection it is proper to state that civil rights, such as are guaranteed by the Constitution against state aggression, cannot be impaired by the wrongful acts of individuals, unsupported by state authority in the shape of laws, customs or judicial or executive proceedings. The wrongful act of an individual, unsupported by any such authority, is simply a private wrong, or a crime of that individual; an invasion of the rights of the injured party, it is true, whether they affect his person, his property or his reputation; but if not sanctioned in some way by the State, or not done under state authority, his rights remain in full force and may presumably be vindicated by resort to the laws of the State for redress. An individual cannot deprive a man of his right to vote, to hold property, to buy and to sell, to sue in the courts or to be a witness or a juror; he may, by force or fraud, interfere with the enjoyment of the right in a particular case; he may commit an assault against the person, or commit murder, or use ruffian violence at the polls, or slander the good name of a fellow citizen; but, unless protected in these wrongful acts by some shield of state law or state authority, he cannot destroy or injure the right; he will only render himself amenable to satisfaction or punishment; and amenable therefore to the laws of the State where the wrongful acts are committed. Hence, in all those cases where the Constitution seeks to protect the rights of the citizen against discriminative and unjust laws of the State by prohibiting such laws, it is not individual offenses, but abrogation and denial of rights, which it denounces, and for which it clothes the Congress with power to provide a remedy. This abrogation and denial of rights, for which the States alone were or could be responsible, was the great seminal and fundamental wrong which was intended to be remedied. And the remedy to be provided must necessarily be predicated upon that wrong. It must assume that in the cases provided for, the evil or wrong actually committed rests upon some state law or state authority for its excuse and perpetration.

Of course, these remarks do not apply to those cases in which Congress is clothed with direct and plenary powers of legislation over the whole subject, accompanied with an express or implied denial of such power to the States, as in the regulation of commerce with foreign Nations, . . . the coining of money, the establishment of postoffices and post-roads, the declaring of war, etc. In these cases, Congress has power to pass laws for regulating the subjects specified in every detail, and the conduct and transactions of individuals in respect thereof. But where a subject is not submitted to the general legislative power of Congress, but is only submitted thereto for the purpose of rendering effective some prohibition against particular state legislation or state action in reference to that subject, the power given is limited by its object, and any legislation by Congress in the matter must necessarily be corrective in its character, adapted to counteract and redress the operation of such prohibited state laws or proceedings of state officers. . . .

But the power of Congress to adopt direct and primary, as distinguished from corrective, legislation on the subject in hand, is sought, in the second place, from the 13th Amendment, which abolishes slavery. . . .

This Amendment, as well as the 14th, is undoubtedly self-executing without any ancillary legislation, so far as its terms are applicable to any existing state of circumstances. By its own unaided force and effect, it abolished slavery and established universal freedom. . . .

The only question under the present head, therefore, is, whether the refusal to any persons of accommodations of an inn or a public conveyance or a place of public amusement, by an individual and without any sanction or support from any state law or regulation, does inflict upon such persons any manner of servitude, or form of slavery, as those terms are understood in this country?

. . . It would be running the slavery argument into the ground, to make it apply to every act of discrimination which a person may see fit to make as to the guests he will entertain, or as to the people he will take into his coach or cab or car, or admit to his concert or theater, or deal with in other matters of intercourse or business. . . .

On the whole we are of the opinion, that no countenance of authority for the passage of the law in question can be found in either the 13th or the 14th Amendment of the Constitution; and no other ground of authority for its passage being suggested, it must necessarily be declared void, at least so far as its operation in the several States is concerned.

Mr. Justice Harlan wrote a dissenting opinion.

UNITED STATES v. GUEST

383 U.S. 745; 86 S. Ct. 1170; 16 L. Ed. 2d 239 (1966)

While it is well settled that the Bill of Rights and the Fourteenth Amendment are not "directed against the action of individuals," it must not be assumed that the citizen enjoys no federal protection against the invasion of his civil rights. Until the 1960s such protection was measured by the scope of two federal statutes passed in the period following the Civil War. The first of these, directed at the actions of private individuals, was Sec. 6 of the Enforcement Act of 1870, which at various times has been known as § 19 of the Criminal Code of 1909, later as § 51 of the U.S. Code of 1926, and is presently known as § 241 of Title 18 of the U.S. Code. This section provides:

"If two or more persons conspire to injure, oppress, threaten or intimidate any citizen in the free exercise or enjoyment of any right or privilege secured to him by the Constitution or laws of the United States, or because of his having so exercised the same; or

"If two or more persons go in disguise on the highway, or on the premises of another, with intent to prevent or hinder his free exercise or enjoyment of any right or privilege so secured—

"They shall be fined not more than $5000 or imprisoned not more than ten years, or both."

Since § 241 is limited to the rights of citizens which come from the national Constitution or laws, it forbids private interference with exactly those things which are "privileges and immunities of citizens of the United States" within the meaning of the Fourteenth Amendment. In fact, it is in construing this statute rather than the Fourteenth Amendment itself that the scope of such "privileges and immunities" has been spelled out by the Court. In Ex parte Yarbrough (1884), § 19 was held applicable to the right to vote in federal elections if the voter is qualified under state law; and in Logan v. United States (1892) it was held to cover the right of a citizen not to be taken by a mob from the custody of a United States marshal and lynched.

If, on the other hand, a person is deprived of his constitutional or statutory rights by a state officer, a different statute comes into play. A state officer is the "state" against which the provisions of the Fourteenth Amendment are directed, and he may be punished not only for abridging the privileges and immunities of a United States citizen, but also for denying any person due process or equal protection of the laws. Congress first provided for the punishment of such acts of state officers in the Civil Rights Act of 1866, and one of the purposes of the Fourteenth Amendment was to provide a constitutional basis for this statute. Reenacted as Sec. 17 of the Enforcement Act of 1870, this statute has been known variously as § 20 of the Criminal Code, § 52 of the U. S. Code, and is presently called § 242 of Title 18 of the U. S. Code. This section provides that:

"Whoever, under color of any law, statute, ordinance, regulation, or custom, willfully subjects any inhabitant of any State, Territory, or District to the deprivation of any rights, privileges, or immunities secured or protected by the Constitution or laws of the United States, or to different punishments, pains, or penalties, on account of such inhabitant being an alien, or by reason of his color, or race, than are prescribed for the punishment of citizens, shall be fined not more than $1,000 or imprisoned not more than one year, or both."

It was not until the Civil Rights Section in the Department of Justice, created in 1939, decided to appeal the Classic case (1941) that the Supreme Court got its first opportunity to interpret § 242. There it held the statute applicable to Classic, a state election official, on the ground that "misuse of power, possessed by virtue of state law and made possible only because the wrongdoer is clothed with the authority of state law, is action taken 'under color of' state law."

In Screws v. United States (1945) the Civil Rights Section invoked the provisions of § 242 for a very different purpose. Screws was sheriff in a county in Georgia. Aided by a deputy and a policeman he arrested Hall, a Negro, late one night for the alleged theft of a tire. There was evidence that Screws had a grudge against Hall and had threatened to "get" him. The three officers handcuffed Hall, brought him to the courthouse, and there proceeded to beat him to death. The state authorities failed to prosecute Screws, and he was thereupon indicted and convicted under the section of the federal statute. The indictment of Screws rested on the theory that the three officers had deprived Hall, under color of the law of Georgia, of rights guaranteed to him by the Fourteenth Amendment: namely, "the right not to be deprived of life without due process of law; the right to be tried upon the charge on which he was arrested, by due process of law and if found guilty to be punished in accordance with the laws of Georgia." The results reached by the Supreme Court in this case were rather confusing. Six justices agreed that the federal statute could validly be applied to the kind of conduct of which Screws was guilty. Five justices, however, ruled that Screws was entitled to a new trial because the trial court had not properly charged the jury that Screws's violation of the statute must be shown to have been "willful." At the new trial Screws was acquitted. The case did, however, extend the authority of the federal government to punish state officers for violations of civil rights which lie within the range of federal protection.

In two cases decided in 1951 (Williams v. United States and United States v. Williams) the Court held that §§ 241 and 242 were mutually exclusive, so that Williams, a police officer, could not be prosecuted under § 241 even though, as a state official, he had denied a person his rights by giving him the "third degree." Four members of the five-man majority agreed that even though Williams was acting under color of law, § 241 was intended to protect only the kind of rights "which Congress can beyond doubt constitutionally secure against interferences by private individuals," rights which can be classified as privileges and immunities of United States citizenship. It was not intended to protect those rights, like the right to be tried by due process of law, which are guaranteed solely against state abridgment. However, both state officers and private persons can be prosecuted under § 241 if, as in the Classic case, the right denied is a privilege of United States citizenship. The importance of this lies in the fact that § 241 carries a penalty of a ten-year prison sentence, while § 242 is limited to one year. The Court did, however, sustain Williams's indictment under § 242. There was no question that he was a state officer and had deprived a citizen, by extorting the confession, of his liberty without due process of law.

The present case grew out of the shotgun murder on a Georgia highway of Lemuel Penn, a Negro educator, who was driving back to Washington after summer duty as a reserve officer. Two of the six members of the alleged conspiracy were tried by the state for murder and acquitted. In October 1964, a federal grand jury returned an indictment charging them with conspiring to violate § 241. The district court dismissed the indictments, but the Supreme Court reversed. In 1966 they were tried for conspiracy, and the two who had been

tried for murder and acquitted by the state were found guilty and sentenced to ten years in prison.

In the companion case of United States v. Price, 18 persons, three of them police officers, were indicted under § 241 and § 242 for the slaying of three civil rights workers near Philadelphia, Mississippi. The district court dismissed the indictments under § 242 of all but the three officers, and all the indictments under § 241. The Supreme Court reinstated the indictments. It conceded that § 242 dealt only with actions taken "under color" of law, but held that "private persons, jointly engaged with state officials in the prohibited action, are acting 'under color' of law for purposes of the statute. To act 'under color' of law does not require that the accused be an officer of the State. It is enough that he is a willful participant in joint activity with the State or its agents. . . . In effect, if the allegations are true, they were participants in official lawlessness, acting in willful concert with state officers and hence under color of law." In sustaining the charges under § 241 the Court reversed what the district court considered the holding in Williams I, that the section applied only to constitutional rights arising from the substantive powers of the federal government. Since Justice Black had concurred in the result of that case on different grounds, the Court considered the question open. "On the basis of an extensive re-examination of the question, we conclude . . . that § 241 must be read as it is written . . . ; that this language includes rights or privileges protected by the Fourteenth Amendment." The defendants were ultimately tried under the indictment and seven of them, including the three police officials, were convicted.

One other statute authorizing federal intervention to protect civil rights was Sec. 4 of the Civil Rights Act of 1875. This provided that "no citizen . . . shall be disqualified for service as grand or petit juror . . . on account of race . . ." and made it a crime for anyone concerned with the summoning of jurors to fail to summon any citizen because of his color. Although the bulk of this statute was held invalid in the Civil Rights Cases (1883), this provision applied to state officers rather than private individuals; and in Ex parte Virginia (1880) the Court held valid under this act the indictment of a county judge who had excluded Negroes from jury service on account of their race.

Mr. Justice **Stewart** delivered the opinion of the Court, saying in part:

II.

The second numbered paragraph of the indictment alleged that the defendants conspired to injure, oppress, threaten, and intimidate Negro citizens of the United States in the free exercise and enjoyment of:

"The right to the equal utilization, without discrimination upon the basis of race, of public facilities in the vicinity of Athens, Georgia, owned, operated or managed by or on behalf of the State of Georgia or any subdivision thereof."

Correctly characterizing this paragraph as embracing rights protected by the Equal Protection Clause of the Fourteenth Amendment, the District Court held as a matter of statutory construction that 18 USC § 241 does not encompass any Fourteenth Amendment rights, and further held as a matter of constitutional law that "any broader construction of § 241 . . . would render it void for indefiniteness." In so holding, the District Court was in error, as our opinion in United States v. Price [1966] makes abundantly clear.

To be sure, Price involves rights under the Due Process Clause, whereas the present case involves rights under the Equal Protection Clause. But no possible reason suggests itself for concluding that § 241—if it protects Fourteenth Amendment rights—protects rights secured by the one Clause but not those secured by the other. We have made clear in Price that when § 241 speaks of "any right or privilege secured . . . by the Constitution or laws of the United States," it means precisely that. . . .

Unlike the indictment in Price, however, the indictment in the present case names no person alleged to have acted in any way under the color of state law. The argument is therefore made that, since there exist no Equal Protection Clause rights against wholly private action, the judgment of the District Court on this branch of the case must be affirmed. On its face, the argument is unexceptionable. The Equal Protection Clause speaks to the State or to those acting under the color of its authority. . . .

It is a commonplace that rights under the Equal Protection Clause itself arise only where there has been involvement of the State or of one acting under the color of its authority. The Equal Protection Clause "does not . . . add any thing to the rights which one citizen has under the Constitution against another." United States v. Cruikshank [1876]. As Mr. Justice Douglas more recently put it, "The Fourteenth Amendment protects the individual against *state action*, not against wrongs done by *individuals*." United States v. Williams [1951] (dissenting opinion). This has been the view of the Court from the beginning. United States v. Cruikshank. . . . It remains the Court's view today. . . .

This is not to say, however, that the involvement of the State need be either exclusive or direct. In a variety of situations the Court has found state action of a nature sufficient to create rights under the Equal Protection Clause even though the participation of the State was peripheral, or its action was only one of several cooperative forces leading to the constitutional violation. See, e.g., Shelley v. Kraemer [1948]. . . .

This case, however, requires no determination of the threshold level that state action must attain in order to create rights under the Equal Protection Clause. This is so because, contrary to the argument of the litigants, the indictment in fact contains an express allegation of state involvement sufficient at least to require the denial of a motion to dismiss. One of the means of accomplish-

ing the object of the conspiracy, according to the indictment, was "By causing the arrest of Negroes by means of false reports that such Negroes had committed criminal acts." In Bell v. Maryland [1964] three members of the Court expressed the view that a private businessman's invocation of state police and judicial action to carry out his own policy of racial discrimination was sufficient to create Equal Protection Clause rights in those against whom the racial discrimination was directed. Three other members of the Court strongly disagreed with that view, and three expressed no opinion on the question. The allegation of the extent of official involvement in the present case is not clear. It may charge no more than co-operative private and state action similar to that involved in Bell, but it may go considerably further. For example, the allegation is broad enough to cover a charge of active connivance by agents of the State in the making of the "false reports," or other conduct amounting to official discrimination clearly sufficient to constitute denial of rights protected by the Equal Protection Clause. Although it is possible that a bill of particulars, or the proof if the case goes to trial, would disclose no co-operative action of that kind by officials of the State, the allegation is enough to prevent dismissal of this branch of the indictment.

III.

The fourth numbered paragraph of the indictment alleged that the defendants conspired to injure, oppress, threaten, and intimidate Negro citizens of the United States in the free exercise and enjoyment of:

"The right to travel freely to and from the State of Georgia and to use highway facilities and other instrumentalities of interstate commerce within the State of Georgia."

The District Court was in error in dismissing the indictment as to this paragraph. The constitutional right to travel from one State to another, and necessarily to use the highways and other instrumentalities of interstate commerce in doing so, occupies a position fundamental to the concept of our Federal Union. It is a right that has been firmly established and repeatedly recognized. . . .

In Edwards v. California [1941] invalidating a California law which impeded the free interstate passage of the indigent, the Court based its reaffirmation of the federal right of interstate travel upon the Commerce Clause. This ground of decision was consistent with precedents firmly establishing that the federal commerce power surely encompasses the movement in interstate commerce of persons as well as commodities. . . . Hoke v. United States [1913]. . . . It is also well settled in our decisions that the federal commerce power authorizes Congress to legislate for the protection of individuals from violations of civil rights that impinge on their free movement in interstate commerce . . . [Heart of] Atlanta Motel v. United States [1964], Katzenbach v. McClung [1964].

Although there have been recurring differences in

emphasis within the Court as to the source of the constitutional right of interstate travel, there is no need here to canvass those differences further. All have agreed that right exists. Its explicit recognition as one of the federal rights protected by what is now 18 USC § 241 goes back at least as far as 1904. . . . We reaffirm it now.

This does not mean, of course, that every criminal conspiracy affecting an individual's right of free interstate passage is within the sanction of 18 USC § 241. A specific intent to interfere with the federal right must be proved, and at a trial the defendants are entitled to a jury instruction phrased in those terms. Screws v. United States [1945]. Thus, for example, a conspiracy to rob an interstate traveler would not, of itself, violate § 241. But if the predominant purpose of the conspiracy is to impede or prevent the exercise of the right of interstate travel, or to oppress a person because of his exercise of that right, then, whether or not motivated by racial discrimination, the conspiracy becomes a proper object of the federal law under which the indictment in this case was brought. Accordingly, it was error to grant the motion to dismiss on this branch of the indictment.

For these reasons, the judgment of the District Court is reversed and the case is remanded to that court for further proceedings consistent with this opinion.

It is so ordered.

Mr. Justice **Clark**, with whom Mr. Justice **Black** and Mr. Justice **Fortas** joined, wrote a concurring opinion.

Mr. Justice **Harlan**, concurring in part and dissenting in part, said in part:

I join Parts I and II of the Court's opinion, but I cannot subscribe to Part III in its full sweep. To the extent that it is there held that 18 USC § 241 (1964 ed.) reaches conspiracies, embracing only the action of private persons, to obstruct or otherwise interfere with the right of citizens freely to engage in interstate travel, I am constrained to dissent. On the other hand, I agree that § 241 does embrace state interference with such interstate travel, and I therefore consider that this aspect of the indictment is sustainable on the reasoning of Part II of the Court's opinion. . . .

[Justice Harlan here considers, and rejects, several alternative arguments under which the right to travel could be protected from private interference.]

V.

If I have succeeded in showing anything in this constitutional exercise, it is that until today there was no federal right to be free from private interference with interstate transit, and very little reason for creating one. Although the Court has ostensibly only "discovered" this private right in the Constitution and then applied § 241 mechanically to punish those who conspire to threaten it, it should be recognized that what the Court has in effect done is to use this all-encompassing criminal statute to fashion federal common-law crimes, forbidden to the federal judiciary since the 1812 decision in United States v. Hudson. My Brother Douglas, dissenting in United States v. Classic [1941], noted well the dangers of the indiscriminate application of the predecessor of § 241: "It is not enough for us to find in the vague penumbra of a statute some offense about which Congress could have legislated, and then to particularize it as a crime because it is highly offensive."

Mr. Justice **Brennan**, with whom the **Chief Justice [Warren]** and Mr. Justice **Douglas** join, concurring in part and dissenting in part, said in part:

. . . I agree with so much of Part II as construes 18 USC § 241 (1964 ed.) to encompass conspiracies to injure, oppress, threaten or intimidate citizens in the free exercise or enjoyment of Fourteenth Amendment rights and holds that, as so construed, § 241 is not void for indefiniteness. I do not agree, however, with the remainder of Part II which holds, as I read the opinion, that a conspiracy to interfere with the exercise of the right to equal utilization of state facilities is not, within the meaning of § 241, a conspiracy to interfere with the exercise of a "right . . . secured . . . by the Constitution" unless discriminatory conduct by state officers is involved in the alleged conspiracy. . . .

I cannot agree with that construction of § 241. I am of the opinion that a conspiracy to interfere with the right to equal utilization of state facilities described in the second numbered paragraph of the indictment is a conspiracy to interfere with a "right . . . secured . . . by the Constitution" within the meaning of § 241—without regard to whether state officers participated in the alleged conspiracy. I believe that § 241 reaches such a private conspiracy, not because the Fourteenth Amendment of its own force prohibits such a conspiracy, but because § 241, as an exercise of congressional power under § 5 of that Amendment, prohibits *all* conspiracies to interfere with the exercise of a "right . . . secured . . . by the Constitution" and because the right to equal utilization of state facilities is a "right . . . secured . . . by the Constitution" within the meaning of that phrase as used in § 241. . . .

SOUTH CAROLINA v. KATZENBACH

383 U. S. 301; 86 S. Ct. 803; 15 L. Ed. 2d 769
(1966)

Within months after the states had ratified the Fifteenth Amendment, Congress passed the Enforcement Act of 1870, the first four sections of which undertook to enforce the right to vote guaranteed by that amendment. In the first two sections guaranteeing the right to vote and punishing interference with a person's registering to vote, the act explicitly forbade discrimination on account of race; but in the last two sections of the act, which punished actual interferences with the voting, these limiting words were omitted so that the law seemed to forbid voting interference even for reasons other than race. Since this was beyond the authority given by the amendment, the Court held these crucial sections void. See *United States v. Reese* (1876).

It was nearly ninety years before Congress tried again. The Civil Rights Act of 1965, held valid in the present case, is the result of nearly a decade of struggle. Timid and experimental, the early laws were limited to federal elections alone and relied almost entirely on the courts for their operation. The Civil Rights Act of 1957 forbade anyone to interfere with a person's right to vote and authorized the Attorney General to seek an injunction to prevent such interference where it was occurring or seemed likely to occur. In *United States v. Raines* (1960) the act was held valid as applied to voting registrars in Georgia who were discriminating on racial grounds.

Failure of these measures to increase black voting substantially led Congress to strengthen them in the Civil Rights Act of 1960, which made it a crime to obstruct the exercise of (voting) rights granted by court order and gave the Attorney General access to voting records for the purpose of determining if a pattern of discrimination existed. In addition, the district courts were authorized both to appoint voting referees to hear complaints and to qualify or to have the voting referees qualify persons to vote in areas where a pattern of discrimination resulted in disfranchising them. Failure to permit a person so qualified to vote was contempt of court.

Continued state resistance, abetted by a lack of aggressiveness on the part of local United States attorneys and district courts, still prevented any marked increase in black voter registration and led to still stronger voting legislation in the Civil Rights Act of 1964. In Title I of this omnibus measure Congress forbade applying different literacy tests to different applicants, prohibited disqualifying applicants for immaterial errors, and made a sixth-grade education in an English-language school prima facie evidence of literacy for purposes of voting in federal elections. Provision was made for getting quick decisions from federal courts in voter registration cases, some of which had dragged on for over a year. But again, state ingenuity in devising delaying tactics kept black registration to a trickle, and again Congress acted.

While the Voting Rights Act of 1965 falls short of providing complete federal election machinery, it harnesses federal power to prevent voting discrimination to a degree never before attempted. Singling out by the use of a ''triggering'' formula those areas in which voting discrimination is most flagrant, it abolishes literacy tests, waives accumulated poll taxes, and forbids the state to institute new voting requirements until the courts or the Attorney General has found them nondiscriminatory. Furthermore, federal examiners can be appointed to list qualified applicants and declare them eligible to vote in all elections, state as well as federal; and federal poll watchers can be assigned to see that their votes are actually counted. If a qualified person is denied access to the polls, United States officials may permit him to cast his ballot and include the vote in the official totals.

Even in areas not singled out by the triggering formula, the Attorney General may institute proceedings to guarantee voting rights, in which case federal examiners and poll watchers may be appointed, all voting tests and devices may be suspended, and the courts may retain jurisdiction of the proceedings to ensure that no new and discriminatory voting rules are adopted.

The only part of the act to be directed primarily at non-Southern voting practices is a section which outlaws forbidding a person to vote because he cannot read and write English. Directed primarily at New York's vast Spanish-speaking Puerto Rican population, the section was introduced by Senators Javits and Kennedy of New York and declares to be literate any person who, in any American flag school and regardless of the language of instruction, has completed the sixth grade, or such higher grade as is used by the state to qualify its voters. In the elections of 1965 Herman Badillo, a Puerto Rican, defeated incumbent Joseph F. Periconi for reelection as Bronx Borough President by a margin of 2,000 votes. Voting in this election were over 4,000 Spanish-speaking voters who had been enfranchised by this provision of the act. Following the election, a three-judge court in the District of Columbia held the section invalid on the ground that the power to set voting qualifications was reserved to the states. The Supreme Court held the restriction valid in *Katzenbach v. Morgan* (1966). It refused to decide whether a requirement of literacy in English, per se, would deny equal protection, but held that the statute was a valid exercise of congressional power under § 5 of the Fourteenth Amendment providing that ''Congress shall have power to enforce, by appropriate legislation, the provisions of this article.'' Thus, while a restrictive state law must be tested against the equal protection clause with the presumption of validity in favor of the state, a federal statute enforcing equal protection is judged by its ''appropriateness,'' with the burden of showing it to be unreasonable resting on its attackers. Clearly this opens up to Congress an almost wholly untried area of power to protect civil rights.

Mr. Chief Justice **Warren** delivered the opinion of the Court, saying in part:

By leave of the Court, South Carolina has filed a bill of complaint, seeking a declaration that selected provisions of the Voting Rights Act of 1965 violate the Federal Constitution, and asking for an injunction against enforcement of these provisions by the Attorney General. Original jurisdiction is founded on the presence of a controversy between a State and a citizen of another State under Art. III, § 2, of the Constitution. . . .

The Voting Rights Act was designed by Congress to banish the blight of racial discrimination in voting, which has infected the electoral process in parts of our country for nearly a century. The Act creates stringent new remedies for voting discrimination where it persists on a pervasive scale, and in addition the statute strengthens existing remedies for pockets of voting discrimination elsewhere in the country. Congress assumed the power to prescribe these remedies from § 2 of the Fifteenth Amendment, which authorizes the National Legislature to effectuate by "appropriate" measures the constitutional prohibition against racial discrimination in voting. We hold that the sections of the Act which are properly before us are an appropriate means for carrying out Congress' constitutional responsibilities and are consonant with all other provisions of the Constitution. We therefore deny South Carolina's request that enforcement of these sections of the Act be enjoined.

I.

The constitutional propriety of the Voting Rights Act of 1965 must be judged with reference to the historical experience which it reflects. Before enacting the measure, Congress explored with great care the problem of racial discrimination in voting. The House and Senate Committees on the Judiciary each held hearings for nine days and received testimony from a total of 67 witnesses. More than three full days were consumed discussing the bill on the floor of the House, while the debate in the Senate covered 26 days in all. At the close of these deliberations, the verdict of both chambers was overwhelming. The House approved the bill by a vote of 328-74, and the measure passed the Senate by a margin of 79-18.

Two points emerge vividly from the voluminous legislative history of the Act contained in the committee hearings and floor debates. First: Congress felt itself confronted by an insidious and pervasive evil which had been perpetuated in certain parts of our country through unremitting and ingenious defiance of the Constitution. Second: Congress concluded that the unsuccessful remedies which it had prescribed in the past would have to be replaced by sterner and more elaborate measures in order to satisfy the clear commands of the Fifteenth Amendment. We pause here to summarize the majority reports of the House and Senate Committees, which document in considerable detail the factual basis for these reactions by Congress. . . . [The Court here summarizes the systematic efforts of Southern states to disfranchise the Negro.]

According to the evidence in recent Justice Department voting suits, . . . [discriminatory application of voting tests is now the principal] method used to bar Negroes from the polls. Discriminatory administration of voting qualifications has been found in all eight Alabama cases, in all nine Louisiana cases, and in all nine Mississippi cases which have gone to final judgment.

Moreover, in almost all of these cases, the courts have held that the discrimination was pursuant to a widespread "pattern or practice." White applicants for registration have often been excused altogether from the literacy and understanding tests or have been given easy versions, have received extensive help from voting officials, and have been registered despite serious errors in their answers. Negroes, on the other hand, have typically been required to pass difficult versions of all the tests, without any outside assistance and without the slightest error. The good-morals requirement is so vague and subjective that it has constituted an open invitation to abuse at the hands of voting officials. Negroes obliged to obtain vouchers from registered voters have found it virtually impossible to comply in areas where almost no Negroes are on the rolls.

In recent years, Congress has repeatedly tried to cope with the problem by facilitating case-by-case litigation against voting discrimination. The Civil Rights Act of 1957 authorized the Attorney General to seek injunctions against public and private interference with the right to vote on racial grounds. Perfecting amendments in the Civil Rights Act of 1960 permitted the joinder of States as parties defendant, gave the Attorney General access to local voting records, and authorized courts to register voters in areas of systematic discrimination. Title I of the Civil Rights Act of 1964 expedited the hearing of voting cases before three-judge courts and outlawed some of the tactics used to disqualify Negroes from voting in federal elections.

Despite the earnest efforts of the Justice Department and of many federal judges, these new laws have done little to cure the problem of voting discrimination. According to estimates by the Attorney General during hearings on the Act, registration of voting-age Negroes in Alabama rose only from 14.2% to 19.4% between 1958 and 1964; in Louisiana it barely inched ahead from 31.7% to 31.8% between 1956 and 1965; and in Mississippi it increased only from 4.4% to 6.4% between 1954 and 1964. In each instance, registration of voting-age whites ran roughly 50 percentage points or more ahead of Negro registration.

The previous legislation has proved ineffective for a number of reasons. Voting suits are unusually onerous to prepare, sometimes requiring as many as 6,000 man-hours spent combing through registration records in preparation for trial. Litigation has been exceedingly slow, in part because of the ample opportunities for delay afforded voting officials and others involved in the proceedings. Even when favorable decisions have finally been obtained, some of the States affected have merely switched to discriminatory devices not covered by the federal decrees or have enacted difficult new tests designed to prolong the existing disparity between white and Negro registration. Alternatively, certain local officials have defied and evaded court orders or have simply closed their registration offices to freeze the voting rolls. The provision of the 1960 law authorizing registration by federal officers has had little impact on local maladministration because of its procedural complexities.

During the hearings and debates on the Act, Selma, Alabama, was repeatedly referred to as the preeminent example of the ineffectiveness of existing legislation. In Dallas County, of which Selma is the seat, there were four years of litigation by the Justice Department and two findings by the federal courts of widespread voting discrimination. Yet in those four years, Negro registration rose only from 156 to 383, although there are approximately 15,000 Negroes of voting age in the county. Any possibility that these figures were attributable to political apathy was dispelled by the protest demonstrations in Selma in the early months of 1965. . . .

II.

The Voting Rights Act of 1965 reflects Congress' firm intention to rid the country of racial discrimination in voting. The heart of the Act is a complex scheme of stringent remedies aimed at areas where voting discrimination has been most flagrant. . . .

At the outset, we emphasize that only some of the many portions of the Act are properly before us. . . .

Coverage Formula

The remedial sections of the Act assailed by South Carolina automatically apply to any State, or to any separate political subdivision such as a county or parish, for which two findings have been made: (1) the Attorney General has determined that on November 1, 1964, it maintained a "test or device," and (2) the Director of the Census has determined that less than 50% of its voting-age residents were registered on November 1, 1964, or voted in the presidential election of November 1964. . . . As used throughout the Act, the phrase "test or device" means any requirement that a registrant or voter must "(1) demonstrate the ability to read, write, understand, or interpret any matter, (2) demonstrate any educational achievement or his knowledge on any particular subject, (3) possess good moral character, or (4) prove his qualifications by the voucher of registered voters or members of any class." § 4 (c). . . .

South Carolina was brought within the coverage formula of the Act on August 7, 1965. . . .

Suspension of Tests

In a State or political subdivision covered by § 4 (b) of the Act, no person may be denied the right to vote in any election because of his failure to comply with a "test or device." § 4 (a).

On account of this provision, South Carolina is temporarily barred from enforcing the portion of its voting laws which requires every applicant for registration to show that he:

"Can both read and write any section of [the State] Constitution submitted to [him] by the registration officer or can show that he owns, and has paid all taxes collectable during the previous year on, property in this State assessed at three hundred dollars or more." . . .

Review of New Rules

In a State or political subdivision covered by § 4 (b) of the Act, no person may be denied the right to vote in any election because of his failure to comply with a voting qualification or procedure different from those in force on November 1, 1964. . . .

Federal Examiners

In any political subdivision covered by § 4 (b) of the Act, the Civil Service Commission shall appoint voting examiners whenever the Attorney General certifies either of the following facts: (1) that he has received meritorious written complaints from at least 20 residents alleging that they have been disenfranchised under color of law because of their race, or (2) that the appointment of examiners is otherwise necessary to effectuate the guarantees of the Fifteenth Amendment. In making the latter determination, the Attorney General must consider, among other factors, whether the registration ratio of non-whites to whites seems reasonably attributable to racial discrimination, or whether there is substantial evidence of good-faith efforts to comply with the Fifteenth Amendment § 6 (b). . . .

The examiners who have been appointed are to test the voting qualifications of applicants according to regulations of the Civil Service Commission prescribing times, places, procedures, and forms. §§ 7 (a) and 9 (b). Any person who meets the voting requirements of state law, insofar as these have not been suspended by the Act, must promptly be placed on a list of eligible voters. . . . Any person listed by an examiner is entitled to vote in all elections held more than 45 days after his name has been transmitted. § 7 (b). . . .

On October 30, 1965, the Attorney General certified the need for federal examiners in two South Carolina counties, and examiners appointed by the Civil Service Commission have been serving there since November 8, 1965. . . .

III.

These provisions of the Voting Rights Act of 1965 are challenged on the fundamental ground that they exceed the powers of Congress and encroach on an area reserved to the States by the Constitution. . . .

Has Congress exercised its powers under the Fifteenth Amendment in an appropriate manner with relation to the States?

The ground rules for resolving this question are clear. The language and purpose of the Fifteenth Amendment, the prior decisions construing its several provisions, and the general doctrines of constitutional interpretation, all point to one fundamental principle. As against the reserved powers of the States, Congress may use any rational means to effectuate the constitutional prohibition of racial discrimination in voting. Cf. our rulings last Term, sustaining Title II of the Civil Rights Act of 1964, in Heart of Atlanta Motel v. United States [1964], and Katzenbach v. McClung [1964]. We turn now to a more detailed description of the standards which govern our review of the Act.

Section 1 of the Fifteenth Amendment declares that "[t]he right of citizens of the United States to vote shall not be denied or abridged by the United States or by any State on account of race, color, or previous condition of servitude." This declaration has always been treated as self-executing and has repeatedly been construed, without further legislative specification, to invalidate state voting qualifications or procedures which are discriminatory on their face or in practice. . . . Guinn v. United States [1915] . . . Smith v. Allwright [1944]. The gist of the matter is that the Fifteenth Amendment supersedes contrary exertions of state power. . . .

South Carolina contends that the cases cited above are precedents only for the authority of the judiciary to strike down state statutes and procedures—that to allow an exercise of this authority by Congress would be to rob the courts of their rightful constitutional role. On the contrary, § 2 of the Fifteenth Amendment expressly declares that "Congress shall have the power to enforce this article by appropriate legislation." By adding this authorization, the Framers indicated that Congress was to be chiefly responsible for implementing the rights created in § 1. . . .

Congress has repeatedly exercised these powers in the past, and its enactments have repeatedly been upheld. For recent examples, see the Civil Rights Act of 1957, which was sustained in United States v. Raines [1960]. . . .

The basic test to be applied in a case involving § 2 of the Fifteenth Amendment is the same as in all cases concerning the express powers of Congress with relation to the reserved powers of the States. Chief Justice Marshall laid down the classic formulation, 50 years before the Fifteenth Amendment was ratified:

"Let the end be legitimate, let it be within the scope of the constitution, and all means which are appropriate, which are plainly adapted to that end, which are not prohibited, but consist with the letter and spirit of the constitution, are constitutional." McCulloch v. Maryland [1819]. . . .

We therefore reject South Carolina's argument that Congress may appropriately do no more than to forbid violations of the Fifteenth Amendment in general terms—that the task of fashioning specific remedies or of applying them to particular localities must necessarily be left entirely to the courts. Congress is not circumscribed by any such artificial rules under § 2 of the Fifteenth Amendment. In the oft-repeated words of Chief

Justice Marshall, referring to another specific legislative authorization in the Constitution, "This power, like all others vested in Congress, is complete in itself, may be exercised to its utmost extent, and acknowledges no limitations, other than are prescribed in the constitution." Gibbons v. Ogden [1824].

IV.

Congress exercised its authority under the Fifteenth Amendment in an inventive manner when it enacted the Voting Rights Act of 1965. First: The measure prescribes remedies for voting discrimination which go into effect without any need for prior adjudication. This was clearly a legitimate response to the problem, for which there is ample precedent under other constitutional provisions. . . . Congress had found that case-by-case litigation was inadequate to combat widespread and persistent discrimination in voting, because of the inordinate amount of time and energy required to overcome the obstructionist tactics invariably encountered in these lawsuits. After enduring nearly a century of systematic resistance to the Fifteenth Amendment, Congress might well decide to shift the advantage of time and inertia from the perpetrators of the evil to its victims. The question remains, of course, whether the specific remedies prescribed in the Act were an appropriate means of combating the evil, and to this question we shall presently address ourselves.

Second: The Act intentionally confines these remedies to a small number of States and political subdivisions which in most instances were familiar to Congress by name. This, too, was a permissible method of dealing with the problem. Congress had learned that substantial voting discrimination presently occurs in certain sections of the country, and it knew no way of accurately forecasting whether the evil might spread elsewhere in the future. In acceptable legislative fashion, Congress chose to limit its attention to the geographic areas where immediate action seemed necessary. . . . The doctrine of the equality of States, invoked by South Carolina, does not bar this approach, for that doctrine applies only to the terms upon which States are admitted to the Union, and not to the remedies for local evils which have subsequently appeared. See Coyle v. Smith [1911]. . . .

Coverage Formula

We now consider the related question of whether the specific States and political subdivisions within § 4 (b) of the Act were an appropriate target for the new remedies. . . . Congress began work with reliable evidence of actual voting discrimination in a great majority of the States and political subdivisions affected by the new remedies of the Act. The formula eventually evolved to describe these areas was relevant to the problem of voting discrimination. . . .

To be specific, the new remedies of the Act are imposed on three States—Alabama, Louisiana, and Mississippi—in which federal courts have repeatedly found substantial voting discrimination. . . .

The areas listed above, for which there was evidence of actual voting discrimination, share two characteristics incorporated by Congress into the coverage formula: the use of tests and devices for voter registration, and a voting rate in the 1964 presidential election at least 12 points below the national average. Tests and devices are relevant to voting discrimination because of their long history as a tool for perpetrating the evil; a low voting rate is pertinent for the obvious reason that widespread disenfranchisement must inevitably affect the number of actual voters. Accordingly, the coverage formula is rational in both practice and theory. It was therefore permissible to impose the new remedies on the few remaining States and political subdivisions covered by the formula, at least in the absence of proof that they have been free of substantial voting discrimination in recent years. . . .

Suspension of Tests

We now arrive at consideration of the specific remedies prescribed by the Act for areas included within the coverage formula. South Carolina assails the temporary suspension of existing voting qualification. . . . The record shows that in most of the States covered by the Act, including South Carolina, various tests and devices have been instituted with the purpose of disenfranchising Negroes, have been framed in such a way as to facilitate this aim, and have been administered in a discriminatory fashion for many years. Under these circumstances, the Fifteenth Amendment has clearly been violated. . . .

The Act suspends literacy tests and similar devices for a period of five years from the last occurrence of substantial voting discrimination. This was a legitimate response to the problem, for which there is ample precedent in Fifteenth Amendment cases. Underlying the response was the feeling that States and political subdivisions which had been allowing white illiterates to vote for years could not sincerely complain about "dilution" of their electorates through the registration of Negro illiterates. Congress knew that continuance of the tests and devices in use at the present time, no matter how fairly administered in the future, would freeze the effect of past discrimination in favor of unqualified white registrants. Congress permissibly rejected the alternative of requiring a complete re-registration of all voters, believing that this would be too harsh on many whites who had enjoyed the franchise for their entire adult lives.

Review of New Rules

The Act suspends new voting regulations pending scrutiny by federal authorities to determine whether their use would violate the Fifteenth Amendment. . . . Congress knew that some of the States covered by § 4 (b) of

the Act had resorted to the extraordinary stratagem of contriving new rules of various kinds for the sole purpose of perpetuating voting discrimination in the face of adverse federal court decrees. Congress had reason to suppose that these States might try similar maneuvers in the future in order to evade the remedies for voting discrimination contained in the Act itself. Under the compulsion of these unique circumstances, Congress responded in a permissibly decisive manner. . . .

Federal Examiners

The Act authorizes the appointment of federal examiners to list qualified applicants who are thereafter entitled to vote, subject to an expeditious challenge procedure. This was clearly an appropriate response to the problem, closely related to remedies authorized in prior cases. . . . In many of the political subdivisions covered by § 4 (b) of the Act, voting officials have persistently employed a variety of procedural tactics to deny Negroes the franchise, often in direct defiance or evasion of federal court decrees. Congress realized that merely to suspend voting rules which have been misused or are subject to misuse might leave this localized evil undisturbed. As for the briskness of the challenge procedure, Congress knew that in some of the areas affected, challenges had been persistently employed to harass registered Negroes. It chose to forestall this abuse, at the same time providing alternative ways for removing persons listed through error or fraud. In addition to the judicial challenge procedure, § 7 (d) allows for the removal of names by the examiner himself, and § 11 (c) makes it a crime to obtain a listing through fraud. . . .

The bill of complaint is dismissed.

Mr. Justice **Black** concurred except as to the validity of § 5.

JONES v. ALFRED H. MAYER CO.

392 U. S. 409; 88 S. Ct. 2186; 20 L. Ed. 2d 1189 (1968)

It is one of the anomalies of our system of government that federal efforts to provide protection for human safety and dignity must be undertaken through what was once called "back-stairs legislation." Under our federal system Congress has no "police power" delegated to it. To provide such protection it must rely on using some power which has been delegated to it. Thus, Title II of the Civil Rights Act of 1964 (see Heart of Atlanta Motel v. United States, 1964) rests upon the commerce power, while the Fair Housing section of the Civil Rights Act of 1968 relies for its validity on the power of Congress to control those who receive its financial help.

During the bitter days of Reconstruction follow-

ing the Civil War, the Radical Republicans, under the leadership of Thaddeus Stevens, made a serious if not wholly altruistic attempt to provide Congress with just such a police power to protect the newly freed Negro. Three constitutional amendments were passed, and to carry them out Congress passed, over the veto of President Johnson, a series of civil rights enforcement acts. The first of these, the Civil Rights Act of 1866, was passed to enforce the provisions of the Thirteenth Amendment abolishing slavery. Section 1 of this act, printed in the case below and now included in §§ 1981 and 1982 of Title 42 of the U. S. Code, declared that "all . . . citizens . . . without regard to any previous condition of slavery . . . shall have the same rights to . . . purchase, lease, sell, hold and convey real and personal property, as is enjoyed by white citizens. . . ." Whether one individual could sue another under the provisions of § 1 was not made explicit, but in § 2 of the act (now § 242 of Title 18 of the U. S. Code) violation of these rights was made a federal crime punishable, where the violator was "acting under color of" state law, by a $1,000 fine and one year in jail. Although the bill became law on April 9, 1866, there was doubt in the minds of many congressmen as to the constitutionality of § 2 punishing for the first time the conduct of state officers, and on June 13, Congress submitted to the states the Fourteenth Amendment to provide a constitutional underpinning for this provision.

The Fourteenth Amendment was ratified by the states in 1868 and the Fifteenth in 1870. Two months later Congress enacted a second civil rights bill known as the Enforcement Act of 1870. This was a catch-all measure which, among other things, provided federal protection for voting, reenacted §§ 1 and 2 of the act of 1866, and in what has become § 241 of Title 18 of the U.S. Code, made it a crime punishable by $5,000 or ten years in jail for "two or more persons" to "conspire together, or go in disguise upon the highway . . . with intent to violate any provision of this act, or to . . . intimidate any citizen with intent to . . . hinder his free exercise . . . of any right or privilege granted or secured to him by the Constitution or laws of the United States."

The result of these statutes was to make it a crime for either a private individual or a state officer to interfere with certain specified civil rights. Then in the Ku Klux Klan Act of 1871, Congress provided a private right of action against a private individual who conspired to deprive anyone of the "equal protection of the laws or of the equal privileges and immunities under the laws," as well as against a state officer who subjected any citizen "to the deprivation of any rights, privileges, or immunities secured by the Constitution. . . ." With the passage of the Revised Statutes of 1874, this privilege and immunities clause was also incorporated into § 242, so that not only rights mentioned in the statute but constitutional rights as well were protected from both state

and private interference. Finally, with the end of the Reconstruction era in sight, Congress passed the Civil Rights Act of 1875, making it both a crime and a civil wrong to deny anyone, on account of race, the "full and equal enjoyment" of public accommodations.

The ensuing decade saw the Supreme Court systematically eviscerate both the newly passed constitutional amendments and the acts passed to enforce them. In a series of cases the Court spelled out its basic assumption that none of the Civil War amendments had been intended to give Congress any new power to enforce individual civil rights. Their only function was to forbid certain state actions. While Congress was given power to enforce the amendments, such enforcement was limited to preventing such state action, and since the amendments limited only states, under no circumstances could the actions of an individual be deemed to violate them. Thus, in the Slaughter-House Cases (1873) the "privileges and immunities" of United States citizenship protected by the Fourteenth Amendment and subsequent statutes were limited to those that Congress, under its delegated powers, had always had power to grant and protect. In United States v. Reese (1876) most of the voting protections of the Enforcement Act were struck down because they were not limited to racial discrimination, and in the Civil Rights Cases (1883), the Civil Rights Act of 1875, punishing discrimination in public accommodations, was held void because it forbade private rather than governmental action.

Only a handful of provisions survived the onslaught. Those forbidding discriminatory action taken "under color of" state law were held to be directed to state action and hence were valid enforcement measures. Those provisions forbidding interference with rights by private individuals, on the other hand, were, like the privileges and immunities of the Fourteenth Amendment, limited to rights in those few areas, such as control over the manner of conducting federal elections, where Congress had power from the original Constitution; see Ex parte Yarbrough (1884).

The Thirteenth Amendment presented the Court with a slightly different problem. Worded to forbid involuntary servitude in any form, and since individuals rather than states had held slaves, the amendment could not reasonably be considered merely a limit upon state action. Two devices, however, permitted the Court to avoid unleashing the tremendous breadth of power latent in the amendment. The first was a refusal to extend the amendment to kinds of servitude "which have from time immemorial been treated as exceptional." Thus in Robertson v. Baldwin (1897), the Court held that seamen who had signed for a voyage aboard ship and deserted could be arrested and returned to the ship; while in the Selective Draft Law Cases (1918) it upheld the "servitude" involved in drafting a person into the armed forces of the United States. Butler v. Perry (1916) held valid on this ground a Florida law requiring that citizens work a specified number of days each year on the county roads and bridges in lieu of the payment of road taxes.

The second and most important was to interpret narrowly the word slavery. Conceding, in the Civil Rights Cases, that Congress had authority to outlaw the "badges of slavery," the Court nevertheless held it would be "running the slavery argument into the ground" to consider such badges as including the private discriminatory conduct of one man toward another. That this also applied to the "make and enforce contracts" guarantees of § 1 of the Civil Rights Act of 1866 was decided in 1906 in Hodges v. United States, discussed in the opinion below, where Negro workmen were intimidated by a group of whites into quitting their jobs.

In the 1960s the Supreme Court suggested subtly that the "back-stairs legislation" approach to civil rights may no longer be needed, and that an overt reliance on the enforcement power granted in the three amendments would be received more sympathetically than it had been before. In upholding the Voting Rights Act of 1965, the Court permitted Congress to substitute federal for state voting machinery where necessary to prevent discrimination, and to outlaw voting qualifications which might not, of themselves, violate the Fourteenth Amendment. These provisions were upheld in South Carolina v. Katzenbach (1966) and Katzenbach v. Morgan (1966). In United States v. Guest (1966), six justices indicated that Congress could protect an individual right to use state facilities; and in the Civil Rights Act of 1968 Congress acted on this suggestion and outlawed interference with "any person because of his race . . . and because he is or has been . . . participating in or enjoying any benefit, service, privilege, program, facility or activity provided or administered by any State or subdivision thereof. . . .

Following the decision in the present case the Court held that a cause of action existed under the old Ku Klux Klan Act of 1871 where a black mistakenly thought to be a civil rights worker was stopped on the highway and beaten up by two armed white men. The law forbids private individuals to deprive other private individuals of the "equal protection of the laws." The Court conceded that "a century of Fourteenth Amendment adjudication has . . . made it understandably difficult to conceive of what might constitute a deprivation of the equal protection of the laws by private persons. Yet there is nothing inherent in the phrase that requires the action working the deprivation to come from the State. . . . . Indeed, the failure to mention any such requisite can be viewed as an important indication of congressional intent to speak in [the act] of all deprivation of 'equal protection of the laws' and 'equal privileges and immunities under the laws,' whatever their source." Nor is the power to control individual conduct limited to the kinds of things traditionally thought of as privileges and immunities of citizenship and hence subject to federal power. Citing Jones v. Alfred H. Mayer Co., the Court found that "Congress was wholly within its powers un-

der § 2 of the Thirteenth Amendment in creating a statutory cause of action for Negro citizens who have been the victims of conspiratorial, racially discriminatory private action aimed at depriving them of the basic rights that the law secures to all free men." See Griffin v. Breckenridge (1971).

Mr. Justice **Stewart** delivered the opinion of the Court, saying in part:

In this case we are called upon to determine the scope and the constitutionality of an Act of Congress, 42 U. S. C. § 1982, which provides that:

"All citizens of the United States shall have the same right, in every State and Territory, as is enjoyed by white citizens thereof to inherit, purchase, lease, sell, hold, and convey real and personal property."

On September 2, 1965, the petitioners filed a complaint in the District Court for the Eastern District of Missouri, alleging that the respondents had refused to sell them a home in the Paddock Woods community of St. Louis County for the sole reason that petitioner Joseph Lee Jones is a Negro. Relying in part upon § 1982, the petitioners sought injunctive and other relief. The District Court sustained the respondents' motion to dismiss the complaint, and the Court of Appeals for the Eighth Circuit affirmed, concluding that § 1982 applies only to state action and does not reach private refusals to sell. We granted certiorari to consider the questions thus presented. For the reasons that follow, we reverse the judgment of the Court of Appeals. We hold that § 1982 bars *all* racial discrimination, private as well as public, in the sale or rental of property, and that the statute, thus construed, is a valid exercise of the power of Congress to enforce the Thirteenth Amendment.

I.

At the outset, it is important to make clear precisely what this case does *not* involve. Whatever else it may be, 42 U. S. C. § 1982 is not a comprehensive open housing law. In sharp contrast to the Fair Housing Title (Title VIII) of the Civil Rights Act of 1968, the statute in this case deals only with racial discrimination and does not address itself to discrimination on grounds of religion or national origin. It does not deal specifically with discrimination in the provision of services or facilities in connection with the sale or rental of a dwelling. It does not prohibit advertising or other representations that indicate discriminatory preferences. It does not refer explicitly to discrimination in financing arrangements or in the provision of brokerage services. It does not empower a federal administrative agency to assist aggrieved parties. It makes no provision for intervention by the Attorney General. And, although it can be enforced by injunction, it contains no provision expressly authorizing a federal court to order the payment of damages.

Thus, although § 1982 contains none of the exemptions that Congress included in the Civil Rights Act of 1968, it would be a serious mistake to suppose that § 1982 in any way diminishes the significance of the law recently enacted by Congress. Indeed, the Senate Subcommittee on Housing and Urban Affairs was informed in hearings held after the Court of Appeals had rendered its decision in this case that § 1982 might well be "a presently valid federal statutory ban against discrimination by private persons in the sale or lease of real property." The Subcommittee was told, however, that even if this Court should so construe § 1982, the existence of that statute would not "eliminate the need for congressional action" to spell out "responsibility on the part of the federal government to enforce the rights it protects." The point was made that, in light of the many difficulties confronted by private litigants seeking to enforce such rights on their own, "legislation is needed to establish federal machinery for enforcement of the rights guaranteed under Section 1982 of Title 42 even if the plaintiffs in Jones v. Alfred H. Mayer Company should prevail in the United States Supreme Court." . . .

. . . Having noted these differences, we turn to a consideration of § 1982 itself. . . .

III.

We begin with the language of the statute itself. In plain and unambiguous terms, § 1982 grants to all citizens, without regard to race or color, "the same right" to purchase and lease property "as is enjoyed by white citizens." As the Court of Appeals in this case evidently recognized, that right can be impaired as effectively by "those who place property on the market" as by the State itself. For, even if the State and its agents lend no support to those who wish to exclude persons from their communities on racial grounds, the fact remains that, whenever property "is placed on the market for whites only, whites have a right denied to Negroes." So long as a Negro citizen who wants to buy or rent a home can be turned away simply because he is not white, he cannot be said to enjoy "the *same* right . . . as is enjoyed by white citizens . . . to . . . purchase [and] lease . . . real and personal property." 42 U. S. C. § 1982. (Emphasis added.)

On its face, therefore, § 1982 appears to prohibit *all* discrimination against Negroes in the sale or rental of property—discrimination by private owners as well as discrimination by public authorities. Indeed, even the respondents seem to concede that, if § 1982 "means what it says"—to use the words of the respondents' brief—then it must encompass every racially motivated refusal to sell or rent and cannot be confined to officially sanctioned segregation in housing. Stressing what they consider to be the revolutionary implications of so literal a reading of § 1982, the respondents argue that Congress

cannot possibly have intended any such result. Our examination of the relevant history, however, persuades us that Congress meant exactly what it said. . . .

V.

The remaining question is whether Congress has power under the Constitution to do what § 1982 purports to do: to prohibit all racial discrimination, private and public, in the sale and rental of property. Our starting point is the Thirteenth Amendment, for it was pursuant to that constitutional provision that Congress originally enacted what is now § 1982. The Amendment consists of two parts. Section 1 states:

"Neither slavery nor involuntary servitude except as a punishment for a crime whereof the party shall have been duly convicted, shall exist within the United States, or any place subject to their jurisdiction." Section 2 provides:

"Congress shall have power to enforce this article by appropriate legislation."

As its text reveals, the Thirteenth Amendment "is not a mere prohibition of State laws establishing or upholding slavery, but an absolute declaration that slavery or involuntary servitude shall not exist in any part of the United States." Civil Rights Cases [1883]. It has never been doubted, therefore, "that the power vested in Congress to enforce the article by appropriate legislation," includes the power to enact laws "direct and primary, operating upon the acts of individuals, whether sanctioned by State legislation or not."

Thus, the fact that § 1982 operates upon the unofficial acts of private individuals, whether or not sanctioned by state law, presents no constitutional problem. If Congress has power under the Thirteenth Amendment to eradicate conditions that prevent Negroes from buying and renting property because of their race or color, then no federal statute calculated to achieve that objective can be thought to exceed the constitutional power of Congress simply because it reaches beyond state action to regulate the conduct of private individuals. The constitutional question in this case, therefore, comes to this: Does the authority of Congress to enforce the Thirteenth Amendment "by appropriate legislation" include the power to eliminate all racial barriers to the acquisition of real and personal property? We think the answer to that question is plainly yes. . . .

. . . Surely Congress has the power under the Thirteenth Amendment rationally to determine what are the badges and the incidents of slavery, and the authority to translate that determination into effective legislation. Nor can we say that the determination Congress has made is an irrational one. For this Court recognized long ago that, whatever else they may have encompassed, the badges and incidents of slavery—its "burdens and disabilities"—included restraints upon "those fundamental rights which are the essence of civil freedom, namely, the same right . . . to inherit, purchase, lease, sell and convey property, as is enjoyed by white citizens." Civil Rights Cases.* Just as the Black Codes, enacted after the Civil War to restrict the free exercise of those rights, were substitutes for the slave system, so the exclusion of Negroes from white communities became a substitute for the Black Codes. And when racial discrimination herds men into ghettos and makes their ability to buy property turn on the color of their skin, then it too is a relic of slavery.

---

*The Court did conclude in the Civil Rights Cases that "the act of . . . the owner of the inn, the public conveyance or place of amusement, refusing . . . accommodation" cannot be "justly regarded as imposing any badge of slavery or servitude upon the applicant." "It would be running the slavery argument into the ground," the Court thought, "to make it apply to every act of discrimination which a person may see fit to make as to the guests he will entertain, or as to the people he will take into his coach or cab or car, or admit to his concert or theatre, or deal with in other matters of intercourse or business." Mr. Justice Harlan dissented, expressing the view that "such discrimination practiced by corporations and individuals in the exercise of their public or quasi-public functions is a badge of servitude the imposition of which Congress may prevent under its power, by appropriate legislation, to enforce the Thirteenth Amendment."

Whatever the present validity of the position taken by the majority on that issue—a question rendered largely academic by Title II of the Civil Rights Act of 1964 (see Heart of Atlanta Motel v. United States [1964]; Katzenbach v. McClung [1964])—we note that the entire Court agreed upon at least one proposition: The Thirteenth Amendment authorizes Congress not only to outlaw all forms of slavery and involuntary servitude but also to eradicate the last vestiges and incidents of a society half slave and half free, securing to all citizens, of every race and color, "the same right to make and enforce contracts, to sue, be parties, give evidence, and to inherit, purchase, lease, sell and convey property, as is enjoyed by white citizens."

In Hodges v. United States [1906], a group of white men had terrorized several Negroes to prevent them from working in a sawmill. The terrorizers were convicted under 18 U. S. C. § 241 . . . of conspiring to prevent the Negroes from exercising the right to contract for employment, a right . . . derived from § 1 of the Civil Rights Act of 1866. . . .

This court reversed the conviction. The majority recognized that "one of the disabilities of slavery, one of the indicia of its existence, was a lack of power to make or perform contracts." And there was no doubt that the defendants had deprived their Negro victims, on racial grounds, of the opportunity to dispose of their labor by contract. Yet the majority said that "no mere personal assault or trespass or appropriation operates to reduce the individual to a condition of slavery," and asserted that only conduct which actually enslaves someone can be subjected to punishment under legislation enacted to enforce the Thirteenth Amendment. . . .

The conclusion of the majority in Hodges rested upon a concept of congressional power under the Thirteenth Amendment irreconcilable with the position taken by every member of this Court in the Civil Rights Cases and incompatible with the history and purpose of the Amendment itself. Insofar as Hodges is inconsistent with our holding today, it is hereby overruled.

Negro citizens North and South, who saw in the Thirteenth Amendment a promise of freedom—freedom to "go and come at pleasure" and to "buy and sell when they please"— would be left with "a mere paper guarantee" if Congress were powerless to assure that a dollar in the hands of a Negro will purchase the same thing as a dollar in the hands of a white man. At the very least, the freedom that Congress is empowered to secure under the Thirteenth Amendment includes the freedom to buy whatever a white man can buy, the right to live wherever a white man can live. If Congress cannot say that being a free man means at least this much, then the Thirteenth Amendment made a promise the Nation cannot keep. . . .

We agree. The judgment is
Reversed.

Mr. Justice **Douglas** wrote a concurring opinion.

Mr. Justice **Harlan**, whom Mr. Justice **White** joins, dissenting, said in part:

The decision in this case appears to me to be most ill-considered and ill-advised.

The petitioners argue that the respondent's racially motivated refusal to sell them a house entitles them to judicial relief on two separate grounds. First, they claim that the respondent acted in violation of 42 U. S. C. § 1982; second, they assert that the respondent's conduct amounted in the circumstances to "state action" and was therefore forbidden by the Fourteenth Amendment even in the absence of any statute. The Court, without reaching the second alleged ground, holds that the petitioners are entitled to relief under 42 U. S. C. § 1982, and that § 1982 is constitutional as legislation appropriate to enforce the Thirteenth Amendment.

For reasons which follow, I believe that the Court's construction of § 1982 as applying to purely private action is almost surely wrong, and at least is open to serious doubt. The issue of the constitutionality of § 1982, as construed by the Court, and of liability under the Fourteenth Amendment alone, also present formidable difficulties. Moreover, the political processes of our own era have, since the date of oral argument in this case, given birth to a civil rights statute embodying "fair housing" provisions which would at the end of this year make available to others, though apparently not to the petitioners themselves, the type of relief which the petitioners now seek. It seems to me that this latter factor so diminishes the public importance of this case that by far the wisest course would be for this Court to refrain from decision and to dismiss the writ as improvidently granted. . . .

7

1992-1993 Cases

SHAW v. RENO

125 L Ed. 2d 511 (1993)

Minorities in the United States have had a long and frequently bitter struggle in their efforts to secure the right to vote. While the passage of the Fifteenth Amendment forbade discrimination against them, those previously disfranchised face a host of devices contrived to keep them from the polls. In addition to brute force, procedural requirements such as literacy or comprehension tests were frequently used to target and screen out minority voters. At the same time grandfather clauses, under which those whose ancestors could vote were exempt from such tests, allowed even illiterate whites to vote.

Under early civil rights statutes, blacks and members of other minority groups could and did challenge state laws and practices that denied them the vote. However, this case-by-case method of addressing discrimination in voter registration proved inadequate to combat the systemic commitment in the South to deny blacks the vote. The Voting Rights Act of 1965 abandoned this approach in favor of a legislatively established presumption that literacy tests or related requirements for registration were being used to discriminate where the voter turnout in any jurisdiction was below 50 percent. The act outlawed directly any voting qualification that discriminated against voters.

Undaunted, legislatures devised other ways to discriminate against voters. To dilute the effect of the mi-

nority vote, they adopted procedures such as at-large elections, changed some offices from elected to appointed, and gerrymandered district boundaries. While minorities could now exercise their right to vote, that vote became diluted.

A "preclearance" requirement included in the act has had the greatest impact in preventing such discriminatory action. This provision requires that in areas where minority voters have historically suffered discrimination, the legislatures must obtain approval from the U. S. Justice Department or the District Court for the District of Columbia before making any changes in the voting laws. Subject to particular scrutiny are changes that "dilute" the minority vote by redrawing district lines so that the votes of some citizens are not accorded the same weight as those of other citizens.

The Court has determined that legislation that can be explained only in terms of race demands strict scrutiny, regardless of legislative intent. This reasoning has been applied not only to voting rights, see Guinn v. United States (1915), but to municipal redistricting as in Gomillion v. Lightfoot (1964). In Mobile v. Bolden (1980) the Court held that a showing of discriminatory intent was required to make out a violation of the Voting Rights Act. Congress responded by amending the act to make it clear that a violation could be proved by a showing that a voting requirement or district lines had a discriminatory effect, even if no proof of discriminatory intent was offered.

In the case printed below, however, the Court was concerned not with the voting rights of minority group members, but with the voting rights of white citizens. The case raised the question of whether actions prescribed by the Justice Department under the Voting Rights Act to protect minority voting rights can themselves violate the constitutional rights of white voters.

Justice **O'Connor** delivered the opinion of the Court, saying in part:

As a result of the 1990 census, North Carolina became entitled to a twelfth seat in the United States House of Representatives. The General Assembly enacted a reapportionment plan that included one majority-black congressional district. After the Attorney General of the United States objected to the plan, the General Assembly passed new legislation creating a second majority-black district. Appellants allege that the revised plan, which contains district boundary lines of dramatically irregular shape, constitutes an unconstitutional racial gerrymander. The question before us is whether appellants have stated a cognizable claim.

I.

The voting age population of North Carolina is approximately ... 20% black. ... The black population is relatively dispersed; blacks constitute a majority of the general population in only 5 of the State's 100 counties. The largest concentrations of black citizens live in the Coastal Plain, primarily in the northern part. ...

The first of the two majority-black districts contained in the revised plan, District 1, is somewhat hook shaped. Centered in the northeast portion of the State, it moves southward until it tapers to a narrow band; then, with finger-like extensions, it reaches far into the southern-most part of the State near the South Carolina border. District 1 has been compared to a "Rorschach inkblot test," and a "bug splattered on a windshield."

The second majority-black district, District 12, is even more unusually shaped. It is approximately 160 miles long and, for much of its length, no wider than the I-85 corridor. It winds in snake-like fashion through tobacco country, financial centers, and manufacturing areas "until it gobbles in enough enclaves of black neighborhoods." ... One state legislator has remarked that " '[i]f you drove down the interstate with both car doors open, you'd kill most of the people in the district.' " ...

... Appellants are five residents of Durham County, North Carolina, all registered to vote in that county. [They] alleged not that the revised plan constituted a political gerrymander, nor that it violated the "one person, one vote" principle, but that the State had created an unconstitutional racial gerrymander.

Appellants ... alleged that the General Assembly deliberately "create[d] two Congressional Districts in which a majority of black voters was concentrated arbitrarily—without regard to any other considerations, such as compactness, contiguousness, geographical boundaries, or political subdivisions," with the purpose "to cre-ate Congressional Districts along racial lines" and to assure the election of two black representatives to Congress. ...

II.

A.

"The right to vote freely for the candidate of one's choice is of the essence of a democratic society . . . ." Reynolds v. Sims [1964]. For much of our Nation's history, that right sadly has been denied to many because of race. The Fifteenth Amendment, ratified in 1870 after a bloody Civil War, promised unequivocally that "[t]he right of citizens of the United States to vote" no longer would be "denied or abridged . . . by any State on account of race, color, or previous condition of servitude."

But "[a] number of states . . . refused to take no for an answer and continued to circumvent the Fifteenth Amendment's prohibition through the use of both subtle and blunt instruments, perpetuating ugly patterns of pervasive racial discrimination." Ostensibly race-neutral devices such as literacy tests with "grandfather" clauses and "good character" provisos were devised to deprive black voters of the franchise. Another of the weapons in the States' arsenal was the racial gerrymander—"the deliberate and arbitrary distortion of district boundaries . . . for [racial] purposes." ... In the 1870s, for example, opponents of Reconstruction in Mississippi "concentrated the bulk of the black population in a 'shoestring' Congressional district running the length of the Mississippi River, leaving five others with white majorities." ... Some 90 years later, Alabama redefined the boundaries of the city of Tuskegee "from a square to an uncouth twenty-eight-sided figure" in a manner that was alleged to exclude black voters, and only black voters, from the city limits. Gomillion v. Lightfoot (1960).

... Congress enacted the Voting Rights Act of 1965 as a dramatic and severe response to the situation. The Act proved immediately successful in ensuring racial minorities access to the voting booth. ...

But it soon became apparent that guaranteeing equal access to the polls would not suffice to root out other racially discriminatory voting practices. ... Drawing on the "one person, one vote" principle, this Court recognized that "[t]he right to vote can be affected by a dilution of voting power as well as by an absolute prohibition on casting a ballot." Where members of a racial minority group vote as a cohesive unit, practices such as multimember or at-large electoral systems can reduce or nullify minority voters' ability, as a group, "to elect the candidate of their choice." Accordingly, the Court held that such schemes violate the Fourteenth Amendment when they are adopted with a discriminatory purpose and have the effect of diluting minority voting strength. ... Congress, too, responded to the problem of vote dilution. In 1982, it amended §2 of the Voting Rights Act to prohibit legislation that *results* in the dilution of a minority group's voting strength, regardless of the legislature's intent. . . .

B.

It is against this background that we confront the questions presented here. . . . Our focus is on appellants' claim that the State engaged in unconstitutional racial gerrymandering. That argument strikes a powerful historical chord: It is unsettling how closely the North Carolina plan resembles the most egregious racial gerrymanders of the past.

An understanding of the nature of appellants' claim is critical to our resolution of the case. In their complaint, appellants did not claim that the General Assembly's reapportionment plan unconstitutionally "diluted" white voting strength. They did not even claim to be white. Rather, appellants' complaint alleged that the deliberate segregation of voters into separate districts on the basis of race violated their constitutional right to participate in a "color-blind" electoral process. [A]ppellants appear to concede that race-conscious redistricting is not always unconstitutional. What appellants object to is redistricting legislation that is so extremely irregular on its face that it rationally can be viewed only as an effort to segregate the races for purposes of voting, without regard for traditional districting principles and without sufficiently compelling justification. For the reasons that follow, we conclude that appellants have stated a claim upon which relief can be granted under the Equal Protection Clause.

III.

A.

The Equal Protection Clause provides that "[n]o State shall . . . deny to any person within its jurisdiction the equal protection of the laws." Its central purpose is to prevent the States from purposefully discriminating between individuals on the basis of race. . . .

These principles apply not only to legislation that contains explicit racial distinctions, but also to those "rare" statutes that, although race-neutral, are, on their face, "unexplainable on grounds other than race." . . .

B.

Appellants contend that redistricting legislation that is so bizarre on its face that it is "unexplainable on grounds other than race" demands the same close scrutiny that we give other state laws that classify citizens by race. Our voting rights precedents support that conclusion. In Guinn v. United States (1914) the Court invalidated under the Fifteenth Amendment a statute that imposed a literacy requirement on voters but contained a "grandfather clause" applicable to individuals and their lineal descendants entitled to vote "on [or prior to] January 1, 1866." [T]he statute was invalid because, on its

face, it could not be explained on grounds other than race.

The Court applied the same reasoning to the "uncouth twenty-eight-sided" municipal boundary line at issue in Gomillion. . . .

. . . Gomillion, in which a tortured municipal boundary line was drawn to exclude black voters, was such a case. So, too, would be a case in which a State concentrated a dispersed minority population in a single district by disregarding traditional districting principles such as compactness, contiguity, and respect for political subdivisions. We emphasize that these criteria are important not because they are constitutionally required—they are not—but because they are objective factors that may serve to defeat a claim that a district has been gerrymandered on racial lines. . . .

. . . Reapportionment is one area in which appearances do matter. A reapportionment plan that includes in one district individuals who belong to the same race, but who are otherwise widely separated by geographical and political boundaries, and who may have little in common with one another but the color of their skin, bears an uncomfortable resemblance to political apartheid. It reinforces the perception that members of the same racial group—regardless of their age, education, economic status, or the community in which the live—think alike, share the same political interests, and will prefer the same candidates at the polls. We have rejected such perceptions elsewhere as impermissible racial stereotypes. . . .

. . . We conclude that a plaintiff challenging a reapportionment statute under the Equal Protection Clause may state a claim by alleging that the legislation, though race-neutral on its face, rationally cannot be understood as anything other than an effort to separate voters into different districts on the basis of race, and that the separation lacks sufficient justification. . . .

C.

The dissenters consider the circumstances of this case "functionally indistinguishable" from multimember districting and at-large voting systems, which are loosely described as "other varieties of gerrymandering." We have considered the constitutionality of these practices and have required plaintiffs to demonstrate that the challenged practice has the purpose and effect of diluting a racial group's voting strength. . . . At-large and multimember schemes, however, do not classify voters on the basis of race. . . .

Justice Souter apparently believes that racial gerrymandering is harmless unless it dilutes a racial group's voting strength. As we have explained, however, reapportionment legislation that cannot be understood as anything other than an effort to classify and separate voters by race injures voters in other ways. It reinforces racial stereotypes and threatens to undermine our system of representative democracy by signaling to elected officials that they represent a particular racial group rather than their constituency as a whole. Justice Souter does not adequately explain why these harms are not cognizable under the Fourteenth Amendment.

The dissenters make two other arguments that cannot be reconciled with our precedents. First, they suggest that a racial gerrymander is functionally equivalent to gerrymanders for nonracial purposes, such as political gerrymanders. This Court has held political gerrymanders to be justiciable under the Equal Protection Clause. ... But nothing in our case law compels the conclusion that racial and political gerrymanders are subject to precisely the same constitutional scrutiny. In fact, our country's long and persistent history of racial discrimination in voting—as well as our Fourteenth Amendment jurisprudence, which always has reserved the strictest scrutiny for discrimination on the basis of race, would seem to compel the opposite conclusion.

Second, Justice Stevens argues that racial gerrymandering poses no constitutional difficulties when district lines are drawn to favor the minority, rather than the majority. We have made clear, however, that equal protection analysis "is not dependent on the race of those burdened or benefited by a particular classification." [Richmond v.] Croson [1989]. ... Indeed, racial classifications receive close scrutiny even when they may be said to burden or benefit the races equally. ...

Finally, nothing in the Court's highly fractured decision in [United Jewish Organizations v. Carey (1977)]— ... which the dissenters evidently believe controls—forecloses the claim we recognize today. ...

... UJO's framework simply does not apply where, as here, a reapportionment plan is alleged to be so irrational on its face that it immediately offends principles of racial equality. UJO set forth a standard under which white voters can establish unconstitutional vote dilution. But it did not purport to overrule Gomillion or Wright. Nothing in the decision precludes white voters (or voters of any other race) from bringing the analytically distinct claim that a reapportionment plan rationally cannot be understood as anything other than an effort to segregate citizens into separate voting districts on the basis of race without sufficient justification. ...

IV.

Justice Souter contends that exacting scrutiny of racial gerrymanders under the Fourteenth Amendment is inappropriate because reapportionment "nearly always require[s] some consideration of race for legitimate reasons." "As long as members of racial groups have [a] commonality of interest" and "racial bloc voting takes place," he argues, "legislators will have to take race into account" in order to comply with the Voting Rights Act. Justice Souter's reasoning is flawed.

Earlier this Term, we unanimously reaffirmed that racial bloc voting and minority-group political cohesion never can be assumed, but specifically must be proved in each case. ... That racial bloc voting or minority political cohesion may be found to exist in *some* cases is no reason to treat *all* racial gerrymanders differently from other kinds of racial classification. Justice Souter apparently views racial gerrymandering of the type presented here as a special category of "benign" racial discrimination that should be subject to relaxed judicial review. ... The very reason that the Equal Protection Clause demands strict scrutiny of all racial classifications is because without it, a court cannot determine whether or not the discrimination truly is "benign." ...

V.

Racial classifications of any sort pose the risk of lasting harm to our society. They reinforce the belief, held by too many for too much of our history, that individuals should be judged by the color of their skin. Racial classifications with respect to voting carry particular dangers. Racial gerrymandering, even for remedial purposes, threatens to carry us further from the goal of a political system in which race no longer matters. It is for these reasons that race-based districting by our state legislatures demands close judicial scrutiny. ...

Justice **White,** with whom Justice **Blackmun** and Justice **Stevens** join, dissenting, said in part:

The facts of this case mirror those presented in United Jewish Organizations of Williamsburgh, Inc. v. Carey (1977) (UJO), where the Court rejected a claim that creation of a majority-minority district violated the Constitution. ... Five of the Justices reasoned that members of the white majority could not plausibly argue that their influence over the political process had been unfairly cancelled ... or that such had been the State's intent. Accordingly, they held that plaintiffs were not entitled to relief under the Constitution's Equal Protection Clause. On the same reasoning, I would affirm the district court's dismissal of appellants' claim in this instance.

The Court today chooses not to overrule UJO, focusing on surface differences, most notably the (admittedly unusual) shape of the newly created district, and imagining an entirely new cause of action. ... The notion that North Carolina's plan, under which whites remain a voting majority in a disproportionate number of congressional districts, and pursuant to which the State has sent its *first* black representatives since Reconstruction to the United States Congress, might have violated appellants' constitutional rights is both a fiction and a departure from settled equal protection principles. Seeing no good reason to engage in either, I dissent.

I.

A.

The grounds for my disagreement with the majority are simply stated: Appellants have not presented a cognizable claim, because they have not alleged a cognizable injury. To date, we have held that only two types of state voting practices could give rise to a constitutional claim. The first involves direct and outright deprivation of the right to vote, for example by means of a poll tax or literacy test. See, e.g., Guinn v. United States (1915). Plainly, this variety is not implicated by appellants' allegations and need not detain us further. The second type of unconstitutional practice is that which "affects the political strength of various groups" ... in violation of the Equal Protection Clause. As for this latter category, we have insisted that members of the political or racial group demonstrate that the challenged action have the intent and effect of unduly diminishing their influence on the political process. Although this severe burden has limited the number of successful suits, it was adopted for sound reasons.

The central explanation has to do with the nature of the redistricting process. As the majority recognizes, "redistricting differs from other kinds of state decision-making in that the legislature always is *aware* of race when it draws district lines, just as it is aware of age, economic status, religious and political persuasion, and a variety of other demographic factors." "Being aware," in this context, is shorthand for "taking into account," and it hardly can be doubted that legislators routinely engage in the business of making electoral predictions based on group characteristics—racial, ethnic, and the like. . . .

As we have said, "it requires no special genius to recognize the political consequences of drawing a district line along one street rather than another." . . . Because extirpating such considerations from the redistricting process is unrealistic, the Court has not invalidated all plans that consciously use race, but rather has looked at their impact.

Redistricting plans also reflect group interests and inevitably are conceived with partisan aims in mind. . . . Moreover, a group's power to affect the political process does not automatically dissipate by virtue of an electoral loss. Accordingly, we have asked that an identifiable group demonstrate more than mere lack of success at the polls to make out a successful gerrymandering claim. . . .

With these considerations in mind, we have limited such claims by insisting upon a showing that "the political processes . . . were not equally open to participation by the group in question—that its members had less opportunity than did other residents in the district to participate in the political processes and to elect legislators of their choice." Indeed, as a brief survey of decisions illustrates, the Court's gerrymandering cases all carry this theme—that it is not mere suffering at the polls but discrimination in the polity with which the Constitution is concerned. . . .

. . . The question in gerrymandering cases is "whether a particular group has been unconstitutionally denied its chance to effectively influence the political process." Thus, "an equal protection violation may be found only where the electoral system *substantially disadvantages certain voters in their opportunity to influence the political process effectively*." (emphasis added). By this, I meant that the group must exhibit "strong in-

dicia of lack of political power and the denial of fair representation," so that it could be said that it has "essentially been shut out of the political process." . . .

To distinguish a claim that alleges that the redistricting scheme has discriminatory intent and effect from one that does not has nothing to do with dividing racial classifications between the "benign" and the malicious—an enterprise which, as the majority notes, the Court has treated with skepticism. Rather, the issue is whether the classification based on race discriminates against *anyone* by denying equal access to the political process. Even members of the Court least inclined to approve of race-based remedial measures have acknowledged the significance of this factor. . . .

B.

The most compelling evidence of the Court's position prior to this day, for it is most directly on point, is UJO. The Court characterizes the decision as "highly fractured," but that should not detract attention from the rejection by a majority in UJO of the claim that the State's intentional creation of majority-minority districts transgressed constitutional norms. As stated above, five Justices were of the view that, absent any contention that the proposed plan was adopted with the intent, or had the effect, of unduly minimizing the white majority's voting strength, the Fourteenth Amendment was not implicated. . . .

. . . It is irrefutable that appellants in this proceeding have failed to state a claim. As was the case in New York, a number of North Carolina's political subdivisions have interfered with black citizens' meaningful exercise of the franchise, and are therefore subject to §§ 4 and 5 of the Voting Rights Act. . . .

In light of this background, it strains credulity to suggest that North Carolina's purpose in creating a second majority-minority district was to discriminate against members of the majority group by "impair[ing] or burden[ing their] opportunity . . . to participate in the political process." . . . There is no question that appellants have not alleged the requisite discriminatory effects. Whites constitute roughly 76 percent of the total population and 79 percent of the voting age population in North Carolina. Yet, under the State's plan, they still constitute a voting majority in 10 (or 83 percent) of the 12 congressional districts. Though they might be dissatisfied at the prospect of casting a vote for a losing candidate—a lot shared by many, including a disproportionate number of minority voters—surely they cannot complain of discriminatory treatment.

II.

The majority attempts to distinguish UJO by imagining a heretofore unknown type of constitutional claim. In its words, "UJO set forth a standard under which white voters can establish unconstitutional vote dilution. . . . Nothing in the decision precludes white voters (or voters of any other race) from bringing the analytically distinct claim that a reapportionment plan rationally cannot be understood as anything other than an effort to segregate citizens into separate voting districts on the basis of race without sufficient justification.'' There is no support for this distinction in UJO, and no authority in the cases relied on by the Court either. More importantly, the majority's submission does not withstand analysis. The logic of its theory appears to be that race-conscious redistricting that ''segregates'' by drawing odd-shaped lines is qualitatively different from race-conscious redistricting that affects groups in some other way. The distinction is without foundation.

A.

The essence of the majority's argument is that UJO dealt with a claim of vote dilution—which required a specific showing of harm—and that cases such as Gomillion v. Lightfoot (1960) . . . dealt with claims of racial segregation—which did not. I read these decisions quite differently. Petitioners' claim in UJO was that the State had ''violated the Fourteenth and Fifteenth Amendments by deliberately revising its reapportionment plan along racial lines.'' . . . In other words, the ''analytically distinct claim'' the majority discovers today was in plain view and did not carry the day for petitioners. The fact that a demonstration of discriminatory effect was required in that case was not a function of the kind of claim that was made. It was a function of the type of injury upon which the Court insisted. . . .

B.

Lacking support in any of the Court's precedents, the majority's novel type of claim also makes no sense. As I understand the theory that is put forth, a redistricting plan that uses race to ''segregate'' voters by drawing ''uncouth'' lines is harmful in a way that a plan that uses race to distribute voters differently is not, for the former ''bears an uncomfortable resemblance to political apartheid.'' The distinction is untenable.

Racial gerrymanders come in various shades: At-large voting schemes . . .; the fragmentation of a minority group among various districts ''so that it is a majority in none,'' . . . ; the ''stacking'' of ''a large minority population concentration . . . with a larger white population'' . . . ; and, finally, the ''concentration of [minority voters] into districts where they constitute an excessive majority.'' . . . In each instance, race is consciously utilized by the legislature for electoral purposes; in each instance, we have put the plaintiff challenging the district lines to the burden of demonstrating that the plan was meant to, and did in fact, exclude an identifiable racial group from participation in the political process.

Not so, apparently, when the districting ''segregates'' by drawing odd-shaped lines. In that case, we are told, such proof no longer is needed. Instead, it is the State that must rebut the allegation that race was taken into account, a fact that, together with the legislators' consideration of ethnic, religious, and other group characteristics, I had thought we practically took for granted. . . .

The other part of the majority's explanation of its holding is related to its simultaneous discomfort and fascination with irregularly shaped districts. Lack of compactness or contiguity, like uncouth district lines, certainly is a helpful indicator that some form of gerrymandering (racial or other) might have taken place and that ''something may be amiss.'' . . .

But while district irregularities may provide strong indicia of a potential gerrymander . . . they have no bearing on whether the plan ultimately is found to violate the Constitution. . . . The majority's contrary view is perplexing in light of its concession that ''compactness or attractiveness has never been held to constitute an independent federal constitutional requirement for state legislative districts.'' It is shortsighted as well, for a regularly shaped district can just as effectively effectuate racially discriminatory gerrymandering as an odd-shaped one. By focusing on looks rather than impact, the majority ''immediately casts attention in the wrong direction—toward superficialities of shape and size, rather than toward the political realities of district composition.'' . . .

IV.

Since I do not agree that petitioners alleged an Equal Protection violation and because the Court of Appeals faithfully followed the Court's prior cases, I dissent and would affirm the judgment below.

Justice **Blackmun**, dissenting, said in part:

I join Justice White's dissenting opinion. I did not join Part IV of his opinion in United Jewish Organizations v. Carey (1977), because I felt that its ''additional argument'' was not necessary to decide that case. I nevertheless agree that the conscious use of race in redistricting does not violate the Equal Protection Clause unless the effect of the redistricting plan is to deny a particular group equal access to the political process or to minimize its voting strength unduly. . . . It is particularly ironic that the case in which today's majority chooses to abandon settled law and to recognize for the first time this ''analytically distinct'' constitutional claim, is a challenge by white voters to the plan under which North Carolina has sent black representatives to Congress for the first time since Reconstruction. I dissent.

Justice **Stevens**, dissenting, said in part:

For the reasons stated by Justice White, the decision of the District Court should be affirmed. I add these comments to emphasize that the two critical facts in this case are undisputed: First, the shape of District 12 is so bizarre that it must have been drawn for the purpose of either advantaging or disadvantaging a cognizable group of voters; and, second, regardless of that shape, it was drawn for the purpose of facilitating the election of a second black representative from North Carolina.

These unarguable facts, which the Court devotes most of its opinion to proving, give rise to three constitutional questions: Does the Constitution impose a requirement of contiguity or compactness on how the States may draw their electoral districts? Does the Equal Protection Clause prevent a State from drawing district boundaries for the purpose of facilitating the election of a member of an identifiable group of voters? And, finally, if the answer to the second question is generally "No," should it be different when the favored group is defined by race? Since I have already written at length about these questions, my negative answer to each can be briefly explained.

The first question is easy. There is no independent constitutional requirement of compactness or contiguity, and the Court's opinion . . . does not suggest otherwise. . . .

As for the second question, I believe that the Equal Protection Clause is violated when the State creates the kind of uncouth district boundaries seen in . . . Gomillion v. Lightfoot (1960), and this case, for the sole purpose of making it more difficult for members of a minority group to win an election. The duty to govern impartially is abused when a group with power over the electoral process defines electoral boundaries solely to enhance its own political strength at the expense of any weaker group. That duty, however, is not violated when the majority acts to facilitate the election of a member of a group that lacks such power because it remains underrepresented in the state legislature. . . . The difference between constitutional and unconstitutional gerrymanders has nothing to do with whether they are based on assumptions about the groups they affect, but whether their purpose is to enhance the power of the group in control of the districting process at the expense of any minority group, and thereby to strengthen the unequal distribution of electoral power. . . .

Finally, we must ask whether otherwise permissible redistricting to benefit an underrepresented minority group becomes impermissible when the minority group is defined by its race. The Court today answers this question in the affirmative, and its answer is wrong. If it is permissible to draw boundaries to provide adequate representation for rural voters, for union members, for Hasidic Jews, for Polish Americans, or for Republicans, it necessarily follows that it is permissible to do the same thing for members of the very minority group whose history in the United States gave birth to the Equal Protection Clause. A contrary conclusion could only be described as perverse.

Accordingly, I respectfully dissent.

Justice **Souter**, dissenting, said in part:

Today, the Court recognizes a new cause of action under which a State's electoral redistricting plan that includes a configuration "so bizarre" that it "rationally cannot be understood as anything other than an effort to separate voters into different districts on the basis of race [without] sufficient justification," will be subjected to strict scrutiny. In my view there is no justification for the Court's determination to depart from our prior decisions by carving out this narrow group of cases for strict scrutiny in place of the review customarily applied in cases dealing with discrimination in electoral districting on the basis of race.

I.

. . . Unlike other contexts in which we have addressed the State's conscious use of race . . . , electoral districting calls for decisions that nearly always require some consideration of race for legitimate reasons where there is a racially mixed population. As long as members of racial groups have the commonality of interest implicit in our ability to talk about concepts like "minority voting strength," and "dilution of minority votes," . . . and as long as racial bloc voting takes place, legislators will have to take race into account in order to avoid dilution of minority voting strength in the districting plans they adopt. One need look no further than the Voting Rights Act to understand that this may be required, and we have held that race may constitutionally be taken into account in order to comply with that Act. . . .

A second distinction between districting and most other governmental decisions in which race has figured is that those other decisions using racial criteria characteristically occur in circumstances in which the use of race to the advantage of one person is necessarily at the obvious expense of a member of a different race. See Richmond v. [Croson] (1989). . . .

In districting, by contrast, the mere placement of an individual in one district instead of another denies no one a right or benefit provided to others. All citizens may register, vote, and be represented. . . . One's constitutional rights are not violated merely because the candidate one supports loses the election or because a group (including a racial group) to which one belongs winds up with a representative from outside that group. . . . "Dilution" thus refers to the effects of districting decisions not on an individual's political power viewed in isolation, but on the political power of a group. This is the reason that the placement of given voters in a given district, even on the basis of race, does not, without more, diminish the effectiveness of the individual as a voter.

II.

Our different approaches to equal protection in electoral districting and nondistricting cases reflect these differences. There is a characteristic coincidence of disadvantageous effect and illegitimate purpose associated with the State's use of race in those situations. . . . Presumably because the legitimate consideration of race in a districting decision is usually inevitable under the Voting Rights Act when communities are racially mixed, however, and because, without more, it does not result in diminished political effectiveness for anyone, we have not taken the approach of applying the usual standard of such heightened "scrutiny" to race-based districting decisions. . . . Under our cases there is in general a requirement that in order to obtain relief under the Fourteenth Amendment, the purpose and effect of the districting must be to devalue the effectiveness of a voter compared to what, as a group member, he would otherwise be able to enjoy. . . .

A consequence of this categorical approach is the absence of any need for further searching "scrutiny" once it has been shown that a given districting decision has a purpose and effect falling within one of those categories. If a cognizable harm like dilution or the abridgment of the right to participate in the electoral process is shown, the districting plan violates the Fourteenth Amendment. If not, it does not. . . .

III.

The Court appears to accept this, and it does not purport to disturb the law of vote dilution in any way. Instead, the Court creates a new "analytically distinct" cause of action, the principal element of which is that a districting plan be "so bizarre on its face," or "irrational on its face," or "extremely irregular on its face," that it "rationally cannot be understood as anything other than an effort to segregate citizens into separate voting districts on the basis of race without sufficient justification." Pleading such an element, the Court holds, suffices without a further allegation of harm, to state a claim upon which relief can be granted under the Fourteenth Amendment. . . .

The Court offers no adequate justification for treating the narrow category of bizarrely shaped district claims differently from other districting claims. The only justification I can imagine would be the preservation of "sound districting principles," such as compactness and contiguity. But . . . we have held that such principles are not constitutionally required. . . . Since there is no justification for the departure here from the principles that continue to govern electoral districting cases generally in accordance with our prior decisions, I would not respond to the seeming egregiousness of the redistricting now before us by untethering the concept of racial gerrymander in such a case from the concept of harm exemplified by dilution. In the absence of an allegation of such harm, I would affirm the judgment of the District Court. I respectfully dissent.

WISCONSIN v. MITCHELL

124 L. Ed. 2d 436 (1993)

In R. A. V. v. St. Paul (1992) the Court invalidated a state law that prohibited the display of symbols known to cause fear or anger in others because of their race, re-ligion or gender. The novel part of the Court's reasoning in that case was the claim that the law was unconstitutional because it was underinclusive. While the Court unanimously held the statute void, the reasoning of the majority that a state can only punish some fighting words if it punishes all fighting words—that it cannot forbid only fighting words it finds particularly harmful— threatens to undermine the very essence of the First Amendment that speech is to be free of state control. R. A. V.'s reasoning suggests that the First Amendment conveys a message of equal treatment: speech may not be prohibited on the basis of content, but it may be prohibited altogether.

Not surprisingly, the doctrinal novelty of R. A. V. was not what caught the nation's attention. The popular press concentrated instead on whether R. A. V. meant that the Court would strike down all laws aimed at combatting the special threat posed by racially motivated attacks. More common than the ordinance struck down in R. A. V. are those, like that challenged in the case below, which increase the penalties for crimes motivated by racial or religious hatred or the gender of the victim.

> Query: *On what basis does the Court distinguish R. A. V.? Does the law here suffer from the same underinclusive problem as the law in R. A. V.? If so, does this case signal a retreat from R. A. V. more novel reasoning?*

Chief Justice **Rehnquist** delivered the opinion of the Court, saying in part:

Respondent Todd Mitchell's sentence for aggravated battery was enhanced because he intentionally selected his victim on account of the victim's race. The question presented in this case is whether this penalty enhancement is prohibited by the First and Fourteenth Amendments. We hold that it is not.

On the evening of October 7, 1989, a group of young black men and boys, including Mitchell, gathered at an apartment complex in Kenosha, Wisconsin. Several members of the group discussed a scene from the motion picture "Mississippi Burning," in which a white man beat a young black boy who was praying. The group moved outside and Mitchell asked them: " 'Do you all feel hyped up to move on some white people?' " Shortly thereafter, a young white boy approached the group on the opposite side of the street where they were standing. As the boy walked by, Mitchell said: " 'You all want to fuck somebody up? There goes a white boy; go get him.' " Mitchell counted to three and pointed in the boy's direction. The group ran towards the boy, beat him severely, and stole his tennis shoes. The boy was rendered unconscious and remained in a coma for four days.

After a jury trial in the Circuit Court for Kenosha County, Mitchell was convicted of aggravated battery. That offense ordinarily carries a maximum sentence of two years' imprisonment. But because the jury found that Mitchell had intentionally selected his victim because of the boy's race, the maximum sentence for

Mitchell's offense was increased to seven years under § 939.645. That provision enhances the maximum penalty for an offense whenever the defendant "intentionally selects the person against whom the crime . . . is committed . . . because of the race, religion, color, disability, sexual orientation, national origin or ancestry of that person. . . ." The Circuit Court sentenced Mitchell to four years' imprisonment for the aggravated battery.

Mitchell unsuccessfully sought postconviction relief in the Circuit Court. Then he appealed his conviction and sentence, challenging the constitutionality of Wisconsin's penalty-enhancement provision on First Amendment grounds. The Wisconsin Court of Appeals rejected Mitchell's challenge, but the Wisconsin Supreme Court reversed. The Supreme Court held that the statute "violates the First Amendment directly by punishing what the legislature has deemed to be offensive thought." It rejected the State's contention "that the statute punishes only the 'conduct' of intentional selection of a victim." According to the court, "the statute punishes the 'because of' aspect of the defendant's selection, the *reason* the defendant selected the victim, the motive behind the selection." (emphasis in original). And under R. A. V. v. St. Paul (1992), "the Wisconsin legislature cannot criminalize bigoted thought with which it disagrees."

The Supreme Court also held that the penalty-enhancement statute was unconstitutionally overbroad. It reasoned that, in order to prove that a defendant intentionally selected his victim because of the victim's protected status, the State would often have to introduce evidence of the defendant's prior speech, such as racial epithets he may have uttered before the commission of the offense. This evidentiary use of protected speech, the court thought, would have a "chilling effect" on those who feared the possibility of prosecution for offenses subject to penalty enhancement. Finally, the court distinguished antidiscrimination laws, which have long been held constitutional, on the ground that the Wisconsin statute punishes the "subjective mental process" of selecting a victim because of his protected status, whereas antidiscrimination laws prohibit "objective acts of discrimination."

We granted certiorari because of the importance of the question presented and the existence of a conflict of authority among state high courts on the constitutionality of statutes similar to Wisconsin's penalty-enhancement provision. We reverse.

Mitchell argues that we are bound by the Wisconsin Supreme Court's conclusion that the statute punishes bigoted thought and not conduct. There is no doubt that we are bound by a state court's construction of a state statute. R. A. V.; . . . Terminiello v. Chicago (1949). In Terminiello, for example, the Illinois courts had defined the term " 'breach of the peace,' " in a city ordinance prohibiting disorderly conduct, to include " 'stirs the public to anger . . . or creates a disturbance.' " We held this construction to be binding on us. But here the Wisconsin Supreme Court did not, strictly speaking, construe the Wisconsin statute in the sense of defining the

meaning of a particular statutory word or phrase. Rather, it merely characterized the "practical effect" of the statute for First Amendment purposes. ("Merely because the statute refers in a literal sense to the intentional 'conduct' of selecting, does not mean the court must turn a blind eye to the intent and practical effect of the law— punishment of motive or thought"). This assessment does not bind us. Once any ambiguities as to the meaning of the statute are resolved, we may form our own judgment as to its operative effect.

The State argues that the statute does not punish bigoted thought, as the Supreme Court of Wisconsin said, but instead punishes only conduct. While this argument is literally correct, it does not dispose of Mitchell's First Amendment challenge. To be sure, our cases reject the "view that an apparently limitless variety of conduct can be labeled 'speech' whenever the person engaging in the conduct intends thereby to express an idea." United States v. O'Brien (1968); . . . Cox v. Louisiana (1956). Thus, a physical assault is not by any stretch of the imagination expressive conduct protected by the First Amendment. See Roberts v. United States Jaycees (1984) ("Violence or other types of potentially expressive activities that produce special harms distinct from their communicative impact . . . are entitled to no constitutional protection"). . . .

But the fact remains that under the Wisconsin statute the same criminal conduct may be more heavily punished if the victim is selected because of his race or other protected status than if no such motive obtained. Thus, although the statute punishes criminal conduct, it enhances the maximum penalty for conduct motivated by a discriminatory point of view more severely than the same conduct engaged in for some other reason or for no reason at all. Because the only reason for the enhancement is the defendant's discriminatory motive for selecting his victim, Mitchell argues (and the Wisconsin Supreme Court held) that the statute violates the First Amendment by punishing offenders' bigoted beliefs.

Traditionally, sentencing judges have considered a wide variety of factors in addition to evidence bearing on guilt in determining what sentence to impose on a convicted defendant. . . . Williams v. New York (1949). The defendant's motive for committing the offense is one important factor. See 1 W. LeFave & A. Scott, Substantive Criminal Law §3.6(b), p. 324 (1986) ("Motives are most relevant when the trial judge sets the defendant's sentence, and it is not uncommon for a defendant to receive a minimum sentence because he was acting with good motives, or a rather high sentence because of his bad motives"); cf. Tison v. Arizona (1987) ("Deeply ingrained in our legal tradition is the idea that the more purposeful is the criminal conduct, the more serious is the offense, and, therefore, the more severely it ought to be punished"). Thus, in many States the commission of a murder, or other capital offense, for pecuniary gain is a separate aggravating circumstance under the capital-sentencing statute.

But it is equally true that a defendant's abstract beliefs, however obnoxious to most people, may not be taken into consideration by a sentencing judge. Dawson v. Delaware (1992). In Dawson, the State introduced evidence at a capital-sentencing hearing that the defendant was a member of a white supremacist prison gang. Because "the evidence proved nothing more than [the defendant's] abstract beliefs," we held that its admission violated the defendant's First Amendment rights. In so holding, however, we emphasized that "the Constitution does not erect a per se barrier to the admission of evidence concerning one's beliefs and associations at sentencing simply because those beliefs and associations are protected by the First Amendment." Thus, in Barclay v. Florida (1983) (plurality opinion), we allowed the sentencing judge to take into account the defendant's racial animus towards his victim. The evidence in that case showed that the defendant's membership in the Black Liberation Army and desire to provoke a "race war" were related to the murder of a white man for which he was convicted. Because "the elements of racial hatred in [the] murder" were relevant to several aggravating factors, we held that the trial judge permissibly took this evidence into account in sentencing the defendant to death.

Mitchell suggests that Dawson and Barclay are inapposite because they did not involve application of a penalty-enhancement provision. But in Barclay we held that it was permissible for the sentencing court to consider the defendant's racial animus in determining whether he should be sentenced to death, surely the most severe "enhancement" of all. And the fact that the Wisconsin Legislature has decided, as a general matter, that bias-motivated offenses warrant greater maximum penalties across the board does not alter the result here. For the primary responsibility for fixing criminal penalties lies with the legislature. Rummel v. Estelle (1980). . . .

Mitchell argues that the Wisconsin penalty-enhancement statute is invalid because it punishes the defendant's discriminatory motive, or reason, for acting. But motive plays the same role under the Wisconsin statute as it does under federal and state antidiscrimination laws, which we have previously upheld against constitutional challenge. See Roberts v. Jaycees [1984]. Title VII, for example, makes it unlawful for an employer to discriminate against an employee "*because* of such individual's race, color, religion, sex, or national origin." (emphasis added). . . .

Nothing in our decision last Term in R. A. V. compels a different result here. That case involved a First Amendment challenge to a municipal ordinance prohibiting the use of " 'fighting words' that insult, or provoke violence, 'on the basis of race, color, creed, religion or gender.' " Because the ordinance only proscribed a class of "fighting words" deemed particularly offensive by the city—i.e., those "that contain . . . messages of 'bias-motivated' hatred,"—we held that it violated the rule against content-based discrimination. But whereas the ordinance struck down in R. A. V. was explicitly directed at expression (i.e., "speech" or "messages," the statute in this case is aimed at conduct unprotected by the First Amendment.

Moreover, the Wisconsin statute singles out for enhancement bias-inspired conduct because this conduct is thought to inflict greater individual and societal harm. For example, according to the State and its amici, bias-motivated crimes are more likely to provoke retaliatory crimes, inflict distinct emotional harms on their victims, and incite community unrest. The State's desire to redress these perceived harms provides an adequate explanation for its penalty-enhancement provision over and above mere disagreement with offenders' beliefs or biases. As Blackstone said long ago, "it is but reasonable that among crimes of different natures those should be most severely punished, which are the most destructive of the public safety and happiness."

Finally, there remains to be considered Mitchell's argument that the Wisconsin statute is unconstitutionally overbroad because of its "chilling effect" on free speech. Mitchell argues (and the Wisconsin Supreme Court agreed) that the statute is "overbroad" because evidence of the defendant's prior speech or associations may be used to prove that the defendant intentionally selected his victim on account of the victim's protected status. Consequently, the argument goes, the statute impermissibly chills free expression with respect to such matters by those concerned about the possibility of enhanced sentences if they should in the future commit a criminal offense covered by the statute. We find no merit in this contention.

The sort of chill envisioned here is far more attenuated and unlikely than that contemplated in traditional "overbreadth" cases. We must conjure up a vision of a Wisconsin citizen suppressing his unpopular bigoted opinions for fear that if he later commits an offense covered by the statute, these opinions will be offered at trial to establish that he selected his victim on account of the victim's protected status, thus qualifying him for penalty-enhancement. To stay within the realm of rationality, we must surely put to one side minor misdemeanor offenses covered by the statute, such as negligent operation of a motor vehicle; for it is difficult, if not impossible, to conceive of a situation where such offenses would be racially motivated. We are left, then, with the prospect of a citizen suppressing his bigoted beliefs for fear that evidence of such beliefs will be introduced against him at trial if he commits a more serious offense against person or property. This is simply too speculative a hypothesis to support Mitchell's overbreadth claim.

The First Amendment, moreover, does not prohibit the evidentiary use of speech to establish the elements of a crime or to prove motive or intent. Evidence of a defendant's previous declarations or statements is commonly admitted in criminal trials subject to evidentiary rules dealing with relevancy, reliability, and the like. Nearly half a century ago, in Haupt v. United States (1947), we rejected a contention similar to that advanced by Mitchell here. Haupt was tried for the offense of treason, which, as defined by the Constitution (Art. III, § 3), may depend very much on proof of motive. To prove that the acts in question were committed out of "adherence to the enemy'' rather than ''parental solicitude,'' the Government introduced evidence of conversations that had taken place long prior to the indictment, some of which consisted of statements showing Haupt's sympathy with Germany and Hitler and hostility towards the United States. We rejected Haupt's argument that this evidence was improperly admitted. While ''such testimony is to be scrutinized with care to be certain the statements are not expressions of mere lawful and permissible difference of opinion with our own government or quite proper appreciation of the land of birth,'' we held that ''these statements . . . clearly were admissible on the question of intent and adherence to the enemy.'' . . .

For the foregoing reasons, we hold that Mitchell's First Amendment rights were not violated by the application of the Wisconsin penalty-enhancement provision in sentencing him. The judgment of the Supreme Court of Wisconsin is therefore reversed, and the case is remanded for further proceedings not inconsistent with this opinion.

It is so ordered.

EMPLOYMENT DIVISION v. SMITH

494 U. S. 872; 110 S. Ct. 1595; 108 L. Ed. 2d 876; (1990)

Over the years the Supreme Court has faced the claims of many religions that the First Amendment's free exercise clause protected their right to engage in religiously required practice, otherwise illegal. Included among these rights were the former requirement of Mormon doctrine that a man have more than one wife, circumstances permitting; of the Jehovah's Witnesses that they not salute the flag because it is tantamount to bowing down to a graven image; and of a pacifist student at a land-grant college that he not be required to take military drill. (See the note to Murdock v. Pennsylvania.)

The Court's earliest approach to such claims was that the free exercise clause protected only belief, not action. Congress was thus deemed free to outlaw religious practices. See Reynolds v. United States (1878), rejecting the Mormon's claim that bigamy laws should not apply to them. Over the years this belief/action distinction was abandoned by the Court because it permitted too much state interference with religious freedom. In Sherbert v. Verner (1963) the Court's new approach was formalized. There the state denied unemployment benefits to a Seventh Day Adventist because she had refused jobs that required her to work on Saturday, the Sabbath in her religion. The requirement that those seeking to collect unemployment benefits be available for Saturday work was a generally applicable state rule and was not adopted to discriminate against religions that celebrated the Sabbath on Saturday. It also involved the regulation of activity, not belief. Moreover, it was not a criminal penalty but merely the denial of a state benefit. Nonetheless, the Court held that the State could not impose a

burden on the exercise of a religious practice, here resting on Saturday, without a compelling state interest. Moreover, even if the state's interest was compelling, it had to try and meet the state interest in some manner that did not interfere with religious activity, if possible. Only when the state's interest was compelling and when there were no feasible alternatives to achieving that interest that did not infringe on religion could the state interfere with religious practice. The Sherbert doctrine was significantly modified by the case below.

The case printed below raised the question whether the First Amendment permits a state to punish religiously motivated peyote use. The Court held that because the State had not targeted peyote use for religious reasons, and because their restriction applied to all who used peyote, the Free Exercise Clause was not violated.

Three years later the Court returned to some of the issues raised by the Smith case in Church of the Lukumi Babalu Aye v. Hialeah (1993). In 1987 the petitioners established in Hialeah, Florida, a Santeria church—a fusion of Roman Catholicism and traditional religions of eastern Africa. Its followers believe in creating a relationship with spirits or ''orishas,'' and one of the primary forms of devotion is animal sacrifice.

In response to the establishment of the church, the city enacted three ordinances. The first prohibited possessing an animal for the purpose of sacrifice, or for food purposes if the animal was to be killed during a ritual. The council restricted application of that ordinance by creating an exception for ''licensed establishments'' to slaughter animals raised expressly for food purposes. The second ordinance made it a crime for anyone to sacrifice an animal within the corporate limits of Hialeah. In both of these ordinances, to sacrifice was defined as ''to unnecessarily kill, torment, torture or mutilate an animal in a public or private ritual or ceremony not for the primary purpose of food consumption.'' The third ordinance prohibited slaughter of animals outside areas zoned specifically for that use, with an exception for the slaughter of small numbers of hogs and cattle, presumably for home consumption.

A unanimous Court struck down the ordinances, reasoning that, unlike the law in the Smith case, the city council's ordinances were neither neutral nor generally applicable. Because these requirements were not met, the city's laws had to be justified by a compelling government interest and the Court found they were not.

The Court found that the laws targeted Santeria religious practices and thus were not neutral. Not only had the city council passed the ordinances soon after the church was established, but the transcript of the city council meeting clearly demonstrated the council's desire to stop this religiously motivated practice. One council member expressly said, ''What can we do to prevent the Church from opening?''

Nor did the ordinances meet the test of general applicability. The city council prohibited the religiously motivated killing of animals while permitting virtually all secular killing, such as hunting, euthanasia, extermination and the slaughter of animals for food. The city made no attempt to explain why religious killing alone was particularly offensive to the interests of public health and prevention of cruelty to animals. By failing to include both religious and secular killing, the ordinances lacked the necessary applicability.

Having found the laws to be neither neutral nor generally applicable, the Court had little trouble finding that they were not justified by a compelling government interest. The state said the laws furthered its interest in the public health and welfare but these interests were not being served by targeting only religious sacrifice.

In a separate concurrence, Justice Scalia argued that only in rare cases should the motives of the legislature be considered, and this was not one of them. What should be considered was the product the legislature produced, regardless of its intent.

Justice Souter, in a separate concurrence, found the complicated analysis of Smith entirely inapplicable in view of the discriminatory nature of the ordinances. In addition, he rejected Smith as violating sound principles of First Amendment law. Smith, he said, held that only those laws whose "object" was to prohibit religious exercise were protected by the First Amendment, neglecting entirely those whose "incidental effect" was to burden religion. He had not sat on the Smith case, but agreed with the dissenters in that case that laws that incidently burdened religion should also be justified by a compelling interest. In addition he pointed out that Smith was inconsistent with Sherbert v. Verner and the cases following Sherbert but that Smith had not overruled Sherbert or its progeny. This "tension" between the precedents, he felt, should be resolved as soon as possible.

Justice Blackmun, writing for himself and Justice O'Connor, argued that a law restricting free exercise of religion should be allowed to stand only in cases where it is the least restrictive means of promoting a compelling government interest. They believe Smith was wrongly decided.

Justice **Scalia** delivered the opinion of the Court, saying in part:

This case requires us to decide whether the Free Exercise Clause of the First Amendment permits the State of Oregon to include religiously inspired peyote use within the reach of its general criminal prohibition on use of that drug, and thus permits the State to deny unemployment benefits to persons dismissed from their jobs because of such religiously inspired use.

I.

Oregon law prohibits the knowing or intentional possession of a "controlled substance" unless the substance has been prescribed by a medical practitioner. The law defines "controlled substance" . . . [to include] the drug peyote, a hallucinogen derived from the plant Lophophora williamsii Lemaire.

Respondents Alfred Smith and Galen Black (hereinafter respondents) were fired from their jobs with a private drug rehabilitation organization because they ingested peyote for sacramental purposes at a ceremony of the Native American Church, of which both are members. When respondents applied to petitioner Employment Division (hereinafter petitioner) for unemployment compensation, they were determined to be ineligible for benefits because they had been discharged for work-related "misconduct." The Oregon Court of Appeals reversed that determination, holding that the denial of benefits violated respondents' free exercise rights under the First Amendment. . . .

On remand, the Oregon Supreme Court held that respondents' religiously inspired use of peyote fell within the prohibition of the Oregon statute, which "makes no exception for the sacramental use" of the drug. It then considered whether that prohibition was valid under the Free Exercise Clause, and concluded that it was not. . . .

II.

Respondents' claim for relief rests on our decisions in Sherbert v. Verner [1963] . . . in which we held that a State could not condition the availability of unemployment insurance on an individual's willingness to forgo conduct required by his religion. . . .

A.

The Free Exercise Clause of the First Amendment, which has been made applicable to the States by incorporation into the Fourteenth Amendment, . . . provides that "Congress shall make no law respecting an establishment of religion, or **prohibiting the free exercise thereof** . . . ." (emphasis added). The free exercise of religion means, first and foremost, the right to believe and profess whatever religious doctrine one desires. Thus, the First Amendment obviously excludes all "governmental regulation of religious beliefs as such." . . .

But the "exercise of religion" often involves not only belief and profession but the performance of (or abstention from) physical acts: assembling with others for a worship service, participating in sacramental use of bread and wine, proselytizing, abstaining from certain foods or certain modes of transportation. It would be true, we think (though no case of ours has involved the point), that a State would be "prohibiting the free exercise [of religion]" if it sought to ban such acts or abstentions only when they are engaged in for religious reasons, or only because of the religious belief that they display. It would doubtless be unconstitutional, for example, to ban the casting of "statues that are to be used for worship purposes," or to prohibit bowing down before a golden calf.

Respondents in the present case, however, seek to carry the meaning of "prohibiting the free exercise [of religion]" one large step further. They contend that their religious motivation for using peyote places them beyond the reach of a criminal law that is not specifically directed at their religious practice, and that is concededly constitutional as applied to those who use the drug for other reasons. They assert, in other words, that "prohibiting the free exercise [of religion]" includes requiring any individual to observe a generally applicable law that requires (or forbids) the performance of an act that his religious belief forbids (or requires). As a textual matter, we do not think the words must be given that meaning. It is no more necessary to regard the collection of a general tax, for example, as "prohibiting the free exercise [of religion]" by those citizens who believe support of organized government to be sinful, than it is to regard the same tax as "abridging the freedom . . . of the press" of those publishing companies that must pay the tax as a condition of staying in business. It is a permissible reading of the text, in the one case as in the other, to say that if prohibiting the exercise of religion (or burdening the activity of printing) is not the object of the tax but merely the incidental effect of a generally applicable and otherwise valid provision, the First Amendment has not been offended. . . .

Our decisions reveal that the latter reading is the correct one. We have never held that an individual's religious beliefs excuse him from compliance with an otherwise valid law prohibiting conduct that the State is free to regulate. On the contrary, the record of more than a century of our free exercise jurisprudence contradicts that proposition. As described succinctly by Justice Frankfurter in Minersville School Dist. Bd. of Ed. v. Gobitis (1940): "Conscientious scruples have not, in the course of the long struggle for religious toleration, relieved the individual from obedience to a general law not aimed at the promotion or restriction of religious beliefs. The mere possession of religious convictions which contradict the relevant concerns of a political society does not relieve the citizen from the discharge of political responsibilities." We first had occasion to assert that principle in Reynolds v. United States (1879), where we rejected the claim that criminal laws against polygamy could not be constitutionally applied to those whose religion commanded the practice. "Laws," we said, "are made for the government of actions, and while they cannot interfere with mere religious belief and opinions, they may with practices. . . . Can a man excuse his practices to the contrary because of his religious belief? To permit this would be to make the professed doctrines of religious belief superior to the law of the land, and in effect to permit every citizen to become a law unto himself."

Subsequent decisions have consistently held that the right of free exercise does not relieve an individual of the obligation to comply with a "valid and neutral law of general applicability on the ground that the law proscribes (or prescribes) conduct that his religion prescribes (or proscribes)." . . .

Our most recent decision involving a neutral, generally applicable regulatory law that compelled activity forbidden by an individual's religion was United States v. Lee [1982]. There, an Amish employer, on behalf of himself and his employees, sought exemption from collection and payment of Social Security taxes on the ground that the Amish faith prohibited participation in governmental support programs. We rejected the claim that an exemption was constitutionally required. There would be no way, we observed, to distinguish the Amish believer's objection to Social Security taxes from the religious objections that others might have to the collection or use of other taxes. "If, for example, a religious adherent believes war is a sin, and if a certain percentage of the federal budget can be identified as devoted to war-related activities, such individuals would have a similarly valid claim to be exempt from paying that percentage of the income tax. The tax system could not function if denominations were allowed to challenge the tax system because tax payments were spent in a manner that violates their religious belief." . . .

The only decisions in which we have held that the First Amendment bars application of a neutral, generally applicable law to religiously motivated action have involved not the Free Exercise Clause alone, but the Free Exercise Clause in conjunction with other constitutional protections, such as freedom of speech and of the press, see Cantwell v. Connecticut [1940] (invalidating a licensing system for religious and charitable solicitations under which the administrator had discretion to deny a license to any cause he deemed nonreligious); Murdock v. Pennsylvania (1943) (invalidating a flat tax on solicitation as applied to the dissemination of religious ideas); Follett v. McCormick (1944) (same), or the right of parents, acknowledged in Pierce v. Society of Sisters (1925), to direct the education of their children, see Wisconsin v. Yoder (1972) (invalidating compulsory school-attendance laws as applied to Amish parents who refused on religious grounds to send their children to school). . . .

The present case does not present such a hybrid situation, but a free exercise claim unconnected with any communicative activity or parental right. Respondents urge us to hold, quite simply, that when otherwise prohibitable conduct is accompanied by religious convictions, not only the convictions but the conduct itself must be free from governmental regulation. We have never held that, and decline to do so now. . . .

B.

Respondents argue that even though exemption from generally applicable criminal laws need not automatically be extended to religiously motivated actors, at least the claim for a religious exemption must be evaluated under the balancing test set forth in Sherbert v. Verner (1963). Under the Sherbert test, governmental actions that substantially burden a religious practice must be justified by a compelling governmental interest. . . . Applying that test we have, on three occasions, invalidated state unemployment compensation rules that conditioned the availability of benefits upon an applicant's willingness to work under conditions forbidden by his religion. See Sherbert v. Verner, supra; Thomas v. Review Bd. of Indiana Employment Security Div. (1981); Hobbie v. Unemployment Appeals Comm'n of Florida (1987). We have never invalidated any governmental action on the basis of the Sherbert test except the denial of unemployment compensation. Although we have sometimes purported to apply the Sherbert test in contexts other than that, we have always found the test satisfied, see United States v. Lee (1982); Gillette v. United States (1971). In recent years we have abstained from applying the Sherbert test (outside the unemployment compensation field) at all. . . .

The "compelling government interest" requirement seems benign, because it is familiar from other fields. But using it as the standard that must be met before the government may accord different treatment on the basis of race . . . or before the government may regulate the content of speech . . . is not remotely comparable to using it for the purpose asserted here. What it produces in those other fields—equality of treatment and an unrestricted flow of contending speech—are constitutional norms; what it would produce here—a private right to ignore generally applicable laws—is a constitutional anomaly.

Nor is it possible to limit the impact of respondents' proposal by requiring a "compelling state interest" only when the conduct prohibited is "central" to the individual's religion. . . . It is no more appropriate for judges to determine the "centrality" of religious beliefs before applying a "compelling interest" test in the free exercise field, than it would be for them to determine the "importance" of ideas before applying the "compelling interest" test in the free speech field. What principle of law or logic can be brought to bear to contradict a believer's assertion that a particular act is "central" to his personal faith? Judging the centrality of different religious practices is akin to the unacceptable "business of evaluating the relative merits of differing religious claims." United States v. Lee. . . .

Values that are protected against government interference through enshrinement in the Bill of Rights are not thereby banished from the political process. Just as a society that believes in the negative protection accorded to the press by the First Amendment is likely to enact laws that affirmatively foster the dissemination of the printed word, so also a society that believes in the negative protection accorded to religious belief can be expected to be solicitous of that value in its legislation as well. It is therefore not surprising that a number of States have made an exception to their drug laws for sacramental peyote use. . . . But to say that a nondiscriminatory religious-practice exemption is permitted, or even that it is desirable, is not to say that it is constitutionally required, and that the appropriate occasions for its creation can be discerned by the courts. It may fairly be said that leaving accommodation to the political process will place at a relative disadvantage those religious practices that are not widely engaged in; but that unavoidable consequence of democratic government must be preferred to a system in which each conscience is a law unto itself or in which judges weigh the social importance of all laws against the centrality of all religious beliefs.

* * *

Because respondents' ingestion of peyote was prohibited under Oregon law, and because that prohibition is constitutional, Oregon may, consistent with the Free Exercise Clause, deny respondents unemployment compensation when their dismissal results from use of the drug. The decision of the Oregon Supreme Court is accordingly reversed.

It is so ordered.

Justice **O'Connor**, with whom Justice **Brennan**, Justice **Marshall**, and Justice **Blackmun** join as to Parts I and II, concurring in the judgment, said in part:*

Although I agree with the result the Court reaches in this case, I cannot join its opinion. In my view, today's holding dramatically departs from well-settled First Amendment jurisprudence, appears unnecessary to resolve the question presented, and is incompatible with our Nation's fundamental commitment to individual religious liberty. . . .

II.

The Court today extracts from our long history of free exercise precedents the single categorical rule that "if prohibiting the exercise of religion . . . is . . . merely the incidental effect of a generally applicable and otherwise valid provision, the First Amendment has not been offended." Indeed, the Court holds that where the law is a generally applicable criminal prohibition, our usual free exercise jurisprudence does not even apply. To reach this sweeping result, however, the Court must not only give a strained reading of the First Amendment but must also disregard our consistent application of free exercise doctrine to cases involving generally applicable regulations that burden religious conduct.

A.

. . . Because the First Amendment does not distinguish between religious belief and religious conduct, conduct motivated by sincere religious belief, like the belief itself, must be at least presumptively protected by the Free Exercise Clause.

The Court today, however, interprets the Clause to permit the government to prohibit, without justification, conduct mandated by an individual's religious beliefs, so long as that prohibition is generally applicable. But a law that prohibits certain conduct—conduct that happens to

---

* Although Justice Brennan, Justice Marshall, and Justice Blackmun join Parts I and II of this opinion, they do not concur in the judgment.

be an act of worship for someone—manifestly does prohibit that person's free exercise of his religion. A person who is barred from engaging in religiously motivated conduct is barred from freely exercising his religion. Moreover, that person is barred from freely exercising his religion regardless of whether the law prohibits the conduct only when engaged in for religious reasons, only by members of that religion, or by all persons. It is difficult to deny that a law that prohibits religiously motivated conduct, even if the law is generally applicable, does not at least implicate First Amendment concerns.

The Court responds that generally applicable laws are "one large step" removed from laws aimed at specific religious practices. The First Amendment, however, does not distinguish between laws that are generally applicable and laws that target particular religious practices. Indeed, few States would be so naive as to enact a law directly prohibiting or burdening a religious practice as such. Our free exercise cases have all concerned generally applicable laws that had the effect of significantly burdening a religious practice. If the First Amendment is to have any vitality, it ought not be construed to cover only the extreme and hypothetical situation in which a State directly targets a religious practice. As we have noted in a slightly different context, " '[s]uch a test has no basis in precedent and relegates a serious First Amendment value to the barest level of minimum scrutiny that the Equal Protection Clause already provides.' " Hobbie v. Unemployment Appeals Comm'n of Florida (1987). . . .

To say that a person's right to free exercise has been burdened, of course, does not mean that he has an absolute right to engage in the conduct. Under our established First Amendment jurisprudence, we have recognized that the freedom to act, unlike the freedom to believe, cannot be absolute. See, e.g., Cantwell [v. Connecticut (1940)]; Reynolds v. United States (1879). Instead, we have respected both the First Amendment's express textual mandate and the governmental interest in regulation of conduct by requiring the government to justify any substantial burden on religiously motivated conduct by a compelling state interest and by means narrowly tailored to achieve that interest. See . . . Wisconsin v. Yoder (1972); . . . Sherbert v. Verner (1963); . . . West Virginia State Bd. of Ed. v. Barnette (1943). The compelling interest test effectuates the First Amendment's command that religious liberty is an independent liberty, that it occupies a preferred position, and that the Court will not permit encroachments upon this liberty, whether direct or indirect, unless required by clear and compelling governmental interests "of the highest order." "Only an especially important governmental interest pursued by narrowly tailored means can justify exacting a sacrifice of First Amendment freedoms as the price for an equal share of the rights, benefits, and privileges enjoyed by other citizens."

The Court attempts to support its narrow reading of the Clause by claiming that "[w]e have never held that an individual's religious beliefs excuse him from compliance with an otherwise valid law prohibiting conduct that the State is free to regulate." But as the Court later notes, as it must, in cases such as Cantwell and Yoder we have in fact interpreted the Free Exercise Clause to forbid application of a generally applicable prohibition to religiously motivated conduct. Indeed, in Yoder we expressly rejected the interpretation the Court now adopts: "[O]ur decisions have rejected the idea that religiously grounded conduct is always outside the protection of the Free Exercise Clause. It is true that activities of individuals, even when religiously based, are often subject to regulation by the States in the exercise of their undoubted power to promote the health, safety, and general welfare, or the Federal Government in the exercise of its delegated powers. But to agree that religiously grounded conduct must often be subject to the broad police power of the State is not to deny that there are areas of conduct protected by the Free Exercise Clause of the First Amendment and thus beyond the power of the State to control, *even under regulations of general applicability.* . . .

"... A regulation neutral on its face may, in its applicaton, nonetheless offend the constitutional requirement for government neutrality if it unduly burdens the free exercise of religion." (emphasis added; citations omitted).

The Court endeavors to escape from our decisions in Cantwell and Yoder by labeling them "hybrid" decisions, but there is no denying that both cases expressly relied on the Free Exercise Clause and that we have consistently regarded those cases as part of the mainstream of our free exercise jurisprudence. Moreover, in each of the other cases cited by the Court to support its categorical rule we rejected the particular constitutional claims before us only after carefully weighing the competing interests. . . .

B.

Respondents, of course, do not contend that their conduct is automatically immune from all governmental regulation simply because it is motivated by their sincere religious beliefs. The Court's rejection of that argument might therefore be regarded as merely harmless dictum. Rather, respondents invoke our traditional compelling interest test to argue that the Free Exercise Clause requires the State to grant them a limited exemption from its general criminal prohibition against the possession of peyote. The Court today, however, denies them even the opportunity to make that argument, concluding that "the sounder approach, and the approach in accord with the vast majority of our precedents, is to hold the [compelling interest] test inapplicable to" challenges to general criminal prohibitions.

In my view, however, the essence of a free exercise claim is relief from a burden imposed by government on religious practices or beliefs, whether the burden is imposed directly through laws that prohibit or compel specific religious practices, or indirectly through laws that, in effect, make abandonment of one's own religion or conformity to the religious beliefs of others the price of an equal place in the civil community. . . .

. . . Once it has been shown that a government regulation or criminal prohibition burdens the free exercise of religion, we have consistently asked the government to demonstrate that unbending application of its regulation to the religious objector "is essential to accomplish an overriding governmental interest," [United States v.] Lee [1982], or represents "the least restrictive means of achieving some compelling state interest." . . . To me, the sounder approach—the approach more consistent with our role as judges to decide each case on its individual merits—is to apply this test in each case to determine whether the burden on the specific plaintiffs before us is constitutionally significant and whether the particular criminal interest asserted by the State before us is compelling. Even if, as an empirical matter, a government's criminal laws might usually serve a compelling interest in health, safety, or public order, the First Amendment at least requires a case-by-case determination of the question, sensitive to the facts of each particular claim. . . . Given the range of conduct that a State might legitimately make criminal, we cannot assume, merely because a law carries criminal sanctions and is generally applicable, that the First Amendment never requires the State to grant a limited exemption for religiously motivated conduct.

Moreover, we have not "rejected" or "declined to apply" the compelling interest test in our recent cases. Recent cases have instead affirmed that test as a fundamental part of our First Amendment doctrine. . . . The cases cited by the Court signal no retreat from our consistent adherence to the compelling interest test. In both Bowen v. Roy [1986] and Lyng v. Northwest Indian Cemetery Protective Assn. (1988), for example, we expressly distinguished Sherbert on the ground that the First Amendment does not "require the Government itself to behave in ways that the individual believes will further his or her spiritual development. . . . The Free Exercise Clause simply cannot be understood to require the Government to conduct its own internal affairs in ways that comport with the religious beliefs of particular citizens." This distinction makes sense because "the Free Exercise Clause is written in terms of what the government cannot do to the individual, not in terms of what the individual can exact from the government." Because the case sub judice, like the other cases in which we have applied Sherbert, plainly falls into the former category, I would apply those established precedents to the facts of this case. . . .

The Court today gives no convincing reason to depart from settled First Amendment jurisprudence. There is nothing talismanic about neutral laws of general applicability or general criminal prohibitions, for laws neutral toward religion can coerce a person to violate his religious conscience or intrude upon his religious duties just as effectively as laws aimed at religion. Although the Court suggests that the compelling interest test, as applied to generally applicable laws, would result in a "constitutional anomaly," the First Amendment unequivocally makes freedom of religion, like freedom from race discrimination and freedom of speech, a "constitutional nor[m]," not an "anomaly." . . . The Court's parade of horribles not only fails as a reason for discarding the compelling interest test, it instead demonstrates just the opposite: that courts have been quite capable of applying our free exercise jurisprudence to strike sensible balances between religious liberty and competing state interests.

Finally, the Court today suggests that the disfavoring of minority religions is an "unavoidable consequence" under our system of government and that accommodation of such religions must be left to the political process. In my view, however, the First Amendment was enacted precisely to protect the rights of those whose religious practices are not shared by the majority and may be viewed with hostility. The history of our free exercise doctrine amply demonstrates the harsh impact majoritarian rule has had on unpopular or emerging religious groups such as the Jehovah's Witnesses and the Amish. Indeed, the words of Justice Jackson in West Virginia State Bd. of Ed. v. Barnette (overruling Minersville School Dist. v. Gobitis (1940)) are apt: "The very purpose of a Bill of Rights was to withdraw certain subjects from the vicissitudes of political controversy, to place them beyond the reach of majorities and officials and to establish them as legal principles to be applied by the courts. One's right to life, liberty, and property, to free speech, a free press, freedom of worship and assembly, and other fundamental rights may not be submitted to vote; they depend on the outcome of no elections." . . .

III. . . .

A.

There is no dispute that Oregon's criminal prohibition of peyote places a severe burden on the ability of respondents to freely exercise their religion. . . .

There is also no dispute that Oregon has a significant interest in enforcing laws that control the possession and use of controlled substances by its citizens. . . .

B.

Thus, the critical question in this case is whether exempting respondents from the State's general criminal prohibition "will unduly interfere with fulfillment of the governmental interest." . . . Although the question is close, I would conclude that uniform application of Oregon's criminal prohibition is "essential to accomplish" its overriding interest in preventing the physical harm caused by the use of a Schedule I controlled substance. Oregon's criminal prohibition represents that State's judgment that the possession and use of controlled substances, even by only one person, is inherently harmful and dangerous. Because the health effects caused by the use of controlled substances exist regardless of the motivation of the user, the use of such substances, even for religious purposes, violates the very purpose of the laws that prohibit them. . . . Moreover, in view of the societal interest in preventing trafficking in controlled substances, uniform application of the criminal prohibition at issue is essential to the effectiveness of Oregon's stated interest in preventing any possession of peyote. Cf. Jacobson v. Massachusetts (1905) (denying exemption from small pox vaccination requirement).

For these reasons, I believe that granting a selective exemption in this case would seriously impair Oregon's compelling interest in prohibiting possession of peyote by its citizens. Under such circumstances, the Free Exercise Clause does not require the State to accommodate respondents' religiously motivated conduct. . . .

Justice **Blackmun,** with whom Justice **Brennan** and Justice **Marshall** join, dissenting, said in part:

This Court over the years painstakingly has developed a consistent and exacting standard to test the constitutionality of a state statute that burdens the free exercise of religion. Such a statute may stand only if the law in general, and the State's refusal to allow a religious exemption in particular, are justified by a compelling interest that cannot be served by less restrictive means.

Until today, I thought this was a settled and inviolate principle of this Court's First Amendment jurisprudence. The majority, however, perfunctorily dismisses it as a "constitutional anomaly." As carefully detailed in Justice O'Connor's concurring opinion, the majority is able to arrive at this view only by mischaracterizing this Court's precedents. The Court discards leading free exercise cases such as Cantwell v. Connecticut (1940), and Wisconsin v. Yoder (1972), as "hybrid." The Court views traditional free exercise analysis as somehow inapplicable to criminal prohibitions (as opposed to conditions on the receipt of benefits), and to state laws of general applicability (as opposed, presumably, to laws that expressly single out religious practices). The Court cites cases in which, due to various exceptional circumstances, we found strict scrutiny inapposite, to hint that the Court has repudiated that standard altogether. In short, it effectuates a wholesale overturning of settled law concerning the Religion Clauses of our Constitution. One hopes that the Court is aware of the consequences, and that its result is not a product of overreaction to the serious problems the country's drug crisis has generated.

This distorted view of our precedents leads the majority to conclude that strict scrutiny of a state law burdening the free exercise of religion is a "luxury" that a well-ordered society cannot afford, and that the repression of minority religions is an "unavoidable consequence of democratic government." I do not believe the Founders thought their dearly bought freedom from religious persecution a "luxury," but an essential element of liberty—and they could not have thought religious intolerance "unavoidable," for they drafted the Religion Clauses precisely in order to avoid that intolerance.

For these reasons, I agree with Justice O'Connor's analysis of the applicable free exercise doctrine, and I join parts I and II of her opinion. As she points out, "the critical question in this case is whether exempting respondents from the State's general criminal prohibition 'will unduly interfere with fulfillment of the governmental interest.' " I do disagree, however, with her specific answer to that question.

I.

In weighing the clear interest of respondents Smith and Black (hereinafter respondents) in the free exercise of their religion against Oregon's asserted interest in enforcing its drug laws, it is important to articulate in precise terms the state interest involved. It is not the State's broad interest in fighting the critical "war on drugs" that must be weighed against respondents' claim, but the State's narrow interest in refusing to make an exception for the religious, ceremonial use of peyote. See Bowen v. Roy (1986) (O'Connor, J., concurring in part and dissenting in part) ("This Court has consistently asked the Government to demonstrate that unbending application of its regulation to the religious objector 'is essential to accomplish an overriding governmental interest,' " quoting Lee.) . . . See Clark, Guidelines for the Free Exercise Clause, 83 Harv. L. Rev. 327, 330-331 (1969) ("The purpose of almost any law can be traced back to one or another of the fundamental concerns of government: public health and safety, public peace and order, defense, revenue. To measure an individual interest directly against one of these rarified values inevitably makes the individual interest appear the less significant"); Pound, A Survey of Social Interests, 57 Harv. L. Rev. 1, 2 (1943) ("When it comes to weighing or valuing claims or demands with respect to other claims or demands, we must be careful to compare them on the same plane . . . [or else] we may decide the question in advance in our very way of putting it").

The State's interest in enforcing its prohibition, in order to be sufficiently compelling to outweigh a free exercise claim, cannot be merely abstract or symbolic. The State cannot plausibly assert that unbending application of a criminal prohibition is essential to fulfill any compelling interest, if it does not, in fact, attempt to enforce that prohibition. In this case, the State actually has not evinced any concrete interest in enforcing its drug laws against religious users of peyote. Oregon has never sought to prosecute respondents, and does not claim that it has made significant enforcement efforts against other religious users of peyote. The State's asserted interest thus amounts only to the symbolic preservation of an unenforced prohibition. But a government interest in "symbolism, even symbolism for so worthy a cause as the abolition of unlawful drugs," . . . cannot suffice to abrogate the constitutional rights of individuals. . . .

The State proclaims an interest in protecting the health and safety of its citizens from the dangers of unlawful drugs. It offers, however, no evidence that the religious use of peyote has ever harmed anyone. The factual findings of other courts cast doubt on the State's assumption that religious use of peyote is harmful. . . .

The fact that peyote is classified as a Schedule I controlled substance does not, by itself, show that any and all uses of peyote, in any circumstance, are inherently harmful and dangerous. The Federal Government, which created the classifications of unlawful drugs from which Oregon's drug laws are derived, apparently does not find peyote so dangerous as to preclude an exemption for religious use. . . .

The carefully circumscribed ritual context in which respondents used peyote is far removed from the irresponsible and unrestricted recreational use of unlawful drugs. The Native American Church's internal restrictions on, and supervision of, its members' use of peyote substantially obviate the State's health and safety concerns. . . .

Moreover, just as in Yoder, the values and interests of those seeking a religious exemption in this case are congruent, to a great degree, with those the State seeks to promote through its drug laws. . . . Not only does the church's doctrine forbid nonreligious use of peyote; it also generally advocates self-reliance, familial responsibility, and abstinence from alcohol. There is considerable evidence that the spiritual and social support provided by the church has been effective in combating the tragic effects of alcoholism on the Native American population. . . . Far from promoting the lawless and irresponsible use of drugs, Native American Church members' spiritual code exemplifies values that Oregon's drug laws are presumably intended to foster.

The State also seeks to support its refusal to make an exception for religious use of peyote by invoking its interest in abolishing drug trafficking. There is, however, practically no illegal traffic in peyote. See . . . DEA Final Order to the effect that total amount of peyote seized and analyzed by federal authorities between 1980 and 1987 was 19.4 pounds . . . .

Finally, the State argues that granting an exception for religious peyote use would erode its interest in the uniform, fair, and certain enforcement of its drug laws.

The State fears that, if it grants an exemption for religious peyote use, a flood of other claims to religious exemptions will follow. . . .

The State's apprehension of a flood of other religious claims is purely speculative. Almost half the States, and the Federal Government, have maintained an exemption for religious peyote use for many years, and apparently have not found themselves overwhelmed by claims to other religious exemptions. . . .

III.

Finally, although I agree with Justice O'Connor that courts should refrain from delving into questions whether, as a matter of religious doctrine, a particular practice is "central" to the religion, I do not think this means that the courts must turn a blind eye to the severe impact of a State's restrictions on the adherents of a minority religion. . . .

Respondents believe, and their sincerity has never been at issue, that the peyote plant embodies their deity, and eating it is an act of worship and communion. Without peyote, they could not enact the essential ritual of their religion. . . .

If Oregon can constitutionally prosecute them for this act of worship, they, like the Amish, may be "forced to migrate to some other and more tolerant region." Yoder. This potentially devastating impact must be viewed in light of the federal policy—reached in reaction to many years of religious persecution and intolerance—of protecting the religious freedom of Native Americans. . . .

IV.

For these reasons, I conclude that Oregon's interest in enforcing its drug laws against religious use of peyote is not sufficiently compelling to outweigh respondents' right to the free exercise of their religion. . . .

I dissent.

Appendix

Constitution
of
the United States

WE THE PEOPLE of the United States, in order to form a more perfect union, establish justice, insure domestic tranquility, provide for the common defense, promote the general welfare, and secure the blessings of liberty to ourselves and our posterity, do ordain and establish this Constitution for the United States of America.

ARTICLE I

SECTION 1. All legislative powers herein granted shall be vested in a Congress of the United States, which shall consist of a Senate and House of Representatives.

SECTION 2. (1) The House of Representatives shall be composed of members chosen every second year by the people of the several States, and the electors in each State shall have the qualifications requisite for electors of the most numerous branch of the State legislature.

(2) No person shall be a Representative who shall not have attained to the age of twenty-five years, and been seven years a citizen of the United States and who shall not, when elected, be an inhabitant of that State in which he shall be chosen.

(3) Representatives and direct taxes* shall be apportioned among the several States which may be included within this Union, according to their respective numbers, which shall be determined by adding to the whole number of free persons, including those bound to service for a term of years, and excluding Indians not taxed, three fifths of all other persons.[†] The actual enumeration shall

be made within three years after the first meeting of the Congress of the United States, and within every subsequent term of ten years, in such manner as they shall by law direct. The number of Representatives shall not excede one for every thirty thousand, but each State shall have at least one Representative; and until such enumeration shall be made, the State of New Hampshire shall be entitled to choose three, Massachusetts eight, Rhode Island and Providence Plantations one, Connecticut five, New York six, New Jersey four, Pennsylvania eight, Delaware one, Maryland six, Virginia ten, North Carolina five, South Carolina five, and Georgia three.

(4) When vacancies happen in the representation from any State, the executive authority thereof shall issue writs of election to fill such vacancies.

(5) The House of Representatives shall choose their Speaker and other officers; and shall have the sole power of impeachment.

SECTION 3 (1) The Senate of the United States shall be composed of two Senators from each State, chosen by the legislature thereof,[‡] for six years; and each Senator shall have one vote.

(2) Immediately after they shall be assembled in consequence of the first election, they shall be divided as equally as may be into three classes. The seats of the

---

*Modified as to income taxes by the 16th Amendment.

[†]Replaced by the 14th Amendment.

[‡]Modified by the 17th Amendment.

Senators of the first class shall be vacated at the expiration of the second year, of the second class at the expiration of the fourth year, and of the third class at the expiration of the sixth year, so that one third may be chosen every second year; and if vacancies happen by resignation, or otherwise, during the recess of the legislature of any State, the executive thereof may make temporary appointments until the next meeting of the legislature, which* shall then fill such vacancies.

(3) No person shall be a Senator who shall not have attained to the age of thirty years, and been nine years a citizen of the United States, and who shall not, when elected, be an inhabitant of that State for which he shall be chosen.

(4) The Vice President of the United States shall be president of the Senate, but shall have no vote, unless they be equally divided.

(5) The Senate shall choose their other officers, and also a president pro tempore, in the absence of the Vice President, or when he shall exercise the office of President of the United States.

(6) The Senate shall have the sole power to try all impeachments. When sitting for that purpose, they shall be on oath or affirmation. When the President of the United States is tried, the Chief Justice shall preside: and no person shall be convicted without the concurrence of two thirds of the members present.

(7) Judgment in cases of impeachment shall not extend further than to removal from office, and disqualification to hold and enjoy any office of honor, trust or profit under the United States: but the party convicted shall nevertheless be liable and subject to indictment, trial, judgment and punishment, according to law.

SECTION 4 (1) The times, places and manner of holding elections for Senators and Representatives, shall be prescribed in each State by the legislature thereof; but the Congress may at any time by law make or alter such regulations, except as to the places of choosing Senators.

(2) The Congress shall assemble at least once in every year, and such meeting shall be on the first Monday in December, unless they shall by law appoint a different day.

SECTION 5 (1) Each House shall be the judge of the elections, returns and qualifications of its own members, and a majority of each shall constitute a quorum to do business; but a smaller number may adjourn from day to day, and may be authorized to compel the attendance of absent members, in such manner, and under such penalties as each House may provide.

(2) Each House may determine the rules of its proceedings, punish its members for disorderly behavior, and, with the concurrence of two thirds, expel a member.

*Modified by the 17th Amendment.

(3) Each House shall keep a journal of its proceedings, and from time to time publish the same, excepting such parts as may in their judgment require secrecy; and the yeas and nays of the members of either House on any question shall, at the desire of one fifth of those present, be entered on the journal.

(4) Neither House, during the session of Congress, shall, without the consent of the other, adjourn for more than three days, nor to any other place than that in which the two Houses shall be sitting.

SECTION 6 (1) The Senators and Representatives shall receive a compensation for their services, to be ascertained by law, and paid out of the Treasury of the United States. They shall in all cases, except treason, felony and breach of the peace, be privileged from arrest during their attendance at the session of their respective Houses, and in going to and returning from the same; and for any speech or debate in either House, they shall not be questioned in any other place.

(2) No Senator or Representative shall, during the time for which he was elected, be appointed to any civil office under the authority of the United States, which shall have been created, or the emoluments whereof shall have been increased during such time, and no person holding any office under the United States, shall be a member of either House during his continuance in office.

SECTION 7 (1) All bills for raising revenue shall originate in the House of Representatives; but the Senate may propose or concur with amendments as on other bills.

(2) Every bill which shall have passed the House of Representatives and the Senate, shall, before it become a law, be presented to the President of the United States; if he approve he shall sign it, but if not he shall return it, with his objections to that House in which it shall have originated, who shall enter the objections at large on their journal, and proceed to reconsider it. If after such reconsideration two thirds of that House shall agree to pass the bill, it shall be sent, together with the objections, to the other house, by which it shall likewise be reconsidered, and if approved by two thirds of that House, it shall become a law. But in all such cases the votes of both Houses shall be determined by yeas and nays, and the names of the persons voting for and against the bill shall be entered on the journal of each House respectively. If any bill shall not be returned by the President within ten days (Sundays excepted) after it shall have been presented to him, the same shall be a law, in like manner as if he had signed it, unless the Congress by their adjournment prevent its return, in which case it shall not be a law.

(3) Every order, resolution, or vote to which the concurrence of the Senate and House of Representatives may be necessary (except on a question of adjournment) shall be presented to the President of the United States; and before the same shall take effect, shall be approved by him, or being disapproved by him, shall be repassed by

two thirds of the Senate and House of Representatives, according to the rules and limitations prescribed in the case of a bill.

SECTION 8 (1) The Congress shall have power to lay and collect taxes, duties, imposts and excises, to pay the debts and provide for the common defense and general welfare of the United States; but all duties, imposts and excises shall be uniform throughout the United States;

(2) To borrow money on the credit of the United States;

(3) To regulate commerce with foreign nations, and among the several States, and with the Indian tribes;

(4) To establish an uniform rule of naturalization, and uniform laws on the subject of bankruptcies throughout the United States;

(5) To coin money, regulate the value thereof, and of foreign coin, and fix the standard of weights and measures

(6) To provide for the punishment of counterfeiting the securities and current coin of the United States;

(7) To establish post offices and post roads;

(8) To promote the progress of science and useful arts, by securing for limited times to authors and inventors the exclusive right to their respective writings and discoveries;

(9) To constitute tribunals inferior to the Supreme Court;

(10) To define and punish piracies and felonies committed on the high seas, and offenses against the law of nations;

(11) To declare war, grant letters of marque and reprisal, and make rules concerning captures on land and water;

(12) To raise and support armies, but no appropriation of money to that use shall be for a longer term than two years;

(13) To provide and maintain a navy;

(14) To make rules for the government and regulation of the land and naval forces;

(15) To provide for calling forth the militia to execute the laws of the Union, suppress insurrections and repel invasions;

(16) To provide for organizing, arming, and disciplining the militia, and for governing such part of them as may be employed in the service of the United States, reserving to the States respectively, the appointment of the officers, and the authority of training the militia according to the discipline prescribed by Congress;

(17) To exercise exclusive legislation in all cases whatsoever, over such district (not exceeding ten miles square) as may, by cession of particular States, and the acceptance of Congress, become the seat of the government of the United States, and to exercise like authority over all places purchased by the consent of the legisla-

ture of the State in which the same shall be, for the erection of forts, magazines, dockyards, and other needful buildings; and

(18) To make all laws which shall be necessary and proper for carrying into execution the foregoing powers, and all other powers vested by this Constitution in the government of the United States, or in any department or officer thereof.

SECTION 9 (1) The migration or importation of such persons as any of the States now existing shall think proper to admit, shall not be prohibited by the Congress prior to the year one thousand eight hundred and eight, but a tax or duty may be imposed on such importation, not exceeding ten dollars for each person.

(2) The privilege of the writ of habeas corpus shall not be suspended, unless when in cases of rebellion or invasion the public safety may require it.

(3) No bill of attainder or ex post facto law shall be passed.

(4) No capitation, or other direct, tax shall be laid, unless in proportion to the census or enumeration herein before directed to be taken.*

(5) No tax or duty shall be laid on articles exported from any State.

(6) No preference shall be given by any regulation of commerce or revenue to the ports of one State over those of another: nor shall vessels bound to, or from, one State, be obliged to enter, clear, or pay duties in another.

(7) No money shall be drawn from the Treasury, but in consequence of appropriations made by law; and a regular statement and account of the receipts and expenditures of all public money shall be published from time to time.

(8) No title of nobility shall be granted by the United States: and no person holding any office of profit or trust under them, shall, without the consent of the Congress, accept of any present, emolument, office, or title, of any kind whatever, from any king, prince, or foreign State.

SECTION 10 (I) No State shall enter into any treaty, alliance, or confederation; grant letters of marque and reprisal; coin money; emit bills of credit; make anything but gold and silver coin a tender in payment of debts; pass any bill of attainder, ex post facto law, or law impairing the obligation of contracts, or grant any title of nobility.

(2) No State shall, without the consent of Congress, lay any imposts or duties on imports or exports, except what may be absolutely necessary for executing its inspection laws; and the net produce of all duties and imposts, laid by any State on imports or exports, shall be for the use of the Treasury of the United States; and all such laws

*Modified by the 16th Amendment.

shall be subject to the revision and control of the Congress.

(3) No State shall, without the consent of Congress, lay any duty of tonnage, keep troops, or ships of war in time of peace, enter into any agreement or compact with another State, or with a foreign power, or engage in war, unless actually invaded, or in such imminent danger as will not admit of delay.

ARTICLE II

SECTION 1 (1) The executive power shall be vested in a President of the United States of America. He shall hold his office during the term of four years, and, together with the Vice President, chosen for the same term, be elected, as follows:

(2) Each State shall appoint, in such manner as the legislature thereof may direct, a number of electors, equal to the whole number of Senators and Representatives to which the State may be entitled in the Congress: but no Senator or Representative, or person holding an office of trust or profit under the United States, shall be appointed an elector.

The electors* shall meet in their respective States, and vote by ballot for two persons, of whom one at least shall not be an inhabitant of the same State with themselves. And they shall make a list of all the persons voted for, and of the number of votes for each; which list they shall sign and certify, and transmit sealed to the seat of the government of the United States, directed to the president of the Senate. The president of the Senate shall, in the presence of the Senate and House of Representatives, open all the certificates, and the votes shall then be counted. The person having the greatest number of votes shall be the President, if such number be a majority of the whole number of electors appointed; and if there be more than one who have such majority, and have an equal number of votes, then the House of Representatives shall immediately choose by ballot one of them for President; and if no person have a majority, then from the five highest on the list the said House shall in like manner choose the President. But in choosing the President, the votes shall be taken by States, the representation from each State having one vote; a quorum for this purpose shall consist of a member or members from two thirds of the States, and a majority of all the States shall be necessary to a choice. In every case, after the choice of the President, the person having the greatest number of votes of the electors shall be the Vice President. But if there should remain two or more who have equal votes, the Senate shall choose from them by ballot the Vice President.

(3) The Congress may determine the time of choosing the electors, and the day on which they shall give their votes; which day shall be the same throughout the United States.

(4) No person except a natural born citizen, or a citizen of the United States, at the time of the adoption of this Constitution, shall be eligible to the office of President; neither shall any person be eligible to that office who shall not have attained to the age of thirty five years, and been fourteen years a resident within the United States.

(5) In the case of the removal of the President from office, or of his death, resignation, or inability to discharge the powers and duties of the said office,† the same shall devolve on the Vice President, and the Congress may by law provide for the case of removal, death, resignation, or inability, both of the President and Vice President, declaring what officer shall then act as president, and such officer shall act accordingly, until the disability be removed, or a President shall be elected.

(6) The President shall, at stated times, receive for his services, a compensation, which shall neither be increased nor diminished during the period for which he shall have been elected, and he shall not receive within that period any other emolument from the United States, or any of them.

(7) Before he enter on the execution of his office, he shall take the following oath or affirmation:—"I do solemnly swear (or affirm) that I will faithfully execute the office of the President of the United States, and will to the best of my ability, preserve, protect and defend the Constitution of the United States."

SECTION 2 (1) The President shall be commander in chief of the army and navy of the United States, and of the militia of the several States, when called into the actual service of the United States; he may require the opinion, in writing, of the principal officer in each of the executive departments, upon any subject relating to the duties of their respective offices, and he shall have power to grant reprieves and pardons for offenses against the United States, except in cases of impeachment.

(2) He shall have power, by and with the advice and consent of the Senate, to make treaties, provided two thirds of the Senators present concur; and he shall nominate, and by and with the advice and consent of the Senate, shall appoint ambassadors, other public ministers and consuls, judges of the Supreme Court, and all other officers of the United States, whose appointments are not herein otherwise provided for, and which shall be established by law: but the Congress may by law vest the appointment of such inferior officers, as they think proper, in the President alone, in the courts of law, or in the heads of departments.

(3) The President shall have power to fill up all vacancies that may happen during the recess of the Senate, by granting commissions which shall expire at the end of their next session.

SECTION 3 He shall from time to time give to the Congress information of the state of the Union, and recom-

---

*This paragraph was replaced in 1804 by the 12th Amendment.

†Modified in 1967 by the 25th Amendment.

mend to their consideration such measures as he shall judge necessary and expedient; he may, on extraordinary occasions, convene both Houses, or either of them, and in case of disagreement between them, with respect to the time of adjournment, he may adjourn them to such time as he shall think proper; he shall receive ambassadors and other public ministers; he shall take care that the laws be faithfully executed, and shall commission all the officers of the United States.

SECTION 4 The President, Vice President and all civil officers of the United States, shall be removed from office on impeachment for, and conviction of, treason, bribery, or other high crimes and misdemeanors.

ARTICLE III

SECTION 1 The judicial power of the United States, shall be vested in one Supreme Court, and in such inferior courts as the Congress may from time to time ordain and establish. The judges, both of the Supreme and inferior courts, shall hold their offices during good behavior, and shall, at stated times, receive for their services, a compensation, which shall not be diminished during their continuance in office.

SECTION 2 (1) The judicial power shall extend to all cases, in law and equity, arising under this Constitution, the laws of the United States, and treaties made, or which shall be made, under their authority;—to all cases affecting ambassadors, other public ministers and consuls;—to all cases of admiralty and maritime jurisdiction;—to controversies to which the United states shall be a party;—to controversies between two or more States;—between a State and citizens of another State;*—between citizens of different States;—between citizens of the same State claiming lands under grants of different States, and between a State, or the citizens thereof, and foreign States, citizens or subjects.

(2) In all cases affecting ambassadors, other public ministers and consuls, and those in which a State shall be party, the Supreme Court shall have original jurisdiction. In all the other cases before mentioned, the Supreme Court shall have appellate jurisdiction, both as to law and fact, with such exceptions, and under such regulations as the Congress shall make.

(3) The trial of all crimes, except in cases of impeachment, shall be by jury; and such trial shall be held in the State where the said crimes shall have been committed; but when not committed within any State, the trial shall be at such place or places as the Congress may by law have directed.

SECTION 3 (1) Treason against the United States, shall consist only in levying war against them, or in adhering to their enemies, giving them aid and comfort. No person shall be convicted of treason unless on the testimony of two witnesses to the same overt act, or on confession in open court.

---

*Restricted by the 11th Amendment.

(2) The Congress shall have power to declare the punishment of treason, but no attainder of treason shall work corruption of blood, or forfeiture except during the life of the person attainted.

ARTICLE IV

SECTION 1 Full faith and credit shall be given in each State to the public acts, records, and judicial proceedings of every other State. And the Congress may by general laws prescribe the manner in which such acts, records and proceedings shall be proved, and the effect thereof.

SECTION 2 (1) The citizens of each State shall be entitled to all privileges and immunities of citizens in the several States.

(2) A person charged in any State with treason, felony, or other crime, who shall flee from justice, and be found in another State, shall on demand of the executive authority of the State from which he fled, be delivered up, to be removed to the State having jurisdiction of the crime.

(3) No person held to service or labor in one State, under the laws thereof, escaping into another, shall, in consequence of any law or regulation therein, be discharged from such service or labor, but shall be delivered up on claim of the party to whom such service or labor may be due.

SECTION 3 (1) New States may be admitted by the Congress into this Union; but no new State shall be formed or erected within the jurisdiction of any other State; nor any State be formed by the junction of two or more States, or parts of States, without the consent of the legislatures of the States concerned as well as of the Congress.

(2) The Congress shall have power to dispose of and make all needful rules and regulations respecting the territory or other property belonging to the United States; and nothing in this Constitution shall be so construed as to prejudice any claims of the United States, or of any particular State.

SECTION 4 The United States shall guarantee to every State in this Union a republican form of government, and shall protect each of them against invasion; and on application of the legislature, or of the executive (when the legislature cannot be convened) against domestic violence.

ARTICLE V

The Congress, whenever two thirds of both Houses shall deem it necessary, shall propose amendments to this Constitution, or, on the application of the legislatures of two thirds of the several States, shall call a convention for proposing amendments, which, in either case, shall be valid to all intents and purposes, as part of this Constitution, when ratified by the legislatures of three fourths of the several States, or by conventions in three fourths thereof, as the one or the other mode of ratification may be proposed by the Congress; Provided that no amendment which may be made prior to the year one thousand eight hundred and eight shall in any manner affect the first and fourth clauses in the ninth section of the first article; and that no State, without its consent, shall be deprived of its equal suffrage in the Senate.

ARTICLE VI

SECTION 1 All debts contracted and engagements entered into, before the adoption of this Constitution, shall be as valid against the United States under this Constitution, as under the Confederation.

SECTION 2 This Constitution, and the laws of the United States which shall be made in pursuance thereof; and all treaties made, or which shall be made, under the authority of the United States, shall be the supreme law of the land; and the judges in every State shall be bound thereby, anything in the constitution or laws of any State to the contrary notwithstanding.

SECTION 3 The Senators and Representatives before mentioned, and the members of the several State legislatures, and all executive and judicial officers, both of the United States and of the several States, shall be bound by oath or affirmation to support this Constitution; but no religious test shall ever be required as a qualification to any office or public trust under the United States.

ARTICLE VII

The ratification of the conventions of nine States, shall be sufficient for the establishment of this Constitution between the States so ratifying the same.

DONE in Convention by the unanimous consent of the States present the seventeenth day of September in the year of our Lord one thousand seven hundred and eighty-seven, and of the independence of the United States of America the twelfth. In witness whereof we have hereunto subscribed our names.
Geo. WASHINGTON—
President and Deputy from Virginia

ARTICLES in addition to and AMENDMENTS of the Constitution of the United States of America, proposed by Congress, and ratified by the legislatures of the several States, pursuant to the fifth article of the original Constitution.

ARTICLE I*

Congress shall make no law respecting an establishment of religion, or prohibiting the free exercise thereof; or abridging the freedom of speech, or of the press; or the right of the people peaceably to assemble, and to petition the govemment for a redress of grievances.

_____
*The first ten Amendments were adopted in 1791.

ARTICLE II

A well regulated militia, being necessary to the security of a free State, the right of the people to keep and bear arms, shall not be infringed.

ARTICLE III

No soldier shall, in time of peace be quartered in any house, without the consent of the owner, nor in time of war, but in a manner to be prescribed by law.

ARTICLE IV

The right of the people to be secure in their persons, houses, papers, effects, against unreasonable searches and seizures, shall not be violated, and no warrants shall issue, but upon probable cause, supported by oath or affirmation, and particularly describing the place to be searched, and the persons or things to be seized.

ARTICLE V

No person shall be held to answer for a capital, or otherwise infamous crime, unless on a presentment or indictment of a grand jury, except in cases arising in the land or naval forces, or in the militia, when in actual service in time of war or public danger; nor shall any person be subject for the same offense to be twice put in jeopardy of life or limb; nor shall be compelled in any criminal case to be a witness against himself, nor be deprived of life, liberty, or property, without due process of law; nor shall private property be taken for public use, without just compensation.

ARTICLE VI

In all criminal prosecutions the accused shall enjoy the right to a speedy and public trial, by an impartial jury of the State and district wherein the crime shall have been committed, which district shall have been previously ascertained by law, and to be informed of the nature and cause of the accusation; to be confronted with the witnesses against him; to have compulsory process for obtaining witnesses in his favor, and to have the assistance of counsel for his defense.

ARTICLE VII

In suits at common law, where the value in controversy shall exceed twenty dollars, the right of trial by jury shall be preserved, and no fact tried by a jury shall be otherwise reexamined in any court of the United States, than according to the rules of the common law.

ARTICLE VIII

Excessive bail shall not be required, nor excessive fines imposed, nor cruel and unusual punishments inflicted.

ARTICLE IX

The enumeration in the Constitution, of certain rights, shall not be construed to deny or disparage others retained by the people.

ARTICLE X

The powers not delegated to the United States by the Constitution, nor prohibited by it to the States, are reserved to the States respectively, or to the people.

ARTICLE XI*

The judicial power of the United States shall not be construed to extend to any suit in law or equity, commenced or prosecuted against one of the United States by citizens of another State, or by citizens or subjects of any foreign State.

ARTICLE XII†

The electors shall meet in their respective States and vote by ballot for President and Vice-President, one of whom, at least, shall not be an inhabitant of the same State with themselves; they shall name in their ballots the person voted for as President, and in distinct ballots the person voted for as Vice-President, and they shall make distinct lists of all persons voted for as President, and of all persons voted for as Vice-President, and of the number of votes for each, which lists they shall sign and certify, and transmit sealed to the seat of the government of the United States, directed to the president of the Senate;—The president of the Senate shall, in the presence of the Senate and House of Representatives, open all the certificates and the votes shall then be counted;—The person having the greatest number of votes for President, shall be the President, if such number be a majority of the whole number of electors appointed; and if no person have such majority, then from the persons having the highest numbers not exceeding three on the list of those voted for as President, the House of Representatives shall choose immediately, by ballot, the President. But in choosing the President, the votes shall be taken by States, the representation from each State having one vote; a quorum for this purpose shall consist of a member or members from two thirds of the States, and a majority of all the States shall be necessary to a choice. And if the House of Representatives shall not choose a President whenever the right of choice shall devolve upon them, before the fourth day of March next following, then the Vice-President shall act as President, as in the case of the death or other constitutional disability of the President.—The person having the greatest number of votes as Vice-President, shall be the Vice-President, if such number be a majority of the whole number of elec-

tors appointed, and if no person have a majority, then from the two highest numbers on the list, the Senate shall choose the Vice-President; a quorum for the purpose shall consist of two thirds of the whole number of Senators, and a majority of the whole number shall be necessary to a choice. But no person constitutionally ineligible to the office of President shall be eligible to that of Vice-President of the United States.

ARTICLE XIII‡

SECTION 1 Neither slavery nor involuntary servitude, except as a punishment for crime whereof the party shall have been duly convicted, shall exist within the United States, or any place subject to their jurisdiction.

SECTION 2 Congress shall have power to enforce this article by appropriate legislation.

ARTICLE XIV**

SECTION 1 All persons born or naturalized in the United States, and subject to the jurisdiction thereof, are citizens of the United States and of the State wherein they reside. No State shall make or enforce any law which shall abridge the privileges or immunities of citizens of the United States; nor shall any State deprive any person of life, liberty, or property, without due process of law; nor deny any person within its jurisdiction the equal protection of the laws.

SECTION 2 Representatives shall be apportioned among the several States according to their respective numbers, counting the whole number of persons in each State, excluding Indians not taxed. But when the right to vote at any election for the choice of electors for President and Vice President of the United States, Representatives in Congress, the executive and judicial offices of a State, or the members of the legislature thereof, is denied to any of the male inhabitants of such State, being twenty-one years of age, and citizens of the United States, or in any way abridged, except for participation in rebellion, or other crime, the basis of representation therein shall be reduced in the proportion which the number of such male citizens shall bear to the whole number of male citizens twenty-one years of age in such State.

SECTION 3 No person shall be a Senator or Representative in Congress, or elector of President and Vice President, or hold any office, civil or military, under the United States, or under any State, who, having previously taken an oath, as a member of Congress, or as an officer of the United States, or as a member of any State legislature, or as an executive or judicial officer of any State, to support the Constitution of the United States, shall have engaged in insurrection or rebellion against the same, or given aid or comfort to the enemies thereof.

---

*Ratified in 1795; proclaimed in 1798.
†Adopted in 1804.

‡Adopted in 1865.
**Adopted in 1868.

But Congress may by a vote of two thirds of each House, remove such disability.

SECTION 4 The validity of the public debt of the United States, authorized by law, including debts incurred for payment of pensions and bounties for services in suppressing insurrection or rebellion, shall not be questioned. But neither the United States nor any State shall assume or pay any debt or obligation incurred in aid of insurrection or rebellion against the United States, or any claim for the loss or emancipation of any slave; but all such debts, obligations and claims shall be held illegal and void.

SECTION 5 The Congress shall have power to enforce, by appropriate legislation, the provision of this article.

ARTICLE XV*

SECTION 1 The right of citizens of the United States to vote shall not be denied or abridged by the United States or by any State on account of race, color, or previous condition of servitude.

SECTION 2 The Congress shall have the power to enforce this article by appropriate legislation.

ARTICLE XVI†

The Congress shall have the power to lay and collect taxes on incomes, from whatever sourced derived, without apportionment among the several States, and without regard to any census or enumeration.

ARTICLE XVII‡

The Senate of the United States shall be composed of two Senators from each State, elected by the people thereof, for six years; and each Senator shall have one vote. The electors in each State shall have the qualifications requisite for electors of the most numerous branch of the State legislatures.

When vacancies happen in the representation of any State in the Senate, the executive authority of such State shall issue writs of election to fill such vacancies: *Provided,* That the legislature of any State may empower the executive thereof to make temporary appointments until the people fill the vacancies by election as the legislature may direct.

This amendment shall not be so construed as to affect the election or term of any Senator chosen before it becomes valid as part of the Constitution.

ARTICLE XVIII**

SECTION 1 After one year from the ratification of this article the manufacture, sale, or transportation of intoxicating liquors within, the importation thereof into, or the exportation thereof from the United States and all territory subject to the jurisdiction thereof for beverage purposes is hereby prohibited.

SECTION 2 The Congress and the several States shall have concurrent power to enforce this article by appropriate legislation.

SECTION 3 This article shall be inoperative unless it shall have been ratified as an amendment to the Constitution by the legislatures of the several States, as provided in the Constitution, within seven years from the date of the submission hereof to the States by the Congress.

ARTICLE XIX††

The right of citizens of the United States to vote shall not be denied or abridged by the United States or by any State on account of sex.

The Congress shall have power to enforce this article by appropriate legislation.

ARTICLE XX‡‡

SECTION 1 The terms of the President and Vice President shall end at noon on the 20th day of January, and the terms of Senators and Representatives at noon on the 3rd day of January, of the years in which such terms would have ended if this article had not been ratified; and the terms of their successors shall then begin.

SECTION 2 The Congress shall assemble at least once in every year, and such meeting shall begin at noon on the 3rd day of January, unless they shall by law appoint a different day.

SECTION 3 If, at the time fixed for the beginning of the term of the President, the President elect shall have died, the Vice President elect shall become President. If a President shall not have been chosen before the time fixed for the beginning of his term, or if the President elect shall have failed to qualify, then the Vice President elect shall act as President until a President shall have qualified; and the Congress may by law provide for the case wherein neither a President elect nor a Vice President elect shall have qualified, declaring who shall then act as President, or the manner in which one who is to act shall be selected, and such person shall act accord-

---

*Adopted in 1870.

†Adopted in 1913.

‡Adopted in 1913

**Adopted in 1919. Repealed by the 21st Amendment.

††Adopted in 1920.

‡‡Adopted in 1933.

ingly until a President or Vice President shall have qualified.

SECTION 4 The Congress may by law provide for the case of the death of any of the persons from whom the House of Representatives may choose a President whenever the right of choice shall have devolved upon them, and for the case of the death of any of the persons from whom the Senate may choose a Vice President whenever the right of choice shall have devolved upon them.

SECTION 5 Sections 1 and 2 shall take effect on the 15th day of October following the ratification of this article.

SECTION 6 This article shall be inoperative unless it shall have been ratified as an amendment to the Constitution by the legislatures of three fourths of the several States within seven years from the date of its submission.

ARTICLE XXI*

SECTION 1 The Eighteenth Article of Amendment to the Constitution of the United States is hereby repealed.

SECTION 2 The transportation or importation into any State, Territory or Possession of the United States for delivery or use therein of intoxicating liquors in violation of the laws thereof is hereby prohibited.

SECTION 3 This article shall be inoperative unless it shall have been ratified as an amendment to the Constitution by conventions in the several States, as provided in the Constitution, within seven years from the date of submission hereof to the States by the Congress.

ARTICLE XXII†

SECTION 1 No person shall be elected to the office of the President more than twice, and no person who has held the office of President, or acted as President, for more than two years of a term to which some other person was elected President shall be elected to the office of the President more than once. But this Article shall not apply to any person holding the office of President when this Article was proposed by the Congress, and shall not prevent any person who may be holding the office of President, or acting as President, during the term within which the Article becomes operative from holding the office of President or acting as President during the remainder of such term.

SECTION 2 This article shall be inoperative unless it shall have been ratified as an amendment to the Constitution by the legislatures of three fourths of the several States within seven years from the date of its submission to the States by the Congress.

ARTICLE XXIII‡

SECTION 1 The District constituting the seat of Government of the United States shall appoint in such manner as the Congress may direct:

A number of electors of President and Vice President equal to the whole number of Senators and Representatives in Congress to which the District would be entitled if it were a State, but in no event more than the least populous State; they shall be in addition to those appointed by the States, but they shall be considered, for the purpose of the election of President and Vice President, to be electors appointed by a State; and they shall meet in the District and perform such duties as provided by the twelfth article of amendment.

SECTION 2 The Congress shall have power to enforce this article by appropriate legislation.

ARTICLE XXIV**

SECTION I The right of citizens of the United States to vote in any primary or other election for President or Vice President, for electors for President or Vice President, or for Senator or Representative in Congress, shall not be denied or abridged by the United States or any State by reason of failure to pay any poll tax or other tax.

SECTION 2 The Congress shall have power to enforce this article by appropriate legislation.

ARTICLE XXV††

SECTION 1 In case of the removal of the President from office or his death or resignation, the Vice President shall become President.

SECTION 2 Whenever there is a vacancy in the office of the Vice President, the President shall nominate a Vice President who shall take the Office upon confirmation by a majority vote of both houses of Congress.

SECTION 3 Whenever the President transmits to the President pro tempore of the Senate and the Speaker of the House of Representatives his written declaration that he is unable to discharge the powers and duties of his office, and until he transmits to them a written declaration to the contrary, such powers and duties shall be discharged by the Vice President as Acting President.

SECTION 4 Whenever the Vice President and a majority of either the principal officers of the executive departments, or of such other body as Congress may by law provide, transmit to the President pro tempore of the Senate and the Speaker of the House of Representatives their written declaration that the President is unable to

---

*Adopted in 1933.

†Adopted in 1951.

‡Adopted in 1961.

**Adopted in 1964.

††Adopted in 1967.

discharge the powers and duties of his office, the Vice President shall immediately assume the powers and duties of the office as Acting President.

Thereafter, when the President transmits to the President pro tempore of the Senate and the Speaker of the House of Representatives his written declaration that no inability exists, he shall resume the powers and duties of his office unless the Vice President and a majority of either the principal officers of the executive department, or of such other body as Congress may by law provide, transmit within four days to the President pro tempore of the Senate and the Speaker of the House of Representatives their written declaration that the President is unable to discharge the powers and duties of his office. Thereupon Congress shall decide the issue, assembling within 48 hours for that purpose if not in session. If the Congress, within 21 days after receipt of the latter written declaration, or, if Congress is not in session, within 21 days after Congress is required to assemble, determines by two-thirds vote of both houses that the President is unable to discharge the powers and duties of his office, the Vice President shall continue to discharge the same as Acting President; otherwise, the President shall resume the powers and duties of his office.

ARTICLE XXVI*

SECTION 1 The right of citizens of the United States, who are eighteen years of age, or older, to vote shall not be denied or abridged by the United States or by any state on account of age.

SECTION 2 The Congress shall have the power to enforce this article by appropriate legislation.

ARTICLE XXVII†

SECTION 1 Equality of rights under the law shall not be denied or abridged by the United States or by any state on account of sex.

SECTION 2 The Congress shall have the power to enforce, by appropriate legislation, the provisions of this article.

SECTION 3 This amendment shall take effect two years after the date of ratification.

---

*Adopted in 1971.

†Proposed to states for ratification March 22, 1972.

Table of Cases

Entries in boldface (with boldface page numbers) indicate the cases reprinted in this volume; italics indicate cases commented on in the editor's notes; ordinary type indicates cases quoted or discussed in the opinions. For convenience, all cases in which the United States is plaintiff are also indexed under the name of the defendant.

Burstyn v. Wilson, 343 U. S. 495 (1952), *210*

Butler v. Michigan, 352 U. S. 380 (1957), *213*

Butler v. Perry, 240 U. S. 328 (1916), *361*

Cabana v. Bullock, 474 U.S. 376 (1986), *145*

Calandra, United States v.

Calder v. Bull, 3 Dall. 387 (1798), 1, *20*

California v. Hodari D., 113 L. Ed. 2d 690 (1991), *129*

California v. Prysock, 453 U. S. 355 (1981), 109-111

Callan v. Wilson, 127 U.S. 540 (1888), 157

Camara v. Municipal Court, 387 U. S. 523 (1967), 116, 167-170

Cantwell v. Connecticut, 310 U. S. 296 (1940), 190, *240*, 377, 379, 381

Cardwell v. Lewis, 417 U. S. 483 (1974), *123*

Carey v. Population Services International, 431 U. S. 678 (1977), 79

Carolene Products Co., United States v.

Carroll v. United States, 267 U. S. 132 (1925), *112, 122, 123, 124*

Cassell v. Texas, 339 U. S. 282 (1950), *299*

Chadwick, United States v.

Chambers v. Florida, 309 U.S. 227 (1940), *49*, 104

Chambers v. Maroney, 399 U. S. 42 (1970), *123*

Chandler v. Florida, 449 U. S. 560 (1981), *235*

Chandler v. Fretag, 348 U. S. 3 (1954), *134*

Chaplinsky v. New Hampshire, 315 U. S. 568 (1942), *188*, 194, 197, 198, 215, *219*, 241

Chapman v. United States, 365 U. S. 610 (1961), 116

Charles River Bridge v. Warren Bridge, 11 Pet. 420 (1837), *11, 20*

Cheff v. Schnackenberg, 384 U. S. 373 (1966), 157

Chicago & S. Air Lines v. Waterman S. S. Corp, 333 U. S. 103 (1948), 225

Chicago, B. & Q. R. Co. v. Chicago, 166 U. S. 226 (1897), *38*, 41

Chicago, B. & Q. R. Co. v. McGuire, 219 U. S. 549 (1911), 33

Chicago, United States v.

Child Labor Case. See Bailey v. Drexel Furniture Co.

Chimel v. California, 395 U. S. 752 (1969), *112, 113*

Chin Loy You, Ex parte, 223 Fed. 833 (1915), 41

Church of the Lukumi Babalu Aye v. Hialeah, 124 L Ed. 2d 472 (1993), *375,*

Civil Rights Cases, 109 U. S. 3 (1883), *301*, 303, *305, 349, 353, 361, 362*, 363, 364

Classic, United States v.

Cleveland v. United States, 329 U. S. 14 (1946), *239*

Cochran v. Louisiana State Board of Education, 281 U. S. 370 (1930), *248*

Cohen v. California, 403 U. S. 15 (1971), *219*

Coker v. Georgia, 433 U. S. 584 (1977), *145*

Cole v. Richardson, 405 U. S. 676 (1972), *167*

Colegrove v. Battin, 413 U. S. 149 (1973), *161*

Committee for Public Education v. Nyquist, 413 U. S. 756 (1973), *252*, 254-257, 269

Committee for Public Education v. Regan, 444 U. S. 646 (1980), *253*

Communist Party v. Subversive Activities Control Board, 367 U. S. 1 (1961), 6, 10, *184*

Connally v. Georgia, 429 U. S. 245 (1977), *45*

Connecticut v. Menillo, 423 U. S. 9 (1975), *67*

Connick v. Myers, 461 U. S. 138 (1983), *166*

Coolidge v. New Hampshire, 403 U. S. 443 (1971), *113, 122*

Corrigan v. Buckley, 271 U. S. 323 (1926), *301*, 304

Cox v. Louisiana, 379 U. S. 536 (1956), *188*, 189-192, 203, 373

Cox v. New Hampshire, 312 U. S. 569 (1941), *200, 201*, 203, 241, *243*

Coyle v. Smith, 221 U. S. 559 (1911), 359

Craig v. Boren, 429 U. S. 190 (1976), *292, 293, 334, 337*, 338, 341

Craig v. Harney, 331 U. S. 367 (1947), *233*

Crawford v. Los Angeles Board of Ed., 458 U. S. 527 (1982), *302*

Cronin v. Adams, 192 U. S. 108 (1904), *333*

Cruikshank, United States v.

Cumming v. County Board of Education, 175 U. S. 528 (1899), *308*, 313

Frost v. Railroad Comm., 271 U. S. 583 (1926), *166*
Frothingham v. Mellon, 262 U. S. 447 (1923), *249*
Fullilove v. Klutznick, 448 U. S. 448 (1980), *324*, 324, 325, 328-332
Furman v. Georgia, 408 U. S. 238 (1972), *2*, *139*,, *140*,, 141-145, *146*, 149, 150

Gallagher v. Crown Kosher Super Market, 366 U. S. 617 (1961), *266*
Galvan v. Press, 347 U. S. 522 (1954), *2*
Gannett Co. v. DePasquale, 443 U. S. 484 (1974), *234*, 235-239
Gardner v. Broderick, 392 U. S. 273 (1968), *167*
Garland, Ex parte, 4 Wall. 333 (1867), *3*, 6, 8
Garner v. Los Angeles Board of Public Works, 341 U. S. 716 (1951), *1*
Garrison v. Louisiana, 379 U. S. 64 (1964), *232*
Garrity v. New Jersey, 385 U. S. 493 (1967), *167*
Gastelum-Quinones v. Kennedy, 374 U. S. 469 (1963), *2*
Gault, In re, 387 U. S. 1 (1967), *54*, 55, 56, 58
Geduldig v. Aiello, 417 U. S. 484 (1974), 333
General Electric v. Gilbert, 429 U. S. 125 (1976), *334*
Gertz v. Welch, 418 U. S. 323 (1974), *232*
Gibbons v. Ogden, 9 Wheat. 1 (1824), 359
Gibson v. Florida Investigation Committee, 372 U. S. 539 (1963), *67*, *189*
Gideon v. Wainwright, 372 U. S. 335 (1963), *47*, *101*, **133**, 155, *342*
Gilbert v. California, 388 U. S. 263 (1967), *50*
Gilbert v. Minnesota, 254 U. S. 325 (1920), *38*, *101*, 181
Gillette v. United States, 401 U. S. 437 (1971), 378
Ginsberg v. New York, 390 U. S. 629 (1968), 215
Ginzburg v. United States, 383 U. S. 463 (1966), *214*, 216
Gitlow v. New York, 268 U.S. 652 (1925), *38*, 41, *43*, *67*, *178*, **179**, 185, 186
Gober v. Birmingham, 373 U. S. 374 (1963), 204
Godfrey v. Georgia, 446 U. S. 420 (1980), *145*
Goesaert v. Cleary, 335 U. S. 464 (1948), **273**, *333*, 336
Goldberg v. Kelly, 397 U. S. 254 (1970), 171
Goldman v. United States, 316 U. S. 129 (1942), *119*, 120, 121
Goldstein v. United States, 316 U.S. 114 (1942), *92*
Gomillion v. Lightfoot, 364 U. S. 339 (1960), *365*,, 366, 367, 370, 371
Gompers v. Buck's Stove & Range Co., 221 U. S. 418 (1911), 179
Gong Lum v. Rice, 275 U. S. 78 (1927), *308*, 313
Gouled v. United States, 255 U. S. 298 (1921), *118*, *119*
Grace, United States v.
Green v. County School Board, 391 U. S. 430 (1968), *312*, 315, 317, 318
Gregg v. Georgia, 428 U. S. 153 (1976), **137**,, *145*, *146*, 148-150
Griffin v. Breckenridge, 403 U. S. 88 (1971), *362*
Griffin v. Illinois, 351 U. S 12 (1956), *46*, 286, *342*, *343*
Griffin v. Maryland, 378 U. S. 130 (1964), *187*
Griffin v. School Board of Prince Edward County, 377 U. S. 218 (1964), *311*
Griggs v. Duke Power Co., 401 U. S. 424 (1971), *322*
Grisham v. Hagan, 361 U. S. 278 (1960), *154*
Griswold v. Connecticut, 381 U. S. 479 (1965), **63**, 67-69, 71, *72*, 72, 80, 169
Groppi v. Wisconsin, 400 U. S. 505 (1971), *153*
Grosjean v. American Press Co., 297 U. S. 233 (1936), 47, 136
Guest, United States v.
Guinn v. United States, 238 U. S. 347 (1915), 359, *365*,, 369

Hague v. CIO, 307 U. S. 496 (1939), 237
Hamilton v. Alabama, 368 U. S. 52 (1961), *101*
Hamilton v. University of California, 293 U. S. 245 (1934), *38*, 43, *239*
Hamm v. Rock Hill, 379 U. S. 306 (1964), *187*, 190
Hannegan v. Esquire, 327 U. S. 146 (1946), 169
Harmelin v. Michigan, 115 L. Ed. 2d 836 (1991), *138,*
Harper v. Virginia Bd. of Elections, 383 U. S. 663 (1966), 283

Massiah v. United States, 377 U. S. 201 (1964), *102*
Maxwell v. Dow, 176 U. S. 581 (1900), 43, *152*, *153*, 156, 155, 157, 159, 163
Mayberry v. Pennsylvania, 400 U. S. 581 (1971), *158*
Mayer v. Chicago, 404 U. S. 189 (1971), *46*, *342*
McAuliffe v. Mayor of New Bedford, 155 Mass. 216 (1892), *166*
McCabe v. Atchison, T. & S. F. Ry. Co., 235 U. S. 151 (1914), *308*, *310*
McCleskey v. Kemp, 95 L. Ed. 2d 262 (1987), 145
McCollum v. Board of Education, 333 U. S. 203 (1948), *248*, *249*, 249-251
McCulloch v. Maryland, 4 Wheat. 316 (1819), 359
McDonald v. Board of Election Comm'rs, 394 U. S. 801 (1969), *281*, 282
McDonald v. United States, 335 U. S. 451 (1948), *112*
McElroy v. United States ex rel. Guagliardo, 361 U. S. 281 (1960), *154*
McGautha v. California, 402 U. S. 183 (1971), *139*,, 141
McGowan v. Maryland, 366 U. S. 420 (1961), 263, *266*, 270, 271, *274*
McKeiver v. Pennsylvania, 403 U. S. 528 (1971), 54, *158*
McLaurin v. Oklahoma State Regents, 339 U. S. 637 (1950), *308*, 309, 313, 314
McLean v. Arkansas Board of Education, 529 F. Supp. 1255 (1982), 261
McNabb v. United States, 318 U. S. 332 (1943), *45*
Meek v. Pittenger, 421 U. S. 349 (1975), *253*
Meese v. Keene, 95 L. Ed 2d 415 (1987), *184*
Memoirs v. Massachusetts, 383 U. S. 413 (1966), *213*, *214*, 215, 216
Metro Broadcasting v. FCC, 107 L Ed. 2d 735 (1990), *324*
Meyer v. Nebraska, 262 U. S. 390 (1923), *38*, 64, 68, 69, 71, 85, 344
Michael H. v. Gerald D., 491 U. S. 110 (1989), 84
Michael M. v. Sonoma County, 450 U. S. 464 (1981), *337*
Michigan v. DeFillippo, 443 U. S. 31 (1979), *128*
Michigan State Police v. Sitz, 496 U. S. 444 (1990), 122
Miller v. California, 413 U. S. 15 (1973), 197, 199, **213**
Milligan, Ex parte, 4 Wall. 2 (1866), *153*, *218*
Milliken v. Bradley, 418 U. S. 717 (1974), *317*
Milliken v. Bradley, 433 U. S. 267 (1977), *318*
Minersville School District v. Gobitis, 310 U. S. 586 (1940), *242*, *243*, 243-247, 377, 380
Minor v. Happersett, 21 Wall. 162 (1875), 285
Miranda v. Arizona, 384 U. S. 436 (1966), *92*, **100**, *107*, *108*, 109-111
Mishkin v. New York, 383 U. S. 502 (1966), 216, 217
Mississippi University for Women v. Hogan, 458 U. S. 718 (1982), *274*, *292*, **337**
Missouri ex rel. Gaines v. Canada, 305 U. S. 337 (1938), 291, *308*, 310, 313
Missouri v. Lewis, 101 U. S. 22 (1880), 36
Mobile v. Bolden, 446 U. S. 55 (1980), *365,*
Monitor Patriot Co. v. Roy, 401 U. S. 265 (1971), *232*
Monroe v. Pape, 365 U. S. 167 (1961), *93*
Mooney v. Holohan, 294 U. S. 103 (1935), *46*
Moore v. Dempsey, 261 U. S. 86 (1923), 44, *45*
Moore v. East Cleveland, 431 U. S. 494 (1977), 73
Moose Lodge No. 107 v. Irvis, 407 U. S. 163 (1972), *302*
Moran v. Burbine, 475 U. S. 412 (1986), *107*
Morehead v. New York ex rel. Tipaldo, 298 U. S. 587 (1936), *32*, 32
Mueller v. Allen, 463 U. S. 388 (1983), *248*, **251**, 263
Mugler v. Kansas, 123 U. S. 623 (1887), *27*, 78
Muller v. Oregon, 208 U. S. 412 (1908), *31*, 33, 336
Munn v. Illinois, 94 U. S. 113 (1877), **19**, *23*, *24*, 26, *38*
Murdock v. Pennsylvania, 319 U. S. 104 (1943), *67*, **239**, *375*,, 377
Murray v. Goldstein, 385 U. S. 816 (1966), *266*
Murray's Lessee v. Hoboken Land & Improvement Co., 18 How. 272 (1856), *35*, 35
Mutual Film Corp. v. Industrial Comm. of Ohio, 236 U. S. 230 (1915), *210*
Myers v. United States, 272 U. S. 52 (1926), 268

NAACP v. Alabama, 357 U. S. 449 (1958), 64, *189*
NAACP v. Alabama, 377 U.S. 288 (1964), *189*

United States v. Place, 462 U. S. 696 (1983), *113*, *124*
United States v. Price, 383 U. S. 787 (1966), *353*, 354
United States v. Rabinowitz, 339 U. S. 56 (1950), *112*
United States v. Raines, 362 U. S. 17 (1960), *356*, 359
United States v. Reese, 92 U. S. 214 (1876), *356*, *361*
United States v. Reynolds, 234 U. S. 1 (1953), 225
United States v. Robinson, 414 U. S. 218 (1973), *113*
United States v. Ross, 456 U. S. 798 (1982), *124*
United States v. Sokolow, 490 U. S. 1 (1989), *114*
United States v. United Mine Workers, 330 U. S. 258 (1947), 205
United States v. Wade, 388 U. S. 218 (1967), *50*, *101*
United States v. Williams, 341 U. S. 70 (1951), *353*, 354
University of California Regents v. Bakke, 438 U. S. 265 (1978), *276*, *323*, *324*, 326, 327, 330, 332

Valley Forge Christian College v. Americans United, 454 U. S. 464 (1982), *249*
Vidal v. Girard's Executors, 2 How. 127 (1884), *249*, *258*
Virginia, Ex parte, 100 U. S. 339 (1880), 152, *298*, 339, *353*
Virginia v. Rives, 100 U. S. 313 (1880), *298*
Von Moltke v. Gillies, 332 U. S. 708 (1948), *134*

Wade, United States v.
Walder v. United States, 374 U. S. 62 (1954), *92*, *102*
Walker v. Birmingham, 388 U. S. 307 (1967), 200
Walker v. Sauvinet, 92 U. S. 90 (1876), 43, *153*
Wallace v. Jaffree, 472 U. S. 38 (1985), *258*, 259, 262, 263, 265
Walz v. Tax Commission, 397 U. S. 664 (1970), *252*, 267, 268, 271
Warden v. Hayden, 387 U. S. 294 (1967), 115-117, *118*, 120
Washington v. Davis, 426 U. S. 229 (1976), 300, 301, *322*
Washington v. Seattle School Dist., 458 U. S. 457 (1982), *302*
Washington v. Texas, 388 U. S. 14 (1967), *153*
Watson v. Memphis, 373 U. S. 526 (1963), *312*
Weaver v. Graham, 450 U. S. 24 (1981), *2*
Weber v. Aetna Casualty & Surety Co., 406 U. S. 164 (1972), 297
Webster v. Reproductive Services, 492 U. S. 490 (1989), *77*,, 83-85, 87
Weeks v. United States, 232 U. S. 383 (1914), 43, 53, **91**, 93-100, *101*, *102*, *118*, 122, *128*
Weems v. United States, 217 U. S. 349 (1910), *138,*
Weinberger v. Wiesenfeld, 420 U. S. 636 (1975), 327, *334*
Wengler v. Druggists Mutual Ins. Co., 446 U. S. 142 (1980), 341
West Coast Hotel v. Parrish, 300 U. S. 379 (1937), **31**, 64, 66, 80, 86, 87
West River Bridge Co. v. Dix, 6 How. 507 (1848), *11*
West v. Louisiana, 194 U. S. 258 (1904), 43
West Virginia State Board of Education v. Barnette, 319 U. S. 624 (1943), 75, *193*, 231, **242**, 379, 380
White v. Maryland, 373 U. S. 59 (1963), *101*
Whitney v. California, 274 U. S. 357 (1927), *179*, *184*, 185, 186
Whitus v. Georgia, 385 U. S. 545 (1967), 300, 301
Widmar v. Vincent, 454 U. S. 263 (1981), *249*, 254, 255
Wilkerson v. Utah, 99 U. S. 130 (1879), *138,*
Wilkinson v. Leland, 2 Pet. 657 (1829), 23
Williams, United States v.
Williams v. Florida, 399 U. S. 78 (1970), 55, 58, **158**, *161*, 162, 164, 165, 163
Williams v. Illinois, 399 U. S. 235 (1970), 286, *342*
Williams v. New York, 337 U. S. 241 (1949), 373
Williams v. Rhodes, 392 U. S. 23 (1968), 282
Williams v. United States, 341 U. S. 97 (1951), *353*
Winship, In re, 397 U. S. 358 (1970), *54*, 55, 162
Winters v. New York, 333 U. S. 507 (1948), *213*
Wisconsin v. Mitchell, 124 L. Ed. 2d 436 (1993), **372,**
Wisconsin v. Yoder, 406 U. S. 205 (1972), 75, *243*, 263, 295, 377, 379, 381, 382
Wise v. Henkel, 220 U. S. 556 (1911), 93